UNDERSTANDING MANAGEMENT

6e

Richard L. Daft

Vanderbilt University

Dorothy Marcic

Vanderbilt University

SOUTH-WESTERN
CENGAGE Learning

Australia • Brazil • Canada • Mexico • Singapore • Spain • United Kingdom • United States

SOUTH-WESTERN
CENGAGE Learning

**Understanding Management,
Sixth Edition**
Richard L. Daft and Dorothy Marcic

VP/Editorial Director: Jack W. Calhoun

Editor-in-Chief: Melissa S. Acuña

Executive Editor: Joe Sabatino

Managing Developmental Editor:
Emma F. Newsom

Executive Marketing Manager:
Kimberly Kanakes

Senior Marketing Coordinator: Sarah Rose

Marketing Manager: Clinton Kernen

Content Project Manager:
Jacquelyn K Featherly

Technology Project Manager:
Kristen Meere

Editorial Assistant: Ruth Belanger

Senior Manufacturing Coordinator:
Doug Wilke

Production House/Compositor:
ICC Macmillan Inc.

Senior Art Director: Tippy McIntosh

Internal Designer: Ke Design

Cover Designer: Tippy McIntosh

Cover Images: Anthony Harvie/Getty

For product information and technology assistance, contact us at
Cengage Learning Customer & Sales Support, 1-800-354-9706

For permission to use material from this text or product,
submit all requests online at **cengage.com/permissions**
Further permissions questions can be emailed to
permissionrequest@cengage.com

ExamView® and ExamView Pro® are registered trademarks of FSCreations, Inc. Windows is a registered trademark of the Microsoft Corporation used herein under license. Macintosh and Power Macintosh are registered trademarks of Apple Computer, Inc. used herein under license.

Library of Congress Control Number: 2007936116

Student Edition 13: 978-0-324-56838-7
Student Edition 10: 0-324-56838-X

Instructor's Edition ISBN 13: 978-0-324-58178-2
Instructor's Edition ISBN 10: 0-324-58178-5

South-Western Cengage Learning
5191 Natorp Boulevard
Mason, OH 45040
USA

Cengage Learning products are represented in Canada by Nelson Education, Ltd.

For your course and learning solutions, visit **academic.cengage.com**

Purchase any of our products at your local college store or at our preferred online store **www.ichapters.com**

Printed in the United States of America
1 2 3 4 5 6 7 12 11 10 09 08

To our daughters Roxanne, Solange and Elizabeth,
who have taught us the importance of good management in every day life.

Managing in Turbulent Times: Spotlight on Innovative Solutions

In light of the dramatic and far-reaching events of the early twenty-first century, the central theme being discussed in the field of management is the pervasiveness of turbulent change and its impact on organizations. This edition of *Understanding Management* was revised to help current and future managers find innovative solutions to the problems that plague today's organizations—whether they are everyday challenges or "once-in-a-lifetime" crises. The world in which most students will work as managers is undergoing a tremendous upheaval. The emergence of crisis management, ethical turmoil, e-business, rapidly changing technologies, globalization, outsourcing, global virtual teams, knowledge management, global supply chains, and other changes place demands on managers that go beyond the techniques and ideas traditionally taught in management courses. Managing in today's turbulent times requires the full breadth of management skills and capabilities. This text provides comprehensive coverage of both traditional management skills and the new competencies needed in a turbulent environment characterized by economic turmoil, political confusion, and general uncertainty.

The traditional world of work assumed the purpose of management was to control and limit people, enforce rules and regulations, seek stability and efficiency, design a top-down hierarchy to direct people, and achieve bottom-line results. To unlock innovative solutions and achieve high performance, however, managers need different skills to engage workers' hearts and minds as well as take advantage of their physical labor. The new workplace asks that managers focus on leading change, on harnessing people's creativity and enthusiasm, on finding shared visions and values, and on sharing information and power. Teamwork, collaboration, participation, and learning are guiding principles that help managers and employees maneuver the difficult terrain of today's turbulent business environment. Managers focus on developing, not controlling, people to adapt to new technologies and extraordinary environmental shifts, and thus achieve high performance and total corporate effectiveness.

My vision for the sixth edition of *Understanding Management* is to explore the newest management ideas for turbulent times in a way that is interesting and valuable to students, while retaining the best of traditional management thinking. To achieve this vision, we have included the most recent management concepts and research as well as showing the contemporary application of management ideas in organizations. We have also added a feature for "new manager" to give students a sense of what will be expected when they become managers. The combination of established scholarship, new ideas, and real-life applications gives students a taste of the energy, challenge, and adventure inherent in the dynamic field of management. The South-Western staff and we have worked together to provide a textbook better than any other at capturing the excitement of organizational management.

We revised *Understanding Management* to provide a book of utmost quality that will create in students both respect for the changing field of management and confidence that they can understand and master it. The textual portion of this book has been enhanced through the engaging, easy-to-understand writing style and the many in-text examples, boxed items, and short exercises that make the concepts come alive for students. The graphic component has been enhanced with several new exhibits and a new set of photo essays that illustrate specific management concepts. The well-chosen photographs provide vivid illustrations and intimate glimpses of management scenes, events, and people. The photos are combined with brief essays that explain how a specific management concept looks and feels. Both the textual and graphic portions of the textbook help students grasp the often abstract and distant world of management.

Spotlight on Innovation: New to the Sixth Edition

The sixth edition of *Understanding Management* is especially focused on the future of management education by identifying and describing emerging ideas and examples of innovative organizations and by providing enhanced learning opportunities for students.

Learning Opportunities

The sixth edition has taken a leap forward in pedagogical features to help students learn what it is like to manage in an organization today. New to this edition is a second New Manager Self Test in each chapter. These short feedback questionnaires give students insight into how they respond to situations and challenges typically faced by real-life managers. End of chapter questions have been thoroughly and carefully revised to encourage critical thinking and application of chapter concepts. The end-of-chapter cases and ethical dilemmas that help students sharpen their diagnostic skills for management problem solving have also been updated. This edition contains 11 new cases and 9 new ethical dilemmas. Seven additional cases and dilemmas have been substantially revised. Other new features include an advice column: Dear Dr. Dorothy, as well as an Action Learning exercises.

Organization

The chapter sequence in *Understanding Management* is organized around the management functions of planning, organizing, leading, and controlling. These four functions effectively encompass both management research and characteristics of the manager's job.

Part One introduces the world of management, including the nature of management, issues related to today's turbulent environment, the learning organization, historical perspectives on management, and the technology-driven workplace.

Part Two examines the environments of management and organizations. This section includes material on the business environment and corporate culture, the global environment, ethics and social responsibility, the natural environment, and the environment of entrepreneurship and small business management.

Part Three presents three chapters on planning, including organizational goal setting and planning, strategy formulation and implementation, and the decision-making process.

Part Four focuses on organizing processes. These chapters describe dimensions of structural design, the design alternatives managers can use to achieve strategic objectives, structural designs for promoting innovation and change, the design and use of the human resource function, and the ways managing diverse employees are significant to the organizing function.

Part Five is devoted to leadership. The section begins with a chapter on organizational behavior, providing grounding in understanding people in organizations. This foundation paves the way for subsequent discussion of leadership, motivating employees, communication, and team management.

Part Six describes the controlling function of management, including basic principles of total quality management, the design of control systems, and information technology.

Chapter Content

Within each chapter, many topics have been added or expanded to address the current issues managers face. Text content has been sharpened to provide greater focus on the key topics that count for management today.

Chapter 1 includes a new section on making the leap from being an individual contributor in the organization to becoming a new manager and getting work done primarily through others. The chapter introduces the skills and competencies needed to effectively manage organizations, including issues such as managing diversity, coping with globalization, new management thinking, historical developments, shifting world of e-business, effective management of the technology-driven workplace, and managing crises. In addition, a new section discusses the emphasis within organizations on innovation as a response to today's turbulent environment.

Chapter 2 contains an updated look at current issues related to the environment and corporate culture, including a section illustrating how managers shape a high-performance culture as an innovative response to a shifting environment.

Chapter 3 includes a new discussion of the growing power of China and India in today's global business environment, and what this means for managers around the world. In addition, the complex issues surrounding globalization are discussed, including a consideration of the current globalization backlash.

Chapter 4 has an expanded discussion of ethical challenges managers face today and the business case for incorporating ethical values in the organization. The chapter also considers global ethical issues, including a discussion of corruption rankings of various countries and a consideration of the growing sustainability movement.

Chapter 5 provides an overview of planning and goal setting, including a close look at crisis planning and how to use scenarios. The chapter's section on planning for high performance has been enhanced by a discussion of the use of executive dashboards to help managers plan in a fast-changing environment and continues its focus on the basics of formulating and implementing strategy and includes a consideration of the challenges of implementing strategy during turbulent times.

Chapter 6's overview of managerial decision making has an expanded discussion of intuition in decision making and the use of brainstorming for group decision making and has been thoroughly updated to incorporate recent trends in information technology, including user-generated content through wikis, blogs, and social networking sites. The chapter explores how these new technologies are being applied within organizations along with traditional information systems. The chapter also discusses e-commerce strategies, the growing use of business intelligence software, and how new IT affects the manager's job.

Chapter 7 discusses basic principles of organizing and describes both traditional and contemporary organization structures in detail. The chapter includes a discussion of organic versus mechanistic structures and when each is more effective, and also contains a description of the virtual network organization form.

Chapter 8 has been thoroughly updated and reorganized to reflect the critical role of managing change and innovation today. The chapter includes new or expanded material on exploration and creativity, the importance of internal and external cooperation, and the growing trend toward open innovation.

Chapter 9 includes a discussion of changes in the social contract between employers and employees. A new section looks at how organizations apply strategic human resource management to help the organization become an employer of choice to attract and retain the best human capital. The chapter has been revised and updated to reflect the most recent thinking on organizational diversity issues and looks at the challenges women and minorities face in organizations, including the current debate about women opting to leave the corporate workforce (the opt-out trend). The chapter also has an expanded discussion of using diversity training to give people the interpersonal and communication skills they need to reap the benefits of diversity.

Chapter 10 contains updated coverage related to personality traits and the use of personality and other assemssment tests in organizations. Exercises throughout the chapter enhance student understanding of organizational behavior topics and their own personalities and attitudes.

Chapter 11 has been reorganized to focus on the styles of leadership that are highly effective today. The chapter emphasizes that leadership can make a difference, often through subtle everyday actions. The discussion of power has been expanded to discuss how leaders exercise power through various interpersonal influence tactics.

Chapter 12 covers the foundations of motivation and also incorporates recent thinking about motivational tools for today, such as the importance of helping employees achieve work-life balance, incorporating fun and learning into the workplace, giving people a chance to fully participate, and helping people find meaning in their work.

Chapter 13 begins with a discussion of how managers facilitate strategic conversations by using communication to direct everyone's attention to the vision, values, and goals of the organization. The chapter explores the foundations of good communication and includes a new section on effective written communication, in recognition of the growing use of e-mail and the need for managers to write clearly and concisely.

Chapter 14 discusses how to lead work teams to effectiveness and includes a new section on using negotiation to manage conflict, including how to reach a win-win solution. The final section of the chapter takes a new look at the positive outcomes of effective teams.

Chapter 15 provides an overview of financial and quality control, including Six Sigma, ISO certification, and a new application of the balanced scorecard, which views employee learning and growth as the foundation of high performance. The chapter also addresses current concerns about corporate governance and finding a proper balance of control and autonomy for employees. The chapter also looks at productivity, lean manufacturing and reduced cycle time.

Appendices

Appendix A is a running discussion of management topics as experienced by one company as it is relevant to the material discussed in that part. Focusing on Costco, the case allows students to follow the managers' and the organizations' problems and solutions in a long-term way.

Appendix B takes a look at entrepreneurial activity on a global basis and examines the reasons entrepreneurship and small business are booming. The chapter continues its focus on practical information regarding small business formation and development, including a look at the challenges of entrepreneurial startups. In addition, a new section discusses the growing interest in *social entrepreneurship,* sometimes called social capitalism.

In addition to the topics listed above, this text integrates coverage of the Internet and new technology into the various topics covered in each chapter. Each chapter also contains a valuable application in an *Spotlight On ...* boxes. Approximately half of these boxes feature a technologically-savvy company or highlight a manager who is using technology to meet the challenges of today's environment. The other half of the *Spotlight On...* boxes describe various unique, innovative, or interesting approaches to managing people for high performance and innovative response, in recognition that human capital is essential for solving today's complex organizational problems. Each chapter also has a *Business Blooper,* describing mistakes companies have made, as well as a *Benchmarking* box, indicating top performing managers and organizations.

Innovative Features

A major goal of this book is to offer better ways of using the textbook medium to convey management knowledge to the reader. To this end, the book includes several innovative features that draw students in and help them contemplate, absorb, and comprehend management concepts. South-Western has brought together a team of experts to create and coordinate color photographs, video cases, beautiful artwork, and supplemental materials for the best management textbook and package on the market.

Chapter Outline and Objectives. Each chapter begins with a clear statement of its learning objectives and an outline of its contents. These devices provide an overview of what is to come and can also be used by students to guide their study and test their understanding and retention of important points.

New Manager's Questions. The text portion of each chapter begins with three questions faced by organization managers. The questions pertain to the topics of the chapter and will heighten students' interest in chapter concepts. In the part of the text relevant to that question, the answer will be given, so that students can compare the "correct" answer to the ones they gave at the beginning of the chapter.

Take Action. The Take Action feature has expanded throughout the chapter. This feature provides a call to action that helps students apply the concepts discussed in the text and see how they would use the idea as a practicing manager. Some of the Take Action features also refer students to the associated New Manager Self Tests, or direct students from the chapter content to relevant end of chapter materials, such as an experiential exercise or an ethical dilemma.

New Manager Self Tests. Two New Manager Self Tests in each chapter of the text provides opportunities for self-assessment and a way for students to experience management issues in a personal way. The change from individual performer to new manager is dramatic, and these self tests provide insight into what to expect and how students might perform in the world of the new manager.

Concept Connection Photo Essays. A key feature of the book is the use of photographs accompanied by detailed photo essay captions that enhance learning. Each caption highlights and illustrates one or more specific concepts from the text to reinforce student understanding of the concepts. While the photos are beautiful to look at, they also convey the vividness, immediacy, and concreteness of management events in today's business world.

Contemporary Examples. Every chapter of the text contains a large number of written examples of management incidents. They are placed at strategic points in the chapter and are designed to illustrate the application of concepts to specific companies. These in-text examples—indicated by an icon in the margin—include well-known U.S. and international companies such as Sony, UPS, Kraft Foods, Lenova, Wal-Mart, BMW, eBay, and LG Electronics, as well as less-well-known companies and not-for-profit organizations such as Remploy Ltd. and Strida (United Kingdom), Barbara K! Enterprises and Manchester Bidwell (U.S.), Esquel Group (Hong Kong), Unión Fenosa (Spain), Mississippi Power Company, the *Los Angeles Times,* and the U.S. Federal Bureau of Investigation (FBI). These examples put students in touch with the real world of organizations so that they can appreciate the value of management concepts.

Spotlight on… Boxes. These features address a specific topic straight from the field of management that is of special interest to students. These boxes may describe a contemporary topic or problem that is relevant to chapter content or they may contain a diagnostic questionnaire or a special example of how managers handle a problem. The boxes heighten student interest in the subject matter and provide an auxiliary view of management issues not typically available in textbooks.

Benchmarking Boxes. Each chapter contains a box that highlights some effective and productive technique or system developed by an outstanding manager or company.

Business Blooper. While most of the book gives students insights into effective management behavior, forgetting common mistakes can be a real loss. Therefore, each chapter describes ineffective decisions or behaviors which have led to disastrous outcomes in companies.

Video Cases. Each chapter conclude with video cases that illustrate the concepts presented in that part. The videos enhance class discussion because students can see the direct application of the management theories they have learned. Companies discussed in the video package include Yahoo, Caterpillar, Cold Stone Creamery, Ford, McDonalds and Allstate. Each video case explores the issues covered in the video, allowing students to synthesize the material they've just viewed. The video cases culminate with several questions that can be used to launch classroom discussion or as homework.

Exhibits. Many aspects of management are research based, and some concepts tend to be abstract and theoretical. To enhance students' awareness and understanding of these concepts, many exhibits have been included throughout the book. These exhibits consolidate key points, indicate relationships among concepts, and visually illustrate concepts. They also make effective use of color to enhance their imagery and appeal.

Glossaries. Learning the management vocabulary is essential to understanding contemporary management. This process is facilitated in three ways. First, key concepts are boldfaced and completely defined where they first appear in the text. Second, brief definitions are set out in the margin for easy review and follow-up. Third, a glossary summarizing all key terms and definitions appears at the end of the book for handy reference.

Chapter Summary and Discussion Questions. Each chapter closes with a summary of key points that students should retain. The discussion questions are a complementary learning tool that will enable students to check their understanding of key issues, to think beyond basic concepts, and to determine areas that require further study. The summary and discussion questions help students discriminate between main and supporting points and provide mechanisms for self-teaching.

End of Chapter Application Opportunities. End-of-chapter exercises called Self Learning, Action Learning, Group Learning and Ethical Dilemma provide opportunities for content application. Students can take self-tests, providng an opportunity to experience management issues in a personal way. These exercises take the form of questionnaires, scenarios, and activities, and many also provide an opportunity for students to work in teams. There are seven new ethical dilemmas in this edition. The exercises are tied into the chapter through the "Take Action" feature that refers students to the end-of-chapter exercises at the appropriate point in the chapter content.

Case for Critical Analysis. Also appearing at the end of each chapter is a brief but substantive case that provides an opportunity for student analysis and class discussion. Some of these cases are about companies whose names students will recognize; others are based on real management events but the identities of companies and managers have been disguised. These cases allow students to sharpen their diagnostic skills for management problem solving. There are eleven new cases in this edition.

Supplementary Materials

Instructor's Manual. Designed to provide support for instructors new to the course, as well as innovative materials for experienced professors, the Instructor's Manual includes Chapter Outlines, annotated learning objectives, Lecture Notes and sample Lecture Outlines. Additionally, the Instructor's Manual includes answers and teaching notes to end of chapter materials, including the continuing case. Each chapter also contains a comprehensive guide for incorporating each of the media elements into the classroom.

Instructor's CD-ROM. Key instructor ancillaries (Instructor's Manual, Test Bank, ExamView and PowerPoint slides) are provided on CD-ROM, giving instructors the ultimate tool for customizing lectures and presentations.

Test Bank. Scrutinized for accuracy, the Test Bank includes more than 2,000 true/false, multiple choice, short answer, and essay questions. Page references are indicated for every question, as are designations of either factual or application so that instructors can provide a balanced set of questions for student exams.

ExamView. Available on the Instructor's Resource CD-ROM, ExamView contains all of the questions in the printed Test Bank. This program is an easy-to-use test creation software compatible with Microsoft Windows. Instructors can add or edit questions, instructions, and answers, and select questions (randomly or numerically) by previewing them on the screen. Instructors can also create and administer quizzes online, whether over the Internet, a local area network (LAN), or a wide area network (WAN).

PowerPoint Lecture Presentation. Available on the Instructor's Resource CD-ROM and the Web site, the PowerPoint Lecture Presentation enables instructors to customize their own multimedia classroom presentation. Containing approximately 350 slides, the package includes figures and tables from the text, as well as outside materials to supplement chapter concepts. Material is organized by chapter, and can be modified or expanded for individual classroom use. PowerPoint slides are also easily printed to create customized Transparency Masters.

JoinIn™ on TurningPoint®. Create a truly interactive classroom environment with this audience response system that operates in conjunction with your PowerPoint presentations. Students can respond to questions, short polls, interactive exercises, or peer review questions. Use this unique tool to take attendance, check student understanding, collect student demographics, and more.

Study Guide. Packed with real-world examples and additional applications for helping students master management concepts, this learning supplement is an excellent resource. For each chapter of the text, the Study Guide includes a summary and completion exercise; a review with multiple choice, true/false, and short answer questions; a mini case with multiple choice questions; management applications; and an experiential exercise that can be assigned as homework or used in class.

Video Package. The video package for *Understanding Management,* 6th Edition, contains On the Job videos created specifically for the 6th edition. Clips are supported by short cases and discussion questions at the end of each chapter. On the Job videos utilize real-world companies to illustrate management concepts as outlined in the text. Focusing on both small and large business, the videos give students an inside perspective on the situations and issues that corporations face. Video cases reinforce what the student has just seen, and provide an opportunity for critical analysis and discussion. Additionally, BizFlix are film clips taken from popular Hollywood movies and integrated into the Sixth Edition.

CengageNOW™ **for Understanding Management.** Discover the ultimate flexibility and control as this fully integrated online teaching and learning system designed by instructors for instructors NOW saves you valuable time and ensures impressive student results. *CengageNOW*™ provides a comprehensive suite of the best in services and resources to help you: Efficiently **plan** your course and student assignments; easily **manage** your gradebook and compare to the latest from AACSB; **teach** with the latest built-in technology, including new videos; **reinforce** understanding with personalized study paths and built-in self-assessments; instantly **assess** students with a customizable test bank that's tagged to AACSB standards to clearly demonstrate how student performance compares to AACSB requirements; and automatically **grade** assignments and compare to **AACSB** requirements. *CengageNOW*™ helps you ensure student comprehension with personalized study paths and built-in self-assessments. A variety of multimedia tools address the variety of learning styles inherent within today's diversity of students. With the proper tools, students take responsibility for their own progress.

Web site (academic.cengage.com/management/daft). Discover a rich array of online teaching and learning management resources that you won't find anywhere else, including interactive learning tools, links to critical management websites, and password-protected teaching resources available for download.

WebTutor is an interactive, web-based, student supplement on WebCT and/or Black-Board that harnesses the power of the Internet to deliver innovative learning aids that actively engage students. The instructor can incorporate WebTutor as an integral part of the course, or the students can use it on their own as a study guide. Benefits to students include automatic and immediate feedback from quizzes and exams; interactive, multimedia rich explanation of concepts; online exercises that reinforce what they've learned; flashcards that include audio support; and greater interaction and involvement through online discussion forums.

Acknowledgments

A gratifying experience for us was working with the team of dedicated professionals at South-Western who were committed to the vision of producing the best management text ever. I am grateful to Joe Sabatino, Executive Editor, whose enthusiasm, creative ideas, assistance, and vision kept this book's spirit alive. Emma Newsom, Managing Developmental Editor, provided superb project coordination and offered excellent ideas and suggestions to help the team meet a demanding and sometimes arduous schedule. Clint Kernen, Marketing Manager, provided keen market knowledge and innovative ideas for instructional support. Jacquelyn Featherly, Content Project Manager, cheerfully and expertly guided me through the production process. Tippy McIntosh contributed her graphic arts skills to create a visually dynamic design. Ruth Belanger, Editorial Assistant, and Sarah Rose, Marketing Coordinator, skillfully pitched in to help keep the project on track. Lynn Lustberg and the team at ICC Macmillan, Inc. deserve a special thank you for their layout expertise and commitment to producing an attractive, high-quality textbook. Jane Woodside skillfully researched and wrote the superb Part Opening features.

Here at Vanderbilt I want to extend special appreciation to my assistant, Barbara Haselton. Barbara provided excellent support and assistance on a variety of projects that gave me time to write. I also want to acknowledge an intellectual debt to my colleagues, Bruce Barry, Ray Friedman, Neta Moye, Rich Oliver, David Owens, Bart Victor, and Tim Vogus. Thanks also to Deans Jim Bradfordand Joe Blackburn who have supported my writing projects and maintained a positive scholarly atmosphere in the school. Special thanks also go to Pat Lane for her continued commitment to the success of these projects. Finally, I want to acknowledge the love and contributions of my wife, Dorothy Marcic. Dorothy has been very supportive during this revision as we share our lives together. I also want to acknowledge my love and support for my five daughters, Danielle, Amy, Roxanne, Solange, and Elizabeth, who make my life special during our precious time together. Thanks also to B. J. and Kaitlyn, and Kaci and Matthew for their warmth and smiles that brighten my life, especially during our days together skiing and on the beach.

R.L.D.

There have been numerous people who have given time and support on this project, including my assistants, Adrienne Ewing-Roush, Karl Cronin and Allison Greer. Friends who gave invaluable support include Peter Neamann, Victoria Marsick, Bob and Debby Rosenfeld, Karen Streets-Anderson, Kathy Diaz, Andi Seals, Adrienne Corn, Mark and Maxine Rossman, Mehr Mansuri, Annie Deardorff, Michael Heitzler, and Shidan Majidi. How can one do such a project without family love and support. My sister, Janet Mittelsteadt is a true friend; my cousins: Marilyn Nowak is a bright light, Michael Shoemaker is the genealogist who has helped me find my own roots, and Katherine Runde is so precious; my Aunt Babe is forever a link to the past. There is no way to imagine my life without my three beautiful daughters: Roxanne, Solange, and Elizabeth, who have taught me more than all my degrees combined. And finally, my husband and partner, Dick Daft, whose collaboration on this book indicates one aspect of our unity and connection.

D. M.

Another group of people who made a major contribution to this textbook are the management experts who provided advice, reviews, answers to questions, and suggestions for changes, insertions, and clarifications. I want to thank each of these colleagues for their valuable feedback and suggestions:

David C. Adams
Manhattanville College

Erin M. Alexander
University of Houston, Clear Lake

Hal Babson
Columbus State Community College

Reuel Barksdale
Columbus State Community College

Gloria Bemben
Finger Lakes Community College

Pat Bernson
County College of Morris

Art Bethke
Northeast Louisiana University

Katharine Bohley
University of Indianapolis

Thomas Butte
Humboldt State University

Peter Bycio
Xavier University, Ohio

Diane Caggiano
Fitchburg State College

Douglas E. Cathon
St. Augustine's College

Jim Ciminskie
Bay de Noc Community College

Dan Connaughton
University of Florida

Bruce Conwers
Kaskaskia College

Byron L. David
The City College of New York

Richard De Luca
William Paterson University

Robert DeDominic
Montana Tech

Sally Dresdow
University of Wisconsin–Green Bay

Diane Duca
Central Washington University

Linn Van Dyne
Michigan State University

Janice Edwards
College of the Rockies

John C. Edwards
East Carolina University

Mary Ann Edwards
College of Mount St. Joseph

Janice M. Feldbauer
Austin Community College

Daryl Fortin
Upper Iowa University

Michael P. Gagnon
New Hampshire Community Technical College

Richard H. Gayor
Antelope Valley College

Dan Geeding
Xavier University, Ohio

James Genseal
Joliet Junior College

Peter Gibson
Becker College

Carol R. Graham
Western Kentucky University

Gary Greene
Manatee Community College

Ken Harris
Indiana University Southeast

Paul Hayes
Coastal Carolina Community College

Dennis Heaton
Maharishi University of Management, Iowa

Jeffrey D. Hines
Davenport College

Bob Hoerber
Westminster College

James N. Holly
University of Wisconsin–Green Bay

Genelle Jacobson
Ridgewater College

C. Joy Jones
Ohio Valley College

Kathleen Jones
University of North Dakota

Sheryl Kae
Lynchburg College

Jordan J. Kaplan
Long Island University

J. Michael Keenan
Western Michigan University

Mary Beth Klinger
College of Southern Maryland

Gloria Komer
Stark State College

Paula C. Kougl
Western Oregon University

Cynthia Krom
Mount St. Mary College

Mukta Kulkarni
University of Texas—San Antonio

William B. Lamb
Millsaps College

Robert E. Ledman
Morehouse College

George Lehma
Bluffton College

Cynthia Lengnick-Hall
University of Texas—San Antonio

Janet C. Luke
Georgia Baptist College of Nursing

Jenna Lundburg
Ithaca College

Walter J. MacMillan
Oral Roberts University

Myrna P. Mandell
California State University, Northridge

Daniel B. Marin
Louisiana State University

Michael Market
Jacksonville State University

Joseph Martelli
University of Findlay

Rachel Mather
Adelphi University

James C. McElroy
Iowa State University

Dennis W. Meyers
Texas State Technical College

Alan N. Miller
University of Nevada, Las Vegas

Irene A. Miller
Southern Illinois University

Micah Mukabi
Essex County College

David W. Murphy
Madisonville Community College

James L. Moseley
Wayne State University

Nora Nurre
Upper Iowa University

Nelson Ocf
Pacific University

Tomas J. Ogazon
St. Thomas University

Alla L. Wilson
University of Wisconsin–Green Bay

Ignatius Yacomb
Loma Linda University

Imad Jim Zbib
Ramapo College of New Jersey

Vic Zimmerman
Pima Community College

Richard L. Daft
Nashville, Tennessee
December 2006

About the Authors

Richard L. Daft, Ph.D., is the Brownlee O. Currey, Jr., Professor of Management in the Owen Graduate School of Management at Vanderbilt University. Professor Daft specializes in the study of organization theory and leadership. Dr. Daft is a Fellow of the Academy of Management and has served on the editorial boards of *Academy of Management Journal, Administrative Science Quarterly,* and *Journal of Management Education.* He was the Associate Editor-in-Chief of *Organization Science* and served for three years as associate editor of *Administrative Science Quarterly.*

Professor Daft has authored or co-authored 12 books, including *Organization Theory and Design* (South-Western, 2007), *The Leadership Experience* (South-Western, 2008) and *What to Study: Generating and Developing Research Questions* (Sage, 1982). He recently published *Fusion Leadership: Unlocking the Subtle Forces That Change People and Organizations* (Berrett-Koehler, 2000, with Robert Lengel). He has also authored dozens of scholarly articles, papers, and chapters. His work has been published in *Administrative Science Quarterly, Academy of Management Journal, Academy of Management Review, Strategic Management Journal, Journal of Management, Accounting Organizations and Society, Management Science, MIS Quarterly, California Management Review,* and *Organizational Behavior Teaching Review.* Professor Daft has been awarded several government research grants to pursue studies of organization design, organizational innovation and change, strategy implementation, and organizational information processing.

Dr. Daft is an active teacher and consultant and has direct management experience. He has taught management, leadership, organizational change, organizational theory, and organizational behavior. He served as associate dean, has been a theatrical producer, and helped manage a start up enterprise. He has been involved in management development and consulting for many companies and government organizations including the American Banking Association, Bell Canada, the National Transportation Research Board, NL Baroid, Nortel, TVA, Pratt & Whitney, State Farm Insurance, Tenneco, the United States Air Force, the U.S. Army, J. C. Bradford & Co., Central Parking System, Entergy Sales and Service, Bristol-Myers Squibb, First American National Bank, and the Vanderbilt University Medical Center.

Dorothy Marcic, Ed.D and M.P.H, is a former faculty member at Vanderbilt University. Dr. Marcic is also a former Fulbright Scholar at the University of Economics in Prague and the Czech Management Center, where she taught courses and did research in leadership, organizational behavior, and cross-cultural management. She teaches courses at the Monterrey Institute of International Studies and the University of Economics, in Prague, and has taught courses or given presentations at the Helsinki School of Economics, Slovenia Management Center, College of Trade in Bulgaria, City University of Slovakia, Landegg Institute in Switzerland, the Swedish Management Association, Technion University in Israel, and the London School of Economics. Other international work includes projects at the Autonomous University in Guadalajara, Mexico, and a training program for the World Health Organization in Guatemala. She has served on the boards of the Organizational Teaching Society, the Health Administration Section of the American Public Health Association, and the Journal of Applied Business Research.

Dr. Marcic has authored 12 books, including *Organizational Behavior: Experiences and Cases* (South-Western Publishing, 6th Edition, 2001), *Management International* (West

Publishing, 1984), *Women and Men in Organizations* (George Washington University, 1984), and *Managing with the Wisdom of Love: Uncovering Virtue in People and Organizations* (Jossey-Bass, 1997), which was rated one of the top ten business books of 1997 by *Management General.* In addition, she has had dozens of articles printed in such publications as *Journal of Management Development, International Quarterly of Community Health Education, Psychological Reports,* and *Executive Development.* She has recently been exploring how to use the arts in the teaching of leadership and has a new book, *RESPECT: Women and Popular Music* (Texere, 2002), the basis for the musical theater production, Respect: A Musical Journey of Women.

Professor Marcic has conducted hundreds of seminars on various business topics and consulted for executives at AT&T Bell Labs; the Governor and Cabinet of North Dakota; the US Air Force; Slovak Management Association; Eurotel; Czech Ministry of Finance; the Cattaraugus Center; USAA Insurance; State Farm Insurance; and the Salt River-Pima Indian Tribe in Arizona.

Brief Contents

Contents

chapter 11   Leadership   408

Appendices

UNDERSTANDING
MANAGEMENT

PART 1

Introduction

Entertainment industry managers have always faced special challenges. Today the digital revolution is profoundly affecting the entire industry, making an already challenging environment even more uncertain. That's because virtually anyone with a computer and Internet access can send high-quality copies of video and audio around the world quickly and cheaply.

The entertainment industry has long made its profits by turning out blockbusters designed to draw huge audiences. However, it's impossible to predict which specific projects will appeal to the often fickle masses. So entertainment industry managers have long spent much of their time overseeing (and surviving) failure.

Journalist Chris Anderson argues in *The Long Tail* that digital age businesses will make their money by offering lots and lots of products, knowing that nearly each and every one will appeal to at least one person. The big money will be in small sales. So the Long Tail theory stands the entertainment industry's current blockbuster-driven business model on its head.

High-performance entertainment industry managers will need to draw on all of their skills as they problem-solve and attempt to seize opportunities in their particularly turbulent, ever-shifting industry.

chapter 1
Innovation for Turbulent Times

Learning Objectives

After studying this chapter, you should be able to:

1 Define *management* and *organization*.

2 Describe the skills needed by an effective manager, and the functions of planning, organizing, leading, and controlling.

3 Understand the personal challenges involved in becoming a new manager in an organization in today's world.

4 Define the roles that managers perform in organizations.

5 Discuss the management competencies needed to deal with today's turbulent environment, including issues such as diversity, globalization, and rapid change.

6 Describe the unique considerations of management in small business and nonprofit organizations.

7 Point out the technological forces affecting organizations.

8 Delineate the new management competencies and how leadership is viewed today.

9 Describe how to management crises and unexpected events.

10 Define *e-business* and *e-commerce*.

11 Understand and explain the ERP and CRM styles.

12 In the context of history, describe the social, political, and economic forces shaping today's management practice.

New Manager's Questions

Please circle your opinion below each of the following statements.

Assess Your Answer

1 I would rather be in a wildly talented rock band with an average manager than a band with above-average talent but outstanding management.

1	2	3	4	5
strongly agree				strongly disagree

2 If I were a manager, the most important part of my job would be to make sure that the company was profitable.

1	2	3	4	5
strongly agree				strongly disagree

3 As the manager in a crisis, I would try to "spin" the truth to make the company look good to customers and investors.

1	2	3	4	5
strongly agree				strongly disagree

In today's turbulent world, managing in times of crisis and confusion is becoming a critical skill for managers in all kinds of organizations, not just companies that have to restore power after a hurricane. Many managers deal with uncertainty and crisis to a lesser extent almost daily. Consider the strife and confusion in the music industry, where traditional recording labels and music stores are battling with the iPod and with online file sharing services that let people download music for free. The once-hot Tower Records declared bankruptcy because of the steep decline in music sales through traditional stores.[1]

Managers in all organizations deal with uncertainty and unexpected events, whether it is something as minor as the loss of a key employee or something as dramatic as a plant explosion. Moreover, the frequency and intensity of crises have increased over the past couple of decades, with a sharp rise in the rate of intentional acts such as product tampering, workplace violence, and terrorism.[2] Solid management skills and actions are keys to helping any organization weather a crisis and remain healthy, inspired, and productive.

The nature of management is to cope with diverse and far-reaching challenges. Managers have to keep pace with ever-advancing technology, find ways to incorporate the Internet and e-business into their strategies and business models, and strive to remain competitive in the face of increasingly tough global competition, uncertain environments, cutbacks in personnel and resources, and massive worldwide economic, political, and social shifts. The growing clout, expertise, and efficiency of China and India, in particular, have many U.S. companies worried. To gain or keep a competitive edge, companies have renewed their emphasis on innovation, shifting from a relentless focus on controlling costs toward investing in the future. In a survey of nearly 1,000 executives in North America, Europe, South America, and Asia, 86 percent agreed that "innovation is more important than cost reduction for long-term success."[3]

The shift toward new ways of working, enabled by technology, places additional demands on today's managers. Many employees are perpetually on the move, juggling laptops, mobile phones, and BlackBerries to keep in electronic touch with customers, teammates, and managers with limited face-to-face contact. In the new world of work, managers need a new approach that relies less on command and control and more on coordination and communication. The field of management is undergoing a revolution that asks managers to do more with less, to engage whole employees, to see change rather than stability as the nature of things, and to inspire vision and cultural values that allow people to create a truly collaborative and productive workplace. This approach differs significantly from a traditional mind-set that emphasizes tight top-down control, employee separation and specialization, and management by impersonal measurement and analysis.

Making a difference as a manager today and tomorrow requires the integration of solid, tried-and-true management skills with innovative approaches that emphasize the human touch, enhance flexibility, and engage employees' hearts and minds as well as their bodies. Successful departments and organizations don't just happen. They are managed to be that way. Managers in every organization have the opportunity to make a difference. For example, Heather Coin made a difference in the Sherman Oaks, California, branch of The Cheesecake Factory when she implemented management changes that reduced turnover from 25 percent to below 10 percent and dramatically increased customer traffic to serve as many as 16,000 customers a week.[4]

And the success of rock groups from the Rolling Stones to U2 to Green Day relies not just on good songs, musical talent, and performance skills but also on solid business management. "We always said it would be pathetic to be good at the music and bad at the business," said Paul McGuinness, U2's band manager. After nearly three decades the Irish rock band is still selling out concerts and moving millions of albums a year by paying attention to some business basics, such as forming a partnership with Apple for a special-edition iPod and collaborating with iTunes to produce the industry's first downloadable version of a box sets.[5] Ray Benson, leader of the Asleep at the Wheel band, learned that he had to balance the

Spotlight on Skills

Asleep at the Wheel

Ray Benson's nine Grammy awards didn't help him keep his band, Asleep at the Wheel, in good financial condition. His creativity and musical abilities weren't enough, he realized. His insight and motivation allowed him to upgrade and transform the band 37 years after it formed.

The Wheel (as its fans call the band) had its first hit in 1975 with a country song, and it opened for big acts such as Tammy Wynette. Famous people heard the band, and *Rolling Stone Magazine* featured an article with the expectation that it would continue. So, like other music stars, Benson spent a lot of money—not on himself, but on the band, which grew to 12 members. "I grossed $1 million and was in debt," he said. "Something wasn't right." Still, Benson bought a recording studio—and attracted big names like Willie Nelson to record there.

Then disco came and the band went. It was a dismal time. The band hit bottom in 2001 when Benson's practice of co-mingling his money with the band's money resulted in big problems when he divorced his wife, who also was the band's business manager. The search for a new manager led to his hiring Peter Schwartz,

who had decade-long experience in a Cajun band. While still a band member, Schwartz's wife went for an MBA. "It shocked me that a traditional business education would address issues important to me in running a band," Peter Schwartz noted. That's when he pursued his own MBA at Harvard.

Schwartz's first tasks were to return the band to an ensemble band—its core mission—and to exploit its niche appeal. He now uses "straight MBS stuff" combined with Benson's creativity. "My job is to guide him in what ideas are going to stick," said Schwartz. "How big is the audience? Is there money in it? In the music business, there really isn't that rigor."

Owning the studio has helped cut production costs and allowed The Wheel to create its own label, with the band finally earning well-deserved royalties, even though sales are less than before. "There are 150,000 people who are passionate enough to spend $100 a year on The Wheel. The Internet allows us to capture that."

Schwartz and Benson teamed to mount a theatrical version of the band and got sponsors to underwrite grants of $700,000. All ticket sales go to the band. Benson finally started making decent money. And it took only 37 years and MBA skills.

SOURCE: Roy Furchgott, "The Band Struts Again, Under an MBA Baton," *The New York Times* (May 16, 2007): H6.

band's creativity with some down-to-earth business sense, as shown in the Spotlight on Skills.

> I would rather be in a wildly talented rock band with an average manager than a band with above-average talent but outstanding management.
>
> ANSWER: It is better to have a stellar management team, as both U2 and Asleep at the Wheel found out.

Assess Your Answer

Managers like these are not unusual. Every day, managers solve difficult problems, turn organizations around, and achieve astonishing performances. To be successful, every organization needs skilled managers.

This textbook introduces and explains the process of management and the changing ways of thinking about the world that are becoming vital for managers of today and tomorrow. By reviewing the actions of some successful and not-so-successful managers, you will learn the fundamentals of management. By the end of this chapter, you will recognize some of the skills that managers use to keep organizations on track, and you will begin to see how managers can achieve astonishing results. By the end of the book, you will understand fundamental management skills for planning, organizing, leading, and controlling a department or an entire organization.

◀ TAKE ACTION

Become a better manager of yourself: Meet deadlines, balance the needs of different courses, and manage a positive relationship with your professors.

CONCEPT CONNECTION

If ever a business emerged out of crisis, it is New York City's Colors, a project of the Restaurant Opportunities Center. Many of the restaurant's employee-owners, immigrants hailing from about 25 different nations, worked in the World Trade Center's North Tower restaurant, Windows on the World, before its destruction on September 11, 2001. They share a strong commitment to a mission of honoring the 73 Windows employees who died, and improving the restaurant industry's working conditions. Yet, good management is necessary to keep people motivated, focused, and productive. **General manager** Stefan Mailvaganam, shown here with head chef Raymond Mohan, says the goal of Colors is to be "a restaurant with a conscience."

In the remainder of this chapter, we will define management and look at the ways in which roles and activities are changing for today's managers. Finally, we will talk about a new kind of workplace that has evolved as a result of changes in technology, globalization, and other forces, and examine how managers can meet the challenges of this new environment.

The Definition of Management

What do managers such as Heather Coin and Paul McGuinness have in common? They get things done through their organizations. Managers create the systems, conditions, and environments that enable organizations to survive and thrive beyond the tenure of any specific supervisor or manager. Jack Welch was CEO of General Electric through 20 amazingly successful years, and some observers worried that GE would falter without him after he left. Yet, the leadership transition to Jeff Immelt in 2001 was as smooth as silk, and in 2005–06 GE once again topped *Fortune* magazine's list of "Most Admired Companies," as well as ranking number one on the *Financial Times'* "Most Respected" survey and *Barron's* ranking of most admired companies.

management
the attainment of organizational goals in an effective and efficient manner through planning, organizing, leading, and controlling organizational resources.

People who have studied GE aren't surprised. The company has thrived for more than a century because managers throughout the years created the ideal environment and conditions: a shared sense of purpose and pride, a passion for change and willingness to take risks, and, most important, an obsession with people and making them the best they can be.

planning
the management function concerned with defining goals for future organizational performance and deciding on the tasks and resources needed to attain them.

The commitment to developing leaders at all levels began in the late 1800s with CEO Charles Coffin, who emphasized that GE's most important product was not lightbulbs or transformers but, rather, managerial talent. Every manager at GE is required to spend a huge amount of time on human resources issues—recruiting, training, appraising, mentoring, and developing leadership talent for the future.[6]

organizing
the management function concerned with assigning tasks, grouping tasks into departments, and allocating resources to departments.

A key aspect of managing is to recognize the role and importance of other people. Early twentieth-century management scholar Mary Parker Follett defined management as "the art of getting things done through people."[7]

More recently, noted management theorist Peter Drucker stated that the job of managers is to give direction to their organizations, provide leadership, and decide how to use organizational resources to accomplish goals.[8] Getting things done through people and other resources and providing leadership and direction are what managers do. These activities apply to top executives such as Bill Gates of Microsoft and Steve Jobs of Apple but also to the leader of an airport security team, a supervisor of an accounting department, or a director of sales and marketing. Moreover, management often is considered universal because it uses organizational resources to accomplish goals and attain high performance in all types of profit and nonprofit organizations.

leading
the management function that involves the use of influence to motivate employees to achieve the organization's goals.

controlling
the management function concerned with monitoring employees' activities, keeping the organization on track toward its goals, and making corrections as needed.

Thus, our definition of **management** is: the attainment of organizational goals in an effective and efficient manner through planning, organizing, leading, and controlling organizational resources. This definition holds two important ideas: (1) the four functions of **planning, organizing, leading,** and **controlling,** and (2) the attainment of organizational goals in an effective and efficient manner. Managers use a multitude of skills to perform these

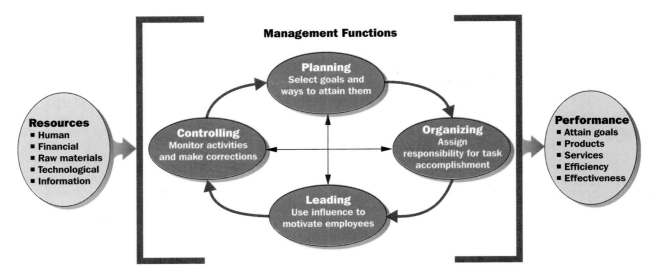

EXHIBIT 1.1

The Process of
Management

functions. Management's conceptual, human, and technical skills are discussed later in the chapter. Exhibit 1.1 illustrates the process of how managers use resources to attain organizational goals. Although some management theorists identify additional management functions, such as staffing, communicating, or decision making, those additional functions will be discussed as subsets of the four primary functions in Exhibit 1.1. Chapters of this book are devoted to the multiple activities and skills associated with each function, as well as to the environment, global competitiveness, and ethics, which influence how managers perform these functions.

Organizational Performance

The definition of management includes the attainment of organizational goals in an efficient and effective manner. Management is important because organizations are important. In an industrialized society where complex technologies dominate, organizations bring together knowledge, people, and raw materials to perform tasks no individual could do alone. Without organizations, how could technology be provided that enables us to share information around the world in an instant; or electricity be produced from huge dams and nuclear power plants; or thousands of videogames, compact discs, and DVDs be made available for our entertainment?

Organizations pervade our society. Most college students will work in an organization— perhaps Cingular Wireless, Toronto General Hospital, Office Depot, or Hollywood Video. College students already are members of several organizations, such as a university or a junior college, YMCA, church, fraternity, or sorority. College students also deal with organizations every day—to renew a driver's license, be treated in a hospital emergency room, buy food from a supermarket, eat in a restaurant, or purchase new clothes. Managers are responsible for these organizations and for seeing that resources are used wisely to attain organizational goals.

Our formal definition of an **organization** is a social entity that is goal-directed and deliberately structured. *Social entity* means being made up of two or more people. *Goal-directed* means designed to achieve some outcome, such as to make a profit (for example, Old Navy, Starbucks), to win pay increases for members (AFL-CIO), to meet spiritual needs (say, the United Methodist Church), or provide social satisfaction (a college sorority, for instance).

◀ **TAKE ACTION**

As a new manager, remember that management means getting things done through other people. You can't do it all yourself. As a manager, your job is to create the environment and conditions that engage other people in goal accomplishment.

organization
a social entity that is goal-directed and deliberately structured.

Deliberately structured means that tasks are divided and responsibility for their performance is assigned to organization members. This definition applies to all organizations, including both profit and nonprofit. Small, offbeat, and nonprofit organizations are more numerous than large, visible corporations—and just as important to society.

Based on our definition of management, the manager's responsibility is to coordinate resources in an effective and efficient manner to accomplish the organization's goals. Organizational **effectiveness** is the extent to which the organization achieves a *stated goal*, or succeeds in accomplishing what it tries to do. Organizational effectiveness means providing a product or service that customers value.

Organizational **efficiency** refers to the amount of resources used to achieve an organizational goal. It is based on how much raw material, money, and people are necessary for producing a given volume of output. Efficiency can be calculated as the amount of resources used to produce a product or service.

Efficiency and effectiveness can both be at high levels in the same organization. During the tough economy of the early 2000s, companies such as Eaton Corporation, which makes hydraulic and electrical devices, struggled to wring as much production as it could from scaled-back factories and a reduced workforce. Managers initiated process improvements, outsourced some work to companies that could do it cheaper, streamlined ordering and shipping procedures, and shifted work to the most efficient assembly lines. At Eaton, these adjustments enabled the company to cut costs and hold the line on prices as well as meet its quality and output goals.[9]

Sometimes, however, managers' efforts to improve efficiency can hurt organizational effectiveness, especially in relation to severe cost-cutting. Some years ago, a former CEO at Delta Airlines dramatically increased cost efficiency by cutting spending on personnel, food, cleaning, and maintenance. These moves temporarily rescued the company from a financial tailspin, but they also precluded Delta from meeting its effectiveness goals. The airline fell to last place among major carriers in on-time performance, the morale of employees sank, and customer complaints about dirty planes and long lines at ticket counters increased by more than 75 percent.[10]

The ultimate responsibility of managers is to achieve high **performance.** This means the attainment of organizational goals by using resources in an efficient and effective manner.

Management Skills

A manager's job is complex and multidimensional and, as we shall see throughout this book, requires a range of skills. Although some management theorists propose a long list of skills, the necessary skills for managing a department or an organization can be summarized in three categories: conceptual, human, and technical.[11] As illustrated in Exhibit 1.2, the application of these skills changes as managers move up in the

effectiveness
the extent to which the organization achieves a stated goal.

efficiency
the use of minimal resources—raw materials, money, and people—to produce a desired volume of output.

performance
the organization's ability to attain its goals by using resources in an efficient and effective manner.

Management Level
Top Managers

Middle Managers

First-Line Managers

Nonmanagers (Individual Contributors)

| Conceptual Skills | Human Skills | Technical Skills |

EXHIBIT 1.2
Relationship of Conceptual, Human, and Technical Skills to Management

organization. Although the degree of each skill necessary at different levels of an organization varies, all managers must possess skills in each of these important areas to perform effectively.

Management Functions

Managers use conceptual, human, and technical skills to perform the four management functions of planning, organizing, leading, and controlling in all organizations—large and small, manufacturing and service, profit and nonprofit, traditional and Internet-based. But not all managers' jobs are the same. Managers are responsible for different departments, work at different levels in the hierarchy, and meet different requirements for achieving high performance.

Twenty-five-year-old Daniel Wheeler is a **first-line** manager in his first management job at Del Monte Foods, where he is involved directly in promoting products, approving packaging sleeves, and organizing sampling events.[12] Kevin Kurtz is a **middle manager** at Lucasfilm, where he works with employees to develop marketing campaigns for some of the entertainment company's hottest films.[13] Domenic Antonellis is CEO of the New England Confectionary Co. (Necco), the company that makes those tiny pastel candy hearts stamped with phrases such as "Be Mine" and "Kiss Me."[14] All three are managers and must contribute to planning, organizing, leading, and controlling their organizations—but in different amounts and ways.

During turbulent times, managers really have to stay on their toes and use all their skills and competencies to benefit the organization and its stakeholders—employees, customers, investors, the community, and so forth. In recent years, numerous, highly publicized examples showed us what happens when managers fail to effectively and ethically apply their skills to meet the demands of an uncertain, rapidly changing world. Companies such as Enron, Tyco, and WorldCom were flying high in the 1990s but came crashing down under the weight of financial scandals. Others, such as Rubbermaid, Kmart, and Xerox, are struggling because of years of management missteps.

Although corporate greed and deceit grab the headlines, many more companies falter or fail less spectacularly. Managers fail to listen to customers, misinterpret signals from the marketplace, or can't build a cohesive team and execute a strategic plan. Over the past several years numerous CEOs, including Carly Fiorina at Hewlett-Packard, Michael Eisner at Disney, and David Pottruck at Charles Schwab Corp., have been ousted because of their failure to implement their strategic plans and improve business results.

Examination of struggling organizations and executives offers a glimpse into the mistakes that managers often make in a turbulent environment.[15] Perhaps the biggest blunder is managers' failure to comprehend and adapt to the rapid pace of change in the world around them. For example, even though Xerox's PARC research center practically invented the personal computer, top managers resisted getting into the computer business until it was too late to even get in the game, much less have a chance at winning. A related problem stems from top managers who create a climate of fear in the organization so people are afraid to tell the truth. Thus, bad news gets hidden, and important signals from the marketplace are missed.

Other critical management missteps include poor communication skills and failure to listen; treating people only as instruments to be used; suppressing dissenting viewpoints; and being unable to build a management team characterized by mutual trust and respect.[16] The financial scandals of the early twenty-first century, from Enron to mutual-fund mismanagement, clearly show what can happen, for instance, when top managers pay more attention to money and Wall Street than they do to their employees and customers.

TAKE ACTION
To be a better manager, learn to listen and treat people with respect.

first-line
managers who are at the first or second management level and are directly responsible for the production of goods and services.

middle manager
managers who work at the mid-levels of the organization and are responsible for major departments.

As another example, consider what happened at *The New York Times* when it became publicly known that Jayson Blair, a rising young reporter, had fabricated and plagiarized many of his stories. Only then did top executives acknowledge the pervasive unhappiness that existed in the newsroom. Executive editor Howell Raines, who had created an environment that favored certain editors and reporters while others were afraid to offer dissenting viewpoints or tell their managers the truth, resigned under pressure following the scandal. The *Times* still is struggling to regain its footing and reclaim its honorable image.[17]

Making the Leap: Becoming a New Manager

Many people who are promoted into a manager position have little idea what the job actually entails and receive little training about how to handle their new role. It's no wonder that, among managers, the first-line supervisors tend to experience the most job burnout and attrition.[18]

Organizations often promote the star performers—those who demonstrate individual expertise in their area of responsibility and have an ability to work well with others—both to reward the individual and to build new talent into the managerial ranks. But making the shift from individual contributor to manager is often tricky. Dianne Baker, an expert nurse who was promoted to supervisor of an outpatient cardiac rehabilitation center, quickly found herself overwhelmed by the challenge of supervising former peers, keeping up with paperwork, and understanding financial and operational issues.[19] Her experience is duplicated every day as new managers struggle with the transition to their new jobs.

One study followed a group of 19 managers over the first year of their managerial careers and found that one key to success is to recognize that becoming a manager involves more than learning a new set of skills. Rather, becoming a manager requires a profound transformation in the way people think of themselves—called personal identity—that includes letting go of deeply held attitudes and habits and learning new ways of thinking.[20] Exhibit 1.3 outlines the transformation from individual performer to manager.

Individual performers are specialists and "doers." Their mind is conditioned to think in terms of performing specific tasks and activities as expertly as possible. The manager, on the other hand, has to be a generalist and learn to coordinate a broad range of activities. Whereas the individual performer strongly identifies with his or her specific tasks, the manager has to identify with the broader organization and industry. In addition, the individual performer gets things done mostly through his or her own efforts, and develops the habit of relying on self rather than others. The manager, though, gets things done through other people. Indeed, one of the most common mistakes that new managers make is wanting to do all the work themselves, rather than delegating to others and developing others' abilities.[21]

EXHIBIT 1.3

Making the Leap from Individual Performer to Manager

From Individual Identity ⟶	To Manager Identity
Specialist, performs specific tasks	Generalist, coordinates diverse tasks
Gets things done through own efforts	Gets things done through others
An individual actor	A network builder
Works relatively independently	Works in highly interdependent manner

SOURCE: Based on Exhibit 1.1, "Transformation of Identity," in Linda A. Hill, *Becoming a Manager: Mastery of a New Identity*, 2nd ed. (Boston, MA: Harvard Business School Press, 2003): 6.

To be a successful manager means thinking in terms of building teams and networks, becoming a motivator and organizer within a highly interdependent system of people and work. Although the distinctions may sound simple in the abstract, they are anything but easy. In essence, becoming a manager means becoming a new person and viewing oneself in a completely new way.

Many new managers have to make the transformation in a "trial by fire," learning on the job as they go, but organizations are beginning to be more responsive to the need for new manager training. The cost to organizations of losing good employees who can't make the transition is greater than the cost of providing training to help new managers cope, learn, and grow. In addition, some of today's organizations are taking great care to select people for managerial positions, including ensuring that each candidate understands what management involves and really wants to be a manager. For example, FedEx offers a training course for aspiring managers called "Is Management for Me?" A career as a manager can be highly rewarding, but it also can be stressful and frustrating.

MANAGER ACTIVITIES

Most new managers are unprepared for the variety of activities that managers routinely perform. One of the most interesting findings about managerial activities is how busy managers are and how hectic the average work-day can be.

Let's visit our Cheesecake Factory manager, Heather Coin, once more. "I really try to keep the plates spinning," Heather says, comparing her management job to a circus act. "If I see a plate slowing down, I go and give it a spin and move on." She arrives at work about 9:30 A.M. and checks the financials for how the restaurant performed the day before. Next comes a staff meeting and various personnel duties. Before and after the lunch shift, she's pitching in with whatever has to be done—making salads in the kitchen, expediting the food, bussing the tables, or talking with guests. After

⟨⟩ CONCEPT CONNECTION

Supported in part by USAID and published by The Killid Group, a media company headquartered in Kabul, *Mursal*, is the first nationally distributed women's magazine in Afghanistan's history. Aimed at average women, most of whom are illiterate because they lack educational opportunities, the publication makes liberal use of photographs to cover a wide range of women's issues. It is the job of middle managers, such as the *Mursal* editors shown here talking with board member Palwasha Hassan, to help realize an organization's strategic goals, which typically are defined by top management.

lunch, from 3:00 P.M. to 4:30 P.M., Heather takes care of administrative duties and paperwork. At 4:30, she holds a shift-change meeting to ensure of a smooth transition from the day crew to the night crew. Throughout the day, Heather also mentors staff members, which she considers the most rewarding part of her job. After the evening rush, she usually heads for home about 10:00 P.M.[22]

Jeff Immelt, CEO of General Electric, claims that he has worked 100 hours a week for the past 24 years. He says the most valuable thing he learned in business school is that "there are 24 hours in a day, and you can use all of them."[23]

Adventures in multitasking. Managerial activity is characterized by variety, fragmentation, and brevity.[24] The widespread and voluminous nature of a manager's involvements leaves little time for quiet reflection. The average time spent on any one activity is less than 9 minutes. Managers shift gears quickly. Significant crises are interspersed with trivial events in no predictable sequence. One example of just two typical hours for general manager Janet Howard follows. Note the frequent interruptions and the brevity and variety of tasks.[25]

7:30 A.M.   Janet arrives at work and begins to plan her day.

7:37 A.M.   A subordinate, Morgan Cook, stops in Janet's office to discuss a customer dinner the previous night and to review the cost-benefit analysis for a proposed customer relationship management-planning system.

◀◀ TAKE ACTION

Notice how much of your day is spent multitasking—cell-phone talking while walking; completing an assignment while instant-messaging.

Spotlight on Skills

Do You Really Want to Be a Manager?

Is management for you? Most people consider becoming a manager to be a positive, forward-looking career move. Indeed, life as a manager offers appealing aspects. But it also holds many challenges, and not everyone will be happy and fulfilled in a management position. Here are some of the issues that would-be managers should consider before deciding they want to pursue a management career:

- *The increased workload.* It isn't unusual for managers to work 70–80 hours per week, and some work even longer hours. A manager's job always starts before a shift and ends hours after the shift is over. When Ray Sarnacki was promoted to manager at an aerospace company, he found himself frustrated by the incessant travel, endless paperwork, and crowded meeting schedule. Eventually he left the job and found happiness in a position earning about one-fifth of his peak managerial salary.

- *The challenge of supervising former peers.* This issue can be one of the toughest for new managers. They frequently struggle to find the right approach. Some try too hard to remain "one of the gang," and others assert their authority too harshly. In almost all cases, the transition from a peer-to-peer relationship to a manager-to-subordinate one is challenging and stressful.

- *The headache of responsibility for other people.* A lot of people get into management because they like the idea of having

power, but the reality is that many managers feel overwhelmed by the responsibility of hiring, supervising, and disciplining others. Laura Kelso, who today thrives on the fast pace and responsibility of being a manager, says that the first time she had to fire someone, she agonized for weeks over how to do it.

- New managers often are astonished at the amount of time it takes to handle "people problems." Kelly Cannell, who quit her job as a manager, puts it this way: "What's the big deal [about managing people]? The big deal is that people are human. . . . To be a good manager, you have to mentor them, listen to their problems, counsel them, and at the end of the day, you still have your own work on your plate. . . . Don't take the responsibility lightly, because no matter what you think, managing people isn't easy."

- *Being caught in the middle.* Except for those in the top echelons, managers find themselves acting as a backstop, caught between upper management and the workforce. Even when managers disagree with the decisions of top executives, they are responsible for implementing them.

For some people, the frustrations of management aren't worth it. For others, management is a fulfilling and satisfying career choice and the emotional rewards can be great. One key to being happy as a manager may be to carefully evaluate whether you can answer yes to the question, "Do I really want to be a manager?"

SOURCES: Erin White, "Learning to Be the Boss," *Wall Street Journal* (November 21, 2005): B1; Jared Sandberg, "Down Over Moving Up: Some New Bosses Find They Hate Their Jobs," *Wall Street Journal* (July 27, 2005): B1; Heath Row, "Is Management for Me? That Is the Question," *Fast Company* (February–March 1998): 50–52; Timothy D. Schellhardt, "Want to Be a Manager? Many People Say No, Calling Job Miserable," *Wall Street Journal* (April 4, 1997): A1, A4; and Matt Murray, "Managing Your Career—The Midcareer Crisis: Am I in This Business to Become a Manager?" *Wall Street Journal* (July 25, 2000): B1.

7:45 A.M.	Janet's administrative assistant, Pat, motions for Janet to pick up the telephone. "Janet, there was serious water damage at the downtown office last night. A pipe broke, causing about $50,000 damage. Everything will be back in shape in three days. Thought you should know."
8:00 A.M.	Pat brings in the mail. She also asks instructions for formatting a report Janet gave her yesterday.
8:14 A.M.	Janet gets a phone call from the accounting manager, who is returning a call from the day before. They talk about an accounting problem.
8:25 A.M.	A Mr. Nance is ushered in. He complains that a sales manager mistreats his employees and something must be done. Janet rearranges her schedule to investigate this claim.
9:00 A.M.	Janet returns to the mail. One letter is from an irate customer. Janet types out a helpful, restrained reply. Pat brings in phone messages.
9:15 A.M.	Janet receives an urgent phone call from Larry Baldwin. They discuss lost business, unhappy subordinates, and a potential promotion.

Life on speed dial. The manager performs a great deal of work at an unrelenting pace.[26] Managers' work is fast-paced and requires great energy. The managers observed by Mintzberg processed 36 pieces of mail each day, attended eight meetings, and took a tour through the building or plant. Technology, such as e-mail, instant messaging, cell phones, and laptops, intensifies the pace. It isn't unusual for a manager to receive hundreds of e-mail messages a day. As soon as a manager's daily calendar is set, unexpected disturbances erupt. New meetings are required. During time away from the office, executives catch up on work-related reading, paperwork, and e-mail.

At O'Hare International Airport in Chicago, an unofficial count one Friday found operations manager Hugh Murphy interacting with about 45 airport employees. In addition, he listened to complaints from local residents regarding airport noise, met with disgruntled executives of a French firm that built the airport's $128 million people-mover system, attempted to soothe a Hispanic city alderman who complained that Mexicana Airlines passengers were being singled out by overzealous tow-truck operators, toured the airport's fire station, and visited the construction site for a new $20 million tower. Murphy's unrelenting pace is typical for managers.[27]

MANAGER ROLES

Mintzberg's observations and subsequent research indicate that diverse manager activities can be organized into 10 roles.[28] A **role** is a set of expectations for a manager's behavior. Exhibit 1.4 provides examples of each of the roles. These roles are divided into three conceptual categories: *informational* (managing by information); *interpersonal* (managing through people); and

TAKE ACTION

Are you ready to step into a job as a new manager? Consider the hectic pace and varied activities managers perform. Are you prepared to make a personal transformation from individual performer to accomplishing work by engaging and coordinating other people. Take the New Manager Self Test to see whether your priorities align with the demands placed on a new manager's job.

role
a set of expectations for one's behavior.

EXHIBIT 1.4
Ten Manager Roles

Category	Role	Activity
Informational	Monitor	Seek and receive information, scan periodicals and reports, maintain personal contacts.
	Disseminator	Forward information to other organization members; send memos and reports, make phone calls.
	Spokesperson	Transmit information to outsiders through speeches, reports, memos.
Interpersonal	Figurehead	Perform ceremonial and symbolic duties such as greeting visitors, signing legal documents.
	Leader	Direct and motivate subordinates; train, counsel, and communicate with subordinates.
	Liaison	Maintain information links both inside and outside organization; use e-mail, phone calls, meetings.
Decisional	Entrepreneur	Initiate improvement projects; identify new ideas, delegate idea responsibility to others.
	Disturbance handler	Take corrective action during disputes or crises; resolve conflicts among subordinates; adapt to environmental crises.
	Resource allocator	Decide who gets resources; schedule, budget, set priorities.
	Negotiator	Represent department during negotiation of union contracts, sales, purchases, budgets; represent departmental interests.

SOURCES: Adapted from Henry Mintzberg, *The Nature of Managerial Work* (New York: Harper & Row, 1973): 92–93; and Henry Mintzberg, "Managerial Work: Analysis from Observation," *Management Science* 18 (1971): B97–B110.

Manager's Role and Reality

Rate each of the following items based on what you think is the appropriate emphasis for that task to your success as a new manager of a department. First, read each item and check either "High Priority" or "Low Priority." Second, go through the list again and change your answers as needed so you score four items as "High Priority" and four as "Low Priority."

	High Priority	Low Priority
1. Spend 50 percent or more of your time in the care and feeding of people.	_____	_____
2. Make sure people understand that you are in control of the department.	_____	_____
3. Use lunches to meet and network with peers in other departments.	_____	_____
4. Implement the changes you believe will improve department performance.	_____	_____
5. Spend as much time as possible talking with and listening to subordinates.	_____	_____
6. Make sure that jobs get out on time.	_____	_____
7. Reach out to your boss to discuss his/her expectations for you and your department.	_____	_____
8. Make sure you set clear expectations and policies for your department.	_____	_____

INTERPRETATION: A big surprise for most new managers is that they are much less in control of things than they expected. New managers typically expect to have power, to be in control, and to be personally responsible for departmental outcomes. In fact, they are dependent on subordinates more than vice-versa, because they now are evaluated on the work of other people rather than on their own work. They have to let go of their identity as an individual performer and immerse themselves into the dynamics of their department. After a year or so, they learn that more than half their time is spent networking and building relationships with other people, especially direct reports. People who fail in their job as new managers typically do so because they had poor working relationships with subordinates, peers, or their boss, or they misjudged management philosophy or cultural values.

Developing good relationships in all directions is typically more important than holding on to old work skills, or emphasizing control and task outcomes. Successful outcomes typically will occur if relationships are solid. Bad relationships may undercut the new manager's efforts.

SCORING: All eight items in the list may be important, but the odd-numbered items are considered more important than the even-numbered items for long-term success as a new manager. If you checked three or four of the odd-numbered items, consider yourself ready for a management position. A successful new manager discovers that a lot of time has to be spent in the care and feeding of people.

SOURCES: Adapted from research findings reported in Linda A. Hill, *Becoming a Manager: How New Managers Master the Challenges of Leadership,* 2nd ed. (Boston, MA: Harvard Business School Press, 2003); and John J. Gabarro, *The Dynamics of Taking Charge* (Boston, MA: Harvard Business School Press, 1987).

decisional (managing through action). Each role represents activities that managers undertake to ultimately accomplish the functions of planning, organizing, leading, and controlling.

Although the components of the manager's job have to be separated to understand the different roles and activities of a manager, it is important to remember that the real job of management cannot be practiced as a set of independent parts; all the roles interact in the real world of management. As Mintzberg says, "The manager who only communicates or only conceives never gets anything done, while the manager who only 'does' ends up doing it all alone."[29]

Managing in Small Businesses and Nonprofit Organizations

Small businesses are growing in importance. Hundreds of small businesses open every month. But the environment for small businesses today is complicated. Globalization, advances in technology, shifting government regulations, and increasing customer demands require that even the smallest businesses have solid management expertise. Small companies sometimes have difficulty developing the managerial dexterity needed to survive in a turbulent environment. In one survey on trends and future developments in small business, nearly half of the respondents indicated that inadequate management skills were a threat to their companies, compared to less than 25 percent of larger organizations.[30] Managing in small businesses and entrepreneurial start-ups will be discussed in detail in Appendix A.

One interesting finding is that managers in small businesses tend to emphasize roles that are different from those of managers in large corporations. Managers in small companies often see their most important role as that of spokesperson, because they must promote the small, growing company to the outside world. The entrepreneur role also is critical in small businesses because managers have to be innovative and help their organizations develop new ideas to remain competitive. Small-business managers tend to rate lower on the leader role and on information-processing roles, compared to their counterparts in large corporations.

Nonprofit organizations also represent a major application of management talent. Salvation Army, Nature Conservancy, Parkland Memorial Hospital, Los Angeles County Museum of Art, Girl Scouts, and Cleveland Orchestra all require excellent management. The functions of planning, organizing, leading, and controlling apply to nonprofits just as they do to business organizations, and managers in nonprofit organizations use similar skills and perform similar activities. The primary difference is that managers in businesses direct their activities toward earning money for the company, while managers in nonprofits direct their efforts toward generating some kind of social impact. The unique characteristics and needs of nonprofit organizations created by this distinction present unique challenges for managers.[31]

Financial resources for nonprofit organizations typically come from government appropriations, grants, and donations rather than from the sale of products or services to customers. In businesses, managers focus on improving the organization's products and services to increase sales revenues. In nonprofits, however, services typically are provided to nonpaying clients, and a major challenge for many organizations is to secure a steady stream of funds to continue operating. Nonprofit managers, committed to serving clients with limited resources, must keep organizational costs as low as possible.[32]

Donors generally want their money to go directly to helping clients rather than for overhead costs. If nonprofit managers can't demonstrate a highly efficient use of resources, they might have a hard time securing additional donations or government appropriations. Although the Sarbanes-Oxley Act (the 2002 corporate governance reform law) doesn't apply to nonprofits, many are adopting its guidelines, striving for more transparency and accountability to boost credibility with constituents and be more competitive when seeking funding.[33]

TAKE ACTION

As a manager, don't make the mistake of always "doing"—you also need to plan and think.

TAKE ACTION

As a nonprofit manager, you will have to balance the mission with efficient use of resources.

In addition, because nonprofit organizations do not have a conventional *bottom line,* managers often struggle with the question of what constitutes results and effectiveness. It is easy to measure dollars and cents, but the metrics of success in nonprofits are much more ambiguous. Managers have to measure intangibles such as "improve public health," "make a difference in the lives of the disenfranchised," or "increase appreciation for the arts." This intangible nature also makes it more difficult to gauge the performance of employees and managers. An added complication is that managers often depend on volunteers and donors, who cannot be supervised and controlled in the same way that a business manager deals with employees.

The roles defined by Mintzberg also apply to nonprofit managers, but these differ somewhat. We might expect managers in nonprofit organizations to place more emphasis on the roles of spokesperson (to "sell" the organization to donors and the public), leader (to build a mission driven community of employees and volunteers), and resource allocator (to distribute government resources or grant funds that often are assigned top-down).

Managers in all organizations—large corporations, small businesses, and nonprofit organizations—carefully integrate and adjust management functions and roles to meet challenges within their own circumstances and keep their organizations healthy. One way in which many organizations are meeting new challenges is through increased use of the Internet. Some government agencies are using the web to cut bureaucracy, improve efficiency, and save money.

Management and the New Workplace

Over the past decade or so, the central theme being discussed in the field of management has been the pervasive changes. Rapid environmental shifts are causing fundamental transformations that have a dramatic impact on the manager's job. These transformations are reflected in the transition to a new workplace, as illustrated in Exhibit 1.5. The primary characteristic of the new workplace is that it centers on bits rather than atoms—information and ideas rather than machines and physical assets. Low-cost computing power means that ideas, documents, movies, music, and all sorts of other data can be zapped around the world at the speed of light. The digitization of business has radically altered the nature of work, employees, and the workplace itself.[34]

TAKE ACTION ▶

To get an idea of information transfer in the workplace, consider how fast and far information moves on platforms such as YouTube and Facebook.

The *old workplace* is characterized by routine, specialized tasks, and standardized control procedures. Employees typically perform their jobs in one company facility, such as an automobile factory in Detroit or an insurance agency in Des Moines. The organization is coordinated and controlled through the vertical hierarchy, and decision-making authority resides with upper-level managers.

In the *new workplace,* by contrast, work is free-flowing and *flexible.* The shift is most obvious in e-commerce and high-tech organizations, which have to respond to changing markets and competition at a second's notice. Numerous other organizations, such as McKinsey & Company, Canada Life, and Nokia, are also incorporating mechanisms to enhance speed and flexibility. *Empowered employees* are expected to seize opportunities and solve problems as they emerge. Structures are flatter, and lower-level employees make decisions based on widespread information and guided by the organization's mission and values.[35]

Knowledge is shared widely rather than hoarded by managers, and people throughout the company keep in touch with a broader range of colleagues via advanced technology. Some organizations, such as Tenary Software, are trying these new models.

The workplace is organized around *networks* rather than rigid hierarchies, and work is often *virtual,* with managers having to supervise and coordinate people who never actually "come to work" in the traditional sense. Thanks to modern information and communications technology, employees can perform their jobs from home

EXHIBIT 1.5
The Transition to a
New Workplace

	The New Workplace	The Old Workplace
Characteristics		
Resources	Bits—information	Atoms—physical assets
Work	Flexible, virtual	Structured, localized
Workers	Empowered employees, free agents	Loyal employees
Forces on Organizations		
Technology	Digital, e-business	Mechanical
Markets	Global, including Internet	Local, domestic
Workforce	Diverse	Homogenous
Values	Change, speed	Stability, efficiency
Events	Turbulent, more frequent crises	Calm, predictable
Management Competencies		
Leadership	Dispersed, empowering	Autocratic
Focus	Connection to customers, employees	Profits
Doing Work	By teams	By individuals
Relationships	Collaboration	Conflict, competition
Design	Experimentation, learning organization	Efficient performance

Tenary Software

A programmer at Tenary Software publicly criticized the CEO's employee incentive plan. Such behavior would be grounds for termination in some companies. Not Tenary, which is run as a democracy among all 19 people, and where every decision must be unanimous. The founders had bad experiences with corporate infighting at other places they worked, so they decided to try something different. As one of the founders and CEO, Brian Robertson has little of the traditional CEO power. "It takes getting beyond your ego," he says.

Champions of this process say it appeals to employees, particularly younger ones, who want more meaning in their jobs. Such a structure, however, might not work at a large company, where giving everyone an equal voice is a logistical problem. Even at Tenary, the first try was a consensus mission statement in 2004, and the company took 2 full days to reach the goal, leaving everyone exhausted.

Since then, the people there have learned a lot. The company shares financial data, including everyone's salary. Changes are proposed, argued, and voted. In 2005, Bill Schofield offered a radical proposal: to slash 15 percent off senior programmers' salaries (which included his own), so junior programmers could get more wages. It was approved.

In 2006, the company hit a sales slump and the employees voted to cut all salaries by 22 percent. When sales increased, they voted to restore salaries. And when the finances of Tenary were healthy once more, it was voted to pay each person what they had lost during the lean months. Robertson believes the example of pay changes shows how the practice really works. Rather than get upset and quit, he said, the staff "used the system to inject feedback and get their needs met."

SOURCE: Jaclyne Badal, "Can a Company be Run as a Democracy?" *Wall Street Journal* (April 23, 2007): B1.

or another remote location, at any time of the day or night.[36] Flexible hours, tele-commuting, and virtual teams are increasingly popular ways of working that require new skills from managers. Using virtual teams allows organizations to use the best people for specific jobs, no matter where they are located, which enables a fast, innovative response to competitive pressures. Teams also may include outside contractors, suppliers, customers, competitors, and *interim managers* who are not affiliated with a specific organization but, instead, work on a project-by-project basis. The valued worker is one who learns quickly, shares knowledge, and is comfortable with risk, change, and ambiguity.

FORCES ON ORGANIZATIONS

The most striking change affecting organizations and management is *technology*. Consider that computing power has roughly doubled every 18 months over the past 30 years while the cost has declined by half or more every 18 months.[37] In addition, the Internet, which was little more than a curiosity to many managers as recently as a decade ago, has transformed the way business is done. Many organizations use *digital networking* technologies to tie together employees and company partners in far-flung operations. Organizations are increasingly shifting significant chunks of what once were considered core functions to outsiders via *outsourcing, joint ventures,* and other complex *alliances.* Companies are becoming interconnected, and managers have to learn how to coordinate relationships with other organizations and influence people who can't be managed and commanded in traditional ways.

The Internet and other new technologies also are tied closely to *globalization.* Although global interconnections bring many opportunities, they also bring new threats, raise new risks, and accelerate complexity and competitiveness. Think about the trend toward *outsourcing* to low-cost providers in other countries. To cut costs, U.S. companies have been sending manufacturing work to other countries for years. Now, work involving high-level knowledge is also being outsourced to countries such as India, Malaysia, and South Africa. India's Wipro Ltd., for example, writes software, performs consulting work, integrates back-office solutions, undertakes systems integration, and handles technical support for some of the biggest corporations in the United States—and does this for 40 percent less than comparable U.S. companies can do the work.[38]

TAKE ACTION ⏩

Practice adapting yourself to changes and new ways of thinking. Rather than arguing, ask questions of others.

Diversity of the population and the workforce in the United States is another fact of life for organizations. The general population of the United States, and thus of the workforce, is growing more ethnically and racially diverse. In addition, generational diversity is a powerful force in today's workplace, with employees of all ages working together on teams and projects in a way rarely seen in the past. In the face of these transformations, organizations are learning to value change, innovation, and speed over stability and efficiency.

The fundamental paradigm during much of the twentieth century was a belief that things can be stable. In contrast, the new paradigm recognizes change and chaos as the natural order of things.[39] Events in today's world are turbulent and unpredictable, with small and large crises occurring frequently. Rock star David Bowie has staked the newest phase of his career on that turbulence (see Bowie Bonds feature on next page).

One way that managers are addressing the complexity of today's world is by renewing their emphasis on innovation. With the power of the Internet, for example, companies have lost much of their ability to control information to consumers and the public, so they are forced to innovate with increasingly better products and services to remain competitive. The intense competition brought about by globalization also spurs companies to keep pace with new technologies and innovative management practices.[40] A report from a group of leading scientists, executives, and educators points to the growing innovation strength of countries such as China and India, which are poised to usurp

diversity
ethnically and racially generational

When David Bowie was a huge rock star in the '70s, complete with flaming groupies, or a reformed punk artist in the '80s, he was never slated to become the smartest entrepreneur in the rock business. Of course, back then he was abusing drugs, which didn't leave him much brainpower for the kinds of deals he is working now. Currently he is so clean that he won't even take Advil because, as he says, "I have such an addictive personality." With his now clear intelligence and ability to be ahead of the times, he has secured continued success.

Influenced by the IPO craze, he raised $55 million by becoming the first big music star to take his music catalog/song royalties public, through 1997's Bowie Bonds. Later he started the high-tech company Ultrastar and his own Internet service provider, which also happens to be his fan club (davidbowie.com). In 2004, Ultrastar created strategic alliances with several other companies, including Circuit City's digital music club MusicNow. Then he started his own record label. Also, he has a short-term distribution agreement with Sony. Bowie's hits include "Let's Dance" and "Space Oddity," and as he reaches age 60, he'll re-release 17 albums and hit the stage again.

His keen sense of the music business environment makes him uneasy about the future. Not certain that he even wants to be on a label in a few years, he thinks it won't work any more by labels and distribution. "The absolute transformation of everything we ever thought about music will take place within 10 years, and nothing is going to be able to stop it . . . I'm truly confident that copyright, for instance, will no longer exist in 10 years, and authorship and intellectual property is in for such a smashing."

Bowie believes he has to take advantage of these last years of the music business as it has been. "You'd better be prepared for doing a lot of touring, because that's the only unique situation that's going to be left." Even with all the changes he expects, he's still looking forward to it. "It's terribly exciting," he says.

SOURCE: Jon Pareles, "David Bowie, 21st Century Entrepreneur," *The New York Times* (June 9, 2002): Section 2, 1 + 30; Anthony Barnes, "Golden Years: Bowie is 60 Tomorrow. And Bigger Than Ever," *The Independent on Sunday* (Jan. 7, 2007): 22.

America's position as an innovation leader. Between the years of 1991 and 2003, research and development spending in China exceeded that in the United States by billions of dollars.[41]

Over the past few years, though, an explosion of attention to innovation roared through U.S. firms. For example, Motorola, which seemed to be on the has-been list in the opening years of the twenty-first century, roared back to life with hot new products such as the RAZR phone, the ROKR, the first combination cell phone and iPod, and the Q phone and e-mail device, designed to compete with the BlackBerry. Motorola CEO Ed Zander is implementing management and cultural changes that support an ongoing process of innovation.[42]

Motorola's changes reflect a broader movement in U.S. firms, seen in companies from General Electric to IBM to Procter & Gamble, as managers are emphasizing creativity and innovation to compete in a new era. General Electric CEO Jeff Immelt, for example, shifted from emphasizing growth through acquisition to pushing growth through technological innovation and providing additional resources for GE's scientific research labs. Procter & Gamble collaborates widely with individual entrepreneurs and other firms, even competitors, to crank out innovative products.[43]

NEW MANAGEMENT COMPETENCIES

In the face of these transitions, managers must rethink their approach to organizing, directing, and motivating employees. Today's best managers give up their command-and-control mind-set to focus on coaching and providing guidance, creating organizations that are fast, flexible, innovative, and relationship-oriented. In many of today's best companies, leadership is dispersed throughout the organization, and managers empower others to gain the benefit of their ideas and creativity.

TAKE ACTION

Read the ethical dilemma at the end of the chapter that pertains to managing in the new workplace. Think about what you would do and how you will solve thorny management problems.

TAKE ACTION

To succeed in the new workplace, you have to learn to network and build collaborative relationships. Expect to manage with little command and control and to master skills including communication, guiding others, and inspiration.

2 If I were a manager, the most important part of my job would be to make sure the company would be profitable.

ANSWER: Today's managers have to pay attention to profits and also the needs of customers and employees.

●●CONCEPT CONNECTION

New York Yankees manager Joe Torre knows how to use new management competencies to build high-performance teams that are capable of winning American League pennants and World Series titles. His management style is built on paradox. He achieves what's best for the team, always his first priority, by paying close attention to each individual's personality and abilities, routinely setting aside time for one-on-one discussions so he can motivate, correct, and encourage. He succeeds in part because he earns player loyalty by tolerating failure and slumps. "To me, managing is about people," says Torre. "Players look to me more for guidance and calmness than anything else."

Success in the new workplace depends on the strength and quality of **collaborative relationships.** Rather than a single-minded focus on profits, today's managers recognize the critical importance of staying connected to employees and customers. New ways of working emphasize collaboration across functions and hierarchical levels as well as with other companies. Team-building skills are crucial. Instead of managing a department of employees, many managers act as team leaders of ever-shifting, temporary projects.

At SEI Investments, the work is distributed among 140 teams. Some are permanent, such as those that serve major customers or focus on specific markets, but many are designed to work on short-term projects or problems. Computer linkups, called *pythons,* drop from the ceiling. As people change assignments, they just unplug their pythons, move their desks and chairs to a new location, plug into a new python, and get to work on the next project.[44]

An important management challenge in the new workplace is to build a **learning organization** by creating an organizational climate that values experimentation and risk taking, applies current technology, tolerates mistakes and failure, and rewards nontraditional thinking and the sharing of knowledge.

Everyone in the organization participates in identifying and solving problems, which enables the organization to continuously experiment, improve, and increase its capability. The role of managers is not to make decisions but, instead, to create learning capability, in which everyone is free to experiment and learn what works best.

TURBULENT TIMES: MANAGING CRISES AND UNEXPECTED EVENTS

learning organization
an organizational climate that values experimentation and risk taking, applies current technology, tolerates mistakes and failure, and rewards nontraditional thinking and the sharing of knowledge.

collaborative relationships
staying connected to employees and customers.

Many managers dream of working in an organization and a world in which life seems relatively calm, orderly, and predictable, but their reality is one of increasing turbulence and disorder. Today's managers and organizations face various levels of crisis every day—from the loss of computer data, to charges of racial discrimination, to a factory fire, to workplace violence. These organizational crises are compounded by crises on a more global level.

Consider a few of the major events that affected U.S. companies within the last few years: the bursting of the dot-com bubble, which led to the failure of thousands of companies and the rapid decline of technology stocks; the crash of Enron as a result of a complex series of unethical and illegal accounting gimmicks, the subsequent investigations of numerous other corporations, and implementation of new corporate governance laws; terrorist attacks in New York City and Washington, DC, that destroyed the World Trade

Center, seriously damaged the Pentagon, killed thousands of people, and interrupted business around the world; the crash of the space shuttle *Columbia* and the ensuing investigation that revealed serious cultural and management problems at NASA; Hurricane Katrina's devastating impact on organizations in New Orleans and the Gulf Coast, as well as numerous companies that do business with them; the removal of spinach from supermarkets because of *e-coli;* and continuing terrorist threats against the United States and its allies—causing companies to hire experts to manage potential crises. Even the Hilton family, Paris's parents, hired a crisis manager after she got arrested and sent to jail.[45] These and other events brought the uncertainty and turbulence of today's world clearly to the forefront of everyone's mind and made crisis management a critical skill for every manager.

Dealing with the unexpected has always been part of the manager's job, but our world has become so fast, interconnected, and complex that unexpected events happen more frequently and more often with greater and more painful consequences. All of the new management skills and competencies we discussed are important to managers in such an environment. Crisis management places further demands on today's managers. Some of the most recent thinking on crisis management suggests the importance of five leadership skills.[46]

1. Stay calm.

2. Be visible.

3. Put people before business.

4. Tell the truth.

5. Know when to get back to business.

Stay calm. A leader's emotions are contagious, so leaders have to stay calm, focused, and optimistic about the future. Perhaps the most important part of a manager's job in a crisis situation is to absorb people's fears and uncertainties. Although managers acknowledge the difficulties, they remain rock-steady and hopeful, which gives comfort, inspiration, and hope to others.

Be visible. When the world becomes ambiguous and frightening to people, they need to feel that someone is in control. After Hurricane Katrina hit New Orleans, Scott Cowen, president of Tulane University, stayed on campus until he was sure that everyone was evacuated and everything that possibly could be done to control the damage was in place.[47] In times of crisis, leadership cannot be delegated. When Russian president Vladimir Putin continued his holiday after the sinking of the submarine Kursk in August 2000, his reputation diminished worldwide.[48]

By contrast, Melvin Wilson of Mississippi Power stayed visible and maintained important networks to deal with a real catastrophe. Imagine that you are a mid-level marketing manager at a public utilities company. One day you're reviewing next year's advertising campaign. A day later you're responsible for coordinating the feeding, housing, and health care of 11,000 repair workers from around the country. That's the situation that Melvin Wilson, a marketing manager for Mississippi Power, found himself in when Hurricane Katrina hit the state in August 2005, wiping out 1,000 miles of power lines, destroying 65 percent of the company's transmission and distribution facilities, damaging 300 transmission towers, and knocking out power for all 195,000 customers. The company had a disaster recovery plan in place, but managers were suddenly thrust into a situation that was twice as bad as the worst-case scenario.

Mississippi Power's corporate headquarters was totally destroyed, its disaster response center flooded and useless. Early recovery work had to be done without access to computers, phones, or basic sanitary facilities. Confusion and chaos reigned. "My day job didn't prepare me for this," Wilson told a reporter in a choked voice as he struggled to find nurses, beds, tetanus shots, laundry service, showers, security services, and food for repair workers.

Other managers, from all levels and divisions, have dealt with similar predicaments. One manager compared the process to managing an Army division at war! Amazingly, Mississippi Power employees got the job done smoothly and efficiently, restoring power in just 12 days, thus meeting the bold target of restoring power by the symbolic date of September 11. The tale of how this was done is one of the great crisis-management stories of modern times, and a lesson for managers in how much can be accomplished quickly when it's managed right.[49]

The managers at Mississippi Power illustrate many of these new management competencies, which enabled the company to execute a swift, ambitious disaster plan and restore power in only 12 days following Hurricane Katrina. Two decades ago, hurricane response was run from the top down, but managers learned that setting priorities from headquarters was ineffective during times of chaos and confusion. Today, decision making has been pushed far down to the level of the substation, and employees are empowered to act within certain guidelines to accomplish a basic mission: "Get the power on."

The corporate culture, based on values of unquestionable trust, superior performance, and total commitment, supports individual initiative and the confidence of management that employees will respond with quick action and on-the-spot innovation. During the disaster recovery, even out-of-state crews working unsupervised were empowered to engineer their own solutions to problems in the field. Networking and team-building skills also are highly valued at Mississippi Power. Middle managers like Melvin Wilson forged networks of relationships throughout the company, with other organizations, and with power company managers in other states, which enabled them to quickly gain access to critical resources and build teams with the right combination of skills. Overall, Mississippi Power reflects the qualities of a learning organization in which employees, from line workers to accountants, are encouraged to experiment, innovate, share knowledge, and solve problems.

Melvin Wilson also illustrates some of the qualities needed for effective crisis management. When he took on the role of "director of storm logistics," he suppressed his own emotions to present a calm and focused persona, which kept employees' emotions directed in a positive way on the job to be done. At the same time, he and other managers made sure that plans were in place to assist employees whose homes were damaged (fortunately, no employees were killed in the storm). Wilson was a highly visible leader throughout the recovery, working 20-hour days and sleeping on the floor. Top leaders were visible as well, meeting with storm directors every day and helping boost the morale of recovery workers.

Leadership during crises and unexpected events is becoming important for all organizations in today's complex world. Managers in crisis situations should stay calm, be visible, put people before business, tell the truth, and know when to get back to business. **Human skills** become critical during times of turbulence and crisis.

human skills
the ability to work with and through other people and to work effectively as a group member.

Put people before business. The companies that weather a crisis best, whether the crisis is large or small, are those in which managers make people and human

Business Blooper

Thomas the Tank Engine

When Thomas the Tank Engine was recalled by the company RC2 because of lead paint issues, it wasn't the first recall. The Oakbrook, Illinois-based company had issued previous recalls on other toys as a result of lead paint. RC2 hasn't yet managed how to be in the spotlight. Crisis-management experts tell companies to be as truthful as possible right away in the midst of a scandal, and to be aggressively forthright in supplying information. RC2 was quiet in the first week. Executives did not return repeated phone calls from the media. But the worst part was when a reporter went to the manufacturing plant in China and was forcibly detained for nine hours.

SOURCE: David Barbaroza and Louise Story, "Train Wreck," *The New York Times* (June 19, 2007): C1 & C4.

feelings their top priority. Ray O'Rourke, managing director for global corporate affairs at Morgan Stanley, put it this way following September 11: "Even though we are a financial services company, we didn't have a financial crisis on our hands; we had a human crisis. After that point, everything was focused on our people."[50]

Tell the truth. Managers should get as much information from as many diverse sources as they can, do their best to determine the facts, and then be open and straightforward about what's going on. After a 17-year-old patient at Duke University Hospital died following a botched organ transplant, hospital managers compounded the organizational crisis by failing to communicate with the media and community for nine full days after the tragedy was reported in the press.[51]

Know when to get back to business. Although managers should first deal with the physical and emotional needs of people, they should get back to business as soon as possible. The company has to keep going, and a natural human tendency makes us want to rebuild and move forward. Rejuvenation of the business is a sign of hope and an inspiration to employees. Moments of crisis also present excellent opportunities for looking forward and using the emotional energy that has emerged to build a better company.

This is a challenging time to be entering the field of management. Throughout this book, you will learn much more about the new workplace, about the new and dynamic roles that managers are playing in the twenty-first century, and about how you can be an effective manager in a complex, ever-changing world.

TAKE ACTION

Don't cover up the truth. People often find out, and then you look the worse for not "fessing up."

The Learning Organization

One of the toughest challenges for managers today is to direct people's focus on adaptive change to meet the demands of a turbulent and rapidly changing environment. Few problems come with ready-made solutions, and they require that people throughout the company think in new ways and learn new values and attitudes.[52] These needs demand a new approach to management and a new kind of organization.

Managers began thinking about the concept of the learning organization after the publication of Peter Senge's book, *The Fifth Discipline: The Art and Practice of Learning Organizations*.[53] Senge described the kind of changes that managers have to undergo to help their organizations adapt to an increasingly chaotic world. These ideas gradually evolved to describe characteristics of the organization itself. No single view describes what the learning organization looks like. The learning organization is an attitude or philosophy about what an organization can become.

TAKE ACTION ▶▶

To foster learning, share information and talk often to people in other units.

DEFINITION OF A LEARNING ORGANIZATION

The learning organization can be defined as one in which everyone is engaged in identifying and solving problems, enabling the organization to continuously experiment, change, and improve, thus increasing its capacity to grow, learn, and achieve its purpose. The essential idea is problem solving, in contrast to the traditional organization designed for efficiency. In the learning organization, all employees look for problems, such as understanding special customer needs. Employees also solve problems, which means putting things together in unique ways to meet a customer's needs.

Many of today's managers are quite aware that sustained competitive advantage can come only by developing the learning capacity of everyone in the organization. This awareness is reflected in a survey conducted by *Strategy Business*. The magazine asked its online subscribers, along with a group of thinkers, educators, interview subjects, and scholars, to vote for the ideas discussed in *Strategy Business* over the last 10 years that they consider most likely to remain relevant for at least the next decade. The concept of the learning organization ranked second on the list of top 10 ideas.[54]

CHARACTERISTICS OF A LEARNING ORGANIZATION

To develop a learning organization, managers make changes in all the subsystems of the organization. Three important adjustments to promote continuous learning are: shifting to a team-based structure, empowering employees, and sharing information. These three characteristics are illustrated in Exhibit 1.6, and each is described here.

Team-based structure. An important value in a learning organization is collaboration and communication across departmental and hierarchical boundaries. Self-directed teams comprise the basic building block of the structure. These teams are made up of employees with different skills who share or rotate jobs to produce an entire product or service. Traditional management tasks are pushed down to lower levels of the organization, with teams often taking responsibility for training, safety, scheduling, and decisions about work methods, pay and reward systems, and coordination with other teams.

Although team leadership is vital, in learning organizations the traditional boss is nearly eliminated. People on the team are given the skills, information, tools, motivation, and authority to make decisions central to the team's performance and to respond creatively and flexibly to new challenges and opportunities that arise.

empowerment
unleashing the power and creativity of employees by giving them the freedom, resources, information, and skills to make decisions and perform effectively.

Employee empowerment. **Empowerment** means unleashing the power and creativity of employees by giving them the freedom, resources, information, and skills to

EXHIBIT 1.6
Elements of a Learning Organization

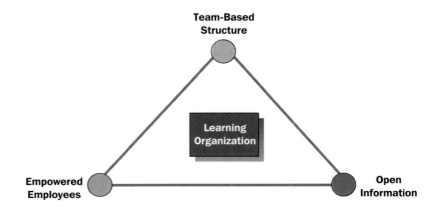

make decisions and perform effectively. Traditional management tries to limit employees, whereas empowerment expands their behavior. Empowerment may be reflected in self-directed work teams, quality circles, job enrichment, and employee-participation groups, as well as through decision-making authority, training, and information so people can perform jobs without close supervision.

In learning organizations, people are a manager's primary source of strength, not a cost to be minimized. Companies that adopt this perspective believe in treating employees well by providing competitive wages and good working conditions, as well as by investing time and money in training programs and opportunities for personal and professional development. In addition, they often provide a sense of employee ownership by sharing gains in productivity and profits.[55]

Open Information. A learning organization is flooded with information. To identify needs and solve problems, people have to be aware of what's going on. They must understand the whole organization as well as their part in it. Formal data about budgets, profits, and departmental expenses are available to everyone. "If you really want to respect individuals," says Solectron Corp.'s Winston Chen, "you've got to let them know how they're doing—and let them know soon enough so they can do something about it."[56]

Managers know that providing too much information is better than providing too little. In addition, managers encourage people throughout the organization to share information. For example, at Viant Inc., which helps companies build and maintain web-based businesses, people are rewarded for their willingness to absorb and share knowledge. Rather than encouraging consultants to hoard specialized knowledge, CEO Bob Gett says, "We value you more for how much information you've given to the guy next to you."[57]

Managing the Technology-Driven Workplace

The shift to the learning organization goes hand-in-hand with the current transition to a technology-driven workplace. The physical world that Frederick Taylor and other proponents of scientific management measured determines less and less of what is valued in organizations and society. Our lives and organizations have been engulfed by information technology. Ideas, information, and relationships are becoming more important than production machinery, physical products, and structured jobs.[58]

Many employees perform much of their work on computers and may be a part of virtual teams, connected electronically to colleagues around the world. Even in factories that produce physical goods, machines have taken over much of the routine and uniform work, freeing workers to use more of their minds and abilities. Managers and employees in today's companies focus on opportunities rather than efficiencies, which requires that they be flexible, creative, and unconstrained by rigid rules and structured tasks.

> **TAKE ACTION**
>
> *Consider how often you buy something at Amazon.com or other online merchants—and that 10 years ago very little was sold on the Web.*

THE SHIFTING WORLD OF E-BUSINESS

Today, much business takes place by digital processes over a computer network rather than in physical space. **E-business** refers to the work an organization does by using electronic linkages (including the Internet) with customers, partners, suppliers, employees, or other key constituents. Organizations that use the Internet or other electronic linkages to communicate with employees or customers are engaged in e-business.

E-commerce is a narrower term. It refers specifically to business exchanges or transactions that occur electronically. E-commerce replaces or enhances the exchange of money and products with the exchange of data and information from one computer to another. Three types of e-commerce are business-to-consumer, business-to-business, and consumer-to-consumer.

e-business
the work an organization does by using electronic linkages (including the Internet) with customers, partners, suppliers, employees, or other key constituents.

e-commerce
refers specifically to business exchanges or transactions that occur electronically.

Companies such as Amazon.com, 800-Flowers, Expedia.com, and Progressive are engaged in what is referred to as **business-to-consumer e-commerce (B2C),** because they sell products and services to consumers over the Internet. Although this type of exchange is probably the most visible expression of e-commerce to the public, the fastest growing area of e-commerce is **business-to-business e-commerce (B2B),** which refers to electronic transactions between organizations. Today, much B2B e-commerce takes place over the Internet.[59]

Large organizations such as Wal-Mart, General Electric, Carrier Corp., General Motors, and Ford Motor Company buy and sell billions of dollars worth of goods and services a year via either public or private Internet linkages.[60] For example, General Motors sells about 300,000 previously owned vehicles a year online through SmartAuction. Ford purchases a large portion of the steel it uses to build cars through e-Steel.[61]

Some companies take e-commerce to high levels to achieve amazing performance through supply chain management. **Supply chain management** refers to managing the sequence of suppliers and purchasers, covering all stages of processing from obtaining raw materials to distributing finished goods to consumers.[62] Dell Computer was a pioneer in the use of end-to-end digital supply-chain networks to keep in touch with customers, take orders, buy components from suppliers, coordinate with manufacturing partners, and ship customized products directly to consumers. This trend is affecting every industry, prompting a group of consultants at a Harvard University conference to conclude that businesses today must either "Dell or be Delled."[63]

The third area of e-commerce, **consumer-to-consumer (C2C),** is made possible when an Internet-based business acts as an intermediary between and among consumers. One of the best-known examples of C2C e-commerce is the web-based auction such as auctions made possible by eBay. Internet auctions create a large electronic marketplace where consumers can buy and sell directly with one another, usually handling nearly the entire transaction via the web. Members of eBay in the United States alone sold approximately $10.6 billion in merchandise during the first 6 months of 2005. Merchandise sales worldwide in the previous year were approximately $36 billion.[64]

Another growing area of C2C commerce is **peer-to-peer (P2P) file-sharing** networks. Companies such as Kazaa and Grokster provide the technology for swapping music, movies, software, and other files. Online music sharing, in particular, has zoomed in popularity, and although music companies and record retailers currently are engaged in a heated battle with file-sharing services, these companies are likely here to stay.[65]

INNOVATIVE TECHNOLOGY IN THE WORKPLACE

New electronic technologies also shape the organization and how it is managed. A century ago, Frederick Taylor described the kind of worker needed in the iron industry: "Now one of the first requirements for a man who is fit to handle pig iron as a regular occupation is that he shall be so stupid and so phlegmatic that he more nearly resembles in his mental makeup the ox than any other type."[66] The philosophy of scientific management was that managers structured and controlled jobs so carefully that thinking on the part of employees wasn't required—indeed, it usually was discouraged.

How different things are today! Many organizations depend on employees' minds more than their physical bodies. In companies where the power of an idea determines success, managers' primary goal is to tap into the creativity and knowledge of every employee.

Technology provides the architecture that supports and reinforces this new workplace. One approach to information management is **enterprise resource planning (ERP),** systems that weave together all of a company's major business functions, such as order processing, product design, purchasing, inventory, manufacturing, distribution, human resources, receipt of payments, and forecasting of future demand.[67]

TAKE ACTION ➔

As a new manager in today's workplace, how would you develop your employees' abilities to think independently, build relationships, and share knowledge? Be prepared to learn to use technology as a tool to tap into the insight and creativity of each person in the organization.

business-to-consumer e-commerce (B2C)
sell products and services to consumers over the Internet.

business-to-business e-commerce (B2B)
electronic transactions between organizations.

supply chain management
managing the sequence of suppliers and purchasers, covering all stages of processing from obtaining raw materials to distributing finished goods to consumers.

consumer-to-consumer (C2C)
an Internet-based business acts as an intermediary between and among consumers.

peer-to-peer (P2P) file-sharing
swapping music, movies, software, and other files.

enterprise resource planning (ERP)
systems that weave together all of a company's major business functions, such as order processing, product design, purchasing, inventory, manufacturing, distribution, human resources, receipt of payments, and forecasting of future demand.

ERP supports a companywide management system in which everyone, from the CEO down to a machine operator on the factory floor, has instant access to critical information. People can see the big picture and act quickly, based on up-to-the-minute information. Thus, ERP also supports management attempts to harness and leverage organizational knowledge.

Peter Drucker coined the term *knowledge work* more than 40 years ago,[68] but only in recent years did managers begin to genuinely recognize knowledge as an important organizational resource that should be managed just as they manage cash flow or raw materials. **Knowledge management** refers to efforts to systematically find, organize, and make available a company's intellectual capital and to foster a culture of continuous learning and knowledge sharing so that a company's activities build on what is already known.[69]

A growing segment of knowledge management is the use of sophisticated **customer relationship management (CRM),** systems that collect and manage large amounts of data about customers and make them available to employees, enabling better decision making and superior customer service. The use of CRM has virtually exploded over the past several years. In Bain and Company's 2005 management tool survey, for example, three out of four companies reported using CRM, up from only 35 percent of companies in 2000, one of the largest and fastest usage increases ever revealed by the survey.[70]

Information technology also is contributing to the rapid growth of **outsourcing**—contracting out selected functions or activities to other organizations that can do the work more cost-efficiently. Today's companies are outsourcing like crazy to free up cash for investment in long-term research and innovation. Outsourcing—along with other trends such as supply chain management, customer relationship management, telecommuting, and virtual teamwork—requires that managers be technologically savvy and also that they learn to manage a complex web of relationships. These relationships might reach far beyond the boundaries of the physical organization; they often are built through flexible e-links between a company and its employees.

Management and Organization

A historical perspective on management provides a context or environment in which to interpret current opportunities and problems. Studying history, however, doesn't mean merely arranging events in chronological order. It means developing an understanding of the impact of societal forces on organizations. Studying history is a way to achieve strategic thinking, see the big picture, and improve conceptual skills. Let's start by examining how social, political, and economic forces have influenced organizations and the practice of management.[71]

INFLUENTIAL FORCES

Social forces refer to those aspects of a culture that guide and influence relationships among people. What do people value? What do people need? What are the standards of behavior among people? These forces shape what is known as the **social contract,** which refers to the unwritten, common rules and perceptions about relationships among people and between employees and management.

A significant social force today is represented by the changing attitudes, ideas, and values of Generation X and Generation Y employees.[72] Generation X employees, those now in their 30s and 40s, have had a profound impact on the workplace, and Generation Y workers (sometimes called Nexters) may have an even greater impact. These young workers, the most-educated generation in the history of the United States, grew up technologically adept and globally conscious.

Unlike many workers of the past, they don't hesitate to question their superiors and challenge the status quo. They want a work environment that is challenging and supportive, with access to cutting-edge technology, opportunities to learn and further their careers

TAKE ACTION
Start to think of knowledge as a product, something you can perfect and make valuable to a customer.

knowledge management
efforts to systematically find, organize, and make available a company's intellectual capital and to foster a culture of continuous learning and knowledge sharing so that a company's activities build on what is already known.

customer relationship management (CRM)
systems that collect and manage large amounts of data about customers and make them available to employees, enabling better decision making and superior customer service.

outsourcing
contracting out selected functions or activities to other organizations that can do the work more cost-efficiently.

social forces
those aspects of a culture that guide and influence relationships among people.

social contract
the unwritten, common rules and perceptions about relationships among people and between employees and management.

and personal goals, and the power to make substantive decisions and changes in the work-place. In addition, Gen X and Gen Y workers have prompted a growing emphasis on work/life balance, reflected in trends such as telecommuting, flextime, shared jobs, and organization-sponsored sabbaticals.

Political forces refers to the influence of political and legal institutions on people and organizations. Political forces include basic assumptions underlying the political system, such as the desirability of self-government, property rights, contract rights, the definition of justice, and the determination of innocence or guilt of a crime. The spread of capitalism throughout the world has altered the business landscape dramatically. The dominance of the free-market system and growing interdependencies among the world's countries require organizations to operate differently and managers to think in new ways. At the same time, strong anti-American sentiments in many parts of the world create challenges for U.S. companies and managers.

Economic forces pertain to the availability, production, and distribution of resources in a society. Governments, military agencies, churches, schools, and business organizations in every society require resources to achieve their goals, and economic forces influence the allocation of scarce resources. Less-developed countries are growing in economic power, and the economy of the United States and other developed countries is shifting dramatically, with the sources of wealth, the fundamentals of distribution, and the nature of economic decision making undergoing significant changes.[73]

Today's economy is based as much on ideas, information, and knowledge as it is on material resources. Supply chains and the distribution of resources have been revolutionized by digital technology. Surplus inventories, which once could trigger recessions, are declining or completely disappearing.

Another economic trend is the boom in small and midsized businesses, including start-ups, which early in the twenty-first century grew at three times the rate of the national economy. "I call it 'the invisible economy,' yet it is *the* economy," says David Birch of Cognetics Inc., a Cambridge, Massachusetts, firm that tracks business formation.[74]

A massive shift in the economy is not without its upheavals, of course. In the early 2000s, years of seemingly endless growth ground to a halt as stock prices fell, particularly for dot-com and technology companies. Numerous Internet-based companies went out of business, and organizations throughout the United States and Canada began laying off hundreds of thousands of workers. This economic downturn, however, also may be a stimulus for even greater technological innovation and small business vitality.

Management practices and perspectives vary in response to these social, political, and economic forces in the larger society. During difficult times, managers look for ideas to help them cope with environmental turbulence and keep their organizations vital. A management tools survey conducted by Bain & Company, for example, reveals a dramatic increase over the past dozen or so years in the variety of management ideas and techniques used by managers.

Challenges such as a tough economy and a rocky stock market, environmental and organizational crises, lingering anxieties over war and terrorism, and the public suspicion and skepticism resulting from corporate scandals leave executives searching for any management tool—new or old—that can help them get the most out of limited resources.[75] This search for guidance is reflected in a proliferation of books, scholarly articles, and conferences dedicated to examining management fashions and trends.[76]

CLASSICAL PERSPECTIVE

Although the practice of management can be traced to 3000 B.C.E. to the first government organizations developed by the Sumerians and Egyptians, the formal study of management is relatively recent.[77] The early study of management as we know it today began with what is now called the **classical perspective**, which emerged during the nineteenth and early twentieth centuries.

political forces
the influence of political and legal institutions on people and organizations.

economic forces
the availability, production, and distribution of resources in a society.

classical perspective
a management perspective that emerged during the nineteenth and early twentieth centuries that emphasized a rational, scientific approach to the study of management and sought to make organizations efficient operating machines.

The factory system that began to appear in the 1800s posed challenges that earlier organizations had not encountered. Problems arose in tooling the plants, organizing managerial structure, training employees (many of them non-English-speaking immigrants), scheduling complex manufacturing operations, and dealing with increased labor dissatisfaction and resulting strikes.

The myriad new problems and the development of large, complex organizations demanded a new approach to coordination and control, and a "new sub-species of economic man—the salaried manager"[78]—was born. Between 1880 and 1920, the number of professional managers in the United States grew from 161,000 to more than 1 million.[79] These professional managers began developing and testing solutions to the mounting challenges of organizing, coordinating, and controlling large numbers of people and increasing worker productivity. Thus began the evolution of modern management with the classical perspective. This perspective contains three subfields, each with a slightly different emphasis: scientific management, bureaucratic organizations, and administrative principles.[80]

Efficiency is everything. The somewhat limited success of organizations in achieving improvements in labor productivity led a young engineer to suggest that the problem lay more in poor management practices than in labor. Frederick Winslow Taylor (1856–1915) insisted that management itself would have to change and, further, that the manner of change could be determined only by scientific study. Hence, the label **scientific management** emerged. Taylor suggested that decisions based on rules of thumb and tradition be replaced with precise procedures developed after careful study of individual situations.[81]

Taylor's philosophy is encapsulated in his statement, "In the past, the man has been first. In the future, the system must be first."[82] The scientific management approach is illustrated by the unloading of iron from rail cars and the reloading of finished steel for the Bethlehem Steel plant in 1898. Taylor calculated that, with the correct movements, tools, and sequencing, each man was capable of loading 47.5 tons per day instead of the typical 12.5 tons. Taylor also worked out an incentive system that paid each man $1.85 a day for meeting the new standard, an increase from the previous rate of $1.15. Productivity at Bethlehem Steel shot up overnight.

These insights helped to establish organizational assumptions that the role of management is to maintain stability and efficiency, with top managers doing the thinking and workers doing what they are told.

How to get organized. Another subfield of the classical perspective took a broader look at the organization. Whereas scientific management focused primarily on the technical core—on work performed on the shop floor—**administrative principles** looked at the design and functioning of the organization as a whole. For example, Henri Fayol proposed fourteen principles of management, such as: "Each subordinate receives orders from only one superior" (unity of command), and "similar activities in an organization should be grouped together under one manager" (unity of

scientific management
precise procedures developed after careful study of individual situations.

administrative principles
the design and functioning of the organization as a whole.

•• •
• •• **CONCEPT CONNECTION**
• • • • • • • • • • • • • • •

Frederick Taylor's scientific management techniques were expanded by automaker Henry Ford, who replaced workers with machines for heavy lifting and moving. One of the first applications of the moving assembly line was the Magneto assembly operation at Ford's Highland Park plant in 1913. Magnetos moved from one worker to the next, reducing production time by half. The same principle was applied to total-car assembly, improving efficiency and reducing worker-hours required to produce a Model-T Ford to less than two. Under this system, a Ford rolled off the assembly line every 10 seconds.

direction). These principles formed the foundation for modern management practice and organization design.

The scientific management and administrative principles approaches were powerful and gave organizations fundamental new ideas for establishing high productivity and increasing prosperity. The administrative principles in particular contributed to the development of bureaucratic organizations, which emphasized designing and managing organizations on an impersonal, rational basis through elements such as clearly defined authority and responsibility, formal record keeping, and uniform application of standard rules. Although the term *bureaucracy* has taken on negative connotations in today's organizations, bureaucratic characteristics worked extremely well for the needs of the Industrial Age.

The term *bureaucracy* has taken on a negative meaning in today's organizations and is associated with endless rules and red tape. We all have been frustrated by waiting in long lines or following seemingly silly procedures. Rules and other bureaucratic procedures, however, provide a standard way of dealing with employees. Everyone gets equal treatment, and everyone knows what the rules are. This foundation enables many organizations to become extremely efficient. UPS serves as a good example.[83]

One problem with the classical perspective is that it failed to consider the social context and human needs. Early work on industrial psychology and human relations received little attention because of the prominence of scientific management. A major breakthrough came, however, with a series of experiments at a Chicago electric company, which came to be known as the Hawthorne Studies. Interpretations of these studies concluded that positive treatment of employees improved their motivation and productivity. Publication of these findings led to a revolution in worker treatment and laid the groundwork for subsequent work examining the treatment of workers, leadership, motivation, and human resource management.

United Parcel Service

The company sometimes called "Big Brown," United Parcel Service (UPS) took on the U.S. Postal Service at its own game—and won. UPS specializes in the delivery of small packages, delivering more than 13 million every business day. In addition, UPS is gaining market share in air service, logistics, and information services. Television commercials asking, "What can Brown do for you?" signify the company's expanding global information services.

Why has Big Brown been so successful? One important factor is the concept of bureaucracy. UPS is bound up in rules and regulations. It teaches drivers an astounding 340 steps for how to correctly deliver a package—such as how to load the truck, how to fasten their seat belts, how to walk, and how to carry their keys. Specific safety rules apply to drivers, loaders, clerks, and managers. Strict dress codes are enforced—clean uniforms (called *browns*) every day, black or brown polished shoes with nonslip soles, no beards, no hair below the collar, and so on. Supervisors conduct 3-minute inspections of drivers each day. The company also has rules specifying cleanliness standards for buildings, trucks, and other properties. No eating or drinking is permitted at employee desks. Every manager is given bound copies of policy books and is expected to use them.

UPS has a well-defined division of labor. Each plant employs specialized drivers, loaders, clerks, washers, sorters, and maintenance personnel. UPS thrives on written records and has been a leader in using new technology to enhance reliability and efficiency. Each driver has a computerized clipboard to track everything from miles per gallon to data on parcel delivery. All drivers have daily worksheets that specify performance goals and work output.

Technical qualification is the criterion for hiring and promotion. The UPS policy book says the leader is expected to have the knowledge and capacity to justify the position of leadership. Favoritism is forbidden. The bureaucratic model works just fine at UPS, "the tightest ship in the shipping business."

Kelly Barron, "Logistics in Brown," *Forbes* (January 10, 2000): 78–83; Scott Kirsner, "Venture Vérité: United Parcel Service," *Wired* (September 1999): 83–96; "UPS," *Atlanta Journal and Constitution* (April 26, 1992): H1; and Kathy Goode, Betty Hahn, and Cindy Seibert, "United Parcel Service: The Brown Giant" (unpublished manuscript, Texas A&M University, 1981).

From a historical perspective, whether the studies were academically sound is of less importance than the fact that they stimulated increased interest in looking at employees as more than extensions of production machinery. The interpretation that employees' output increased when managers treated them in a positive manner started a revolution in worker treatment for improving organizational productivity. Despite flawed methodology or inaccurate conclusions, the findings provided the impetus for the human relations movement.

IBM, one of the earliest proponents of a human relations approach, shaped management theory and practice for well over a quarter century. The company's belief that attention to human relations is the best approach for increasing productivity still persists today.[84]

HUMAN RESOURCES PERSPECTIVE

The human relations movement initially espoused a *dairy farm* view of management: Contented cows give more milk, so satisfied workers will give more work. Gradually, views with deeper content began to emerge. The **human resources perspective** maintained an interest in worker participation and considerate leadership but shifted the emphasis to the daily tasks that people perform. The human resources perspective combines prescriptions for design of job tasks with theories of motivation.[85] In the human resources view, jobs are designed so tasks are not perceived as dehumanizing or demeaning but, instead, allow workers to use their full potential. Two of the best-known contributors to the human resources perspective were Abraham Maslow and Douglas McGregor.

Abraham Maslow (1908–1970), a practicing psychologist, observed that his patients' problems usually stemmed from an inability to satisfy their needs. Thus, he generalized his work and suggested a hierarchy of needs. Maslow's hierarchy started with physiological needs and progressed to safety, belongingness, esteem, and, finally, self-actualization needs.

Douglas McGregor (1906–1964), during the time he was president of Antioch College in Ohio, had become frustrated with the early simplistic human relations notions. He challenged both the classical perspective and the early human relations assumptions about human behavior. Based on his experiences as a manager and consultant, his training as a psychologist, and the work of Maslow, McGregor formulated his Theory X and Theory Y.[86] McGregor believed that the classical perspective was based on Theory X assumptions about workers and posited that a slightly modified version of Theory X fit early human relations ideas. In short, he believed that the human relations ideas of the time did not go far enough. McGregor proposed Theory Y as a more realistic view of workers for guiding management thinking.

The point of Theory Y is that organizations can take advantage of the imagination and intellect of all their employees. Employees will exercise self-control and will contribute to organizational goals when given the opportunity. A few companies today still use Theory X management, but many are using Theory Y techniques.

BEHAVIORAL SCIENCES APPROACH

The **behavioral sciences approach** develops theories about human behavior based on scientific methods and study. Behavioral science draws from sociology, psychology, anthropology, economics, and other disciplines to understand employee behavior and interaction in an organizational setting. The approach can be seen in practically every organization. When General Electric conducts research to determine the best set of tests, interviews, and employee profiles to use when selecting new employees, it is applying behavioral science techniques. When Circuit City electronics stores train new managers in the techniques of employee motivation, most of the theories and findings are rooted in behavioral science research.

human resources perspective
combines prescriptions for design of job tasks with theories of motivation.

behavioral sciences approach
a subfield of the humanistic management perspective that applies social science in an organizational context drawing from economics, psychology and other disciplines.

NEW MANAGER SELF TEST

Evolution of Style

This questionnaire asks you to describe yourself. For each item, write the number "4" next to the phrase that best describes you, "3" to the item that is next best, and on down to "1" for the item that is least like you.

1. My strongest skills are:

_____ **a.** Analytical skills

_____ **b.** Interpersonal skills

_____ **c.** Political skills

_____ **d.** Flair for drama

2. The best way to describe me is:

_____ **a.** Technical expert

_____ **b.** Good listener

_____ **c.** Skilled negotiator

_____ **d.** Inspirational leader

3. What has helped me the most to be successful is my ability to:

_____ **a.** Make good decisions

_____ **b.** Coach and develop people

_____ **c.** Build strong alliances and a power base

_____ **d.** Inspire and excite others

4. The thing people are most likely to notice about me is my:

_____ **a.** Attention to detail

_____ **b.** Concern for people

_____ **c.** Ability to succeed in the face of conflict and opposition

_____ **d.** Charisma

5. My most important leadership trait is:

_____ **a.** Clear, logical thinking

_____ **b.** Caring and support for others

_____ **c.** Toughness and aggressiveness

_____ **d.** Imagination and creativity

6. I am best described as:

_____ **a.** An analyst

_____ **b.** A humanist

_____ **c.** A politician

_____ **d.** A visionary

INTERPRETATION: New managers typically view their world through one or more mental frames of reference. (1) The *structural frame of reference* sees the organization as a machine that can be economically efficient and that provides a manager with formal authority to achieve goals. This manager frame became strong during the era of scientific management and bureaucratic administration. (2) The *human resource frame* sees the organization as people, with manager emphasis on support, empowerment, and belonging. This manager frame gained importance with the rise of the humanistic perspective. (3) The *political frame* sees the organization as a competition for resources to achieve goals, with manager emphasis on negotiation and hallway coalition building. This frame reflects the need within systems theory to have all parts working together. (4) The *symbolic frame* of reference sees the organization as theater—a place to achieve dreams—with manager emphasis on symbols, vision, culture, and inspiration. This manager frame is important for learning organizations.

Which frame reflects your way of viewing the world? The first two frames of reference—structural and human resource—are more important for new managers. These two frames usually are mastered first. As new managers gain experience and move up the organization, they should acquire political skills and also learn to use symbols for communication. New managers must not be stuck for years in one way of viewing the organization, because that may limit their progress. Many new managers evolve through, and master, each of the four frames as they become more skilled and experienced.

SCORING: A higher score represents your way of viewing the organization and will influence your management style. Compute your scores as follows:

ST = 1a + 2a + 3a + 4a + 5a + 6a = _____

HR = 1b + 2b + 3b + 4b + 5b + 6b = _____

PL = 1c + 2c + 3c + 4c + 5c + 6c = _____

SY = 1d + 2d + 3d + 4d + 5d + 6d = _____

Nevertheless, the hierarchical system and bureaucratic approaches that came about during the Industrial Revolution remained the primary approach to organization design and functioning well into the 1970s and 1980s. In general, this approach worked well for most organizations until the past few decades. During the 1980s, however, it began to lead to problems. Increased competition, especially on a global scale, changed the playing field. North American companies had to find a better way. The 1980s produced new corporate cultures that valued lean staff, flexibility, rapid response to the customer, motivated employees, caring for customers, and quality products.

Over the past two decades, the world of organizations has undergone even more profound and far-reaching changes. The Internet and other advances in information technology, globalization, rapid social and economic changes, and other challenges from the environment call for new management perspectives and more flexible approaches to organization design.

Don't forget the environment. Many problems arise when all organizations are treated as similar, which was the case with scientific management and administrative principles approaches that attempted to design all organizations the same. The structures and systems that work in the retail division of a conglomerate will not be appropriate for the manufacturing division. The organization charts and financial procedures that are best for an entrepreneurial Internet firm such as eBay or MaMaMedia will not work for a large food processing plant.

Contingency means that one thing depends on other things, and for organizations to be effective, there must be a "goodness of fit" between their structure and the conditions in their external environment. What works in one setting may not work in another setting. There is not one best way. Contingency theory means "it depends." For example, some organizations have a certain environment, use a routine technology, and desire efficiency. In this situation, a management approach that uses bureaucratic control procedures, a hierarchical structure, and formal communication would be appropriate. Likewise,

contingency
one thing depends on other things, and for organizations to be effective, there must be a "goodness of fit" between their structure and the conditions in their external environment.

Signet Painting Inc.

Consider how Signet Painting Inc. taps into the full potential of every worker by operating from Theory Y assumptions. A painting contractor might seem an unlikely place to look for modern management techniques, but Signet Painting is on the cutting edge in creating a work environment that affords workers self-esteem and significance as well as a paycheck. Twin brothers Larry and Garry Gehrke started searching for a new approach to managing workers when the company grew so large that they couldn't be involved personally in every project. They began by giving crew leaders the power and authority to make decisions on a job, such as reordering supplies without supervisor approval.

The Gehrkes found a number of ways to involve workers and offer them opportunities to share their best knowledge and skills. One approach is a policy committee made up of volunteers who meet to brainstorm solutions to problems they encounter in the field. Managers also strive to incorporate employees' interests and past work experience into their jobs so that each person has the opportunity to make a unique contribution. "Every person wants to feel like they have the knowledge of what they're doing…," says foreman Derrick Borsheim. "I ask my crew questions like, 'What do you think? What should I do?' And I use their ideas."

Chief operating officer Julie Gehrke says that when the management team gave employees in the field more power and authority to make decisions and control their own jobs, it totally changed people's workplace identity. Managers set clear boundaries, rules, and systems, and then trust workers to carry out their responsibilities professionally and reliably. The application of Theory Y assumptions at Signet Painting has given employees a new sense of pride and ownership in their work. Gehrke says, "When I come into the office on Monday morning and hear one of our painters giving an orientation to a new hire and expounding on what a great company this is to work for, I feel triumphant."

Julie Gehrke, "Power to the Painters," *Painting and Wallcovering Contractor* (September–October 2003): 84.

free-flowing management processes work best in an uncertain environment with nonroutine technology. The correct management approach is contingent on the organization's situation.

Today, almost all organizations operate in highly uncertain environments. Thus, we are involved in a significant period of transition, in which concepts of organizations and management are changing as dramatically as they changed with the dawning of the Industrial Revolution.

TOTAL QUALITY MANAGEMENT

TAKE ACTION ▶

Try doing equally well in all courses, and you might see how this contingency theory works!

The quality movement in Japan emerged partly as a result of American influence after World War II. The ideas of W. Edwards Deming, known as the "father of the quality movement," were scoffed at in the United States initially, but the Japanese embraced his theories and modified them to help rebuild their industries into world powers.[87] Japanese companies achieved a significant departure from the American model by gradually shifting from an inspection-oriented approach to quality control toward an approach emphasizing employee involvement in the prevention of quality problems.[88]

During the 1980s and into the 1990s, **total quality management (TQM),** which focuses on managing the total organization to deliver quality to customers, was at the forefront in helping managers deal with global competition. The approach infuses quality values throughout every activity within a company, with front-line workers intimately involved in the process. Four significant elements of quality management are employee involvement, focus on the customer, benchmarking, and continuous improvement.

Employee involvement means that TQM requires companywide participation in quality control. All employees are focused on the customer; TQM companies find out what customers want and try to meet their needs and expectations. *Benchmarking* refers to a process whereby companies find out how others do something better than they do and then try to imitate or improve on it. *Continuous improvement* is the implementation of small, incremental improvements in all areas of the organization on an ongoing basis.

TAKE ACTION ▶

Benchmark your papers and assignments so you can become a better student.

TQM is not a quick fix, but companies such as General Electric, Texas Instruments, Procter & Gamble, and DuPont achieved astonishing results in efficiency, quality, and customer satisfaction through total quality management.[89] TQM is still an important part of today's organizations, and managers consider benchmarking in particular to be a highly effective and satisfying management technique.[90]

Some of today's companies pursue highly ambitious quality goals to demonstrate their commitment to improving quality. For example, *Six Sigma*, popularized by Motorola and General Electric, specifies a goal of no more than 3.4 defects per million parts. But the term also refers to a broad quality control approach that emphasizes a disciplined and relentless pursuit of higher quality and lower costs. TQM is discussed in detail in Chapter 15.

total quality management (TQM) focuses on managing the total organization to deliver quality to customers.

Summary

High performance requires the efficient and effective use of organizational resources through the four management functions of planning, organizing, leading, and controlling. To perform the four functions, managers need three skills—conceptual, human, and technical.

Two characteristics of managerial work are: (1) Managerial activities involve variety, fragmentation, and brevity; and (2) managers perform a great deal of work at an unrelenting pace. Managers are expected to perform activities associated with their informational, interpersonal, and decisional roles.

These management characteristics apply to small businesses, entrepreneurial start-ups, and nonprofit organizations just as they do in large corporations. In addition, they are being applied in a new workplace and a rapidly changing world. In the new workplace, work is free-flowing and flexible to encourage speed and adaptation, and empowered employees are expected to seize opportunities and solve problems.

The workplace is organized around networks rather than vertical hierarchies, and work is often virtual. These changing characteristics result from forces such as advances in technology and e-business, globalization, increased diversity, and a growing emphasis on innovation, change, and speed over stability and efficiency. Managers need new skills and competencies in this new environment. Leadership is dispersed and empowering. Customer relationships are critical, and most work is done by teams that work directly with customers. In the new workplace, managers focus on building relationships, which may include customers, partners, and suppliers. In addition, they strive to build learning capability throughout the organization.

Three major perspectives on management evolved since the late 1800s—the classical, the human resources, and the behavior approach. Each perspective encompasses several specialized subfields. Recent extensions of those perspectives include systems theory, the contingency view, and total quality management (TQM). The most recent thinking about organizations was brought about by today's turbulent times and the shift to a new workplace. Many managers are redesigning their companies toward the learning organization, which fully engages all employees in identifying and solving problems. The learning organization is characterized by a team-based structure, empowered employees, and open information. The learning organization represents a substantial departure from the traditional management hierarchy.

The shift to a learning organization goes hand-in-hand with today's transition to a technology-driven workplace. Ideas, information, and relationships are becoming more important than production machinery and physical assets, which require new approaches to management. E-business is burgeoning as more economic activity takes place over digital computer networks rather than in physical space, and supply chain management is a priority. Other management tools used in the digital workplace include enterprise resource planning, knowledge management, customer relationship management, and outsourcing. These approaches require managers to think in new ways about the role of employees, customers, and partners. Today's best managers value employees for their ability to think, build relationships, and share knowledge—quite different from the scientific management perspective of a century ago.

Discussion Questions

1. What do you think about having a manager's responsibility in today's world, characterized by uncertainty, ambiguity, and sudden changes or threats from the environment? Describe some skills and qualities that are important to managers under these conditions.

2. Assume that you are a project manager at a biotechnology company, working with managers from research, production, and marketing on a major product modification. You notice that every memo you receive from the marketing manager has been copied to senior management. At every company function, she spends time talking to the big shots. You also are aware that sometimes when you and the other project members are slaving away over the project, she is playing golf with senior managers. What is your evaluation of her behavior? As project manager, what do you do?

3. Jeff Immelt of GE said that the most valuable thing he learned in business school was that "there are 24 hours in a day, and you can use all of them." Do you agree or disagree? What are some of the advantages to this approach to being a manager? What are some of the drawbacks?

4. Why do some organizations seem to have a new CEO every year or two, whereas others have top leaders who stay with the company for many years (e.g., Jack Welch's 20 years as CEO at General Electric)? What factors about the manager or about the company might account for this difference?

5. What is the difference between efficiency and effectiveness? Which is more important for performance? Can managers improve both simultaneously?

6. You are a bright, hard-working entry-level manager who fully intends to rise through the ranks. Your performance evaluation gives you high marks for your technical skills but low marks when it comes to people skills. Do you think people skills can be learned, or do you need to rethink your career path? If people skills can be learned, how would you go about it?

8. A college professor told her students, "The purpose of a management course is to teach students about management, not to teach them to be managers." Do you agree or disagree with this statement? Why?

9. Discuss some of the ways that organizations and jobs changed over the past decade. What changes do you anticipate over the next 10 years? How might these changes affect the manager's job and the skills a manager needs to be successful?

10. Based on your experience at work or school, describe some ways in which the principles of scientific management and bureaucracy are still used in organizations.

Do you believe these characteristics will ever cease to be a part of organizational life? Discuss.

11. A management professor once said that for successful management, studying the present was most important, studying the past was next, and studying the future was least important. Do you agree? Why?

12. Why can new information such as produced in the Hawthorne Studies give rise to a major turning point in the history of management even if the idea is later shown to be in error? Discuss.

13. Which of the characteristics of learning organizations do you find most appealing? As a manager, which would be hardest for you to adopt? Why?

14. As organizations become more technology-driven, which do you think will become more important—managing the human element of the organization or managing the technology? Why?

Dear Dr. Dorothy

I work 30 hours a week at a nearby auto rental center and have managed to organize classes around my work schedule. Two months ago I was promoted to shift supervisor, which is awesome. In my new job I have to schedule and supervise counter and phone employees, and also the maintenance and security people. Plus I must step in with difficult customers, and I have to reconcile financial figures at the end of the shift. Here's the problem: I have to stay late, usually two to three hours every day. My employees just can't handle customers at night, so I end up spending a lot of time handling this rather than my new management tasks. If I don't do something soon, I'm going to have to either quit my job or drop out of school.

Cloneless in Wichita

Dear Cloneless,

You have the new manager disease: can't-let-go-itis. You no doubt got promoted because you breezed through customer interactions in a way that left customers happy and time to spare. Now, though, dear friend, your job is to *manage* the work of others, not do it yourself. Making the shift from doer to *manager* is more complicated than most college students (or other grown-ups, for that matter) appreciate. But you have an incessant desire to do that which you have done well.

Because you got promoted, Dr. Dorothy can feel confident that you are not deluding yourself about how well you handle the customers. You have to learn to let go and allow your employees to do their jobs themselves rather than have you meddle, which is precisely how they see it—take Dr. Dorothy's word for it. If you see that they are not talking to customers the way you want, coach them, or send them to training. And if they are really bad, fire them! Before you do that, however, make sure the real problem is not your own need to control and to have things done your way. Dr. Dorothy assures you that if you learn to let go, delegate, and empower, this will make you a better person in other relationships, too.

Self Learning

Management Aptitude Questionnaire

Rate each of the following statements according to the following scale:

1 I am never like this.

2 I am rarely like this.

3 I am sometimes like this.

4 I am often like this.

5 I am always like this.

1. When I have a number of tasks or homework to do, I set priorities and organize the work around deadlines.	1	2	3	4	5
2. Most people would describe me as a good listener.	1	2	3	4	5
3. When I am deciding on a specific course of action for myself (such as hobbies to pursue, languages to study, which job to take, special projects to be involved in), I typically consider the long-term (3 years or more) implications of what I would choose to do.	1	2	3	4	5
4. I prefer technical or quantitative courses to those involving literature, psychology, or sociology.	1	2	3	4	5
5. When I have a serious disagreement with someone, I hang in there and talk it out until it is completely resolved.	1	2	3	4	5
6. When I have a project or assignment, I really get into the details rather than the "big picture" issues.	1	2	3	4	5
7. I would rather sit in front of my computer than spend a lot of time with people.	1	2	3	4	5
8. I try to include others in activities or discussions.	1	2	3	4	5
9. When I take a course, I relate what I am learning to other courses I took or concepts I learned elsewhere.	1	2	3	4	5
10. When somebody makes a mistake, I want to correct the person and let her or him know the proper answer or approach.	1	2	3	4	5
11. I think it is better to be efficient with my time when talking with someone, rather than worry about the other person's needs, so I can get on with my real work.	1	2	3	4	5
12. I know my long-term vision of career, family, and other activities and have thought it over carefully.	1	2	3	4	5
13. When solving problems, I would much rather analyze some data or statistics than meet with a group of people.	1	2	3	4	5
14. When I am working on a group project and someone doesn't pull a fair share of the load, I am more likely to complain to my friends rather than confront the slacker.	1	2	3	4	5
15. Talking about ideas or concepts can get me really enthused or excited.	1	2	3	4	5
16. The type of management course for which this book is used is a waste of time.	1	2	3	4	5
17. I think it is better to be polite and not to hurt people's feelings.	1	2	3	4	5
18. Data or things interest me more than people.	1	2	3	4	5

Scoring and Interpretation

Subtract your scores for questions 6, 10, 14, and 17 from the number 6, and then add the total points for the following sections:

1, 3, 6, 9, 12, 15	Conceptual skills total score	_____
2, 5, 8, 10, 14, 17	Human skills total score	_____
4, 7, 11, 13, 16, 18	Technical skills total score	_____

These skills are three abilities needed to be a good manager. Ideally, a manager should be strong (though not necessarily equal) in all three. Anyone who is noticeably weaker in any of the skills should take courses and read to build up that skill.

Group Learning

A. The Absolute Worst Manager

1. By yourself, think of two managers you have had—the best and the worst. Briefly describe each.

   The best manager I ever had was . . .

   The worst manager I ever had was . . .

2. Divide into groups of 5–7 members. Share your experiences. Each group should choose a couple of examples to share with the whole group. Complete the table below as a group.

	management principle followed or broken	skills evident or missing	lessons to be learned	advice you would give managers
The best managers				
The worst managers				

1. What are the common problems that managers have?

2. Prepare a list of "words of wisdom" you would give as a presentation to a group of managers. What are some basic principles they should use to be effective?

©2001 Dorothy Marcic. Do not reprint without permission.

Action Learning

1. Make plans to interview two different managers, a younger one and an older one, and preferably in two different professions.

2. Ask them questions such as:

   a. How did you get to your current job? What was your career path?

   b. What did you want to be when you were younger?

   c. What do you find most satisfying about your work? Most frustrating?

   d. What were the biggest surprises after you chose this career?

   e. What were, and are, the biggest obstacles to your moving ahead in your career?

   f. What is a typical work day?

   g. What advice would you give to college students who want to go into this profession?

3. Write a short (2–3 page) paper, comparing the two people you interviewed. What were their similarities? differences? Did age make a difference? If they were different genders, did that make a difference? What insights did you gain?

4. Your instructor may ask you to form small groups and discuss your findings. Be prepared to share with them the whole class.

Ethical Dilemma

Can Management Afford to Look the Other Way?

Harry Rull had been with Shellington Pharmaceuticals for 30 years. After a tour of duty in the various plants and 7 years overseas, Harry was back at headquarters, looking forward to his new role as vice president of U.S. marketing.

Two weeks into his new job, Harry received some unsettling news about one of the managers under his supervision. Over casual lunch conversation, the director of human resources mentioned that Harry should expect a phone call about Roger Jacobs, manager of new product development. Jacobs had a history of being "pretty horrible" to his subor-

dinates, she said, and one disgruntled employee asked to speak to someone in senior management. After lunch, Harry did some follow-up work. Jacobs's performance reviews had been stellar, but his personnel file also contained a large number of notes documenting charges of Jacobs's mistreatment of subordinates. The complaints ranged from "inappropriate and derogatory remarks" to subsequently dropped charges of sexual harassment. What was more disturbing was that the amount as well as the severity of complaints had increased with each of Jacobs's 10 years with Shellington.

When Harry questioned the company president about the issue, he was told, "Yeah, he's had some problems, but you can't replace someone with an eye for new products. You're a bottom-line guy. You understand why we let these things slide."

Not sure how to handle the situation, Harry met briefly with Jacobs and reminded him to "keep the team's morale up."

Just after the meeting, Sally Barton from HR called to let him know that the problem she'd mentioned over lunch had been worked out. She warned, however, that another employee had now come forward demanding that her complaints be addressed by senior management.

What Would You Do?

1. Ignore the problem. Jacobs's contributions to new product development are too valuable to risk losing him, and the problems over the past 10 years have always worked themselves out anyway. No sense starting something that could make you look bad.

2. Launch a full-scale investigation of employee complaints about Jacobs, and make Jacobs aware that the documented history over the past 10 years has put him on thin ice.

3. Meet with Jacobs and the employee to try to resolve the current issue. Then start working with Sally Barton and other senior managers to develop stronger policies regarding sexual harassment and treatment of employees, including clear-cut procedures for handling complaints.

SOURCE: Based on Doug Wallace, "A Talent for Mismanagement: What Would You Do?" *Business Ethics*, 2 (November–December 1992): 3–4.

Case for Critical Analysis

Elektra Products, Inc.

Barbara Russell, a manufacturing vice president, walked into the monthly companywide meeting with a light step and a hopefulness she hadn't felt in a long time. The company's new, dynamic CEO was going to announce a new era of employee involvement and empowerment at Elektra Products, an 80-year-old, publicly held company that once had been a leading manufacturer and retailer of electrical products and supplies. In recent years, the company experienced a host of problems: Market share was declining in the face of increased foreign and domestic competition; new product ideas were few and far between; departments such as manufacturing and sales barely spoke to one another; morale was at an all-time low, and many employees were actively seeking other jobs. Everyone needed a dose of hope.

Martin Griffin, who had been hired to revive the failing company, briskly opened the meeting with a challenge: "As we face increasing competition, we need new ideas, new energy, new spirit to make this company great. And the source for this change is you—each one of you."

Then he went on to explain that under the new empowerment campaign, employees would be getting more information about how the company was run and would be able to work with their fellow employees in new and creative ways. Martin proclaimed a new era of trust and cooperation at Elektra Products.

Barbara felt the excitement stirring within her; but as she looked around the room, she saw many of the other employees, including her friend Simon, rolling their eyes. "Just another pile of corporate crap," Simon said later. "One minute they try downsizing, the next reengineering. Then they dabble in restructuring. Now Martin wants to push empowerment. Garbage like empowerment isn't a substitute for hard work and a little faith in the people who have been with this company for years. We made it great once, and we can do it again. Just get out of our way."

Simon had been a manufacturing engineer with Elektra Products for more than 20 years. Barbara knew he was extremely loyal to the company, but he—and a lot of others like him—were going to be an obstacle to the empowerment efforts.

Top management assigned selected managers to several problem-solving teams to come up with ideas for implementing the empowerment campaign. Barbara enjoyed her assignment as team leader of the manufacturing team, working on ideas to improve how retail stores got the merchandise they needed when they needed it. The team thrived, and trust blossomed among the members. They even spent nights and weekends working to complete their report. They were proud of their ideas, which they believed were innovative but easily achievable: Permit a manager to follow a product from design through sales to customers; allow salespeople to refund up to $500 worth of merchandise on the spot; make information available to salespeople about future products; and swap sales and manufacturing personnel for short periods to let them get to know one another's jobs.

When the team presented its report to the department heads, Martin Griffin was enthusiastic. But shortly into the meeting he had to excuse himself because of a late-breaking deal with a major hardware store chain. With Martin absent, the department heads rapidly formed a wall of resistance. The director of human resources complained that the ideas for personnel changes would destroy the carefully crafted job categories that had just been completed. The finance department argued that allowing salespeople to make $500 refunds would create a gold mine for unethical customers and salespeople. The legal department warned that providing information to salespeople about future products would invite industrial spying.

The team members were stunned. As Barbara mulled over the latest turn of events, she considered her options: Keep her mouth shut; take a chance and confront Martin about her sincerity in making empowerment work; push slowly for reform and work for gradual support from the other teams; or look for another job and leave a company that she really cares about. Barbara realized that she was looking at no easy choices and no easy answers.

Questions

1. How might top management have done a better job changing Elektra Products into a new kind of organiza-

tion? What might they do now to get the empowerment process back on track?

2. Can you think of ways in which Barbara could have avoided the problems that her team faced in the meeting with department heads?

3. If you were Barbara, what would you do now? Why?

SOURCE: Based on Lawrence R. Rothstein, "The Empowerment Effort That Came Undone," *Harvard Business Review* (January–February 1995): 20–31.

BIZ FLIX

8 Mile

Jimmy "B-Rabbit" Smith, Jr. (Eminem) wants to be a successful rapper and to prove that a white man can create moving sounds. He works days at a plant run by the North Detroit Stamping Company and pursues his music at night, sometimes on the plant's grounds. The film's title refers to Detroit's northern city boundary which divides Detroit's white and African American populations. This film gives a gritty look at Detroit's hip-hop culture in 1995 and Jimmy's desire to be accepted by it. Eminem's original songs "Lose Yourself" and "8 Mile" received Golden Globe and Academy Award nominations.

This scene is an edited composite of two brief sequences involving the stamping plant. The first half of the scene appears early in the film as part of "The Franchise" sequence. The second half appears in the last 25 minutes of the film as

part of the "Papa Doc Payback" sequence. In the first part of the scene, Jimmy's car won't start so he rides the city bus to work and arrives late. The second part occurs after he is beaten by Papa Doc (Anthony Mackie) and Papa Doc's gang. Jimmy's mother (Kim Basinger) returns to their trailer and tells him she won $3,200 at bingo. The film continues to its end with Jimmy's last battle (a rapper competition).

What to Watch for and Ask Yourself

1. What is your perception of the quality of Jimmy's job and his work environment?

2. What is the quality of Jimmy's relationship with Manny, his foreman (Paul Bates)? Does it change? If it does, why?

3. How would you react to this type of work experience?

VIDEO CASE

Managing in Turbulent Times at Second City Theater

Imagine you have prepared for weeks for this moment. All eyes are on you and everyone is counting on you to make the most of this meeting. You must respond instantly and effectively to the changes in the interaction, affirm all participants and their ideas, and direct it towards a successful conclusion. And your partner is asking you to bark like a dog.

While many business meetings contain elements of this scenario, the most likely context is a Second City Theater production of improvisational and sketch comedy. Managers today are expected to deal with uncertainty, unexpected events, diversity, and change. They must demonstrate flexibility, foster trust, and engage the hearts and minds of employees. The managers at Second City have a leg up in developing these skills and dealing with these situations because Second City has been doing it for years . . . on stage.

Since its inception in 1953, Second City has been the nation's most renowned creator of improvisational comedy acts based on the spontaneous interaction of actors and audience, and sketch comedy akin to those seen on television shows such as Saturday Night Live. Its accolades include the production of an Emmy Award winning TV series, multiple, national touring groups, and a long list of infamous alumni including Chris Farley, Tina Fey, Mike Meyers, Halle Barry, Bill Murray, and many others who have gone on to prominent careers in TV, theater, and film.

One key to Second City's success is the unified goal of furthering the art form of improvisational, satire, and revue comedy. From that goal, the managers of Second City have taken the organization many places, diversifying its reach. In 1975, owner and executive producer, Andrew Alexander, started the Second City television series (SCTV) in response to the new trend of television sketch comedy and the creation of Saturday Night Live in 1975. Later, the company opened the Second City Training Center, an educational center offering classes in improvisation, acting, writing, and other skills, as well as a summer camp. In addition to its theater in Chicago, Second City has theaters in Toronto, Vegas, Detroit, Denver, and Los Angeles, as well as national touring companies. Most recently, managers at Second City saw a need within corporations for staff trainings grounded in building trust, communication, presentation, team-building, and improvisational skills. Understanding Second City's background and specialization in just these areas, they opened the corporate communications division which provides trainings in the areas of internal communications, external marketing and branding, and learning development.

With its focus on human skills, Second City demonstrates all of the qualities of a learning organization. The managers at Second City foster a climate where experimentation and learning is encouraged. As Andrew Alexander says, "there is a culture of encouraging failure." Just like the actors on stage, employees at Second City are expected to share their thoughts and opinions and in turn, to support and build on the ideas of others. This non-traditional environment inspires trust, innovation, and teamwork amongst the many levels of the organization. Through careful planning and management, Second City has directed this unleashing of creative energy to take the company to the next level. As Kelly Leonard, vice president of Second City Theater said, "Don't stop the creativity."

Questions

1. Many students of the Second City Training Center are businesspeople looking to gain skills for the corporate context. What skills from the world of improvisational comedy would be valuable to a business manager?

2. In what way does the focus of a learning organization address the transition to a new workplace as outlined in Exhibit 1.5?

3. What do you think would be the challenges of a manager in a learning organization? Why?

PART 2

The Environment

Translate video and audio into digital files and then find a way to compress them so they can be transmitted reasonably quickly. Add personal computers and Internet access, develop high-speed broadband, and keep lowering costs. It all adds up to a digital revolution that has the entertainment industry scrambling to reinvent itself.

Digital technology has fundamentally changed the industry's relationship with customers. Consumers now have many, many choices: They can visit a social networking site, watch TV, or download a movie (legally or illegally). Not so long ago, a few corporations were in control. Today, consumers have seized power.

The most important legal issues are piracy and privacy. The music and film industries have been hit hard by piracy, especially file-sharing practiced by people who don't see themselves as thieves. And privacy advocates feel threatened by the ability of Web-based operations to gather huge amounts of data on individuals for marketing purposes.

The continuing rapid advances in digital technology make it a sure bet that this external environmental factor will be shaking things up in the entertainment industry and keeping competition in a constant state of flux for some time to come.

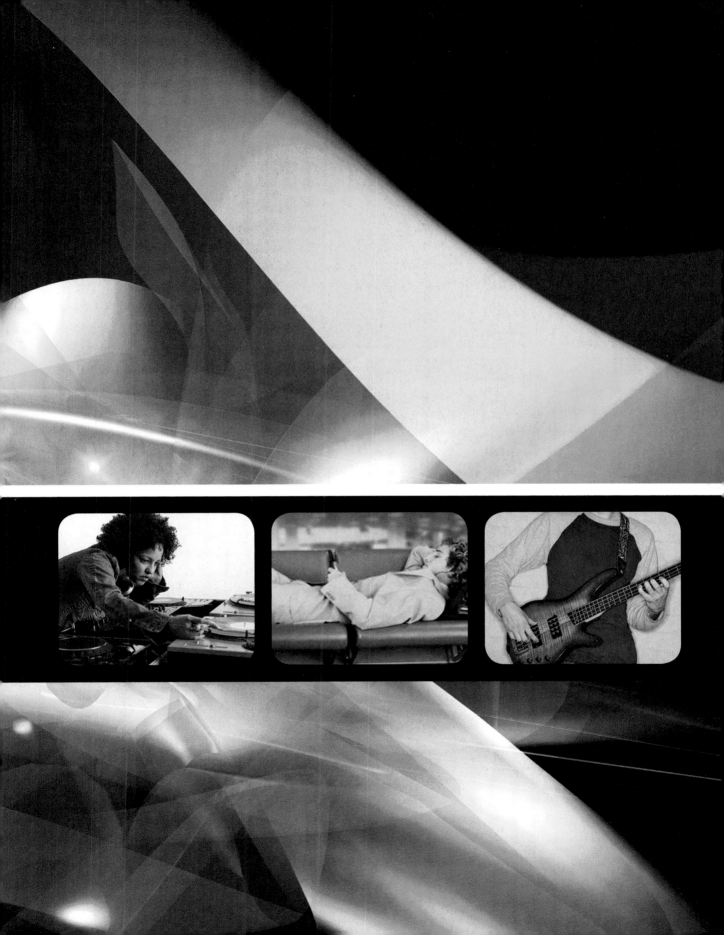

chapter 2

The Environment and Corporate Culture

Learning Objectives

After studying this chapter, you should be able to:

1 Describe the general and task environments and the dimensions of each.

2 Explain the strategies managers use to help organizations adapt to an uncertain or turbulent environment.

3 Define corporate culture and give organizational examples.

4 Explain organizational symbols, stories, heroes, slogans, and ceremonies and their relationship to corporate culture.

5 Describe how corporate culture relates to the environment.

6 Define a cultural leader and explain the tools a cultural leader uses to create a high-performance culture.

New Manager's Questions

Please circle your opinion below each of the following statements. ★ Assess Your Answer

1 I think sales companies should be allowed to send out large catalogs, because it can increase revenues.

1	2	3	4	5
strongly agree				strongly disagree

2 I like my job to have a good deal of stability.

1	2	3	4	5
strongly agree				strongly disagree

3 When I get a new job, I should be accepted for who I am and they should let me be myself.

1	2	3	4	5
strongly agree				strongly disagree

In high-tech industries, environmental conditions are volatile. Microsoft currently is in a situation similar to the one Xerox faced in the early 1990s. Xerox was dominant in its industry for many years, but managers missed cues from the environment and got blindsided by rivals Canon and Ricoh when they began selling comparable copy machines at lower prices. Moreover, Xerox failed to keep pace with changing methods of document management and had no new products to fill the gaps in the declining copy business. Consequently, the company struggled for more than decade to find its footing in a vastly changed world. Current CEO Anne Mulcahy has used her management skills to mastermind a hot turnaround at Xerox and get the company moving forward again.[1] Similar to Xerox, Microsoft has held a dominant position for nearly 30 years, but the environment is shifting dramatically, and Microsoft will have to change significantly to remain competitive.

Yet, an organization doesn't have to be high-tech to be devastated by shifts in the environment. Dixon Ticonderoga Company, which makes pencils, once had a large share of the U.S. market. Today, though, the majority of pencils sold in the United States come from overseas, compared to only 16 percent a decade ago.[2]

In the toy industry, Mattel lost 20 percent of its share of the worldwide fashion doll market when rival MGA Entertainment created a hip new line of dolls called Bratz. Mattel failed to recognize that preteen girls are maturing more quickly and want dolls that look like their pop star idols. Mattel eventually came out with a rival line of dolls for preteens called My Scene, but the damage was already done. Barbie, the top fashion doll for more than 40 years, fell from her pedestal virtually overnight.[3]

Government actions and red tape also can affect an organization's environment and create problems. The 2002 Sarbanes-Oxley corporate governance law is making life more complicated for managers in all organizations. Scandals in the mutual fund industry prompted the SEC to propose a ban on special incentive payments to brokerage firms. The beef and dairy industries in the United States were hurt by increased rules and restrictions following the discovery of mad cow disease in Washington state. And consider thousands of public schools that use a common land snail called *Helix aspera* as a major unit in their science curricula. The U.S. Department of Agriculture's unexpected ban on the interstate transport of the snails threw school science programs into disarray around the nation.[4]

The environment surprises many managers and leaves them unable to adapt their companies to new competition, shifting consumer interests, or new technologies. The study of management traditionally focused on factors within the organization—a *closed* systems view—such as leading, motivating, and controlling employees. The classical, behavioral, and management science schools described in Chapter 1 looked at internal aspects of organizations over which managers have direct control. These views are accurate but incomplete. To be effective, managers must monitor and respond to the environment—an *open systems* view. The events that have the greatest impact on an organization typically originate in the external environment. In addition, globalization and worldwide societal turbulence affect companies in new ways, making the international environment of growing concern to managers everywhere.

This chapter explores in detail components of the external environment and how they affect the organization. We also examine a major part of the organization's internal environment—corporate culture. Corporate culture is shaped by the external environment and is an important part of the context within which managers do their jobs.

TAKE ACTION ➡

As a manager, read and follow the news to keep up on coming changes.

The External Environment

The tremendous and far-reaching changes occurring in today's world can be understood by defining and examining components of the external environment. The external **organizational environment** includes all elements existing outside the boundary of the organization that have the potential to affect the organization.[5] The environment includes

organizational environment
all elements existing outside the organization's boundaries that have the potential to affect the organization.

Talk about asking for trouble. The U.S. toy industry is dominated by giants—Mattel, Habro, Fisher Price, Little Tykes, and so on. With so many failed start-ups in recent years (anyone remember Purple Moon?), it would be foolish for a new company to introduce a toy that would compete with the big guys, wouldn't it? Not to mention that educational toys usually don't make money.

Luckily, Mike Wood and Jim Marggraff at LeapFrog didn't know that. When high-paid law partner Wood got frustrated looking for materials to teach his 3-year-old to read, he started building an electronic toy that would help children make sounds that corresponded to letters of the alphabet. Clumsy prototype in hand, he got an order for 40,000 units from Toys "R" Us. That was enough for him to bid the law firm goodbye, raise $800,000 from friends and family, and start his own company, LeapFrog. After a series of follow-up toys, Wood took $40 million for a majority stake in his company to Knowledge Universe, owned by Michael Milken (former junk bond king of the '80s) and others.

That's when Jim Marggraff entered the picture. He had left a lucrative job at Cisco Systems to launch his innovative globe that had an interactive pen-like pointer. Marggraff's pointer together with Wood's unit ultimately became LeapPad, a paper book placed on top of a pad that looks like an Etch-a-Sketch. When the kid touches the pen to the paper, the book "talks" that word.

Still, there were all those big toy companies to worry about. Few companies lived to tell about it. In a market dominated by GameBoy, Pokemon, and Playstation, the odds were against LeapFrog. Still, its $49.99 LeapPad became the bestselling plaything in 2000, outdoing even the red-hot Razor Skooter. Good things just kept happening. Revenues have been strong—more than $200 million. With Wal-Mart and Toys "R" Us the biggest customers, LeapFrog is trying to increase sales to schools, boosted by a study showing that its products help early literacy.

With only two products in 1995, the company now has 100 interactive toys involving everything from math to music. Leapfrog has introduced a talking-pen computer with character-recognition software. The $99 Fly allows teens and tweens to draw a piano and then play it, or translate words from English to Spanish. Its design includes elements of a calculator, notepad, and alarm clock. With this new product, Leapfrog is growing with its customers, allowing them to keep buying their products as they get older. Now they can Fly.

SOURCES: Jim Milliott, "Leapfrog IPO Looks to Raise $150 million," *Publisher's Weekly* (May 6, 2002): 13; Edward C. Baig, "Will Pen be Mightier Than Other Toys?" *USA Today* (Jan 18, 2005): B.3; "BWR Begins Tracking LeapFrog Enterprises, Inc.," *M2 Presswire* (March 2, 2007): 1; "Ready, Set, Leap Program from LeapFrog Schoolhouse Shows Critical Gains in Early Literacy," *Business Wire* (April 16, 2007): 1.

LeapFrog

competitors, resources, technology, and economic conditions that influence the organization. It does not include events so far removed from the organization that their impact is not perceived.

The organization's external environment can be further conceptualized as having two layers—general and task environments. The **general environment** is the outer layer that is widely dispersed and affects organizations indirectly. It includes social, demographic, and economic factors that influence all organizations about equally. Increases in the inflation rate or the percentage of dual-career couples in the workforce are illustrative of the organization's general environment. These events do not directly change day-to-day operations, but they do affect all organizations eventually.

One impact of the environment is that as parents become more educated and more affluent, they place higher demands on educational toys, a situation one company is exploiting.

The **task environment** is closer to the organization and includes the sectors that conduct day-to-day transactions with the organization and directly influence its basic operations and performance. This environment generally is considered to include competitors, suppliers, and customers.

The organization also has an **internal environment,** which includes the elements within the organization's boundaries. The internal environment is composed of current employees, management, and especially corporate culture, which defines employee

general environment
the layer of the external environment that affects the organization indirectly.

task environment
the layer of the external environment that directly influences the organization's operations and performance.

internal environment
the environment that includes the elements within the organization's boundaries.

EXHIBIT 2.1

Location of the
Organization's
General, Task, and
Internal Environments

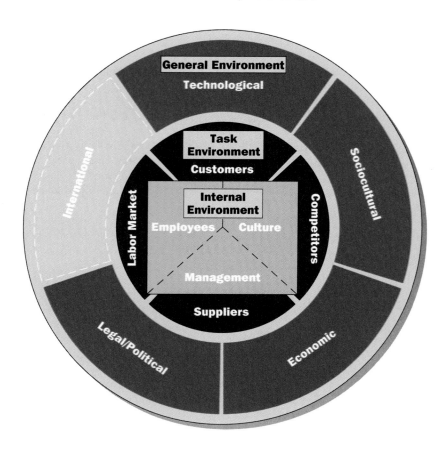

behavior in the internal environment and how well the organization will adapt to the external environment.

Exhibit 2.1 illustrates the relationship among the general, task, and internal environments. As an open system, the organization draws resources from the external environment and releases goods and services back to it. We now will discuss the two layers of the external environment in more detail. Then we will discuss corporate culture, the key element in the internal environment. Other aspects of the internal environment, such as structure and technology, will be covered in Parts Three and Four of this book.

GENERAL ENVIRONMENT

The general environment represents the outer layer of the environment. These dimensions influence the organization over time but often are not involved in day-to-day transactions with it. The dimensions of the general environment include international, technological, sociocultural, economic, and legal-political.

International. The **international dimension** of the external environment represents events originating in foreign countries as well as opportunities for U.S. companies in other countries. Note in Exhibit 2.1 that the international dimension represents a context that influences all other aspects of the external environment. The international environment provides new competitors, customers, and suppliers and shapes social, technological, and economic trends, as well.

Today, every company has to compete on a global basis. High-quality, low-priced automobiles from Japan and Korea have changed the American automobile industry permanently.

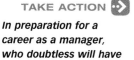

TAKE ACTION

In preparation for a career as a manager, who doubtless will have to deal with employees and customers from different cultures, seek out foreign students and spend time with them, learning to get along with people who are different from you.

international dimension
the portion of the external environment that represents events originating in foreign countries, as well as opportunities for U.S. companies in other countries.

In cell phones and handhelds, U.S.–based companies face stiff competition from Korea's Samsung, Finland's Nokia, and Taiwan's High Tech Computer (HTC) Corporation. For many U.S. companies, such as Starbucks and Wal-Mart, domestic markets have become saturated, and the only potential for growth lies overseas. E-commerce organizations, too, are making international expansion a priority. The U.S. share of worldwide e-commerce is falling as foreign companies set up their own e-commerce ventures.

The most dramatic change in the international environment in recent years is the shift of economic power to China and India. Together, these countries have the population, brainpower, and dynamism to transform the twenty-first–century global economy. If things continue on the current track, analysts predict that India will overtake Germany as the world's third-largest economy within three decades, and that China will overtake the United States as number one by mid-century. In China, per-capita income has tripled in a generation, and leaders are building the infrastructure for decades of expansion, as reflected in the country's hunger for raw materials. In 2005, China represented roughly 47 percent of the global cement consumption, 30 percent of coal, and 26 percent of crude steel. No one can predict the future, but it is clear that however things in India and China shake out, U.S. and other Western firms clearly have no choice but to pay attention.

CONCEPT CONNECTION

"The big idea behind fair trade is that you can actually make globalization work for the poor," says Paul Rice, founder and CEO of TransFair USA. TransFair is the only U.S. organization authorized to grant the Fair Trade logo to products made from a growing list of crops, such as coffee, cocoa, and sugar, for which farmers in developing countries have been paid a fair price. The Oakland, California-based nonprofit is influencing the **international dimension** of today's business environment by helping to increase the sales of fair trade products around the world. Rice says that adhering to TransFair standards is just good business as the global environment grows increasingly important.

The global environment represents a complex, ever-changing, and uneven playing field compared to the domestic environment. To remain competitive, managers who are used to thinking only about the domestic environment must learn new rules. When operating globally, managers have to consider legal, political, sociocultural, and economic factors, not only in their home countries but in various other countries as well. For example, the rising consumer class in China and India plays a growing role in setting the standards for high-tech products and services such as cell phones, multimedia gadgets, and wireless web services.[6]

Chapter 3 describes how today's businesses are operating in an increasingly borderless world and examines in detail how the management in a global environment differs from the management of domestic operations. Perhaps the hardest lesson for managers in the United States to learn is that they do not always know best. U.S. decision makers know little about issues and competition in foreign countries, and many pay little attention to cultural factors, which is a sure route to failure.

One study found that only 28 percent of surveyed executives from the United States think multi-cultural experience is important.[7] U.S. arrogance is a shortcut to failure. An observer of emerging companies in India issues a wake-up call: "Once they learn to sell at Indian prices with world quality, they can compete anywhere."[8]

Benchmarking

iPhones

New technologies have created increased expectations of what a cell phone ought to do. Even before iPhones went on sale in June 2007, Apple's CEO Steven Jobs was changing people's perception of a cell phone from a fast way to make a call to a hip and cool media-friendly apparatus. As a result, he's required cell phone companies and Hollywood moguls to hungrily chase iPhone's trail or risk being left behind. Cellular phone companies are hustling to find ways to compete with iPhone's amazing touch screen and its ability to watch YouTube through a WiFi network. This has scared broadband companies, who wonder if iPhone will make them irrelevant one day soon.

Jobs has pushed some reluctant companies. Just a couple of years ago, Motorola refused to develop a phone with a touch screen. And though wireless has been around for 20 years, most companies have kept its complex nature in the products they develop.

"Steven Jobs and the Apple team come at it from a different perspective," says Glenn Lurie of AT&T. They have a history of turning complicated technology into simple designs. Plus this wouldn't be the first time Jobs has changed an industry. When the iPod came out in 2002, it was a serious block to the illegal song downloading that had become way too common.

Apple is trying to get movie companies to allow more downloads onto the iPhone. Other areas also need work. The current status of providing news, entertainment, and sports on cell phones is dismal, at best, and is the "antithesis of what's happening on the Web," says John Smelzer, of Fox Interactive Media. "Any device that replicates the experience online is good for the entire industry. It will help us reach a mass audience."

SOURCE: Saura M. Holson, "Hollywood Seeks Way to Fit Its Content into the Realm of the iPhone," *The New York Times* (June 25, 2007): C1 & C8.

Technological. The **technological dimension** includes scientific and technological advancements in a specific industry as well as in society at large. In recent years, this dimension created massive changes for organizations in all industries. Twenty years ago, many organizations didn't even use desktop computers. Today, computer networks, Internet access, handheld devices, videoconferencing capabilities, cell phones, fax machines, and laptops are the minimum tools for doing business.

A new generation of handhelds allows users to check their corporate e-mail, daily calendars, business contacts, and even customer orders from anywhere there's a wireless network. Cell phones now can switch seamlessly between cellular networks and corporate WiFi connections. Some companies hand out wireless key fobs with continually updated security codes that enable employees to log on to their corporate networks and securely view data or write e-mails from any PC with a broadband connection.[9]

Other technological advances also will affect organizations and managers. Decoding of the human genome could lead to revolutionary medical advances. Cloning technology and stem cell research are raising both scientific and ethical concerns. Nanotechnology, which refers to manipulating matter at its tiniest scale, is moving from the research lab to the marketplace. Although only a few products incorporated nanoparticles in 2005, within a few years, nanotechnology could affect every industry.

General Electric is researching how nanoceramics can make turbines more efficient. Medical researchers are looking at the potential for portable labs that offer instant analysis for everything from diabetes to HIV. Nanoparticles could someday give us golf balls designed to fly straight, army fatigues that resist chemical weapons, dent-free automobiles, and super-charged fuel cells that could replace fossil-fuel engines. Some 1,200 nanotechnology start-ups have emerged around the world, and smart managers at established organizations such as 3M, Dow Chemical, Samsung, NASA, Intel, Johnson & Johnson, and IBM are investing research dollars in this technological breakthrough.[10]

TAKE ACTION ▶▶

Our generation is technologically savvy. But even greater technological innovations will come down the line. Make it your business to stay on top of the new technologies, no matter what age you are.

technological dimension
the dimension of the general environment that includes scientific and technological advancements in the industry and society at large.

Sociocultural. The **sociocultural dimension** of the general environment represents the demographic characteristics as well as the norms, customs, and values of the general population. Important sociocultural characteristics are geographical distribution and population density, age, and education levels. Today's demographic profiles are the foundation of tomorrow's workforce and consumers. Forecasters see increased globalization of both consumer markets and the labor supply, with increasing diversity both within organizations and consumer markets.[11] Consider the following key demographic trends in the United States:

CONCEPT CONNECTION

Want to get the best out of Generation Y employees? Why not let your current Gen Y workers show you how? That's what Monarch Mountain, a ski and snowboard area near Salida, Colorado, does. As millions of GenY employees flood the job market, companies are finding ways to adapt to this shift in the **sociocultural dimension** of the environment. At Monarch, young employees, not managers, talk with prospective hires to answer questions and address their concerns from the perspective of the job seeker. Through the "First Responder" program, the employee provides a realistic picture of what it's like to work at Monarch and often becomes a mentor if the candidate is hired.

1. The United States is experiencing the largest influx of immigrants in more than a century. By 2050, non-Hispanic whites will make up only about half of the population, down from 74 percent in 1995 and 69 percent in 2004. Hispanics are expected to make up about a quarter of the U.S. population.[12]

2. People are staying in the workforce longer, and many members of the huge post–World War II baby-boom generation are choosing to work well past traditional retirement age. At the same time, the 76 million or so members of Generation Y, which rivals the baby-boom generation in size, are beginning to flood the job market. For the first time, a significant number of organizations are dealing with four generations working side-by-side.[13]

3. The fastest-growing type of living arrangement is single-father households, which rose 62 percent in 10 years, even though two-parent and single-mother households are still much more numerous.[14]

4. In an unprecedented demographic shift, married couple households have slipped from 80 percent in the 1950s to just over 50 percent in 2003. Couples with kids total just 25 percent, with the number projected to drop to 20 percent by 2010. By that year, 30 percent of homes are expected to be inhabited by someone who lives alone.[15]

Demographic trends affect organizations in other countries just as powerfully. Japan, Italy, and Germany are all faced with an aging workforce and customer base as a result of years of declining birth rates. In both Italy and Japan, the proportion of people over the age of 65 reached 20 percent in 2006.[16]

The sociocultural dimension also includes societal norms and values. The low-carb craze replaced the low-fat craze, spurring restaurants to alter their menus and supermarkets to revise their product mix. Even the Girl Scouts were affected, as sales declined about 10 percent during the 2004 cookie season.[17] Handgun manufacturers in the United States have been tugged back and forth as public acceptance and support of guns in the home fell in the wake of tragic school shootings, then surged following terrorist attacks in the United States.

Economic. The **economic dimension** represents the general economic health of the country or region in which the organization operates. Consumer purchasing power, the unemployment rate, and interest rates are part of an organization's economic environment.

sociocultural dimension
the dimension of the general environment representing the demographic characteristics, norms, customs, and values of the population within which the organization operates.

economic dimension
the dimension of the general environment representing the overall economic health of the country or region in which the organization operates.

Spotlight on Skills

The Ties That Bind

With its low labor costs and huge potential market, China is luring thousands of U.S. companies in search of growth opportunities. Yet, University of New Haven's Usha C. V. Haley found that only one-third of multinationals doing business in China have actually turned a profit. One reason that Western businesses fall short of expectations, experts agree, is that they fail to grasp the centuries-old concept of *guanxi* that lies at the heart of Chinese culture. At its simplest level, guanxi is a supportive, mutually beneficial connection between two people. Eventually, those personal relationships are linked together into a network, and it is through these networks that business gets done. Anyone considering doing business in China should keep in mind the following basic rules:

- **Business is always personal.** It is impossible to translate "don't take it so personally—it's only business" into Chinese. Western managers tend to believe that if they conclude a successful transaction, a good business relationship will follow. The development of a personal relationship is an added bonus, but not really necessary when it comes to getting things done. In the Chinese business world, though, a personal relationship must be in place before managers even consider entering a business transaction. Western managers doing business in China should cultivate personal relationships—both during and outside of business hours. Accept any and all social invitations—for drinks, a meal, or even a potentially embarrassing visit to a karaoke bar.
- **Don't skip the small talk.** Getting right down to business and bypassing the small talk during a meeting might seem like an efficient use of time to an American manager. To the Chinese, however, this approach neglects the all-important work of forging an emotional bond. Be aware that the real purpose of your initial meetings with potential business partners is to begin building a relationship, so keep your patience if the deal you're planning to discuss never even comes up.

- **Remember that relationships are not short-term.** The work of establishing and nurturing guanxi relationships in China is never done. Western managers must put aside their usual focus on short-term results and recognize that it takes a long time for foreigners to be accepted into a guanxi network. Often, foreign companies must prove their trustworthiness and reliability over time. For example, firms that weathered the political instability that culminated in the 1989 student protests in Tiananmen Square found it much easier to do business afterward.

- **Make contact frequently.** Some experts recommend hiring ethnic Chinese staff members and then letting them do the heavy lifting of relationship-building. Others emphasize that Westerners themselves should put plenty of time and energy into forging links with Chinese contacts; those efforts will pay off because the contacts can smooth the way by tapping into their own guanxi networks. Whatever the strategy, contact should be frequent and personal. And be sure to keep careful track of the contacts you make. In China, any and all relationships are bound to be important at some point in time.

SOURCES: Michelle Dammon Loyalka, "Doing Business in China," *BusinessWeek Online* (January 6, 2006), www.businessweek.com/smallbiz/; "Guanxi," *Wikipedia*, http://en.wikipedia.org/wiki/Guanxi; Los Angeles Chinese Learning Center, "Chinese Business Culture," http://chinese-school.netfirms.com/guanxi.html; and Beijing British Embassy, "Golden Hints for Doing Business in China," http://chinese-school.netfirms.com/goldenhints.html

Because organizations today are operating in a global environment, the economic dimension has become exceedingly complex and creates enormous uncertainty for managers. The economies of countries are tied together more closely now. For example, the economic recession in the early 2000s and the decline of consumer confidence in the United States affected economies and organizations around the world. Similarly, economic problems in Asia and Europe had a tremendous impact on companies and the stock market in the United States.

One significant trend in the economic environment of late is the frequency of mergers and acquisitions. Citibank and Travelers merged to form Citigroup, IBM purchased PricewaterhouseCoopers Consulting, and Cingular acquired AT&T Wireless. In the toy industry, the three largest toy makers—Hasbro, Mattel, and Tyco—gobbled up at least a dozen smaller competitors within a few years. At the same time, a tremendous vitality is evident in the small business sector of the economy. Entrepreneurial start-ups are a significant aspect of today's U.S. economy, as will be discussed in Appendix A.

Legal-Political. The **legal-political dimension** includes government regulations at the local, state, and federal levels, as well as political activities designed to influence company behavior. The U.S. political system encourages capitalism, and the government tries not to overregulate business. Government laws, however, do specify rules of the game. The federal government influences organizations through the Occupational Safety and Health Administration (OSHA), Environmental Protection Agency (EPA), fair trade practices, libel statutes allowing lawsuits against business, consumer protection legislation, product safety requirements, import and export restrictions, and information and labeling requirements.

Many organizations also have to contend with government and legal issues in other countries. The European Union (EU) adopted environmental and consumer protection rules that are costing American companies hundreds of millions of dollars a year. Companies such as Hewlett-Packard, Ford Motor Company, and General Electric have to pick up the bill for recycling the products they sell in the EU, for example.[18]

Managers also must recognize a variety of **pressure groups** that work within the legal-political framework to influence companies to behave in socially responsible ways. Environmental activists have targeted Victoria's Secret, L.L.Bean, and other companies for wasteful catalog-printing practices that the activists say contribute to the stripping of endangered forests.[19]

Tobacco companies today are certainly feeling the far-reaching power of antismoking groups. Middle-aged activists who once protested the Vietnam War have gone to battle to keep Wal-Mart from "destroying the quality of small-town life." Some groups also attacked the giant retailer on environmental issues, which likely will be one of the strongest pressure points in coming years.[20]

Two of the hottest current issues for pressure groups that also are related to environmental concerns are biotechnology and world trade. Environmental and human rights protesters disrupted World Trade Organization meetings and meetings of the World Bank and the International Monetary Fund to protest a system of worldwide integration that has food, goods, people, and capital freely moving across borders. This current international issue will be discussed in more detail in Chapter 3.

TASK ENVIRONMENT

As described earlier, the task environment includes those sectors that have a direct working relationship with the organization. These include customers, competitors, suppliers, and the labor market.

Customers. People and organizations in the environment that acquire goods or services from the organization are its **customers.** As recipients of the organization's output, customers are important because they determine the organization's success. Patients are the customers of hospitals, students the customers of schools, and travelers the customers of airlines. Many companies are searching for ways to reach the coveted teen and youth market by tying marketing messages into online social networks such as MySpace.com and Facebook.com. With high school and college students representing a $375 billion consumer-spending market, this is serious business for managers at companies such as Target, Apple, Coca-Cola, and Walt Disney. Apple sponsors an Apple-lovers group on Facebook.com, giving away iPod Shuffles in weekly contests. Target has sponsored a group on MySpace.com that features a 15-year-old professional snowboarder wearing a Target logo on his helmet.[21]

legal-political dimension
the dimension of the general environment that includes federal, state, and local government regulations and political activities designed to influence company behavior.

pressure group
an interest group that works within the legal-political framework to influence companies to behave in socially responsible ways.

customers
people and organizations in the environment who acquire goods or services from the organization.

TAKE ACTION

Have you ever been flamed? Or has someone passed along a secret e-mail of yours to someone else—or 100 other people? Imagine the power that thousands of angry consumers have toward one company!

TAKE ACTION

As a new manager, you can get a leg up by paying attention to the external environment and international events. Stay in tune with what's going on in the general environment, including social, economic, technological, and political trends. Pay particular attention to the task environment, including your customers, competitors, and suppliers. Be sure to connect the dots among the things you see.

competitors
other organizations in the same industry or type of business that provide goods or services to the same set of customers.

suppliers
people and organizations who provide the raw materials the organization uses to produce its output.

labor market
the people available for hire by the organization.

Customers today have more power because of the Internet, which presents threats as well as opportunities for managers. Today's customers can directly affect the organization's reputation and sales, for example, through gripe sites such as *walmartsucks.com*, where customers and sales associates cyber-vent about the nation's largest retailer, and *untied.com*, where United Airlines employees and disgruntled fliers rail against the air carrier.

"In this new information environment," says Kyle Shannon, CEO of e-commerce consultant Agency.com, "you've got to assume everyone knows everything."[22]

Competitors. Other organizations in the same industry or type of business that provide goods or services to the same set of customers are referred to as **competitors.** Each industry is characterized by specific competitive issues. The recording industry differs from the steel industry and the pharmaceutical industry.

Competitive wars are being waged worldwide in all industries. Coke and Pepsi continue to battle it out for the soft-drink market. UPS and FedEx fight the overnight delivery wars. Home Depot and Lowe's brawl in the retail home improvement market, trying to out-do one another in terms of price, service, and selection.[23] In the travel and tourism industry, Internet companies such as Expedia.com and Hotels.com have hurt the big hotel chains. These chains are fighting back by undercutting the brokers' prices on the hotels' own websites. In addition, five of the largest chains banded together to create Travelweb.com, which is aimed directly at the online brokers.[24] When celebrities become part of the competition, it often puts an unfair burden on other players, as shown in the Spotlight on Skills feature.

Suppliers. The raw materials the organization uses to produce its output are provided by **suppliers.** A steel mill requires iron ore, machines, and financial resources. A small, private university may utilize hundreds of suppliers for paper, pencils, cafeteria food, computers, trucks, fuel, electricity, and textbooks. Companies from toolmakers to construction firms and auto manufacturers were hurt in 2004 by an unanticipated jump in the price of steel from suppliers. Just as they were starting to see an upturn in their business, the cost of raw materials jumped 30 percent in a two-month period.[25]

Consider also that China now produces more than 85 percent of the Vitamin C used by companies in the United States. An agreement among China's four largest producers led to an increase in the price of Vitamin C from $3 a kilogram to as high as $9 a kilogram.[26]

Many companies are using fewer suppliers and trying to build good relationships with them so they will receive high-quality parts and materials at lower prices. The relationship between manufacturers and suppliers traditionally has been an adversarial one, but managers are finding that cooperation is the key to saving money, maintaining quality, and speeding products to market.

Labor market. The **labor market** represents people in the environment who can be hired to work for the organization. Every organization needs a supply of trained, qualified personnel. Unions, employee associations, and the availability of certain classes of employees can influence the organization's labor market. Curent labor market forces affecting organizations include (1) the growing need for computer-literate knowledge workers; (2) the

Spotlight on Skills

Mary Kate and Ashley Olsen

Talented designer Philip Lim worked for ten years in other designers' studios before he got his own label, which now sells at Neiman Marcus. So when he recently was awarded the highest honor for emerging talent in the fashion industry, he must have felt some hesitation when his statuette was handed to him by two self-described designers—Mary Kate and Ashley Olsen. These turning-21 ubiquitous twins are introducing a soon-to-be competing collection, and they would really like to someday receive the same honor awarded Lim.

"You think, 'Wow, how unfair!'" Lim said before the awards, after he read about the twins' plans to extend their $1.4 billion fashion, marketing, and lip-gloss empire into the trendy clothing market. In a tuxedo he sewed himself for the ceremony, Lim talked about the frustration within his peer-group, facing an assault of celebrity competing labels. Previously, the Olsens'

markets were teens buying at Wal-Mart, but as emerging adults, they now are going after the high-end designer segment and named their line Elizabeth and James (after their non-famous siblings).

The paradox is that for many years designers courted celebrities as customers and even encouraged those who moonlighted as designers, such as Jennifer Lopez and Sean Combs. Now young designers are questioning this phenomenon. Though Lim's collection is expected to gross $30 million this year, he says it is virtually impossible for new, non-celebrity designers to survive in the business, when lines of Combs and Lopez grossed $100 million in their first years.

"Celebrities have made it harder for real designers," said Vera Wang, who won the fashion council's top award in 1995, after two decades in the industry. Says another successful designer, "We live in a media-crazed culture, where it's all about celebrity."

SOURCE: Eric Wilson, "Stealing the Scene along with the Store," *The New York Times* (June 7, 2007): E1 & E6.

necessity for continuous investment in human resources through recruitment, education, and training to meet the competitive demands of the borderless world; and (3) the effects of international trading blocs, automation, outsourcing, and shifting facility location upon labor dislocations, which creates unused labor pools in some areas and labor shortages in others.

Changes in these various sectors of the general and task environments can give rise to tremendous challenges, especially for organizations operating in complex, rapidly changing industries. Nortel Networks, a Canadian company with multiple U.S. offices, is an example of an organization operating in a highly complex environment.

Nortel Networks. The external environment for Nortel Networks is illustrated in Exhibit 2.2. The Canadian-based company began in 1895 as a manufacturer of telephones and has reinvented itself many times to keep up with changes in the environment. In the late 1990s, the company transformed itself into a major player in wireless technology and equipment for connecting businesses and individuals to the Internet. In 1997, the company was about to be run over by rivals, such as Cisco Systems, who were focused on Internet gear. Then-CEO John Roth knew he had to do something bold to respond to changes in the technological environment. A name change to Nortel Networks symbolized and reinforced the company's new goal of providing unified network solutions to customers worldwide.

One response to the competitive environment was to spend billions of dollars to acquire data and voice networking companies, including Bay Networks (which makes Internet and data equipment), Cambrian Systems (a hot maker of optical technology), Periphonics (maker of voice-response systems), and Clarify (customer relationship management software). These companies brought Nortel top-notch technology, helping the company snatch customers away from rivals Cisco and Lucent Technologies. In addition, even during rough economic times, Nortel kept spending nearly 20 percent of its revenues on research and development to keep pace with changing technology.

EXHIBIT 2.2

The External
Environment of Nortel

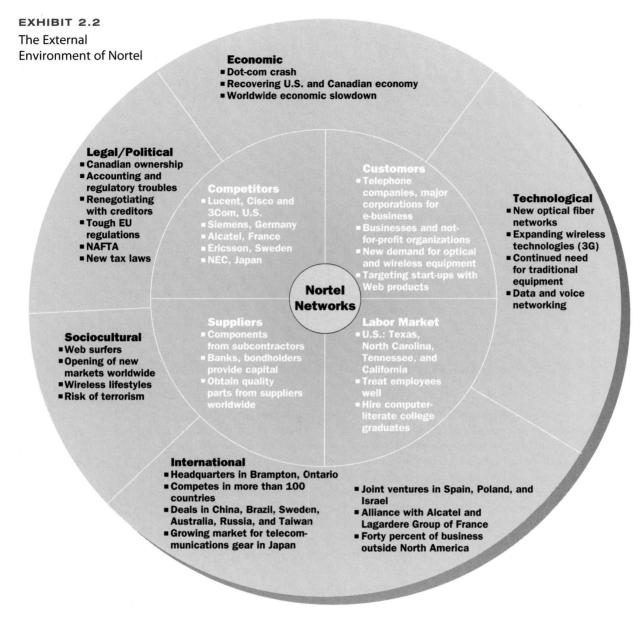

Economic
- Dot-com crash
- Recovering U.S. and Canadian economy
- Worldwide economic slowdown

Legal/Political
- Canadian ownership
- Accounting and regulatory troubles
- Renegotiating with creditors
- Tough EU regulations
- NAFTA
- New tax laws

Competitors
- Lucent, Cisco and 3Com, U.S.
- Siemens, Germany
- Alcatel, France
- Ericsson, Sweden
- NEC, Japan

Customers
- Telephone companies, major corporations for e-business
- Businesses and not-for-profit organizations
- New demand for optical and wireless equipment
- Targeting start-ups with Web products

Technological
- New optical fiber networks
- Expanding wireless technologies (3G)
- Continued need for traditional equipment
- Data and voice networking

Nortel Networks

Sociocultural
- Web surfers
- Opening of new markets worldwide
- Wireless lifestyles
- Risk of terrorism

Suppliers
- Components from subcontractors
- Banks, bondholders provide capital
- Obtain quality parts from suppliers worldwide

Labor Market
- U.S.: Texas, North Carolina, Tennessee, and California
- Treat employees well
- Hire computer-literate college graduates

International
- Headquarters in Brampton, Ontario
- Competes in more than 100 countries
- Deals in China, Brazil, Sweden, Australia, Russia, and Taiwan
- Growing market for telecommunications gear in Japan
- Joint ventures in Spain, Poland, and Israel
- Alliance with Alcatel and Lagardere Group of France
- Forty percent of business outside North America

SOURCES: W. C. Symonds, J. B. Levine, N. Gross, and P. Coy, "High-Tech Star: Northern Telecom Is Challenging Even AT&T," *BusinessWeek* (July 27, 1992): 54–58; I. Austen, "Hooked on the Net," *Canadian Business* (June 26–July 10, 1998): 95–103; J. Weber with A. Reinhardt and P. Burrows, "Racing Ahead at Nortel," *BusinessWeek* (November 8, 1999): 93–99; "Nortel's Waffling Continues: First Job Cuts, Then Product Lines, and Now the CEO," *Telephony* (May 21, 2001): 12; and M. Heinzl, "Nortel's Profits of 499 Million Exceeds Forecast," *Wall Street Journal* (January 30, 2004): B4.

Internationally, Nortel made impressive inroads in Taiwan, China, Brazil, Mexico, Colombia, Japan, and Sweden, among other countries. It also won customers by recognizing the continuing need for traditional equipment and offering hybrid gear that combines old telephone technology with new Internet features, allowing companies to make the transition from the old to the new. Bold new technologies for Nortel include optical systems that move voice and data at the speed of light and third-generation wireless networks (3G), which zap data and video from phone to phone. Nortel is considered a leader in wireless gear and won contracts from Verizon Communications and Orange SA, a unit of France Telecom, to supply equipment that sends phone calls as packets of digital data like that used over the Internet.

Companies moving in a Net-speed environment risk a hard landing, and when the demand for Internet equipment slumped in the early 2000s, Nortel's business was devastated. The company cut more than two-thirds of its workforce and closed dozens of plants and offices. An accounting scandal that led to fraud investigations and senior executive dismissals made things even worse. At one point, Nortel's stock was trading for less than a dollar. By early 2006, though, positive changes in the economic environment, along with a savvy new CEO, put Nortel back on an uphill swing. Analysts predicted that the company would outdo major competitor Lucent in sales growth and other financial metrics. As one analyst said, however, "It's a tough business," and Nortel's managers have to stay on their toes to help the organization cope in an ever-changing, difficult environment.[27]

The Organization–Environment Relationship

Why do organizations care so much about factors in the external environment? The reason is that the environment creates uncertainty for organization managers, and they must respond by designing the organization to adapt to the environment.

ENVIRONMENTAL UNCERTAINTY

To be effective, organizations must manage environmental uncertainty. *Uncertainty* means that managers do not have sufficient information about environmental factors to understand and predict environmental needs and changes.[28] As indicated in Exhibit 2.3, environmental characteristics that influence uncertainty are the number of factors that affect the organization and the extent to which those factors change. A large multinational such as Nortel Networks has thousands of factors in the external environment creating uncertainty for managers. When external factors change rapidly, the organization experiences high uncertainty. Examples are telecommunications and aerospace firms, computer and electronics companies, and e-commerce organizations that sell products and services over the Internet. Companies have to make an effort to adapt to the rapid changes in the environment. When an organization deals with only a few external factors and these factors are relatively stable, such as for soft-drink bottlers or food processors, managers experience low uncertainty and can devote less attention to external issues.

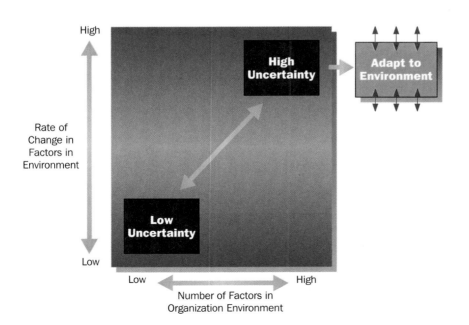

EXHIBIT 2.3

The External Environment and Uncertainty

2 I like my job to have a good deal of stability.

ANSWER: With each passing year, the environment for organizations gets more unpredictable, which results in jobs being increasingly less predictable. Even so, some industries and sectors have relatively more stability. When looking for a job, be honest with yourself about how much stability you need, and then make that one of the considerations when evaluating different positions.

CONCEPT CONNECTION

A consumer focus group in Mexico evaluates Campbell's soups, reviewing qualities such as packaging, preparation, appearance, and taste. The passage of NAFTA broadened market opportunities in Mexico, where nearly 9 billion servings of soup are consumed each year. Marketing executives act as **boundary spanners** to test reactions and assess whether products meet local needs. Boundary spanning provided competitive intelligence that Mexican consumers like convenient dry-soup varieties as well as condensed and ready-to-serve soups.

boundary-spanning roles

roles assumed by people and/or departments that link and coordinate the organization with key elements in the external environment.

ADAPTING TO THE ENVIRONMENT

If an organization faces increased uncertainty with respect to competition, customers, suppliers, or government regulations, managers can use several strategies to adapt to these changes, including **boundary-spanning roles,** interorganizational partnerships, and mergers or joint ventures.

People in departments such as marketing and purchasing span the boundary to work with customers and suppliers, both face-to-face and through market research. Some organizations are staying in touch with customers through the Internet, such as by monitoring gripe sites, communicating with customers on company websites, and contracting with market-research firms that use the web to monitor rapidly changing marketplace trends.[29] Another approach to boundary spanning is the use of *business intelligence,* which results from using sophisticated software to search through large amounts of internal and external data to spot patterns, trends, and relationships that might be significant. For example, Verizon uses business intelligence software to actively monitor customer interactions and fix problems almost immediately.[30]

Boundary spanning is an increasingly important task in organizations because environmental shifts can happen so quickly in today's world. To make good decisions, managers need good information about their competitors, customers, and other elements of the environment. Thus, the most successful companies involve everyone in boundary-spanning activities. People at the grassroots often can see and interpret significant changes sooner than managers who are more removed from the day-to-day work.[31] But top executives, too, have to stay in tune with the environment. Tom Stemberg, CEO of Staples, visits a competitor's store once a week and shares what he learns with others on the management team.[32] Perceiving environmental shifts that could impact the organization isn't always easy. Managers must learn to not only interpret the data right in front of them but also to see weak signals on the periphery and answer the question, "What don't we know that might matter?"[33]

NEW MANAGER SELF TEST

Manager Mind and the Environment

Does your mind fit an uncertain environment? Think back to how you thought or behaved at a time when you were in a formal or informal leadership position. Please answer whether each of the following items was "Mostly True" or "Mostly False" for you.

	Mostly True	Mostly False
1. Enjoyed hearing about new ideas even when working toward a deadline.	_____	_____
2. Welcomed unusual viewpoints of others even if we were working under pressure.	_____	_____
3. Made it a point to attend industry trade shows and company events.	_____	_____
4. Specifically encouraged others to express opposing ideas and arguments.	_____	_____
5. Asked "dumb" questions.	_____	_____
6. Always offered comments on the meaning of data or issues.	_____	_____
7. Expressed a controversial opinion to bosses and peers.	_____	_____
8. Suggested ways of improving my and others' ways of doing things.	_____	_____

INTERPRETATION: In an organization in a highly uncertain environment, everything seems to be changing. In that case, an important quality for a new manager is "mindfulness," which includes the qualities of being open-minded and an independent thinker. In a stable environment, a closed-minded manager may perform okay because much work can be done in the same old way. In an uncertain environment, even a new manager has to facilitate new thinking, new ideas, and new ways of working. A high score on the preceding items suggests higher mindfulness and a better fit with an uncertain environment.

SCORING: Give yourself one point for each item you marked as "Mostly True." If you scored less than 5, you might want to start your career as a manager in a stable environment rather than an unstable environment. A score of 5 or above suggests a higher level of mindfulness and a better fit for a new manager in an organization with an uncertain environment.

SOURCES: The questions are based on ideas from R. L. Daft and R. M. Lengel, *Fusion Leadership* (San Francisco: Berrett Koehler, 2000): Chapter 4; B. Bass and B. Avolio, *Multifactor Leadership Questionnaire*, 2nd ed. (Mind Garden, Inc); and Karl E. Weick and Kathleen M. Sutcliffe, *Managing the Unexpected: Assuring High Performance in an Age of Complexity* (San Francisco: Jossey–Bass, 2001).

Managers are shifting from an adversarial orientation to a partnership orientation, as summarized in Exhibit 2.4. The new paradigm is based on trust and the ability of partners to work out equitable solutions to conflicts so everyone profits from the relationship. Managers work to reduce costs and add value to both sides rather than try to get all the benefits for their own company. The new model also is characterized by a high level of

EXHIBIT 2.4

The Shift to a
Partnership Paradigm

From Adversarial Orientation →	To Partnership Orientation
• Suspicion, competition, arm's length	• Trust, value added to both sides
• Price, efficiency, own profits	• Equity, fair dealing, everyone profits
• Information and feedback limited	• E-business links to share information and conduct digital transactions
• Lawsuits to resolve conflict	• Close coordination; virtual teams and people onsite
• Minimal involvement and up-front investment	• Involvement in partner's product design and production
• Short-term contracts	• Long-term contracts
• Contracts limit the relationship	• Business assistance goes beyond the contract

TAKE ACTION

Read the ethical dilemma at the end of the chapter, pertaining to competitive intelligence. Do you have the courage to risk your job over the inappropriate use of confidential information?

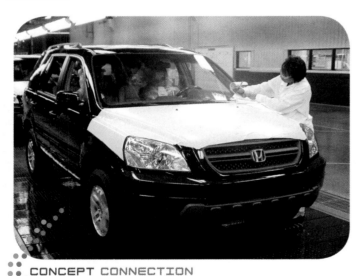

•• **CONCEPT CONNECTION**

Equality is at the heart of Japanese automaker Honda's **corporate culture,** and visible manifestations of the cultural values are everywhere. For example, facilities such as this automobile manufacturing plant in Lincoln, Alabama, have open offices, no assigned parking spaces, and the 4,500 employees, called *associates,* all eat in the same cafeteria and call each other by their first names. Everyone, from the president on down, comes to work, walks into the locker room, and changes into a gleaming white two-piece uniform emblazoned with the Honda insignia. It's no accident that it's hard to tell the managers from the front-line workers.

information sharing, including e-business linkages for automatic ordering, payments, and other transactions.

In addition, person-to-person interaction provides corrective feedback and solves problems. People from other companies may be onsite or participate in virtual teams to enable close coordination. Partners frequently are involved in one another's product design and production, and they are committed for the long term. It is not unusual for business partners to help one another, even outside of what is specified in the contract.[34]

A step beyond strategic partnerships is for companies to become involved in mergers or joint ventures to reduce environmental uncertainty. A **merger** occurs when two or more organizations combine to become one. For example, Wells Fargo merged with Norwest Corp. to form the nation's fourth largest banking corporation. A **joint venture** involves a strategic alliance or program by two or more organizations. A joint venture typically occurs when a project is too complex, expensive, or uncertain for one firm to handle alone. Oprah Winfrey's Harpo Inc. formed a joint venture with Hearst Magazines to launch *O, The Oprah Magazine.*[35]

The Internal Environment: Corporate Culture

The internal environment within which managers work includes corporate culture, production technology, organization structure, and physical facilities. Of these, corporate culture surfaces as extremely important to competitive advantage. The internal culture must fit the needs of the external environment and company strategy. With this fit,

merger
the combining of two or more organizations into one.

joint venture
a strategic alliance or program by two or more organizations.

**Assess Your Answer**

3 When I get a new job, I should be accepted for who I am and allowed to be myself.

ANSWER: Each organization has its own culture, its own assumptions and expectations of behavior. To succeed, you should spend time observing the culture and try to adapt to it, without giving up any of your own core values.

highly committed employees create a high-performance organization that is tough to beat.[36]

Most people don't think about culture; it's just "how we do things around here" or "the way things are here." But managers have to think about culture because it typically plays a significant role in organizational success. The concept of culture has been of growing concern to managers since the 1980s, as turbulence in the external environment has grown, often requiring new values and attitudes. Organizational culture has been defined and studied in many and varied ways. For the purposes of this chapter, we define **culture** as the set of key values, beliefs, understandings, and norms shared by members of an organization.[37] The concept of culture helps managers understand the hidden, complex aspects of organizational life. Culture is a pattern of shared values and assumptions about how things are done within the organization. Members learn this pattern as they cope with external and internal problems and teach it to new members as the correct way to perceive, think, and feel.

Culture can be analyzed at three levels, as illustrated in Exhibit 2.5, with each level becoming less obvious.[38] At the surface level are visible artifacts, which include things such as manner of dress, patterns of behavior, physical symbols, organizational ceremonies, and office layout. Visible artifacts are all the things one can see, hear, and observe by watching members of the organization. At a deeper level are the expressed values and beliefs, which are not observable but can be discerned from how people explain and justify what they do.

Members of the organization hold these values at a conscious level. They can be interpreted from the stories, language, and symbols organization members use to represent them.

Some values become so deeply embedded in a culture that members no longer are consciously aware of them. These basic, underlying assumptions and beliefs are the essence of culture and subconsciously guide behavior and decisions. In some organizations, a basic

◀◦▸ TAKE ACTION

As a new manager, you will have to learn to span the boundary to other units that influence your success. As you progress to higher management positions, you will learn how to use interorganizational partnerships, and even mergers or joint ventures, to help your organization adapt and stay competitive in a shifting environment.

culture
the set of key values, beliefs, understandings, and norms that members of an organization share.

EXHIBIT 2.5

Levels of Corporate Culture

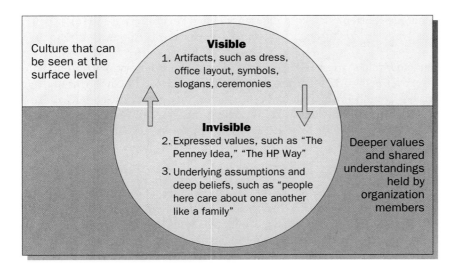

Culture that can be seen at the surface level

Visible
1. Artifacts, such as dress, office layout, symbols, slogans, ceremonies

Invisible
2. Expressed values, such as "The Penney Idea," "The HP Way"

3. Underlying assumptions and deep beliefs, such as "people here care about one another like a family"

Deeper values and shared understandings held by organization members assumption might be that people are essentially lazy and will shirk their duties whenever possible; thus, employees are closely supervised and given little freedom, and colleagues frequently are suspicious of one another. More enlightened organizations operate on the basic assumption that people want to do a good job. In these organizations, employees are given more freedom and responsibility and colleagues trust one another and work cooperatively. Take the New Manager Self Test see how well you might do in a new organizational culture.

The fundamental values that characterize an organization's culture can be understood through the visible manifestations of symbols, stories, heroes, slogans, and ceremonies.

SYMBOLS

A **symbol** is an object, act, or event that conveys meaning to others. Symbols can be considered a rich, nonverbal language that vibrantly conveys the organization's important values concerning how people relate to one another and interact with the environment.[39] For example, managers at a New York–based start-up that provides Internet solutions to local television broadcasters wanted a way to symbolize the company's unofficial mantra of "drilling down to solve problems." They bought a dented old drill for $2 and dubbed it The Team Drill. Each month, the drill is presented to a different employee in recognition of exceptional work, and the employee personalizes the drill in some way before passing it on to the next winner.[40]

Buildings and office layout also can be symbolic. The headquarters of RadioShack Corp. used to have 22 separate entrances and five parking lots, with employees higher up the hierarchy having more convenient parking and building access. When the company built its new headquarters, top managers asked that it be designed with one parking garage and a single front door for all 2,400 employees. The door spills onto a "main street" corridor that connects all departments. Executives who once took a private elevator to their top floor, marble-clad suite now ride the elevator with everyone else and are located close to rank-and-file employees. The new headquarters symbolizes RadioShack's new cultural values of egalitarianism, horizontal collaboration, teamwork, and innovation.[41]

STORIES

A **story** is a narrative based on true events and is repeated frequently and shared among organizational employees. Stories are told to new employees to keep the organization's primary values alive. One of Nordstrom's primary means of emphasizing the importance of customer service is through corporate storytelling. An example is the story about a sales representative who took back a customer's two-year-old blouse with no questions asked.[42]

A frequently told story at UPS concerns an employee who, without authorization, ordered an extra Boeing 737 to ensure timely delivery of a load of Christmas packages that had been left behind in the holiday rush. As the story goes, rather than punishing the worker, UPS rewarded his initiative. By telling this story, UPS workers communicate that the company stands behind its commitment to worker autonomy and customer service.[43]

HEROES

A **hero** is a figure who exemplifies the deeds, character, and attributes of a strong culture. Heroes are role models for employees to follow. Sometimes heroes are real, such as the female security supervisor who once challenged IBM's chairman because he wasn't carrying the appropriate clearance identification to enter a security area.[44] Other times they are symbolic, such as the mythical sales representative at Robinson Jewelers

symbol
an object, act, or event that conveys meaning to others.

story
a narrative based on true events that is repeated frequently and is shared among organizational employees.

hero
a figure who exemplifies the deeds, character, and attributes of a strong corporate culture.

Organization Culture

How good are you at adapting to a new organizational culture? Are you ready for an environment that is different from what you've become accustomed to?

	Mostly True	Mostly False
1. Carefully observed how others interacted before I developed work relationships.	_____	_____
2. Listened and did not talk much in work meetings for the first month or two.	_____	_____
3. Followed the norms of coming to work on time and leaving on time.	_____	_____
4. Tried to be a good "company citizen," meaning that I did work without complaining and volunteered for extra work.	_____	_____
5. Spent time getting to know clerical and support staff and treating them as valuable people.	_____	_____
6. Observed norms of how conflicts are handled and tried to behave similarly.	_____	_____
7. Learned to ask more questions and truly listen to the answers, to learn about the people I work with and the company itself.	_____	_____
8. Never spend energy to prove "I am right."	_____	_____

INTERPRETATION: Starting a new job requires more than technical skills. It also requires the ability to adapt and thrive in the new culture. A common reason for failure in a new job is being unaware or unconcerned about the culture of the new company.

SCORING: Give yourself one point for each "Mostly True" answer. If you scored 4 or less, you need to take stock and really spend energy getting to know the new culture. If you scored 5 or 6, you might do all right, but still need some work. Scoring 7 or 8 shows that you are in command of organizational culture issues.

who delivered a wedding ring directly to the church because the ring had been ordered late.

The deeds of heroes are out of the ordinary, but not so far out as to be unattainable by other employees. Heroes show how to do the right thing in the organization. Companies with strong cultures take advantage of achievements to define heroes who uphold key values.

At 3M Corp., top managers keep alive the heroes who developed projects that were killed by top management. One hero was a vice president who was fired earlier in his career for persisting with a new product even after his boss had told him, "That's a stupid idea.

Stop!" After the worker was fired, he would not leave. He stayed in an unused office, working without a salary on the new product idea. Eventually he was rehired, the idea succeeded, and he was promoted to vice president. The lesson of this hero as a major element in 3M's culture is to persist at what you believe in.[45]

SLOGANS

TAKE ACTION ⏩

What are the slogans on your campus? List as many as you can. What does that tell you about what the culture values?

A **slogan** is a phrase or sentence that succinctly expresses a key corporate value. Many companies use a slogan or saying to convey special meaning to employees. H. Ross Perot of Electronic Data Systems established the philosophy of hiring the best people he could find and noted how difficult it was to find them. His motto was, "Eagles don't flock. You gather them one at a time."

Averitt Express uses the slogan "Our driving force is people" to express its commitment to treating employees and customers well. Cultural values also can be discerned in written public statements, such as corporate mission statements or other formal statements that express the core values of the organization. The mission statement for Hallmark Cards, for example, emphasizes values of excellence, ethical and moral conduct in all relationships, business innovation, and corporate social responsibility.[46]

CEREMONIES

A **ceremony** is a planned activity at a special event that is conducted for the benefit of an audience. Managers hold ceremonies to provide dramatic examples of company values. Ceremonies are special occasions that reinforce valued accomplishments, create a bond among people by allowing them to share an important event, and anoint and celebrate heroes.[47] Wal-Mart founder Sam Walton initiated a ceremony in 1962 that thrives to this day and remains the heartbeat of Wal-Mart's culture.[48]

In summary, organizational culture represents the values, norms, understandings, and basic assumptions that employees share, and these values are signified by symbols, stories, heroes, slogans, and ceremonies. Managers help define important symbols, stories, and heroes to shape the culture.

Environment and Culture

TAKE ACTION ⏩

As a new manager, you will have to pay attention to culture. Recognize the ways in which cultural values can help or hurt your department's performance. Consciously shape adaptive values through the use of symbols, stories, heroes, ceremonies, and slogans.

A big influence on internal corporate culture is the external environment. Cultures can vary widely across organizations; however, organizations within the same industry often reveal similar cultural characteristics because they are operating in similar environments.[49] The internal culture should embody what it takes to succeed in the environment. If the external environment requires extraordinary customer service, the culture should encourage good service. If it calls for careful technical decision making, cultural values should reinforce managerial decision making.

ADAPTIVE CULTURES

slogan
a phrase or sentence that succinctly expresses a key corporate value.

ceremony
a planned activity at a special event that is conducted for the benefit of an audience.

Harvard University researched 207 U.S. firms to illustrate the critical relationship between corporate culture and the external environment. The study found that a strong corporate culture alone did not ensure business success unless the culture encouraged healthy adaptation to the external environment. Adaptive corporate cultures have values and behaviors different from unadaptive corporate cultures. In adaptive cultures, managers are concerned about customers and the internal people and processes that bring about useful change. In unadaptive corporate cultures, managers are concerned about themselves, and their values tend to discourage risk taking and change. Thus, a strong culture alone is not enough because an unhealthy culture may encourage the organization to march resolutely in the wrong direction. Healthy cultures help companies adapt to the environment.[50]

TYPES OF CULTURES

In considering what cultural values are important for the organization, managers consider the external environment as well as the company's strategy and goals. Studies suggest that the right fit between culture, strategy, and the environment is associated with four categories or types of culture. These categories are based on two dimensions: (1) the extent to which the external environment requires flexibility or stability; and (2) the extent to which a company's strategic focus is internal or external. The four categories associated with these differences are adaptability, achievement, involvement, and consistency.[51]

The **adaptability culture** emerges in an environment that requires fast response and high-risk decision making. Managers encourage values that support the company's ability to rapidly detect, interpret, and translate signals from the environment into new behavior responses. Employees have autonomy to make decisions and act freely to meet new needs, and responsiveness to customers is highly valued. Managers also actively create change by encouraging and rewarding creativity, experimentation, and risk taking.

Lush Cosmetics, a fast-growing maker of shampoos, lotions, and bath products made from fresh ingredients such as mangoes and avocados, provides a good example of an adaptability culture. A guiding motto at the company is: "We reserve the right to make mistakes." Founder and CEO Mark Constantine is passionately devoted to change and encourages employees to break boundaries, experiment, and take risks. The company kills

adaptability culture
a culture characterized by values that support the company's ability to interpret and translate signals from the environment into new behavior responses.

Valero

When Hurricane Katrina hit New Orleans in late August 2005, companies throughout the region set their disaster plans into action. But few matched the heroic efforts put forth by employees at Valero's St. Charles oil refinery. Just eight days after the storm, the St. Charles facility was up and running, while a competitor's plant across the road was weeks away from getting back online. During the same time period, St. Charles's disaster crew managed to locate every one of the plant's 570 employees.

Part of the credit goes to Valero's family-like, let's-get-it-done-together culture, which has given Valero a distinctive edge during an era of cut-throat global competition in the oil industry. As CEO Bill Greehey transformed Valero, once primarily a natural-gas-pipeline company, into the nation's largest oil refinery business, he also instilled a culture in which people care about one another and the company. Many of the refineries that Valero bought were old and run-down. After buying a refinery, Greehey's first steps were to assure people that their jobs were secure, bring in new safety equipment, and promise employees that if they would work hard, he would put them first, before shareholders and customers. Employees held up their end of the bargain, and so did Greehey.

Greehey maintains a strict no-layoff policy, believing that people need to feel secure in their jobs to perform at their best. "I see this cycle with companies where they fire and they hire and they fire and they hire," he says. "Fear does not motivate people." Of course, Greehey occasionally has to do some firing of his own—specifically, he'll fire any executive who is condescending or uses profanity when addressing subordinates. Although employees and even many at upper management levels call him "Mr. Greehey," the CEO doesn't put himself above his employees. He'll work side by side with them, chat with them about their jobs and ideas for the company, and listen compassionately as they describe their problems. He set up a Valero SAFE fund, which grants employees up to $10,000 in aid following a disaster.

Putting employees first has engendered amazing loyalty and dedication. When Greehey visited the St. Charles facility after Katrina, he was surprised to be greeted at a giant tent with a standing ovation. Even in the aftermath of a hurricane, the employees had held to their tradition of throwing a plant-wide barbecue lunch whenever Greehey visits a plant.

"Right now morale is so high in this refinery that you can't get at it with a space shuttle," an electrical superintendent at St. Charles said. "Valero has been giving away gas, chain saws, putting up trailers for the employees. They've kept every employee paid. Other refineries shut down and stopped paying. What else can you ask?"

Janet Guyon, "The Soul of a Moneymaking Machine," *Fortune* (October 3, 2005): 113–120.

off a third of its product line every year to offer new and offbeat products.[52] Other companies in the cosmetics industry, as well as those involved in electronics, e-commerce, and fashion, often use an adaptability culture because they must move quickly in response to rapid changes in the environment.

The **achievement culture** is suited to organizations that are concerned with serving specific customers in the external environment but without the intense need for flexibility and rapid change. This results-oriented culture values competitiveness, aggressiveness, personal initiative, and willingness to work long and hard to achieve results. An emphasis on winning and achieving specific ambitious goals is the glue that holds the organization together.[53]

Siebel Systems, which sells complex software systems, thrives on an achievement culture. Professionalism and aggressiveness are core values. Employees are forbidden to eat at their desks or to decorate with more than one or two personal photographs. People who succeed at Siebel are focused, competitive, and driven to win. Those who perform and meet stringent goals are rewarded handsomely; those who don't are fired.[54]

The **involvement culture** emphasizes an internal focus on the involvement and participation of employees to adapt rapidly to changing needs from the environment. This culture places high value on meeting employees' needs, and the organization may be characterized as having a caring, family-like atmosphere. Managers emphasize values such as cooperation, consideration of employees and customers alike, and avoiding status differences.

Consider the involvement culture at Valero, which is partly responsible for helping the company become the top oil refinery in the United States.

Some managers might think putting employees ahead of customers and shareholders is nice, but not very good for business. But at Valero, a strong involvement culture based on putting employees first has paid off in terms of high employee performance and rising market share, profits, and shareholder value.[55]

The final category of culture, the **consistency culture,** uses an internal focus and a consistency orientation for a stable environment. Value is placed on following the rules and being thrifty, and the culture supports and rewards a methodical, rational, orderly way of doing things. In today's fast-changing world, few companies operate in a stable environment, and most managers are shifting toward cultures that are more flexible and in tune with changes in the environment.

But one thriving company, Pacific Edge Software, successfully implemented elements of a consistency culture, ensuring that all its projects are on time and on budget. The husband-and-wife team of Lisa Hjorten and Scott Fuller implanted a culture of order, discipline, and control from the moment they founded the company. The emphasis on order and focus means that employees can generally go home by 6:00 P.M. rather than work all night to finish an important project. Hjorten insists that the company's culture isn't rigid or uptight, just *careful*. Although sometimes being careful means being slow, so far Pacific Edge has managed to keep pace with the demands of the external environment.[56]

Each of these four categories of culture can be successful. In addition, organizations usually have values that fall into more than one category. The relative emphasis on various cultural values depends on the needs of the environment and the organization's focus. Managers are responsible for instilling the cultural values the organization must have to be successful in its environment.

Shaping Corporate Culture for Innovative Response

Research conducted by a Stanford University professor indicates that the one factor that increases a company's value the most is people and how they are treated.[57] In addition, surveys found that CEOs cite organizational culture as their most important mechanism for attracting, motivating, and retaining talented employees, a capability they consider the

TAKE ACTION ⦿

How would you characterize the cultures in your courses— adaptability, achievement, or involvement cultures? What about your student clubs? Where you live?

achievement culture
a results-oriented culture that values competitiveness, personal initiative, and achievement.

involvement culture
a culture that places high value on meeting the needs of employees and values cooperation and equality.

consistency culture
a culture that values and rewards a methodical, rational, orderly way of doing things.

single best predictor of overall organizational excellence.[58] In a survey of Canadian senior executives, fully 82 percent indicated that they believe culture and financial performance are directly correlated.[59]

Corporate culture plays a key role in creating an organizational climate that enables learning and innovative responses to threats from the external environment, challenging new opportunities, or organizational crises. Managers, however, realize that they can't focus all their effort on values. They also must be committed to solid business performance.

MANAGING THE HIGH-PERFORMANCE CULTURE

Companies that succeed in a turbulent world are those that pay careful attention to cultural values *and* business performance. Cultural values can energize and motivate employees by appealing to higher ideals and unifying people around shared goals. In addition, values boost performance by shaping and guiding employee behavior, so that everyone's actions are aligned with strategic priorities.[60] Exhibit 2.6 illustrates four organizational outcomes based on the relative attention managers pay to cultural values and business performance.[61]

A company in Quadrant A pays little attention to either values or business results and is unlikely to survive for long. Managers in Quadrant B organizations are highly focused on creating a strong cohesive culture, but they don't tie organizational values directly to goals and desired business results. When cultural values aren't connected to business performance, they aren't likely to benefit the organization during hard times. For example, Levi Strauss placed a high premium on values, even tying part of managers' pay to how well they toed the values line. The problem was that top executives lost sight of the business performance side of the issue. Thus, when Levi jeans began losing market share to new, hip rivals, the company was unable to adapt quickly to the changing environment.[62]

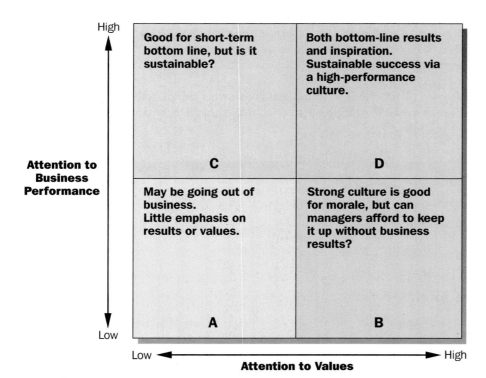

EXHIBIT 2.6

Combining Culture and Performance

SOURCE: Adapted from Jeff Rosenthal and Mary Ann Masarech, "High-Performance Cultures: How Values Can Drive Business Results," *Journal of Organizational Excellence* (Spring 2003): 3–18.

Quadrant C represents organizations that are focused primarily on bottom-line results and pay little attention to organizational values.

Quadrant C courses would have students engage in cut-throat competition for grades. The teacher doesn't care about the people, only how well they do on assignments and tests. This approach may be profitable in the short run, but the success is difficult to sustain over the long term because the "glue" that holds the organization together—shared cultural values—is missing.

Think about the numerous get-rich-quick goals of dot-com entrepreneurs. Thousands of companies that sprang up in the late 1990s were aimed primarily at fast growth and quick profits, with little effort to build a solid organization based on long-term mission and values. When the crash came, these companies failed. Those that survived typically were companies with strong cultural values that helped them weather the storm. For example, both eBay and Amazon.com managers paid careful attention to organizational culture, as did smaller e-commerce companies such as Canada's Mediagrif Interactive Technologies, an online B2B brokerage that allows businesses to meet online and trade their goods.[63]

Finally, companies in Quadrant D emphasize both culture and solid business performance as drivers of organizational success. Managers in these organizations align values with the company's day-to-day operations—hiring practices, performance management, budgeting, criteria for promotions and rewards, and so forth. A 2004 study of corporate values by Booz Allen Hamilton and the Aspen Institute found that managers in companies that report superior financial results typically emphasize values and link them directly to the way they run the organization.[64]

A good example is the fast-growing Umpqua Bank, which expanded from 11 branches and $140 million in assets in 1994 to 92 branches and $5 billion in assets nine years later. At Umpqua, every element of the culture is directed to serving customers, and every aspect of operations reflects the cultural values.

Consider training programs. To avoid the "it's not my job" attitude that infects many banks, managers devised the "universal associate" program, which trains every bank staffer in every task so a teller can take a mortgage application and a loan officer can process your checking account deposit. Employees are empowered to make their own decisions about how to satisfy customers, and branches have free reign to devise unique ways to coddle the clientele in their particular location.

Umpqua also carefully measures and rewards the cultural values it wants to maintain. The bank's executive vice president of cultural enhancement devised a software program

Business Blooper

Hewlett-Packard

Carly Fiorina's leadership style at Hewlett-Packard illustrates the danger of focusing only on results and not on culture. Carly Fiorina was the much-trumpeted CEO of Hewlett-Packard, the first woman appointed as CEO of a *Fortune* 100 company. Coming from high visibility as CEO of Lucent Technologies, she was charged with changing and updating HP, one of the first high-tech companies, a firm that many were saying was too stodgy to compete in tumultuous times.

Fiorina's style was big and attention-seeking. She held big forums with huge video screens hung high, showing her image—with a Tony Robbins headset microphone. Her forums kept her from roaming the halls connecting with employees. She tried to force a centralized style on a decentralized structure, a marketing culture on a deeply-entrenched engineering culture. Finally, after 5½ years, Carly Fiorina was asked to resign in early February 2005, the result of HP's culture rejecting her style.

SOURCE: Claudia H. Deutsch, "Carl Fiorina? He'd Probably Be Out of Work, Too," *The New York Times* (February 13, 2005): 5.

that measures how cultural values are connected to performance, which the bank calls "return on quality" (ROQ). The ROQ scores for each branch and department are posted every month, and they serve as the basis for determining incentives and rewards.[65]

Quadrant D organizations represent the **high-performance culture,** a culture that (1) is based on a solid organizational mission or purpose, (2) embodies shared adaptive values that guide decisions and business practices, and (3) encourages individual employee ownership of both bottom-line results and the organization's cultural backbone.[66]

One of the most important things that managers do is to create and influence organizational culture to meet strategic goals, because culture has a significant impact on performance. In *Corporate Culture and Performance,* Kotter and Heskett provided evidence that companies that intentionally managed cultural values outperformed similar companies that did not. Research has validated that some elements of corporate culture are positively correlated with higher financial performance.[67] A good example is Caterpillar Inc., which developed a Cultural Assessment Process (CAP) to measure and manage how effectively the culture contributes to organizational effectiveness. The assessment gave top executives hard data documenting millions of dollars in savings attributed directly to cultural factors.[68]

high-performance culture
a culture based on a solid organizational mission or purpose in which adaptive values guide decisions and business practices and encourage individual employee ownership of both bottom-line results and the organization's cultural backbone.

Spotlight on
Leadership

It's All About Power (and Responsibility) to the People

Feeling all too burdened by responsibility, 24-year-old Ricardo Semler created a new vision for the culture of his family's business in 1983, while he was recuperating from a stress-related illness. When Semler had taken over Brazil-based Semco Corp. from his father in 1980 as a freshly minted Harvard MBA (one of the youngest ever to earn the prestigious degree), the company was manufacturing equipment for a Brazilian shipbuilding industry that was in abysmal shape. As Semco's president and majority owner, Semler fired most of the top management and used a series of strategic acquisitions to steer the company into more viable markets. Ironically, as the company's fortunes began to revive, Semler's own health took a nosedive.

As he lay in a hospital bed, Semler had a vision for a new way to manage—by relinquishing control to his employees. Thus began a five-year process of building a radically democratic culture based on open information and employee participation. Semler started modestly—letting employees choose their uniform color, for example—and eventually moved to create egalitarian project teams with complete responsibility for specific projects, total authority regarding how to perform them, and the opportunity for team members to pocket a substantial percentage of any profits generated. Today, self-directed teams form the basis of the company's loose, flexible organizational structure. People typically have a chance to choose what projects they will work on, based on how they think they can best make a contribution.

Semco bestows few job titles and has only three management levels: counselors (the name Semler now goes by), partners, and associates. The CEO position rotates every 6 months among the counselors. Workers set their own hours, elect and evaluate supervisors, and have major input into how they are compensated, with some actually setting their own pay rates. All financial information, including salaries, is available to everyone, and any employee is eligible to attend any meeting, including board meetings, where two seats are reserved for employees on a first-come, first-served basis.

The result of applying these rather radical cultural values is that Semco has not only survived but prospered in Brazil's often chaotic economic and political climate. The conglomerate now produces a diverse range of products and services, from manufacturing giant oil pumps to participating in mail-processing joint ventures. Its revenues grew from $4 million in 1982 to approximately $240 million in 2005.

"It's about competitive advantage," Semler says. "Once you stop trying to control employees", he insists, "you release the powerful twin forces of self-discipline and peer pressure. Performance becomes the only criterion for success. At Semco, treating employees like responsible adults is just good business."

SOURCES: Lawrence Fisher, "Ricardo Semler Won't Take Control," *Strategy + Business* (Winter 2005): 78–88; Simon Caulkin, "Who's in Charge Here? No One," *Observer* (April 29, 2003), http://observer .guardian.co.uk; "Ricardo Semler," *Wikipedia,* http://en.wikipedia.org; Nick Easen, "Interview with Ricardo Semler," *CNN.com* (June 14, 2004), http://edition.cnn.com; and Lancourt, Joan and Charles Savage, "Organizational Transformation and the Changing Role of the Human Resource Function," *Compensation & Benefits Management* (Autumn 1995).

CULTURAL LEADERSHIP

TAKE ACTION ➡️

Have you had a course where everyone works really hard because they respect the teacher, who is a smart and approachable person with high standards? Try to emulate that person.

A primary way in which managers shape cultural norms and values to build a high-performance culture is by being a **cultural leader.** Managers must *overcommunicate* to ensure that employees understand the new culture values, and they signal these values in actions as well as words.

A cultural leader defines and uses signals and symbols to influence corporate culture. Cultural leaders influence culture in two key areas:

1. *The cultural leader articulates a vision for the organizational culture that employees can believe in.* The leader defines and communicates central values that employees believe in and will rally around. Values are tied to a clear and compelling mission, or core purpose.

2. *The cultural leader heeds the day-to-day activities that reinforce the cultural vision.* The leader makes sure that work procedures and reward systems match and reinforce the values. Actions speak louder than words, so cultural leaders "walk their talk."[69]

Leaders can create a culture that brings people together by ensuring that people have a voice in what the important values should be. Managers at United Stationers built a new, adaptive culture from the ground up by asking all 6,000 globally dispersed employees to help define the values that would be the building blocks of the culture.[70]

Managers widely communicate the cultural values through words and actions. Values statements that aren't reinforced by management behavior are meaningless or even harmful to employees and the organization. Consider Enron, whose values statement included things like communication, respect, and integrity. Managers' actions at the corporation clearly belied those stated values.[71]

For values to guide the organization, managers have to model them every day. Canada's WestJet Airlines, which ranked in a survey as having Canada's most admired corporate culture, provides an illustration. WestJet employees (called simply "people" at WestJet) regularly see CEO Clive Beddoe and other top leaders putting the values of equality, teamwork, participation, and customer service into action. At the end of a flight, for example, everyone on hand pitches in to pick up garbage—even the CEO.

cultural leader
a manager who uses signals and symbols to influence corporate culture.

Top executives spend much of their time chatting informally with employees and customers, and they regularly send notes of thanks to people who have gone above and beyond the call of duty. Top executives have been known to visit the call center on Christmas Day to pitch in and to thank people for working on the holiday. Managers don't receive perks over and above anyone else; they get no assigned parking spaces and no club memberships. Every person at WestJet is treated like first-class, exactly the way leaders want employees to treat every passenger on a WestJet flight.[72]

Cultural leaders also uphold their commitment to values during difficult times or crises, as illustrated by the example of Bill Greehey at Valero earlier in this chapter. On *Fortune* magazine's list of "100 Best Companies to Work For," Valero zoomed from Number 23 to Number 3 based on its treatment of employees following the devastating 2005 hurricanes. Despite the costs, Valero kept people on the payroll throughout the crisis, set up special booths to feed volunteers, and donated $1 million to the American Red Cross for hurricane relief efforts.[73] Upholding the cultural values helps organizations weather a crisis and come out stronger on the other side.

Creating and maintaining a high-performance culture is not easy in today's turbulent environment and changing workplace, but through their words—and particularly their actions—cultural leaders let everyone in the organization know what really counts.

CONCEPT CONNECTION

Eileen Fisher's award-winning company makes simple, comfortable clothing for women following the firm's mission to support collaboration, individual growth, and social consciousness.

Summary

Events in the external environment significantly influence organizational behavior and performance. The external environment consists of two layers: the general environment and the task environment. The general environment has technological, sociocultural, economic, legal-political, and international dimensions. The task environment includes customers, competitors, suppliers, and the labor market. Management techniques for helping the organization adapt to the environment include boundary-spanning roles, interorganizational partnerships, and mergers and joint ventures.

A major internal element for helping organizations adapt to the environment is culture. Corporate culture is an important part of the internal organizational environment and includes the key values, beliefs, understandings, and norms that organization members share. Organizational activities that illustrate corporate culture include symbols, stories, heroes, slogans, and ceremonies. For the organization to be effective, corporate culture should be aligned with organizational strategy and the needs of the external environment. Four types of culture are adaptability, achievement, involvement, and consistency. Strong cultures are effective when they enable an organization to meet strategic goals and adapt to changes in the external environment.

Culture can have a significant impact on organizational performance. Effective managers emphasize both values and business results to create a high-performance culture, enabling the organization to consistently achieve solid business performance through the actions of motivated employees who are aligned with the company's mission and goals. Managers create and sustain adaptive high-performance cultures through cultural leadership. They define and articulate important values that are tied to a clear and compelling mission, and they widely communicate and uphold the values through their words and particularly their actions. Work procedures, budgeting, decision making, reward systems, and other day-to-day activities are aligned with the cultural values.

Discussion Questions

1. What can you do now as a student—both inside and outside the classroom—to train yourself to be a more effective manager in an increasingly global business environment?

2. Would the task environment for a cell phone company contain the same elements as that for a government welfare agency? Discuss.

3. What do you think are the major forces in the external environment that create uncertainty for organizations today? Do the forces you identified typically arise in the task environment or in the general environment?

4. Contemporary best-selling management books often argue that customers are the most important element in the external environment. Do you agree? In what company situations might this statement be untrue?

5. Why do you think many managers are surprised by environmental changes and unable to help their organizations adapt? Can a manager ever be prepared for an environmental change as dramatic as that experienced by airlines in the United States following the September 11, 2001, terrorist attacks in New York and Washington? If so, how?

6. Why are interorganizational partnerships so important for today's companies? What elements in the current environment might contribute to either an increase or a decrease in interorganizational collaboration? Discuss.

7. Consider the chairs you have seen in an office. How do the assistant's chair, the manager's chair, and executive's chair differ? What do the differences mean?

8. Why are symbols important to a corporate culture? Do stories, heroes, slogans, and ceremonies have symbolic value? Discuss.

9. Both China and India are rising economic powers. How might your approach to doing business with Communist China be different from your approach to doing business with India, the world's most populous democracy? In which country would you expect to encounter the most rules? The most bureaucracy?

10. General Electric is famous for firing the lowest-performing 10 percent of its managers each year. With its strict no-layoff policy, Valero Energy believes that people need to feel secure in their jobs to perform their best. Yet, both are high-performing companies. How do you account for the success of such opposite philosophies?

Dear Dr. Dorothy

Two months ago I was happy as a clam working in marketing research. Then I got an offer I couldn't refuse in another company. This is my first experience as a manager, and some days I wish I had stayed in my old job. Now I'm stuck with 18 employees who are totally lazy. All they want to do is go to meetings and talk everything over, again and again. When I try to say something about getting their work done, they give me dirty looks and say, "This is the work." And they don't seem to give me the respect I deserve as their supervisor. I'm afraid to take this to my boss because I notice that he spends a lot of time in meetings, too. And he seems to like wasting time, just like the others. How can I get these employees to be serious about their work?

Clock-watcher

Dear Clock-watcher,

You are suffering from culture shock, the same as if you had traveled to Moscow, Russia, and found the native people were not at all like what you left back in Moscow, Idaho. Dr. Dorothy must remind you, however, that just because some behaviors were normal back in your "home" company does not make different behaviors in your new locale of a suspicious and lowly nature. You no doubt were in an "Achievement Culture" back there and have started your formidable climb to the top at an "Involvement Culture," where people spend a lot of time building consensus, where respect for one another is of utmost importance, and where status differences are negligible. Therefore, Dr. Dorothy advises you to re-read your management textbook on corporate culture, learn to be a better listener and team player, and spend the next two months observing how things get done. During this time, try to refrain from being judgmental and self-righteous, because Dr. Dorothy assures you that these behaviors are never attractive.

Self Learning

Working in an Adaptive Culture

Think of a specific full-time job you have held. Please respond to the following statements according to your perception of the *managers above you* in that job. Circle a number on the 1–5 scale based on the extent to which you agree with each statement about the managers above you: 5 Strongly agree; 4 Agree; 3 Neither agree nor disagree; 2 Disagree; 1 Strongly disagree.

	1	2	3	4	5
1. Good ideas received serious consideration from management above me.	1	2	3	4	5
2. Management above me was interested in ideas and suggestions from people at my level in the organization.	1	2	3	4	5
3. When suggestions were made to management above me, these received fair evaluation.	1	2	3	4	5
4. Management did not expect me to challenge or change the status quo.	1	2	3	4	5
5. Management specifically encouraged me to bring about improvements in my workplace.	1	2	3	4	5
6. Management above me took action on recommendations from people at my level.	1	2	3	4	5
7. Management rewarded me for correcting problems.	1	2	3	4	5
8. Management clearly expected me to improve work unit procedures and practices.	1	2	3	4	5
9. I felt free to make recommendations to management above me to change existing practices.	1	2	3	4	5
10. Good ideas did not get communicated upward because management above me was not approachable.	1	2	3	4	5

Scoring and Interpretation

To compute your score: Subtract from 6 each of your scores for questions 4 and 10. Using your adjusted scores, add the numbers for all 10 questions to give you the total score. Divide that number by 10 to get your average score: _____.

An adaptive culture is shaped by the values and actions of top and middle managers. When managers actively encourage and welcome change initiatives from below, the organization will be infused with values for change. These 10 statements measure your management's openness to change. A typical average score for management openness to change is about 3. If your average score was 4 or higher, your organization expressed strong cultural values of adaptation. If your average score was 2 or below, the culture was probably unadaptive.

Thinking about your job, is the level of management openness to change correct for the organization? Why? Compare your scores to those of another student, and take turns describing what it was like working for the managers above your jobs. Do you sense a relationship between job satisfaction and your management's openness to change? What specific management characteristics and corporate values explain the openness scores in the two jobs?

SOURCES: S. J. Ashford, N. P. Rothbard, S. K. Piderit, and J. E. Dutton, "Out on a Limb: The Role of Context and Impression Management in Issue Selling," *Administrative Science Quarterly* 43 (1998): 23–57; and E. W. Morrison and C. C. Phelps, "Taking Charge at Work: Extrarole Efforts to Initiate Workplace Change," *Academy of Management Journal* 42 (1999): 403–419.

Group Learning

5-Minute Mini-Change Exercise
Coping with a Continuously Changing World

On a separate sheet of paper, list every password, code, ID number, etc. you have that you have to use on a regular basis. Include both personal and professional code numbers. Be sure to destroy the paper after completing the exercise!
Example: x12345   PC password at work

Questions to Discuss:

- What was the frequency distribution of number of passwords in the class?
- How many people have passwords they cannot remember?
- How do people keep track of all these passwords?
- Do these information management strategies vary by:
  - Age?
  - Gender?
  - Job type/education background?
  - Other characteristics?
- What are the implications of information overload for management?

Developed by Anne H. Reilly, Professor of Management, Loyola University. Used with Permission.

Action Learning

Answer the following questions yourself:

1. How do you spend a typical day? Weekend?

2. What kind of music do you listen to? How do you listen to it? How many favorite groups do you have? Name some.

3. How much time do you spend on the phone or online each day?

4. What do you expect to do when you are 25 (or 35, if older) years old?

5. When (if ever) do you expect to marry and have kids?

6. What is dating like now?

7. Do your parents support you financially? If so, how much does it cost them roughly per year, including things such as tuition, room and board, etc.?

8. How old do you expect to be before your parents don't support you at all financially, other than occasional birthday or holiday gifts?

9. Do you work while going to school? If so, how much and what type of work?

10. If you've had several jobs, describe the differences.

11. How do you spend your disposable income?

12. How often do you travel? To where? Who pays?

After you've answered these questions, go to your parents or two other similarly aged adults (male and female) and ask them:

Think back to when you were about the age of the person asking you the questions and respond in terms of your life back then.

13. How did you spend a typical day? Weekend?

14. What kind of music did you listen to? How did you listen to it? How many favorite groups did you have? Name some.

15. How much time did you spend on the phone each day?

16. What did you expect to do when you were 25 years old?

17. When did you get married and have kids?

18. What was dating like back then?

19. How long did your parents support you financially? If they did so during college, how much did it cost them

roughly per year, including things such as tuition, room and board, etc.?

20. At what age did your parents stop supporting you financially, other than occasional birthday or holiday gifts?

21. Did you work while going to school (high school and/or college)? If so, how much, and what type of work?

22. What's the difference between the jobs you had back then and now? Is your worklife more or less predictable?

23. How did you spend your disposable income?

24. How often did you travel? To where? Who paid?

Write a brief paper describing the differences between your world and your parents at that age. What were the biggest differences?

Your instructor may ask you to participate in a class discussion about this.

Ethical Dilemma

Competitive Intelligence Predicament

Miquel Vasquez was proud of his job as a new product manager for a biotechnology start-up, and he enjoyed the high stakes and tough decisions that went along with the job. But as he sat in his den after a long day, he was troubled, struggling over what had happened earlier that day and the information he now possessed.

Just before lunch, Miquel's boss had handed him a stack of private strategic documents from their closest competitor. It was a competitive intelligence gold mine—product plans, pricing strategies, partnership agreements, and other documents, most clearly marked "proprietary and confidential." When Miquel asked where the documents came from, his boss told him, with a touch of pride, that he had taken them off the competing firm's server. "I got into a private section of their intranet and downloaded everything that looked interesting," he said.

Later, realizing that Miquel was suspicious, the boss would say only that he had obtained "electronic access" via a colleague and had not personally broken any passwords. Maybe not, Miquel thought to himself, but this situation wouldn't pass the *60 Minutes* test. If word of this acquisition of a competitor's confidential data ever got out to the press, the company's reputation would be ruined.

Miquel didn't feel good about using these materials. He spent the afternoon searching for answers to his dilemma

but found no clear company policies or regulations that offered any guidance. His sense of fair play told him that to use the information was unethical, if not downright illegal. What bothered him even more was the knowledge that this kind of thing might happen again. Using this confidential information would certainly give him and his company a competitive advantage, but Miquel wasn't sure he wanted to work for a firm that would stoop to such tactics.

What Would You Do?

1. Go ahead and use the documents to the company's benefit, but make clear to your boss that you don't want him passing confidential information to you in the future. If he threatens to fire you, threaten to leak the news to the press.

2. Confront your boss privately, and let him know that you're uncomfortable with how the documents were obtained and what possessing them says about the company's culture. In addition to the question of the legality of using the information, point out that it is a public relations nightmare waiting to happen.

3. Talk to the company's legal counsel, and contact the Society of Competitive Intelligence Professionals for guidance. Then, with their opinions and facts to back you up, go to your boss.

SOURCE: Adapted from Kent Weber, "Gold Mine or Fool's Gold?" *Business Ethics* (January–February 2001): 18.

Case for Critical Analysis

Rio Grande Supply Co.

Jasper Hennings, president of Rio Grande Supply Co., knew full well that a company's top executives were largely responsible for determining a firm's corporate culture. That's why he took such personal pride in the culture of his Texas-based wholesale plumbing supply company. It didn't just pay lip service to the values it espoused: integrity, honesty, and respect for each individual employee. His management team set a good example by living those principles—at least that's what he'd believed until the other day.

The importance that Jasper attached to respecting each individual was apparent in the company's Internet use policy. It was abundantly clear that employees weren't to use Rio Grande's computers for anything except business-related activities. But Jasper himself had vetoed the inclusion of what was becoming a standard provision in such policies that management had the right to access and review anything the employees created, stored, sent, or received on company equipment. He cut short any talk of installing software filters that would prevent abuse of the corporate computer system. Still, the company reserved the right to take disciplinary action, including possible termination, and to press criminal charges if an employee was found to have violated the policy.

So how was Jasper to square his cherished assumptions about his management team with what he'd just discovered? Henry Darger, his hard-working chief of operations and a member of his church, had summarily fired a female employee for having accessed another worker's e-mail surreptitiously. She hadn't taken her dismissal well. "Just ask Darger what he's up to when he shuts his office door," she snarled as she stormed out of Jasper's office. She voiced what Jasper hoped was an idle threat to hire a lawyer.

When Jasper asked Henry what the fired employee could possibly have meant, tears began to roll down the operations chief's face. He admitted that ever since a young nephew had committed suicide the year before and a business he'd helped his wife start had failed, he'd increasingly been seeking escape from his troubles by logging onto adult pornography sites. At first, he'd indulged at home, but of late he'd found himself spending hours at work visiting pornographic sites, the more explicit the better.

Jasper was stunned. After a few speechless minutes, he told Henry to take the rest of the day off, go home, and think things over.

The president himself needed the afternoon to gather his wits. How should he handle this turn of events? On the one hand, Henry's immediate dismissal of the woman who'd tapped into another employee's e-mail when the operations chief was violating the Internet policy himself was hypocritical, to say the least. The person charged with enforcing that policy should be held to the highest standards. On the other hand, Jasper knew that Rio Grande employees routinely used computers at their desks to check personal e-mail, do banking transactions, check the weather, or make vacation arrangements. The company had turned a blind eye because it didn't seem worth the effort of enforcing the hard-and-fast policy for such minor infractions. Besides, Henry was a valued, if clearly troubled, employee. Replacing him would be costly and difficult. If Jasper decided to keep him on, the president clearly had no choice but to cross the line and get involved in Henry's private life, and he would be treating Darger differently from the treatment the female employee received.

When he met with Henry again the first thing in the morning, he had to have a plan of action.

Questions

1. What environmental factors contributed to the situation Jasper Hennings faces? What factors should Jasper consider when deciding on his course of action?

2. Analyze Rio Grande's culture. In addition to the expressed cultural values and beliefs, what other subconscious values and beliefs do you detect? Are conflicting values present? When values are in conflict, how would you decide which ones take precedence?

3. Assume you are Jasper. What are the first two action steps you would take to handle the Henry Darger situation? How would your role as a cultural leader influence your decision? What message will your solution send to the other managers and rank-and-file employees?

SOURCES: Based on Willard P. Green, "Pornography at Work," *Business Ethics* (Summer 2003): 19; Patrick Marley, "Porn-Viewing Parole Agent Regains Job," *Milwaukee Journal Sentinel* (January 24, 2006): http://www.jsonline.com/story/idex.aspx?id=387492; "Sample Internet Policies for Businesses and Organizations," *Websense,* http:// www.websense-sales.com/internet-access-policy.html; and Art Lambert, "Technology in the Workplace: A Recipe for Legal Trouble," *Workforce* (February 14, 2005): http://www.workforce.com/archive/article/23/95/08.php

Backdraft

Two brothers follow in the footsteps of their late father, a legendary Chicago firefighter, and join the department. Stephen "Bull" McCaffrey (Kurt Russell) joins first and rises to the rank of lieutenant. Younger brother Brian (William Baldwin) joins later and becomes a member of Bull's Company 17. Sibling rivalry tarnishes their work relationships, but they continue to successfully fight Chicago fires. Add a plot element about a mysterious arsonist and you have the basis of an ordinary film. The film, however, rises above its otherwise formulaic plot thanks to great acting and amazing special effects. The intense, unprecedented special effects give the viewer an unparalleled experience of what it is like to fight a fire. Chicago firefighters applauded the realism of the fire scenes.[1]

This scene appears early in the film as part of "The First Day" sequence. Brian McCaffrey has graduated from the fire academy, and the fire department has assigned him to his brother's company. This scene shows him fighting his first real fire at a garment factory. The film continues with Company 17 fighting the fire and Brian receiving some harsh first-day lessons.

What to Watch for and Ask Yourself

1. What elements of the Chicago fire department culture does this scene show? Does the scene show any cultural artifacts or symbols? If it does, what are they?

2. Does the scene show any values that guide the firefighters' behavior?

3. What does Brian McCaffrey learn on his first day at work?

[1] J. Craddock, Ed. *VideoHound's Golden Movie Retriever*, (Farmington Hills, MI: The Gale Group, Inc.), 2000.

The Environment and Corporate Culture at Caterpillar

Not satisfied with merely watching the external environment shift and change at ever-increasing speed, Caterpillar's top management saw the need for both stability and flexibility within their internal environment. Despite their industry-leading position, management was not content to sit back and wait for the next big externally driven change to hit, so they began to explore the company's internal dynamics.

In January 2003, Caterpillar launched a key six Sigma project, which found compelling evidence that having Enterprise Values, and putting them into practice, would make for a better performing company. They determined that the values outlined in their existing Code of Conduct fit the bill nicely, but management realized that simply having an official Code of Conduct would not ensure its universal buy-in throughout the organization.

The next step was to bring Caterpillar's core values to the fore by reinforcing them with a fresh coat of paint, and greatly increasing employee access to the message. If the values were a background hum before, CAT cranked up the volume so that none could ignore it. Their plan to create a global recipe for values-based behavior ultimately led to companywide distribution of the booklet ***Our Values in Action—Caterpillar's Worldwide Code of Conduct***. To help support this lynchpin of their newly redefined culture, they put up a dedicated website, and printed the Code in 14 languages, to reflect and embrace the diversity of their global workforce. Management at all levels spread the message, and positively reinforced the supporting behaviors increasingly displayed among employees. Upper management stayed visible and on-message throughout. They believed that if employees saw them "walk the talk" consistently, it would motivate and inspire them.

In preparation for launching their new ad campaign, Caterpillar issued something new to all of its employees, amidst an atmosphere of celebration: ***The CAT Manifesto***. It drew a direct correlation between CAT employees just doing their job, and the easing of human suffering through progress. They wanted their employees to feel that each of them was personally responsible for making the world a better place, and to feel pride when they experienced the new billboards, print ads, and radio spots. Caterpillar's "The World: In Progress" campaign carried this notion into the external environment, with graphic images that powerfully suggested moving toward the future, and sparse but effective copy such as "Caterpillar: Today's Work. Tomorrow's World."

These initiatives served to redefine Caterpillar's values for both management and employees, and continue to encourage the kind of corporate culture that upper management has envisioned. When organization members feel that their employer's actions are clearly aligned with its stated values, it is reflected in increased returns and retention. A quick look at Caterpillar's numbers suggests that they are indeed "walking the talk."

Questions

1. Caterpillar went to a great deal of effort to clarify its organizational values, and get employees from 120 facilities in 23 countries on the same page. Why did they do this?

2. How can Caterpillar's corporate culture, which springs from the organization's internal environment, impact the external environment?

3. What are the most essential core values that should be integrated into your organization's corporate culture? Why?

chapter 3

The Global Environment

New Manager's Questions

Please circle your opinion below each of the following statements.

Assess Your Answer

1 I have no desire to live abroad, or to work overseas, even for a short while.

| 1 | 2 | 3 | 4 | 5 |

strongly agree   strongly disagree

2 I would never want to be part of a business operation in a place with political instability.

| 1 | 2 | 3 | 4 | 5 |

strongly agree   strongly disagree

3 I really admire cultures that are high-achieving.

| 1 | 2 | 3 | 4 | 5 |

strongly agree   strongly disagree

Sitting in his Texas college dorm room in 1984, Michael Dell had a powerful insight: Why not sell personal computers directly to consumers rather than going through distributors or retailers? Dell Computer Corporation was born, and the computer industry has never been the same. Now Dell is striving to apply its ultra-efficient processes to shake up the Chinese computer industry the same way it did in the United States. But things got off to a shaky start. The company encountered problems ranging from language barriers and cultural resistance to tough competition from Lenova, a Chinese firm that is becoming a global player in PCs and services. Even the term *direct sales* was a problem for Dell, translating into a Chinese term used primarily to describe illegal pyramid marketing schemes. The language glitch was solved, but by sticking to its direct sales model, Dell is losing Chinese customers who typically want to see and touch products before they buy.

With 4,800 retail outlets, Lenova long has been the market leader in China and now is making a global push with the purchase of IBM's PC unit. Dell lost its most experienced Asia-Pacific executive when Lenova snared Dell's Asia chief Bill Amelio as its new CEO. Amelio and Lenova chairman Yang Yuanqing vowed that Lenova wouldn't cede the Asia market to Dell. Lenova managers are gunning for Dell in its established markets as well. The company invested $60 million to become China's first Olympic sponsor and provider of computers to the 2006 Turin games and for the Beijing Summer Olympics in 2008. "It's a coming-out party to say, 'Here's Lenova; we're a global brand, and we're here to stay,'" said Amelio.[1]

Dell was unprepared for the difficulties it is facing in China and is outgunned by Lenova, which has a 20.4 percent market share in Asia and 4,800 retail outlets in China alone. Some observers believe that Lenova eventually could challenge Dell's lead globally, which illustrates the growing power of Chinese companies in international business. Behind the scenes, Lenova is scrambling to cut its costs to match Dell's efficiency and has begun dealing with large customers directly rather than through distributors.

After going it alone for almost ten years, Dell finally formed a partnership with Gome, China's biggest electronic retailer, to sell computers in its stores. Dell had problems courting consumers and businesses in smaller cities, where demand is growing faster, and therefore ran into trouble competing with Lenovo. Direct sales in China are a problem because few Chinese customers use credit cards, for example. Dell was loath to break with its successful model, but establishing "a presence on the street" through kiosks or retailers, or perhaps by partnering with a local company, was necessary for Dell to compete successfully with the hometown leader in this new market.[2]

Dell's core U.S. market is saturated, and its biggest potential for growth lies in emerging markets such as China. But managers at Dell are learning, as other companies have, that they may have to adjust how the company operates to succeed in a new country or region.

Wal-Mart, for example, has faced significant challenges in Germany, where the giant U.S. firm is still a secondary player after 10 years of effort. The German market is dominated by local retail chains that cater to local tastes and are familiar with tough union rules and labor laws in that country. Wal-Mart also struggled in South America and Japan, partly because of managers' proclivity for doing things the Wal-Mart way without adequately considering local customs.

Other large, successful U.S. businesses, including FedEx and Nike, also found that "the rest of the world is not the United States of America," as one FedEx competitor put it. Yet these companies recognize that international expansion is necessary despite the risks. Companies such as McDonald's, IBM, Coca-Cola, Kellogg, Texas Instruments, and Gillette rely on international business for a substantial portion of their sales and profits. Internet-based companies headquartered in the United States, such as Amazon, Yahoo!, eBay, and America Online, also are rapidly expanding internationally and are finding that, even on the Web, going global is fraught with difficulties. These and other online companies encounter problems ranging from cultural blunders to violations of foreign laws. All organizations face special problems in trying to tailor their products, services, and business management to the unique needs of foreign countries—but if they succeed, the whole world is their marketplace.

How important is international business to the study of management? If you aren't thinking international, you're not thinking business management. It's that serious. Rapid advances in technology and communications have made the international dimension an increasingly important part of the external environment discussed in Chapter 2. Isolation from international forces is no longer possible. The future of our businesses and our societies will be shaped by global rather than local relationships.[3]

Today's companies can locate different parts of the organization wherever it makes the most business sense—top leadership in one place, technical brainpower and production in other locales. Virtual connections enable close, rapid coordination and communication among people working in different parts of the world, so it is no longer necessary to keep all operations in one place. Samsung, the Korean electronics giant, moved its semiconductor-making facilities to the Silicon Valley to be closer to the best scientific brains in the industry. Canada's Nortel Networks selected a location in the southwest of England as its world manufacturing center for a new fixed-access radio product. Siemens of Germany has moved its electronic ultrasound division to the United States, and the U.S. company DuPont shifted its electronic operations headquarters to Japan.[4] Many of today's organizations also outsource certain functions to contractors in other countries as easily as if the contractor were located next door.

These examples indicate that the environment for companies is becoming extremely complex and extremely competitive. Less-developed countries are challenging mature countries in a number of industries. China is the world's largest maker of consumer electronics and rapidly and expertly is moving into biotechnology, computer manufacturing, and semiconductors. At least 19 advanced new semiconductor plants are in or nearing operation in China.[5] The pace of innovation in India is startling, in industries as diverse as precision manufacturing, health care, and pharmaceuticals, and some observers see the beginnings of hypercompetitive multinationals in that country.[6]

This chapter introduces basic concepts about the global environment and international management. First we consider the difficulty that managers have operating in an increasingly borderless world. We address challenges—economic, legal-political, and sociocultural—facing companies within the global business environment. Then we discuss multinational corporations and touch on the various types of strategies and techniques needed for entering and succeeding in foreign markets.

A Borderless World

Why do companies such as Dell, FedEx, and eBay want to pursue a global strategy, despite difficulties, failures, and losses? They recognize that business is becoming a unified, global field as trade

CONCEPT CONNECTION

Today's companies compete in a borderless world. Procter & Gamble's sales in Southeast Asia make up a rapidly growing percentage of the company's worldwide sales. These shoppers are purchasing P&G's diaper products, Pampers, in Malaysia.

Tortasperu

By using computers and cakes, Edwin San Roman and his wife, Maria del Carmen Vucetich, came up with an idea to service a waiting market—Peruvian expatriates around the work, particularly in the United States. For example, Pedro in Los Angeles could visit the Tortas Peru website (www.tortasperu.com) and order a home-baked cake, as a way of showing his love to his Peruvian family. Finding women to bake the cakes was no problem. Through Vucetich's network, she found women all over the country, most of whom needed to earn extra money but found it difficult to work outside the home. Orders would be sent to the women from the website via e-mail.

Even though few people in Peru have computers, the country is well-covered with Internet cafés, where women can access their own e-mail accounts. These women would make the cake to order and personally deliver it to the Peruvian loved one of the customer. Average cost: $25. Because a large percentage of the customers consisted of Peruvians living in the United States, payment was made by having them send a check to an American address. The checks didn't clear for several days, however, and sometimes the cake arrived too late for the special event. Customers were losing interest. But other means of payment were not common in Peru. Roman and Vucetich realized that if they did not figure out some other solution that would meet customers' needs and be implementable in Peru, their short-lived business would turn to crumbs.

Then Roman was asked to speak at a virtual seminar on tourism in Peru. One of the other speakers was using a credit card system that was workable in Peru, so Roman immediately signed up that service. In addition, the company still takes personal checks sent to the U.S. address or does bank transfers. With a way to collect money, Tortas Peru was able to expand to seven Peruvian cities and promises to deliver a cake to any of those cities within 72 hours after the order is placed. Plus, they take a digital picture of the cake being delivered and send it back to the customer in the United States.

Tortas Peru is such a successful business model that when it entered the 2001 Stockholm Challenge with 62 other contenders for the New Economy Award, it was the only winner. More important, it not only provides a service to Peruvian expatriates but also provides much needed foreign exchange money as income to Peruvian housewives who don't have to leave their homes—or their cake pans.

SOURCES: "UN: Opportunities Rising for Women in E-commerce, but Glass Ceiling Remains to be Broken," *M2 Presswire* (Nov. 19, 2002): p. 1; Cecilia Ng and Swasti Mitter, "Gender and the Digital Economy: Perspectives from the Developing World" (Thousand Oaks, CA: Sage Publications, 2005).

barriers fall, communication becomes faster and cheaper, and consumer tastes in everything from clothing to cellular phones converge. Thomas Middelhoff of Germany's Bertelsmann AG, which purchased U.S. publisher Random House, put it this way: "There are no German and American companies. There are only successful and unsuccessful companies."[7]

In addition, for many companies today, the only potential for significant growth lies overseas. The demand for raw materials such as steel, aluminum, cement, and copper has slowed in the United States but is booming in countries such as China, India, and Brazil.[8] For online companies, too, going global is a key to growth. The number of residential Internet subscribers in China is growing significantly faster than that of the United States. Western Europe and Japan together account for a huge share of the world's e-commerce revenue.[9]

TAKE ACTION ►

As a new manager, learn to "think globally," reading about international issues, taking an interest in and networking with international people.

Companies that think globally have a competitive edge. Consider the U.S. movie industry, where global markets used to be an afterthought. Not any more. The success of *Crouching Tiger, Hidden Dragon* in both Asian and U.S. markets spurred movie studios to take a broader view. Squeezed at the box office in the United States, studios such as New Line Cinemas, Columbia Pictures, Disney, and Universal are busily striking deals to co-produce foreign language films designed primarily for foreign markets that are experiencing a booming demand. The box-office share for local films in Russia, for example, nearly tripled in 2004.[10] Movement of people around the world, as immigrants to a new country, can now create business opportunities.

The reality of today's borderless companies means that consumers no longer can tell from which country they're buying. U.S.-based Ford Motor Company owns Sweden's Volvo.

Spotlight on Skills

Cross-Cultural Communication

American managers often are at a disadvantage when doing business overseas. This is partly because they lack foreign language skills. Also, they are inexperienced in dealing with other cultures and less-than-ideal living conditions. This results in many mistakes—mistakes that could easily be avoided. When managers are prepared and trained for cross-cultural interactions, studies show that their productivity increases by 30 percent.

The manager's attitude is perhaps the most important factor in success. Managers who go abroad with a sense of "wonder" about the new culture are better off than those with a judgmental view of "If it's different, my culture must be better." Seeing differences as new and interesting is more productive than being critical. One way is to begin to *appreciate* rather than *evaluate* cultural differences. These evaluations lead to an "us versus them" approach, which never sits well with the locals.

Though every culture has its own way of communicating, some basic principles to follow in international business relations are:

1. Always show respect and listen carefully. Don't be in a hurry to finish the "business." Many other cultures value the social component of these interactions.
2. Try to gain an appreciation for the differences between Hofsede's "masculine" and feminine" cultures [discussed later in this chapter]. American masculine business behaviors include high achievement, acquisition of material goods, and efficiency. Cultures with more feminine cultures value relationships, leisure time with family, and developing a sense of community. Don't mistake this more feminine approach with lack of motivation. Similarly, cultures that value "being and inner spiritual development" rather than compulsively "doing" are not necessarily inferior.
3. Try hard not to think that your way is the best. This can come across as arrogance and rubs salt in deep wounds in some lesser-developed countries.
4. Emphasize points of agreement.
5. When disagreements arise, check on the perceived definitions of words. Often a huge or a subtle difference in meaning is causing the problem. You both actually may be trying to say the same thing.
6. Save face and "give" face as well, for this can be a way of showing honor to others.

7. Don't go alone. Take someone who knows the culture or language better than you. If you are discussing in English and the others are familiar with the language, you might be surprised how much they miss. Often, taking an excellent translator along is a good investment.
8. Don't assume that the other country views leadership the same as you do. In many other cultures, "empowerment" seems more like anarchy and the result of an ineffectual manager.
9. Don't lose your temper.
10. Don't embarrass anyone in front of others. Even if you meant it as a joke, it likely won't be taken that way.
11. Avoid clique-building, and try to interact with the locals as much as possible. Americans tend to hang together in packs or tribes, which is not welcoming to the locals.
12. Be aware that most Asian countries are "high-context cultures," based on a complicated system of relationships and moral codes (some of which might not seem "moral" to you), while the United States is "low-context," meaning that people are more direct and rely on legal codes.
13. Leave the common American task-oriented, fast-paced style at home. Effectively transferring skills to other cultures requires patient nonjudgmentalism. Hasty criticisms of the foreigner's ideas only serve to shut down that person and close the door to meaningful interactions.
14. Some countries, such as Israel, however, are even more fast-paced, and people there get impatient with Americans' small talk.
15. Also be sensitive to the difference between the North American low-context culture—in which employees are encouraged to be self-reliant—and high-context cultures (much of Asia, Africa, South America), in which workers expect warmly supportive relationships with their American supervisors and co-workers.
16. If you travel to the increasingly visited out-of-the-way locations, learn to tolerate unpredictability and go without what you may consider basic amenities. Avoid complaining to business clients about poor phone service, lack of hot (or any, for that matter!) water, erratic availability of electricity, or unsavory food. Just remember you are a guest, and act with the grace that goes along with that role.

SOURCES: Peter Cowley and Barbara E. Hanna, *Language & Culture* (Jan. 2005): 1–17; Pui-Wing Tam, "Culture Course," *Wall Street Journal* (May 25, 2004): B1 & B12; "Improved Cross-cultural Communication Increases Global Sourcing, Productivity, Accenture Study Finds," *Business Wire* (July 12, 2006): 1.

	1. Domestic	2. International	3. Multinational	4. Global
Strategic Orientation	Domestically oriented	Export-oriented, multidomestic	Multinational	Global
Stage of Development	Initial foreign involvement	Competitive positioning	Explosion of international operations	Global
Cultural Sensitivity	Of little importance	Very important	Somewhat important	Critically important
Manager Assumptions	"One best way"	"Many good ways"	"The least-cost way"	"Many good ways"

SOURCE: Based on Nancy J. Adler, *International Dimensions of Organizational Behavior*, 4th ed. (Cincinnati, OH: South-Western, 2002), 8–9.

EXHIBIT 3.1

Four Stages of Globalization

TAKE ACTION

Take advantage of any opportunity you can to do international internships or take school trips over breaks or summers. The world of work will continue to value those with international experience.

Toyota is a Japanese company, but it has manufactured more than 10 million vehicles in North American factories. The technology behind Intel's Centrino wireless components was born in a lab in Haifa, Israel. Chinese researchers designed the microprocessors that control the pitch of the blade on General Electric's giant wind turbines.

Companies can participate in the international arena on a variety of levels. The process of globalization typically passes through four distinct stages, as illustrated in Exhibit 3.1.

For today's managers, international experience is fast becoming a requisite. A survey of the 700 largest U.S. companies by *Chief Executive* and the executive search firm Spencer Stuart found that the percentage of CEOs with international experience jumped from 21 percent in 2002 to 30 percent the following year.[11] Increasingly, managers at lower levels also are expected to know a second or third language and have international experience.

Young managers who want their careers to move forward recognize the importance of global experience. According to Harvard Business School professor Christopher Bartlett, author of *Managing Across Borders*, people should try to get global exposure when they are young, to build skills and networks that will grow throughout their careers. "If you've lived your whole life in the United States," he says, "you don't have as much sensitivity to all sorts of opportunities."[12]

Assess Your Answer

✱

1 I have no desire to live abroad, or to work overseas, even for a short while.

ANSWER: To advance in a career, young managers should strongly consider an international assignment.

global outsourcing
engaging in the international division of labor so as to obtain the cheapest sources of labor and supplies regardless of country; also called *global sourcing*.

Getting Started Internationally

Organizations have a couple of ways to become involved internationally. One is to seek cheaper sources of materials or labor offshore, which is called *offshoring* or **global outsourcing.** Another way is to develop markets for finished products outside their home

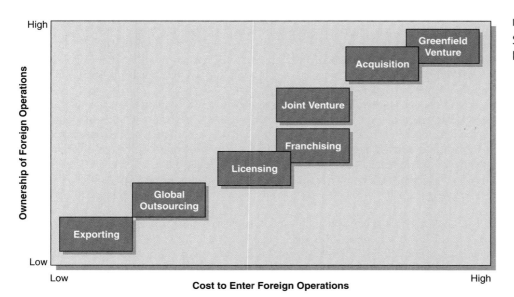

EXHIBIT 3.2

Strategies for Entering
International Markets

countries, which may include **exporting, licensing,** and **direct investing.** These **market entry strategies** represent alternative ways to sell products and services in foreign markets. Most firms begin with exporting and work up to direct investment. Exhibit 3.2 shows the strategies companies can use to enter foreign markets.

OUTSOURCING

In recent years, millions of low-tech jobs such as textile manufacturing have been outsourced to low-wage countries. The Internet and plunging telecommunications costs are enabling companies to outsource more and higher-level work as well.[13]

Service companies are getting in on the outsourcing trend as well. U.S. data-processing companies use high-speed data lines to ship document images to Mexico and India, where 45,000 workers do everything from processing airline tickets to screening credit card applications. British banks have transferred back-office operations to companies in China and India, as well.[14]

EXPORTING

With exporting, the corporation maintains its production facilities within the home nation and transfers its products for sale in foreign countries.[15] Exporting enables a company to market its products in other countries at modest resource cost and with limited risk. Exporting does entail numerous problems based on physical distances, government regulations, foreign currencies, and cultural differences, but it is less expensive than committing the firm's own capital to building plants in host countries.

A form of exporting to less-developed countries is called **countertrade,** which is the barter of products for products rather than the sale of products for currency. Many less-developed countries have products to exchange but have no foreign currency. An estimated 20 percent of world trade is countertrade.

FRANCHISING

Franchising is a special form of licensing in which the franchisee buys a complete package of materials and services, including equipment, products, product ingredients, trademark and trade name rights, managerial advice, and a standardized operating system. Whereas with licensing a licensee generally keeps its own company name and operating

exporting
an entry strategy in which the organization maintains its production facilities within its home country and transfers its products for sale in foreign countries.

licensing
an entry strategy in which an organization in one country makes certain resources available to companies in another to be able to participate in the production and sale of its products abroad.

direct investing
an entry strategy in which the organization is involved in managing its production facilities in a foreign country.

market entry strategies
organizational strategies for entering a foreign market.

countertrade
the barter of products for other products rather than their sale for currency.

franchising
a form of licensing in which an organization provides its foreign franchisees with a complete package of materials and services.

Li & Fung

If you buy a shirt at Guess or the Limited, chances are that it was outsourced through Li & Fung in Hong Kong. Run by Harvard graduates and Hong Kong natives William and Victor Fung, Li & Fung has no machines, no factories, no fabrics. The Fungs deal only in information. And they work with 7,500 suppliers in 38 countries, taking orders from companies such as Abercrombie & Fitch, Disney, Levi Strauss, and American Eagle Outfitters.

"There are no secrets to manufacturing," says Managing Director William. "A shirt is a shirt." Instead, they build on proprietary information, such as how to make that shirt faster or more efficiently.

When an order comes in, the Fungs use personalized websites to fine-tune the specifications with the customer. Taking that information and feeding it into their own intranet, they are able to find the best supplier of raw materials and the best factories to assemble them. An order for pants from an American brand ended up this way. Fabric was woven in China, because it could do dark green dyes. Fasteners were done in Hong Kong and Korea for durability. Then these were shipped to Guatemala for sewing.

"For simple things like pants with four seams, Guatemala is great," says division manager Ada Liu. With its proximity to the United States, delivery takes only a few days. If Guatemala has production problems, Li & Fung can tap into its extensive database to find another place. As the order progresses, customers can make last-minute changes on the company website.

As recently as a decade ago, when the company was run by phone and fax, Li & Fung would get an order for 50,000 cargo pants and have it delivered 5 months later, instead of the few weeks it takes today. Now, with customers online making adjustments to color or cutting immediately, there are fewer mistakes and unhappy customers. Because this new system has increased productivity, profits rose 21 percent to HK $502 million. The company's success has allowed the Fungs to make a $120 million acquisition in the health and beauty industry, as a means to diversify.

Until a few years ago, stores changed their clothes four times a year for each season. In this new economy, some rotate their clothes every week!

SOURCE: Joanne Lee-Young and Megan Barnett, "Furiously Fast Fashions," *The Industry Standard* (June 11, 2001): 72–79; Li & Fung Ltd., *Wall Street Journal Asia* (June 18, 2007): 9.

CONCEPT CONNECTION

While vacationing in Thailand in 1988, former art student Henry Jacobson was impressed by the luster of the hand-woven silk ties, unlike any he'd seen back home. Soon after returning to the United States, he and Mulberry Neckwear co-founder Katie Smith introduced Thai silk ties to the U.S. market. The ties caught on. In 2006, the privately held Mulberry, headquartered in Richmond, California, had estimated sales of $60 million. The company uses global outsourcing, working with contractors in China, Italy, and Korea to produce ties designed in the United States from Thai and Korean silk. Here, a Thai silk factory worker spins spools of thread.

systems, a franchise takes the name and systems of the franchisor. For example, Anheuser-Busch licenses the right to brew and distribute Budweiser beer to several breweries, including Labatt in Canada and Kirin in Japan, but these breweries retain their own company names, identities, and autonomy.

In contrast, a Burger King franchise anywhere in the world is a Burger King, and managers use standard procedures designed by the franchisor. The fast-food chains are some of the best-known franchisors. KFC, Burger King, Wendy's, and McDonald's outlets are found in almost every large city in the world. The story often is told of the Japanese child visiting Los Angeles who excitedly pointed out to his parents, "They have McDonald's in America."

Licensing and franchising offer a business firm relatively easy access to international markets at low cost, but they limit its participation in and control over the development of those markets.

CHINA INC.

Just as managers at Delphi are looking to China as the wave of the future, many companies today are going straight to China or India as a first step into international business. As we discussed, business in both countries is booming, and U.S. and European companies are taking advantage of opportunities for all of the tactics we've discussed here—outsourcing, exporting, licensing, and direct investment. In 2003, foreign companies invested more in business in China than they spent anywhere else in the world.[16] Multinationals based in the United States and Europe are manufacturing more and more products in China using design, software, and services from India. This trend prompted one business writer to coin the term "Chindia" to reflect the combined power of the two countries in the international dimension.[17]

Outsourcing is perhaps the most widespread approach to international involvement in China and India. China manufactures an ever-growing percentage of the industrial and consumer products sold in the United States—and in other countries as well. China produces more clothes, shoes, toys, television sets, DVD players, and cell phones than any other country. Manufacturers there also are moving into higher-ticket items such as automobiles, computers, and parts for Boeing 757s. China can manufacture almost any product at a much lower cost than in the West. For its part, India is a rising power in software design, services, and precision engineering.

JPMorgan Chase announced plans to move 30 percent of its investment bank back-office and support staff functions to India by the end of 2007 to take advantage of the low cost of highly educated workers.[18] Nearly 50 percent of microchip engineering for Conexant Systems, a California company that makes the intricate brains behind Internet access for home computers and satellite-connection set-top boxes for televisions, is done in India.[19]

Many large organizations also are developing joint ventures or building subsidiaries in China and India. Cummins Engine was one of the earliest U.S. firms to open plants in both countries.

The International Business Environment

International management is defined as the management of business operations conducted in more than one country. The fundamental tasks of business management, including financing, production, and distribution of products and services, do not change in any substantive way when a firm is transacting business across international borders. The basic management functions of planning, organizing, leading, and controlling are the same whether a company operates domestically or internationally. But managers will experience

international management
the management of business operations conducted in more than one country.

Business Blooper

Aeroflot

A passenger on Russia's Aeroflot airline got tired of the sloppy service he was receiving from two flight attendants, who had sampled from the liquor tray and were way over the legal limit. After more frustration dealing with the drunk attendants, he asked if there was a sober employee who would be able to serve him. The response may indicate a need for customer service training. The two intoxicated crew members beat him up.

SOURCE: Adam Horowitz, Mark Athitakis, Mark Lasswell, and Owen Thomas, "101 Dumbest Moments in Business," *Business 2.0* (Jan/Feb. 2005): pp. 103–112.

EXHIBIT 3.3

Key Factors in
the International
Environment

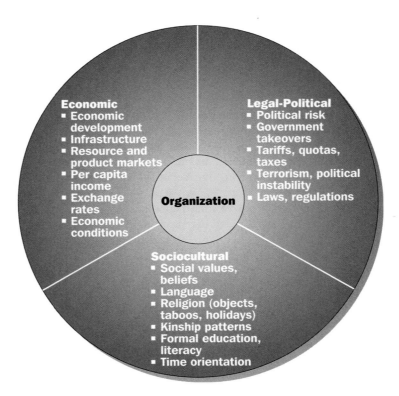

more difficulty and risks when performing these management functions on an international scale. Consider the following blunders:

- When U.S. chicken entrepreneur Frank Purdue translated a successful advertising slogan into Spanish, "It takes a tough man to make a tender chicken" came out as "It takes a virile man to make a chicken affectionate."[20]

- It took McDonald's more than a year to figure out that Hindus in India do not eat beef. The company's sales took off only after McDonald's started using lamb to make burgers that were sold in India.[21]

- In Africa, the labels on bottles show pictures of what is inside so illiterate shoppers can know what they're buying. When a baby-food company showed a picture of an infant on its label, the product didn't sell very well.[22]

- United Airlines discovered that even colors can doom a product. The airline handed out white carnations when it started flying from Hong Kong, only to discover that to many Asians, these flowers represent death and bad luck.[23]

Some of these examples seem humorous, but there's nothing funny about them to managers trying to operate in a highly competitive global environment. What should managers of emerging global companies look for to avoid obvious international mistakes? When they are comparing one country with another, the economic, legal-political, and sociocultural sectors present the greatest difficulties. Key factors to understand in the international environment are summarized in Exhibit 3.3.

The Economic Environment

The economic environment represents the economic conditions in the country where the international organization operates. This part of the environment includes factors such as economic development, infrastructure, resource and product markets, and exchange rates, each of which is discussed next. In addition, factors such as inflation, interest rates, and economic growth are part of the international economic environment.

ECONOMIC DEVELOPMENT

Economic development differs widely among the countries and regions of the world. Countries can be categorized as either *developing* or *developed*. Developing countries are referred to as *less-developed countries (LDCs)*. The criterion traditionally used to classify countries as developed or developing is *per-capita income*, which is the income generated by the nation's production of goods and services divided by total population.

The developing countries have low per-capita incomes. LDCs generally are located in Asia, Africa, and South America. Developed countries generally are located in North America, Europe, and Japan. Most international business firms are headquartered in the wealthier, economically advanced countries, but smart managers are investing heavily in Asia, Eastern Europe, Latin America, and Africa.[24] These companies face risks and challenges today, but they stand to reap huge benefits in the future.

INFRASTRUCTURE

A country's physical facilities that support economic activities make up its **infrastructure**, which includes transportation facilities such as airports, highways, and railroads; energy-producing facilities such as utilities and power plants; and communication facilities such as telephone lines and radio stations. Companies operating in LDCs must contend with lower levels of technology and perplexing logistical, distribution, and communication problems. Undeveloped infrastructures represent opportunities for some firms, such as United Technologies Corporation, based in Hartford, Connecticut, whose businesses include jet engines, air-conditioning and heating systems, and elevators.

As countries such as China, Russia, and Vietnam open their markets, new buildings need elevators and air and heat systems, and opening remote regions for commerce requires more jet engines and helicopters.[25] Cellular telephone companies have found tremendous opportunities in LDCs, where land lines are still limited. China has the world's biggest base of cell phone subscribers at 350 million, and the number is expected to grow to near 600 million by 2009.[26]

RESOURCE AND PRODUCT MARKETS

When operating in another country, company managers must evaluate the market demand for their products. If market demand is high, managers may choose to export products to that country. To develop plants, however, resource markets for providing needed raw materials and labor must be available. For example, the greatest challenge for McDonald's, which sells Big Macs on every continent except Antarctica, is to obtain supplies of everything from potatoes to hamburger buns to plastic straws. At McDonald's in Cracow, the burgers come from a Polish plant, partly owned by Chicago-based OSI Industries; the onions come from Fresno, California; the buns come from a production and

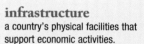
infrastructure
a country's physical facilities that support economic activities.

CONCEPT CONNECTION

While working as a New York investment banker, Bangladesh native Iqbal Quadir realized that connectivity equals productivity. He also knew that his impoverished homeland was one of the least connected places on earth. That prompted him to collaborate with countryman Muhammad Yunus, Grameen Bank founder and 2006 Nobel Peace Prize winner, to create Village Phone. Entrepreneurs, mostly women, use Grameen Bank microloans to purchase cell phones. "Telephone ladies," such as Monwara Begum pictured here, then earn the money to repay the debt by providing phone service to fellow villagers. Village Phone results in thousands of new small businesses, as well as an improved communication infrastructure that makes a wide range of economic development possible.

Qara Argentina

New college grad Amanda Knauer knew she would have a tough time landing the job of her dreams, one that would combine fashion design and foreign travel, so she designed her own company. Heading for Buenos Aires, Argentina, sometimes called the Paris of South America, with one suitcase, $45,000 in the bank, and only a rudimentary knowledge of Spanish, she didn't take long to find what she was looking for: Argentine leather. Soon she launched Qara Angentina, which makes luxury hand-crafted calfskin wallets and messenger bags, targeted to the 25–40-year-old urban male.

Starting a business anywhere is a challenge, but in another country it's monumental. "Everything reverts to the cultural divide," says Knauer, "which is also what makes it interesting." She stressed the importance of leaving your own culture behind and not doing business as an American. "You have to observe and immerse yourself and study the Argentine way of doing business and more or less mimic it," she said.

Learning that she had to get an Argentine partner, she contacted a lawyer, incorporated her business in both countries, and found the right kind of "silent partner." She found it difficult to get manufacturers to create products at the high luxury standard she wanted, so she opened her own facility. Within a few months, she had rented space in downtown Buenos Aires, found second-hand machines, and hired artisans. Six of her seven employees are Argentine. Only the public relations person is a fellow American expatriate.

Getting the Argentine artisans to produce what she needs has been a challenge, and she's had to retrain them. "They're used to working for quantity instead of quality, and I'm asking for the opposite." Her goods sell anywhere from $65 to $650. Though many of her sales are online, she sells through a boutique in Manhattan (Foley + Corinna) and plans to open another one in Buenos Aires. "It's important to be on shelves," she says. "People really like touching and smelling leather."

SOURCE: Tara Siegel Bernard, "Entrepreneur Heads Far South to Launch Firm," *Wall Street Journal* (Feb. 21, 2006): B6.

distribution center near Moscow; and the potatoes come from a plant in Aldrup, Germany.[27] American Amanda Knauer found high-quality raw materials in South America, where she set up her own business.

EXCHANGE RATES

Exchange rate is the rate at which one country's currency is exchanged for another country's. Volatility in exchange rates is a major concern for companies doing business internationally.[28] Changes in the exchange rate can have major implications for the profitability of international operations that exchange millions of dollars into other currencies every day.[29] For example, assume that the U.S. dollar is exchanged for 0.8 euros. If the dollar increases in value to 0.9 euros, U.S. goods will be more expensive in France because more euros will be required to buy a dollar's worth of U.S. goods. It will be more difficult to export U.S. goods to France, and profits will be slim. If the dollar drops to a value of 0.7 euros, by contrast, U.S. goods will be cheaper in France and can be exported at a profit.

The Legal-Political Environment

When going international, businesses must deal with unfamiliar political systems, as well as with more government supervision and regulation. Government officials and the general public often view foreign companies as outsiders or even intruders, and are suspicious of their impact on economic independence and political sovereignty. Some of the major legal-political concerns affecting international business are political risk, political instability, and laws and regulations.

POLITICAL RISK AND INSTABILITY

A company's **political risk** is defined as its risk of loss of assets, earning power, or managerial control because of politically based events or actions by host governments.[30] An

---

TAKE ACTION ▶

When you travel overseas, never buy foreign money on the streets. In many places this is illegal and you can end up in jail, or you might end up with counterfeit money. Use regular banks, legal money changers, or ATMs.

exchange rate
the rate at which one country's currency is exchanged for another country's.

political risk
a company's risk of loss of assets, earning power, or managerial control as a result of politically based events or actions by host governments.

example is Brazil's pressuring of its agencies and citizens to adopt open-source software, which could severely hurt Microsoft and other software companies.[31] Political risk also includes government takeovers of property and acts of violence directed against a firm's properties or employees. In Mexico, business executives and their families are prime targets for gangs of kidnappers, many of which reportedly are led by state and local police. A Japanese tire company, for example, paid a $1 million ransom after its CEO's daughter was kidnapped. Estimates are that big companies in Mexico typically spend between 5 and 15 percent of their annual budgets on security.[32]

Companies operating in other countries also formulate special plans and programs to guard against unexpected losses. Executives at Tricon, which owns KFC and Pizza Hut restaurants, monitor events through an international security service to stay on top of potential hot spots.[33] Some companies buy political risk insurance, and political risk analysis has emerged as a critical component of environmental assessment for multinational organizations.[34]

To reduce uncertainty, organizations sometimes also rely on the *Index of Economic Freedom*, which ranks countries according to the impact that political intervention has on business decisions, and the *Corruption Perception Index*, which assesses 91 countries according to the level of perceived corruption in government and public administration.[35] Although most companies would prefer to do business in stable countries, some of the greatest growth opportunities lie in areas characterized by **political instability.**

CONCEPT CONNECTION

Despite the political risk, political instability, and the local laws and regulations of countries such as Morocco, the Coca-Cola Company earns about 80 percent of its profits from markets outside North America. The soft-drink company suffered in global markets after complaints of tainted products from Belgium bottling plants. Managers are busily trying to rebuild relationships because of the importance of international sales.

2 I would never want to be part of a business operation in a place with political instability.

 Assess Your Answer

ANSWER: Though doing business in countries with political instability is risky, it can offer some of the highest financial returns.

LAWS AND REGULATIONS

Government laws and regulations differ from country to country and make doing business a true challenge for international firms. Host governments have myriad laws concerning libel statutes, consumer protection, information and labeling, employment and safety, and wages. International companies must learn these rules and regulations and abide by them. In addition, the Internet increases the impact of foreign laws on U.S. companies because it expands the potential for doing business on a global basis.

The Sociocultural Environment

A nation's culture encompasses the shared knowledge, beliefs, and values, as well as the common modes of behavior and ways of thinking, among members of a society. Cultural factors can be more perplexing than political and economic factors. When working or living in a foreign country, cultural clashes can emerge in some unusual ways.

political instability
events such as riots, revolutions, or government upheavals that affect the operations of an international company.

Miss Pakistan Earth

Neelam Nourani won the Miss Pakistani Earth competition without wearing a swimsuit, so as not to offend Muslim sensibilities about revealing women's bodies. Judges were instructed to speculate whether the contestants had "nice healthy bodies" underneath their roomy trouser-tunic costumes. Nourani would have to buy a swimsuit to compete in the international Miss Earth contest.

Along with other concerns in Muslim countries, there has been some pressure to "develop." Along with fast food, beauty contests have become a measure of Westernization, shunned by some countries, such as Malaysia and Indonesia, which contain the world's largest Muslim populations. Others try to adapt it to the Muslim way.

That was Muhammed Usman's idea in 1994 when he saw rival India take the Miss World and Miss Universe crowns. Both countries have nuclear weapons, reasoned Usman. "Why not beauty queens?" So he hooked up with the Miss Earth contest, which has a "green theme," and "beauties for a cause."

With family and friends as investors, Usman held the first contest in 2002, and 73 people showed up to watch the 18 contestants sing and dance or recite Urdu poetry. Britney Spears' fan Noorani presented a disco Pakistani song in her energetic performance. Other contests were held in 2003 and 2004. Today there are also Miss Pakistan and Miss Pakistan World contests.

Winner Nourani had to hire bodyguards on her promotional tour to protect herself from Islamic extremists. "In Pakistan, if you take part in beauty contests," she says, "you're considered a scandalous woman."

Afghani Zohra Yusof Daoud would like to see that changed. An activist for women's rights living in California, she was the 1972 Miss Afghanistan. She wants the world to see that Afghani women are more than faceless burka-wearers. But it will have to "incorporate Muslim values," she notes, not sure how that can be done. Having spent some of her formative years in the United States, Nourani has a Western frankness that made her an outcast among the contestants. "We're Allah's creation," she says. "We have a right to represent womanhood."

SOURCES: Mei Fong, "For a Muslim Woman from Two Cultures, Swimsuits Are Tricky—Born in Pakistan, Raised in US, Neelam Nourani Nervously Dips into Beauty Pageants," *Wall Street Journal* (March 22, 2002): A1+A6; "Beauty Queen's Calendar Image Draws Hate Titles," *Gulf News* (Jan 23, 2007): 1.

SOCIAL VALUES

Culture is intangible, pervasive, and difficult for outsiders to learn. One way that managers can comprehend local cultures and deal with them effectively is to understand differences in social values.

In research that included 116,000 IBM employees in 40 countries, Geert Hofstede identified four dimensions of national value systems that influence organizational and employee working relationships.[36] Examples of how countries rate on the four dimensions are shown in Exhibit 3.4.

power distance
the degree to which people accept inequality in power among institutions, organizations, and people.

uncertainty avoidance
a value characterized by people's intolerance for ambiguity and the resulting support for beliefs that promise certainty and conformity.

individualism
a preference for a loosely knit social framework in which individuals are expected to take care of themselves.

collectivism
a preference for a tightly knit social framework in which individuals look after one another, and organizations protect their members' interests.

1. *Power distance.* High **power distance** means that people accept inequality in power among institutions, organizations, and people. Low power distance means that people expect equality in power. Countries that value high power distance are Malaysia, the Philippines, and Panama. Countries that value low power distance are Denmark, Austria, and Israel.

2. *Uncertainty avoidance.* High **uncertainty avoidance** means that members of a society feel uncomfortable with uncertainty and ambiguity and thus support beliefs that promise certainty and conformity. Low uncertainty avoidance means that people have high tolerance for the unstructured, the unclear, and the unpredictable. Countries with high uncertainty avoidance include Greece, Portugal, and Uruguay. Countries with a value of low uncertainty avoidance values are Singapore and Jamaica.

3. *Individualism and collectivism.* **Individualism** reflects the value of a loosely knit social framework in which individuals are expected to take care of themselves. **Collectivism** denotes a preference for a tightly knit social framework in which individuals look after one another, and organizations protect their members' interests.

EXHIBIT 3.4
Rank Orderings of
Ten Countries along
Four Dimensions
of National Value
Systems

Country	Power Distance[a]	Uncertainty Avoidance[b]	Individualism[c]	Masculinity[d]
Australia	7	7	2	5
Costa Rica	8 (tie)	2 (tie)	10	9
France	3	2 (tie)	4	7
West Germany	8 (tie)	5	5	3
India	2	9	6	6
Japan	5	1	7	1
Mexico	1	4	8	2
Sweden	10	10	3	10
Thailand	4	6	9	8
United States	6	8	1	4

a1 = highest power distance
10 = lowest power distance
b1 = highest uncertainty avoidance
10 = lowest uncertainty avoidance

c1 = highest individualism
10 = lowest individualism
d1 = highest masculinity
10 = lowest masculinity

SOURCES: From Dorothy Marcic, *Organizational Behavior and Cases*, 4th ed. (St. Paul, MN: West, 1995), based on Geert Hofstede, *Culture's Consequences* (London: Sage Publications, 1984); and *Cultures and Organizations: Software of the Mind* (New York: McGraw-Hill, 1991).

 TAKE ACTION

Remember: People from some Eastern countries value obligations with their families above all else, while Americans have fewer family obligations but more workplace obligations. It all evens out.

masculinity
a cultural preference for achievement, heroism, assertiveness, work centrality, and material success.

femininity
a cultural preference for relationships, cooperation, group decision making, and quality of life.

long-term orientation
a greater concern for the future and high value on thrift and perseverance.

short-term orientation
a concern with the past and present and a high value on meeting social obligations.

Countries with individualist values include the United States, Canada, Great Britain, and Australia. Countries with collectivist values are Guatemala, Ecuador, and China.

4. *Masculinity/femininity.* **Masculinity** represents a preference for achievement, heroism, assertiveness, work centrality (with resulting high stress), and material success. **Femininity** reflects the values of relationships, cooperation, group decision making, and quality of life. Societies with strong masculine values are Japan, Austria, Mexico, and Germany.

Countries with feminine values are Sweden, Norway, Denmark, and France. In masculine and feminine cultures, men and women alike subscribe to the dominant value.

Hofstede and his colleagues later identified a fifth dimension, long-term orientation versus short-term orientation. The **long-term orientation,** found in China and other Asian countries, includes a greater concern for the future, with high values of thrift and perseverance. A **short-term orientation,** found in Russia and West Africa, is more concerned with the past and the present and places a high value on tradition and meeting social obligations.[37] Researchers continue to explore and expand on Hofstede's findings. In the last 25 years, more than 1,400 articles and numerous books have been published on individualism and collectivism alone.[38]

3 I really admire cultures that are high-achieving.

Assess Your Answer

ANSWER: Cultures that value relationships rather than material success usually have stronger families and community life. Neither orientation is better. They are just different.

TAKE ACTION ➡️

Read the manager's ethics.

Research by the GLOBE Project extends Hofstede's assessment and offers a broader understanding for today's managers. The GLOBE (Global Leadership and Organizational Behavior Effectiveness) project used data collected from 18,000 managers in 62 countries to identify nine dimensions that explain cultural differences, including those identified by Hofstede.[39]

1. *Assertiveness.* A high value on assertiveness means that a society encourages toughness and competitiveness. Low assertiveness means that people value tenderness and concern for others over being competitive.

2. *Future orientation.* Similar to Hofstede's time orientation, this dimension refers to the extent to which a society encourages and rewards planning for the future over short-term results and quick gratification.

3. *Uncertainty avoidance.* As with Hofstede's study, this dimension gauges the degree to which members of a society feel uncomfortable with uncertainty and ambiguity.

4. *Gender differentiation.* This dimension refers to the extent to which a society maximizes gender role differences. In countries with low gender differentiation, such as Denmark, women typically have a higher status and stronger role in decision making. Countries with high gender differentiation accord men higher social, political, and economic status.

5. *Power distance.* This dimension is the same as Hofstede's and refers to the degree to which people expect and accept equality or inequality in relationships and institutions.

6. *Societal collectivism.* This term defines the degree to which practices in institutions such as schools, businesses, and other social organizations encourage a tightly knit collectivist society, in which people are an important part of a group, or a highly individualistic society.

7. *Individual collectivism.* Rather than looking at how societal organizations favor individualism versus collectivism, this dimension looks at the degree to which individuals take pride in being members of a family, close circle of friends, team, or organization.

8. *Performance orientation.* A society with a high performance orientation emphasizes performance and rewards people for performance improvements and excellence. A low performance orientation means that people pay less attention to performance and more attention to loyalty, belonging, and background.

9. *Humane orientation.* The final dimension refers to the degree to which a society encourages and rewards people for being fair, altruistic, generous, and caring. A country that

Business Blooper

Cameron Diaz

Cameron Diaz, who is the voice of Fiona in the *Shrek* movies, offended Peruvian people while filming an episode of MTV Canada. The actress carried an olive-green handbag with a large red star emblazoned on its side, along with Chinese characters for the words, "Serve the People," the famous slogan for former communist leader Mao Zedong. These words are a lightning rod to the Peruvian people, who were terrorized during the '80s and '90s by the Maoist Shining Path movement. Almost 70,000 people died during that time. Although the bags are trendy fashion accessories in some places, a Peruvian prominent human rights activist said Diaz should have been more sensitive to a concept that is associated with many victims in that country.

SOURCE: "People in the News," *The Tennessean* (June 24, 2007): 2A.

EXHIBIT 3.5
Examples of Country
Rankings on Selected
GLOBE Value
Dimensions

Dimension	Low	Medium	High
Assertiveness	Sweden	Egypt	Spain
	Switzerland	Iceland	United States
	Japan	France	Germany (former East)
Future Orientation	Russia	Slovenia	Denmark
	Italy	Australia	Canada
	Kuwait	India	Singapore
Gender Differentiation	Sweden	Italy	South Korea
	Denmark	Brazil	Egypt
	Poland	Netherlands	China
Performance Orientation	Russia	Israel	United States
	Greece	England	Taiwan
	Venezuela	Japan	Hong Kong
Humane Orientation	Germany	New Zealand	Indonesia
	France	Sweden	Egypt
	Singapore	United States	Iceland

SOURCE: Mansour Javidan and Robert J. House, "Cultural Acumen for the Global Manager: Lessons from Project GLOBE," *Organizational Dynamics 29*, no. 4 (2001: 289–305.

is high on humane orientation places high value on helping others and being kind. A country that is low in this orientation expects people to take care of themselves. Self-enhancement and gratification are of high importance.

Exhibit 3.5 gives examples of how some countries rank on several of the GLOBE dimensions. These dimensions offer managers an added tool for identifying and managing cultural differences. Although Hofstede's dimensions are still valid, the GLOBE research provides a more comprehensive view of cultural similarities and differences.

Social values greatly influence organizational functioning and management styles. Consider the difficulty that managers encountered when implementing self-directed work teams in Mexico. As shown in Exhibit 3.4, Mexico is characterized by very high power distance and a relatively low tolerance for uncertainty—characteristics that often conflict with the American concept of teamwork, which emphasizes shared power and authority, with team members working on a variety of problems without formal guidelines, rules, and structure.

Many workers in Mexico, as well as in France and Mediterranean countries, expect organizations to be hierarchical. In Russia, people are good at working in groups and like competing as a team rather than individually. Organizations in Germany and other central European countries typically strive to be impersonal, well-oiled machines. Effective management styles differ in each country, depending on cultural characteristics.[40]

OTHER CULTURAL CHARACTERISTICS

Other cultural characteristics that influence international organizations are language, religion, attitudes, social organization, and education. Some countries, such as India, are characterized by *linguistic pluralism,* meaning that several languages exist within the country. Other countries rely heavily on spoken versus written language. Religion includes sacred objects, philosophical attitudes toward life, taboos, and rituals. Attitudes toward achievement, work, and people can all affect organizational productivity.

TAKE ACTION

Understanding national culture is just as important as paying attention to economic and political matters when working in or with a foreign country. Take the New Manager's Self-Test to gain insight into your own cultural beliefs and values.

Spotlight on Skills

How Well Do You Play the Culture Game?

How good are you at understanding cross-cultural differences in communication and etiquette? For fun, see how many of the following questions you can answer correctly. The answers appear at the end.

1. You want to do business with a Greek company, but the representative insists on examining every detail of your proposal for several hours. This time-consuming detail means that the Greek representative:
   a. Doesn't trust the accuracy of your proposal
   b. Is being polite and really doesn't want to go ahead with the deal
   c. Is signaling you to consider a more reasonable offer but doesn't want to ask directly
   d. Is uncomfortable with detailed proposals and would prefer a simple handshake
   e. Is showing good manners and respect to you and your proposal

2. Male guests in many Latin American countries often give their visitors an *abrazzo* when greeting them. An *abrazzo* is:
   a. A light kiss on the nose
   b. A special gift, usually wine or food
   c. Clapping hands in the air as the visitor approaches
   d. A strong embrace, or a kiss with hand on shoulder
   e. A firm two-handed handshake, lasting almost a minute

3. Japanese clients visit you at your office for a major meeting. Where should the top Japanese official be seated?
   a. Closest to the door
   b. As close to the middle of the room as possible
   c. Anywhere in the room; seating location isn't important to Japanese businesspeople
   d. Somewhere away from the door with a piece of artwork behind him or her
   e. Always beside rather than facing the host

4. One of the most universal gestures is:
   a. A pat on the back (congratulations)
   b. A smile (happiness or politeness)
   c. Scratching your chin (thinking)
   d. Closing your eyes (boredom)
   e. Arm up, shaking back and forth (waving)

5. While visiting a German client, you compliment the client's beautiful pen set. What probably will happen?
   a. The client will insist very strongly that you take it
   b. The client will tell you where to buy such a pen set at a good price

   c. The client will accept the compliment and get on with business
   d. The client probably will get upset that you aren't paying attention to the business at hand
   e. The client will totally ignore the comment

6. Managers from which country are least likely to tolerate someone being 5 minutes late for an appointment?
   a. United States
   b. Australia
   c. Brazil
   d. Sweden
   e. Saudi Arabia

7. In which of the following countries are office arrangements NOT usually an indicator of the person's status?
   a. United Kingdom
   b. Germany
   c. Saudi Arabia
   d. China
   e. United States

8. In many Asian cultures, a direct order such as "Get me the Amex report" is most likely to be given by:
   a. Senior management to most subordinates
   b. A junior employee to a peer
   c. Senior management only to very junior employees
   d. Junior employees to outsiders
   e. None of the above

9. In the United States, scratching one's head usually means that the person is confused or skeptical. In Russia, it means:
   a. "You're crazy!"
   b. "I'm listening carefully."
   c. "I want to get to know you better."
   d. "I'm confused or skeptical."
   e. None of the above

10. A polite way to give your business card to a Japanese business person is:
   a. Casually, after several hours of getting to know the person
   b. When first meeting, presenting your card with both hands
   c. At the very end of the first meeting
   d. Casually during the meeting, with the information down to show humility
   e. Never; it is considered rude in Japan to give business cards.

SOURCES: Steven L. McShane and Mary Ann Von Glinow, *Organizational Behavior: Emerging Realities for the Workplace Revolution*, 3rd ed. (New York: McGraw-Hill/Irwin, 2004); "Cross-Cultural Communication Game," developed by Steven L. McShane, based on material in R. Axtell, *Gestures: The Do's and Taboos of Body Language Around the World* (New York: Wiley, 1991); R. Mead, *Cross-Cultural Management Communication* (Chichester, UK: Wiley, 1990): chapter 7; and J.V. Thill and C. L. Bovée, *Excellence in Business Communication* (New York: McGraw-Hill, 1995): chapter 17.

Answers

1. e; 2. d; 3. d; 4. b; 5. c; 6. d; 7. c; 8. c; 9. d; 10. b

NEW MANAGER SELF TEST

Cultural Beliefs and Values

To help you understand how behaviors in culture follow from values and beliefs, respond to the statements below. Your instructor may ask you to bring these to class for a subgroups discussion to find common themes, followed by a class discussion.

	Mostly True			Mostly False	
1. I know people who believe in reincarnation and karma and have had discussions with these people or read books on the topics.	1	2	3	4	5
2. I have a grasp of concepts surrounding the idea of "infidels."	1	2	3	4	5
3. I have tried to understand the difference between fate and free will and have had meaningful discussions with others about this topic.	1	2	3	4	5
4. I understand my own cultural value of having either a passive orientation or an action orientation to life; I have thought about the ramifications of this value.	1	2	3	4	5
5. I have talked to people or read articles relating to the ideologies of certain ethnic or racial groups being seen as inferior and others as superior. I have thought through the consequences of this type of thinking.	1	2	3	4	5
6. I have noted the difference in certain cultures of old people being revered, versus other cultures in which youth is cultivated.	1	2	3	4	5
7. I can see that some cultures value aesthetics and others value material abundance.	1	2	3	4	5
8. I know people who think that men are superior and others who think that women are superior, and I've had discussions with both types of people.	1	2	3	4	5

INTERPRETATION: This test helps identify how broad your thinking is; that is, have you challenged the values that come with your own culture? Or are you confined to the kinds of thought patterns that you grew up with? As the world becomes smaller and smaller, it will become even more important for people to understand (though not necessarily agree with) values and ways of thinking in other cultures.

SCORING: If you scored "Mostly True" on six or more of these statements, you have broken out of your own cultural patterns and are moving toward a more global way of thinking. If you scored three or less, you need to expand your horizons. Start reading books about other cultures and novels by authors in other countries, and initiate discussions of important issues with people from other cultures.

Adapted from Christopher Taylor, University of Arizona.

One study found that the prevalent American attitude that treats employees as resources to be used (an *instrumental* attitude toward people) can be a strong impediment to business success in countries where people are valued as an end in themselves rather than as a means to an end (a *humanistic* attitude). U.S. companies sometimes use instrumental human resource policies that conflict with local humanistic values.[41]

Ethnocentrism, which refers to a natural tendency of people to regard their own culture as superior and to downgrade or dismiss other cultural values, can be found in all countries. Strong ethnocentric attitudes within a country make it difficult for foreign firms to operate there.

Other factors include social organization, such as status systems, kinship and families, social institutions, and opportunities for social mobility. Education influences the literacy level, the availability of qualified employees, and the predominance of primary or secondary education degrees.

American managers are regularly accused of an ethnocentric attitude that assumes that the American way is the best way. At an executive training seminar at IMD, a business school in Lausanne, Switzerland, managers from Europe expressed a mixture of admiration and disdain for U.S. managers. "They admire the financial results," says J. Peter Killing, an IMD professor, "but when they meet managers from the United States, they see that even these educated, affluent Americans don't speak any language besides English, don't know how or when to eat and drink properly, and don't know anything about European history, let alone geography."[42]

As business grows increasingly global, U.S. managers are learning that cultural differences cannot be ignored if international operations are to succeed. Coke had to withdraw its two-liter bottle from the Spanish market after discovering that compartments of Spanish refrigerators were too small for it. Wal-Mart goofed by stocking footballs in Brazil, a country where soccer rules.[43] Companies can improve their success by paying attention to culture. U.S. companies could take a lesson from South Korean appliance maker LG Electronics, which rules in emerging markets.

International Trade Alliances

One of the most visible changes in the international business environment in recent years has been the development of regional trading alliances and international trade agreements. These developments are significantly shaping global trade.

GATT AND THE WORLD TRADE ORGANIZATION

The General Agreement on Tariffs and Trade (GATT), signed by 23 nations in 1947, started as a set of rules to ensure nondiscrimination, clear procedures, the negotiation of disputes, and the participation of lesser-developed countries in international trade. GATT and its successor, the World Trade Organization (WTO), primarily use tariff concessions as a tool to increase trade. Member countries agree to limit the level of tariffs they will impose on imports from other members. The **most favored nation** clause calls for each member country to grant to every other member country the most favorable treatment it accords to any country with respect to imports and exports.[44]

GATT sponsored eight rounds of international trade negotiations aimed at reducing trade restrictions. The 1986 to 1994 Uruguay Round (the first to be named for a developing country) involved 125 countries and cut more tariffs than ever before. The Round's multilateral trade agreement, which took effect January 1, 1995, was the most comprehensive pact since the original 1947 agreement. It boldly moved the world closer to global free trade by calling for establishment of the WTO. The WTO represents the maturation of GATT into a permanent global institution that can monitor international trade and has legal authority to arbitrate disputes on some 400 trade issues. As of December 11, 2005, 149 countries were members of the WTO.[45]

TAKE ACTION ▶

Notice your own tendencies towards ethnocentrism. When you see people from another culture dressing, eating, or interacting differently, are you immediately critical, or do you curiously wonder why they behave so? If you were to travel to a Buddhist or Hindu country, would you insist on ostentatiously celebrating Christmas or some other religious holiday?

TAKE ACTION ▶

Start watching more foreign movies, and notice how people interact, what values are important to the characters, what outcomes are desired. Watching foreign movies from a variety of countries will help you manage cross-cultural situations.

ethnocentrism
a cultural attitude marked by the tendency to regard one's own culture as superior to others.

most favored nation
a term describing a GATT clause that calls for member countries to grant other member countries the most favorable treatment they accord any country concerning imports and exports.

The goal of the WTO is to guide—and sometime urge—the nations of the world toward free trade and open markets.[46] The WTO encompasses the GATT and all its agreements, as well as various other agreements related to trade in services and intellectual property issues in world trade. As a permanent membership organization, the WTO is bringing greater trade liberalization in goods, information, technological developments, and services; stronger enforcement of rules and regulations; and more power to resolve disputes. The power of the WTO, however, is partly responsible for a growing backlash against global trade. An increasing number of individuals and public interest groups are protesting that global trade locks poor people into poverty and harms wages, jobs, and the environment.

EUROPEAN UNION

Formed in 1957 to improve economic and social conditions among its members, the European Economic Community, now called the European Union (EU), has grown to the 25-nation alliance illustrated in Exhibit 3.6. The biggest expansion came in 2004, when the EU welcomed 10 new members from southern and eastern Europe: Cyprus, the Czech Republic, Estonia, Hungary, Latvia, Lithuania, Malta, Poland, Slovakia, and Slovenia. In addition, Bulgaria, Romania, and Turkey have opened membership negotiations. A treaty signed in early 2003 formalized new rules and policies to ensure that the EU can continue to function efficiently with 25 or more members.[47]

EXHIBIT 3.6

The Nations of the European Union

Another aspect of significance to countries operating globally is the European Union's monetary revolution and the introduction of the euro. In January 2002, the **euro,** a single European currency, replaced national currencies in 12 member countries and unified a huge marketplace, creating a competitive economy second only to the United States.[48] Belgium, Germany, Greece, France, Spain, Italy, Ireland, the Netherlands, Austria, Finland, Portugal, and Luxembourg traded their deutschemarks, francs, lira, and other currencies to adopt the euro, a currency with a single exchange rate. The United Kingdom thus far has refused to accept the euro, in part because of a sense of nationalism, but many believe that the United Kingdom and new EU members eventually will adopt the currency.

The implications of a single European currency are enormous, within as well as outside Europe. Because it potentially replaces up to 25 European domestic currencies, the euro will affect legal contracts, financial management, sales and marketing tactics, manufacturing, distribution, payroll, pensions, training, taxes, and information management systems. Every corporation that does business in or with EU countries will feel the impact.[49] In addition, the EU is likely to speed deregulation, which already has reordered Europe's corporate and competitive landscape.

NORTH AMERICAN FREE TRADE AGREEMENT (NAFTA)

The North American Free Trade Agreement, which went into effect January 1, 1994, merged the United States, Canada, and Mexico into a mega market with more than 421 million consumers. The agreement breaks down tariffs and trade restrictions on most agricultural and manufactured products over a 15-year period. The treaty built on the 1989 U.S.–Canada agreement and was intended to spur growth and investment, increase exports, and expand jobs in all three nations.[50]

Between 1994 and 2004, U.S. trade with Mexico increased more than threefold, while trade with Canada also rose dramatically.[51] NAFTA spurred the entry of small businesses into the global arena. Jeff Victor, general manager of Treatment Products, Ltd., which makes car cleaners and waxes, credits NAFTA for his surging export volume. Prior to the pact, Mexican tariffs as high as 20 percent made it impossible for the Chicago-based company to expand its presence south of the border.[52]

On the tenth anniversary of the agreement in January 2004, opinions concerning the benefits of NAFTA seemed to be as divided as they were when talks began. Some people call it a spectacular success, and others brand it as a dismal failure.[53] Although NAFTA has not lived up to its grand expectations, experts stress that it increased trade, investment, and income and continues to enable companies in all three countries to compete more effectively with rival Asian and European firms.[54]

THE GLOBALIZATION BACKLASH

As the world becomes increasingly interconnected, a backlash over globalization is occurring. Perhaps the first highly visible antiglobalization protest took place at the meeting of the World Trade Organization (WTO) in Seattle, Washington, in the fall of 1999, where business and political leaders were caught off guard by the strong sentiments. Since then, protesters have converged on both the International Monetary Fund (IMF) and the World Bank. These three organizations sometimes are referred to as the *Iron Triangle* of globalization.

A primary concern is the loss of jobs as companies expand their offshoring activities by exporting more and more work to countries with lower wages.[55] Consider, for example, that a 26-year-old engineer in Bangalore, India, designs next-generation mobile phone chips at a Texas Instruments research center for a salary of $10,000 a year. Boeing used aeronautical specialists in Russia to design luggage bins and wing parts for planes. These people make about $650 a month, compared to counterparts in the United States making $6,000 a

euro
a single European currency that has replaced the currencies of 12 European nations.

month. IBM shifted thousands of high-paying programming jobs to cheap-labor sites in China, India, and Brazil.[56]

The transfer of jobs such as making shoes, clothing, and toys began two decades ago. Today, services and knowledge work are rapidly moving to developing countries. Outsourcing of white-collar jobs to India jumped 60 percent in 2003 compared to the year before. An analyst at Forrester Research Inc. predicts that at least 3.3 million mostly white-collar jobs and $136 billion in wages will shift from the United States to low-wage countries by 2015.[57]

Activists charge that globalization not only hurts people who lose their jobs in the United States but also contributes to worldwide environmental destruction and locks poor people in developing nations into a web of poverty and suffering.[58] Political leaders struggle to assure the public of the advantages of globalization and free trade,[59] with President George W. Bush admonishing those who oppose globalization as "no friends to the poor." Business leaders, meanwhile, insist that the economic benefits flow back to the U.S. economy in the form of lower prices, expanded markets, and increased profits that can fund innovation.[60]

Yet, the antiglobalization fervor keeps getting hotter—and is not likely to dissipate any time soon. Managers who once saw antiglobalists as a fringe group are starting to pay attention to their growing concerns. In the end, it is not whether globalization is good or bad, but how business and government can work together to ensure that the advantages of a global world are shared fully and fairly.

Managing in a Global Environment

Managers working in foreign countries often face tremendous personal difficulties. In addition, they must be sensitive to cultural subtleties and understand that the ways to provide proper leadership, decision making, motivation, and control vary in different cultures. A clue to the complexity of working internationally comes from a study of the factors that contribute to failures by global managers. Based on extensive interviews with global managers, researchers found that personal traits, the specific cultural context, or management mistakes by the organization all could contribute to failure in an international assignment.[61]

DEVELOPING CULTURAL INTELLIGENCE

When managing in a foreign country, the need for personal learning and growth is crucial. The managers who will be most successful in foreign assignments are culturally flexible and able to adapt readily to new situations and ways of doing things. Managers working internationally must have **cultural intelligence (CQ)**, the ability to use reasoning and observation skills to interpret unfamiliar gestures and situations and devise appropriate behavioral responses.[62] A manager working in a foreign country must study the language and learn as much as possible about local norms, customs, beliefs, and taboos.

That information alone, however, cannot prepare the manager for every conceivable situation. Developing a high level of CQ enables a person to interpret unfamiliar situations and adapt quickly. Rather than a list of global "do's and don'ts," CQ is a practical learning approach that enables a person to ferret out clues to a culture's shared understandings and respond to new situations in culturally appropriate ways.

Cultural intelligence consists of three components that work together: cognitive, emotional, and physical.[63] The *cognitive* component involves a person's observational and learning skills and the ability to pick up on clues to understanding. The *emotional* aspect concerns one's self-confidence and self-motivation. A manager has to believe in his or her ability to understand and assimilate into a different culture. Difficulties and setbacks are triggers to work harder, not a cause to give up. Working in a foreign environment is stressful, and most managers in foreign assignments face a period of homesickness, loneliness, and culture shock from being immersed suddenly in a culture with completely different languages, foods, values, beliefs, and ways of doing things.

TAKE ACTION

Before going on to the next discussion, find out your CQ by answering the questions in the New Manager's Self-Test. Your answers will indicate your level of cultural intelligence and help you relate to the concepts that follow. As a new manager, you should begin to develop cultural intelligence for other countries.

TAKE ACTION

How many of your friends are a different color than you, come from other countries, practice other religions, are from a different socioeconomic class? How prepared are you to work with them?

cultural intelligence (CQ)
a person's ability to use reasoning and observation skills to interpret unfamiliar gestures and situations and devise appropriate behavioral responses.

Cultural Intelligence

Most new managers start out with a focus on their local department. The job of a manager demands a lot, and before long your activities will include situations that will test your knowledge and capacity for dealing with people from other national cultures. Are you ready? To find out, think about your experiences in other countries or with people from other countries. To what extent does each of the following statements characterize your behavior? Please answer each of the following items as "Mostly True" or "Mostly False" for you.

	Mostly True			Mostly False	
1. I plan how I'm going to relate to people from a different culture before I meet them.	1	2	3	4	5
2. I understand the religious beliefs of other cultures.	1	2	3	4	5
3. When I visit a new culture, I can quickly sense whether something is going well or badly.	1	2	3	4	5
4. I seek out opportunities to interact with people from different cultures.	1	2	3	4	5
5. I can adapt to living in a different culture with relative ease.	1	2	3	4	5
6. I am confident that I can befriend locals in a culture that is unfamiliar to me.	1	2	3	4	5
7. I change my speech style (e.g., accent, tone) when a cross-cultural interaction requires it.	1	2	3	4	5
8. I alter my facial expressions and gestures as needed to facilitate cross-culture interaction.	1	2	3	4	5
9. I am quick to change the way I behave when a cross-culture encounter seems to require it.	1	2	3	4	5

INTERPRETATION AND SCORING: Each statement pertains to some aspect of *cultural intelligence.* Statements 1–3 pertain to the head (*cognitive* CQ subscale), questions 4–6 to the heart (*emotional CQ* subscale), and statements 7–9 to the body (*physical CQ* subscale). If you have sufficient international experience and CQ to have answered "Mostly True" to two of three statements for each subscale or six of nine for all the statements, consider yourself at a high level of CQ for a new manager. If you scored one or fewer "Mostly True" on each subscale or three or fewer for all nine statements, it is time for you to learn more about other national cultures. Hone your observational skills and learn to pick up on clues about how people from a different country respond to various situations. Be open to new ideas, and develop empathy for people who are different from you.

SOURCES: Based on P. Christopher Earley and Elaine Mosakowski, "Cultural Intelligence," *Harvard Business Review* (October 2004): 139–146; and Lynn Van Dyne and Soon Ang, "Cultural Intelligence: An Essential Capability for Individuals in Contemporary Organizations," unpublished working paper (June 2005).

Culture shock is the term referring to the frustration and anxiety that result from constantly being subjected to strange and unfamiliar cues about what to do and how to do it. A person with high CQ is able to move quickly through this initial period of culture shock.

The third component of CQ, the *physical,* refers to a person's ability to shift his or her speech patterns, expressions, and body language to be in tune with people from a different culture. Most managers aren't equally strong in all three areas, but maximizing cultural intelligence requires that they draw upon all three facets. In a sense, CQ requires that the head, heart, and body work in concert.

High CQ also requires that a manager be open and receptive to new ideas and approaches. One study found that people who adapt to global management most readily are those who have grown up learning how to understand, empathize, and work with others who are different from themselves. For example, Singaporeans consistently hear English and Chinese spoken side by side. The Dutch have to learn English, German, and French, as well as Dutch, to interact and trade with their economically dominant neighbors. English Canadians must be well-versed in American culture and politics and also have to consider the views and ideas of French Canadians, who, in turn, must learn to think like North Americans, member of a global French community, Canadians, and Quebecois.[64] People in the United States who have grown up without this kind of language and cultural diversity typically have more difficulties with foreign assignments, but willing managers from any country can learn to open their minds and appreciate other viewpoints.

MANAGING CROSS-CULTURALLY

Which two of the following three items go together: a panda, a banana, and a monkey? If you said a monkey and a banana, you answered like a majority of Asians. If you said a panda and a monkey, you answered like a majority of people in Western Europe and the United States. Where Westerners see distinct categories (animals), Asians see relationships (monkeys eat bananas).[65] Although this test is not definitive, it illustrates an important reality for managers: The cultural differences in how people think and see the world affect working relationships. To be effective on an international level, managers have to interpret the culture of the country and organization in which they are working and acquire the sensitivity required to avoid making costly cultural blunders.[66]

In addition to developing cultural intelligence, managers can prepare for foreign assignments by understanding how the country differs in terms of the Hofstede and GLOBE social values discussed earlier in this chapter. These values greatly influence how a manager should interact with subordinates and colleagues in the new assignment. For example, the United States scores extremely high on individualism, and, to be successful, a U.S. manager working in a country such as Japan, which scores high on collectivism, will have to modify his or her approach to leading and controlling.

Leading. In relationship-oriented societies that rank high on collectivism, such as those in Asia, the Arab world, and Latin America, leaders typically take a warm, personalized approach with employees. One of the greatest difficulties U.S. leaders encounter in doing business in China, for example, is failing to recognize that to the Chinese, any relationship is a personal relationship.[67] Managers are expected to have periodic social visits with workers, inquiring about their morale and health. Sometimes the socializing can be excessive, as shown in the Benchmarking feature. Leaders should be especially careful about how and in what context they criticize others. To Asians, Africans, Arabs, and Latin Americans, the loss of self-respect brings dishonor to themselves and their families. The principle of *saving face* is highly important in some cultures.

TAKE ACTION

When you return from an extended time abroad, you experience reverse culture shock, *which means adapting back to your own culture—which is often more difficult than going away*.

culture shock
feelings of confusion, disorientation, and anxiety that result from being immersed in a foreign culture.

Alcohol in Korea

It's a time-honored practice in Korea for managers to take their teams on twice-weekly drinking bouts after work. In one case, the boss kept urging the employees to drink more and more, but the 29-year-old female graphic artist kept protesting that her limit was two beers.

"Either you drink, or you'll get it from me tomorrow," warned the boss. Rather than lose her job, she drank but finally couldn't take it any longer. She quit and sued.

In a precedent-setting ruling, the Seoul High Court said it was illegal to force subordinates to drink alcohol, saying that the manager was guilty of "violation of human dignity." The dramatic increase of women in the professional workforce has forced companies to change some of their practices. Heretofore, the typical scenario started with dinner, washed down with Korea's vodka, then more alcohol at a beer hall, followed by lots of whiskey in a drunken, singer-filled karaoke hall. Hundreds of inebriated dark-suited men stumbling toward taxis became part of Seoul's nightscape. Drinking together was seen as essential to the bonding necessary to do an excellent job the next day at work.

Male and female managers alike report that the incidence of drinking is reduced when women join the team. "My boss used to be about 'let's drink 'til we die,' reported We Sujung, a 31-year-old employee at a shipping company. "The women got together and complained about the drinking and the pressure to drink. So things changed last year. Now we sometimes go to musicals or movies instead."

Similarly, the practice of excessive alcohol consumption is questioned when a foreigner arrives on an assignment, is taken out in the evening, and then often says something like, "Man, people drink like crazy here!" The drinking culture is reinforced in interviews, where applicants are asked if they drink. Everyone knows the correct answer to that one.

In the trial, the employee told of cases when she left early and was ordered back to party and drink, usually until dawn. The boss justified his behavior, saying that subordinates needed to bond, a need he took so seriously that he often paid for the alcohol himself. He called the female employee a weirdo. "I'm the victim," he complained.

SOURCE: Norimitse Onishi, "As Women Rise, Corporate Korea Corks the Bottle, *The New York Times* (June 10, 2007): 1 & 4,

Decision Making. In the United States, on the one hand, mid-level managers may discuss a problem and give the boss a recommendation. On the other hand, managers in Iran, which reflects South Asian cultural values, expect the boss to make a decision and issue specific instructions.[68] In Mexico, employees often don't understand participatory decision making. Mexico ranks extremely high on power distance, and many workers expect managers to exercise their power in making decisions and issuing orders. American managers working in Mexico have been advised to explain a decision rarely lest workers perceive this as a sign of weakness.[69]

In contrast, managers in many Arab and African nations are expected to use consultative decision making in the extreme.

Motivating. Motivation must fit the incentives within the culture. One study, for example, confirmed that intrinsic factors such as challenge, recognition, and the work itself are less effective in countries that value high power distance. Possibly workers in these cultures perceive manager recognition and support as manipulative and, therefore, demotivating.[70] In places such as the United States and the United Kingdom, by contrast, intrinsic factors can be highly motivating. In Japan, which values collectivism, employees are motivated to satisfy the company. A financial bonus for star performance would be humiliating to employees from Japan, China, or Ecuador.

An American executive in Japan offered a holiday trip to the top salesperson, but the employees weren't interested. After he realized that the Japanese are motivated in groups, he changed the reward to a trip for everyone if together they would achieve the sales target. They did. Managers in Latin America, Africa, and the Middle East improve

TAKE ACTION »

Don't get frustrated with people in high power-distance countries if they don't take initiative or want to make decisions. Just realize that their culture is different. They don't have to be like you. Remember the saying, "When in Rome, do as the Romans do."

employees' motivation by showing respect for them as individuals with needs and interests outside of work.[71]

Controlling. When things go wrong, managers in foreign countries often are unable to get rid of employees who do not work out. Consider the following research finding: When asked what to do about an employee whose work had been sub par for a year after 15 years of exemplary performance, 75 percent of Americans and Canadians said "fire her"; only 20 percent of Singaporeans and Koreans chose that solution.[72] In Europe, Mexico, and Indonesia, as well, to hire and fire based on performance seems unnaturally brutal. In addition, workers in some countries are protected by strong labor laws and union rules.

In foreign cultures, managers also should not control the wrong things. A Sears manager in Hong Kong insisted that employees come to work on time instead of 15 minutes late. The employees did exactly as they were told, but they also left on time instead of working into the evening as they had previously. As a result, a lot of work was left unfinished. The manager eventually told the employees to go back to their old ways. His attempt at control had a negative effect.

As a means of learning across borders, here is a poem that addresses cultural differences.

An Asian View of Cultural Differences

Eastern Perspective	Western Perspective
We live in time.	You live in space.
We are always at rest.	You are always on the move.
We are passive.	You are aggressive.
We like to contemplate.	You like to act.
We accept the world as it is.	You try to change the world according to your blueprint.
We live in peace with nature.	You try to impose your will in her.
Religion is our first love.	Technology is your passion.
We delight to think about the meaning of life.	You delight in physics.
We believe in freedom of silence.	You believe in freedom of speech.
We lapse into meditation.	You strive for articulation.
We marry first, then love.	You love first, then marry.
Our marriage is the beginning of a love affair.	Your marriage is the happy end of a romance.
It is an indissoluble bond.	It is a contract.
Our love is mute.	Your love is vocal.
We try to conceal it from the world.	You delight in showing it to others.
Self-denial is the secret to our survival.	Self-assertiveness is the key to your success.
We are taught from the cradle to want less and less.	You are urged every day to want more and more.
We glorify austerity and renunciation.	You emphasize gracious living and enjoyment.
In the sunset years of life we renounce the world and prepare for the hereafter.	You retire to enjoy the fruits of your labor.

SOURCE: Dr. Mai Van Trang, Indochinese Materials Center

Summary

Successful companies are expanding their business overseas and competing with foreign companies on their home turf. Major alternatives for serving foreign markets are exporting, licensing, franchising, and direct investing through joint ventures or wholly owned subsidiaries. Business in the global arena involves special risks and difficulties because of complicated economic, legal-political, and sociocultural forces. Moreover, the global environment is changing rapidly, as illustrated by the emergence of the World Trade Organization (WTO), the European Union (EU), the North American Free Trade Agreement (NAFTA), and other emerging trade alliances. Expansion of free-trade policies has sparked a globalization backlash among people who are fearful of losing their jobs and economic security, as well as those who believe that economic globalization hurts poor people worldwide.

Much of the growth in international business has been carried out by large businesses called multinational corporations (MNCs) These large companies exist in an almost borderless world, encouraging the free flow of ideas, products, manufacturing, and marketing among countries to achieve the greatest efficiencies. Managers in MNCs, as well as those in much smaller companies doing business internationally, face many challenges and must develop a high level of cultural intelligence (CQ) to be successful. CQ, which involves a cognitive component (head), an emotional component (heart), and a physical component (body), helps managers interpret unfamiliar situations and devise culturally appropriate responses. Social and cultural values differ widely across cultures and influence appropriate patterns of leadership, decision making, motivation, and managerial control.

Discussion Questions

1. What specifically would the experience of living and working in another country contribute to your skills and effectiveness as a manager in your own country?

2. What might be some long-term ramifications of the war in Iraq for U.S. managers and companies operating internationally?

3. What do you think is your strongest component of cultural intelligence? Your weakest? How would you go about shoring up your weaknesses?

4. What steps could a company take to avoid making product design and marketing mistakes when introducing new products into East Germany? How would you go about hiring a plant manager for a facility you are planning to build in East Germany?

5. Should a multinational corporation operate as a tightly integrated, worldwide business system, or would it be more effective to let each national subsidiary operate autonomously?

6. What does it mean to say that the world is becoming *borderless?* That large companies are *stateless?*

7. Two U.S. companies are competing to take over a large factory in the Czech Republic. One delegation tours the facility and asks questions about how the plant might be run more efficiently. The other delegation focuses on ways to improve working conditions and produce a better product. Which delegation do you think is more likely to succeed with the plant? Why? What information would you want to collect to decide whether to acquire the plant for your company?

8. What is meant by the cultural values of individualism and power distance? How might these values affect organization design and management processes? Why do people from countries that are more collectivistic see individualism as selfish?

9. How do you think trade alliances such as NAFTA, the EU, and others might affect you as a future manager?

Dear Dr. Dorothy

I just got sent on a plum assignment overseas. It's so cool the way they gave me this management assignment in my company's Southeast Asia manufacturing plant. It's really exciting to be here, even if the food is extremely different and people seem to be everywhere.

Here's my question: Nine office employees report to me, and they are all nice people and good workers. It's just that when we have meetings and I ask for their advice, they don't say anything. I learned in business school that having employees giving ideas was a good thing for morale. So why isn't it working here?

Just Wondering in Jakarta

Dear Wondering,

Dr. Dorothy suspects that you must have skipped the chapter in your management textbook about cross-cultural differences. Shame on you! What the book would have said is that Southeast Asia has a greater power distance than most Western countries such as the United States. Therefore, these workers expect their bosses to have more authority than what you probably are used to (that is, unless in the likely event you've had a tyrant for a boss). They see you as the Big Guy, the Decider. When you ask their advice, they think you don't know what you are doing. Dr. Dorothy has no way of knowing if this is true, but since you obviously did not study all your books, she wonders if you also are not doing enough preparation for your job abroad. Learn that culture, and work from its strengths. In any event, skip the participative management, as you are in the wrong culture.

Self Learning

Rate Your Global Management Potential

A global environment requires that managers learn to deal effectively with people and ideas from a variety of cultures. How well prepared are you to be a global manager? Read the following statements and circle the number on the response scale that reflects most closely how well the statement describes you.

	Good Description							Poor Description		
1. I reach out to people from different cultures.	10	9	8	7	6	5	4	3	2	1
2. I frequently attend seminars and lectures about other cultures or international topics.	10	9	8	7	6	5	4	3	2	1
3. I believe female expatriates can be equally as effective as male expatriates.	10	9	8	7	6	5	4	3	2	1
4. I have a basic knowledge about several countries in addition to my native country.	10	9	8	7	6	5	4	3	2	1
5. I have good listening and empathy skills.	10	9	8	7	6	5	4	3	2	1
6. I have spent more than two weeks traveling or working in another country.	10	9	8	7	6	5	4	3	2	1
7. I easily adapt to the different work ethics of students from other cultures when we are involved in a team project.	10	9	8	7	6	5	4	3	2	1
8. I can speak a foreign language.	10	9	8	7	6	5	4	3	2	1
9. I know which countries tend to cluster into similar sociocultural and economic groupings.	10	9	8	7	6	5	4	3	2	1
10. I feel capable of assessing different cultures on the basis of power distance, uncertainty avoidance, individualism, and masculinity.	10	9	8	7	6	5	4	3	2	1

Total Score: _____

Scoring and Interpretation

Add up the total points for the 10 statements. If you scored 81–100 points, you have a great capacity for developing good global management skills. A score of 61–80 points indicates that you have potential but may lack skills in certain areas, such as language or foreign experience. A score of 60 or less means that you need to do some serious work to improve your potential for global management. Regardless of your total score, go back over each item and make a plan of action to increase scores of less than 5 on any question.

SOURCE: Based in part on "How Well Do You Exhibit Good Intercultural Management Skills?" in John W. Newstrom and Keith Davis, *Organizational Behavior: Human Behavior at Work* (Boston, MA: McGraw-Hill Irwin, 2002): 415–416.

Group Learning

Test Your Global IQ

1. Complete the test below on your own. Do NOT look up the answers.

2. In class, the instructor will divide you into groups of 3–4 and ask you to come up with group scores.

3. Only after you've done all of them as a group, look up the correct answers.

4. How well did your group do? Was it better than any of the individuals?

5. After hearing how other groups in your class did, how would you rate your group in terms of Global IQ?

How aware are you of the rest of the planet? If you will be working internationally, the more you know about the world, the more successful you are likely to be.

1. Which six countries make up more than half of the world's population?

   1.   4.
   2.   5.
   3.   6.

2. Which six most commonly spoken first languages account for one-third of the total world population:

   1.   4.
   2.   5.
   3.   6.

3. How many living languages (those still spoken) are there in the world?

   a. 683
   b. 2,600
   c. 6,800

4. How many nations were there in 2005?

   a. 293
   b. 193
   c. 93

5. The proportion of people in the world over age 60 will increase _____ percent by 2050.

6. The number of people who have immigrated from poorer countries to developed ones has been _____ per year in recent years.

7. Between 1970 and 2000, the number of people in the world suffering from malnutrition:

   a. declined
   b. remained about the same
   c. increased

8. Between 1960 and 1987, the world spent approximately $10 trillion on health care. How much did the world spend on military?

   a. $7 trillion
   b. $10 trillion
   c. $17 trillion
   d. $25 trillion

9. According to the United Nations, what percentage of the world's work (paid and unpaid) is done by women?

   a. 1/3
   b. 1/2
   c. 2/3
   d. 3/4

10. Women make up _____% of the world's illiterates.

11. In some African countries, ___% of women have suffered female genital mutilation.

12. According to the United Nations, what percentage of the world's income is earned by women?

   a. 1/10
   b. 3/10
   c. 5/10
   d. 7/10

13. The nations of Africa, Asia, Latin America, and the Middle East, often referred to as the Third World, contain about 78% of the world's population. What percentage of the world's monetary income do they possess?

   a. 10%
   b. 20%
   c. 30%
   d. 40%

14. Americans constitute approximately 5% of the world's population. What percentage of the world's resources do Americans consume?

   a. 15%
   b. 25%
   c. 35%
   d. 45%

15. Which city has the worst air pollution—New York, Mexico City, or Moscow?

16. The total output of the world economy was $6.3 trillion in 1950. What was it in 2000?

17. The number of host computers on the Internet grew by _____% between 1990 and 2000.

18. Which three countries have the highest rate of HIV infection? Which country had the greatest decrease of cases?

19. The world's urban population will grow from 2.86 billion to _____ billion in 2030.

20. The average amount of water used per day by a person living in Ethiopia, Eritrea, Djibouti, Gambia, Somalia, Mali, Mozambique, Tanzania, or Uganda, is the same as people in a developed country:

    a. Making a pot of tea (1 liter)

    b. Cleaning their teeth with the tap running (10 liters)

    c. Filling up a dishwasher (65 liters)

    d. Taking a bath (200 liters)

21. Sixty-five million girls do not go to school. What's the main reason behind their exclusion from education?

    a. Girls are less intelligent than boys

    b. In many countries it's illegal for girls to go to school

    c. Poverty takes a greater toll on girls

    d. Girls drop out earlier to get married and have babies

22. Which country gives the least aid as a proportion of GDP?

    a. U.S.A.

    b. Saudi Arabia

    c. Japan

    d. Switzerland

23. If the world were represented by 100 people, fill in the blanks below to indicate what percentage:

    _____ would be Asian

    _____ would be non-white

    _____ would be non-Christian

    _____ would live in substandard housing

    _____ would be illiterate

    _____ would have a college education

    _____ would own a computer

24. True or False: In the developed world, the population is aging, meaning that there are fewer young people for each retiring adult; but in the developing countries, there are relatively more young people.

25. Russia controls what percentage of the world's energy supply?

    a. 15%

    b. 25%

    c. 40%

26. Which is the biggest trading partner of the United States?

    a. Canada

    b. China

    c. Mexico

27. In Asia, how many city dwellers will be added by 2030?

    a. 600 million

    b. 850 million

    c. 1 billion

28. Which city will have the highest population numbers in 20 years?

    a. Los Angeles

    b. Mumbai

    c. Tokyo

29. Each year, how much money do Mexican immigrants send back to Mexico each year to family members?

    a. $900 million

    b. $3 billion

    c. $20 billion

SOURCES: "What's Your Global IQ?" *Newsweek* (July 2/July 9, 2007): 36–37; World Economic and Social Survey 2007, E/2007/50/Rev.1, United Nations, 2007; United Nations website, 2007; "State of the World Quiz," *BBC News This World*, Feb. 2, 2005; *The UN-HABITAT Report*, United Nations, 2004; *The State of the World's Cities Report 200/2005*, World Watch 2005/06.

Action Learning

Global Economy Scavenger Hunt

To gain a perspective on the pervasiveness of the global economy, you will be asked to find a number of things and bring them back to class.

1. Divide into teams of 4–6 members.

2. Each team is to bring items to a future class from the list on the following page.

3. On that day in class, each team will give a 2-minute presentation on the items that were the most difficult to find or the most interesting, as well as answer the questions at the end of the exercise.

4. How many countries did your team get items from? How many for the entire class?

List for scavenger hunt:

1. Brochures of Annual Reports of four multinational corporations.

2. Evidence from three local businesses to show that they do business internationally.

3. A retail store that sells only "Made in America."

4. Ten toys or games that originated in other countries.

5. Five toys or games that had components from one country and were assembled in another—or somehow were developed in more than one country.

6. Food items from 25 different countries.

7. Articles of clothing from 15 different countries.

8. List of books sold in your town from authors of 12 different countries. Where were the books published? Who translated them?

9. List of 12 films in the past five years that starred someone from another country.

10. List of five films in the past 5 years that had multinational crews and locations. Include at least one that was co-produced by two or more countries.

11. Descriptions of interviews from 5 foreigners (not from your team or the class) asking them what six things they like about the United States and six things they don't like.

12. A list of eight places where a language other than English is displayed (on a bulletin board, poster, etc.).

13. Two maps of the world drawn before 1900.

14. Five items in your town that were manufactured in another country that were not made in that country 6 years ago.

Questions for Discussion

1. What did you learn about the reach of global manufacturing from this assignment?

2. Based on your hunt/research, which industries seem to be the most global? Which are the least?

3. Which countries were represented more often? Which least?

4. What did you learn about the United States and its position in the world?

Adapted from: Jan Drum, Steve Hughes, and George Otero, "Global Scavenger Hunt," in *Global Winners* (Yarmouth, ME: Intercultural Press, 1994): 21–23.

Ethical Dilemma

AH Biotech

Dr. Abraham Hassan knew he couldn't put off the decision any longer. AH Biotech, the Bound Brook, New Jersey-based company started up by this psychiatrist-turned-entrepreneur, had developed a novel drug that seemed to promise long-term relief from panic attacks. If it gained FDA approval, it would be the company's first product. It was now time for large-scale clinical trials. But where should AH Biotech conduct those tests?

David Berger, who headed up research and development, was certain that he already knew the answer to that question: Albania. "Look—doing these trials in Albania will be quicker, easier, and a lot cheaper than doing them in the States," he pointed out. "What's not to like?"

Dr. Hassan had to concede that Berger's arguments were sound. If they did trials in the United States, AH Biotech would spend considerable time and money advertising for patients and then finding physicians who'd be willing to serve as clinical trial investigators. Rounding up U.S. doctors prepared to take on that job was getting increasingly difficult. They just didn't want to take time out of their busy practices to do the testing, not to mention all the record keeping such a study entailed.

In Albania, it was an entirely different story. It was one of the poorest, if not *the* poorest, Eastern European country, with a barely functioning health care system. Albanian physicians and patients would arrive at AH Biotech's doorstep pleading to take part. Physicians there could earn much better money as clinical investigators for a U.S. company than they could actually practicing medicine, and patients saw signing up as test subjects as their best chance for receiving any treatment at all, let alone cutting-edge Western medicine. All of these factors meant that the company could count on realizing at least a 25 percent savings, maybe more, by running the tests overseas.

What's not to like? As the Egyptian-born CEO of a start-up biotech company with investors and employees hoping for its first marketable drug, Dr. Hassan found there was absolutely nothing not to like. But when he thought like a U.S.-trained physician, he felt qualms. If he used U.S. test subjects, he knew they'd likely continue to receive the drug until it was approved. At that point, most would have insurance covering most of the costs of their prescriptions. But he already knew that it wasn't going to make any sense to market the drug in a poor country like Albania, so when the study was over, he'd have to cut off treatment. Sure, he conceded, panic attacks usually weren't fatal. But he knew how debilitating these sudden bouts of feeling completely terrified were—the pounding heart, chest pain, choking sensation, and nausea. The severity and unpredictability of these attacks often made a normal life all but impossible. How could he offer people dramatic relief and then snatch it away?

What Would You Do?

1. Do the clinical trials in Albania. You'll be able to bring the drug to market faster and cheaper, which will be good for AH Biotech's employees and investors and good for the millions of people who suffer from anxiety attacks.

2. Do the clinical trials in the United States. Even though it certainly will be more expensive and time-consuming, you'll feel as if you're living up to the part of the Hippocratic Oath that instructed you to "prescribe regimens for the good of my patients according to my ability and my judgment and never do harm to anyone."

3. Do the clinical trials in Albania, and if the drug is approved, use part of the profits to set up a compassionate-use program in Albania, even though setting up a distribution system and training doctors to administer the drug, monitor patients for adverse effects, and track results will entail considerable expense.

SOURCES: Based on Gina Kolata, "Companies Facing Ethical Issue as Drugs Are Tested Overseas," *The New York Times* (March 5, 2004): A1; and Julie Schmit, "Costs, Regulations Move More Drug Tests Outside USA," *USA Today* (June 16, 2005), http://www.usatoday.com/money/industries/health/drugs/2005-05-16-drug-trials-usat_x.htm

Case for Critical Analysis

Shui Fabrics

Ray Betzell, general manager for the past five years of a joint venture between Ohio-based Rocky River Industries and Shanghai Fabric Ltd., was feeling caught in the middle these days. As he looked out over Shanghai's modern, gleaming skyline from his corner office, Ray knew that his Chinese deputy general manager, Chiu Wai, couldn't be more pleased with the way things were going. Ten years ago Rocky River had launched Shui Fabrics, a 50–50 joint venture between the U.S. textile manufacturer and the Chinese company, to produce, dye, and coat fabric for sale to both Chinese and international sportswear manufacturers.

After many obstacles, considerable red tape, and several money-losing years, the joint venture was fulfilling Chiu Wai's expectations—and those of the local government and party officials who were keeping careful tabs on the enterprise—much more quickly than he'd anticipated. By providing jobs to close to 3,000 people, Shui was making a real contribution to the local economy. Job creation was no small accomplishment in a country where outside experts estimated that the actual (as opposed to the official) unemployment rate routinely hovered at 20 percent.

From Chiu Wai's point of view, Shui was generating just the right level of profit—not too little and, just as important, not too much. With so many U.S.–Chinese joint ventures still operating in the red, Chiu Wai saw no reason why Ray's American bosses shouldn't be more than satisfied with their 5 percent annual return on investment. But those earnings weren't going to land him in hot water with local authorities, many of whom still viewed profits made by Western companies on Chinese soil as one more instance of exploitation in a long history of foreign attempts at domination.

If Chiu Wai had been eavesdropping on the conversation Ray just had with Rocky River president Paul Danvers, the Chinese manager certainly would have been dismayed. Ray, who'd thoroughly enjoyed his time in China, was painfully aware of the quiet frustration in his boss's voice as it traveled over the phone lines from the other side of the world. To be sure, Paul conceded, Shui had cut Rocky River's labor costs, given the company access to the potentially huge Chinese market, and helped inoculate the firm against the uncertainty surrounding the periodic, often contentious U.S.–Chinese textile trade negotiations. Current U.S. tariffs and quotas could change at any time.

"But a 5 percent ROI is pathetic," Paul complained. "And we've been stuck there for three years now. At this point, I'd expected to be looking at something more on the order of 20 percent." He pointed out that greater efficiency plus incorporating more sophisticated technology would allow Shui to reduce its workforce substantially and put it on the road to a more acceptable ROI. "I'm well aware of the fact that the Chinese work for a fraction of what we'd have to pay American workers, and I do appreciate the pressure the government is putting on you guys. But still, it doesn't make any sense for us to hire more workers than we would in a comparable U.S. plant."

After an uncomfortable silence, during which Ray tried and failed to imagine broaching the subject of possible layoffs to his Chinese counterparts, he heard Paul ask the question he'd been dreading: "I'm beginning to think it's time to pull the plug on Shui. Is there any way you can see to turn this around, Ray, or should we start thinking about other options? Staying in China is a given, but there has to be a better way to do it."

Questions

1. How would you characterize the main economic, legal-political, and sociocultural differences influencing the relationship between the partners in Shui Fabrics? What GLOBE Project dimensions would help you

understand the differences in Chinese and American perspectives illustrated in the case?

2. How would you define Shui's core problem? Are sociocultural differences the main underlying cause of this problem? Why or why not? How would you handle the conflict with your boss back in the United States?

3. If you were Ray Betzell, what other options to the 50–50 joint venture would you consider for manufacturing textiles in China? Make the argument that one of these options is more likely to meet Rocky River's expectations than the partnership already in place.

SOURCES: Based on Katherine Xin and Vladimir Pucik, "Trouble in Paradise," *Harvard Business Review* (August 2003): 27–35; Lillian McClanaghan and Rosalie Tung, "Summary of 'Negotiating and Building Effective Working Relationships with People in China,'"(presentation by Sidney Rittenberg to Pacific Region Forum on Business and Management Communication at Simon Fraser University at Harbour Centre, Vancouver, B.C., 21 March 1991), http://www.cic.sfu.ca/forum/rittenbe.html; and Charles Wolfe Jr., "China's Rising Unemployment Challenge," Rand Corporation Web Page\July 7, 2004), http://www.rand.org/commentary/070704AWSJ.html

BIZ FLIX

Mr. Baseball

The New York Yankees trade aging baseball player Jack Elliot (Tom Selleck) to the Chunichi Dragons, a Japanese team. This lighthearted comedy traces Elliot's bungling entry into Japanese culture where he almost loses everything including Hiroko Uchiyama (Aya Takanashi). As Elliot slowly begins to understand Japanese culture and Japanese baseball, he finally is accepted by his teammates. This film shows many examples of Japanese culture, especially their love for baseball.

Unknown to her father, Hiroko and Jack develop an intimate relationship. Meanwhile, Jack does not know that Hiroko's father is "The Chief" (Ken Takakura), the manager of the Chunichi Dragons. This scene takes place after "The Chief" has removed Jack from a baseball game. The scene shows Jack dining with Hiroko and her grandmother (Mineko Yorozuya), grandfather (Jun Hamamura), and father.

What to Watch for and Ask Yourself

1. Does Jack Elliot behave as if he had had cross-cultural training before arriving in Japan?

2. Is he culturally sensitive or insensitive?

3. What do you propose that Jack Elliot do for the rest of his time in Japan?

VIDEO CASE

The Global Environment at Yahoo!

The Internet provides a way to connect with people the world over that is unlike any other. Traditional methods of reaching a potential customer, such as print, radio, and television ads, simply can't match its scale or versatility. Managers face a formidable challenge in creating e-business models for their companies that take full advantage of the opportunities that the medium provides, while building in some measure of flexibility to cope with technological change. As a business model exists to establish an organization's position within the value chain, an e-business model establishes the value chain position in terms of the way operations are integrated with the Web.

Yahoo! (www.yahoo.com) is a true e-business model implementation success story. What started as the hobby of two grad students in 1994 has become the most trafficked Internet destination in the world, with half of all Internet users having visited at least one of Yahoo!'s global network of branded properties.

The company's e-business model is, as of this writing, in transition. Yahoo! has long attracted users by offering enticing free content in 13 different languages, paid for by advertising that appears with the content. Most of Yahoo!'s revenue has been driven by its marketing services, like Yahoo! Search Marketing. This pioneering arm of the company came up with the Pay-Per-Click (PPC) idea in 1998, which revolutionized the way advertising is implemented online. The advertiser-supported free content model has worked well for them for quite some time.

Since 2001, Yahoo! has been implementing a subscription-based model under the banner of Premium Services, while gradually transforming free content into pay content. By November 2006, there were 250 million email users with a yahoo.com account, making up half of all web-based mail users worldwide. Anyone with Internet access has been able to get an ad-supported basic account for free, but Yahoo! offers premium features for those willing to pay for an upgraded account. Most do not upgrade. As more of its services go pay-to-play, the question must be asked: Can Yahoo! add enough value to its content to convince users to stick and subscribe in force, rather than migrate to a free alternative?

There are over a billion Internet users worldwide, divided roughly in thirds between English speakers, non-English European language speakers, and those who speak an Asian tongue. Fifty percent of them have visited at least one Yahoo! site—that's a lot of impressions, and a tremendous opportunity to gain new regular users. In January 2007, Yahoo! implemented a sweeping reorganization to address this opportunity. As competitors like Google continue to take bites out of Yahoo!'s pie while seizing hot properties like YouTube and MySpace, the Yahoo! management team faces perhaps the most critical decisions in the company's history.

Questions

1. What are some of the ways that businesses, both domestically and abroad, can take advantage of the Internet's inherently global nature?

2. As Yahoo! shifts focus from free content toward gaining paid subscribers, what do you predict the outcome will be?

3. What are some strategies that Yahoo!, or any other top-ranked business, can use to keep its edge and remain in a top market slot amid increased global competition?

chapter 4

Ethics and Social Responsibility

Learning Objectives

After studying this chapter, you should be able to:

1 Define ethics and explain how ethical behavior relates to behavior governed by law and free choice.

2 Explain the utilitarian, individualism, moral-rights, and justice approaches for evaluating ethical behavior.

3 Describe how both individual and organizational factors shape ethical decision making.

4 Define corporate social responsibility and how to evaluate it along economic, legal, ethical, and discretionary criteria.

5 Describe four organizational approaches to environmental responsibility, and explain the philosophy of sustainability.

6 Discuss how ethical organizations are created through ethical leadership and organizational structures and systems.

7 Identify important stakeholders for an organization and discuss how managers balance the interests of various stakeholders.

New Manager's Questions

Please circle your opinion below each of the following statements.

Assess Your Answer

1 If some action is legal, it is also ethical.

| 1 | 2 | 3 | 4 | 5 |

strongly agree   strongly disagree

2 It's wrong to be a snitch, a tattler, even if it's about telling on your company, when it is doing something illegal or immoral.

| 1 | 2 | 3 | 4 | 5 |

strongly agree   strongly disagree

3 It's not the manager's job to solve problems in the outside world.

| 1 | 2 | 3 | 4 | 5 |

strongly agree   strongly disagree

chapter outline

What Is Managerial Ethics?

Criteria for Ethical Decision Making
Utilitarian Approach
Individualism Approach
Moral-Rights Approach
Justice Approach

Factors Affecting Ethical Choices
The Manager
The Organization

What Is Social Responsibility?

Organizational Stakeholders

The Ethic of Sustainability and the Natural Environment

Evaluating Corporate Social Responsibility
Economic Responsibilities
Legal Responsibilities
Ethical Responsibilities
Discretionary Responsibilities

Managing Company Ethics and Social Responsibility
Ethical Individuals
Ethical Leadership
Organizational Structures and Systems
Whistle-Blowing

Ethical Challenges in Turbulent Times
The Business Case for Ethics and Social Responsibility

Determining what is right can be difficult for managers. Thus, ethics always has been a concern. Recent widespread moral lapses and corporate financial scandals, however, bring the topic to the forefront and pressure managers in large and small companies alike to put ethics near the top of their list of priorities. Corporations are rushing to adopt stringent codes of ethics, strengthen ethical and legal safeguards, and develop socially responsible policies.

Although every decade sees its share of corporate, political, and social villains, the pervasiveness of ethical lapses in the early 2000s was astounding. Once-respected firms such as Enron, Arthur Andersen, WorldCom, Tyco, and HealthSouth became synonymous with greed, deceit, and financial chicanery. No wonder a public poll found that 79 percent of respondents believe questionable business practices are widespread. Fewer than one-third said they think most CEOs are honest.[2] Moreover, more than 20 percent of U.S. employees surveyed report having first-hand knowledge of managers making false or misleading promises to customers, discriminating in hiring or promotions, and violating employees' rights.[3]

But positive news can be found too. After Hurricane Katrina devastated the Gulf Coast, Kaiser Permanente donated $2 million to the Centers for Disease Control and Prevention Foundation, and it set aside an additional $1 million for long-term recovery efforts. The insurance company St. Paul Travelers works with neighborhood organizations to fund financial literacy programs in low-income areas. And each year, Computer Associates pairs 75 employee volunteers with 75 employees from major customers to build playgrounds in needy areas.[4] A number of companies have begun tying managers' pay to ethical factors, such as how well they treat employees or how effectively they live up to the stated corporate values.

This chapter expands on the ideas about environment, corporate culture, and the international environment discussed in Chapters 2 and 3. We first focus on the topic of ethical values, which builds on the idea of corporate culture. Then we examine corporate relationships to the external environment as reflected in social responsibility. Ethics and social responsibility are hot topics in corporate America, and we will discuss fundamental approaches that help managers think through ethical issues. Understanding ethical approaches helps managers build a solid foundation on which to base future decision making.

ethics
the code of moral principles and values that governs the behaviors of a person or group with respect to what is right or wrong.

CONCEPT CONNECTION

Protective Life Corporation shows its commitment to ethics through its corporate strategy: "Offer great products at highly competitive prices and provide the kind of attentive service we'd hope to get from others." Treating others the way you want to be treated is one approach to making ethically responsible decisions and handling ethical dilemmas. Insurance companies, however, often have to rely on a **utilitarian approach** to ethical decision making that considers how to provide the greatest good to the greatest number of policyholders.

What Is Managerial Ethics?

Ethics is difficult to define in a precise way. In a general sense, **ethics** is the code of moral principles and values that governs the behaviors of a person or group with respect to what is right or wrong. Ethics sets standards as to what is good or bad in conduct and decision making.[5] Ethics deals with internal values that are a part of corporate culture and shapes decisions concerning social responsibility with respect to the external environment. An ethical issue is present in a situation when the actions of a person or organization may harm or benefit others.[6] Ethics can be more clearly understood when compared with behaviors governed by laws and by free choice.

Exhibit 4.1 illustrates that human behavior falls into three categories. The first is codified law, in which values and standards are written into the legal system and enforceable in the courts. In this area, lawmakers set rules that people and corporations

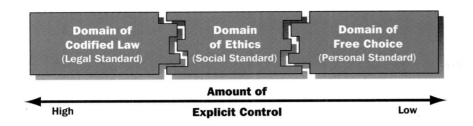

EXHIBIT 4.1

Three Domains of
Human Action

must follow in a certain way, such as obtaining licenses for cars or paying corporate taxes. The courts alleged that Enron executives broke the law, for example, by manipulating financial results, such as using off-balance-sheet partnerships to improperly create income and hide debt.[7] The domain of free choice, at the opposite end of the scale, pertains to behavior about which the law has no say and for which an individual or organization enjoys complete freedom. Examples of free choice are a manager's choice of where to eat lunch and a music company's choice of the number of CDs to release.

Between these domains lies the area of ethics. This domain has no specific laws, yet it does have standards of conduct based on shared principles and values about moral conduct that guide an individual or company. Executives at Enron, for example, did not break any specific laws by encouraging employees to buy more shares of stock even when they believed the company was in financial trouble and the price of the shares was likely to decline. This behavior, however, was a clear violation of the executives' ethical responsibilities to employees.[8] These managers were acting based on their own interests rather than their duties to employees and other stakeholders. In the domain of free choice, obedience is strictly to oneself. In the domain of codified law, obedience is to laws prescribed by the legal system. In the domain of ethical behavior, obedience is to unenforceable norms and standards about which the individual or company is aware. An ethically acceptable decision is both legally and morally acceptable to the larger community.

TAKE ACTION

Try to do the right thing, the ethical thing, rather than just following "the law."

1 If some action is legal, it is also ethical.

ANSWER: Actions can be legal and yet highly unethical, though behaviors often are both legal and ethical.

Assess Your Answer

Many companies and individuals get into trouble with the simplified view that choices are governed by either law or free choice. This way of thinking leads people to mistakenly assume that if it's not illegal, it must be ethical, as if this third domain didn't exist.[9] A better option is to recognize the domain of ethics and accept moral values as a powerful force for good that can regulate behaviors both inside and outside corporations. As principles of ethics and social responsibility are more widely recognized, companies can use codes of ethics and their corporate cultures to govern behavior, thereby eliminating the need for additional laws and avoiding the problems of unfettered choice.

Because ethical standards are not codified, disagreements and dilemmas about proper behavior often occur. Ethics is always about making decisions, and some issues are difficult to resolve. An **ethical dilemma** arises in a situation concerning right or wrong when values are in conflict.[10] Right and wrong cannot be clearly identified, as shown in the Business Blooper.

ethical dilemma
a situation that arises when all alternative choices or behaviors are deemed undesirable because of potentially negative consequences, making it difficult to distinguish right from wrong.

Business Blooper

Spyware

Nobody wants to pay for anything on the Internet, right? That's why, to pay their bills, companies that make toolbars, media players, screensavers, and cyber-toys end up going to spyware companies for some revenue. To make matters worse, some of the spyware is so insidious that even after it is uninstalled, the program comes back like the sorcerer's apprentice.

Eliot Spitzer, former Attorney General of New York, finally indicted a major spyware company, Direct Revenue. The defense? The programs are easy to uninstall and users are warned—never mind that such warning comes only through a baffling set of links. Plus, the company says, what it did was legal.

SOURCE: Patty Waldmeir, "We, the People, are Winning the Spyware Game," *Financial Times* (May 4, 2006): 7.

The individual who must make an ethical choice in an organization is the *moral agent*.[11] Consider the dilemmas facing a moral agent in the following situations:

- Your company requires a terrorist watch list screening for all new customers, which takes approximately 24 hours from the time an order is placed. You can close a lucrative deal with a potential long-term customer if you agree to ship the products overnight, even though that means the required watch list screening will have to be done after the fact.[12]

- As a sales manager for a major pharmaceuticals company, you've been asked to promote a new drug that costs $2,500 per dose. You've read the reports saying the drug is only 1 percent more effective than an alternative drug that costs less than one-fourth as much. Can you in good conscience aggressively promote the $2,500-per-dose drug? If you don't, could lives be lost that might have been saved with that 1 percent increase in effectiveness?

- Your company is hoping to build a new overseas manufacturing plant. You could save about $5 million by not installing standard pollution control equipment that is required in the United States. The plant will employ many local workers in a poor country where jobs are scarce. Your research shows that pollutants from the factory potentially could damage the local fishing industry. Yet, building the factory with the pollution control equipment will likely make the plant too expensive to build.[13]

- You are the accounting manager of a division that is $15,000 below profit targets. Approximately $20,000 of office supplies were delivered on December 21. The accounting rule is to pay expenses when incurred. The division general manager asks you not to record the invoice until February.

- You have been collaborating with a fellow manager on an important project. One afternoon you walk into his office a bit earlier than scheduled and see sexually explicit images on his computer monitor. The company has a zero-tolerance sexual harassment policy, as well as strict guidelines regarding personal use of the Internet. Your colleague was in his own office and not bothering anyone else, though.[14]

These kinds of dilemmas and issues fall squarely in the domain of ethics. Now let's turn to approaches to ethical decision making that provide criteria for understanding and resolving these difficult issues.

Criteria for Ethical Decision Making

Most ethical dilemmas involve a conflict between the needs of the part and of the whole—the individual versus the organization or the organization versus society as a whole. For example, should a company implement mandatory alcohol and drug testing for employees, which might benefit the organization as a whole but reduce the individual freedom of employees? Or should products that fail to meet tough FDA standards be exported to other countries where government standards are lower, benefiting the company but potentially harming world citizens?

Sometimes ethical decisions entail a conflict between two groups. For example, should the potential for local health problems resulting from a company's effluents take precedence over the jobs it creates as the town's leading employer? What about baseball, in which some players evidently benefit from steroid use? Even though the substance is banned, there has yet to be an all-out effort to stop the practice, indicating some moral ambivalence about the practice.

Managers faced with these kinds of tough ethical choices often benefit from a normative strategy—one based on norms and values—to guide their decision making. Normative ethics uses several approaches to describe values for guiding ethical decision making. Four of these approaches that are relevant to managers are the utilitarian approach, the individualism approach, the moral-rights approach, and the justice approach.[15]

UTILITARIAN APPROACH

The **utilitarian approach,** espoused by nineteenth-century philosophers Jeremy Bentham and John Stuart Mill, holds that moral behavior produces the greatest good for the greatest number. Under this approach, a decision maker is expected to consider the effect of each decision alternative on all parties and select the one that optimizes the satisfaction for the greatest number of people. Because actual computations can be complex, simplifying

utilitarian approach
the ethical concept that moral behaviors produce the greatest good for the greatest number.

Steroids in Sports

After New York Yankees Jason Giambi was accused of using steroids and virtually confessed, the practice still is believed to be common—and only recently being discussed. "At least half the guys are using steroids," said National League Most Valued Player Ken Caminiti, who was the first high-profile player to admit to a long-whispered-about practice. That estimate had been affirmed earlier by Boston Red Sox pitcher Curt Schilling, who added, "Is that a problem? It depends on what you consider a problem. It certainly has tainted records, there's no doubt about that."

Congressional hearings on the matter have caused some stars to fall. The once-popular former St. Louis Cardinals' Mark McGwire was so evasive about whether he used steroids that a lot of people are disappointed in the man who had an unprecedented 70-homer season. A Missouri congressman even wants McGwire's name taken off a highway named for him. Medical records of Sammy Sosa and Rafael Palmiero were subpoenaed. Power hitter Barry Bonds' attorney said that Bonds would not testify before the panel if he would risk incriminating himself. Do you think that means he's guilty, or what?

A former New York Mets clubhouse assistant has admitted that he widely distributed steroids to major league players between 1995 and 2005. In addition, Jose Canseco said he used steroids and named other users also. He said that baseball managers and owners knew about the common use of steroids. What gets forgotten is how steroids benefit only the players who cheat, as opposed to smaller ballparks or a lower mound, which benefit all players equally.

Unlike basketball, football, and hockey, major league baseball does no drug testing. But with so many record-breaking players, it is widely assumed that steroids have been used freely. Steroid use has health risks for heart and liver damage and even strokes. NFL star Lyle Alzado went public in 1992 about his brain cancer being caused by long-time steroid use.

So why take the risks? Because steroid use increases muscle mass and can lead to better performance and, hence, high contract dollars. Replying to the concerns, Schilling said, "If you can get an advantage somewhere, even if it involves crossing an ethical line, people will do it. Home runs are money."

Caminiti said that the practice is so prevalent that players who don't do it put themselves at a disadvantage. One of the biggest hurdles in drug testing has been the baseball players themselves, through their union. The tide may be turning, though. Diamondback first baseman Mark Grace says players finally are getting fed up with inflated statistics and record-breaking. "I personally would love to see it banned."

SOURCE: "Baseball Whiffs," *Chicago Tribune*, March 19, 2005, p. 28; Dave Anderson, "Putting the Con Back in Confession," *The New York Times* (February 11, 2005): C15 & C17; Juliet Macur and David Sanger, "Baseball Steroid Panel Asks Active Players to Appear," *The New York Times* (May 5, 2007): A1.

them is considered appropriate. For example, a simple economic frame of reference could be used by calculating dollar costs and dollar benefits.

TAKE ACTION ⟶
Make decisions that benefit others, not just yourself.

Also, a decision could be made that considers only the people who are affected directly by the decision, not those who are affected indirectly. The utilitarian ethic is cited as the basis for the trend among companies to monitor employees' use of the Internet and to police personal habits such as alcohol and tobacco consumption, because such behavior affects the entire workplace.[16] The utilitarian ethic also can be used to explain managers' decision at Northfield Laboratories to continue clinical trials of a product that has showed some troubling results and raises red flags.[17]

By emphasizing the potential benefits to many over the risks to a few, Northfield managers reflect a decision-making approach based in the utilitarian ethic. The FDA reflects a utilitarian approach as well by allowing experimental treatments on trauma patients who frequently are incapable of giving informed consent. A spokesperson said that without the FDA rule allowing such trials, experiments would be impossible and the larger society wouldn't benefit from advances in trauma care.

INDIVIDUALISM APPROACH

The **individualism approach** contends that acts are moral when they promote the individual's best long-term interests. Individual self-direction is paramount, and external forces that restrict self-direction should be severely limited.[18] Individuals calculate the best long-term advantage to themselves as a measure of how good a decision is. The action that is intended to produce a higher ratio of good to bad for the individual compared with other alternatives is the right one. In theory, with everyone pursuing self-direction, the greater good ultimately is served because people learn to accommodate each other in their own long-term interest.

Individualism is believed to lead to honesty and integrity because that works best in the long run. Lying and cheating for immediate self-interest just causes business associates to lie and cheat in return. Thus, individualism ultimately leads to behavior toward others that fits standards of behavior people want toward themselves.[19] One value of understanding this approach is to recognize short-term variations if they are proposed. People might argue for short-term self-interest based on individualism, but that misses the point. Because individualism is easily misinterpreted to support immediate self-gain, it is not popular in the highly organized and group-oriented society of today. Dozens of disgraced top executives from WorldCom, Enron, Tyco, and other companies demonstrate the flaws of the individualism approach. This approach is closest to the domain of free choice described in Exhibit 4.1.

MORAL-RIGHTS APPROACH

individualism approach
the ethical concept that acts are moral when they promote the individual's best long-term interests, which ultimately leads to the greater good.

moral-rights approach
the ethical concept that moral decisions are those that best maintain the rights of those people affected by them.

The **moral-rights approach** asserts that human beings have fundamental rights and liberties that cannot be taken away by an individual's decision. Thus, an ethically correct decision is one that best maintains the rights of those affected by it.

Six moral rights should be considered during decision making:

1. *The right of free consent.* Individuals are to be treated only as they knowingly and freely consent to be treated.

2. *The right to privacy.* Individuals can choose to do as they please away from work and have control of information about their private life.

3. *The right of freedom of conscience.* Individuals may refrain from carrying out any order that violates their moral or religious norms.

4. *The right of free speech.* Individuals may criticize truthfully the ethics or legality of actions of others.

5. *The right to due process.* Individuals have a right to an impartial hearing and fair treatment.

6. *The right to life and safety.* Individuals have a right to live without endangerment or violation of their health and safety.

To make ethical decisions, managers have to avoid interfering with the fundamental rights of others. Some people might construe Northfield's clinical trials on trauma patients described earlier, for example, as a violation of the right to free consent. A decision to eavesdrop on employees violates the right to privacy. Sexual harassment is unethical because it violates the right to freedom of conscience. The right of free speech would support whistle-blowers who call attention to illegal or inappropriate actions within a company.

JUSTICE APPROACH

The **justice approach** holds that moral decisions must be based on standards of equity, fairness, and impartiality. Three types of justice are of concern to managers.

- **Distributive justice** requires that different treatment of people not be based on arbitrary characteristics. Individuals who are similar in ways that are relevant to a decision should be treated similarly. Thus, men and women should not receive different salaries if they are performing the same job. People who differ in a substantive way, however, such as job skills or job responsibility, can be treated differently in proportion to the differences in skills or responsibility among them. This difference should have a clear relationship to organizational goals and tasks.

- **Procedural justice** requires that rules be administered fairly. Rules should be stated clearly and be enforced consistently and impartially.

- **Compensatory justice** means that individuals should be compensated for the cost of their injuries by the party responsible. Moreover, individuals should not be held responsible for matters over which they have no control.

The justice approach is closest to the thinking underlying the domain of law in Exhibit 4.1, because it assumes that justice is applied through rules and regulations. This theory does not require complex calculations such as those demanded by a utilitarian approach, nor does it justify self-interest as the individualism approach does. Managers are expected to define attributes on which different treatment of employees is acceptable. Questions such as how minority workers should be compensated for past discrimination are extremely difficult. The justice approach, however, does justify the ethical behavior of efforts to correct past wrongs, playing fair under the rules, and insisting on job-relevant differences as the basis for different levels of pay or promotion opportunities. Most of the laws guiding human resource management (Chapter 9) are based on the justice approach.

Understanding these various approaches is only a first step. Managers still have to consider how to apply them. The approaches offer general principles that managers can recognize as useful in making ethical decisions.

Factors Affecting Ethical Choices

When managers are accused of lying, cheating, or stealing, the blame is usually is placed on the individual or on the company situation. Most people believe that individuals make ethical choices because of individual integrity, which is true, but it is not the whole story. Ethical or unethical business practices usually reflect the values, attitudes, beliefs, and behavior patterns of the organizational culture; thus, ethics is as much an organizational as a personal issue.[20] Let's examine how both the manager and the organization shape ethical decision making,[21] as shown in the Benchmarking Box.

TAKE ACTION
Take time to make decisions so you treat others fairly, with justice.

justice approach
the ethical concept that moral decisions must be based on standards of equity, fairness, and impartiality.

distributive justice
the concept that different treatment of people should not be based on arbitrary characteristics. In the case of substantive differences, people should be treated differently in proportion to the differences among them.

procedural justice
the concept that rules should be clearly stated and consistently and impartially enforced.

compensatory justice
the concept that individuals should be compensated for the cost of their injuries by the party responsible and also that individuals should not be held responsible for matters over which they have no control.

Benchmarking

Challenging the Boss on Ethical Issues

Many of today's top executives are renewing an emphasis on ethics in light of serious ethical lapses that have tarnished the reputations and hurt the performance of previously respected and successful companies. Yet keeping an organization in ethical line is an ongoing challenge, and it requires that people at all levels be willing to stand up for what they think is right. Challenging the boss or other senior leaders on potentially unethical behaviors is particularly unnerving for most people. Here are some tips for talking to the boss about an ethically questionable decision or action. Following these guidelines can increase the odds that you'll be heard and your opinions will be seriously considered.

- **Do your research.** Marshal any facts and figures that support your position on the issue at hand, and develop an alternative policy or course of action that you can suggest at the appropriate time. Prepare succinct answers to any questions you anticipate being asked about your plan.

- **Begin the meeting by giving your boss the floor.** Make sure that you really do understand what the decision or policy is and the reasons behind it. Ask open-ended questions, and listen actively, showing through both your responses and your body language that you're listening seriously and trying to understand the other person's position. In particular, seek out information about what the senior manager sees as the decision's or policy's benefits as well as any potential downsides. It will give you information that you can use later to highlight how your plan can produce similar benefits while avoiding the potential disadvantages.

- **Pay attention to your word choice and demeanor.** No matter how strongly you feel about the matter, don't rant and rave about it. You're more likely to be heard if you remain calm, objective, and professional. Try to disagree without making it personal. Avoid phrases such as "You're wrong," "You can't," "You should," or "How could you?" to prevent triggering the other person's automatic defense mechanisms.

- **Take care how you suggest your alternative solution.** Introduce your plan with phrases such as, "Here's another way to look at this" or, "What would you think about. . . . ?" Check for your superior's reactions by explicitly asking for feedback and by being sensitive to body language clues. Point out the potential negative consequences of implementing decisions that might be construed as unethical by customers, shareholders, suppliers, or the public.

- **Be patient.** Don't demand a resolution on the spot. During your conversation, you may realize that your plan requires some work, or your boss might just need time to digest the information and opinions you've presented. It's often a good idea to ask for a follow-up meeting.

If the decision or action being considered is clearly unethical or potentially illegal and this meeting doesn't provide a quick resolution, you might have to take your concerns to higher levels, or even blow the whistle to someone outside the organization who can make sure the organization stays in line. Most managers, however, don't want to take actions that will harm the organization, its people, or the community. In many cases, questionable ethical issues can be resolved through open and honest communication. That, however, requires that people have the courage—and develop the skills—to confront their superiors in a calm and rational way.

SOURCE: Kevin Daley, "How to Disagree: Go Up Against Your Boss or a Senior Executive and Live to Tell the Tale," *T&D* (April 2004); Diane Moore, "How to Disagree with Your Boss—and Keep Your Job," *Toronto Star* (November 12, 2003); "How to Disagree with Your Boss," *WikiHow,* http://wiki.ehow.com/Disagree-With-Your-Boss; and "How to Confront Your Boss Constructively," *The Buzz* (October 23–29, 1996), www.hardatwork.com/Buzz/ten.html

THE MANAGER

Managers bring specific personality and behavioral traits to the job. Personal needs, family influence, and religious background all shape a manager's value system. Specific personality characteristics, such as ego strength, self-confidence, and a strong sense of independence, may enable managers to make ethical decisions.

One important personal trait is the stage of moral development.[22] A simplified version of one model of personal moral development is shown in Exhibit 4.2. At the *preconventional*

EXHIBIT 4.2
Three Levels of
Personal Moral
Development

Level 3: Postconventional

Follows self-chosen principles of justice and right. Aware that people hold different values and seeks creative solutions to ethical dilemmas. Balances concern for individual with concern for common good.

Level 2: Conventional

Lives up to expectations of others. Fulfills duties and obligations of social system. Upholds laws.

Level 1: Preconventional

Follows rules to avoid punishment. Acts in own interest. Obedience for its own sake.

Leadership Style:	Autocratic/coercive	Guiding/encouraging, team oriented	Transforming, or servant leadership
Employee Behavior:	Task accomplishment	Work group collaboration	Empowered employees, full participation

SOURCE: Based on L. Kohlberg, "Moral Stages and Moralization: The Cognitive-Developmental Approach," in *Moral Development and Behavior: Theory, Research, and Social Issues*, ed. T. Lickona (New York: Holt, Rinehart, and Winston, 1976): 31–53; and Jill W. Graham, "Leadership, Moral Development and Citizenship Behavior," *Business Ethics Quarterly* 5, no. 1 (January 1995): 43–54.

level, individuals are concerned with external rewards and punishments and obey authority to avoid detrimental personal consequences. In an organizational context, this level may be associated with managers who use an autocratic or coercive leadership style, with employees oriented toward dependable accomplishment of specific tasks.

At level two, called the *conventional level*, people learn to conform to the expectations of good behavior as defined by colleagues, family, friends, and society. Meeting social and interpersonal obligations is important. Work group collaboration is the preferred manner for accomplishing organizational goals, and managers use a leadership style that encourages interpersonal relationships and cooperation.

At the *postconventional*, or *principled*, level, individuals are guided by an internal set of values and standards and even will disobey rules or laws that violate these principles. Internal values become more important than the expectations of significant others. An example of the postconventional or principled approach comes from World War II. When the *USS Indianapolis*

CONCEPT CONNECTION

Oprah Winfrey is an Emmy-winning television talk show host, heads multimedia empire Harpo Productions, and personally is worth an estimated $1.5 billion. Yet, Winfrey is motivated not by a desire for influence, power, or money but by her "calling"—a mission to serve others by uplifting, enlightening, encouraging, and transforming how people see themselves. Winfrey demonstrates the postconventional level of moral development. Rather than listening to "the voice of the world," she says she listens to "the still small voice" inside that tells her what to do based on her deep moral values and standards of integrity. Winfrey evaluates every staff idea in terms of how it connects to service to others.

Spotlight on
Leadership

Skateboarding Street Art

Shepard Fairey likes to think of himself as a rebel, a maverick. The 34 year-old is one of his generation's most notorious and prolific street artists. Originally designing art around skateboarding as a fine art medium, he split with his long-time creative partner and started his own marketing design firm, Studio Number One (see www.subliminalprojects.com). He has been invited to speak at conferences and travels to Japan with his wife to visit a shop that sells clothing with his images. He works with huge business firms that hope Fairey can connect them to a much-desired demographic.

But Fairey can't stay away from bad-boy stuff. He and his friends went to New York's Chinatown one night and went "bombing," as they call it. Finding a blank billboard, Fairey managed to get to the roof of the building with an 8-foot rolled poster and some paste. He managed to affix the image, but someone called the police and he was arrested for criminal mischief and trespassing. He spent 48 hours in jail—his ninth bust.

Even with that rapsheet, he gets courted by mainstream firms. His previous company, BLK/MRKT, worked with Mountain Dew, Levi's, Sunkist, Dr. Pepper, and Universal Pictures. After he posted bail, he had work to do, including designs for Express Jeans and Obey Giant clothing, based on his long-held Obey Giant images. These companies like him because they have trouble reaching the elusive demographic of young males, who are difficult to target, watch little television, and are cynical toward normal advertisements. When young people take Fairey's posters or stickers and put them on their own bulletin boards, the advertisers know the campaign worked.

How can you achieve this kind of success? Fairey says it's instinct, like Louis Armstrong's response when he was asked to define jazz: "If you have to ask, you'll never know."

Often clients are vague with Fairey: "Make it cool," they say. "Make it urban." He retorts: "Urban like hip-hop, like black? Or urban like disaffected suburban white graffiti kids?" Then they get more specific.

Fairey's former company BLK/MRKT took in $1 million per year and it won't be long before Studio Number One follows suit. He despises ads that insult the customer, that are unintelligent.

But how can Fairey remain true to his street image when he is raking in the dough from the fat multinationals? He's not alone. Many entrepreneurs struggle with issues of integrity— the conflict between what they really want to do and what the market is going to pay them to do. "Sometimes I feel like a double agent," he says. He wants to do work that is fun, with clients that can be hip, and he does have his boundaries: no tobacco companies. If he could make over the advertising world so all marketing materials were smart, creative, and art-like, that would be great. He says, "it sounds pretty utopian to me." Still, he's got his enemies, people who think he isn't true to his street roots. Some of them have defaced his graffiti. They think that "if you do anything besides street art, you're a sellout," says Fairey.

SOURCE: Rob Walker, *Buzz Guru, Inc. Magazine* (March 2004): 105–109; "Artist Turns Up Nose as Bomb Ploy Flops," *New York Daily News* (June 23, 2007): 23.

sank after being torpedoed, one Navy pilot disobeyed orders and risked his life to save men who were being picked off by sharks. The pilot was operating from the highest level of moral development in attempting the rescue despite a direct order from superiors.

Assess Your Answer

2 It's wrong to be a snitch, a tattler, even if it's about telling on your company, when it is doing something illegal or immoral.

ANSWER: It takes courage, and often a higher level of ethical development to go against strong authority in the company and report illegal behavior. Rather than calling these people "whistle-blowers," which has a negative connotation, why not call them "conscience-seekers?"

When managers operate from this highest level of development, they use transformative or servant leadership, focusing on the needs of followers and encouraging others to think for themselves and to engage in higher levels of moral reasoning. Employees are empowered and given opportunities for constructive participation in governance of the organization.

The great majority of managers operate at level two, the conventional level. A few have not advanced beyond level one. Only about 20 percent of American adults reach the level-three stage of moral development. People at level three are able to act in an independent, ethical manner regardless of expectations from others inside or outside the organization. Managers at level three of moral development will make ethical decisions whatever the organizational consequences for them.

TAKE ACTION

Listen to your conscience and take moral actions. Independently investigate where the truth lies and what is the right thing to do.

NEW MANAGER SELF TEST

Manager Courage

Probably not right away, but soon enough in your duties as a new manager, you will be confronted with a situation that will test the strength of your moral beliefs or your sense of justice. Are your ready? To find out, think about times when you were part of a student group or work group. To what extent does each of the following statements characterize your behavior? Please respond to each of the following statements as Mostly True or Mostly False for you.

	Mostly True			Mostly False	
1. I risked substantial personal loss to achieve the vision.	1	2	3	4	5
2. I took personal risks to defend my beliefs.	1	2	3	4	5
3. I would say no to inappropriate things even if I had a lot to lose.	1	2	3	4	5
4. My significant actions were linked to higher values.	1	2	3	4	5
5. I easily acted against the opinions and approval of others.	1	2	3	4	5
6. I quickly told people the truth as I saw it, even when it was negative.	1	2	3	4	5
7. I spoke out against group or organizational injustice.	1	2	3	4	5
8. I acted according to my conscience even if I would lose stature.	1	2	3	4	5

INTERPRETATION: Each question pertains to some aspect of displaying courage in a group situation, which often reflects a person's level of *moral development*. A person at the *postconventional* level might answer the questions as "Mostly True," and someone at a *preconventional* level might answer many as "Mostly False." Think about what influences your moral behavior and decisions, such as the need for success or approval. Study the behavior of others whom you consider to be moral individuals. As a new manager, how might you increase your courage?

SCORING: Count the number of checkmarks for "Mostly True." If you scored five or more, congratulations! That behavior would enable you to become a courageous manager about moral issues. A score below four indicates that you may avoid difficult issues or have not been in situations that challenged your moral courage. Study the specific questions for which you scored "Mostly True" and "Mostly False" to learn more about your specific strengths and weaknesses.

One interesting study indicates that most researchers fail to account for the different ways in which women view social reality and develop psychologically and have thus consistently classified women as being stuck at lower levels of development. Researcher Carol Gilligan suggested that the moral domain be enlarged to include responsibility and care in relationships. Women may, in general, perceive moral complexities more astutely than men and make moral decisions based not on a set of absolute rights and wrongs but on principles of not causing harm to others.[23]

Globalization makes ethical issues even more complicated for today's managers.[24] For example, although tolerance for bribery is waning, bribes are still considered a normal part of doing business in many foreign countries. Transparency International, an international organization that monitors corruption, publishes an annual report ranking countries according to how many bribes are offered by their international businesses. Exhibit 4.3 shows results of the organization's most recent available report. International businesses based in countries such as Russia, China, Taiwan, and South Korea were found to be using bribes "on an exceptional and intolerable scale." Multinational firms in the United States, Japan, France, and Spain, however, also revealed a relatively high propensity to pay bribes overseas.[25]

American managers working in foreign countries require sensitivity and an openness to other systems, as well as the fortitude to resolve these difficult issues. Companies that don't oil the wheels of contract negotiations in foreign countries can put themselves at a competitive disadvantage, yet managers walk a fine line when making deals overseas. Although U.S. laws allow certain types of payments, tough federal antibribery laws also are in place. Goldman Sachs got preapproval from the U.S. Justice Department and the Securities and Exchange Commission (SEC) before agreeing to pay a $67 million fee to Beijing power brokers to facilitate a joint venture in China.[26] But many other companies, including Monsanto, ScheringPlough, and IBM, have gotten into trouble with the SEC for using incentives to facilitate foreign deals.

THE ORGANIZATION

Rarely can ethical or unethical corporate actions be attributed solely to the personal values of a single manager. The values adopted within the organization are important, especially when we understand that most people are at the level-two stage of moral development,

TAKE ACTION ⊙➔

Complete the the New Manager Self-Test below pertaining to ethical work environments. With what level of ethical climate are you most comfortable? As a manager, how might you improve the ethical climate of a department for which you are responsible?

EXHIBIT 4.3

The Transparency International Bribe Payers Index 2002

A score of 10 represents zero propensity to pay bribes, while a score of 0 reflects very high levels of bribery.

Rank		Score	Rank		Score
1	Australia	8.5	12	France	5.5
2	Sweden	8.4	13	United States	5.3
2 (tie)	Switzerland	8.4	13 (tie)	Japan	5.3
4	Austria	8.2	15	Malaysia	4.3
5	Canada	8.1	15 (tie)	Hong Kong	4.3
6	Netherlands	7.8	17	Italy	4.1
6 (tie)	Belgium	7.8	18	South Korea	3.9
8	United Kingdom	6.9	19	Taiwan	3.8
9	Singapore	6.3	20	People's Republic of China	3.5
9 (tie)	Germany	6.3	21	Russia	3.2
11	Spain	5.8			

SOURCE: Transparency International, www.transparency.org.

which means they believe their duty is to fulfill obligations and expectations of others. Consider, for example, how David Myers slid into trouble at WorldCom, which disintegrated in an $11 billion fraud scandal.[27]

Research verifies that these values strongly influence employee actions and decision making.[28] In particular, corporate culture, as described in Chapter 3, lets employees

Ethical Work Climates

Answer the following questions by checking true or false, whichever best describes an organization for which you have worked.

	Mostly True	Mostly False
1. What is the best for everyone in the company is the major consideration here.	_____	_____
2. Our major concern is always what is best for the other person.	_____	_____
3. People are expected to comply with the law and professional standards over and above other considerations.	_____	_____
4. In this company, the first consideration is whether a decision violates any law.	_____	_____
5. It is very important to follow the company's rules and procedures here.	_____	_____
6. People in this company strictly obey the company policies.	_____	_____
7. In this company, people are mostly out for themselves.	_____	_____
8. People are expected to do anything to further the company's interests, regardless of the consequences.	_____	_____
9. In this company, people are guided by their own personal ethics.	_____	_____
10. Each person in this company decides for himself or herself what is right and wrong.	_____	_____

SCORING: Give yourself one point for each "mostly true." Subtract each of your scores for questions 7 and 8 from the number 6. Then, add up your adjusted scores for all ten questions: _____. These questions measure the dimensions of an organization's ethical climate. Questions 1 and 2 measure caring for people, questions 3 and 4 measure lawfulness, questions 5 and 6 measure rules adherence, questions 7 and 8 measure emphasis on financial and company performance, and questions 9 and 10 measure individual independence. A total score of 8 to 10 indicates a very positive ethical climate. A score from 5 to 7 indicates above-average ethical climate. A score from 3 and 4 indicates a below-average ethical climate, and a score of 0 to 2 indicates a very poor ethical climate.

Go back over the questions and think about changes that you could have made to improve the ethical climate in the organization. Discuss with other students what you could do as a manager to improve ethics in future companies you work for.

SOURCE: Based on Bart Victor and John B. Cullen, "The Organizational Bases of Ethical Work Climates," *Administrative Science Quarterly* 33 (1988), 101–125.

EXHIBIT 4.4

Questions for Analyzing a Company's Cultural Impact on Ethics

1. Identify the organization's heroes. What values do they represent? Given an ambiguous ethical dilemma, what decision would they make and why?
2. What are some important organizational rituals? How do they encourage or discourage ethical behavior? Who gets the awards, people of integrity or individuals who use unethical methods to attain success?
3. What are the ethical messages sent to new entrants into the organization—must they obey authority at all costs, or is questioning authority acceptable or even desirable?
4. Does analysis of organizational stories and myths reveal individuals who stand up for what's right, or is conformity the valued characteristic? Do people get fired or promoted in these stories?
5. Does language exist for discussing ethical concerns? Is this language routinely incorporated and encouraged in business decision making?
6. What informal socialization processes exist, and what norms for ethical/unethical behavior do they promote?

SOURCE: Linda Klebe Treviño, "A Cultural Perspective on Changing and Developing Organizational Ethics," in *Research in Organizational Change and Development*, ed. R. Woodman and W. Pasmore (Greenwich, CT: JAI Press, 1990): 4.

TAKE ACTION ▶

As a new manager, be prepared to build or enforce an ethical culture in your area of responsibility. Remember that managers make decisions within the norms of their interactions with others. Make sure that your values and the organization's values support and encourage doing the right thing.

know what beliefs and behaviors the company supports and those it will not tolerate. If unethical behavior is tolerated or even encouraged, it becomes routine. In many companies, employees believe that if they do not go along, their jobs will be in jeopardy or they will not fit in.[29]

Culture can be examined to see the kinds of ethical signals transmitted to employees. Exhibit 4.4 lists questions to ask to understand the cultural system. High ethical standards can be affirmed and communicated through public awards and ceremonies. Heroes provide role models that can either support or refute ethical decision making. Culture is not the only aspect of an organization that influences ethics, but it is a major force because it defines company values. Other aspects of the organization, such as explicit rules and policies, the reward system, the extent to which the company cares for its people, the selection system, emphasis on legal and professional standards, and leadership and decision processes, also can affect ethical values and manager decision making.[30]

What Is Social Responsibility?

Now let's turn to the issue of social responsibility. In one sense, the concept of social responsibility, like ethics, is easy to understand: It means distinguishing right from wrong and doing right. It means being a good corporate citizen. The formal definition of **corporate social responsibility** is management's obligation to make choices and take actions that will contribute to the welfare and interests of society as well as the organization.[31]

As straightforward as this definition seems, social responsibility can be a difficult concept to grasp because different people have different beliefs as to which actions improve society's welfare.[32] To make matters worse, social responsibility covers a range of issues, many of which are ambiguous with respect to right or wrong. If a bank deposits the money from a trust fund into a low-interest account for 90 days, from which it makes a substantial profit, is it being a responsible corporate citizen? How about two companies engaging in intense competition? Is it socially responsible for the stronger corporation to drive the weaker one into bankruptcy or a forced merger?

Or consider companies such as Chiquita, Kmart, and Dana Corporation, all of which declared bankruptcy—which is perfectly legal—to avoid mounting financial obligations to suppliers, labor unions, or competitors. These examples contain moral, legal, and economic considerations that make socially responsible behavior hard to define. A company's impact on the natural environment also must be taken into consideration.

corporate social responsibility
the obligation of organization management to make decisions and take actions that will enhance the welfare and interests of society as well as the organization.

Organizational Stakeholders

One reason for the difficulty in understanding corporate social responsibility is that managers must confront the question, "Responsibility to whom?" Recall from Chapter 3 that the organization's environment consists of several sectors in both the task and general environment. From a social responsibility perspective, enlightened organizations view the internal and external environment as a variety of stakeholders.

A **stakeholder** is any group within or outside the organization that has a stake in the organization's performance. Each stakeholder has a different criterion of responsiveness because it has a different interest in the organization.[33] For example, Wal-Mart uses aggressive bargaining tactics with suppliers so it is able to provide low prices for customers. Some stakeholders see this type of corporate behavior as responsible because the greater efficiency benefits customers and forces.

Others, however, argue that the aggressive tactics are unethical and socially irresponsible because they force U.S. manufacturers to lay off workers, close factories, and outsource from low-wage countries. For instance, Wal-Mart now purchases about 10 percent of all Chinese imports to the United States, and company executives are considering increasing their China purchases significantly over the next five years, which critics charge will hurt American companies and workers even more. One supplier said clothing is being sold so cheaply at Wal-Mart that many U.S. companies could not compete even if they were to pay their employees nothing.[34]

The organization's performance affects stakeholders, but stakeholders also can have a tremendous effect on the organization's performance and success. Consider the case of Monsanto, a leading competitor in the life sciences industry.

Other important stakeholders are the government and the community, which have become increasingly important in recent years. Most corporations exist only under the proper charter and licenses and operate within the limits of safety laws, environmental protection requirements, antitrust regulations, antibribery legislation, and other laws and regulations in the government sector. The community includes local government, the natural and physical environments, and the quality of life provided for residents. Special interest groups, still another stakeholder, may include trade associations, political action committees, professional associations, and consumerists.

stakeholder
any group within or outside the organization that has a stake in the organization's performance.

Monsanto

The company's genetic seed business has been the target of controversy and protest. European consumers rebelled against a perceived imposition of unlabeled, genetically modified food ingredients. Research institutes and other organizations took offense at what they perceived as Monsanto's arrogant approach to the new business. Activist groups accused the company of creating "Frankenstein foods."

Partly as a result of these public sentiments, investor confidence in the company waned and the stock took a downhill slide. To make matters even worse, in seeking to sell genetically modified seeds in Indonesia, managers allegedly bribed government officials, which got Monsanto into hot water with the U.S. Securities and Exchange Commission.

The leadership has promised an ongoing dialogue between Monsanto managers and various stakeholder constituencies. The company paid $1.5 million to settle the SEC charges and is voluntarily cooperating with regulatory investigators. If Monsanto managers cannot effectively manage critical stakeholder relationships, Monsanto is not likely to survive as a business.[35]

Exhibit 4.5 illustrates important stakeholders for Monsanto. Most organizations are similarly influenced by a variety of stakeholder groups. Investors and shareholders, employees, customers, and suppliers are considered primary stakeholders, without whom the organization cannot survive. Investors, shareholders, and suppliers' interests are served by managerial efficiency—that is, use of resources to achieve profits. Employees expect work satisfaction, pay, and good supervision. Customers are concerned with decisions about the quality, safety, and availability of goods and services. When any primary stakeholder group becomes seriously dissatisfied, the organization's viability is threatened.[36]

EXHIBIT 4.5

Major Stakeholders
Relevant to Monsanto
Company

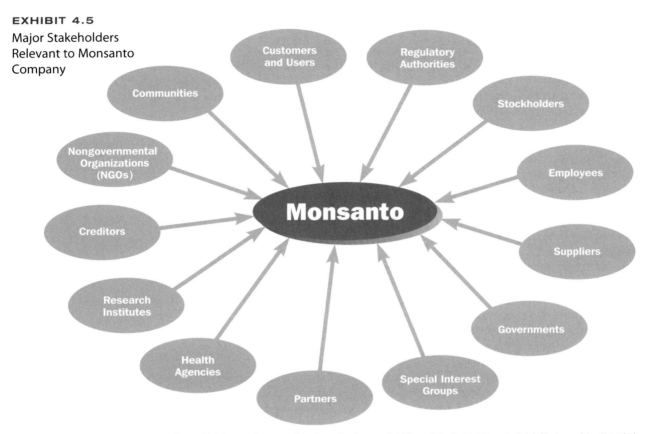

SOURCES: Based on information in D. Wheeler, B. Colbert, and R. E. Freeman, "Focusing on Value: Reconciling Corporate Social Responsibility, Sustainability, and a Stakeholder Approach in a Networked World," *Journal of General Management* 28, no. 3 (Spring 2003): 1–28; and J. E. Post, L. E. Preston, and S. Sachs.

Socially responsible organizations consider the effects of their actions on all stakeholder groups and may also invest in a number of philanthropic causes that benefit stakeholders. Cummins Engine, for example, funds the development of schools in China and India, where it has facilities, and has purchased biodiverse forest land in Mexico to demonstrate the company's commitment to the natural environment.[37] Bristol-Myers Squibb provides funding for health clinics in areas of Texas, California, and Florida to hire *promotoras de salud*, or peer health educators, to help fight Type 2 diabetes in the Hispanic population.[38]

Today, special interest groups continue to be one of the largest stakeholder concerns that companies face. Environmental responsibility has become a primary issue as business and the public alike acknowledge the damage that has been done to our natural environment.

Assess Your Answer   3 It's not the manager's job to solve problems in the outside world.

ANSWER: A company is a "citizen" of the country in which it resides, as well as a citizen of the world. And just as ordinary citizens should be concerned about issues regarding the environment, or community-harming problems such as extreme poverty, companies should be aware and take actions that are decent, yet reasonable.

The Ethic of Sustainability and the Natural Environment

When the first Earth Day celebration was held in 1970, most managers considered environmentalists to be an extremist fringe group and felt little need to respond to environmental concerns.[39] Today environmental issues have become a hot topic among business leaders, and managers and organizations in all industries are jumping on the environmental bandwagon.

One model uses the phrase *shades of green* to evaluate a company's commitment to environmental responsibility.[40] The various shades, which represent a company's approach to addressing environmental concerns, are illustrated in Exhibit 4.6. With a *legal approach*, the organization does just what is necessary to satisfy legal requirements. In general, managers and the company show little concern for environmental issues.

For example, Willamette Industries of Portland, Oregon, agreed to install $7.4 million worth of pollution control equipment in its 13 factories to comply

CONCEPT CONNECTION

Bob Smet, an Alcoa Power Generating Inc. (APGI) natural resources specialist, talks to Badin, North Carolina, elementary school students as part of parent company Alcoa Inc.'s "Taking Action" initiative. This annual employee volunteer program represents only one facet of the company's commitment to sustainable development. Alcoa's *2020 Strategic Framework for Sustainability* spells out goals for integrating sustainability principles into its ongoing operations and establishes specific benchmarks. The World Economic Forum named Alcoa one of the world's most sustainable corporations. In recognition of its 80 percent reduction of greenhouse gas per fluorocarbon, *Business Week* and The Climate Group cited the world's leading aluminum producer as a top "green" company of the decade.

EXHIBIT 4.6

The Shades of Corporate Green

Activist Approach
Sustainability; Actively conserve the environment

Stakeholder Approach
Address multiple stakeholder concerns

Market Approach
Respond to customers

Legal Approach
Satisfy legal requirements regarding environmental conservation

SOURCE: Based on R.E. Freeman, J. Pierce, and R. Dodd, *Shades of Green: Ethics and the Environment* (New York: Oxford University Press, 1995).

White Dog Enterprises

Judy Wicks provides environmentally friendly products and also uses green energy for her restaurant. She got into the restaurant business by accident—literally. Having just left her first husband (with whom she founded Urban Outfitters), she was driving her car in Philadelphia when she ran a light and rammed into another car. Broke and jobless, she poured out her heart to a bystander on the street who happened to own a nearby restaurant—and he needed a waitress. Wicks stayed there for 13 years, and was promoted to manager at La Terrasse. Toward the end, she was running a muffin shop out of her house down the street. When the expected offer to be co-owner of the restaurant didn't materialize, she finished serving breakfast one day, quit La Terrasse, and expanded White Dog Café's menu—something she has done for 24 years.

Wicks' efforts to make the world a better place include being the first Pennsylvania business run on electricity generated from wind power. Believing in building up the local economy, she gets her meats and vegetables from local organic farms, and she often helps them with small loans to buy supplies. She welcomes debates, even with the green business world, where she often proclaims, "Businesses should not grow bigger!"

Seeing business as a way of life rather than merely a means for profit, she compares her feelings for White Dog to the way farmers feel about their land. When she hit age 60, though, she decided that she wanted a larger sphere of operation. While embarking on a plan to give employees ownership of the café, which did $4.5 million in sales in a recent year, she's now giving employees full decision-making power and will ease out completely over the next decade. She'll spend her time traveling around the world, preaching the Gospel of Good Business and working on a book. "That's the kind of thing I feel is the best use of my time as an elder," she says.

SOURCE: Jess McCuan, "Entrepreneurs We Love: Judy Wicks, Inc.," *Magazine* (April 2004):142; Diana Marder, "Top Dog Easing Out," *Philadelphia Enquirer* (Nov. 9, 2006): F1.

with Environmental Protection Agency requirements. The move came only after Willamette was fined a whopping $11.2 million for violating emissions standards.[41]

The next shade, the *market approach*, represents a growing awareness of and sensitivity to environmental concerns, primarily to satisfy customers. A company might provide environmentally friendly products because customers want them, for instance, not necessarily because of strong management commitment to the environment.

A further step is to respond to multiple demands from the environment. The *stakeholder approach* means that companies attempt to answer the environmental concerns of various stakeholder groups, such as customers, the local community, business partners, and special interest groups. Ontario Power Generation, Shell, and Alcan Aluminum are among the large companies that are partnering with Environmental Defense to reduce greenhouse gases.[42] The move comes in response to growing concerns among customers, communities where the companies operate, and environmental groups, as well as recognition that emissions are likely to be regulated by government actions.

Finally, at the highest level of green, organizations take an *activist approach* to environmental issues by actively searching for ways to conserve the Earth's resources. A growing number of companies around the world are embracing a revolutionary idea called **sustainability** or *sustainable development*. Sustainability refers to economic development that generates wealth and meets the needs of the current generation while saving the environment so future generations can meet their needs as well.[43] With a philosophy of sustainability, managers weave environmental and social concerns into every strategic decision, revise policies and procedures to support sustainability efforts, and measure their progress toward sustainability goals.

The mission of New Leaf Paper Company, for example, is to inspire the paper industry to move toward sustainability. New Leaf developed a paper called EcoBook 100, made from 100 percent post-consumer waste processed without chlorine, which was used for the Canadian printing of *Harry Potter and the Order of the Phoenix*. The small San Francisco-based company is having a big impact on the industry by tying its success closely to its

sustainability
economic development that meets the needs of the current population while preserving the environment for the needs of future generations.

environmental goals. Part of managers' time is devoted to educating printers, designers, paper merchants, and even competing companies on the uses and benefits of environmentally responsible paper. New Leaf generated $4 million in sales in its first year (1999) and expected revenues in 2005 of more than $18 million. Rather than being worried about increased competition from other firms' jumping on the green bandwagon, New Leaf managers are delighted because it means the industry is shifting toward sustainability.[44]

Even large U.S. organizations as diverse as DuPont, McDonald's, and UPS are grappling with issues related to sustainability. McDonald's, for example, buys some of its energy from renewable sources, has stopped buying poultry treated with antibiotics, and offers incentives to suppliers that support sustainable practices.[45] The UPS fleet now includes about 2,000 alternative-fuel vehicles, which emit 35 percent less pollution than standard diesel engines.[46] DuPont developed biodegradable materials for plastic silverware, a stretchable fabric called Sorona made partially from corn, and a housing insulation wrap that saves far more energy than is required to produce it. The company's new vision is to eventually manage a collection of businesses that can go on forever without depleting any natural resources.[47]

Despite these impressive advances, few U.S. firms have fully embraced the principles of sustainability, as reflected in a resistance to adopting ISO 14001 standards.[48] ISO 14001 is an international environmental management system that aims to boost the sustainability agenda. To become ISO 14001-compliant, firms develop policies, procedures, and systems that will continually reduce the organization's impact on the natural environment. Sustainability argues that organizations can find innovative ways to create wealth at the same time they are preserving natural resources. ZipCar, for example, rents cars by the hour, 24 hours a day, with no paperwork. By reducing private car usage, ZipCar contributes to reduced emissions and reduced load on the nation's transit infrastructure.[49]

Evaluating Corporate Social Responsibility

A model for evaluating corporate social performance is presented in Exhibit 4.7. The model indicates that total corporate social responsibility can be subdivided into four primary criteria: economic, legal, ethical, and discretionary responsibilities.[50] These four criteria fit together to form the whole of a company's social responsiveness. Managers and organizations typically are involved in several issues at the same time, and a company's ethical and discretionary responsibilities are increasingly considered to be as important as economic and legal issues. Social responsibility has become an integral topic on the corporate agenda in light of corporate scandals, concerns about globalization, and a growing mistrust of business.[51]

Note the similarity between the categories in Exhibit 4.7 and those in Exhibit 4.1. In both cases, ethical issues are located between the areas of legal and freely discretionary responsibilities. Exhibit 4.7 also has an economic category, because profits are a major reason for corporations' existence.

EXHIBIT 4.7

Criteria of Corporate Social Performance

Total Corporate Social Responsibility

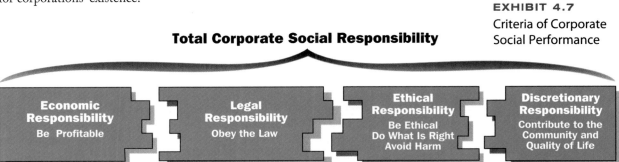

SOURCES: Based on Archie B. Carroll, "A Three-Dimensional Conceptual Model of Corporate Performance," *Academy of Management Review* 4 (1979), 499; A.B. Carroll, "The Pyramid of Corporate Social Responsibility: Toward the Moral Management of Corporate Stakeholders," *Business Horizons* 34 (July–August 1991), 42; and Mark S. Schwartz and Archie B. Carroll, "Corporate Social Responsibility: A Three-Domain Approach," *Business Ethics Quarterly* 13, no. 4 (2003), 503–530.

ECONOMIC RESPONSIBILITIES

The first criterion of social responsibility is *economic responsibility*. The business institution is, above all, the basic economic unit of society. Its responsibility is to produce the goods and services that society wants and to maximize profits for its owners and shareholders. Economic responsibility, carried to the extreme, is called the *profit-maximizing view,* advocated by Nobel economist Milton Friedman. This view argues that the corporation should be operated on a profit-oriented basis, with its sole mission to increase its profits as long as it stays within the rules of the game.[52]

T. J. Rodgers, CEO of Cypress Semiconductor, is a strong proponent of the profit-maximizing view. Rodgers believes that businesses should exist for one purpose: to make a profit. He points out, though, that the long-term pursuit of profits necessitates being a good corporate citizen.[53] The purely profit-maximizing view is no longer considered an adequate criterion of performance in Canada, the United States, and Europe. This approach means that economic gain is the only social responsibility and can lead companies into trouble.

LEGAL RESPONSIBILITIES

All modern societies lay down ground rules, laws, and regulations that businesses are expected to follow. *Legal responsibility* defines what society deems as important with respect to appropriate corporate behavior.[54] Businesses are expected to fulfill their economic goals within the legal framework. Legal requirements are imposed by local town councils, state legislators, and federal regulatory agencies.

Organizations that knowingly break the law are poor performers in this category. Managers at numerous companies learned in recent years that organizations and managers ultimately pay for ignoring legal responsibilities. Between mid-2002 and mid-2005, the U.S. Justice Department charged more than 900 individuals in more than 400 corporate fraud cases.[55] Other examples of illegal acts by corporations include intentionally selling defective goods, performing unnecessary repairs or procedures, and billing clients for work not done. Tenet Healthcare paid $54 million to settle a federal lawsuit charging that one of its hospitals was cheating Medicare by performing unnecessary cardiac procedures.[56] The press release in Exhibit 4.8 describes the punishment imposed on another company that broke the law.

ETHICAL RESPONSIBILITIES

Ethical responsibility includes behaviors that are not necessarily codified into law and may not serve the corporation's direct economic interests. As described earlier in this chapter, to be *ethical,* organization decision makers should act with equity, fairness, and impartiality, respect the rights of individuals, and provide different treatment of individuals only when relevant to the organization's goals and tasks.[57] *Unethical* behavior occurs when decisions enable an individual or company to gain at the expense of other people or society as a whole.

TAKE ACTION ▶

Read the ethical dilemma on page 147 that pertains to legal and ethical responsibilities. How important is it to you to protect the natural environment?

One firm in the food packaging industry, for example, ordered tens of thousands of dollars in goods from a supplier, even though managers knew the company's finances were shaky and it might never pay for them. As another example, a doctor at Louisiana State University Health Sciences Center got into trouble for accepting significant annual payments from a medical device company and heavily promoting its products to his patients.[58]

DISCRETIONARY RESPONSIBILITIES

discretionary responsibility
organizational responsibility that is voluntary and guided by the organization's desire to make social contributions not mandated by economics, law, or ethics.

Discretionary responsibility is purely voluntary and is guided by a company's desire to make social contributions not mandated by economics, law, or ethics. Discretionary activities include generous philanthropic contributions that offer no payback to the company and are not expected. An example of discretionary behavior occurred when Emigrant Savings deposited $1,000 into the accounts of customers living in areas hit hardest by Hurricane Katrina. CEO Howard Milstein thought only a few hundred customers lived in the area, but he stuck by his decision even when he learned that the number of customers was nearly 1,000. The total donation cut straight into the company's bottom line, but Milstein believed it was

EXHIBIT 4.8
One Company's
Punishment for
Breaking the Law

Headquarters Press Release
Washington, DC

Date Published:	07/12/2001
Title:	WASHINGTON STATE/ALASKA COMPANY SENTENCED IN ASBESTOS CASE

**FOR RELEASE: THURSDAY, JULY 12, 2001
WASHINGTON STATE/ALASKA COMPANY SENTENCED IN
ASBESTOS CASE**

Luke C. Hester 202-564-7818 / hester.luke@epa.gov

On June 27, Great Pacific Seafood, a Washington State corporation operating in Alaska, and its General Manager, Roger D. Stiles, were sentenced for violations of the Clean Air Act. Great Pacific Seafood was sentenced to serve five years probation, pay a $75,000 fine, pay $7,000 in restitution, publish a public apology statement in the local newspaper and adopt an environmental management program. Stiles was sentenced to pay a $5,000 fine, perform 120 hours of community service, and serve two to three years probation. Great Pacific Seafood and Stiles pleaded guilty to having five of its employees directly or indirectly exposed to asbestos fibers without the proper training, equipment or protective clothing. The hazardous nature of abatement was never disclosed to two of the employees. Failure to follow asbestos work practices can expose workers to the inhalation of airborne asbestos fibers which can cause lung cancer, a lung disease known as "asbestosis" and mesothelioma, a cancer of the chest and abdominal cavities. This case was investigated by the EPA Criminal Investigation Division, the FBI and the Alaska State Occupational Safety and Health Administration. Technical assistance was provided by the EPA Office of Air Quality. The case was prosecuted by the U.S. Attorney's Office in Anchorage.

R-105 ###

the right thing to do.[59] Discretionary responsibility is the highest criterion of social responsibility because it goes beyond societal expectations to contribute to the community's welfare.

Managing Company Ethics and Social Responsibility

Many managers are concerned with improving the ethical climate and social responsiveness of their companies. As one expert on the topic of ethics said, "Management is responsible for creating and sustaining conditions in which people are likely to behave themselves."[60] Managers can take active steps to ensure that the company stays on an ethical footing. As discussed earlier in this chapter, ethical business practices depend on individual managers as well as the organization's values, policies, and practices. Exhibit 4.9 illustrates the three pillars that support an ethical organization.[61]

TAKE ACTION
Remember that your company has to make a profit, but is also expected to be a good citizen and follow the law, as well as being moral.

ETHICAL INDIVIDUALS

Managers who are essentially ethical individuals make up the first pillar. These individuals possess honesty and integrity, which is reflected in their behavior and decisions. People inside and outside the organization trust them because they can be relied upon to follow the standards of fairness, treat people right, and be ethical in their dealings with others. Ethical individuals strive for a high level of moral development, as discussed earlier in the chapter.

EXHIBIT 4.9

The Three Pillars of an
Ethical Organization

The Ethical Organization

Ethical Individuals
- Act with integrity
- Behave honestly
- Inspire trust
- Treat people right
- Play fair
- Have high level of moral development

Ethical Leadership
- Be a role model
- Uphold ethical values in the organization
- Communicate about ethics and values
- Reward ethical behavior
- Swiftly discipline unethical behavior

Structures and Systems
- Corporate culture
- Code of ethics
- Ethics committee
- Chief ethics officer
- Ethics training
- Whistle-blowing mechanisms

SOURCE: Adapted from Linda Klebe Treviño, Laura Pincus Hartman, and Michael Brown, "Moral Person and Moral Manager," *California Management Review* 42, no. 4 (Summer 2000), 128–142.

TAKE ACTION

Go to the Manager's Self Learning on page 146 that pertains to ethical dilemmas and decisions.

Being a moral person and making ethical decisions is not enough, though. Ethical managers also encourage the moral development of others.[62] They find ways to focus the entire organization's attention on ethical values and create an organizational environment that encourages, guides, and supports the ethical behavior of all employees. Two additional pillars are needed to provide a strong foundation for an ethical organization: ethical leadership and organizational structures and systems.

ETHICAL LEADERSHIP

TAKE ACTION

Be aware that as a leader, others look to you as a role model for ethical behavior.

In a study of ethics policy and practice in successful ethical companies, no point emerged more clearly than the crucial role of leadership.[63] If people don't hear about ethical values from top leaders, they get the idea that ethics is not important in the organization. Employees are acutely aware of their leaders' ethical lapses, and the company grapevine quickly communicates situations in which top managers choose an expedient action over an ethical one.[64]

Lower-level managers and first-line supervisors perhaps are even more important as role models for ethical behavior, because they are the leaders whom employees see and work with on a daily basis. These managers can strongly influence the ethical climate in the organization by adhering to high ethical standards in their own behavior and decisions. In addition, these leaders articulate the desired ethical values and help others embody and reflect those values.[65]

Using performance reviews and rewards effectively is a powerful way for managers to signal that ethics counts. Managers also take a stand against unethical behavior. Consistently rewarding ethical behavior and disciplining unethical conduct at all levels of the company is a critical component of providing ethical leadership.[66]

Spotlight on Skills

Avoiding Prison Time

Patrick Kuhse knows the dangers of not being ethical. After spending 4 years in the federal penitentiary, Patrick Kuhse wants to warn college students that lapses in ethical behavior can be dangerous. His quest for money and a feeling of invincibility—common in young people, he says—were part of the reason he bribed a public official while working at a financial planning company. To avoid prosecution, he fled to Costa Rica, but soon realized he didn't want to live as an outlaw and turned himself in to the American Embassy.

Now he gives talks at universities whenever he can. Maybe he can help prevent others from making the same mistakes. You do a little here, cut a little there, he says, and pretty soon you see the world differently. Whether it's music sharing or plagiarizing, students make ethical decisions that shape their future mind-set. Unethical behavior looks more and more all right.

Sometimes you get a job, sign an ethics statement, and then your boss takes you into another room and says, "Now this is the way we really do this here." That's why Kuhse thinks college students need to learn the old adage: Money isn't everything.

Kuhse advises to surround yourself with mentors, people of integrity whom you trust—parents, siblings, spouse. Then listen to them. "I was relatively okay," he says, "until I stopped listening to my mom and my wife." When he speaks to students, he looks intently and says, "Anyone want to follow in my footsteps?" Before they can answer, he continues, "If you mess up, admit it and move forward."

SOURCE: Zachary Mesenbourg, "Speaker Challenges Students' Ethics," *Post-Standard* (April 23, 2004): C6; "Ex-Con Offers Firsthand Greed Lesson," *St. Joseph News-Press* (Nov. 30, 2006).

Kathryn Reimann, a senior vice president at American Express, recalls the impact one senior executive had on the ethical tone of the organization. The leader heard reports that one of the company's top performers was mistreating subordinates. After he verified the reports, the executive publicly fired the manager and emphasized that no amount of business success could make up for that kind of behavior. The willingness to fire a top performer because of his unethical treatment of employees made a strong statement that ethics was important at American Express.[67]

ORGANIZATIONAL STRUCTURES AND SYSTEMS

The third pillar of ethical organizations is the set of tools that managers use to shape values and promote ethical behavior throughout the organization. Three of these tools are codes of ethics, ethical structures, and mechanisms for supporting whistle-blowers.

Code of Ethics. A **code of ethics** is a formal statement of the company's values concerning ethics and social issues. It communicates to employees what the company stands for. Codes of ethics tend to exist as two types: principle-based statements and policy-based statements.

Principle-based statements are designed to affect corporate culture; they define fundamental values and contain general language about company responsibilities, quality of products, and treatment of employees. General statements of principle are often called *corporate credos*. A good example is Johnson & Johnson's "The Credo."

Policy-based statements generally outline the procedures to be used in specific ethical situations. These situations include marketing practices, conflicts of interest, observance of laws, proprietary information, political gifts, and equal opportunities. Examples of policy-based statements are Boeing's "Business Conduct Guidelines," Chemical Bank's "Code of Ethics," GTE's "Code of Business Ethics" and "Anti-Trust and Conflict of Interest Guidelines," and Norton's "Norton Policy on Business Ethics."[68]

TAKE ACTION

Go to Johnson & Johnson's website at www.jnj.com/home and click on "View Our Credo," which is available in 36 languages. For more than 60 years, the Credo has guided Johnson & Johnson's managers in making decisions that honor the company's responsibilities to employees, customers, the community, and stockholders.

code of ethics
a formal statement of the organization's values regarding ethics and social issues.

Milwaukee Journal Sentinel Guidelines

In recent years, charges of plagiarism and other ethical violations cast a spotlight on newspaper publishers and other media outlets. As a result, many companies put renewed emphasis on journalistic standards of integrity.

Executives at Journal Communications, the parent company of *The Milwaukee Journal Sentinel,* hope the company's clear and comprehensive code of ethics will reinforce the public's trust as well as prevent ethical misconduct. This excerpt from the opening sections of the code outlines some broad provisions for what the company stands for:

> Journal Communications and its subsidiaries operate in a complex and changing society. The actions of the company's employees, officers and directors clearly affect other members of that society. Therefore, every employee has an obligation to conduct the day-to-day business of the company in conformity with the highest ethical standards and in accordance with the various laws and regulations that govern modern business operations. . . .

Journal Communications' ethical standards embrace not only the letter of the law but also the spirit of the law. To that end, we must apply plain old-fashioned honesty and decency to every aspect of our job. We must never sacrifice ethics for expediency. Broadly put, we should treat others fairly and with respect.

If faced with an ethical question, we should ask:

- Is this action legal?
- Does it comply with company policies and/or good business conduct?
- Is it something I would not want my supervisors, fellow employees, subordinates or family to know about?
- Is it something I would not want the general public to know about?

We must not condone illegal or unethical behavior . . . by failing to report it, regardless of an employee's level of authority. . . . The company will protect us if we bring unethical activity to its attention.

The *Journal's* code of ethics also includes statements concerning respect for people, respect for the company, conflicts of interest, unfair competition, relationships with customers, suppliers and news sources, confidential information, and accepting gifts and favors.

Journal Communications—Code of Ethics, from Codes of Ethics Online, The Center for the Study of Ethics in the Professions, Illinois Institute of Technology, www.iit.edu/departments/csep/ PublicWWW/codes/index.html

Codes of ethics state the values or behaviors expected and those that will not be tolerated, backed up by management action. Because of the number of scandals in the financial services industry, a group convened by the American Academy of Arts and Sciences suggested that Wall Street should have a broad ethics code similar to the millennia-old Hippocratic oath for doctors. With numerous areas open to ethical abuses and the pressures that investment bankers face when millions of dollars are at stake, the group, which includes some of the most respected leaders on Wall Street, believes a code could serve as a guide for managers facing thorny ethical issues.[69]

Many financial institutions, of course, have their own individual corporate codes. A survey of *Fortune* 1,000 companies found that 98 percent address issues of ethics and business conduct in formal corporate documents, and 78 percent of those have separate codes of ethics that are widely distributed.[70] When top management supports and enforces these codes, including rewards for compliance and discipline for violation, ethics codes can boost a company's ethical climate.[71] The code of ethics for *The Milwaukee Journal Sentinel* gives employees some guidelines for dealing with ethical questions.[72]

By giving people some guidelines for confronting ethical questions and promising protection from recriminations for people who report wrongdoing, the *Journal's* code of ethics gives all employees the responsibility and the right to maintain the organization's ethical climate.

ETHICAL STRUCTURES

Ethical structures represent the various systems, positions, and programs a company can undertake to implement ethical behavior. An **ethics committee** is a group of executives appointed to oversee company ethics. The committee provides rulings on questionable ethical issues. The ethics committee assumes responsibility for disciplining wrongdoers, which is essential if the organization is to directly influence employee behavior.

For example, Motorola's Ethics Compliance Committee is charged with interpreting, clarifying, and communicating the company's code of ethics and with adjudicating suspected code violations. Many companies, such as Sears, Northrop Grumman, and Columbia/HCA Healthcare, set up ethics offices with full-time staff to ensure that ethical standards are an integral part of company operations. These offices are headed by a **chief ethics officer,** a company executive who oversees all aspects of ethics and legal compliance, including establishing and broadly communicating standards, ethics training, dealing with exceptions or problems, and advising senior managers in the ethical and compliance aspects of decisions.[73]

The title of *chief ethics officer* was almost unheard of a decade ago, but highly publicized ethical and legal problems faced by companies in recent years sparked a growing demand for these ethics specialists. The Ethics and Compliance Officers Association, a trade group, reports that membership soared to more than 1,250 companies, up from about half that number in 2002.[74] Most ethics offices also work as counseling centers to help employees resolve difficult ethical issues. A toll-free confidential hotline allows employees to report questionable behavior as well as seek guidance concerning ethical dilemmas.

Ethics training programs also help employees deal with ethical questions and translate the values stated in a code of ethics into everyday behavior.[75] Training programs are an important supplement to a written code of ethics. General Electric implemented a strong compliance and ethics training program for all 320,000 employees worldwide. Much of the training is conducted online, with employees able to test themselves on how they would handle thorny ethical issues.

In addition, small-group meetings give people a chance to ask questions and discuss ethical dilemmas or questionable actions. Every quarter, each of GE's business units reports to headquarters the percentage of division employees who completed training sessions and the percentage that have read and signed off on the company's ethics guide, "Spirit and Letter."[76]

At McMurray Publishing Company in Phoenix, all employees attend a *weekly* meeting on workplace ethics. In these meetings the discussion centers on how to handle ethical dilemmas and how to resolve conflicting values.[77]

A strong ethics program is important, but it is no guarantee against lapses. Enron could boast of a well-developed ethics program, for example, but managers failed to live up to it. Enron's problems sent a warning to other managers and organizations. It is not enough to *have* an impressive ethics program. The ethics program must be merged with day-to-day operations, encouraging ethical decisions throughout the company.

WHISTLE-BLOWING

Employee disclosure of illegal, immoral, or illegitimate practices on the employer's part is called **whistle-blowing**.[78] No organization can rely exclusively on codes of conduct and ethical structures to prevent all unethical behavior.

Holding organizations accountable depends to some extent on individuals who are willing to blow the whistle if they detect illegal, dangerous, or unethical activities. Whistle-blowers often report wrongdoing to outsiders, such as regulatory agencies, senators, or newspaper reporters. Some firms have instituted innovative programs and confidential

ethics committee
a group of executives assigned to oversee the organization's ethics by ruling on questionable issues and disciplining violators.

chief ethics officer
a company executive who oversees ethics and legal compliance.

ethics training
training programs to help employees deal with ethical questions and values.

whistle-blowing
the disclosure by an employee of illegal, immoral, or illegitimate practices by the organization.

CONCEPT CONNECTION

A Supreme Court case started with a Birmingham, Alabama, high school coach whose girls' basketball team played in a shabby gym that clearly was inferior to the one the boys' team used. After Roderick Jackson complained repeatedly to the school system that his team was being denied equal access to facilities, equipment, and funding, he lost his coaching position. Jackson filed suit under Title IX, which prohibits gender discrimination by educational institutions receiving federal funds. Here, Jackson stands flanked by his attorneys in front of the Supreme Court. By a 5-4 decision, the Court expanded the scope of Title IX not only to protect direct victims of discrimination but also to shield whistle-blowers such as Jackson from retaliation.

hotlines to encourage and support internal whistle-blowing. For this practice to be an effective ethical safeguard, however, companies must view whistle-blowing as a benefit to the company and make dedicated efforts to protect whistle-blowers.[79]

Without effective protective measures, whistle-blowers suffer. Although whistle-blowing has become widespread in recent years, it still is risky for employees, who can lose their jobs, be ostracized by co-workers, or be transferred to lower-level positions. Consider what happened when Linda Kimble reported that the car rental agency where she worked was pushing the sale of insurance to customers who already had coverage. Within a few weeks after making the complaint to top managers, Kimble was fired.

The 2002 Sarbanes-Oxley Act provides some safety for whistle-blowers like Kimble. People fired for reporting wrongdoing can file a complaint under the law and are eligible for back pay, attorney's fees, and a chance to get their old job back, as Kimble did. The impact of the legislation is still unclear, but many whistle-blowers fear that they will suffer even more hostility if they return to the job after winning a case under Sarbanes-Oxley.[80]

Many managers still look upon whistle-blowers as disgruntled employees who aren't good team players. Yet, to maintain high ethical standards, organizations need people who are willing to point out wrongdoing. Managers can be trained to view whistle-blowing as a benefit rather than a threat, and systems can be set up to effectively protect employees who report illegal or unethical activities.

Ethical Challenges in Turbulent Times

The problem of lax ethical standards in business is nothing new, but in recent years it seems to have escalated. In addition, public reaction has been swift and unforgiving. Any ethical misstep can cost a company its reputation and hurt its profitability and performance. Within months after Martha Stewart was charged with insider trading, her company's market capitalization plummeted $400 million, although Martha and her company managed to survive the scandal and her stint in jail. Companies such as Nike and Gap have been hurt by accusations of exploitative labor practices in Third World factories. Oil companies have been targeted for allegedly abusing the environment and contributing to a host of social ills in developing nations, and pharmaceutical firms have been accused of hurting the world's poor by pricing drugs out of their reach. Organizational stakeholders, including employees, shareholders, governments, and the general community, are taking a keen interest in how managers run their businesses.

One reason for the proliferation of ethical lapses is the turbulence of our times. Things move so fast that managers who aren't firmly grounded in ethical values can find themselves making poor choices simply because they don't have the time to carefully weigh the situation and exercise considered judgment. When organizations operate in highly competitive industries, rapidly changing markets, and complex cultural and social environments, a strong corporate culture that emphasizes ethical behavior becomes even more important because it guides people to do the right thing even in the face of confusion and change.[81]

THE BUSINESS CASE FOR ETHICS
AND SOCIAL RESPONSIBILITY

The scandals that have rocked the corporate world prompted new demands from government legislators, stockholders, management experts, and the general public. One consultant argued in a recent *Wall Street Journal* column that the current regulatory climate distracts managers from doing what's good for business.[82] But the combination of a turbulent domestic environment, globalization of business, and increasing public scrutiny convinces many managers that paying attention to ethics and social responsibility is as much of a business issue as paying attention to costs, profits, and growth.

Beyond maintaining high ethical standards, top managers at a growing number of companies recognize how to target their social responsibility efforts in ways that also benefit the business. After Hurricane Katrina, for example, rather than giving a general gift, employees of Papa John's spent weeks in a pizza trailer handing out thousands of free 6-inch pies, which benefited local residents and relief workers while also promoting the company's product. Home Depot identified affordable housing for low-income families as its primary social initiative, working collaboratively with Habitat for Humanity. Hundreds of thousands of would-be Home Depot customers participate as volunteers in the housing projects and how-to clinics. Starbucks builds social responsibility into its business model by paying hourly employees above minimum wage, buying fair-trade coffee, and negotiating long-term contracts with coffee growers who farm in environmentally friendly ways. These efforts make good business sense at the same time they build the image of these companies as good corporate citizens.[83] One organization in Spain, Unión Fenosa, pioneered the concept of corporate social responsibility as a business issue.[84]

Social sustainability refers to interacting with the community in which a company does business in a way that makes money for the company but also improves the long-term well-being of the community. In the United States, various stakeholders are increasingly pushing new reporting initiatives connected to the sustainability movement that emphasize *the triple bottom line* of economic, social, and environmental performance. Naturally, the relationship of a corporation's ethics and social responsibility to its financial performance concerns both managers and management scholars and has generated a lively debate.[85]

Unión Fenosa

Unión Fenosa is a large Spanish business group that does business in three major industries: energy, consulting services, and telecommunications. The company's approach to corporate social responsibility—called "complicity with the environment"—emerged during the 1980s when Unión Fenosa was building power stations in isolated areas and providing consulting services to other companies moving into developing countries.

Former head engineer José Luis Castro recalls that the company had to essentially build an entire community around a developing power station to serve the personal and social needs of engineers, technicians, local workers, and their families. From the beginning, productivity and progress in business was seen to go hand-in-hand with the well-being of the community. Thus began Unión Fenosa's concept of "complicity with the environment" as a key to business success. The company sees its success as tied inextricably to the well-being of not only shareholders but also workers, suppliers, and the immediate environment in which the company is working.

Although altruism influences Unión Fenosa's philanthropy to some extent, top leaders emphasize that it's really a business issue: The survival of the company is based on its ability to involve itself with the local community in a way that makes money for the company at the same time it makes the community better than it was before. Unión Fenosa executives believe that a concern with *social sustainability* is essential for a company to remain competitive and successful.

Cristina Simón, Juan Luis Martínez, and Ana Agüero, "Solidarity Day at Unión Fenosa in Spain," *Business Horizons* 48 (2005): 161–168.

One concern of managers is whether good citizenship will hurt performance. After all, ethics programs and social responsibility cost money. A number of studies, undertaken to determine whether heightened ethical and social responsiveness increases or decreases financial performance, provided varying results but generally found a small positive relationship between social responsibility and financial performance.[86] For example, a study of the financial performance of large U.S. corporations considered "best corporate citizens" found that they enjoy both superior reputations and superior financial performance.[87] Similarly, Governance Metrics International, an independent corporate governance ratings agency in New York, found that the stocks of companies with more selfless principles perform better than those run in a self-serving manner. Top-ranked companies such as Pfizer, Johnson Controls, and Sunoco also outperformed lower-ranking companies in measures such as return on assets, return on investment, and return on capital.[88] Although results from these studies are not proof, they indicate that use of resources for ethics and social responsibility does not hurt companies.[89] Moreover, one survey found that 70 percent of global CEOs believe corporate social responsibility is vital to their companies' profitability.[90]

Companies also are making an effort to measure the nonfinancial factors that create value. Researchers find, for example, that people prefer to work for companies that demonstrate a high level of ethics and social responsibility; these organizations can attract and retain high-quality employees.[91] Customers pay attention, too. A study by Walker Research indicates that, price and quality being equal, two-thirds of customers say they would switch brands to do business with a company that is ethical and socially responsible.[92] Enlightened companies realize that integrity and trust are essential to sustain successful and profitable business relationships with an increasingly connected web of employees, customers, suppliers, and partners. Although doing the right thing might not always be profitable in the short run, many managers believe it can provide a competitive advantage by developing a level of trust that money can't buy.[93]

Summary

Ethics and social responsibility are hot topics for today's managers. The ethical domain of behavior pertains to values of right and wrong. Ethical decisions and behavior typically are guided by a value system. Four value-based approaches that serve as criteria for ethical decision making are utilitarian, individualism, moral-rights, and justice. For an individual manager, the ability to make correct ethical choices will depend on both individual and organizational characteristics. An important individual characteristic is the level of moral development. Corporate culture is an organizational characteristic that influences ethical behavior. Strong ethical cultures become more important in turbulent environments because they help people make the right choices in the face of confusion and rapid change.

Corporate social responsibility concerns a company's values toward society. How can organizations be good corporate citizens? The model for evaluating social performance uses four criteria: economic, legal, ethical, and discretionary. Evaluating corporate social behavior often requires assessing its impact on organizational stakeholders.

An issue of growing concern is the responsibility to our natural environment. Organizations may take a legal, market, stakeholder, or activist approach to addressing environmental concerns. Sustainability is a growing movement that emphasizes economic development that meets the needs of today while preserving resources for the future.

Ethical organizations are supported by three pillars: ethical individuals, ethical leadership, and organizational structures and systems, including codes of ethics, ethics committees, chief ethics officers, training programs, and mechanisms to protect whistle-blowers. Companies that are ethical and socially responsible perform as well as—and often better than—those that are not socially responsible. Smart managers are finding ways to target their social responsibility efforts in ways that benefit the business. After years of scandal, many managers are recognizing that managing ethics and social responsibility is just as important as paying attention to costs, profits, and growth.

Discussion Questions

1. Dr. Martin Luther King, Jr., said, "As long as there is poverty in the world, I can never be rich. . . . As long as diseases are rampant, I can never be healthy. . . . I can never be what I ought to be until you are what you ought to be." Discuss this quote with respect to the material in this chapter. Would this idea be true for corporations, too?

2. Environmentalists are trying to pass laws involving oil spills that would remove all liability limits for the oil companies. This change would punish corporations financially. Is this approach the best way to influence companies to be socially responsible?

3. Choose two of the dilemmas listed on page 147. First apply the utilitarian approach to ethical decision making in each situation, and then apply the moral-rights approach. Did you reach the same or different conclusions depending on the approach used? Which do you think is generally the better approach for managers to use?

4. Imagine yourself in a situation of being encouraged to inflate your expense account. Do you think your choice would be more affected by your individual moral development or by the cultural values of the company for which you work? Explain.

5. Is it socially responsible for organizations to undertake political activity or join with others in a trade association to influence the government? Discuss.

6. Was it ethical during the 1990s for automobile manufacturers to attempt to accommodate an ever-increasing consumer appetite for SUVs with their low fuel efficiency? Was it good business?

7. A noted business executive said, "A company's first obligation is to be profitable. Unprofitable enterprises can't afford to be socially responsible." Do you agree? Discuss.

8. Do you believe it is ethical for companies to compile portfolios of personal information about their website visitors without informing them? What about organizations monitoring their employees' use of the Web? Discuss.

9. Which do you think would be more effective for shaping long-term ethical behavior in an organization: a written code of ethics combined with ethics training or strong ethical leadership? Which would have more impact on you? Why?

10. Lincoln Electric considers customers and employees to be more important stakeholders than shareholders. Is it appropriate for management to define some stakeholders as more important than others? Should all stakeholders be considered equal?

11. Do you think a social entrepreneur can run a profitable business with a primary goal of improving society? Discuss.

Dear Dr. Dorothy

We have a group paper assignment in one of my courses, and it counts as 40 percent of our final grade. It's a really tough course and the teacher gives us assignments like we were graduate students. The paper we have to do is nearly impossible to figure out. One of our group members has a friend at another university who did a similar paper, and he says he can get that paper for us to "adapt" and turn in. I'm not sure if I feel good about this, though I can see the point. The assignment is way too hard, the paper counts for too much of our grade, and two of the people in the group will lose their merit scholarships if they don't get an "A" in this course. Should I go along with what they want to do?

Torn Apart

Dear Torn,

And torn you should be. Dr. Dorothy sincerely hopes you don't take these slackers' advice in other areas of your life. Imagine a similar scenario. You need to have a place to live and the rents are way, way too high, "forcing" you to take someone else's money. Seem farfetched? Not if you think of a term paper as intellectual "property." When you pass off others' property as your own (even with their permission), you are perpetrating fraud. Plus, it shows that you and your group members are at a low level of ethical development, in the preconventional stage. And who wants to admit to that?

In the case of the paper, all Dr. Dorothy hears are excuses on why your group can't manage the assignment. Dr. Dorothy warns you that if this style of behavior becomes a habit, you will have much difficulty succeeding in your career—and in life. In short, get your group to write its own paper. You can practice your persuasion skills.

Self Learning

Ethical Dilemmas

Write down your responses to the situations below. Your instructor may ask you to either turn in your answers or may conduct a discussion about these ethical dilemmas.

1. An employee whose mother is very sick starts slacking in her work, causing other employees to stay later to get all the tasks done. If you were her boss, what would you do?

2. You see a student cheating during an exam, a test for which you have studied several weeks. That student gets a higher grade than you. What do you do? Would you feel differently about it if he got a lower grade?

3. Your mother is an executive at a record company. Sales have declined in the last two years, mostly because of music piracy and illegal downloads. You see lots of students downloading songs illegally. You know this affects your mother's income, and ultimately your inheritance. What do you do?

4. Your group has a difficult assignment, part of which is a paper. One student announces that a friend of his did a similar paper at another university and is willing to let your group copy that paper. What do you do?

5. A friend of yours has found a way to sneak in to the local movie theater without paying and invites you along. What do you do?

Group Learning

1. In groups of 4–7 students, discuss the case below, rank ordering the five choices for strategies.

2. As a group, determine which of the ethical approaches (utilitarian, individualism, moral-rights, and justice) relate to each of the five choices.

3. Groups report their rankings to the large class and the instructor facilitates discussion on ethical frameworks.

Case Study

You are the head seismologist of one of the top research institutions in the country. A new machine that you helped develop has determined that a damaging earthquake is imminent in a nearby state in three days. Your new equipment can predict earthquakes with an 80% reliability. The area the earthquake is likely to strike has great population density and many bridges and tall buildings, some of them so-called "projects."

You reported your findings to the director of your institute, but nothing has been done. You now have two days until the earthquake and you must decide what to do. Here are the options:

1. You should be careful about your findings. After all, there is a 20% chance you are wrong and you could create unnecessary chaos, not to mention your career is at stake.

2. You must immediately inform all of the media. Everyone should know and be able to prepare for the possible disaster.

3. Calculate the costs of damage expected from the quake, both in damaged buildings and lost lives. Compare this with the cost of falsely predicting the quake and all the costs associated with the chaos that would result. Compare these two figures and decide which is greater.

4. Look back and see how other earthquake threats have been treated. Was there bias in terms of warning people in richer vs. poorer regions? What is the fair thing to do in this less-than affluent area?

SOURCE: Adapted from Mark Mallinger, "Decisive Decision-Making: An Exercise Using Ethical Frameworks," *Journal of Management Education*, 21 (3), 1997, 411–17.

Action Learning

1. Find six newspaper articles from the past six months relating to someone violating business ethics, corruption in business or someone in an organization violating a law.

2. Summarize each article.

3. Are there similar themes?

4. Do the accused seem repentive or defensive?

5. From what you have read, what conditions led to the ethics or legal breach?

6. What would you do as a manager to prevent such behavior in your organization?

7. Your instructor may conduct a discussion on these issues.

Ethical Dilemma

Should We Go Beyond the Law?

Nathan Rosillo stared out his office window at the lazy curves and lush, green, flower-lined banks of the Dutch Valley River. He'd grown up near here and envisioned the day his children would enjoy the river as he had as a child. But now his own company might make that a risky proposition.

Nathan is a key product developer at Chem-Tech Corporation, an industry leader. Despite its competitive position, Chem-Tech experienced several quarters of dismal financial performance. Nathan and his team developed a new lubricant product that the company sees as the turning point in its declining fortunes. Top executives are thrilled that they can produce the new product at a significant cost savings because of recent changes in environmental regulations. Regulatory agencies loosened requirements on reducing and recycling wastes, which means that Chem-Tech now can release waste directly into the Dutch Valley River.

Nathan is as eager as anyone to see Chem-Tech survive this economic downturn, but he doesn't think this route is the way to do it. He expressed his opposition regarding the waste dumping to both the plant manager and his direct supervisor, Martin Feldman. Martin previously supported Nathan, but this time was different. The plant manager, too, turned a deaf ear. "We're meeting government standards," he said. "It's up to them to protect the water. It's up to us to make a profit and stay in business."

Frustrated and confused, Nathan turned away from the window, his prime office view mocking his inability to protect the river he prized. He knew the manufacturing vice president would be visiting the plant next week. Maybe if he were to talk with her, she would agree that the decision to dump waste materials in the river was ethically and socially irresponsible. But if she didn't, he would be skating on thin ice. His supervisor had already had accused him of not being a team player. Maybe he should be a passive bystander—after all, the company isn't breaking any laws.

What Would You Do?

1. Talk to the manufacturing vice president and emphasize the responsibility Chem-Tech has as an industry leader to set an example. Present her with a recommendation that Chem-Tech participate in voluntary pollution-reduction as a marketing tool, positioning itself as the environmentally friendly choice.

2. Mind your own business and just do your job. The company isn't breaking any laws, and if ChemTech's economic situation doesn't improve, a lot of people will be thrown out of work.

3. Call the local environmental advocacy group and get it to stage a protest of the company.

SOURCE: Adapted from Janet Q. Evans, "What Do You Do: What If Polluting Is Legal?" *Business Ethics* (Fall 2002): 20.

Case for Critical Analysis

Empress Luxury Lines

From what computer technician Kevin Pfeiffer just told him, Antonio Melendez thought top management at Empress Luxury Lines finally had found a way to fund the computer system upgrade he'd been requesting ever since he'd taken the job two years ago.

It began innocently enough, Kevin said. When he reported to the luxury cruise line's corporate headquarters, his supervisor, Phil Bailey, informed him that the computer system had been hit by a power surge during the fierce thunderstorms that rolled through southern Florida the night before. "Check out the damage, and report directly back to me," Phil instructed.

When Kevin delivered what he thought would be good news—the damaged underground wires and computer circuits could be repaired to the tune of about $15,000—he couldn't understand why Phil looked so deflated. "Go out to the reception area. I've got to call Roger," Phil snapped, referring to Empress's CFO—and Antonio's boss. In a few minutes, Phil called Kevin back into the office and instructed

him to dig up nearly all the underground wire and cable and haul it all off before the insurance adjustor would appear. If Kevin were to carry out Phil's orders, he knew the costs would balloon astronomically to about a half-million dollars—a tidy sum that would go a long way toward covering the costs of a computer system upgrade, as Phil pointed out.

Kevin took a deep breath and refused, even though he was still considered a new hire and on probation. When Antonio congratulated Kevin on his integrity, the technician shook his head. "Didn't really matter," he said. "On my way back to my cubicle, Matt passed me on his way to do the deed."

Antonio could guess at the motivation behind the scam. During the 1990s, Empress had increased its fleet of ships in response to the healthy demand for its luxury cruises during the stock market bubble. But the bubble burst, the nation was traumatized by September 11, and some of the vacationers who did venture onto cruises were felled by an outbreak of the Norwalk virus. Bookings fell off precipitously. To top it off, the 2005 hurricanes hit, forcing Empress to write piles of refund checks for its Caribbean and Gulf cruises while coping with steep increases in fuel costs. Seriously sagging earnings explained why Antonio's requests for that system upgrade went unheeded.

He also could guess at the likely consequences if he were to choose to do the right thing. Since taking the job, he'd heard rumors that Empress successfully defrauded insurance companies before he arrived. He dismissed them at the time, but now he wasn't so sure. No confidential mechanism was in place for employees to report wrongdoing internally, and no protections were available for whistle-blowers. Shaken, Antonio wasn't feeling at all confident that, even if he bypassed the CFO, he would find upper-level management eager to thwart the scheme. He had a hunch that the person most likely to be penalized would be the whistle-blower.

"I debated about just calling the insurance company," Kevin said, "but I decided to come to you first."

So what should Antonio do? Should he advise Kevin to go ahead and report Empress to the insurance company? Or should he treat Kevin's communication as confidential and deal with the situation himself, in effect putting only his own job in jeopardy? And really, considering the high degree of personal risk and the low probability that the problem actually would be addressed, should he sweep the problem under the rug?

Questions

1. When determining his obligations to his subordinate, Kevin Pfeiffer, what decision would Antonio Melendez most likely reach were he to apply the utilitarian approach to decision making? What conclusions probably would result if he were to employ the individualism approach?

2. Put yourself in Antonio's position and decide realistically what you would do. Is your response at a preconventional, conventional, or postconventional level of moral development? How do you feel about your response?

3. If Antonio or Kevin were fired because they reported Empress's fraud, would they be justified in removing all traces of their employment at the cruise line from their resumes so they won't have to explain to a prospective employer why they were fired? Why or why not?

SOURCES: Based on Don Soeken, "On Witnessing a Fraud," *Business Ethics* (Summer 2004): 14; Amy Tao, "Have Cruise Lines Weathered the Storm?" *BusinessWeek Online* (September 11, 2003), http://www.businessweek.com/bwdaily/dnflash/sep2003/nf20030911_6693_db014.htm; and Joan Dubinsky, "A Word to the Whistle-Blower," *Workforce* (July 2002): 28.

BIZ FLIX

Emperor's Club

William Hundert (Kevin Kline), a professor at Saint Benedict's preparatory school, believes in teaching his students about living a principled life as well as teaching them his beloved classical literature. Hundert's principled ways are challenged, however, by a new student, Sedgewick Bell (Emile Hirsch). Bell's behavior during the 73rd annual Julius Caesar competition causes Hundert to suspect that Bell leads a less than principled life.

Years later Hundert is the honored guest of his former student Sedgewick Bell (Joel Gretsch) at Bell's estate. Depaak Mehta (Rahul Khanna), Bell, and Louis Masoudi (Patrick Dempsey) compete in a reenactment of the Julius Caesar competition. Bell wins the competition, but Hundert notices that Bell is wearing an earpiece. Earlier in the film Hundert had suspected that the young Bell also wore an earpiece during the competition, but Headmaster Woodbridge (Edward Herrmann) had pressed him to ignore his suspicion.

This scene appears at the end of the film. It is an edited portion of the competition reenactment. Bell announced his candidacy for the U.S. Senate just before talking to Hundert in the bathroom. He carefully described his commitment to specific values that he would pursue if elected.

What to Watch for and Ask Yourself

1. Does William Hundert describe a specific type of life that one should lead? If so, what are its elements?

2. Does Sedgewick Bell lead that type of life? Is he committed to any specific ethical view or theory?

3. What consequences or effects do you predict for Sedgewick Bell because of the way he chooses to live his life?

Ethics and Social Responsibility at British Petroleum

While stories of greedy and unscrupulous business executives have dominated the business news during the last few years, one innovative leader for BP (BP) has been at the forefront of social responsibility by demonstrating a commitment to preserving the world's fragile environment. Lord John Browne, Group Chief Executive to the second largest company in the world, earning him more than $30,000 a day, is consistently recognized as one of the 100 most influential British executives, according to the British Newspaper *The Times*. Browne is keenly aware of BP's responsibility to protect and preserve the earth's fragile environment. As a top executive, he sets the tone for BP's culture of environmental responsibility.

Environmental issues are a growing concern among businesses worldwide. In particular, energy companies face tough scrutiny by their customers and stakeholders to make socially and ethically responsible decisions. But environmental responsibility represents a realm in which varying stakeholders have differing beliefs as to what constitutes an improvement in social welfare. A crucial question is whether energy companies are responsible for encouraging the energy conservation and sustainable alternatives that are necessary to reducing environmental degradation in any meaningful way. When making decisions about the future of BP, Lord Browne must weigh BP's legal, ethical, economic, and discretionary responsibilities. Recognizing a rapidly increasing demand for energy worldwide, Browne is committed to taking BP "beyond petroleum," although the burden of this increased demand still falls to hydrocarbon-based sources, such as oil and natural gas. And while BP continues to grow its oil and gas production by 5% per year, Browne's concerns are clear: "The real challenge is the potential impact of burning ever greater volumes of hydrocarbons on the world's climate." But Browne feels, "business is at the heart of the process of taking scientific advances and transforming them into technology . . . which can alter the lives of individuals and whole communities, and which can protect the environment." And he is putting his—and BP's—money where his mouth is.

In 2002, under Lord Browne's leadership, BP succeeded in reducing its carbon emissions by 10%, well beyond the 5.2% suggested by the Kyoto treaty. But, this is still far less than the 60% reductions recommended by scientists as necessary to stabilize climate change. Since 2002, BP has begun several innovative initiatives to help preserve the environment and reverse damaging trends. These include using a process called carbon sequestration in which carbon, produced by natural gas production, is trapped before it can be released into the atmosphere. It then is injected back into reservoirs below ground where it does less harm to the environment. BP estimates this project will prevent the release of 17 million tons of CO_2. Further, BP has created an emissions trading system, similar to market-driven emissions exchanges, to allocate resources as efficiently as possible.

While BP is the leading investor of solar energies at 17% of the world market, its investment in renewable energies is still well below that of its investment in hydrocarbon-based sources. BP has made great strides in furthering socially and environmentally responsible practices. Whether these efforts are considered enough are up for personal and community ethical debate.

Questions

1. Who are BP's stakeholders? How might each view BP's environmental practices?

2. Where does BP fall on the Shades of Corporate Green chart in Exhibit 4.6? Why?

3. With oil and gas production growing by 5% a year, BP will not be able to keep its emissions at the 2002 level. In the video, one BP executive argues that BP should be allowed to increase its emission levels based on "credit" from its sizable emission reductions and its promotion of "cleaner" energy forms such as natural gas in previously coal-based markets. Do you think this is socially responsible? Why or why not?

PART 3
Planning

Figuring out the rules of a dramatically new game in the digital age is a daunting challenge for TV network strategic managers.

Until relatively recently, major networks broadcast a limited selection of programs, essentially dictating what viewers watched and when. Because commercials allowed advertisers to reach millions of people, they supported the programming. Digital technology changes all that. Today's viewers watch shows on TVs, computers, or iPods. They can buy current episodes or old favorites from online stores, such as Apple's iTunes. They can also use sophisticated new digital video recorders to replay shows broadcast from moments to months ago. Digital technology shifts power from broadcasters to consumers. Those consumers want complete control, unlimited choice, and personalized content. And the revolution is by no means over. Many predict that television and the Internet will soon converge.

Networks face fundamental questions as they formulate strategies in this fast-changing environment. What should programs look like? How can networks generate revenue? Who are their competitors? Should networks compete or form partnerships? What business are they in? One thing is certain: There will be no shortage of opportunities for network managers to hone their decision-making skills.

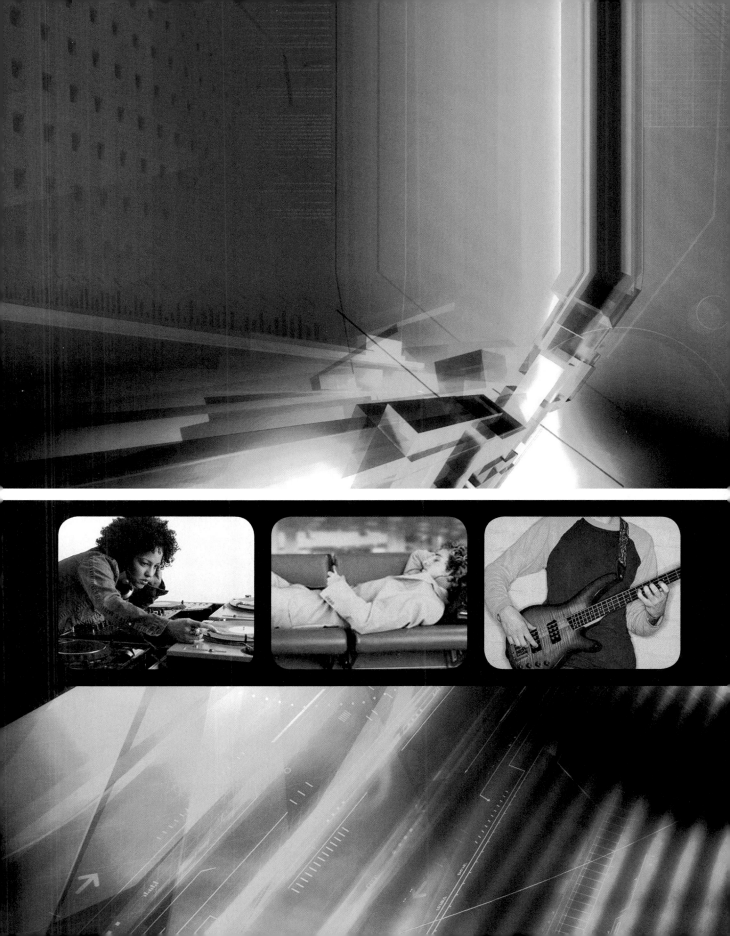

chapter 5

Planning and Goal Setting

Learning Objectives

After studying this chapter, you should be able to:

1 Define goals and plans and explain the relationship between them.

2 Explain the concept of organizational mission and how it influences goal setting and planning.

3 Describe the types of goals an organization should have and why they resemble a hierarchy.

4 Define the characteristics of effective goals.

5 Describe the four essential steps in the MBO process.

6 Explain the difference between single-use plans and standing plans.

7 Describe and explain the importance of the three stages of crisis management planning.

8 Summarize the guidelines for high-performance planning in a fast-changing environment.

9 Define the components of strategic management.

10 Describe the strategic planning process and SWOT analysis.

11 Describe business-level strategies, including Porter's competitive forces and strategies and partnership strategies.

12 Explain the major considerations in formulating functional strategies.

13 Discuss the organizational dimensions used for implementing strategy.

New Manager's Questions

Please circle your opinion below each of the following statements.

Assess Your Answer

1 It is better to have a flexible and loose plan, so you can easily adapt as you go along.

1	2	3	4	5
strongly agree				strongly disagree

2 It's a good idea to make the product or service available to as many customers as possible.

1	2	3	4	5
strongly agree				strongly disagree

3 Top managers should get together and develop and plan and then announce it to employees.

1	2	3	4	5
strongly agree				strongly disagree

One of the primary responsibilities of managers is to decide where the organization should go in the future and how to get it there. Without clear goals and plans, employees cannot perform up to their potential and the organization flounders.

In some organizations, typically small ones, planning is informal. In others, managers follow a well-defined planning framework. The company establishes a basic mission and develops formal goals and strategic plans for carrying it out. Companies such as Royal Dutch/Shell, IBM, and United Way undertake a strategic planning exercise each year— reviewing their missions, goals, and plans to meet environmental changes or the expectations of important stakeholders such as the community, owners, or customers. Many of these companies also develop *contingency plans* or *scenarios* for unexpected circumstances and *disaster recovery plans* for what the organization would do in the event of a major disaster such as a hurricane, earthquake, or terrorist attack.

Of the four management functions—planning, organizing, leading, and controlling— described in Chapter 1, planning is considered the most fundamental. Everything else stems from planning. Yet planning also is the most controversial management function. How do managers plan for the future in a constantly changing environment? As we discussed in Chapter 1, most organizations are facing turbulence and uncertainty. The economic, political, and social turmoil of recent years has left many managers wondering how to cope and has sparked a renewed interest in organizational planning, particularly planning for unexpected problems and events. Yet planning cannot read an uncertain future. Planning cannot tame a turbulent environment. A statement by General Colin Powell, former U.S. Secretary of State, offers a warning for managers: "No battle plan survives contact with the enemy."[1]

In this chapter we will explore the process of planning and consider how managers develop effective plans that can grow and change to meet new conditions. Special attention is given to goal setting, for that is where planning starts. Then, we discuss the various types of plans that managers use to help the organization achieve those goals, including a section on crisis management planning. Finally, we examine new approaches to planning that emphasize the involvement of employees, customers, partners, and other stakeholders in strategic thinking and execution. In Chapter 6, we look at management decision making. Proper decision-making techniques are crucial to selecting the organization's goals, plans, and strategic options.

TAKE ACTION ⏩

Practice planning every day. Make a list of your goals for the day, for the week, and eventually it will become second nature.

Overview of Goals and Plans

Goals and plans have become general concepts in our society. A **goal** is a desired future state that the organization attempts to realize.[2] Goals are important because organizations exist for a purpose and goals define and state that purpose. A **plan** is a blueprint for goal achievement and specifies the necessary resource allocations, schedules, tasks, and other actions. Goals specify future ends; plans specify today's means. The word **planning** usually incorporates both ideas; it means determining the organization's goals and defining the means for achieving them.[3]

Exhibit 5.1 illustrates the levels of goals and plans in an organization. The planning process starts with a formal mission that defines the basic purpose of the organization, especially for external audiences. The mission is the basis for the strategic (company) level of goals and plans, which in turn shapes the tactical (divisional) level and the operational (departmental) level.[4]

Top managers typically are responsible for establishing *strategic* goals and plans that reflect a commitment to both organizational efficiency and effectiveness, as described in Chapter 1. *Tactical* goals and plans are the responsibility of middle managers, such as the heads of major divisions or functional units. A division manager formulates tactical plans that focus on the major actions the division must take to fulfill its part in the strategic plan set by top management. *Operational* plans identify the specific procedures or processes needed at lower levels of

goal
a desired future state that the organization attempts to realize.

plan
a blueprint specifying the resource allocations, schedules, and other actions necessary for attaining goals.

planning
the act of determining the organization's goals and the means for achieving them.

EXHIBIT 5.1
Levels of Goals/Plans
and Their Importance

the organization, such as individual departments and employees. Front-line managers and supervisors develop operational plans that focus on specific tasks and processes and that help to meet tactical and strategic goals. Planning at each level supports the other levels.

Purposes of Goals and Plans

The complexity of today's environment and uncertainty about the future overwhelm many managers and cause them to focus on operational issues and short-term results rather than long-term goals and plans. Planning, however, generally positively affects a company's performance.[5] In addition to improving financial and operational performance, developing explicit goals and plans at each level illustrated in Exhibit 5.1 is important because of the external and internal messages they send. These messages go to both external and internal audiences and provide important benefits for the organization:[6]

- *Legitimacy.* An organization's mission describes what the organization stands for and its reason for existence. It symbolizes legitimacy to external audiences such as investors, customers, suppliers, and the local community. The mission helps them look on the company in a favorable light.

     Companies have to guard their reputations, as evidenced by recent criticism of Wal-Mart. After years of ignoring critics, who targeted the company for everything from its labor practices to its environmental impact to its tactics with suppliers, managers launched a massive public relations campaign to try to mend relationships. As society's expectations of Wal-Mart change, the company's mission of bringing everyday low prices to average people is being fine-tuned to emphasize a strong commitment to doing business in an ethical and socially responsible way.[7]

     A strong mission also has an impact on employees, enabling them to become committed to the organization because they identify with its overall purpose and reason for existence. One of the traits often cited by employees in *Fortune* magazine's list of the "100 Best Companies to Work For" is a sense of purpose and meaning.[8] For example, at

TAKE ACTION

Before reading the rest of this chapter, learn about your personal goal-setting behavior by completing the items in the New Manager Self Test.

Does Goal Setting Fit Your Management Style?

How do your work habits fit with making plans and setting goals? Respond to the following as they apply to your work or study behavior. Please indicate whether each item is "Mostly True" or "Mostly False" for you.

	Mostly True	Mostly False
1. I have clear, specific goals in several areas.	_____	_____
2. I have a definite outcome in life that I want to achieve.	_____	_____
3. I prefer general goals to specific goals.	_____	_____
4. I work better without specific deadlines.	_____	_____
5. I set aside time each day or week to plan my work.	_____	_____
6. I am clear about the measures that indicate when I have achieved a goal.	_____	_____
7. I work better when I set more challenging goals for myself.	_____	_____
8. I help other people clarify and define their goals.	_____	_____

INTERPRETATION: An important part of a new manager's job is setting goals, measuring results, and reviewing progress for their department and their subordinates. Goal setting can be learned. Most organizations have goal setting and review systems that new managers use. The preceding statements indicate the extent to which you already have adopted the disciplined use of goals in your life and work. Not everyone thrives under a disciplined goal-setting system, but as a new manager, setting goals and assessing results are tools that will enhance your impact.

SCORING: Award yourself one point for each item you marked as "Mostly True" except items 3 and 4. For items 3 and 4 give yourself one point for each one you marked "Mostly False." If you scored 4 or less, you might want to evaluate and begin to change your goal-setting behavior. Research indicates that setting clear, specific, and challenging goals in key areas will produce better performance. A score of 5 or higher suggests a positive level of goal-setting behavior and better preparation for a new manager's role in an organization.

mutual fund company Vanguard, helping people pay for a happy retirement is a guiding mission for employees.

- *Source of motivation and commitment.* Goals and plans facilitate employees' identification with the organization and help motivate them by reducing uncertainty and clarifying what they should accomplish. At Boeing, the manufacturing department has a goal of moving a plane, once the wings and landing gear are attached, along the assembly line and out the door in only 5 days.

Managers are revising processes and procedures, mechanics are coming up with innovative machine adjustments, and assembly-line workers are trying new techniques to meet this ambitious goal.[9] Lack of a clear goal can damage employees' motivation and commitment because people don't understand what they're working toward. Whereas a goal provides the "why" of an organization or subunit's existence, a plan tells the "how." A plan lets employees know what actions to undertake to achieve the goal.

1 It is better to have a flexible and loose plan so you can easily adapt it as you go along.

ANSWER: Though flexibility is important, it is better to have clarity in your plans, because it reduces anxiety in employees, who may be demotivated by what seems to them as an ambiguous plan. One option might be to allow employees to develop the details of their own plans. This helps them gain ownership of the process and still allows for clarity.

- *Resource allocation.* Goals help managers decide where they should allocate resources, such as employees, money, and equipment. For example, DuPont has a goal of generating 25 percent of revenues from renewable resources by 2010. This goal lets managers know that they must use resources to develop renewable and biodegradable materials, acquire businesses that produce products with renewable resources, and buy equipment that reduces waste, emissions, and energy usage.

  As another example, following the new goals of fighting domestic terrorism, the Federal Bureau of Investigation (FBI) pulled more than 600 agents off their regular beats and reassigned them to terrorist-related cases. The FBI also is allocating resources to rebuild an archaic computer network, open foreign offices, and form terrorism task forces.[10]

- *Guides to action.* Goals and plans provide a sense of direction. They direct attention to specific targets and direct employee efforts toward important outcomes. Managers at Guitar Center, one of the fastest-growing retailers in the United States, emphasize sales growth. Sales teams at every Guitar Center store are given sales goals each morning, and employees do whatever they have to, short of losing the company money, to meet the targets. The fast-growing retailer's unwritten mantra of "Take the deal" means that salespeople are trained to take any profitable deal, even at razor-thin margins, to meet daily sales targets.[11]

- *Rationale for decisions.* Through goal setting and planning, managers learn what the organization is trying to accomplish. They can make decisions to ensure that internal policies, roles, performance, structure, products, and expenditures will be made in accordance with desired outcomes. Decisions throughout the organization will be in alignment with the plan.

- *Standard of performance.* Because goals define the desired outcomes for the organization, they also serve as performance criteria. They provide a standard of assessment. If an organization wishes to grow by 15 percent and actual growth is 17 percent, managers will have exceeded their prescribed standard.

The overall planning process prevents managers from thinking merely in terms of day-to-day activities. When organizations drift away from goals and plans, they typically get into trouble.

Goals in Organizations

Setting goals starts with top managers. The overall planning process begins with a mission statement and strategic goals for the organization as a whole.

ORGANIZATIONAL MISSION

At the top of the goal hierarchy is the **mission**—the organization's reason for existence. The mission describes the organization's values, aspirations, and reason for being.

mission
the organization's reason for existence.

The Bristol-Myers Squibb Pledge

Our company's mission is to extend and enhance human life by providing the highest-quality pharmaceutical and related health care products.

We pledge—to our patients and customers, to our employees and partners, to our shareholders and neighbors, and to the world we serve— to act on our belief that the priceless ingredient of every product is the honor and integrity of its maker.

Bristol-Myers Squibb Company

TAKE ACTION

Decide on your personal mission: What is your purpose in life?

mission statement
a broadly stated definition of the organization's basic business scope and operations that distinguishes it from similar types of organizations.

strategic goals
broad statements of where the organization wants to be in the future; they pertain to the organization as a whole rather than to specific divisions or departments.

strategic plans
the action steps by which an organization intends to attain strategic goals.

tactical goals
goals that define the outcomes that major divisions and departments must achieve for the organization to reach its overall goals.

tactical plans
plans designed to help execute major strategic plans and to accomplish a specific part of the company's strategy.

A well-defined mission is the basis for development of all subsequent goals and plans. Without a clear mission, goals and plans may be developed haphazardly and not take the organization in the direction it should be going.

The formal **mission statement** is a broadly stated definition of purpose that distinguishes the organization from others of a similar type. A well-designed mission statement can enhance employee motivation and organizational performance.[12] The content of a mission statement often focuses on the market and customers and identifies desired fields of endeavor. Some mission statements describe company characteristics such as corporate values, product quality, location of facilities, and attitude toward employees. Mission statements often reveal the company's philosophy as well as purpose. An example is the mission statement for Bristol-Myers Squibb Company, presented in Exhibit 5.2. Such short, straightforward mission statements describe basic business activities and purposes, as well as the values that guide the company. Another example of this type of mission statement is that of State Farm Insurance.

State Farm's mission is to help people manage the risks of everyday life, recover from the unexpected, and realize their dreams.

> We are people who make it our business to be like a good neighbor; who built a premier company by selling and keeping promises through our marketing partnership; who bring diverse talents and experiences to our work of serving the State Farm customer.
> Our success is built on a foundation of shared values—quality service and relationships, mutual trust, integrity, and financial strength.[13]

Mission statements such as those of Bristol-Myers Squibb and State Farm let employees, as well as customers, suppliers, and stockholders, know the company's stated purpose and values.

GOALS AND PLANS

Broad statements describing where the organization wants to be in the future are called **strategic goals.** They pertain to the organization as a whole rather than to specific divisions or departments. Strategic goals often are called *official goals,* because they are the stated intentions of what the organization wants to achieve. For example, a strategic goal for the Wm. Wrigley Jr. Co., which for more than 100 years made only gum, now is to become a major player in the broader candy market.[14]

Strategic plans define the action steps by which the company intends to attain strategic goals. The strategic plan is the blueprint that defines the organizational activities and resource allocations—in the form of cash, personnel, space, and facilities—required for meeting these targets. Strategic planning tends to be long-term and may define organizational action steps from 2 to 5 years in the future.

The purpose of strategic plans is to turn organizational goals into realities within that time period. Elements of the strategic plan at Wrigley, for example, included acquiring candy brands from food companies such as Kraft and investing in a global innovation center.

As another example, consider the strategic goals and plans at Nintendo in the Benchmarking Box below.

After strategic goals are formulated, the next step is to define **tactical goals,** the results that major divisions and departments within the organization intend to achieve. These goals apply to middle management and describe what major subunits must do for the organization to achieve its overall goals.

Tactical plans are designed to help execute the major strategic plans and to accomplish a specific part of the company's strategy.[15] Tactical plans

CONCEPT CONNECTION

In 2001, California fashion house BCBG Max Azria Group was facing possible bankruptcy. Its strategic goal was clear: growth. But its expansion had gone awry. Undeterred, CEO Max Azria hired Ben Malka as president. Together they formulated a new strategic plan, obtained $53 million in financing, and got to work. BCBG introduced new lines, concluded licensing agreements, and dramatically increased the number of retail outlets worldwide through acquisitions and by opening new stores. In 2006, BCBG expected to realize $1 billion in sales for the first time. Here Azria and his wife Lubov, a BCBG creative designer, acknowledge applause at a New York fashion show.

Benchmarking

Nintendo's Wii

After the flop of GameCube, Nintendo decided to change its strategy and asked previously stonewalled software developers to create games for the Wii. Previously, Nintendo had big hits with Donkey Kong and Super Mario Brothers, always making its own games while cold-shouldering game software developers. Even with sleek designs, the company was outsold by Sony PlayStation. Then came the flop known as GameCube, and Nintendo learned that it must change its approach. To the surprise of almost everyone, Nintendo started courting game developers, even showing up at Namco Bandai Games headquarters and handing employees the unique wand-like controllers. Nintendo asked Namco to develop games for the Wii, so that both companies could make money.

Nintendo's strategy has two parts.

1. Make the Wii less expensive and easier to play than the competitors, in hopes of attracting a broader range of customers, even those completely new to game machines. Wii may not have the graphics and speed of PlayStation 3, but it does have new ideas, such as the wireless motion detector, which actually gets players up and jumping around.

2. Get game developers to make more games than they did previously for Nintendo, which had preferred to write its own games. Now Nintendo is more forthcoming with permissions and codes for outside developers, resulting in 25 percent more games for Wii than PlayStation 3. This was in contrast to PlayStation 2, which had almost 1,500 titles, while GameCube had only 271.

"Nintendo is determined not to repeat past mistakes," said game analyst Masashi Morita. "It is taking a whole new approach with Wii."

Has it worked? Consider the history: Whereas SonyPlaystation 2 outsold GameBox six to one, the Wii has sold twice as many as SonyPlaystation 3. Nintendo's profits jumped 77 percent in 2007. "Being cool toward other game developers didn't work," says a Tokyo analyst. "Nintendo has learned that it pays to be friendly."

SOURCE: Martin Fackler, "Putting the We back in Wii," *The New York Times* (June 8, 2007): C1 & C4.

typically have a shorter time horizon than strategic plans—covering the next year or so. The word *tactical* originally comes from the military. In a business or nonprofit organization, tactical plans define what major departments and organizational subunits will do to implement the organization's strategic plan.

For example, the overall strategic plan of a large florist might involve becoming the Number 1 telephone and Internet-based purveyor of flowers, which requires high-volume sales during peak seasons such as Valentine's Day and Mother's Day. Human resource managers will develop tactical plans to ensure that the company has the dedicated order takers and customer service representatives it needs during these critical periods.

Tactical plans might include cross-training employees so they can switch to different jobs as departmental needs change, allowing order takers to transfer to jobs at headquarters during off-peak times to prevent burnout, and using regular order takers to train and supervise temporary workers during peak seasons.[16] These actions help top managers implement their overall strategic plan. Normally, it is the middle manager's job to take the broad strategic plan and identify specific tactical plans.

The results expected from departments, work groups, and individuals are the **operational goals.** They are precise and measurable. Examples of operational goals are: "Process 150 sales applications each week"; "Achieve 90 percent of deliveries on time"; "Reduce overtime by 10 percent next month"; "Develop two new online courses in accounting." An example of an operational goal at the Internal Revenue Service (IRS) is to "give accurate responses to 85 percent of taxpayer questions."[17]

Operational plans are developed at the lower levels of the organization to specify action steps toward achieving operational goals and to support tactical plans. The operational plan is the department manager's tool for daily and weekly operations. Goals are stated in quantitative terms, and the department plan describes how goals will be achieved. Operational planning specifies plans for department managers, supervisors, and individual employees.

Schedules are an important component of operational planning. Schedules define precise time frames for the completion of each operational goal required to meet the organization's tactical and strategic goals. Operational planning also must be coordinated with the budget, because resources must be allocated for desired activities. For example, Apogee Enterprises, a window and glass fabricator with 150 small divisions, is rigorous in operational planning and budgeting. Committees are set up to review and challenge budgets, profit plans, and proposed expenditures. Assigning the dollars makes the operational plan work for everything from hiring new salespeople to increasing travel expenses.

ALIGNMENT OF GOALS

Effectively designed organizational goals are aligned into a hierarchy in which the achievement of goals at low levels permits the attainment of high-level goals, also called a *means-ends chain*. Achievement of operational goals leads to the achievement of tactical goals, which in turn leads to the attainment of strategic goals. Organizational performance is an outcome of how well these interdependent elements are aligned, so that individuals, teams, departments, and so forth are working in concert to attain specific goals that ultimately help the organization fulfill its mission.[18] Traditionally, strategic goals are considered the responsibility of top management, tactical goals that of middle management, and operational goals that of first-line supervisors and workers.

Today, some companies are pushing greater involvement of all employees in goal setting and planning at each level. Microsoft, facing greater competition and new threats from the shifting technological and economic environment, developed a goal-setting process that emphasizes individual commitments and alignment of goals.

An example of a goal hierarchy is illustrated in Exhibit 5.3. Note how the strategic goal of "excellent service to customers" translates into "Open one new sales office" and "Respond to customer inquiries within two hours" at lower management levels.

operational goals
specific, measurable results expected from departments, work groups, and individuals within the organization.

operational plans
plans developed at the organization's lower levels that specify action steps toward achieving operational goals and that support tactical planning activities.

Mission

Manufacture both standard and custom metal products
for various applications in the machine tool industry

EXHIBIT 5.3

Hierarchy of Goals
for a Manufacturing
Organization

Strategic Goals

President
12% return on investment
5% growth
No employee layoffs
Excellent service to customers

Tactical Goals

Finance V.P.	**Production V.P.**	**Marketing V.P.**
Keep outstanding accounts below $500,000	Manufacture 1,200,000 products at average cost of $19	Sell 1,200,000 units at average price of $27
Keep borrowing below $1,250,000	Increase manufacturing productivity by 2%	Introduce 1 new product line
Provide monthly budget statements for departments	Resolve employee grievances within 3 working days	Increase sales by 5% in new market areas
Have delinquent accounts of no more than 2% of total		Open 1 new sales office
		Attain market share of 19%

Operational Goals

Accounts Receivable Manager	**Supervisor—Automatic Machines**	**Sales Manager—Region 1**
Issue invoices within 5 days of sale	Produce 150,000 standard units at average cost of $16	Respond to customer inquiries within 2 hours
Check new customers' credit within 1 working day	Have machine downtime of less than 7%	Meet sales quota of 120,600 units
Allow no account to be overdue more than 5 months	Respond to employee grievances within 24 hours	Work with salespeople to:
Call delinquent accounts weekly		Visit 1 new customer each day
		Call on each large customer every 4 weeks
		Call on each small customer every 8 weeks

Managers at Microsoft Corporation have long stressed that the achievement of individual goals is what enables the company to achieve high performance. As the company faced new challenges, managers decided to review the goal-setting process to make sure it was contributing to a culture of performance and accountability.

Each year, employees at all levels are asked to develop individual performance goals and discuss them with their managers. One area of concern discovered in the review was that most employee goals were stated as hopes or aspirations rather than as real commitments. Moreover, it often was difficult to see an alignment between individual goals and broader team, departmental, divisional, and company goals. Top leaders first changed the terminology they used by asking employees and managers to develop a list of *commitments*. Next they involved everyone in training to help people establish commitments that would be in alignment.

The training was designed so everyone first would receive clarity of the mission and commitments (goals) of the corporation. The commitments then were cascaded down to the divisional, departmental, team, and ultimately individual level.[19]

Microsoft executives are monitoring the new goal-setting process and providing continuing training and guidance to make sure that the goals stay in alignment and help the company carry out its mission.

Microsoft

Karyll N. Shaw, "Changing the Goal-Setting Process at Microsoft," *Academy of Management Executive* 18, no. 4 (November 2004): 139–142.

Criteria for Effective Goals

To ensure goal-setting benefits for the organization, certain characteristics and guidelines should be adopted. The characteristics of both goals and the goal-setting process are listed in Exhibit 5.4. These characteristics pertain to organizational goals at the strategic, tactical, and operational levels:

- *Specific and measurable.* When possible, goals should be expressed in quantitative terms, such as increasing profits by 2 percent, having zero incomplete sales order forms, decreasing scrap by 1 percent, or increasing average teacher effectiveness ratings from 3.5 to 3.7. Although not all goals can be expressed in numerical terms, vague goals have little motivating power for employees. By necessity, goals are qualitative as well as quantitative, especially at the top of the organization. The key point is that the goals be defined precisely and allow for measurable progress.

TAKE ACTION ▶

Make your goals measurable, so that you can know when you achieve them.

- *Cover key result areas.* Goals cannot be set for every aspect of employee behavior or organizational performance. If they were, their sheer number would render them meaningless. Instead, managers establish goals based on the idea of *choice and clarity*. A few carefully chosen, clear, and direct goals can be aimed more powerfully at organizational attention, energy, and resources.[20] Managers should identify a few key result areas—perhaps up to four or five for any organizational department or job. Key result areas are activities that contribute most to company performance and competitiveness.[21] Most companies take a balanced approach to goal setting. For example, Northern States Power Co. tracks measurements in four key areas: financial performance, customer service and satisfaction, internal processes, and innovation and learning.[22]

- *Challenging but realistic.* Goals should be challenging but not unreasonably difficult. When goals are unrealistic, they set up employees for failure and a decrease in employee morale. For example, one team at a Texas-based company that was recognized as tops in the organization had its quota raised by 65 percent, an impossible goal to reach, while lesser-performing teams had their targets raised by only 15 percent. Members of the high-performing team were so discouraged that most of them began looking for other jobs.[23] If goals are too easy, however, employees may not feel motivated.
  Stretch goals are extremely ambitious but realistic goals that challenge employees to meet high standards. An example comes from 3M, where top managers set a goal that 30 percent of sales must come from products introduced during the past 4 years (the old standard was 25 percent). Setting ambitious goals helps to keep 3M churning out innovative new products—more than 500 in one recent year alone—and has entrenched the company as a leader in some of today's most dynamic markets.[24] The key to attaining effective stretch goals is to ensure that goals are set within the existing resource base, not beyond departments' time, equipment, or financial resources.

- *Defined time period.* Goals should specify the time period over which they will be achieved. A time period is a deadline stating the date against which goal attainment will be measured. A goal of implementing a new customer relationship management system, for instance, might have a deadline of September 1, 2008. If a strategic goal involves a 2- to 3-year time

EXHIBIT 5.4

Characteristics of Effective Goal Setting

Goal Characteristics

- Specific and measurable
- Cover key result areas
- Challenging but realistic
- Defined time period
- Linked to rewards

horizon, specific dates for achieving parts of it can be set up. For example, strategic sales goals could be established on a 3-year time horizon, with a $100 million target in year one, a $129 million target in year two, and a $165 million target in year three.

- *Linked to rewards.* The ultimate impact of goals depends on the extent to which salary increases, promotions, and awards are based on goal achievement. Employees pay attention to what is noticed and rewarded in the organization, and people who attain goals should be rewarded for doing so. Rewards give meaning and significance to goals and help commit employees to achieving goals. Managers also should remember that failure to attain goals often relates to factors outside employees' control. For example, failure to achieve a financial goal may be associated with a drop in market demand because of an industry recession; thus, an employee could not be expected to reach that goal. A reward still might be appropriate if the employee partially achieves goals under difficult circumstances.[25]

Planning Types

Managers use strategic, tactical, and operational goals to direct employees and resources toward achieving specific outcomes that enable the organization to perform efficiently and effectively. They take a number of planning approaches, among the most popular of which are management by objectives, single-use plans, standing plans, and contingency plans.

MANAGEMENT BY OBJECTIVES

Management by objectives (MBO) is a method whereby managers and employees define goals for every department, project, and person and use them to monitor subsequent performance.[26] A model of the essential steps of the MBO process is presented in Exhibit 5.5. Four major activities must occur for MBO to be successful:[27]

1. *Set goals.* This step is the most difficult in MBO. Setting goals involves employees at all levels and looks beyond day-to-day activities to answer the question: "What are we trying to accomplish?" A good goal is concrete and realistic, provides a specific target and time frame, and assigns responsibility. Goals may be quantitative or qualitative. Quantitative goals are described in numerical terms, such as: "Salesperson Jones will obtain 16 new accounts in December." Qualitative goals use statements such as, "Marketing will reduce complaints by improving customer service next year." Goals should be jointly derived. Mutual agreement between employee and supervisor creates the strongest commitment to achieving goals. In the case of teams, all team members may participate in setting goals.

management by objectives (MBO)
a method of management whereby managers and employees define goals for every department, project, and person and use them to monitor subsequent performance.

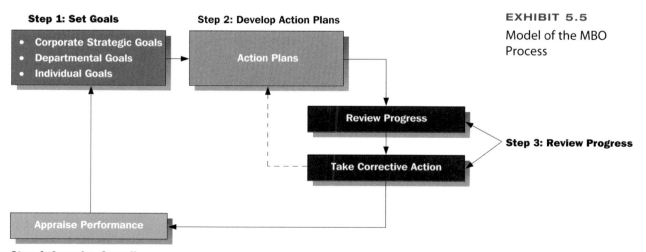

Step 1: Set Goals
- Corporate Strategic Goals
- Departmental Goals
- Individual Goals

Step 2: Develop Action Plans
Action Plans

Review Progress

Step 3: Review Progress

Take Corrective Action

Appraise Performance

Step 4: Appraise Overall Performance

EXHIBIT 5.5

Model of the MBO Process

2. *Develop action plans.* An action plan defines the course of action needed to achieve the stated goals. Action plans are made for individuals as well as departments.

3. *Review progress.* A periodic progress review is important to ensure that action plans are working. These reviews can take place informally between managers and subordinates, and the organization may wish to conduct 3-, 6-, or 9-month reviews during the year. This periodic checkup allows managers and employees to see whether they are on target or whether corrective action is needed.

TAKE ACTION ⏩

Review your goals periodically to see how you are doing and if you would be wise to adjust them.

Managers and employees should not be locked into predefined behavior and must be willing to take whatever steps are necessary to produce meaningful results. The point of MBO is to achieve goals. The action plan can be changed whenever goals are not being met.

4. *Appraise overall performance.* The final step in MBO is to carefully evaluate whether the annual goals have been achieved for individuals and departments. Success or failure to achieve goals can become part of the performance appraisal system and the designation of salary increases and other rewards. The appraisal of departmental and overall corporate performance shapes the goals for the next year. The MBO cycle repeats itself annually.

Many companies, including Intel, Tenneco, Black & Decker, and DuPont, have adopted MBO, and most managers consider MBO as an effective management tool.[28] Managers believe they are better oriented toward achieving goals when they are using MBOs. In recent years, the U.S. Congress required that federal agencies adopt a type of MBO system to encourage government employees to achieve specific outcomes.[29] Like any system, MBO achieves benefits when it is used properly but results in problems when it is used improperly. The benefits and problems of MBOs are summarized in Exhibit 5.6.

Benefits of the MBO process can be many. Corporate goals are more likely to be achieved when they focus on manager and employee efforts. Using a performance measurement system such as MBO helps employees see how their jobs and performance contribute to the business, giving them a sense of ownership and commitment.[30] Performance is improved when employees are committed to attaining the goal, are motivated because they help decide what is expected, and are free to be resourceful. Goals at lower levels are aligned with and enable the attainment of goals at top management levels.

Problems with MBO arise when the company faces rapid change. The environment and internal activities must have some stability for performance to be measured and compared against goals. Setting new goals every few months allows no time for action plans and appraisal to take effect. Also, poor employer–employee relations reduce effectiveness because

EXHIBIT 5.6

MBO Benefits and Problems

Benefits of MBO	Problems with MBO
1. Manager and employee efforts are focused on activities that will lead to goal attainment.	1. Constant change prevents MBO from taking hold.
2. Performance can be improved at all company levels.	2. An environment of poor employer–employee relations reduces MBO effectiveness.
3. Employees are motivated.	3. Strategic goals may be displaced by operational goals.
4. Departmental and individual goals are aligned with company goals.	4. Mechanistic organizations and values that discourage participation can harm the MBO process.
	5. Too much paperwork saps MBO energy.

of an element of distrust that may be present between managers and workers. Sometimes goal "displacement" occurs if employees concentrate exclusively on their operational goals to the detriment of other teams or departments. Overemphasis on operational goals can harm the attainment of overall goals.

Another problem arises in mechanistic organizations characterized by rigidly defined tasks and rules that may not be compatible with the emphasis of MBOs on mutual determination of goals by employee and supervisor. In addition, when participation is discouraged, employees will lack the training and values to set goals jointly with employers. Finally, if MBO becomes a process of filling out annual paperwork rather than energizing employees to achieve goals, it becomes an empty exercise. Once the paperwork is completed, employees forget about the goals, perhaps even resenting the paperwork in the first place.

SINGLE-USE AND STANDING PLANS

Single-use plans are developed to achieve a set of goals that are not likely to be repeated in the future. **Standing plans** are ongoing plans that provide guidance for tasks performed repeatedly within the organization. Exhibit 5.7 outlines the major types of single-use and standing plans. Single-use plans typically include both programs and projects. The primary standing plans are organizational policies, rules, and procedures. Standing plans generally pertain to matters such as employee illness, absences, smoking, discipline, hiring, and dismissal.

single-use plans
plans that are developed to achieve a set of goals that are unlikely to be repeated in the future.

standing plans
ongoing plans that are used to provide guidance for tasks performed repeatedly within the organization.

Single-Use Plans	Standing Plans
Program • Plans for attaining a one-time organizational goal • Major undertaking that may take several years to complete • Large in scope; may be associated with several projects **Examples:** Building a new headquarters Converting all paper files to digital **Project** • Also a set of plans for attaining a onetime goal • Smaller in scope and complexity than a program; shorter in horizon • Often one part of a larger program **Examples:** Renovating the office Setting up a company intranet	**Policy** • Broad in scope—general guide to action • Based on organization's overall goals/strategic plan • Defines boundaries within which to make decisions **Examples:** Sexual harassment policies Internet and e-mail usage policies **Rule** • Narrow in scope • Describes how a specific action is to be performed • May apply to specific setting **Examples:** No eating rule in areas of company where employees are visible to the public **Procedure** • Sometimes called a standard operating procedure • Defines a precise series of steps to attain certain goals **Examples:** Procedures for issuing refunds Procedures for handling employee grievances

EXHIBIT 5.7

Major Types of Single-Use and Standing Plans

TAKE ACTION ➡

If things don't work out as expected, try something different.

CONTINGENCY PLANS

When organizations are operating in a highly uncertain environment or dealing with long-time horizons, planning can seem like a waste of time sometimes. In fact, strict plans may even hinder rather than help an organization's performance in the face of rapid technological, social, economic, or other environmental change. In these cases, managers may want to develop multiple future alternatives to help them form more flexible plans.

Contingency plans define company responses to be taken in the case of emergencies, setbacks, or unexpected conditions.

To develop contingency plans, managers identify important factors in the environment, such as possible economic downturns, declining markets, increases in cost of supplies, new technological developments, or safety accidents. Managers then forecast a range of alternative responses to the most likely high-impact contingencies, focusing on the worst case.[31] For example, if sales fall 20 percent and prices drop 8 percent, what will the company do? Managers could develop contingency plans that include layoffs, emergency budgets, new sales efforts, or new markets. A real-life example comes from FedEx, which has to cope with some kind of unexpected disruption to its

CONCEPT CONNECTION

A desert flare marks the area where geologists discovered Libya's rich Zilten oilfield in the 1950's. At their peak in 1970, Libyan oil fields operated by Occidental Petroleum were producing 660,000 barrels a day, more than the company's total oil production in 2003. Today, with economic sanctions against Libya lifted by the U.S. government, big oil companies such as Occidental, Chevron Texaco, and Exxon Mobil are ready again to do business with Libya's National Oil Corporation. Yet, the current environment of terrorist threats and general uncertainty means that managers have to be prepared for whatever might happen. They are busy developing contingency plans to define how their companies will respond in case of unexpected setbacks associated with renewed Libyan operations. Companies are willing to take the risks because the potential rewards are huge.

service somewhere in the world on a daily basis. In 2005, for example, managers activated contingency plans related to more than two dozen tropical storms, an air traffic controller strike in France, and a blackout in Los Angeles. The company also has contingency plans in place for events such as labor strikes, social upheavals in foreign countries, or incidents of terrorism.[32]

Planning in a Turbulent Environment

Today, contingency planning takes on a whole new urgency as increasing turbulence and uncertainty shake the business world. Managers must renew their emphasis on bracing for unexpected—even unimaginable—events. Two recent extensions of contingency planning are *building scenarios* and *crisis planning*.

BUILDING SCENARIOS

One way managers cope with greater uncertainty is with a forecasting technique known as scenario building. **Scenario building** involves looking at current trends and discontinuities and visualizing future possibilities. Rather than looking only at history and thinking about what has been, managers think about what *could be*. The events that cause the most damage to companies are those that no one even conceived of, such as the collapse of the World Trade Center towers in New York from the terrorist attack.

contingency plans
plans that define company responses to specific situations, such as emergencies, setbacks, or unexpected conditions.

scenario building
looking at trends and discontinuities and imagining possible alternative futures to build a framework within which unexpected future events can be managed.

Top executives around the globe are discovering that casual e-mail messages can come back to haunt them—in court. The American Management Association (AMA) surveyed 1,100 companies and found that 14 percent of them had been ordered to disclose e-mail messages. Eight brokerage firms were fined $8 million for not keeping and producing e-mail in accordance with SEC guidelines. Some companies have had to pay millions of dollars to settle sexual harassment lawsuits arising from inappropriate e-mail.

As with any powerful tool, e-mail has the potential to be hazardous, backfiring not only on the employee but on the organization as well. Experts say a formal written policy is the best way for a company to protect itself and offer some tips for managers in developing effective policies governing the use of e-mail.

- *Make clear that all e-mail and its contents are the property of the company.* Many experts recommend warning employees that the company reserves the right to read any messages transmitted over its system. "Employees need to understand that a company can access employees' e-mail at any time without advance notice or consent," says lawyer Pam Reeves. This rule helps to discourage frivolous e-mails and those that might be considered crude and offensive.
- *Tie the policy to the company's sexual harassment policy or other policies governing employee behavior on the job.* In almost all sexual harassment cases, judges have ruled that the use of e-mail is considered part of the workplace environment.
- *Establish clear guidelines on matters such as the use of e-mail for jokes and other nonwork-related communications, the sending of confidential messages, and how to handle junk e-mail.* At Prudential Insurance, for example, employees are prohibited from using company e-mail to share jokes, photographs, or any kind of nonbusiness information.
- *Establish guidelines for deleting or retaining messages.* Retention periods of 30 to 90 days for routine messages are typical. Most organizations also set up a centralized archive for retaining essential e-mail messages.
- *Consider having policies pop up on users' screens when they log on.* Be sure to remind employees that e-mail belongs to the employer and may be monitored.

Even deleted e-mails usually can be tracked down by a computer forensics expert. An effective policy is the best step that companies can take to manage the potential risks of e-mail abuse.

SOURCES: "E-Mail: The DNA of Office Crimes," *Electric Perspectives* 28, no. 5 (September–October 2003): 4; Marcia Stepanek with Steve Hamm, "When the Devil is in the E-Mails," *BusinessWeek* (June 8, 1998): 72–74; Joseph McCafferty, "The Phantom Menace," *CFO* (June 1999): 89–91; and "Many Company Internet and E-Mail Policies Are Worth Revising," *Kiplinger Letter* (February 21, 2003): 1.

Regulating E-Mail in the Workplace

Although managers can't predict the future, they can rehearse a framework within which to manage future events.[33] With scenario building, a broad base of managers mentally rehearses different scenarios, anticipating various changes that could impact the organization. Scenarios are like stories that offer alternative vivid pictures of what the future will be like and how managers will respond. Typically, two to five scenarios are developed for each set of factors, ranging from the most optimistic to the most pessimistic view.[34] Scenario building forces managers to mentally rehearse what they would do if their best-laid plans collapse.

Royal Dutch/Shell has long used scenario building to help managers navigate the turbulence and uncertainty of the oil industry. One scenario that Shell managers rehearsed in 1970, for example, involved an imagined accident in Saudi Arabia that severed an oil pipeline, which in turn decreased supply. The market reacted by increasing oil prices, which allowed OPEC nations to pump less oil and make more money.

This story caused managers to reexamine the standard assumptions about oil price and supply and imagine what would happen and how they would respond if OPEC were to increase prices. Nothing in the exercise told Shell managers to expect an embargo, but by rehearsing this scenario, they were much more prepared than the competition when OPEC announced its first oil embargo in October 1973. This speedy response to a massive shift in the environment enabled Shell to move in two years from being the world's eighth largest oil company to being number two.[35]

TAKE ACTION

As a new manager, get in the mind-set of scenario planning. Go to http://www.shell.com/scenarios, where Shell Oil publishes the outline of its annual scenario planning exercise, and http://www.cia.gov/nic, where the National Intelligence Council pictures possible futures for the year 2020.

CONCEPT CONNECTION

This looks harmless, doesn't it? But three people died and nearly 200 became ill after E. coli-contaminated spinach grown in central California reached consumers throughout the United States. Government and the food industry activated crisis management plans to contain the public health menace. Producers voluntarily recalled spinach products, grocers swept shelves clear of bagged spinach, and the FDA worked tirelessly to determine the cause. Various groups also proposed future prevention measures. Some advocated more stringent government regulation, and others argued for producers to do more product testing and a better job of tracking produce from field to table.

CRISIS PLANNING

Some unexpected events are so sudden and devastating that they require immediate response. Consider events such as the November 12, 2001, crash of American Airlines Flight 587 in a New York neighborhood that already had been devastated by terrorist attacks, the 1993 deaths from e-coli bacteria in Jack-in-the-Box hamburgers, or the 2003 crash of the *Columbia* space shuttle. Companies, too, face many smaller crises that call for rapid response, such as the conviction of Martha Stewart, chair of Martha Stewart Living Omnimedia, on charges of insider trading; allegations of tainted Coca-Cola in Belgium; or charges that Tyson Foods hired illegal immigrants to work in its processing plants. Crises have become expected in our organizations.[36]

Although crises differ, a carefully thought-out and coordinated crisis plan can be used to respond to any disaster. In addition, crisis planning reduces the incidence of trouble, much like putting a good lock on a door reduces burglaries.[37]

Exhibit 5.8 outlines the three essential stages of crisis management.[38] The

EXHIBIT 5.8

Three Stages of Crisis Management

Prevention
- Build relationships.
- Detect signals from environment.

Preparation
- Designate crisis management team and spokesperson.
- Create detailed crisis management plan.
- Set up effective communications system.

Containment
- Rapid response: Activate the crisis management plan.
- Get the awful truth out.
- Meet safety and emotional needs.
- Return to business.

SOURCE: Based on information in W. Timothy Coombs, *Ongoing Crisis Communication: Planning, Managing, and Responding* (Thousand Oaks, CA: Sage Publications, 1999).

prevention stage involves activities that managers undertake to try to prevent crises from happening and to detect warning signs of potential crises. The preparation stage includes all the detailed planning to handle a crisis when it arises. Containment focuses on the organization's response to an actual crisis and any follow-up concerns.

Prevention. Although unexpected events and disasters will happen, managers should do everything they can to prevent crises. Critical to prevention is to build trusting relationships with key stakeholders such as employees, customers, suppliers, governments, unions, and the community. By developing favorable relationships, managers often can prevent crises from happening and can respond more effectively to those that cannot be avoided. For example, organizations that have open, trusting relationships with employees and unions may avoid crippling labor strikes.

Good communication also helps managers identify problems early so they do not turn into major issues. Coca-Cola suffered a major crisis in Europe because it failed to respond quickly to reports of "foul-smelling" Coke in Belgium. A former CEO observed that every problem the company has faced in recent years "can be traced to a singular cause: We neglected our relationships."[39]

TAKE ACTION
Prevent crises through communicating frequently, building trust, and careful planning.

Preparation. The three steps in the preparation stage are

1. designating a crisis management team and spokesperson,

2. creating a detailed crisis management plan, and

3. setting up an effective communications system.

Some companies are setting up crisis management offices, with high-level leaders who report directly to the CEO.[40] Although these offices are in charge of crisis management, people throughout the company must be involved. The crisis management team, for example, is a cross-functional group of people who are designated to swing into action if a crisis erupts. The organization also should designate a spokesperson who will be the voice of the company during the crisis.[41] In many cases this person is the top leader. Organizations, however, typically assign more than one spokesperson so someone else will be prepared if the top leader is not available.

The **crisis management plan (CMP)** is a detailed, written plan that specifies the steps to be taken, and by whom, if a crisis arises. The CMP should include the steps for dealing with various types of crises—natural disasters such as fires or earthquakes, normal accidents such as economic crises or industrial accidents, and abnormal events such as product tampering or acts of terrorism.[42]

Morgan Stanley Dean Witter, the World Trade Center's largest tenant with 3,700 employees, adopted a crisis management plan for abnormal events after bomb threats during the Persian Gulf War in 1991. Top managers credit its detailed evacuation procedures for saving the lives of all but six employees during the September 11, 2001, terrorist attack.[43] A key point is that a crisis management plan should be a living, changing document that is regularly reviewed, practiced, and updated as needed.

Containment. Some crises are inevitable no matter how well prepared an organization is. When a crisis hits, a rapid response is crucial. Training and practice enable the team to implement the crisis management plan immediately. In addition, the organization should "get the awful truth out" to employees and the public as soon as possible.[44] At this stage, the organization must speak with one voice so people do not get conflicting stories about what's going on and what the organization is doing about it.

After ensuring people's physical safety, if necessary, during a crisis, the next step should be to respond to the emotional needs of employees, customers, and the public. Presenting

crisis management plan (CMP)
a detailed, written plan that specifies the steps to be taken, and by whom, if a crisis arises.

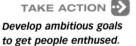
facts and statistics to try to downplay the disaster inevitably backfires because it does not meet people's emotional need to feel that someone cares about them and what the disaster has meant to their lives.

Organizations strive to give people a sense of security and hope by getting back to business quickly. Companies that cannot get up and running within 10 days after any major crisis are not likely to stay in business.[45] People want to feel that they are going to have a job and be able to take care of their families. Managers also use a time of crisis to bolster their prevention abilities and be better prepared in the future. Executives at Home Depot do a postmortem after each catastrophic event to learn how to better prepare for the next one.[46]

A crisis also is an important time for companies to strengthen their stakeholder relationships. By being open and honest about the crisis and putting people first, organizations build stronger bonds with employees, customers, and other stakeholders, and they gain a reputation as a trustworthy company.

Planning for High Performance

The purpose of planning and goal setting is to help the organization achieve high performance. Overall organizational performance depends on achieving outcomes identified by the planning process. The process of planning is changing to be more in tune with a rapidly changing environment. Traditionally, strategy and planning have been the domain of top managers. Today, managers involve people throughout the organization, which can spur higher performance because people understand the goals and plans and buy into them.

In a complex and competitive business environment, strategic thinking and execution become the expectation of every employee.[47] Planning comes alive when employees are involved in setting goals and determining the means to reach them. Here are some guidelines for planning in the new workplace.

1. *Start with a strong mission and vision.* Planning for high performance requires flexibility. Employees may have to adapt their plans to meet new needs and respond to changes in the environment. During times of turbulence or uncertainty, a powerful sense of purpose (mission) and direction for the future (vision) become even more important. Without a strong mission and vision to guide employees' thinking and behavior, the resources of a fast-moving company can quickly become uncoordinated, with employees pursuing radically different plans and activities. A compelling mission and vision also can increase employee commitment and motivation, which are vital to helping organizations compete in a rapidly shifting environment.[48]

 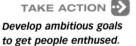
2. *Set stretch goals for excellence.* Stretch goals are highly ambitious goals that are so clear, compelling, and imaginative that they fire up employees and engender excellence. Stretch goals enable people to think in new ways because they are so far beyond the current levels that people don't know how to reach them. At the same time, though, as we discussed earlier, the goals must be seen as achievable or employees will be discouraged and demotivated.[49] Stretch goals are extremely important today because things move fast.

A company that focuses on gradual, incremental improvements in products, processes, or systems will be left behind. Managers can use stretch goals to compel employees to think in new ways that lead to bold, innovative breakthroughs. Motorola used stretch goals to achieve *Six Sigma* quality which now has become the standard for numerous companies. Managers first set a goal of a tenfold increase in quality over a two-year period. After this goal was met, the company set a new stretch goal of a hundredfold improvement over a four-year period.[50]

 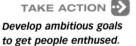
3. *Embrace event-driven planning.* In rapidly shifting environments, managers have to be in tune with what's happening *right now*, rather than concentrating only on long-range goals and plans. Long-range strategic planning is not abandoned but is accompanied by event-driven planning, which responds to the current reality of what

Calendar-Driven Planning	Event-Driven Planning
Is based on time	Is based on events—small and large
Produces a document	Produces a sequential process
Is declared	Is evolutionary and interactive
Focuses on goals	Focuses on process
Creates obstacles to change once set	Allows for continuous change
Creates strategy implementers	Creates organizationwide strategists

EXHIBIT 5.9
Comparing Two
Planning Styles

SOURCE: Chuck Martin, "How to Plan for the Short Term," book excerpt from Chuck Martin, *Managing for the Short Term* (New York: Doubleday, 2002), in *CIO* (September 15, 2002), 90–97.

the environment and the marketplace demand.[51] Exhibit 5.9 compares traditional calendar-driven planning to event-driven planning.

Event-driven planning is a continuous, sequential process rather than a staid planning document. It is evolutionary and interactive, taking advantage of unforeseen events to shift the company as needed to improve performance. Event-driven planning allows for flexibility to adapt to market forces or other shifts in the environment rather than being tied to a plan that no longer works.

For example, Redix International, a software development firm, has a long-term plan for items it wants to incorporate into the software. But the plan is modified at least four or five times a year. The shifts in direction are based on weekly discussions that president and CEO Randall King has with key Redix managers, where they examine what demands from clients indicate about where the marketplace is going.[52]

4. *Use performance dashboards.* People need a way to see how plans are progressing and gauge their progress toward achieving goals. Companies began using business performance dashboards as a way for executives to keep track of key performance metrics, such as sales in relation to targets, number of products on back order, or percentage of customer service calls resolved within specified time periods. Today, dashboards are evolving into organization-wide systems that help align and track goals across the enterprise. The true power of dashboards comes from deploying them throughout the company, even on the factory floor, so all employees can track progress toward goals, notice when things are falling short, and find innovative ways to get back on course toward reaching the specified targets.

At Emergency Medical Associates, a physician-owned medical group that manages emergency rooms for hospitals in New York and New Jersey, dashboards enable the staff to note when performance thresholds related to patient wait times, for example, aren't being met at various hospitals.[53] Some dashboard systems also incorporate software that enables users to perform what-if scenarios to evaluate the impact of various alternatives for meeting goals.

5. *Organize temporary task forces.* A **planning task force** is a temporary group of managers and employees who take responsibility for developing a strategic plan. Many of today's companies use interdepartmental task forces to help establish goals and make plans for achieving them. The task force often includes outside stakeholders as well, such as customers, suppliers, strategic partners, investors, or even members of the general community. Today's companies concentrate on satisfying the needs and interests of all stakeholder groups, so they bring these stakeholders into the planning and goal-setting process.[54] LendLease, an Australian real estate and financial services company, for example, involves numerous stakeholders, including community advocates and potential customers, in the planning process for every new project it undertakes.[55]

6. *Recognize that planning still starts and stops at the top.* Top managers create a mission and vision worthy of employees' best efforts, which provides a framework for planning

event-driven planning
evolutionary planning that responds to the current reality of what the environment and the marketplace demand.

planning task force
a group of managers and employees who develop a strategic plan.

and goal setting. Even though planning is decentralized, top managers must show support and commitment to the planning process. Top managers also accept responsibility when planning and goal setting are ineffective, rather than blaming the failure on lower-level managers or employees.

Thinking Strategically

Strategic management is considered a specific type of planning. Strategic planning in for-profit business organizations typically pertains to competitive actions in the marketplace. In nonprofit organizations such as the Red Cross and the Salvation Army, strategic planning pertains to events in the external environment. The final responsibility for strategy rests with top managers and the chief executive.

For an organization to succeed, the CEO must be actively involved in making the tough choices and trade-offs that define and support strategy.[56] In addition, senior executives at companies such as General Electric, 3M, and Johnson & Johnson want middle- and low-level managers to think strategically. Some companies also are finding ways to get front-line workers involved in strategic thinking and planning.

Strategic thinking means to take the long-term view and to see the big picture, including the organization and the competitive environment, and to consider how they fit together. Understanding the strategy concept, levels of strategy, and strategy formulation versus implementation is an important start toward strategic thinking.

WHAT IS STRATEGIC MANAGEMENT?

Strategic management is the set of decisions and actions used to formulate and implement strategies that will provide a competitively superior fit between the organization and its environment so as to achieve organizational goals.[57] Managers ask questions such as: What changes and trends are taking place in the competitive environment? Who are our competitors, and what are their strengths and weaknesses? Who are our customers? What products or services should we offer, and how can we offer them most efficiently? What does the future hold for our industry, and how can we change the rules of the game? Answers to these questions help managers make choices about how to position their organizations in the environment with respect to rival companies.[58]

Superior organizational performance is not a matter of luck. It is determined by the choices managers make. Top executives use strategic management to define an overall direction for the organization—the firm's grand strategy.

PURPOSE OF STRATEGY

Within the overall grand strategy of an organization, executives define an explicit **strategy,** the plan of action that describes resource allocation and activities for dealing with the

TAKE ACTION ▸

As a potential new manager, practice thinking strategically by studying your department's or your organization's environment, market, and competitors. Think about what the long-term future might hold and how you think the company can best be positioned to stay competitive.

strategic management
a specific type of planning in for-profit business organizations; typically pertains to competitive actions in the marketplace.

strategy
plan of action that describes resource allocation and activities for dealing with the environment, achieving a competitive advantage, and attaining the organization's goals.

Business Blooper

Hollywood Ratings

Hollywood's strategy to make lots of R-rated films doesn't translate to higher revenues. Studies show that the highest grossing and most profitable movies are G-rated,

earning about 150% of the profits of R movies. Yet, of all the films produced each year, only about 3% are G, 22% are P or P-G, and 55% are R. But don't despair. It looks like more G-movies are on the way. Hail to Harry Potter and Bambi!

SOURCE: David Germain, "A Boom Year for G Films," *The Record* (July 5, 2002): 8; Michael Booth, "Please, More Family Films?" *Denver Post* (January 29, 2006): F1.

environment, achieving a competitive advantage, and attaining the organization's goals. **Competitive advantage** refers to what sets the organization apart from others and provides it with a distinctive edge for meeting customer needs in the marketplace. The essence of formulating strategy is to choose how the organization will be different.[59]

Managers make decisions about whether the company will perform different activities or will execute similar activities differently than competitors do. Strategy necessarily changes over time to fit environmental conditions, but to remain competitive, companies develop strategies that emphasize core competencies, develop synergy, and create value for customers.

Core Competence. A company's **core competence** is something the organization does especially well in comparison to its competitors. A core competence represents a competitive advantage because the company acquires expertise that competitors do not have. A core competence may be in the area of superior research and development, expert technological know-how, process efficiency, or exceptional customer service.[60]

At VF, a large apparel company that owns Vanity Fair, Nautica, Wrangler, and The North Face, strategy focuses on the company's core competencies of operational efficiency and merchandising know-how. When VF bought The North Face, for example, its distribution systems were so poor that stores were getting ski apparel at the end of winter and camping gear at the end of summer. The company's operating profit margin was minus 35 percent. Managers at VF revamped The North Face's sourcing, distribution, and financial systems, and within 5 years doubled sales to $500 million and improved profit margins to a healthy 13 percent. "For VF it was easy, and it's not easy for everybody" one retail analyst said, referring to the company's application of its core competencies.[61]

Gaylord Hotels, which has large hotel and conference centers in several states, as well as the Opryland complex near Nashville, Tennessee, thrives based on a strategy of superior service for large group meetings.[62] Robinson Helicopter succeeds through superior technological know-how for building small, two-seater helicopters used for everything from police patrols in Los Angeles to herding cattle in Australia.[63] In each case, leaders identified what their company does especially well and built strategy around it.

Synergy. Organizational parts interacting to produce a joint effect that is greater than the sum of the parts acting alone is called **synergy.** The organization may attain a special advantage with respect to cost, market power, technology, or management skill. When managed properly, synergy can create additional value with existing resources, which provides a big boost to the bottom line.[64]

Synergy was one motivation for the FedEx acquisition of Kinko's Inc. in 2004, to bring together package delivery with full-service counters. But the merger has not gone as well as planned and the company has retooled its strategy by focusing on different customers (small- and medium-sized businesses, mobile professionals and convention centers/hotels). In addition, more stores are being opened. While the company had only opened about 20 stores a year previously, in 2007 it opened 100 and plans to double and triple that in the next two years.[65]

Synergy also can be obtained through good relations with suppliers or by strong alliances among companies. Yahoo!, for example, uses partnerships, such as a deal with Verizon Communications, to boost its number of paying subscribers to nearly 12 million.[66]

Delivering Value. Delivering value to the customer is at the heart of strategy. **Value** can be defined as the combination of benefits received and costs paid.

Managers help their companies create value by devising strategies that exploit core competencies and attain synergy. To compete with the rising clout of satellite television, for example, cable companies such as Adelphia and Charter Communications are trying to provide better value with cable value packages that offer a combination of basic cable,

TAKE ACTION
Make sure that the customer gets good value.

competitive advantage
what sets the organization apart from others and provides it with a distinctive edge for meeting customer needs in the marketplace.

core competence
something the organization does especially well in comparison to its competitors.

synergy
a joint effect that is greater than the sum of the parts acting alone.

value
the combination of benefits received and costs paid.

Spotlight on
Collaboration

Facebook

Facebook started on college campuses, and after it opened its dorm rooms to non-students, its membership skyrocketed in 12 months from 13 to 24 million active members and was 50 million by late 2007. MySpace is twice as large and crafted a different reputation, fostering creativity by imposing few restrictions and allowing members to bring in tools from other providers, such as slide shows. In contrast, Facebook kept a tight reign on members and did not allow users to customize pages with tools from other companies. Through this practice, Facebook pages retained a uniform look and underlined its main goal of facilitating online communication with friends.

Now that's shifting. Facebook has been changing its face, so to speak, and permits users to listen to or recommend music, play games, and post Amazon book reviews without ever leaving the site. This move allows more creativity and also makes it easier for spammers, which blurs Facebook's identity. But Facebook's 23-year-old CEO Mark Zuckerberg is thinking big and is positioning the company as an Internet "social operating system," desiring to be at the center of its members' online experience, much like Microsoft Windows does with PC users. His strategy has paid off. Turning down $1 billion from Yahoo in 2006, the following year Zuckerberg closed a deal giving Microsoft a 1.6 percent share for $240 million, valuing the company at $15 billion and retaining a 20 percent share for himself.

With advertisers spending $1.2 billion worldwide on social-networking advertising in 2007, Facebook's revenues were anticipated to increase by creating synergy with companies that can contribute features and then advertise as well. Venture capitalist Peter Thiel sees this as an important development, though fraught with risks. "The company is taking a massive gamble. There are a lot of things that could go wrong," he says.

SOURCE: Brad Stone, "Facebook Goes off the Campus," *The New York Times* (May 25, 2007): C1.

Save-A-Lot

Consider how Save-A-Lot has grown into one of the most successful grocery chains in the United States with a strategy based on exploiting core competencies, building synergy, and providing value to customers. When most supermarket executives look at the inner city, they see peeling paint, low-income customers, rampant crime, and low profits. Save-A-Lot looks at the inner city and sees opportunity. Save-A-Lot was started in the late 1970s, when Bill Moran noticed that low-income and rural areas were served poorly by large supermarkets. Moran began opening small stores in low-rent areas and stocking them with a limited number of low-priced staples. He hand-wrote price signs and built crude shelves out of particle board. He made his own labels from low-quality paper, which suppliers then slapped on generic products.

Save-A-Lot has thrived ever since by using its core competency of cost efficiency, which enables the stores to sell goods at prices 40 percent lower than major supermarkets. Unlike the typical supermarket, which is about 45,000 square feet, Save-A-Lot stores use a compact 16,000-square-foot, no-frills format, target areas with dirt-cheap rent, and court households earning less than $35,000 a year. Save-A-Lot stores don't have bakeries, pharmacies, or grocery baggers. Labor costs are kept ultra low. For example, whereas most grocery managers want employees to keep displays well-stocked and tidy, Save-A-Lot managers tell employees to let the displays sell down before restocking.

Save-A-Lot has obtained synergy by developing good relationships with a few core suppliers. Most supermarkets charge manufacturers slotting fees to put their products on shelves, but not Save-A-Lot. In addition, the company doesn't ask suppliers to take back damaged goods. It just sticks up a hand-written "Oops" sign and marks prices even lower.

Customers love it. Now even branded food makers want a slice of the Save-A-Lot pie. Procter & Gamble, for example, developed a lower-priced version of Folgers, and the chain also sells a low-priced brand of cheese from Kraft and a cereal from General Mills.

The value that customers get from Save-A-Lot is based not just on low prices but also on convenience and quality. Doc Otis Roper, who makes $8 an hour as a recycling worker, says Save-A-Lot is a blessing for its combination of low prices and convenience. He used to have to ride the bus to buy groceries or shop at convenience stores where prices were high and quality low. Now he walks five blocks to Save-A-Lot and gets quality goods at a price even lower than Wal-Mart's.

Janet Adamy, "Bare Essentials; To Find Growth, No-Frills Grocer Goes Where Other Chains Won't," *Wall Street Journal* (August 30, 2005): A1, A8.

digital premium channels, video on demand, and high-speed Internet for a reduced cost. The Swedish retailer IKEA has become a global cult brand by offering beautiful, functional products at modest cost, thus delivering superior value to customers.[67]

The Strategic Management Process

The overall strategic management process is illustrated in Exhibit 5.10. It begins when executives evaluate their current position with respect to mission, goals, and strategies. Then they scan the organization's internal and external environments and identify strategic factors that might require change. Internal or external events might indicate a need to redefine the mission or goals or to formulate a new strategy at the corporate, business, or functional level. The final stage in the strategic management process is to implement the new strategy.

STRATEGY FORMULATION VERSUS IMPLEMENTATION

Strategy formulation involves the planning and decision making that lead to establishment of the firm's goals and development of a specific strategic plan.[68] Strategy formulation may include assessing the external environment and internal problems and integrating the results into goals and strategy. This process is in contrast to **strategy implementation,** which is the use of managerial and organizational tools to direct resources toward accomplishing strategic results.[69] Strategy implementation is the administration and execution of the strategic plan. Managers may use persuasion, new equipment, changes in organizational structure, or a revised reward system to ensure that employees and resources are utilized to make formulated strategy a reality.

SITUATION ANALYSIS

Formulating strategy often begins with an assessment of the internal and external factors that will affect the organization's competitive situation. **Situation analysis** typically

TAKE ACTION

As a new manager, identify the core competence of your team or department and identify ways that it can contribute to the overall organization's strategy. Who are your team's or department's customers, and how can you deliver value?

strategy formulation
the planning and decision making that lead to establishment of the firm's goals and development of a specific strategic plan.

strategy implementation
the use of managerial and organizational tools to direct resources toward accomplishing strategic results.

situation analysis
an evaluation that typically includes a search for SWOT—strengths, weaknesses, opportunities, and threats—that affect organizational performance.

EXHIBIT 5.10

The Strategic Management Process

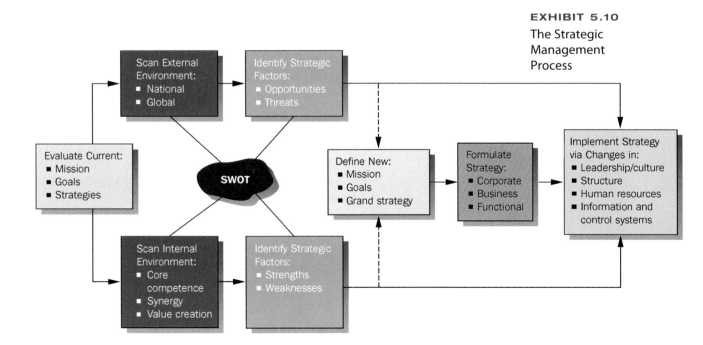

includes a search for SWOT—strengths, weaknesses, opportunities, and threats—that affect organizational performance. Situation analysis is important to all companies but is crucial to those considering globalization because of the diverse environments in which they will operate.

External information about opportunities and threats may be obtained from a variety of sources, including customers, government reports, professional journals, suppliers, bankers, friends in other organizations, consultants, and association meetings. Many firms hire special scanning organizations to provide them with newspaper clippings, Internet research, and analyses of relevant domestic and global trends. In addition, many companies are hiring competitive intelligence professionals to scope out competitors, as we discussed in Chapter 2.

Executives acquire information about internal strengths and weaknesses from a variety of reports, including budgets, financial ratios, profit-and-loss statements, and surveys of employee attitudes and satisfaction. Managers spend 80 percent of their time giving and receiving information. Through frequent face-to-face discussions and meetings with people at all levels of the hierarchy, executives build an understanding of the company's internal strengths and weaknesses.

Internal Strengths and Weaknesses. *Strengths* are positive internal characteristics that the organization can exploit to achieve its strategic performance goals. *Weaknesses* are internal characteristics that might inhibit or restrict the organization's performance. Some examples of what executives evaluate to interpret strengths and weaknesses are given in Exhibit 5.11. The information sought typically pertains to specific functions such as marketing, finance, production, and R&D. Internal analysis also examines overall organization structure, management competence and quality, and human resource

TAKE ACTION ▶

When considering a strategy, look carefully at strengths, weaknesses, opportunities, and threats. Don't just jump into a course of action.

EXHIBIT 5.11
Checklist for Analyzing Organizational Strengths and Weaknesses

Management and Organization	Marketing	Human Resources
Management quality	Distribution channels	Employee experience, education
Staff quality	Market share	Union status
Degree of centralization	Advertising efficiency	Turnover, absenteeism
Organization charts	Customer satisfaction	Work satisfaction
Planning, information, control systems	Product quality	Grievances
	Service reputation	
	Sales force turnover	

Finance	Production	Research and Development
Profit margin	Plant location	Basic applied research
Debt-equity ratio	Machinery obsolescence	Laboratory capabilities
Inventory ratio	Purchasing system	Research programs
Return on investment	Quality control	New-product innovations
Credit rating	Productivity/efficiency	Technology innovations

characteristics. Based on their understanding of these areas, managers can determine their strengths or weaknesses compared to other companies.

External Opportunities and Threats.

Threats are characteristics of the external environment that may prevent the organization from achieving its strategic goals. *Opportunities* are characteristics of the external environment that have the potential to help the organization achieve or exceed its strategic goals. Executives evaluate the external environment with information about the nine sectors described in Chapter 2.

The task environment sectors, the most relevant to strategic behavior, include the behavior of competitors, customers, suppliers, and the labor supply. The general environment contains those sectors that have an indirect influence on the organization but nevertheless must be understood and incorporated into strategic behavior. The general environment includes technological developments, the economy, legal-political and international events, and sociocultural changes. Additional areas that might reveal opportunities or threats include pressure groups, interest groups, creditors, natural resources, and potentially competitive industries.

CONCEPT CONNECTION

The effects of this oil fire in Iraq were felt thousands of miles away—in the executive suites at companies such as United Airlines, the number two air carrier in the United States. Uncertainty about oil costs and supplies is a significant external threat to the nation's airlines. Other threats that United faces as it struggles to recover from bankruptcy are stiff competition from low-cost carriers and the ever-lingering threat of terrorism.

Kraft Foods

Kraft Foods provides an example of how situation analysis can be used to help executives formulate the correct strategy. Kraft has some of the most recognizable brand names in the grocery store, but the giant food company has been facing some difficult challenges in recent years. To get things back on track, managers are evaluating the company by looking at strengths, weaknesses, opportunities, and threats (SWOT).

Kraft's greatest *strengths* are its powerful brands, its positive reputation, its track record as an innovator, and a well-funded R&D budget. Its biggest *weaknesses* include the loss of top management talent in recent years and a sluggish response to environmental changes.

Several major *threats* have been building for a couple of years. The first is that less-expensive, private-label brands are successfully stealing market share from Kraft's core brands such as Kraft Singles cheese slices, Maxwell House coffee, Oscar Mayer beef cold cuts, and Ritz crackers. At the same time, other major food companies have responded more quickly to growing consumer demands for less fattening, more healthful food choices. PepsiCo, for example, began cutting trans-fats from Doritos, Tostitos, and Cheetos—and saw sales increase by 28 percent.

A third threat to Kraft is that more people are eating ready-made lunches rather than consuming home-prepared lunch foods such as sandwiches made of cheese and cold cuts. Kraft managers recognize *opportunities* in the environment, as well, however. Trends show that Americans are looking for more snack foods and comfort foods, which presents a golden opportunity for Kraft, whose name for many Americans is almost synonymous with comfort food.

What does SWOT analysis suggest for Kraft's future strategy? Kraft managers will try to capitalize on the company's strengths by investing research dollars to develop healthier snack and prepackaged lunch foods, such as lower-fat versions of its popular "Lunchables." To bolster core brands, Kraft has pumped an additional $200 million into its multibillion-dollar marketing and advertising budget. Managers also are exploring vending opportunities for giant Kraft-branded machines that churn out ready-made food at movie theaters, shopping malls, and other public venues.[70]

Pallavi Gogoi, "The Heat in Kraft's Kitchen; Cheap Rivals and Demands for Leaner Fare Close In," *BusinessWeek* (August 4, 2003): 82; and Shelly Branch, "Critical Curds; At Kraft, Making Cheese 'Fun' Is Serious Business," *Wall Street Journal* (May 31, 2002): A1, A6.

Formulating Business-Level Strategy

One model for formulating strategy, Porter's competitive strategies, provides a framework for business unit competitive action. Michael E. Porter studied a number of business organizations and proposed that business-level strategies are the result of five competitive forces in the company's environment.[71] More recently he examined the impact of the Internet on business-level strategy.[72] New web-based technology is influencing industries in both positive and negative ways, and understanding this impact is essential for managers to accurately analyze their competitive environments and design appropriate strategic actions.

Exhibit 5.12 illustrates the competitive forces in a company's environment and indicates some ways that Internet technology is affecting each area. These forces help to determine a company's position vis-à-vis competitors in the industry environment.

1. *Potential new entrants.* Examples of two potential barriers to entry that can keep out new competitors are *capital requirements* and *economies of scale.* Entering the automobile industry, for instance, is far more costly than starting a specialized mail-order business. In general, Internet technology has made it much easier for new companies to enter an industry by curtailing the need for organizational elements such as an established sales force, physical assets such as buildings and machinery, and access to existing supplier and sales channels.

EXHIBIT 5.12

Porter's Five Forces Affecting Industry Competition

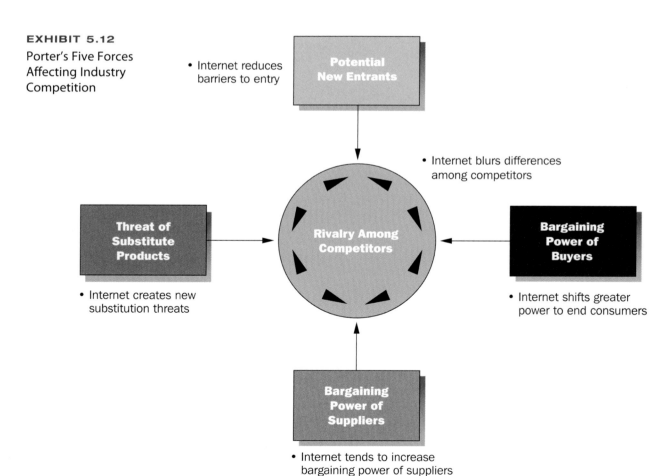

SOURCES: Based on Michael E. Porter, *Competitive Strategy: Techniques for Analyzing Industries and Competitors* (New York: Free Press, 1980); and Michael E. Porter, "Strategy and the Internet," *Harvard Business Review* (March 2001): 63–78.

2. *Bargaining power of buyers.* Informed customers become empowered customers. The Internet provides easy access to a wide array of information about products, services, and competitors, thereby greatly increasing the bargaining power of end consumers. For example, a customer shopping for a car can gather extensive information about various options, such as wholesale prices for new cars or average value for used vehicles, detailed specifications, repair records, and even whether a used car has ever been involved in an accident.

3. *Bargaining power of suppliers.* The concentration of suppliers and the availability of substitute suppliers are significant factors in determining supplier power. The sole supplier of engines to a manufacturer of small airplanes will have great power, for example. The impact of the Internet in this area can be both positive and negative. That is, procurement over the Web tends to give a company greater power over suppliers, but the Web also gives suppliers access to more customers, as well as the ability to reach end users. Overall, the Internet tends to raise the bargaining power of suppliers.

4. *Threat of substitute products.* The power of alternatives and substitutes for a company's product may be affected by changes in cost or in trends, such as increased health consciousness, which deflect buyer loyalty. Companies in the sugar industry suffered from the growing popularity of sugar substitutes. Manufacturers of aerosol spray cans lost business as environmentally conscious consumers chose other products. The Internet created threats of new substitutes by enabling new approaches to meeting customer needs. For example, offers of low-cost airline tickets over the Internet hurt traditional travel agencies.

5. *Rivalry among competitors.* As illustrated in Exhibit 5.13, rivalry among competitors is influenced by the preceding four forces, as well as by cost and product differentiation. With the leveling force of the Internet and information technology, many companies have more difficulty finding ways to distinguish themselves from their competitors, which intensifies rivalry.

Porter referred to the "advertising slugfest" when describing the scrambling and jockeying for position that often occurs among fierce rivals within an industry. Famous examples include the competitive rivalry between Pepsi and Coke, between UPS and FedEx, and between Home Depot and Lowe's. The rivalry between Gillette Company (which has been purchased by Procter & Gamble) and Schick, the number two maker of razors (now owned by Energizer), may become just as heated. Although Gillette is still way ahead, introduction of the Schick Quattro and a massive advertising campaign helped Schick's 2003 sales grow 149 percent while Gillette's razor sales slipped. In the two years after the Quattro was introduced, Schick's market share for replacement blades jumped 6 percent while Gillette's declined. In the fall of 2005, Schick brought out a battery-powered version of Quattro, aimed directly at stealing market share from Gillette's M3Power. Gillette took the next shot with its announcement of the new Fusion five-blade razor.[73]

◄·· TAKE ACTION

As a new manager, examine the competitive forces affecting your organization. As a lower-level manager, what can you do as to help the firm find or keep its competitive edge through a differentiation, cost leadership, or focus strategy?

EXHIBIT 5.13

Types of Organizational Change

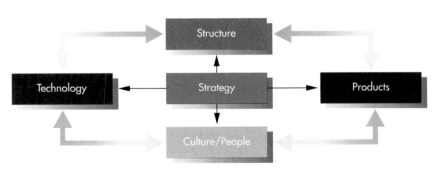

SOURCE: Based on Harold J. Leavitt, "Applied Organizational Change in Industry: Structural, Technical, and Human Approaches," in *New Perspectives in Organization Research*, ed. W. W. Cooper, H. J. Leavitt, and M. W. Shelly II (New York: Wiley, 1964), 55–74.

COMPETITIVE STRATEGIES

In finding its competitive edge within these five forces, Porter suggests that a company can adopt one of three strategies: differentiation, cost leadership, or focus. The organizational characteristics typically associated with each strategy are summarized in Exhibit 5.14.

Differentiation. The **differentiation strategy** involves an attempt to distinguish the firm's products or services from others in the industry. The organization may use advertising, distinctive product features, exceptional service, or new technology to achieve a product perceived as unique. The differentiation strategy can be profitable because customers are loyal and will pay high prices for the product. Examples of products that have benefited from a differentiation strategy are Harley-Davidson motorcycles, Snapper lawn equipment, and Gore-Tex fabrics, all of which are perceived as distinctive in their markets.

When lawn equipment maker Simplicity bought Snapper, for example, one of the first things that executives did was to pull Snapper products out of Wal-Mart. Whereas most manufacturers do whatever they can to sell through the giant retailer, Simplicity's managers recognized that selling mowers at Wal-Mart was incompatible with their strategy, which

differentiation strategy
an attempt to distinguish the firm's products or services from others in the industry.

EXHIBIT 5.14

Organizational Characteristics of Porter's Competitive Strategies

Strategy	Organizational Characteristics
Differentiation	Acts in a flexible, loosely knit way, with strong coordination among departments
	Strong capability in basic rewards
	Creative flair, thinks "out of the box"
	Strong marketing abilities
	Rewards employee innovation
	Corporate reputation for quality or technological leadership
Cost Leadership	Strong central authority; tight cost controls
	Maintains standard operating procedures
	Easy-to-use manufacturing technologies
	Highly efficient procurement and distribution systems
	Close supervision, finite employee empowerment
Focus	Frequent, detailed control reports
	May use combination of above policies directed at particular strategic target
	Values and rewards flexibility and customer intimacy
	Measures cost of providing service and maintaining customer loyalty
	Pushes empowerment to employees with customer contact

SOURCES: Based on Michael E. Porter, *Competitive Strategy: Techniques for Analyzing Industries and Competitors* (New York: The Free Press: 1980); Michael Treacy and Fred Wiersema, "How Market Leaders Keep Their Edge," *Fortune* (February 6, 1995): 88–98; and Michael A. Hitt, R. Duane Ireland, and Robert E. Hoskisson, *Strategic Management* (St. Paul, MN: West, 1995): 100–113.

Spotlight on Skills

White Stripes

Jack White didn't want to be like anyone else. As singer-guitarist of the White Stripes band, he made sure the image was unique and well-planned, whether it involved musical arrangements or the black-white-red color scheme. Jack White enters a room like the "real thing," along with the drummer, black-and-red-clad ex-wife Meg White. Most indie-rock tastemakers want bands that look like they do, but Jack White goes more for smoke and mirrors, the strategy that caused detractors to relegate White Stripes to the category of gimmickry. Jack believes his attention to the funky details are what makes the band successful. "Everything from your haircut to your clothes to the type of instrument you play to the melody of a song to the rhythm—they're all tricks to get people to pay attention," he said.

Having been ripped off by small record labels, White Stripes doesn't mind being with a major record company. This doesn't mean the band will go mainstream, as most bands covet. White Stripes is sticking to its indie-roots. The most recent album, "Icky Thump," is a more traditional sound for the band. White said, "There are songs on this album that could easily have been on

our first," adding that the Beatles created a nearly impossible expectation of reinvention for rock groups. Fans want to hear some new and a lot of the familiar songs, says Jack.

Formerly a young, aspiring film maker, Jack changed to music, but he runs his operation much like a director would, creating a whole universe from casting to costumes to props. Almost everything White Stripes does, then, is strategic and premeditated, but not the music. "Things happen song by song and by accident," he notes. "If you admit to the song that you aren't in control, then some good things start to happen."

Success can be measured by the tours, which started in small clubs and now include arenas. Jack still is surprised that a two-person band can keep the audience interested for more than three songs. In addition to urban tours, the band is going to outer-Canadian areas such as Yellowknife and Nunavut, not knowing if anyone has even heard of White Stripes there. Jack welcomes new audiences, with a strategy of having major-market cities pay for the tour and then become experimental artists in the new locations. On the last South American tour, Jack said, "Like, do we even have fans here in Chile?" The band was sold out. Some fans even brought homemade White Stripes t-shirts.

SOURCE: Alan Light, "Still True to the Red, White and Black," *The New York Times*, June 10, 2007, 26.

emphasizes quality, dependability, durability, and cachet rather than high volume and low cost. Customers can buy a lawn mower at Wal-Mart for less than a hundred bucks, but the least expensive Snapper is about $350 and is built to last for decades.[74] Service companies such as Starbucks, Whole Foods Market, and IKEA also use a differentiation strategy.

Companies that pursue a differentiation strategy typically require strong marketing abilities, a creative flair, and a reputation for leadership.[75] A differentiation strategy can reduce rivalry with competitors if buyers are loyal to a company's brand. Successful differentiation also can reduce the bargaining power of large buyers by making other products less attractive, which also helps the firm fight off threats of substitute products. In addition, differentiation erects entry barriers in the form of customer loyalty, which a new entrant into the market would have difficulty overcoming.

Cost Leadership. With a **cost leadership strategy,** the organization aggressively seeks efficient facilities, pursues cost reductions, and uses tight cost controls to produce products more efficiently than competitors do. A low-cost position means that the company can undercut competitors' prices and still offer comparable quality and earn a reasonable profit. Comfort Inn and Motel 6 are examples of low-priced alternatives to Four Seasons and Marriott. Enterprise Rent-A-Car is a low-priced alternative to Hertz.

Being a low-cost producer provides a successful strategy to defend against the five competitive forces in Exhibit 5.13. For example, the most efficient, low-cost company is in the best position to succeed in a price war while still making a profit. Likewise, the low-cost producer is protected from powerful customers and suppliers because customers cannot find lower prices elsewhere and other buyers would have less slack for price negotiation

cost leadership strategy
an aggressive attempt to seek efficient facilities, pursue cost reductions, and use tight cost controls to produce products more efficiently than competitors.

TAKE ACTION

To succeed, try to differentiate your product—or have highly competitive prices.

with suppliers. If substitute products or new entrants come onto the scene, the low-cost producer is better positioned than higher-cost rivals to prevent loss of market share. The low price acts as a barrier against new entrants and substitute products.[76]

Focus. With a **focus strategy,** the organization concentrates on a specific regional market or buyer group. The company uses either a differentiation approach or a cost leadership approach, but only for a narrow target market. Save-A-Lot, described earlier, uses a focused cost leadership strategy, placing its stores in low-income areas. Another example is low-cost leader Southwest Airlines, which was founded in 1971 to serve only three cities—Dallas, Houston, and San Antonio—and didn't fly outside of Texas for the first 8 years of its history. Managers aimed for controlled growth, gradually moving into new geographic areas where Southwest could provide short-haul service from city to city. Through a focus strategy, Southwest was able to grow rapidly and expand to other markets.[77]

Edward Jones Investments, a St. Louis-based brokerage house, uses a focused differentiation strategy, building its business in rural and small-town America and providing clients with conservative, long-term investment advice. According to management consultant Peter Drucker, the safety-first orientation means that Edward Jones delivers a product "that no Wall Street house has ever sold before: peace of mind."[78]

Assess Your Answer

2 It's a good idea to make the product or service available to as many customers as possible.

ANSWER: Creating a target market is almost always more effective. If you try to sell to everybody, you might end up impacting no one. This can be compared to light focused through a magnifying glass, which can create fire, while dissipated light has little effect.

Managers think carefully about which strategy will provide their company with its competitive advantage. Gibson Guitar Corp., famous in the music world for its innovative, high-quality products, found that switching to a low-cost strategy to compete against Japanese rivals such as Yamaha and Ibanez actually hurt the company. When managers realized that people wanted Gibson products because of its reputation, not its price, the company went back to a differentiation strategy and invested in new technology and marketing.[79]

In his studies, Porter found that some businesses did not consciously adopt one of these three strategies and were stuck with no strategic advantage. Without a strategic advantage,

focus strategy
concentration on a specific regional market or buyer group.

businesses earned below-average profits compared to those that used differentiation, cost leadership, or focus strategies. Similarly, a five-year study of management practices in hundreds of businesses, referred to as the *Evergreen Project,* found that a clear strategic direction was a key factor that distinguished winners from losers.[80]

Because the Internet is having such a profound impact on the competitive environment in all industries, companies now, more than ever, must distinguish themselves through careful strategic positioning in the marketplace.[81] The Internet tends to erode both cost leadership advantages and differentiation advantages by providing new tools for managing costs and giving consumers greater access to comparison shopping. Nevertheless, managers can find ways to incorporate the Internet into their strategic approaches in a way that provides unique value to customers in an efficient way. Sears, for example, uses the Web to showcase its line of Kenmore appliances, building the brand's reputation by providing detailed information in a relatively inexpensive way.[82]

PARTNERSHIP STRATEGIES

So far we have been discussing strategies that are based on how to compete with other companies. An alternative approach to strategy emphasizes **collaboration.** In some situations, companies can achieve competitive advantage by cooperating with other firms rather than competing with them. Partnership strategies are becoming increasingly popular as firms in all industries join with other organizations to promote innovation, expand markets, and pursue joint goals. At one time, partnering was a strategy adopted primarily by small firms that required greater marketing muscle or international access. Today, however, it has become a way of life for most companies, large and small. The question no longer is whether to collaborate but, rather, where, how much, and with whom to collaborate.[83]

Competition and cooperation often are present at the same time. Procter & Gamble and Clorox are fierce rivals in cleaning products and water purification, but both companies profited by collaborating on a new plastic wrap. P&G researchers invented a wrap that seals tightly only where it is pressed, but P&G didn't have a plastic wrap category. Managers negotiated a joint venture with Clorox to market the wrap under the well-established Glad brand name, and Glad Press & Seal became one of the company's most popular products. The two competitors continued the collaboration with the introduction of Glad Force Flex trash bags, which make use of a stretchable plastic invented in P&G's labs.[84]

The Internet is both driving and supporting the move toward partnership thinking. The ability to rapidly and smoothly conduct transactions, communicate information, exchange ideas, and collaborate on complex projects via the Internet means that companies such as Citigroup, Dow Chemical, and Herman Miller have been able to enter entirely new businesses by partnering in business areas that previously were unimaginable.[85] Many companies, including Target, Circuit City, Lands' End, and

collaboration
cooperating with other firms rather than competing with them.

•• CONCEPT CONNECTION
How do you compete with the likes of Nike? For Under Armour Inc., the phenomenally successful Baltimore company that manufactures high-performance, moisture-wicking athletic apparel, the key is *partnership strategies*. Pictured here are company founder Kevin Plank and Auburn University athletics director Jay Jacob announcing a five-year, $10.6 million *preferred supplier contract,* similar to deals the company has struck with Texas Tech and the University of Maryland. In addition, the upstart company has fueled its soaring sales by using *strategic business partnerships,* including the one with national retailers such as Dick's Sporting Goods Inc. Dick's now features Under Armour "concept shops" in several stores.

Golfsmith International, are gaining a stronger online presence by partnering with Amazon. com. Amazon maintains the site and processes the orders, and the retailers fill the orders from their own warehouses. The arrangement gives Amazon a new source of revenue and frees the retailers to focus on their bricks-and-mortar business while also gaining new customers online.[86]

Mutual dependencies and partnerships have become a fact of life, but the extent of collaboration varies. Organizations can choose to build cooperative relationships in many ways, such as through preferred suppliers, strategic business partnering, joint ventures, or mergers and acquisitions. Exhibit 5.14 illustrates these major types of strategic business relationships according to the amount of collaboration involved. With preferred supplier relationships, a company such as Wal-Mart, for example, develops a special relationship with a key supplier such as Procter & Gamble, which eliminates intermediaries by sharing complete information and reducing the costs of salespeople and distributors. Preferred supplier arrangements provide long-term security for both organizations, but the level of collaboration is relatively low.

Strategic business partnering requires a higher level of collaboration. Five of the largest hotel chains—Marriott International, Hilton Hotels Corp., Six Continents, Hyatt Corp., and Starwood Hotels and Resorts Worldwide Inc.—partnered to create their own website, Travelweb.com, to combat the growing power of intermediaries such as Expedia and Hotels. com. According to one senior vice president, the hotels felt a need to "take back our room product, and . . . sell it the way we want to sell it and maximize our revenues." At the same time, some chains are striving to build more beneficial partnerships with the third-party brokers.[87]

Still more collaboration is reflected in **joint ventures,** which are separate entities created with two or more active firms as sponsors. For example, International Truck and Engine Corporation has a joint venture with Ford Motor Company to build midsized trucks and diesel engine parts.[88] MTV Networks originally was created as a joint venture of Warner Communications and American Express. In a joint venture, organizations share the risks and costs associated with the new venture.

Mergers and acquisitions represent the ultimate step in collaborative relationships. U.S. business has been in the midst of a tremendous merger and acquisition boom. Consider the frenzied deal-making in the telecom industry alone. Sprint acquired Nextel, and Verizon Communications purchased MCI. SBC Communications Inc. acquired AT&T and took over the storied brand name, then announced plans to buy BellSouth, making AT&T once again the giant in the telecommunications industry.[89]

Using these various partnership strategies, today's companies simultaneously embrace competition *and* cooperation. Few companies can go it alone under the constant onslaught of international competition, changing technology, and new regulations. Most businesses choose a combination of competitive and partnership strategies that add to their overall sustainable advantage.[90]

Strategy Implementation and Control

The final step in the strategic management process is implementation—how strategy is put into action. Some people argue that strategy implementation is the most difficult and important part of strategic management.[91] No matter how brilliant the formulated strategy, the organization will not benefit if it is not implemented skillfully. Today's competitive environment requires growing recognition of the need for more dynamic approaches to implementing strategies.[92]

Strategy is not a static, analytical process. It requires vision, intuition, and employee participation. Effective strategy implementation requires that all aspects of the organization be in congruence with the strategy and that every individual's efforts be coordinated toward accomplishing strategic goals.[93]

joint ventures
separate entities created with two or more active firms as sponsors, and the organizations share the associated risks and costs.

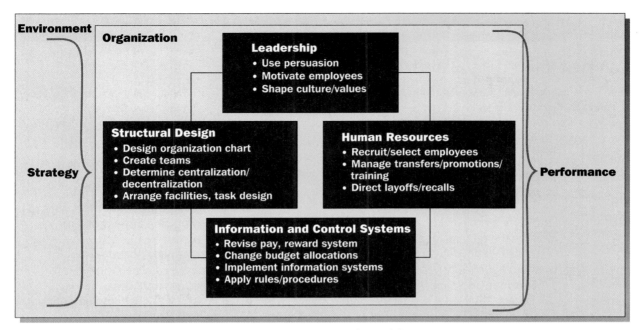

SOURCE: Adapted from Jay R. Galbraith and Robert K. Kazanjian, *Strategy Implementation: Structure, Systems, and Process*, 2d ed. (St. Paul, MN: West, 1986): 115. Used with permission.

EXHIBIT 5.15
Tools for Putting Strategy into Action

INFORMATION AND CONTROL SYSTEMS

Strategy implementation involves using several tools—parts of the firm that can be adjusted to put strategy into action—as illustrated in Exhibit 5.15. Once a new strategy is selected, it is implemented through changes in leadership, structure, information and control systems, and human resources.[94] Implementation involves regularly making difficult decisions about doing things in a way that supports rather than undermines the organization's chosen strategic approach. The remaining chapters of this book examine in detail topics including leadership, organizational structure, information and control systems, and human resource management.

LEADERSHIP

The primary key to successful strategy implementation is leadership, the ability to influence people to adopt the new behaviors needed for strategy implementation. An integral part of implementing strategy is to build consensus. People throughout the organization must believe in the new strategy and have a strong commitment to achieving the vision and goals. **Leadership** means using persuasion, motivating employees, and shaping culture and values to support the new strategy.

Managers can make speeches to employees, build coalitions of people who support the new strategic direction, and persuade middle managers to go along with their vision for the company. At IBM, for example, CEO Sam Palmisano uses leadership to align people throughout the organization with a new strategy aimed at getting IBM intimately involved in revamping and even running customers' business operations. To implement the new approach, Palmisano dismantled the executive committee that previously presided over strategic initiatives and replaced it with committees made up of people from all over the company. He's investing tons of money to teach managers at all levels how to lead rather than control their staffs. And he's talking to people all over the company, appealing to their sense of pride and uniting them behind this new vision and strategy.[95] With a clear sense of direction and a shared purpose, employees feel motivated, challenged, and empowered to pursue new strategic goals.

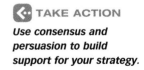 **TAKE ACTION**
Use consensus and persuasion to build support for your strategy.

leadership
the ability to influence people to adopt the new behaviors needed for strategy implementation.

NEW MANAGER SELF TEST

What Is Your Strategy Strength?

As a new manager, what are your strengths in strategy formulation and implementation? To find out, think about how you handle challenges and issues in your school or job. Then mark (a) or (b) for each of the following items, depending on which is more descriptive of your behavior. There are no right or wrong answers. Respond to each item as it best describes how you respond to work situations.

1. When keeping records, I tend to
   _____ **a.** be careful about documentation.
   _____ **b.** be haphazard about documentation.

2. If I run a group or a project, I
   _____ **a.** have the general idea and let others figure out how to do the tasks.
   _____ **b.** try to figure out specific goals, timelines, and expected outcomes.

3. My thinking style could be more accurately described as
   _____ **a.** linear thinker, going from A to B to C.
   _____ **b.** thinking like a grasshopper, hopping from one idea to another.

4. In my office or home, things are
   _____ **a.** here and there in various piles.
   _____ **b.** laid out neatly or at least in reasonable order.

5. I take pride in developing
   _____ **a.** ways to overcome a barrier to a solution.
   _____ **b.** new hypotheses about the underlying cause of a problem.

6. I can best help strategy by encouraging
   _____ **a.** openness to a wide range of assumptions and ideas.
   _____ **b.** thoroughness when implementing new ideas.

7. One of my strengths is
   _____ **a.** commitment to making things work.
   _____ **b.** commitment to a dream for the future.

8. I am most effective when I emphasize
   _____ **a.** inventing original solutions.
   _____ **b.** making practical improvements.

SCORING AND INTERPRETATION: For *Strategic Formulator* strength, score one point for each (a) answer for items 2, 4, 6, and 8, and for each (b) answer for items 1, 3, 5, and 7. For *Strategic Implementer* strength, score one point for each (b) answer for questions 2, 4, 6, and 8, and for each (a) answer for questions 1, 3, 5, and 7. Which of your two scores is higher, and by how much? The higher score indicates your strategy strength.

New managers with implementer strengths tend to work within the situation and improve it by making it more efficient and reliable. Leaders with the formulator strength push toward out-of-the-box strategies and like to seek dramatic breakthroughs. Both styles are essential to strategic management. Strategic formulators often use their skills to create entirely new strategies, and strategic implementers often work with strategic improvements and implementation.

If the difference between your two scores is 2 or less, you have a balanced formulator/implementer style and work well in both arenas. If the difference is 4–5, you have a moderately strong style and probably work best in the area of your strength. And if the difference is 7–8, you have a distinctive strength and almost certainly would want to work in the area of your strength rather than in the opposite domain.

SOURCES: Adapted from Dorothy Marcic and Joe Seltzer, *Organizational Behavior: Experiences and Cases* (Cincinnati, OH: South-Western, 1998): 284–287, and William Miller, *Innovation Styles* (Global Creativity Corporation, 1997).

Another way in which leaders build consensus and commitment is through broad participation. When people participate in strategy formulation, implementation is easier because managers and employees already understand the reasons for the new strategy and feel more committed to it.

3 Top managers should get together and develop a plan, then announce it to employees.

ANSWER: It is much more effective to involve employees either in the development of goals or at least in meetings that have a great deal of two-way communication. Engaging employees in meaningful discussions regarding the goals helps to gain commitment and can increase motivation levels greatly.

HUMAN RESOURCES

The organization's *human resources* are its employees. The human resource function recruits, selects, trains, transfers, promotes, and lays off employees to achieve strategic goals. Training employees helps them understand the purpose and importance of a new strategy or helps them develop the necessary skills and behaviors.

New strategies involve change, which naturally generates resistance. Sometimes employees have to be let go and replaced. One newspaper shifted its strategy from an evening paper to a morning paper to compete with a large newspaper from a nearby city. The new strategy required a change from working daytimes to working from 1:00 p.m. to about midnight or so. The change fostered resentment and resistance among department heads. To implement the plan, 80 percent of the department heads had to be let go because they refused to cooperate. New people were recruited and placed in those positions, and the morning newspaper strategy became a resounding success.[96]

At IBM, employees in administration and computer repair were let go by the thousands. They were replaced by people who are skilled in business operations as well as technology.[97]

Implementation during Turbulent Times

The challenges of implementing strategy continue to escalate with the increased complexity and turbulence in today's business environment. Many managers are confident that they have found the right strategy to provide a competitive advantage, but they are less optimistic about their ability to implement it. Three issues that are particularly critical for implementing strategy during turbulent times are a global mind-set, paying close attention to corporate culture, and embracing the Internet and other information technologies.

GLOBAL MIND-SET

To implement strategies on a global scale, managers have to adopt a global mind-set and be aware of various implementation issues. Flexibility and openness emerge as mandatory leadership skills. Structural issues are more complex as managers struggle to find the proper mix to achieve the desired level of global integration and local responsiveness, as discussed earlier. Information, control, and reward systems have to fit the values and incentives within the local cultures. Finally, the recruitment, training, transfer, promotion, and layoff of international human resources create an array of problems not confronted in North America. To be effective internationally, managers have to apply a global perspective to strategy implementation.

For example, one well-respected multinational firm formed a task force of U.S. employees to review and revise workforce policies in connection with a new strategy.

Employees from different levels and functional areas met for months and sent employee surveys to all U.S.-based facilities to obtain wider input. Top executives reviewed and approved the final draft. They were surprised when the streamlined workforce manual, which reduced the number of policies from 120 to 10 core policies, met with resistance and even hostility by the overseas units. Managers' lack of a global mind-set led them to assume incorrectly that the international units would accept whatever was handed down from U.S. headquarters.

CORPORATE CULTURE

At the same time that managers need a global mind-set, they have to create and maintain a cohesive corporate culture that supports the strategy. *Culture* is the link between strategy and performance outcomes, and different culture styles are better suited to different strategic directions.[98] Recall our discussion of different types of culture and the high-performance culture from Chapter 2. A study of the world's most admired companies, as reported annually in *Fortune* magazine, found that managers in these organizations pay close attention to culture and to the values that contribute to strategic success.[99] Managers want to develop a culture that is oriented toward performance—encouraging everyone to adopt the behaviors and attitudes needed to meet the company's strategic goals and holding everyone responsible for success.[100]

An example comes from Ansys, a developer of engineering simulation products used to predict product design behavior in manufacturing operations. Ansys has more than two dozen sales offices on three continents and a network of partners in 40 countries. Serving diverse customers around the world with superior technology requires a commitment to a global mind-set as well as a culture of intense customer focus. Ansys managers built a family-like, high-performance culture that embraces customers as well as employees. Employees are committed to the vision of meeting customers' emerging technology needs. Because people feel appreciated and cared about, they feel safe taking risks that lead to better products and better service. A key aspect is, as one executive put it, "giving people enough leeway, enough rope, but not letting them hang themselves." Employees are empowered with decision-making authority, but the company has in place systems that prevent people from possibly taking a hard fall.[101]

INFORMATION TECHNOLOGY

A final concern for managers implementing strategy during turbulent times is to incorporate the Internet and other information technology. For example, Dell pioneered the use of an online system to let customers configure computers to their exact specifications and submit the order over the Web, saving the cost of salespeople. Many firms now use online mass customization to decrease costs while enhancing their product mix and building their brand reputation.[102]

Another company that uses the Internet successfully to implement strategy is independent toy retailer Kazoo & Company. Owner Diane Nelson competes with giant retailers such as Wal-Mart by using a differentiation strategy that focuses primarily on selling educational, nonviolent toys. She considered franchising as a way to grow the business but decided that expanding via a website would better enable the company to maintain its distinctiveness. Kazoo.com quickly became a go-to site for people seeking specialty toys, and Nelson negotiated deals with some vendors that will send products directly to customers who order online. About 40 percent of Kazoo's business now is online, and at least a quarter of that comes from overseas.[103]

Summary

An organization exists for a single, overriding purpose known as its *mission*—the basis for strategic goals and plans. Goals within the organization are aligned in a hierarchical fashion, beginning with strategic goals, followed by tactical and operational goals. Plans are defined similarly, with strategic, tactical, and operational plans to achieve the goals. Other goal concepts include characteristics of effective goals and goal-setting behavior.

Among the several types of plans are strategic, tactical, operational, single-use, standing, and contingency plans, as well as management by objectives (MBO). Two extensions of contingency planning are scenario building and crisis planning. Scenarios, alternative vivid pictures of what the future might be like, provide a framework for managers to cope with unexpected or unpredictable events. Crisis planning involves the stages of prevention, preparation, and containment.

In the past, planning was almost always done entirely by top managers, by consultants, or by central planning departments. During turbulent times, decentralized planning means that people throughout the organization are involved in establishing dynamic plans that can meet rapidly changing needs in the environment. Guidelines for planning in a turbulent environment include starting with a powerful mission and vision, setting stretch goals for excellence, embracing event-driven planning, using performance dashboards, and organizing temporary task forces that may include outside stakeholders. Planning is evolutionary, and plans are adapted continually to meet new needs and changing markets. Top managers, however, still are responsible for providing a guiding mission and vision for the future and creating a solid framework for planning and goal setting.

Strategic management begins with an evaluation of the organization's current mission, goals, and strategy. This evaluation is followed by situation analysis (called SWOT analysis), which examines opportunities and threats in the external environment as well as strengths and weaknesses within the organization. Situation analysis leads to the formulation of explicit strategies, which indicate how the company intends to achieve a competitive advantage. Managers formulate strategies that focus on core competencies, develop synergy, and create value.

An approach to business-level strategy is based on Porter's competitive forces and strategies. The Internet is having a profound impact on the competitive environment, and managers should consider its influence when analyzing these five competitive forces and formulating business strategies. An alternative approach to strategic thought emphasizes cooperation rather than competition. Partnership strategies include preferred supplier arrangements, strategic business partnering, joint ventures, and mergers and acquisitions. Most of today's companies choose a mix of competitive and partnership strategies. Once business strategies have been formulated, functional strategies for supporting them can be developed.

Even the most creative strategies have no value if they cannot be translated into action. Implementation is the most important and most difficult part of strategy. Managers implement strategy by aligning all parts of the organization to be in congruence with the new strategy. Three areas of concentration for strategy implementation are leadership, information and control systems, and human resources. Additional issues for managers in today's turbulent and complex environment require adopting a global mind-set, paying close attention to corporate culture, and embracing use of the Internet in implementation.

Discussion Questions

1. Companies such as Wal-Mart and Valero Energy Corp. were days ahead of FEMA in responding to relief operations after Katrina and Rita devastated the Gulf Coast in the fall of 2005. Why do you think they were able to respond more quickly? What types of planning would help federal, state, and local governments prepare for unexpected events?

2. How might having a clear, written mission statement benefit a small organization? Write a brief mission statement for a local business with which you are familiar.

3. What strategic plans could the college or university at which you are taking this management course adopt to compete for students in the marketplace? Would these plans depend on the school's goals?

4. If you were a top manager of a medium-sized real estate sales agency, would you use MBO? If so, give examples of goals you might set for managers and sales agents.

5. How do you think planning in today's organizations compares to planning 25 years ago? Do you think planning becomes more important or less important in a world where everything is changing rapidly and crises are a regular part of organizational life? Why?

6. Assume that Southern University decides to (1) raise its admission standards, and (2) initiate a business fair to which local townspeople will be invited. What types of plans might it use to carry out these two activities?

7. Come up with a stretch goal for some aspect of your own life. How do you determine if pursuing a stretch goal makes sense to you?

8. Perform a situation analysis (SWOT) for the school or university you attend. Do you think university administrators consider the same factors when devising their strategy?

9. Using Porter's competitive strategies, how would you describe the strategies of Wal-Mart, Bloomingdale's, and Target? Do any of these companies also use partnership strategies? Discuss.

10. Describe how the Internet increases the bargaining power of consumers, one of Porter's five competitive forces. Have you felt increased power as a consumer because of the Internet? Explain.

Dear Dr. Dorothy

I share an office cubicle with Matthew, who leaves his stuff all over the place, sometimes on my floor space and even my desk. The smell of his stale coffee is awful, and I don't like looking at his moldy donuts. It's hard to work in this mess! Matthew hates it when I ask him to clean up, and he quotes the company trainer from our orientation program, who talked about the need for flexibility and creativity in our workplace. Am I inflexible? What should I do?

Irritated in Tallahassee

Dear Irritated,

It's hard for Dr. Dorothy to tell from your letter if you are inflexible in life, but in this case it's more a matter of calling a slob a slob. The requirement for companies to be flexible and creative doesn't include allowing a workspace to become a pig's place. You have every right to expect a minimum level of neatness in your work area, though Dr. Dorothy must caution you to do some self-reflection and determine whether you are compulsively organized.

Though difficult to face, if you are a bit neurotic, lighten up! If you determine that you are relatively normal (though who is, really, these days?), go to Matthew and try to negotiate a "Officemate Contract" that would include not only a minimum level of tidiness but also things such as how loud to talk on the phone, looking at things on the other's desk, taking messages, etc.

You may need a trusted third-party facilitator from HR so neither of you will start hurling obscenities. In the event Matthew refuses to discuss such a contract or your negotiations create more calamity than clarity, you should ask to be transferred to a different, and hopefully more work-inducing, cubicle.

Next time, plan ahead and collaborate on the contract *before* you start sharing office space. Better yet, Dr. Dorothy recommends that you work very hard so one day you will have your own office and no longer will be stuck in a cubicle.

Self Learning

Company Crime Wave

Senior managers in your organization are concerned about internal theft. Your department has been assigned the task of writing an ethics policy that defines employee theft and prescribes penalties. Stealing goods is easily classified as theft, but other activities are more ambiguous. Before writing the policy, go through the following list and decide which behaviors should be defined as stealing and whether penalties should apply. Discuss the items with your department members until reaching agreement. Classify each item as an example of (1) theft, (2) acceptable behavior, or (3) in between with respect to written policy. Is it theft when an employee

- Gets paid for overtime not worked?
- Takes a longer lunch or coffee break than authorized?
- Punches a time card for another?
- Comes in late or leaves early?

- Fakes injury to receive workers' compensation?
- Takes care of personal business on company time?
- Occasionally uses company copying machines or makes long-distance telephone calls for personal purposes?
- Takes a few stamps, pens, or other supplies for personal use?
- Takes money from the petty cash drawer?
- Uses company vehicles or tools for his or her own purposes but returns them?

- Damages merchandise so a cohort can purchase it at a discount?
- Accepts a gift from a supplier?

Now consider those items rated "in between." Do these items represent ethical issues as defined in Chapter 4? How should these items be handled in the company's written policy?

Group Learning

Course Goal Setting

Consider goals for yourself regarding doing well in this course. What do you need to do in order to get a good grade? Goals should be according the criteria for effective goals listed in this chapter. In addition, you need a system to monitor your progress, such as the table below, which shows the types of goals you may choose to select for yourself.

1. Complete the table below on your own. Fill in each cell, writing down what you have done to achieve that goal. For example, under define vocabulary words, what would you need to remember those? Would you have to read them over six times, or write them down on flash cards, etc? List what you plan to do and/or did for each week. You also can add items of your own at the bottom of the table.

2. In groups of 3 or 4, compare your goals and what you need to do to achieve your goals.

3. How similar and different were the implementation strategies of group members? Which ones seem most likely to be most effective?

Goals	Class weeks			
	first week (from now)	second week	third week	fourth week
1. 100% attendance				
2. Class notes				
3. Read assigned chapters				
4. Outline chapters				
5. Define margin terms				
6. Answer end-of-chapter Discussion Questions				
7. Complete Self Learning				
8. Class participation				
9.				
10.				

Your instructor may ask you to turn in your monitor sheets at the end of the course.

copyright © 1996 by Dorothy Marcic.

SOURCE: Nancy C. Morey, "Applying Goal Setting in the Classroom, *The Organizational Behavior Teaching Review* 11, no. 4 (1986–87): 53–59.

Action Learning

Developing Strategy for a Small Business

Instructions: In groups of 4–6, select a local business with which you (or group members) are familiar. Complete the following activities.

	Internal (within company)	External (outside company)
Positive	Strengths:	Opportunities:
Negative	Weaknesses:	Threats:

Activity 1 Perform a SWOT analysis for the business.

SWOT Analysis for _____ (name of company)

Activity 2 Write a statement of the business's current strategy.

Activity 3 Decide on a goal you would like the business to achieve in 2 years, and write a statement of proposed strategy for achieving that goal.

Activity 4 Write a statement describing how the proposed strategy will be implemented.

Activity 5 What have you learned from this exercise?

Ethical Dilemma

Inspire Learning Corp.

When the idea first occurred to her, it seemed like such a win-win situation. Now she wasn't so sure. Marge Brygay was a hard-working sales rep for Inspire Learning Corporation, a company intent on becoming the top educational software provider in 5 years. That newly adopted strategic goal translated into an ambitious million-dollar sales target for each of Inspire's sales reps. At the beginning of the fiscal year, her share of the sales department's operational goal seemed entirely reasonable to Marge. She believed in Inspire's products. The company had developed innovative, highly regarded math, language, science, and social studies programs for the K–12 market.

What set the software apart was a foundation in truly cutting-edge research. Marge had seen for herself how Inspire programs could engage whole classrooms of normally unmotivated kids, and the significant rise in test scores on those increasingly important standardized tests bore out her subjective impressions.

But now, just days before the end of the year, Marge's sales were $1,000 short of her million-dollar goal. The sale that would have put her comfortably over the top fell through because of last-minute cuts in one large school system's budget. At first she was nearly overwhelmed with frustration, but then it occurred to her that if she were to contribute $1,000 to Central High, the inner-city high school in her territory probably most in need of what she had for sale, the school could purchase the software and put her over the top.

Her scheme certainly would benefit Central High students. Achieving her sales goal would make Inspire happy, and it wouldn't harm her, either professionally or financially. Reaching the goal would earn her a $10,000 bonus check that would come in handy when the time would come to write out that first tuition check for her oldest child, who had just been accepted to a well-known, private university.

Initially this it seemed like the ideal solution all the way around. The more she thought about it, though, the more it didn't sit well with her conscience. Time was running out. She had to decide what to do.

What Would You Do?

1. Donate the $1,000 to Central High, and consider the $10,000 bonus a good return on your gift.

2. Accept the fact you didn't quite make your sales goal this year. Figure out ways to work smarter next year to increase the odds of achieving your target.

3. Don't make the donation, but investigate whether any other ways were available to help Central High raise the funds that would allow the school to purchase the much-needed educational software.

SOURCE: Based on Shel Horowitz, "Should Mary Buy Her Own Bonus?" *Business Ethics* (Summer 2005): 34.

Case for Critical Analysis

H.I.D.

Consultant Keith Houck strode into the conference room in Bill Collins's wake. Bill, the president of H.I.D., had hired Keith to help the hotel company's management team with strategic planning. Wasting no time, Bill introduced Keith to human resources director Karen Setz, marketing head Tony Briggs, hotel operations chief Dave King, and accountant Art Johnson. Already written in large block letters on an easel in the front of the room was the company's 10-year-old mission statement: "H.I.D. strives to exceed the expectations of our guests by providing excellent value in well-run hotels located off the beaten track. In this way, we will meet our profit, quality, and growth goals."

Keith, of course, had digested all of the background materials that the president had sent him, so he knew the company currently owned 21 properties—the original 10 Holiday Inns and 2 Quality Inns, all in Georgia, plus 8 hotels in Canada and a property in the Caribbean, acquired since Bill assumed the presidency 5 years ago. Keith also was well aware that even though H.I.D. was a reasonably profitable company, Bill wasn't satisfied.

The consultant started the ball rolling by asking each person in the room to describe his or her vision for domestic operations over the next 10 years. How many hotels should H.I.D. own? Where should they be located, and what should the target market be? As the managers shared their views, Keith summarized their answers on the flip chart.

The consultant wasn't surprised that Bill's goals were the most ambitious. He advocated for an intermediate goal of adding 27 properties in 5 years and a long-term goal of 50 in 10 years. The other managers didn't come close, calling for only 15 hotels to be added in 5 years and no more than 20 over a decade. The H.I.D. senior managers just sat and stared at the figures.

Keith asked for reactions. After an uncomfortable silence, Dave was the first to jump into the fray. "We can't build something like five hotels a year. We would outpace our income. And we couldn't run them—certainly not given our current staffing. I don't see how we could afford to hire the people we'd need." Art nodded in agreement.

"You know, we've always concentrated on medium-priced hotels in smaller towns where we don't have much competition," Tony pointed out.

Karen jumped in. "Well, do we need to think about moving to bigger towns now, like maybe Jacksonville? We've got one property in Atlanta already. Maybe we should look into building another one there."

"Why stick so close to home?" Bill asked. "You know, we're already looking at the possibility of going to Jacksonville. But why stop there? We've got an interesting opportunity out in California, and we might have another one in New Jersey."

Keith was beginning to fully appreciate the breadth and depth of the job he had on his hands. He looked at the mission statement, reviewed the list of current properties, and realized, as he listened to the managers, that nothing really matched up. So now what should he do?

Questions

1. What are the causes of the confusion confronting Keith Houck? Is H.I.D. ready to formulate a strategic plan? Why or why not?

2. If you were Keith Houck, what questions would you ask the managers? What steps would you recommend in your effort to help H.I.D. successfully formulate strategic goals and plans?

3. If you were Bill Collins, what might you have done differently during your tenure as H.I.D. president?

SOURCE: Based on a case provided by James Higgins.

BIZ FLIX

The Bourne Identity

Jason Bourne (Matt Damon) cannot remember who he is, but others believe he is an international assassin. Bourne tries to learn his identity with the help of his new friend and lover Marie (Franka Potente). Meanwhile, while CIA agents pursue him across Europe trying to kill him, Bourne slowly discovers that he is an extremely well-trained and lethal agent. The story, which is loosely based on Robert Ludlum's 1981 novel, was previously filmed in 1988 as a television miniseries starring Richard Chamberlain.

This scene is an edited version of the "Bourne's Game" sequence near the end of the film. Jason Bourne kills the hired assassin who tried to kill him the day after Jason and Marie arrived at the home of Eamon (Tim Dutton). Eamon is Marie's friend but is a stranger to Jason. Jason uses the dead man's cell phone after returning to his apartment in Paris,

France. He presses the redial button, which connects him to Conklin (Chris Cooper), the CIA manager who is looking for him. Listen carefully to Jason's conversation with Conklin as he walks along the right bank of the Seine River in Paris.

What to Watch for and Ask Yourself

1. Does Jason Bourne describe a plan to Conklin? If he does, what are the plan's elements? What is Bourne's goal?

2. Does Bourne assess the plan's execution to determine if it conforms to his goal? If so, what does he-do?

3. Was Bourne's plan successfully carried out? Why or why not? How does this scene relate to organizational strategic planning?

VIDEO CASE

Planning and Goal Setting at Cold Stone Creamery

Cake batter mixed with sprinkles and chocolate chips, doused with marshmallows. Did you ever think something as fun as ice cream could be so serious? Donald and Susan Sutherland, founders of Cold Stone Creamery are very serious about providing the "Ultimate Ice Cream Experience." They started in 1988 with a passion to serve the world's best ice cream, opening the first Cold Stone Creamery in Tempe, Arizona. Now, with more than 1,300 stores, people everywhere have become serious about ice cream.

Cold Stone Creamery isn't just selling ice cream, it is creating an experience. Freshly made ice cream in a dizzying array of unique flavors is folded together with any topping: nuts, fruits, candy, cookies, brownies, or others on a frozen granite stone while staff sing and dance for tips, mixing to the beat of the tune. These are not servers but artists. You can customize your "Creation" to any combination you can dream up, or choose from a menu of Cold Stone Original Creations, wild concoctions of ice cream decadence. Today, Cold Stone is the number 3 scoop shop chain, outselling Ben & Jerry's and Haagen-Dazs. It got there with a song and a dance and a careful plan.

Cold Stone started with a mission: "We will make people happy around the world by selling the highest quality, most creative ice cream experience with passion, excellence, and innovation." This is what drives every member of the company and defines their daily activity. It is the reason people come to work at Cold Stone. From that mission, the company's top executives set a company-wide goal of becoming America's number 1 best selling ice cream by December 31st, 2009. With careful planning, they created a strategic plan, their Pyramid of Success 2010, and broke this down into what it would mean for every member of the company to reach this goal. From the marketing department, to the creamery, to the staff 'on the stone,' they translated this goal into tactical and operational plans. In doing so, Cold Stone ensured that every employee knows what he or she is working towards and is empowered to make decisions that support that goal. The singing staff know that whatever they can do to get one more customer and 'make them happy' contributes to making Cold Stone #1.

The purpose of Cold Stone's Pyramid of Success 2010 is, as with all goal setting, to achieve high performance. But it is particularly successful because of a number of its characteristics.

From the company-wide goal to the organizational goals, each one is numerically defined and measurable. The marketing team can track its progress towards increasing sales by $100,000 over the next three years, the developers know how close they are to opening another 600 stores, and the front-line staff can count how many customers they brought in that day. Besides being measurable, each of these goals is meaningful to the employee and speaks to their area of focus. They are also within a defined time period, which helps in planning and resource allocation. The management of Cold Stone conducted large amounts of research and market analysis in determining these goals. They are a challenge to the company as a whole, but realistic and reachable. And further, the goals are linked to rewards, so every employee knows what waits for them on the other side of success.

Throughout their race to be #1, Cold Stone Creamery remains true to the "ice cream dram" of the Sutherlands to provide the "Ultimate Ice Cream Experience." They continue to be ice cream innovators, "redefining plain old regular ice cream into something truly extraordinary." In the works is a line of breakfast flavors that includes French Toast, Cinnabon, and Blueberry Muffin. In this culture of experimentation, they are also toying with Twinkie ice cream and Pop-Tart ice cream sandwiches. Each new flavor, like those before it, will continue to produce smiles and move Cold Stone ever closer to being #1.

Questions

1. Does Cold Stone Creamery represent a high performance approach to planning? Why or why not?

2. Cold Stone's Pyramid of Success 2010 represents an example of a single use plan. What might be a standing plan for a procedure for a staff 'on the stone'?

3. Locate Cold Stone's Pyramid of Success 2010 on their website and explain how it provides each of the benefits listed under "Purposes of Goals and Plans".

chapter 6

Decision Making

Learning Objectives

After studying this chapter, you should be able to:

1 Explain why decision making is an important component of good management.

2 Explain the difference between programmed and nonprogrammed decisions and the decision characteristics of risk, uncertainty, and ambiguity.

3 Describe the classical, administrative, and political models of decision making and their applications.

4 Identify the six steps used in managerial decision making.

5 Explain four personal decision styles used by managers.

6 Discuss the advantages and disadvantages of participative decision making.

7 Identify techniques for improving decision making in today's turbulent environment.

8 Describe the importance of information technology (IT) for organizations and the attributes of quality information.

New Manager's Questions

Please circle your opinion below each of the following statements.

Assess Your Answer

1 When a manager makes a well-reasoned decision, the next course of action is implementation.

1	2	3	4	5
strongly agree				strongly disagree

2 It is almost always better to get participation from others when making a decision.

1	2	3	4	5
strongly agree				strongly disagree

3 The increased technology in the workplace keeps people too disconnected from one another, making it harder to get their jobs done.

1	2	3	4	5
strongly agree				strongly disagree

Every organization grows, prospers, or fails as a result of decisions by its managers, and top executives make difficult decisions every day. Managers often are referred to as *decision makers*. Although many of their important decisions are strategic, such as Yang's decision whether to build a new factory, managers also make decisions about every other aspect of an organization, including structure, control systems, responses to the environment, and human resources. Managers scout for problems, make decisions for solving them, and monitor the consequences to see whether additional decisions are required. Good decision making is a vital part of good management because decisions determine how the organization solves its problems, allocates resources, and accomplishes its goals.

The business world is full of evidence of both good and bad decisions. For example, CEO Robert Iger is revamping Disney's "Old Media" image with his decision to make popular television programs from ABC and other Disney channels available free of charge on the Web, a first in the industry.[1] Cadillac managers ditched stuffy golf and yachting sponsorships and instead tied in with top Hollywood movies, a decision that boosted sales by 43 percent.[2] On the other hand, Maytag's decision to introduce the Neptune Drying Center was a complete flop. The new $1,200 product was hyped as a breakthrough in laundry, but the six-foot tall Drying Center wouldn't fit into most people's existing laundry rooms. Or, consider the decision of Timex managers to replace the classic tag line, "It takes a licking and keeps on ticking," with the bland "Life is ticking." The desire to modernize their company's image led Timex managers to ditch one of the most recognizable advertising slogans in the world in favor of a lame and rather depressing new one.[3] Decision making is not easy. It must be done amid ever-changing factors, unclear information, and conflicting points of view.

Chapter 5 described strategic planning. This chapter explores the decision process that underlies strategic planning. Plans and strategies are arrived at through decision making; the better the decision making, the better the strategic planning. First, we examine decision characteristics, and then we look at decision-making models and the steps executives should take when making important decisions. The chapter also examines participative decision making and discusses techniques for improving decision making in today's organizations. Later in the chapter, we will explore the management of IT and e-business. We begin by developing a basic understanding of IT and the types of information systems frequently used in organizations. Then, the chapter will look at the growing use of the Internet and e-business, including a discussion of fundamental e-business strategies, business-to-business marketplaces, use of IT in business operations, and the importance of knowledge management.

Types of Decisions and Problems

A **decision** is a choice made from available alternatives. For example, an accounting manager's selection among Colin, Tasha, and Carlos for the position of junior auditor is a decision. Many people assume that making a choice is the major part of decision making, but it is only a part.

Decision making is the process of identifying problems and opportunities and then resolving them. Decision making involves effort both before and after the actual choice. Thus, the decision as to whether to select Colin, Tasha, or Carlos requires the accounting manager to ascertain whether a new junior auditor is needed, determine the availability of potential job candidates, interview candidates to acquire necessary information, select one candidate, and follow up with the socialization of the new employee into the organization to ensure the decision's success.

decision
a choice made from available alternatives.

decision making
the process of identifying problems and opportunities and then resolving them.

PROGRAMMED AND NONPROGRAMMED DECISIONS

Management decisions typically fall into one of two categories: programmed and nonprogrammed. **Programmed decisions** involve situations that have occurred often enough to enable decision rules to be developed and applied in the future.[4] Programmed decisions are made in response to recurring organizational problems. The decision to reorder paper and other office supplies when inventories drop to a certain level is a programmed decision. Other programmed decisions concern the types of skills required to fill certain jobs, the reorder point for manufacturing inventory, exception reporting for expenditures 10 percent or more over budget, and selection of freight routes for product deliveries. After managers formulate decision rules, subordinates and others can make the decision, freeing managers for other tasks.

Nonprogrammed decisions are made in response to situations that are unique, are poorly defined and largely unstructured, and have important consequences for the organization. Many nonprogrammed decisions involve strategic planning because uncertainty is great, and decisions are complex. Decisions to build a new factory, develop a new product or service, enter a new geographical market, or relocate headquarters to another city are all nonprogrammed decisions. One good example of a nonprogrammed decision is ExxonMobil's decision to form a consortium to drill for oil in Siberia. One of the largest foreign investments in Russia, the consortium committed $4.5 billion before pumping the first barrel and expects a total capital cost of $12+ billion. The venture could produce 250,000 barrels a day, about 10 percent of ExxonMobil's global production. But if things go wrong, the oil giant, which has already invested some $4 billion, will take a crippling hit. At General Motors, top executives are facing multiple, enormously complex nonprogrammed decisions. The company has been rapidly losing market share, and 2005 losses totaled $10.6 billion. The giant corporation is also subject to six Securities and Exchange Commission (SEC) probes; is entangled in the impending bankruptcy of its largest supplier, Delphi; and is burdened by massive health care and unionized labor costs. Top GM executives have to analyze complex problems, evaluate alternatives, and make decisions about the best way to reverse GM's sagging fortunes and keep the company out of bankruptcy.[5]

CERTAINTY, RISK, UNCERTAINTY, AND AMBIGUITY

One primary difference between programmed and nonprogrammed decisions relates to the degree of certainty or uncertainty that managers deal with in making the decision. In a perfect world, managers would have all the information necessary for making decisions. In reality, however, some things are unknowable; thus, some decisions will fail to solve the problem or attain the desired outcome. Managers try to obtain information about decision alternatives that will reduce decision uncertainty. Every decision situation can be organized on a scale according to the availability of information and the possibility of failure. The four positions on the scale are certainty, risk, uncertainty, and ambiguity, as illustrated in Exhibit 6.1. Whereas programmed decisions can be made in situations involving certainty, many situations that managers deal with every day involve at least some degree of uncertainty and require nonprogrammed decision making.

Certainty. **Certainty** means that all the information the decision maker needs is fully available.[6] Managers have information on operating conditions, resource costs or constraints, and each course of action and possible outcome. For example, if a company considers a $10,000 investment in new equipment that it knows for certain will yield $4,000 in cost savings per year over the next five years, managers can calculate a before-tax

programmed decision
a decision made in response to a situation that has occurred often enough to enable decision rules to be developed and applied in the future.

nonprogrammed decision
a decision made in response to a situation that is unique, is poorly defined and largely unstructured, and has important consequences for the organization.

certainty
the situation in which all the information the decision maker needs is fully available.

EXHIBIT 6.1

Conditions That
Affect the Possibility
of Decision Failure

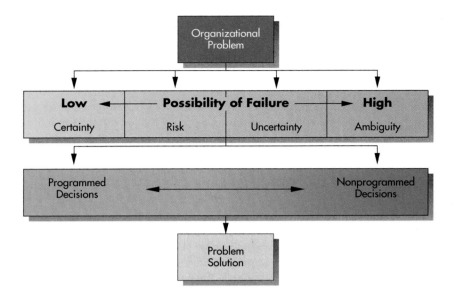

rate of return of about 40 percent. If managers compare this investment with one that will yield only $3,000 per year in cost savings, they can confidently select the 40 percent return. However, few decisions are certain in the real world. Most contain risk or uncertainty.

Risk. **Risk** means that a decision has clear-cut goals and that good information is available, but the future outcomes associated with each alternative are subject to chance. However, enough information is available to allow the probability of a successful outcome for each alternative to be estimated.[7] Statistical analysis might be used to calculate the probabilities of success or failure. The measure of risk captures the possibility that future events will render the alternative unsuccessful. For example, to make restaurant location decisions, McDonald's can analyze potential customer demographics, traffic patterns, supply logistics, and the local competition, and come up with reasonably good forecasts of how successful a restaurant will be in each possible location.[8]

Uncertainty. **Uncertainty** means that managers know which goals they want to achieve, but information about alternatives and future events is incomplete. Managers do not have enough information to be clear about alternatives or to estimate their risk. Factors that may affect a decision, such as price, production costs, volume, or future interest rates are difficult to analyze and predict. Managers may have to make assumptions from which to forge the decision even though it will be wrong if the assumptions are incorrect. Managers may have to come up with creative approaches to alternatives and use personal judgment to determine which alternative is best.

Managers at Wolters Kluwer, a leader in online information services based in The Netherlands, faced uncertainty as they considered ways to spark growth. The company had historically grown through acquisition, but that strategy had reached its limit. CEO Nancy McKinstry and other top managers talked with customers, analyzed the industry and Wolters Kluwer's market position and capabilities, and decided to shift the company toward growing through internal development of new products and services. Wolters Kluwer didn't have a track record in internal growth, and analysts were skeptical. Decisions about how to finance the internal development were complex and unclear, involving such

risk
a situation in which a decision has clear-cut goals, and good information is available, but the future outcomes associated with each alternative are subject to chance.

uncertainty
the situation that occurs when managers know which goals they want to achieve, but information about alternatives and future events is incomplete.

considerations as staff reductions, restructuring of departments and divisions, and shifting operations to lower-cost facilities. Furthermore, decisions had to be made about which new and existing products to fund and at what levels.[9] These decisions and others like them have no clear-cut solutions and require that managers rely on creativity, judgment, intuition, and experience to craft a response.

Many decisions made under uncertainty do not produce the desired results, but managers face uncertainty every day. They find creative ways to cope with uncertainty to make more effective decisions.

Ambiguity. **Ambiguity** is by far the most difficult decision situation. Ambiguity means that the goals to be achieved or the problem to be solved is unclear, alternatives are difficult to define, and information about outcomes is unavailable.[10] Ambiguity is what students would feel if an instructor created student groups, told each group to complete a project, but gave the groups no topic, direction, or guidelines whatsoever. Ambiguity has been called a *wicked decision problem*. Managers have a difficult time coming to grips with the issues. Wicked problems are associated with manager conflicts over goals and decision alternatives, rapidly changing circumstances, fuzzy information, and unclear linkages among decision elements.[11] Sometimes managers will come up with a "solution" only to realize that they hadn't clearly defined the real problem to begin with.[12] One example of a wicked decision problem was when managers at Ford Motor Company and Firestone confronted the problem of tires used on the Ford Explorer coming apart on the road, causing deadly blowouts and rollovers. Just defining the problem and whether the tire itself or the design of the Explorer was at fault was the first hurdle. Information was fuzzy and fast-changing, and managers were in conflict over how to handle the problem. Neither side dealt effectively with this decision situation, and the reputations of both companies suffered as a result. Fortunately, most decisions are not characterized by ambiguity. But when they are, managers must conjure up goals and develop reasonable scenarios for decision alternatives in the absence of information.

TAKE ACTION

When faced with a difficult and ambiguous decision, develop a "Worst Case Scenario" for each of the possible choices to help you determine which course of action you want to take.

Decision-Making Models

The approach managers use to make decisions usually falls into one of three types—the classical model, the administrative model, or the political model. The choice of model depends on the manager's personal preference, whether the decision is programmed or nonprogrammed, and the extent to which the decision is characterized by risk, uncertainty, or ambiguity.

CLASSICAL MODEL

The **classical model** of decision making is based on economic assumptions. This model has arisen within the management literature because managers are expected to make decisions that are economically sensible and in the organization's best economic interests. The four assumptions underlying this model are as follows:

1. The decision maker operates to accomplish goals that are known and agreed upon. Problems are precisely formulated and defined.

2. The decision maker strives for conditions of certainty, gathering complete information. All alternatives and the potential results of each are calculated.

3. Criteria for evaluating alternatives are known. The decision maker selects the alternative that will maximize the economic return to the organization.

4. The decision maker is rational and uses logic to assign values, order preferences, evaluate alternatives, and make the decision that will maximize the attainment of organizational goals.

ambiguity
a condition in which the goals to be achieved or the problem to be solved is unclear, alternatives are difficult to define, and information about outcomes is unavailable.

classical model
a decision-making model based on the assumption that managers should make logical decisions that will be in the organization's best economic interests.

The classical model of decision making is considered to be **normative,** which means it defines how a decision maker *should* make decisions. It does not describe how managers actually make decisions so much as it provides guidelines on how to reach an ideal outcome for the organization. The value of the classical model has been its ability to help decision makers be more rational. Many managers rely solely on intuition and personal preferences for making decisions.[13] For example, during this era of rising medical costs, decisions in hospitals and medical centers about who gets scarce resources such as expensive procedures and drugs are usually made on an ad hoc basis. Administrators at the University of Texas Medical Branch, however, are using the classical model to provide some clear guidelines and rules that can be consistently applied. A committee of administrators, doctors, and mid-level staffers codified a top-to-bottom system for allocating medical services. Patients without insurance must pay upfront to see a doctor. Strict rules bar expensive drugs being given to patients who can't pay for them. Screeners see patients as soon as they come in and follow clear, rational procedures for determining who is eligible for what services. A special fund can pay for drugs that are off-limits to poor patients, but approval has to come from the chief medical director, who often uses cost-benefit analysis to make her decisions. The hospital's rationing system is controversial. However, top managers argue that it helps the institution impartially care for the poor at the same time it adheres to rational budget restrictions needed to keep the institution financially solid.[14]

In many respects, the classical model represents an "ideal" model of decision making that is often unattainable by real people in real organizations. It is most valuable when applied to programmed decisions and to decisions characterized by certainty or risk because relevant information is available, and probabilities can be calculated. For example, new analytical software programs automate many programmed decisions, such as freezing the account of a customer who has failed to make payments, determining the cellular phone service plan that is most appropriate for a particular customer, or sorting insurance claims so that cases are handled most efficiently.[15] Airlines use automated systems to optimize seat pricing, flight scheduling, and crew assignment decisions. GE Energy Rentals uses a system that captures financial and organizational information about customers to help managers evaluate risks and make credit decisions. The system has enabled the division to reduce costs, increase processing time, and improve cash flow. In the retail industry, software programs analyze current and historical sales data to help companies such as The Home Depot and Gap decide when, where, and how much to mark down prices.[16]

normative
an approach that defines how a decision maker should make decisions and provides guidelines for reaching an ideal outcome for the organization.

NBC

For television viewers, news and entertainment is the primary function of the NBC network. But for NBC managers, one of the biggest concerns is optimizing the advertising schedule. Each year, managers have to develop a detailed advertising plan and a schedule that meets advertisers' desires in terms of cost, target audience, program mix, and other factors. At the same time, the schedule has to get the most revenues for the available amount of inventory (advertising slots).

Creating an advertising plan and schedule can be extremely complex, with numerous decision constraints and variables, such as product conflict restraints, airtime availability restraints, client requirements, or management restrictions. NBC offices use a computerized system that quickly and efficiently makes optimal use of advertising slots. When an advertiser makes a request, planners enter all the information into the system, including the budgeted amount the customer is willing to pay for a total package of commercials, the number of people the advertiser wants to reach, the targeted demographic characteristics, how the budget is to be distributed over four quarters of the year, the number of weeks in the program year, the unit lengths of commercials, the specific shows the advertiser is interested in, and so forth. Management ranks the shows and weeks of the year by their importance, and these data are also entered into the system, along with the availability of advertising slots during each week and other constraints. The system formulates an advertising plan that uses the least amount of premium inventory subject to meeting client requirements, saving millions of dollars of premium inventory, which can be used to lure new advertisers who will pay high fees to advertise on the hottest shows.[17]

The growth of quantitative decision techniques that use computers has expanded the use of the classical approach. Quantitative techniques include such things as decision trees, payoff matrices, break-even analysis, linear programming, forecasting, and operations research models. The NBC television network uses a computer-based system to create optimum advertising schedules.

ADMINISTRATIVE MODEL

The **administrative model** of decision making describes how managers actually make decisions in difficult situations, such as those characterized by nonprogrammed decisions, uncertainty, and ambiguity. Many management decisions are not sufficiently programmable to lend themselves to any degree of quantification. Managers are unable to make economically rational decisions even if they want to.[18]

Bounded Rationality and Satisficing.
The administrative model of decision making is based on the work of Herbert A. Simon. Simon proposed two concepts that were instrumental in shaping the administrative model: bounded rationality and satisficing. **Bounded rationality** means that people have limits, or boundaries, on how rational they can be. The organization is incredibly complex, and managers have the time and ability to process only a limited amount of information with which to make decisions.[19] Because managers do not have the time or cognitive ability to process complete information about complex decisions, they must satisfice. **Satisficing** means that decision makers choose the first solution alternative that satisfies minimal decision criteria.

administrative model
a decision-making model that describes how managers actually make decisions in situations characterized by nonprogrammed decisions, uncertainty, and ambiguity.

bounded rationality
the concept that people have the time and cognitive ability to process only a limited amount of information on which to base decisions.

satisficing
to choose the first solution alternative that satisfies minimal decision criteria, regardless of whether better solutions are presumed to exist.

Spotlight on Skills

InPhonic

David Steinberg left college with a degree in economics, average grades, and a path to fill his father's desired career path: going to law school. A dyslexic who changes words from "anecdotally" to "anitdotally," he got a job clipping newspaper items and came across an ad to sell life insurance door-to-door. Steinberg told his father about the job. The old man flipped at the thought of his son putting off law school for a year, so Steinberg beseeched his stepfather, Irv Siegel, who realized the importance of the young man learning to sell. During his 18 months hawking insurance, he was promoted to manager and made a ton of money. Just when he thought he'd found his niche in life, he found a bright yellow coupon for a free cell phone and immediately drove to the store, asking how they could possibly make any money. The saleswoman told him she got paid $300 for each phone activation, and the phones cost her $150. Steinberg immediately saw the business opportunity. "Wow, you make $150 each time you give away one of these for free?" He turned to his friend as they walked out and said, "I'm in the wrong business."

His stepfather wouldn't loan him money to start a business, believing he needed to work with an experienced pro who would mentor him in the business. But Steinberg was too impatient and started the business anyway. Without any money for a store and unable to get a carrier to sign him as a dealer, he began in his basement, subcontracting with a another dealer—with whom the stepfather vouched for his creditworthiness.

With five friends from his insurance company, he went door-to-door, and soon they were selling upwards of $300,000 a month, more than the dealer they represented. Siegel co-signed a loan so that Steinberg could open a storefront for Cellular One. He was only 23 years old. Six years later, he had built it up to 58 locations. Growing so fast, they needed some high-powered management. Enter old friend Brad LaTour, who wanted to start his own business. At lunch, Steinberg convinced him otherwise with: "If you take this job, I will make you a success," writing it down on a napkin and signing it.

The business is humming along, becoming one of the nation's leading online retailers selling wireless devices and services, but it takes a lot of work. Steinberg's wife says she would be happier if he worked a normal 40-hour week and made only a "nice income."

SOURCE: Ian Mount, "The Great Persuader," *Inc. Magazine* (March 2005): p. 93; "InPhonic calls on QlikTech for business analysis," *Business Wire* (June 4, 2007): p. 1.

Rather than pursuing all alternatives to identify the single solution that will maximize economic returns, managers will opt for the first solution that appears to solve the problem, even if better solutions are presumed to exist. The decision maker cannot justify the time and expense of obtaining complete information.[20]

An example of both bounded rationality and satisficing occurs when a manager on a business trip spills coffee on her blouse just before an important meeting. She will run to a nearby clothing store and buy the first satisfactory replacement she finds. Having neither the time nor the opportunity to explore all the blouses in town, she satisfices by choosing a blouse that will solve the immediate problem. In a similar fashion, managers sometimes generate alternatives for complex problems only until they find one they believe will work. For example, several years ago, then-CEO William Smithburg of Quaker attempted to thwart takeover attempts but had limited options. He satisficed with a quick decision to acquire Snapple, thinking he could use the debt acquired in the deal to discourage a takeover. The acquisition had the potential to solve the problem at hand; thus, Smithburg looked no further for possibly better alternatives.[21] David Steinberg was too impatient for any kind of decision making other than satisficing, but it served him well, as shown here.

The administrative model relies on assumptions different from those of the classical model and focuses on organizational factors that influence individual decisions. It is more realistic than the classical model for complex, nonprogrammed decisions. According to the administrative model:

1. Decision goals often are vague, conflicting, and lack consensus among managers. Managers often are unaware of problems or opportunities that exist in the organization.

2. Rational procedures are not always used, and, when they are, they are confined to a simplistic view of the problem that does not capture the complexity of real organizational events.

3. Managers' searches for alternatives are limited because of human, information, and resource constraints.

4. Most managers settle for a satisficing rather than a maximizing solution, partly because they have limited information and partly because they have only vague criteria for what constitutes a maximizing solution.

The administrative model is considered to be **descriptive,** meaning that it describes how managers actually make decisions in complex situations rather than dictating how they *should* make decisions according to a theoretical ideal. The administrative model recognizes the human and environmental limitations that affect the degree to which managers can pursue a rational decision-making process.

Intuition. Another aspect of administrative decision making is intuition. **Intuition** represents a quick apprehension of a decision situation based on past experience but without conscious thought.[22] Intuitive decision making is not arbitrary or irrational because it is based on years of practice and hands-on experience that enable managers to quickly identify solutions without going through painstaking computations. In today's fast-paced, turbulent business environment, intuition plays an increasingly important role in decision making. A survey of managers conducted by Christian and Timbers found that nearly half of executives say they rely more on intuition than on rational analysis to run their companies.[23]

Cognitive psychologist Gary Klein studied how people make good decisions using their intuition under extreme time pressure and uncertainty.[24] Klein found that intuition begins with *recognition*. When people build a depth of experience and knowledge in a particular area, the right decision often comes quickly and effortlessly as a recognition of information that has been largely forgotten by the conscious mind. For example,

---

TAKE ACTION ➡️

Remember that "Perfection is the enemy of greatness," in order to not become paralyzed in decision making by seeking unrealistically great outcomes.

descriptive
an approach that describes how managers actually make decisions rather than how they should.

intuition
the immediate comprehension of a decision situation based on past experience but without conscious thought.

firefighters make decisions by recognizing what is typical or abnormal about a fire, based on their experience. Similarly, in the business world, managers continuously perceive and process information that they may not consciously be aware of, and their base of knowledge and experience helps them make decisions that may be characterized by uncertainty and ambiguity.

Research by a growing number of psychologists and neuroscientists affirms the power of our unconscious minds in making decisions. Studies of intuition indicate that the unconscious mind has cognitive abilities that sometimes surpass those of the conscious mind.[25] Howard Schultz turned Starbucks into a household name by following his intuition that the leisurely *caffe* model he observed in Italy would work in the United States. Jerry Jones based his decision to buy the losing Dallas Cowboys on intuition, and then made a series of further intuitive decisions that turned the team back into a winner.[26] Another example comes from the Fox television network, where prime-time ratings were dismal until Steven Chao came up with *America's Most Wanted* and *Cops.* Initially, everyone hated the idea of these raw, crime-oriented shows, but Chao and his boss Barry Diller stuck with their gut feelings and pushed the projects.[27]

CONCEPT CONNECTION

"Lots of people hear what I'm doing and think, 'That's a crazy idea!'" says Russell Simmons. The successful entrepreneur, who heads the New York-based media firm, Rush Communications Inc., has relied on his **intuition** to build a half-billion dollar empire on one profitable "crazy idea" after another. It all began with his belief that he could go mainstream with the vibrant rap music he heard in African American neighborhoods. In 1983, he started the pioneering hip-hop Def Jam record label, launching the careers of Beastie Boys, LL Cool J, and Run-DMC, among others. He's since moved on to successful ventures in fashion, media, consumer products, and finance.

However, many other examples show intuitive decisions that failed, and scholarly studies emphasize that managers should take a cautious approach, applying intuition under the right circumstances and in the right way rather than considering it a magical way to make important decisions.[28] Managers may walk a fine line between two extremes: on the one hand, making arbitrary decisions without careful study, and on the other, relying obsessively on rational analysis. One is not better than the other, and managers need to take a balanced approach by considering both rationality and intuition as important components of effective decision making.[29]

POLITICAL MODEL

The third model of decision making is useful for making nonprogrammed decisions when conditions are uncertain, information is limited, and managers may disagree about what goals to pursue or what course of action to take. Most organizational decisions involve many managers who are pursuing different goals, and they have to talk with one another to share information and reach an agreement. Managers often engage in coalition building for making complex organizational decisions. A **coalition** is an informal alliance among managers who support a specific goal. *Coalition building* is the process of forming alliances among managers. In other words, a manager who supports a specific alternative, such as increasing the corporation's growth by acquiring another company, talks informally to other executives and tries to persuade them to support the decision.

The political model closely resembles the real environment in which most managers and decision makers operate. For example, interviews with CEOs in high-tech industries found that they strived to use some type of rational process in making decisions, but the

TAKE ACTION

Practice collaborating and developing alliances because good ideas are not enough—you will need to build coalitions. When the outcomes are not predictable, managers gain support through discussion, negotiation, and bargaining. Without a coalition, a powerful individual or group could derail the decision-making process. Coalition building gives several managers an opportunity to contribute to decision making, enhancing their commitment to the alternative that is ultimately adopted.[30]

coalition
an informal alliance among managers who support a specific goal.

way they actually decided things was through a complex interaction with other managers, subordinates, environmental factors, and organizational events.[31] Decisions are complex and involve many people, information is often ambiguous, and disagreement and conflict over problems and solutions are normal. The political model begins with four basic assumptions:

1. Organizations are made up of groups with diverse interests, goals, and values. Managers disagree about problem priorities and may not understand or share the goals and interests of other managers.

2. Information is ambiguous and incomplete. The attempt to be rational is limited by the complexity of many problems as well as personal and organizational constraints.

3. Managers do not have the time, resources, or mental capacity to identify all dimensions of the problem and process all relevant information. Managers talk to each other and exchange viewpoints to gather information and reduce ambiguity.

4. Managers engage in the push and pull of debate to decide goals and discuss alternatives. Decisions are the result of bargaining and discussion among coalition members.

Assess Your Answer

1 When a manager makes a well-reasoned decision, the next course of action is implementation.

ANSWER: One of the most common mistakes is for a manager to move ahead on a course of action without getting support from colleagues and subordinates. It is usually necessary to build a coalition before implementation.

An example of the political model was when AOL chief executive Jonathan Miller built a coalition to support the development of a Yahoo-like free Web site. Opposition to offering AOL's rich content for free was strong, but Miller talked with other executives and formed a coalition that supported the move as the best way to rejuvenate the declining AOL in the shifting Internet service business. The decision proved to be a turning point, making AOL once more a relevant force on the Web and enticing tech titans such as Google and Microsoft as potential partners.[32]

The inability of leaders to build coalitions often makes it difficult or impossible for managers to get their decisions implemented. Hershell Ezrin resigned as CEO of Canada's Speedy Muffler King because he was unable to build a coalition of managers who supported his decisions for change at the troubled company. Many senior-level executives resented Ezrin's appointment and refused to go along with his ideas for reviving the company.[33] Similarly, former U.S. Treasury Secretary Lawrence Summers took the job as president of Harvard University in 2001 with plans for shaking up many of the university's long-time ways of doing things. However, his inability to build a coalition to support his changes led Summers to resign five years later with the campus in turmoil and few of his desired changes effectively implemented.[34]

The key dimensions of the classical, administrative, and political models are listed in Exhibit 6.2. Research into decision-making procedures found rational, classical procedures to be associated with high performance for organizations in stable environments. However, administrative and political decision-making procedures and intuition have been associated with high performance in unstable environments in which decisions must be made rapidly and under more difficult conditions.[35]

TAKE ACTION

As a new manager, use your political skills to reach a decision in the midst of disagreement about goals or problem solutions. Talk with other managers or employees and negotiate to gain support for the goal or solution you favor. Learn to compromise and to support others when appropriate.

EXHIBIT 6.2

Characteristics of Classical, Administrative, and Political Decision-Making Models

Classical Model	Administrative Model	Political Model
Clear-cut problem and goals	Vague problem and goals	Pluralistic; conflicting goals
Condition of certainty	Condition of uncertainty	Condition of uncertainty/ ambiguity
Full information about alternatives and their outcomes	Limited information about alternatives and their outcomes	Inconsistent viewpoints; ambiguous information
Rational choice by individual for maximizing outcomes	Satisficing choice for resolving problem using intuition	Bargaining and discussion among coalition members

Decision-Making Steps

Whether a decision is programmed or nonprogrammed and regardless of managers' choice of the classical, administrative, or political model of decision making, six steps typically are associated with effective decision processes. These steps are summarized in Exhibit 6.3.

RECOGNITION OF DECISION REQUIREMENT

Managers confront a decision requirement in the form of either a problem or an opportunity. A **problem** occurs when organizational accomplishment is less than established goals. Some aspect of performance is unsatisfactory. An **opportunity** exists when managers see potential accomplishment that exceeds specified current goals. Managers see the

problem
a situation in which organizational accomplishments have failed to meet established goals.

opportunity
a situation in which managers see potential organizational accomplishments that exceed current goals.

EXHIBIT 6.3

Six Steps in the Managerial Decision-Making Process

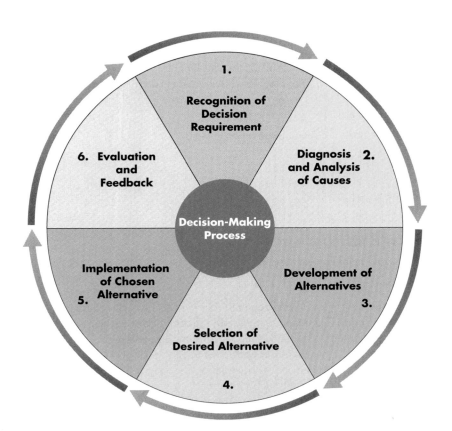

1. Recognition of Decision Requirement
2. Diagnosis and Analysis of Causes
3. Development of Alternatives
4. Selection of Desired Alternative
5. Implementation of Chosen Alternative
6. Evaluation and Feedback

Decision-Making Process

Jon Bon Jovi is a rock star and entrepreneur, who co-owns the Philadelphia Soul, an expansion team of the Arena Football League (AFL). Bon Jovi and his partner, businessman Craig Spencer, spotted an **opportunity** to capitalize on Bon Jovi's personality and fame, as well as his savvy marketing skills, by acquiring the franchise. Bon Jovi personally made decisions such as naming the team the Soul (because "anybody can have soul," he says) and creating a mascot (the Soul Man), and he is actively involved in decisions regarding everything from advertising budgets to where to place the autograph tables after a game. Today, the Soul leads the AFL in ticket sales, advertising sales, and merchandising revenue.

possibility of enhancing performance beyond current levels. Oprah Winfrey's agent saw opportunities for her that she never dreamed of, as described in the Spotlight on Collaboration box.

Awareness of a problem or opportunity is the first step in the decision sequence and requires surveillance of the internal and external environment for issues that merit executive attention.[36] This process resembles the military concept of gathering intelligence. Managers scan the world around them to determine whether the organization is satisfactorily progressing toward its goals.

Some information comes from periodic financial reports, performance reports, and other sources that are designed to discover problems before they become too serious. Managers also take advantage of informal sources. They talk to other managers, gather opinions on how things are going, and seek advice on which problems should be tackled or which opportunities embraced.[37] Recognizing decision requirements is difficult because it often means integrating bits and pieces of information in novel ways. For example, the failure of U.S. intelligence leaders to recognize the imminent threat of Al Qaeda prior to the September 11, 2001, terrorist attacks has been attributed partly to the lack of systems that could help leaders put together myriad snippets of information that pointed to the problem.[38]

DIAGNOSIS AND ANALYSIS OF CAUSES

After a problem or opportunity comes to a manager's attention, the understanding of the situation should be refined. **Diagnosis** is the step in the decision-making process in which managers analyze underlying causal factors associated with the decision situation. Managers make a mistake here if they jump right into generating alternatives without first exploring the cause of the problem more deeply.

Kepner and Tregoe, who conducted extensive studies of manager decision making, recommend that managers ask a series of questions to specify underlying causes, including the following:

- What is the state of disequilibrium affecting us?
- When did it occur?
- Where did it occur?
- How did it occur?
- To whom did it occur?
- What is the urgency of the problem?
- What is the interconnectedness of events?
- What result came from which activity?[39]

diagnosis
the step in the decision-making process in which managers analyze underlying causal factors associated with the decision situation.

Such questions help specify what actually happened and why. Managers at General Motors are struggling to diagnose the underlying factors in the company's recent troubles. The problem is an urgent one, with sales, profits, market share, and the stock price all plummeting, and the giant corporation on the verge of bankruptcy. Managers are examining the multitude of problems facing GM, tracing the pattern of the decline, and looking at the interconnectedness of issues such as changing consumer tastes in vehicles, surging gas prices that make trucks and SUVs less appealing, the rising burden of retiree benefits

Spotlight on

Collaboration

Oprah, Inc.

With her Oprah Brand designed around the mantra, "You are responsible for your own life," it might seem strange that Oprah Winfrey describes her decision making as "leaps of faith" and that she embraces a management-by-instinct style. But that's not the whole story. The other part of the picture is about her former business manager, Jeff Jacobs, who was president of Oprah's company, Harpo, Inc, until he left in 2002 to go back to his law practice and to teach law at Loyola University. He was a young entertainment lawyer when the t-shirt and flip-flop wearing Oprah asked for help in 1984 with a new contract. With an instinct for business potential, Jacobs convinced her to invest in herself, rather than remaining an actor-for-hire, where most entertainers are. Together they formed Harpo Entertainment in 1986, and her company has soared since.

While Oprah develops her themes and images, Jacobs worked behind the scenes keeping the business running and making tough decisions. For every gut instinct Oprah has, it was backed up with Jacobs' realistic business experience and knowing when to "multipurpose the content." Still, Oprah has a strong sense of her mission and her decisions follow her purpose and values. Sometimes her wishes clash with business concerns. She has the *O Magazine* table of contents on page 2, rather than the more common 22. Advertisers prefer for people to wade through their glossy ads before finding the table of contents, but Oprah wouldn't have it. "Let's put the readers first," she commanded.

Her model has propelled her to the top of *Forbes Magazine's* Celebrity 100 list, not only because of her wealth but also due to her influence, soon to be stronger, with two reality shows in the works.

Oprah tries to live her message, to be strong, courageous, and a good role model. She has yet to make the decision to give up control of her brand—Oprah—unlike Martha Stewart who sold her name rights to the now Chapter 11ed K-Mart, and also took her company public. Oprah feels strongly about maintaining her self in the process. "If I lost control of the business, I'd lost myself or at least the ability to be myself. Owning is a way to be myself." She deeply regrets her decision, based on financial gain, to sell rights to Oprah reruns. "It's not a commodity. It's my soul. It's who I am."

SOURCE: Patricia Sellers, "The Business of Being Oprah," *Fortune* (April 1, 2002): pp. 50–64; Tom Walker, "Oprah Winfrey No. 1 on *Forbes'* list of Celebrities," *Atlanta Journal-Constitution* (June 26, 2007): p. B2.

promised to workers in more profitable times, increased competition and the growth of auto manufacturing in low-cost countries such as China, excess factory capacity and high costs, poor headquarters planning, and weak control systems that allowed the company to drift further and further into crisis.[40]

DEVELOPMENT OF ALTERNATIVES

After the problem or opportunity has been recognized and analyzed, decision makers begin to consider taking action. The next stage is to generate possible alternative solutions that will respond to the needs of the situation and correct the underlying causes. Studies find that limiting the search for alternatives is a primary cause of decision failure in organizations.[41]

For a programmed decision, feasible alternatives are easy to identify and, in fact, usually are already available within the organization's rules and procedures. Nonprogrammed decisions, however, require developing new courses of action that will meet the company's needs. For decisions made under conditions of high uncertainty, managers may develop only one or two custom solutions that will satisfice for handling the problem.

TAKE ACTION ▶▶

Always come up with several options to solve problems, so that you can reasonably choose among them.

Decision alternatives can be thought of as the tools for reducing the difference between the organization's current and desired performance. For example, to improve sales at fast-food giant McDonald's, executives considered alternatives such as using mystery shoppers and unannounced inspections to improve quality and service, motivating demoralized franchisees to get them to invest in new equipment and programs, taking R&D out of the test kitchen and encouraging franchisees to help come up with successful new menu items, and closing some stores to avoid cannibalizing its own sales.[42]

SELECTION OF DESIRED ALTERNATIVE

After feasible alternatives are developed, one must be selected. The decision choice is the selection of the most promising of several alternative courses of action. The best alternative is one in which the solution best fits the overall goals and values of the organization and achieves the desired results using the fewest resources.[43] The manager tries to select the choice with the least amount of risk and uncertainty. Because some risk is inherent for most nonprogrammed decisions, managers try to gauge prospects for success. Under conditions of uncertainty, they might rely on their intuition and experience to estimate whether a given course of action is likely to succeed. Basing choices on overall goals and values can also effectively guide the selection of alternatives. Recall from Chapter 2 Valero Energy's decision to keep everyone on the payroll after Hurricane Katrina hit the Gulf Coast, while other refineries shut down and laid off workers. For Valero managers, the choice was easy based on values of putting employees first. Valero's values-based decision making helped the company zoom from number 23 to number 3 on *Fortune* magazine's list of best companies to work for—and enabled Valero to get back to business weeks faster than competitors.[44]

Choosing among alternatives also depends on managers' personality factors and willingness to accept risk and uncertainty. For example, **risk propensity** is the willingness to undertake risk with the opportunity of gaining an increased payoff. The level of risk a manager is willing to accept will influence the analysis of cost and benefits to be derived from any decision. Consider the situations in Exhibit 6.4. In each situation, which alternative would you choose? A person with a low-risk propensity would tend to take assured moderate returns by going for a tie score, building a domestic plant, or pursuing a career as a physician. A risk taker would go for the victory, build a plant in a foreign country, or embark on an acting career.

risk propensity
the willingness to undertake risk with the opportunity of gaining an increased payoff.

EXHIBIT 6.4
Decision Alternatives with Different Levels of Risk

For each of the following decisions, which alternative would you choose?

1. In the final seconds of a game with the college's traditional rival, the coach of a college football team may choose a play that has a 95 percent chance of producing a tie score or one with a 30 percent chance of leading to victory or to sure defeat if it fails.

2. The president of a Canadian company must decide whether to build a new plant within Canada that has a 90 percent chance of producing a modest return on investment or to build it in a foreign country with an unstable political history. The latter alternative has a 40 percent chance of failing, but the returns would be enormous if it succeeded.

3. A college senior with considerable acting talent must choose a career. She has the opportunity to go on to medical school and become a physician, a career in which she is 80 percent likely to succeed. She would rather be an actress but realizes that the opportunity for success is only 20 percent.

IMPLEMENTATION OF CHOSEN ALTERNATIVE

The **implementation** stage involves the use of managerial, administrative, and persuasive abilities to ensure that the chosen alternative is carried out. This step is similar to the idea of strategic implementation. The ultimate success of the chosen alternative depends on whether it can be translated into action.[45] Sometimes an alternative never becomes reality because managers lack the resources or energy needed to make things happen. Implementation may require discussion with people affected by the decision. Communication, motivation, and leadership skills must be used to see that the decision is carried out. When employees see that managers follow up on their decisions by tracking implementation success, they are more committed to positive action.[46]

At Boeing Commercial Airplanes, CEO Alan R. Mulally engineered a remarkable turnaround by skillfully implementing decisions that reduced waste, streamlined production lines, and moved Boeing into breakthrough technologies for new planes.[47] If managers lack the ability or desire to implement decisions, the chosen alternative cannot be carried out to benefit the organization.

EVALUATION AND FEEDBACK

In the evaluation stage of the decision process, decision makers gather information that tells them how well the decision was implemented and whether it was effective in achieving its goals. For example, Tandy executives evaluated their decision to open computer centers for businesses, and feedback revealed poor sales performance. Feedback indicated that implementation was unsuccessful, and computer centers were closed so Tandy could focus on its successful Radio Shack retail stores.

Feedback is important because decision making is a continuous, neverending process. Decision making is not completed when an executive or board of directors votes yes or no. Feedback provides decision makers with information that can precipitate a new decision cycle. The decision may fail, thus generating a new analysis of the problem, evaluation of

TAKE ACTION

When you make a decision, develop the mental discipline to carry it out.

implementation
the step in the decision-making process that involves using managerial, administrative, and persuasive abilities to translate the chosen alternative into action.

Tom's of Maine

Tom's of Maine, known for its all-natural personal hygiene products, saw an opportunity to expand its line with a new natural deodorant. However, the opportunity quickly became a problem when the deodorant worked only half of the time with half of the customers who used it, and its all-recyclable plastic dials were prone to breakage.

The problem of the failed deodorant led founder Tom Chappell and other managers to analyze and diagnose what went wrong. They finally determined that the company's product-development process had run amok. The same group of merry product developers was responsible from conception to launch of the product. They were so attached to the product that they failed to test it properly or consider potential problems, becoming instead "a mutual admiration society." Managers considered several alternatives for solving the problem. The decision to publicly admit the problem and recall the deodorant was an easy one for Chappell, who runs his company on principles of fairness and honesty. Not only did the company apologize to its customers, but it also listened to their complaints and suggestions. Chappell himself helped answer calls and letters. Even though the recall cost the company $400,000 and led to a stream of negative publicity, it ultimately helped improve relationships with customers.

Evaluation and feedback also led Tom's of Maine to set up *acorn groups,* from which it hopes mighty oaks of successful products will grow. Acorn groups are cross-departmental teams that will shepherd new products from beginning to end. The cross-functional teams are a mechanism for catching problems—and new opportunities—that ordinarily would be missed. They pass on their ideas and findings to senior managers and the product-development team.

Tom's was able to turn a problem into an opportunity, thanks to evaluation and feedback. Not only did the disaster ultimately help the company solidify relationships with customers, but it also led to a formal mechanism for learning and sharing ideas—something the company did not have before.[48]

TAKE ACTION ▶

If something you try fails, do an "after-action review" to evaluate what went wrong and what you would do differently next time.

TAKE ACTION ▶

Did you know that decision behavior differs markedly between new managers and successful senior executives? To understand how, complete the New Manager Self Test on page 213.

alternatives, and selection of a new alternative. Many big problems are solved by trying several alternatives in sequence, each providing modest improvement. Feedback is the part of monitoring that assesses whether a new decision needs to be made.

To illustrate the overall decision-making process, including evaluation and feedback, we can look at the decision to introduce a new deodorant at Tom's of Maine.

Tom's of Maine's decision illustrates all the decision steps, and the process ultimately ended in success. Strategic decisions always contain some risk, but feedback and follow-up decisions can help get companies back on track. By learning from their decision mistakes, managers and companies can turn problems into opportunities.

Personal Decision Framework

Imagine you were a manager at Tom's of Maine, Boeing Commercial Airplanes, a local movie theater, or the public library. How would you go about making important decisions that might shape the future of your department or company? So far, we have discussed a number of factors that affect how managers make decisions. For example, decisions may be programmed or nonprogrammed, situations are characterized by various levels of uncertainty, and managers may use the classical, administrative, or political models of decision making. In addition, the decision-making process follows six recognized steps.

However, not all managers go about making decisions in the same way. In fact, significant differences distinguish the ways in which individual managers may approach problems and make decisions concerning them. These differences can be explained by the concept of personal **decision styles.** Exhibit 6.5 illustrates the role of personal style in the decision-making process. Personal decision style refers to distinctions among people with respect to how they perceive problems and make decisions. Research identified four major decision styles: directive, analytical, conceptual, and behavioral.[49]

1. The *directive style* is used by people who prefer simple, clear-cut solutions to problems. Managers who use this style often make decisions quickly because they do not like to deal with a lot of information and may consider only one or two alternatives. People who prefer the directive style generally are efficient and rational and prefer to rely on existing rules or procedures for making decisions.

2. Managers with an *analytical style* like to consider complex solutions based on as much data as they can gather. These individuals carefully consider alternatives and often base their decisions on objective, rational data from management control systems and other sources. They search for the best possible decision based on the information available.

3. People who tend toward a *conceptual style* also like to consider a broad amount of information. However, they are more socially oriented than those with an analytical style and like to talk to others about the problem and possible alternatives for solving it. Managers using a conceptual style consider many broad alternatives, rely on information from both people and systems, and like to solve problems creatively.

4. The *behavioral style* is often the style adopted by managers having a deep concern for others as individuals. Managers using this style like to talk to people one on one and understand their feelings about the problem and the effect of a given decision upon

decision styles
differences among people with respect to how they perceive problems and make decisions.

EXHIBIT 6.5

Personal Decision Framework

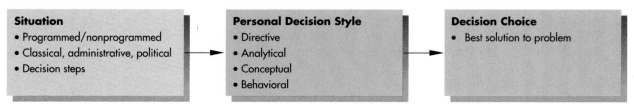

Your Decision-Making Behavior

How do you make decisions? You probably make decisions automatically and without realizing that people have diverse decision-making behaviors, which they bring to management positions. Think back to how you make decisions in your personal, student, or work life, especially where other people are involved. Answer whether each of the following items is Mostly True or Mostly False for you.

	Mostly True				Mostly False
1. I like to decide quickly and move on to the next thing.	1	2	3	4	5
2. I would use my authority to make the decision if certain I was right.	1	2	3	4	5
3. I appreciate decisiveness.	1	2	3	4	5
4. There is usually one correct solution to a problem.	1	2	3	4	5
5. I identify everyone who needs to be involved in the decision.	1	2	3	4	5
6. I explicitly seek conflicting perspectives.	1	2	3	4	5
7. I use discussion strategies to reach a solution.	1	2	3	4	5
8. I look for different meanings when faced with a great deal of data.	1	2	3	4	5
9. I take time to reason things through and use systematic logic.	1	2	3	4	5

INTERPRETATION: New managers typically use a different decision behavior from seasoned executives. The decision behavior of a successful CEO may be almost the opposite of a first-level supervisor. The difference is due partly to the types of decisions and partly to learning what works at each level. New managers typically start out with a more directive, decisive, command-oriented behavior and gradually move toward more openness, diversity of viewpoints, and interactions with others as they move up the hierarchy.

SCORING: All 9 items in the list reflect appropriate decision-making behavior, but items 1–4 are more typical of new managers. Items 5–8 are typical of successful senior manager decision making. Item 9 is considered part of good decision making at all levels. If you checked Mostly True for three or four of items 1–4 and 9, consider yourself typical of a new manager. If you checked Mostly True for three or four of items 5–8 and 9, you are using behavior consistent with top managers. If you checked a similar number of both sets of items, your behavior is probably flexible and balanced.

them. People with a behavioral style usually are concerned with the personal development of others and may make decisions that help others achieve their goals.

Many managers have a dominant decision style. One example is Jeff Zucker at NBC Entertainment. Zucker uses a primarily conceptual style, which makes him well suited to the television industry. He consults with dozens of programmers about possible new shows and likes to consider many broad alternatives before making decisions.[50] However, managers frequently use several different styles or a combination of styles in making the varied decisions they confront daily. A manager might use a directive style for deciding on which printing company to use for new business cards, yet shift to a more conceptual style when handling an interdepartmental conflict. The most effective managers are able to shift among styles as needed to meet the situation. Being aware of one's dominant decision style can help a manager avoid making critical mistakes when his or her usual style may be inappropriate to the problem at hand.

Increasing Participation in Decision Making

Managers do make some decisions as individuals, but decision makers more often are part of a group. Major decisions in the business world rarely are made entirely by an individual. Effective decision making often depends on whether managers involve the right people in the right ways in helping to solve problems. One model that provides guidance for practicing managers was originally developed by Victor Vroom and Arthur Jago.[51]

THE VROOM-JAGO MODEL

The **Vroom-Jago model** helps a manager gauge the appropriate amount of participation by subordinates in making a specific decision. The model has three major components: leader participation styles, a set of diagnostic questions with which to analyze a decision situation, and a series of decision rules.

Vroom-Jago model
a model designed to help managers gauge the amount of subordinate participation in decision making.

Leader Participation Styles. The model employs five levels of subordinate participation in decision making, ranging from highly autocratic (leader decides alone) to highly democratic (leader delegates to group), as illustrated in Exhibit 6.6.[52] The exhibit

EXHIBIT 6.6
Five Leader
Participation Styles

Area of Influence by Leader				Area of Freedom for Group
Decide	**Consult Individually**	**Consult Group**	**Facilitate**	**Delegate**
You make the decision alone and either announce or "sell" it to the group. You may use your expertise in collecting information that you deem relevant to the problem from the group or others.	You present the problem to the group members individually, get their suggestions, and make the decision.	You present the problem to the group members in a meeting, get their suggestions, and make the decision.	You present the problem to the group in a meeting. You act as facilitator, defining the problem to be solved and the boundaries within which the decision must be made. Your objective is to get concurrence on a decision. Above all, you take care to show that your ideas are not given any greater weight than those of others simply because of your position.	You permit the group to make the decision within prescribed limits. The group undertakes the identification and diagnosis of the problem, develops alternative procedures for solving it, and decides on one or more alternative solutions. Though you play no direct role in the group's deliberations unless explicitly asked, your role is an important one behind the scenes, providing needed resources and encouragement.

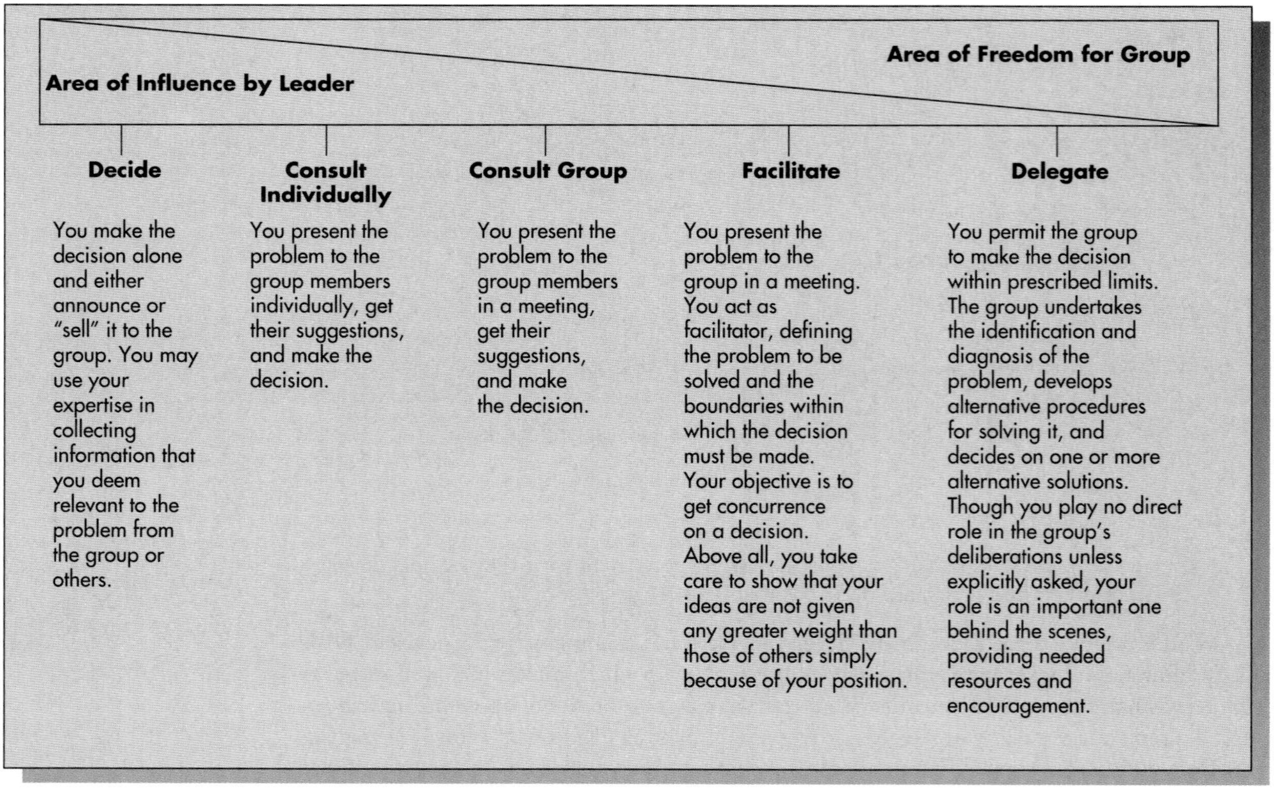

SOURCE: Victor H. Vroom, "Leadership and the Decision-Making Process," *Organizational Dynamics* 28, no. 4 (Spring 2000): pp. 82–94. This exhibit is Vroom's adaptation of Tannenbaum and Schmidt's Taxonomy. Used with permission.

shows five decision styles, starting with the leader making the decision alone (Decide); presenting the problem to subordinates individually for their suggestions and then making the decision (Consult Individually); presenting the problem to subordinates as a group, collectively obtaining their ideas and suggestions, then making the decision (Consult Group); sharing the problem with subordinates as a group and acting as a facilitator to help the group arrive at a decision (Facilitate); or delegating the problem and permitting the group to make the decision within prescribed limits (Delegate).

Diagnostic Questions. How does a manager decide which of the five decision styles to use? The appropriate degree of decision participation depends on a number of situational factors, such as the required level of decision quality, the level of leader or subordinate expertise, and the importance of having subordinates commit to the decision. Leaders can analyze the appropriate degree of participation by answering seven diagnostic questions.

1. *Decision significance: How significant is this decision for the project or organization?* If the quality of the decision is highly important to the success of the project or organization, the leader has to be actively involved.

2. *Importance of commitment: How important is subordinate commitment to carrying out the decision?* If implementation requires a high level of commitment to the decision, leaders should involve subordinates in the decision process.

3. *Leader expertise: What is the level of the leader's expertise in relation to the problem?* If the leader does not have a high amount of information, knowledge, or expertise, the leader should involve subordinates to obtain it.

4. *Likelihood of commitment: If the leader were to make the decision alone, would subordinates have high or low commitment to the decision?* If subordinates typically go along with whatever the leader decides, their involvement in the decision-making process will be less important.

5. *Group support for goals: What is the degree of subordinate support for the team's or organization's objectives at stake in this decision?* If subordinates have low support for the goals of the organization, the leader should not allow the group to make the decision alone.

6. *Group expertise: What is the level of group members' knowledge and expertise in relation to the problem?* If subordinates have a high level of expertise in relation to the problem, more responsibility for the decision can be delegated to them.

7. *Team competence: How skilled and committed are group members to working together as a team to solve problems?* When subordinates have high skills and high desire to work together cooperatively to solve problems, more responsibility for decision making can be delegated to them.

These questions seem detailed, but considering these seven situational factors can quickly narrow the options and point to the appropriate level of group participation in decision making.

Selecting a Decision Style. The decision matrix in Exhibit 6.7 allows a manager to adopt a participation style by answering the diagnostic questions in sequence. The manager enters the matrix at the left-hand side, at Problem Statement, and considers the seven situational questions in sequence from left to right, answering high (H) or low (L) to each one and avoiding crossing any horizontal lines. The first question would be: *How significant is this decision for the project or organization?* If the answer is High, the leader proceeds to importance of commitment: *How important is subordinate commitment to carrying out the decision?* An answer of High leads to a question about leader expertise: *What is the level of the leader's expertise in relation to the problem?* If the leader's knowledge and expertise is High, the leader next considers

EXHIBIT 6.7

Vroom-Jago Decision Model for Determining an Appropriate Decision-Making Style—Group Problems

Instructions: The matrix operates like a funnel. You start at the left with a specific decision problem in mind. The column headings denote situational factors which may or may not be present in that problem. You progress by selecting High or Low (H or L) for each relevant situational factor. Proceed down the funnel, judging only those situational factors for which a judgement is called for, until you reach the recommended process.

Decision Significance?	Importance or Commitment?	Leader Expertise?	Likelihood of Commitment?	Group Support?	Group Expertise?	Team Competence?	
H	H	H	H	–	–	–	Decide
			L	H	H	H	Delegate
						L	Consult (Group)
					L	–	Consult (Group)
				L	–	–	Consult (Group)
		L	H	H	H	H	Facilitate
						L	Consult (Individually)
					L	–	Consult (Individually)
				L	–	–	Consult (Individually)
			L	H	H	H	Facilitate
						L	Consult (Group)
					L	–	Consult (Group)
				L	–	–	Consult (Group)
	L	H	–	–	–	–	Decide
		L	–	H	H	H	Facilitate
						L	Consult (Individually)
					L	–	Consult (Individually)
				L	–	–	Consult (Individually)
L	H	–	H	–	–	–	Decide
			L	–	–	H	Delegate
						L	Facilitate
	L	–	–	–	–	–	Decide

(Left vertical label: PROBLEM STATEMENT)

SOURCE: Victor H. Vroom "Leadership and the Decision-Making Process," *Organizational Dynamics* 28, no. 4 (Spring 2000): pp. 82–94. Used with permission.

likelihood of commitment: *If the leader were to make the decision alone, how likely is it that subordinates would be committed to the decision?* A high likelihood that subordinates would be committed means the decision matrix leads directly to the Decide style of decision making, in which the leader makes the decision alone and presents it to the group.

The Vroom-Jago model has been criticized as being less than perfect,[53] but it is useful to managers, and the body of supportive research is growing.[54] Managers can use the model to make timely, high-quality decisions. Consider the application of the model to the following hypothetical problem.

The Vroom-Jago model in Exhibit 6.7 shows that Robbins used the correct decision style. Moving from left to right in Exhibit 6.7, the questions and answers are as follows: *How significant is the decision?* Definitely high. The company's future might be at stake. *How important is subordinate commitment to the decision?* Also high. The team members must support and implement Robbins' solution. *What is the level of Robbins's*

TAKE ACTION ▸

When making a decision, ask yourself how important is employee commitment, in order to determine if you should make the decision alone or with the group.

W hen Madison Manufacturing won a coveted contract from a large auto manufacturer to produce an engine to power their flagship sports car, Dave Robbins was thrilled to be selected as project manager. This project dramatically enhanced the reputation of Madison, and Robbins and his team of engineers took great pride in their work. However, their enthusiasm was dashed by a recent report of serious engine problems in cars delivered to customers. Taking quick action, the auto manufacturer suspended sales of the sports car, halted current production, and notified owners of the current model not to drive the car. Everyone involved knows this situation is a disaster. Unless the engine problem is solved quickly, Madison Manufacturing could be exposed to extended litigation. In addition, Madison's valued relationship with one of the world's largest auto manufacturers would likely be lost forever.

As the project manager, Robbins spent two weeks in the field inspecting the seized engines and the auto plant where they were installed. Based on this extensive research, Robbins has some pretty good ideas about what is causing the problem, but he knows members of his team who may have stronger expertise for solving it. In addition, while he was in the field, other team members were carefully evaluating the operations and practices in Madison's plant where the engine is manufactured. Therefore, Robbins chooses to get the team together and discuss the problem before making his final decision. The group meets for several hours, discussing the problem in detail and sharing their varied perspectives, including the information Robbins and team members gathered. Following the group session, Robbins makes his decision, which will be presented at the team meeting the following morning, after which testing and correction of the engine problem will begin.[55]

> **Madison Manufacturing**

information and expertise? Probably low. Even though he has spent several weeks researching the seized engines, other team members have additional information and expertise that needs to be considered. *If Robbins makes the decision on his own, would team members have high or low commitment to it?* The answer to this question is probably also low. Even though team members respect Robbins, they take pride in their work as a team and know Robbins does not have complete information. This leads to the question, *What is the degree of subordinate support for the team's or organization's objectives at stake in this decision?* Definitely high. This leads to the question, *What is the level of group members' knowledge and expertise in relation to the problem?* The answer to this question is low, which leads to the Consult Group decision style, as described earlier in Exhibit 6.6. Thus, Robbins used the style that would be recommended by the Vroom-Jago model.

In many situations, several decision styles might be equally acceptable. However, smart managers are encouraging greater employee participation in solving problems whenever possible. The use of new knowledge management technologies allows for accessing the ideas and knowledge of a much broader group of people, both inside and outside the organization.[56] Broad participation often leads to better decisions. Involving others in decision making also contributes to individual and organizational learning, which is critical for rapid decision making in a turbulent environment.

2 It is almost always better to get participation from others when making a decision.

ANSWER: Increasingly, because of more turbulent times, participation is desirable, but there are situations where participation either takes too much time, or there is a sensitive quality issue. The truly effective manager will look at each situation and make a determination on which style is most appropriate.

NEW DECISION APPROACHES FOR TURBULENT TIMES

The ability to make fast, widely supported, high-quality decisions on a frequent basis is a critical skill in today's fast-moving organizations.[57] In many industries, the rate of competitive and technological change is so extreme that opportunities are fleeting, clear and complete information is seldom available, and the cost of a slow decision means lost business or even company failure. Do these factors mean managers should make the majority of decisions on their own? No. The rapid pace of the business environment calls for just the opposite—that is, for people throughout the organization to be involved in decision making and have the information, skills, and freedom they need to respond immediately to problems and questions. Business is taking a lesson from today's military. For example, the U.S. Army, once considered the ultimate example of a rigid, top-down organization, is pushing information and decision making to junior officers in the field. Fighting a fluid, fast-moving, and fast-changing terrorist network means that people who are knowledgeable about the local situation have to make quick decisions, learning through trial and error and sometimes departing from standard Army procedures. Junior leaders rely on a strong set of core values and a clear understanding of the mission to craft creative solutions to problems that the Army might never have encountered before.[58]

Similarly, in today's fast-moving businesses, people often have to act first and analyze later.[59] Top managers do not have the time to evaluate options for every decision, conduct research, develop alternatives, and tell people what to do and how to do it. When speed matters, a slow decision may be as ineffective as the wrong decision, and companies can learn to make decisions fast. Effective decision making under turbulent conditions relies on the following guidelines.

Start with Brainstorming. One of the best-known techniques for rapidly generating creative alternatives is **brainstorming.** Brainstorming uses a face-to-face interactive group to spontaneously suggest a wide range of alternatives for decision making. The keys to effective brainstorming are that people can build on one another's ideas; all ideas are acceptable, no matter how crazy they seem; and criticism and evaluation are not allowed. The goal is to generate as many ideas as possible. Brainstorming has been found to be highly effective for quickly generating a wide range of alternate solutions to a problem, but it does have some drawbacks. For one, people in a group often want to conform to what others are saying, a problem sometimes referred to as *groupthink*. Others may be concerned about pleasing the boss or impressing colleagues. In addition, many creative people simply have social inhibitions that limit their participation in a group session or make it difficult to come up with ideas in a group setting. In fact, one study found that when four people are asked to "brainstorm" individually, they typically come up with twice as many ideas as a group of four brainstorming together.

One approach, electronic brainstorming, takes advantage of the group approach while overcoming some disadvantages. **Electronic brainstorming,** sometimes called *brainwriting*, brings people together in an interactive group over a computer network.[60] One member writes an idea, another reads it and adds other ideas, and so on. Studies show that electronic brainstorming generates about 40 percent more ideas than individuals brainstorming alone, and 25 to 200 percent more ideas than regular brainstorming groups, depending on group size.[61] Why? Because the process is anonymous, so the sky's the limit in terms of what people feel free to say. People can write down their ideas immediately, avoiding the possibility that a good idea might slip away while the person is waiting for a chance to speak in a face-to-face group. Social inhibitions and concerns are avoided, which typically allows for a broader range of participation. Another advantage is that electronic brainstorming can potentially be done with groups made up of employees from around the world, further increasing the diversity of alternatives.

brainstorming
a technique that uses a face-to-face group to spontaneously suggest a broad range of alternatives for decision making.

electronic brainstorming
bringing people together in an interactive group over a computer network to suggest alternatives; sometimes called *brainwriting*.

Learn, Don't Punish. Decisions made under conditions of uncertainty and time pressure produce many errors, but smart managers are willing to take the risk in the spirit of trial and error. If a chosen decision alternative fails, the organization can learn from it and try another alternative that better fits the situation. Each failure provides new information and learning. People throughout the organization are encouraged to engage in *experimentation,* which means taking risks and learning from their mistakes. Good managers know that every time a person makes a decision, whether it turns out to have positive or negative consequences, it helps the employee learn and be a better decision maker the next time around. By making mistakes, people gain valuable experience and knowledge to perform more effectively in the future. PSS World Medical of Jacksonville, Florida, encourages people to take initiative and try new things with a policy of never firing anyone for an honest mistake. In addition, PSS promises to find another, more appropriate job in the company for any employee who is failing in his or her current position. This "soft landing" policy fosters a climate in which mistakes and failure are viewed as opportunities to learn and improve.[62]

CONCEPT CONNECTION

The decisions Whole Foods Market chairman John Mackey likes best are the ones he doesn't have to make. The philosophy at Whole Foods, the Austin, Texas-based natural foods grocer, is that, whenever possible, decisions should be made by those closest to where they're carried out. Ideally, that means in the stores themselves by a team of employees, who decide everything from who gets hired to what products to carry. Curtis Hellman, pictured here, is part of a team that serves beer and barbeque at the chain's flagship store in Austin. Whole Foods' emphasis on **group decision making** reflects new decision-making processes for today's turbulent times.

When people are afraid to make mistakes, the company is stuck. For example, when Robert Crandall led American Airlines, he built a culture in which any problem that caused a flight delay was followed by finding someone to blame. People became so scared of making a mistake that whenever something went wrong, no one was willing to jump in and try to fix the problem. In contrast, Southwest Airlines uses what it calls *team delay,* which means a flight delay is everyone's problem. This puts the emphasis on fixing the problem rather than on finding an individual to blame.[63] In a turbulent environment, managers do not use mistakes and failure to create a climate of fear. Instead, they encourage people to take risks and move ahead with the decision process, despite the potential for errors.

Know When to Bail. Even though managers encourage risk taking and learning from mistakes, they also aren't hesitant to pull the plug on something that is not working. Research found that organizations often continue to invest time and money in a solution despite strong evidence that it is not appropriate. This tendency is referred to as **escalating commitment.** Managers might block or distort negative information because they don't want to be responsible for a bad decision, or they might simply refuse to accept that their solution is wrong. A study in Europe verified that even highly successful managers often miss or ignore warning signals because they become committed to a decision and believe if they persevere it will pay off.[64] As companies face increasing competition, complexity, and change, it is important that managers don't get so attached to their own ideas that they're unwilling to recognize when to move on. According to Stanford University professor Robert Sutton, the key to successful creative decision making is to "fail early, fail often, and pull the plug early."[65]

TAKE ACTION

If someone makes a mistake, use it as a chance to learn, not to criticize.

escalating commitment
continuing to invest time and resources in a failing decision.

Practice the Five Whys. One way to encourage good decision making under high uncertainty is to get people to think more broadly and deeply about problems rather than going with a superficial understanding and a first response. However, this approach doesn't mean people have to spend hours analyzing a problem and gathering research. One simple procedure adopted by a number of leading companies is known as the *five whys*.[66] For every problem, employees learn to ask "Why?" not just once, but five times. The first *why* generally produces a superficial explanation for the problem, and each subsequent *why* probes deeper into the causes of the problem and potential solutions. The point of the *five whys* is to improve how people think about problems and generate alternatives for solving them.

Engage in Rigorous Debate. An important key to better decision making under conditions of uncertainty is to encourage a rigorous debate of the issue at hand.[67] Good managers recognize that constructive conflict based on divergent points of view can bring a problem into focus, clarify people's ideas, stimulate creative thinking, create a broader understanding of issues and alternatives, and improve decision quality.[68] Chuck Knight, the former CEO of Emerson Electric, always sparked heated debates during strategic planning meetings. Knight believed rigorous debate gave people a clearer picture of the competitive landscape and forced managers to look at all sides of an issue, helping them reach better decisions.[69]

Stimulating rigorous debate can be done in several ways. One way is by ensuring that the group is diverse in terms of age and gender, functional area of expertise, hierarchical level, and experience with the business. Some groups assign a **devil's advocate,** who has the role of challenging the assumptions and assertions made by the group.[70] The devil's advocate may force the group to rethink its approach to the problem and avoid reaching premature conclusions. Jeffrey McKeever, CEO of MicroAge, often plays the devil's advocate, changing his position in the middle of a debate to ensure that other executives don't just go along with his opinions.[71] Another approach is to have group members develop as many alternatives as they can as quickly as they can.[72] It allows the team to work with multiple alternatives and encourages people to advocate ideas they might not prefer simply to encourage debate. Still another way to encourage constructive conflict is to use a technique called **point-counterpoint,** which breaks a decision-making group into two subgroups and assigns them different, often competing responsibilities.[73] The groups then develop and exchange proposals and discuss and debate the various options until they arrive at a common set of understandings and recommendations.

Decision making in today's high-speed, complex environment is one of the most important—and most challenging—responsibilities for managers. By using brainstorming, learning from mistakes rather than assigning blame, knowing when to bail, practicing the *five whys,* and engaging in rigorous debate, managers can improve the quality and effectiveness of their organizational decisions.

Information Technology Has Changed Everything

devil's advocate
a decision-making technique in which an individual is assigned the role of challenging the assumptions and assertions made by the group to prevent premature consensus.

point-counterpoint
a decision-making technique in which people are assigned to express competing points of view.

The Internet, little more than a curiosity to many managers just a decade ago, now influences their lives and jobs in myriad ways. Managers at Arch Coal use the Internet and GPS networking to monitor and manage major mining equipment. Trinchero Family Estates, producer of Sutter Hill wines, uses an online system to track the processing of grapes from harvesting to bottling to selling. And the American Society for the Prevention of Cruelty to Animals used the Web to quickly recruit volunteers after Hurricane Katrina—even though the organization had never before recruited volunteers in its 130-year history.[74] Some companies, such as Wal-Mart, are profiting by using Web sites to sell more products, but they are also discovering that the Internet has drawbacks.

Almost every company uses the Internet to some extent as part of its information technology (IT) system. The strategic use of IT is one of the defining aspects of organizational success in today's world. Managers use information systems that rely on a massive data warehouse to make decisions about what to stock, how to price and promote it, and when to reorder or discontinue items. Handheld scanners enable managers to keep close tabs on inventory and monitor sales; at the end of each workday, orders for new merchandise are sent by computer to headquarters, where they are automatically organized and sent to regional distribution centers, which have electronic linkages with key suppliers for reordering. A recent innovation is using tiny chips with identification numbers on shipments of products (called radio-frequency identification, or RFID), which enables close tracking of inventory all through the supply chain. At Wal-Mart headquarters, top executives analyze buying patterns and other information, enabling them to spot problems or opportunities and convey the information to stores.[75] Numerous other companies, in industries from manufacturing to entertainment, as well as not-for-profit and government organizations, are using IT to get closer to customers, enter new markets, and streamline business processes.

IT and e-business have changed the way people and organizations work and thus present new challenges for managers. The Internet continues to disrupt and transform the traditional ways of business as well as convulse entire industries by giving advantages to nimble upstarts. Yet existing businesses are using e-business to cut costs, increase efficiency, improve customer service, speed up innovation, and improve productivity.[76] This section explores the management of IT and e-business. We begin by looking at the management implications of using advanced IT. Next, we examine some recent technology trends and the types of information systems frequently used in organizations. Then, the section looks at the growing use of the Internet and e-business, including a discussion of fundamental e-business strategies, business-to-business marketplaces, use of IT in business operations, and the importance of knowledge management.

An organization's **information technology (IT)** consists of the hardware, software, telecommunications, database management, and other technologies it uses to store data and make them available in the form of information for organizational decision making. IT, including the use of the Internet for e-business, can enable managers to be better connected with employees, the environment, and each other. In general, IT has positive implications for the practice of management, although it can also present problems. Some specific implications of IT for managers, as shown in Exhibit 6.8, include enhanced collaboration, improved employee effectiveness, increased efficiency, empowered employees, and potential information overload.

BOUNDARIES DISSOLVE; COLLABORATION REIGNS

Walk into the video conference room at Infosys Technologies, a leader in India's outsourcing and software industry, and the first thing you'll see is a wall-size flat-screen television. On that screen, Infosys can hold virtual meetings of the key players from its entire global supply chain for any project at any time of the day or night. For example, American designers could be onscreen talking to their Indian software writers and their Asian manufacturers all at once.[77] Time, distance, and other boundaries between individuals, departments, and organizations are irrelevant in today's business world. Collaboration is what it's all about.

One of the most significant advantages of using advanced IT is that it enhances collaboration both within the organization and with customers, suppliers, and partners. As historian Thomas L. Friedman puts it, "Wherever you look today . . . hierarchies are being flattened and value is being created less and less within vertical silos and more and more through horizontal collaboration within companies, between companies, and among individuals."[78] IT can connect employees around the world for the sharing and exchange of information and ideas. The emphasis on using IT rather than personal travel for

information technology (IT)
the hardware, software, telecommunications, database management, and other technologies used to store, process, and distribute information.

EXHIBIT 6.8
Implications
of Information
Technology for
Managers

collaboration is a response to reduced travel budgets and rising airfares, concern over incidents such as international terrorism, and the need for speed in today's global marketplace.[79] Sometimes flattening the hierarchy can have negative effects, as shown in the Business Blooper.

PEOPLE DO BETTER WORK

IT can provide employees with all kinds of information about their customers, competitors, markets, and service, as well as enable them to instantly share information and insights with colleagues. In addition, with time and geographic boundaries dissolving, a team can work throughout the day on a project in Switzerland and, while they sleep, a team in the United States can continue where the Swiss team left off.

Business Blooper

Harassing E-Mails?

Be careful who you list as a friend on the next Web site you see, or you may land in jail on harassment charges. That's what happened to Shannon Michelle O'Dell after she was fired from her job at Ford Custom Homes in Franklin, Tennessee. Almost immediately, her former supervisor started getting a barrage of magazines, e-mails, music, books, and phone calls from companies that found her through contact information left on a Web site. Police traced it back to O'Dell, who simply said she went to a Web site that let's you sign up for free offers and coupons. When the site asked for a friend's name, O'Dell listed her boss. "I didn't know that would happen," says O'Dell, and that she didn't mean for her boss to be overwhelmed with e-mail offers. The police were not impressed with her excuse and booked her into County Jail.

SOURCE: Mitchell Kline, "E-mail, Calls to Ex-Boss Land Woman in Hot Water," *The Tennessean* (June 26, 2007): p. B1.

In general, IT enables managers to design jobs to provide people with more intellectual engagement and more challenging work. The availability of IT does not guarantee increased job performance, but when implemented and used appropriately, it can have a dramatic influence on employee effectiveness. For example, an Internet system at Continental Airlines alerts the company when planes arrive late and assesses passengers' needs, enabling employees to delay the departure of other flights or send carts to make connections easier for passengers. Continental's various systems for analyzing data to improve customer service helped the company move into the top ranks in terms of customer satisfaction, after being dead last in the industry during the 1990s.[80]

THINGS ARE MORE EFFICIENT

IT can significantly speed work processes, cut costs, and increase efficiency. McDonald's is experimenting with a system that allows workers at a call center in Santa Maria, California, to remotely take drive-through orders from 40 restaurants scattered around the United States, in places such as Honolulu, Hawaii; Gulfport, Mississippi; and Gillette, Wyoming. The orders are zapped back to the restaurant via the Internet to be filled, and most customers have no idea their order has just traveled hundreds or thousands of miles. The system saves just a few seconds per order, but over the course of time at a busy drive-through, that adds up to significant cost savings and increased sales.[81]

Sweeping away administrative paperwork, automating mundane tasks, and standardizing services are other advantages of IT. For example, at IBM, automating customer service helped reduce the number of call center employees and saved $750 million in one year alone. Intermountain Health Care, based in Salt Lake City, Utah, automated its pharmacies in the 1990s and is now applying IT to standardize medical care, resulting in fewer mistakes, greater consistency in applying the latest medical advances, and lower costs.

EMPLOYEES ARE ENGAGED

IT is profoundly affecting the way organizations are structured. With IT, managers can change the locus of knowledge by providing information to people who would not otherwise receive it. Lower-level employees are increasingly challenged with more information and more interesting jobs. Nurses, bellhops, truck drivers, utility repair workers, and warehouse staffers all need easy access to information to do their jobs well in today's fast-paced environment.[82]

3 The increased technology in the workplace keeps people too disconnected from one another, making it harder to get their jobs done.

ANSWER: Technology can actually bring people closer together, if used properly, though not necessarily face-to-face. Communication can exist with more people, keeping a larger group in the loop. Because of the increased efficiencies, it can actually allow for more interaction time.

IT enables decisions to be made by the employees who are in the best position to implement them and monitor their effects. For example, the U.S. Army is using new technology that pushes information about battlefield conditions, the latest intelligence on the enemy, and so forth, down the line to the lower troops. Armed with better data and trained to see patterns in the barrage of information, lieutenants in the field are making more of the decisions once made by commanders.[83] Avnet, a computer systems, component, and embedded subsystems manufacturer, uses an IT system that pushes data on orders, shipment schedules,

NEW MANAGER SELF TEST

Brain Hemispheric Dominance

The questions that follow ask you to describe your behavior. For each question, check the answer that best describes you.

1. I am usually running late for class or other appointments:

_____ a. Yes

_____ b. No

2. When taking a test I prefer:

_____ a. Subjective questions (discussion or essay)

_____ b. Objective questions (multiple choice)

3. When making decisions, I typically:

_____ a. Go with my gut—what feels right

_____ b. Carefully weigh each option

4. When solving a problem, I would more likely:

_____ a. Take a walk, mull things over, then discuss

_____ b. Write down alternatives, prioritize them, then pick the best

5. I consider time spent daydreaming as:

_____ a. A viable tool for planning my future

_____ b. A waste of time

6. To remember directions, I typically:

_____ a. Visualize the information

_____ b. Make notes

7. My work style is mostly:

_____ a. Juggle several things at once

_____ b. Concentrate on one task at a time until complete

8. My desk, work area, or laundry area are typically:

_____ a. Cluttered

_____ b. Neat and organized

INTERPRETATION AND SCORING: People have two thinking processes—one visual and intuitive in the right half of the brain, and the other verbal and analytical in the left half of the brain. As a new manager, the thinking process you prefer predisposes you to certain types of knowledge and information—visual dashboards vs. written reports, tacit suggestions vs. quantitative data—as effective input to your thinking and decision making.

Count the number of checked "a" items and "b" items. Each "a" represents right-brain processing, and each "b" represents left-brain processing. If you scored 6 or higher on either, you have a distinct processing style. If you checked less than 6 for either, you probably have a balanced style. New managers typically need left-brain processing to handle data and to justify decisions. At middle and upper management levels, right-brain processing enables visionary thinking and strategic insights.

SOURCE: Adapted from Carolyn Hopper, *Practicing Management Skills* (New York: Houghton Mifflin, 2003); and Jacquelyn Wonder and Priscilla Donovan, "Mind Openers," *Self* (March 1984).

and dates by which the company will cease manufacturing certain products directly to front-line sales teams, who use this information to modify their work practices and improve customer service.[84]

PEOPLE CAN SUFFER FROM INFORMATION OVERLOAD

Getting data and information to people who need it and can use it to improve their performance and decision-making is important, but it's possible to have too much of a good thing. One major problem associated with advances in technology is that the company can become a quagmire of information, with employees so overwhelmed by the sheer volume that they are unable to sort out the valuable from the useless.[85]

In many cases, the ability to produce data and information is outstripping employees' ability to process it. One British psychologist claims to have identified a new mental disorder caused by too much information; he has termed it *information fatigue syndrome*.[86] IT is a primary culprit in contributing to this new "disease." However, managers have the ability to alleviate the problem and improve information quality. The first step is to ensure that suppliers of IT and CIOs work closely with employees to identify the kinds of questions they must answer and the kinds of data and information they really need. Specialists often are enamored with the volume of data a system can produce and overlook the need to provide small amounts of quality information in a timely and useful manner for decision making. Top executives should be actively involved in setting limits by focusing the organization on key strategies and on the critical questions that must be answered to pursue those strategies.[87]

The Evolving World of IT

IT changes rapidly, and organizations that want to stay competitive are adopting new technologies and approaches to improve their operations. However, most organizations merge new IT applications with existing operational and management information systems.

A NEW GENERATION OF IT

The force that is fueling growth on the Internet today isn't a bunch of dot-com startups or even long-established companies making waves in the online world. Instead, power has shifted to the individual, with blogs and social networking becoming the most explosive outbreaks in the world of IT since the emergence of the Internet itself.[88] A **blog** is a running Web log that allows an individual to post opinions and ideas about anything from the weather and dating relationships to a company's products, management, or business practices. There were an estimated 60 million bloggers in mid-2006, and the number was growing.[89] Smart managers are paying attention to the phenomenon. For example, before announcing a major investment in energy efficient technology, managers at General Electric engaged with environmental bloggers to build support. Companies such as Microsoft and Cingular Wireless have enlisted the aid of bloggers to spread the word about new products or services.[90] An entire industry is springing up to help companies navigate the new world of blogs, such as monitoring what is being said about the company, implementing damage control strategies, and tracking what the majority of the world is thinking, minute by minute, to help the organization respond to emerging trends and opportunities.[91]

Social networking, also referred to as *social media* or *user generated content,* is an extension of blogs.[92] Sites such as MySpace, Facebook, and Friendster provide an unprecedented peer-to-peer communication channel, where people interact in an online community, sharing personal information and photos, producing and sharing all sorts of information and opinions, or unifying activists and raising funds. MySpace, now owned by News Corp., had 72 million members within only two years, with an estimated quarter of a million more signing up every day. A new social networking site, TagWorld, which is being referred to as the "MySpace killer" by bloggers, could grow even bigger. TagWorld offers an expanded range of services, including not only blogging but a multipage site, a gigabyte of storage, a music player, classifieds, and photo- and video-sharing capabilities. In addition, TagWorld gathers and provides real-time information, such as allowing a musician who posts his music online to see exactly who is listening and where. This real-time information and automated feedback makes TagWorld especially valuable to businesses for spotting trends, marketing products and services, and other activities.

blog
web log that allows individuals to post opinions and ideas.

social networking
online interaction in a community format where people share personal information and photos, produce and share all sorts of information and opinions, or unify activists and raise funds.

CONCEPT CONNECTION

Just how completely will the Internet and IT revolutionize banking? Start-ups such as everbank.com believe there's a place for branchless, Internet-only "click banks." Everbank.com offers full banking and brokerage services 24 hours a day, and without the expense of building and staffing offices, it can offer customers higher interest rates than its brick-and-mortar competitors. To be sure, Everbank does have to overcome security concerns, compensate for the lack of ATM machines, and compete against improved online services at traditional banks. Still, managers such as CEO Frank Trotter, pictured here, think the new Web bank can prosper by targeting affluent, computer-savvy professionals who value its time-saving convenience.

Single-use social networks, such as YouTube (video), Craigslist (classified ads), and Wikipedia (encyclopedia articles) are also growing in popularity. On YouTube's Web site, for example, individual users post more than 60,000 video clips a day, many of them home-shot, and consumers all over the world are viewing them at a rate of 70 million times a day.[93] NBC Universal, which originally demanded that YouTube take down clips of its programming, decided to join the trend rather than fight it, announcing that it would make promotional clips of popular shows available on the site and holding contests for users to submit their own promotional videos for certain shows.[94]

Blogs and social networking sites have the potential to shake up every business, government, and nonprofit organization in the world, for good or ill. Smart managers and organizations are searching for ways to use the power of these innovations to their advantage and minimize the damage or disruptions they might bring.

DATA VERSUS INFORMATION

A central purpose of both operations information systems and management information systems is to translate *data* into *information*. **Data** are raw facts and figures that in and of themselves may not be useful. To be useful, data must be processed into finished **information**—that is, data that have been converted into a meaningful and useful context for specific users. New software and systems can help managers effectively identify and access useful information. For example, American Greetings Corporation, which sells greeting cards, might gather *data* about demographics in various parts of the country. These data are then translated into *information;* for example, stores in Florida require an enormous assortment of greeting cards directed at grandson, granddaughter, niece, and nephew, while stores in some other parts of the country might need a larger percentage of slightly irreverent, youth-oriented products.[95]

data
raw, unsummarized, and unanalyzed facts and figures.

information
data that have been converted into a meaningful and useful context for the receiver.

operations information system
a computer-based information system that supports a company's day-to-day operations.

Types of Information Systems

Organizations typically incorporate new and emerging tools into their existing IT systems. Most managers appreciate the value of making information readily available and easily shared with those who need it in some kind of formal, computer-based information system. Such a system combines hardware, software, and human resources to support organizational information and communication needs. One way to distinguish among the many types of information systems is to focus on the functions they perform and the people they serve in an organization. **Operations information systems** support information-processing needs of a business's day-to-day operations, as well as low-level operations management functions. Management information systems typically support the strategic decision-making needs of higher-level managers.

OPERATIONS INFORMATION SYSTEMS

A variety of tools referred to as operations information systems support the information-processing needs related to a business's day-to-day operations. Types of operations' information systems include transaction-processing systems, process control systems, and office automation systems. Each of these supports daily operations and decisions that typically are made by nonmanagement employees or lower-level managers.

Transaction-processing systems (TPSs) record and process data resulting from business operations, including such data as sales to customers, purchases from suppliers, inventory changes, and wages to employees. A TPS collects data from these transactions and stores them in a database. Employees use the database to produce reports and other information, such as customer statements and employee paychecks. Most of an organization's reports are generated from these databases. Transaction-processing systems identify, collect, and organize the fundamental information from which an organization operates.

While a transaction-processing system keeps track of the size, type, and financial consequences of the organization's transactions, companies also need information about the quantity and quality of their production activities. Therefore, they may use process control systems to monitor and control ongoing physical processes. For example, petroleum refineries, pulp and paper mills, food manufacturing plants, and electric power plants use **process control systems** with special sensing devices that monitor and record physical phenomena such as temperature or pressure changes. The system relays the measurements or sensor-detected data to a computer for processing; employees and operations managers can check the data to look for problems requiring action.

Office automation systems combine modern hardware and software such as word processors, desktop publishers, e-mail, and teleconferencing to handle the tasks of publishing and distributing information. Office automation systems can also use data from other operations systems to transform manual accounting procedures to electronic media or to automatically make programmed decisions, as described earlier in this chapter. Some banks, for example, use automated systems to make credit decisions. Cellular phone companies use automation to determine the best service package for a particular customer.[96] Merrill Lynch uses office automation to electronically manage consultants' travel and entertainment expenses, cutting the time it takes to process a report and issue reimbursement from six weeks to four days and slashing the average cost of processing a report from $25 to only a few bucks.[97] These systems enable businesses to streamline office tasks, reduce errors, and improve customer service. In this way, office automation systems support the other kinds of information systems.

Operations information systems aid organizational decision makers in many ways and across various settings. For example, Enterprise Rent-A-Car's Automated Rental Management System (ARMS) provides front-line employees with up-to-the-minute information that enables them to provide exceptional service to each customer. ARMS helps Enterprise keep track of the millions of transactions the company logs every hour. If a customer visits a branch office and requests a certain kind of car, the agent can immediately determine whether one is available anywhere in the city. Insurance companies such as Geico can also link their claims systems directly to Enterprise's automated rental system, book a reservation, and send payments electronically, eliminating the need for paper invoices and checks.[98]

MANAGEMENT INFORMATION SYSTEMS

A **management information system (MIS)** is a computer-based system that provides information and support for effective managerial decision making. The basic elements of a management information system are illustrated in Exhibit 6.9. The MIS is supported by the organization's operations information systems and by organizational databases (and frequently databases of external data as well). Management information systems typically include reporting systems, decision support systems, executive information

---

TAKE ACTION

As a manager, find ways to get more information that can help you measure how well the organization is doing.

---

transaction-processing system (TPS)
a type of operations information system that records and processes data resulting from routine business transactions such as sales, purchases, and payroll.

process control system
a computer system that monitors and controls ongoing physical processes, such as temperature or pressure changes.

office automation systems
systems that combine modern hardware and software to handle the tasks of publishing and distributing information.

management information system (MIS)
a computer-based system that provides information and support for effective managerial decision making.

EXHIBIT 6.9

Basic Elements
of Management
Information Systems

Internet
a global collection of computer networks linked together for the exchange of data and information.

World Wide Web (WWW)
a collection of central servers for accessing information on the Internet.

e-business
any business that takes place by digital processes over a computer network rather than in physical space.

e-commerce
business exchanges or transactions that occur electronically.

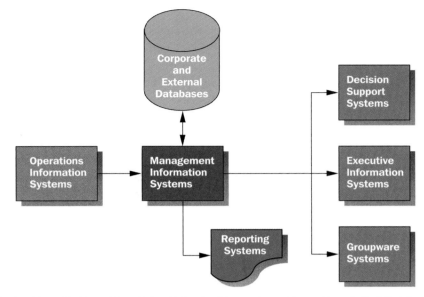

SOURCE: Adapted from Ralph M. Stair and George W. Reynolds, *Principles of Information Systems: A Managerial Approach*, 4th ed. (Cambridge, MA: Course Technology, 1999): 391.

CONCEPT CONNECTION

The next stop in the **evolving world of IT** is Web 2.0, a term that's been coined to refer to Web-based services such as social networking and wikis. This *Newsweek* cover from spring 2006 reflects Web 2.0's basic philosophy of putting the *"we"* in *Web* with sites such as the social networking site MySpace and the video-sharing service YouTube. Entrepreneurs all over the world are tapping into the Web's ability to help people in far-flung locations share, collaborate, socialize, and form communities. They're setting up new Web businesses staffed by only a handful of people, inviting users to create and organize the site's content.

systems, and groupware, each of which will be explained in this section.

MISs typically support strategic decision-making needs of mid-level and top management. However, as technology becomes more widely accessible, more employees are wired into networks, and organizations push decision making downward.

The Internet and E-Business

In recent years, most organizations have incorporated the Internet as part of their IT strategy.[99] The **Internet** is a global collection of computer networks linked together for the exchange of data and information. The Internet became accessible as a public information and communications tool after Tim Berners-Lee, a researcher at CERN (Centre Européan pour la Recherche Nucléaire) in Geneva, Switzerland, designed software for the original **World Wide Web (WWW),** a user-friendly interface that today allows people to easily communicate with each other and with the Internet via a set of central servers.[100]

Both business and nonprofit organizations quickly realized the potential of the Internet for expanding their operations globally, improving business processes, reaching new customers, and making the most of their resources. Exhibit 6.10 shows the opening Web page for IKEA, a Swedish furniture retailer with more than 200 stores around the world and a thriving catalog and Internet business.

E-business has begun to flourish. **E-business** can be defined as any business that takes place by digital processes over a computer network rather than in physical space. Most commonly today, it refers to electronic linkages over the Internet with customers, partners, suppliers, employees, or other key constituents. **E-commerce** is a more limited term that refers specifically to business exchanges or transactions that occur electronically.

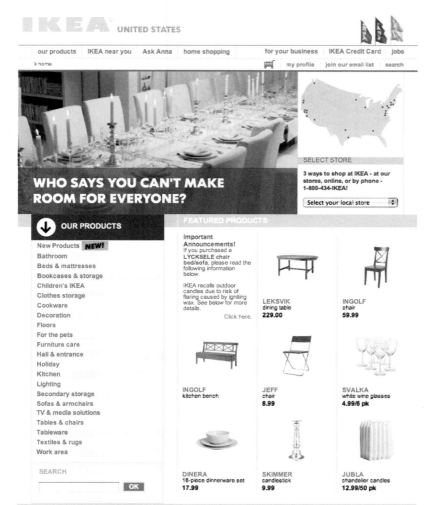

EXHIBIT 6.10

Opening Page of the
Web Site for IKEA

Benchmarking

String Cheese Incident

Most bands focus primarily on their music, the creativity, and the soul. Not String Cheese Incident. The Boulder-based jazzy band improvises its music but not its business. The five-member band has developed a loyal following during the past 14 years of nonstop touring. During a time when the music business was cutting back, when piracy was eating into album sales, String Cheese Incident built a $15 million dollar business (selling 590,000 albums) that now employs 45 people.

The secret: exploiting the Internet, including selling downloads of live concerts. "Our goal from the beginning," says bass player Keith Moseley, "was to control our own destiny and to maintain artistic control." Interestingly, they were that way from the start, always seeing the band as a serious business opportunity. Taking advantage of all the people they came in contact with on the road, they grilled successful musicians about how they managed their careers, from tour operations to record deals. And they weren't impressed with the answers because they saw the music business model was falling apart. Band manager Jeremy Stein says, "We wanted a new model for ourselves."

String Cheese Incident looked to the one great business-model band, The Grateful Dead, which built brand loyalty by catering to its die-hard fans with low ticket prices and permission to tape concerts. String Cheese Incident wanted to do that with one advantage: the Internet. Live shows bring in 50 percent of their revenue, and they now sell a major portion of their tickets online (after settling a lawsuit against Ticketmaster). Customers can save 10 percent by booking through String Cheese Incident rather than Ticketmaster. Then they set up their own travel agency, which helps fans plan trips to their concerts, as well as concerts of 20 other bands. It's all about putting themselves in their fans' shoes and making the whole experience easier. It must be working, because there are many fans like 35-year-old real estate agent Pjef Grantham, who's attended way more than 200 "incidents" (translation: concerts) worldwide since 1996. His motto: "First in line, last to leave."

Benefiting most from the Internet is online album sales, which account for 20 percent of the band's CD sales, and it is a much more profitable deal than selling in retail stores. Last year, the band started selling downloads of its concerts for $10 each on its Web site (http://www.stringcheeseincident.com). Even though piracy is a threat, they are going to carry on offering the cheap downloads. "We're going to continue to make music available, even if that means giving it away," says Moseley. "The more people are exposed to our music, the better it is for the band."

SOURCE: David Kushner, "String Theory," *FSB* (January 2005): pp. 95–96; Johnny Lehndorff, "Five Questions for Pjef Grantham," *Rocky Mountain News* (March 21, 2007): p. 17.

Some organizations are set up as e-businesses that are run completely over the Internet, such as eBay, Amazon.com, Expedia, and Yahoo!. These companies would not exist without the Internet. However, most traditional, established organizations, including General Electric, the City of Madison, Wisconsin; Target stores; and the U.S. Postal Service, also make extensive use of the Internet, and we will focus on these types of organizations in the remainder of this section. The goal of e-business for established organizations is to digitalize as much of the business as possible to make the organization more efficient and effective. Companies are using the Internet and the Web for everything from filing expense reports and calculating daily sales to connecting directly with suppliers for the exchange of information and ordering of parts.[101] Indie rock band String Cheese Incident has used the Internet to create a highly profitable venture.

First, each organization operates an **intranet,** an internal communications system that uses the technology and standards of the Internet but is accessible only to people within the company. The next component is a system that allows the separate companies to share data and information. Two options are an electronic data interchange network or an extranet. **Electronic data interchange (EDI)** networks link the computer systems of buyers and sellers to allow the transmission of structured data primarily for ordering, distribution, and payables and receivables.[102] An **extranet** is an external communications system that uses the Internet and is shared by two or more organizations. With an extranet, each organization moves certain data outside of its private intranet, but makes the data

intranet
an internal communications system that uses the technology and standards of the Internet but is accessible only to people within the organization.

electronic data interchange (EDI)
a network that links the computer systems of buyers and sellers to allow the transmission of structured data primarily for ordering, distribution, and payables and receivables.

extranet
an external communications system that uses the Internet and is shared by two or more organizations.

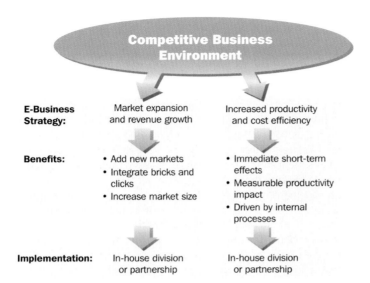

EXHIBIT 6.11

Strategies for
Engaging Clicks
with Bricks

available only to the other companies sharing the extranet. The final piece of the overall system is the Internet, which is accessible to the general public. Organizations make some information available to the public through their Web sites, which may include products or services offered for sale. For example, at IKEA's Web site, consumers can chat with an automated online assistant, use room planning tools for interior design, and order furniture and other products.

E-BUSINESS STRATEGIES

The first step toward a successful e-business is for managers to determine why they need such a business to begin with.[103] Failure to align the e-business initiative with corporate strategy can lead to e-business failure. Two basic strategic approaches for traditional organizations setting up an Internet operation are illustrated in Exhibit 6.11. Some companies embrace e-business primarily to expand into new markets and reach new customers. Others use e-business as a route to increased productivity and cost efficiency. As shown in the exhibit, these strategies are implemented either by setting up an in-house Internet division or by partnering with other organizations to handle online activities.

Market Expansion. An Internet division allows a company to establish direct links to customers and expand into new markets. The organization can provide access around the clock to a worldwide market and thus reach new customers. ESPN.com, for example, is the biggest Internet draw for sports, attracting a devoted audience of 18- to 34-year-old men, which is an audience that is less and less interested in traditional television. The site's ESPN360, a customizable high-speed service, offers super-sharp video clips of everything from *SportsCenter* to poker tournaments, as well as behind-the-scenes coverage. To reach young viewers, other television networks, including Comedy Central; E. W. Scripps Networks, which owns HGTV and the Food Network; CBS Broadcasting; and NBC Universal, are also launching high-speed broadband channels to deliver short videos, pilots of new shows, or abbreviated and behind-the-scenes looks.[104] Print media organizations use Web sites to reach new customers, as well. *Radar* magazine is taking an innovative approach by launching a Web site to build a market *before* publishing the magazine itself.

It remains to be seen whether *Radar* will succeed in any form—print or online. Efforts have just begun to build a market for the new publication. For established firms, the market expansion strategy is competitively sustainable because the e-business division works in conjunction with a conventional bricks-and-mortar company. For example, The Finish

 **TAKE ACTION**

Go to the ethical dilemma on page 241 that pertains to using the Internet for market expansion.

Radar

In the summer of 2006, an intriguing new Web site turned up on the Internet. A click on http://www.radarmagazine.com revealed an above-ground stone crypt, from which protrudes a hand holding a copy of *Radar* magazine. *Radar* was first introduced in 2003 but ran out of cash and closed after only two issues. But the Web site says it all: "Hard to Kill. Radar Rises Again. Online This Summer—On Newsstands 2007."

With an infusion of cash from publishing and real estate mogul Mortimer B. Zuckerman and financier Jeffrey Epstein, managers are reviving *Radar* as an irreverent, fun, urban-oriented publication aimed at 25- to 39-year-olds. But this time around, they decided to take a fresh approach by introducing a Web page long before the first issue is published. Maer Roshan, *Radar's* editor, and Elinore Carmody, senior vice president and chief marketing and sales officer, say easing into the marketplace with a Web site will help promote the magazine to its target audience, as well as take some pressure off the first print issue. "We don't want to be a one-hit wonder," Carmody says. "Slower is better when you launch." Managers and editors hope the Web site will build buzz and lure advertisers, who are increasingly diverting money from print media to the Web.

Radar's Web site will continue after the magazine emerges in print form, showcasing a series of features and offering fresh takes daily on news, gossip, and social or cultural events. With all the resources and energy going into the Web site, some question why *Radar* wants to publish a traditional magazine at all. Yet *Radar* believes there's still a place for magazines that allow for in-depth stories. "And," Roshan says, "there is just something tactilely great about the way paper feels and the way pictures look" in a magazine. Time will tell whether the marketplace agrees.[105]

Line, a retailer of athletic clothing, footwear, and accessories, sells products online but also uses the Web site as a way to drive more traffic into its stores.[106]

Productivity and Efficiency. With this approach, the e-business initiative is seen primarily as a way to improve the bottom line by increasing productivity and cutting costs. An automaker, for example, might use e-business to reduce the cost of ordering and tracking parts and supplies and to implement just-in-time manufacturing. GM has implemented wireless Internet technology to increase productivity in 90 of its plants, where Wi-Fi devices are mounted on forklifts and used by assembly workers to track the movement of engine parts and car seats tagged with tiny chips that emit electronic signals.[107] At Nibco, a manufacturer of piping products, 12 plants and distribution centers automatically share data on inventory and orders, resulting in about 70 percent of orders being automated. The technology has enabled Nibco to trim its inventory by 13 percent, as well as respond more quickly to changes in orders from customers.[108]

Several studies attest to real and significant gains in productivity from e-business, and productivity gains from U.S. businesses were projected to reach $450 billion by 2005.[109] Even the smallest companies can realize gains. Rather than purchasing parts from a local supplier at premium rates, a small firm can access a worldwide market and find the best price, or negotiate better terms with the local supplier.[110] Service firms and government agencies can benefit too. New York City became the first city to use the Internet to settle personal injury claims more efficiently. Using NYC Comptroller's Cybersettle Service, lawyers submit blind offers until a match is hit. If an agreement can't be reached, the parties go back to face-to-face negotiations. The city saved $17 million in less than 2 years by settling 1,137 out of 7,000 claims online, and reduced settlement times from 4 years to 9 months.[111]

IMPLEMENTING E-BUSINESS STRATEGIES

When traditional organizations such as Nibco, CBS Broadcasting, or General Motors Corporation want to establish an Internet division, managers have to decide how best to integrate bricks and clicks—that is, how to blend their traditional operations with an Internet initiative.[112] One approach is to set up an *in-house division*. This approach offers tight integration between the online business and the organization's traditional operation. Managers create a separate department or unit within the company that functions within the structure and guidance of the traditional organization. This approach gives the new division several advantages by piggybacking on the established company, including brand recognition, purchasing leverage with suppliers, shared customer information, and marketing opportunities. Office Depot, for example, launched an online unit for market expansion as a tightly integrated in-house part of its overall operation. Managers and employees within the company are assigned to the unit to handle Web site maintenance, product offerings, order fulfillment, customer service, and other aspects of the online business.[113]

A second approach is through *partnerships,* such as joint ventures or alliances. Safeway partnered with the British supermarket chain Tesco, described in the previous chapter, to establish its online grocery business in the United States. Safeway first tried to go it alone but found that it needed the expertise of an established online player with a proven business model.[114] In many cases, a traditional company will partner with an established Internet firm to reach a broader customer base or to handle activities such as customer service, order fulfillment, and Web site maintenance. Companies such as Linens 'n Things, Timberland, and Reebok partner with GSI Commerce, which stores goods, takes orders, and then picks, packs, and ships orders directly to customers. The bricks-and-mortar companies get the expertise and services of a world-class Internet business without having to hire more people with IT expertise and build the capabilities themselves.[115]

GOING INTERNATIONAL

When businesses were first rushing to set up Web sites, managers envisioned easily doing business all over the world. Soon, though, they awakened to the reality that national boundaries matter just as much as they ever did. The global e-market can't be approached as if it were one homogeneous piece.[116] Organizations that want to succeed with international e-business are tailoring their Web sites to address differences in language, regulations, payment systems, and consumer preferences in different parts of the world. For example, Yahoo!, Amazon, Dell, Walt Disney, and the National Football League have all set up country-specific sites in the local language. Washingtonpost.com gives its news a broader global flavor during the overnight hours when international readers frequent the site. eBay is struggling with currency issues, as it has alienated many potential users in other countries by quoting prices only in U.S. dollars. And companies with online stores are finding that they may need to offer a different product mix and discounts tailored to local preferences. The Internet is a powerful way to reach customers and partners around the world, and managers are learning to address the cross-national challenges that come with serving a worldwide market.

E-MARKETPLACES

The biggest boom in e-commerce has been in business-to-business (B2B) transactions, or buying and selling between companies. B2B transactions are at $2.4 trillion and growing, according to Forrester Research Inc.[117] One significant trend is the development of **B2B marketplaces,** in which an intermediary sets up an electronic marketplace where buyers and sellers meet, acting as a hub for B2B commerce. Exhibit 6.12 illustrates a B2B marketplace, where many different sellers offer products and services to many different buyers through a *hub,* or online portal. Conducting business through a Web marketplace can mean lower transaction costs, more favorable negotiations, and productivity gains for both buyers and sellers. For example, defense contractor United Technologies buys around $450 million worth of metals, motors, and other products annually via an e-marketplace and gets prices about 15 percent less than what it once paid.[118] Whirlpool uses Rearden Commerce, an online marketplace that is the world's largest hub for services, to book travel arrangements, make restaurant reservations for managers, schedule shipping, and arrange

B2B marketplace
an electronic marketplace set up by an intermediary where buyers and sellers meet.

EXHIBIT 6.12

B2B Marketplace
Model

Many sellers offer products and services through an intermediary to many buyers.

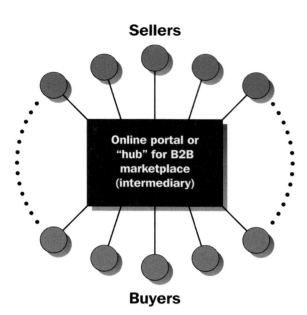

Sellers

Online portal or "hub" for B2B marketplace (intermediary)

Buyers

other services. Within the first two months of using the system, shipping department employees saved 10 percent and cut the time spent arranging for shipping by 52 percent.[119]

eBay, which started out as a marketplace primarily for consumers, has also expanded into B2B commerce. Reliable Tools, Inc., a machine tool shop, tried listing a few items on eBay in late 1998, including items such as a $7,000, 2,300-pound milling machine. The items "sold like ice cream in August," and sales on eBay now make up about 75 percent of Reliable's overall business. Pioneers such as Reliable spurred eBay to set up an industrial products marketplace, which is now on track to top $500 million in annual gross sales.[120] The success of eBay has created an entirely new kind of marketplace, where both individuals and businesses are buying and selling billions of dollars worth of goods a year. A Canadian organization, Mediagrif Interactive Technologies, is giving eBay a run for its money in the B2B marketplace. Mediagrif focuses its efforts entirely on B2B exchanges in markets such as used computer parts, routers and switches, automotive parts, medical equipment, and other areas.[121]

In addition to open, public B2B marketplaces such as eBay, Mediagrif, and AutoTradeCenter, where dealers buy about 100,000 used cars a year, some companies set up private marketplaces to link with a specially invited group of suppliers and partners.[122] For example, General Motors spends billions a year on public marketplaces, but it also operates its own private marketplace, GMSupplyPower, to share proprietary information with thousands of its parts suppliers. E-marketplaces can bring efficiencies to many operations, but some companies find that they don't offer the personal touch their type of business needs.

CONCEPT CONNECTION

The BMW subsidiary MINI offers customers a voice in everything from personalizing their credit cards to designing their cars. BMW Financial Services' MINI Platinum Visa cardholders can customize the MINI image that graces their card by accessing the Web page, shown here. There they can choose from four body styles, 36 different wheels, 21 body colors, and 24 roof options. Similar software allows individuals to customize their actual MINI vehicles. "No two MINIs are exactly alike," the MINI Web site proclaims. This type of collaborative customer experience is the next step in CRM, as companies court Internet-savvy Gen X and Gen Y consumers.

CUSTOMER RELATIONSHIP MANAGEMENT

In addition to better internal information management and information sharing with suppliers and other organizations, companies are using e-business solutions to build stronger customer relationships. One approach is **customer relationship management (CRM) systems** that help companies track potential customers, follow customers' interactions with the firm, and allow employees to call up a customer's past sales and service records, outstanding orders, or unresolved problems.[123] According to a 2005 study by Gartner Group, 60 percent of mid-sized businesses had plans to adopt or expand their CRM usage, while only 2 percent of surveyed companies had no plans for using this technology.[124]

Today, CRM tools are evolving to provide "collaborative customer experiences."[125] Whereas the traditional CRM model gives the organization insight into customers, the new approach provides for a two-way relationship that also gives customers transparency into company thinking. This means that, rather than having employees provide what they *think* customers want and need, employees and customers will jointly craft the customer experience, with the customer, rather than the company, defining what value means.

Increasingly, what distinguishes an organization from its competitors are its knowledge resources, such as product ideas and the ability to identify and find solutions to customers' problems. Exhibit 6.13 lists examples of how CRM and other IT can shorten the distance between customers and the organization, contributing to organizational success through customer loyalty, superior service, better information gathering, and organizational learning.

TURNING DATA AND INFORMATION INTO KNOWLEDGE

The Internet also plays a key role in the recent emphasis managers are putting on **knowledge management,** the efforts to systematically gather knowledge, make it widely available throughout the organization, and foster a culture of learning. Some researchers believe that intellectual capital will soon be the primary way in which businesses measure their value.[126] Therefore, managers see knowledge as an important resource to manage, just as they manage cash flow, raw materials, and other resources. An effective knowledge management system may incorporate a variety of technologies, supported by leadership that values learning, an organizational structure that supports communication and information sharing, and processes for managing change.[127] Two specific technologies that facilitate knowledge management are business intelligence software and corporate intranets or networks. The use of new

customer relationship management (CRM) systems
systems that help companies track customers' interactions with the firm and allow employees to call up information on past transactions.

knowledge management
the process of systematically gathering knowledge, making it widely available throughout the organization, and fostering a culture of learning.

EXHIBIT 6.13

Competitive Advantages Gained from Customer Relationship Management (CRM) Systems

Competitive Advantage	Example
• Increase in customer loyalty	Full information about customer profile and previous requests or preferences is instantly available to sales and service representatives when a customer calls.
• Superior service	Customer representatives can provide personalized service and offer new products and services based on customer's purchasing history.
• Superior information gathering and knowledge sharing	The system is updated each time a customer contacts the organization, whether the contact is in person, by phone, or via the Web. Sales, marketing, service support, and technical support have access to shared database.
• Organizational learning	Managers can analyze patterns to solve problems and anticipate new ones.

business intelligence software helps organizations make sense out of huge amounts of data. These programs combine related pieces of information to create knowledge. Knowledge that can be codified, written down, and contained in databases is referred to as *explicit knowledge*. However, much organizational knowledge is unstructured and resides in people's heads. This *tacit knowledge* cannot be captured in a database, making it difficult to formalize and transmit. Intranets and knowledge-sharing networks can support the spread of tacit knowledge.

Intranets. Many companies are building knowledge management portals on the corporate intranet to give employees an easier way to access and share information. A **knowledge management portal** is a single, personalized point of access for employees to access multiple sources of information on the corporate intranet. Intranets can give people access to explicit knowledge that may be stored in databases, but the greatest value of intranets for knowledge management is increasing the transfer of tacit knowledge. For example, Xerox tried to codify the knowledge of its service technicians and embed it in an expert decision system that was installed in the copiers. The idea was that technicians could be guided by the system and complete repairs more quickly, sometimes even off-site. However, the project failed because it did not take into account the tacit knowledge—the nuances and details—that could not be codified. After a study found that service techs shared their knowledge primarily by telling "war stories," Xerox developed an intranet system called *Eureka* to link 25,000 field service representatives. Eureka, which enables technicians to electronically share war stories and tips for repairing copiers, has cut average repair time by 50 percent.[128]

Organizations typically combine several technologies to facilitate the sharing and transfer of both tacit and explicit knowledge. For example, to spur sharing of explicit knowledge, a leading steel company set up a centralized data warehouse containing the financial and operational performance data and standards for each business unit. Managers can use business intelligence and other decision tools to identify performance gaps and make changes as needed. The company also enables tacit knowledge transfer through an intranet-based document management system, combined with Web conferencing systems, where worldwide experts can exchange ideas.[129] Similarly, when employees of Barclays Global Investors are working on proposals from large customers who require answers to hundreds of complex questions, they can access the knowledge network to reuse answers from previous similar proposals. In addition, employees set up online workspaces to tap into subject experts who can collaborate to help answer new kinds of queries and complete proposals faster.[130]

Overall, IT, including e-business and knowledge management systems, can enable managers to be better connected with employees, customers, partners, and each other.

knowledge management portal
a single point of access for employees to multiple sources of information that provides personalized access on the corporate intranet.

Summary

This chapter made several important points about the process of organizational decision making. The study of decision making is important because it describes how managers make successful strategic and operational decisions. Managers must confront many types of decisions, including programmed and nonprogrammed, and these decisions differ according to the amount of risk, uncertainty, and ambiguity in the environment.

Three decision-making approaches were described: the classical model, the administrative model, and the political model. The classical model explains how managers should make decisions to maximize economic efficiency. The administrative model describes how managers actually make nonprogrammed, uncertain decisions with skills that include intuition. The political model relates to making nonprogrammed decisions when conditions are uncertain, information is limited and ambiguous, and managers are in conflict about what goals to pursue or what course of action to take. Managers have to engage in discussion and coalition building to reach agreement for decisions.

Decision making should involve six basic steps: problem recognition, diagnosis of causes, development of alternatives, choice of an alternative, implementation of the alternative, and feedback and evaluation. Another factor affecting decision making is the manager's personal decision style. The four major decision styles are directive, analytical, conceptual, and behavioral.

The Vroom-Jago model can be used by managers to determine when a decision calls for group participation. Involving others in decision making contributes to individual and organizational learning, which is critical during turbulent times and in high-tech industries. Decisions often have to be made quickly and with limited information. Managers can use the following guidelines: start with brainstorming; learn, don't punish; know when to bail; practice the five whys; and engage in rigorous debate. These techniques improve the quality and effectiveness of decision making in today's turbulent business environment.

IT and e-business are changing the way people and organizations work. Specific implications of IT include enhanced collaboration, more effective employees, increased efficiency, empowered employees, and potential information overload.

New IT tools include blogs, wikis, social networking, peer-to-peer file sharing, and group project management services. These new tools are used in conjunction with information systems that gather huge amounts of data and transform them into useful information for decision makers. Operations information systems, including transaction-processing systems, process control systems, and office automation systems, support daily business operations and the needs of low-level managers. Management information systems, including information reporting systems, decision support systems, and executive information systems, typically support the decision-making needs of middle- and upper-level managers. Collaborative work systems allow groups of managers or employees to share information, collaborate electronically, and have access to computer-based support data for group decision making and problem solving.

Most organizations have incorporated the Internet and e-business as part of their IT strategy. Traditional organizations use an online division primarily for market expansion or to increase productivity and reduce costs. Two primary ways e-business strategies are implemented are through an in-house dot-com division or by partnering with other organizations for the Internet business. Companies are also benefiting from participation in e-marketplaces, where many different sellers offer products and services to many different buyers through an online hub.

Discussion Questions

1. You are a busy partner in a legal firm, and an experienced secretary complains of continued headaches, drowsiness, dry throat, and occasional spells of fatigue and flu. She tells you she believes air quality in the building is bad and would like something to be done. How would you respond?

2. Why do you think decision making is considered a fundamental part of management effectiveness?

3. Explain the difference between risk and ambiguity. How might decision making differ for a risky versus ambiguous situation?

4. Analyze three decisions you made over the past six months. Which of these were programmed and which were nonprogrammed? Which model—the classical, administrative, or political—best describes the approach you took to make each decision?

5. What opportunities and potential problems are posed by the formation of more than one coalition within an organization, each one advocating a different direction or alternatives? What steps can you take as a manager to make sure that dueling coalitions result in constructive discussion rather than dissension?

6. The Vroom-Jago model for group decision making has been criticized as being less than perfect. What do you think are the major criticisms of the model?

7. As a new, entry-level manager, how important is it to find ways to compensate for your relative lack of experience when trying to determine which alternative before you is most likely to succeed? What are some ways you can meet this challenge?

8. List some possible advantages and disadvantages to using computer technology for managerial decision making.

9. Do you think intuition is a valid approach to making decisions in an organization? Why or why not? How might intuition be combined with a rational decision approach?

10. Do you see a conflict between today's emphasis on risk taking and learning and the six steps in Exhibit 6.3 that are associated with effective decision making? Discuss.

11. What do you think is your dominant decision style? Which style are you most comfortable using? Which style feels least comfortable? What are the implications for the type of job you might want to seek?

12. What do you see as the advantages and disadvantages of electronic brainstorming versus face-to-face brainstorming?

13. What types of IT do you as a student use on a regular basis? How might your life be different if this technology were not available to you?

14. If you were a manager in charge of new product marketing, what are some ways you might harness the power of blogs and social networking sites to help market your latest products?

15. Define the difference between explicit knowledge and tacit knowledge and give an example of each from your own experience. How can knowledge management systems be designed to promote the sharing of both explicit and tacit knowledge?

16. Do you believe information overload is a problem for today's students? For managers or employees in an organization where you have worked? How might people deal with information overload?

Dear Dr. Dorothy

I never knew management would be so difficult. It looked so easy before I got promoted. Now I see the hard work and daily grind that goes into it. My big problem is that I have a bunch of employees who think they know better than me. How can they, when they don't have all the information? And someone is always coming in to my office to tell me how we could have done something better. Really, how do I get them to mind their own business?

Under Siege in Sacramento

Dear Under Siege,

Really, to you! Dr. Dorothy feels she must remind you that giving feedback is your subordinates' business, especially when it involves projects they've been working on. You need to focus on excellence rather than your own ego enhancement. Results will be that much better with more input from the group.

And what, pray tell, is going on, Dr. Dorothy wonders, that your employees are so in the dark, that they have so little information? Shame on you for keeping the knowledge to yourself! No wonder they are in your office so often. They want to know what is going on. Here is Dr. Dorothy's advice: a) Hold weekly meetings where you talk AND you listen; b) At these meetings, share information with them, even more than you think they need, because your tendency is to withhold; c) Sincerely ask for their input and feedback; and d) This is VERY IMPORTANT, do not get defensive; listen and accept the feedback graciously; do not go back to your office and complain about what they said, either to yourself or someone else; learn to appreciate their input. Dr. Dorothy assures you if you do these things, you will likely have better results and less stress.

Self Learning

What's Your Personal Decision Style?

Read each of the following questions and circle the answer that best describes you. Think about how you typically act in a work or school situation and mark the answer that first comes to mind. There are no right or wrong answers.

1. In performing my job or class work, I look for:
  a. practical results
  b. the best solution
  c. creative approaches or ideas
  d. good working conditions

2. I enjoy jobs that:
  a. are technical and well-defined
  b. have a lot of variety
  c. allow me to be independent and creative
  d. involve working closely with others

3. The people I most enjoy working with are:
  a. energetic and ambitious
  b. capable and organized
  c. open to new ideas
  d. agreeable and trusting

4. When I have a problem, I usually:
  a. rely on what has worked in the past
  b. apply *careful analysis*
  c. consider a variety of *creative approaches*
  d. seek consensus with others

5. I am especially good at:
   a. remembering dates and facts
   b. solving complex problems
   c. seeing many possible solutions
   d. getting along with others

6. When I don't have much time, I:
   a. make decisions and act quickly
   b. follow established plans or priorities
   c. take my time and refuse to be pressured
   d. ask others for guidance and support

7. In social situations, I generally:
   a. talk to others
   b. think about what's being discussed
   c. observe
   d. listen to the conversation

8. Other people consider me:
   a. aggressive
   b. disciplined
   c. creative
   d. supportive

9. What I dislike most is:
   a. not being in control
   b. doing boring work
   c. following rules
   d. being rejected by others

10. The decisions I make are usually:
   a. direct and practical
   b. systematic or abstract
   c. broad and flexible
   d. sensitive to others' needs

Scoring and Interpretation

These questions rate your personal decision style, as described in the text and listed in Exhibit 6.5.

Count the number of *a* answers. They provide your *directive* score.
Count the number of *b* answers for your *analytical* score.
The number of *c* answers is your *conceptual* score.
The number of *d* answers is your *behavioral* score.

What is your dominant decision style? Are you surprised, or does this result reflect the style you thought you used most often?

SOURCE: Adapted from Alan J. Rowe and Richard O. Mason, *Managing with Style: A Guide to Understanding, Assessing, and Improving Decision Making* (San Francisco: Jossey-Bass, 1987): 40–41.

Group Learning

An Ancient Tale

1. Read the introduction and case study, and answer the questions.
2. In groups of three or four, discuss your answers.
3. As a group, report to the whole class and then engage in an instructor-led discussion of the issues raised.

INTRODUCTION

To understand, analyze, and improve organizations, we must carefully think through the issue of who is responsible for what activities in different organizational settings. Often we hold responsible someone who has no control over the outcome, or we fail to teach or train someone who could make the vital difference.

To explore this issue, the following exercise could be conducted on either an individual or group basis. It provides an opportunity to see how different individuals assign responsibility for an event. It is also a good opportunity to discuss the concept of organizational boundaries (what is the organization, who is in or out, etc.).

Case Study

You should read the short story and respond quickly to the first three questions. Then take a little more time on questions four through six. The results, criteria, and implications could then be discussed in groups.

Long ago in an ancient kingdom, there lived a princess who was very young and very beautiful. The princess, recently married, lived in a large and luxurious castle with her husband, a powerful and wealthy lord. The young princess was not content, however, to sit and eat strawberries by herself while her husband took frequent and long journeys to neighboring kingdoms. She felt neglected and soon became quite unhappy. One day, while she was alone in the castle gardens, a handsome vagabond rode out of the forest bordering the castle. He spied the beautiful princess, quickly won her heart, and carried her away with him.

Following a day of dalliance, the young princess found herself ruthlessly abandoned by the vagabond. She then discovered that the only way back to the castle led through the bewitched forest of the wicked sorcerer. Fearing to venture into the forest alone, she sought out her kind and wise godfather. She explained her plight, begged forgiveness of the godfather, and asked his assistance in returning home before her husband returned. The godfather, however, surprised and shocked at her behavior, refused forgiveness and denied her any assistance. Discouraged but still determined, the princess disguised her identity and sought the help of the most noble of all the kingdom's knights. After hearing the sad story, the knight pledged his unfailing aid—for a modest fee. But alas, the princess had no money, and the knight rode away to save other damsels.

The beautiful princess had no one else from whom she might seek help and decided to brave the great peril alone. She followed the safest path she knew, but when she was almost through the forest, the wicked sorcerer spied her and caused her to be devoured by the fire-breathing dragon.

1. Who was inside the organization and who was outside? Where were the boundaries?

2. Who is most responsible for the death of the beautiful princess?

3. Who is next most responsible? Least responsible?

4. What is your criterion for the preceding decisions?

5. What interventions would you suggest to prevent a recurrence?

6. What are the implications for *organizational development and change?*

Character	Most Responsible	Next Most Responsible	Least Responsible
Princess			
Husband			
Vagabond			
Godfather			
Knight			
Sorcerer			

Check one character in each column.

Action Learning

1. Prior to class, interview four people (two students and two managers) on how they make decisions. Ask them the following:

   a. What types of decisions do you make every day? Only occasionally?

   b. What is the process you use to make a decision?

   c. Does the process change whether it is a minor everyday decision versus an important life decision?

   d. What do you do to learn from the outcomes of your decisions, in terms of how to make decisions in the future?

   e. Give an example of a good decision and a poor one.

2. Come to class prepared to talk about your interviews.

3. Your instructor may divide you into groups to share your information.

4. What decision-making theories are relevant for the processes used by your interviewees?

5. What did you learn from this exercise that will help you make more effective decisions?

Ethical Dilemma

Manipulative or Not?

As head of the marketing department for Butter Crisp Snack Foods, 55-year-old Frank Bellows has been forced to learn a lot about the Internet in recent years. Although he initially resisted the new technology, Frank has gradually come to appreciate the potential of the Internet for serving existing customers and reaching potential new ones. In fact, he has been one of the biggest supporters of the company's increasing use of the Internet to stay in touch with customers.

However, something about this new plan just doesn't feel right. At this morning's meeting, Keith Deakins, Butter Crisp's CEO, announced that the company would soon be launching a Web site geared specifically to children. Although Deakins has the authority to approve the site on his own, he has asked all department heads to review the site and give their approval for its launch. He then turned the meeting over to the IT team that developed the new site, which will offer games and interactive educational activities. The team pointed out that although it will be clear that Butter Crisp is the sponsor of the site, the site will not include advertising of Butter Crisp products. So far, so good, Frank thinks. However, he knows that two of the young hot-shot employees in his department have been helping to develop the site and that they provided a list of questions that children will be asked to answer online. Just to enter the Web site, for example, a user must provide name, address, gender, e-mail address, and favorite TV show. In return, users receive "Crisp Cash," a form of virtual money that they can turn in for toys, games, Butter Crisp samples, and other prizes. After they enter the site, children can earn more Crisp Cash by providing other information about themselves and their families.

Frank watched the demonstration and agreed that the Web site does indeed have solid educational content. However, he is concerned about the tactics for gathering information from children when that information will almost certainly be used for marketing purposes. So far, it seems that the other department heads are solidly in favor of launching the Web site. Frank is wondering whether he can sign his approval with a clear conscience. He also knows that several groups, including the national PTA and the Center for Media Education, are calling for stricter governmental controls regarding collecting information from children via the Internet.

What Would You Do?

1. Stop worrying about it. There's nothing illegal about what Butter Crisp is proposing to do, and the company will closely guard any personal information gathered. Children can't be harmed in any way by using the new Web site.

2. Begin talking with other managers and try to build a coalition in support of some stricter controls, such as requiring parental permission to enter areas of the site that offer Crisp Cash in exchange for personal information.

3. Contact the Center for Media Education and tell them you suspect Butter Crisp intends to use the Web site to conduct marketing research. The Center might be able to apply pressure that would make it uncomfortable enough for Deakins to pull the plug on the new kids' Web site.

SOURCE: Based on Denise Gellene, "Internet Marketing to Kids Is Seen as a Web of Deceit," *Los Angeles Times* (March 29, 1996): pp. A1, A20.

Case for Critical Analysis

Pinnacle Machine Tool Co.

Don Anglos had to decide whether to trust his gut or his head, and he had to make that decision by next week's board meeting. Either way, he knew he was bound to make at least a member or two of his senior management team unhappy.

The question at hand was whether Pinnacle Co., the small, publicly held Indiana-based machine tool company he led as CEO, should attempt to acquire Hoilman Inc. Hoilman was a company known for the cutting-edge sensor technology and communications software it had developed to monitor robotics equipment. Anglos had just heard a credible rumor that one of Pinnacle's chief competitors was planning a hostile takeover of the company. Coincidentally, Don Anglos knew Hoilman well because he had recently held exploratory talks about the possibility of a joint venture designed to develop similar technology capable of monitoring a broad range of manufacturing equipment. The joint venture did not work out. But now, by acquiring Hoilman, Pinnacle could develop software that transmitted real-time information on its customers' equipment, enabling it to set itself apart by providing top-notch service far more sophisticated than its current standard maintenance and service contracts.

Don, a hard-charging 48-year-old, firmly believed that bigger was better. It was a premise that had served his Greek immigrant father well as he built a multimillion-dollar business from nothing by acquiring one commercial laundry after another. The CEO had to admit, though, that getting bigger in the machine tool industry, currently a slow-growing sector facing increasing competition from low-priced foreign manufacturers, was going to be a challenge. Still, he had been convinced to sign on as Pinnacle's CEO four years ago not only because the company had relatively healthy earnings but also because his sixth sense told him the company had growth potential. He hadn't been entirely sure where that potential lay, but he was a problem-solver with a proven track record of successfully spotting new market opportunities. In the past, he acted on hunches, which had paid off handsomely.

So far, Anglos had managed to modestly nudge Pinnacle's revenue growth and increase its market share through aggressive pricing that successfully kept customers from switching to several potential foreign rivals. But those moves inevitably chipped away at the company's healthy profit margins. In any case, he recognized he'd taken the company down that road as far as he could. It was time for a real change in strategy. Instead of concentrating on manufacturing, he wanted to transform Pinnacle into a high-tech service company. Such a drastic metamorphosis was going to require a new, service-oriented corporate culture, he admitted, but it was the only way he could see achieving the growth and profitability he envisioned. Acquiring Hoilman looked like a good place to start, but this option would be gone if Hoilman sold out to another firm.

Jennifer Banks, services division head, was enthusiastic about both the acquisition and the new strategy. "Acquiring Hoilman is the chance of a lifetime," she crowed. Not all the senior managers agreed. In particular, CFO Sam Lodge advanced arguments against the acquisition that were hard to dismiss. The timing was wrong, he insisted. Pinnacle's recent drop in profitability hadn't escaped Wall Street's attention, and the further negative impact on earnings that would result from the Hoilman acquisition wasn't likely to make already wary investors feel any better. But then Sam shocked Don by offering an even more fundamental critique. "Getting into the service business is a mistake, Don. It's what everybody's doing right now. Just look at the number of our competitors who've already taken steps to break into the services market. What makes you think we'll come out on top? And when I look at our customers, I just don't see any evidence that even if they wanted to, they could afford to buy any add-on services any time soon."

With such a big decision, Don's head had to agree with Lodge's position, which was based on his usual CFO thoroughness with number crunching. But his gut wasn't so sure. Sometimes, he thought, you just have to go with your instincts. And his instincts were chomping at the bit to go after Hoilman.

Questions

1. What steps in the decision-making process have Don Anglos and Pinnacle taken? Which ones have they not completed?

2. Which decision-making style best describes Don's approach: directive, analytical, conceptual, or behavioral? Which style best describes Sam Lodge's approach?

3. What leadership style is Anglos employing? Is it the participation style you'd recommend based on a Vroom-Jago analysis of the situation? Why or why not?

4. Would you recommend that Pinnacle attempt to acquire Hoilman? If so, why? If not, what alternatives would you suggest?

SOURCE: Based on Paul Hemp, "Growing for Broke," *Harvard Business Review* (September 2002): pp. 27–37.

BIZ FLIX

Dr. Seuss' How the Grinch Stole Christmas

Readers and lovers of Dr. Seuss's original tale may be put off by Ron Howard's loose adaptation of the story. Whoville, a magical, mythical land that exists inside a snowflake, features two types of life: the Whos who love Christmas and the Grinch (Jim Carrey) who hates it. Cindy Lou Who (Taylor Momsen) tries to bring the Grinch back to Yuletide celebrations, an effort that backfires on all involved. Sparkling special effects will dazzle most viewers and likely distract them from the film's departures from the original story.

This scene is an edited version of the "Second Thoughts" sequence early in the film. Just before this scene, fearless Cindy Lou entered the Grinch's lair to invite him to be the Holiday Cheermeister at the Whobilation One-thousand Celebration. In typical Grinch fashion, he pulls the trap door on Cindy Lou who unceremoniously slides out of his lair to land on a snowy Whoville street. The Grinch now must decide whether to accept the invitation. The film continues with the Cheermeister award ceremony.

What to Watch for and Ask Yourself

1. What are the Grinch's decision alternatives or options?
2. What decision criteria does the Grinch use to choose from the alternatives?
3. Describe the steps in the Grinch's decision-making process.

Managerial Decision-Making, Organizational Planning, and Goal Setting at McDonald's

The "hit by a bus scenario" is something that any company's board of directors must consider carefully. The idea is that a successor must be agreed upon; someone well equipped to take the reigns of the company, should a CEO die suddenly. Most companies plan for an interim successor, a substitute CEO who can occupy the spot until a permanent appointee is chosen. It is understandable that a company might not have a permanent replacement in the wings, as the "hit by a bus" scenario is possible, but certainly seems improbable. The likelihood of losing the newly appointed CEO shortly thereafter seems downright unthinkable. How many companies would have a *second* succession candidate in mind?

Jim Cantalupo, favoring improvement over expansion, was the superstar who brought McDonald's back into the light after a dark period for the company's earnings. He died suddenly at a big McDonald's conference in April 2004, prompting the board that had appointed him just the year before to quickly assemble. Hours later, they announced that COO Charlie Bell was the new CEO. Conference attendees, shocked and saddened by the news of Cantalupo's passing, were nevertheless impressed that the board had acted so quickly and decisively. Two weeks later, Bell was diagnosed with colon cancer. Both his family and the board of directors hoped for the best, but prepared for the worst. In January 2005, Jim Skinner became the third CEO in under a year.

By immediately appointing new successors, McDonald's managed to avoid the fallout that often accompanies the sudden loss of a leader. The organization kept its momentum going, and was rewarded with a confident internal environment and continued earnings growth. What is especially impressive about this scenario is not just that both successors were decided on without interruption to the business, but that they were so capable of stepping into the role. Jim Cantalupo had been with the organization since 1974, and rose from entry-level accountant to head of International Operations before he took the top spot. Charlie Bell had been with the company for almost thirty years himself, and had made history by fast-tracking through the company's ranks in Australia at a young age. Skinner joined McDonald's in 1971 as a manager trainee, and eventually became a key player in McDonald's global presence. These men were not only qualified for the role, they were prepared to excel in it at a moment's notice.

The fact that McDonald's was so well prepared for the unthinkable made a lot of organizations re-examine their own leadership development efforts. Cultivating internal talent in a focused, meaningful way can provide essential strength in the darkest of times.

Questions

1. When a company's succession plan names an interim CEO, it buys time to decide on a permanent replacement. What are some of the risks a company might face during this process?

2. When an organization is faced with unexpected change, what can managers do to help insure that they make the right choices?

3. During Jim Cantalupo's brief tenure as CEO, McDonald's stock shot up 49 percent. When the company announced his replacement within a day of losing him, the share price rose again. With Cantalupo gone, why would stock go up again so soon?

In the entertainment industry, innovation has a short shelf life. Take Netflix, for example.

In the late 1990s, Netflix, the online digital video disc (DVD) rental company, hit upon its groundbreaking, highly successful service innovation. A flat monthly fee lets customers use its well-designed Web site to pick DVDs from among 80,000 titles. Netflix ships selections in handy postage-paid envelopes that customers then use to return them. There are no late fees.

But Netflix can't afford to rest on its laurels. It's had to fight off competitors such as Blockbuster and Wal-Mart, plus there are movie download sites and new products springing up as well as set-top devices hitting the market. They access movies by connecting TVs directly to the Internet.

How does Netflix foster innovation? It has an organizational structure with few layers and little hierarchy. It also works hard to attract exceptional employees and then holds them to high standards. "In many companies adequate performance gets a modest raise," lectures the company's Web site sternly. "At Netflix, adequate performance gets a generous severance package."

Change demands innovation, and innovation requires adaptive, flexible organizations populated with the right employees.

Designing Adaptive Organizations

Learning Objectives

After studying this chapter, you should be able to:

1 Discuss the fundamental characteristics of organizing, including such concepts as work specialization, chain of command, span of management, and centralization versus decentralization.

2 Describe functional and divisional approaches to structure.

3 Explain the matrix approach to structure and its application to both domestic and international organizations.

4 Describe the contemporary team and virtual network structures and why they are being adopted by organizations.

5 Explain why organizations need coordination across departments and hierarchical levels, and describe mechanisms for achieving coordination.

6 Identify how structure can be used to achieve an organization's strategic goals.

7 Ilustrate how organization structure can be designed to fit environmental uncertainty.

8 Define production technology (manufacturing, service, and digital) and explain how it influences organization structure.

New Manager's Questions

Please circle your opinion below each of the following statements.

Assess Your Answer

1 Managers should give employees the choice to work on whatever they want, so that motivation stays high.

1	2	3	4	5
strongly agree				strongly disagree

2 If people make mistakes on the job, they shouldn't be punished.

1	2	3	4	5
strongly agree				strongly disagree

3 It is better for one person to be in charge of making decisions.

1	2	3	4	5
strongly agree				strongly disagree

Nissan Motors was in trouble. Executive Carlos Ghosn saw that managers did not have clearly defined areas of responsibility and authority, as well as poor communications between various departments. The problem confronting Carlos Ghosn at Nissan is largely one of structural design. Ghosn wants to use elements of structure to define authority and responsibility for managers, promote accountability, and improve coordination so that Nissan can bring out new products and regain a competitive edge. Every firm wrestles with the problem of how to organize. Reorganization often is necessary to reflect a new strategy, changing market conditions, or innovative technology. In recent years, many companies, including American Express, IBM, Microsoft, Hewlett-Packard, and Ford Motor Co., have realigned departmental groupings, chains of command, and horizontal coordination mechanisms to attain new strategic goals. Structure is a powerful tool for reaching strategic goals, and a strategy's success often is determined by its fit with organization structure.

organizing
the deployment of organizational resources to achieve strategic goals.

Many companies have found a need to make structural changes that are compatible with use of the Internet for e-business, which requires stronger horizontal coordination. Brady Corporation, a Milwaukee-based manufacturer of identification and safety products, reorganized to increase cross-functional collaboration in connection with the rollout of a new system that links customers, distributors, and suppliers over the Internet.[1] Ford Motor Company used a horizontal team approach to design and build the Escape Hybrid, bringing the first hybrid SUV to market in record time.[2] Companies are increasingly using outsourcing as a structural option, as the Internet has expanded the types of activities firms can farm out to subcontractors. WuXi Pharmatech in Shanghai, China, for example, not only manufactures drugs but does laboratory and drug development work for most of the large pharmaceutical firms in the United States and Europe. Drug makers such as Roche Holding of Switzerland, GlaxoSmithKline of Britain, and Eli Lilly of the United States are also outsourcing clinical trial work to low-wage countries such as India, a practice that is raising both economic and ethical concerns.[3] Some of today's companies operate as virtual network organizations, limiting themselves to a few core activities and letting outside specialists handle everything else. Each of these organizations is using fundamental concepts of organizing. **Organizing** is the deployment of organizational resources to achieve strategic goals. The deployment of resources is reflected in the organization's division of labor into specific departments and jobs, formal lines of authority, and mechanisms for coordinating diverse organization tasks.

Organizing is important because it follows from strategy—the topic of Part 3. Strategy defines *what* to do; organizing defines *how* to do it. Organization structure is a tool that managers use to harness resources for getting things done. Part 4 explains the variety of organizing principles and concepts used by managers. This chapter covers fundamental concepts that apply to all organizations and departments, including organizing the vertical structure and using mechanisms for

CONCEPT CONNECTION

Successful artist Shepard Fairey has proven himself to be an effective manager too. Fairey runs his own marketing design firm, Studio Number One, a studio that designs unique graphics and logos used in untraditional advertising campaigns, and on labels for clothing, soft drinks, and other products. Fairey manages a creative team of seven full-time employees and a handful of part-timers and interns. Even in a small organization such as this, **organizing** is a critical part of good management. Fairey has to be sure people are assigned and coordinated to do all the various jobs necessary to satisfy clients such as Express, Levi's, and Dr. Pepper/Seven Up. The right **organization structure** enables Studio Number One to be "fast, deadline-sensitive, and responsive."

horizontal coordination. The chapter also examines how managers tailor the various elements of structural design to the organization's situation. Chapter 8 discusses how organizations can be structured to facilitate innovation and change. Chapter 9 consider how to use human resources to the best advantage within the organization's structure.

Organizing the Vertical Structure

The organizing process leads to the creation of organization structure, which defines how tasks are divided and resources deployed. **Organization structure** is defined as (1) the set of formal tasks assigned to individuals and departments; (2) formal reporting relationships, including lines of authority, decision responsibility, number of hierarchical levels, and span of managers' control; and (3) the design of systems to ensure effective coordination of employees across departments.[4]

The set of formal tasks and formal reporting relationships provides a framework for vertical control of the organization. The characteristics of vertical structure are portrayed in the **organization chart**, which is the visual representation of an organization's structure.

A sample organization chart for a water bottling plant is illustrated in Exhibit 7.1. The plant has four major departments—Accounting, Human Resources, Production, and Marketing. The organization chart delineates the chain of command, indicates departmental tasks and how they fit together, and provides order and logic for the organization. Every employee has an appointed task, line of authority, and decision responsibility. The following sections discuss several important features of vertical structure in more detail.

◀ TAKE ACTION

Make an organization chart of the place you work, so that you can understand reporting relationships.

organization structure
the framework in which the organization defines how tasks are divided, resources are deployed, and departments are coordinated.

organization chart
the visual representation of an organization's structure.

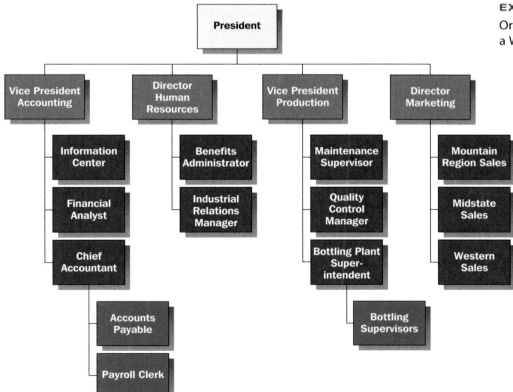

EXHIBIT 7.1

Organization Chart for a Water Bottling Plant

WORK SPECIALIZATION

Organizations perform a wide variety of tasks. A fundamental principle is that work can be performed more efficiently if employees are allowed to specialize.[5] **Work specialization,** sometimes called *division of labor,* is the degree to which organizational tasks are subdivided into separate jobs. Work specialization in Exhibit 7.1 is illustrated by the separation of production tasks into bottling, quality control, and maintenance. Employees within each department perform only the tasks relevant to their specialized function. When work specialization is extensive, employees specialize in a single task. Jobs tend to be small, but they can be performed efficiently. Work specialization is readily visible on an automobile assembly line where each employee performs the same task over and over again. It would not be efficient to have a single employee build the entire automobile or even perform a large number of unrelated jobs.

> **Assess Your Answer** ✱
>
> **1** Managers should give employees the choice to work on whatever they want, so that motivation stays high.
>
> ANSWER: Work needs to be organized with some thought about how to get the work done best, which may include specialization. It will help motivation, however, to give employees some choices in what work they do and how to do it. Depending on the type of task, this may or may not be possible.

Despite the apparent advantages of specialization, many organizations are moving away from this principle. With too much specialization, employees are isolated and do only a single, boring job. Many companies are enlarging jobs to provide greater challenges or assigning teams so that employees can rotate among the several jobs performed by the team. One company that has followed work specialization, though, is Kate Spade, as described in the Spotlight on Skills box.

CHAIN OF COMMAND

The **chain of command** is an unbroken line of authority that links all persons in an organization and shows who reports to whom. It is associated with two underlying principles. *Unity of command* means that each employee is held accountable to only one supervisor. The *scalar principle* refers to a clearly defined line of authority in the organization that includes all employees. Authority and responsibility for different tasks should be distinct. All persons in the organization should know to whom they report as well as the successive management levels all the way to the top. In Exhibit 7.1 shown earlier, the payroll clerk reports to the chief accountant, who in turn reports to the vice president, who in turn reports to the company president.

AUTHORITY, RESPONSIBILITY, AND DELEGATION

The chain of command illustrates the authority structure of the organization. **Authority** is the formal and legitimate right of a manager to make decisions, issue orders, and allocate resources to achieve organizationally desired outcomes. Authority is distinguished by three characteristics:[6]

1. *Authority is vested in organizational positions, not people.* Managers have authority because of the positions they hold, and other people in the same positions would have the same authority.

2. *Authority is accepted by subordinates.* Although authority flows top-down through the organization's hierarchy, subordinates comply because they believe that managers

work specialization
the degree to which organizational tasks are subdivided into individual jobs; also called division of labor.

chain of command
an unbroken line of authority that links all individuals in the organization and specifies who reports to whom.

authority
the formal and legitimate right of a manager to make decisions, issue orders, and allocate resources to achieve organizationally desired outcomes.

Spotlight on Skills

Kate Spade

Kate Spade never thought she'd be a designer. She wanted to work in publishing. After college at Arizona State University (where she met her future husband, Andy), she went to New York and got a job as an editorial assistant at *Mademoiselle* for $14,500 per year. Soon Andy followed, and they got a tiny apartment in SoHo. Andy moved up the career ladder in advertising agencies. Kate was so successful that by 28 she was senior fashion editor for accessories, but she didn't want to keep doing the same thing. She told Andy, "I just want something that will keep me busy." A temporary thing. He suggested she launch a line of accessories. She was flabbergasted and didn't know where to start, but Andy kept prodding her. It was the process they would continue for 10 years: Andy with a bold vision and Kate as the more conservative who executes his idea with great style and attention to detail. Their deal was he would work to pay rent and provide startup capital, while she would get the business going.

Starting with a purse was, she says, "kind of random." As a fashion stylist, she had looked for unusual accessories that weren't there. Purses were all blacks and browns back in 1993. With no fashion training, Kate was scared to take on design, but

Andy kept urging her on. She made a prototype out of construction paper and found a sewer to make a sample—a simple burlap square. After a few more samples, they went to the Accessories Circuit show in New York and signed up the three hottest retailers: Fred Segal, Barneys, and Charivari. Refusing outside money, Andy kept working at the ad agency, until finally they started making enough money for him to work full time at the company.

Structuring the workload was a challenge. Andy loved the creative role, but he took on the CEO role, even though he had little experience or interest in the operational side.

By 1999, Neiman Marcus and Saks adopted the lines for their stores, making revenues soar. Further, Neiman bought a 56 percent share for $34. Andy and Kate Spade built a business that is now worth $175 million. Splitting the responsibilities was smart. Even though Andy didn't want to be CEO, he turned out to have the right aptitude. Now that Kate is pregnant again, they are both reassessing their priorities. First on the board: Hire a new CEO and give Kate and Andy some much-needed breathing space. And space for their three-year-old daughter, who has taught Kate to relax. "It has made me less precious," she says, "more fly-by-the-seat-of-my pants." Good thing she designs purses and shoes.

SOURCE: Linda Tischler, "Power Couple," *Fast Company*, (March 2005): 44–51; "I am what I am," *Sunday Times* (London), (Feb. 18, 2007): 7.

have a legitimate right to issue orders. The *acceptance theory of authority* argues that a manager has authority only if subordinates choose to accept his or her commands. If subordinates refuse to obey because the order is outside their zone of acceptance, a manager's authority disappears.[7]

3. *Authority flows down the vertical hierarchy.* Positions at the top of the hierarchy are vested with more formal authority than are positions at the bottom.

Responsibility is the flip side of the authority coin. **Responsibility** is the duty to perform the task or activity as assigned. Typically, managers are assigned authority commensurate with responsibility. When managers have responsibility for task outcomes but little authority, the job is possible but difficult. They rely on persuasion and luck. When managers have authority exceeding responsibility, they may become tyrants, using authority toward frivolous outcomes.[8]

Accountability is the mechanism through which authority and responsibility are brought into alignment. **Accountability** means that the people with authority and responsibility are subject to reporting and justifying task outcomes to those above them in the chain of command.[9] For organizations to function well, everyone needs to know what they are accountable for and accept the responsibility and authority for performing it. Accountability can be built into the organization structure. For example, at Whirlpool, incentive programs tailored to different hierarchical levels provide strict accountability. Performance of all

 **TAKE ACTION**

Go to the ethical dilemma on page 282 that pertains to issues of authority, responsibility, and delegation.

responsibility
the duty to perform the task or activity an employee has been assigned.

accountability
the fact that the people with authority and responsibility are subject to reporting and justifying task outcomes to those above them in the chain of command.

Caterpillar, Inc.

Caterpillar, which makes large construction equipment, engines, and power systems, had almost total control of its markets until the mid-1980s, when a combination of global recession and runaway inflation opened the door to a host of new competitors, including Japan's Komatsu. The unanticipated surge of competition almost put Cat under, and the company was losing $1 million a day seven days a week in 1983 and 1984.

When George Schaefer took over as CEO, he and other top managers decided to undertake a major transformation to make sure Cat wasn't caught flat-footed again. They started with structure. One major problem Schaefer saw was that the organization didn't have clear accountability. Schaefer pushed authority, responsibility, and accountability dramatically downward by reorganizing Caterpillar into several new business divisions that would be judged on divisional profitability. Business units could now design their own products, develop their own manufacturing processes, and set their own prices rather than getting permission or directives from headquarters. The division managers were strictly accountable for how they used their new decision-making authority. Each division was judged on profitability and return on assets (ROA), and any division that couldn't demonstrate 15 percent ROA was subject to elimination. The CEO held regular meetings with each division president and kept notes of what they said they would achieve. Then at the next meeting, he would review each manager's performance compared to his or her commitments. The compensation plan was also overhauled to base individual managers' bonuses on meeting divisional plan targets.

Previously, if things went wrong, division managers would blame headquarters. The clear accountability of the new structure forced people to find solutions to their problems rather than assigning blame.[10]

managers is monitored, and bonus payments are tied to successful outcomes. Another example comes from Caterpillar Inc., which got hammered by new competition in the mid-1980s and reorganized to build in accountability.

Assess Your Answer

2 If people make mistakes on the job, they shouldn't be punished.

ANSWER: Punishment is a strong word. When something goes wrong, there needs to be someone who is *accountable*. This actually prevents mistakes because people feel more responsible for success. Punishing and blaming are not often effective, but accountability, if done right, is.

Some top managers at Caterpillar had trouble letting go of authority and responsibility in the new structure because they were used to calling all the shots. Another important concept related to authority is delegation.[11] **Delegation** is the process managers use to transfer authority and responsibility to positions below them in the hierarchy. Most organizations today encourage managers to delegate authority to the lowest possible level to provide maximum flexibility to meet customer needs and adapt to the environment. However, as at Caterpillar, many managers find delegation difficult.

Line Authority and Staff Authority. An important distinction in many organizations is between line authority and staff authority, reflecting whether managers work in line departments or staff departments in the organization's structure. *Line departments* perform tasks that reflect the organization's primary goal and mission. In a software company, line departments make and sell the product. In an Internet-based company, line departments develop and manage online offerings and sales. *Staff departments* include all those that provide specialized skills in support of line departments. Staff departments have

delegation
the process managers use to transfer authority and responsibility to positions below them in the hierarchy.

an advisory relationship with line departments and typically include marketing, labor relations, research, accounting, and human resources.

Line authority means that people in management positions have formal authority to direct and control immediate subordinates. **Staff authority** is narrower and includes the right to advise, recommend, and counsel in the staff specialists' area of expertise. Staff authority is a communication relationship; staff specialists advise managers in technical areas. For example, the finance department of a manufacturing firm would have staff authority to coordinate with line departments about which accounting forms to use to facilitate equipment purchases and standardize payroll services.

SPAN OF MANAGEMENT

The **span of management** is the number of employees reporting to a supervisor. Sometimes called the *span of control*, this characteristic of structure determines how closely a supervisor can monitor subordinates. Traditional views of organization design recommended a

CONCEPT CONNECTION

Prior to the early 1990s, there were seven management layers at Electric Boat Corporation's Quonset Point facility in Rhode Island, which fabricates and assembles U.S. Navy nuclear submarines. This **tall structure** resulted in high costs and a lengthy chain of command that slowed decision making. After the General Dynamics Corporation subsidiary reengineered itself into a **flat structure** with only three layers, overhead and indirect labor costs were cut by 50 percent, and communications, efficiency, and productivity all improved. The Best Manufacturing Practice (BPM) Center of Excellence ranks Electric Boat's practices as among the best. BPM is a partnership of the Office of Naval Research, the Commerce Department, and the University of Maryland.

span of management of about seven subordinates per manager. However, many lean organizations today have spans of management as high as 30, 40, and even higher. For example, at Consolidated Diesel's team-based engine assembly plant, the span of management is 100.[12] Research over the past 40 or so years shows that span of management varies widely and that several factors influence the span.[13] Generally, when supervisors must be closely involved with subordinates, the span should be small, and when supervisors need little involvement with subordinates, it can be large. The following factors are associated with less supervisor involvement and thus larger spans of control:

1. Work performed by subordinates is stable and routine.
2. Subordinates perform similar work tasks.
3. Subordinates are concentrated in a single location.
4. Subordinates are highly trained and need little direction in performing tasks.
5. Rules and procedures defining task activities are available.
6. Support systems and personnel are available for the manager.
7. Little time is required in nonsupervisory activities such as coordination with other departments or planning.
8. Managers' personal preferences and styles favor a large span.

The average span of control used in an organization determines whether the structure is tall or flat. A **tall structure** has an overall narrow span and more hierarchical levels. A **flat structure** has a wide span, is horizontally dispersed, and has fewer hierarchical levels.

line authority
a form of authority in which individuals in management positions have the formal power to direct and control immediate subordinates.

staff authority
a form of authority granted to staff specialists in their area of expertise.

span of management
the number of employees reporting to a supervisor; also called *span of control*.

tall structure
a management structure characterized by an overall narrow span of management and a relatively large number of hierarchical levels.

flat structure
a management structure characterized by an overall broad span of control and relatively few hierarchical levels.

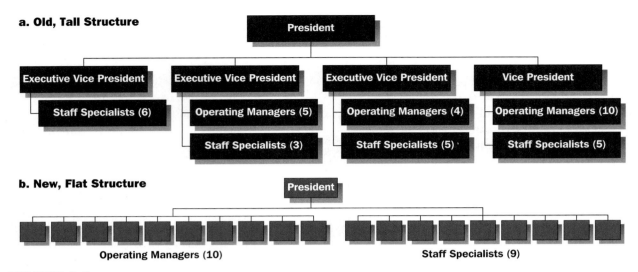

a. Old, Tall Structure

b. New, Flat Structure

Operating Managers (10)   Staff Specialists (9)

EXHIBIT 7.2

Reorganization to Increase Span of Management for President of an International Metals Company

Having too many hierarchical levels and narrow spans of control is a common structural problem for organizations. The result may be routine decisions that are made too high in the organization, which pulls higher-level executives away from important long-range strategic issues. It also limits the creativity and innovativeness of lower-level managers in solving problems.[14] The trend in recent years has been toward wider spans of control as a way to facilitate delegation.[15] One study of 300 large U.S. corporations found that the average number of division heads reporting directly to the CEO tripled between 1986 and 1999.[16] Exhibit 7.2 illustrates how an international metals company was reorganized. The multi-level set of managers shown in panel *a* was replaced with 10 operating managers and 9 staff specialists reporting directly to the CEO, as shown in panel *b*. The CEO welcomed this wide span of 19 management subordinates because it fit his style, his management team was top quality and needed little supervision, and they were all located on the same floor of an office building.

CENTRALIZATION AND DECENTRALIZATION

Centralization and decentralization pertain to the hierarchical level at which decisions are made. **Centralization** means that decision authority is located near the top of the organization. With **decentralization**, decision authority is pushed downward to lower organization levels. Organizations may have to experiment to find the correct hierarchical level at which to make decisions.

In the United States and Canada, the trend over the past 30 years has been toward greater decentralization of organizations. Decentralization is believed to relieve the burden on top managers, make greater use of employees' skills and abilities, ensure that decisions are made close to the action by well-informed people, and permit more rapid response to external changes.

However, this trend does not mean that every organization should decentralize all decisions. Managers should diagnose the organizational situation and select the decision-making level that will best meet the organization's needs. Factors that typically influence centralization versus decentralization are as follows:

1. *Greater change and uncertainty in the environment are usually associated with decentralization.* A good example of how decentralization can help cope with rapid change and uncertainty occurred following Hurricane Katrina. Recall from the Chapter 1 opening example how Mississippi Power restored power in just 12 days thanks largely to a decentralized management system that empowered

centralization
the location of decision authority near top organizational levels.

decentralization
the location of decision authority near lower organizational levels.

people at the electrical substations to make rapid on-the-spot decisions. Similarly, decentralized decision making at UPS enabled trucks to keep running on time in New York after the September 2001 terrorist attacks.[17] With the world rapidly changing, you could expect information management to be decentralized, as it is in Wikipedia's model, described in the Benchmarking box.

2. *The amount of centralization or decentralization should fit the firm's strategy.* For example, Johnson & Johnson gives almost complete authority to its 180 operating companies to develop and market their own products. Decentralization fits the corporate strategy of empowerment that gets each division close to customers so it can speedily adapt to their needs.[18] Taking the opposite approach, Procter & Gamble recentralized some of its operations to take a more focused approach and leverage the giant company's capabilities across business units.[19]

3. *In times of crisis or risk of company failure, authority may be centralized at the top.* When Honda could not get agreement among divisions about new car models, President Nobuhiko Kawamoto made the decision himself.[20]

TAKE ACTION

As a manager, carefully determine which areas you can decentralize and which should be centralized. Take a moment to complete the New Manager Self Test on centralization/decentralization characteristics.

NEW MANAGER SELF TEST

How Decentralized are You?

	Mostly True				Mostly False
1. If I am the leader, I want to know everything that is going on.	1	2	3	4	5
2. Insubordination, or questioning a leader, is wrong.	1	2	3	4	5
3. It is better to have one person make all the decisions.	1	2	3	4	5
4. Having subgroups make their own decisions gets very confusing.	1	2	3	4	5
5. The more input into decision making the better.	1	2	3	4	5
6. It's often good for the group to decide rather than the leader.	1	2	3	4	5
7. Letting subgroups make their own goals and decisions is best.	1	2	3	4	5
8. Subordinates often know better how to solve a problem than their supervisor.	1	2	3	4	5

INTERPRETATION AND SCORING

Give yourself one point for each mostly true answer (1 or 2); give yourself zero points if you chose 3, 4 or 5.

Items 1-4 are related to centralized decision making. If you scored 3-4 here and 0-1 on items 5-8, then you prefer centralized decision making.

Items 5-8 relate to decentralized decision making. If you scored 3-4 here and 0-1 on items 1-4, you are high on decentralized decision making. The ideal score would be to have a mixture of both centralized and decentralized.

Benchmarking

Wikipedia

Not long after the news broke that six young men had been arrested for an alleged plot to blow up Fort Dix, Wikipedia contributor CltFn started at seven in the morning writing a "stub" (a placeholder) called, "Fort Dix Terror Plot." A few minutes later Gracenotes joined the process. Over the next several hours, a growing pack of contributors started adding to the story, while in constant contact with another group of self-appointed editors. Soon, Gracenotes (real name: Matthew Gruen) added and corrected the stub some 59 times until it was quite presentable and went onto the front page of Wikipedia. Around midnight, Gruen signed off, went to bed and awoke the next morning to head off to junior high school.

Started in 2001, Wikipedia is a global online encyclopedia available in 250 languages, with 1.8 million articles in English alone. Depending on your bent, it is either one of the great-est inventions in information or the death knell of intellectual rigor. The process by which Wikipedia gets its articles "right," is a constant rewriting and editing, in such an egalitarian fashion that is seems impossible that it could be accurate, especially about events unfolding in real time. To be sure, mistakes have been made; people have "conned" the system. But they are usually found out and corrected very quickly.

Wikipedia's structure is the most decentralized imaginable, and with the chaotic system that has emerged, it is amazing anything gets done. And yet it does, by thousands of motivated contributors. Founder and watcher Jimmy Wales isn't even sure who all these contributors are, but that fits with its decentralized culture. Wikipedians are passionately committed to weeding out the subjectivity in one another's writing, policing bias in others and remarkably, in themselves. No one seems to know where they learned to do this. But one thing is certain: They are teaching it to each other.

SOURCE: Jonathan Dee, "All the news that's fit to print out," *New York Times Magazine* (July 1, 2007): 34–39.

Assess Your Answer

3 It is better for one person to be in charge of making decisions.

ANSWER: It all depends. In a crisis, yes, one person is best, but under normal conditions, it is generally better if people have at least input or are part of the actual decision-making team.

Departmentalization

Another fundamental characteristic of organization structure is **departmentalization,** which is the basis for grouping positions into departments and departments into the total organization. Managers make choices about how to use the chain of command to group people together to perform their work. Five approaches to structural design reflect different uses of the chain of command in departmentalization, as illustrated in Exhibit 7.3. The functional, divisional, and matrix are traditional approaches that rely on the chain of command to define departmental groupings and reporting relationships along the hierarchy. Two innovative approaches are the use of teams and virtual networks, which have emerged to meet changing organizational needs in a turbulent global environment.

The basic difference among structures illustrated in Exhibit 7.3 is the way in which employees are departmentalized and to whom they report.[21] Each structural approach is described in detail in the following sections.

departmentalization
the basis on which individuals are grouped into departments and departments into the total organization.

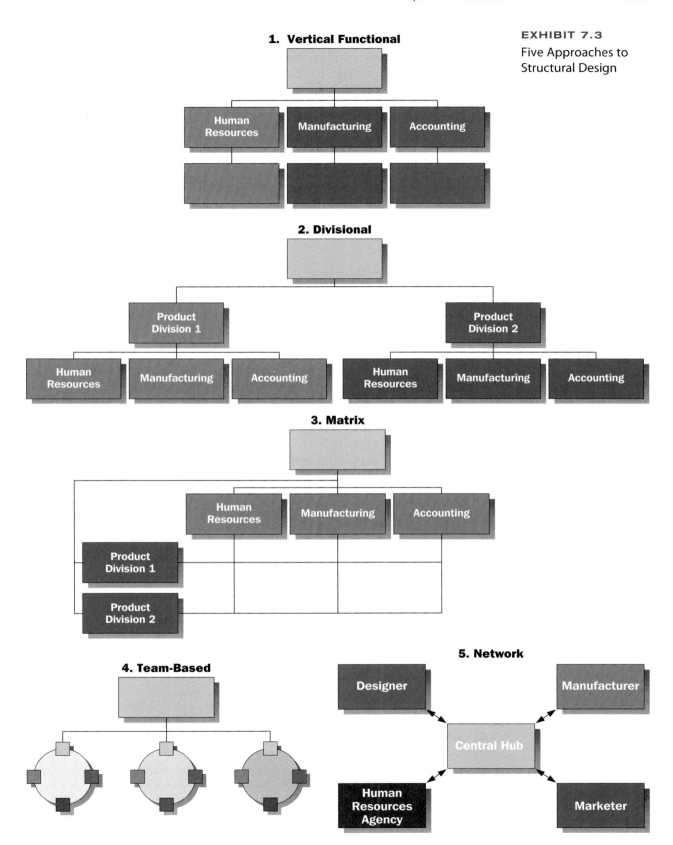

1. Vertical Functional

Human Resources | Manufacturing | Accounting

EXHIBIT 7.3
Five Approaches to
Structural Design

2. Divisional

Product Division 1 — Human Resources | Manufacturing | Accounting

Product Division 2 — Human Resources | Manufacturing | Accounting

3. Matrix

Human Resources | Manufacturing | Accounting

Product Division 1

Product Division 2

4. Team-Based

5. Network

Designer

Manufacturer

Central Hub

Human Resources Agency

Marketer

VERTICAL FUNCTIONAL APPROACH

What It Is. **Functional structure** is the grouping of positions into departments based on similar skills, expertise, work activities, and resource use. A functional structure can be thought of as departmentalization by organizational resources because each type of functional activity—accounting, human resources, engineering, manufacturing—represents specific resources for performing the organization's task. People, facilities, and other resources representing a common function are grouped into a single department. One example is Blue Bell Creameries, which relies on in-depth expertise in its various functional departments to produce high-quality ice creams for a limited regional market. The quality control department, for example, tests all incoming ingredients and ensures that only the best go into Blue Bell's ice cream. Quality inspectors also test outgoing products, and because of their years of experience, can detect the slightest deviation from expected quality. Blue Bell also has functional departments such as sales, production, maintenance, distribution, research and development, and finance.[22]

TAKE ACTION

When developing teams, try having people learn one another's jobs, as it gives you more flexibility and keeps the workers more interested in their work.

How It Works. Refer to Exhibit 7.1 (see page 249) for an example of a functional structure. The major departments under the president are groupings of similar expertise and resources, such as accounting, human resources, production, and marketing. Each of the functional departments is concerned with the organization as a whole. The marketing department is responsible for all sales and marketing, for example, and the accounting department handles financial issues for the entire company.

The functional structure is a strong vertical design. Information flows up and down the vertical hierarchy, and the chain of command converges at the top of the organization. In a functional structure, people within a department communicate primarily with others in the same department to coordinate work and accomplish tasks or implement decisions that are passed down the hierarchy. Managers and employees are compatible because of similar training and expertise. Typically, rules and procedures govern the duties and responsibilities of each employee, and employees at lower hierarchical levels accept the right of those higher in the hierarchy to make decisions and issue orders.

DIVISIONAL APPROACH

What It Is. In contrast to the functional approach, in which people are grouped by common skills and resources, the **divisional structure** occurs when departments are grouped together based on organizational outputs. The divisional structure is sometimes called a *product structure, program structure,* or *self-contained unit structure.* Each of these terms means essentially the same thing: Diverse departments are brought together to produce a single organizational output, whether it be a product, a program, or a service to a single customer.

Most large corporations have separate divisions that perform different tasks, use different technologies, or serve different customers. When a huge organization produces products for different markets, the divisional structure works because each division is an autonomous business. Microsoft has reorganized into three business divisions: Platform Products & Services (which includes Windows and MSN); Business (including Office and Business Solutions products); and Entertainment & Devices (Xbox games, Windows mobile, and Microsoft TV). Each unit is headed by a president who is accountable for the performance of the division, and each contains the functions of a standalone company, doing its own product development, sales, marketing, and finance. Facing new competitive threats from Google and makers of the free Linux operating system, top executives initiated the restructuring to help Microsoft be more flexible and nimble in developing and delivering new products. The structure groups together products and services that depend on similar technologies, and at the same time, it enables more rapid decision making and less red tape at the giant corporation.[23]

functional structure
the grouping of positions into departments based on similar skills, expertise, and resource use.

divisional structure
an organization structure in which departments are grouped based on similar organizational outputs.

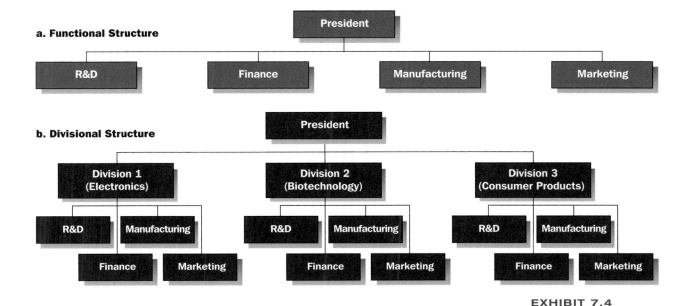

EXHIBIT 7.4
Functional Versus
Divisional Structures

How It Works. Functional and divisional structures are illustrated in Exhibit 7.4. In the divisional structure, divisions are created as self-contained units with separate functional departments for each division. For example, in Exhibit 7.4, each functional department resource needed to produce the product is assigned to each division. Whereas in a functional structure, all engineers are grouped together and work on all products, in a divisional structure, separate engineering departments are created within each division. Each department is smaller and focuses on a single product line or customer segment. Departments are duplicated across product lines.

The primary difference between divisional and functional structures is that the chain of command from each function converges lower in the hierarchy. In a divisional structure, differences of opinion among research and development, marketing, manufacturing, and finance would be resolved at the divisional level rather than by the president. Thus, the divisional structure encourages decentralization. Decision making is pushed down at least one level in the hierarchy, freeing the president and other top managers for strategic planning.

GEOGRAPHIC- OR CUSTOMER-BASED DIVISIONS

An alternative for assigning divisional responsibility is to group company activities by geographic region or customer group. For example, the Internal Revenue Service shifted to a structure focused on four distinct taxpayer (customer) groups: individuals, small businesses, corporations, and nonprofit or government agencies.[24] A global geographic structure is illustrated in Exhibit 7.5. In this structure, all functions in a specific country or region report to the same division manager. The structure focuses company activities on local market conditions. Competitive advantage may come from the production or sale of a product or service adapted to a given country or region. Colgate-Palmolive Company is organized into regional divisions in North America, Europe, Latin America, the Far East, and the South Pacific.[25] The structure works for Colgate because personal care products often need to be tailored to cultural values and local customs.

Large nonprofit organizations such as the United Way, National Council of YMCAs, Habitat for Humanity International, and the Girl Scouts of the USA also frequently use a type of geographical structure, with a central headquarters and semiautonomous local units. The national organization provides brand recognition, coordinates fund-raising services,

EXHIBIT 7.5

Geographic-Based
Global Organization
Structure

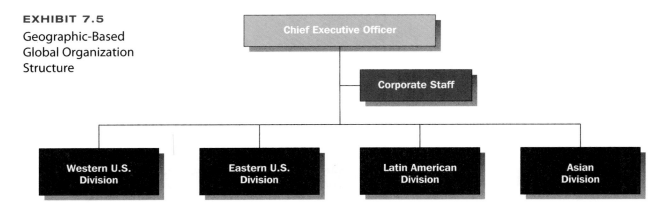

and handles some shared administrative functions, while day-to-day control and decision making are decentralized to local or regional units.[26]

MATRIX APPROACH

What It Is. The **matrix approach** combines aspects of both functional and divisional structures simultaneously in the same part of the organization. The matrix structure evolved as a way to improve horizontal coordination and information sharing.[27] One unique feature of the matrix is that it has dual lines of authority. In Exhibit 7.6, the functional hierarchy of authority runs vertically, and the divisional hierarchy of authority runs horizontally. The vertical structure provides traditional control within functional departments, and the horizontal structure provides coordination across departments. The matrix structure therefore supports a formal chain of command for both functional (vertical) and divisional (horizontal) relationships. As a result of this dual structure, some employees actually report to two supervisors simultaneously.

matrix approach
an organization structure that uses functional and divisional chains of command simultaneously in the same part of the organization.

EXHIBIT 7.6

Dual-Authority
Structure in a Matrix
Organization

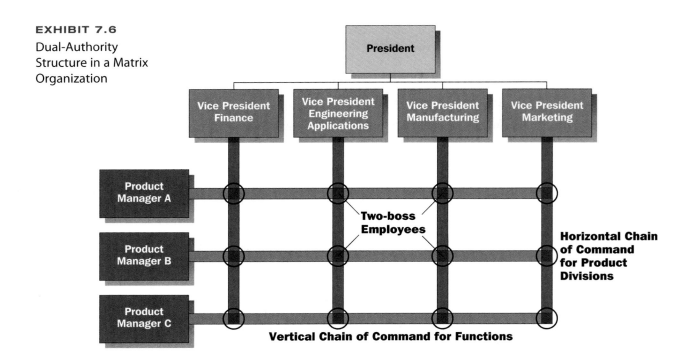

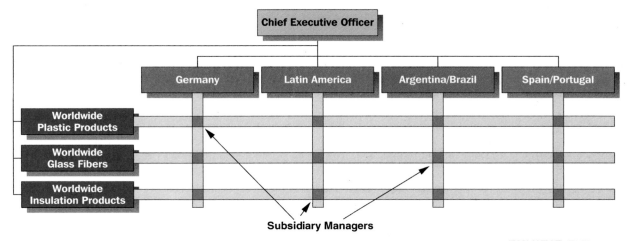

Subsidiary Managers

How It Works. The dual lines of authority make the matrix unique. To see how the matrix works, consider the global matrix structure illustrated in Exhibit 7.7. The two lines of authority are geographic and product. The geographic boss in Germany coordinates all subsidiaries in Germany, and the plastics products boss coordinates the manufacturing and sale of plastics products around the world. Managers of local subsidiary companies in Germany would report to two superiors, both the country boss and the product boss. The dual authority structure violates the unity-of-command concept described earlier in this chapter but is necessary to give equal emphasis to both functional and divisional lines of authority. Dual lines of authority can be confusing, but after managers learn to use this structure, the matrix provides excellent coordination simultaneously for each geographic region and each product line.

The success of the matrix structure depends on the abilities of people in key matrix roles. **Two-boss employees,** those who report to two supervisors simultaneously, must resolve conflicting demands from the matrix bosses. They must confront senior managers and reach joint decisions. They need excellent human relations skills with which to confront managers and resolve conflicts. The **matrix boss** is the product or functional boss, who is responsible for one side of the matrix. The top leader is responsible for the entire matrix. The **top leader** oversees both the product and functional chains of command. His or her responsibility is to maintain a power balance between the two sides of the matrix. If disputes arise between them, the problem will be kicked upstairs to the top leader.[28]

TEAM APPROACH

What It Is. Probably the most widespread trend in departmentalization in recent years has been the implementation of team concepts. The vertical chain of command is a powerful means of control, but passing all decisions up the hierarchy takes too long and keeps responsibility at the top. The team approach gives managers a way to delegate authority, push responsibility to lower levels, and be more flexible and responsive in the competitive global environment.

How It Works. One approach to using teams in organizations is through **cross-functional teams,** which consist of employees from various functional departments who are responsible to meet as a team and resolve mutual problems. Team members typically still report to their functional departments, but they also report to the team, one member of whom may be the leader. Cross-functional teams are used to provide needed horizontal coordination to complement an existing divisional or functional structure. A frequent use of cross-functional teams is for change projects, such as a new product or service innovation.

two-boss employees
employees who report to two supervisors simultaneously.

matrix boss
the product or functional boss, responsible for one side of the matrix.

top leader
the overseer of both the product and functional chains of command, responsible for the entire matrix.

cross-functional teams
a group of employees from various functional departments that meet as a team to resolve mutual problems.

A cross-functional team of mechanics, flight attendants, reservations agents, ramp workers, luggage attendants, and aircraft cleaners, for example, collaborated to plan and design a new low-fare airline for US Airways.[29]

The second approach is to use **permanent teams,** groups of employees who are brought together in a way similar to a formal department. Each team brings together employees from all functional areas focused on a specific task or project, such as parts supply and logistics for an automobile plant. Emphasis is on horizontal communication and information sharing because representatives from all functions are coordinating their work and skills to complete a specific organizational task. Authority is pushed down to lower levels, and front-line employees are often given the freedom to make decisions and take action on their own. Team members may share or rotate team leadership. With a **team-based structure,** the entire organization is made up of horizontal teams that coordinate their work and work directly with customers to accomplish the organization's goals. Imagination Ltd., Britain's largest design firm, is based entirely on teamwork. Imagination puts together a diverse team at the beginning of each new project it undertakes, whether it be creating the lighting for Disney cruise ships or redesigning the packaging for Ericsson's cell phone products. The team then works closely with the client throughout the project.[30] Imagination Ltd. has managed to make every project a smooth, seamless experience by building a culture that supports teamwork.

permanent teams
a group of participants from several functions who are permanently assigned to solve ongoing problems of common interest.

team-based structure
structure in which the entire organization is made up of horizontal teams that coordinate their activities and work directly with customers to accomplish the organization's goals.

Spotlight on
Collaboration

Teams Work at Imagination Ltd.

The essence of teamwork is that people contribute selflessly, putting the good of the whole above their own individual interests. It doesn't always work that way, but London-based Imagination Ltd., Europe's largest independent design and communications agency, seems to have found the secret ingredient to seamless teamwork. According to Adrian Caddy, Imagination's creative director: "The culture at Imagination is this: You can articulate your ideas without fear."

Imagination Ltd. has made a name for itself by producing award-winning, often highly theatrical programs. For example, in February 2006, it staged a launch event for the *Harry Potter and the Prisoner of Azkaban* DVD and video by inviting 800 guests to an historic London building where it had re-created four movie sets, among them the Great Hall at the Hogwarts School of Witchcraft and Wizardry. Accomplishing such feats are teams of designers, architects, lighting experts, writers, theater people, film directors, and artists, in addition to IT specialists, marketing experts, and other functional specialties. By having employees with a wide range of skills, the company is able to put together a diverse team to provide each client with a new approach to its design problems. Imagination is

deliberately nonhierarchical; only four people have formal titles, and on most project teams, no one is really in charge. Teams meet weekly, and everyone participates in every meeting from the very beginning, so there is no perception that any particular talent is primary—or secondary. Information technology specialists, production people, and client-contact personnel are just as much a part of the team as the creative types. In addition, each person is expected to come up with ideas outside his or her area of expertise. The philosophy is that people at Imagination must be willing to *make* all kinds of suggestions and also to *take* all kinds of suggestions. So many ideas get batted around, revised, and adapted at the weekly meetings that no one can claim ownership of a particular element of the project. The team also works closely with the client as a source of ideas and inspiration.

Talent and respect help to make the system work. Imagination hires its people carefully, based not only on the quality of their work but also on their open-mindedness and curiosity about the world beyond their functional area of expertise. Then, the company makes sure everyone's work is so closely integrated that people gain an understanding and respect for what others do. "The integrated approach breeds respect for one another," says writer Chris White. "When you work alone, or in isolation within your discipline, you can get an overblown sense of your own importance to a project."

SOURCES: Charles Fishman, "Total Teamwork: Imagination Ltd.," *Fast Company* (April 2000): 156–168; and Kelly Wardle, "Confetti: Imagination Creates One Enchanted Evening," *Special Events* (February 1, 2006), http://specialevents.com/corporate.

THE VIRTUAL NETWORK APPROACH

What It Is. The most recent approach to departmentalization extends the idea of horizontal coordination and collaboration beyond the boundaries of the organization. In a variety of industries, vertically integrated, hierarchical organizations are giving way to loosely interconnected groups of companies with permeable boundaries.[31] *Outsourcing,* which means farming out certain activities, such as manufacturing or credit processing, has become a significant trend. In addition, partnerships, alliances, and other complex collaborative forms are now a leading approach to accomplishing strategic goals. In the music industry, firms such as Vivendi Universal and Sony have formed networks of alliances with Internet service providers, digital retailers, software firms, and other companies to bring music to customers in new ways.[32] Some organizations take this networking approach to the extreme to create an innovative structure. The **virtual network structure** means that the firm subcontracts most of its major functions to separate companies and coordinates their activities from a small headquarters organization.[33] Indian telecom company Bharti Tele-Ventures Ltd., for example, outsources everything except marketing and customer management.[34]

How It Works. The organization may be viewed as a central hub surrounded by a network of outside specialists, as illustrated in Exhibit 7.8. Rather than being housed under one roof, services such as accounting, design, manufacturing, and distribution are outsourced to separate organizations that are connected electronically to the central office.[35] Networked computer systems, collaborative software, and the Internet enable organizations to exchange data and information so rapidly and smoothly that a loosely connected network of suppliers, manufacturers, assemblers, and distributors can look and act like one seamless company.

The idea behind networks is that a company can concentrate on what it does best and contract out other activities to companies with distinctive competence in those specific areas, which enables a company to do more with less.[36] The Birmingham, England-based company, Strida, provides an example of the virtual network approach.

With a network structure such as that used at Strida, it is difficult to answer the question, "Where is the organization?" in traditional terms. The different organizational parts may be spread all over the world. They are drawn together contractually and coordinated electronically, creating a new form of organization. Much like building blocks, parts of the network can be added or taken away to meet changing needs.[37]

A similar approach to networking is called the **modular approach,** in which a manufacturing company uses outside suppliers to provide entire chunks of a product, which are then assembled into a final product by a handful of workers. The Canadian firm Bombardier's new Continental business jet is made up of about a dozen huge modular components

virtual network structure
an organization structure that disaggregates major functions to separate companies that are brokered by a small headquarters organization.

modular approach
the process by which a manufacturing company uses outside suppliers to provide large components of the product, which are then assembled into a final product by a few workers.

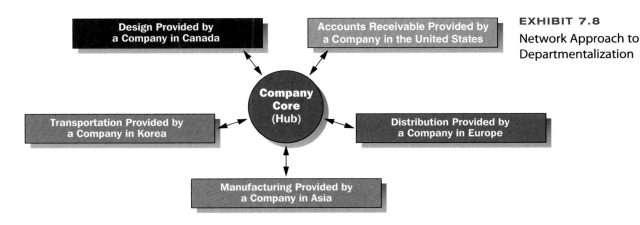

EXHIBIT 7.8
Network Approach to Departmentalization

Strida

How do two people run an entire company that sells thousands of high-tech folding bicycles all over the world? Steedman Bass and Bill Bennet do it with a virtual network approach that outsources design, manufacturing, customer service, logistics, accounting, and just about everything else to other organizations.

Bass, an avid cyclist, got into the bicycle business when he and his partner Bennet bought the struggling British company Strida, which was having trouble making enough quality bicycles to meet even minimum orders. The partners soon realized why Strida was struggling. The design for the folding bicycle was a clever engineering idea, but it was a manufacturing nightmare. Bass and Bennet immediately turned over production engineering and new product development to an American bicycle designer, still with intentions of building the bikes at the Birmingham factory. However, a large order from Italy sent them looking for other options. Eventually, they transferred all manufacturing to Ming Cycle Company of Taiwan, which builds the bikes with parts sourced from parts manufacturers in Taiwan and mainland China.

Finally, the last piece of the puzzle was to contract with a company in Birmingham that would take over everything else—from marketing to distribution. Bass and Bennet concentrate their energies on managing the partnerships that make the network function smoothly.[38]

from all over the world: the engines from the United States; the nose and cockpit from Canada; the mid-fuselage from Northern Ireland; the tail from Taiwan; the wings from Japan; and so forth.[39] Automobile plants, including General Motors, Ford, Volkswagen, and DaimlerChrysler, are leaders in using the modular approach. The modular approach hands off responsibility for engineering and production of entire sections of an automobile, such as the chassis or interior, to outside suppliers. Suppliers design a module, making some of the parts themselves and subcontracting others. These modules are delivered right to the assembly line, where a handful of employees bolt them together into a finished vehicle.[40]

ADVANTAGES AND DISADVANTAGES OF EACH STRUCTURE

Each of these approaches to departmentalization—functional, divisional, matrix, team, and virtual network—has strengths and weaknesses. The major advantages and disadvantages of each are listed in Exhibit 7.9.

Functional Approach. Grouping employees by common task permits economies of scale and efficient resource use. For example, at American Airlines, all IT people work in the same, large department. They have the expertise and skills to handle almost any IT problem for the organization. Large, functionally based departments enhance the development of in-depth skills because people work on a variety of related problems and are associated with other experts within their own department. Because the chain of command converges at the top, the functional structure also provides a way to centralize decision making and provide unified direction from top managers. The primary disadvantages reflect barriers that exist across departments. Because people are separated into distinct departments, communication and coordination across functions are often poor, causing a slow response to environmental changes. Innovation and change require involvement of several departments. Another problem is that decisions involving more than one department may pile up at the top of the organization and be delayed.

Divisional Approach. By dividing employees and resources along divisional lines, the organization will be flexible and responsive to change because each unit is small and tuned in to its environment. By having employees working on a single product line, the concern for customers' needs is high. Coordination across functional departments is better because

Structural Approach	Advantages	Disadvantages
Functional	Efficient use of resources; economies of scale In-depth skill specialization and development Top manager direction and control	Poor communication across functional departments Slow response to external changes; lagging innovation Decisions concentrated at top of hierarchy, creating delay
Divisional	Fast response, flexibility in unstable environment Fosters concern for customer needs Excellent coordination across functional departments	Duplication of resources across divisions Less technical depth and specialization Poor coordination across divisions
Matrix	More efficient use of resources than single hierarchy Flexibility, adaptability to changing environment Interdisciplinary cooperation, expertise available to all divisions	Frustration and confusion from dual chain of command High conflict between two sides of the matrix Many meetings, more discussion than action
Team	Reduced barriers among departments, increased compromise Shorter response time, quicker decisions Better morale, enthusiasm from employee involvement	Dual loyalties and conflict Time and resources spent on meetings Unplanned decentralization
Virtual Network	Can draw on expertise worldwide Highly flexible and responsive Reduced overhead costs	Lack of control; weak boundaries Greater demands on managers Employee loyalty weakened

EXHIBIT 7.9

Structural Advantages and Disadvantages

employees are grouped together in a single location and committed to one product line. Great coordination exists *within* divisions; however, coordination *across* divisions is often poor. Problems occurred at Hewlett-Packard, for example, when autonomous divisions went in opposite directions. The software produced in one division did not fit the hardware produced in another. Thus, the divisional structure was realigned to establish adequate coordination across divisions. Another major disadvantage is the duplication of resources and the high cost of running separate divisions. Instead of a single research department in which all research people use a single facility, each division may have its own research facility. The organization loses efficiency and economies of scale. In addition, the small size of departments within each division may result in a lack of technical specialization, expertise, and training.

Matrix Approach. The matrix structure is controversial because of the dual chain of command. However, the matrix can be highly effective in a complex, rapidly changing environment in which the organization needs to be flexible and adaptable.[41] The conflict and frequent meetings generated by the matrix allow new issues to be raised and resolved. The matrix structure makes efficient use of human resources because specialists can be transferred from one division to another. The major problem is the confusion and frustration caused by the dual chain of command. Matrix bosses and two-boss employees have difficulty with the dual reporting relationships. The matrix structure also can generate high conflict because it pits divisional against functional goals in a domestic structure, or product line versus country goals in a global structure. Rivalry between the two sides of the matrix can be exceedingly difficult for two-boss employees to manage. This problem leads to the third disadvantage: time lost to meetings and discussions devoted to resolving this conflict. Often the matrix structure leads to more discussion than action because different

 **TAKE ACTION**

As a new manager, understand the advantages and disadvantages of each approach to departmentalization. Recognize how each structure can provide benefits but might not be appropriate for every organization and situation.

goals and points of view are being addressed. Managers may spend a great deal of time co-ordinating meetings and assignments, which takes time away from core work activities.[42]

Team Approach. The team concept breaks down barriers across departments and improves cooperation. Team members know one another's problems and compromise rather than blindly pursue their own goals. The team concept also enables the organization to more quickly adapt to customer requests and environmental changes and speeds decision making because decisions need not go to the top of the hierarchy for approval. Another big advantage is the morale boost. Employees are enthusiastic about their involvement in bigger projects rather than narrow departmental tasks. At video games company Ubisoft, for example, each studio is set up so that teams of employees and managers work collaboratively to develop new games. Employees don't make a lot of money, but they're motivated by the freedom they have to propose new ideas and put them into action.[43]

However, the team approach has disadvantages as well. Employees may be enthusiastic about team participation, but they may also experience conflicts and dual loyalties. A cross-functional team may make different demands on members than do their department managers, and members who participate in more than one team must resolve these conflicts. A large amount of time is devoted to meetings, thus increasing coordination time. Unless the organization truly needs teams to coordinate complex projects and adapt to the environment, it will lose production efficiency with them. Finally, the team approach may cause too much decentralization. Senior department managers who traditionally made decisions might feel left out when a team moves ahead on its own. Team members often do not see the big picture of the corporation and may make decisions that are good for their group but bad for the organization as a whole.

Virtual Network Approach. The biggest advantages to a virtual network approach are flexibility and competitiveness on a global scale. The extreme flexibility of a network approach is illustrated by today's "war on terrorism." Most experts agree that the primary reason the insurgency is so difficult to fight is that it is a far-flung collection of groups that share a specific mission but are free to act on their own. "Attack any single part of it, and the rest carries on largely untouched," wrote one journalist after talking with U.S. and Iraqi officials. "It cannot be decapitated because the insurgency, for the most part, has no head."[44] One response is for the United States and its allies to organize into networks to quickly change course, put new people in place as needed, and respond to situations and challenges as they emerge.[45]

Today's business organizations can also benefit from a flexible network approach that lets them shift resources and respond quickly. A network organization can draw on resources and expertise worldwide to achieve the best quality and price and can sell its products and services worldwide. Flexibility comes from the ability to hire whatever services are needed and to change a few months later without constraints from owning plant, equipment, and facilities. The organization can continually redefine itself to fit new product and market opportunities. This structure is perhaps the leanest of all organization forms because little supervision is required. Large teams of staff specialists and administrators are not needed. A network organization may have only 2 or 3 levels of hierarchy, compared with 10 or more in traditional organizations.[46]

One of the major disadvantages is lack of hands-on control. Managers do not have all operations under one roof and must rely on contracts, coordination, negotiation, and electronic linkages to hold things together. Each partner in the network necessarily acts in its own self-interest. The weak and ambiguous boundaries create higher uncertainty and greater demands on managers for defining shared goals, coordinating activities, managing relationships, and keeping people focused and motivated.[47] Finally, in this type of organization, employee loyalty can weaken. Employees might feel they can be replaced by contract services. A cohesive corporate culture is less likely to develop, and turnover tends to be higher because emotional commitment between organization and employee is weak.

Organizing for Horizontal Coordination

One reason for the growing use of teams and networks is that many companies are recognizing the limits of traditional vertical organization structures in today's fast-shifting environment. In general, the trend is toward breaking down barriers between departments, and many companies are moving toward horizontal structures based on work processes rather than departmental functions.[48] However, regardless of the type of structure, every organization needs mechanisms for horizontal integration and coordination. The structure of an organization is not complete without designing the horizontal as well as the vertical dimensions of structure.[49]

THE NEED FOR COORDINATION

As organizations grow and evolve, two things happen. First, new positions and departments are added to deal with factors in the external environment or with new strategic needs. For example, in recent years, most colleges and universities established in-house legal departments to cope with increasing government regulations and a greater threat of lawsuits in today's society. Whereas small schools once relied on outside law firms, legal counsel is now considered crucial to the everyday operation of a college or university.[50] Many organizations establish IT departments to manage the proliferation of new information systems. As companies add positions and departments to meet changing needs, they grow more complex, with hundreds of positions and departments performing incredibly diverse activities.

Second, senior managers have to find a way to tie all of these departments together. The formal chain of command and the supervision it provides is effective, but it is not enough. The organization needs systems to process information and enable communication among people in different departments and at different levels. **Coordination** refers to the quality of collaboration across departments. Without coordination, a company's left hand will not act in concert with the right hand, causing problems and conflicts. Coordination is required regardless of whether the organization has a functional, divisional, or team structure.

Without a major effort at coordination, an organization may be like Chrysler Corporation in the 1980s when Lee Iacocca took over:

> What I found at Chrysler were 35 vice presidents, each with his own turf. . . . I couldn't believe, for example, that the guy running engineering departments wasn't in constant touch with his counterpart in manufacturing. But that's how it was. Everybody worked independently. I took one look at that system, and I almost threw up. That's when I knew I was in really deep trouble.
>
> I'd call in a guy from engineering, and he'd stand there dumbfounded when I'd explain to him that we had a design problem or some other hitch in the engineering-manufacturing relationship. He might have the ability to invent a brilliant piece of engineering that would save us a lot of money. He might come up with a terrific new design. There was only one problem: He didn't know that the manufacturing people couldn't build it. Why? Because he had never talked to them about it. Nobody at Chrysler seemed to understand that interaction among the different functions in a company is absolutely critical. People in engineering and manufacturing almost have to be sleeping together. These guys weren't even flirting![51]

If one thing changed at Chrysler in the years before Iacocca retired, it was improved coordination. Cooperation among engineering, marketing, and manufacturing enabled the rapid design and production of the Chrysler PT Cruiser, for example.

TAKE ACTION

Remember that the more departments you have, the more time you need to devote to the various departments talking to one another. Employees identify with their immediate department or team, taking its interest to heart, and may not want to compromise with other units for the good of the organization as a whole.

coordination
the quality of collaboration across departments.

EXHIBIT 7.10

Evolution of
Organization
Structures

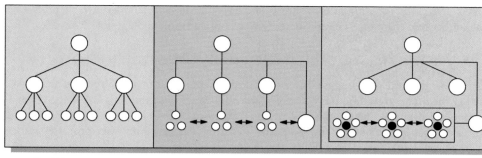

Traditional Vertical Structure   **Cross-Functional Teams and Project Managers**   **Reengineering to Horizontal Teams**

The problem of coordination is amplified in the international arena because organizational units are differentiated not only by goals and work activities but by geographical distance, time differences, cultural values, and perhaps language as well. How can managers ensure that needed coordination will take place in their company, both domestically and globally? Coordination is the outcome of information and cooperation. Managers can design systems and structures to promote horizontal coordination. For example, to support its global strategy, Whirlpool decentralized its operations, giving more authority and responsibility to teams of designers and engineers in developing countries such as Brazil, and established outsourcing relationships with manufacturers in China and India.[52] Exhibit 7.10 illustrates the evolution of organizational structures, with a growing emphasis on horizontal coordination. Although the vertical functional structure is effective in stable environments, it does not provide the horizontal coordination needed in times of rapid change. Innovations such as cross-functional teams, task forces, and project managers work within the vertical structure but provide a means to increase horizontal communication and cooperation. The next stage involves reengineering to structure the organization into teams working on horizontal processes. The vertical hierarchy is flattened, with perhaps only a few senior executives in traditional support functions such as finance and human resources. Challenges with international structures are illustrated in the following Business Blooper about Starbucks.

Business Blooper

Starbucks

Starbucks sells itself as the fair-trade champion in North America, saying it typically pays a lot more money to farmers than they get from other buyers, sometimes twice as much. Their website says while averages are $0.55-$0.70 per pound, Starbucks pays usually $1.20 per pound for coffee. Tell that to coffee farmers in Ethiopia, a place that Starbucks itself says is the birthplace for coffee. Ethiopia wants to trademark the names of its most famous coffee regions: Harar, Sidamo and Yirgacheffe, names that Starbucks uses on its own packaging. Starbucks tried over months to convince Ethiopia not to get the trademarks, saying it wasn't a good business decision. But the country wants to take more control over the promotion and distribution of one of its prime exports, with the end result to secure a better price for its farmers. Growers in one region receive only $0.75 per pound, while Starbucks sells the coffee at $26 per pound. Ethiopian officials are wondering how to address what they see as an unfair price gap, hoping to guarantee poor farmers a more reasonable return, and they have started accusing Starbucks of "coffee colonialism."

SOURCE: Janet Adamy and Roger Thurow, "Ethiopia battles Starbucks over rights to coffee names," *Wall Street Journal* (March 2, 2007): A1.

TASK FORCES, TEAMS, AND PROJECT MANAGEMENT

A **task force** is a temporary team or committee designed to solve a short-term problem involving several departments.[53] Task force members represent their departments and share information that enables coordination. For example, the Shawmut National Corporation created a task force in human resources to consolidate all employment services into a single area. The task force looked at job banks, referral programs, employment procedures, and applicant tracking systems; found ways to perform these functions for all Shawmut's divisions in one human resource department; and then disbanded.[54] In addition to creating task forces, companies also set up *cross-functional teams*, as described earlier. A cross-functional team furthers horizontal coordination because participants from several departments meet regularly to solve ongoing problems of common interest.[55] This team is similar to a task force except that it works with continuing rather than temporary problems and might exist for several years.

CONCEPT CONNECTION

Frito-Lay, a subsidiary of PepsiCo Inc., introduced Lay's Cool Guacamole potato chips and Doritos Guacamole tortilla chips in 2003. A **task force** that included members of Adelante, the Frito-Lay network for Hispanic employees, helped develop both products. In the photo, Frito-Lay researchers and Adelante members check the quality of the new guacamole chips.

Team members think in terms of working together for the good of the whole rather than just for their own department. For example, top executives at one large consumer products company had to hold frequent marathon meetings to resolve conflicts among functional units. Functional managers were focused on achieving departmental goals and were engaged in little communication across units. Resolving the conflicts that arose was time-consuming and arduous for everyone involved. Establishing a cross-functional team solved the problem by ensuring regular horizontal communication and cooperation regarding common issues and problems.[56]

Companies also use project managers to increase coordination between functional departments. A **project manager** is a person who is responsible for coordinating the activities of several departments for the completion of a specific project.[57] Project managers are critical today because many organizations are continually reinventing themselves, creating flexible structures, and working on projects with an ever-changing assortment of people and organizations.[58] Project managers might work on several different projects at one time and might have to move in and out of new projects at a moment's notice.

The distinctive feature of the project manager position is that the person is not a member of one of the departments being coordinated. Project managers are located outside of the departments and have responsibility for coordinating several departments to achieve desired project outcomes. For example, General Mills, Procter & Gamble, and General Foods all use product managers to coordinate their product lines. A manager is assigned to each line, such as Cheerios, Bisquick, and Hamburger Helper. Product managers set budget goals, marketing targets, and strategies, and obtain the

task force
a temporary team or committee formed to solve a specific short-term problem involving several departments.

project manager
a person responsible for coordinating the activities of several departments on a full-time basis for the completion of a specific project.

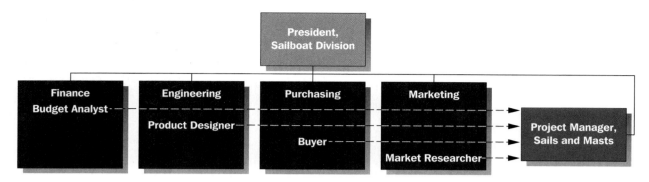

EXHIBIT 7.11

Example of Project
Manager Relationships
to Other Departments

cooperation from advertising, production, and sales personnel needed for implementing product strategy.

In some organizations, project managers are included on the organization chart, as illustrated in Exhibit 7.11. The project manager is drawn to one side of the chart to indicate authority over the project but not over the people assigned to it. Dashed lines to the project manager indicate responsibility for coordination and communication with assigned team members, but department managers retain line authority over functional employees.

Project managers might also have titles such as product manager, integrator, program manager, or process owner. Project managers need excellent people skills.

They use expertise and persuasion to achieve coordination among various departments, and their jobs involve getting people together, listening, building trust, confronting problems, and resolving conflicts and disputes in the best interest of the project and the organization. Many organizations move to a stronger horizontal approach such as the use of permanent teams, project managers, or process owners after going through a redesign procedure called reengineering.

REENGINEERING

Reengineering, sometimes called *business process reengineering,* is the radical redesign of business processes to achieve dramatic improvements in cost, quality, service, and speed.[59] Because the focus of reengineering is on process rather than function, reengineering generally leads to a shift away from a strong vertical structure to one emphasizing stronger horizontal coordination and greater flexibility in responding to changes in the environment.

Reengineering changes the way managers think about how work is done in their organizations. Rather than focusing on narrow jobs structured into distinct, functional departments, they emphasize core processes that cut horizontally across the company and involve teams of employees working to provide value directly to customers.[60] A **process** is an organized group of related tasks and activities that work together to transform inputs into outputs and create value. Common examples of processes include new product development, order fulfillment, and customer service.[61]

Reengineering frequently involves a shift to a horizontal team-based structure, as described earlier in this chapter. All the people who work on a particular process have easy access to one another so they can easily communicate and coordinate their efforts, share knowledge, and provide value directly to customers.[62] For example, reengineering at Texas Instruments led to the formation of product development teams that became the fundamental organizational unit. Each team is made up of people drawn from engineering, marketing, and other departments, and takes full responsibility for a product from conception through launch.[63]

reengineering
the radical redesign of business processes to achieve dramatic improvements in cost, quality, service, and speed.

process
an organized group of related tasks and activities that work together to transform inputs into outputs and create value.

The Pentagon can act quickly to move thousands of tons of humanitarian aid material or hundreds of thousands of troops, but until recently, sending employees on routine travel has been a different story. Before Pentagon travelers could even board a bus, they had to secure numerous approvals and fill out reams of paperwork. Coming home wasn't any easier—the average traveler spent six hours preparing vouchers for reimbursement following a trip.

The Department of Defense set up a task force to reengineer the cumbersome travel system, aiming to make it cheaper, more efficient, and more customer friendly. The reengineered system reduces the steps in the pretravel process from an astounding 11 to only 4, as shown in Exhibit 7.12. Travel budgets and authority to approve travel requests and vouchers, which traditionally rested in the budget channels of the various service commands, were transferred to local supervisors. Travelers make all their arrangements through a commercial travel office, which prepares a "should-cost" estimate for each trip. This document is all a traveler needs before, during, and after a trip. With a supervisor's signature, it becomes a travel authorization; during travel, it serves as an itinerary; after amendments to reflect variations from plans, it becomes an expense report. Other travel expenses and needed cash or travelers' checks can be charged to a government-issued travel card, with payment made directly to the travel card company through electronic funds transfer.[64]

U.S. Department of Defense

Reengineering can also squeeze out the dead space and time lags in work flows, as illustrated by reengineering of the travel system at the U.S. Department of Defense.

As illustrated by this example, reengineering can lead to stunning results, but, like all business ideas, it has its drawbacks. Simply defining the organization's key business processes can be mind-boggling. AT&T's Network Systems division started with a list of 130 processes and then began working to pare them down to 13 core ones.[65] Organizations often have difficulty realigning power relationships and management processes to support work redesign and thus do not reap the intended benefits of reengineering. According to some estimates, 70 percent of reengineering efforts fail to reach their intended goals.[66] Because reengineering is expensive, time consuming, and usually painful, it seems best suited to companies that are facing serious competitive threats.

EXHIBIT 7.12

Reengineering the Travel System—U.S. Department of Defense

Steps in the Pretravel Process—Old System

1. Identify need to travel
2. Prepare request for orders
3. Prepare cost estimate
4. Identify source of funding
5. Obtain requesting official's signature
6. Get budget office and reviewing official's signatures
7. Get approving official's signature
8. Finance office checks funds availability and updates accounting
9. Obtain travel advance
10. Obtain ticket from CTO or agency transportation office
11. CTO bills for tickets

Steps in the Pretravel Process—Reengineered System

1. Identify need to travel and notify commercial travel office (CTO)
2. CTO team provides "should-cost" estimate and complete travel package
3. Supervisor approves and funds trip; computer updates accounting automatically
4. Computer issues travel advance inform requested

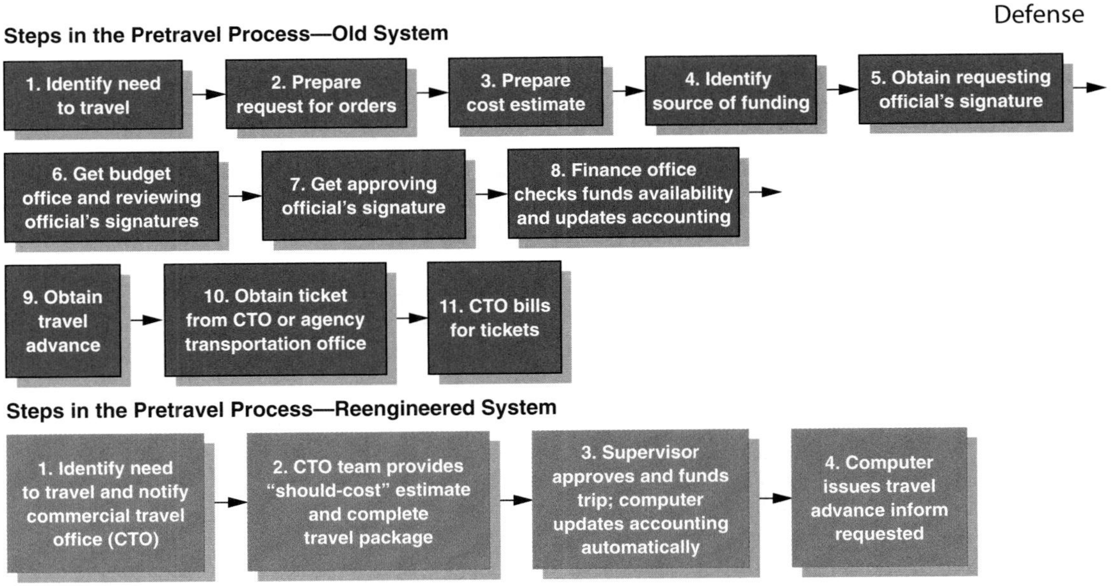

SOURCE: Richard Koonce, "Reengineering the Travel Game," *Government Executive* (May 1995), 28–34, 69–70.

Authority Role Models

An organization's structure is based on authority. Beliefs about authority for a new manager are often based on experiences in your first authority figures and role models—Mom and Dad. To understand your authority role models, answer each of the following items as Mostly True or Mostly False for you. Think in terms about each statement as it applies to the parent or parents who made primary decisions about raising you.

	Mostly True			Mostly False	
1. My parent(s) believed that children should get their way in the family as often as the parents do.	1	2	3	4	5
2. When a family policy was established, my parent(s) discussed the reasoning behind it with the children.	1	2	3	4	5
3. My parent(s) believed it was for my own good if I was made to conform to what they thought was right.	1	2	3	4	5
4. My parents felt we should make up our own minds about what we wanted to do even if we did not agree with them.	1	2	3	4	5
5. My parent(s) directed my activities through reasoning and discussion.	1	2	3	4	5
6. My parent(s) was clear about who was the boss in the family.	1	2	3	4	5
7. My parent(s) allowed me to decide most things for myself without a lot of direction.	1	2	3	4	5
8. My parent(s) took the children's opinions into consideration when making family decisions.	1	2	3	4	5
9. If I didn't meet parental rules and expectations, I could expect to be punished.	1	2	3	4	5

INTERPRETATION AND SCORING: Each question pertains to one of three subscales of **parental authority.** Questions 1, 4, and 7 reflect *permissive* parental authority, questions 2, 5, and 8 indicate *flexible* authority, and questions 3, 6, and 9 indicate *authoritarian* parental authority. The subscale for which you checked more items Mostly True may reveal personal beliefs from your early role models that shape your comfort with authority as a new manager. *Authoritarian* beliefs typically would fit in a traditional vertical hierarchy. *Flexible* authority beliefs typically would fit with horizontal organizing, such as managing teams, projects, and reengineering. Because most organizations thrive on structure, *permissive* beliefs may be insufficient to enforce accountability under any structure. How do you think your childhood role models affect your authority beliefs? Remember, this questionnaire is just a guide because your current beliefs about authority may not directly reflect your childhood experiences.

SOURCE: Adapted from John R. Buri, "Parental Authority Questionnaire," *Journal of Personality and Social Assessment* 57 (1991): 110–119.

Factors Shaping Structure

Despite the trend toward horizontal design, vertical hierarchies continue to thrive because they often provide important benefits for organizations.[67] How do managers know whether to design a structure that emphasizes the formal, vertical hierarchy or one with an emphasis on horizontal communication and collaboration? The answer lies in the contingency factors that influence organization structure. Research on organization design shows that structure depends on a variety of *contingencies,* as defined in Chapter 1. The right structure is designed to "fit" the contingency factors of strategy, environment, and production technology, as illustrated in Exhibit 7.13. These three areas are changing quite dramatically for most organizations, creating a need for stronger horizontal coordination.

STRUCTURE FOLLOWS STRATEGY

In Chapter 5, we discussed several strategies that business firms can adopt. Two strategies proposed by Porter are differentiation and cost leadership.[68] With a differentiation strategy, the organization attempts to develop innovative products unique to the market. With a cost leadership strategy, the organization strives for internal efficiency. The strategies of cost leadership versus differentiation typically require different structural approaches. A recent study demonstrated that business performance is strongly influenced by how well the company's structure is aligned with its strategic intent, so managers strive to pick strategies and structures that are congruent.[69]

Exhibit 7.14 shows a simplified continuum that illustrates how structural approaches are associated with strategic goals. The pure functional structure is appropriate for achieving internal efficiency goals. The vertical functional structure uses task specialization and a strict chain of command to gain efficient use of scarce resources, but it does not enable the organization to be flexible or innovative. In contrast, horizontal teams are appropriate when the primary goal is innovation and flexibility. Each team is small, is able to be responsive, and has the people and resources necessary for performing its task. The flexible horizontal structure enables organizations to differentiate themselves and respond quickly to the demands of a shifting environment but at the expense of efficient resource use. New strategies also shape structure in government organizations. Under financial pressure to cut costs and political pressure to keep customers happy, Departments of Motor Vehicles are farming out DMV business whenever possible by building strong partnerships with other companies. For example, in most states, auto dealers register new cars on site when they are sold.[70]

Exhibit 7.14 also illustrates how other forms of structure represent intermediate steps on the organization's path to efficiency or innovation. The functional structure with cross-functional teams and project managers provides greater coordination and flexibility than the pure functional structure. The divisional structure promotes differentiation because each division can focus on specific products and customers, although divisions tend to be larger and less flexible than small teams. Exhibit 7.14 does not include all possible structures,

TAKE ACTION

As a manager, remember if your strategy changes, you need to revisit the structure to make sure it is appropriate.

EXHIBIT 7.13

Contingency Factors That Influence Organization Structure

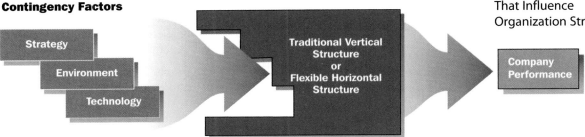

Contingency Factors

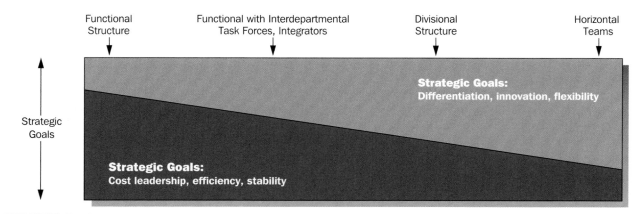

| Functional Structure | Functional with Interdepartmental Task Forces, Integrators | Divisional Structure | Horizontal Teams |

Strategic Goals

Strategic Goals:
Differentiation, innovation, flexibility

Strategic Goals:
Cost leadership, efficiency, stability

EXHIBIT 7.14

Relationship of Strategic Goals to Structural Approach

but it illustrates how structures can be used to facilitate the strategic goals of cost leadership or differentiation.

STRUCTURE REFLECTS THE ENVIRONMENT

In Chapter 2, we discussed the nature of environmental uncertainty. Environmental uncertainty means that decision makers have difficulty acquiring good information and predicting external changes. Uncertainty occurs when the external environment is rapidly changing and complex. An uncertain environment causes three things to happen within an organization.

1. *Increased differences occur among departments.* In an uncertain environment, each major department—marketing, manufacturing, research and development—focuses on the task and environmental sectors for which it is responsible and hence distinguishes itself from the others with respect to goals, task orientation, and time horizon.[71] Departments work autonomously. These factors create barriers among departments.

2. *The organization needs increased coordination to keep departments working together.* Additional differences require more emphasis on horizontal coordination to link departments and overcome differences in departmental goals and orientations.

3. *The organization must adapt to change.* The organization must maintain a flexible, responsive posture toward the environment. Changes in products and technology require cooperation among departments, which means additional emphasis on coordination through the use of teams, project managers, and horizontal information processing.[72]

The terms *mechanistic* and *organic* can be used to explain structural responses to the external environment.[73] When the environment is stable, the organization uses a mechanistic system. It typically has

CONCEPT CONNECTION

There is nothing like the approach of a fighter jet with a landing speed of 150 miles per hour to shake up an organization—especially if you're standing on a small, moving flight deck, such as that of the *USS Dwight D. Eisenhower.* Here, crew members on the nuclear aircraft supercarrier practice a waveoff, signaling to an FA-18 Hornet pilot that he or she should take another pass before touching down. The crew adapts to the high-stakes, **uncertain environment** surrounding the orchestrated take-offs and landings of high-speed planes by shifting from a **mechanistic** to an **organic** system that allows for flexibility and rapid response.

STRUCTURE

	Vertical	Horizontal
Uncertain (Unstable)	**Incorrect Fit:** Vertical structure in uncertain environment Mechanistic structure too tight	**Correct Fit:** Horizontal structure in uncertain environment
Certain (Stable)	**Correct Fit:** Vertical structure in certain environment	**Incorrect Fit:** Horizontal structure in certain environment Organic structure too loose

ENVIRONMENT

EXHIBIT 7.15

Relationship Between Environment and Structure

a rigid, vertical, centralized structure, with most decisions made at the top. The organization is highly specialized and characterized by rules, procedures, and a clear hierarchy of authority. In rapidly changing environments, however, the organization tends to be much looser, free-flowing, and adaptive, using an organic system. The structure is more horizontal and decision-making authority is decentralized. People at lower levels have more responsibility and authority for solving problems, enabling the organization to be more fluid and adaptable to changes in the environment.[74]

The contingency relationship between environmental uncertainty and structural approach is illustrated in Exhibit 7.15. When the external environment is stable, the organization can succeed with a mechanistic structure that emphasizes vertical control. With little need for change, flexibility, or intense coordination, the structure can emphasize specialization and centralized decision making. When environmental uncertainty is high, however, a flexible organic structure that emphasizes lateral relationships such as teams and horizontal projects is appropriate. Vertical structure characteristics such as specialization and centralization should be downplayed. In an uncertain environment, the organization figures things out as it goes along, departments must cooperate, and decisions should be decentralized to the teams and task forces working on specific problems. The flight deck of the *USS Dwight D. Eisenhower,* a nuclear-powered aircraft carrier, provides an excellent example of the relationship between structure and the environment.

TAKE ACTION

Go to the experiential exercise on page 280 that pertains to organic versus mechanistic structure.

USS Dwight D. Eisenhower

Launching or landing a plane from the oil-slicked deck of a nuclear-powered aircraft carrier, such as the *USS Dwight D. Eisenhower,* is a tricky, finely balanced procedure. A sudden wind shift, a mechanical breakdown, or the slightest miscommunications could spell disaster. Yet, surprisingly, flight deck operations generally run as smooth as silk, and accidents are quite rare. The reason for this has a lot to do with organizational structure.

At first glance, a nuclear aircraft carrier is structured in a rigid, hierarchical way—the captain issues orders to commanders, who direct lieutenants, who pass orders on to ensigns, and on down the hierarchy. Within a strict chain of command, people are expected to follow orders promptly and without question. Manuals detail standard operating procedures for everything. But an interesting thing happens in times of high demand, such as the launching and recovery of planes during real or simulated wartime. In this different environment, the hierarchy dissolves, and a loosely organized, collaborative structure in which sailors and officers work together as colleagues takes its place. People discuss and negotiate the best procedure to use, and everyone typically follows the lead of whoever has the most experience and knowledge in a particular area, no matter the person's rank or job title.

During this time, no one is thinking about job descriptions, authority, or chain of command; they are just thinking about getting the job done safely. Planes landing every 60 seconds leave no time to send messages up the chain of command and wait for decisions to come down from the top. Anyone who notices a problem is expected to respond quickly, and each member of the crew has the power—and the obligation—to shut down flight operations immediately if the circumstances warrant it.[75]

Researchers studied this ability to glide smoothly from a rigid, hierarchical structure to a loosely structured, horizontal one, not only on aircraft carriers but in other organizations that need to be exceptionally responsive to environmental changes—for example, air-traffic controllers or workers at nuclear power plants. The hierarchical side helps keep discipline and ensure adherence to rules that have been developed and tested over many years to cope with expected and well-understood problems and situations. However, during times of complexity and high uncertainty, the most effective structure is one that loosens the lines of command and enables people to work across departmental and hierarchical lines to anticipate and avoid problems.[76]

Not all organizations have to be as super-responsive to the environment as the *USS Dwight D. Eisenhower,* but using the correct structure for the environment is important for businesses as well. When managers use the wrong structure for the environment, reduced performance results. A rigid, vertical structure in an uncertain environment prevents the organization from adapting to change. Likewise, a loose, horizontal structure in a stable environment is inefficient. Too many resources are devoted to meetings and discussions when employees could be more productive focusing on specialized tasks.

STRUCTURE FITS THE TECHNOLOGY

Technology includes the knowledge, tools, techniques, and activities used to transform organizational inputs into outputs.[77] Technology includes machinery, employee skills, and work procedures. A useful way to think about technology is as production activities. The production activities may be to produce steel castings, television programs, or computer software. Technologies vary between manufacturing and service organizations. In addition, new digital technology has an impact on structure.

Woodward's Manufacturing Technology. The most influential research into the relationship between manufacturing technology and organization structure was conducted by Joan Woodward, a British industrial sociologist.[78] She gathered data from 100 British firms to determine whether basic structural characteristics, such as administrative overhead, span of control, and centralization, were different across firms. She found that manufacturing firms could be categorized according to three basic types of production technology:

1. *Small-batch and unit production.* **Small-batch production** firms produce goods in batches of one or a few products designed to customer specification. Each customer orders a unique product. This technology also is used to make large, one-of-a-kind products, such as computer-controlled machines. Small-batch manufacturing is close to traditional skilled-craft work because human beings are a large part of the process. Examples of items produced through small-batch manufacturing include custom clothing, special-order machine tools, space capsules, satellites, and submarines.

2. *Large-batch and mass production.* **Mass production** technology is distinguished by standardized production runs. A large volume of products is produced, and all customers receive the same product. Standard products go into inventory for sale as customers need them. This technology makes greater use of machines than does small-batch production. Machines are designed to do most of the physical work, and employees complement the machinery. Examples of mass production are automobile assembly lines and the large-batch techniques used to produce tobacco products and textiles.

3. *Continuous process production.* In **continuous process production**, the entire work flow is mechanized in a sophisticated and complex form of production technology. Because the process runs continuously, it has no starting and stopping. Human operators are not part of actual production because machinery does all of

small-batch production
a type of technology that involves the production of goods in batches of one or a few products designed to customer specification.

mass production
a type of technology characterized by the production of a large volume of products with the same specifications.

continuous process production
a type of technology involving mechanization of the entire work flow and nonstop production.

	Manufacturing Technology		
	Small Batch	**Mass Production**	**Continuous Process**
Technical Complexity of Production Technology:	Low	Medium	High
Organization Structure:			
Centralization	Low	High	Low
Top administrator ratio	Low	Medium	High
Indirect/direct labor ratio	1/9	1/4	1/1
Supervisor span of control	23	48	15
Communication:			
Written (vertical)	Low	High	Low
Verbal (horizontal)	High	Low	High
Overall structure	Organic	Mechanistic	Organic

SOURCE: Based on Joan Woodward, *Industrial Organizations: Theory and Practice* (London: Oxford University Press, 1965).

the work. Human operators simply read dials, fix machines that break down, and manage the production process. Examples of continuous process technologies are chemical plants, distilleries, petroleum refineries, and nuclear power plants.

The difference among the three manufacturing technologies is called **technical complexity.** Technical complexity is the degree to which machinery is involved in the production to the exclusion of people. With a complex technology, employees are hardly needed except to monitor the machines.

The structural characteristics associated with each type of manufacturing technology are illustrated in Exhibit 7.16. Note that centralization is high for mass production technology and low for continuous process. Unlike small-batch and continuous process production, standardized mass-production machinery requires centralized decision making and well-defined rules and procedures. The administrative ratio and the percentage of indirect labor required also increase with technological complexity. Because the production process is nonroutine, closer supervision is needed. More indirect labor in the form of maintenance people is required because of the machinery's complexity; thus, the indirect/direct labor ratio is high. Span of control for first-line supervisors is greatest for mass production. On an assembly line, jobs are so routinized that a supervisor can handle an average of 48 employees. The number of employees per supervisor in small-batch and continuous process production is lower because closer supervision is needed. Overall, small-batch and continuous process firms have somewhat loose, flexible structures (organic), and mass production firms have tight vertical structures (mechanistic).

The important conclusion about manufacturing technology was described by Woodward as follows: "Different technologies impose different kinds of demands on individuals and organizations, and these demands have to be met through an appropriate structure."[79] Woodward found that the relationship between structure and technology was directly related to company performance. Low-performing firms tended to deviate from the preferred structural form, often adopting a structure appropriate for another type of technology. High-performing organizations had characteristics similar to those listed in Exhibit 7.16.

TAKE ACTION

As a manager, always consider technical complexity when deciding on what structure to use.

technical complexity
the degree to which complex machinery is involved in the production process to the exclusion of people.

Service Technology. Service organizations are increasingly important in North America. For the past two decades, more people have been employed in service organizations than in manufacturing firms. Examples of service organizations include consulting companies, law firms, brokerage houses, airlines, hotels, advertising companies, amusement parks, and educational organizations. In addition, service technology characterizes many departments in large corporations, even manufacturing firms. In a manufacturing company such as Ford Motor Company, the legal, human resources, finance, and market research departments all provide service. Thus, the structure and design of these departments reflect their own service technology rather than the manufacturing plant's technology. **Service technology** can be defined as follows:

1. *Intangible output.* The output of a service firm is intangible. Services are perishable and, unlike physical products, cannot be stored in inventory. The service is either consumed immediately or lost forever. Manufactured products are produced at one point in time and can be stored until sold at another time.

2. *Direct contact with customers.* Employees and customers interact directly to provide and purchase the service. Production and consumption are simultaneous. Service firm employees have direct contact with customers. In a manufacturing firm, technical employees are separated from customers, and hence no direct interactions occur.[80]

One distinct feature of service technology that directly influences structure is the need for employees to be close to the customer.[81] Structural characteristics are similar to those for continuous manufacturing technology, shown in Exhibit 7.16. Service firms tend to be flexible, informal, and decentralized. Horizontal communication is high because employees must share information and resources to serve customers and solve problems. Services also are dispersed; hence each unit is often small and located geographically close to customers. For example, banks, hotels, fast-food franchises, and doctors' offices disperse their facilities into regional and local offices to provide faster and better service to customers.

Some services can be broken down into explicit steps, so that employees can follow set rules and procedures. For example, McDonald's has standard procedures for serving customers, and Marriott has standard procedures for cleaning hotel rooms. When services can be standardized, a tight centralized structure can be effective, but service firms in general tend to be more organic, flexible, and decentralized.

Digital Technology. **Digital technology** is characterized by use of the Internet and other digital processes to conduct or support business online. E-commerce organizations such as Amazon.com, which sells books and other products to consumers over the Internet; eBay, an online auction site; Google, an Internet search engine; and Priceline.com, which allows consumers to name their own prices and then negotiates electronically with its partner organizations on behalf of the consumer, are all examples of firms based on digital technology. In addition, large companies such as General Electric, Dell Inc., and Ford Motor Company are involved in business-to-business commerce, using digital technology to conduct transactions with suppliers and partners.

Like service firms, organizations based on digital technology tend to be flexible and decentralized. Horizontal communication and collaboration are typically high, and these companies may frequently be involved in virtual network arrangements. Digital technology is driving the move toward horizontal forms that link customers, suppliers, and partners into the organizational network, with everyone working together as if they were one organization. People may use electronic connections to link themselves together into teams. For example, an employee may send an e-mail to people both within and outside the organization who can help with a particular customer problem and quickly form a virtual team to develop a solution.[82] In other words, digital technology encourages *boundarylessness,* where information and work activities flow freely among various organizational participants.

TAKE ACTION ▶

As a new manager, recognize how structure fits the contingency factors of strategy, environment, and technology. Design the right mix of structural characteristics to fit the contingency factors.

---

service technology
technology characterized by intangible outputs and direct contact between employees and customers.

digital technology
technology characterized by use of the Internet and other digital processes to conduct or support business operations.

Centralization is low, and employees are empowered to work in teams to meet fast-changing needs. Verbal and electronic communication is high, both up and down as well as across the organization because up-to-the-minute information is essential. In the digital world, advantage comes from seeing first and moving fastest, which requires extraordinary openness and flexibility.[83]

Summary

This chapter introduced a number of important organizing concepts. Fundamental characteristics of organization structure include work specialization, chain of command, authority and responsibility, span of management, and centralization and decentralization. These dimensions represent the vertical hierarchy and define how authority and responsibility are distributed.

Another major concept is departmentalization, which describes how organization employees are grouped. Three traditional approaches are functional, divisional, and matrix; contemporary approaches are team and virtual network structures. The functional approach groups employees by common skills and tasks. The opposite structure is divisional, which groups people by organizational output so that each division has a mix of functional skills and tasks. The matrix structure uses two chains of command simultaneously, and some employees have two bosses. The team approach uses permanent teams and cross-functional teams to achieve better coordination and employee commitment than is possible with a pure functional structure. The network approach means that a firm concentrates on what it does best and subcontracts other functions to separate organizations that are connected to the headquarters electronically. Each organization form has advantages and disadvantages and can be used by managers to meet the needs of the competitive situation. In addition, managers adjust elements of the vertical structure, such as the degree of centralization or decentralization, to meet changing needs.

As organizations grow, they add new departments, functions, and hierarchical levels. A major problem for management is how to tie the whole organization together. Horizontal coordination mechanisms provide coordination across departments and include reengineering, task forces, project managers, and horizontal teams.

Contingency factors of strategy, environment, and production technology influence the correct structural approach. When a firm's strategy is to differentiate its products or services, an organic flexible structure using teams, decentralization, and empowered employees is appropriate. A mechanistic structure is appropriate for a low-cost strategy. Similarly, the structure needs to be looser and more flexible when environmental uncertainty is high. For manufacturing firms, small-batch, continuous process, and flexible manufacturing technologies tend to be structured loosely, whereas a tighter vertical structure is appropriate for mass production. Service technologies are people oriented, and firms are located geographically close to dispersed customers. In general, services have more flexible, horizontal structures, with decentralized decision making. Similarly, organizations based on new digital technology are typically horizontally structured and highly decentralized.

Discussion Questions

1. Sandra Holt, manager of Electronics Assembly, asked Hector Cruz, her senior technician, to handle things in the department while Sandra worked on the budget. She needed peace and quiet for at least a week to complete her figures. After 10 days, Sandra discovered that Hector had hired a senior secretary, not realizing that Sandra had promised interviews to two other people. Evaluate Sandra's approach to delegation.

2. Many experts note that organizations have been making greater use of teams in recent years. What factors might account for this trend?

3. An organizational consultant was heard to say, "Some aspect of functional structure appears in every organization." Do you agree? Explain.

4. The divisional structure is often considered almost the opposite of a functional structure. Do you agree? Briefly explain the major differences in these two approaches to departmentalization.

5. Some people argue that the matrix structure should be adopted only as a last resort because the dual chains of command can create more problems than they solve. Discuss. Do you agree or disagree? Why?

6. What is the virtual network approach to structure? Is the use of authority and responsibility different compared with other forms of departmentalization? Explain.

7. The Hay Group published a report that some managers have personalities suited to horizontal relationships

such as project management that achieve results with little formal authority. Other managers are more suited to operating roles with much formal authority in a vertical structure. In what type of structure—functional, matrix, team, or virtual network—would you feel most comfortable managing? Which structure would be the most challenging for you? Give your reasons.

8. Experts say that organizations are becoming increasingly decentralized, with authority, decision-making responsibility, and accountability being pushed farther down into the organization. How will this trend affect what will be asked of you as a new manager? The chapter suggested that structure should be designed to fit strategy. Some theorists argue that strategy should be designed to fit the organization's structure. With which theory do you agree? Explain.

9. Carnival Cruise Lines provides pleasure cruises to the masses. Carnival has several ships and works on high volume/low price rather than offering luxury cruises.

What would you predict about the organization structure of a Carnival Cruise ship compared with a company that had smaller ships for wealthy customers? Discuss why an organization in an uncertain environment requires more horizontal relationships than one in a certain environment.

10. What is the difference between manufacturing and service technology? How would you classify a university, a local discount store, and a nursery school? How would you expect the structure of a service organization to differ from that of a manufacturing organization?

11. What impact does the growing use of digital technology have on organizational structure? Would you expect the structure of an Internet-based organization such as eBay, which operates almost entirely online, to be different from a bricks-and-mortar company such as General Electric that uses the Internet for business-to-business transactions with vendors? Why or why not?

Dear Dr. Dorothy

I got promoted last year to a management position, and my employees are driving me nuts! They won't do what I ask, miss deadlines, and make so many mistakes I can hardly believe they get a paycheck from the company. I end up having to redo their work for them. If I don't my bosses will get on my case, and I might get fired. But I don't have time to do their work and mine, nor do I have time to keep explaining to them how to do their work. They are grownups, aren't they? Why is it so hard to find good help?

Tired of Yelling

Dear Tired,

Dr. Dorothy thinks you need to take some deep breaths and repeat to yourself, "I will learn to delegate, I will learn to delegate." You have the classic new manager delgatitis condition. You think you can do the work so much better, and you constantly get frustrated when employees prove that is true. If these people are that awful, maybe they should get fired. On the other hand, Dr. Dorothy wonders how you got promoted with such a negative attitude toward others. After all, management is getting work done through OTHERS. If you were meant to do it alone, you wouldn't have subordinates. Get a grip and try some new behaviors. Talk to your subordinates—in a CALM voice—and ask them how you can help them get their work done. Dr. Dorothy thinks they will tell you to back off, that your hovering makes them nervous and less productive. Plus when you do their work for them, it is demoralizing. Help them get some meaning in their work rather than you demeaning them.

Self Learning

Organic Versus Mechanistic Organization Structure

Interview an employee at your university, such as a department head or secretary. Have the employee answer the following 13 questions about his or her job and organizational conditions. Then, answer the same set of questions for a job you have held.

Disagree Strongly   1 2 3 4 5   Agree Strongly

1. Your work would be considered routine.   **1 2 3 4 5**

2. A clearly known way is established to do the major tasks you encounter.   **1 2 3 4 5**

3. Your work has high variety and frequent exceptions.   **1 2 3 4 5**

4. Communications from above consist of information and advice rather than instructions and directions.
1 2 3 4 5

5. You have the support of peers and your supervisor to do your job well.   **1 2 3 4 5**

6. You seldom exchange ideas or information with people doing other kinds of jobs.   **1 2 3 4 5**

7. Decisions relevant to your work are made above you and passed down.   **1 2 3 4 5**

8. People at your level frequently have to figure out for themselves what their jobs are for the day.   **1 2 3 4 5**

9. Lines of authority are clear and precisely defined.
1 2 3 4 5

10. Leadership tends to be democratic rather than autocratic in style.   **1 2 3 4 5**

11. Job descriptions are written and up-to-date for each job.   **1 2 3 4 5**

12. People understand each other's jobs and often do different tasks.   **1 2 3 4 5**

13. A manual of policies and procedures is available to use when a problem arises.   **1 2 3 4 5**

Scoring and Interpretation

To obtain the total score, subtract the scores for questions 1, 2, 6, 7, 9, 11, and 13 from the number 6 and total the adjusted scores.

Total Score, Employee: _____

Total Score, You: _____

Compare the total score for a place you have worked to the score of the university employee you interviewed. A total score of 52 or above suggests that you or the other respondent is working in an organic organization. The score reflects a loose, flexible structure that is often associated with uncertain environments and small-batch or service technology. People working in this structure feel empowered. Many organizations today are moving in the direction of flexible structures and empowerment.

A score of 26 or below suggests a mechanistic structure. This structure uses traditional control and functional specialization, which often occurs in a certain environment, a stable organization, and routine or mass-production technology. People in this structure may feel controlled and constrained.

Discuss the pros and cons of organic versus mechanistic structure. Does the structure of the employee you interviewed fit the nature of the organization's environment, strategic goals, and technology? How about the structure for your own workplace? How might you redesign the structure to make the work organization more effective?

Group Learning

Family Business

You are the parent of 10 children and have just used your inheritance to acquire a medium-sized pharmaceutical company. Last year's sales were down 18 percent from the previous year. In fact, the past three years have been real losers. You want to clean house of current managers over the next 10 years and bring your children into the business. Being a loving parent, you agree to send your children to college to educate each of them in one functional specialty. The 10 children are actually 5 sets of twins exactly a year apart. The first set will begin college this fall, followed by the remaining sets the next 4 years. The big decision is which specialty each child should study. You want to have the most important functions taken over by your children as soon as possible, so you will ask the older children to study the most important areas.

Your task right now is to rank in order of priority the functions to which your children will be assigned and develop reasons for your ranking.

The 10 functions follow:

Distribution

Manufacturing

Market Research

New-Product Development

Human Resources

Product Promotion

Quality Assurance

Sales

Legal and Governmental Affairs

Office of the Controller

1. Analyze your reasons for how functional priority relates to the company's environmental/strategic needs.

2. In groups of 4 to 6, now rank the functions. Discuss the problem until group members agree on a single ranking.

3. How does the group's reasoning and ranking differ from your original thinking?

4. What did you learn about organization structure and design from this exercise?

Action Learning

You and Organization Structure

Background

Organization is a way of gaining some power against an unreliable environment. The environment provides the organization with inputs, which include raw materials, human resources, and financial resources. There is a service or product to produce that involves technology. The output goes to clients, a group that must be nurtured. The complexities of the environment and the technology determine the complexity of the organization.

To better understand the importance of organization structure in your life, do the following assignment in groups of 4 to 6 members.

Select one of the following situations to organize. Imagine you are the CEO and have to design the organization for maximum efficiency and effectiveness.

a. The registration process at your university or college

b. A new fast-food franchise

c. A sports rental in an ocean/ski/snowboard resort area, such as jet skis, and so on

d. A bakery

e. The process for getting a parking ticket at your university.

Ask yourself the following questions to complete the assignment.

Understanding the organization:

1. Write down the mission or purpose of the organization in a few sentences.

2. What are the specific things to be done to accomplish the mission?

3. Based on the specifics in #2, develop an organization chart. Each position in the chart will perform a specific task or is responsible for a certain outcome.

4. Add duties to each job position in the chart. These will be the job descriptions.

5. How can you make sure people in each position will work together?

6. What level of skill and abilities is required at each position and level to hire the right persons?

7. Make a list of the decisions that would have to be made as you developed your organization.

8. Who is responsible for customer satisfaction? How will you know if customers' needs are met?

9. How will information flow within the organization?

10. After you have completed the preceding items, go to the type of organization you designed. Spend some time there as a group and bring your results along. Discuss with your group each item, trying to determine if this organization is similar or different in structure to what you have proposed.

SOURCE: Adapted from "Organizing," in Donald D. White and H. William Vroman, *Action in Organizations*, 2e. (Boston: Allyn and Bacon): 154.

Your instructor may ask you to turn in a paper with your results and/or make a presentation to the class.

Ethical Dilemma

A Matter of Delegation

Tom Harrington loved his job as an assistant quality-control officer for Rockingham Toys. After six months of unemployment, he was anxious to make a good impression on his boss, Frank Golopolus. One of his new responsibilities was ensuring that new product lines met federal safety guidelines. Rockingham had made several manufacturing changes over the past year. Golopolus and the rest of the quality-control team had been working 60-hour weeks to troubleshoot the new production process.

Harrington was aware of numerous changes in product safety guidelines that he knew would impact the new Rockingham toys. Golopolus was also aware of the guidelines, but he was taking no action to implement them. Harrington wasn't sure whether his boss expected him to implement the new procedures. The ultimate responsibility belonged to his boss, and Harrington was concerned about moving ahead on his own. To cover for his boss, he continued to avoid the questions he received from the factory floor, but he was beginning to wonder whether Rockingham would have time to make changes with the Christmas season rapidly approaching.

Harrington felt loyalty to Golopolus for giving him a job and didn't want to alienate him by interfering. However, he was beginning to worry about what might happen if he didn't act. Rockingham had a fine product safety reputation and was rarely challenged on matters of quality. Should he question Golopolus about implementing the new safety guidelines?

What Would You Do?

1. Prepare a memo to Golopolus, summarizing the new safety guidelines that affect the Rockingham product line and requesting his authorization for implementation.

2. Mind your own business. Golopolus hasn't said anything about the new guidelines and you don't want to overstep your authority. You've been unemployed and need this job.

3. Send copies of the reports anonymously to the operations manager, who is Golopolus's boss.

SOURCE: Based on Doug Wallace, "The Man Who Knew Too Much," *Business Ethics*, 2 (March–April 1993): 7–8.

Case for Critical Analysis

FMB&T

Marshall Pinkard, president and CEO of FMB&T, a growing California-based regional commercial and consumer retail bank, clicked on an e-mail from Ayishia Coles. Ayishia was the bright, hard-working, self-confident woman who'd recently come onboard as the bank's executive vice president and chief information officer. The fact that the person in Coles's position in the company's traditional vertical organization now reported directly to him and was a full-fledged member of the executive committee reflected FMB&T's recognition of just how important information technology was to all aspects of its increasingly competitive business. The successful, leading-edge banks were the ones using information technology not only to operate efficiently but also to help them focus more effectively on customer needs. Marshall settled back to read what he expected would be a report on how she was settling in. He was sadly mistaken.

After a few months on the job, Ayishia Coles was frustrated. What she needed from him, she wrote, was a clear statement of her responsibilities and authority. The way Ayishia saw it, the relationship between information technology and the bank's other business units was muddled, often causing considerable confusion, friction, and inefficiency. Typically, someone from retail banking or marketing, for example, came to her department with a poorly defined problem, such as how to link up checking account records with investment records, and they always expected a solution the same day. What made the situation even more vexing was that more often than not, the problem crossed organizational lines. She found that generally the more work units the problem affected, the less likely it was that any single unit took responsibility for defining exactly what they wanted IT to do. Who exactly was supposed to be getting all these units together and coordinating requests? When she tried to step into the breach and act as a facilitator, unit managers usually didn't welcome her efforts.

Despite the vagueness of their requests, the work units still expected IT to come up with a solution—and come up with it quickly. All of these expectations seemed almost calculated to drive the methodical IT folks mad. Before taking on a problem, they wanted to make sure they thoroughly understood all of its dimensions so that the solution would fit seamlessly into the existing systems. This coordination took time that other parts of the bank weren't willing to give IT.

In addition, Ayishia knew the IT staff was increasingly feeling underused. The staff wanted to identify opportunities for dazzling new IT developments to contribute to business strategies, but it found itself limited to applications work. Ayishia's greatest concern was the president of a large regional branch who was actively campaigning to locate decentralized IT departments in each large branch under branch authority so that work would be completed faster to meet branch needs. He said it would be better to let work units coordinate their own IT departments rather than run everything though corporate IT. Under that scenario, Ayishia Coles's department could end up one-half its current size.

Marshall leaned back in his high-backed executive chair and sighed. At the very least, he needed to clarify Ayishia's authority and responsibilities as she had asked him to do. But he recognized that the new vice president was talking about a much larger can of worms. Was it time to rethink the bank's entire organizational structure?

Questions

1. What are the main organizational causes of the frustration that Ayishia Coles feels?

2. If you were Marshall Pinkard, how would you address both Ayishia's request for clarification about her authority and responsibilities and the underlying problems her e-mail brings to his attention? Can the problems be addressed with minor adjustments, or would you need to consider a drastic overhaul of the bank's organizational structure? What environmental and technological factors would influence your decision?

3. Sketch a general chart for the type of organization that you think would work best for IT at FMB&T.

SOURCES: Based on Perry Glasser, "In CIOs We Trust," *CIO Enterprise* (June 15, 1999): 34–44; Stephanie Overby, "What Really Matters: Staying in the Game," *CIO Magazine* (October 1, 2004), www.cio.com/archive/100104/role.html; and Alenka Grealish, "Banking Trends in 2005 That Will Make A Difference," *Bank Systems & Technology* (December 14, 2004), www.banktech.com/news/showarticle.jhtml?articleid=55301770.

BIZ FLIX

The Paper

This engaging film shows the ethical dilemmas and stress of producing the *New York Sun,* a daily metropolitan newspaper. Metro Editor Henry Hackett (Michael Keaton) races against the clock to publish a story about a major police scandal that could send two young African American men to jail. He is in constant conflict with Managing Editor Alicia Clark (Glenn Close) who is more concerned about controlling the budget than about running accurate stories. Hackett is also under constant pressure from his wife Marty (Marisa Tomei), who is pregnant with their first child. While Hackett tries to get his story, Marty urges him to take a less demanding job at *The Sentinel.*

This scene is an edited version of the "The Managing Editor" sequence, which occurs early in *The Paper.* It shows a staff meeting that takes place the day after the *Sun* missed a story about a murder and other shootings with racial overtones. Instead, the *Sun* ran a front-page story about parking problems. At the meeting, Senior Editor Bernie White (Robert Duvall) discusses his preferences in front-page stories.

What to Watch for and Ask Yourself

1. Senior Editor Bernie White wants to reach a specific goal with the next edition of the *New York Sun.* What is this goal?

2. What method of departmentalization best describes the organizational structure at the *Sun:* functional, product, customer, geographic, or matrix? Explain your choice.

3. Is the organizational structure of the *Sun* appropriate for reaching White's goal? Why or why not?

VIDEO CASE

Designing Adaptive Organizations at Boyne USA Resorts

What did it take for a one-man operation to expand into the largest privately owned ski and golf corporation in the country? The answer is vision, passion, and the persistence of one special entrepreneur.

Detroit native, Everett Kircher, moved to northern Michigan in 1947 and purchased the land (for the price of $1) necessary to start his first ski resort known today as Boyne Mountain. His roles as president and CEO were not eclipsed by his roles as chief engineer, head chef and director of marketing and finance. His success was also fueled by his inventions of many industry "firsts" in snowmaking, snow-grooming equipment and ski lift technology.

He practiced a traditional **chain of command** in a vertical organizational structure. Like most entrepreneurs, every decision came from Everett Kircher's desk. As his company expanded during the 1950s and '60s from skiing to golf resorts and real estate, additional people were needed to manage the different locations. For Everett, it was the very beginnings of a partial decentralization of his leadership and decision-making. Over the next 50 years of expansion, this change would prove profitable.

Today, Boyne USA Resorts hosts seven major four-season resorts across America from Michigan to Washington State. The natural beauty of each resort continues to draw sport and travel enthusiasts nationally and internationally. Through excellence in management practices, sport and leisure enthusiasts of all ages embrace the Boyne "way of life."

In 2002, Everett Kircher died at the age of 85 but his legacy lives on. Boyne USA's reorganization in 2004 paved the way for the "Boyne Brand" to grow while maintaining organizational integrity. This system was designed with key managers for accountability, control, and information flow in order to make critical decisions.

General managers known as "Mayors of Towns" were hired at each resort location to oversee operations. In addition, vice presidents known as "subject matter experts," were also hired. These experts are passionate and knowledgeable in their specific fields of expertise, for example, food and beverage, retail, etc. The VP's share critical information with the general managers to help each resort operation. The general managers fold these experts into the decision-making process and help provide policy.

This streamlining of information helps general managers integrate the VP's knowledge in any areas of weakness. In addition, if one resort was doing well in a particular area, that knowledge could be also be shared and applied throughout branches of Boyne East and West.

Boyne's projections for the future are as ambitious as Everett Kircher's dream. By diversifying their resorts throughout North America they are stronger than many of their competitors. Weather-dependent industries must constantly adapt new marketing strategies. The launch of a new attraction, Boyne Mountain's indoor *"Avalanche Waterpark,"* is designed to increase the year-round market accustomed to Boyne's state-of-the-art facilities.

This family-owned company grew from revenues of $40 million in 1990 to over $200 million in 2005. Now entering their 60th year, Boyne USA Resorts' approach to organizational structure is intentional, proactive, and always subject to change.

Questions

1. Why was further decentralization necessary to Boyne's future in spite of the success with Everett Kircher at the helm of a vertical structure?

2. What do you think Boyne's organizational structure formally became after Everett Kircher's death in 2002.

3. Give an example of how Boyne USA's organizational structure supports three key areas: (a) strategy, (b) environment, and (c) technology.

Change and Innovation

Learning Objectives

After studying this chapter, you should be able to:

1 Define organizational change, and explain the forces driving innovation and change in today's organizations.

2 Identify the three innovation strategies managers implement for changing products and technologies.

3 Explain the value of creativity, idea incubators, horizontal linkages, open innovation, idea champions, and new-venture teams for innovation.

4 Discuss why changes in people and culture are critical to any change process.

5 Define organization development (OD) and large group interventions.

6 Explain the OD stages of unfreezing, changing, and refreezing.

7 Describe the sequence of change activities that must be performed for change to be successful.

8 Identify sources of resistance to change.

9 Explain force-field analysis and other implementation tactics that can be used to overcome resistance.

New Manager's Questions

Please circle your opinion below each of the following statements. **Assess Your Answer**

1 When a company makes a new product, the main concern after that is marketing it well.

1	2	3	4	5
strongly agree				strongly disagree

2 The most important way for a company to be innovative is to encourage lots of creative ideas.

1	2	3	4	5
strongly agree				strongly disagree

3 Changing an organization is not as hard as people make it out to be.

1	2	3	4	5
strongly agree				strongly disagree

Every organization at some time faces the need to change quickly and dramatically to survive in a changing environment. Many firms in the United States, Europe, and Japan recognize the need for greater product and service innovation to keep pace with technological and societal advances and compete with the growing power of companies in China and other developing countries. Rather than focusing on ways to improve efficiency and cut costs, today's companies are rewiring their organizations for creativity and innovation. Some observers of business trends suggest that the *knowledge economy* of the late 1900s and early 2000s is rapidly being transformed into the *creativity economy*. As more high-level knowledge work is outsourced to less-developed countries, companies in the United States, Europe, and Japan are evolving to the next level—generating economic value from creativity, imagination, and innovation.[1]

Turbulent Times and the Changing Workplace

Today's organizations face an almost continual need for change. Sometimes, forces outside the organization bring about changes, such as when a powerful retailer such as Wal-Mart demands annual price cuts, or when a key supplier goes out of business. Many U.S. companies revised their procedures to comply with provisions of the Sarbanes-Oxley corporate governance reform law. In China, organizations feel pressure from the government to increase wages to help workers cope with rising food costs. At the same time, costs of steel and other raw materials are skyrocketing for Chinese companies seeking to expand their businesses.[2] These outside forces compel managers to look for greater efficiencies in operations and other changes to keep their organizations profitable. Other times, managers within the company want to initiate major changes, such as forming employee-participation teams, introducing new products, or instituting new training systems, but they don't know how to make the change successful. Organizations must embrace many types of change. Businesses must develop improved production technologies, create new products and services desired in the marketplace, implement new administrative systems, and upgrade employees' skills. Companies such as Samsung, Apple, Toyota, and General Electric implement all of these changes and more.

How important is organizational change? Consider this: The parents of today's college students grew up without e-mail, digital cameras, video on demand, laptop computers, iPods, laser checkout systems, and online shopping. As companies that produce the new products and services prosper, many companies are caught with outdated products and failed technologies. Today's successful companies are constantly innovating. For example, Johnson & Johnson Pharmaceuticals uses biosimulation software from Entelos that compiles all known information about a disease such as diabetes or asthma and runs extensive virtual tests of new drug candidates. With a new-drug failure rate of 50 percent even at the last stage of clinical trials, the process helps scientists cut the time and expense of early testing and focus their efforts on the most promising prospects. Telephone companies such as AT&T are investing in technology to push deeper into the television and broadband markets. Automakers Chrysler, General Motors, and Toyota are perfecting fuel-cell power systems that could make today's internal combustion engine as obsolete as the steam locomotive.[3] Computer companies are developing computers that are smart enough to configure themselves, balance huge workloads, and know how to anticipate and fix problems before they happen.[4] Organizations that change successfully are both profitable and admired.

CONCEPT CONNECTION

Starbucks leaders realize that the Seattle-based chain's current business model won't continue to meet their goals for growth, so they're searching for ways to reinvent the company. This **internal force for change** has led the company to branch into entertainment, such as by experimenting with self-service CD burners in test stores, like the one pictured here. Starbucks has also released music compilation CDs, marketed audio books, produced a feature-length film, and reached an agreement with Apple that allows customers to purchase a variety of Starbucks' titles from the iTunes store.

Assess Your Answer

1 When a company makes a new product, the main concern after that is marketing it well.

ANSWER: Marketing a product and marketing effectively are vital to success. But that is not all a company needs to worry about. If new products are not innovated and brought to market, the company is likely to gradually fail over time.

Organizational change is defined as the adoption of a new idea or behavior by an organization.[5] In this chapter, we look at how organizations can be designed to respond to the environment through internal change and development. First we look at two key aspects of change in organizations: introducing new products and technologies and changing people and culture. Then we examine the basic forces for change and present a model for planned organizational change. Finally, we discuss how managers implement change, including overcoming resistance.

Changing Things: New Products and Technologies

Competition is more intense than ever before, and companies are driven by a new innovation imperative. The past decade's attention to efficiency in operations is no longer enough to keep organizations successful in a new, hypercompetitive environment. To thrive, companies must innovate more—and more quickly—than ever. One vital area for innovation is introducing new products and technologies.

A **product change** is a change in the organization's product or service outputs. Product and service innovation is the primary way in which organizations adapt to changes in markets, technology, and competition.[6] Examples of new products include Apple's iPhone and the iPod Hi-Fi, Glad Force Flex trash bags, the Motorola RAzr 2 V8 cell phone, and The Smart ForTwo car. The introduction of *e-file*, which allows online filing of tax returns, by the U.S. Internal Revenue Service (IRS) is an example of a new service innovation. Product changes are related to changes in the technology of the organization. Not all product changes are good ideas, as show in the Business Blooper box.

A **technology change** is a change in the organization's production process—how the organization does its work. Technology changes are designed to make the production of a product or service more efficient. The adoption of automatic mail sorting machines by the U.S. Postal Service is one example of a technology change.

organizational change
the adoption of a new idea or behavior by an organization.

product change
a change in the organization's product or service outputs.

technology change
a change that pertains to the organization's production process.

Business Blooper

Nestlé KitKat

KitKat candy bars (invented in 1935) are practically an institution in England. Everyone loves them and has them with their afternoon tea. Global sales were $1.6 million. Then the company reached too far, tried too many new flavors, and revenues fell in two years by 18 percent. The company's costly new introduction of a premium bar, Double Cream, was the straw that broke the camel's back. With hefty advertising costs and minimum shelf space, Nestlé couldn't support the more than 20 brands it had in the United Kingdom. With cutbacks necessary, Nestlé reduced advertising and fired sales staff. But customers revolted when they reduced the amount of chocolate in the traditional KitKat. That was going just a tad too far.

SOURCE: Deborah Ball, "Spoiling the Recipe," *Wall Street Journal* (July 6, 2006): A1.

EXHIBIT 8.1

Three Innovative Strategies for New Products and Technologies

Exploration	Cooperation	Entrepreneurship
• Creativity • Experimentation • Idea incubators	• Horizontal coordination mechanisms • Customers, partners • Open innovation	• Idea champions • New venture teams • Skunkworks • New venture fund

SOURCE: Based on Patrick Reinmoeller and Nicole van Baardwijk, "The Link Between Diversity and Resilience," *MIT Sloan Management Review* (Summer 2005): 61–65.

Three critical innovation strategies for changing products and technologies are illustrated in Exhibit 8.1.[7] The first strategy, *exploration,* involves designing the organization to encourage creativity and the initiation of new ideas. The strategy of *cooperation* refers to creating conditions and systems to facilitate internal and external coordination and knowledge sharing. Finally, *entrepreneurship* means that managers put in place processes and structures to ensure that new ideas are carried forward for acceptance and implementation.

EXPLORATION

Exploration is the stage where ideas for new products and technologies are born. Managers design the organization for exploration by establishing conditions that encourage creativity and allow new ideas to spring forth. **Creativity,** which refers to the generation of novel ideas that might meet perceived needs or respond to opportunities for the organization, is the essential first step in innovation.[8] People noted for their creativity include Edwin Land, who invented the Polaroid camera; Richard Tait and Whit Alexander, who came up with the idea for the mega-hit board game Cranium; and Swiss engineer George de Mestral, who created Velcro after noticing the tiny hooks on the burrs caught on his wool socks. Each of these people saw unique and creative opportunities in a familiar situation.

Characteristics of highly creative people are illustrated in the left-hand column of Exhibit 8.2. Creative people often are known for originality, open-mindedness, curiosity, a focused approach to problem solving, persistence, a relaxed and playful attitude, and receptivity to new ideas.[9] Creativity can also be designed into organizations. Companies or departments within companies can be organized to be creative and initiate ideas for change. Most companies want more highly creative employees and often seek to hire creative individuals. However, the individual is only part of the story, and each of us has some potential for creativity. Managers are responsible for creating a work environment that allows creativity to flourish.[10]

The characteristics of creative organizations correspond to those of individuals, as illustrated in the right-hand column of Exhibit 8.2. Creative organizations are loosely structured. People find themselves in a situation of ambiguity, assignments are vague, territories overlap, tasks are poorly defined, and much work is done through teams. Managers strive to involve employees in a varied range of projects, so that people are not stuck in the

creativity
the generation of novel ideas that might meet perceived needs or offer opportunities for the organization.

Assess Your Answer

2 The most important way for a company to be innovative is to encourage lots of creative ideas.

ANSWER: Without stimulating new and even outlandish ideas, a company's capacity to innovate will be greatly reduced. Perhaps equally important, though, is organizing to sustain innovation. Without such a structure, most of the creative ideas will not come to fruition.

The Creative Individual	The Creative Organization or Department
1. Conceptual fluency Open-mindedness	1. Open channels of communication Contact with outside sources Overlapping territories; cross-polination of ideas across disciplines Suggestion systems, brainstorming, freewheeling discussions
2. Originality	2. Assigning nonspecialists to problems Eccentricity allowed Hiring outside your comfort zone
3. Less authority Independence Self-confidence	3. Decentralization, loosely defined positions, loose control Acceptance of mistakes; rewarding risk-taking People encouraged to challenge their bosses
4. Playfulness Undisciplined exploration Curiosity	4. Freedom to choose and pursue problems Not a tight ship, playful culture, doing the impractical Freedom to discuss ideas; long time horizon
5. Persistence Commitment Focused approach	5. Resources allocated to creative personnel and projects without immediate payoff Reward system encourages innovation Absolution of peripheral responsibilities

EXHIBIT 8.2

Characteristics of Creative People and Organizations

SOURCES: Based on Gary A. Steiner, ed., *The Creative Organization* (Chicago: University of Chicago Press, 1965): 16–18; Rosabeth Moss Kanter, "The Middle Manager as Innovator," *Harvard Business Review* (July–August 1982): 104–105; James Brian Quinn, "Managing Innovation: Controlled Chaos," *Harvard Business Review* (May–June 1985): 73–84; Robert I. Sutton, "The Weird Rules of Creativity," *Harvard Business Review* (September 2001): 94–103; and Bridget Finn, "Playbook: Brainstorming for Better Brainstorming," *Business 2.0* (April 2005): 109–114.

rhythm of routine jobs, and they drive out the fear of making mistakes that can inhibit creative thinking.[11] Creative organizations have an internal culture of playfulness, freedom, challenge, and grassroots participation.[12] They harness all potential sources of new ideas.

Advertising agency Leo Burnett holds a regular "Inspire Me" day, when one team takes the rest of the department out to do something totally unrelated to advertising. One team took the group to a Mexican wrestling match, where team members showed up in costumes and masks like some of the more ardent wrestling fans. One idea that grew out of the experience was a new slogan for The Score, a sports network: "The Score: Home for the Hardcore."[13] To keep creativity alive at Google, managers let people spend 20 percent of their time working on any project they choose, even if the project doesn't tie in with the company's central mission. Many Google managers hold open office hours two or three times a week, when anyone can come by to bat around ideas.[14]

The most creative companies embrace risk and encourage employees to experiment and make mistakes. At software company Intuit, managers in the various divisions hold free-association sessions at least once a week, where people can propose all sorts of seemingly kooky ideas without embarrassment or fear.[15] One manager at Intel used to throw a dinner party every month for the "failure of the month," demonstrating to people that failure was an inevitable and accepted part of risk-taking.[16] Jim Read, president of the Read Corporation, says, "When my employees make mistakes trying to improve something, I give them a round of applause. No mistakes mean no new products. If they ever become afraid to make one, my company is doomed."[17]

 **TAKE ACTION**

As a new manager, you can inspire people to be more creative by giving them opportunities to explore ideas outside their regular jobs and encouraging them to experiment and take risks. Be open-minded and willing to listen to "crazy ideas," and let people know it's okay to make mistakes.

TAKE ACTION ▶

Go to the self-learning exercise on page 313 that pertains to creativity in organizations.

Another popular way to encourage new ideas within the organization is the **idea incubator.** An idea incubator provides a safe harbor where ideas from employees throughout the company can be developed without interference from company bureaucracy or politics.[18] The great value of an internal idea incubator is that an employee with a good idea has a specific place to go to develop it, rather than having to shop the idea all over the company and hope someone pays attention. Companies as diverse as Boeing, Adobe Systems, Ball Aerospace, UPS, and Ziff Davis are using incubators to quickly produce products and services related to the company's core business.[19]

COOPERATION

Another important aspect of innovation is providing mechanisms for both internal and external coordination. Ideas for product and technology innovations typically originate at lower levels of the organization and need to flow horizontally across departments. Implementation of an innovation typically requires changes in behavior across several departments. In addition, people and organizations outside the firm can be rich sources of innovative ideas. Lack of innovation is widely recognized as one of the biggest problems facing today's businesses. Consider that 72 percent of top executives surveyed by *BusinessWeek* and the Boston Consulting Group reported that innovation is a top priority, yet almost half said they are dissatisfied with their results in that area.[20] Thus, many companies are undergoing a transformation in the way they find and use new ideas, focusing on improving both internal and external coordination.

INTERNAL COORDINATION

Successful innovation requires expertise from several departments simultaneously, and failed innovation is often the result of failed cooperation.[21] Companies that successfully innovate usually have the following characteristics:

1. People in marketing have a good understanding of customer needs.

2. Technical specialists are aware of recent technological developments and make effective use of new technology.

3. Members from key departments—research, manufacturing, marketing—cooperate in the development of the new product.[22]

One approach to successful innovation is called the **horizontal linkage model,** which is illustrated in the center circle of Exhibit 8.3.[23] The model shows that the research, manufacturing, and sales and marketing departments within an organization must simultaneously contribute to new products and technologies. People from these departments meet frequently in teams and task forces to share ideas and solve problems. For example, research people inform marketing of new technical developments to learn whether they will be useful to customers. Marketing people pass customer complaints to research to use in the design of new products and to manufacturing people to develop new ideas for improving production speed and quality. Manufacturing informs other departments concerning whether a product idea can be manufactured within cost limits.

The appliance-maker Electrolux was struggling with spiraling costs and shrinking market share until CEO Hans Straberg introduced a new approach to product development that has designers, engineers, marketers, and production people working side-by-side to come up with hot new products such as the Pronto cordless stick vacuum, which gained a 50 percent market share in Europe within two years. "We never used to create new products together," says engineer Giuseppe Frucco. "The designers would come up with something and then tell us to build it." The new horizontal approach saves both time and money at Electrolux by avoiding the technical glitches that crop up as a new design moves through the development process.[24]

idea incubator
an in-house program that provides a safe harbor where ideas from employees throughout the organization can be developed without interference from company bureaucracy or politics.

horizontal linkage model
an approach to product change that emphasizes shared development of innovations among several departments.

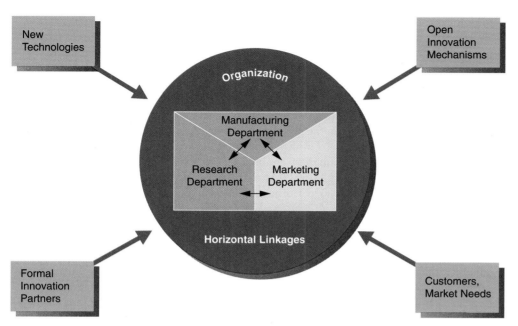

EXHIBIT 8.3
Coordination Model
for Innovation

The horizontal linkage model is increasingly important in today's high-pressure business environment that requires developing and commercializing products and services incredibly fast. Sprinting to market with a new product requires a *parallel approach*, or *simultaneous linkage*, among departments. This kind of teamwork is similar to a rugby match wherein players run together, passing the ball back and forth as they move downfield.[25] Speed is emerging as a pivotal strategic weapon in the global marketplace for a wide variety of industries.[26] Stockholm's H&M (Hennes & Mauritz) has become one of the hottest fashion retailers around because it can spot trends and rush items into stores in as little as 3 weeks. Nissan cut the time it takes to get a new car to market from 21 months to about 10.[27] Some companies use fast-cycle teams to deliver products and services faster than competitors, giving them a significant strategic advantage. A **fast-cycle team** is a multifunctional, and sometimes multinational, team that works under stringent timelines and is provided with high levels of resources and empowerment to accomplish an accelerated product development project.[28]

fast-cycle team
a multifunctional team that is provided with high levels of resources and empowerment to accomplish an accelerated product development project.

EXTERNAL COORDINATION

Exhibit 8.3 also illustrates that organizations look outside their boundaries to find and develop new ideas. Engineers and researchers stay aware of new technological developments. Marketing personnel pay attention to shifting market conditions and customer needs. Some organizations build formal strategic partnerships such as alliances and joint ventures to improve innovation success. Outsourcing partnerships can help companies get things done incredibly fast.

CONCEPT CONNECTION

How does eBay keep coming up with new approaches to business and new sources of income? By tapping into the collective intelligence of customers, employees, and outsiders. "It is far better to have an army of a million than a command and control system," said eBay CEO Meg Whitman, referring to eBay's approach of letting buyers and sellers largely determine how the company operates. eBay has thrived on this process of **open innovation,** reflected in the slogan "The power of all of us," which adorned the stage at the 2006 eBay Live convention in Las Vegas, shown here. The convention drew around 15,000 eBayers from around the world.

TAKE ACTION ⏩

Even as a new manager, you can make sure people are communicating and cooperating across organizational boundaries. Implement mechanisms to help your team or department members stay in touch with what's happening in other departments and in the marketplace.

open innovation
extending the search for and commercialization of new ideas beyond the boundaries of the organization.

Some leading cell phone makers, for example, work with outsourcing partner Cellon Inc. to take a new phone model from design to market in five months. Cellon, with operations in China, keeps a half-dozen basic designs that it can quickly customize for a particular client. Then, the company works with local manufacturers to rapidly move designs into production. People want hot new phones, and the life cycle of a cell phone model is about 9 months. Companies can't afford the 12 to 18 months it typically takes to develop a new model from scratch.[29]

Today's most successful companies are including customers, strategic partners, suppliers, and other outsiders directly in the product and service development process. One of the hottest trends is *open innovation*.[30] Think of Google, which opened its mapping technology to the public, allowing programmers to combine Google's maps with anything from real estate listings to local poker game sites.[31] At online game designer Linden Lab's Second Life, players have the freedom to create just about everything, from new characters to buildings to whole new games.[32]

In the past, most businesses generated their own ideas in house and then developed, manufactured, marketed, and distributed them, a closed innovation approach. Today, though, forward-looking companies are trying a different method. **Open innovation** means extending the search for and commercializing new ideas beyond the boundaries of the organization and even beyond the boundaries of the industry. Smart companies find and use ideas from anywhere within and outside the organization.[33] Procter & Gamble, not so long ago a stodgy consumer products company, has become one of the country's hottest innovators and a role model for the open innovation process.

Connecting with customers is also a critical aspect of open innovation. At companies such as P&G and Electrolux, rather than relying on focus groups, researchers now spend time with people in their homes, watching how they wash their dishes or clean their floors, and asking questions about their habits and frustrations with household chores. P&G's CEO makes 10 to 15 visits a year to watch women applying their beauty products or doing their laundry.[34]

In line with the new way of thinking we discussed in Chapter 1, which sees partnership and collaboration as more important than independence and competition, the boundaries between an organization and its environment are becoming porous, so that ideas flow back

Procter & Gamble (P&G)

Swiffer Wet Jet. Crest Whitestrips. Mr. Clean Magic Reach. Downy Wrinkle Releaser. Iams Dental Defense. Olay Regenerist. They're some of Procter & Gamble's best-selling products—and all of them were developed in whole or in part by someone outside of P&G. The technology that helps P&G's Swiffer products pick up so much dust and debris came from a competitor in Japan. The Crest Spin Brush was invented by a small entrepreneurial firm in Cleveland.

Procter & Gamble CEO A. G. Lafley set a goal to get 50 percent of the company's innovation from outside the organization, up from about 35 percent in 2004 and only 10 percent in 2000. P&G developed a detailed, well-organized process for open innovation with its Connect + Develop (C + D) initiative, which taps into networks of inventors, scientists, academics, partners, and suppliers to embrace the collective brains of the world. "Inventors are evenly distributed in the population," says Lafley, "and we're as likely to find invention in a garage as in our labs." One technique is to contract with external "innovation sourcing" firms such as NineSigma Inc. and InnoCentive, which link companies with outside inventors, problem solvers, academic researchers, and small entrepreneurial companies. When P&G was looking for an antiwrinkling spray that consumers could use on cotton clothing, NineSigma used the Web to blast out queries to about 6,000 people, eventually signing two of them to contracts. InnoCentive's 80,000 independent inventors provided solutions to more than one-third of the two dozen requests P&G submitted. But P&G doesn't just look for extensions of its current product categories. An important part of its open innovation process is networking with external scientists in totally new areas that could lead to totally new businesses.

Between 2002 and 2004, P&G raised its new product success rate from 70 percent to 90 percent, thanks largely to the Connect + Develop initiative. At the same time, R&D spending as a percentage of sales decreased because of the more efficient and effective innovation process.[35]

and forth among different people and companies that engage in partnerships, joint ventures, licensing agreements, and other alliances. Japanese high-tech firms, such as Fujitsu, for example, are achieving rapid innovation by building strategic innovation communities that link managers from all levels with partners, customers, and other outsiders for developing new products. Similarly, in the United States, external collaboration and innovation networking were key to IBM's reemergence as a technology powerhouse.[36]

ENTREPRENEURSHIP

The third aspect of product and technology innovation is creating mechanisms to make sure new ideas are carried forward, accepted, and implemented. Here is where idea champions come in. The formal definition of an **idea champion** is a person who sees the need for and champions productive change within the organization. Wendy Black of Best Western International championed the idea of coordinating the corporate mailings to the company's 2,800 hoteliers into a single packet every two weeks. Some hotels were receiving three special mailings a day from different departments. Her idea saved $600,000 a year in postage alone.[37]

Remember: Change does not occur by itself. Personal energy and effort are required to successfully promote a new idea. Often a new idea is rejected by management. Champions are passionately committed to a new product or idea despite rejection by others. Robert Vincent was fired twice by two different division managers at a semiconductor company. Both times, he convinced the president and chairman of the board to reinstate him to continue working on his idea for an airbag sensor that measures acceleration and deceleration. He couldn't get approval for research funding, so Vincent pushed to complete another project in half the time and used the savings to support the new product development.[38] At Kyocera Wireless, lead engineer Gary Koerper was a champion for the Smartphone. When he couldn't get his company's testing department to validate the new product, he had an outside firm do the testing for him—at a cost of about $30,000—without approval from Kyocera management. After the Smartphone was approved and went into production, demand was so great the company could barely keep up.[39]

Championing an idea successfully requires roles in organizations, as illustrated in Exhibit 8.4. Sometimes a single person may play two or more of these roles, but successful innovation in most companies involves an interplay of different people, each adopting one role. The *inventor* comes up with a new idea and understands its technical value but has neither the ability nor the interest to promote it for acceptance within the organization. The *champion* believes in the idea, confronts the organizational realities of costs and benefits, and gains the political and financial support needed to bring it to reality. The *sponsor* is a high-level manager who approves the idea, protects the idea, and removes major organizational barriers to acceptance. The *critic* counterbalances the zeal of the champion by challenging the concept and providing a reality test against hard-nosed criteria. The critic prevents people in the other roles from adopting a

idea champion
a person who sees the need for and champions productive change within the organization.

EXHIBIT 8.4
Four Roles in Organizational Change

Inventor	**Champion**	**Sponsor**	**Critic**
Develops and understands technical aspects of idea	Believes in idea	High-level manager who removes organizational barriers	Provides reality test
Does not know how to win support for the idea or make a business of it	Visualizes benefits	Approves and protects idea within organization	Looks for shortcomings
	Confronts organizational realities of cost, benefits		Defines hard-nosed criteria that idea must pass
	Obtains financial and political support		
	Overcomes obstacles		

SOURCES: Based on Harold L. Angle and Andrew H. Van de Ven, "Suggestions for Managing the Innovation Journey," in *Research in the Management of Innovation: The Minnesota Studies*, ed. A. H. Van de Ven, H. L. Angle, and Marshall Scott Poole (Cambridge, MA: Ballinger/Harper & Row, 1989); and Jay R. Galbraith, "Designing the Innovating Organization," *Organizational Dynamics* (Winter 1982): 5–25.

Benchmarking

Netflix

Reed Hastings sold his first company for $525 million when he was just 36, after which he settled into a leisurely life in education, politics, and philanthropy. Then he was forced to pay a $40 late fee for one video, and he balked at the idea of paying a late fee greater than the cost of buying a new video. It bothered him so much, he started to think other people might be bothered too and would join a DVD club the same way they might join a health club, with monthly fees. No one thought the idea had any merit, that people would rent movies through the mail. "It was precisely because it was a contrarian idea that enabled us to get ahead of our competition," he said.

In the first few years, Netflix wasn't much unlike a video store, only via mail. Subscription fees began the next year, and later a browsing tool was used that figures out what kind of movies someone wants, based on only three previous selections. Customers create a list, and Netflix sends the first three that are available, in envelopes to be reused when mailing them back, postage prepaid.

In 1990, there was only one distribution center, in San Francisco, and it took a long time to get the videos because of distance. Now the company has 30 distribution centers in the United States, so any of the 80,000 titles can reach customers faster. But even with increasing revenues, Netflix was still losing money in 2000, and another $50 million had to be raised. Luckily, business grew enough to have positive cash flow by 2001, and it went public in 2002. Now it is the world's largest online movie rental company. Perhaps Netflix's most successful new feature is allowing subscribers to instantly watch movies on their PC, within 30 seconds.

The biggest challenges now are new competitors Amazon, Wal-Mart, and Blockbuster, who saw how successful and profitable Netflix was. Hastings is grateful they didn't enter the field four years ago, when Netflix was still shaky. Still, he feels confident, despite others' wariness. After all, he proved them wrong once before. As he put it, "To be doubted and be successful is particularly satisfying."

SOURCE: Gary Rivlin, "Does the kid stay in the picture?" *The New York Times* (Feb. 22, 2005): E1 and E8; "Netflix instant-watching feature scores 5 million viewings in first 6 months," *PR Newswire* (July 10, 2007): 1.

---

bad idea.[40] Reed Hastings was inventor, champion, and critic all in one, as is often the case in small-business startups, as described in the Benchmarking box.

Managers can directly influence whether champions will flourish. When Texas Instruments studied 50 of its new-product introductions, a surprising fact emerged: Without exception, every new product that failed lacked a zealous champion. In contrast, most of the new products that succeeded had a champion. Managers made an immediate decision: No new product would be approved unless someone championed it. Research confirms that successful new ideas are generally those that are backed by someone who believes in the idea wholeheartedly and is determined to convince others of its value.[41]

Another way to facilitate entrepreneurship is through a **new-venture team.** A new-venture team is a unit separate from the rest of the organization that is responsible for developing and initiating a major innovation.[42] Motorola's successful Razr cell phone was developed in an innovation lab 50 miles from employees' regular offices in the company's traditional research and development facility. Team members were free from the distractions of their everyday routines and were given the autonomy to implement product ideas without the usual process of running things past regional managers.[43] Whenever BMW Group begins developing a new car, the project's team members—from engineering, design, production, marketing, purchasing, and finance—are relocated to a separate Research and Innovation Center, where they work collaboratively to speed the new product to market.[44] New-venture teams give free rein to members' creativity because their separate facilities and location unleash people from the restrictions imposed by organizational rules and procedures. These teams typically are small, loosely structured, and flexible, reflecting the characteristics of creative organizations described in Exhibit 8.2.

One variation of a new-venture team is called a **skunkworks.**[45] A skunkworks is a separate small, informal, highly autonomous, and often secretive group that focuses on breakthrough ideas for the business. The original skunkworks, which still exists, was created by

TAKE ACTION ▶

As a new manager, have the courage to promote useful change. Are you an idea champion for changes or new ideas you believe in? To find out, complete the New Manager Self Test on page 297.

new-venture team
a unit separate from the mainstream of the organization that is responsible for developing and initiating innovations.

skunkworks
a separate small, informal, highly autonomous, and often secretive group that focuses on breakthrough ideas for the business.

Lockheed Martin more than 50 years ago. The essence of a skunkworks is that highly talented people are given the time and freedom to let creativity reign.[46] The laser printer was invented by a Xerox researcher who was transferred to a skunkworks, the Xerox Palo Alto Research Center (PARC), after his ideas about using lasers were stifled within the company for being "too impractical and expensive."[47] IBM is launching entirely new businesses by using the skunkworks concept. Managers identify emerging business

NEW MANAGER SELF TEST

Taking Charge of Change

As a new manager, do you have what it takes to be an idea champion? Will you initiate change? Think of a job you held for a period of time. Answer the following questions according to your behaviors and perspective on that job. Please answer whether each item is Mostly True or Mostly False for you.

	Mostly True	Mostly False
1. I often tried to adopt improved procedures for doing my job.	_____	_____
2. I felt a personal sense of responsibility to bring about change in my workplace.	_____	_____
3. I often tried to institute new work methods that were more effective for the company.	_____	_____
4. I often tried to change organizational rules or policies that were nonproductive or counterproductive.	_____	_____
5. It was up to me to bring about improvement in my workplace.	_____	_____
6. I often made constructive suggestions for improving how things operated.	_____	_____
7. I often tried to implement new ideas for pressing organizational problems.	_____	_____
8. I often tried to introduce new structures, technologies, or approaches to improve efficiency.	_____	_____

SCORING AND INTERPRETATION: An important part of a new manager's job is to facilitate improvements through innovation and change. Will you be a champion for change? Your answers to the questions may indicate the extent to which you have a natural inclination toward taking charge of change. Not everyone thrives in a position of initiating change, but as a new manager, initiating change within the first six months will enhance your impact.

Give yourself one point for each mostly true answer. If you scored 4 or less, you may not have been flexing your change muscles on the job. You may need to become more active at taking charge of change. Moreover, you may need to be in a more favorable change situation. Research indicates that a job with open-minded management where change is believed likely to succeed and is rewarded increases a person's initiative. So the organization in which you are a new manager plus your own inclination will influence your initiation of change. A score of 5 or more suggests a positive level of previous change initiation behavior and solid preparation for a new manager role as an idea champion.

SOURCE: Based on Elizabeth W. Morrison and Corey C. Phelps, "Taking charge at work: Extra role efforts to initiate workplace change," *Academy of Management Journal* 42 (1999): 403–419.

opportunities (EBOs) that have the potential to become profitable businesses in the next five to seven years, and then put a senior leader in charge of building the business, often with only a few hand-picked colleagues. A digital media EBO, which helps companies manage video, audio, and still images, has grown into a $1.7 billion business in only three years.[48]

A related idea is the **new-venture fund,** which provides resources from which individuals and groups can draw to develop new ideas, products, or businesses. At 3M, scientists can apply for Genesis Grants to work on innovative project ideas. 3M awards from 12 to 20 of these grants each year, ranging from $50,000 to $100,000 each, for researchers to hire supplemental staff, acquire equipment, or whatever is needed to develop the new idea. Intel has been highly successful with Intel Capital, which provides new-venture funds to both employees and outside organizations to develop promising ideas. An Intel employee came up with the idea for liquid crystal on silicon, a technology that lowers the cost of big-screen TV projection. "We took an individual who had an idea, gave him money to pursue it, and turned it into a business," said Intel CEO Craig Barrett.[49]

Changing People and Culture

All successful changes involve changes in people and culture as well. For example, getting products to market fast requires that people learn to work collaboratively. Changes in people and culture pertain to how employees think—changes in mind-set. **People change** pertains to just a few employees, such as sending a handful of middle managers to a training course to improve their leadership skills. **Culture change** pertains to the organization as a whole, such as when the IRS shifted its basic mind-set from an organization focused on collection and compliance to one dedicated to informing, educating, and serving customers (taxpayers).[50] In the business world, Jeff Immelt at General Electric strives to replace GE's famous obsession with bottom-line results with a new culture of risk-taking, bold thinking, and creative energy.

Culture change of the magnitude at GE is not easy. Indeed, executives routinely report that improving people and corporate culture is their most difficult job.[51] Two specific tools for changing people and culture are training and development programs, and organizational development (OD).

TAKE ACTION ▷
Go to the ethical dilemma on page 314 that pertains to structural change.

new-venture fund
a fund providing resources from which individuals and groups can draw to develop new ideas, products, or businesses.

people change
a change in the attitudes and behaviors of a few employees in the organization.

culture change
a major shift in the norms, values, attitudes, and mind-set of the entire organization.

General Electric

General Electric, long revered as a hard-driving company focused on cost-cutting and process efficiency, evaluated and rewarded its managers based on the continual improvement of operations and their ability to achieve bottom-line results. Since he took over as CEO, however, Jeff Immelt has been on a mission to change that efficiency and productivity-oriented culture to one wired for creativity, risk-taking, and innovation.

In today's environment, Immelt knows that efficiency is not enough. To shift the culture toward one of bold thinking and creative energy, Immelt tossed out some of GE's longstanding traditions and began evaluating top executives on innovation-oriented traits such as "external focus" and "imagination and courage." Bonuses are now linked to a manager's ability to generate new ideas, improve customer satisfaction, and boost sales. In a gathering called the Commercial Council, top executives hold monthly phone meetings and meet in person each quarter to talk about new ideas and new markets. Division heads are expected to submit at least three "Imagination Breakthrough" proposals a year that go before the council for evaluation and possible funding. Immelt already committed at least $5 billion to breakthrough projects that take GE into a new line of business, geographic region, or customer base. He also spent big bucks to beef up GE's research facilities and create other structural mechanisms that foster a culture of creativity and imagination. Some executives hold "idea jams," where people from various divisions brainstorm ideas. A "virtual idea box" allows people to brainstorm and submit ideas over the Internet.

Immelt knows this massive cultural shift is difficult for most of GE's managers and employees. "These guys just aren't dreamer types," said one consultant about GE's workforce. "It almost seems painful to them, like a waste of time." Immelt, though, believes the culture change is essential to keep GE relevant and thriving in the changing world of the 21st century.[52]

3 Changing an organization is not as hard as people make it out to be.

ANSWER: Organization change is very difficult, in fact more difficult than most managers realize. If not done correctly, the department or unit will revert back to its old behaviors. Change that is lasting takes a long time, much longer than the short programs usually initiated.

TRAINING AND DEVELOPMENT

Training is one of the most frequently used approaches to changing people's mind-sets. A company might offer training programs to large blocks of employees on subjects such as teamwork, diversity, emotional intelligence, quality circles, communication skills, or participative management. General Electric, for example, initiated new courses in marketing and idea generation to help shift attitudes and values. Training and development programs aimed at changing individual behavior and interpersonal skills are a big business for consultants, universities, and training firms.

Some companies particularly emphasize training and development for managers, with the idea that the behavior and attitudes of managers will influence people throughout the organization and lead to culture change. A number of Silicon Valley companies, including Intel, Advanced Micro Devices (AMD), and Sun Microsystems, regularly send managers to the Growth and Leadership Center (GLC), where they learn to use emotional intelligence to build better relationships. Nick Kepler, director of technology development at AMD, was surprised to learn how his emotionless approach to work was intimidating people and destroying the rapport needed to shift to a culture based on collaborative teamwork.[53]

Leading companies also want to provide training and development opportunities for everyone. An excellent example of training is First Data Corp., which uses a multifaceted, team-based approach first initiated by CFO Kim Patmore to boost morale among finance personnel.[54] First Data's "Extreme Teams" bring together employees from all hierarchical levels to organize departmental training and development programs for each of First Data's six regional finance units. One team is charged with organizing a mentoring program that pairs less-experienced personnel with seasoned managers who support and encourage them to make changes needed to further their own and the organization's well-being. Another team focuses on a program called *Fast Tracks*, an annual two-day seminar that brings people from all areas and levels of the company together to learn skills such as communication or conflict resolution.

organization development (OD)
the application of behavioral science techniques to improve an organization's health and effectiveness through its ability to cope with environmental changes, improve internal relationships, and increase learning and problem-solving capabilities.

•••• CONCEPT CONNECTION
Organization development (OD) specialists have long recognized that fun can be a powerful tool in the serious business of **team building.** Here, Target Corporation store employees engage in some group problem solving. While holding hands, each member must wriggle through two hula hoops without breaking the human chain. Such noncompetitive games not only break the ice but also give team members practice in working cooperatively to achieve a common goal.

ORGANIZATION DEVELOPMENT

Organization development (OD) is a planned, systematic process of change that uses behavioral science knowledge and techniques to improve an organization's health and effectiveness through its ability to adapt to the environment, improve internal relationships, and increase learning and problem-solving capabilities.[55] OD focuses on the human and social aspects of the organization and works to change attitudes and relationships among employees, helping to strengthen the organization's capacity for adaptation and renewal.[56]

OD can help managers address at least three types of current problems:[57]

1. *Mergers/acquisitions.* The disappointing financial results of many mergers and acquisitions are caused by the failure of executives to determine whether the administrative style and corporate culture of the two companies fit. Executives may concentrate on potential synergies in technology, products, marketing, and control systems but fail to recognize that two firms may have widely different values, beliefs, and practices. These differences create stress and anxiety for employees, and these negative emotions affect future performance. Cultural differences should be evaluated during the acquisition process, and OD experts can be used to smooth the integration of two firms.

2. *Organizational decline/revitalization.* Organizations undergoing a period of decline and revitalization experience a variety of problems, including a low level of trust, lack of innovation, high turnover, and high levels of conflict and stress. The period of transition requires opposite behaviors, including confronting stress, creating open communication, and fostering creative innovation to emerge with high levels of productivity. OD techniques can contribute greatly to cultural revitalization by managing conflicts, fostering commitment, and facilitating communication.

3. *Conflict management.* Conflict can occur at any time and place within a healthy organization. For example, a product team for the introduction of a new software package was formed at a computer company. Made up of strong-willed individuals, the team made little progress because members could not agree on project goals. At a manufacturing firm, salespeople promised delivery dates to customers that were in conflict with shop supervisor priorities for assembling customer orders. In a publishing company, two managers disliked each other intensely. They argued at meetings, lobbied politically against each other, and hurt the achievement of both departments. Organization development efforts can help resolve these kinds of conflicts, as well as conflicts that are related to growing diversity and the global nature of today's organizations.

Organization development can be used to solve the types of problems just described and many others. However, to be truly valuable to companies and employees, organization development practitioners go beyond looking at ways to settle specific problems. Instead, they become involved in broader issues that contribute to improving organizational life, such as encouraging a sense of community, pushing for an organizational climate of openness and trust, and making sure the company provides employees with opportunities for personal growth and development.[58] At Great Britain's General Communications Headquarters, OD specialists helped managers transform a rigid, insular culture into a flexible and collaborative one designed for the twenty-first century, as described next. Specialized techniques have been developed to help meet OD goals.

OD ACTIVITIES

A number of OD activities have emerged in recent years. Three of the most popular and effective are the following:

1. *Team-building activities.* **Team building** enhances the cohesiveness and success of organizational groups and teams. For example, a series of OD exercises can be used with members of cross-departmental teams to help them learn to act and function as a team. An OD expert can work with team members to increase their communication skills, facilitate their ability to confront one another, and help them accept common goals.

2. *Survey-feedback activities.* **Survey feedback** begins with a questionnaire distributed to employees on values, climate, participation, leadership, and group cohesion within their

team building
a type of OD intervention that enhances the cohesiveness of departments by helping members learn to function as a team.

survey feedback
a type of OD intervention in which questionnaires on organizational climate and other factors are distributed among employees and their results reported back to them by a change agent.

Spotlight on
Collaboration

The Spies Who Came in from the Cold

Transforming the secretive culture of Great Britain's General Communications Headquarters (GCHQ) wasn't easy. It took the concerted efforts of computer experts, OD specialists, and the architects and builders responsible for the "Doughnut," the GCHQ's award-winning headquarters in Cheltenham.

The U.S. National Security Agency's counterpart, GCHQ produces intelligence obtained largely by intercepting phone calls, e-mail, and other electronic signals originating throughout the world. It's also charged with keeping government communication and information systems safe from cybercriminals, terrorists, and other saboteurs. Up until the late 1990s, staff members worked in a structured, compartmentalized hierarchy. Employees not only didn't talk to outsiders about their work, they didn't even share information with co-workers who didn't have a clear "need to know."

It made sense during the Cold War, but the Cold War has been over for nearly a decade. GCHQ now faces global threats, especially from decentralized terrorist networks, as well as the challenge of monitoring and securing communication systems revolutionized by digital technology. Recognizing that GCHQ had to become more agile, top executives consolidated its technological infrastructure but soon realized that a flexible, responsive infrastructure meant little without an equally flexible, responsive culture. They needed to create cross-functional, multidisciplinary teams engaged in collaborative learning and knowledge sharing.

In 1998, GCHQ called on outside OD consultants to help create and implement *Lead 21*, a project designed to promote a new collaborative, flexible culture and give people practice in the new ways of working. Initially, consultants and GCHQ executives believed training senior managers in the desired behaviors was enough because those behaviors would trickle down through the organization. They quickly saw a need to expand the project, first to middle managers in 1999 and then to the remaining 3,000 staff members the following year.

Top leaders also realized early on that the physical environment—50 buildings located several miles apart—was hindering the shift to a collaborative culture, so they began planning for a new headquarters. The result is the Doughnut, a $615 million, million-square-foot, ring-shaped building completed in 2003. Architects designed the facility to encourage interaction and collaboration. For example, all three main entrances empty onto a circular "street," a common corridor surrounding an interior garden. The corridor provides access to the open-plan workstations, occupied by almost everyone—including senior managers—so that employees are likely to bump into colleagues from all levels and departments. Employees not only don't have conventional offices, they don't even have their own desks. They simply log onto a workstation wherever it makes the most sense for the task at hand, and their computer files and phone calls automatically find them.

Has this cultural retooling produced the desired results? The spy organization offers outsiders only limited information. But it will say that in contrast to September 2001, when it took a full three months to install a response team, it took only 24 hours to get a team up and running when terrorist-planted explosions ripped through London in 2005.

SOURCES: GCHQ Corporate Development and Corporate Communications Teams, "GCHQ: The Change Journey" (July 2003), http://www.gchq.gov.uk/press/publications.html; Steve Crabb, "Out in the Open," *People Management* (October 13, 2005); Chartered Institute of Personnel and Development, "Removing Barriers and Encouraging Collaborative Learning at GCHQ," http://www.cipd.co.uk/helpingpeoplelearn/researchinpractice_3.asp#section7; Dave Barista, "Spy Central," *Building Design & Construction* (August 2004): 34ff; and Richard Norton-Taylor, "The Doughnut, the Less Secretive Weapon in the Fight Against International Terrorism," *The Guardian* (June 10, 2003).

---

organization. After the survey is completed, an OD consultant meets with groups of employees to provide feedback about their responses and the problems identified. Employees are engaged in problem solving based on the data.

3. *Large-group interventions.* In recent years, the need for bringing about fundamental organizational change in today's complex, fast-changing world prompted a growing interest in applications of OD techniques to large group settings.[59] The **large-group intervention** approach brings together participants from all parts of the organization—often including key stakeholders from outside the organization as well—to discuss problems or opportunities and plan for change. A large-group intervention might involve 50 to 500 people and last several days. The idea is to include everyone who has a stake in the change, gather perspectives from all parts of the system, and enable people to create a collective future through sustained, guided dialogue.

large-group intervention
an approach that brings together participants from all parts of the organization (and may include key outside stakeholders as well) to discuss problems or opportunities and plan for major change.

EXHIBIT 8.5

OD Approaches to Culture Change

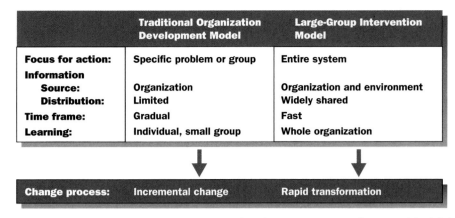

	Traditional Organization Development Model	Large-Group Intervention Model
Focus for action:	Specific problem or group	Entire system
Information Source: Distribution:	Organization Limited	Organization and environment Widely shared
Time frame:	Gradual	Fast
Learning:	Individual, small group	Whole organization
Change process:	Incremental change	Rapid transformation

SOURCE: Adapted from Barbara Benedict Bunker and Billie T. Alban, "Conclusion: What Makes Large Group Interventions Effective," *Journal of Applied Behavioral Science* 28, no. 4 (December 1992): 579–591.

Large-group interventions reflect a significant shift in the approach to organizational change from earlier OD concepts and approaches. Exhibit 8.5 lists the primary differences between the traditional OD model and the large-scale intervention model of organizational change.[60] In the newer approach, the focus is on the entire system, which takes into account the organization's interaction with its environment. The source of information for discussion is expanded to include customers, suppliers, community members, and even competitors, and this information is shared widely so that everyone has the same picture of the organization and its environment. The acceleration of change when the entire system is involved can be remarkable. In addition, learning occurs across all parts of the organization simultaneously, rather than in individuals, small groups, or business units. The result is that the large-group approach offers greater possibilities for fundamental, radical transformation of the entire culture, whereas the traditional approach creates incremental change in a few individuals or small groups at a time.

Large-group interventions represent a significant shift in the way leaders think about change and reflect an increasing awareness of the importance of dealing with the entire system, including external stakeholders, in any significant change effort.

OD STEPS

OD experts acknowledge that changes in corporate culture and human behavior are tough to accomplish and require major effort. The theory underlying OD proposes three distinct stages for achieving behavioral and attitudinal change: (1) unfreezing, (2) changing, and (3) refreezing.[61]

The first stage, **unfreezing,** means that people throughout the organization are made aware of problems and the need for change. This stage creates the motivation for people to change their attitudes and behaviors. Unfreezing may begin when managers present information that shows discrepancies between desired behaviors or performance and the current state of affairs. In addition, managers need to establish a sense of urgency to unfreeze people and create an openness and willingness to change. The unfreezing stage is often associated with *diagnosis,* which uses an outside expert called a *change agent.* The **change agent** is an OD specialist who performs a systematic diagnosis of the organization and identifies work-related problems. He or she gathers and analyzes data through personal interviews, questionnaires, and observations of meetings. The diagnosis helps determine the extent of organizational problems and helps unfreeze managers by making them aware of problems in their behavior.

The second stage, **changing,** occurs when individuals experiment with new behavior and learn new skills to be used in the workplace. This process is sometimes known as

---

TAKE ACTION

As a new manager, look for and implement training opportunities that can help people shift their attitudes, beliefs, and behaviors toward what is needed for team, department, and organization success. Use OD consultants and techniques such as team building, survey feedback, and large-group intervention for widespread change.

unfreezing
the stage of organization development in which participants are made aware of problems to increase their willingness to change their behavior.

change agent
an OD specialist who contracts with an organization to facilitate change.

changing
the intervention stage of organization development in which individuals experiment with new workplace behavior.

intervention, during which the change agent implements a specific plan for training managers and employees. The changing stage might involve a number of specific steps.[62] For example, managers put together a coalition of people with the will and power to guide the change, create a vision for change that everyone can believe in, and widely communicate the vision and plans for change throughout the company. In addition, successful change involves using emotion as well as logic to persuade people and empowering employees to act on the plan and accomplish the desired changes.

The third stage, **refreezing,** occurs when individuals acquire new attitudes or values and are rewarded for them by the organization. The impact of new behaviors is evaluated and reinforced. The change agent supplies new data that show positive changes in performance. Managers may provide updated data to employees that demonstrate positive changes in individual and organizational performance. Top executives celebrate successes and reward positive behavioral changes. At this stage, changes are institutionalized in the organizational culture, so that employees begin to view the changes as a normal, integral part of how the organization operates. Employees may also participate in refresher courses to maintain and reinforce the new behaviors.

Model of Planned Organizational Change

Change does not happen easily, but change can be managed. By observing external trends, patterns, and needs, managers use planned change to help the organization adapt to external problems and opportunities.[63] When organizations are caught flat-footed, failing to anticipate or respond to new needs, management is at fault.

An overall model for planned change is presented in Exhibit 8.6. Three events make up the change sequence: (1) internal and external forces for change exist; (2) organization managers monitor these forces and become aware of a need for change; and (3) the required change is implemented. How each of these activities is handled depends on the organization and managers' styles.

We now turn to a brief discussion of the specific activities associated with the first two events—forces for change and the perceived need for the organization to respond. Later, we will discuss change implementation.

FORCES FOR CHANGE

Forces for organizational change exist both in the external environment and within the organization.

Environmental Forces. As described in Chapters 3 and 4, external forces originate in all environmental sectors, including customers, competitors, technology, economic forces, and the international arena. For example, shifts in customer tastes led McDonald's,

refreezing
the reinforcement stage of organization development in which individuals acquire a desired new skill or attitude and are rewarded for it by the organization.

EXHIBIT 8.6

Model of Change
Sequence of Events

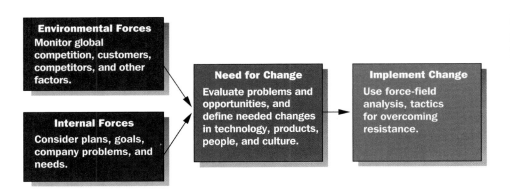

Spotlight on
Technology

Sundance Channel's
Second Life

Vincent Tibbett might work for Sundance Channel, but don't try taking him to lunch because he only exists in virtual reality, as an electronic avatar who can only be found on Sundance's popular online virtual community, Second Life. Others have followed suit, setting up camp in virtual communities, hoping browsers may discover their programming online. Sundance and Showtime have plopped themselves into existing worlds, while MTV is creating its own. What was science fiction just a few years ago is here: the unification of watching television's passive act with the interactive ability of the Web.

Even traditional networks are watching. Says CBS's president of CBS Interactive Quincy Smith, "You want to be in this because you know, as a content provider, that this is where the future is going." But where it is going is in dispute. Older networks want carefully monitored experience for customers, while the newer players favor no restrictions. Second Life people think there is no such thing as too much freedom and autonomy. "We're free and crazy and chaotic," says one executive. "They are too controlled." MTV, on the other hand, thinks the ideal is a balance of rules, guidance, and freedom, and getting the right mix is the trick.

Revenue comes from advertisers, who set up shop in the virtual reality. And just like people buy things in real stores, so they do in the virtual worlds. The information advertisers get is excruciatingly detailed. How many people stopped into a particular store, how many looked at product X, what type of people were they, and how many actually bought it? "It's scary actually," says MTV vice-president Jeff Yapp. "It's like Google on steroids."

Developers have high hopes, and at the same time, they know they must make these worlds more user friendly. If done right, the experience is compelling for viewers. One executive said, "I've never been involved with a technology where you can make people say 'Aha!' so consistently."

SOURCE: Dave Itzkoff, "A Brave New World for TV? Virtually," *The New York Times* (June 24, 2007): AR1 and AR28.

the giant purveyor of burgers and fries, to begin offering salads, fruit, whole grain muffins, and grilled chicken sandwiches that are perceived as healthier.[64] Changes in technology and the health care needs of customers caused Medtronic to shift how it views medical devices, from simply providing therapy to monitoring a patient's health condition. The company's cardioverter-defibrillators, for example, can now send information to a secure server, allowing medical personnel to review the patient's condition in real time and identify any problems.[65] Increased competition spurred Microsoft to change how it designs and builds software. With competitors such as Google rapidly introducing innovative software products over the Internet, Microsoft had to find a faster, more flexible way to bring out a new version of Windows onto which new features can be added one by one over time.[66] Technology has also forced television networks and stations to venture into new territory, as shown in the Spotlight in Technology box.

Internal Forces. Internal forces for change arise from internal activities and decisions. If top managers select a goal of rapid company growth, internal actions will have to be changed to meet that growth. New departments or technologies will be created and additional people hired to pursue growth opportunities. To support growth goals at 3M, CEO James McNerney revved up the company's product innovation with a new approach to research and development.

Take a moment to complete the New Manager Self Test on openness to change.

By changing the company's approach to R&D, McNerney and Wendling got 3M's sales and profits growing again. New business strategies, shifts in the labor pool, demands from

Is Your Company Creative?

An effective way to assess the creative climate of an organization for which you have worked is to fill out the following questionnaire. Answer each question based on your work experience in that firm. Discuss the results with members of your group, and talk about whether changing the firm along the dimensions in the questions would make it more creative.

Instructions: Answer each of the following questions mostly true or mostly false.

	Mostly True	Mostly False
1. We are encouraged to seek help anywhere inside or outside the organization with new ideas for our work unit.	_____	_____
2. Assistance is provided to develop ideas into proposals for management review.	_____	_____
3. Our performance reviews encourage risky, creative efforts, ideas, and actions.	_____	_____
4. We are encouraged to fill our minds with new information by attending professional meetings and trade fairs, visiting customers, and so on.	_____	_____
5. Our meetings are designed to allow people to free-wheel, brainstorm, and generate ideas.	_____	_____
6. All members contribute ideas during meetings.	_____	_____
7. Meetings often involve much spontaneity and humor.	_____	_____
8. We discuss how company structure and our actions help or spoil creativity within our work unit.	_____	_____
9. During meetings, the chair is rotated among members.	_____	_____
10. Everyone in the work unit receives training in creativity techniques and maintaining a creative climate.	_____	_____

SCORING AND INTERPRETATION

Add your total score for all 10 questions: _____

   Give yourself one point for each mostly true answer; give yourself zero points if you choose Mostly False. To measure how effectively your organization fosters creativity, use the following scale:

Highly effective: 8–10

Moderately effective: 5–7

Moderately ineffective: 3–4

Ineffective: 0–3

SOURCE: Adapted from Edward Glassman, *Creativity Handbook: Idea Triggers and Sparks That Work* (Chapel Hill, NC: LCS Press, 1990). Used by permission.

3M

How could it be? 3M, a century-old icon of American innovation, was looking a little tired when James McNerney took over as CEO. Sales and profits were stalled. What's worse, though, was that scientists seemed to be so focused on their current markets that the company was no longer creating breakthrough products. Scotchgard and Post-it Notes were all well and good—but where were the pioneering products that could keep 3M growing?

McNerney asked Larry Wendling, the vice president in charge of 3M's central research and development (R&D) lab, to shake things up. He did it by stripping "technologies of the present" from R&D's priorities and reorganizing scientists around fast-growth "technologies of the future." The company's R&D system, with 12 separate research units each focused on specific target markets, worked fine for launching families of new products from existing product lines, but it gave researchers little incentive to look beyond them. Wendling reorganized R&D so that the majority of 3M scientists were assigned to the major business units. A core group at central R&D was charged specifically with working on breakthrough research.

Today, the products that are driving 3M's growth are coming primarily from nanotechnology, an area that has proven the hardest for many companies to get out of the research lab. Scotchgard and Post-it Notes are still big sellers, but 3M is now pulling in $500 million a year in sales of nanotech-based products such as natural-looking dental fillings, super-conductive power cables, ultra-bright cell phone displays, and filters that prevent nosy onlookers from seeing your laptop screen. 3M is currently the world's biggest manufacturer of nanotech materials, controlling more than a third of the global market.[67]

unions, and production inefficiencies all can generate a force to which management must respond with change. Production inefficiencies at Chrysler U.S. factories, for example, prompted managers to initiate a total overhaul of the assembly process, resulting in a new, flexible assembly system that makes extensive use of robots and allows for building more than one type of vehicle on a single assembly line. The flexibility can keep Chrysler's plants running at full capacity, enabling the company to increase profits.[68]

NEED FOR CHANGE

As indicated in Exhibit 8.6, external or internal forces translate into a perceived need for change within the organization. Many people are not willing to change unless they perceive a problem or a crisis. Managers at Humana Inc., for example, changed how the company sells health insurance after losing more than 100,000 private health insurance members in 2005 due to a rapid decrease in the number of small and midsized companies providing benefits to their employees.[69] In many cases, however, it is not a crisis that prompts change. Most problems are subtle, so managers have to recognize and then make others aware of the need for change.[70]

One way managers sense a need for change is through the appearance of a **performance gap**—a disparity between existing and desired performance levels. They then try to create a sense of urgency so that others in the organization will recognize and understand the need for change. For example, the chief component-purchasing manager at Nokia noticed that order numbers for some of the computer chips it purchased from Philips Electronics weren't adding up, and he discovered that a fire at Philips' Albuquerque, New Mexico, plant had delayed production. The manager moved quickly to alert top managers, engineers, and others throughout the company that Nokia could be caught short of chips unless it took action. Within weeks, a crisis team had redesigned chips, found new suppliers, and restored the chip supply line. In contrast, managers at a competing firm that also purchased chips from Philips, had the same information but failed to recognize or create a sense of crisis for change, which left the company millions of chips short of what it needed to produce a key product.[71]

Recall from Chapter 5 the discussion of SWOT analysis. Managers are responsible for monitoring threats and opportunities in the external environment as well as strengths and

performance gap
a disparity between existing and desired performance levels.

weaknesses within the organization to determine whether a need for change exists. Managers in every company must be alert to problems and opportunities because the perceived need for change sets the stage for subsequent actions that create a new product or technology. Big problems are easy to spot. Sensitive monitoring systems are needed to detect gradual changes that can fool managers into thinking their company is doing fine. An organization may be in greater danger when the environment changes slowly because managers may fail to trigger an organizational response. Failing to use planned change to meet small needs can place the organization in hot water, as illustrated in the following passage:

> When frogs are placed in a boiling pail of water, they jump out—they don't want to boil to death. However, when frogs are placed in a cold pail of water, and the pail is placed on a stove with the heat turned very low, over time the frogs will boil to death.[72]

Implementing Change

The final step to be managed in the change process is *implementation*. A new, creative idea will not benefit the organization until it is in place and being fully used. One frustration for managers is that employees often seem to resist change for no apparent reason. To effectively manage the implementation process, managers should be aware of the reasons people resist change and use techniques to enlist employee cooperation. Major, corporate-wide changes can be particularly challenging.

RESISTANCE TO CHANGE

Idea champions often discover that other employees are unenthusiastic about their new ideas. Members of a new-venture group may be surprised when managers in the regular organization do not support or approve their innovations. Managers and employees not involved in an innovation often seem to prefer the status quo. Employees appear to resist change for several reasons, and understanding them can help managers implement change more effectively.

Self-Interest. People typically resist a change they believe will take away something of value. A proposed change in job design, structure, or technology may lead to a real or perceived loss of power, prestige, pay, or company benefits. The fear of personal loss is perhaps the biggest obstacle to organizational change.[73] For example, when FedEx first expanded into ground transportation to be more competitive with UPS, the company's express air service employees felt threatened. Managers smoothly implemented the change by being aware of this possibility and taking steps to alleviate the concerns. Similarly, the acquisition of Kinko's required FedEx managers to recognize that the self-interest of Kinko's employees could trigger some resistance to changes in the organization.[74]

Lack of Understanding and Trust. Employees often distrust the intentions behind a change or do not understand the intended purpose of a change. If previous working relationships with an idea champion have been negative, resistance may occur. One manager had a habit of initiating a change in the financial reporting system about every 12 months and then losing interest and not following through. After the third time, employees no longer went along with the change because they did not trust the manager's intention to follow through to their benefit.

Uncertainty. *Uncertainty* is the lack of information about future events. It represents a fear of the unknown. Uncertainty is especially threatening for employees who have a low tolerance for change and fear anything out of the ordinary. They do not know how a change will affect them and worry about whether they will be able to meet the demands of a new procedure or technology.[75] For example, union leaders at an American auto manufacturer resisted the introduction of employee participation programs. They were uncertain about how the program would affect their status and thus initially opposed it.

Different Assessments and Goals. Another reason for resistance to change is that people who will be affected by an innovation may assess the situation differently from an idea champion or new-venture group. Critics frequently voice legitimate disagreements over the proposed benefits of a change. Managers in each department pursue different goals, and an innovation may detract from performance and goal achievement for some departments. For example, if marketing gets the new product it wants for customers, the cost of manufacturing may increase, and the manufacturing superintendent thus will resist. Resistance may call attention to problems with the innovation. At a consumer products company in Racine, Wisconsin, middle managers resisted the introduction of a new employee program that turned out to be a bad idea. The managers truly believed that the program would do more harm than good.[76]

These reasons for resistance are legitimate in the eyes of employees affected by the change. The best procedure for managers is not to ignore resistance but to diagnose the reasons and design strategies to gain acceptance by users.[77] Strategies for overcoming resistance to change typically involve two approaches: the analysis of resistance through the force-field technique and the use of selective implementation tactics to overcome resistance.

FORCE-FIELD ANALYSIS

Force-field analysis grew from the work of Kurt Lewin, who proposed that change was a result of the competition between *driving forces* and *restraining forces*.[78] Driving forces can be thought of as problems or opportunities that provide motivation for change within the organization. Restraining forces are the various barriers to change, such as a lack of resources, resistance from middle managers, or inadequate employee skills. When a change is introduced, management should analyze both the forces that drive change (problems and opportunities) and the forces that resist it (barriers to change). By selectively removing forces that restrain change, the driving forces will be strong enough to enable implementation, as illustrated by the move from A to B in Exhibit 8.7. As barriers are reduced or removed, behavior will shift to incorporate the desired changes.

Just-in-time (JIT) inventory control systems schedule materials to arrive at a company just as they are needed on the production line. In an Ohio manufacturing company, management's analysis showed that the driving forces (opportunities) associated with the implementation of JIT were (1) the large cost savings from reduced inventories, (2) savings

force-field analysis
the process of determining which forces drive and which resist a proposed change.

EXHIBIT 8.7

Using Force-Field Analysis to Change from a Traditional to a Just-in-Time Inventory System

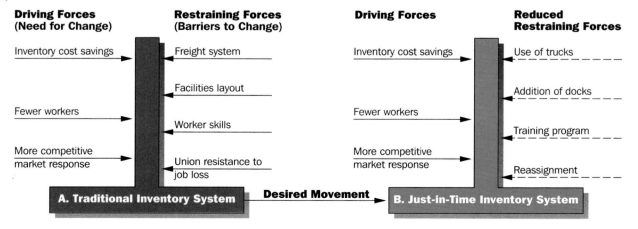

Driving Forces (Need for Change)	Restraining Forces (Barriers to Change)	Driving Forces	Reduced Restraining Forces
Inventory cost savings	Freight system	Inventory cost savings	Use of trucks
	Facilities layout		Addition of docks
Fewer workers	Worker skills	Fewer workers	Training program
More competitive market response	Union resistance to job loss	More competitive market response	Reassignment
A. Traditional Inventory System	**Desired Movement** →	**B. Just-in-Time Inventory System**	

from needing fewer workers to handle the inventory, and (3) a quicker, more competitive market response for the company. Restraining forces (barriers) discovered by managers were (1) a freight system that was too slow to deliver inventory on time, (2) a facility layout that emphasized inventory maintenance over new deliveries, (3) worker skills inappropriate for handling rapid inventory deployment, and (4) union resistance to loss of jobs. The driving forces were not sufficient to overcome the restraining forces.

To shift the behavior to JIT, managers attacked the barriers. An analysis of the freight system showed that delivery by truck provided the flexibility and quickness needed to schedule inventory arrival at a specific time each day. The problem with facility layout was met by adding four new loading docks. Inappropriate worker skills were attacked with a training program to instruct workers in JIT methods and in assembling products with uninspected parts. Union resistance was overcome by agreeing to reassign workers no longer needed for maintaining inventory to jobs in another plant. With the restraining forces reduced, the driving forces were sufficient to allow the JIT system to be implemented.

IMPLEMENTATION TACTICS

The other approach to managing implementation is to adopt specific tactics to overcome employee resistance. For example, resistance to change may be overcome by educating employees or inviting them to participate in implementing the change. Researchers have studied various methods for dealing with resistance to change. The following five tactics, summarized in Exhibit 8.8, have proven successful.[79]

Communication and Education. *Communication* and *education* are used when solid information about the change is needed by users and others who may resist implementation. Education is especially important when the change involves new technical knowledge or users are unfamiliar with the idea. Canadian Airlines International spent a year and a half preparing and training employees before changing its entire reservations, airport, cargo, and financial systems as part of a new "Service Quality" strategy. Smooth implementation resulted from this intensive training and communications effort, which involved 50,000 tasks, 12,000 people, and 26 classrooms around the world.[80] Managers should also remember that implementing change requires speaking to people's hearts (touching their feelings) as well as to their minds (communicating facts). Emotion is a key component in persuading and influencing others. People are much more likely to change their behavior when they both understand the rational reasons for doing so and see a picture of change that influences their feelings.[81]

Participation. *Participation* involves users and potential resisters in designing the change. This approach is time consuming, but it pays off because users understand and become committed to the change. Participation also helps managers determine potential

CONCEPT CONNECTION

Implementing change, especially when workers are unionized, often requires **negotiation.** For instance, managers at Goodyear Tire & Rubber Co. concluded that the company needed to pull out of some of its private label business to compete with low-cost foreign producers, but this would lead to plant closings. After having made major concessions several years earlier to help the ailing tire manufacturer get back on track, the United Steelworkers union was adamantly opposed to further job losses. Despite months of talks, the two sides failed to reach an agreement and 15,000 USW members went on strike in October 2006.

EXHIBIT 8.8

Tactics for Overcoming
Resistance to Change

Approach	When to Use
Communication, education	• Change is technical. • Users need accurate information and analysis to understand change.
Participation	• Users need to feel involved. • Design requires information from others. • Users have power to resist.
Negotiation	• Group has power over implementation. • Group will lose out in the change.
Coercion	• A crisis exists. • Initiators clearly have power. • Other implementation techniques have failed.
Top management support	• Change involves multiple departments or reallocation of resources. • Users doubt legitimacy of change.

SOURCE: Based on J. P. Kotter and L. A. Schlesinger, "Choosing Strategies for Change," *Harvard Business Review* 57 (March–April 1979): 106–114.

problems and understand the differences in perceptions of change among employees.[82] When General Motors tried to implement a new management appraisal system for supervisors in its Adrian, Michigan, plant, it met with immediate resistance. Rebuffed by the lack of cooperation, top managers proceeded more slowly, involving supervisors in the design of the new appraisal system. Through participation in system design, managers understood what the new approach was all about and dropped their resistance to it.

Negotiation. Negotiation is a more formal means of achieving cooperation. *Negotiation* uses formal bargaining to win acceptance and approval of a desired change. For example, if the marketing department fears losing power if a new management structure is implemented, top managers may negotiate with marketing to reach a resolution. Companies that have strong unions frequently must formally negotiate change with the unions. The change may become part of the union contract reflecting the agreement of both parties.

Coercion. *Coercion* means that managers use formal power to force employees to change. Resisters are told to accept the change or lose rewards or even their jobs. In most cases, this approach should not be used because employees feel like victims, are angry at change managers, and may even sabotage the changes. However, coercion may be necessary in crisis situations when a rapid response is urgent. For example, a number of top managers at Coca-Cola had to be reassigned or let go after they refused to go along with a new CEO's changes for revitalizing the sluggish corporation.[83]

Top Management Support. The visible support of top management also helps overcome resistance to change. *Top management support* symbolizes to all employees that the change is important for the organization. Top management support is especially important when a change involves multiple departments or when resources are being reallocated among

Remploy, the U.K.'s top employer of disabled people, owns 82 manufacturing sites that make a diverse range of products, including car headrests, school furniture, and protective clothing for military and civil use. Top managers set some audacious growth goals—to increase staff from 12,500 to 25,000 and triple output within four years, but they knew meeting the goals would require massive changes in how work was done. To ensure success, Remploy used a team of internal consultants to identify the weakest link in a production process, fix it, and then move on to whatever emerged as the next weakest link.

Remploy Ltd.

The entire change process was at first frightening and confusing to Remploy's workers, 90 percent of whom have some sort of disability. However, by communicating with employees, providing training, and closely involving them in the change process, the implementation occurred smoothly. For example, at Remploy's Stirling site, top executives made sure factory manager Margaret Harrison understood the program and could communicate its importance to the plant workers. Harrison and the consultants trained people on the factory floor to look for ways to improve day-to-day work processes. "The more we involved the shopfloor people, the more they bought into it because they were part of the decision-making process," Harrison said. As people saw their ideas implemented, they proposed even more solutions. One worker, for example, suggested sticking colored tape on the machinists' tables to ensure absolute accuracy while speeding up the process. Another group repositioned a huge overhanging machine so that shopfloor workers could see one another, communicate more easily, and pitch in to overcome any workflow slowdowns.

These changes helped Remploy achieve a 5 percent increase in its profit margin and the first growth in business in more than a decade. "If you think, 'I can do this a different way,' you approach the team leaders and tell them," machinist Helen Galloway said. "It's all teamwork. Change is frightening but, because we all have a say, we feel more confident making those changes."[84]

departments. Fred Smith, the founder of FedEx, got personally involved in communicating about the addition of ground shipping services. By giving talks on the corporate television network, going on road trips, and communicating via e-mail and newsletters, Smith signaled that the change was important to the company's future success. Without top management support, changes can get bogged down in squabbling among departments. Moreover, when change agents fail to enlist the support of top executives, these leaders can inadvertently undercut the change project by issuing contradictory orders.

The example of Remploy Ltd. above illustrates how smart implementation techniques can smooth the change process.

Communication and participation were the key to smooth implementation of significant changes at Remploy's factories. When managers use appropriate implementation techniques, resistance to change softens and the change process proceeds more quickly and smoothly.

Summary

Change is inevitable in organizations. This chapter discussed the techniques available for managing the change process. Two key aspects of change in organizations are changing products and technologies, and changing people and culture. Three essential innovation strategies for changing products and technologies are exploration, cooperation, and entrepreneurship. Exploration involves designing the organization to promote creativity, imagination, and idea generation. Cooperation requires mechanisms for internal coordination, such as horizontal linkages across departments, and mechanisms for connecting with external parties. One popular approach is open innovation, which extends the search for and commercialization of ideas beyond the boundaries of the organization. Entrepreneurship includes encouraging idea champions and establishing new-venture teams, skunkworks, and new-venture funds.

People and culture changes pertain to the skills, behaviors, and attitudes of employees. Training and organization development are important approaches to changing people's mindsets and corporate culture. The OD process entails three steps—unfreezing (diagnosis of the problem), the actual change (intervention), and refreezing (reinforcement of new attitudes and behaviors). Popular OD techniques include team building, survey feedback, and large-group interventions.

Managers should think of change as having three elements—the forces for change, the perceived need for change, and the implementation of change. Forces for change can originate either within or outside the firm, and managers are responsible for monitoring events that may require a planned organizational response. The final step is implementation. Managers should be prepared to encounter resistance to change. Some typical reasons for resistance include self-interest, lack of trust, uncertainty, and conflicting goals. Force-field analysis is one technique for diagnosing barriers, which often can be removed. Managers can also draw on the implementation tactics of communication, participation, negotiation, coercion, or top management support.

Discussion Questions

1. Times of shared crisis, such as the September 11, 2001, terrorist attack on the World Trade Center or the Gulf Coast hurricanes in 2005, can induce many companies that have been bitter rivals to put their competitive spirit aside and focus on cooperation and courtesy. Do you believe this type of change will be a lasting one? Discuss.

2. A manager of an international chemical company said that few new products in her company were successful. What would you advise the manager to do to help increase the company's success rate?

3. What is meant by the terms *internal* and *external forces for change*? Which forces do you think are causes of change in a university? In a pharmaceuticals firm?

4. As a manager, how would you deal with resistance to change when you suspect employee fears of job loss are well founded?

5. How might businesses use the Internet to identify untapped customer needs through open innovation? What do you see as the major advantages and disadvantages of the open innovation approach?

6. Why do organizations experience resistance to change? What techniques can managers use to overcome resistance?

7. Explain force-field analysis. Use examples from your own experience to analyze the driving and restraining forces for a change.

8. Which role or roles—the inventor, champion, sponsor, or critic—would you most like to play in the innovation process? Which roles would you be least comfortable playing? Why do you think idea champions are so essential to the initiation of change?

9. You are a manager, and you believe the expense reimbursement system for salespeople is far too slow, taking weeks instead of days. How would you go about convincing other managers that this problem needs to be addressed?

10. Do the underlying values of organization development differ from assumptions associated with other types of change? Discuss.

11. How do large-group interventions differ from OD techniques such as team building and survey feedback?

Dear Dr. Dorothy

I've been working in a high-tech firm for several years and am a new supervisor. The work is great, pay is decent, and my co-workers are cool. The only problem is nothing stays the same. I thought it was bad before, but it's even worse as a supervisor. Really, I just get adjusted to a new team, a new cubicle, and WHAM! Everything gets changed. It's like we play musical offices every few months. And now, I'm the one who has to make office assignments, or tell people their work is completely different, or maybe that they just got laid off. My head is dizzy from all these moves and new work assignments. Will it get better?

Whiplashed in Santa Cruz

Dear Whiplashed,

Has no one bothered to tell you we live in an ever-changing world? And need Dr. Dorothy remind you that high-tech is the changiest of them all? Really, if you want work stability, try civil service, though even that is less constant than it used to be. For high-tech companies to stay in business and beat the competition, they have to hustle and flow, which means employees have to constantly learn, adjust, modify, and alter. You say it's worse as a supervisor. Well, I'm sure your mother told you, "If you can't take the heat, get out of the kitchen." Dr. Dorothy agrees with your mother. If you can't take the stress of management, go back to taking orders rather than giving them.

Self Learning

Innovation Climate

To examine differences in the level of innovation encouragement in organizations, you will be asked to rate two different organizations. You may choose one in which you have worked or the university. The other should be someone else's workplace, such as a family member, friend, or acquaintance. Therefore, you will have to interview that person to answer the following questions. You should put your own answers in column A, your interviewee's answers in column B, and finally, what you think would be the "ideal" in column C.

Use the following scale of 1–5: 1 = Don't agree at all to 5 = Agree completely

Innovation Measures Item of Measure	Column A Your Org.	Column B Other Org.	Column C Your Ideal
1. Creativity is encouraged here.*			
2. People are allowed to solve the same problems in different ways.*			
3. I get free time to pursue creative ideas.#			
4. The organization publicly recognizes and also rewards those who are innovative.#			
5. Our organization is flexible and always open to change.*			

Below score items on the opposite scale: 1 = Agree completely through 5 = Don't agree at all

6. The primary job of people here is to follow orders that come from the top.*			
7. The best way to get along here is to think and act like the others.*			
8. This place seems to be more concerned with the status quo than with change.*			
9. People are rewarded more if they don't rock the boat.#			
10. New ideas are great, but we don't have enough people or money to carry them out.#			

NOTE: *Starred items indicate the organization's innovation climate.
#Pound sign items show "resource support."

1. What comparisons about innovative climates can you make from these two organizations?

2. How might productivity differ when there is a climate that supports versus a climate that does not support innovation?

3. Which type of place would you rather work? Why?

SOURCE: Adapted from Susanne G. Scott and Reginald A. Bruce, "Determinants of innovative behavior: A path model of individual innovation in the workplace," *Academy of Management Journal* 37 (3) (1994): 580–607.

Group Learning

ABS Crisis

You are the internal OD consultant brought in by your company, ABS. There is an urgent problem that must be solved by the managers within a week. Because the company is near bankruptcy, your skills as a consultant are very important, as you may be able to save the company. You must help facilitate the managers to reach a decision concerning the following situation.

Case: In the past two years, the ABS Specialized Machinery Movers has suffered revenue losses because of increased competition and rising energy costs. ABS is known a premier company in the industry offering quality expertise and customer service. The company recently offered a low bid on a complex machinery-moving project. The company badly needed to generate revenue given its losses and offered the bid knowing that profit margins would be low unless drastic measures were taken. Upon winning the bid, the management set about to cut as many costs as possible to control costs on this low bid and increase the profit margin. The ABS president believed that if this project did not produce profits, the company would likely have to close.

One option is to cut labor costs by hiring illegal aliens. The project managers and supervisors for the job have years of experience and expertise; however, many of the laborers do not necessarily have to be highly skilled. The president and management are aware that it is unlawful to hire illegal immigrants; however, they also know the laws regarding this issue are not enforced. Additionally, they are concerned that they may be putting unskilled workers at safety risk in this often hazardous line of work. The threat of losing the company remains of highest concern to the president and upper management. Decisions must be made soon because the project's beginning date is only 25 days ahead. After consulting with your colleagues, you feel the best course of action is to put the managers through a force-field analysis (see page 308). Follow the chart provided on page 308, with blank space where you can write in the driving forces and restraining forces.

1. On your own, fill in the chart with Driving and Restraining Forces of the ABS case.

2. In groups of 4–6, discuss these issues, and come up with your group's Driving and Restraining Forces.

3. Choose a spokesperson to present your results to the entire class.

SOURCE: By Jennie Carter Thomas and Harry N. Hollis, Belmont University. Used with permission.

Action Learning

1. Find two people to interview who have gone through an organization change in recent years.

2. Ask them the following questions:

   a. Describe the organization before the change: What was the work like, how did people get along with one another, was the culture friendly, how did management treat employees, and so on?

   b. Who wanted the change? How was the decision made to bring about the change?

   c. Was an outside consultant brought in to help with the change? If not, who managed the change? How did the change process work? Was it effective?

   d. Describe the company after the change, using similar criteria from question #a.

3. Write a short paper describing the similarities and differences in the two situations.

4. What conclusions would you draw on organization change from what you learned in these two interviews?

5. Your instructor may ask you to discuss your findings in groups, or as part of a class discussion.

Ethical Dilemma

Crowdsourcing

Last year, when Ai-Lan Nguyen told her friend, Greg Barnwell, that Asheville, North Carolina-based Off the Hook Tees, was going to experiment with crowdsourcing, he warned her she wouldn't like the results. Now, as she was about to walk into a meeting called to decide whether to adopt this new business model, she was afraid her friend had been right.

Crowdsourcing uses the Internet to invite anyone, professionals and amateurs alike, to perform tasks such as product design that employees usually perform. In exchange, contributors receive recognition—but little or no pay. Ai-Lan, as vice president of operations for Off the Hook, a company specializing in witty T-shirts aimed at young adults, upheld the values of founder Chris Woodhouse, who like Ai-Lan was a graphic artist. Before he sold the company, the founder always insisted that T-shirts be well designed by top-notch graphic artists to make sure each screen print was a work of art. Those graphic artists reported to Ai-Lan.

During the past 18 months, Off the Hook's sales stagnated for the first time in its history. The crowdsourcing experiment was the latest in a series of attempts to jumpstart sales growth. Last spring, Off the Hook issued its first open call for T-shirt designs and then posted the entries on the Web so people could vote for their favorites. The top five vote-getters were handed over to the in-house designers, who tweaked the submissions until they met the company's usual quality standards.

When CEO Rob Taylor first announced the company's foray into crowdsourcing, Ai-Lan found herself reassuring the designers that their positions were not in jeopardy. Now Ai-Lan was all but certain she would have to go back on her word. Not only had the crowdsourced tees sold well, but Rob had put a handful of winning designs directly into production, bypassing the design department altogether. Customers didn't notice the difference.

Ai-Lan concluded that Rob was ready to adopt some form of the Web-based crowdsourcing because it made T-shirt design more responsive to consumer desires. Practically speaking, it reduced the uncertainty that surrounded new designs, and it dramatically lowered costs. The people who won the competitions were delighted with the exposure it gave them.

However, when Ai-Lan looked at the crowdsourced shirts with her graphic artist's eye, she felt that the designs were competent, but none achieved the aesthetic standards attained by her in-house designers. Crowdsourcing essentially replaced training and expertise with public opinion. That made the artist in her uncomfortable.

More distressing, it was beginning to look as if Greg had been right when he'd told her that his working definition of crowdsourcing was "a billion amateurs want your job." It was easy to see that if Off the Hook adopted crowdsourcing, she would be handing out pink slips to most of her design people, long-time employees whose work she admired. "Sure, crowdsourcing costs the company less, but what about the human cost?" Greg asked.

What future course should Ai-Lan argue for at the meeting? And what personal decisions did she face if Off the Hook decided to put the crowd completely in charge when it came to T-shirt design?

What Would You Do?

1. Go to the meeting and argue for abandoning crowdsourcing for now in favor of maintaining the artistic integrity and values that Off the Hook has always stood for.

2. Accept the reality that because Off the Hook's CEO Rob Taylor strongly favors crowdsourcing, it's a fait accompli. Be a team player and help work out the details of the new design approach. Prepare to lay off graphic designers as needed.

3. Accept the fact that converting Off the Hook to a crowdsourcing business model is inevitable, but because it violates your own personal values, start looking for a new job elsewhere.

SOURCES: Based on Paul Boutin, "Crowdsourcing: Consumers as Creators," *BusinessWeek Online* (July 13, 2006), http://www.businessweek.com/innovate/content/jul2006/id20060713_55844.htm?campaign_id=search; Jeff Howe, "The Rise of Crowdsourcing," *Wired* (June 2006), http://www.wired.com/wired/archive/14.06/crowds.html; and Jeff Howe, Crowdsourcing Blog, http://www.crowdsourcing.com.

Case for Critical Analysis

Southern Discomfort

Jim Malesckowski remembers the call of two weeks ago as if he just put down the telephone receiver. "I just read your analysis and I want you to get down to Mexico right away," Jack Ripon, his boss and CEO, had blurted in his ear. "You know we can't make the plant in Oconomo work anymore—the costs are just too high. So go down there, check out what our operational costs would be if we move, and report back to me in a week."

At that moment, Jim felt as if a shiv had been stuck in his side, just below the rib cage. As president of the Wisconsin Specialty Products Division of Lamprey, Inc., he knew quite well the challenge of dealing with high-cost labor in a third-generation, unionized U.S. manufacturing plant. And although he had done the analysis that led to his boss's knee-jerk response, the call still stunned him. There were 520 people who made a living at Lamprey's Oconomo facility, and if it closed, most of them wouldn't have a journeyman's prayer of finding another job in the town of 9,000 people.

Instead of the $16-per-hour average wage paid at the Oconomo plant, the wages paid to the Mexican workers—who lived in a town without sanitation and with an unbelievably toxic effluent from industrial pollution—would amount to about $1.60 an hour on average. That's a savings of nearly $15 million a year for Lamprey, to be offset in part by increased costs for training, transportation, and other matters.

After two days of talking with Mexican government representatives and managers of other companies in the town, Jim had enough information to develop a set of comparative figures of production and shipping costs. On the way home, he started to outline the report, knowing full well that unless some miracle occurred, he would be ushering in a blizzard of pink slips for people he had come to appreciate.

The plant in Oconomo had been in operation since 1921, making special apparel for persons suffering injuries and other medical conditions. Jim had often talked with employees who would recount stories about their fathers or grandfathers working in the same Lamprey company plant—the last of the original manufacturing operations in town.

But friendship aside, competitors had already edged past Lamprey in terms of price and were dangerously close to overtaking it in product quality. Although both Jim and the plant manager had tried to convince the union to accept lower wages, union leaders resisted. In fact, on one occasion when Jim and the plant manager tried to discuss a cell manufacturing approach, which would cross-train employees to perform up to three different jobs, local union leaders could barely restrain their anger. Yet probing beyond the fray, Jim sensed the fear that lurked under the union reps' gruff exterior. He sensed their vulnerability but could not break through the reactionary bark that protected it.

A week has passed, and Jim just submitted his report to his boss. Although he didn't specifically bring up the point, it was apparent that Lamprey could put its investment dollars in a bank and receive a better return than what its Oconomo operation is currently producing.

Tomorrow, he'll discuss the report with the CEO. Jim doesn't want to be responsible for the plant's dismantling, an act he personally believes would be wrong as long as there's a chance its costs can be lowered. "But Ripon's right," he says to himself. "The costs are too high, the union's unwilling to cooperate, and the company needs to make a better return on its investment if it's to continue at all. It sounds right but feels wrong. What should I do?"

Questions

1. What forces for change are evident at the Oconomo plant?

2. What is the primary type of change needed—changing "things" or changing the "people and culture?" Can the Wisconsin plant be saved by changing things alone, by changing people and culture, or must both be changed? Explain your answer.

3. What do you think is the major underlying cause of the union leaders' resistance to change? If you were Jim Malesckowski, what implementation tactics would you use to try to convince union members to change to save the Wisconsin plant?

SOURCE: Doug Wallace, "What Would You Do?" *Business Ethics* (March/April 1996): 52–53. Reprinted with permission.

BIZ FLIX

Apollo 13

This film dramatically portrays the Apollo 13 mission to the moon that almost ended in disaster. Only innovative problem solving and decision making amid massive ambiguity saved the crew. Almost any scene dramatically makes this point. Flight Director Gene Kranz wrote a book describing the mission and the actions that prevented disaster.

A zero gravity simulator, a KC-135 four-engine jet aircraft (NASA's "Vomit Comet"), helped create the film's realistic weightless scenes. These scenes required 600 parabolic loops over 10 days of filming.[1] See the later Biz Flix exercise for a discussion of another scene from *Apollo 13*.

This scene is a composite built from portions of the "Carbon Dioxide Problem" sequence, which occurs a little after the midway point of the film, and parts of the "With Every Breath . . ." sequence, which appears about seven minutes later. The scene's first part follows the nearly complete shutdown of the Apollo 13 module to save battery power. Mission Control has detected rising carbon dioxide levels in the module, which could kill the astronauts if NASA engineers on the ground cannot solve the problem. The film continues with the Apollo 13 crew building a carbon dioxide filter designed by the engineers.

What to Watch for and Ask Yourself

1. What is the problem in this scene?

2. What are the engineers' options for solving the problem?

3. Does this scene show innovation and innovative behavior? If so, in what form?

[1] J. Craddock, Ed. *VideoHound's Golden Movie Retriever*, (Farmington Hills, MI: The Gale Group, Inc.), 2000.

Change and Innovation at Hard Rock

At the close of 2006, British gaming company Rank Group made a deal with the Seminole Tribe of Florida to sell its stake in the Hard Rock business, to the tune of $965 million dollars. The deal covered ownership of the Hard Rock brand name, 124 Hard Rock Cafes and stores located around the world, 8 hotels, and two Hard Rock Live concert venues.

The Rank Group was going through tough times before it put its stake in the Hard Rock business on the auction block. It was swimming in debt, and Rank stock had taken a beating on the market. Although the chain had been profitable, the Rank Group felt its demands had taken too much focus off of their gambling interests, and that selling it would give them renewed focus. The money Rank made from the sale put the company into the black again, enabled a dividend payout to its investors, and better prepared them financially to take advantage of the UK's recent deregulation of the gambling industry.

The Hard Rock acquisition marks the first time on record that a Native American tribe has purchased such a large international corporation. It was not the first time the Seminole tribe made history. Despite efforts in the early 1800s by U.S. Army and militia forces to destroy the tribe or force them to yield, they never surrendered, and remain the only American Indian tribe who never signed a peace treaty. The Seminole Tribe was the first to win the right to build a tax-free gambling hall on Indian land, a move that changed the economic landscape for Native American tribes forever. Ownership of Hard Rock now gives the savvy tribe a full-blown international presence.

The Hard Rock Cafe business stands to truly benefit from the change. It has always turned a profit, and the most impressive earnings by far have been driven by the two Seminole Hard Rock Casino hotels that the Seminole Tribe opened in 2004. The Tribe stated that it intends to expand operations into new territory, and will look into adding casinos to existing Hard Rock hotels.

All parties involved in the deal can expect big changes in the near future. The Rank Group got less for Hard Rock than many analysts and investors expected, and it may take a while for the company's stock, and investor confidence, to improve. Being newly in the black, however, gives them options. The Seminole Tribe of Florida now runs a large international operation, and must learn a new suite of best practices in order to propel the brand, and the tribe, into the future. Hard Rock's current staff and patrons must adapt to any changes the company's new owners throw at them.

Questions

1. The Seminole Tribe of Florida has had a long history of overcoming adversity in their little corner of the world. What sort of resistance might Hard Rock's new owners face when initiating organizational change?

2. What measures can Hard Rock's new owners take to reassure staff and investors that they are in good hands?

3. Name some basic steps that upper management should take as they assess the best possible direction in which to take the company.

chapter 9

Human Resources and Diversity

Learning Objectives

After studying this chapter, you should be able to:

1 Explain the role of human resource management in organizational strategic planning.

2 Describe federal legislation and societal trends that influence human resource management.

3 Explain what the changing social contract between organizations and employees means for workers and human resource managers.

4 Describe the tools managers use to recruit and select employees.

5 Explain how organizations maintain a workforce through the administration of wages and salaries, benefits, and terminations.

6 Explain the dimensions of employee diversity and why ethnorelativism is the appropriate attitude for today's organizations.

7 Explain affirmative action and why factors such as the glass ceiling have kept it from being more successful.

8 Explain the importance of addressing sexual harassment in the workplace.

New Manager's Questions

Please circle your opinion below each of the following statements.

★ Assess Your Answer

1 Managers need to have a prime focus on the bottom line, on the financial well being of the company.

1	2	3	4	5
strongly agree				strongly disagree

2 Hiring people to work for a company is about the economic contract between employer and employee.

1	2	3	4	5
strongly agree				strongly disagree

3 The increasing number of foreign workers at U.S. companies needs to give a lot of attention to learning the U.S. culture and adapting.

1	2	3	4	5
strongly agree				strongly disagree

Hiring and retaining quality employees is one of the most urgent concerns of today's managers.[1] The people who make up an organization give the company its primary source of competitive advantage, and human resource management plays a key role in finding and developing the organization's people as human resources that contribute to and directly affect company success. The term **human resource management (HRM)** refers to the design and application of formal systems in an organization to ensure the effective and efficient use of human talent to accomplish organizational goals.[2] This system includes activities undertaken to attract, develop, and maintain an effective workforce. The situation at UPS's Buffalo distribution center provides a dramatic example of the challenges managers face every day. Every hour or so throughout the night, big brown trucks back into the bays at UPS's distribution center in Buffalo, New York, where part-time workers load, unload, and sort packages at a rate of 1,200 boxes an hour. A typical employee handles a box every three seconds. The packages don't stop until the shift is over, which allows little time for friendly banter and chitchat, even if you could hear over the din of the belts and ramps that carry packages through the cavernous 270,000-square-foot warehouse. It's not the easiest job in the world, and many people don't stick around for long. When Jennifer Shroeger arrived in Buffalo as the new district manager, the attrition rate of part-time workers, who account for half of Buffalo's workforce, was 50 percent a year. With people deserting at that rate, hiring and training costs were through the roof, not to mention the slowdown in operations caused by continually training new workers.[3] Shroeger worked with the HR department to solve the problem of high turnover at the Buffalo distribution center, dramatically cutting the attrition rate to a low 6 percent. Managers realized that retaining employees had a lot to do with how those people were selected in the first place. Previously, UPS basically hired the first applicant who walked in and was capable of handling heavy packages. Shroeger decided they needed to start asking what the applicant was looking for in the job. Many of those hired as part-timers were really looking for full-time jobs, which rarely opened up. After a few months, these people realized their chances of full-time work were slim, so they'd move on. UPS started giving realistic job previews, emphasizing not only the hard, intimidating environment of the warehouse but also the fact that these positions were part-time jobs and short shifts that were never going to be anything else. The upside to this aspect of the job is that it is perfect for students, mothers, and other people who genuinely *want* to work only part-time. But hiring those people meant UPS needed to build in flexibility. Students and mothers, for example, tend to need more occasional days off or frequent changes in their schedule. Instead of just saying "we can't do that," HRM started looking for ways the company could do it. Other changes involved improved training and mentoring for new employees, handled by part-time shift supervisors who understood the problems of the work environment. The supervisors themselves also got upgraded training in communication skills, motivation, and flexibility to meet the needs of diverse workers. A final, important aspect of the new strategy was to accept that most people they hired wouldn't want to load and unload boxes for their entire careers. "Instead of worrying about them leaving, we should be taking an interest in their future," Shroeger says. "I'd like for all of those part-time workers to graduate from college and start their own businesses—and become UPS customers."[4]

Managers at Electronic Arts, the world's largest maker of computer games, include a commitment to human resources as one of the company's four worldwide goals. They have to, in a company where the creativity and mind power of artists, designers, model makers, mathematicians, and filmmakers determines strategic success, and the competition for talent is intense.[5] HRM is equally important for government and nonprofit organizations. For example, public schools in the United States are facing a severe teacher shortage, with HRM directors struggling with how to fill an estimated 2.2 million teacher vacancies over the next decade. Many are trying innovative programs such as recruiting in foreign countries, establishing relationships with leaders at top universities, and having

human resource management (HRM)
activities undertaken to attract, develop, and maintain an effective workforce within an organization.

their most motivated and enthusiastic teachers work with university students considering teaching careers.[6]

Over the past decade, HRM has shed its old "personnel" image and gained recognition as a vital player in corporate strategy.[7] Increasingly, large corporations are outsourcing routine HR administrative activities, freeing HRM staff from time-consuming paperwork and enabling them to take on more strategic responsibilities. In 2003, human resources (HR) topped Gartner Inc.'s list of most commonly outsourced business activities.[8] Today's best HR departments not only support the organization's strategic objective but actively pursue an ongoing, integrated plan for furthering the organization's performance.[9] HR managers are key players on the executive team. Research has found that effective HRM has a positive impact on strategic performance, including higher employee productivity and stronger financial results.[10]

CONCEPT CONNECTION

With a booming economy, the Republic of Ireland had employers looking for workers. Poland, on the other hand, had plenty of workers looking for jobs. The result was the Warsaw job fair pictured here, an example of how **globalization** affects **human resource management.** Because both countries are EU members, Irish construction companies were free to come to the Polish capital in search of the engineers, project managers, and skilled carpenters they needed. Polish applicants flocked to the job fair from all over the country, seeking to escape high unemployment and a job market where the take-home pay for even an experienced engineer is roughly $800 a month.

Today, all managers need to be skilled in the basics of HRM. Flatter organizations often require that managers throughout the organization play an active role in recruiting and selecting the right personnel, developing effective training programs, or creating appropriate performance appraisal systems. HRM professionals act to guide and assist line managers in managing their human resources to achieve the organization's strategic goals.

The Strategic Role of Human Resource Management

 **TAKE ACTION**

Remember that employees are an important asset of the company.

The strategic approach to HRM recognizes three key elements. First, as we just discussed, all managers are HR managers. For example, at IBM every manager is expected to pay attention to the development and satisfaction of subordinates. Line managers use surveys, career planning, performance appraisal, and compensation to encourage commitment to IBM.[11] Second, employees are viewed as assets. Employees, not buildings and machinery, give a company its competitive advantage. How a company manages its workforce may be the single most important factor in sustained competitive success.[12]

Third, HRM is a matching process, integrating the organization's strategy and goals with the correct approach to managing the firm's human capital.[13] Current strategic issues of particular concern to managers include the following:

- Becoming more competitive on a global basis
- Improving quality, innovation, and customer service
- Managing mergers and acquisitions
- Applying new information technology for e-business

All of these strategic decisions determine a company's need for skills and employees.

This chapter examines the three primary goals of HRM as illustrated in Exhibit 9.1. HRM activities and goals do not take place inside a vacuum but within the context of issues and

EXHIBIT 9.1
Strategic Human
Resource Management

factors affecting the entire organization, such as globalization, changing technology and the shift to knowledge work, a growing need for rapid innovation, quick shifts in markets and the external environment, societal trends, government regulations, and changes in the organization's culture, structure, strategy, and goals.

The three broad HRM activities outlined in Exhibit 9.1 are to attract an effective workforce, develop the workforce to its potential, and maintain the workforce over the long term.[14] Achieving these goals requires skills in planning, recruiting, training, performance appraisal, wage and salary administration, benefit programs, and even termination. Each of the activities in Exhibit 9.1 will be discussed in this chapter.

Environmental Influences on HRM

"Our strength is the quality of our people."

"Our people are our most important resource."

These often-repeated statements by executives emphasize the importance of HRM. HR managers must find, recruit, train, nurture, and retain the best people.[15] Without the right people, the brightest idea or management trend—whether virtual teams, e-business, or flexible compensation—is doomed to failure. In addition, when employees don't feel valued, usually they are not willing to give their best to the company and often leave to find a more supportive work environment. For these reasons, it is important that HR executives be involved in competitive strategy. HR managers also interpret federal legislation and respond to the changing nature of careers and work relationships.

COMPETITIVE STRATEGY

HRM contributes directly to the bottom line, because it is the organization's human assets—its people—that meet or fail to meet strategic goals. To keep companies competitive, HRM is changing in three primary ways: focusing on building human capital, developing global HR strategies, and using information technology.

Building Human Capital. Today, more than ever, strategic decisions are related to HR considerations. In many companies, especially those that rely more on employee

1 Managers need to have a prime focus on the bottom line, on the financial well being of the company.

ANSWER: Paying attention to the bottom line is important, but managers must remember that people and HRM issues are directly related to financial success. Too often, managers only look at numbers and forget that people are part of the system and part of the success or failure of that system.

information, creativity, knowledge, and service rather than on production machinery, success depends on the ability to manage *human capital*.[16] **Human capital** refers to the economic value of the combined knowledge, experience, skills, and capabilities of employees.[17] To build human capital, HRM develops strategies for finding the best talent, enhancing their skills and knowledge with training programs and opportunities for personal and professional development, and providing compensation and benefits that enhance the sharing of knowledge and appropriately reward people for their contributions to the organization.

One organization that recognizes the strategic role of HRM in getting employees mobilized to meet goals is The Home Depot, the nation's largest home improvement retail chain.

Home Depot's HRM team often uses data-driven research to develop human capital initiatives. For example, data showed that senior workers had fewer absences and stayed with their jobs longer, so the company signed a recruiting partnership with the American Association of Retired Persons (AARP). Surveys revealed that employees prefer semiannual bonuses to annual ones, so the HRM department made the switch.[18] These types of initiatives, combined with opportunities for personal and professional development, help create an environment that gives highly talented people compelling reasons to stay.

Another concern related to human capital for HRM managers is building *social capital*, which refers to the quality of interactions among employees and whether they share a common perspective.[19] In organizations with a high degree of social capital, for example, relationships are based on honesty, trust, and respect, and people cooperate smoothly to achieve shared goals and outcomes.

TAKE ACTION

Don't hire people just because they are available. Get the right person for the job.

human capital
the economic value of the knowledge, experience, skills, and capabilities of employees.

The Home Depot

One of first moves Bob Narelli made as the previous CEO of The Home Depot was to hire a highly visible, experienced HR executive to immediately dive into leading major strategy and change initiatives. As executive vice president of HR, Dennis Donavan reports directly to the CEO, has the second-highest salary in the company, and holds one of the most powerful positions in the giant corporation. It's a reflection of the importance Nardelli puts on building human capital.

The Home Depot relies on the quality of its employees' interactions with customers to stay on top in its business. More than 325,000 employees interact with customers at a rate of 3 billion times a year, often at a personal level, helping them select bathroom fixtures or discussing how to repair a garbage disposal. When Nardelli took over as CEO, those human interactions were beginning to show signs of strain due to rapid growth. Donovan and his HR team came up with 300 different strategic change projects to initiate over a three-year period, many of them designed to strengthen management and leadership skills. Because store managers are so critical to achieving corporate goals, for example, the HR department created a learning forum for district and store-level managers, and within only a few months had put nearly 1,800 store managers through a weeklong intensive leadership program. Today, thanks to Donovan, every Home Depot store has its own HR manager who works directly with the store manager to facilitate hiring and developing store-level employees, including creating staff education seminars and e-learning kiosks.

The Home Depot is on the cutting edge in involving HRM managers in all areas of business decision making, whether it be ongoing operational concerns, changes in the market, or long-term strategic initiatives. In fact, many of the company's most important strategic initiatives have been initiated and led by the HR department.[20]

Information Technology. Information technology is transforming HRM and helping to meet the challenges of today's global environment. A study of the transition from traditional HR to e-HR found that the Internet and information technology significantly affects every area of HRM, from recruiting, to training and career development, to retention strategies.[21] A **human resource information system** is an integrated computer system designed to provide data and information used in HR planning and decision making. The most basic use is the automation of administrative duties such as handling pay, benefits, and retirement plans, which is convenient for employees and can lead to significant cost savings for the organization.

Federal Legislation. Over the past 40 years, a number of federal laws have been passed to ensure equal employment opportunity (EEO). Some of the most significant legislation and executive orders are summarized in Exhibit 9.2. The point of the laws is to stop discriminatory practices that are unfair to specific groups and to define enforcement

human resource information system
an integrated computer system designed to provide data and information used in HR planning and decision making.

EXHIBIT 9.2
Major Federal Laws Related to Human Resource Management

Federal Law	Year	Provisions
Equal Opportunity/Discrimination Laws		
Civil Rights Act	1991	Provides for possible compensatory and punitive damages plus traditional back pay for cases of intentional discrimination brought under title VII of the 1964 Civil Rights Act. Shifts the burden of proof to the employer.
Americans with Disabilities Act	1990	Prohibits discrimination against qualified individuals by employers on the basis of disability and demands that "reasonable accommodations" be provided for the disabled to allow performance of duties.
Vocational Rehabilitation Act	1973	Prohibits discrimination based on physical or mental disability and requires that employees be informed about affirmative action plans.
Age Discrimination in Employment Act (ADEA)	1967 (amended 1978, 1986)	Prohibits age discrimination and restricts mandatory retirement.
Civil Rights Act, Title VII	1964	Prohibits discrimination in employment on the basis of race, religion, color, sex, or national origin.
Compensation/Benefits Laws		
Health Insurance Portability and Accountability Act (HIPPA)	1996	Allows employees to switch health insurance plans when changing jobs and get the new coverage regardless of preexisting health conditions; prohibits group plans from dropping a sick employee.
Family and Medical Leave Act	1993	Requires employers to provide up to 12 weeks unpaid leave for childbirth, adoption, or family emergencies.
Equal Pay Act	1963	Prohibits sex differences in pay for substantially equal work.
Health/Safety Laws		
Consolidated Omnibus Budget Reconciliation Act (COBRA)	1985	Requires continued health insurance coverage (paid by employee) following termination.
Occupational Safety and Health Act (OSHA)	1970	Establishes mandatory safety and health standards in organizations.

agencies for these laws. EEO legislation attempts to balance the pay given to men and women; provide employment opportunities without regard to race, religion, national origin, and gender; ensure fair treatment for employees of all ages; and avoid discrimination against disabled individuals.

The Equal Employment Opportunity Commission (EEOC) created by the Civil Rights Act of 1964 initiates investigations in response to complaints concerning discrimination. The EEOC is the major agency involved with employment discrimination. **Discrimination** occurs when some applicants are hired or promoted based on criteria that are not job relevant. For example, refusing to hire a black applicant for a job he is qualified to fill or paying a woman a lower wage than a man for the same work are discriminatory acts. When discrimination is found, remedies include providing back pay and taking affirmative action. **Affirmative action** requires that an employer take positive steps to guarantee equal employment opportunities for people within protected groups. An affirmative action plan is a formal document that can be reviewed by employees and enforcement agencies. The goal of organizational affirmative action is to reduce or eliminate internal inequities among affected employee groups.

Failure to comply with EEO legislation can result in substantial fines and penalties for employers. Suits for discriminatory practices can cover a broad range of employee complaints. One issue of growing concern is *sexual harassment,* which is also a violation of Title VII of the Civil Rights Act. The EEOC guidelines specify that behavior such as unwelcome advances, requests for sexual favors, and other verbal and physical conduct of a sexual nature becomes sexual harassment when submission to the conduct is tied to continued employment or advancement or when the behavior creates an intimidating, hostile, or offensive work environment.[22] Sexual harassment will be discussed in more detail later in the chapter.

Exhibit 9.2 also lists the major federal laws related to compensation and benefits and health and safety issues. The scope of HR legislation is increasing at federal, state, and municipal levels. The working rights and conditions of women, minorities, older employees, and the disabled will likely receive increasing legislative attention in the future.

The Changing Nature of Careers

Another current issue is the changing nature of careers. HRM can benefit employees and organizations by responding to recent changes in the relationship between employers and employees and new ways of working such as telecommuting, job sharing, outsourcing, and virtual teams.

THE CHANGING SOCIAL CONTRACT

In the old social contract between organization and employee, the employee could contribute ability, education, loyalty, and commitment and expect in return that the company would provide wages and benefits, work, advancement, and training throughout the employee's working life. But volatile changes in the environment have disrupted this contract. As many organizations downsized, significant numbers of employees were eliminated. Employees who are left may feel little stability. In a fast-moving company, a person is hired and assigned to a project. The project changes over time, as do the person's tasks. Then the person is assigned to another project and then to still another.

These new projects require working with different groups and leaders and schedules, and people may be working in a virtual environment, where they rarely see their colleagues face to face.[23] Careers no longer progress up a vertical hierarchy but move across jobs horizontally. In many of today's companies, everyone is expected to be a self-motivated worker, with excellent interpersonal relationships, who is continuously acquiring new skills.

 TAKE ACTION

Learn to be flexible and work with various people in different teams.

discrimination
the hiring or promoting of applicants based on criteria that are not job relevant.

affirmative action
a policy requiring employers to take positive steps to guarantee equal employment opportunities for people within protected groups.

EXHIBIT 9.3
The Changing Social Contract

	New Contract	Old Contract
Employee	• Employability, personal responsibility • Partner in business improvement • Learning	• Job security • A cog in the machine • Knowing
Employer	• Continuous learning, lateral career movement, incentive compensation • Creative development opportunities • Challenging assignments • Information and resources	• Traditional compensation package • Standard training programs • Routine jobs • Limited information

SOURCES: Based on Louisa Wah, "The New Workplace Paradox," *Management Review* (January 1998): 7; and Douglas T. Hall and Jonathan E. Moss, "The New Protean Career Contract: Helping Organizations and Employees Adapt," *Organizational Dynamics* (Winter 1998): 22–37.

Exhibit 9.3 lists some elements of the new social contract. The new contract is based on the concept of employability rather than lifetime employment. Individuals manage their own careers; the organization no longer takes care of them or guarantees employment. Companies agree to pay somewhat higher wages and invest in creative training and development opportunities so that people will be more employable when the company no longer needs their services. Employees take more responsibility and control in their jobs, becoming partners in business improvement rather than cogs in a machine. In return, the organization provides challenging work assignments as well as information and resources to enable people to continually learn new skills. The new contract can provide many opportunities for employees to be more involved and express new aspects of themselves.

However, many employees are not prepared for new levels of cooperation or responsibility on the job. In addition, some companies take the new approach as an excuse to treat employees as economic factors to be used when needed and then let go. This attitude leads to a decline in morale and commitment in organizations, as well as a decline in performance. Studies in the United States and China found lower employee and firm performance and decreased commitment in companies where the interaction between employer and employee is treated as a contract-like economic exchange rather than a genuine human and social relationship.[24] In general, it is harder than it was in the past to gain an employee's full commitment and enthusiasm. One study found that even though most workers feel they are contributing to their companies' success, they are increasingly skeptical that their hard work is being fully recognized and appreciated.[25] Some companies find it hard to keep good workers because of diminished employee trust.

 Assess Your Answer

2 Hiring people to work for a company is about the economic contract between employer and employee.

ANSWER: In addition to the economic contract is the equally important social contract. If people feel they are not appreciated and are seen as replaceable machine parts, their motivation and loyalty will be diminished.

An important challenge for HRM is revising performance evaluation, training, compensation, and reward practices to be compatible with the new social contract. In addition, smart organizations contribute to employees' long-term success by offering extensive professional training and development opportunities, career information and assessment, and career coaching.[26] These programs help to preserve trust and enhance the organization's social capital. Even when employees are let go or voluntarily leave, they often maintain feelings of goodwill toward the company. Sometimes people leave because stress is too great.

HR ISSUES IN THE NEW WORKPLACE

The rapid change and turbulence in today's business environment bring significant new challenges for HRM. Some important current issues are becoming an employer of choice, responding to the increasing use of teams and project management, addressing the needs of temporary employees and virtual workers, acknowledging growing employee demands for work-life balance, and humanely managing downsizing.

BECOMING AN EMPLOYER OF CHOICE

The old social contract may be broken for good, but today's best companies recognize the importance of treating people right and thinking for the long term rather than looking for quick fixes based on an economic exchange relationship with employees. An *employer of choice* is a company that is highly attractive to potential employees because of HR practices that focus not just on tangible benefits such as pay and profit sharing but also on intangibles (such as work/life balance, a trust-based work climate, and a healthy corporate culture), and that embraces a long-term view to solving immediate problems.[27] To engage people and spur high commitment and performance, an employer of choice chooses a carefully balanced set of HR strategies, policies, and practices that are tailored to the organization's own unique goals and needs. Motek Software, for example, has a strict 9 A.M. to 5 P.M. policy and gives employees a full month of vacation each year. Founder and CEO Ann Price wants the best and brightest IT workers, and she doesn't want them to burn out and leave after a couple of years. The consulting and training firm, IHS Help Desk, on the other hand, doesn't expect people to stay more than a couple of years. People work long hours, but IHS keeps them motivated and builds social capital by offering plenty of training and career development opportunities.[28]

Teams and Projects. The advent of *teams* and *project management* is a major trend in today's workplace. People who used to work alone on the shop floor, in the advertising department, or in middle management are now thrown into teams and succeed as part of a group. Each member of the team acts like a manager, becoming responsible for quality standards, scheduling, and even hiring and firing other team members. With the emphasis on projects, the distinctions between job categories and descriptions are collapsing. Many of today's workers straddle functional and departmental boundaries and handle multiple tasks and responsibilities.[29]

Temporary Employees. In the opening years of the twenty-first century, the largest employer in the United States was a temporary employment agency, Manpower Inc.[30] Temporary agencies grew rapidly during the 1990s, and early 2000s, and millions of employees today are in temporary firm placements. People in these temporary jobs do everything from data entry, to project management, to becoming the interim CEO. Although in the past, most temporary workers were in clerical and manufacturing positions, in recent years, demand has grown for professionals, particularly financial analysts, interim managers, information technology specialists, accountants, product managers, and operations experts.[31] **Contingent workers** are people who work for an organization but

CONCEPT CONNECTION

It is technology—such as laptops, home computers, and broadband—that makes **telecommuting** possible. But it's social and cultural trends that make its continuing growth probable. For example, many employees believe telecommuting makes it easier to achieve **work-life balance,** whereas employers find the new arrangement expands their labor pool and cuts overhead expenses. The federal government has encouraged the practice as well because fewer commuters means improved air quality and reduced energy consumption. So managers will continue to find themselves dealing with the issues telecommuting raises: Just how do you select, train, monitor, and reward employees you very rarely see?

◀ TAKE ACTION

As a new manager, appreciate the opportunities that are offered by the new social contract. Allow people to make genuine contributions of their talents to the organization, and provide them with challenging work and opportunities to learn new skills they can transfer to other jobs in the future.

contingent workers people who work for an organization but not on a permanent or full-time basis, including temporary placements, contracted professionals, or leased employees.

not on a permanent or full-time basis. These workers include temporary placements, contracted professionals, leased employees, or part-time workers. One estimate is that contingent workers make up at least 25 percent of the U.S. workforce.[32] The use of contingent workers means reduced payroll and benefit costs, as well as increased flexibility for both employers and employees.

Technology. Related trends are virtual teams and telecommuting. Some **virtual teams** are made up entirely of people who are hired on a project-by-project basis. Team members are geographically or organizationally dispersed and rarely meet face to face, doing their work instead through advanced information technologies and collaborative software. **Telecommuting** means using computers and telecommunications equipment to do work without going to an office. TeleService Resources has more than 25 telephone agents who work entirely from home, using state-of-the-art call-center technology that provides seamless interaction with TSR's Dallas–Fort Worth call center.[33] Millions of people in the United States and Europe telecommute on a regular or occasional basis.[34] Wireless Internet devices, laptops, cell phones, and fax machines make it possible for people to work just about anywhere. A growing aspect of this phenomenon is called *extreme telecommuting,* which means that people live and work in countries far away from the organization's physical location. For example, Paolo Concini works from his home in Bali, Indonesia, even though his company's offices are located in China and Europe.[35]

Work/Life Balance. Telecommuting is one way organizations are helping employees lead more balanced lives. By working part of the time from home, for example, parents can avoid some of the conflicts they often feel in coordinating their work and family responsibilities. *Flexible scheduling* for regular employees is also important in today's workplace. Approximately 27 percent of the U.S. workforce has flexible hours. When and where an employee does the job is becoming less important. In addition, broad work/life balance initiatives play a critical role in retention strategy, partly in response to the shift in expectations among young employees.[36]

Typically, Gen Y employees work smart and work hard on the job, but they refuse to let work be their whole life. Unlike their parents, who placed a high priority on career, Gen Y workers expect the job to accommodate their personal lives.[37]

Many managers recognize that individuals may have personal needs that require special attention. Some HR responses include benefits such as on-site gym facilities and childcare, assistance with arranging childcare and eldercare, and paid leaves or sabbaticals. Work-life balance is often necessary in the dating process, as shown in the Spotlight on Collaboration box.

Downsizing. In some cases, organizations have more people than they need and have to let some employees go. **Downsizing,** which refers to an intentional, planned reduction in the size of a company's workforce, is a reality for many of today's companies. In the first three years of the twenty-first century, for example, employers cut some 2.7 million jobs.[38] Some researchers found that massive downsizing often failed to achieve the intended benefits and, in some cases, significantly harmed the organization.[39] Unless HRM departments effectively and humanely manage the downsizing process, layoffs can lead to decreased morale and performance. Managers can smooth the downsizing process by regularly communicating with employees and providing them with as much information as possible, providing assistance to workers who will lose their jobs, and using training and development to help address the emotional needs of remaining employees to enable them to cope with new or additional responsibilities.[40]

These various issues present many challenges for organizations and HRM, such as new ways of recruiting and compensation that address the interests and needs of contingent and

TAKE ACTION ▶
As a manager, be mindful of your employees' need to achieve balance in their lives. Generation Y workers are a fast-growing segment of the workforce.

virtual team
a team made up of members who are geographically or organizationally dispersed, rarely meet face to face, and do their work using advanced information technologies.

telecommuting
using computers and telecommunications equipment to perform work from home or another remote location.

downsizing
intentional, planned reduction in the size of a company's workforce.

SOURCE: Sue Shellenbarger, "Dinner and a PowerPoint?" *Wall Street Journal* (June 28, 2007): D1-2.

Spotlight on Collaboration

Laptop Dating

Young entrepreneurs such as Patricia Handschiegel, find themselves so immersed in their work that a typical date involves dinner, followed by both parties taking out their laptops and working for a few hours and then doing dessert. "We laugh and have a great time," she says, admitting it doesn't sound like fun. But for her, it's either that or no social life. Without bringing the laptop along, "I probably wouldn't have left the house or office" for any man.

Working vacations have led to working dates, fueled by wall-to-wall hours in many jobs, as well as the fact that all-consuming entrepreneurial ventures are being started by younger and younger people. Add this to compatibility indices: matching work ethics. Scott Friedman finds that relationships where the woman isn't as busy as he is generally tank. If after dinner, he'd want to get some work done, "it was uncomfortable for me because I knew she was just waiting for me to spend time with her," he says.

Letting work intrude on dates can be a way of avoiding emotional intimacy, says therapist Ian Kerner. Working on a date is indicative of an inability to have a relationship be first in someone's life. Also, working can get in the way of communication, says relationship author Michael French. "The values we associate with work success are very different from the values we associate with relationship success," he says.

Those who want working dates should be clear up front. Let the other party know you have a deadline and won't be available 100 percent of time. But also say what time you will stop work and watch a DVD or have dessert. Finding someone with similar work habits can be the foundation for a good relationship. Clothing designer Liz Dennis found that when first dating George Allen, who worked in a private equity firm. After dinner, he'd work on this computer or take conference calls, while she chose fabric swatches. Working side-by-side led to marriage in 2005. Now they even type one another's e-mails. "For us," Liz Dennis Allen says, "It has definitely worked out."

---

virtual workers, new training methods that help people work cross-functionally, or new ways to retain valuable employees. All of these concerns are taken into consideration as HR managers work toward the three primary HR goals described earlier: attracting, developing, and maintaining an effective workforce.

Attracting an Effective Workforce

The first goal of HRM is to attract individuals who show signs of becoming valued, productive, and satisfied employees. The first step in attracting an effective workforce involves HR planning, in which managers or HRM professionals predict the need for new employees based on the types of vacancies that exist, as illustrated in Exhibit 9.4. The second step is to use recruiting procedures to communicate with potential applicants. The third step is to select from the applicants those persons believed to be the best potential contributors to the organization. Finally, the new employee is welcomed into the organization.

Underlying the organization's effort to attract employees is a matching model. With the **matching model,** the organization and the individual attempt to match the needs, interests, and values that they offer each other.[41] HRM professionals attempt to identify a correct match. For example, a small software developer might require long hours from creative, technically skilled employees. In return, it can offer freedom from bureaucracy, tolerance of idiosyncrasies, and potentially high pay. A large manufacturer can offer employment security and stability, but it might have more rules and regulations and require greater skills for "getting approval from the higher-ups." The individual who would thrive working for the software developer might feel stymied and unhappy working for a large manufacturer. Both the company and the employee are interested in finding a good match.

matching model
an employee selection approach in which the organization and the applicant attempt to match each other's needs, interests, and values.

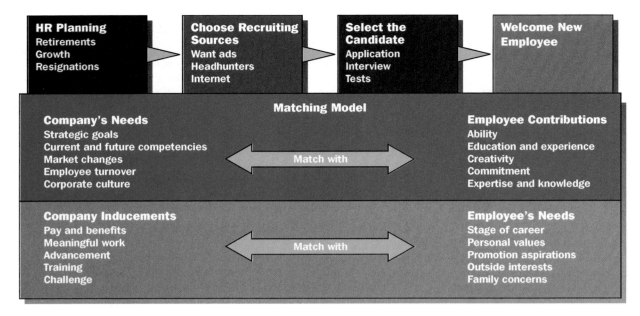

EXHIBIT 9.4

Attracting an Effective Workforce

A new approach, called *job sculpting*, attempts to match people to jobs that enable them to fulfill deeply embedded life interests.[42] This matching effort often requires that HR managers play detective to find out what really makes a person happy. The idea is that people can fulfill deep-seated needs and interests on the job, which will induce them to stay with the organization.

HUMAN RESOURCE PLANNING

Human resource planning is the forecasting of HR needs and the projected matching of individuals with expected vacancies. HR planning begins with several questions:

- What new technologies are emerging, and how will these affect the work system?
- What is the volume of the business likely to be in the next 5 to 10 years?
- What is the turnover rate, and how much, if any, is avoidable?

The responses to these questions are used to formulate specific questions pertaining to HR activities, such as the following:

- How many senior managers will we need during this time period?
- What types of engineers will we need, and how many?
- Are persons with adequate computer skills available for meeting our projected needs?
- How many administrative personnel—technicians, IT specialists—will we need to support the additional managers and engineers?
- Can we use temporary, contingent, or virtual workers to handle some tasks?[43]

Answers to these questions help define the direction for the organization's HRM strategy. For example, if forecasting suggests a strong upcoming need for more technically trained individuals, the organization can (1) define the jobs and skills needed in some detail, (2) hire and train recruiters to look for the specified skills, and (3) provide new training for existing employees. By anticipating future HR needs, the organization can prepare itself to meet competitive challenges more effectively than organizations that react to problems only as they arise.

human resource planning
the forecasting of HR needs and the projected matching of individuals with expected job vacancies.

recruiting
the activities or practices that define the desired characteristics of applicants for specific jobs.

job analysis
the systematic process of gathering and interpreting information about the essential duties, tasks, and responsibilities of a job.

RECRUITING

Recruiting is defined as "activities or practices that define the characteristics of applicants to whom selection procedures are ultimately applied."[44] Today, recruiting is sometimes referred to as *talent acquisition* to reflect the importance of the human factor in the organization's success.[45] Although we frequently think of campus recruiting as a typical recruiting activity, many organizations use *internal recruiting,* or *promote-from-within* policies, to fill their high-level positions.[46] At oil field services company Schlumberger, Ltd., for example, current employees are given preference when a position opens. Eighty percent of top managers have been moved up the ranks based on the promote-from-within philosophy; many of them started fresh out of school as field engineers.[47] Internal recruiting has several advantages: It is less costly than an external search, and it generates higher employee commitment, development, and satisfaction because it offers opportunities for career advancement to employees rather than outsiders.

Frequently, however, *external recruiting*—recruiting newcomers from outside the organization—is advantageous. Applicants are available through a variety of outside sources, including advertising, state employment services, online recruiting services, private employment agencies *(headhunters)*, job fairs, and employee referrals.

Assessing Organizational Needs. An important step in recruiting is to get a clear picture of what kinds of people the organization needs. Basic building blocks of HRM include job analysis, job descriptions, and job specifications. **Job analysis** is a systematic process of gathering and interpreting information about the essential duties, tasks, and responsibilities of a job, as well as about the context within which the job is performed.[48] To perform job analysis, managers or specialists ask about work activities and work flow, the degree of supervision given and received in the job, knowledge and skills needed, performance standards, working conditions, and so forth. The manager then prepares a written **job description,** which is a clear and concise summary of the specific tasks, duties, and responsibilities, and **job specification,** which outlines the knowledge, skills, education, physical abilities, and other characteristics needed to adequately perform the job.

Job analysis helps organizations recruit the right kind of people and match them to appropriate jobs. For example, to enhance internal recruiting, Sara Lee Corporation identified 6 functional areas and 24 significant skills that it wants its finance executives to develop, as illustrated in Exhibit 9.5. Managers are tracked on their development and moved into other positions to help them acquire the needed skills.[49] New software programs and Web-based, on-demand subscription services are aiding today's companies in more efficiently and effectively recruiting and matching the right candidates with the right jobs.

Realistic Job Previews. Job analysis also helps enhance recruiting effectiveness by enabling the creation of **realistic job previews.** A realistic job preview (RJP) gives applicants all pertinent and realistic information—positive and negative—about the job

●●●● CONCEPT CONNECTION ●●●●

This ad from *Black Enterprise* magazine enhances **external recruiting** by giving potential applicants a **realistic job preview.** The applicant must possess critical skills such as speaking a foreign language, have a four-year college degree plus three years of professional work experience, be willing to live anywhere on assignment, be between the ages of 23 and 36, and be able to pass "a rigorous physical fitness test." If you possess these requirements, you can even apply online at http://www.fbijobs.com.

job description
a concise summary of the specific tasks and responsibilities of a particular job.

job specification
an outline of the knowledge, skills, education, and physical abilities needed to adequately perform a job.

realistic job preview (RJP)
a recruiting approach that gives applicants all pertinent and realistic information about the job and the organization.

EXHIBIT 9.5

Sara Lee's Required Skills for Finance Executives

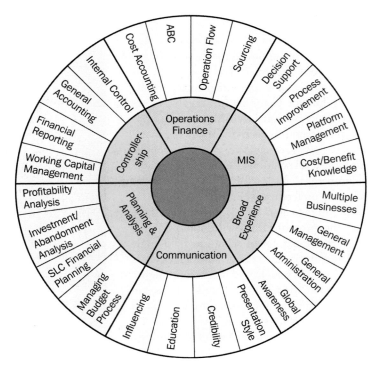

SOURCE: Victoria Griffith, "When Only Internal Expertise Will Do," *CFO* (October 1998): 95–96, 102.

and the organization.[50] RJPs enhance employee satisfaction and reduce turnover because they facilitate matching individuals, jobs, and organizations. Individuals have a better basis on which to determine their suitability to the organization and "self-select" into or out of positions based on full information.

Legal Considerations. Organizations must ensure that their recruiting practices conform to the law. As discussed earlier in this chapter, EEO laws stipulate that recruiting and hiring decisions cannot discriminate on the basis of race, national origin, religion, or gender. The Americans with Disabilities Act underscored the need for well-written job descriptions and specifications that accurately reflect the mental and physical dimensions of jobs, so that people with disabilities will not be discriminated against. *Affirmative action* refers to the use of goals, timetables, or other methods in recruiting to promote the hiring, development, and retention of *protected groups*—persons historically underrepresented in the workplace. For example, a city might establish a goal of recruiting one black firefighter for every white firefighter until the proportion of black firefighters is commensurate with the black population in the community.

Most large companies try to comply with affirmative action and EEO guidelines. Prudential Insurance Company's policy is presented in Exhibit 9.6. Prudential actively recruits employees and takes affirmative action steps to recruit individuals from all walks of life.

E-cruiting. One of the fastest-growing approaches to recruiting is use of the Internet for recruiting, or *e-cruiting*.[51] Recruiting job applicants online dramatically extends the organization's recruiting reach, offering access to a wider pool of applicants and saving time and money. Besides posting job openings on company websites, many organizations use commercial recruiting sites such as Monster.com, where job seekers can post their résumés, and companies can search for qualified applicants. In addition, as competition for high-quality employees heats up, new online companies, such as Jobster and JobThread, emerge

EXHIBIT 9.6

Prudential's Corporate
Recruiting Policy

An Equal Opportunity Employer

Prudential recruits, hires, trains, promotes, and compensates individuals without regard to race, color, religion or creed, age, sex, marital status, national origin, ancestry, liability for service in the armed forces of the United States, status as a special disabled veteran or veteran of the Vietnam era, or physical or mental handicap.

This is official company policy because: · we believe it is right
                                        · it makes good business sense
                                        · it is the law

We are also committed to an ongoing program of affirmative action in which members of underrepresented groups are actively sought out and employed for opportunities in all parts and at all levels of the company. In employing people from all walks of life, Prudential gains access to the full experience of our diverse society.

to help companies search for "passive candidates," people who aren't looking for jobs but might be the best fit for a company's opening. Expedia calls it "anti-inbox recruiting." Instead of waiting until it has job openings, it uses Jobster to build up a ready supply of passive prospects who have the skills and experience the company might need.[52]

Companies as diverse as Deloitte Touche Tohmatsu, Cisco Systems, and Atkinsson Congregational Church use the Web for recruiting. Organizations have not given up their traditional recruiting strategies, but the Internet gives HR managers new tools for searching the world to find the best available talent.

Other Recent Approaches to Recruiting. Organizations are finding other ways to enhance their recruiting success. One highly effective approach is getting referrals from current employees. A company's employees often know of someone who would be qualified for a position and fit in with the organization's culture. Many organizations offer cash awards to employees who submit names of people who subsequently accept employment because referral by current employees is one of the cheapest and most reliable methods of external recruiting.[53] NewsMarket, a New York-city based company that distributes broadcast-standard video clips over the Internet, shelled out $10,000 in cash awards to employees who referred candidates in 2005. Referrals generate about 40 percent of the new hires at NewsMarket.[54] At many of today's top companies, managers emphasize that recruiting is part of everyone's job.

Having employees assist with recruiting has the added bonus of providing potential candidates with a realistic job preview. At the Container Store, employees share with customers what it's like to work for the company. They want people to know the positive and potentially negative aspects of the job because it's important to get people who will fit in.

Some companies turn to nontraditional sources to find dedicated employees, particularly in a tight labor market. For example, when Walker Harris couldn't find workers for his ice company on the west side of Chicago, Harris Ice, he began hiring former prison inmates, many of whom have turned out to be reliable, loyal employees.[55] Manufacturer Dee Zee, which makes aluminum truck accessories in a factory in Des Moines, Iowa, found a source of hard-working employees among refugees from Bosnia, Vietnam, and Kosovo.[56] Since 1998, Bank of America has hired and trained more than 3,000 former welfare recipients in positions that offer the potential for promotions and long-term careers. Numerous companies recruit older workers, who typically have lower turnover rates, especially for part-time jobs. The Home Depot offers "snowbird specials"—winter work in Florida and summers in Maine. Border's Bookstores entices retired teachers with book discounts and reading and discussion groups.[57] Recruiting on a global basis is on the rise, as well. Public schools are recruiting teachers from overseas. High-tech companies are looking for qualified workers in foreign countries because they cannot find people with the right skills in the United States.[58]

SELECTING

The next step for managers is to select desired employees from the pool of recruited applicants. In the **selection** process, employers assess applicants' characteristics in an attempt to determine the "fit" between the job and applicant characteristics.

Several selection devices are used for assessing applicant qualifications. The most frequently used are the application form, interview, employment test, and assessment center. Studies indicate that the greater the skill requirements and work demands of an open position, the greater the number and variety of selection tools the organization will use.[59] HR professionals may use a combination of devices to obtain a valid prediction of employee job performance. **Validity** refers to the relationship between a person's score on a selection device and that person's future job performance. A valid selection procedure will provide high scores that correspond to subsequent high job performance. One way to determine fit is to look at your customer base.

APPLICATION FORM

The **application form** is used to collect information about the applicant's education, previous job experience, and other background characteristics. Research in the life insurance industry shows that biographical information inventories can validly predict future job success.[60]

One pitfall to be avoided is the inclusion of questions that are irrelevant to job success. In line with affirmative action, the application form should not ask questions that will create an adverse impact on protected groups unless the questions are clearly related to the job.[61] For example, employers should not ask whether the applicant rents or owns his or her own home because (1) an applicant's response might adversely affect his or her chances at the job, (2) minorities and women may be less likely to own a home, and (3) home ownership is probably unrelated to job performance. By contrast, the CPA exam is relevant to job performance in a CPA firm; thus, it is appropriate to ask whether an applicant for employment has passed the CPA exam, even if only one-half of all female or minority applicants have done so versus nine-tenths of male applicants.

INTERVIEW

The *interview* serves as a two-way communication channel that allows both the organization and the applicant to collect information that would otherwise be difficult to obtain. This selection technique is used in almost every job category in nearly every organization. It is another area where the organization can get into legal trouble if the interviewer asks questions that violate EEO guidelines. Exhibit 9.7 lists some examples of appropriate and inappropriate interview questions.

Although widely used, the interview is not generally a valid predictor of job performance. Studies of interviewing suggest that people tend to make snap judgments of others within the first few seconds of meeting them and only rarely change their opinions based on anything that occurs in the interview.[62] However, the interview as a selection tool has high *face validity*. That is, it seems valid to employers, and managers prefer to hire someone only after they have been through some form of interview, preferably face to face.

Today's organizations are trying different approaches to overcome the limitations of the interview. Some put candidates through a series of interviews, each one conducted by a different person and each one probing a different aspect of the candidate. At Microsoft, for example, interviewers include HRM professionals, managers of the appropriate functional department, peers, and people outside the department who are well grounded in the corporate culture.[63] Other companies, including Virginia Power and Philip Morris USA, use

selection
the process of determining the skills, abilities, and other attributes a person needs to perform a particular job.

validity
the relationship between an applicant's score on a selection device and his or her future job performance.

application form
a device for collecting information about an applicant's education, previous job experience, and other background characteristics.

People on the Bus

As a new manager, how much emphasis will you give to getting the right people on your team? How much emphasis on people is needed? Find out by answering the following questions based on your expectations and beliefs for handling the people part of your management job. Please indicate whether each item is Mostly True or Mostly False for you.

	Mostly True				Mostly False
1. I will readily fire someone who isn't working out for the interests of the organization.	1	2	3	4	5
2. Selecting the right people for a winning business team is as important to me as it is to a winning sports team.	1	2	3	4	5
3. I expect to spend 40 percent to 60 percent of my management time on issues such as recruiting, developing, and placing people.	1	2	3	4	5
4. I will paint a realistic picture of negative job aspects that will help scare off the wrong people for the job.	1	2	3	4	5
5. My priority as a manager is first to hire the right people, second to put people in the right positions, and third to then decide strategy and vision.	1	2	3	4	5
6. With the right people on my team, problems of motivation and supervision will largely go away.	1	2	3	4	5
7. I expect that hiring the right people is a lengthy and arduous process.	1	2	3	4	5
8. I view firing someone as helping them find the place where they belong to find fulfillment.	1	2	3	4	5

SCORING AND INTERPRETATION: Most new managers are shocked at the large amount of time, effort, and skill required to recruit, place, and retain the right people. In recent years, the importance of "getting the right people on the bus" has been described in popular business books such as *Good to Great* and *Execution*. The right people can make an organization great; the wrong people can be catastrophic. Many of the questions are based on the ideas expressed in recent popular books.

Give yourself one point for each mostly true answer (choosing 1 or 2); give yourself zero points if you choose 3, 4 or 5. If you scored 4 or less, you may be in for a shock as a new manager. People issues will take up most of your time, and if you don't handle people correctly, your effectiveness will suffer. You should learn how to get the right people on the bus, and how to get the wrong people off the bus. The faster you learn these lessons, the better new manager you will be. A score of 5 or more suggests you have the right understanding and expectations for becoming a manager and dealing with people on the bus.

SOURCES: Based on ideas presented in Jim Collins, *Good to Great: Why Some Companies Make the Leap . . . and Others Don't* (New York: Harper Business, 2001); and other publications.

EXHIBIT 9.7

Employment Applications and Interviews: What Can You Ask?

Category	Okay to Ask	Inappropriate or Illegal to Ask
National origin	• The applicant's name • If applicant has ever worked under a different name	• The origin of applicant's name • Applicant's ancestry/ethnicity
Race	• Nothing	• Race or color of skin
Disabilities	• Whether applicant has any disabilities that might inhibit performance of job	• If applicant has any physical or mental defects • If applicant has ever filed workers' compensation claim
Age	• If applicant is over 18	• Applicant's age • When applicant graduated from high school
Religion	• Nothing	• Applicant's religious affiliation • What religious holidays applicant observes
Criminal record	• If applicant has ever been convicted of a crime	• If applicant has ever been arrested
Marital/family status	• Nothing	• Marital status, number of children or planned children • Childcare arrangements
Education and experience	• Where applicant went to school • Prior work experience	• When applicant graduated • Hobbies
Citizenship	• If applicant has a legal right to work in the United States	• If applicant is a citizen of another country

SOURCES: Based on "Appropriate and Inappropriate Interview Questions," in George Bohlander, Scott Snell, and Arthur Sherman, *Managing Human Resources*, 12th ed. (Cincinnati, OH: South-Western, 2001): 207; and "Guidelines to Lawful and Unlawful Preemployment Inquiries," Appendix E, in Robert L. Mathis and John H. Jackson, *Human Resource Management*, 2nd ed. (Cincinnati, OH: South-Western, 2002): 189–190.

TAKE ACTION ⊙⟩

As a new manager, get the right people in the right jobs by assessing your team's or department's needs, offering realistic job previews, using a variety of recruiting methods, and striving to match the needs and interests of the individual to those of the organization. It is typically wise to use a variety of selection tools. For lower-skilled jobs, an application and brief interview might be enough, but higher-skilled jobs call for a combination of interviews, aptitude and skills tests, and assessment exercises.

employment test
a written or computer-based test designed to measure a particular attribute such as intelligence or aptitude.

panel interviews, in which the candidate meets with several interviewers who take turns asking questions, to increase interview validity.[64] The Container Store, described earlier, uses group interviews, in which as many as 10 candidates are asked to make a pitch for a product that solves a particular organization challenge. This approach gives managers a chance to see how people function as part of a team.[65]

Some organizations also supplement traditional interviewing information with *computer-based interviews.* This type of interview typically requires a candidate to answer a series of multiple-choice questions tailored to the specific job. The answers are compared to an ideal profile or to a profile developed on the basis of other candidates. Companies such as Pinkerton Security, Coopers & Lybrand, and Pic 'n Pay Shoe Stores found computer-based interviews to be valuable for searching out information regarding the applicant's honesty, work attitude, drug history, candor, dependability, and self-motivation.[66] Sometimes the interview actually starts online, as shown in the Spotlight on Skills box.

Employment Test. **Employment tests** may include intelligence tests, aptitude and ability tests, and personality inventories, particularly those shown to be valid predictors. Many companies today are particularly interested in personality inventories that measure such characteristics as openness to learning, initiative, responsibility, creativity, and emotional stability. Brian Kautz of Arnold Logistics uses a Web-based personality assessment called the Predictive Index (PI) to hire good employees for Arnold's IT department. The PI, originally developed in the 1950s, provides information about the working conditions that are most rewarding to an applicant and that make the person the most motivated and productive. The test is based on the notion that different types of jobs require different personality characteristics and behaviors.[67]

Assessment Center. First developed by psychologists at AT&T, assessment centers are used to select individuals with high potential for managerial careers by such organizations as IBM, General Electric, and JCPenney.[68] **Assessment centers** present a series of managerial situations to groups of applicants over, say, a two- or three-day period. One technique is the *in-basket simulation,* which requires the applicant to play the role of a manager who must decide how to respond to 10 memos in his or her in-basket within a two-hour period. Panels of two or three trained judges observe the applicant's decisions and assess the extent to which they reflect interpersonal, communication, and problem-solving skills.

Assessment centers have proven to be valid predictors of managerial success, and some organizations now use them for hiring front-line workers as well. Mercury Communications in England uses an assessment center to select customer assistants. Applicants participate in simulated exercises with customers and in various other exercises designed to assess their listening skills, customer sensitivity, and ability to cope under pressure.[69]

Developing an Effective Workforce

Following selection, the next goal of HRM is to develop employees into an effective workforce. Development includes training and performance appraisal.

assessment center
a technique for selecting individuals with high managerial potential based on their performance on a series of simulated managerial tasks.

TAKE ACTION ⟩⟩

Remember that insufficient training is one reason many employees fail on the job.

TRAINING AND DEVELOPMENT

Training and development represent a planned effort by an organization to facilitate employees' learning of job-related skills and behaviors.[70] Organizations spent some $51.1 billion for training in 2005. The training budget of IBM alone in that year was $750 million.[71] The most common method of training is on-the-job training. In **on-the-job training (OJT),** an experienced employee is asked to take a new employee "under his or her wing" and show the newcomer how to perform job duties. OJT has many advantages, such as few out-of-pocket costs for training facilities, materials, or instructor fees and easy transfer of learning back to the job. When implemented well, OJT is considered the fastest and most effective means of facilitating learning in the workplace.[72] One type of OJT involves moving people to various types of jobs within the organization, where they work with experienced employees to learn different tasks. This *cross-training* may place an employee in a new position for as short a time as a few hours or for as long as a year, enabling the employee to develop new skills and giving the organization greater flexibility.

Another type of on-the-job training is *mentoring,* which means a more experienced employee is paired with a newcomer or a less-experienced worker to provide guidance, support, and learning opportunities. Other frequently used training methods include the following:

- *Orientation training,* in which newcomers are introduced to the organization's culture, standards, and goals.

- *Classroom training,* including lectures, films, audiovisual techniques, and simulations—makes up approximately 70 percent of all formal corporate training.[73]

- *Self-directed learning,* also called programmed instruction, which involves the use of books, manuals, or computers to provide subject matter in highly organized and logical sequences that require employees to answer a series of questions about the material.

- *Computer-based training,* sometimes called *e-training,* including computer-assisted instruction, Web-based training, and teletraining. As with self-directed learning, the employee works at his or her own pace, and instruction is individualized, but the training program is interactive, and more complex, nonstructured information can be communicated.[74] E-training has soared in recent years because it offers cost savings to organizations and allows people to learn at their own pace.[74]

Exhibit 9.8 shows the most frequently used types and methods of training in today's organizations.

Corporate Universities. A recent popular approach to training and development is the corporate university. A **corporate university** is an in-house training and education facility that offers broad-based learning opportunities for employees—and frequently for customers, suppliers, and strategic partners as well—throughout their careers.[75] One well-known corporate university is Hamburger University, McDonald's worldwide training center, which has been in existence for more than 40 years. Numerous other companies, including IBM, FedEx, General Electric, Intel, Harley-Davidson, and Capital One, pump millions of dollars into corporate universities to continually build human capital.[76] Employees at Caterpillar attend courses at Caterpillar University, which combines e-training, classroom sessions, and hands-on training activities. The U.S. Department of Defense runs Defense Acquisition University to provide ongoing training to 129,000 military and civilian workers in acquisitions, technology, and logistics.[77] Although corporate universities have extended their reach with new technology that enables distance learning via videoconferencing and online education, most emphasize the importance of classroom interaction.[78]

Promotion from Within. Another way to further employee development is through promotion from within, which helps companies retain valuable people. This

on-the-job training (OJT)
a type of training in which an experienced employee "adopts" a new employee to teach him or her how to perform job duties.

corporate university
an in-house training and education facility that offers broad-based learning opportunities for employees.

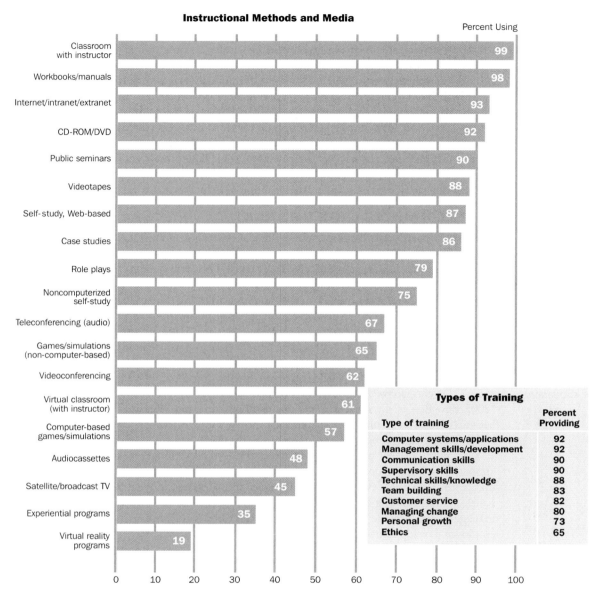

Instructional Methods and Media

Percent Using

Method	Percent
Classroom with instructor	99
Workbooks/manuals	98
Internet/intranet/extranet	93
CD-ROM/DVD	92
Public seminars	90
Videotapes	88
Self-study, Web-based	87
Case studies	86
Role plays	79
Noncomputerized self-study	75
Teleconferencing (audio)	67
Games/simulations (non-computer-based)	65
Videoconferencing	62
Virtual classroom (with instructor)	61
Computer-based games/simulations	57
Audiocassettes	48
Satellite/broadcast TV	45
Experiential programs	35
Virtual reality programs	19

Types of Training

Type of training	Percent Providing
Computer systems/applications	92
Management skills/development	92
Communication skills	90
Supervisory skills	90
Technical skills/knowledge	88
Team building	83
Customer service	82
Managing change	80
Personal growth	73
Ethics	65

SOURCE: Methods data from Tammy Galvin, "2003 Industry Report," *Training* (October 2003): 21+. Reprinted with permission from the October 2003 issue of *Training* magazine, Copyright 2003, Bill Communications, Minneapolis, Minn. All rights reserved. Not for resales. Types data from Holly Dolezalek, "2005 Industry Report," *Training* (December 2005): 14–28.

EXHIBIT 9.8

Types and Methods of Training

provides challenging assignments, prescribes new responsibilities, and helps employees grow by expanding and developing their abilities. The Peebles Hydro Hotel in Scotland is passionate about promoting from within as a way to retain good people and give them opportunities for growth. A maid has been promoted to head housekeeper, a wine waitress to restaurant head, and a student worker to deputy manager. The hotel also provides constant training in all areas. These techniques, combined with a commitment to job flexibility, have helped the hotel retain high-quality workers at a time when others in the tourism and hospitality industry are suffering from a shortage of skilled labor. Staff members with 10, 15, or even 20 years of service aren't uncommon at Hydro.[79]

Workforce Optimization. A related approach is **workforce optimization,** which can be defined as putting the right person in the right place at the right time.[80] With

workforce optimization
implementing strategies to put the right people in the right jobs, make the best use of employee talent and skills, and develop human capital for the future.

today's emphasis on managing and building human capital, HR professionals are pursuing a range of strategies that help organizations make the best use of the talent they have and effectively develop that talent for the future. New software programs and information technology can help identify people with the right mix of skills to tackle a new project, for example, as well as pinpoint where to move staff internally to ensure they have opportunities for growth and development. IBM is a leader in workforce optimization with a technology-based staff-deployment tool it calls the Workforce Management Initiative. One use of the system is as a sort of in-house recruiting tool that lets managers search for employees with the precise skills needed for particular projects. However, the system's greatest impact is that it helps HR professionals and managers analyze what skills employees have, see how those talents match up with current and anticipated needs in the business and technology environment, and devise job transfers and other training to help close skills gaps.[81]

PERFORMANCE APPRAISAL

Performance appraisal comprises the steps of observing and assessing employee performance, recording the assessment, and providing feedback to the employee. During performance appraisal, skillful managers give feedback and praise concerning the acceptable elements of the employee's performance. They also describe performance areas that need improvement. Employees can use this information to change their job performance.

TAKE ACTION ‣›
Remember that more frequent feedback to employees is more effective than the once-a-year evaluation.

Performance appraisal can also reward high performers with merit pay, recognition, and other rewards. However, the most recent thinking is that linking performance appraisal to rewards has unintended consequences. The idea is that performance appraisal should be ongoing, not something that is done once a year as part of a consideration of raises. At go2call.com, a provider of VOIP (voice over Internet protocol) phone services, people are reviewed every two weeks. Founders John Nix and Larry Speer were ranked among the 15 "2005 Best Bosses" by *Fortune Small Business* magazine and Winning Workplaces, partly because of innovative practices that let their mostly young workers know how they're doing and how they can get better.[82]

Generally, HRM professionals concentrate on two things to make performance appraisal a positive force in their organizations: (1) the accurate assessment of performance through the development and application of assessment systems such as rating scales, and (2) training managers to effectively use the performance appraisal interview, so managers can provide feedback that will reinforce good performance and motivate employee development.

Assessing Performance Accurately. To obtain an accurate performance rating, managers acknowledge that jobs are multidimensional and performance thus may be multidimensional as well. For example, a sports broadcaster might perform well on the job-knowledge dimension; that is, she or he might be able to report facts and figures about the players and describe which rule applies when there is a questionable play on the field. But the same broadcaster might not perform as well on another dimension, such as communication. The person might be unable to express the information in a colorful way that interests the audience or might interrupt the other broadcasters.

For performance to be rated accurately, the appraisal system should require the rater to assess each relevant performance dimension. A multidimensional form increases the usefulness of the performance appraisal and facilitates employee growth and development.

performance appraisal
the process of observing and evaluating an employee's performance, recording the assessment, and providing feedback to the employee.

360-degree feedback
a process that uses multiple raters, including self-rating, to appraise employee performance and guide development.

A recent trend in performance appraisal is called **360-degree feedback,** a process that uses multiple raters, including self-rating, as a way to increase awareness of strengths and weaknesses and guide employee development. Members of the appraisal group may include supervisors, co-workers, and customers, as well as the individual, thus providing appraisal of the employee from a variety of perspectives.[83] One study found that 26 percent of companies used some type of multirater performance appraisal.[84]

Another alternative performance-evaluation method is the *performance review ranking system*.[85] This method grew quite popular over the past several years, with as many as one third of U.S. corporations using some type of forced ranking system.[86] However, because these systems essentially evaluate employees by pitting them against one another, the method is increasingly coming under fire. As most commonly used, a manager evaluates his or her direct reports relative to one another and categorizes each on a scale, such as A = outstanding performance, B = high-middle performance, or C = in need of improvement. Most companies routinely fire those managers falling in the bottom 10 percent of the ranking. Proponents say the technique provides an effective way to assess performance and offer guidance for employee development. But critics of these systems, sometimes called *rank and yank,* argue that they are based on subjective judgments, produce skewed results, and discriminate against employees who are "different" from the mainstream. A class-action lawsuit charges that Ford's ranking system discriminates against older managers. Use of the system has also triggered employee lawsuits at Conoco and Microsoft, and employment lawyers warn that other suits will follow.[87]

In addition, critics warn that ranking systems significantly hinder collaboration and risk taking, which are increasingly important for today's companies striving for innovation. One recent study found that forced rankings that include firing the bottom 5 or 10 percent can lead to a dramatic improvement in organizational performance in the short term, but the benefits dissipate over several years as people become focused on competing with one another rather than improving the business.[88] Many companies, including General Electric, the most famous advocate of forced rankings in recent years, are building more flexibility into the performance review ranking system, and some are abandoning it altogether.[89]

Despite these concerns, the appropriate use of performance ranking has been useful for many companies, especially as a short-term way to improve performance. A forced ranking system instituted by new HR director Priscilla Vacassin, for instance, has been one key to helping the British banking firm Abbey recover from years of sluggish performance.[90] A variation of the system is helping U.S. restaurant chain Applebee's retain quality workers in the high-turnover restaurant business.

Performance Evaluation Errors. Although we would like to believe that every manager assesses employees' performance in a careful and bias-free manner, researchers have identified several rating problems.[91] One of the most dangerous

---

Applebee's

Most people working in fast-food and casual dining restaurants don't stay long. Turnover of hourly employees is a perpetual problem, averaging more than 200 percent a year in the casual dining sector for the past 30 years. Applebee's managers wanted to reduce their turnover rate, but they also wanted to focus their retention efforts on the best people.

A key aspect of the new retention strategy was the Applebee's Performance Management system, called ApplePM. ApplePM took performance appraisal to the Web, making it easier for managers to complete the evaluations and—more importantly—put the results to good use. Twice a year, each hourly employee conducts a self-evaluation that covers nine areas: appearance, reliability, fun (including the ability to tolerate frustration), ability, guest service, willingness to be a team player, initiative, stamina, and cooperation. The store manager does the same for each employee; then they meet, compare results, and discuss areas for improvement. But the feedback loop doesn't end there. With a few mouse clicks, the manager looks at how each employee ranks with respect to all others in the restaurant, separating employees into the top 20 percent, the middle 60 percent, and the bottom 20 percent.

The system is not the basis for firing low-ranking employees, but they usually leave soon enough anyway. Its value lies in helping managers focus their retention efforts on the top 20 percent, who have management potential, and provide training and development opportunities to the middle 60 percent, who have the potential to move up the ranking. Concentrating on certain employees is paying off for Applebee's. The turnover rate dropped almost 50 percentage points within less than two years.[92]

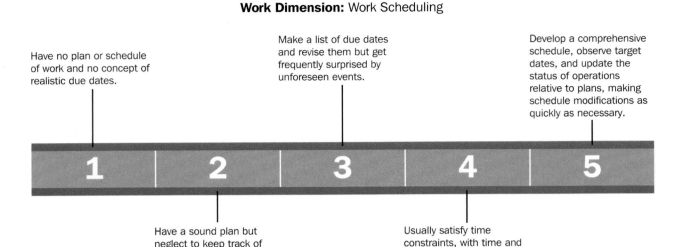

Job: Production Line Supervisor
Work Dimension: Work Scheduling

Have no plan or schedule of work and no concept of realistic due dates.

Make a list of due dates and revise them but get frequently surprised by unforeseen events.

Develop a comprehensive schedule, observe target dates, and update the status of operations relative to plans, making schedule modifications as quickly as necessary.

1   2   3   4   5

Have a sound plan but neglect to keep track of target dates or to report schedule slippages or other problems as they occur.

Usually satisfy time constraints, with time and cost overruns coming up infrequently.

EXHIBIT 9.9

Example of a Behaviorally Anchored Rating Scale

SOURCES: Based on J. P. Campbell, M. D. Dunnette, R. D. Arvey, and L. V. Hellervik, "The Development and Evaluation of Behaviorally Based Rating Scales," *Journal of Applied Psychology* 57 (1973): 15–22; and Francine Alexander, "Performance Appraisals," *Small Business Reports* (March 1989): 20–29.

stereotyping
placing an employee into a class or category based on one or a few traits or characteristics.

halo effect
a type of rating error that occurs when an employee receives the same rating on all dimensions regardless of his or her performance on individual ones.

behaviorally anchored rating scale (BARS)
a rating technique that relates an employee's performance to specific job-related incidents.

compensation
monetary payments (wages, salaries) and nonmonetary goods/commodities (benefits, vacations) used to reward employees.

is **stereotyping,** which occurs when a rater places an employee into a class or category based on one or a few traits or characteristics—for example, stereotyping an older worker as slower and more difficult to train. Another rating error is the **halo effect,** in which a manager gives an employee the same rating on all dimensions even if his or her performance is good on some dimensions and poor on others.

One approach to overcome performance evaluation errors is to use a behavior-based rating technique, such as the behaviorally anchored rating scale. The **behaviorally anchored rating scale (BARS)** is developed from critical incidents pertaining to job performance. Each job performance scale is anchored with specific behavioral statements that describe varying degrees of performance. By relating employee performance to specific incidents, raters can more accurately evaluate an employee's performance.[93]

Exhibit 9.9 illustrates the BARS method for evaluating a production line supervisor. The production supervisor's job can be broken down into several dimensions, such as equipment maintenance, employee training, or work scheduling. A BARS should be developed for each dimension. The dimension in Exhibit 9.9 is work scheduling. Good performance is represented by a 4 or 5 on the scale and unacceptable performance as a 1 or 2. If a production supervisor's job has eight dimensions, the total performance evaluation will be the sum of the scores for each of eight scales.

Maintaining an Effective Workforce

Now we turn to the topic of how managers and HRM professionals maintain a workforce that has been recruited and developed. Maintenance of the current workforce involves compensation, wage and salary systems, benefits, and occasional terminations.

COMPENSATION

The term **compensation** refers to (1) all monetary payments and (2) all goods or commodities used in lieu of money to reward employees.[94] An organization's compensation structure includes wages and/or salaries and benefits such as health insurance, paid vacations, or employee fitness centers. Developing an effective compensation system is an important part of HRM because it helps to attract and retain talented workers. In addition, a company's compensation system has an impact on strategic performance.[95] HR managers design the pay and benefits systems to fit company strategy and to provide compensation equity.

Wage and Salary Systems.
Ideally, management's strategy for the organization should be a critical determinant of the features and operations of the pay system.[96] For example, managers may have the goal of maintaining or improving profitability or market share by stimulating employee performance. Thus, they should design and use a merit pay system rather than a system based on other criteria such as seniority.

The most common approach to employee compensation is *job-based pay,* which means linking compensation to the specific tasks an employee performs. However, these systems present several problems. For one thing, job-based pay may fail to reward the type of learning behavior needed for the organization to adapt and survive in today's environment. In addition, these systems reinforce an emphasis on organizational hierarchy and centralized decision making and control, which are inconsistent with the growing emphasis on employee participation and increased responsibility.[97]

Skill-based pay systems are becoming increasingly popular in both large and small companies, including Sherwin-Williams, au Bon Pain, and Quaker Oats. Employees with higher skill levels receive higher pay than those with lower skill levels. At the Quaker Oats pet food plant in Topeka, Kansas, for example, employees might start at something like $8.75 per hour but reach a top hourly rate of $14.50 when they master a series of skills.[98] Also called *competency-based pay,* skill-based pay systems encourage employees to develop their skills and competencies, thus making them more valuable to the organization as well as more employable if they leave their current jobs.

Compensation Equity.
Whether the organization uses job-based pay or skill-based pay, good managers strive to maintain a sense of fairness and equity within the pay structure and thereby fortify employee morale. **Job evaluation** refers to the process of determining the value or worth of jobs within an organization through an examination of job content. Job evaluation techniques enable managers to compare similar and dissimilar jobs and to determine internally equitable pay rates—that is, pay rates that employees believe are fair compared with those for other jobs in the organization.

Organizations also want to make sure their pay rates are fair compared to other companies. HRM managers may obtain **wage and salary surveys** that show what other organizations pay incumbents in jobs that match a sample of "key" jobs selected by the organization. These surveys are available from a number of sources, including the U.S. Bureau of Labor Statistics National Compensation Survey.

Pay-for-Performance.
Many of today's organizations develop compensation plans based on a *pay-for-performance standard* to raise productivity and cut labor costs in a competitive global environment. **Pay-for-performance,** also called *incentive pay*, means tying at least part of compensation to employee effort and performance, whether it be through merit-based pay, bonuses, team incentives, or various gainsharing or profit-sharing plans. Data show that, while growth in base wages is slowing in many industries, the use of pay-for-performance has steadily increased since the early 1990s, with approximately 70 percent of companies now offering some form of incentive pay.[99] The U.S. Congress and President Bush recently called for implementing performance-based pay in agencies of the federal government. The seniority-based pay system used by most federal agencies has come under intense scrutiny in recent years, with critics arguing that it creates an environment where poor performers tend to stay, and the best and brightest leave out of frustration.

TAKE ACTION

As a manager, keep in mind that low pay often means higher turnover, which costs you more money.

job evaluation
the process of determining the value of jobs within an organization through an examination of job content.

wage and salary surveys
surveys that show what other organizations pay incumbents in jobs that match a sample of "key" jobs selected by the organization.

pay-for-performance
incentive pay that ties at least part of compensation to employee effort and performance.

A survey conducted by the Office of Personnel Management found that only one in four federal employees believe adequate steps are taken to deal with poor performers, and only two in five think strong performers are appropriately recognized and rewarded.[100]

With pay-for-performance, incentives are aligned with the behaviors needed to help the organization achieve its strategic goals. Employees have an incentive to make the company more efficient and profitable because if goals are not met, no bonuses are paid.

BENEFITS

The best HR managers know that a compensation package requires more than money. Although wage/salary is an important component, it is only a part. Equally important are the benefits offered by the organization. Benefits make up 40 percent of labor costs in the United States.[101]

Some benefits are required by law, such as Social Security, unemployment compensation, and workers' compensation. In addition, companies with 50 or more employees are required by the Family and Medical Leave Act to give up to 12 weeks of unpaid leave for such things as the birth or adoption of a child, the serious illness of a spouse or family member, or an employee's serious illness. Other types of benefits, such as health insurance, vacations, and such things as on-site daycare or fitness centers are not required by law but are provided by organizations to maintain an effective workforce. At Aegis Living, a chain of assisted living centers based in Redmond, Washington, CEO Dwayne Clark uses benefits to keep turnover of low-paid patient care staff to a low 34 percent (the average annual turnover rate in assisted living is 93 percent). Clark offers Appreciation Days for employees to take days off and negotiates with suppliers and prospective vendors to provide perks such as discounted massages and haircuts, special mortgage interest rates, and prepared meals from community kitchens.[102]

One reason benefits make up such a large portion of the compensation package is that health care costs continue to increase. Many organizations are requiring that employees absorb a greater share of the cost of medical benefits, such as through higher co-payments and deductibles. Microsoft, for example, recently sliced health care benefits by requiring a higher co-pay on prescription drugs.[103]

Computerization cuts the time and expense of administering benefits programs tremendously. At many companies, such as Wells Fargo and LG&E Energy, employees access their benefits package through an intranet, creating a "self-service" benefits administration.[104] This access also enables employees to change their benefits selections easily. Today's organizations realize that the "one-size-fits-all" benefits package is no longer appropriate, so they frequently offer *cafeteria-plan benefits packages* that allow employees to select the benefits of greatest value to them.[105] Other companies use surveys to determine which combination of fixed benefits is most desirable. The benefits packages provided by large companies attempt to meet the needs of all employees.

TERMINATION

Despite the best efforts of line managers and HRM professionals, the organization will lose employees. Some will retire, others will depart voluntarily for other jobs, and still others will be forced out through mergers and cutbacks or for poor performance.

The value of termination for maintaining an effective workforce is twofold. First, employees who are poor performers can be dismissed. Productive employees often resent disruptive, low-performing employees who are allowed to stay with the company and receive pay and benefits comparable to theirs. Second, employers can use exit interviews as a valuable HR tool, regardless of whether the employee leaves voluntarily or is forced out. An **exit interview** is an interview conducted with departing employees to determine why they are leaving. The value of the exit interview is to provide an inexpensive way to learn about pockets of dissatisfaction within the organization and hence reduce future turnover. The

---

TAKE ACTION ▶

Even as a new manager, play a role in how people are compensated. Consider skill-based pay systems and incentive pay to encourage high performers. Don't be dismayed if some people have to be let go. If people have to be laid off or fired, do it humanely.

---

exit interview
an interview conducted with departing employees to determine the reasons for their termination.

oil services giant Schlumberger includes an exit interview as part of a full-scale investigation of every departure, with the results posted online so managers all around the company can get insight into problems.[106] However, in many cases, employees who leave voluntarily are reluctant to air uncomfortable complaints or discuss their real reasons for leaving. Companies such as T-Mobile, Campbell Soup, and Conair found that having people complete an online exit questionnaire yields more open and honest information. When people have negative things to say about managers or the company, the online format is a chance to speak their mind without having to do it in a face-to-face meeting.[107]

For companies experiencing downsizing through mergers or because of global competition or a shifting economy, often a large number of managers and workers are terminated at the same time. In these cases, enlightened companies try to find a smooth transition for departing employees. For example, General Electric laid off employees in three gradual steps. It also set up a reemployment center to assist employees in finding new jobs or in learning new skills. It provided counseling in how to write a résumé and conduct a job search. Additionally, GE placed an advertisement in local newspapers saying that these employees were available.[108] By showing genuine concern in helping laid-off employees, a company communicates the value of human resources and helps maintain a positive corporate culture.

Diversity In Organizations

Many managers are finding innovative ways to integrate diversity initiatives into their organizations. These initiatives teach current employees to value differences, direct corporate recruiting efforts, influence supplier decisions, and provide development training for women and minorities. Smart managers value diversity and enforce the value in day-to-day decision making.

In the United States, today's companies reflect the country's image as a melting pot but with a difference. In the past, the United States was a place where people of different national origins, ethnicities, races, and religions came together and blended to resemble one another. Opportunities for advancement were limited to those workers who easily fit into the mainstream of the larger culture. Some immigrants chose desperate measures to fit in, such as abandoning their native languages, changing their last names, and sacrificing their own unique cultures. In essence, everyone in workplace organizations was encouraged to share similar beliefs, values, and lifestyles despite differences in gender, race, and ethnicity.[109]

Now organizations recognize that everyone is not the same and that the differences people bring to the workplace are valuable.[110] Rather than expecting all employees to adopt similar attitudes and values, managers are learning that these differences enable their companies to compete globally and to tap into rich sources of new talent. Although diversity in North America has been a reality for some time, genuine efforts to accept and *manage* diverse people began only in recent years. Exhibit 9.10 lists some interesting milestones in the history of corporate diversity.

The following sections introduce the topic of diversity, its causes, and its consequences. We look at some of the challenges minorities face, ways managers deal with workforce diversity, and organizational responses to create an environment that welcomes and values diverse employees. The chapter also considers issues of sexual harassment, global diversity, and new approaches to managing diversity in today's workplace.

Valuing Diversity

Top managers say their companies value diversity for a number of reasons, such as to give the organization access to a broader range of opinions and viewpoints, to spur greater creativity and innovation, to reflect an increasingly diverse customer base, to obtain the best talent in a competitive environment, and to more effectively compete in a global

EXHIBIT 9.10

Some Milestones in the History of Corporate Diversity in the United States

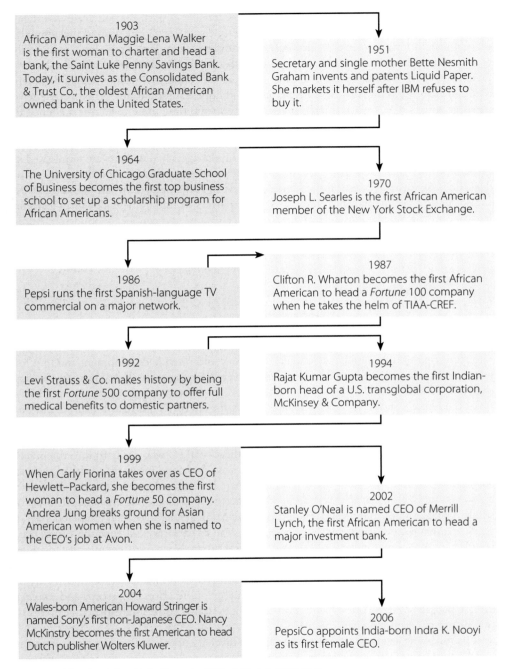

1903
African American Maggie Lena Walker is the first woman to charter and head a bank, the Saint Luke Penny Savings Bank. Today, it survives as the Consolidated Bank & Trust Co., the oldest African American owned bank in the United States.

1951
Secretary and single mother Bette Nesmith Graham invents and patents Liquid Paper. She markets it herself after IBM refuses to buy it.

1964
The University of Chicago Graduate School of Business becomes the first top business school to set up a scholarship program for African Americans.

1970
Joseph L. Searles is the first African American member of the New York Stock Exchange.

1986
Pepsi runs the first Spanish-language TV commercial on a major network.

1987
Clifton R. Wharton becomes the first African American to head a *Fortune* 100 company when he takes the helm of TIAA-CREF.

1992
Levi Strauss & Co. makes history by being the first *Fortune* 500 company to offer full medical benefits to domestic partners.

1994
Rajat Kumar Gupta becomes the first Indian-born head of a U.S. transglobal corporation, McKinsey & Company.

1999
When Carly Fiorina takes over as CEO of Hewlett–Packard, she becomes the first woman to head a *Fortune* 50 company. Andrea Jung breaks ground for Asian American women when she is named to the CEO's job at Avon.

2002
Stanley O'Neal is named CEO of Merrill Lynch, the first African American to head a major investment bank.

2004
Wales-born American Howard Stringer is named Sony's first non-Japanese CEO. Nancy McKinstry becomes the first American to head Dutch publisher Wolters Kluwer.

2006
PepsiCo appoints India-born Indra K. Nooyi as its first female CEO.

SOURCE: "Spotlight on Diversity," special advertising section, *MBA Jungle* (March–April 2003): 58–61.

marketplace.[111] A recent study of diversity management in the United Kingdom, Scandinavia, and Continental Europe found managers reporting similar motives, as well as a desire to enhance the company's image and to improve employee satisfaction.[112] A survey commissioned by *The New York Times* found that 91 percent of job seekers think diversity programs make a company a better place to work, and nearly all minority job seekers said they would prefer to work in a diverse workplace.[113] In a survey by the Society for Human Resource Management and *Fortune* magazine, more than 70 percent of HR executives indicated that diversity has enhanced their organizations' recruitment efforts and improved the overall corporate culture.[114]

However, many managers are ill-prepared to handle diversity issues. Many Americans grew up in racially unmixed neighborhoods and had little exposure to people substantially different from themselves.[115] The challenge is particularly great when working with people from other countries and cultures. One recent challenge at IBM involved a new immigrant, a Muslim woman who was required to have a photo taken for a company identification badge. She protested that her religious beliefs required that, as a married woman, she wear a veil and not expose her face to men in public. A typical American manager, schooled in traditional management training, might insist that she have the photo taken or hit the door. Fortunately, IBM has a well-developed diversity program, and managers worked out a satisfactory compromise.[116] Consider some other mistakes that American managers could easily make:[117]

- To reward a Vietnamese employee's high performance, her manager promoted her, placing her at the same level as her husband, who also worked at the factory. Rather than being pleased, the worker became upset and declined the promotion because Vietnamese husbands are expected to have a higher status than their wives.

- A manager, having learned that a friendly pat on the arm or back would make workers feel good, took every chance to touch his subordinates. His Asian employees hated being touched and thus started avoiding him, and several asked for transfers.

- A manager declined a gift offered by a new employee, an immigrant who wanted to show gratitude for her job. He was concerned about ethics and explained the company's policy about not accepting gifts. The employee was so insulted she quit.

These issues related to cultural diversity are difficult and real. Similar complicated issues occur for managers in other countries. For example, the United Kingdom and other European countries are facing a growing diversity challenge because of a recent influx of immigrants. A scan of the classifieds in any major newspaper in the United Kingdom finds numerous advertisements for skilled diversity management leaders.[118] Before discussing how companies handle the challenges of diversity, let's define *diversity* and explore people's attitudes toward it.

ATTITUDES TOWARD DIVERSITY

Valuing diversity by recognizing, welcoming, and cultivating differences among people so they can develop their unique talents and be effective organizational members is difficult to achieve. **Ethnocentrism** is the belief that one's own group and subculture are inherently superior to other groups and cultures. Ethnocentrism makes it difficult to value diversity. Viewing one's own culture as the best culture is a natural tendency among most people. Moreover, the business world still tends to reflect the values, behaviors, and assumptions based on the experiences of a rather homogeneous, white, middle-class, male workforce. Most theories of management presume that workers share similar values, beliefs, motivations, and attitudes about work and life in general. These theories presume one set of behaviors best helps an organization to be productive and effective and therefore should be adopted by all employees.[119]

Ethnocentric viewpoints and a standard set of cultural practices produce a **monoculture,** a culture that accepts only one way of doing things and one set of values and beliefs, which can cause problems for minority employees. People of color, women, gay people, the disabled, the elderly, and other diverse employees may feel undue pressure to conform, may be victims of stereotyping attitudes, and may be presumed deficient because they are different. White, heterosexual men, many of whom themselves do not fit the notion of the "ideal" employee, may also feel uncomfortable with the monoculture and resent stereotypes that label white males as racists and sexists. Valuing diversity means ensuring that *all* people are given equal opportunities in the workplace.[120]

 **TAKE ACTION**

Go to the New Manager Self Test on page 356 that pertains to attitudes toward diversity.

TAKE ACTION

Try to remember that another culture's way of doing something may have validity; it's just different.

ethnocentrism
the belief that one's own group or subculture is inherently superior to other groups or cultures.

monoculture
a culture that accepts only one way of doing things and one set of values and beliefs.

The goal for organizations seeking cultural diversity is pluralism rather than a monoculture and ethnorelativism rather than ethnocentrism. **Ethnorelativism** is the belief that groups and subcultures are inherently equal. **Pluralism** means that an organization accommodates several subcultures. Movement toward pluralism seeks to fully integrate into the organization the employees who otherwise would feel isolated and ignored.

Most of today's organizations are applying conscious efforts to shift from a monoculture perspective to one of pluralism. Consider a recent report from the National Bureau of Economic Research, entitled "Are Greg and Emily More Employable than Lakisha and Jamal?," which shows that employers often unconsciously discriminate against job applicants based solely on the Afrocentric or black-sounding names on their resume. In interviews prior to the research, most HR managers surveyed said they expected only a small gap, and some expected to find a pattern of reverse discrimination. The results showed instead that white-sounding names got 50 percent more callbacks than black-sounding names, even when skills and experience were equal.[121]

TAKE ACTION ➡

Remember that most discrimination is not overt but rather unconscious; therefore, even if you don't realize you are discriminating, you might still be.

This type of discrimination is often not intentional but is based on deep-seated personal biases and deep-rooted organizational assumptions. Many managers are not even aware of their own "culture" and don't see that they are specifically failing to hire, develop, and promote minorities, women, or others who are different from themselves.[122] In addition, employees in a monoculture may not be aware of their biases and the negative stereotypes they apply toward people who represent diverse groups. Through effective training, people can be helped to accept different ways of thinking and behaving, the first step away from narrow, ethnocentric thinking. Ultimately, employees are able to integrate diverse cultures, which means that judgments of appropriateness, goodness, badness, and morality are no longer applied to racial or cultural differences. These differences are experienced as essential, natural, and joyful, enabling an organization to enjoy true pluralism and take advantage of diverse human resources.[123]

One organization that is making a firm commitment to break out of monoculture thinking is Hyatt hotels, which has a diversity council made up of employees and managers from different parts of the company and representing different cultural and ethnic backgrounds. The council meets three times a year to review how well the company is recognizing, developing, and promoting minorities. For managers at Hyatt, 15 percent of their bonus is dependent on meeting specific diversity goals.[124]

TAKE ACTION ➡

As a new manager, adopt a viewpoint that accepts all groups and subcultures as inherently equal. Appreciate the differences that people bring to the workplace and consciously work toward hiring, developing, and promoting diverse people.

The Changing Workplace

Diversity is no longer just the right thing to do; it has become a business imperative and perhaps the single most important factor of the twenty-first century for organizational performance.[125] One reason is the dramatic change taking place in the workplace, in our society, and in the economic environment. These changes include globalization and the changing workforce and customer base.[126] Earlier chapters described the impact of global competition on business in North America. Competition is intense. At least 70 percent of all U.S. businesses are engaged directly in competition with companies overseas. Companies that ignore diversity have a hard time competing in today's multicultural global environment. As Ted Childs, director of diversity at IBM, puts it, "Diversity is the bridge between the workplace and the marketplace."[127]

Companies that succeed in this environment adopt radical new ways of doing business, with sensitivity toward the needs of different cultural practices. Consider the consulting firm McKinsey & Co. In the 1970s, most consultants were American, but by the turn of the century, McKinsey's chief partner was a foreign national (Rajat Gupta from India), only 40 percent of consultants were American, and the firm's foreign-born consultants came from 40 different countries.[128] Many other companies based in the United States reflect a similar mix of native- and foreign-born managers. The other dominant trend

ethnorelativism
the belief that groups and subcultures are inherently equal.

pluralism
an environment in which the organization accommodates several subcultures, including employees who would otherwise feel isolated and ignored.

is the changing composition of the workforce and the customer base. The average worker is older now, and many more women, people of color, and immigrants are seeking job and advancement opportunities. The demographics of the U.S. population are shifting dramatically. The people who used to be called minorities now make up a majority of the U.S. population. Nonwhite residents are the majority in 48 of the nation's 100 largest cities, as they are in New Mexico, Hawaii, the District of Columbia, and California—the largest consumer market in the country. Hispanics, African Americans, and Asian Americans together represent $1.5 trillion in annual purchasing power.[129] During the 1990s, the foreign-born population of the United States nearly doubled, and immigrants now number more than 34 million, meaning that almost one in eight people living in the United States was born in another country, the highest percentage since the 1920s.[130] The U.S. Bureau of Labor Statistics indicates that by 2008, women and minorities are expected to make up fully 70 percent of the new entrants into the workforce.[131] So far, the ability of organizations to manage diversity has not kept pace with these demographic trends, thus creating a number of significant challenges for minority workers and managers.

TAKE ACTION

As a manager, always notice the changing landscape of your customer demographics.

3 The increasing number of foreign workers at U.S. companies needs to give a lot of attention to learning the U.S. culture and adapting.

ANSWER: Although foreign-born workers do need to adapt, the companies must also learn to adjust to having people with various languages and practices in their workforces.

★ Assess Your Answer

CHALLENGES MINORITIES FACE

A one-best-way approach leads to a mind-set that views difference as deficiency or dysfunction. For many career women and minorities, their experience suggests that no matter how many college degrees they earn, how many hours they work, how they dress, or how much effort and enthusiasm they invest, they are never perceived as "having the right stuff." If the standard of quality were based, for instance, on being white and male, anything else would be seen as deficient. This dilemma often is difficult for white men to understand because most of them are not intentionally racist and sexist. As one observer points out, you would need to be nonwhite to understand what it is like to have people assume a subordinate is your superior simply because he is white, or to lose a sale after the customer sees you in person and finds out you're not Caucasian.[132]

Although blatant discrimination is not as widespread as in the past, bias in the workplace often shows up in subtle ways: a lack of choice assignments, the disregard by a subordinate of a minority manager's directions, or the ignoring of comments made by women and minorities at meetings. A survey by Korn Ferry International found that 59 percent of minority managers surveyed had observed a racially motivated double standard in the delegation of assignments.[133] Their perceptions are supported by a study that showed minority managers spend more time in the "bullpen" waiting for their chance and then have to prove themselves over and over again with each new assignment. Another recent study found that white managers gave more negative performance ratings to black leaders and white subordinates and more positive ratings to white leaders and black subordinates, affirming the widespread acceptance of these employees in their stereotypical roles.[134] Minority employees typically feel that they have to put in longer hours and extra effort to achieve the same status as their white colleagues. "It's not enough to be as good as the next person," says Bruce Gordon, president of Bell Atlantic's enterprise group. "We have to be better."[135]

MANAGEMENT CHALLENGES

What do these factors mean for managers who are responsible for creating a workplace that offers fulfilling work, opportunities for professional development and career advancement, and respect for all individuals? Inappropriate behavior by employees lands squarely at the door of the organization's top executives. Managers can look at different areas of the organization to see how well they are doing in creating a workplace that values and supports all people. Exhibit 9.11 illustrates some of the key areas of management challenge for dealing with a diverse workforce. Managers focus on these issues to see how well they are addressing the needs and concerns of diverse employees. One step is to ensure that their organizations' HR systems are designed to be bias-free, dropping the perception of the middle-aged white male as the ideal employee. Consider how the FBI expanded its recruiting efforts.

Recruiting and career development are only one part of the HR challenge. For example, the increased career involvement of women represents an enormous opportunity to organizations, but it also means managers must deal with issues such as work-family conflicts, dual-career couples, and sexual harassment. Providing reasonable accommodation for disabled employees requires more than putting in a handicap access ramp. Demands for equal opportunities for the physically and mentally disabled are growing, and most companies have done little to respond. "When it comes to dealing with the disabled, we are about where we were with race in the 1970s," says David Thomas, a professor of organizational

EXHIBIT 9.11

Management
Challenges for a
Culturally Diverse
Workforce

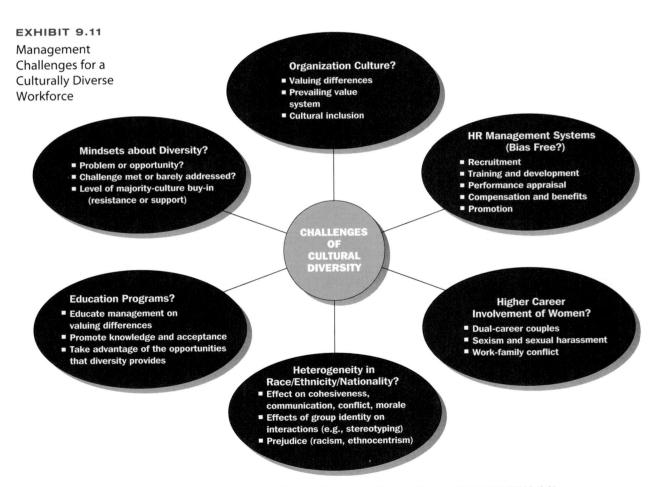

SOURCE: Taylor H. Cox and Stacy Blake, "Managing Cultural Diversity: Implications for Organizational Competitiveness," *Academy of Management Executive* 5, no. 3 (1991): 45–56.

How does the FBI gain credibility and obtain the information it needs to investigate and solve crimes? One way is by looking and thinking like the people in the communities where it seeks information. Not so long ago, if you were a woman or member of a minority group, you didn't stand a chance of becoming an FBI agent. Today, though, the agency's goal is to reflect the diversity of U.S. society. Each of the FBI's 56 field offices gets a report card on how well they've done in terms of making their offices reflective of the community. Each office is responsible for bringing minorities on board and providing them with advancement opportunities.

In addition, the FBI's national recruitment office was launched specifically to develop programs for recruiting women and minorities. One innovative initiative was the EdVenture Partners Collegiate Marketing Program, which worked with two historically black universities. The program gave students college credit and funding to devise and implement a local marketing plan for the FBI. As a result of the program, the agency received 360 minority applications. "In many cases, the students' perceptions about the FBI were totally changed," says Gwen Hubbard, acting chief of the national recruitment office. "Initially, we were not viewed as an employer of choice by the diverse student populations." The EdVenture Partners program is being expanded to eight colleges and universities. Another initiative is a minority summer intern program, which started with 21 full-time student interns and is being expanded to at least 40.

These programs on the national level, along with emphasis in the field offices on reflecting the local communities, ensure that the FBI recruits diverse candidates. Today, the FBI has thousands of female and minority agents. Top leaders are also focusing on ways to make sure those people have full opportunity to move up the ranks so that there is diversity at leadership levels as well.[136]

behavior and HRM at Harvard Business School.[137] In fact, employment rates for disabled people dropped 30 percent between 1990 and 2004. And for the most part, the workers who do find jobs are tracked into low-skill, low-pay jobs rather than being allowed to fully participate in training and educational programs available to other employees.[138] One company bucking that trend is Habitat International, a manufacturer of carpet and turf based in Chattanooga, Tennessee. David Morris, Habitat's owner and CEO, admits that giving disabled workers a chance originally "had to be forced down my throat." Today, though, nearly every employee at the company, including some managers, has a physical or mental disability. Performance and quality have gone up at Habitat and turnover and absenteeism have gone down since Morris began hiring people with disabilities. The plant's defect rate, for example, is less than one-half of 1 percent, and every order is delivered on time.[139]

The growing immigrant population presents other challenges. Whereas in previous generations most foreign-born immigrants came from Western Europe, 84 percent of recent immigrants come from Asia and Latin America.[140] These immigrants come to the United States with a wide range of backgrounds, often without adequate skills in using English. Organizations must face not only the issues of dealing with race, ethnicity, and nationality to provide a prejudice-free workplace but also develop sufficient educational programs to help immigrants acquire the technical and customer service skills required in a service economy.

Current Debates About Affirmative Action

Affirmative action refers to government-mandated programs that focus on providing opportunities to women and members of minority groups who previously faced discrimination. It is not the same thing as diversity, but affirmative action has facilitated greater recruitment, retention, and promotion of minorities and women. Affirmative action has made workplaces much more fair and equitable. However, research shows that full integration of women and racial minorities into organizations is still nearly a decade away.[141] Despite affirmative action's successes, salaries and promotion opportunities for women and minorities continue to lag behind those of white males.

Affirmative action was developed in response to conditions 40 years ago. Adult white males dominated the workforce, and economic conditions were stable and improving. Because of widespread prejudice and discrimination, legal and social coercion were necessary to allow women, people of color, immigrants, and other minorities to become part of the economic system.[142]

Affirmative action is highly controversial today. The economic and social environment has changed tremendously since the 1960s. "Minority" groups have become the majority in large U.S. cities. More than half of the U.S. workforce consists of women and minorities, and the economic climate changes rapidly as a result of globalization. Some members of nonprotected groups argue that affirmative action is no longer needed and that it leads to *reverse discrimination*. Even the intended beneficiaries of affirmative action programs often disagree as to their value, and some believe these programs do more harm than good. One reason may be the *stigma of incompetence* that often is associated with affirmative action hires. One study found that both working managers and students consistently rated people portrayed as affirmative action hires as less competent and recommended lower salary increases than for those not associated with affirmative action.[143] In addition, people who perceive that they were hired because of affirmative action requirements may demonstrate negative self-perceptions and negative views of the organization, which leads to lower performance and reinforces the opinions of others that they are less competent.[144]

Recent court decisions weakened affirmative action's clout while still upholding its value. For example, the Supreme Court preserved affirmative action policies as a means of achieving diversity in universities but barred the use of point systems that might favor minority candidates.[145] Other court decisions have also limited the use of certain affirmative action practices for hiring and college admissions. In general, though, the courts support the continued use of affirmative action as a means of giving women and minority groups equal access to opportunities. In addition, according to a Gallup poll conducted to coincide with the 50th anniversary of the *Brown v. Board of Education* ruling that declared school segregation unconstitutional, 57 percent of Americans support the continued use of affirmative action.[146]

glass ceiling
an invisible barrier that separates women and minorities from top management positions.

CONCEPT CONNECTION

As Indian-born Indra Nooyi, pictured here, once observed, "If you are a woman, and especially a person-of-color woman, there are two strikes against you. Immigrant, person of color, and woman—three strikes against you." She has certainly overcome the odds. *Fortune* named Nooyi its 2006 most powerful woman in business shortly after she became PepsiCo's CEO. How did she break through the **glass ceiling?** There's her considerable talent and powerful work ethic, of course. But she also benefited from PepsiCo's supportive culture and commitment to diversity. Under her predecessor, Steve Reinemund, half of all new hires were women or ethnic minorities, a policy spurred by the company's desire to have its workforce reflect its increasingly global customers.

THE GLASS CEILING

The **glass ceiling** is an invisible barrier that separates women and minorities from top management positions. They can look up through the ceiling and see top management, but prevailing attitudes and stereotypes are invisible obstacles to their own advancement.

In addition, women and minorities are often excluded from informal manager networks and often don't get access to the type of general and line management experience that is required for moving to the top.[147] Research suggests the existence of *glass walls* that

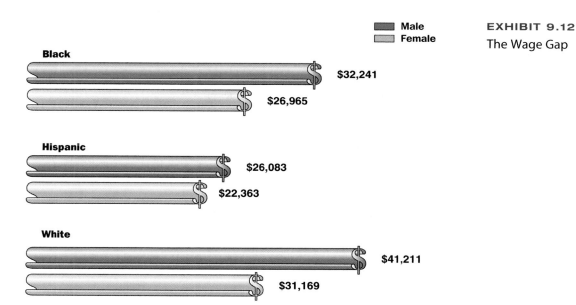

EXHIBIT 9.12

The Wage Gap

Male
Female

Black
$32,241
$26,965

Hispanic
$26,083
$22,363

White
$41,211
$31,169

SOURCE: U.S. Census Bureau, Current Population Survey, 2004 Annual Social and Economic Supplement, reported in "2000 Median Annual Earnings by Race and Sex," http://www.infoplease.com/ipa/A0197814.html.

serve as invisible barriers to important lateral movement within the organization. Glass walls, such as exclusion from manager networks, bar experience in areas such as line supervision that would enable women and minorities to advance vertically.[148]

Evidence that the glass ceiling persists is the distribution of women and minorities, who are clustered at the bottom levels of the corporate hierarchy. Among minority groups, women have made the biggest strides in recent years, but they still represent only 15.7 percent of corporate officers in America's 500 largest companies, up from 12.5 percent in 2000 and 8.7 percent in 1995.[149] In 2006, only eight *Fortune* 500 companies had female CEOs. And both male and female African Americans and Hispanics continue to hold only a small percentage of all management positions in the United States.[150]

Women and minorities also make less money. As shown in Exhibit 9.12, black men earn about 22 percent less, white women 24 percent less, and Hispanic men 37 percent less than white males. Minority women fare even worse, with black women earning 35 percent less and Hispanic women 46 percent less than white males.[151]

Another sensitive issue related to the glass ceiling is homosexuals in the workplace. Many gay men and lesbians believe they will not be accepted as they are and risk losing their jobs or their chances for advancement. Gay employees of color are particularly hesitant to disclose their sexual orientation at work because by doing so they risk a double dose of discrimination.[152] Although some examples of openly gay corporate leaders can be found, such as David Geffen, co-founder of DreamWorks SKG, and Ford Vice Chairman Allan D. Gilmour, most managers still believe staying in the closet is the only way they can succeed at work. Thus, gays and lesbians often fabricate heterosexual identities to keep their jobs or avoid running into the glass ceiling they see other employees encounter.

THE OPT-OUT TREND

Many women are never hitting the glass ceiling because they choose to get off the fast track long before it comes into view. In recent years, an ongoing discussion concerns something referred to as the *opt-out trend*. In a recent survey of nearly 2,500 women and

653 men, 37 percent of highly qualified women report that they voluntarily left the workforce at some point in their careers, compared to only 24 percent of similarly qualified men.[153]

Quite a debate rages over the reasons for the larger number of women who drop out of mainstream careers. Opt-out proponents say women are deciding that corporate success isn't worth the price in terms of reduced family and personal time, greater stress, and negative health effects.[154] Women don't want corporate power and status in the same way that men do, and clawing one's way up the corporate ladder has become less appealing. For example, Marge Magner left her job as CEO of Citigroup's Consumer Group after suffering both the death of her mother and a personal life-changing accident in the same year. In evaluating her reasons, Magner said she realized that "life is about everything, not just the work." For many women today, the high-pressure climb to the top is just not worth it. Some are opting out to be stay-at-home moms, while others want to continue working but just not in the kind of fast-paced, competitive, aggressive environment that exists in most corporations. Some researchers who study the opt-out trend say that most women just don't want to work as hard and competitively as most men want to work.[155]

Critics, however, argue that this view is just another way to blame women themselves for the dearth of female managers at higher levels.[156] Vanessa Castagna, for example, left JCPenney after decades with the company not because she wanted more family or personal time but because she kept getting passed over for top jobs.[157] Although some women are voluntarily leaving the fast track, many more genuinely want to move up the corporate ladder but find their paths blocked. Fifty-five percent of executive women surveyed by Catalyst said they aspire to senior leadership levels.[158] In addition, a survey of 103 women voluntarily leaving executive jobs in *Fortune* 1000 companies found that corporate culture was cited as the number 1 reason for leaving.[159] The greatest disadvantages of women leaders stem largely from prejudicial attitudes and a heavily male-oriented corporate culture.[160] Some years ago, when Procter & Gamble asked the female executives it considered "regretted losses" (that is, high performers the company wanted to retain) why they left their jobs, the most common answer was that they didn't feel valued by the company.[161] Top-level corporate culture evolves around white, heterosexual, American males, who tend to hire and promote people who look, act, and think like them. Compatibility in thought and behavior plays an important role at higher levels of organizations. For example, among women who managed to break through the glass ceiling, fully 96 percent said adapting to a predominantly white male culture was necessary for their success.[162]

THE FEMALE ADVANTAGE

Some people think women might actually be better managers, partly because of a more collaborative, less hierarchical, relationship-oriented approach that is in tune with today's global and multicultural environment.[163] As attitudes and values change with changing generations, the qualities women seem to naturally possess may lead to a gradual role reversal in organizations. For example, a stunning gender reversal is taking place in U.S. education, with girls taking over almost every leadership role from kindergarten to graduate school. In addition, women of all races and ethnic groups are outpacing men in earning bachelor's and master's degrees. In 2005, women made up 57 percent of undergraduate college students. The gender gap in some states is even wider, with Maine reporting the greatest gap, with 154 women for every 100 men in the state's colleges and universities.[164] Among 25- to 29-year-olds, 32 percent of women have college degrees, compared to 27 percent of men. Women are rapidly closing the M.D. and Ph.D. gap, and they make up about half of all U.S. law students, half of all undergraduate business majors, and about 30 percent of MBA candidates. Overall, women's participation in both the labor force and civic affairs steadily increased since the mid-1950s, while men's participation has slowly but steadily declined.[165]

According to James Gabarino, an author and professor of human development at Cornell University, women are "better able to deliver in terms of what modern society requires of people—paying attention, abiding by rules, being verbally competent, and dealing with interpersonal relationships in offices."[166] His observation is supported by the fact that female managers are typically rated higher by subordinates on interpersonal skills as well as on factors such as task behavior, communication, ability to motivate others, and goal accomplishment.[167] Recent research found a correlation between balanced gender composition in companies (that is, roughly equal male and female representation) and higher organizational performance. Moreover, a study by Catalyst indicates that organizations with the highest percentage of women in top management financially outperform, by about 35 percent, those with the lowest percentage of women in higher-level jobs.[168] It seems that women should be marching right to the top of the corporate hierarchy, but prevailing attitudes, values, and perceptions in organizations create barriers and a glass ceiling.

Current Responses to Diversity

Today's companies are searching for inclusive practices that go well beyond affirmative action to confront the obstacles that prevent women and minorities from advancing to senior management positions. Procter & Gamble, for example, dramatically improved its retention of women and increased the number who moved into senior level positions by offering time-management training and greater flexibility that enabled more women to accept career-oriented line management jobs.[169] When the Boston-based law firm Mintz Levin Cohn Ferris Glovsky & Popeo decided to build an employment law practice in Washington, the partners determined to create a diverse, inclusive environment by hiring many minority lawyers for senior positions from the start. The goal is to create a "critical mass" of people who can serve as role models and mentors for younger minority lawyers who typically find it difficult to move up the ranks and become partners in large law firms.[170]

To prepare for and respond to an increasingly diverse business climate, managers in most companies are also expanding the organization's emphasis on diversity beyond race and gender to consider such factors as ethnicity, age, physical ability, religion, and sexual orientation. Generational diversity is a key concern for managers in many of today's companies, with four generations working side-by-side, each with a different mind-set and different expectations. "In my career, I was trained not to start a meeting without an agenda," says 55-year-old manager J. Robert Carr. "Gen Yers make up the agenda as they go along."[171]

After managers create and define a vision for a diverse workplace, they can analyze and assess the current culture and systems within the organization. Actions to develop an inclusive workplace that values and respects all people include three major steps: (1) building a corporate culture that values diversity; (2) changing structures, policies, and systems to support diversity; and (3) providing diversity awareness training.

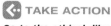

TAKE ACTION

Go to the ethical dilemma on page 363 that pertains to cultural and religious differences in the workplace.

Defining New Relationships in Organizations

One outcome of diversity is an increased incidence of close personal relationships in the workplace, which can have both positive and negative results for employees as well as the organization. Two issues of concern are emotional intimacy and sexual harassment.

NEW MANAGER SELF TEST

Subtle Biases

As a new manager, your day-to-day behavior will send signals about your biases and values. Some personal biases are active and well known to yourself and others. Other biases are more subtle, and the following questions may provide some hints about where you are biased and don't know it. Please answer whether each item is Mostly True or Mostly False for you.

	Mostly True				Mostly False
1. I prefer to be in work teams with people who think like me.	1	2	3	4	5
2. I have avoided talking about culture differences with people I met from different cultures because I didn't want to say the wrong thing.	1	2	3	4	5
3. My mind has jumped to a conclusion without first hearing all sides of a story.	1	2	3	4	5
4. The first thing I notice about people is the physical characteristics that make them different from the norm.	1	2	3	4	5
5. Before I hire someone, I have a picture in mind of what they should look like.	1	2	3	4	5
6. I typically ignore movies, magazines, and TV programs that are targeted toward groups and values that are different from mine.	1	2	3	4	5
7. When someone makes a bigoted remark or joke, I don't confront them about it.	1	2	3	4	5
8. I prefer to not discuss sensitive topics such as race, age, gender, sexuality, or religion at work.	1	2	3	4	5
9. There are people I like but I would feel uncomfortable inviting them to be with my family or close friends.	1	2	3	4	5

SCORING AND INTERPRETATION: Give yourself one point for each mostly true answer (choosing 1 or 2); give yourself zero points if you choose 3, 4 or 5. The ideal score is 0, but few people reach the ideal. Each question reflects an element of "passive bias," which can cause people different from you to feel ignored or disrespected by you. Passive bias may be more insidious than active discrimination because it excludes people from opportunities for expression and interaction. If you scored 5 or more, you should take a careful look at how you think and act toward people different from yourself. The sooner you learn to actively include diverse views and people, the better new manager you will be.

SOURCE: Based on Lawrence Otis Graham, *Proversity: Getting Past Face Values and Finding the Soul of People* (New York: John Wiley & Sons, 1997).

EMOTIONAL INTIMACY

Close emotional relationships, particularly between men and women, often have been discouraged in companies for fear that they would disrupt the balance of power and threaten organizational stability.[172] This opinion grew out of the assumption that organizations are designed for rationality and efficiency, which were best achieved in a nonemotional environment.

However, a recent study of friendships in organizations sheds interesting light on this issue.[173] Managers and workers responded to a survey about emotionally intimate relationships with both male and female co-workers. Many men and women reported having close relationships with an opposite-sex co-worker. Called *nonromantic love relationships,* the friendships resulted in trust, respect, constructive feedback, and support in achieving work goals. Intimate friendships did not necessarily become romantic, and they affected each person's job and career in a positive way. Rather than causing problems, nonromantic love relationships, according to the study, affected work teams in a positive manner because conflict was reduced. Men reported somewhat greater benefit than women from these relationships, perhaps because the men had fewer close relationships outside the workplace upon which to depend.

However, when such relationships *do* become romantic or sexual in nature, real problems can result. Romances that require the most attention from managers are those that arise between a supervisor and a subordinate. These relationships often lead to morale problems among other staff members, complaints of favoritism, and questions about the supervisor's intentions or judgment. Harry Stonecipher was ousted as CEO of Boeing Corporation in 2005 after the board learned of an extramarital affair with a female executive. However, office romances in general are tolerated far more today than in the past. Some companies, including Xerox and IBM, have formal

 **TAKE** **ACTION**

As a manager, be careful not to cross boundaries with employees at work, because having too close a relationship with one employee can cause demotivation with others.

Business Blooper

The $38 Million Affair

It's one thing to have a fling, but when you are CEO, the costs can be high. For Harry Stonecipher, it was $38 million, losing a stock award when he was forced out of the company. In some companies, the CEO might keep his job, but he's lost the respect of the workforce because it is often (correctly) seen that the boss is unfairly favoring his lover. Boeing CEO Harry Stonecipher, age 68, sent his paramour a raunchy e-mail, which somehow fell into unintended hands. When confronted, Stonecipher immediately confessed to Chairman Lew Platt but denied that he used the affair to enhance the 48-year-old divorced woman's career and salary. Stonecipher had an illustrious career but lost it all at the end for an eight-week relationship. A month later, his wife of 50 years filed for divorce.

Still, it put the man who is the chief ethics enforcer in a bad light, and he was asked to resign. Such behavior sends

up red flags in the defense industry. Stonecipher had come out of retirement in 2003 to successfully revive Boeing after a series of ethical scandals, including bribery and dirty tricks that sent two executives to jail, not to mention a still-unsettled sexual harassment class-action suit. Stonecipher came to clean up the place, and he was improving the company's image, having won the support of Wall Street and the business community with his reforms. His own downfall was brought about by the very system he put in place to prevent other ethical lapses. What's surprising is Stonecipher's lapse of judgment, sending such graphic e-mails in a monitored system that had already been punished for e-mails about unethical actions. One of the board members asked the ethics director, "How can you administer an ethics program for 160,000 employees if it's perceived that your CEO is above the rules?"

SOURCE: Lynn Lunsford, Andy Passtor, and Joann S. Lublin, "Boeings' CEO Forced to Resign Over His Affair with Employee," *Wall Street Journal* (March 8, 2005): A1 & A8; Cecil Johnson, "What Is Happening to America's CEO's?" *St. Louis Post-Dispatch* (June 15, 2007): B5.

policies that allow romantic relationships between employees as long as neither party directly reports to the other. Surveys show that approximately 25 percent of sexual harassment policies now include guidelines about office relationships, and 70 percent of companies surveyed have policies prohibiting romantic relationships between a superior and a subordinate.[174]

SEXUAL HARASSMENT

Although psychological closeness between men and women in the workplace may be a positive experience, sexual harassment is not. Sexual harassment is illegal. As a form of sexual discrimination, sexual harassment in the workplace is a violation of Title VII of the 1964 Civil Rights Act. Sexual harassment in the classroom is a violation of Title VIII of the Education Amendment of 1972. The following list categorizes various forms of sexual harassment as defined by one university:

- *Generalized.* This form involves sexual remarks and actions that are not intended to lead to sexual activity but that are directed toward a co-worker based solely on gender and reflect on the entire group.

- *Inappropriate/offensive.* Though not sexually threatening, it causes discomfort in a co-worker, whose reaction in avoiding the harasser may limit his or her freedom and ability to function in the workplace.

- *Solicitation with promise of reward.* This action treads a fine line as an attempt to "purchase" sex, with the potential for criminal prosecution.

- *Coercion with threat of punishment.* The harasser coerces a co-worker into sexual activity by using the threat of power (through recommendations, grades, promotions, and so on) to jeopardize the victim's career.

- *Sexual crimes and misdemeanors.* The highest level of sexual harassment, these acts would, if reported to the police, be considered felony crimes and misdemeanors.[175]

Statistics in Canada indicate that between 40 and 70 percent of women and about 5 percent of men have been sexually harassed at work.[176] The situation in the United States is just as dire. Over a recent 10-year period, the EEOC shows a 150 percent increase in the number of sexual harassment cases filed annually.[177] About 10 percent of those were filed by males. The Supreme Court held that same-sex harassment as well as harassment of men by female co-workers is just as illegal as the harassment of women by men. In the suit that prompted the Court's decision, a male oil-rig worker claimed he was singled out by other members of the all-male crew for crude sex play, unwanted touching, and threats of rape.[178] A growing number of men are urging recognition that sexual harassment is not just a woman's problem.[179]

Because the corporate world is dominated by a male culture, however, sexual harassment affects women to a much greater extent. Companies such as Dow Chemical, Xerox, and *The New York Times* have been swift to fire employees for circulating pornographic images, surfing pornographic websites, or sending offensive e-mails.[180]

TAKE ACTION ▶

As a new manager, be careful about a romantic involvement in the workplace. In particular, steer clear of such relationships with superiors or subordinates, which is a slippery ethical area. Know what sexual harassment means, and make sure everyone in your team or department understands that sexual harassment is disrespectful and against the law.

Global Diversity

Globalization is a reality for today's companies. As stated in a report from the Hudson Institute, *Workforce 2020,* "The rest of the world matters to a degree that it never did in the past."[181] For example, Google, which employs about 4,000 people worldwide, has seen a tremendous increase in the number of immigrants working in its U.S. headquarters. This realization prompted leaders to take a new approach to the company cafeteria, as described in this chapter's Benchmarking box.

Benchmarking

Google Chow

As Google's first food guru, chef Charlie Ayers had plenty of opportunity to indulge his penchant for varied, eclectic flavors. When hired in 1999, Ayers oversaw food services for only about 50 employees. By the time he departed in 2005, he left behind 100 chefs serving more than 2,000 meals a day at the Googleplex, Google's Mountain View, California, headquarters. Google offers expertly prepared meals, free of charge, to all its employees.

Today, those employees arrive from all corners of the world, and the cafeteria offerings reflect that diversity. Ayers's eclectic tastes and the needs of an increasingly diverse workforce meshed nicely. He created his own dishes, searched all types of restaurants for new recipes, and often got some of his best ideas from foreign-born employees. For example, a Filipino accountant offered a recipe for chicken *adobo,* a popular dish from her native country. Scattered around the Googleplex are cafes specializing in Southwestern, Italian, California-Mediterranean, and vegetarian cuisines. And because more and more Googlers originally hail from Asia, employees can find sushi at the Japanese-themed Pacific Café or Thai red curry beef at the East Meets West Café.

Google cafeteria fare has such a sterling reputation it's rumored that Yahoo! employees working nearby sneak onto campus just to grab a bite. Whether that rumor is true or not, the company indisputably stands at the forefront of organizations that believe in paying careful attention to their corporate cafeteria offerings. For Google, the company's $6 million plus annual food budget is an investment in productivity.

Why? First of all, by offering appetizing cuisine on campus, the company saves people the time and trouble of driving to an eatery, as well as provides a place for them to mingle informally. In addition, serving all employees the kind of tasty food usually reserved for swank executive dining rooms sends a clear message that Google values its human capital. Even more fundamentally, Google managers believe that what you eat literally affects your work. Indeed, the company requires that its chefs not only keep people well fed but also provide healthy foods that leave them feeling energized when they get up from the table.

Last, but not least, along with companies such as REI and Nintendo, Google believes food can be a tool for supporting an inclusive workplace. The diversity of options gives people a chance to try new things and learn more about their co-workers. And when people just need a little comfort and familiarity? Nothing takes the edge off of working in a foreign country, Google knows, like eating food that reminds you of home.

SOURCES: Jim Carlton, "Dig In," *Wall Street Journal* (November 14, 2005): R9; Tony DiRomualdo, "Is Google's Cafeteria a Competitive Weapon?" *Wisconsin Technology Network* (August 30, 2005), http://wistechnology.com/article.php?id=2190; Marc Ramirez, "Tray Chic: At Work, Cool Cafeterias, Imaginative Menus," *The Seattle Times* (November 21, 2005), http://seattletimes.nwsource.com/html/living/2002634266_cafes21.html?pageid=display-in-the-news.module&pageregion=itn-body.

Summary

This chapter described several important points about HRM in organizations. All managers are responsible for HR, and most organizations have an HR department that works with line managers to ensure a productive workforce. HRM plays a key strategic role in today's organizations. HRM is changing in three ways to keep today's organizations competitive—focusing on human and social capital; globalizing HR systems, policies, and structures; and using information technology to help achieve strategic HR goals. The HR department must also implement procedures to reflect federal and state legislation and respond to changes in working relationships and career directions. The old social contract of the employee being loyal to the company and the company taking care of the employee until retirement no longer holds. Employees are responsible for managing their own careers. Although many people still follow a traditional management career path, others look for new opportunities as contingent workers, telecommuters, project managers, and virtual employees. Other current issues of concern to HRM are becoming an employer of choice, implementing work-life balance initiatives, and humanely managing downsizing.

The first goal of HRM is to attract an effective workforce through HR planning, recruiting, and employee selection. The second is to develop an effective workforce. Newcomers are introduced to the organization and to their jobs through orientation and training programs. Moreover, employees are evaluated through performance appraisal programs. The third goal is to maintain an effective workforce through wage and salary systems, benefits packages, and termination procedures. In many organizations, information technology is being used to more effectively meet all three of these important HR goals.

Several important ideas pertain to workforce diversity, which is the inclusion of people with different human qualities and from different cultural groups. Dimensions of diversity are both primary, such as age, gender, and race; and secondary, such as education, marital status, and income. Ethnocentric attitudes generally produce a monoculture that accepts only one way of doing things and one set of values and beliefs, thereby excluding nontraditional employees from full participation. Minority employees face several significant challenges in the workplace.

Affirmative action programs have been successful in gaining employment for women and minorities, but the glass ceiling has kept many from obtaining top management positions. Another result of increased diversity in organizations is the opportunity for emotional intimacy and friendships between men and women that are beneficial to all parties. However, even though emotional connections are a positive outcome, sexual harassment has become a serious problem for today's managers.

Discussion Questions

1. It is the year 2018. In your company, central planning has given way to frontline decision making, and bureaucracy has given way to teamwork. Shopfloor workers use handheld computers and robots. A labor shortage currently affects many job openings, and the few applicants you do attract lack skills to work in teams, make their own production decisions, or use sophisticated technology. As vice president of HRM since 2006, what should you have done to prepare for this situation?

2. If you were asked to advise a private company about its equal employment opportunity responsibilities, what two points would you emphasize as most important?

3. How might the HR activities of recruiting, performance appraisal, and compensation be related to corporate strategy?

4. Think back to your own job experience. What HRM activities described in this chapter were performed for the job you filled? Which ones were absent?

5. How "valid" do you think the information obtained from a personal interview versus an employment test versus an assessment center would be for predicting effective job performance for a college professor? For an assembly-line worker in a manufacturing plant? Discuss.

6. How do you think the growing use of telecommuters, contingent workers, and virtual teams affect HRM? How can managers improve recruiting and retention of these new kinds of employees?

7. If you are in charge of training and development, which training option or options—such as OTJ, cross-training, classroom, self-directed, or computer-based—would

you be likely to choose for your company's production line manager? A customer service representative? An entry-level accountant?

8. If you were to draw up a telecommuting contract with an employee, what would it look like? Include considerations such as job description, compensation and benefits, performance measures, training, and grounds for dismissal.

9. How would you go about deciding whether to use a job-based, skills-based, or pay-for-performance compensation plan for employees in a textile manufacturing plant? For wait staff in a restaurant? For salespeople in an insurance company?

10. What purpose do exit interviews serve for HRM?

11. If you were a senior manager at a company such as Mitsubishi, Allstate Insurance, or Wal-Mart, how would you address the challenges faced by minority employees?

12. What is the glass ceiling, and why do you think it has proven to be such a barrier for women and minorities?

13. In preparing an organization to accept diversity, do you think it is more important to change the corporate culture or to change structures and policies? Explain.

14. Why do you think a large number of women are *opting out* of corporate management? Discuss whether this trend is likely to continue over the next 10 years.

15. You are a manager at an organization that has decided it needs a more diverse workforce. What steps or techniques will you use to accomplish this goal? What steps will you take to retain diverse employees once you have successfully recruited them?

Dear Dr. Dorothy

I work in a graphics-design house and recently got promoted to management in a different department. My colleagues are cool, and my boss is great, except about one thing. In the two evaluations I've had, he rates me as "above average," even though I work my butt off and spend extra hours getting all the work done. He doesn't seem to notice. Joshua, one of my fellow-managers, though, goes fishing with the boss every weekend, often when I'm in the office making sure the projects are all managed well. As far as I can tell, Joshua does no better than me in the work, but he sure does better on schmoozing, so he gets "superior" ratings from the boss. I'd like to spend time with the boss outside of work, too, but I am female, and he is married, and I think that might look suspect. What should I do?

Fishless in Wyoming

Dear Fishless,

Dr. Dorothy has no way of objectively knowing whether your work is equal to Joshua's or not. You merely believing this to be the case is not sufficient evidence. Perhaps your work *is* better than his, perhaps not. Your work could be actually inferior, too. Why are you spending so many more hours than Joshua? Are you less efficient in your work? Dr. Dorothy wonders if you spend too much time complaining to colleagues about your unfair treatment, rather than doing your work. Let's assume for now your work is as good as Joshua's, except for one vital area: You are not as good of a networker. And need Dr. Dorothy remind you how important it is for managers to create positive networks? Shame on you for forgetting this vital principle. Because Joshua has done better in managing his relationships with the boss, Dr. Dorothy believes Joshua is being evaluated according to the halo effect, which means his work is seen in a more positive light. You need to develop a more positive relationship with the boss, too, despite your fears surrounding his marital status. There are more ways to interact with the boss than throwing anglers into the lake. Offer to take the boss out to lunch or to a business breakfast. Invite he and his wife to your place for a dinner party. Send birthday cards to his kids. But don't stop with the boss. Start networking with other colleagues; otherwise, Dr. Dorothy fears you will be complaining about a similar situation in five years.

Self Learning

How Tolerant Are You?

For each of the following questions, circle the answer that best describes you.

1. Most of your friends
   a. are very similar to you.
   b. are very different from you and from each other.
   c. are like you in some respects but different in others.

2. When someone does something you disapprove of, you
   a. break off the relationship.
   b. tell how you feel but keep in touch.
   c. tell yourself it matters little and behave as you always have.

3. Which virtue is most important to you?
   a. kindness
   b. objectivity
   c. obedience

4. When it comes to beliefs, you
   a. do all you can to make others see things the same way you do.
   b. actively advance your point of view but stop short of argument.
   c. keep your feelings to yourself.

5. Would you hire a person who has had emotional problems?
   a. No
   b. Yes, provided the person shows evidence of complete recovery
   c. Yes, if the person is suitable for the job

6. Do you voluntarily read material that supports views different from your own?
   a. Never
   b. Sometimes
   c. Often

7. You react to old people with
   a. patience.
   b. annoyance.
   c. sometimes a, sometimes b.

8. Do you agree with the statement, "What is right and wrong depends upon the time, place, and circumstance"?
   a. Strongly agree
   b. Agree to a point
   c. Strongly disagree

9. Would you marry someone from a different race?
   a. Yes
   b. No
   c. Probably not

10. If someone in your family were homosexual, you would
    a. view this as a problem and try to change the person to a heterosexual orientation.
    b. accept the person as a homosexual with no change in feelings or treatment.
    c. avoid or reject the person.

11. You react to little children with
    a. patience.
    b. annoyance.
    c. sometimes a, sometimes b.

12. Other people's personal habits annoy you
    a. often.
    b. not at all.
    c. only if extreme.

13. If you stay in a household run differently from yours (cleanliness, manners, meals, and other customs), you
    a. adapt readily.
    b. quickly become uncomfortable and irritated.
    c. adjust for a while, but not for long.

14. Which statement do you agree with most?
    a. We should avoid judging others because no one can fully understand the motives of another person.
    b. People are responsible for their actions and have to accept the consequences.
    c. Both motives and actions are important when considering questions of right and wrong.

SCORING AND INTERPRETATION

Circle your score for each of the answers and total the scores:

1. a = 4; b = 0; c = 2
2. a = 4; b = 2; c = 0
3. a = 0; b = 2; c = 4
4. a = 4; b = 2; c = 0

5. a = 4; b = 2; c = 0
6. a = 4; b = 2; c = 0
7. a = 0; b = 4; c = 2
8. a = 0; b = 2; c = 4

9. a = 0; b = 4; c = 2
10. a = 2; b = 0; c = 4
11. a = 0; b = 4; c = 2
12. a = 4; b = 0; c = 2

13. a = 0; b = 4; c = 2
14. a = 0; b = 4; c = 2

Total Score

0–14: If you score 14 or below, you are a very tolerant person and dealing with diversity comes easily to you.

15–28: You are basically a tolerant person, and others think of you as tolerant. In general, diversity presents few problems for you; you may be broad-minded in some areas and have less tolerant ideas in other areas of life, such as attitudes toward older people or male-female social roles.

29–42: You are less tolerant than most people and should work on developing greater tolerance of people different from you. Your low tolerance level could affect your business or personal relationships.

43–56: You have a very low tolerance for diversity. The only people you are likely to respect are those with beliefs similar to your own. You reflect a level of intolerance that could cause difficulties in today's multicultural business environment.

SOURCE: Adapted from the Tolerance Scale by Maria Heiselman, Naomi Miller, and Bob Schlorman, Northern Kentucky University, 1982. In George Manning, Kent Curtis, and Steve McMillen, *Building Community: The Human Side of Work*, (Cincinnati, OH: Thomson Executive Press, 1996): 272–277.

Group Learning

Hiring and Evaluating using Core Competencies

1. Form groups of four to seven members. Develop a list of "core competencies" for the job of student in this course. List the core competencies here.

   1.   5.

   2.   6.

   3.   7.

   4.   8.

2. Which of these are the most important four?

   1.   3.

   2.   4.

3. What questions would you ask a potential employee/student to determine if that person could be successful in this class, based on the four most important core competencies? (Interviewing)

   1.

   2.

   3.

   4.

4. What learning experiences would you develop to enhance those core competencies? (Training and development)

   1.

   2.

   3.

   4.

5. How would you evaluate or measure the success of a student in this class, based on the four core competencies? (Performance evaluation)

   1.

   2.

   3.

   4.

Action Learning

Interview Questions

1. Meet with four or five people who have recently gone through job interviews. Ask them what questions they were asked and list those on a sheet of paper. Note if questions were asked to more than one of these people, that is, how many people were asked that type of question. Find out which questions they found uncomfortable or invasive, and ask them how they responded to those questions.

2. Your instructor may ask you to form groups of three to five people. If so, come up with a composite list of questions. Refer to Exhibit 9.7 to see which of the questions should not have been asked.

3. How did people answer difficult questions?

4. Be prepared to make a presentation to the entire class.

5. The instructor may lead a discussion about appropriate interview questions and how to respond to them.

Ethical Dilemma

Sunset Prayers

Frank Piechowski, plant manager for a Minnesota North Woods Appliance Corp. refrigerator plant, just received his instructions from the vice president for manufacturing. He was to hire 40 more temporary workers through Twin Cities Staffing, the local labor agency North Woods used. Frank already knew from past experience that most, if not all, of the new hires available to work the assembly line would be Muslim Somali refugees, people who had immigrated to Minnesota from their war-torn native country en masse over the past 15 years.

North Woods, like all appliance manufacturers, was trying to survive in a highly competitive, mature industry. Appliance companies were competing mainly on price. The entrance of large chains such as Best Buy and Home Depot only intensified the price wars, not to mention that consumers could easily do comparison shopping before leaving home by logging onto the Internet. The pressure to keep production costs low was considerable.

That's where the Somali workers came in. In an effort to keep labor costs low, North Woods was relying more and more on temporary workers rather than increasing the ranks of permanent employees. Frank was quite pleased with the Somalis already at work on the assembly line. Although few in number, they were responsible, hardworking, and willing to work for the wages he could afford to pay.

It was the first time this son of Polish immigrants had ever come into contact with Muslims, but so far, it had gone well. Frank had established a good working relationship with the Somalis' spokesperson, Halima Adan, who explained that unlike most Western faiths, Islamic religious practices were inextricably woven into everyday life. So together, they worked out ways to accommodate Muslim customs. Frank authorized changes in the plant's cafeteria menu so the Somali workers had more options that conformed to their dietary restrictions, and he allowed women to wear traditional clothing as long as they weren't violating safety standards.

After learning that the Somalis would need to perform at least some of the ceremonial washing and prayers they were required to do five times a day during work hours, the plant manager set aside a quiet, clean room where they could observe their 15-minute rituals during their breaks and at sunset. The Maghrib sunset prayers second shift workers had to perform were disruptive to a smooth work flow. Compared to their midday and afternoon rituals, the Muslim faithful had considerably less leeway as to when they said the sunset prayers, and of course, the sun set at a slightly different time each day. But so far, they'd all coped.

But what was he going to do about the sunset prayers with an influx of 40 Somali workers that would dramatically increase the number of people who would need to leave the line to pray? Was it time to modify his policy? He knew that Title VII of the Civil Rights Act required that he make "reasonable" accommodations to his employees' religious practices unless doing so would impose an "undue hardship" on the employer. Had he reached the point where the accommodations Halima Adan would probably request crossed the line from reasonable to unreasonable? But if he changed his policy, did he risk alienating his workforce?

What Would You Do?

1. Continue the current policy that leaves it up to the Muslim workers as to when they leave the assembly line to perform their sunset rituals.

2. Try to hire the fewest possible Muslim workers so the work line will be efficient on second shift.

3. Ask the Muslim workers to delay their sunset prayers until a regularly scheduled break occurs, pointing out that North Woods is primarily a place of business, not a house of worship.

SOURCES: Based on Rob Johnson, "30 Muslim Workers Fired for Praying on Job at Dell," *The Tennessean* (March 10, 2005), http://tennessean.com/local/archives/05/03/66733769.shtml?Element_ID= 66733769; Anayat Durrani, "Religious Accommodation for Muslim Employees," *Workforce.com*, http://www.workforce.com/archive/feature/22/26/98/index.php?ht=muslim%20muslim; U.S. Equal Employment Opportunity Commission, "Questions and Answers about Employer Responsibilities Concerning the Employment of Muslims, Arabs, South Asians, and Sikhs," http://www.eeoc.gov/facts/backlash-employer.html; and U.S. Department of Commerce, Office of Health and Consumer Goods, "2005 Appliance Industry Outlook," *Trade.gov*, http://www.ita.doc.gov/td/ocg/outlook05_appliances.pdf.

Case for Critical Analysis

Waterway Industries

Lee Carter and her husband, Jack Schiffer, became two of Waterway Industries most valuable managers almost by accident. But now, if the snatch of conversation CEO Cyrus Maher just overheard on his way to get coffee meant what he thought it did, he was in danger of losing the very people who'd contributed most to Waterway's recent growth surge.

Cyrus had met Lee and Jack, both paddling enthusiasts, when he was advisor to a university outing club. Lee had been majoring in marketing at the time, while Jack was studying engineering. He took a liking to the young couple and offered them part-time work at Waterways, then a small manufacturer of high-quality canoes in upstate New York. After graduation, the newlyweds decided to stay on full-time and take a breather before launching their demanding professional careers. That was 10 years ago.

When Lee and Jack joined Waterway, they found a laid-back atmosphere. Even as Waterway had grown steadily over the years, it continued to attract shopfloor employees who loved water sports and enjoyed making quality products they themselves used in their off-hours. Workers spent time good-naturedly horsing around with each other, but they got their work done on time. In fact, on nice days, they often completed their tasks early so they could leave by mid-afternoon and get some canoeing in before dark.

In late 2003, Lee took a hard look at the slowing demand for canoes and the rapidly growing kayak market. "Cyrus," she asked, "have you ever thought about making kayaks?" Intrigued, Cyrus gave Lee and Jack the go-ahead to see what they could do. Jack responded by designing a compact, inexpensive, lightweight kayak that immediately found favor among baby boomers looking for a way to have some fun. Lee established a formal marketing department to drive sales. That's when things really took off. Many Waterway canoe customers placed sizable kayak orders, and a number of private labels asked Cyrus to make kayaks for their companies.

Energized by their success, Cyrus, Lee, Jack (who'd recently been named design department head), and other Waterway managers developed a long-range strategic plan that called for aggressive growth, new product designs, and nationwide marketing and distribution by 2008. These ambitious plans resulted in an increased workload and a faster-paced work environment. Waterway managers provided employees across-the-board pay raises.

In Cyrus's opinion, the pay increases were more than reasonable, but lately he has heard complaints, both from the shopfloor and from managers. He is dealing with compensation issues the way he always has—on a case-by-case basis. When a plant manager suggested top hourly performers receive additional wage increases, Cyrus turned it down, contending that Waterway's wages were in line with other manufacturers in rural New York. Shortly afterwards, a new automotive parts plant offering a slightly higher wage lured away three of Waterway's best workers.

When the company's CFO threatened to leave unless his compensation package included profit-sharing, Cyrus appeased him with a pay increase and extra vacation. But Lee and Jack have been more insistent. What they feel they deserve, in view of their contribution to the company's growth, is a share in the profits. He turned them down, and now, if he heard correctly, they are considering a lucrative job offer from a competing company.

What should the CEO do? He sees Lee and Jack's point of view but would the other managers understand if he granted the couple the part ownership in the company he'd denied the others? And how would the hourly workers react?

Questions

1. Does Waterway's current compensation system seem to fit the company's strategy of aggressive growth and product innovation? How might it be changed to achieve a better fit?

2. Specifically, how would you gather the data and design a competitive compensation system for Waterway? Would your approach be different for hourly workers versus managers? Would you treat all managers equally?

3. How might nonfinancial incentives play a role in helping Waterway retain hourly shop workers? How can they help keep aggressive and ambitious professionals such as Lee and Jack?

SOURCES: Based on Robert D. Nicoson, "Growing Pains," *Harvard Business Review* (July–August 1996): 20–36.

BIZ FLIX

Bowfinger

This film, which brought Steve Martin and Eddie Murphy together for the first time, offers a funny look at Hollywood film-making. Bobby Bowfinger (Martin), perhaps the least successful director in films, wants to produce a low-budget film with top star Kit Ramsey (Murphy). Bowfinger's problem: how to recruit a crew and cast with almost no budget while tricking Kit into appearing in his film.

Bowfinger interviews several candidates for the Kit Ramsey lookalike role. He rejects everyone until Jifferson (Jiff) Ramsey (also played by Murphy) auditions. This scene is an edited version of "The Look-alike" sequence early in the film. It includes Jiff's audition, interview, and a brief look at his first day at work.

What to Watch for and Ask Yourself

1. Does Bobby Bowfinger have a set of valid selection criteria for filling the role of a Kit Ramsey look-alike? Does Bowfinger apply the criteria uniformly to each applicant?

2. Is Jiff Ramsey a good person-job fit in the screen role of Kit Ramsey?

3. Do you predict that Jiff Ramsey will be successful as a Kit Ramsey substitute?

VIDEO CASE

Human Resource Management at Allstate

Most successful companies agree that their greatest asset is their employees. It is the knowledge, skills, experience, and creativity of their human capital that keeps successful companies at the forefront of their industries. Talented employees, performing to their full potential, are what give these companies their competitive edge. To attract, retain, and develop this crucial capital, takes comprehensive human resource management. And with today's swiftly changing labor culture, human resource managers must stay on top of management and compensation trends to remain competitive.

We all know "you're in good hands with Allstate." And Allstate has a lot of hands. With over 70,000 employees, Allstate is committed to attracting and retaining the top professionals in their industry while creating a workforce that reflects the diversity of their customer base. Of Allstate's many employees, 29.4% are minorities, 58.9% are women, and within management, over 40 percent are women and nearly 20 percent come from one of five minority groups. As Ed Liddy, Allstate's chairman and CEO said, "Our competitive advantage is our people and our people are diverse . . . Diversity is a strength and a strategy through which the company will continue to realize its growth goals."

Allstate's human resource management philosophy reflects the change in the social contract of today's workforce. Their challenging and collaborative work environment encourages individual accountability, innovative thinking, and continuous learning. They provide challenging positions that are engaging and meaningful to their employees and reward employees' efforts on a pay for performance basis. Allstate also offers a comprehensive compensation package that encourages employees to balance their work and personal life and pursue career opportunities.

Allstate makes a huge investment in their employees. In 2005, Allstate spent $3.3 billion on employee compensation, payroll taxes, welfare, and benefits. In addition to the standard benefits package of insurance, retirement, profit-sharing, and time off compensation, Allstate has a number of other benefits that contribute to their overall Work/Life Strategy. These include the option for flexible work arrangements, on-site childcare at headquarters, adoption reimbursement, and other perks such as on-site dry-cleaning, oil change, salon, postal and catering services at their headquarters. Not only is Allstate committed to attracting and retaining quality employees, they also foster personal and professional growth. Allstate has numerous education programs which include mentoring programs, on-site undergraduate, MBA and professional courses, tuition reimbursement, and education loans for employees and their families. They also have in-house training such as the Talent Acceleration Program, which develops leadership early in employee's careers, and the Learning Resource network which connects employees to more than 6,000 learning activities that help them develop new business, interpersonal, technical, and leadership skills. Allstate encourages their employees to live complete lives, giving back to their families and communities. More than 50% of Allstate employees participate in the company's Helping Hands program and the Allstate Foundation awards $500 grants to nonprofit organizations where Allstate employees volunteer. With a donation matching program, Allstate also contributed $9.5 million to various community development agencies.

Allstate's investment in its human resources has met with great success. Not only is Allstate the nation's largest publicly held personal lines insurer, but the satisfaction rate from its annual employee satisfaction survey was 88%. The employees of Allstate are clearly in good hands.

Questions

1. Imagine you are considering a job at Allstate. Use the matching model to determine if it would be good fit. Why or why not?

2. In what way does Allstate's human resource management philosophy adhere to the new social contract between organization and employee?

3. What are the benefits for a pay-for-performance-based system versus a seniority-based pay system?

If there was ever an industry in need of transformational leadership, it's today's record business. Columbia Records hopes it's found just such a leader in Rick Rubin, named co-chair of the Sony division in 2007.

Arguably the most visionary producer of the past 20 years, Rubin co-founded hip-hop record label Def Jam. However, unlike many record company executives, he has no background in sound engineering, music, business, or law. His most important credential is that he's a passionate fan. Known for his unusually supportive, egalitarian leadership style, the shaggy Rubin sees his role as nurturing creative people so they can do their best and create art.

Until recently, powerful record company executives decided what music got created. But now musicians are using computer software to produce their own high-quality recordings, and consumers are flocking to file-sharing sites and online stores. CD sales are dropping fast as listeners download singles and create their own CDs of personal favorites. So Rubin has his work cut out for him as he tries to help Columbia rethink its mission, strategy, and structure and come up with badly needed innovative products and technologies.

Dynamics of Behavior in Organizations

chapter outline

Managers' attitudes, and their ability to understand and shape the attitudes of employees, can profoundly affect the workplace and influence employee motivation, morale, and job performance. People differ in many ways. Some are quiet and shy while others are gregarious; some are thoughtful and serious while others are impulsive and fun loving. Employees—and managers—bring their individual differences to work each day. Differences in attitudes, values, personality, and behavior influence how people interpret an assignment, whether they like to be told what to do, how they handle challenges, and how they interact with others. People are an organization's most valuable resource—and the source of some of managers' most difficult problems. Three basic leadership skills are at the core of identifying and solving people problems: (1) diagnosing, or gaining insight into the situation a manager is trying to influence; (2) adapting individual behavior and resources to meet the needs of the situation; and (3) communicating in a way that others can understand and accept. Thus, managers need insight about individual differences to understand what a behavioral situation is now and what it may be in the future.

To handle this responsibility, managers need to understand the principles of organizational behavior—that is, the ways individuals and groups tend to act in organizations. By increasing their knowledge of individual differences in the areas of attitudes, personality, perception, learning, and stress management, managers can understand and lead employees and colleagues through many workplace challenges. This chapter introduces basic principles of organizational behavior in each of these areas.

Organizational Behavior

Organizational behavior, commonly called OB, is an interdisciplinary field dedicated to the study of human attitudes, behavior, and performance in organizations. OB draws concepts from many disciplines, including psychology, sociology, cultural anthropology, industrial engineering, economics, ethics, and vocational counseling, as well as the discipline of management. The concepts and principles of organizational behavior are important to managers because in every organization, human beings ultimately make the decisions that control how the organization acquires and uses resources. Those people may cooperate with, compete with, support, or undermine one another. Their beliefs and feelings about themselves, their co-workers, and the organization shape what they do and how well they do it. People can distract the organization from its strategy by engaging in conflict and misunderstandings, or they can pool their diverse talents and perspectives to accomplish much more as a group than they could ever do as individuals.

By understanding what causes people to behave as they do, managers can exercise leadership to achieve positive outcomes. By creating a positive environment, for example, managers can foster **organizational citizenship,** which refers to the tendency of people to help one another and put in extra effort that goes beyond job requirements to contribute to the organization's success.

An employee demonstrates organizational citizenship by being helpful to co-workers and customers, doing extra work when necessary, and looking for ways to improve products and procedures. These behaviors enhance the organization's performance and help to build *social capital,* as described in Chapter 9.[1] Organizational citizenship contributes to positive relationships both within the organization and with customers, leading to a high level of social capital and smooth organizational functioning. Managers can encourage organizational citizenship by applying their knowledge of human behavior, such as selecting people with positive attitudes and personalities, helping them see how they can contribute, and enabling them to learn from and cope with workplace challenges.

ATTITUDES

Most students have probably heard the expression that someone "has an attitude problem," which means some consistent quality about the person affects his or her behavior in a

TAKE ACTION ▶

No matter what job you have, strive to be a good corporate citizen, work hard, get along with others, and be the kind of colleague others want to work with.

organizational behavior
an interdisciplinary field dedicated to the study of how individuals and groups tend to act in organizations.

organizational citizenship
work behavior that goes beyond job requirements and contributes as needed to the organization's success.

negative way. An employee with an attitude problem might be hard to get along with, might constantly gripe and cause problems, and might persistently resist new ideas. We all seem to know intuitively what an attitude is, but we do not consciously think about how strongly attitudes affect our behavior. Defined formally, an **attitude** is an evaluation—either positive or negative—that predisposes a person to act in a certain way. Understanding employee attitudes is important to managers because attitudes determine how people perceive the work environment, interact with others, and behave on the job. Emerging research is revealing the importance of positive attitudes to both individual and organizational success. For example, studies have found that the characteristic most common to top executives is an optimistic attitude. People rise to the top because they have the ability to see opportunities where others see problems and can instill in others a sense of hope and possibility for the future.[2]

Good managers strive to develop and reinforce positive attitudes among all employees because happy, positive people are healthier, more effective, and more productive.[3] A person who has the attitude "I love my work; it's challenging and fun" will typically tackle work-related problems cheerfully, whereas one who comes to work with the attitude "I hate my job" is not likely to show much enthusiasm or commitment to solving problems. Some companies, such as David's Bridal, the nation's largest bridal-store chain, are applying scientific research to improve employee attitudes—and sales performance.

As the example at David's Bridal shows, sometimes negative attitudes can result from characteristics of the job, such as a high stress level, but managers can find ways to help people have more positive attitudes. Managers should pay attention to negative attitudes because they can be both the result of underlying problems in the workplace as well as a contributor to forthcoming problems.[4]

Components of Attitudes.

One important step for managers is recognizing and understanding the *components* of attitudes, which is particularly important when attempting to change attitudes.

Behavioral scientists consider attitudes to have three components: cognitions (thoughts), affect (feelings), and behavior.[5] The cognitive component of an attitude includes the beliefs, opinions, and information the person has about the object of the attitude, such as knowledge of what a job entails and opinions about personal abilities. The affective component is the person's emotions or feelings about the object of the attitude, such as enjoying or hating a job. The behavioral component of an attitude is the person's intention to behave toward the object of the attitude in a certain way. Exhibit 10.1 illustrates the three components of a positive attitude toward one's job. The cognitive element is the conscious thought that "my job is interesting and challenging." The affective element is the feeling that "I love this job." These elements, in turn, are related to the behavioral component—an employee might arrive at work early because he or she is happy with the job.

Often, when we think about attitudes, we focus on the cognitive component. However, it is important for managers to remember the other components as well. The emotional (affective) component is often the stronger factor in affecting behavior. When people feel strongly about something, the affective component may influence them to act in a certain way no matter what someone does to change their thoughts or opinions. Recall the

CONCEPT CONNECTION

Baseball legend Hank Aaron is still hitting home runs. Aaron has successfully made the transition from sports to business and built a BMW dealership from the ground up that now ranks in the top 50% in sales for BMW of North America, with revenue growth of 54.6% last year. Aaron's **positive attitude** played a large role in his success, first as a baseball player and now as a business leader. "I believed if I could just get into something and keep it growing, I could do well. That's when I looked at myself and said I was a businessman."

attitude
a cognitive and affective evaluation that predisposes a person to act in a certain way.

David's Bridal

Planning a wedding can be one of the most joyful experiences in a woman's life—and one of the most nerve-wracking. The salespeople at David's Bridal, a 267-store chain owned by Federated Department Stores, bear the brunt of these intense emotions. For many, dealing with those emotions can be overwhelming and exhausting, translating into negative attitudes and impatience with already-stressed customers.

Managers turned to new research on happiness to help employees cope and develop more positive attitudes. Adaptiv Learning Systems, based in King of Prussia, Pennsylvania, conducted a pilot training program in four stores based on the work of psychologist Martin Seligman. Salespeople were taught how to feel more cheerful with techniques such as "emotion regulation," "impulse control," and "learned optimism." They learned coping techniques to use when dealing with a harried, indecisive bride-to-be, such as making a mental list of the top five things that bring them joy. These techniques enable salespeople to be more calm and centered, which helps customers stay calm and centered as well. That attitude/behavior translates into better sales, meaning employees make better commissions, which in turn contributes to more positive attitudes toward the job.

The success of the pilot project spurred David's Bridal to consider various training options, such as online training, to expand the strategies to all of the company's 3,000 employees.[6]

discussion of idea champions in Chapter 8. When someone is passionate about a new idea, he or she may go to great lengths to implement it, even when colleagues and superiors say the idea is stupid. Another example is an employee who is furious about being asked to work overtime on his birthday. The supervisor might present clear, rational reasons for the need to put in extra hours, but the employee might still act based on his anger—by failing

EXHIBIT 10.1

Components of an Attitude

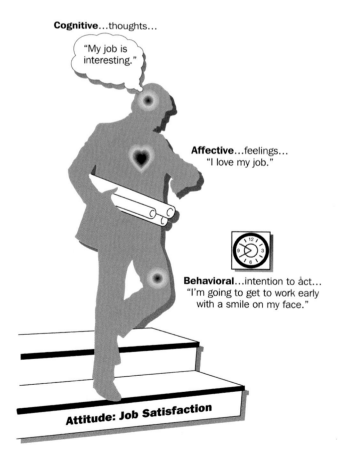

Cognitive...thoughts...

"My job is interesting."

Affective...feelings...
"I love my job."

Behavioral...intention to act...
"I'm going to get to work early with a smile on my face."

Attitude: Job Satisfaction

to cooperate, lashing out at co-workers, or even quitting. In cases such as these, effective leadership includes addressing the emotions associated with the attitude. Are employees so excited that their judgment may be clouded or so discouraged that they have given up trying? If nothing else, the manager probably needs to be aware of situations that involve strong emotions and give employees a chance to vent their feelings appropriately.

As a general rule, changing just one component—cognitions, affect, or behavior—can contribute to an overall change in attitude. Suppose a manager concludes that some employees have the attitude that the manager should make all the decisions affecting the department, but the manager prefers that employees assume more decision-making responsibility. To change the underlying attitude, the manager would consider whether to educate employees about the areas in which they can make good decisions (changing the cognitive component), build enthusiasm with pep talks about the satisfaction of employee empowerment (changing the affective component), or simply insist that employees make their own decisions (behavioral component) with the expectation that, after they experience the advantages of decision-making authority, they will begin to like it.

High-Performance Work Attitudes. The attitudes of most interest to managers are those related to work, especially attitudes that influence how well employees perform. To lead employees effectively, managers logically seek to cultivate the kinds of attitudes that are associated with high performance. Two attitudes that might relate to high performance are satisfaction with one's job and commitment to the organization.

Job Satisfaction. A positive attitude toward one's job is called **job satisfaction.** In general, people experience this attitude when their work matches their needs and interests, when working conditions and rewards (such as pay) are satisfactory, when they like

their co-workers, and when they have positive relationships with supervisors. You can take the quiz in Exhibit 10.2 to better understand some of the factors that contribute to job satisfaction.

Many managers believe job satisfaction is important because they think satisfied employees will do better work. In fact, research shows that the link between satisfaction and performance is generally small and is influenced by other factors.[7] For example, the importance of satisfaction varies according to the amount of control the employee has; employees doing routine tasks may produce about the same output no matter how they feel about the job. However, one internal study at Sears found a clear link between employee satisfaction, customer satisfaction, and revenue. In particular, employees' attitudes about whether their workloads were manageable and well organized ranked among the top 10 indicators of company performance.[8]

Managers of today's knowledge workers often rely on job satisfaction to keep motivation and enthusiasm for the

job satisfaction
a positive attitude toward one's job.

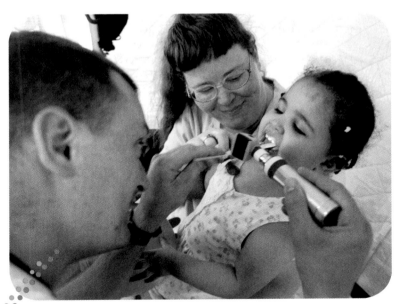

CONCEPT CONNECTION

"To shake the hand of someone who was nearly dead—there's no feeling like that in the world." That's how one physician assistant (PA) explained why he finds the profession so fulfilling. **Job satisfaction** is extraordinarily high for PAs, such as Jim Johnson, shown here helping patients in a makeshift medical tent after Hurricane Katrina hit Gulfport, Mississippi. A recent survey reported that 90 percent would make the same career choice all over again. In addition to good pay and flexible working conditions, PAs relish the autonomy of the job, a chance to help others, the challenge of diagnosing and treating a variety of ailments, and working as part of a team.

Think of a job—either a current or previous job—that was important to you, and then answer the following questions with respect to how satisfied you were with that job. Please answer the six questions with a number 1–5 that reflects the extent of your satisfaction.

1 = Very dissatisfied   3 = Neutral   5 = Very satisfied
2 = Dissatisfied   4 = Satisfied

1. Overall, how satisfied are you with your job?	1	2	3	4	5
2. How satisfied are you with the opportunities to learn new things?	1	2	3	4	5
3. How satisfied are you with your boss?	1	2	3	4	5
4. How satisfied are you with the people in your work group?	1	2	3	4	5
5. How satisfied are you with the amount of pay you receive?	1	2	3	4	5
6. How satisfied are you with the advancement you are making in the organization?	1	2	3	4	5

Scoring and Interpretation: Add up your responses to the six questions to obtain your total score: _____. The questions represent various aspects of satisfaction that an employee may experience on a job. If your score is 24 or above, you probably feel satisfied with the job. If your score is 12 or below, you probably do not feel satisfied. What is your level of performance in your job, and is your performance related to your level of satisfaction?

SOURCES: These questions were adapted from Daniel R. Denison, *Corporate Culture and Organizational Effectiveness* (New York: John Wiley, 1990); and John D. Cook, Susan J. Hepworth, Toby D. Wall, and Peter B. Warr, *The Experience of Work: A Compendium and Review of 249 Measures and their Use* (San Diego, CA: Academic Press, 1981).

EXHIBIT 10.2
Rate Your Job Satisfaction

organization high. Organizations don't want to lose talented, highly skilled workers. In addition, most managers care about their employees and simply want them to feel good about their work—and almost everyone prefers being around people who have positive attitudes. Regrettably, a survey by International Survey Research found that Gen X employees, those who are carrying the weight of much of today's knowledge work, are the least satisfied of all demographic groups.[9] Managers play an important role in whether employees have positive or negative attitudes toward their jobs.[10]

Assess Your Answer

1 Job satisfaction is about getting a good paycheck and liking the work you do.

ANSWER: Job satisfaction usually requires a number of things, such as decent pay, liking the work itself, but also having a good boss, positive relationships with co-workers, and some control over the job itself and working conditions.

ORGANIZATIONAL COMMITMENT

Organizational commitment refers to an employee's loyalty to and engagement with the organization. An employee with a high degree of organizational commitment is likely to say *we* when talking about the company. Such a person likes being a part of the organization and tries to contribute to its success. This attitude is illustrated by an incident at the A. W. Chesterton Company, a Massachusetts manufacturer of mechanical seals and pumps. When two Chesterton pumps that supply water on Navy ship *USS John F. Kennedy* failed on a Saturday night just before the ship's scheduled departure, Todd Robinson, the leader of the team that produces the seals, swung into action. He and his fiancée, who also works for Chesterton, worked through the night to make new seals and deliver them to be installed before the ship left port.[11]

organizational commitment
loyalty to and heavy involvement in one's organization.

Most managers want to enjoy the benefits of loyal, committed employees, including low turnover and willingness to do more than the job's basic requirements. In addition, results of a survey of more than 650,000 employees in global organizations suggest that companies

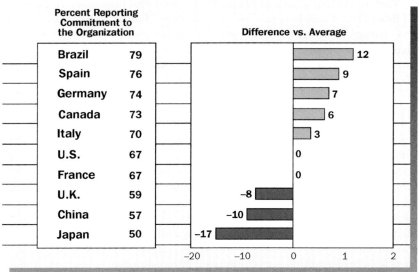

Shaded difference bar denotes a statistically significant difference.

EXHIBIT 10.3

Variations in Organizational Commitment: The World's 10 Largest Economies

with committed employees perform better. The study found that companies with highly committed employees outperformed the industry average over a 12-month period by 6 percent, whereas those with low levels of commitment underperformed the average by 9 percent.[12] Alarmingly, levels of commitment in the United States are significantly lower than those in half of the world's other large economies, as illustrated in Exhibit 10.3. U.S. employees are less committed than those in Brazil, Spain, Germany, Canada, and Italy. This low level of organizational commitment puts U.S. firms at a serious disadvantage in the global marketplace.[13]

The high motivation and engagement that comes with organizational commitment is essential to the success of organizations that depend on employees' ideas and creativity. Trust in management's decisions and integrity is an important component of organizational commitment.[14] Unfortunately, in recent years, many employees have lost that trust, resulting in a decline in commitment. Just 28 percent of employees surveyed by *Fast Company* magazine said they think the CEO of their company has integrity. Another recent survey by Ajilon Professional Staffing found that only 29 percent of employees believe their boss truly cares about them and looks out for their interests.[15]

Managers can promote organizational commitment by keeping employees informed, giving them a say in decisions, providing the necessary training and other resources that enable them to succeed, treating them fairly, and offering rewards they value. For example, recent studies suggest that employee commitment in today's workplace is strongly correlated with initiatives and benefits that help people balance their work and personal lives.[16]

Conflicts Among Attitudes. Sometimes people discover that their attitudes conflict with one another or are not reflected in behavior. For example, a person's high level of organizational commitment might conflict with a commitment to family members. If employees routinely work evenings and weekends, their long hours and dedication to the job might conflict with their belief that family ties are important. This conflict can create a state of **cognitive dissonance,** a psychological discomfort that occurs when individuals recognize inconsistencies in their own attitudes and behaviors.[17] The theory of cognitive dissonance, developed by social psychologist Leon Festinger in the 1950s, says that people want to behave in accordance with their attitudes and usually will take corrective action to alleviate the dissonance and achieve balance.

 TAKE ACTION

As a manager, if you want committed employees, make sure you are acting in a trustworthy fashion.

cognitive dissonance
a condition in which two attitudes or a behavior and an attitude conflict.

In the case of working overtime, people who can control their hours might restructure responsibilities so that they have time for both work and family. In contrast, those who are unable to restructure workloads might develop an unfavorable attitude toward the employer, reducing their organizational commitment. They might resolve their dissonance by saying they would like to spend more time with their kids but their unreasonable employer demands that they work too many hours.

Perception

Another critical aspect of understanding behavior is perception. **Perception** is the cognitive process people use to make sense out of the environment by selecting, organizing, and interpreting information from the environment. Attitudes affect perceptions, and vice versa. For example, a person might have developed the attitude that managers are insensitive and arrogant, based on a pattern of perceiving arrogant and insensitive behavior from managers over a period of time. If the person moves to a new job, this attitude will continue to affect the way this person perceives superiors in the new environment, even though managers in the new workplace might take great pains to understand and respond to employees' needs.

Because of individual differences in attitudes, personality, values, interests, and so forth, people often "see" the same thing in different ways. A class that is boring to one student might be fascinating to another. One student might perceive an assignment to be challenging and stimulating, whereas another might find it a silly waste of time. Referring to the topic of diversity discussed in Chapter 9, many African Americans perceive that blacks are regularly discriminated against, whereas many white employees perceive that blacks are given special opportunities in the workplace.[18] Similarly, in a survey of financial profession executives, 40 percent of women perceive that women face a "glass ceiling" that keeps them from reaching top management levels, while only 10 percent of men share that perception.[19]

We can think of perception as a step-by-step process, as shown in Exhibit 10.4. First, we observe information (sensory data) from the environment through our senses: taste, smell, hearing, sight, and touch. Next, our mind screens the data and selects only the items we will process further. Third, we organize the selected data into meaningful patterns for interpretation and response. Most differences in perception among people at work are related to how they select and organize sensory data. You can experience differences in perceptual organization by looking at the visuals in Exhibit 10.5. What do you see in part *a* of Exhibit 10.5? Most people see this as a dog, but others see only a series of unrelated ink-blots. Some people will see the figure in part *b* as a beautiful young woman, whereas others will see an old one. Now look at part *c*. How many blocks do you see—six or seven? Some people have to turn the figure upside down before they can see seven blocks. These visuals illustrate how complex perception is. Perception has a lot to do with how we view workplace interactions. Someone with a large ego will expect special treatment and would tend to see equal treatment as more-or-less unfair.

PERCEPTUAL SELECTIVITY

We all are aware of our environment, but not everything in it is equally important to our perception of it. We tune in to some data (e.g., a familiar voice off in the distance) and tune out other data (e.g., paper shuffling next to us). People are bombarded by so much sensory data that it is impossible to process it all. The brain's solution is to run the data through a

TAKE ACTION

Always remember that your reactions to some incident will not necessarily be the same as others.

perception
the cognitive process people use to make sense out of the environment by selecting, organizing, and interpreting information.

EXHIBIT 10.4

The Perception Process

| Observing information via the senses | → | Screening the information and selecting what to process | → | Organizing the selected data into patterns for interpretation and response |

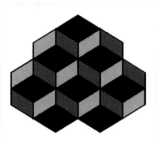

a. Do you see the dog?　　**b.** Old woman or young woman?　　**c.** How many blocks?

perceptual filter that retains some parts and eliminates others. **Perceptual selectivity** is the process by which individuals screen and select the various objects and stimuli that vie for their attention. Certain stimuli catch their attention, and others do not.

People typically focus on stimuli that satisfy their needs and that are consistent with their attitudes, values, and personality. For example, employees who need positive feedback to feel good about themselves might pick up on positive statements made by a supervisor but tune out most negative comments. A supervisor could use this understanding to tailor feedback in a positive way to help the employee improve work performance. The influence of needs on perception has been studied in laboratory experiments and found to have a strong impact on what people perceive.[20]

Characteristics of the stimuli themselves also affect perceptual selectivity. People tend to notice stimuli that stand out against other stimuli or that are more intense than surrounding stimuli. Examples are a loud noise in a quiet room or a bright red dress at a party where most women are wearing basic black. People also tend to notice things that are familiar to them, such as a familiar voice in a crowd, as well as things that are new or different from their previous experiences. In addition, *primacy* and *recency* are important to perceptual selectivity. People pay relatively greater attention to sensory data that occur toward the beginning of an event or toward the end. Primacy supports the old truism that first impressions really do count, whether it be on a job interview, meeting a date's parents, or participating in a new social group. Recency reflects the reality that the last impression might be a lasting impression. For example, Malaysian Airlines discovered its value in building customer loyalty. A woman traveling with a nine-month-old might find the flight itself an exhausting blur, but one such traveler enthusiastically told people for years how Malaysian Airlines flight attendants helped her with baggage collection and ground transportation.[21]

As these examples show, perceptual selectivity is a complex filtering process. Managers can use an understanding of perceptual selectivity to obtain clues about why one person sees things differently from others, and they can apply the principles to their own communications and actions, especially when they want to attract or focus attention.

PERCEPTUAL DISTORTIONS

After people select the sensory data to be perceived, they begin grouping the data into recognizable patterns. Perceptual organization is the process by which people organize or categorize stimuli according to their own frame of reference. Of particular concern in the work environment are **perceptual distortions,** errors in perceptual judgment that arise from inaccuracies in any part of the perceptual process.

Some types of errors are so common that managers should become familiar with them. These include stereotyping, the halo effect, projection, and perceptual defense. Managers who recognize these perceptual distortions can better adjust their perceptions to more closely match objective reality.

EXHIBIT 10.5
Perception—What Do You See?

TAKE ACTION
Remember that other people will not always hear everything you say, especially if it is difficult information.

perceptual selectivity
the process by which individuals screen and select the various stimuli that vie for their attention.

perceptual distortions
errors in perceptual judgment that arise from inaccuracies in any part of the perceptual process.

TAKE ACTION ▶

As a manager, avoid having some employees become your "favorites" because it causes other workers to withdraw emotionally from their work.

Stereotyping is the tendency to assign an individual to a group or broad category (e.g., female, black, elderly; or male, white, disabled) and then to attribute widely held generalizations about the group to the individual. Thus, someone meets a new colleague, sees he is in a wheelchair, assigns him to the category "physically disabled," and attributes to this colleague generalizations she believes about people with disabilities, which may include a belief that he is less able than other co-workers. However, the person's inability to walk should not be seen as indicative of lesser abilities in other areas. Indeed, the assumption of limitations may not only offend him, but it also prevents the person making the stereotypical judgment from benefiting from the many ways in which this person can contribute. Stereotyping prevents people from truly knowing those they classify in this way. In addition, negative stereotypes prevent talented people from advancing in an organization and fully contributing their talents to the organization's success.

The **halo effect** occurs when the perceiver develops an overall impression of a person or situation based on one characteristic, either favorable or unfavorable. In other words, a halo blinds the perceiver to other characteristics that should be used in generating a more complete assessment. The halo effect can play a significant role in performance appraisal, as we discussed in Chapter 9. For example, a person with an outstanding attendance record may be assessed as responsible, industrious, and highly productive; another person with less-than-average attendance may be assessed as a poor performer. Either assessment may be true, but it is the manager's job to be sure the assessment is based on complete information about all job-related characteristics and not just his preferences for good attendance.

Projection is the tendency of perceivers to see their own personal traits in other people; that is, they project their own needs, feelings, values, and attitudes into their judgment of others. A manager who is achievement oriented might assume that subordinates are as well. This assumption might cause the manager to restructure jobs to be less routine and more challenging, without regard for employees' actual satisfaction. The best guards against errors based on projection are self-awareness and empathy.

Perceptual defense is the tendency of perceivers to protect themselves against ideas, objects, or people that are threatening. People perceive things that are satisfying and pleasant but tend to disregard things that are disturbing and unpleasant. In essence, people develop blind spots in the perceptual process so that negative sensory data do not hurt them. For example, the director of a nonprofit educational organization in Tennessee hated dealing with conflict because he had grown up with parents who constantly argued and often put him in the middle of their arguments. The director consistently overlooked discord among staff members until things would reach a boiling point. When the blowup occurred, the director would be shocked and dismayed because he had truly perceived that everything was going smoothly among the staff. Recognizing perceptual blind spots can help people develop a clearer picture of reality.

stereotyping
the tendency to assign an individual to a group or broad category and then attribute generalizations about the group to the individual.

halo effect
an overall impression of a person or situation based on one characteristic, either favorable or unfavorable.

projection
the tendency to see one's own personal traits in other people.

perceptual defense
the tendency of perceivers to protect themselves by disregarding ideas, objects, or people that are threatening to them.

Business Blooper

Cisco

Cisco CEO John Chambers had his own problems with perceptual distortions. The day before he spent $89 million to buy router maker Procket, he proudly announced,

"I'm not going to buy another router company for a router. I could not be more comfortable with our router strategy."

SOURCE: Adam Horowitz, et al, "101 Dumbest Moments in Business," *Business 2.0* (Jan/Feb. 2005): 106.

ATTRIBUTIONS

As people organize what they perceive, they often draw conclusions, such as about an object or a person. Among the judgments people make as part of the perceptual process are attributions. **Attributions** are judgments about what caused a person's behavior—something about the person or something about the situation. An *internal attribution* says characteristics of the person led to the behavior. ("My boss yelled at me because he's impatient and doesn't listen.") An *external attribution* says something about the situation caused the person's behavior. ("My boss yelled at me because I missed the deadline, and the customer is upset.") Attributions are important because they help people decide how to handle a situation. In the case of the boss yelling, a person who blames the yelling on the boss's personality will view the boss as the problem and might cope by avoiding the boss. In contrast, someone who blames the yelling on the situation might try to help prevent such situations in the future.

Social scientists have studied the attributions people make and identified three factors that influence whether an attribution will be external or internal.[22] These three factors are illustrated in Exhibit 10.6.

1. *Distinctiveness.* Whether the behavior is unusual for that person (in contrast to a person displaying the same kind of behavior in many situations). If the behavior is distinctive, the perceiver probably will make an *external* attribution.

2. *Consistency.* Whether the person being observed has a history of behaving in the same way. People generally make *internal* attributions about consistent behavior.

3. *Consensus.* Whether other people tend to respond to similar situations in the same way. A person who has observed others handle similar situations in the same way will likely make an *external* attribution; that is, it will seem that the situation produces the type of behavior observed.

In addition to these general rules, people tend to have biases that they apply when making attributions. When evaluating others, we tend to underestimate the influence of

attributions
judgments about what caused a person's behavior—either characteristics of the person or of the situation.

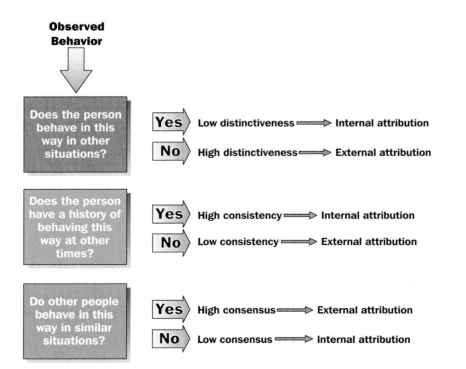

EXHIBIT 10.6

Factors Influencing Whether Attributions Are Internal or External

external factors and overestimate the influence of internal factors. This tendency is called the **fundamental attribution error.** Consider the case of someone being promoted to CEO. Employees, outsiders, and the media generally focus on the characteristics of the person that allowed him or her to achieve the promotion. In reality, however, the selection of that person might have been heavily influenced by external factors, such as business conditions creating a need for someone with a strong financial or marketing background at that particular time.

Another bias that distorts attributions involves attributions we make about our own behavior. People tend to overestimate the contribution of internal factors to their successes and overestimate the contribution of external factors to their failures. This tendency, called the **self-serving bias,** means people give themselves too much credit for what they do well and give external forces too much blame when they fail. Thus, if your manager says you don't communicate well enough, and you think your manager doesn't listen well enough, the truth may actually lie somewhere in between.

Personality and Behavior

Another area of particular interest to organizational behavior is personality. In recent years, many employers showed heightened interest in matching people's personalities to the needs of the job and the organization.

In the workplace, we find people whose behavior is consistently pleasant or aggressive or stubborn in a variety of situations. An individual's **personality** is the set of characteristics that underlie a relatively stable pattern of behavior in response to ideas, objects, or people in the environment. Understanding personality can help managers predict how a person might act in a particular situation. Managers who appreciate the ways their employees' personalities differ have insight into what kinds of leadership behavior will be most influential.

PERSONALITY TRAITS

In common usage, people think of personality in terms of traits, the fairly consistent characteristics a person exhibits. Researchers investigated whether any traits stand up to scientific scrutiny. Although investigators examined thousands of traits over the years, their findings fit into five general dimensions that describe personality. These dimensions, often called the "Big Five" personality factors, are illustrated in Exhibit 10.7.[23] Each factor may contain a wide range of specific traits. The **Big Five personality factors** describe an individual's extroversion, agreeableness, conscientiousness, emotional stability, and openness to experience:

1. *Extroversion.* The degree to which a person is outgoing, sociable, assertive, and comfortable with interpersonal relationships.

2. *Agreeableness.* The degree to which a person is able to get along with others by being good-natured, likable, cooperative, forgiving, understanding, and trusting.

3. *Conscientiousness.* The degree to which a person is focused on a few goals, thus behaving in ways that are responsible, dependable, persistent, and achievement oriented.

4. *Emotional stability.* The degree to which a person is calm, enthusiastic, and self-confident, rather than tense, depressed, moody, or insecure.

5. *Openness to experience.* The degree to which a person has a broad range of interests and is imaginative, creative, artistically sensitive, and willing to consider new ideas.

As illustrated in the exhibit, these factors represent a continuum. That is, a person may have a low, moderate, or high degree of each quality. Answer the questions in Exhibit 10.7 to see where you fall on the Big Five scale for each of the factors. Having a moderate-to-high degree of each of the Big Five personality factors is considered desirable for a wide range of employees, but this isn't always a key to success. For example, having an outgoing, sociable personality (extroversion) is considered desirable for managers, but many successful top leaders, including

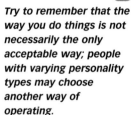

TAKE ACTION
Try to remember that the way you do things is not necessarily the only acceptable way; people with varying personality types may choose another way of operating.

fundamental attribution error
the tendency to underestimate the influence of external factors on another's behavior and to overestimate the influence of internal factors.

self-serving bias
the tendency to overestimate the contribution of internal factors to one's successes and the contribution of external factors to one's failures.

personality
the set of characteristics that underlies a relatively stable pattern of behavior in response to ideas, objects, or people in the environment.

Big Five personality factors
dimensions that describe an individual's extroversion, agreeableness, conscientiousness, emotional stability, and openness to experience.

Each individual's collection of personality traits is different; it is what makes us unique. But, although each *collection* of traits varies, we all share many common traits. The following phrases describe various traits and behaviors. Rate how accurately each statement describes you, based on a scale of 1 to 5, with 1 being very inaccurate and 5 very accurate. Describe yourself as you are now, not as you wish to be. There are no right or wrong answers.

	1	2	3	4	5
	Very Inaccurate			Very Accurate	

Extroversion

	1	2	3	4	5
I am usually the life of the party.	1	2	3	4	5
I feel comfortable around people.	1	2	3	4	5
I am talkative.	1	2	3	4	5

Neuroticism (Low Emotional Stability)

	1	2	3	4	5
I often feel critical of myself.	1	2	3	4	5
I often envy others.	1	2	3	4	5
I am temperamental.	1	2	3	4	5

Agreeableness

	1	2	3	4	5
I am kind and sympathetic.	1	2	3	4	5
I have a good word for everyone.	1	2	3	4	5
I never insult people.	1	2	3	4	5

Openness to New Experiences

	1	2	3	4	5
I am imaginative.	1	2	3	4	5
I prefer to vote for liberal political candidates.	1	2	3	4	5
I really like art.	1	2	3	4	5

Conscientiousness

	1	2	3	4	5
I am systematic and efficient.	1	2	3	4	5
I pay attention to details.	1	2	3	4	5
I am always prepared for class.	1	2	3	4	5

Which are your most prominent traits? For fun and discussion, compare your responses with those of classmates.

EXHIBIT 10.7

The Big Five Personality Traits

Bill Gates, Charles Schwab, and Steven Spielberg, are introverts, people who become drained by social encounters and need time alone to reflect and recharge their batteries.

One study found that 4 in 10 top executives test out to be introverts.[24] Thus, the quality of extroversion is not as significant as is often presumed. Traits of agreeableness, on the other hand, seem to be particularly important in today's collaborative organizations. The days are over when a hard-driving manager can run roughshod over others to earn a promotion. Companies want managers who work smoothly with others and get help from lots of people inside and outside the organization. Today's successful CEOs are not the tough guys of the past but those men and women who know how to get people to like and trust them. Philip Purcell was forced out as CEO of Morgan Stanley largely because he was a remote, autocratic leader who treated many employees with contempt and failed to build positive relationships with clients. Purcell had little goodwill to back him up when things started going against him. Many people just didn't like him. In contrast, Procter & Gamble, CEO A. G. Lafley stresses good relationships with employees, suppliers, partners, and customers as a key to effective management.[25]

2 Managers should be outgoing and agreeable.

Assess Your Answer

ANSWER: Not all managers need to be outgoing, but getting along with others (agreeability) is essential.

One recent book argues that the secret to success in work and in life is *likability*. We all know we're more willing to do something for someone we like than for someone we don't, whether a teammate, a neighbor, a professor, or a supervisor. Managers can increase their likeability by developing traits of agreeableness, including being friendly and cooperative, understanding other people in a genuine way, and striving to make people feel positive about themselves.[26]

Many companies, including JCPenney, DuPont, Toys"R"Us, and the Union Pacific Railroad, use personality testing to hire, evaluate, or promote employees. Surveys show that at least 30 percent of organizations use some kind of personality testing for hiring.[27] American MultiCinema (AMC), one of the largest theater chains in the United States, looks for front-line workers with high conscientiousness and high emotional stability.[28] Marriott Hotels looks for people who score high on conscientiousness and agreeableness because they believe these individuals will provide better service to guests.[29] Companies also use personality testing for managers. Hewlett-Packard, Dell Computer, and General Electric all put candidates for top positions through testing, interviews with psychologists, or both to see whether they have the "right stuff" for the job.[30] Executives at franchises such as Little Gym International and Yum Brands, which owns Pizza Hut, KFC, and Taco Bell, are using personality testing to make sure potential franchisees can fit into their system and be successful.[31] As described in the Spotlight on Skills box, a growing number of entrepreneurs are using sophisticated personality testing to match singles through online dating services. eHarmony, for example, claims to have facilitated 30,000 marriages by matching people based on their compatible personalities.

Despite growing use of personality tests, little hard evidence shows them to be valid predictors of job or relationship success. The long-term tracking of data of romantic matchmaking sites has been referred to as "the early days of a social experiment of unprecedented proportions, involving millions of couples and possibly extending over the course of generations."[32] Similarly, scientific evidence for the valid use of personality testing for job success is still years away.

CONCEPT CONNECTION

Managers at One Georgia Bank routinely refer to their personality test results to gauge their progress toward improving the skills or personal characteristics that need work. CEO Willard Lewis firmly believes in the value of **personality testing** to help him gauge whether job applicants have the optimal traits for the position and to aid employees in their personal development. He's not alone. A 2005 Society for Human Resource Management survey revealed that more than a third of the respondents were already using behavioral or personality assessments, with more organizations planning to incorporate such tests in the near future.

EMOTIONAL INTELLIGENCE

In recent years, new insights into personality are emerging through research in the area of *emotional intelligence*. Emotional intelligence (EQ) includes four basic components:[33]

1. *Self-awareness.* The basis for all the other components is being aware of what you are feeling. People who are in touch with their feelings are better able to guide their own lives and actions. A high degree of self-awareness means you can accurately assess your own strengths and limitations and have a healthy sense of self-confidence. Companies have become highly successful by helping people become more self-aware, as shown in the Spotlight on Skills box.

2. *Self-management.* The ability to control disruptive or harmful emotions and balance one's moods so that worry, anxiety, fear, or anger do not cloud thinking and get in the way of what needs to be done. People who are skilled at self-management remain optimistic and hopeful despite setbacks and obstacles. This ability is crucial for pursuing long-term goals. For example, MetLife found that applicants who failed the regular sales aptitude test but scored high on optimism made 21 percent more sales in their first year and 57 percent more in their second year than those who passed the sales test but scored high on pessimism.[34]

3. *Social awareness.* The ability to understand others and practice *empathy,* which means being able to put yourself in someone else's shoes, to recognize what

Spotlight on Skills

eHarmony.com and PerfectMatch.com

"Experience for yourself the magic and joy of true compatibility," Dr. Neil Clark Warren urges television viewers in his commercials for eHarmony.com, an online dating service with a mission to create happy, lasting marriages. Millions of people think that sounds like a good idea, and according to eHarmony, more than 30,000 marriages have resulted from the service.

The online dating industry has grown into a half-billion dollar industry in just over 10 years. In recent years, personality tests have been central to some of these organizations' strategies. Companies such as eHarmony, Chemistry.com, and PerfectMatch.com use them to pursue so-called serious daters, people whose search for lasting relationships means they're more likely to become subscribers. Increasingly, companies enlist social scientists to help devise personality tests they hope will make the quest for a soul mate more efficient and successful.

After administering a test and determining an individual's personality traits, the companies use the results, along with other information, to match the member up with compatible prospective partners, saving subscribers the time and trouble of wading through volumes of online personal ads. Each company bases its assessment tools and matching process on their varying theories of what makes successful relationships tick. Sociologist Pepper Schwartz helped PerfectMatch.com develop its Duet Total Compatibility System, with its relatively brief 48-question test. The survey focuses on eight specific personality traits, such as romantic impulsivity, personal energy, and decision making, and then takes both a couple's similarities and differences into account during the matching process. Over at Chemistry.com, a Match.com offshoot, anthropologist Helen Fisher helped translate her theory that all personalities are literally chemical in nature into a 146-question test that categorizes people into four personality types. For example, Directors are testosterone-driven, whereas Negotiators tend to run on estrogen. Builders are ruled by their serotonin, and Explorers by their dopamine. Each of these ruling chemicals, according to Fisher's theory, generates specific personality characteristics. "My hypothesis is that we're unconsciously drawn to chemical personalities that complement our type," she says.

And finally, eHarmony's Compatibility Matching System employs an exhaustive 436-question instrument. The personality survey is based on founder Neil Clark Warren's past professional experience and his company's own research into long-lived marriages. Warren, who holds both divinity and clinical psychology degrees, believes the unions most likely to succeed are those between people who share at least 10 of the 29 personality traits eHarmony measures.

Does the approach work? So far, the only company to track relationships it's helped create is eHarmony. Claiming to have helped bring about 16,000 marriages in 2005 alone, the company conducted an in-house study it says showed eHarmony couples enjoyed higher levels of marital satisfaction than those who had met through other channels. But most observers say it's too soon to tell whether using personality tests really will increase your odds of finding your one true love.

SOURCES: Lori Gottlieb, "How Do I Love Thee?" *The Atlantic Monthly* (March 2006): 58–70; Rachel Lehmann-Haupt, "Is the Right Chemistry a Click Nearer?" *The New York Times* (February 12, 2006): Sec. 9, 2; Christopher Palmeri "Dr. Warren's Lonely Hearts Club," *BusinessWeek Online* (February 20, 2006), www.businessweek.com/magazine/content/06_08/b3972111.htm?campaign_id=search; and Alex Salkever, "Finding Love Online, Version 2.0," *BusinessWeek Online* (June 10, 2003), www.businessweek.com/technology/content/jun2003/tc20030610_4294_tc104.htm?campaign_id=search.

Assess Your Answer

3 As a manager, if one of your employees offends you, the best thing is to really let them have it, to teach them a lesson.

ANSWER: Having control of one's emotions and reactions is very important for today's managers. Rather than react in a mode of "showing them" or "getting back" at someone, a manager should carefully consider the best way to resolve an interpersonal problem. How can the problem be solved in a way that people will learn the most, in hopes of avoiding a similar problem in the future?

others are feeling without them needing to tell you. People with social awareness are capable of understanding divergent points of view and interacting effectively with many different types of people.

4. *Relationship awareness.* The ability to connect to others, build positive relationships, respond to the emotions of others, and influence others. People with relationship

TAKE ACTION

As a new manager, one thing that influences your EQ, agreeableness, and other behavior is self-confidence—an important foundation for a good manager. Take the New Manager Self-Test below to see how your level of self-confidence may affect your behavior as a new manager.

awareness know how to listen and communicate clearly, and they treat others with compassion and respect.

Studies find a positive relationship between job performance and high degrees of emotional intelligence in a variety of jobs. Numerous organizations, including the U.S. Air Force and Canada Life, use EQ tests to measure such things as self-awareness, ability to empathize, and capacity to build positive relationships.[35] EQ seems to be particularly important for jobs that require a high degree of social interaction, which includes managers, who are responsible for influencing others and building positive attitudes and relationships in the organization. Managers with low emotional intelligence can undermine employee morale and harm the organization.

At times of great change or crisis, managers rely on a high EQ level to help employees cope with the anxiety and stress they may be experiencing. In the United States, fears of terrorism, devastating natural disasters such as Hurricane Katrina, anxiety and sorrow over

---

NEW MANAGER SELF TEST

Self-Confidence

Self-confidence is the foundation for many behaviors of a new manager. To learn something about your level of self-confidence, answer the following questions. Please answer whether each item is Mostly True or Mostly False for you.

	Mostly True				Mostly False
1. I have a lot of confidence in my decisions.	1	2	3	4	5
2. I would like to change some things about myself.	1	2	3	4	5
3. I am satisfied with my appearance and personality.	1	2	3	4	5
4. I would be nervous about meeting important people.	1	2	3	4	5
5. I come across as a positive person.	1	2	3	4	5
6. I sometimes think of myself as a failure.	1	2	3	4	5
7. I am able to do things as well as most people.	1	2	3	4	5
8. I find it difficult to believe nice things someone says about me.	1	2	3	4	5

SCORING AND INTERPRETATION: Many good things come from self-confidence. If new managers lack self-confidence, they are more likely to avoid difficult decisions and confrontations and may tend to overcontrol subordinates, which is called micromanaging. A lack of self-confidence also leads to less sharing of information and less time hiring and developing capable people. Self-confident managers, by contrast, can more easily delegate responsibility, take risks, give credit to others, confront problems, and assert themselves for the good of their team.

Give yourself one point for each *odd-numbered* item marked as a Mostly True answer (choosing 1 or 2) and give yourself one point for each *even-numbered* item marked as a Mostly False answer (choosing 3, 4, or 5). If you scored three or less, your self-confidence may not be very high. You might want to practice new behavior in problematic areas to develop greater confidence. A score of six or above suggests a higher level of self-confidence and a solid foundation on which to begin your career as a new manager.

Spotlight on Skills

What's Your Crisis EQ?

Threats of terrorist attacks. Downsizing. The SARS virus. Company failures. Anthrax in the mail. Stock market crashes. Rapid technological changes. Information overload. The turbulence of today's world has left lingering psychological and emotional damage in workplaces all across the United States, as well as in the rest of the world. When even a minor crisis hits an organization, uncertainty and fear are high. Today's managers need the skills to help people deal with their emotions and return to a more normal work routine. Although managers cannot take the place of professional counselors, they can use patience, flexibility, and understanding to assist people through a crisis. Here are some important elements of crisis EQ for managers:

- Be visible and provide as much up-to-date, accurate information as possible about what's going on in the company and the industry. Rumor control is critical.
- Find simple ways to get employees together. Order pizza for the entire staff. Invite telecommuters to come in to the office so they can connect with others and have a chance to share their emotions.

- Give employees room to be human. It is natural for people to feel anger and other strong emotions, so allow those feelings to be expressed as long as they aren't directed at other employees.
- Publicize the company's charitable endeavors, and make employees aware of the various opportunities both within and outside the organization to volunteer and donate to charity.
- Thank employees in person and with handwritten notes when they go above and beyond the call of duty during a difficult time.
- Recognize that routine, structured work can help people heal. Postpone major, long-term projects and decisions to the extent possible, and break work into shorter, more manageable tasks. Listen to employees and determine what they need to help them return to a normal work life.
- Provide professional counseling services for people who need it. Those with a history of alcohol abuse, trouble at home, or previous mental or emotional problems are especially at risk, but anyone who has trouble gradually returning to his or her previous level of work may need outside counseling.

SOURCES: Based on Matthew Boyle, "Nothing Really Matters," *Fortune* (October 15, 2001): 261–264; and Sue Shellenbarger, "Readers Face Dilemma Over How Far to Alter Post-Attack Workplace," *Wall Street Journal* (October 31, 2001): B1.

the war in Iraq, and continuing economic hardship for many people all make meeting the psychological and emotional needs of employees a new role for managers. Following are some elements of EQ that are particularly important in times of crisis and turmoil. It is important to remember that EQ is not an in-born personality characteristic, but something that can be learned and developed.[36]

ATTITUDES AND BEHAVIORS INFLUENCED BY PERSONALITY

An individual's personality influences a wide variety of work-related attitudes and behaviors. Four that are of particular interest to managers are locus of control, authoritarianism, Machiavellianism, and problem-solving styles.

Locus of Control. People differ in terms of what they tend to accredit as the cause of their success or failure. Their **locus of control** defines whether they place the primary responsibility within themselves or on outside forces.[37] Some people believe that their own actions strongly influence what happens to them. They feel in control of their own fate. These individuals have a high *internal* locus of control. Other people believe that events in their lives occur because of chance, luck, or outside people and events. They feel more like pawns of their fate. These individuals have a high *external* locus of control. Many top leaders of e-commerce and high-tech organizations possess a high internal locus of control. These managers have to cope with rapid change and uncertainty associated with Internet business. They must believe that they and their employees can counter the negative impact

locus of control
the tendency to place the primary responsibility for one's success or failure either within oneself (internally) or on outside forces (externally).

TAKE ACTION ➡

Strive to take responsibility for your actions, rather than always blaming others or the situation (external locus).

of outside forces and events. John Chambers, CEO of Cisco Systems, is a good example. Despite a tough economy and a drastically diminished stock price in the early 2000s, Chambers maintained his belief that Cisco can defeat any challenge thrown its way.[38] A person with a high external locus of control would likely feel overwhelmed trying to make the rapid decisions and changes needed to keep pace with the industry, particularly when environmental conditions are unstable.

Research on locus of control shows real differences in behavior across a wide range of settings. People with an internal locus of control are easier to motivate because they believe the rewards are the result of their behavior. They are better able to handle complex information and problem solving and are more achievement oriented, but are also more independent and therefore more difficult to manage. By contrast, people with an external locus of control are harder to motivate, less involved in their jobs, more likely to blame others when faced with a poor performance evaluation, but also more compliant and conforming and, therefore, easier to manage.[39]

Do you believe luck plays an important role in your life, or do you feel that you control your own fate? To find out more about your locus of control, read the instructions and complete the following New Manager Self Test.

Authoritarianism. **Authoritarianism** is the belief that power and status differences should exist within the organization.[40] Individuals high in authoritarianism tend to be concerned with power and toughness, obey recognized authority above them, stick to conventional values, critically judge others, and oppose the use of subjective feelings. The degree to which managers possess authoritarianism will influence how they wield and share power. The degree to which employees possess authoritarianism will influence how they react to their managers. If a manager and employees differ in their degree of authoritarianism, the manager may have difficulty leading effectively. The trend toward empowerment and shifts in expectations among younger employees for more equitable relationships contribute to a decline in strict authoritarianism in many organizations.

Machiavellianism. Another personality dimension that is helpful in understanding work behavior is **Machiavellianism,** which is characterized by the acquisition of power and the manipulation of other people for purely personal gain. Machiavellianism is named after Niccolo Machiavelli, a 16th-century author who wrote *The Prince,* a book for noblemen of the day on how to acquire and use power.[41] Psychologists developed instruments to measure a person's Machiavellianism (Mach) orientation.[42] Research shows that high Machs are predisposed to being pragmatic, capable of lying to achieve personal goals, more likely to win in win-lose situations, and more likely to persuade than be persuaded.[43]

Different situations may require people who demonstrate one or the other type of behavior. In loosely structured situations, high Machs actively take control, whereas low Machs accept the direction given by others. Low Machs thrive in highly structured situations, and high Machs perform in a detached, disinterested way. High Machs are particularly good in jobs that require bargaining skills or that involve substantial rewards for winning.[44]

Problem-Solving Styles and the Myers-Briggs Type Indicator.
Managers also need to understand that individuals differ in the way they solve problems and make decisions. One approach to understanding problem-solving styles grew out of the work of psychologist Carl Jung. Jung believed differences resulted from our preferences in how we go about gathering and evaluating information.[45] According to Jung, gathering information and evaluating information are separate activities. People gather information either by *sensation* or *intuition* but not by both simultaneously. Sensation-type people would rather work with known facts and hard data and prefer routine and

authoritarianism
the belief that power and status differences should exist within the organization.

Machiavellianism
the tendency to direct much of one's behavior toward the acquisition of power and the manipulation of other people for personal gain.

NEW MANAGER SELF TEST

Your Locus of Control

This questionnaire is designed to measure locus-of-control beliefs. Researchers using this questionnaire in a study of college students found a mean of 51.8 for men and 52.2 for women, with a standard deviation of 6 for each. The higher your score on this questionnaire, the more you tend to believe that you are generally responsible for what happens to you; in other words, higher scores are associated with internal locus of control. Low scores are associated with external locus of control. Scoring low indicates that you tend to believe that forces beyond your control, such as powerful other people, fate, or chance, are responsible for what happens to you.

For each of these 10 questions, indicate the extent to which you agree or disagree using the following scale:

1 = Strongly disagree   3 = Slightly disagree   5 = Slightly agree   7 = Strongly agree

2 = Disagree   4 = Neither disagree nor agree   6 = Agree

1. When I get what I want, it is usually because I worked hard for it.   `1   2   3   4   5   6   7`

2. When I make plans, I am almost certain to make them work.   `1   2   3   4   5   6   7`

3. I prefer games involving some luck over games requiring pure skill.   `1   2   3   4   5   6   7`

4. I can learn almost anything if I set my mind to it.   `1   2   3   4   5   6   7`

5. My major accomplishments are entirely due to my hard work and ability.   `1   2   3   4   5   6   7`

6. I usually don't set goals because I have a hard time following through on them.   `1   2   3   4   5   6   7`

7. Competition discourages excellence.   `1   2   3   4   5   6   7`

8. Often people get ahead just by being lucky.   `1   2   3   4   5   6   7`

9. On any sort of exam or competition, I like to know how well I do relative to everyone else.   `1   2   3   4   5   6   7`

10. It's pointless to keep working on something that's too difficult for me.   `1   2   3   4   5   6   7`

SCORING AND INTERPRETATION

To determine your score, reverse the values you selected for questions 3, 6, 7, 8, and 10 (1 = 7, 2 = 6, 3 = 5, 4 = 4, 5 = 3, 6 = 2, 7 = 1). For example, if you strongly disagree with the statement in question 3, you would have given it a value of 1. Change this value to a 7. Reverse the scores in a similar manner for questions 6, 7, 8, and 10. Now add the point values for all 10 questions together.

Your score _____

SOURCES: Adapted from J. M. Burger, *Personality: Theory and Research* (Belmont, CA: Wadsworth, 1986): 400–401, cited in D. Hellriegel, J. W. Slocum, Jr., and R. W. Woodman, *Organizational Behavior*, 6th ed. (St. Paul, MN: West, 1992): 97–100. Original source: D. L. Paulhus, "Sphere-Specific Measures of Perceived Control," *Journal of Personality and Social Psychology*, 44 (June, 1983): 1253–1265.

Personal Style	Action Tendencies	Likely Occupations
Sensation-Thinking	• Emphasizes details, facts, certainty • Is a decisive, applied thinker • Focuses on short-term, realistic goals • Develops rules and regulations for judging performance	• Accounting • Production • Computer programming • Market research • Engineering
Intuitive-Thinking	• Prefers dealing with theoretical or technical problems • Is a creative, progressive, perceptive thinker • Focuses on possibilities using impersonal analysis • Is able to consider a number of options and problems simultaneously	• Systems design • Systems analysis • Law • Middle/top management • Teaching business, economics
Sensation-Feeling	• Shows concern for current, real-life human problems • Is pragmatic, analytical, methodical, and conscientious • Emphasizes detailed facts about people rather than tasks • Focuses on structuring organizations for the benefit of people	• Directing supervisor • Counseling • Negotiating • Selling • Interviewing
Intuitive-Feeling	• Avoids specifics • Is charismatic, participative, people oriented, and helpful • Focuses on general views, broad themes, and feelings • Decentralizes decision making, develops few rules and regulations	• Public relations • Advertising • Human Resources • Politics • Customer service

EXHIBIT 10.8

Four Problem-Solving Styles

order in gathering information. Intuitive-type people would rather look for possibilities than work with facts and prefer solving new problems and using abstract concepts.

Evaluating information involves making judgments about the information a person has gathered. People evaluate information by *thinking* or *feeling*. These represent the extremes in orientation. Thinking-type individuals base their judgments on impersonal analysis, using reason and logic rather than personal values or emotional aspects of the situation. Feeling-type individuals base their judgments more on personal feelings such as harmony and tend to make decisions that result in approval from others.

According to Jung, only one of the four functions—sensation, intuition, thinking, or feeling—is dominant in an individual. However, the dominant function usually is backed up by one of the functions from the other set of paired opposites. Exhibit 10.8 shows the four problem-solving styles that result from these matchups, as well as occupations that people with each style tend to prefer.

Two additional sets of paired opposites not directly related to problem solving are *introversion–extroversion* and *judging–perceiving*. Introverts gain energy by focusing on personal thoughts and feelings, whereas extroverts gain energy from being around others and interacting with others. On the judging versus perceiving dimension, people with a judging preference like certainty and closure and tend to make decisions quickly based on available data. Perceiving people, on the other hand, enjoy ambiguity, dislike deadlines, and may change their minds several times as they gather large amounts of data and information to make decisions.

A widely used personality test that measures how people differ on all four of Jung's sets of paired opposites is the **Myers–Briggs Type Indicator (MBTI)**. The MBTI measures a person's preferences for introversion versus extroversion, sensation versus intuition, thinking versus feeling, and judging versus perceiving. The various combinations of these four preferences result in 16 unique personality types.

Each of the 16 different personality types can have positive and negative consequences for behavior. Based on the limited research that has been done, the two preferences that seem to be most strongly associated with effective management in a variety of organizations

TAKE ACTION

Go to the experiential exercise on page 400 that pertains to evaluating your Myers–Briggs personality type.

Myers–Briggs Type Indicator (MBTI)

personality test that measures a person's preference for introversion versus extroversion, sensation versus intuition, thinking versus feeling, and judging versus perceiving.

When Kurt Swogger arrived at Dow Chemical's plastics business in 1991, it took anywhere from 6 to 15 years to launch a new product—and the unit hadn't launched a single one for 3 years. Today, a new product launch takes just 2 to 4 years, and Swogger's R&D team has launched 13 product hits over the past decade.

Dow Chemical

How did Swogger lead such an amazing transformation? By making sure people were doing the jobs they were best suited for. The simple fact, Swogger says, "is that some [people] do development better than others. The biggest obstacle to launching great new products was not having the right people in the right jobs." Swogger began reassigning people based on his intuition and insight, distinguishing pure inventors from those who could add value later in the game and still others who were best at marketing the new products. Swogger says he was right-on about 60 percent of the time. If someone didn't work out after six months, he'd put them in another assignment.

Seeking a better way to determine people's strengths, Swogger turned to a former Dow employee, Greg Stevens, who now owns a consulting firm. Stevens and Swogger used the Myers–Briggs Type Indicator (MBTI), predicting which types would be best suited to each stage of the product development and launch cycles. After administering the test to current and former Dow plastics employees, they found some startling results. In 1991, when Swogger came on board, the match between the right personality type and the right role was only 29 percent. By 2001, thanks to Swogger's great instincts, the rate had jumped to 93 percent.

Swogger's next step is to administer the MBTI to new hires, so the job match is right to begin with. He believes the MBTI can help him assign people to jobs that match their natural thinking and problem-solving styles, leading to happier employees and higher organizational performance.[46]

Other organizations also use the MBTI, with 89 of the *Fortune* 100 companies recently reporting that they use the test in hiring and promotion decisions.[47] Matching the right people to the right jobs is an important responsibility for managers, whether they do it based on intuition and experience or by using personality tests such as the MBTI. Managers strive to create a good fit between the people and the jobs they are asked to do.

and industries are thinking and judging.[48] However, people with other preferences can also be good managers. One advantage of understanding your natural preferences is to maximize your innate strengths and abilities. Dow Chemical manager Kurt Swogger believes the MBTI can help put people in the right jobs—where they will be happiest and make the strongest contribution to the organization.

person–job fit
the extent to which a person's ability and personality match the requirements of a job.

PERSON–JOB FIT

Given the wide variation among personalities and among jobs, an important responsibility of managers is to try to match employee and job characteristics so that work is done by people who are well suited to do it. This goal requires that managers be clear about what they expect employees to do and have a sense of the kinds of people who would succeed at various types of assignments. The extent to which a person's ability and personality match the requirements of a job is called **person–job fit.** When managers achieve person–job fit, employees are more likely to contribute and have higher levels of job satisfaction and commitment.[49]

 **CONCEPT CONNECTION**

Andrew Field, who owns a $10.3 million printing services company, PrintingForLess.com, uses dogs to help him create the **person–environment fit** when hiring new employees. Every day for five years, Jessie (far left), Field's Border collie and black Labrador mix, has accompanied him to work. The idea caught on and as many as eight dogs frequent the company offices. With rules such as owner accountability, a dog review board, and a dog-approval process, employees find that the dogs are a great release for stress. Field says that the dog policy helps him make good hires; candidates who respond favorably to the canine rule are likely to fit in with the office culture.

Benchmarking

Teach for America

Trying to hire the right graduates to send into inner-city high-risk schools is not child's play, but the Peace Corps-like program Teach for America is doing a pretty good job. First off, they try to convince top students to temporarily shelve their career goals and head toward one of the country's most troubled schools. During the application process, seniors who compete are subjected to hours of tests and interviews, all designed to measure their perseverance, organizational skills, and resilience—traits known to be critical because those hired get only five weeks of intense teacher training before they get thrust into the South Bronx or some other equally poor location. Founder Wendy Kopp doesn't soften the potential problems. "It can be really overwhelming and depressing," she cautions. "We all have bad days, and people who teach in Teach for America probably have more bad days than most."

It might sound like a recipe for disaster, but Kopp has turned this 18 year-old nonprofit into a model for social change success. Last year 19,000 students, including 10 percent of Yale and Dartmouth's senior classes, applied to Teach for America, and 2,400 were hired. This makes it one of the country's largest employers of college seniors. The selection program is so effective that companies are now riding on its coattails. J.P. Morgan found they were competing for the same top grads, so they've formed a strategic recruiting alliance with TFA, staging joint events at colleges and offering job deferral, bonuses, and relocation costs. "We want employees who are committed to serving the community as well as to serving shareholders," said J.P. Morgan's David Puth. Goldman Sachs is hoping for a similar alliance with TFA because, as COO of Human Capital Management Edie Hunt says, "One of the few jobs that people pass up Goldman Sach offers for is Teach for America." Similarly Amgen is partnering with the nonprofit, using it as a benchmark to redesign the bank's recruiting. Says VP Shannon McFayden, "We think TFA is the best college recruiting organization in the US."

SOURCE: Patricia Sellers, "The Recruiter," *Fortune* (Nov. 27, 2006): 87–90.

The importance of person–job fit became especially apparent during the dot-com heyday of the late 1990s. People who rushed to Internet companies in hopes of finding a new challenge—or making a quick buck—found themselves floundering in jobs for which they were unsuited. One manager recruited by a leading executive search firm lasted less than two hours at his new job. The search firm, a division of Russell Reynolds Associates, later developed a "Web Factor" diagnostic to help determine whether people have the right personality for the Internet, including such things as a tolerance for risk and uncertainty, an obsession with learning, and a willingness to do whatever needs doing, regardless of job title.[50]

TAKE ACTION ⏩

Look for the kind of job that uses your strengths, rather than weaknesses; find the type of work that you really love.

As a manager, determining which candidates will have the best fit to the job is a real challenge and one done successfully by Teach for America, as shown in the Benchmarking box.

A related concern is *person–environment fit,* which looks not only at whether the person and job are suited to one another but also at how well the individual will fit in the overall organizational environment. An employee who is by nature strongly authoritarian, for example, would have a hard time in an organization such as W. L. Gore and Associates, which has few rules, no hierarchy, no fixed or assigned authority, and no bosses. Many of today's organizations pay attention to person–environment fit from the beginning of the recruitment process. Texas Instruments' website includes an area called Fit Check that evaluates personality types anonymously and gives prospective job candidates a chance to evaluate for themselves whether they would be a good match with the company.[51]

Learning

Years of schooling condition many of us to think that learning is something students do in response to teachers in a classroom. With this view, in the managerial world of time deadlines and concrete action, learning seems remote—even irrelevant. However, successful managers need specific knowledge and skills as well as the ability to adapt to changes in the world around them. Managers have to learn.

Learning is a change in behavior or performance that occurs as the result of experience. Experience may take the form of observing others, reading or listening to sources of information, or experiencing the consequences of one's own behavior. This important way of adapting to events is linked to individual differences in attitudes, perception, and personality.

Two individuals who undergo similar experiences—for example, a business transfer to a foreign country—probably will differ in how they adapt their behaviors to (that is, learn from) the experience. In other words, each person learns in a different way.

THE LEARNING PROCESS

One model of the learning process, shown in Exhibit 10.9, depicts learning as a four-stage cycle.[52] First, a person encounters a concrete experience. This event is followed by thinking and reflective observation, which leads to abstract conceptualization and, in turn, to active experimentation. The results of the experimentation generate new experiences, and the cycle repeats.

The Best Buy chain of consumer electronics superstores owes its birth to the learning process of its founder, Richard M. Schulze. In the 1960s, Schulze built a stereo store called Sound of Music into a chain of nine stores in and near St. Paul, Minnesota. However, a tornado destroyed his largest and most profitable store, so he held a massive clearance sale in the parking lot. So many shoppers descended on the lot that they caused traffic to back up for two miles. Reflecting on this experience, Schulze saw great demand for a store featuring large selection and low prices, backed by heavy advertising. He tried out his idea by launching his first Best Buy superstore. Today, Best Buy has nearly 800 retail stores in the United States and Canada, as well as a thriving online division.[53]

The arrows in the model of the learning process in Exhibit 10.9 indicate that this process is a recurring cycle. People continually test their conceptualizations and adapt them as a result of their personal reflections and observations about their experiences.

learning
a change in behavior or performance that occurs as the result of experience.

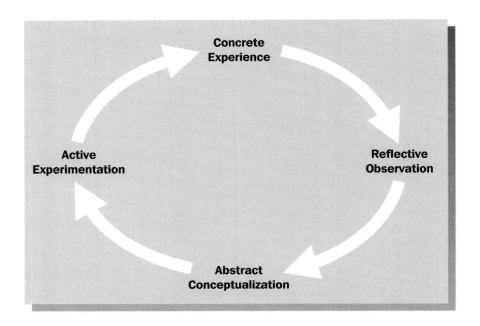

EXHIBIT 10.9
The Experiential Learning Cycle

LEARNING STYLES

Individuals develop personal learning styles that vary in terms of how much they emphasize each stage of the learning cycle. These differences occur because the learning process is directed by individual needs and goals. For example, an engineer might place greater emphasis on abstract concepts, whereas a salesperson might emphasize concrete experiences. Because of these preferences, personal learning styles typically have strong and weak points.

Questionnaires can assess a person's strong and weak points as a learner by measuring the relative emphasis the person places on each of the four learning stages shown in Exhibit 10.9: concrete experience, reflective observation, abstract conceptualization, and active experimentation. Some people have a tendency to overemphasize one stage of the learning process or to avoid some aspects of learning. Not many people have totally balanced profiles, but the key to effective learning is competence in each of the four stages when it is needed.

Researchers identified four fundamental learning styles that combine elements of the four stages of the learning cycle.[54] Exhibit 10.10 summarizes the characteristics and dominant learning abilities of these four styles, labeled Diverger, Assimilator, Converger, and Accommodator. The exhibit also lists occupations that frequently attract individuals with each of the learning styles. For example, people whose dominant style is Accommodator are often drawn to sales and marketing. A good example is Gertrude Boyle, who took over Columbia Sportswear after the death of her husband. She and her son, Tim, propelled the company from sales of $13 million to $358 million over a 13-year period by observing what competitors were doing and actively experimenting to find a novel sales approach. The 74-year-old Gert Boyle decided to star in her own "Tough Mother" ads as a way to distinguish the company from competitors who advertised their products worn by fit, young models. Boyle believes in constantly pushing herself and her company, questioning everything, and trying new ideas.[55] Exhibit 10.10 lists other likely occupations for Divergers, Assimilators, Convergers, and Accommodators.

TAKE ACTION ▶

As a manager, remember that some employees learn by reading and learning concepts, whereas others need to "do" in order to learn.

TAKE ACTION ▶

As a new manager, determine your natural learning style to understand how you approach problems and strive for a balance among the four learning stages shown in Exhibit 10.9.

EXHIBIT 10.10

Learning Style Types

Learning Style Type	Dominant Learning Abilities	Learning Characteristics	Likely Occupations
Diverger	• Concrete experience • Reflective observation	• Is good at generating ideas, seeing a situation from multiple perspectives, and being aware of meaning and value • Tends to be interested in people, culture, and the arts	• Human resource management • Counseling • Organization development specialist
Assimilator	• Abstract conceptualization • Reflective observation	• Is good at inductive reasoning, creating theoretical models, and combining disparate observations into an integrated explanation • Tends to be less concerned with people than ideas and abstract concepts.	• Research • Strategic planning
Converger	• Abstract conceptualization • Active experimentation	• Is good at decisiveness, practical application of ideas, and hypothetical deductive reasoning • Prefers dealing with technical tasks rather than interpersonal issues	• Engineering
Accommodator	• Concrete experience • Active experimentation	• Is good at implementing decisions, carrying out plans, and getting involved in new experiences • Tends to be at ease with people but may be seen as impatient or pushy	• Marketing • Sales

CONTINUOUS LEARNING

To thrive in today's turbulent business climate, individuals and organizations must be continuous learners. For individuals, continuous learning entails looking for opportunities to learn from classes, reading, and talking to others, as well as looking for the lessons in life's experiences. One manager who embodies the spirit of continuous learning is Larry Ricciardi, senior vice president and corporate counsel at IBM. Ricciardi is an avid traveler and voracious reader who likes to study art, literature, and history. In addition, Ricciardi likes to add supermarket tabloids to his daily fare of the *Wall Street Journal*. On business trips, he scouts out side trips to exotic or interesting sites so he can learn something new.[56] Ricciardi never knows when he might be able to apply a new idea or understanding to improve his life, his job, or his organization.

For organizations, continuous learning involves the processes and systems through which the organization enables its people to learn, share their growing knowledge, and apply it to their work. In an organization in which continuous learning is taking place, employees actively apply comments from customers, news about competitors, training programs, and more to increase their knowledge and improve the organization's practices. For example, at the Mayo Clinic, doctors are expected to consult with doctors in other departments, with the patient, and with anyone else inside or outside the clinic who might help with any aspect of the patient's problem.[57] The emphasis on teamwork, openness, and collaboration keeps learning strong at Mayo.

Managers can foster continuous learning by consciously stopping from time to time and asking, "What can we learn from this experience?" They can allow employees time to attend training and reflect on their experiences. Recognizing that experience can be the best teacher, managers should focus on how they and their employees can learn from mistakes, rather than fostering a climate in which employees hide mistakes because they fear being punished for them. Managers also encourage organizational learning by establishing information systems that enable people to share knowledge and learn in new ways. Information technology was discussed in detail in Chapter 6. As individuals, managers can help themselves and set an example for their employees by being continuous learners, listening to others, reading widely, and reflecting on what they observe. Can leaders really learn and change their own behavior?

Stress and Stress Management

Just as organizations can support or discourage learning, organizational characteristics also interact with individual differences to influence other behaviors. In every organization, these characteristics include sources of stress. Formally defined, **stress** is an individual's physiological and emotional response to external stimuli that place physical or psychological demands on the individual and create uncertainty and lack of personal control when important outcomes are at stake.[58] These stimuli, called *stressors,* produce some combination of frustration (the inability to achieve a goal, such as the inability to meet a deadline because of inadequate resources) and anxiety (such as the fear of being disciplined for not meeting deadlines).

People's responses to stressors vary according to their personalities, the resources available to help them cope, and the context in which the stress occurs. Thus, a looming deadline will feel different depending on the degree to which the individual enjoys a challenge, the willingness of co-workers to team up and help each other succeed, and family members' understanding of an employee's need to work extra hours, among other factors.

When the level of stress is low relative to a person's coping resources, stress can be a positive force, stimulating desirable change and achievement. However, too much stress is associated with many negative consequences, including sleep disturbances, drug and alcohol abuse, headaches, ulcers, high blood pressure, and heart disease. People who are

 TAKE ACTION

Go to the ethical dilemma on page 405 that pertains to organizational sources of stress.

stress
a physiological and emotional response to stimuli that place physical or psychological demands on an individual.

experiencing the ill effects of too much stress may become irritable or withdraw from interactions with their co-workers, take excess time off, and have more health problems. For example, a recent study of manufacturing workers in Bangladesh found a significant connection between job stress and absenteeism. Another study of 46,000 workers in the United States found that health care costs are 147 percent higher for individuals who are stressed or depressed.[59] People suffering from stress are less productive and may leave the organization. Clearly, too much stress is harmful to employees as well as to companies.

TYPE A AND TYPE B BEHAVIOR

Researchers observed that some people seem to be more vulnerable than others to the ill effects of stress. From studies of stress-related heart disease, they categorized people as having behavior patterns called Type A and Type B.[60] The **Type A behavior** pattern includes extreme competitiveness, impatience, aggressiveness, and devotion to work. In contrast, people with a **Type B behavior** pattern exhibit less of these behaviors. They consequently experience less conflict with other people and a more balanced, relaxed lifestyle. Type A people tend to experience more stress-related illness than Type B people.

Most Type A individuals are high-energy people and may seek positions of power and responsibility. One example is John Haughom, senior vice president for health care improvement at PeaceHealth, a network of private hospitals in the Pacific Northwest. When Haughom was in charge of establishing an information network of community-wide medical records to support patient care, he typically began his day at 6 A.M. and worked until 11 P.M. His days were a blur of conference calls, meetings, and e-mail exchanges. "I could move mountains if I put my mind to it," he says. "That's what good executives do."[61]

By pacing themselves and learning control and intelligent use of their natural high-energy tendencies, Type A individuals can be powerful forces for innovation and leadership within their organizations, as John Haughom has been at Peace-Health. However, many Type A personalities cause stress-related problems for themselves and sometimes for those around them. Haughom eventually reached burnout. He couldn't sleep, he began snapping at colleagues, and he finally took a sabbatical and learned to lead a more balanced life.[62] Type B individuals typically live with less stress unless they are in high-stress situations. A number of factors can cause stress in the workplace, even for people who are not naturally prone to high stress.

CAUSES OF WORK STRESS

Workplace stress is skyrocketing worldwide. A recent World Congress on Health and Safety at Work presented studies suggesting that job-related stress may be as big a danger to the world's people as chemical and biological hazards.[63] In the United States, the number of people who say they are overworked has risen from 28 percent in 2001 to 44 percent in 2005, and one-third of Americans between the ages of 25 and 39 say they feel burned out by their jobs. The U.K.'s Health and Safety Executive says that half a million people in the United Kingdom are ill because of workplace stress, and stress-related illnesses are second only to back pain as a cause of work absences. In India, growing numbers of young software professionals and call-center workers are falling prey to depression, anxiety, and other mental illnesses because of increasing workplace stress.[64]

TAKE ACTION ➔

If you are a Type A person with a high-stress job, take a relaxing vacation; if you are a Type B with a low-key job, then you can do the seven-countries-in-five-days kind of trip.

Type A behavior
behavior pattern characterized by extreme competitiveness, impatience, aggressiveness, and devotion to work.

Type B behavior
behavior pattern that lacks Type A characteristics and includes a more balanced, relaxed lifestyle.

CONCEPT CONNECTION

Sylvia Weinstock is founder of Sylvia Weinstock Cakes in New York City, known for celebrity wedding cakes, including those for Catherine Zeta-Jones, Liam Neeson, and Donald Trump. Weinstock, named "New York's reigning cake diva" by *InStyle* magazine, loves her job but feels the stress of **task demands.** "This is an obsessive business because of the intensity and personal value that everyone places on their occasion," she says. "And I honor that. I fret. I worry. And unless I heard that the cake arrived happy, I'm checking that phone all the time."

Most people have a general idea of what a stressful job is like: difficult, uncomfortable, exhausting, even frightening. Managers can better cope with their own stress and establish ways for the organization to help employees cope if they define the conditions that tend to produce work stress. One way to identify work stressors is to think about stress caused by the demands of job tasks and stress caused by interpersonal pressures and conflicts.

- *Task demands* are stressors arising from the tasks required of a person holding a particular job. Some kinds of decisions are inherently stressful: those made under time pressure, those that have serious consequences, and those that must be made with incomplete information. For example, emergency room doctors are under tremendous stress as a result of the task demands of their jobs. They regularly have to make quick decisions based on limited information that may determine whether a patient lives or dies. Almost all jobs, especially those of managers, have some level of stress associated with task demands. Task demands also sometimes cause stress because of **role ambiguity,** which means that people are unclear about what task behaviors are expected of them.

- *Interpersonal demands* are stressors associated with relationships in the organization. Although in some cases interpersonal relationships can alleviate stress, they also can be a source of stress when the group puts pressure on an individual or when conflicts arise between individuals. Managers can resolve many conflicts using techniques that will be discussed in Chapter 14. **Role conflict** occurs when an individual perceives incompatible demands from others. Managers often feel role conflict because the demands of their superiors conflict with those of the employees in their department. They may be expected to support employees and provide them with opportunities to experiment and be creative, while at the same time top executives are demanding a consistent level of output that leaves little time for creativity and experimentation.

Almost everyone experiences some degree of job stress associated with these factors. For example, consider the stress caused by task demands on Verizon's call center representatives.

The situation for call center representatives in other countries, who are handling calls for U.S.-based companies such as American Express, Citibank, Sprint, and IBM, can be even more stressful. There, the high stress caused by task demands is compounded by interpersonal issues, primarily "hate calls" from American customers angry over the loss of U.S. jobs. A survey by the Indian magazine *Dataquest* found that most call center employees find these calls "psychologically disturbing" and identify them as a major cause of job stress.[65]

TAKE ACTION

As a new manager, learn to recognize the conditions that cause stress and then try to alleviate unnecessary or excessive stress for employees.

role ambiguity
uncertainty about what behaviors are expected of a person in a particular role.

role conflict
incompatible demands of different roles.

Roland G. Collins Jr. loves his job as a call center representative for Verizon Communications. He enjoys connecting with customers; he makes good money, and he has good benefits. But he admits that it's not the job for everyone. About a third of the 100 or so calls a representative handles each day are stressful. Besides dealing with irate customers and handling calls regarding billing or other problems, representatives have to be able to rattle off Verizon's string of products and services, including terms and rates, and try to sell them to each and every call. It doesn't matter how angry or rude the customer on the other end of the line—pushing new services is a key requirement of the job.

What makes matters worse is that representatives often have to do these tasks under observation. Managers routinely sit next to a representative or listen in on a call to check whether the rep has hit on nearly 80 different points required in every customer contact. Call center reps must meet precise performance specifications, and managers defend the observation practice as a way to ensure consistency and better customer service. However, employees almost always find the experience adds to their stress level. For some employees, particularly inexperienced ones, an observation can create a panic situation, causing heart pounding and profuse sweating, which, in turn, creates even greater stress.[66]

Verizon Communications

INNOVATIVE RESPONSES TO STRESS MANAGEMENT

Organizations that want to challenge their employees and stay competitive in a fast-changing environment will never be stress-free. But because many consequences of stress are negative, managers need to make stress management a priority. In Britain, lawmakers implemented a new requirement that employers meet certain conditions that help to manage workplace stress, such as ensuring that employees are not exposed to a poor physical work environment, have the necessary skills and training to meet their job requirements, and are given a chance to offer input into the way their work is done.[67]

A variety of techniques can help individuals manage stress. Among the most basic strategies are those that help people stay healthy: exercising regularly, getting plenty of rest, and eating a healthful diet.

Although individuals can pursue stress management strategies on their own, today's enlightened companies support healthy habits to help people manage stress and be more productive. Stress costs businesses billions of dollars a year in absenteeism, lower productivity, staff turnover, accidents, and higher health insurance and workers' compensation costs.[68] In today's workplace, taking care of employees has become a business as well as an ethical priority.

Supporting employees can be as simple as encouraging people to take regular breaks and vacations. Consider that more than a third of U.S. employees surveyed by the Families and Work Institute currently don't take their full allotment of vacation time.[69] Some companies, including BellSouth, First Union, and Tribble Creative Group, also have designated *quiet rooms* or meditation centers where employees can take short, calming breaks at any time they feel the need.[70] The time off is a valuable investment when it allows employees to approach their work with renewed energy and a fresh perspective.

Companies develop other programs aimed at helping employees reduce stress and lead healthier, more balanced lives. Some have wellness programs that provide access to nutrition counseling and exercise facilities. A worldwide study of wellness programs conducted by the Canadian government found that for each dollar spent, the company gets from $1.95 to $3.75 return payback from benefits.[71] Other organizations create broad work–life balance initiatives that may include flexible work options such as telecommuting and flexible hours, as well as benefits such as onsite daycare, fitness centers, and personal services, such as pickup and delivery of dry cleaning. *Daily flextime* is considered by many employees to be the most effective work–life practice, which means giving employees the freedom to vary their hours as needed, such as leaving early to take an elderly parent shopping or taking time off to attend a child's school play.[72]

The study of organizational behavior reminds managers that employees are *human* resources with human needs. By acknowledging the personal aspects of employees' lives, work–life practices communicate that managers and the organization care about employees. In addition, managers' attitudes make a tremendous difference in whether employees are stressed out and unhappy or relaxed, energetic, and productive.

TAKE ACTION ▶

To avoid overstress, eat well, exercise, sleep adequately and make sure you have a good emotional support system.

Summary

The principles of organizational behavior describe how people as individuals and groups behave and affect the performance of the organization as a whole. Desirable work-related attitudes include job satisfaction and organizational commitment. Employees' and managers' attitudes can strongly influence employee motivation, performance, and productivity. Three components of attitudes are cognitions, emotions, and behavior.

Attitudes affect people's perceptions, and vice versa. Individuals often "see" things in different ways. The perceptual process includes perceptual selectivity and perceptual organization. Perceptual distortions, such as stereotyping, the halo effect, projection, and perceptual defense, are errors in judgment that can arise from inaccuracies in the perception process. Attributions are judgments that individuals make about whether a person's behavior was caused by internal or external factors.

Another area of interest is personality, the set of characteristics that underlie a relatively stable pattern of behavior. One way to think about personality is the Big Five personality traits of extroversion, agreeableness, conscientiousness, emotional stability, and openness to experience. Some important work-related attitudes and behaviors influenced by personality are locus of control, authoritarianism, Machiavellianism, and problem-solving styles. A widely used personality test is the Myers–Briggs Type Indicator. Managers want to find a good person–job fit by ensuring that a person's personality, attitudes, skills, abilities, and problem-solving styles match the requirements of the job and the organizational environment. New insight into personality has been gained through research in the area of emotional intelligence (EQ). Emotional intelligence includes the components of self-awareness, self-management, social awareness, and relationship management.

Even though people's personalities may be relatively stable, individuals can learn new behaviors. Learning refers to a change in behavior or performance that occurs as a result of experience. The learning process goes through a four-stage cycle, and individual learning styles differ. Four learning styles are Diverger, Assimilator, Converger, and Accommodator. Rapid changes in today's marketplace create a need for ongoing learning. They may also create greater stress for many of today's workers. The causes of work stress include task demands and interpersonal demands. Individuals and organizations can alleviate the negative effects of stress by engaging in a variety of techniques for stress management.

Discussion Questions

1. If you were trying to change a subordinate's attitude, which approach do you think would be more effective: changing cognition, affect, or behavior? Why? Why is it important for managers to have an understanding of organizational behavior? Do you think a knowledge of OB might be more important at some managerial levels than at others? Discuss.

2. In what ways might the cognitive and affective components of attitude influence the behavior of employees who are faced with learning an entirely new set of computer-related skills to retain their jobs at a manufacturing facility?

3. Suggest a way that managers might be able to use their understanding of perceptual selectivity and organization to communicate more effectively with subordinates. What steps might managers at a company that is about to merge with another company take to promote organizational commitment among employees?

4. In the Big Five personality factors, extroversion is considered a "good" quality to have. Why might introversion be an equally positive quality?

5. Why do you think surveys show that Generation X employees (those born between 1961 and 1981) experience the least job satisfaction of all demographic groups? Do you expect this finding to be true throughout their careers?

6. What is meant by perceptual selectivity? Explain some characteristics of the perceiver and of the stimuli that might affect perception?

7. Which of the four components of EQ do you consider most important to an effective manager in today's world? Why?

8. How might understanding whether an employee has an internal or an external locus of control help a manager better communicate with, motivate, and lead the employee?

9. You are a manager, and you realize that one of your employees repeatedly teases co-workers born in India that they come from a backward country with pagan beliefs. How would you decide whether it's necessary to respond to the situation? If you decide to intervene, what would your response be? Why is it important for managers to achieve person–job fit when they are hiring employees?

10. Review Exhibit 10.10. Which learning style best characterizes you? How can you use this understanding to improve your learning ability? To improve your management skills?

11. Describe a time when you experienced role ambiguity or role conflict. What stress management techniques did you use to cope with the stress this situation created?

12. Why do you think workplace stress seems to be skyrocketing? Do you think it is a trend that will continue? Explain the reasons for your answer. Do you think it is the responsibility of managers and organizations to help employees manage stress? Why or why not?

Dear Dr. Dorothy

As a new manager, I am learning a lot. One thing is that there are different kinds of people. All of my subordinates have been in their jobs longer than I have, and their behaviors, well, let's just say sometimes I feel like I am back in junior high school. Two people in particular trouble me. They are very controlling and are not nice to people who march to a different drummer, as they say. Sometimes I think they are bullies, and I've seen them really be mean to co-workers who disagree with their ideas. It really hurts the morale of the group because lots of people are plain afraid of them. What should I do?

Walking on eggshells in Washington

Dear Walking,

Dr. Dorothy thinks you might be leaving out one important fact: that YOU are afraid of these two bullies. Otherwise, you would have already taken care of the problem and not be asking for advice. These two sound like classic High Mach types, whose currency is power and who wield it ruthlessly. They operate best in loosely structured environments, where they get little, if any, consequence for their damaging behaviors. Clearly, your predecessor was not into consequences. Your job as boss is to make them feel some effects to their negative interactions. If they keep getting away with it, they'll keep doing it, and the morale will continue to plummet. High Machs usually need loosely structured systems to operate, so get some controls in place. Dr. Dorothy urges you to take control of the environment, because if you don't, they will.

Self Learning

Personality Assessment: Jung's Typology and the Myers-Briggs Type Indicator

For each of the following items, circle either a or b. In some cases, both a and b may apply to you. You should decide which is more like you, even if it is only slightly more true.

1. I would rather
   a. solve a new and complicated problem.
   b. work on something that I have done before.

2. I like to
   a. work alone in a quiet place.
   b. be where "the action" is.

3. I want a boss who
   a. establishes and applies criteria in decisions.
   b. considers individual needs and makes exceptions.

4. When I work on a project, I
   a. like to finish it and get some closure.
   b. often leave it open for possible change.

5. When making a decision, the most important considerations are
   a. rational thoughts, ideas, and data.
   b. people's feelings and values.

6. On a project, I tend to
   a. think it over and over before deciding how to proceed.
   b. start working on it right away, thinking about it as I go along.

7. When working on a project, I prefer to
   a. maintain as much control as possible.
   b. explore various options.

8. In my work, I prefer to
   a. work on several projects at a time, and learn as much as possible about each one.
   b. have one project that is challenging and keeps me busy.

9. I often
   a. make lists and plans whenever I start something and hate to seriously alter my plans.
   b. avoid plans and just let things progress as I work on them.

10. When discussing a problem with colleagues, it is easy for me
    a. to see "the big picture."
    b. to grasp the specifics of the situation.

11. When the phone rings in my office or at home, I usually
    a. consider it an interruption.
    b. don't mind answering it.

12. The word that describes me better is
    a. analytical.
    b. empathetic.

13. When I am working on an assignment, I tend to
    a. work steadily and consistently.
    b. work in bursts of energy with "downtime" in between.

14. When I listen to someone talk on a subject, I usually try to
    a. relate it to my own experience and see whether it fits.
    b. assess and analyze the message.

15. When I come up with new ideas, I generally
    a. "go for it."
    b. like to contemplate the ideas some more.

16. When working on a project, I prefer to
    a. narrow the scope so it is clearly defined.
    b. broaden the scope to include related aspects.

17. When I read something, I usually
    a. confine my thoughts to what is written there.
    b. read between the lines and relate the words to other ideas.

18. When I have to make a decision in a hurry, I often
    a. feel uncomfortable and wish I had more information.
    b. am able to do so with available data.

19. In a meeting, I tend to
    a. continue formulating my ideas as I talk about them.
    b. speak out only after I have carefully thought the issue through.

20. In work, I prefer spending a great deal of time on issues of
    a. ideas.
    b. people.

21. In meetings, I am most often annoyed with people who
    a. come up with many sketchy ideas.
    b. lengthen the meeting with many practical details.

22. I tend to be
    a. a morning person.
    b. a night owl.

23. My style in preparing for a meeting is
    a. to be willing to go in and be responsive.
    b. to be fully prepared and sketch an outline of the meeting.

24. In meetings, I would prefer for people to
    a. display a fuller range of emotions.
    b. be more task-oriented.

25. I would rather work for an organization where
    a. my job was intellectually stimulating.
    b. I was committed to its goals and mission.

26. On weekends, I tend to
    a. plan what I will do.
    b. just see what happens and decide as I go along.

27. I am more
    a. outgoing.
    b. contemplative.

28. I would rather work for a boss who is
    a. full of new ideas.
    b. practical.

In the following, choose the word in each pair that appeals to you more:

29. a. Social
    b. Theoretical

30. a. Ingenuity
    b. Practicality

31. a. Organized
    b. Adaptable

32. a. Active
    b. Concentration

Scoring and Interpretation

Count one point for each of the following items that you circled in the inventory.

	Score for I (Introversion)	**Score for E** (Extroversion)	**Score for S** (Sensing)	**Score for N** (Intuition)
	2a	2b	1b	1a
	6a	6b	10b	10a
	11a	11b	13a	13b
	15b	15a	16a	16b
	19b	19a	17a	17b
	22a	22b	21a	21b
	27b	27a	28b	28a
	32b	32a	30b	30a
Totals	_____	_____	_____	_____

Circle the one with more points:
I or E
(If tied on I/E, don't count #11.)

Circle the one with more points:
S or N
(If tied on S/N, don't count #16.)

	Score for T (Thinking)	**Score for F** (Feeling)	**Score for J** (Judging)	**Score for P** (Perceiving)
	3a	3b	4a	4b
	5a	5b	7a	7b
	12a	12b	8b	8a
	14b	14a	9a	9b
	20a	20b	18b	18a
	24b	24a	23b	23a
	25a	25b	26a	26b
	29b	29a	31a	31b
Totals	_____	_____	_____	_____

Circle the one with more points:
T or F
(If tied on T/F, don't count #24.)

Circle the one with more points:
J or P
(If tied on J/P, don't count #23.)

Your Score Is: I or E _____ S or N _____ T or F _____ J or P _____

Your MBTI type is _____ (example: INTJ; ESFP; etc.)

Characteristics Frequently Associated with Each Myers-Briggs Type

Sensing Types		Intuitive Types	

Introverts

ISTJ

Quiet, serious, earn success by thoroughness and dependability. Practical, matter-of-fact, realistic, and responsible. Decide logically what should be done and work toward it steadily, regardless of distractions. Take pleasure in making everything orderly and organized—their work, their home, their life. Value traditions and loyalty.

ISFJ

Quiet, friendly, responsible, and conscientious. Committed and steady in meeting their obligations. Thorough, painstaking, and accurate. Loyal, considerate, notice and remember specifics about people who are important to them, concerned with how others feel. Strive to create an orderly and harmonious environment at work and at home.

INFJ

Seek meaning and connection in ideas, relationships, and material possessions. Want to understand what motivates people and are insightful about others. Conscientious and committed to their firm values. Develop a clear vision about how best to serve the common good. Organized and decisive in implementing their vision.

INTJ

Have original minds and great drive for implementing their ideas and achieving their goals. Quickly see patterns in external events and develop long-range explanatory perspectives. When committed, organize a job and carry it through. Skeptical and independent, have high standards of competence and performance—for themselves and others.

ISTP

Tolerant and flexible, quiet observers until a problem appears, then act quickly to find workable solutions. Analyze what makes things work and readily get through large amounts of data to isolate the core of practical problems. Interested in cause and effect, organize facts using logical principles, value efficiency.

ISFP

Quiet, friendly, sensitive, and kind. Enjoy the present moment, what's going on around them. Like to have their own space and to work within their own time frame. Loyal and committed to their values and to people who are important to them. Dislike disagreements and conflicts, do not force their opinions or values on others.

INFP

Idealistic, loyal to their values and to people who are important to them. Want an external life that is congruent with their values. Curious, quick to see possibilities, can be catalysts for implementing ideas. Seek to understand people and to help them fulfill their potential. Adaptable, flexible, and accepting unless a value is threatened.

INTP

Seek to develop logical explanations for everything that interests them. Theoretical and abstract, interested more in ideas than in social interaction. Quiet, contained, flexible, and adaptable. Have unusual ability to focus in depth to solve problems in their area of interest. Skeptical, sometimes critical, always analytical.

Extraverts

ESTP

Flexible and tolerant, they take a pragmatic approach focused on immediate results. Theories and conceptual explanations bore them—they want to act energetically to solve the problem. Focus on the here-and-now, spontaneous, enjoy each moment that they can be active with others. Enjoy material comforts and style. Learn best through doing.

ESFP

Outgoing, friendly, and accepting. Exuberant lovers of life, people, and material comforts. Enjoy working with others to make things happen. Bring common sense and a realistic approach to their work, and make work fun. Flexible and spontaneous, adapt readily to new people and environments. Learn best by trying a new skill with other people.

ENFP

Warmly enthusiastic and imaginative. See life as full of possibilities. Make connections between events and information very quickly, and confidently proceed based on the patterns they see. Want a lot of affirmation from others, and readily give appreciation and support. Spontaneous and flexible, often rely on their ability to improvise and their verbal fluency.

ENTP

Quick, ingenious, stimulating, alert, and outspoken. Resourceful in solving new and challenging problems. Adept at generating conceptual possibilities and then analyzing them strategically. Good at reading other people. Bored by routine, will seldom do the same thing the same way, apt to turn to one new interest after another.

ESTJ

Practical, realistic, matter-of-fact. Decisive, quickly move to implement decisions. Organize projects and people to get things done, focus on getting results in the most efficient way possible. Take care of routine details. Have a clear set of logical standards, systematically follow them and want others to also. Forceful in implementing their plans.

ESFJ

Warmhearted, conscientious, and cooperative. Want harmony in their environment, work with determination to establish it. Like to work with others to complete tasks accurately and on time. Loyal, follow through even in small matters. Notice what others need in their day-by-day lives and try to provide it. Want to be appreciated for who they are and for what they contribute.

ENFJ

Warm, empathetic, responsive, and responsible. Highly attuned to the emotions, needs, and motivations of others. Find potential in everyone, want to help others fulfill their potential. May act as catalysts for individual and group growth. Loyal, responsive to praise and criticism. Sociable, facilitate others in a group, and provide inspiring leadership.

ENTJ

Frank, decisive, assume leadership readily. Quickly see illogical and inefficient procedures and policies, develop and implement comprehensive systems to solve organizational problems. Enjoy long-term planning and goal setting. Usually well informed, well read, enjoy expanding their knowledge and passing it on to others. Forceful in presenting their ideas.

The Myers-Briggs Type Indicator (MBTI), based on the work of psychologist Carl Jung, is the most widely used personality assessment instrument in the world. The MBTI, which was described in the chapter text, identifies 16 different "types," shown with their dominant characteristics provided here. Remember that no one is a pure type; however, each individual has preferences for introversion versus extroversion, sensing versus intuition, thinking versus feeling, and judging versus perceiving. Read the description of your type as determined by your scores in the survey. Do you believe the description fits your personality?

SOURCE: From *Organizational Behavior: Experience and Cases,* 4th ed. by Dorothy Marcic. © 1995. Reprinted with permission of South-Western, a division of Thomson Learning, http://www.thomsonrights.com.

Group Learning

An Ancient Tale

1. Read the introduction and case study and answer the questions.

2. In groups of 3–4 discuss your answers.

3. Groups report to the whole class and the instructor leads a discussion on the issues raised.

Introduction

To understand, analyze, and improve organizations, we must carefully think through the issue of who is responsible for what activities in different organizational settings. Often we hold responsible someone who has no control over the outcome, or we fail to teach or train someone who could make the vital difference.

To explore this issue, the following exercise could be conducted on either an individual or group basis. It provides an opportunity to see how different individuals assign responsibility for an event. It is also a good opportunity to discuss the concept of organizational boundaries (what is the organization, who is in or out, etc.)

Case Study

You should read the short story and respond quickly to the first three questions. Then take a little more time on questions four through six. The results, criteria, and implications could then be discussed in groups.

Long ago in an ancient kingdom there lived a princess who was very young and very beautiful. The princess, recently married, lived in a large and luxurious castle with her husband, a powerful and wealthy lord. The young princess was not content, however, to sit and eat strawberries by herself while her husband took frequent and long journeys to neighboring kingdoms. She felt neglected and soon became quite unhappy. One day, while she was alone in the castle gardens, a handsome vagabond rode out of the forest bordering the castle. He spied the beautiful princess, quickly won her heart, and carried her away with him.

Following a day of dalliance, the young princess found herself ruthlessly abandoned by the vagabond. She then discovered that the only way back to the castle led through the bewitched forest of the wicked sorcerer. Fearing to venture into the forest alone, she sought out her kind and wise godfather. She explained her plight, begged forgiveness of the godfather, and asked his assistance in returning home before her husband returned. The godfather, however, surprised and shocked at her behavior, refused forgiveness and denied her any assistance. Discouraged but still determined, the princess disguised her identity and sought the help of the most noble of all the kingdom's knights. After hearing the sad story, the knight pledged his unfailing aid—for a modest fee. But alas, the princess had no money and the knight rode away to save other damsels.

The beautiful princess had no one else from whom she might seek help, and decided to brave the great peril alone. She followed the safest path she knew, but when she was almost through the forest, the wicked sorcerer spied her and caused her to be devoured by the fire-breathing dragon.

1. Who was inside the organization and who was outside? Where were the boundaries?

2. Who is most responsible for the death of the beautiful princess?

3. Who is next most responsible? Least responsible?

4. What is your criterion for the above decisions?

5. What interventions would you suggest to prevent a recurrence?

6. What are the implications for *organizational development and change?*

Character	Most Responsible	Next Most Responsible	Least Responsible
Princess			
Husband			
Vagabond			
Godfather			
Knight			
Sorcerer			

Check one character in each column.

Action Learning

1. Find two people to interview who have gone through an organization change in recent years.

2. Ask them the following questions:
   a. Describe the organization before the change: What was the work like? How did people get along with one another? Was the culture friendly? How did management treat employees?

   b. Who wanted the change? How was the decision made to bring about the change?

   c. Was an outside consultant brought in to help with the change? If not, who managed the change? How did the change process work? Was it effective?

   d. Describe the company after the change, using similar criteria from question #a.

3. Write a short paper describing the similarities and differences in the two situations.

4. What conclusions would you draw on organization change from what you learned in these two interviews?

5. Your instructor may ask you to discuss your findings in groups, or as part of a class discussion.

Ethical Dilemma

Should I Fudge the Numbers?

Sara MacIntosh recently joined MicroPhone, a large telecommunications company, to take over the implementation of a massive customer service training project. The program was created by Kristin Cole, head of human resources and Sara's new boss. According to the grapevine, Kristin was hoping this project alone would give her the "star quality" she needed to earn a coveted promotion. Industry competition was heating up, and MicroPhone's strategy called for being the best at customer service, which meant having the most highly trained people in the industry, especially those who worked directly with customers. Kristin's new training program called for an average of one full week of intense customer service training for each of 3,000 people and had a price tag of about $40 million.

Kristin put together a team of overworked staffers to develop the training program, but now she needed someone well qualified and dedicated to manage and implement the project. Sara, with eight years of experience, a long list of accomplishments, and advanced degrees in finance and organizational behavior, seemed perfect for the job. However, during a thorough review of the proposal, Sara discovered some assumptions built into the formulas that raised red flags. She approached Dan Sotal, the team's coordinator, about her concerns, but the more Dan tried to explain how the financial projections were derived, the more Sara realized that Kristin's proposal was seriously flawed. No matter how she tried to work them out, the most that could be squeezed out of the $40 million budget was 20 hours of training per person, not the 40 hours everyone expected for such a high price tag.

Sara knew that, although the proposal had been largely developed before she came on board, it would bear her signature. As she carefully described the problems with the proposal to Kristin and outlined the potentially devastating consequences, Kristin impatiently tapped her pencil. Finally, she stood up, leaned forward, and interrupted Sara, quietly saying, "Sara, make the numbers work so that it adds up to 40 hours and stays within the $40 million budget." Sara glanced up and replied, "I don't think it can be done unless we either change the number of employees who are to be trained or the cost figure. . . ." Kristin's smile froze on her face and her eyes began to snap as she again interrupted. "I don't think you understand what I'm saying. We have too much at stake here. *Make the previous numbers work.*" Stunned, Sara belatedly began to realize that Kristin was ordering her to fudge the numbers. She felt an anxiety attack coming on as she wondered what she should do.

What Would You Do?

1. Make the previous numbers work. Kristin and the entire team have put massive amounts of time into the project, and they all expect you to be a team player. You don't want to let them down. Besides, this project is a great opportunity for you in a highly visible position.

2. Stick to your principles, and refuse to fudge the numbers. Tell Kristin you will work overtime to help develop an alternate proposal that stays within the budget by providing more training to employees who work directly with customers and fewer training hours for those who don't have direct customer contact.

3. Go to the team and tell them what you've been asked to do. If they refuse to support you, threaten to reveal the true numbers to the CEO and board members.

SOURCE: Adapted from Doug Wallace, "Fudge the Numbers or Leave," *Business Ethics* (May–June 1996): 58–59. Adapted with permission.

Case for Critical Analysis

Reflex Systems

As the plane took off from the L.A. airport for Chicago and home, Henry Rankin tried to unwind, something that didn't come naturally to the Reflex Systems software engineer. He needed time to think, and the flight from Los Angeles was a welcome relief. He went to L.A. to help two members of his project team solve technical glitches in software. Rankin had been pushing himself and his team hard for three months now, and he didn't know when they would get a break. Rankin was responsible for the technical implementation of the new customer relationship management (CRM) software being installed for western and eastern sales offices in L.A. and Chicago. The software was badly needed to improve follow-up sales for his company, Reflex Systems. Reflex sold exercise equipment to high schools and colleges through a national force of 310 salespeople. Reflex also sold products to small- and medium-sized businesses for recreation centers.

Rankin knew CEO Mike Frazer saw the new CRM software as the answer to one of the exercise equipment manufacturer's most persistent problems. Even though Reflex's low prices generated healthy sales, follow-up service was spotty. Consequently, getting repeat business from customers—high schools, colleges, and corporate recreation centers—was an uphill battle. Excited by the prospect of finally removing this major roadblock, Frazer ordered the CRM software installed in just 10 weeks, a goal Rankin privately thought was unrealistic. He also felt the project budget wasn't adequate. Rankin thought about meeting the next day with his three Chicago team members and about the status update he would give his boss, Nicole Dyer, the senior vice president for information technology. Rankin remembered that Dyer had scheduled 10 weeks for the CRM project. He had always been a top performer by driving himself hard and had been in his management position three years now. He was good with technology but was frustrated when members of his five-person team didn't seem as committed. Dyer told him last week that she didn't feel a sense of urgency from his team. How could she think that? Rankin requested that team members work evenings and weekends because the budget was too tight to fill a vacant position. They agreed to put in the hours, although they didn't seem enthusiastic.

Still, Frazer was the boss, so if he wanted the job done in 10 weeks, Rankin would do everything in his power to deliver, even if it meant the entire team worked nights and weekends. He wasn't asking any more of his subordinates than he was asking of himself, as he frequently reminded them when they came to him with bloodshot eyes and complained about the hours. Rankin thought back to a flight one month ago when he returned to Chicago from L.A. Sally Phillips sat next to him. Phillips was one of five members on Rankin's team and told him she had an offer from a well-known competitor. The money was less, but she was interested in the quality-of-life aspect of the company. Phillips asked for feedback on how she was doing and about her career prospects at Reflex. Rankin said he didn't want her to leave, but what more could he say? She got along well with people, but she wasn't as technically gifted as some on the team. Rankin needed her help to finish the project, and he told her so. Two weeks later she turned in her letter of resignation, and now the team was shorthanded. Rankin was also aware that his own possible promotion in two years, when Nicole Dyer was eligible for retirement, depended on his success with this project. He would just take up the slack himself. He loved studying, analyzing, and solving technical problems when he could get time alone.

Henry Rankin knew that Nicole Dyer had noticed a lack of commitment on the part of the team members. He wondered whether she had discussed the team's performance with Frazer as well. Rankin hadn't noticed any other problems, but he recalled his partner on the project, Sam Matheny, saying that two Chicago team members, Bob Finley and Lynne Johnston, were avoiding each other. How did Sam know that? Matheny was in charge of nontechnical sales implementation of the CRM project, which meant training salespeople, redesigning sales procedures, updating customer records, and so forth. Rankin called Finley and Johnston to his office and said he expected them to get along for the good of the project. Finley said he had overreacted to Johnston from lack of sleep and wondered when the project would be over. Rankin wasn't certain because of all the problems with both software and hardware, but he said the project shouldn't last more than another month.

As the plane taxied to the gate, an exhausted Rankin couldn't quell his growing fears that as the deadline fast approached, the project team was crumbling. How could he meet that deadline? As the plane taxied to the gate at Chicago, Rankin wondered about the project's success. Was there more to managing this team than working hard and pushing others hard? Even he was tired. Maybe he would ask his wife when he got home. He hadn't seen her or the kids for a week, but they had not complained.

Questions

1. What personality and behavior characteristics does Henry Rankin exhibit? Do you think these traits contribute to a good person–job fit for him? If you were an executive coach hired to help Rankin be a better manager, what would you say to him? Why?

2. Does Rankin display Type A or Type B behavior? What are the causes of stress for his team?

3. If you were Rankin, how would you have handled your team members (Sally Phillips, Bob Finley, and Lynne Johnston)? Be specific. What insights or behaviors would make Rankin a better manager?

BIZ FLIX

The Breakfast Club

John Hughes's careful look at teenage culture in a suburban high school outside Chicago focuses on a group of teenagers from the school's subcultures. They start their Saturday detention with nothing in common. Over the day they learn each others' most inner secrets. The highly memorable characters—the Jock, the Princess, the Criminal, the Kook, and the Brain—leave lasting impressions. (If you have seen the film, try to recall which actor or actress played each character.)

This scene shows the detainees at lunchtime. It is an edited version of the "Lunch Time" sequence that appears in the first third of the film. Carefully study each character's behavior to answer the questions below.

What to Watch for and Ask Yourself

1. Which Big Five personality dimensions describe each character in this scene?

2. Which characters show positive affectivity? Which show negative affectivity?

3. Are any of these characters Type A personalities or Type B personalities? If so, which ones?

VIDEO CASE

Dynamics of Behavior in Organizations at Zingerman's

The people who create the delightful Zingerman's Experience in Ann Arbor, Michigan for their customers' dining pleasure are on a mission: To make customers' lives more enjoyable with remarkably flavored food, great service, great finances, and a great work environment. The masterful mixing, stirring, and blending of the talents, skills, passion, and behavior of 400 people (closer to 1,000 people during the peak holiday season) has created the legendary Zingerman's Community of Businesses, named "The Coolest Small Business in America" by *Inc. Magazine*.

The people of Zingerman's are not only students and connoisseurs of traditional foods, from which they craft remarkably flavored recipes. They are also students and connoisseurs of people. Ari Weinzweig, one of the co-founders of the original Zingerman's Deli in 1982, puts it this way: "People don't need our food at the price point that is required to prepare and serve it. They have to be educated to appreciate traditional recipes and foods. We not only have a passion for food, we have a passion for education and we have a passion for service."

To build and lead this level of service to their customers, the leaders, managers, and staff of all of Zingerman's Community of Businesses believe that outstanding service to customers is the result of outstanding service to one another. Zingerman's subscribes to Servant Leadership, which means that the managing partners are in service to all the managers. The managers are in service to all the people on the staff. They all feel that the staff will not provide a better service experience to customers than that which they themselves experience with one another.

What it takes to lead, inspire, and organize this level of dedication to service in every cell of the Zingerman's Experience is a passion that begins with the founders and is taught, nurtured, and developed in the hearts of everyone who is on the Zingerman's team. Zingerman's seeks to recruit people with an easy smile and a high level of emotional intelligence: self awareness, self management, social awareness, and relationship awareness, which leads to high work ethic, interest in learning, self direction and ownership ability, and enthusiasm for what they are doing.

Zingerman's is an organization that then gives people an opportunity to make a difference, an impact on the organization. They ask people to get involved. When people think they are making a difference, they are making a difference. That is the recipe that inspires the organizational behavior in the Zingerman's Community of Businesses.

Questions

1. What is the connection between great work environment and organizational behavior at Zingerman's?

2. Why is there a high premium placed on staff education and on customer education at Zingerman's?

3. Why does Zingerman's seek to recruit emotionally intelligent people?

chapter 11

Leadership

Learning Objectives

After studying this chapter, you should be able to:

1 Define leadership, and explain its importance for organizations.

2 Describe how leadership is changing in today's organizations.

3 Identify personal characteristics associated with effective leaders.

4 Define task-oriented behavior and people-oriented behavior, and explain how these categories are used to evaluate and adapt leadership style.

5 Describe Hersey and Blanchard's situational theory and its application to subordinate participation.

6 Explain the path–goal model of leadership.

7 Discuss how leadership fits the organizational situation and how organizational characteristics can substitute for leadership behaviors.

8 Describe transformational leadership and when it should be used.

9 Identify the five sources of leader power and the tactics leaders use to influence others.

10 Explain servant leadership and moral leadership and their importance in contemporary organizations.

New Manager's Questions

Please circle your opinion below each of the following statements. **★ Assess Your Answer**

1 A strong, healthy ego helps a leader to be more effective and to take charge.

1	2	3	4	5
strongly agree				strongly disagree

2 Good leaders are participative, engaged, and supportive.

1	2	3	4	5
strongly agree				strongly disagree

3 Leaders should amass as much power as they can; it helps them get things done.

1	2	3	4	5
strongly agree				strongly disagree

The attitudes and behaviors of leaders, as we explored in the previous chapter, play an important role in shaping employee attitudes, such as their job satisfaction and organizational commitment. Yet there are as many variations among leaders as there are among other individuals, and many different styles of leadership can be effective.

Different leaders behave in different ways depending on their individual differences as well as their followers' needs and the organizational situation. For example, contrast the styles of Pat McGovern, founder and chair of International Data Group, a technology publishing and research firm that owns magazines such as *CIO*, *PC World*, and *Computerworld*, with that of Tom Siebel, CEO of software company Siebel Systems. McGovern treats each employee to lunch at the Ritz on his or her tenth anniversary with IDG to emphasize how important each employee is to the success of the company. He personally thanks almost every person in every business unit once a year, which takes about a month of his time. Managers provide him with a list of accomplishments for all their direct reports, which McGovern memorizes the night before his visit so he can congratulate people on specific accomplishments. In addition to appreciating and caring about employees, McGovern also shows that he believes in them by decentralizing decision making so that people have the autonomy to make their own decisions about how best to accomplish organizational goals. Tom Siebel, in contrast, is known as a disciplined and dispassionate manager who remains somewhat aloof from his employees and likes to maintain strict control over every aspect of the business. He enforces a dress code, sets tough goals and standards, and holds people strictly accountable. "We go to work to realize our professional ambitions, not to have a good time," Siebel says.[1] Both Siebel and McGovern have been successful as leaders, although their styles are quite different.

This chapter explores one of the most widely discussed and researched topics in management—leadership. Here we define leadership and explore the differences between leadership and management. We look at some important leadership approaches for contemporary organizations, as well as examine trait, behavioral, and contingency theories of leadership effectiveness, discuss charismatic and transformational leadership, and consider how leaders use power and influence to get things done. The final section of the chapter discusses servant leadership and moral leadership, which are two enduring approaches that have received renewed emphasis in recent years. Chapters 12–14 will look in detail at many of the functions of leadership, including employee motivation, communication, and encouraging teamwork.

The Nature of Leadership

No topic is probably more important to organizational success today than leadership. Leadership matters. In most situations, a team, military unit, or volunteer organization is only as good as its leader. Consider the situation in Iraq, as U.S. military advisors strive to build Iraqi forces that can take over security duties without support from coalition troops. Many trainers say they encounter excellent individual soldiers and junior leaders but that many of the senior commanders are stuck in old authoritarian patterns that undermine their units. Whether an Iraqi unit succeeds or fails often comes down to one person—its commander—so advisors are putting emphasis on finding and strengthening good leaders.[2] Top leaders make a difference in business organizations as well. Baron Partners Fund, which picks stocks based largely on an evaluation of companies' senior executives, was the best-performing diversified stock fund of 2004, with a return of 42 percent. Manager Ron Baron says top leaders who are smart, honorable, and treat their employees right typically lead their companies to greater financial success and greater shareholder returns.[3]

The concept of leadership continues to evolve as the needs of organizations change. Among all the ideas and writings about leadership, three aspects stand out—people, influence, and goals. Leadership occurs among people, involves the use of influence,

Spotlight on Skills

Seven—or Five—Leadership Habits of Spongebob Squarepants

A new leader is emerging. He lives with his pet snail, Gary, in a pineapple at the bottom of the ocean and adores his fry-cook job at the Krusty Krab. Spongebob seems to get into trouble a lot. In fact, that is his gift. He hangs out with his starfish pal, Patrick, and his thrill-seeking friend Sandy Cheeks, a squirrel. Spongebob has had some harrowing experiences and has learned important leadership skills:

1. Be resilient. Today it's all about the globalization and learning multicultural skills. When Spongebob is marooned in a frightening abyss, he is forced to find his willpower and resources to learn a new dialect, find some chow, and maneuver his way back to Bikini Bottom. (Episode: "Rock Bottom")
2. Recruit the finest. When he learns that his superhero friends and crime fighters Mermaidman and Barnacleboy have been relegated to a nursing home, Spongebob convinces them to come out of retirement to fulfill their destinies: ward off evildoers from Goo Lagoon. (Episode: "Mermaidman and Barnacleboy")
3. No resting on laurels. Spongebob is in a rut but a good one. After becoming Employee of the Month 26 times straight, he feels himself at risk of losing the title. He compulsively strives to outcook, outclean, and outwork rival Squidward. "Having pride in your work," says Spongebob, "is the only thing that makes it all worthwhile." (Episode: "Employee of the Month")
4. Innovate and innovate. Good leaders are those that follow the rules, while great leaders change them. Spongebob suggests multicolored "pretty patties," which are rejected by management. Undaunted, he sets out on his own, becoming a wild success. Showing cool business savvy, he sells his idea in the nick of time. (Episode: "Patty Hype")
5. Recognize employees' limits. To cut costs, Mr. Krab, the ultimate miser, charges workers for infractions such as "existing" and "breathing." Squidward and Spongebob complain, and they are fired, causing them to "dismantle the establishment," an objective they take literally. (Episode: "Squid of Strike")

SOURCE: Lucas Conley, "Leadership secrets of Spongebob Squarepants," *Fast Company* (Sept 2004): 45; L. A. Johnson, "Hands-off bosses get better workers, work," *Pittsburgh Post-Gazette* (July 3, 2007): 2D.

and is used to attain goals.[4] *Influence* means that the relationship among people is not passive. Moreover, influence is designed to achieve some end or goal. Thus, **leadership** as defined here is the ability to influence people toward the attainment of goals. This definition captures the idea that leaders are involved with other people in the achievement of goals.

Leadership is reciprocal, occurring *among* people.[5] Leadership is a "people" activity, distinct from administrative paper shuffling or problem-solving activities. Leadership is dynamic and involves the use of power to influence people and get things done. Role models for leadership can come from wide and varied sources, as shown in the Spotlight on Skills.

Leadership for Contemporary Times

The environmental context in which leadership is practiced influences which approach might be most effective, as well as what kinds of leaders are most admired by society. The technology, economic conditions, labor conditions, and social and cultural mores of the times all play a role. A significant influence on leadership styles in recent years is the turbulence and uncertainty of the environment in which most organizations are operating. Ethical and economic difficulties, corporate governance concerns, globalization, changes in technology, new ways of working, shifting employee expectations, and significant social transitions have contributed to a shift in how we think about and practice leadership.

Of particular interest for leadership in contemporary times is a *post-heroic approach* that focuses on the subtle, unseen, and often unrewarded acts that good leaders perform every

 **TAKE ACTION**

Go to the ethical dilemma on page 438 that pertains to post-heroic leadership for turbulent times.

leadership
the ability to influence people toward the attainment of organizational goals.

day, rather than on the grand accomplishments of celebrated business heroes.[6] During the 1980s and 1990s, leadership became equated with larger-than-life personalities, strong egos, and personal ambitions. In contrast, the post-heroic leader's major characteristic is humility.[7] **Humility** means being unpretentious and modest rather than arrogant and prideful. Humble leaders don't have to be in the center of things. They quietly build strong, enduring companies by developing and supporting others rather than touting their own abilities and accomplishments. Two approaches that are in tune with post-heroic leadership for today's times are Level 5 leadership and interactive leadership, a style that is commonly used by women leaders.

LEVEL 5 LEADERSHIP

A recent five-year study conducted by Jim Collins and his research associates identified the critical importance of what Collins calls *Level 5 leadership* in transforming companies from merely good to truly great organizations.[8] As described in his book *Good to Great: Why Some Companies Make the Leap . . . and Others Don't,* Level 5 leadership refers to the highest level in a hierarchy of manager capabilities, as illustrated in Exhibit 11.1. A key characteristic of Level 5 leaders is an almost complete lack of ego, coupled with a fierce resolve to do what is best for the organization. In contrast to the view of great leaders as larger-than-life personalities with strong egos and big ambitions, Level 5 leaders often seem shy and unpretentious. Although they accept full responsibility for mistakes, poor results, or failures, Level 5 leaders give credit for successes to other people. For example, Joseph F. Cullman III, former CEO of Philip Morris, staunchly refused to accept credit for the company's long-term success, citing his great colleagues, successors, and predecessors as the reason for the accomplishments. Another example is Darwin E. Smith. When he was promoted to CEO of Kimberly-Clark, Smith questioned whether the board really wanted to appoint him because he didn't believe he had the qualifications a CEO needed.

Despite their personal humility, Level 5 leaders have a strong will to do whatever it takes to produce great and lasting results for their organizations. They are extremely

humility
being unpretentious and modest rather than arrogant and prideful.

EXHIBIT 11.1
The Level 5 Leadership Hierarchy

Level 5: The Level 5 Leader
Builds an enduring great organization through a combination of personal humility and professional resolve.

Level 4: The Effective Executive
Builds widespread commitment to a clear and compelling vision; stimulates people to high performance.

Level 3: Competent Manager
Sets plans and organizes people for the efficient and effective pursuit of objectives.

Level 2: Contributing Team Member
Contributes to the achievement of team goals; works effectively with others in a group.

Level 1: Highly Capable Individual
Productive contributor; offers talent, knowledge, skills, and good work habits as an individual employee.

SOURCE: "The Level 5 Leadership Hierarchy" from *Good to Great: Why Some Companies Make the Leap . . . and Others Don't,* by Jim Collins. Reprinted by permission of HarperCollins Publishers, Inc.

Assess Your Answer

1 A strong, healthy ego helps a leader to be more effective and to take charge.

ANSWER: Current research has shown that egoless leaders are actually the most effective and create the most productive/profitable companies.

ambitious for their companies rather than for themselves. This goal becomes highly evident in the area of succession planning. Level 5 leaders develop a solid corps of leaders throughout the organization, so that when they leave the company, it can continue to thrive and grow even stronger. Egocentric leaders, by contrast, often set their successors up for failure because it will be a testament to their own greatness if the company doesn't perform well without them. Rather than an organization built around "a genius with a thousand helpers," Level 5 leaders build an organization with many strong leaders who can step forward and continue the company's success. These leaders want everyone in the organization to develop to their fullest potential.

WOMEN'S WAYS OF LEADING

The focus on minimizing personal ambition and developing others is also a hallmark of *interactive leadership*, which has been found to be common among female leaders. Research indicates that women's style of leadership is typically different from most men's and is particularly suited to today's organizations.[9] Using data from actual performance evaluations, one study found that when rated by peers, subordinates, and bosses, female managers score significantly higher than men on abilities such as motivating others, fostering communication, and listening.[10]

Interactive leadership means that the leader favors a consensual and collaborative process, and influence derives from relationships rather than position power and formal authority.[11] For example, Nancy Hawthorne, former chief financial officer at Continental Cablevision Inc., felt that her role as a leader was to delegate tasks and authority to others and to help them be more effective. "I was being traffic cop and coach and facilitator," Hawthorne says. "I was always into building a department that hummed."[12] Similarly, Terri Kelly, who took over as CEO of W. L. Gore in 2005, says her goal is to provide overall direction and guidance, not to micromanage and tell people how to do their jobs.[13] It is important to note that men can be interactive leaders as well, as demonstrated by the example of Pat McGovern of International Data Group earlier in the chapter. For McGovern, having personal contact with employees and letting them know they're appreciated is a primary responsibility of leaders. The characteristics associated with interactive leadership are emerging as valuable qualities for both male and female leaders in today's workplace. Values associated with interactive leadership include personal humility, inclusion, relationship building, and caring.

Leadership Versus Management

Much has been written in recent years about the leadership role of managers. Management and leadership are both important to organizations. Effective managers have to be leaders, too, because distinctive qualities are associated with management and leadership that provide different strengths for the organization, as illustrated in Exhibit 11.2. As shown in the exhibit, management and leadership reflect two different sets of qualities and skills that frequently overlap within a single individual. A person might have more of one set of qualities than the other, but ideally a manager develops a balance of both manager and leader qualities.

interactive leadership
a leadership style characterized by values such as inclusion, collaboration, relationship building, and caring.

EXHIBIT 11.2

Leader and Manager Qualities

LEADER QUALITIES

MANAGER QUALITIES

SOUL
Visionary
Passionate
Creative
Flexible
Inspiring
Innovative
Courageous
Imaginative
Experimental
Initiates change
Personal power

MIND
Rational
Consulting
Persistent
Problem solving
Tough-minded
Analytical
Structured
Deliberate
Authoritative
Stabilizing
Position power

SOURCE: Based on Genevieve Capowski, "Anatomy of a Leader: Where Are the Leaders of Tomorrow?" *Management Review* (March 1994): 12.

traits
distinguishing personal characteristics, such as intelligence, values, and appearance.

CONCEPT CONNECTION

Joanna B. Meiseles, president and founder of Snip-its Corp., a $1.5 million children's haircutting chain based in Natick, Massachusetts, demonstrates many of the **personal traits** associated with effective leadership. For example, she displayed intelligence, ability, knowledge, and judgment by knowing that to make her company successful, it had to be unique. Everything about Snip-its is tailored to children. Snip-its characters perch on a hot pink and lime green entry arch, games and stories are loaded on funky quasi-anthropomorphic computers at every cutting station, and the Magic Box dispenses a prize in exchange for a swatch of hair at the end of a visit.

A primary distinction between management and leadership is that management promotes stability, order, and problem solving within the existing organizational structure and systems. Leadership promotes vision, creativity, and change. In other words, "a manager takes care of where you are; a leader takes you to a new place."[14] Leadership means questioning the status quo so that outdated, unproductive, or socially irresponsible norms can be replaced to meet new challenges.

Leadership Traits

Early efforts to understand leadership success focused on the leader's personal characteristics or traits. **Traits** are the distinguishing personal characteristics of a leader, such as intelligence, values, self-confidence, and appearance. The early research focused on leaders who had achieved a level of greatness, and hence was referred to as the *Great Man* approach. The idea was relatively simple: Find out what made these people great, and select future leaders who already exhibited the same traits or could be trained to develop them. Generally, early research found only a weak relationship between personal traits and leader success.[15]

In recent years, interest in examining leadership traits has reemerged. In addition to personality traits, physical, social, and work-related characteristics of leaders have been studied.[16] Exhibit 11.3 summarizes the physical, social, and personal leadership characteristics that have received the greatest research support. However, these characteristics do not stand alone. The appropriateness of a trait or set of traits depends on the leadership situation. The same traits do not apply to every organization or situation. Further studies expand the understanding of leadership beyond

NEW MANAGER SELF TEST

Interpersonal Patterns

The majority of a new manager's work is accomplished through interpersonal relationships. To understand your relationship pattern, consider the following verbs. These 20 verbs describe some of the ways people feel and act from time to time. Think about your behavior in groups. How do you feel and act in groups? Check the five verbs that best describe your behavior in groups as you see it.

_____ acquiesce	_____ coordinate	_____ lead
_____ advise	_____ criticize	_____ oblige
_____ agree	_____ direct	_____ relinquish
_____ analyze	_____ disapprove	_____ resist
_____ assist	_____ evade	_____ retreat
_____ concede	_____ initiate	_____ withdraw
_____ concur	_____ judge	

Two underlying patterns of interpersonal behavior are represented in the preceding list: *dominance* (authority or control) and *sociability* (intimacy or friendliness). Most individuals tend either to like to control things (high dominance) or to let others control things (low dominance). Similarly, most persons tend either to be warm and personal (high sociability) or to be somewhat distant and impersonal (low sociability). In the following diagram, circle the five verbs in the list that you used to describe yourself. The set of 10 verbs in either horizontal row (sociability dimension) or vertical column (dominance dimension) in which 3 or more are circled represents your tendency in interpersonal behavior.

	High Dominance	**Low Dominance**
High Sociability	advises	acquiesces
	coordinates	agrees
	directs	assists
	initiates	concurs
	leads	obliges
Low Sociability	analyzes	concedes
	criticizes	evades
	disapproves	relinquishes
	judges	retreats
	resists	withdraws

Your behavior pattern suggested in the diagram is a clue to your interpersonal style as a new manager. Which of the four quadrants provides the best description of you? Is that the type of leader you aspire to become? Generally speaking, the high sociability and high dominance pattern reflects the type of leader to which many new managers aspire. How does your pattern correspond to the Level 5 and interactive leadership patterns described in the text?

SOURCE: David W. Johnson and Frank P. Johnson, *Joining Together: Group Theory and Group Skills*, 8th ed. (New York: Allyn and Bacon, 2003): 189–190. Used with permission.

the personal traits of the individual to focus on the dynamics of the relationship between leaders and followers.

Behavioral Approaches

The inability to define effective leadership based solely on traits led to an interest in looking at the behavior of leaders and how it might contribute to leadership success or failure. Perhaps any leader can adopt the correct behavior with appropriate training. Two basic

 TAKE ACTION

To be a good manager, you must organize resources; to be a good leader, you must help others to follow the vision.

Physical Characteristics	**Personality**	**Work-Related Characteristics**
Energy	Self-confidence	Achievement drive, desire to excel
Physical stamina	Honesty and integrity	Conscientiousness in pursuit of goals
	Enthusiasm	Persistence against obstacles, tenacity
	Desire to lead	
	Independence	
Intelligence and Ability	**Social Characteristics**	**Social Background**
Intelligence, cognitive ability	Sociability, interpersonal skills	Education
Knowledge	Cooperativeness	Mobility
Judgment, decisiveness	Ability to enlist cooperation	
	Tact, diplomacy	

SOURCES: Based on Bernard M. Bass, *Bass & Stogdill's Handbook of Leadership: Theory, Research, and Managerial Applications,* 3rd ed. (New York: The Free Press, 1990): 80–81; and S. A. Kirkpatrick and E. A. Locke, "Leadership: Do Traits Matter?" *Academy of Management Executive* 5, no. 2 (1991): 48–60.

EXHIBIT 11.3

Personal
Characteristics
of Leaders

leadership behaviors identified as important for leadership are *task-oriented behavior* and *people-oriented behavior.* These two *metacategories,* or broadly defined behavior categories, were found to be applicable to effective leadership in a variety of situations and time periods.[17] Although they are not the only important leadership behaviors, concern for tasks and concern for people must be shown at some reasonable level. Thus, many approaches to understanding leadership use these metacategories as a basis for study and comparison. Important research programs on leadership behavior were conducted at Ohio State University, University of Michigan, and University of Texas.

OHIO STATE STUDIES

Researchers at Ohio State University surveyed leaders to study hundreds of dimensions of leader behavior.[18] They identified two major behaviors, called consideration and initiating structure.

Consideration falls in the category of people-oriented behavior and is the extent to which the leader is mindful of subordinates, respects their ideas and feelings, and establishes mutual trust. Considerate leaders are friendly, provide open communication, develop teamwork, and are oriented toward their subordinates' welfare.

Initiating structure is the degree of task behavior, that is, the extent to which the leader is task oriented and directs subordinate work activities toward goal attainment. Leaders with this style typically give instructions, spend time planning, emphasize deadlines, and provide explicit schedules of work activities.

Consideration and initiating structure are independent of each other, which means that a leader with a high degree of consideration may be either high or low on initiating structure. A leader may have any of four styles: high initiating structure–low consideration, high initiating structure–high consideration, low initiating structure–low consideration, or low initiating structure–high consideration. The Ohio State research found that the high consideration–high initiating structure style achieved better performance and greater satisfaction than the other leader styles. The value of the high–high style is illustrated by Brigadier General Michael P. Mulqueen, who retired from the U.S. Marine Corps to head up the Greater Chicago Food Depository. Mulqueen runs the depository like a business rather than a typical nonprofit. He stresses efficiency and is as demanding as any corporate CEO in organizing and directing people toward achieving the organization's goals. Yet Mulqueen knows that leaders don't get people to rally around them simply by issuing orders. He's never intimidating, and he's always willing to listen to other people's ideas, allow people autonomy in how they accomplish goals, and show appreciation and respect. Mulqueen's high consideration–high initiating structure

TAKE ACTION

As a manager, work to have both consideration and structure—to achieve balance.

consideration
a type of behavior that describes the extent to which the leader is sensitive to subordinates, respects their ideas and feelings, and establishes mutual trust.

initiating structure
a type of leader behavior that describes the extent to which the leader is task oriented and directs subordinate work activities toward goal attainment.

The last time the De La Salle Spartans lost a football game was December 7, 1991. Since then, coach Bob LaDouceur has led his team of players, many of whom are derided as "undersized" and "untalented," to one victory after another, year after year. Despite competing against bigger schools and tougher players, the De La Salle Spartans just keep on winning.

De La Salle is a small, private parochial school in Concord, California. Years ago, LaDouceur sized up his team of a few, small demoralized players and made a decision. He was going to teach these guys what it takes to win, and then make it a day-to-day process. LaDouceur directs close attention to the tasks needed to accomplish the goal of winning. He keeps his players on a year-round strength and conditioning program. Each practice is methodical, and LaDouceur constantly tells his players to leave every practice just a little bit better than they were when it started. He teaches players to make up for what they lack in size and talent with intelligence and wit.

However, the coach hasn't just institutionalized the process of drills, workouts, and practices. He has also institutionalized a process of building bonds and intimacy among his players. "If a team has no soul," LaDouceur says, "you're just wasting your time." Tasks are important, but for LaDouceur, people always come first. "It's not about how we're getting better physically, it's about how we're getting better as people," he says. During the off season, players go camping and rafting together and volunteer for community service. When the season starts, the team attends chapel together for readings and songs. After every practice, a dinner is held at a player's home.

Then comes what LaDouceur's considers his central task and his main goal for the team. As tensions build during the season, players are encouraged to speak their hearts, to confess their fears and shortcomings, and to talk about their commitments and expectations of themselves for the next game. On Thursday night before Friday games, LaDouceur doesn't give a typical locker room speech. He talks about the "L word." "*Love.* Why is that word so hard to say?" he asks his players. And then he waits—as long as it takes—until a few players overcome their embarrassment enough to say it.

SOURCE: Don Wallace, "The Soul of a Sports Machine," *Fast Company* (October 2003): 100–102; and Neil Hayes, *When the Game Stands Tall. The Story of the De La Salle Spartans and Football's Longest Winning Streak* (Berkeley, CA: Frog, Ltd./North Atlantic Books, 2005).

The De La Salle Spartans Win with Soul

leadership approach has turned the Greater Chicago Food Depository into one of the nation's most effective hunger-relief agencies.[19] Successful pro football coaches also often use a high–high style.[20] For example, coaches have to keep players focused on winning football games by scheduling structured practices, emphasizing careful planning, and so forth. However, the best coaches are those who genuinely care about and show concern for their players. At the top of this page is a profile of Bob Ladouceur, the coach of an extraordinary high school football team, who personifies the high–high leadership style.

Some research, however, indicates that the high–high style is not necessarily the best. These studies suggest that effective leaders may be high on consideration and low on initiating structure or low on consideration and high on initiating structure, depending on the situation.[21]

MICHIGAN STUDIES

Studies at the University of Michigan at about the same time took a different approach by comparing the behavior of effective and ineffective supervisors.[22] The most effective supervisors were those who focused on the subordinates' human needs to "build effective work groups with high performance goals." The Michigan researchers used the term *employee-centered leaders* for leaders who established high performance goals and displayed supportive behavior toward subordinates. The less-effective leaders were called *job-centered leaders;* these leaders tended to be less concerned with goal achievement and human needs in favor of meeting schedules, keeping costs low, and achieving production efficiency.

THE LEADERSHIP GRID

Building on the work of the Ohio State and Michigan studies, Blake and Mouton of the University of Texas proposed a two-dimensional leadership theory called the

EXHIBIT 11.4

The Leadership Grid®
Figure

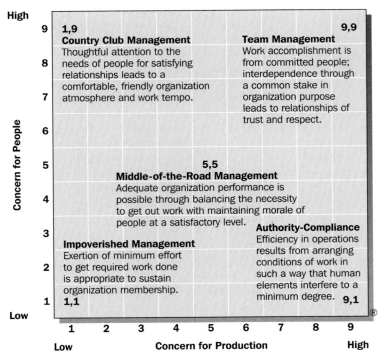

SOURCE: The Leadership Grid® figure, Paternalism figure and Opportunism from *Leadership Dilemmas-Grid Solutions*, by Robert R. Blake and Anne Adams McCanse (formerly the Managerial Grid by Robert R. Blace and Jase S. Mouton). (Houston: Gulf Publishing Company). (Grid figure: p. 29, Paternalism figure: p. 30, Opportunism figure: p. 31). Copyright © 1991, by Blake and Mouton, and Scientific Methods, Inc. Reproduced by permission of the owners.

leadership grid.[23] The two-dimensional model and five of its seven major management styles are depicted in Exhibit 11.4. Each axis on the grid is a nine-point scale, with 1 meaning low concern and 9 high concern.

Team management (9,9) often is considered the most effective style and is recommended for managers because organization members work together to accomplish tasks. *Country club management* (1,9) occurs when primary emphasis is given to people rather than to work outputs. *Authority-compliance management* (9,1) occurs when efficiency in operations is the dominant orientation. *Middle-of-the-road management* (5,5) reflects a moderate amount of concern for both people and production. *Impoverished management* (1,1) means the absence of a management philosophy; managers exert little effort toward interpersonal relationships or work accomplishment.

The next group of theories builds on the leader–follower relationship of behavioral approaches to explore how organizational situations affect the leader's approach.

Contingency Approaches

Several models of leadership explain the relationship between leadership styles and specific situations. They are termed **contingency approaches** and include the situational theory of Hersey and Blanchard, the leadership model developed by Fiedler and his associates, the path–goal theory presented by Evans and House, and the substitutes-for-leadership concept.

HERSEY AND BLANCHARD'S SITUATIONAL THEORY

The **situational theory** of leadership is an interesting extension of the behavioral theories summarized in the leadership grid (see Exhibit 11.4). Hersey and Blanchard's approach focuses a great deal of attention on the characteristics of followers in determining appropriate

TAKE ACTION ➡

As a leader, try to find the right kind of style for each situation.

leadership grid
a two-dimensional leadership theory that measures the leader's concern for people and for production.

contingency approach
a model of leadership that describes the relationship between leadership styles and specific organizational situations.

situational theory
a contingency approach to leadership that links the leader's behavioral style with the task readiness of subordinates.

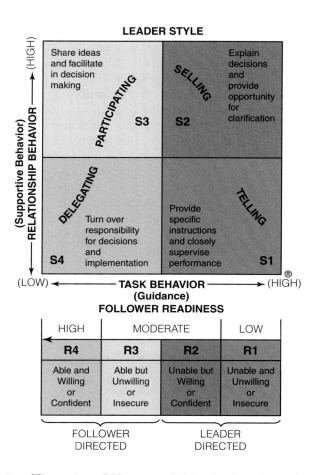

EXHIBIT 11.5

Hersey and Blanchard's
Situational Theory of
Leadership

leadership behavior. The point of Hersey and Blanchard is that subordinates vary in readiness level. People low in task readiness because of little ability or training, or insecurity, need a different leadership style than those who are high in readiness and have good ability, skills, confidence, and willingness to work.[24] According to the situational theory, a leader can adopt one of four leadership styles, based on a combination of relationship (concern for people) and task (concern for production) behavior. The appropriate style depends on the readiness level of followers.

Exhibit 11.5 summarizes the relationship between leader style and follower readiness. The *telling style* reflects a high concern for tasks and a low concern for people and relationships. This highly directive style involves giving explicit directions about how tasks should be accomplished. The *selling style* is based on a high concern for both people and tasks. With this approach, the leader explains decisions and gives subordinates a chance to ask questions and gain clarity and understanding about work tasks. The next leader behavior style, the *participating style*, is based on a combination of high concern for people and relationships and low concern for production tasks. The leader shares ideas with subordinates, gives them a chance to participate, and facilitates decision making. The fourth style, the *delegating style*, reflects a low concern for both relationships and tasks. This leader style provides little direction and little support because the leader turns over responsibility for decisions and their implementation to subordinates.

The bell-shaped curve in Exhibit 11.5 is called a prescriptive curve because it indicates when each leader style should be used. The readiness level of followers is indicated in the lower part of the Exhibit. R1 is low readiness, and R4 represents high readiness. The telling style is for low readiness followers because people are unable or unwilling because of poor ability and skills, little experience, or insecurity, to take responsibility for their own task behavior. The leader is specific, telling people exactly what to do, how to do it, and when. The selling and participating styles work for followers at moderate readiness levels. For example, followers might lack some education and experience for the job but have high confidence, interest, and willingness to learn. As shown in the exhibit, the selling style is effective in this situation because it involves giving direction but also includes seeking input from others and clarifying tasks rather than simply instructing that they be performed. When followers have the necessary skills and experience but are somewhat insecure in their abilities or lack high willingness, the participating style enables the leader to guide followers' development and act as a resource for advice and assistance. When followers demonstrate high readiness, that is, they have high levels of education, experience, and readiness to accept responsibility for their own task behavior, the delegating style can effectively be used. Because of the high readiness level of followers, the leader can delegate responsibility for decisions and their implementation to subordinates who have the skills, abilities, and positive attitudes to follow through. The leader provides a general goal and sufficient authority to do the task as followers see fit.

To apply the Hersey and Blanchard model, the leader diagnoses the readiness level of followers and adopts the appropriate style—telling, selling, participating, or delegating. Using the incorrect style can hurt morale and performance. When president of Harvard University, former U.S. Treasury Secretary Lawrence Summers, tried to use a primarily telling style with followers who were at high readiness levels, it led to serious conflict with some faculty members and eventual demands for his ouster.

Summers employed an assertive top-down style with followers who think of themselves not as employees but as partners in an academic enterprise. Faculty members at Harvard have long been accustomed to decentralized, democratic decision making and having a say in matters such as department mergers or new programs of study. Summers made many decisions on his own that followers thought should be put to a faculty vote. Although students in general supported Summers, the conflicts and a vote of no-confidence from some faculty convinced Summers to resign with many of his goals and plans for the university unrealized.[25]

TAKE ACTION

As a leader, only use the delegating style if the group has enough training, education, and experience; otherwise, it can be a disaster.

FIEDLER'S CONTINGENCY THEORY

Whereas Hersey and Blanchard focused on the characteristics of followers, Fiedler and his associates looked at some other elements of the organizational situation to assess when one leadership style is more effective than another.[26] The starting point for Fiedler's theory is the extent to which the leader's style is task oriented or relationship (people) oriented. Fiedler considered a person's leadership style to be relatively fixed and difficult to change; therefore, the basic idea is to match the leader's style with the situation most favorable for that person's effectiveness. By diagnosing leadership style and the organizational situation, the correct fit can be arranged.

Situation: Favorable or Unfavorable? The suitability of a person's leadership style is determined by whether the situation is favorable or unfavorable to the leader. The favorability of a leadership situation can be analyzed in terms of three elements: the quality of relationships between leader and followers, the degree of task structure, and the extent to which the leader has formal authority over followers.[27]

For example, a situation would be considered *highly favorable* to the leader when leader–member relationships are positive, tasks are highly structured, and the leader has formal authority over followers. In this situation, followers trust, respect, and have confidence in the leader. The group's tasks are clearly defined, involve specific procedures, and have clear, explicit goals. In addition, the leader has formal authority to direct and evaluate followers, along with the power to reward or punish. A situation would be considered *highly unfavorable* to the leader when leader–member relationships are poor, tasks are highly unstructured, and the leader has little formal authority. In a highly unfavorable situation, followers have little respect for or confidence and trust in the leader. Tasks are vague and ill-defined, lacking in clear-cut procedures and guidelines. The leader has little formal authority to direct subordinates and does not have the power to issue rewards or punishments.

MATCHING LEADER STYLE TO THE SITUATION

Combining the three situational characteristics yields a variety of leadership situations, ranging from highly favorable to highly unfavorable. When Fiedler examined the relationships among leadership style and situational favorability, he found the pattern shown in Exhibit 11.6. Task-oriented leaders are more effective when the situation is either highly favorable or highly unfavorable. Relationship-oriented leaders are more effective in situations of moderate favorability. Basketball coaches must be task-focused to get the job done. Read the following "High School Coaches" segment to see if you think the situation is favorable or unfavorable.

The task-oriented leader excels in the favorable situation because everyone gets along, the task is clear, and the leader has power; all that is needed is for someone to lead the charge and provide direction. Similarly, if the situation is highly unfavorable to the leader, a great deal of structure and task direction is needed. A strong leader will define task structure and establish authority over subordinates. Because leader–member relations are poor anyway, a strong task orientation will make no difference in the leader's popularity.

The relationship-oriented leader performs better in situations of intermediate favorability because human relations skills are important in achieving high group performance. In these situations, the leader may be moderately well liked, have some power, and supervise jobs that contain some ambiguity. A leader with good interpersonal skills can create a positive group atmosphere that will improve relationships, clarify task structure, and establish position power.

A leader, then, needs to know two things to use Fiedler's contingency theory. First, the leader should know whether he or she has a relationship- or task-oriented style. Second, the leader should diagnose the situation and determine whether leader–member relations, task structure, and position power are favorable or unfavorable.

High School Coaches

Is it leadership, or is it abuse? That's the controversy now in high school sports. Some years ago, everyone expected coaches to yell at players, criticize their mistakes, raising their voices and their hands. "It used to be that sports was the last bastion for emotionally confrontational treatment, and usually players years later look back at it as something they valued, a badge of honor," says high school basketball coach Dennis King. Now those same coaches are seen as politically incorrect, needing sensitivity training and anger management. Coach King sees it as a "trend that is seen in all aspects of society."

A new breed of parent is complaining. Philip George has two daughters in Smyrna High School soccer, and he thinks that what some call negative reinforcement crosses the line. "No one at our school deserves to be abused," he says. His idea: Continued and unrelenting verbal abuse to diminish a kid is no way to treat kids. Soccer coach Pete Dakis agrees and resigned after several complaints from parents. Other coaches have been fired or resigned in recent years for similar reasons, including several in New Jersey.

Tennessee high school sports administrator Chris Madewell is only 33 and not too many years away from his days as high school athlete. But he sees changes. "Something as simple as grabbing a kid by the helmet and just talking to him, something like that was pretty normal when I was in school. And now you are kind of wary of it," because of negative ramifications.

There are parents, though, who feel that coaches raising their voice and calling them names is teaching them important life lessons. Shelbyville girls basketball coach Rick Insell knows he has to treat every player differently. Some can handle rougher treatment, in fact, they need it. Others need a more gentle approach. It's contingency leadership for athletes.

SOURCE: Jessica Hopp, "Tough line to draw for coaches," *Tennessean,* (March 6, 2005): 19A-20A; "A coach's words: Schools must prohibit verbal abuse of players," *The Record* (May 16, 2007): L08.

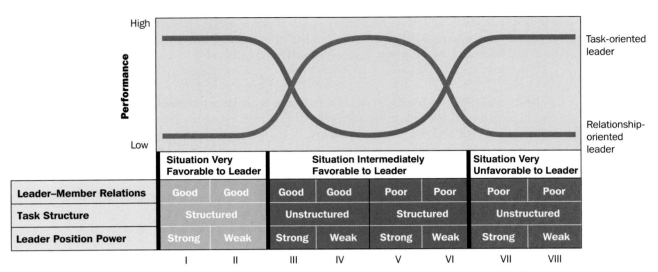

	Situation Very Favorable to Leader		Situation Intermediately Favorable to Leader				Situation Very Unfavorable to Leader	
Leader–Member Relations	Good	Good	Good	Good	Poor	Poor	Poor	Poor
Task Structure	Structured		Unstructured		Structured		Unstructured	
Leader Position Power	Strong	Weak	Strong	Weak	Strong	Weak	Strong	Weak
	I	II	III	IV	V	VI	VII	VIII

SOURCE: Based on Fred E. Fiedler, "The Effects of Leadership Training and Experience: A Contingency Model Interpretation," *Administrative Science Quarterly* 17 (1972): 455.

EXHIBIT 11.6

How Leader Style Fits the Situation

Fiedler believed fitting leader style to the situation can yield big dividends in profits and efficiency.[28] On the other hand, the model has also been criticized.[29] For one thing, some researchers have challenged the idea that leaders cannot adjust their styles as situational characteristics change. Despite criticisms, Fiedler's model has continued to influence leadership studies. Fiedler's research called attention to the importance of finding the correct fit between leadership style and the situation.

NEW MANAGER SELF TEST

Least Preferred Co-Worker (LPC)

Take a moment to complete the following inventory that measures your leadership style according to Fiedler's model.

Think of another student you have worked with that you have trouble liking—the one person you hope is not on your team again. Circle a number on each scale below, with your circle showing how close to which word you would describe this person.

My least-preferred co-worker is:

open	1	2	3	4	5	6	7	8	guarded
quarrelsome	8	7	6	5	4	3	2	1	harmonious
efficient	1	2	3	4	5	6	7	8	inefficient
self-assured	1	2	3	4	5	6	7	8	hesitant
gloomy	8	7	6	5	4	3	2	1	cheerful

Total in
Each column   __   __   __   __   __   __   __   __

Add the totals from each column. The total number will be between 5 and 40. Place the Grand Total here: ____

Interpretation: If you describe the least preferred co-worker using positive concepts (and your grand total is between 5 and 20), you are considered relationship oriented, that is, a leader who cares about and is sensitive to other people's feelings. Conversely, if you use negative concepts to describe the least preferred coworker (and your grand total is 21–40), you are considered task oriented—that is, a leader who places greater value on task activities than on people. The lower your score, the more relationship oriented you are, and the greater your score, the more task oriented you are.

PATH–GOAL THEORY

Another contingency approach to leadership is called the path–goal theory.[30] According to the **path–goal theory,** the leader's responsibility is to increase followers' motivation and clarify the path to attain personal and organizational goals.[31] This model includes two sets of contingencies: leader behavior and the use of rewards to meet subordinates' needs.[32] In the Fiedler theory, the assumption would be to switch leaders as situations change, but the path–goal theory suggests that leaders can switch their behaviors to match the situation.

path–goal theory
a contingency approach to leadership specifying that the leader's responsibility is to increase subordinates' motivation by clarifying the behaviors necessary for task accomplishment and rewards.

2 Good leaders are participative, engaged, and supportive.

✳ **Assess Your Answer**

ANSWER: It all depends on the situation. Some circumstances call for a more authoritarian leader; others call for more participation. Part of the leader's job is to monitor the situation and make judgments on which style is better for each situation.

Leader Behavior. The path–goal theory suggests a fourfold classification of leader behaviors.[33] These classifications are the types of leader behavior the leader can adopt and include supportive, directive, achievement-oriented, and participative styles.

Supportive leadership involves leader behavior that shows concern for subordinates' well being and personal needs. Leadership behavior is open, friendly, and approachable, and the leader creates a team climate and treats subordinates as equals. Supportive leadership is similar to the consideration, people-centered, or relationship-oriented leadership described earlier.

Directive leadership occurs when the leader tells subordinates exactly what they are supposed to do. Leader behavior includes planning, making schedules, setting performance goals and behavior standards, and stressing adherence to rules and regulations. Directive leadership behavior is similar to the initiating-structure, job-centered, or task-oriented leadership style described earlier.

Participative leadership means that the leader consults with his or her subordinates about decisions. Leader behavior includes asking for opinions and suggestions, encouraging participation in decision making, and meeting with subordinates in their workplaces. The participative leader encourages group discussion and written suggestions.

Achievement-oriented leadership occurs when the leader sets clear and challenging goals for subordinates. Leader behavior stresses high-quality performance

CONCEPT CONNECTION

Southwest Airlines co-founder and chairman Herb Kelleher (shown here celebrating Southwest's new Philadelphia service with Ben Franklin) firmly believes that it's free-flowing communication that makes **participative leadership** possible. Southwest encourages employees to talk to anyone at anytime about anything on their minds. In addition to sending notes or e-mails, workers get the chance to share their opinions and ask questions when executives drop in on them periodically. When Gary Kelly, Kelleher's successor as CEO, visited an employee lounge at Chicago's Midway Airport, a mechanic who owns Southwest stock took him aside. "What's happening here?" he asked, pointing to stock quotes on a computer screen. "That's my retirement, and it's not moving."

Benchmarking

Teach for America

Something like a two-letter word "no" has never stopped Wendy Kopp from marching ahead, even when one of her Princeton professors gave her some icy feedback when she proposed starting a sort-of Peace Corps for teachers. "My dear Ms. Kopp," he responded, "you are quite evidently deranged."

Good thing she didn't listen to him because Teach for America (TFA) has become one of the most respected educational programs in the United States, with applications from nearly 10 percent of Columbia's and Duke's graduates. TFA only selects one out of every eight candidates. And results? In various studies, principals see TFA members as more effective than other beginning teachers, and TFA teachers were found to get higher math than peers.

Kopp never aspired to be running a huge corporation. All she wanted to do was reform public education. When she got to Princeton, she started to see the failures in the educational system and began organizing conferences on educational reform. It became so important to her that she wrote her senior thesis on

the subject: "A Plan and Argument for the Creation of a National Teacher Corps," followed by a letter to then President George H. W. Bush, asking him to start a national teacher corp, which elicited an impersonal rejection letter.

Like we said, "no" never stops her. Despite her shyness, she got on the phone and managed to garner support from various CEOs for her vision. Here she was, a lone young woman making cold calls to strangers. And they gave her money! The first year's budget was $2.5 million, enough to get 500 teachers started. Several years later, the grants dried up, and most people would have thrown in the towel. Not Kopp. She got her executive team together and developed a new plan, cutting the budget and laying off 60 people. They had to strengthen the management team, set priorities, and diversify funding. The turn-around year was 1996 when some billionaires got interested. TFA raised $25 million in four months. And now, the extended plan is for the 12,000 alums to move into leadership positions in schools. All because Wendy Kopp had a dream and wouldn't give up. Says one major donor, "I'm bowled over by Wendy's absolute belief that TFA can change the world."

SOURCES: Elizabeth Weiss Green, "Heeding a teaching moment," *US News & World Report* (Oct. 30, 2006): 84; Patricia Sellers, "The Recruiter," *Fortune* (Nov. 27, 2006): 87–90.

---

and improvement over current performance. Wendy Koop is an achievement-oriented leader, as described in the Benchmarking box.

Achievement-oriented leaders also show confidence in subordinates and assist them in learning how to achieve high goals.

The four types of leader behavior are not considered ingrained personality traits as in the Fiedler theory; rather, they reflect types of behavior that every leader is able to adopt, depending on the situation.

Use of Rewards. Recall that the leader's responsibility is to clarify the path to rewards for subordinates or to increase the value of rewards to enhance satisfaction and job performance. In some situations, the leader works with subordinates to help them acquire the skills and confidence needed to perform tasks and achieve rewards already available. In others, the leader may develop new rewards to meet the specific needs of subordinates.

Exhibit 11.7 illustrates four examples of how leadership behavior is tailored to the situation. In the first example situation, the subordinate lacks confidence; thus, the supportive leadership style provides the social support with which to encourage the subordinate to undertake the behavior needed to do the work and receive the rewards. In the second situation, the job is ambiguous, and the employee is not performing effectively. Directive leadership behavior is used to give instructions and clarify the task so that the follower will know how to accomplish it and receive rewards. In the third situation, the subordinate is unchallenged by the task; thus, an achievement-oriented behavior is used to set higher goals. In the fourth situation, an incorrect reward is given to a subordinate, and the participative leadership style is used to change this situation. By discussing the subordinates' needs, the leader is able to identify the correct reward for task accomplishment and help

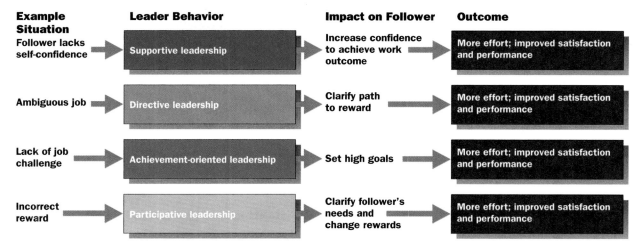

Example Situation	Leader Behavior	Impact on Follower	Outcome
Follower lacks self-confidence	Supportive leadership	Increase confidence to achieve work outcome	More effort; improved satisfaction and performance
Ambiguous job	Directive leadership	Clarify path to reward	More effort; improved satisfaction and performance
Lack of job challenge	Achievement-oriented leadership	Set high goals	More effort; improved satisfaction and performance
Incorrect reward	Participative leadership	Clarify follower's needs and change rewards	More effort; improved satisfaction and performance

SOURCE: Adapted from Gary A. Yukl, *Leadership in Organizations* (Englewood Cliffs, NJ: Prentice Hall, 1981): 146–112.

EXHIBIT 11.7

Path–Goal Situations and Preferred Leader Behaviors

people know how to achieve the reward. In all four cases, the outcome of fitting the leadership behavior to the situation produces greater employee effort by either clarifying how subordinates can receive rewards or changing the rewards to fit their needs.

At The Home Depot, CEO Bob Nardelli reinvigorated employee morale—and retail sales—with his achievement-oriented leadership, which cascaded down from headquarters to the store level.

Nardelli's achievement-oriented leadership was successful because it encouraged every manager in the organization to focus on keeping people challenged and motivated to reach goals.[34] Path–goal theorizing can be complex, but much of the research on it has been encouraging.[35] Using the model to specify precise relationships and make exact predictions about employee outcomes may be difficult, but the four types of leader behavior and the

 **TAKE ACTION**

As a leader, get to know your people and their needs; don't treat everyone exactly the same—but be careful not to show favorites.

T hings seemed a little shaky when new CEO Bob Nardelli first started imposing high goals, order, and discipline at The Home Depot, the nation's second-largest retailer next to Wal-Mart. Many store managers, who were used to a more relaxed approach, left the company, and investors sent the stock price plummeting.

But Nardelli knew what he was after. Instead of a retail chain where employees were becoming complacent and bored, he wanted a company full of enterprising people who thrive on challenge, responsibility, and recognition. Nardelli slowly began building a cadre of talented people, from top to bottom, and instituting a "no-bull performance culture" that gives people challenging goals and generous rewards for achieving them. Rigorous talent assessments, new approaches to hiring, new performance measurement systems, and programs such as the Store Leadership Program and Accelerated Leadership Program enhanced employee skills and reduced turnover. Nardelli could monitor stores in real time via computer, and he spent one week a quarter as a "mystery shopper," popping in unannounced to as many as 10 stores a day. He made clear to employees that he's not trying to "catch anybody," he just wanted to see the store from the eyes of customers and help people do a better job of serving them.

Nardelli's achievement-oriented leadership helped to increase sales from $45.7 billion to about $80 billion within five years, increase earnings per share by 20 percent annually, and gave the retailer an edge in new segments such as the $410 billion professional construction market. "His real ability," says Jack Welch, who was Nardelli's boss at General Electric, "is to motivate lots of people around a mission, excite them about it, and make it happen."

The Home Depot

Variable		Task-Oriented Leadership	People-Oriented Leadership
Organizational variables	Group cohesiveness	Substitutes for	Substitutes for
	Formalization	Substitutes for	No effect on
	Inflexibility	Neutralizes	No effect on
	Low position power	Neutralizes	Neutralizes
	Physical separation	Neutralizes	Neutralizes
Task characteristics	Highly structured task	Substitutes for	No effect on
	Automatic feedback	Substitutes for	No effect on
	Intrinsic satisfaction	No effect on	Substitutes for
Group characteristics	Professionalism	Substitutes for	Substitutes for
	Training/experience	Substitutes for	No effect on

EXHIBIT 11.8

Substitutes and Neutralizers for Leadership

ideas for fitting them to situational contingencies provide a useful way for leaders to think about motivating subordinates.

SUBSTITUTES FOR LEADERSHIP

The contingency leadership approaches considered so far focus on the leaders' style, the subordinates' nature, and the situation's characteristics. The final contingency approach suggests that situational variables can be so powerful that they actually substitute for or neutralize the need for leadership.[36] This approach outlines those organizational settings in which a leadership style is unimportant or unnecessary.

Exhibit 11.8 shows the situational variables that tend to substitute for or neutralize leadership characteristics. A **substitute** for leadership makes the leadership style unnecessary or redundant. For example, highly professional subordinates who know how to do their tasks do not need a leader who initiates structure for them and tells them what to do. A **neutralizer** counteracts the leadership style and prevents the leader from displaying certain behaviors. For example, if a leader has absolutely no position power or is physically removed from subordinates, the leader's ability to give directions to subordinates is greatly reduced.

Situational variables in Exhibit 11.8 include characteristics of the group, the task, and the organization itself. When followers are highly professional and experienced, both leadership styles are less important. People do not need much direction or consideration. With respect to task characteristics, highly structured tasks substitute for a task-oriented style, and a satisfying task substitutes for a people-oriented style. With respect to the organization itself, group cohesiveness substitutes for both leader styles. Formalized rules and procedures substitute for leader task orientation. Physical separation of leader and subordinate neutralizes both leadership styles.

The value of the situations described in Exhibit 11.8 is that they help leaders avoid leadership overkill. Leaders should adopt a style with which to complement the organizational situation.

Consider the work situation for bank tellers. A bank teller performs highly structured tasks, follows clear written rules and procedures, and has little flexibility in terms of how to do the work. The head teller should not adopt a task-oriented style because the organization already provides structure and direction. The head teller should concentrate on a people-oriented style to provide a more pleasant work environment. In other organizations, if group cohesiveness or intrinsic satisfaction meets employees' social needs, the leader is free to concentrate on task-oriented behaviors. The leader can adopt a style complementary to the organizational situation to ensure that both task needs and people needs of the work group will be met.

TAKE ACTION ⏩

As a leader, only be as much of a leader as the situation demands. Remember that professional employees typically need less leadership.

substitute

a situational variable that makes a leadership style unnecessary or redundant.

neutralizer

a situational variable that counteracts a leadership style and prevents the leader from displaying certain behaviors.

Leading Change

In Chapter 1, we defined management to include the functions of leading, planning, organizing, and controlling. But recent work on leadership has begun to distinguish leadership as something more: a quality that inspires and motivates people beyond their normal levels of performance. We are living in an era when leadership is needed more than ever. The environment today is turbulent, and organizations need to shift direction quickly to keep pace.[37] Leaders in many organizations have had to reconceptualize almost every aspect of how they do business to meet the needs of increasingly demanding customers, keep employees motivated and satisfied, and remain competitive in a rapidly changing global environment.

Research finds that some leadership approaches are more effective than others for bringing about change in organizations. Two types of leadership with a substantial impact are charismatic and transformational. These types of leadership are best understood in comparison to *transactional leadership*.[38] **Transactional leaders** clarify the role and task requirements of subordinates, initiate structure, provide appropriate rewards, and try to be considerate to and meet the social needs of subordinates. The transactional leader's ability to satisfy subordinates may improve productivity. Transactional leaders excel at management functions. They are hardworking, tolerant, and fair minded. They take pride in keeping things running smoothly and efficiently. Transactional leaders often

CONCEPT CONNECTION

The real magic behind e-tailing company Amazon.com is the **visionary leadership** of founder and CEO Jeff Bezos. His passion and enthusiasm was the key to getting investors to give him millions of dollars in financing. Bezos continued to inspire employees with his vision of a new kind of retailer as the company struggled for years before finally achieving profitability. He keeps Amazon innovative with bold moves, such as his new vision to use Amazon's technological, operations, and logistics expertise to provide services to other companies and entrepreneurs. The company plans to rent out just about everything it uses to run its own business, from warehouse space to spare computing capacity and data storage.

stress the impersonal aspects of performance, such as plans, schedules, and budgets. They have a sense of commitment to the organization and conform to organizational norms and values. Transactional leadership is important to all organizations, but leading change requires a different approach.

CHARISMATIC AND VISIONARY LEADERSHIP

Charismatic leadership goes beyond transactional leadership techniques. Charisma has been referred to as "a fire that ignites followers' energy and commitment, producing results above and beyond the call of duty."[39] The **charismatic leader** has the ability to inspire and motivate people to do more than they would normally do, despite obstacles and personal sacrifice. Followers transcend their own self-interests for the sake of the team, department, or organization. The impact of charismatic leaders is normally from (1) stating a lofty vision of an imagined future that employees identify with, (2) shaping a corporate value system for which everyone stands, and (3) trusting subordinates and earning their

transactional leader
a leader who clarifies subordinates' role and task requirements, initiates structure, provides rewards, and displays consideration for subordinates.

charismatic leader
a leader who has the ability to motivate subordinates to transcend their expected performance.

Spotlight on Skills

Are You a Charismatic Leader?

If you were the head of a major department in a corporation, how important would each of the following activities be to you? Answer yes or no to indicate whether you would strive to perform each activity.

1. Help subordinates clarify goals and how to reach them.
2. Give people a sense of mission and overall purpose.
3. Help get jobs out on time.
4. Look for the new product or service opportunities.
5. Use policies and procedures as guides for problem solving.
6. Promote unconventional beliefs and values.
7. Give monetary rewards in exchange for high performance from subordinates.
8. Command respect from everyone in the department.
9. Work alone to accomplish important tasks.
10. Suggest new and unique ways of doing things.
11. Give credit to people who do their jobs well.
12. Inspire loyalty to yourself and to the organization.
13. Establish procedures to help the department operate smoothly.
14. Use ideas to motivate others.
15. Set reasonable limits on new approaches.
16. Demonstrate social nonconformity.

The even-numbered items represent behaviors and activities of charismatic leaders. Charismatic leaders are personally involved in shaping ideas, goals, and direction of change. They use an intuitive approach to develop fresh ideas for old problems and seek new directions for the department or organization. The odd-numbered items are considered more traditional management activities, or what would be called *transactional leadership*. Managers respond to organizational problems in an impersonal way, make rational decisions, and coordinate and facilitate the work of others. If you answered yes to more even-numbered than odd-numbered items, you may be a potential charismatic leader.

SOURCES: Based on "Have You Got It?" a quiz that appeared in Patricia Sellers, "What Exactly Is Charisma?" *Fortune* (January 15, 1996): 68–75; Bernard M. Bass, *Leadership and Performance Beyond Expectations* (New York: Free Press, 1985); and Lawton R. Burns and Selwyn W. Becker, "Leadership and Managership," in S. Shortell and A. Kaluzny (eds.), *Health Care Management* (New York: Wiley, 1986).

complete trust in return.[40] Charismatic leaders tend to be less predictable than transactional leaders. They create an atmosphere of change, and they may be obsessed by visionary ideas that excite, stimulate, and drive other people to work hard.

Charismatic leaders are often skilled in the art of *visionary leadership*. A **vision** is an attractive, ideal future that is credible yet not readily attainable. Vision is an important component of both charismatic and transformational leadership. Visionary leaders speak to the hearts of employees, letting them be part of something bigger than themselves. Where others see obstacles or failures, they see possibility and hope.

TAKE ACTION ⊕

As a leader, strive to help create a compelling vision and bring others along to follow the vision.

Charismatic leaders typically have a strong vision for the future, almost an obsession, and they can motivate others to help realize it.[41] These leaders have an emotional impact on subordinates because they strongly believe in the vision and can communicate it to others in a way that makes the vision real, personal, and meaningful. Charismatic and transformational leaders are passionate about a vision. This chapter's Spotlight on Skills segment provides a short quiz to help you determine whether you have the potential to be a charismatic leader.

Charismatic leaders include Mother Theresa, Adolf Hitler, Sam Walton, Alexander the Great, Ronald Reagan, David Koresh, Martin Luther King Jr., and Osama bin Laden. Charisma can be used for positive outcomes that benefit the group, but it can also be used for self-serving purposes that lead to deception, manipulation, and exploitation of others. When charismatic leaders respond to organizational problems in terms of the needs of the entire group rather than their own emotional needs, they can have a powerful, positive influence on organizational performance.[42] Visionary leaders who don't develop enough infrastructure, or who spread themselves too thin, can run into serious problems, as shown in the Business Blooper.

vision
an attractive, ideal future that is credible yet not readily attainable.

Business **Blooper**

George Clooney/Steven Soderbergh

Actor and director George Clooney knows he's not curing cancer or feeding the starving masses. "Anyone who thinks this stuff lasts and is permanent, to me, is an idiot." Still, he's putting his heart and soul into "Section Eight," a movie production company he started with Stephen Soderbergh, who won Academy Awards for "Traffic" and "Erin Brockovich." Section Eight aspires to a more maverick goal, to be more innovative—like Francis Ford Coppola and Stanley Kubrick. Section Eight's philosophy is simple: Provide a wide berth for directors and protect them from the inevitable studio meddling. They want to give new directors a place and a voice in an increasingly hostile studio system that only wants worldwide blockbusters. Yet Clooney and Soderbergh themselves are being crushed under the weight of correspondence, studio meetings, and project development. Their creativity stifled, Soderbergh went forth with duds like *Solaris* and *The Good German*. There were too many distractions. "If you dragged me into court for paying too little attention, I'd be in jail," says Soderbergh. "It's a huge, huge learning curve with a lot of human wreckage left behind." Finally it got too much for them. With *Ocean's Thirteen* Section Eight's last film, the company officially closed in 2006. "It was too much work," says Soderbergh. "Maybe we didn't understand what was involved. I just can't be a producer anymore."

SOURCE: Laura M. Holson, "Confessions of a perplexed mind," *The New York Times* (Jan. 17, 2005): C1; James Mottram, "Steven Soderbergh: Success dies like videotape," *Belfast Telegraph* (March 9, 2007): 1.

TRANSFORMATIONAL LEADERS

Transformational leaders are similar to charismatic leaders but are distinguished by their special ability to bring about innovation and change by recognizing followers' needs and concerns, helping them look at old problems in new ways, and encouraging them to question the status quo. Transformational leaders inspire followers not just to believe in the leader personally but to believe in their own potential to imagine and create a better future for the organization. Transformational leaders create significant change in both followers and the organization.[43] They have the ability to lead changes in the organization's mission, strategy, structure, and culture, as well as to promote innovation in products and technologies. Transformational leaders do not rely solely on tangible rules and incentives to control specific transactions with followers. They focus on intangible qualities such as vision, shared values, and ideas to build relationships, give larger meaning to diverse activities, and find common ground to enlist followers in the change process.[44]

A recent study confirmed that transformational leadership has a positive impact on follower development and follower performance. Moreover, transformational leadership skills can be learned and are not ingrained personality characteristics.[45] However, some personality traits may make it easier for a leader to display transformational leadership behaviors. For example, studies of transformational leadership have found that the trait of agreeableness, as discussed in the previous chapter, is positively associated with transformational leaders.[46] In addition, transformational leaders are typically emotionally stable and positively engaged with the world around them, and they have a strong ability to recognize and understand others' emotions.[47] These characteristics are not surprising considering that these leaders accomplish change by building networks of positive relationships.

Richard Kovacevich, who steered midsized Norwest Corp. (now Wells Fargo & Co.) through numerous acquisitions to make it one of the largest and most powerful banking companies in the United States, is an excellent example of a transformational leader.

Kovacevich's leadership style puts accountability for success in the hands of each and every employee. He leads with slogans such as, "Mind share plus heart share equals market share." Although some people might think it sounds hokey, Kovacevich and his employees don't care. It is the substance behind the slogans that matters. Kovacevich believes it's not

TAKE ACTION

To be a transformational leader, work at building networks of positive relationships.

transformational leader
a leader distinguished by a special ability to bring about innovation and change.

TAKE ACTION

As a leader, use coercive power rarely; if you use it too much, you will create a culture of fear.

what employees know that is important but whether they care. Employees are rewarded for putting both their hearts and minds into their work. Kovacevich spends a lot of time out in the field, meeting employees, patting backs, and giving pep talks. He likes to personally remind people on the front lines that they are the heart and soul of Wells Fargo, and that only through their efforts can the company succeed.[48]

Power and Influence

Recall our definition of leadership, which is the ability to influence people to achieve goals. Particularly for leaders involved in major change initiatives, the effective and appropriate use of power is crucial. One way to understand how leaders get things done is to look at the sources of leader power and the interpersonal influence tactics leaders use.

Power is the potential ability to influence the behavior of others.[49] Sometimes the terms *power* and *influence* are used synonymously, but the two are distinct in important ways. Basically, **influence** is the effect a person's actions have on the attitudes, values, beliefs, or behavior of others. Whereas power is the capacity to cause a change in a person, influence may be thought of as the degree of actual change.

Power results from an interaction of leader and followers. Some power comes from an individual's position in the organization. Power may also come from personal sources that are not as invested in the organization, such as a leader's personal interests, goals, and values. Within organizations, five sources of power are typical: legitimate, reward, coercive, expert, and referent.

UPS employees joke that when Mike Eskew became CEO, he'd only worked for the company for 30 years. This bit of office humor reflects UPS's long-standing promote-from-within approach to management development. Most UPS managers gain **expert power** by working their way up from the bottom. For example, when Eskew arrived as a young industrial engineer, his first assignment was to redraw a parking lot so it could accommodate more trucks. Today, he's using his thorough understanding of the business to help move the $43 billion company from package delivery into global supply chain management.

POSITION POWER

The traditional manager's power comes from the organization. The manager's position gives him or her the power to reward or punish subordinates to influence their behavior. Legitimate power, reward power, and coercive power are all forms of position power used by managers to change employee behavior.

Legitimate Power. Power coming from a formal management position in an organization and the authority granted to it is called **legitimate power.** After a person has been selected as a supervisor, most workers understand that they are obligated to follow his or her direction with respect to work activities. Subordinates accept this source of power as legitimate, which is why they comply.

Reward Power. Another kind of power, **reward power,** stems from the authority to bestow rewards on other people. Managers may have access to formal rewards, such as pay increases or promotions. They also have at their disposal such rewards as praise, attention, and recognition. Managers can use rewards to influence subordinates' behavior.

Coercive Power. The opposite of reward power is **coercive power:** It refers to the authority to punish or recommend punishment. Managers have coercive power when they have the right to fire or demote employees, criticize, or withdraw pay increases.

For example, if Sanjay, a salesperson, does not perform as expected, his supervisor has the coercive power to criticize him, reprimand him, put a negative letter in his file, and hurt his chance for a raise.

power
the potential ability to influence others' behavior.

influence
the effect a person's actions have on the attitudes, values, beliefs, or behavior of others.

legitimate power
power that stems from a formal management position in an organization and the authority granted to it.

reward power
power that results from the authority to bestow rewards on other people.

coercive power
power that stems from the authority to punish or recommend punishment.

PERSONAL POWER

In contrast to the external sources of position power, personal power most often comes from internal sources, such as a person's special knowledge or personal characteristics.

A good example of personal power is Charles Firneno, math teacher and football coach at Benjamin Franklin High School in New Orleans. After the school was devastated by Hurricane Katrina in 2005, and no one could get through to inspect the damage, Firneno took it upon himself to get things rolling. A former U.S. Marine helicopter pilot, Firneno put on his uniform and convinced National Guardsmen to let him through. Firneno laid out a plan for fixing the building and began mobilizing people to help. Although before the flood, Firneno had been held in rather low esteem by his faculty colleagues with more advanced degrees, his commitment, knowledge, skills, and ability to mobilize people in a crisis quickly won the support and respect of teachers, parents, and community volunteers. Soon, Firneno was handed an extra set of keys to the building and the principal's authorization to spend school funds as he saw fit, helping to get the school open in record time.[50] Firneno's power came from his special knowledge and skills and from his personal commitment to the school, rather than from a formal position of authority.

Personal power is the primary tool of the leader, and it is becoming increasingly important as more businesses are run by teams of workers who are less tolerant of authoritarian management.[51] Two types of personal power are expert power and referent power.

Expert Power. Power resulting from a leader's special knowledge or skill regarding the tasks performed by followers is referred to as **expert power.** When the leader is a true expert, subordinates go along with recommendations because of his or her superior knowledge. Leaders at supervisory levels often have experience in the production process that gains them promotion. At top management levels, however, leaders may lack expert power because subordinates know more about technical details than they do.

Referent Power. The last kind of power, **referent power,** comes from a leader's personal characteristics that command followers' identification, respect, and admiration so they want to emulate the leader. Referent power does not depend on a formal title or position. When workers admire a supervisor because of the way she deals with them, the influence is based on referent power. Referent power is most visible in the area of charismatic leadership. In social and religious movements, for example, we often see charismatic leaders who emerge and gain a tremendous following based solely on their personal power.

 **TAKE ACTION**

As a new manager, build your personal power by strengthening your knowledge and skills and by developing positive relationships.

expert power
power that stems from special knowledge of or skill in the tasks performed by subordinates.

referent power
power that results from characteristics that command subordinates' identification with, respect and admiration for, and desire to emulate the leader.

3 Leaders should amass as much power as they can; it helps them get things done.

ANSWER: Leaders do need power, but all types, not just position or coercive power, which is too often what new leaders go after. Increasing expert and referent power are very important.

★ Assess Your Answer

INTERPERSONAL INFLUENCE TACTICS

The next question is how leaders use their power to implement decisions and facilitate change. Leaders often use a combination of influence strategies, and people who are perceived as having greater power and influence typically are those who use a wider variety of tactics. One survey of a few hundred leaders identified more than 4,000 different techniques these people used to influence others.[52]

EXHIBIT 11.9

Seven Interpersonal Influence Tactics for Leaders

> 1. Use rational persuasion.
> 2. Make people like you.
> 3. Rely on the rule of reciprocity.
> 4. Develop allies.
> 5. Be assertive—ask for what you want.
> 6. Make use of higher authority.
> 7. Reward the behaviors you want.

However, these tactics fall into basic categories that rely on understanding the principles that cause people to change their behavior and attitudes. Exhibit 11.9 lists seven principles for asserting influence. Notice that most of these involve the use of personal power rather than relying solely on position power or the use of rewards and punishments.[53]

1. *Use rational persuasion.* The most frequently used influence strategy is to use facts, data, and logical argument to persuade others that a proposed idea, request, or decision is appropriate. Using rational persuasion can often be highly effective because most people have faith in facts and analysis.[54] Rational persuasion is most successful when a leader has technical knowledge and expertise related to the issue at hand (expert power), although referent power is also used. That is, in addition to facts and figures, people also have to believe in the leader's credibility.

2. *Make people like you.* Recall our discussion of *likeability* from the previous chapter. People would rather say yes to someone they like than to someone they don't. Effective leaders strive to create goodwill and favorable impressions. When a leader shows consideration and respect, treats people fairly, and demonstrates trust in others, people are more likely to want to help and support the leader by doing what he or she asks. In addition, most people like a leader who makes them feel good about themselves, so leaders should never underestimate the power of praise.

3. *Rely on the rule of reciprocity.* Leaders can influence others through the exchange of benefits and favors. Leaders share what they have—whether it is time, resources, services, or emotional support. The feeling among people is nearly universal that others should be paid back for what they do, in one form or another. This unwritten "rule of reciprocity" means that leaders who do favors for others can expect that others will do favors for them in return.[55]

4. *Develop allies.* Effective leaders develop networks of allies, people who can help the leader accomplish his or her goals. Leaders talk with followers and others outside of formal meetings to understand their needs and concerns as well as to explain problems and describe the leader's point of view. They strive to reach a meeting of minds with others about the best approach to a problem or decision.[56]

5. *Ask for what you want.* Another way to influence others is to make a direct and personal request. Leaders have to be explicit about what they want, or they aren't likely to get it. An explicit proposal is sometimes accepted simply because others have no better alternative. Also, a clear proposal or alternative will often receive support if other options are less well defined.

6. *Make use of higher authority.* Sometimes to get things done, leaders have to use their formal authority, as well as gain the support of people at higher levels to back them up. However, research has found that the key to successful use of formal authority is to be knowledgeable, credible, and trustworthy—that is, to demonstrate expert and referent power as well as legitimate power. Managers who become known for their expertise, who are honest and straightforward with others, and who inspire trust can exert greater influence than those who simply issue orders.[57]

7. *Reward the behaviors you want.* Leaders can also use organizational rewards and punishments to influence others' behavior. The use of punishment in organizations is controversial,

but negative consequences almost always occur for inappropriate or undesirable behavior. Leaders should not rely solely on reward and punishment as a means for influencing others, but combined with other tactics that involve the use of personal power, rewards can be highly effective. At General Electric, for example, CEO Jeff Immelt is having success in shifting managers' behavior by using rewards for managers who demonstrate an ability to come up with innovative ideas and improve customer service and satisfaction.[58]

Research indicates that people rate leaders as "more effective" when they are perceived to use a variety of influence tactics. But not all managers use influence in the same way. Studies have found that leaders in human resources, for example, tend to use softer, more subtle approaches such as building goodwill, using favors, and developing allies, whereas those in finance are inclined to use harder, more direct tactics such as formal authority and assertiveness.[59]

Enduring Leadership Approaches

To close our chapter, let's look at two timeless leadership approaches that are gaining renewed attention in today's environment of ethical scandals and weakened employee trust. Characteristics of servant leadership and moral leadership can be successfully used by leaders in all situations to make a positive difference.

SERVANT LEADERSHIP

Some leaders operate from the assumption that work exists for the development of the worker as much as the worker exists to do the work.[60] For example, a young David Packard, who cofounded Hewlett-Packard, made a spectacle of himself in 1949 by standing up in a roomful of business leaders and arguing that companies had a responsibility to recognize the dignity and worth of their employees and share the wealth with those who helped to create it.[61]

The concept of servant leadership, first described by Robert Greenleaf, is leadership upside down, because leaders transcend self-interest to serve others and the organization.[62] **Servant leaders** operate on two levels: for the fulfillment of their subordinates' goals and needs and for the realization of the larger purpose or mission of their organization. Servant leaders give things away—power, ideas, information, recognition, credit for accomplishments, even money. Harry Stine, founder of Stine Seed Company in Adel, Iowa, casually announced to his employees at the company's annual post-harvest luncheon that they would each receive $1,000 for each year they had worked at the company. For some loyal workers, that amounted to a $20,000 bonus.[63] Servant leaders truly value other people. They are trustworthy, and they trust others. They encourage participation, share power, enhance others' self-worth, and unleash people's creativity, full commitment, and natural impulse to learn and contribute. Servant leaders can bring their followers' higher motives to the work and connect their hearts to the organizational mission and goals.

Servant leaders often work in the nonprofit world because it offers a natural way to apply their leadership drive and skills to serve others. But servant leaders also succeed in business. George Merck believed the purpose of a corporation was to do something useful. At Merck & Co., he insisted that people always come before profits. By insisting on serving people rather than profits, Merck shaped a company that averaged 15 percent earnings growth for an amazing 75 years.[64]

MORAL LEADERSHIP

Another enduring issue in leadership is its moral component. Because leadership can be used for good or evil, to help or to harm others, all leadership has a moral component. Leaders carry a tremendous responsibility to use their power wisely and ethically. Sadly, in recent years, too many have chosen to act from self-interest and greed rather than behaving in ways that serve and uplift others. The disheartening ethical climate in American business has led to a renewed interest in moral leadership. **Moral leadership** is about distinguishing

> **TAKE ACTION**
> *As a leader, see yourself as serving your employees; you are there to meet their needs.*

> **servant leader**
> a leader who works to fulfill subordinates' needs and goals as well as to achieve the organization's larger mission.

> **moral leadership**
> distinguishing right from wrong and choosing to do right in the practice of leadership.

right from wrong and choosing to do right. It means seeking the just, the honest, the good, and the decent behavior in the practice of leadership.[65] Moral leaders remember that business is about values, not just economic performance.

Distinguishing the right thing to do is not always easy, and doing it is sometimes even harder. Leaders are often faced with right-versus-right decisions, in which several responsibilities conflict with one another.[66] Commitments to superiors, for example, may mean a leader feels the need to hide unpleasant news about pending layoffs from followers. Moral leaders strive to find the moral answer or compromise, rather than taking the easy way out. Consider Katherine Graham, the long-time leader of *The Washington Post*, when she was confronted with a decision in 1971 about what to do with the Pentagon Papers, a leaked Defense Department study that showed Nixon administration deceptions about the Vietnam War. Graham admitted she was terrified—she knew she was risking the whole company on the decision, possibly inviting prosecution under the Espionage Act, and jeopardizing thousands of employees' jobs. She decided to go ahead with the story, and reporters Bob Woodward and Carl Bernstein made Watergate—and *The Washington Post*—a household name.[67]

Clearly, moral leadership requires **courage,** the ability to step forward through fear and act on one's values and conscience. Leaders often behave unethically simply because they lack courage. Most people want to be liked, and it is easy to do the wrong thing to fit in or impress others. One example might be a leader who holds his tongue to "fit in with the guys" when colleagues are telling sexually or racially offensive jokes. Moral leaders summon the fortitude to do the right thing, even if it is unpopular. Standing up for what is right is the primary way in which leaders create an environment of honesty, trust, and integrity in the organization.

TAKE ACTION ⏵

When in a moral dilemma, think of what is the right thing to do, rather than only the most financially beneficial.

---

courage
The ability to step forward through fear and act on one's values and conscience.

Summary

This chapter covered several important ideas about leadership. The concept of leadership continues to evolve and change with the changing times. Of particular interest in today's turbulent environment is a post-heroic leadership approach. Two significant concepts in line with the post-heroic approach are Level 5 leadership and interactive leadership, which is common among women leaders. Level 5 leaders are characterized by personal humility combined with a strong determination to build a great organization that will thrive beyond the leader's direct influence. Interactive leadership emphasizes relationships and helping others develop to their highest potential and may be particularly well-suited to today's workplace.

The early research on leadership focused on personal traits such as intelligence, energy, and appearance. Later, research attention shifted to leadership behaviors that are appropriate to the organizational situation. Behavioral approaches dominated the early work in this area; task-oriented behavior and people-oriented behavior were suggested as essential behaviors that lead work groups toward high performance. The Ohio State and Michigan approaches and the managerial grid are in this category. Contingency approaches include Hersey and Blanchard's situational theory, Fiedler's theory, the path–goal model, and the substitutes-for-leadership concept.

Leadership concepts have evolved from the transactional approach to charismatic and transformational leadership behaviors. Charismatic leadership is the ability to articulate a vision and motivate followers to make it a reality. Transformational leadership extends charismatic qualities to guide and foster dramatic organizational change. Leadership involves the use of power to influence others. Five types of power are legitimate, reward, coercive, expert, and referent. Leaders rely more on personal power than position power, and they use a variety of interpersonal influence tactics to implement decisions and accomplish goals. Two enduring leadership approaches are servant leadership and moral leadership. Servant leaders facilitate the growth, goals, and development of others to liberate their best qualities in pursuing the organization's mission. Moral leadership means seeking to do the honest and decent thing in the practice of leadership. Leaders can make a positive difference by applying characteristics of servant and moral leadership.

Discussion Questions

1. Do you think leadership style is fixed and unchangeable for a leader or flexible and adaptable? Discuss.

2. Suggest some personal traits that you believe would be useful to a business leader today. Are these traits more valuable in some situations than in others?

3. What is the difference between trait theories and behavioral theories of leadership?

4. Suggest the sources of power that would be available to a leader of a student government organization. What sources of power may not be available? To be effective, should student leaders keep power to themselves or delegate power to other students?

5. What skills and abilities does a manager need to lead effectively in a virtual environment? Do you believe a leader with a consideration style or an initiating-structure style would be more successful as a virtual leader? Explain your answer.

6. What is transformational leadership? Give examples of organizational situations that would call for transformational, transactional, or charismatic leadership.

7. How does Level 5 leadership differ from the concept of servant leadership? Do you believe anyone has the potential to become a Level 5 leader? Discuss.

8. Do you think leadership is more important or less important in today's flatter, team-based organizations? Are some leadership styles better suited to such organizations as opposed to traditional hierarchical organizations? Explain.

9. Consider the leadership position of a senior partner in a law firm. What task, subordinate, and organizational factors might serve as substitutes for leadership in this situation?

10. Do you see yourself as having leader qualities or manager qualities? Do you think you will become a better leader/manager by developing the characteristics you already have or by trying to develop the characteristics you don't have? Discuss.

Dear Dr. Dorothy

My boss sent me to a "Leadership for New Managers" training program. It was fun to travel and stay in a nice hotel, and the program was interesting. But some things I'm having trouble implementing. The instructor told us we should get as much power as we can, and he gave us some strategies. One of them is about making people wait for you, to show how important you are. Another is to take up more space at the lunch table, or to sit at the head of the table in the conference room, and to talk more than anyone else, to try and be the center of attention. Maybe I am not leader-material because I just can't see myself doing these things. Should I quit my job?

Wondering-if-I-have-it in Walla Walla

Dear Wondering,

Dr. Dorothy thinks rather than quit your job, you should dust off some of the management books you read in college, anything that might have talked about how power is more than domination, and how sustainable power means you respect other people, while you are busy networking and developing power through social relationships. The ideas you were taught fit more into a 1980s seminar, and author Wayne Dyer would be proud. But Dr. Dorothy thinks the person who should quit the job is that instructor. This is the new millennium, after all, and you need to put your energies into collaboration (creating allies) and continuous learning, creating situations for reciprocity, becoming more likable, becoming better at asking for what you want, and increasing your expert and referent powers, not measuring how much real estate you are taking up in the restaurant.

Self Learning

T–P Leadership Questionnaire: An Assessment of Style

Some leaders deal with general directions, leaving details to subordinates. Other leaders focus on specific details with the expectation that subordinates will carry out orders. Depending on the situation, both approaches may be effective. The important issue is the ability to identify relevant dimensions of the situation and behave accordingly. Through this questionnaire, you can identify your relative emphasis on two dimensions of leadership: task orientation (T) and people orientation (P). These approaches are not opposites; and an individual can rate high or low on either or both.

Directions: The following items describe aspects of leadership behavior. Respond to each item according to the way you would most likely act if you were the leader of a work group. Circle whether you would most likely behave in the described way: always (A), frequently (F), occasionally (O), seldom (S), or never (N).

	A	F	O	S	N
1. I would most likely act as the spokesperson of the group.	A	F	O	S	N
2. I would encourage overtime work.	A	F	O	S	N
3. I would allow members complete freedom in their work.	A	F	O	S	N
4. I would encourage the use of uniform procedures.	A	F	O	S	N
5. I would permit members to use their own judgment in solving problems.	A	F	O	S	N
6. I would stress being ahead of competing groups.	A	F	O	S	N
7. I would speak as a representative of the group.	A	F	O	S	N
8. I would needle members for greater effort.	A	F	O	S	N
9. I would try out my ideas in the group.	A	F	O	S	N
10. I would let members do their work the way they think best.	A	F	O	S	N
11. I would be working hard for a promotion.	A	F	O	S	N
12. I would tolerate postponement and uncertainty.	A	F	O	S	N
13. I would speak for the group if visitors were present.	A	F	O	S	N
14. I would keep the work moving at a rapid pace.	A	F	O	S	N
15. I would turn the members loose on a job and let them go to it.	A	F	O	S	N
16. I would settle conflicts when they occur in the group.	A	F	O	S	N
17. I would get swamped by details.	A	F	O	S	N
18. I would represent the group at outside meetings.	A	F	O	S	N

19. I would be reluctant to allow the members any freedom of action.	**A**	**F**	**O**	**S**	**N**
20. I would decide what should be done and how it should be done.	**A**	**F**	**O**	**S**	**N**
21. I would push for increased production.	**A**	**F**	**O**	**S**	**N**
22. I would let some members have authority that I could keep.	**A**	**F**	**O**	**S**	**N**
23. Things would usually turn out as I had predicted.	**A**	**F**	**O**	**S**	**N**
24. I would allow the group a high degree of initiative.	**A**	**F**	**O**	**S**	**N**
25. I would assign group members to particular tasks.	**A**	**F**	**O**	**S**	**N**
26. I would be willing to make changes.	**A**	**F**	**O**	**S**	**N**
27. I would ask the members to work harder.	**A**	**F**	**O**	**S**	**N**
28. I would trust the group members to exercise good judgment.	**A**	**F**	**O**	**S**	**N**
29. I would schedule the work to be done.	**A**	**F**	**O**	**S**	**N**
30. I would refuse to explain my actions.	**A**	**F**	**O**	**S**	**N**
31. I would persuade others that my ideas are to their advantage.	**A**	**F**	**O**	**S**	**N**
32. I would permit the group to set its own pace.	**A**	**F**	**O**	**S**	**N**
33. I would urge the group to beat its previous record.	**A**	**F**	**O**	**S**	**N**
34. I would act without consulting the group.	**A**	**F**	**O**	**S**	**N**
35. I would ask that group members follow standard rules and regulations.	**A**	**F**	**O**	**S**	**N**

T_____ **P**_____

Scoring and Interpretation

The T–P Leadership Questionnaire is scored as follows:

a. Circle the statements numbered 8, 12, 17, 18, 19, 30, 34, and 35.

b. Write the number 1 in front of the circled number if you responded S (seldom) or N (never) to that statement.

c. Also write a number 1 in front of the statement numbers not circled if you responded A (always) or F (frequently).

d. Circle the number 1s that you have written in front of the following statements: 3, 5, 8, 10, 15, 18, 19, 22, 24, 26, 28, 30, 32, 34, and 35.

e. Count the circled number 1s. This total is your score for concern for people. Record the score in the blank following the letter P at the end of the questionnaire.

f. Count the uncircled number 1s. This total is your score for concern for task. Record this number in the blank following the letter T.

SOURCE: The T–P Leadership Questionnaire was adapted by J. B. Ritchie and P. Thompson in *Organization and People* (New York: West, 1984). Copyright 1969 by the American Educational Research Association. Adapted by permission of the publisher.

Group Learning

Assumptions About Leaders

Individually complete the following sentences:

1. A leader must always …
2. Leaders should never …
3. The best leader I ever had did …
4. The worst leader I ever had did …
5. When I am doing a good job as a leader, I …
6. I am afraid of leaders who …
7. I would follow a leader who …
8. I am repelled by leaders who …

9. Some people think they are good leaders, but they are not because they …
10. I want to be the kind of leader who …

In groups of four to six, discuss the following:

A. What did you learn about your own assumptions about leadership?

B. Trace those assumptions back to theories on leadership in this chapter.

C. What were common themes in your group?

SOURCE: Copyright 2000 by Dorothy Marcic.

Action Learning

1. Find three people who have had bosses or CEOs who were either charismatic or transformational.

   a. Ask them to describe what the leader was like, what were the values, the behaviors?

   b. Ask them to contrast those charismatic/transformational leaders with an ineffective boss or CEO they worked with.

   c. What were the differences in behavior? How did the behavior of the ineffective leaders impact the organization?

   d. Ask them to give a few sentences on how they would compare the transformational/charismatic leader to the ineffective one.

2. Your instructor may ask you to write a paper on this subject or bring this information to class and be prepared to discuss it.

3. What did you learn about transformational and charismatic leadership from this assignment? Did it agree with what the textbook described?

Ethical Dilemma

Too Much of a Good Thing?

Not long ago, Jessica Armstrong, vice president of administration for Delaware Valley Chemical Inc., a New Jersey-based multinational company, made a point of stopping by department head Darius Harris's office and lavishly praising him for his volunteer work with an after-school program for disadvantaged children in a nearby urban neighborhood. Now she was about to summon him to her office so she could take him to task for dedication to the same volunteer work.

It was Carolyn Clark, Harris's secretary, who'd alerted her to the problem. "Darius told the community center he'd take responsibility for a fundraising mass mailing. And then he asked me to edit the letter he'd drafted, make all the copies, stuff the envelopes, and get it into the mail—most of this on my own time," she reported, still obviously indignant.

"When I told him, 'I'm sorry, but that's not my job,' he looked me straight in the eye and asked when I'd like to schedule my upcoming performance appraisal."

Several of Harris's subordinates also volunteered with the program. After chatting with them, Armstrong concluded most were volunteering out of a desire to stay on the boss's good side. It was time to talk to Harris.

"Oh, come on," responded Harris impatiently when Armstrong confronted him. "Yes, I asked for her help as a personal favor to me. But I only brought up the appraisal because I was going out of town, and we needed to set some time aside to do the evaluation." Harris went on to talk about how important working for the after-school program was to him personally. "I grew up in that neighborhood, and if it hadn't been for the people at the center, I wouldn't be here today," he said. Besides, even if he had pressured employees to help out—and he wasn't saying he had—didn't all the emphasis the company was putting on employee volunteerism make it okay to use employees' time and company resources?

After Harris left, Armstrong thought about the conversation. There was no question Delaware Valley actively encouraged employee volunteerism—and not just because it was the right thing to do. It was a chemical company with a couple of unfortunate accidental spills in its recent past that caused environmental damage and community anger.

Volunteering had the potential to help employees acquire new skills, create a sense of camaraderie, and play a role in recruiting and retaining talented people. But most of all, it gave a badly needed boost to the company's public image. Recently, Delaware Valley took every opportunity to publicize its employees' extracurricular community work on its website and in company publications. And the company created the annual Delaware Prize, which granted cash awards ranging from $1,000 to $5,000 to outstanding volunteers.

So now that Armstrong had talked with everyone concerned, just what was she going to do about the dispute between Darius Harris and Carolyn Clark?

What Would You Do?

1. Tell Carolyn Clark that employee volunteerism is important to the company and that while her performance evaluation will not be affected by her decision, she should consider helping Harris because it is an opportunity to help a worthy community project.

2. Tell Darius Harris that the employee volunteer program is just that: a volunteer program. Even though the company sees volunteerism as an important piece of its campaign to repair its tarnished image, employees must be free to choose whether to volunteer. He should not ask for the help of his direct reports with the after-school program.

3. Discipline Darius Harris for coercing his subordinates to spend their own time on his volunteer work at the community after-school program. This action will send a signal that coercing employees is a clear violation of leadership authority.

Case for Critical Analysis

Mountain West Health Plans Inc.

"Be careful what you wish for," thought Martin Quinn, senior vice president for service and operations for the Denver-based health insurance company, Mountain West Health Plans, Inc. When there was an opening for a new director of customer service last year due to Evelyn Gustafson's retirement, he'd seen it as the perfect opportunity to bring someone in to control the ever-increasing costs of the labor-intensive department. He'd been certain he had found just the person in Erik Rasmussen, a young man in his late twenties with a shiny new bachelor's degree in business administration.

A tall, unflappable woman, Evelyn Gustafson consistently showed warmth and concern toward her mostly female, nonunionized employees as they sat in their noisy cubicles, fielding call after call about Mountain West's products, benefits, eligibility, and claims. Because she had worked her way up from a customer service representative position herself, she could look her subordinates right in the eye after they'd fielded a string of stressful calls and tell them she knew exactly how they felt. She did her best to offset the low pay by accommodating the women's needs with flexible scheduling, giving them frequent breaks, and offering plenty of training opportunities that kept them up-to-date in the health company's changing products and in the latest problem-solving and customer service techniques.

Her motto was "Always put yourself in the subscriber's shoes." She urged representatives to take the time necessary to thoroughly understand the subscriber's problem and do their best to see that it was completely resolved by the call's completion. Their job was important, she told them. Subscribers counted on them to help them negotiate the often Byzantine complexities of their coverage. Evelyn's subordinates adored her, as demonstrated by the 10 percent turnover rate, compared to the typical 25 to 45 percent rate for customer service representatives. Mountain West subscribers were generally satisfied, although Quinn did hear some occasional grumbling about the length of time customers spent on hold.

However, whatever her virtues, Gustafson firmly resisted all attempts to increase efficiency and lower costs in a department where salaries accounted for close to 70 percent of the budget. That's where Erik Rasmussen came in. Upper-level management charged him with the task of bringing costs under control. Eager to do well in his first management position, the hard-working, no-nonsense young man made increasing the number of calls per hour each representative handled a priority. For the first time ever, the company measured the representatives' performance against statistical standards that emphasized speed, recorded the customer service calls, and used software that generated automated work schedules based on historical information and projected need. Efficient, not flexible, scheduling was the goal. In addition, the company cut back on training.

The results, Martin Quinn had to admit, were mixed. With more efficient scheduling and clear performance standards in place, calls per hour increased dramatically, and subscribers spent far less time on hold. The department's costs were finally heading downwards, but department morale was spiraling downwards as well, with the turnover rate currently at 30 percent and climbing. And Quinn was beginning to hear more complaints from subscribers who'd received inaccurate information from inexperienced or representatives who sounded rushed.

It was time for Rasmussen's first performance review. Quinn knew the young manager was about to walk into his office ready to proudly recite the facts and figures that documented the department's increased efficiency. What kind of an evaluation was he going to give Rasmussen? Should he recommend some mid-course corrections?

Questions

1. How would you describe Evelyn Gustafson's leadership style? What were its strengths and weaknesses? What were the sources of her influence?

2. How would you describe Erik Rasmussen's leadership style as he tried to effect change? What are its strengths and weaknesses? What are the sources of his influence?

3. If you were Martin Quinn, would you recommend modifications in Erik Rasmussen's leadership style that you would like him to adopt? Do you think it will be possible for Rasmussen to make the necessary changes? If not, why not? If you do think change is possible, how would you recommend the desired changes be facilitated?

SOURCES: Based on Gary Yukl, *Leadership in Organizations*, 4th ed. (Englewood Cliffs, NJ: Prentice Hall, 1998): 66–67; and "Telephone Call Centers: The Factory Floors of the 21st Century," *Knowledge@ Wharton* (April 10, 2002): http://knowledge.wharton.upenn.edu/index.cfm?fa=viewArticle&ID=540.

BIZ FLIX

U-571

This action-packed thriller deals with a U.S. submarine crew's efforts to retrieve an Enigma encryption device from a disabled German submarine during World War II. After the crew gets the device, the U.S. submarine sinks, and they must use the German submarine to escape from enemy destroyers. The film's almost nonstop action and extraordinary special effects will look and sound best with a home theater system.

This scene is an edited composite of the "To Be a Captain" sequence early in the film. The S33, an older U.S. submarine, is embarking on a secret mission. Before departure, the S33's officers receive a briefing on their mission from Office of Naval Intelligence representatives on board. Executive officer Lt. Andrew Tyler (Matthew McConaughey) reports on the submarine's status to Lt. Commander Mike Dahlgren (Bill Paxton). The film continues with the S33 finding the disabled German submarine.

What to Watch for and Ask Yourself

1. What aspects of leadership does Dahlgren say are important for a submarine commander?

2. Which leadership behaviors or traits does he emphasize?

3. Are these traits or behaviors right for this situation? Why or why not?

Leadership at McDonald's

Do you want fries with that? This ubiquitous phrase is heard by nearly 50 million people in more than 119 countries each day. McDonald's has achieved the status of one of the most recognizable franchises across the globe through a mixture of successful marketing, consistent service and products, and strong leadership.

Ray Kroc was a visionary leader. He saw the potential for standardizing an efficient, systematized restaurant model and replicating it across the country. He began as the distributor of the mechanized milk shake maker, the Multimixer. At the McDonald's hamburger stand in California, Kroc saw a restaurant that used not one, but eight Multimixers and served a record number of people in the shortest amount of time imaginable. He proposed the idea of opening up several such restaurants to the brothers Dick and Mac McDonald, and in 1955, Kroc opened the first McDonald's in Des Plaines, Illinois. The rest is history.

Not only was Kroc a visionary leader who inspired others with his charisma, he possessed a strong initiating structure. He is quoted as saying, "If you've got time to lean, you've got time to clean," which highlights his goal-oriented and task-focused leadership style that still exists today. McDonalds' global business strategy—Plan to Win—encompasses five areas: place, products, price, promotion, and people. Part of the commitment to people is providing employees the resources to get their jobs done. This includes adequately staffing restaurants to allow for a good customer experience as well as to provide schedule flexibility, providing employees the proper tools to serve the customer, and training employees in job skills including customer service, responsibility, teamwork, time management, problem-solving, and communication at Hamburger University. Such a philosophy follows the Path–Goal theory of increasing employee motivation through clarifying desired behaviors and company goals. This philosophy has proven successful in producing future leadership for McDonald's, as over 40% of its top management started as crew members, including CEO Jim Skinner.

Another side of McDonalds' Plan to Win embodies the more people-oriented facet of consideration-based leadership. McDonald's espouses a commitment to investing in the growth and job satisfaction of its employees so they can realize their full potential. This includes a commitment to an inclusive, supportive workplace environment that recognizes and rewards good performance. Managers are encouraged to treat employees as they would want to be treated, act as coaches as opposed to policemen, promote teamwork, and communicate openly, listening to understand, and valuing others' opinions.

Like many successful organizations, McDonald's has found great success by promoting a corporate leadership style that combines a high initiating structure and high consideration. Such a combination will allow them to weather the next 50 years of selling Big Macs.

Questions

1. Where does the leadership at McDonald's fall on the Leadership Grid in Exhibit 11.4? Explain your answer.
2. What are the benefits of a corporate leadership strategy?
3. As a leader in the first years of McDonald's, what kind of power did Ray Kroc have?

chapter 12

Motivation

Learning Objectives

After studying this chapter, you should be able to:

1 Define *motivation* and explain the difference between current approaches and traditional approaches to motivation.

2 Identify and describe content theories of motivation based on employee needs.

3 Identify and explain process theories of motivation.

4 Describe reinforcement theory and how it can be used to motivate employees.

5 Discuss major approaches to job design and how job design influences motivation.

6 Explain how empowerment heightens employee motivation.

7 Describe ways that managers can create a sense of meaning and importance for employees at work.

New Manager's Questions

Please circle your opinion below each of the following statements.

Assess Your Answer

1 Money is the most important motivator for employees.

1	2	3	4	5
strongly agree				strongly disagree

2 A strong need for power is necessary to develop your career.

1	2	3	4	5
strongly agree				strongly disagree

3 Too much feedback can be harmful to workers' productivity.

1	2	3	4	5
strongly agree				strongly disagree

TAKE ACTION ▶

As a manager, always learn what motivates each individual who works for you, remembering that different people have different motivators.

motivation
the arousal, direction, and persistence of behavior.

intrinsic reward
the satisfaction received in the process of performing an action.

Motivation is a challenge for managers because motivation arises from within employees and typically differs for each person. For example, Janice Rennie makes $350,000 a year selling residential real estate in Toronto; she attributes her success to the fact that she likes to listen carefully to clients and then find houses to meet their needs. Greg Storey is a skilled machinist who is challenged by writing programs for numerically controlled machines. After dropping out of college, he swept floors in a machine shop and was motivated to learn to run the machines. Frances Blais sells educational books and software. She is a top salesperson, but she doesn't care about the $50,000-plus commissions: "I'm not even thinking money when I'm selling. I'm really on a crusade to help children read well." In stark contrast, Rob Michaels gets sick to his stomach before he goes to work. Rob is a telephone salesperson who spends all day trying to get people to buy products they do not need, and the rejections are painful. His motivation is money; he earned $120,000 in the past year and cannot make nearly that much doing anything else.[1]

Rob is motivated by money, Janice by her love of listening and problem solving, Frances by the desire to help children read, and Greg by the challenge of mastering numerically controlled machinery. Each person is motivated to perform, yet each has different reasons for performing. With such diverse motivations, it is a challenge for managers to motivate employees toward common organizational goals.

This chapter reviews theories and models of employee motivation. First we examine various perspectives on motivation and consider several models that describe the employee needs and processes associated with motivation. We discuss goal-setting theory and the reinforcement perspective on motivation, as well as examine how *job design*—changing the structure of the work itself—can affect employee satisfaction and productivity. Finally, we discuss the trend of *empowerment*, where authority and decision making are delegated to subordinates to increase employee motivation, and look at how managers can imbue work with a sense of meaning to inspire and motivate employees to higher performance.

The Concept of Motivation

Most of us get up in the morning, go to school or work, and behave in ways that are predictably our own. We respond to our environment and the people in it with little thought as to why we work hard, enjoy certain classes, or find some recreational activities so much fun. Yet all these behaviors are motivated by something. **Motivation** refers to the forces either within or external to a person that arouse enthusiasm and persistence to pursue a certain course of action. Employee motivation affects productivity, and part of a manager's job is to channel motivation toward the accomplishment of organizational goals.[2] The study of motivation helps managers understand what prompts people to initiate action, what influences their choice of action, and why they persist in that action over time.

A simple model of human motivation is illustrated in Exhibit 12.1. People have basic *needs*—for food, achievement, or monetary gain—that translate into an internal tension that motivates specific behaviors with which to fulfill the need. To the extent that the behavior is successful, the person is rewarded in the sense that the need is satisfied. The reward also informs the person that the behavior was appropriate and can be used again in the future.

Rewards are of two types: intrinsic and extrinsic. **Intrinsic rewards** are the satisfactions a person receives in the process of performing a particular action. The completion of a complex task may bestow a pleasant

• • CONCEPT CONNECTION

Managers at Albertson's believe that creating a work environment that is rich in opportunity, challenge, and reward **motivates employees** and is key to the company's success. By providing clear goals and objectives, performance reviews, formal and informal education programs, functional training, lateral promotions, and individual mentoring, managers help employees, such as Raymond Harlan (photo), find both **intrinsic** and **extrinsic rewards** in their work. Harlan has been assisting shoppers and winning hearts at Albertson's Acme supermarket in Philadelphia since the store opened in 1999. "He's the 'Mayor of Acme,'" says store director Dan Houck.

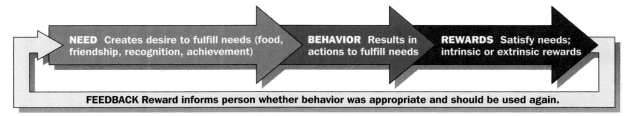

EXHIBIT 12.1
A Simple Model of
Motivation

feeling of accomplishment, or solving a problem that benefits others may fulfill a personal mission. For example, Frances Blais sells educational materials for the intrinsic reward of helping children read well. **Extrinsic rewards** are given by another person, typically a manager, and include promotions, pay increases, and bonuses. They originate externally, as a result of pleasing others. Rob Michaels, who hates his sales job, nevertheless is motivated by the extrinsic reward of high pay. Although extrinsic rewards are important, good managers strive to help people achieve intrinsic rewards as well. The most talented and innovative employees are rarely motivated exclusively by rewards such as money and benefits, or even praise and recognition. Instead, they seek satisfaction from the work itself.[3] For example, at Google, people are motivated by an idealistic goal of providing "automated universal transference," which basically means unifying data and information around the world and totally obliterating language barriers via the Internet. People are energized by the psychic rewards they get from working on intellectually stimulating and challenging technical problems, as well as by the potentially beneficial global impact of their work.[4]

The importance of motivation as illustrated in Exhibit 12.1 is that it can lead to behaviors that reflect high performance within organizations. Studies have found that high employee motivation goes hand-in-hand with high organizational performance and profits.[5] Managers can use motivation theory to help satisfy employees' needs and simultaneously encourage high work performance. With massive layoffs in many U.S. organizations in recent years and a decline in trust of corporate leadership, managers are struggling to keep employees focused and motivated. Finding and keeping talented workers is a growing challenge. Managers have to find the right combination of motivational techniques and rewards to keep people satisfied and productive in a variety of organizational situations.

TAKE ACTION
Know yourself well enough to understand if you are more motivated by intrinsic or extrinsic rewards.

Foundations of Motivation

A manager's assumptions about employee motivation and the use of rewards depend on his or her perspective on motivation. Four distinct perspectives on employee motivation have evolved: the traditional approach, the human relations approach, the human resource approach, and the contemporary approach.[6]

TRADITIONAL APPROACH

The study of employee motivation really began with the work of Frederick W. Taylor on scientific management. Recall from Chapter 1 that scientific management pertains to the systematic analysis of an employee's job for the purpose of increasing efficiency. Economic rewards are provided to employees for high performance. The emphasis on pay evolved into the notion of the *economic man*—people would work harder for higher pay. This approach led to the development of incentive pay systems, in which people were paid strictly on the quantity and quality of their work outputs.

HUMAN RELATIONS APPROACH

The economic man was gradually replaced by a more sociable employee in managers' minds. Beginning with the landmark Hawthorne studies at a Western Electric plant, as

extrinsic reward
a reward given by another person.

NEW MANAGER SELF TEST

Employee Engagement

The term *employee engagement* is becoming popular in the corporate world. To learn what engagement means, answer the following questions twice—(1) once for a course you both enjoyed and performed well in and (2) a second time for a course you did not enjoy and performed poorly in. Mark a "1" to indicate whether each item is Mostly True or Mostly False for the course you enjoyed and performed well in. Mark a "2" to indicate whether each item is Mostly True or Mostly False for the course you did not enjoy and performed poorly in.

	Mostly True	Mostly False
1. I made sure to study on a regular basis.	_____	_____
2. I put forth effort.	_____	_____
3. I found ways to make the course material relevant to my life.	_____	_____
4. I found ways to make the course interesting to me.	_____	_____
5. I raised my hand in class.	_____	_____
6. I had fun in class.	_____	_____
7. I participated actively in small group discussions.	_____	_____
8. I helped fellow students.	_____	_____

INTERPRETATION AND SCORING: Engagement means that people involve and express themselves in their work, going beyond the minimum effort required. Engagement typically has a positive relationship with both personal satisfaction and performance. If this relationship was true for your classes, the number of "1s" in the Mostly True column will be higher than the number of "2s." You might expect a score of 6 or higher for a course in which you were engaged, and possibly 3 or lower if you were disengaged.

The challenge for a new manager is to learn to engage subordinates in the same way your instructors in your favorite classes were able to engage you. Teaching is similar to managing. What techniques did your instructors use to engage students? Which techniques can you use to engage your people when you become a new manager?

SOURCE: Questions based on Mitchell M. Handelsman, William L. Briggs, Nora Sullivan, and Annette Towler, "A Measure of College Student Course Engagement," *Journal of Educational Research* 98 (January/February 2005): 184–191.

described in Chapter 1, noneconomic rewards, such as congenial work groups that met social needs, seemed more important than money as a motivator of work behavior.[7] For the first time, workers were studied as people, and the concept of *social man* was born.

HUMAN RESOURCE APPROACH

The human resource approach carries the concepts of economic man and social man further to introduce the concept of the *whole person*. Human resource theory suggests that employees are complex and motivated by many factors. For example, the work by McGregor on Theory X and Theory Y described in Chapter 1 argued that people want to do a good job and that work is as natural and healthy as play. Proponents of the human resource approach

Spotlight on Skills

GFOUR Theatrical Productions

Managing musical theater on or off-Broadway is not so different from running other businesses. Alan Glist, a founder and co-chairman of GFOUR Productions, spent most of his career manufacturing and selling clothing through 30 retail locations. Alan learned if you want a highly motivated workforce, you must treat each person special. After selling the garment business, he and his wife Kathi founded GFOUR, a theatrical production company, with Ken Greenblatt, GFOUR's other co-chairman, and Sandra Greenblatt. Their first Broadway production was a lesson on how people were treated. During auditions, singers were cut off after a few notes, with a rude "Next!" Kathi, Alan, Ken, and Sandra decided they would build a different kind of company. And they have, as proven by employees' reactions. "We are all one family," say several cast members. As musical director Dale Grogan noted, "Going to work was an utter joy. And it was that way from the beginning."

"It all starts with the audition process," said Kathi. "That's where our 'Producing with a Heart' begins. We treat them respectfully, letting them finish their song and then talk to them." Casting the right people—team players—is vital. "Even if someone is very talented, we won't hire them if they have an attitude, or seem like a diva," says Ken. Afterwards each noncasted person is called, explained why they weren't cast and what they could work on. "This is not standard practice," says Alan, "and we often get criticized for spending too much time, but we think it's worth it."

On opening night, there's a big post-show celebration. Ken, Alan, and Kathi all give short speeches, and then Alan thanks every person involved in the show, including costumers, marketers, and group sales. Such a celebration with acknowledgement of each and every contributor helps create high motivation and loyalty.

Even with 12 to 15 concurrently running productions (some of which have won Broadway's prestigious Tony Award), they visit each one to mark milestones, to celebrate. For example, they go to each 100th performance and bring the crew—the stage manager, lighting guy, sound person, those behind-the-scenes workers who are vital to the success but that hardly ever get recognized—on stage to thank them. Also, they take the cast out for lunch to talk over concerns and to build relationships. "They put themselves on the line for us every day," says Kathi. "They are out there creating the successes every day, and we want to show them we care."

SOURCES: Alan and Kathi Glist, personal interviews, June 2007; Ken Greenblatt, personal interview, June 2007; Dale Grogan, email message, July 2007.

believed that earlier approaches had tried to manipulate employees through economic or social rewards. By assuming that employees are competent and able to make major contributions, managers can enhance organizational performance. The human resource approach laid the groundwork for contemporary perspectives on employee motivation. Seeing employees as real people is one strength of GFOUR Theatrical Productions, as shown in the Spotlight on Skills box.

CONTEMPORARY APPROACH

The contemporary approach to employee motivation is dominated by three types of theories, each of which will be discussed in the following sections. The first are *content theories*, which stress the analysis of underlying human needs. Content theories provide insight into the needs of people in organizations and help managers understand how needs can be satisfied in the workplace. *Process theories* concern the thought processes that influence behavior. They focus on how people seek rewards in work circumstances. *Reinforcement theories* focus on employee learning of desired work behaviors. In Exhibit 12.1, content theories focus on the concepts in the first box, process theories on those in the second, and reinforcement theories on those in the third.

Content Perspectives on Motivation

Content theories emphasize the needs that motivate people. At any point in time, people have basic needs such as those for monetary reward, achievement, or recognition. These needs translate into an internal drive that motivates specific behaviors in an attempt to

content theories
a group of theories that emphasize the needs that motivate people.

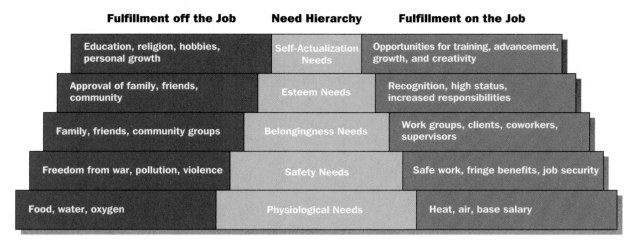

EXHIBIT 12.2

Maslow's Hierarchy
of Needs

fulfill the needs. In other words, our needs are like a hidden catalog of the things we want and will work to get. To the extent that managers understand employees' needs, they can design reward systems to meet them and direct employees' energies and priorities toward attaining organizational goals.

HIERARCHY OF NEEDS THEORY

Probably the most famous content theory was developed by Abraham Maslow.[8] Maslow's **hierarchy of needs theory** proposes that people are motivated by multiple needs and that these needs exist in a hierarchical order, as illustrated in Exhibit 12.2. Maslow identified five general types of motivating needs in order of ascendance:

1. *Physiological needs.* These most basic human physical needs include food, water, and oxygen. In the organizational setting, they are reflected in the needs for adequate heat, air, and base salary to ensure survival.

2. *Safety needs.* These needs include a safe and secure physical and emotional environment and freedom from threats—that is, for freedom from violence and for an orderly society. In an organizational workplace, safety needs reflect the needs for safe jobs, fringe benefits, and job security.

3. *Belongingness needs.* These needs reflect the desire to be accepted by one's peers, have friendships, be part of a group, and be loved. In the organization, these needs influence the desire for good relationships with co-workers, participation in a work group, and a positive relationship with supervisors.

4. *Esteem needs.* These needs relate to the desire for a positive self-image and to receive attention, recognition, and appreciation from others. Within organizations, esteem needs reflect a motivation for recognition, an increase in responsibility, high status, and credit for contributions to the organization.

5. *Self-actualization needs.* These needs include the need for self-fulfillment, which is the highest need category. They concern developing one's full potential, increasing one's competence, and becoming a better person. Self-actualization needs can be met in the organization by providing people with opportunities to grow, be creative, and acquire training for challenging assignments and advancement.

hierarchy of needs theory
a content theory that proposes that people are motivated by five categories of needs—physiological, safety, belongingness, esteem, and self-actualization—that exist in a hierarchical order.

According to Maslow's theory, low-order needs take priority—they must be satisfied before higher-order needs are activated. The needs are satisfied in sequence: Physiological needs come before safety needs, safety needs before social needs, and so on. A person desiring physical safety will devote efforts to securing a safer environment and will not be concerned with esteem needs or self-actualization needs. When a need is satisfied, it declines in importance, and the next higher need is activated.

A study of employees in the manufacturing department of a major health care company in the United Kingdom provides some support for Maslow's theory. Most line workers emphasized that they worked at the company primarily because of the good pay, benefits, and job security. Thus, employees' lower-level physiological and safety needs were being met. When questioned about their motivation, employees indicated the importance of positive social relationships with both peers and supervisors (belongingness needs) and a desire for greater respect and recognition from management (esteem needs).[9]

ERG THEORY

Clayton Alderfer proposed a modification of Maslow's theory in an effort to simplify it and respond to criticisms of its lack of empirical verification.[10] His **ERG theory** identified three categories of needs:

1. *Existence needs.* The needs for physical well-being.
2. *Relatedness needs.* The needs for satisfactory relationships with others.
3. *Growth needs.* The needs that focus on the development of human potential and the desire for personal growth and increased competence.

The ERG model and Maslow's need hierarchy are similar because both are in hierarchical form and presume that individuals move up the hierarchy one step at a time. However, Alderfer reduced the number of need categories to three and proposed that movement up the hierarchy is more complex, reflecting a **frustration-regression principle,** namely, that failure to meet a high-order need may trigger a regression to an already fulfilled lower-order need. Thus, a worker who cannot fulfill a need for personal growth may revert to a lower-order need and redirect efforts toward making a lot of money. The ERG model therefore is less rigid than Maslow's need hierarchy, suggesting that individuals may move down as well as up the hierarchy, depending on their ability to satisfy needs.

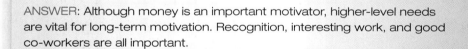

1 Money is the most important motivator for employees.

ANSWER: Although money is an important motivator, higher-level needs are vital for long-term motivation. Recognition, interesting work, and good co-workers are all important.

⁕ Assess Your Answer

Need hierarchy theory helps explain why organizations find ways to recognize employees, encourage their participation in decision making, and give them opportunities to make significant contributions to the organization and society. For example, Sterling Bank, with headquarters in Houston, Texas, no longer uses *bank tellers*. These positions are now front-line managers who are expected to make decisions and contribute ideas for improving the business.[11] USAA, which offers insurance, mutual funds, and banking services to 5 million members of the military and their families, provides another example.

A recent survey found that employees who contribute ideas at work, such as those at USAA, are more likely to feel valued, committed, and motivated. In addition, when employees' ideas are implemented and recognized, a motivational effect often ripples throughout the workforce.[12]

ERG theory
a modification of the needs hierarchy theory that proposes three categories of needs: existence, relatedness, and growth.

frustration-regression principle
the idea that failure to meet a high-order need may cause a regression to an already satisfied lower-order need.

USAA

USAA's customer service agents are on the front lines in helping families challenged by war and overseas deployment manage their financial responsibilities. Managers recognize that the most important factor in the company's success is the relationship between USAA members and these front-line employees.

To make sure that relationship is a good one, USAA treats customer service reps, who are often considered the lowest rung on the corporate ladder, like professionals. People have a real sense that they're making life just a little easier for military members and their families, which instills them with a feeling of pride and accomplishment. Employees are organized into small, tightly knit "expert teams" and are encouraged to suggest changes that will benefit customers. One service rep suggested that the company offer insurance premium billing timed to coincide with the military's bi-weekly paychecks. Service reps don't have scripts to follow, and calls aren't timed. Employees know they can take whatever time they need to give the customer the best possible service.

Giving people the opportunity to make real contributions has paid off. In a study by Forrester Research, 81 percent of USAA customers said they believe the company does what's best for them, rather than what's best for the bottom line. Compare that to about 20 percent of customers for financial services firms such as JPMorgan Chase and Citibank.[13]

Many companies are finding that creating a humane work environment that allows people to achieve a balance between work and personal life is also a great high-level motivator. Flexibility in the workplace, including options such as telecommuting, flexible hours, and job sharing, is highly valued by today's employees because it enables them to manage their work and personal responsibilities. Flexibility is good for organizations too. Employees who have control over their work schedules are significantly less likely to suffer job burnout and are more highly committed to their employers, as shown in Exhibit 12.3. This idea was supported by a survey conducted at Deloitte, which found that client service professionals cited workplace flexibility as a strong reason for wanting to stay with the firm. Another study at Prudential Insurance found that work-life satisfaction and work flexibility directly correlated to job satisfaction, organizational commitment, and employee retention.[14]

Making work fun can play a role in creating this balance. One psychologist recently updated Maslow's hierarchy of needs for a new generation and included the need to have fun as a substantial motivator for today's employees.[15] Having fun at work relieves stress and

EXHIBIT 12.3

The Motivational Benefits of Job Flexibility

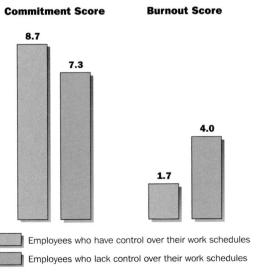

SOURCE: WFD Consulting data, as reported in Karol Rose, "Work-Life Effectiveness," *Fortune* (September 29, 2003): S1–S17.

enables people to feel more "whole," rather than feeling that their personal lives are totally separate from their work lives. Something as simple as a manager's choice of language can create a lighter, more fun environment. Research suggests the use of phrases such as "Play around with this . . . Explore the possibility of . . . Have fun with . . . Don't worry about little mistakes . . . View this as a game . . ." and so forth can effectively build elements of fun and playfulness into a workplace.[16]

TWO-FACTOR THEORY

Frederick Herzberg developed another popular theory of motivation called the *two-factor theory*.[17] Herzberg interviewed hundreds of workers about times when they were highly motivated to work and other times when they were dissatisfied and unmotivated at work. His findings suggested that the work characteristics associated with dissatisfaction were quite different from those pertaining to satisfaction, which prompted the notion that two factors influence work motivation.

The two-factor theory is illustrated in Exhibit 12.4. The center of the scale is neutral, meaning that workers are neither satisfied nor dissatisfied. Herzberg believed that two entirely separate dimensions contribute to an employee's behavior at work. The first, called **hygiene factors,** involves the presence or absence of job dissatisfiers, such as working conditions, pay, company policies, and interpersonal relationships. When hygiene factors are poor, work is dissatisfying. However, good hygiene factors simply remove the dissatisfaction; they do not in themselves cause people to become highly satisfied and motivated in their work.

The second set of factors does influence job satisfaction. **Motivators** focus on high-level needs and include achievement, recognition, responsibility, and opportunity for growth. Herzberg believed that when motivators are absent, workers are neutral toward work, but when motivators are present, workers are highly motivated and satisfied. Thus, hygiene factors and motivators represent two distinct factors that influence motivation. Hygiene factors

TAKE ACTION

As a manager, remember that some people are motivated by money, and others by interesting work and recognition.

hygiene factors
factors that involve the presence or absence of job dissatisfiers, including working conditions, pay, company policies, and interpersonal relationships.

motivators
factors that influence job satisfaction based on fulfillment of high-level needs such as achievement, recognition, responsibility, and opportunity for growth.

Highly Satisfied

Area of Satisfaction

Motivators

Achievement
Recognition
Responsibility
Work itself
Personal growth

Motivators influence level of satisfaction.

Neither Satisfied nor Dissatisfied

Area of Dissatisfaction

Hygiene Factors

Working conditions
Pay and security
Company policies
Supervisors
Interpersonal relationships

Hygiene factors influence level of dissatisfaction.

Highly Dissatisfied

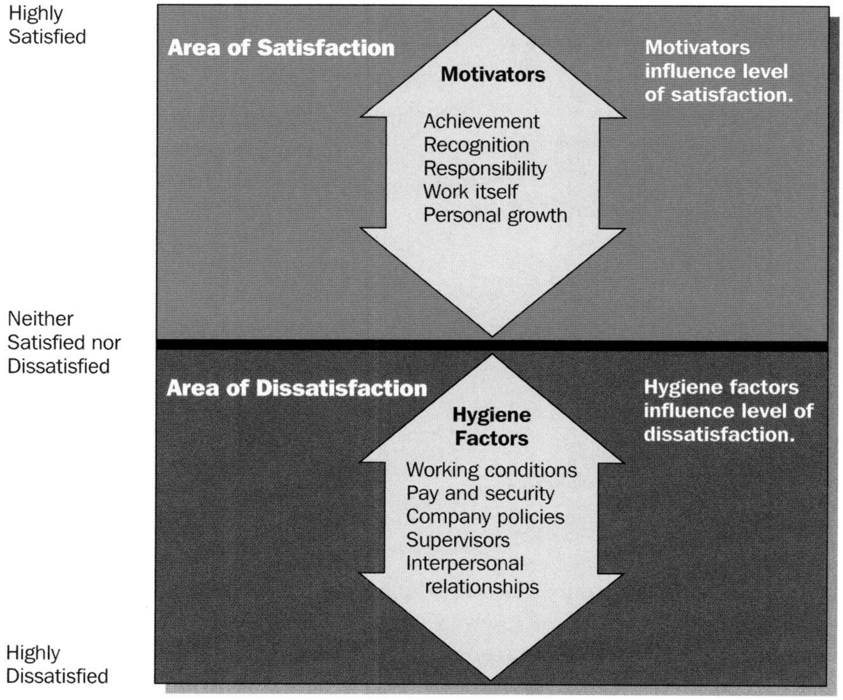

EXHIBIT 12.4

Herzberg's Two-Factor Theory

work only in the area of dissatisfaction. Unsafe working conditions or a noisy work environment will cause people to be dissatisfied, but their correction will not lead to a high level of motivation and satisfaction. Motivators such as challenge, responsibility, and recognition must be in place before employees will be highly motivated to excel at their work.

The implication of the two-factor theory for managers is clear. On one hand, providing hygiene factors will eliminate employee dissatisfaction but will not motivate workers to high achievement levels. On the other hand, recognition, challenge, and opportunities for personal growth are powerful motivators and will promote high satisfaction and performance. The manager's role is to remove dissatisfiers—that is, to provide hygiene factors sufficient to meet basic needs—and then to use motivators to meet higher-level needs and propel employees toward greater achievement and satisfaction.

CONCEPT CONNECTION

According to General Electric CEO Jeffrey Immelt, people who succeed at GE are usually those who have a strong **need for achievement** or **need for affiliation**. "We lose people who just want to make a lot of money, or just want to be powerful. But if you like building stuff, and you like who you work with, this is a pretty energizing place to work." Immelt is counting on those highly motivated employees as he tries to steer the multinational conglomerate toward unprecedented growth by transforming it into a customer-driven company that thrives on innovation as well as superior productivity.

ACQUIRED NEEDS THEORY

The final content theory was developed by David McClelland. The *acquired needs theory* proposes that certain types of needs are acquired during the individual's lifetime. In other words, people are not born with these needs but may learn them through their life experiences.[18] The three needs most frequently studied are these:

1. *Need for achievement.* The desire to accomplish something difficult, attain a high standard of success, master complex tasks, and surpass others.

2. *Need for affiliation.* The desire to form close personal relationships, avoid conflict, and establish warm friendships.

3. *Need for power.* The desire to influence or control others, be responsible for others, and have authority over others.

Assess Your Answer

2 A strong need for power is necessary to develop your career.

ANSWER: Too strong a need for power can get in the way of doing a good job because it often means the person is more concerned about "winning" than about doing the best job.

Early life experiences determine whether people acquire these needs. If children are encouraged to do things for themselves and receive reinforcement, they will acquire a need to achieve. If they are reinforced for forming warm human relationships, they will develop a need for affiliation. If they get satisfaction from controlling others, they will acquire a need for power.

NEW MANAGER SELF TEST

Manifest Needs

Circle one letter for each item, depending on how you are most of the time.

1. At work or in class, I would rather work
   a. Alone
   b. In a group

2. When working on a project, I usually
   a. Spend a great deal of time so it is really good
   b. Try to just make it acceptable

3. In a group,
   a. I really try to be a leader
   b. I let others take the lead

4. With a project, I prefer
   a. To do it my way
   b. To see how others have done it or want it done

5. My goals at work or school are usually to
   a. Be good enough to get by
   b. To outperform others

6. When there is a disagreement, I usually
   a. Refrain from saying much if people I like are arguing against my opinion
   b. Speak my mind

7. In a group,
   a. I let the ideas or recommendations develop naturally
   b. I try to influence those in the group to my opinion

8. At work, I pretty much
   a. Keep to myself and get the work done
   b. Enjoy chatting with other people

9. At work or school, I usually
   a. Avoid risks
   b. Stick my neck out and take moderate risks to get ahead

10. Regarding rules and regulations, I generally
    a. Follow them unless there is a compelling reason not to
    b. Disregard them if they get in the way of freedom

11. When involved in sports or other games, I usually play
    a. To have a good time
    b. To win or at least to do better than I have previously

12. When working on a project, I like to
    a. Have a lot of say in the outcome
    b. Be an accepted "team player"

(Continued)

13. In my work life, I often
   a. Make certain I give adequate time to my personal life (family, friends, etc.)
   b. Get so over-scheduled I have less time for my personal life

14. When I am working with other people, I usually want to
   a. Do better than they do
   b. Organize and direct the activities of the others

SCORING

Score one point in the following categories if you marked the appropriate letter.

N Aut	n Power	n Ach	n Aff
1a	3a	2a	1b
4a	5b	9b	6a
6b	7b	11b	8b
8a	12a	13b	12b
10b	14b	14a	13a

Totals

In the 1930s, Henry Murray developed a theory on motivation and personality, which was further developed by David Mc-Clelland. Four needs were identified, need for autonomy (n Aut); need for power (n Pow), need for achievement (n Ach), and need for affiliation (n Aff). The four needs coexist in each person at varying levels. N Aut determines the requirement to do things alone, with a minimum of outside supervision. N Pow relates to the desire to be in charge, in control, giving orders. N Ach describes the desire to excel, to accomplish goals, to do better than others. Finally, n Aff is someone's need to be part of a group to be accepted and liked. The maximum in each category is 5, so whichever you score the most in, that is your greatest tendency. There are no "right" or "wrong" answers. Each combination of strengths works best in some situations.

For more than 20 years, McClelland studied human needs and their implications for management. People with a high need for achievement are frequently entrepreneurs. The parents of social entrepreneur Bill Strickland, the charismatic leader who established Manchester Bidwell, described in the previous chapter, always encouraged him to follow his dreams. When he wanted to go south to work with the Freedom Riders in the 1960s, they supported him. His plans for tearing up the family basement and making a photography studio were met with equal enthusiasm. Strickland thus developed a need for *achievement* that enabled him to accomplish amazing results later in life.[19] People who have a high need for *affiliation* are successful integrators, whose job is to coordinate the work of several departments in an organization.[20] Integrators include brand managers and project managers who must have excellent people skills. People high in need for affiliation are able to establish positive working relationships with others.

A high need for *power* often is associated with successful attainment of top levels in the organizational hierarchy. For example, McClelland studied managers at AT&T for 16 years and found that those with a high need for power were more likely to follow a path of continued promotion over time. More than half of the employees at the top levels had a high need for power. In contrast, managers with a high need for achievement but a low need for power tended to peak earlier in their careers and at a lower level. The reason is that achievement needs can be met through the task itself, but power needs can be met only by ascending to a level at which a person has power over others.

In summary, content theories focus on people's underlying needs and label those particular needs that motivate behavior. The hierarchy of needs theory, the ERG theory, the two-factor theory, and the acquired needs theory all help managers understand what motivates people. In this way, managers can design work to meet needs and hence elicit appropriate and successful work behaviors.

Process Perspectives on Motivation

Process theories explain how people select behavioral actions to meet their needs and determine whether their choices were successful. The two basic process theories are equity theory and expectancy theory.

EQUITY THEORY

Equity theory focuses on individuals' perceptions of how fairly they are treated compared with others. Developed by J. Stacy Adams, equity theory proposes that people are motivated to seek social equity in the rewards they expect for performance.[21]

According to equity theory, if people perceive their compensation as equal to what others receive for similar contributions, they will believe that their treatment is fair and equitable. People evaluate equity by a ratio of inputs to outcomes. Inputs to a job include education, experience, effort, and ability. Outcomes from a job include pay, recognition, benefits, and promotions. The input-to-outcome ratio may be compared to another person in the work group or to a perceived group average. A state of **equity** exists whenever the ratio of one person's outcomes to inputs equals the ratio of another's outcomes to inputs.

Inequity occurs when the input-to-outcome ratios are out of balance, such as when a person with a high level of education or experience receives the same salary as a new, less-educated employee. Interestingly, perceived inequity also occurs in the other direction. Thus, if an employee discovers she is making more money than other people who contribute the same inputs to the company, she may feel the need to correct the inequity by working harder, getting more education, or considering lower pay. Studies of the brain have shown that people get less satisfaction from money they receive without having to earn it than they do from money they work to receive.[22] Perceived inequity creates tensions within individuals that motivate them to bring equity into balance.[23]

The most common methods for reducing a perceived inequity are these:

- *Change inputs.* A person may choose to increase or decrease his or her inputs to the organization. For example, underpaid individuals may reduce their level of effort or increase their absenteeism. Overpaid people may increase their effort on the job.

- *Change outcomes.* A person may change his or her outcomes. An underpaid person may request a salary increase or a bigger office. A union may try to improve wages and working conditions to be consistent with a comparable union whose members make more money.

- *Distort perceptions.* Research suggests that people may distort perceptions of equity if they are unable to change inputs or outcomes. They may artificially increase the status attached to their jobs or distort others' perceived rewards to bring equity into balance.

- *Leave the job.* People who feel inequitably treated may decide to leave their jobs rather than suffer the inequity of being underpaid or overpaid. In their new jobs, they expect to find a more favorable balance of rewards.

The implication of equity theory for managers is that employees indeed evaluate the perceived equity of their rewards compared to others'. An increase in salary or a promotion will have no motivational effect if it is perceived as inequitable relative to that of other employees.

process theories
a group of theories that explain how employees select behaviors with which to meet their needs and determine whether their choices were successful.

equity theory
a process theory that focuses on individuals' perceptions of how fairly they are treated relative to others.

equity
a situation that exists when the ratio of one person's outcomes to inputs equals that of another's.

At Meadowcliff Elementary School in Little Rock, Arkansas, principal Karen Carter used the ideas of equity theory to devise a bonus system for teachers. Carter implemented several new programs designed to improve student learning, and she wanted to reward teachers for their efforts. To avoid fears of bias or favoritism, Carter and the Public Education Foundation of Little Rock decided to use Stanford Achievement Test results as a basis for bonuses. For each student whose Stanford score rose up to 4 percent over the course of the year, the teacher involved would get $100; 5 percent to 9 percent, $200; 10 percent to 14 percent, $300; and more than 15 percent, $400. The school's scores on the test rose by an average of 17 percent over the course of the year. The base line test gave teachers a way to analyze individual students' strengths and weaknesses and tailor instruction for each student. And because teachers felt the bonus system was equitable, it proved to be a powerful incentive. Administrators think the bonus system is helping to retain the best teachers at Meadowcliff, which serves primarily low-income students.[24] If bonuses were based on subjective judgment, some teachers would likely be concerned that rewards were not being distributed equitably.

Inequitable pay puts pressure on employees that is sometimes almost too great to bear. They attempt to change their work habits, try to change the system, or leave the job.[25] Consider Deb Allen, who went into the office on a weekend to catch up on work and found a document accidentally left on the copy machine. When she saw that some new hires were earning $200,000 more than their counterparts with more experience, and that "a noted screw-up" was making more than highly competent people, Allen began questioning why she was working on weekends for less pay than many others were receiving. Allen became so demoralized by the inequity that she quit her job three months later.[26]

TAKE ACTION ▶

As a new manager, don't play favorites, such as regularly praising some while overlooking others making similar contributions.

EXPECTANCY THEORY

Expectancy theory suggests that motivation depends on individuals' expectations about their ability to perform tasks and receive desired rewards. Expectancy theory is associated with the work of Victor Vroom, although a number of scholars have made contributions in this area.[27] Expectancy theory is concerned not with identifying types of needs but with the thinking process that individuals use to achieve rewards. Consider Amy Huang, a university student with a strong desire for a B in her accounting course. Amy has a C+ average and one more exam to take. Amy's motivation to study for that last exam will be influenced by (1) the expectation that hard study will lead to an A on the exam and (2) the expectation that an A on the exam will result in a B for the course. If Amy believes she cannot get an A on the exam or that receiving an A will not lead to a B for the course, she will not be motivated to study exceptionally hard.

TAKE ACTION ▶

Remember, if you believe that hard work will help you achieve your goals, you will be more likely to work hard.

expectancy theory
a process theory that proposes that motivation depends on individuals' expectations about their ability to perform tasks and receive desired rewards.

$E \rightarrow P$ **expectancy**
expectancy that putting effort into a given task will lead to high performance.

$P \rightarrow O$ **expectancy**
expectancy that successful performance of a task will lead to the desired outcome.

Elements of Expectancy Theory. Expectancy theory is based on the relationship among the individual's *effort*, the individual's *performance*, and the desirability of *outcomes* associated with high performance. These elements and the relationships among them are illustrated in Exhibit 12.5. The keys to expectancy theory are the expectancies for the relationships among effort, performance, and the value of the outcomes to the individual.

$E \rightarrow P$ **expectancy** involves determining whether putting effort into a task will lead to high performance. For this expectancy to be high, the individual must have the ability, previous experience, and necessary machinery, tools, and opportunity to perform. For Amy Huang to get a B in the accounting course, the $E \rightarrow P$ expectancy is high if Amy truly believes that with hard work, she can get an A on the final exam. If Amy believes she has neither the ability nor the opportunity to achieve high performance, the expectancy will be low, and so will be her motivation.

$P \rightarrow O$ **expectancy** involves determining whether successful performance will lead to the desired outcome. In the case of a person who is motivated to win a job-related award,

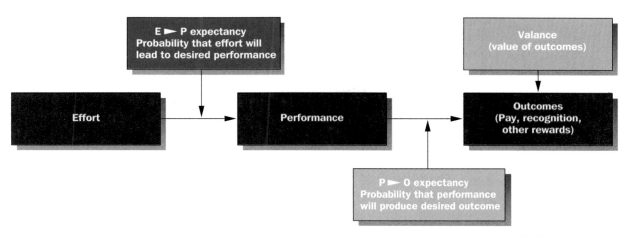

EXHIBIT 12.5

Major Elements of
Expectancy Theory

this expectancy concerns the belief that high performance will truly lead to the award. If the $P \rightarrow O$ expectancy is high, the individual will be more highly motivated. If the expectancy is that high performance will not produce the desired outcome, motivation will be lower. If an A on the final exam is likely to produce a B in the accounting course, Amy Huang's $P \rightarrow O$ expectancy will be high. Amy might talk to the professor to see whether an A will be sufficient to earn her a B in the course. If not, she will be less motivated to study hard for the final exam.

Valence is the value of outcomes, or attraction to outcomes, for the individual. If the outcomes that are available from high effort and good performance are not valued by employees, motivation will be low. Likewise, if outcomes have a high value, motivation will be higher.

Expectancy theory attempts not to define specific types of needs or rewards but only to establish that they exist and may be different for every individual. One employee might want to be promoted to a position of increased responsibility, and another might have high valence for good relationships with peers. Consequently, the first person will be motivated to work hard for a promotion and the second for the opportunity of a team position that will keep him or her associated with a group. Recent studies by the Gallup Organization substantiate the idea that rewards need to be individualized to be motivating. A recent finding from the U.S. Department of Labor shows that the number 1 reason people leave their jobs is because they "don't feel appreciated." Yet Gallup's analysis of 10,000 work groups in 30 industries found that making people feel appreciated depends on finding the right kind of reward for each individual. Some people prefer tangible rewards or gifts, whereas others place high value on words of recognition. In addition, some want public recognition, whereas others prefer to be quietly praised by someone they admire and respect.[28] Many of today's managers are also finding that praise and recognition from one's peers often means more than a pat on the back from a supervisor, so they are implementing peer-recognition programs that encourage employees to applaud one another for accomplishments.[29]

A simple sales department example illustrates how the expectancy model in Exhibit 12.5 works. If Carlos, a salesperson at the Diamond Gift Shop, believes that increased selling effort will lead to higher personal sales, we can say that he has a high $E \rightarrow P$ expectancy. Moreover, if Carlos also believes that higher personal sales will lead to a promotion or pay raise, we can say that he has a high $P \rightarrow O$ expectancy. Finally, if Carlos places a high value on the promotion or pay raise, valence is high, and he will have a high motivational force. On the other hand, if either the $E \rightarrow P$ or $P \rightarrow O$ expectancy is low, or if the money or promotion has low valence for Carlos, the overall motivational force will be low. For an employee to be highly motivated, all three factors in the expectancy model must be high.[30]

valence
the value or attraction an individual
has for an outcome.

Implications for Managers. The expectancy theory of motivation is similar to the path–goal theory of leadership described in Chapter 11. Both theories are personalized to subordinates' needs and goals. Managers' responsibility is to help subordinates meet their needs and at the same time attain organizational goals. Managers try to find a match between a subordinate's skills and abilities, job demands, and available rewards. To increase motivation, managers can clarify individuals' needs, define the outcomes available from the organization, and ensure that each individual has the ability and support (namely, time and equipment) needed to attain outcomes.

Some companies use expectancy theory principles by designing incentive systems that identify desired organizational outcomes and give everyone the same shot at getting the rewards. The trick is to design a system that fits with employees' abilities and needs. When goal-setting isn't used, results can be disastrous, as shown in the Business Blooper.

GOAL-SETTING THEORY

Recall from Chapter 5 our discussion of the importance and purposes of goals. Numerous studies have shown that people are more motivated when they have specific targets or objectives to work toward.[31] You have probably noticed in your own life that you are more motivated when you have a specific goal, such as making an A on a final exam, losing 10 pounds before spring break, or earning enough money during the summer to buy a used car.

Business Blooper

Guns N' Roses

Back before the band members of Guns 'N Roses were multi-platinum superstars, producer Tom Zutaut signed them to Geffen records. By 2001, he had left the label but was coaxed back to try and work with Axl Rose, the only original remaining member of the band, to nudge him to finish the much-waited, "Chinese Democracy." Rose had started the album in 1994, but got waylaid by personal demons. Gossip had him focused on plastic surgery and past-life regression therapy, not to mention lawsuits. Axl Rose isn't the only musician to ever drag his feet. But the irony is that the very musician who cast himself as the "master of predatory Hollywood" in his 1991 hit song, "Welcome to the Jungle," is now seen as the master of the music industry's largest white elephant. As time wore on, a horrible truth emerged: The more record companies rely on musicians like Rose, the less they can be controlled.

By 1994, the band had dispersed, victim to drug abuse, on-stage tantrums, and lyric controversies. But they reconvened for the new album, and Rose made himself leader, albeit more of a dictator. Not much got done. Because the band was still selling lots of old albums, no one seemed to mind. Leadership changed at Geffen; it was bought by Seagram. When the original band dispersed again, Geffen records sent CDs to Rose, asking him to listen for people he might want to work with. He ran over the CDs with his car. One day Geffen talent agent Todd Sullivan tried to gently encourage Rose to pull together a lot of recorded riffs and song fragments into complete compositions. The next day Geffen CEO pulled Sullivan off the project.

The record company kept paying Rose a million here, a million there, to keep on with the project, but he had built so many walls around himself that he became extremely isolated. Rose requested a specialized piece of equipment that cost about $150,000 to rent for two years and only used it 30 days. His pattern for years has been some flurried activity, then creative chaos, and finally isolation. Label executives improbably believed if they just brought in the right producer, the album would get done. But Rose's work (or lack of it) has outlasted scores of label managers, producers, and even the corporate structure that first hired him. In fact, the entire music recording industry has consolidated and is more bottom-line driven than ever. So despite millions of dollars over budget with to-date costs of $13 million, "Chinese Democracy," is not even on the release schedule anymore. China itself will probably have democracy before the record comes out. Record executives have learned it is better to invest in reliable musicians, those who have a proven track record and are known to meet deadlines. A gifted musician, but moody man often unable to follow-through is now seen as an unmanageable variable in anybody's business plan.

SOURCE: Jeff Leeds, "The most expensive album never made," *New York Times* (March 6, 2005): AR1, 28 and 32; Jason Bracelin, "Pray these long shots don't cross finish line," *Las Vegas Review-Journal* (June 26, 2007): 1E.

Goal-setting theory, described by Edwin Locke and Gary Latham, proposes that managers can increase motivation by setting specific, challenging goals that are accepted as valid by subordinates, and then helping people track their progress toward goal achievement by providing timely feedback. The four key components of goal-setting theory include the following:[32]

- *Goal specificity* refers to the degree to which goals are concrete and unambiguous. Specific goals such as "Visit one new customer each day," or "Sell $1,000 worth of merchandise a week" are more motivating than vague goals such as "Keep in touch with new customers" or "Increase merchandise sales." The first, critical step in any pay-for-performance system is to clearly define exactly what managers want people to accomplish. Lack of clear, specific goals is a major cause of the failure of incentive plans in many organizations.[33]

- In terms of *goal difficulty,* hard goals are more motivating than easy ones. Easy goals provide little challenge for employees and don't require them to increase their output. Highly ambitious but achievable goals ask people to stretch their abilities.

- *Goal acceptance* means that employees have to "buy into" the goals and be committed to them. Managers often find that having people participate in setting goals is a good way to increase acceptance and commitment. At Aluminio del Caroni, a state-owned aluminum company in southeastern Venezuela, plant workers felt a renewed sense of commitment when top leaders implemented a *co-management* initiative that has managers and lower-level employees working together to set budgets, determine goals, and make decisions. "The managers and the workers are running this business together," said one employee who spends his days shoveling molten aluminum down a channel from an industrial oven to a cast. "It gives us the motivation to work hard." [34]

- Finally, the component of *feedback* means that people get information about how well they are doing in progressing toward goal achievement. It is important for managers to provide performance feedback on a regular, ongoing basis. However, self-feedback, where people are able to monitor their own progress toward a goal, has been found to be an even stronger motivator than external feedback.[35]

TAKE ACTION

As a manager, give regular and meaningful feedback to employees.

Managers at Advanced Circuits of Aurora, Colorado, which makes custom-printed circuit boards, steer employee performance toward goals by giving everyone ongoing numerical feedback about every aspect of the business. Employees are so fired up that they check the data on the intranet throughout the day as if they were checking the latest sports scores. The system enables people to track their progress toward achieving goals, such as reaching sales targets or solving customer problems within specified time limits. "The more goals we get, the better it is for us," says employee Barb Frevert. "The more we do for Ron, the more he does for us."[36]

Why does goal setting increase motivation? For one thing, it enables people to focus their energies in the right direction. People know what to work toward, so they can direct their efforts toward the most important activities to accomplish the goals. Goals also energize behavior because people feel compelled to develop plans and strategies that keep them focused on achieving the target. Specific, difficult goals provide a challenge and encourage people to put forth high levels of effort. In addition, when goals are achieved, pride and

goal-setting theory
a motivation theory in which specific, challenging goals increase motivation and performance when the goals are accepted by subordinates and these subordinates receive feedback to indicate their progress toward goal achievement.

3 Too much feedback can be harmful to workers' productivity.

ANSWER: Honest, matter-of-fact feedback helps workers know when they are doing well or not making the mark. Too much feedback is only a problem if it is given in a negative, punitive manner.

Assess Your Answer

Best Buy

Darrell Owens just got out of the hospital. What put him there, he believes, was staying up three days straight to finish a report that was unexpectedly due for his employer, Best Buy, the nation's largest and highly successful consumer electronics retailer. Owens got a big bonus and a vacation for his extraordinary efforts, but now he's wondering whether it was worth it. Traci Tobias, who manages travel reimbursements, is sneaking out the door in the mornings to avoid the guilt she feels when her young children beg her to stay for breakfast and cry when she can't. She is feeling less commitment to her job as the sacrifices she makes for it seem greater and greater. Jennifer Janssen in finance recently discovered she is pregnant and is considering leaving her job. A manager in the human resources department, Cali Ressler, noticed an alarming trend at Best Buy: increasing turnover, signs of weakening organizational commitment, and more employees, especially women, accepting the reduced pay and prestige of part-time positions because they need more flexibility than a full-time position allows. Best Buy expects a lot from its people, and the company culture has always glorified long hours and personal sacrifice. Like other companies, Best Buy is searching for an edge in an increasingly competitive global environment.[37]

The problem at Best Buy headquarters is that many experienced employees are losing their drive. Best Buy executives are continually looking for ways to do things better, faster, and cheaper than the competition, but they realize that simply pushing for greater productivity is not the key to reviving employee morale and motivation. This situation can be a problem even for the most successful and admired of organizations, when experienced, valuable employees lose the motivation and commitment they once felt, causing a decline in their performance. One secret for success in organizations is motivated and enthusiastic employees.

At Best Buy headquarters, experienced employees were beginning to lose their motivation, and managers wisely recognized this situation as a danger to Best Buy's competitiveness. The answer was an innovative work-life balance initiative known as ROWE (Results-Oriented Work Environment), which means that people can work when and where they like, as long as they get the job done. The experiment started in one division where morale and motivation were dismal. Hourly employees, such as data entry clerks and claims processors, were disgruntled, saying that punching a time clock made them feel like unruly children who had to be kept in line. Under the ROWE system, those employees now focus on how many forms they can process in a week, rather than on the time it takes them to do it (they still keep track of their hours because of federal overtime regulations). The experiment in that division showed some remarkable results. Under ROWE, turnover in the first three months of employment fell from 14 percent to 0, job satisfaction increased 10 percent, and team-performance scores rose 13 percent. These results spurred executives to make the ROWE system available companywide. ROWE has proved to be a great high-level motivator at Best Buy.[38]

---

reinforcement theory
a motivation theory based on the relationship between a given behavior and its consequences.

behavior modification
the set of techniques by which reinforcement theory is used to modify human behavior.

law of effect
the assumption that positively reinforced behavior tends to be repeated, and unreinforced or negatively reinforced behavior tends to be inhibited.

reinforcement
anything that causes a given behavior to be repeated or inhibited.

---

satisfaction increase, contributing to higher motivation and morale.[39] One company that learned to use these principles is Best Buy.

Reinforcement Perspective on Motivation

The reinforcement approach to employee motivation sidesteps the issues of employee needs and thinking processes described in the content and process theories. **Reinforcement theory** simply looks at the relationship between behavior and its consequences. It focuses on changing or modifying employees' on-the-job behavior through the appropriate use of immediate rewards and punishments.

REINFORCEMENT TOOLS

Behavior modification is the name given to the set of techniques by which reinforcement theory is used to modify human behavior.[40] The basic assumption underlying behavior modification is the **law of effect,** which states that behavior that is positively reinforced tends to be repeated, and behavior that is not reinforced tends not to be repeated. **Reinforcement** is defined as anything that causes a certain behavior to be repeated or inhibited. The four reinforcement tools are positive reinforcement, avoidance learning, punishment, and extinction. Each type of reinforcement is a consequence of either a pleasant or unpleasant event being applied or withdrawn following a person's behavior. The four types of reinforcement are summarized in Exhibit 12.6.

Positive Reinforcement. *Positive reinforcement* is the administration of a pleasant and rewarding consequence following a desired behavior. A good example of positive reinforcement is immediate praise for an employee who arrives on time or does a little extra work. The pleasant consequence will increase the likelihood of the excellent work behavior occurring again. Studies have shown that positive reinforcement does help to improve performance. In addition, nonfinancial reinforcements such as positive feedback, social recognition, and attention are just as effective as financial incentives.[41] Indeed, many people consider factors other than money to be more important. Nelson Motivation Inc. con-

Farm managers often use a **fixed-rate reinforcement schedule** by basing a fruit or vegetable picker's pay on the amount he or she harvests. A variation on this individual piece-rate system is a relative incentive plan that bases each worker's pay on the ratio of the individual's productivity to average productivity among all co-workers. A study of Eastern and Central European pickers in the United Kingdom found that workers' productivity declined under the relative plan. Researchers theorized that fast workers didn't want to hurt their slower colleagues, so they reduced their efforts. The study authors suggested a team-based scheme—where everyone's pay increased if the team did well—would be more effective.

ducted a survey of 750 employees across various industries to assess the value they placed on various rewards. Cash and other monetary awards came in dead last. The most valued rewards involved praise and manager support and involvement.[42]

Avoidance Learning. *Avoidance learning* is the removal of an unpleasant consequence following a desired behavior. Avoidance learning is sometimes called *negative reinforcement*. Employees learn to do the right thing by avoiding unpleasant situations.

EXHIBIT 12.6

Changing Behavior with Reinforcement

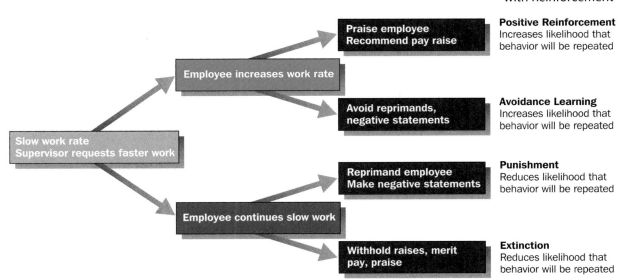

Positive Reinforcement
Increases likelihood that behavior will be repeated

Avoidance Learning
Increases likelihood that behavior will be repeated

Punishment
Reduces likelihood that behavior will be repeated

Extinction
Reduces likelihood that behavior will be repeated

Praise employee
Recommend pay raise

Employee increases work rate

Avoid reprimands, negative statements

Slow work rate
Supervisor requests faster work

Reprimand employee
Make negative statements

Employee continues slow work

Withhold raises, merit pay, praise

SOURCE: Based on Richard L. Daft and Richard M. Steers, *Organizations: A Micro/Macro Approach* (Glenview, IL: Scott, Foresman, 1986): 109.

Avoidance learning occurs when a supervisor stops criticizing or reprimanding an employee after the incorrect behavior has stopped.

Punishment. *Punishment* is the imposition of unpleasant outcomes on an employee. Punishment typically occurs following undesirable behavior. For example, a supervisor may berate an employee for performing a task incorrectly. The supervisor expects that the negative outcome will serve as a punishment and reduce the likelihood of the behavior recurring. The use of punishment in organizations is controversial and often criticized because it fails to indicate the correct behavior. However, almost all managers report that they find it necessary to occasionally impose forms of punishment ranging from verbal reprimands to employee suspensions or firings.[43]

Extinction. *Extinction* is the withdrawal of a positive reward. Whereas with punishment, the supervisor imposes an unpleasant outcome such as a reprimand, extinction involves withholding pay raises, bonuses, praise, or other positive outcomes. The idea is that behavior that is not positively reinforced will be less likely to occur in the future. For example, if a perpetually tardy employee fails to receive praise and pay raises, he or she will begin to realize that the behavior is not producing desired outcomes. The behavior will gradually disappear if it is continually not reinforced.

Executives can use aspects of reinforcement theory to shape employees' behavior. Garry Ridge, CEO of WD-40 Company, which makes the popular lubricant used for everything from loosening bolts to removing scuff marks from floors, wanted to encourage people to talk about their failures so the company could learn from them. He offered prizes to anyone who would e-mail and share their "learning moments," and each respondent would have the chance to win an all-expenses paid vacation. The positive reinforcement, combined with the company's "blame-free" policy, motivated people to share ideas that have helped WD-40 keep learning and growing.[44]

SCHEDULES OF REINFORCEMENT

A great deal of research into reinforcement theory suggests that the timing of reinforcement has an impact on how quickly employees learn and respond with the desired behavior. **Schedules of reinforcement** pertain to the frequency with which and intervals over which reinforcement occurs. A reinforcement schedule can be selected to have maximum impact on employees' job behavior. Five basic types of reinforcement schedules include continuous and four types of partial reinforcement.

Continuous Reinforcement. With a **continuous reinforcement schedule,** every occurrence of the desired behavior is reinforced. This schedule can be especially effective in the early stages of learning new types of behavior because every attempt has a pleasant consequence. Some companies use a continuous reinforcement schedule by offering people cash, game tokens, or points that can be redeemed for prizes each time they perform the desired behavior. LDF Sales & Distributing tried a program called "The Snowfly Slots," developed by management professor Brooks Mitchell, to cut inventory losses. Workers received tokens each time they double-checked the quantity of a shipment. Since it started using Snowfly, the company saved $31,000 a year when inventory losses fell 50 percent. Many companies are developing continuous reinforcement programs so that employees make a clear connection between their behavior and the desired reward.[45]

Partial Reinforcement. However, in the real world of organizations, it is often impossible to reinforce every correct behavior. With a **partial reinforcement schedule,** the reinforcement is administered only after some occurrences of the correct behavior.

schedule of reinforcement
the frequency with which and intervals over which reinforcement occurs.

continuous reinforcement schedule
a schedule in which every occurrence of the desired behavior is reinforced.

partial reinforcement schedule
a schedule in which only some occurrences of the desired behavior are reinforced.

Schedule of Reinforcement	Nature of Reinforcement	Effect on Behavior When Applied	Effect on Behavior When Withdrawn	Example
Continuous	Reward given after each desired behavior	Leads to fast learning of new behavior	Rapid extinction	Praise
Fixed-interval	Reward given at fixed time intervals	Leads to average and irregular performance	Rapid extinction	Weekly paycheck
Fixed-ratio	Reward given at fixed amounts of output	Quickly leads to very high and stable performance	Rapid extinction	Piece-rate pay system
Variable-interval	Reward given at variable times	Leads to moderately high and stable performance	Slow extinction	Performance appraisal and awards given at random times each month
Variable-ratio	Reward given at variable amounts of output	Leads to very high performance	Slow extinction	Sales bonus tied to number of sales calls, with random checks

EXHIBIT 12.7

Schedules of Reinforcement

The schedules of reinforcement are illustrated in Exhibit 12.7. Continuous reinforcement is most effective for establishing new learning, but behavior is vulnerable to extinction. Partial reinforcement schedules are more effective for maintaining behavior over extended time periods. The most powerful is the variable-ratio schedule because employee behavior will persist for a long time due to the random administration of reinforcement only after a long interval.[46]

Reinforcement also works at such organizations as Campbell Soup Co., Emery Air Freight, Emerald Packaging, Michigan Bell, and PSS World Medical because managers reward the desired behaviors. They tell employees what they can do to receive rewards, tell them what they are doing wrong, distribute rewards equitably, tailor rewards to behaviors, and keep in mind that failure to reward deserving behavior has an equally powerful impact on employees.

Reward and punishment motivational practices dominate organizations. According to the Society for Human Resource Management, 84 percent of all companies in the United States offer some type of monetary or nonmonetary reward system, and 69 percent offer incentive pay, such as bonuses, based on an employee's performance.[47] However, in other studies, more than 80 percent of employers with incentive programs have reported that their programs are only somewhat successful or not working at all.[48] Despite the testimonies of organizations that enjoy successful incentive programs, criticism of these "carrot-and-stick" methods is growing, as discussed in the Spotlight on Skills box.

Job Design for Motivation

A *job* in an organization is a unit of work that a single employee is responsible for performing. A job could include writing tickets for parking violators in New York City, performing MRIs at Salt Lake Regional Medical Center, reading meters for Pacific Gas and Electric, or doing long-range planning for The WB Television Network. Jobs are an important consideration for motivation because performing their components may provide rewards that meet employees' needs. An assembly-line worker may install the same bolt over and over, whereas an emergency room physician may provide each trauma victim with a unique treatment package. Managers need to know what aspects of a job provide motivation as well as how to compensate for routine tasks that have little inherent satisfaction. **Job design** is the application of motivational theories to the structure of work for improving

TAKE ACTION

As a new manager, remember reward and punishment practices are extrinsic and only motivate so far, and you need intrinsic rewards too.

TAKE ACTION

As a leader, think about how you can design jobs more effectively to keep your employees more motivated.

job design
the application of motivational theories to the structure of work for improving productivity and satisfaction.

Spotlight on Skills

The Carrot-and-Stick Controversy

Everybody thought Rob Rodin was crazy when he decided to wipe out all individual incentives for his sales force at Marshall Industries, a large distributor of electronic components based in El Monte, California. He did away with all bonuses, commissions, vacations, and other awards and rewards. All salespeople would receive a base salary plus the opportunity for profit sharing, which would be the same percent of salary for everyone, based on the entire company's performance. Six years later, Rodin says productivity per person has tripled at the company, but still he gets questions and criticism about his decision.

Rodin is standing right in the middle of a big controversy in modern management. Do financial and other rewards really motivate the kind of behavior organizations want and need? A growing number of critics say no, arguing that carrot-and-stick approaches are a holdover from the Industrial Age and are inappropriate and ineffective in today's economy. Today's workplace demands innovation and creativity from everyone—behaviors that rarely are inspired by money or other financial incentives. Reasons for criticism of carrot-and-stick approaches include the following:

1. *Extrinsic rewards diminish intrinsic rewards.* When people are motivated to seek an extrinsic reward, whether it be a bonus, an award, or the approval of a supervisor, generally they focus on the reward rather than on the work they do to achieve it. Thus, the intrinsic satisfaction people receive from performing their jobs actually declines. When people lack intrinsic rewards in their work, their performance stays just adequate to achieve the reward offered. In the worst case, employees may cover up mistakes or cheat to achieve the reward. One study found that teachers who were rewarded for increasing test scores frequently used various forms of cheating, for example.

2. *Extrinsic rewards are temporary.* Offering outside incentives may ensure short-term success but not long-term high performance. When employees are focused only on the reward, they lose interest in their work. Without personal interest, the potential for exploration, creativity, and innovation disappears. Although the current deadline or goal may be met, better ways of working and serving customers will not be discovered, and the company's long-term success will be affected.

3. *Extrinsic rewards assume people are driven by lower-level needs.* Rewards such as bonuses, pay increases, and even praise presume that the primary reason people initiate and persist in behavior is to satisfy lower-level needs. However, behavior also is based on yearnings for self-expression and on feelings of self-esteem and self-worth. Typical individual incentive programs don't reflect and encourage the myriad behaviors that are motivated by people's need to express themselves and realize their higher needs for growth and fulfillment.

As Rob Rodin discovered at Marshall Industries, today's organizations need employees who are motivated to think, experiment, and continuously search for ways to solve new problems. Alfie Kohn, one of the most vocal critics of carrot-and-stick approaches, offers the following advice to managers regarding how to pay employees: "Pay well, pay fairly, and then do everything you can to get money off people's minds." Indeed some evidence indicates that money is not primarily what people work for. Managers should understand the limits of extrinsic motivators and work to satisfy employees' higher, as well as lower, needs. To be motivated, employees need jobs that offer self-satisfaction in addition to a yearly pay raise.

SOURCES: Alfie Kohn, "Incentives Can Be Bad for Business," *Inc.* (January 1998): 93–94; A. J. Vogl, "Carrots, Sticks, and Self-Deception" (an interview with Alfie Kohn), *Across the Board* (January 1994): 39–44; Geoffrey Colvin, "What Money Makes You Do," *Fortune* (August 17, 1998): 213–214; and Jeffrey Pfeffer, "Sins of Commission," *Business 2.0* (May 2004): 56.

---

productivity and satisfaction. Approaches to job design are generally classified as job simplification, job rotation, job enlargement, and job enrichment.

JOB SIMPLIFICATION

Job simplification pursues task efficiency by reducing the number of tasks one person must do. Job simplification is based on principles drawn from scientific management and industrial engineering. Tasks are designed to be simple, repetitive, and standardized. As complexity is stripped from a job, the worker has more time to concentrate on doing more of the same routine task. Workers with low skill levels can perform the job, and the organization achieves a high level of efficiency. Indeed, workers are interchangeable because they

job simplification
a job design whose purpose is to improve task efficiency by reducing the number of tasks a single person must do.

need little training or skill and exercise little judgment. As a motivational technique, however, job simplification has failed. People dislike routine and boring jobs and react in a number of negative ways, including sabotage, absenteeism, and unionization.

JOB ROTATION

Job rotation systematically moves employees from one job to another, thereby increasing the number of different tasks an employee performs without increasing the complexity of any one job. For example, an autoworker might install windshields one week and front bumpers the next. Job rotation still takes advantage of engineering efficiencies, but it provides variety and stimulation for employees. Although employees might find the new job interesting at first, the novelty soon wears off as the repetitive work is mastered.

Companies such as The Home Depot, Motorola, 1-800-Flowers, and Dayton Hudson have built on the notion of job rotation to train a flexible workforce. As companies break away from ossified job categories, workers can perform several jobs, thereby reducing labor costs and giving people opportunities to develop new skills. At The Home Depot, for example, workers scattered throughout the company's vast chain of stores can get a taste of the corporate climate by working at in-store support centers, while associate managers can dirty their hands out on the sales floor.[49] Job rotation also gives companies greater flexibility. One production worker might shift among the jobs of drill operator, punch operator, and assembler, depending on the company's need at the moment. Some unions have resisted the idea, but many now go along, realizing that it helps the company be more competitive.[50]

JOB ENLARGEMENT

Job enlargement combines a series of tasks into one new, broader job. This type of design is a response to the dissatisfaction of employees with oversimplified jobs. Instead of only one job, an employee may be responsible for three or four and will have more time to do them. Job enlargement provides job variety and a greater challenge for employees. At Maytag, jobs were enlarged when work was redesigned so that workers assembled an entire water pump rather than doing each part as it reached them on the assembly line. Similarly, rather than just changing the oil at a Precision Tune location, a mechanic changes the oil, greases the car, airs the tires, and checks fluid levels, battery, air filter, and so forth. Then, the same employee is responsible for consulting with the customer about routine maintenance or any problems he or she sees with the vehicle.

JOB ENRICHMENT

Recall the discussion of Maslow's need hierarchy and Herzberg's two-factor theory. Rather than just changing the number and frequency of tasks a worker performs, **job enrichment** incorporates high-level motivators into the work, including job responsibility, recognition, and opportunities for growth, learning, and achievement. In an enriched job, employees have control over the resources necessary for performing it, make decisions on how to do the work, experience personal growth, and set their own work pace. Research shows that when jobs are designed to be controlled more by employees than by managers, people typically feel a greater sense of involvement, commitment, and motivation, which in turn contributes to higher morale, lower turnover, and stronger organizational performance.[51]

Many companies have undertaken job enrichment programs to increase employees' involvement, motivation, and job satisfaction. At Ralcorp's cereal manufacturing plant in Sparks, Nevada, for example, managers

job rotation
a job design that systematically moves employees from one job to another to provide them with variety and stimulation.

job enlargement
a job design that combines a series of tasks into one new, broader job to give employees variety and challenge.

job enrichment
a job design that incorporates achievement, recognition, and other high-level motivators into the work.

CONCEPT CONNECTION

At the Frito-Lay plant in Lubbock, Texas, Julia Garcia used to just pack bags of chips into cardboard cartons. Today, she's interviewing new hires, refusing products that don't meet quality standards, and sending home excess workers if machines shut down. Hourly workers have been enjoying the benefits of **job enlargement** and **job enrichment** since Frito-Lay introduced work teams six years ago. Garcia's 11-member potato chip team is responsible for everything from potato processing to equipment maintenance.

enriched jobs by combining several packing positions into a single job and cross-training employees to operate all of the packing line's equipment. In addition, assembly-line employees screen, interview, and train all new hires. They are responsible for managing the production flow to and from their upstream and downstream partners, making daily decisions that affect their work, managing quality, and contributing to continuous improvement. Enriched jobs have improved employee motivation and satisfaction, and the company has benefited from higher long-term productivity, reduced costs, and happier, more motivated employees.[52]

JOB CHARACTERISTICS MODEL

One significant approach to job design is the job characteristics model developed by Richard Hackman and Greg Oldham.[53] Hackman and Oldham's research concerned **work redesign**, which is defined as altering jobs to increase both the quality of employees' work experience and their productivity. Hackman and Oldham's research into the design of hundreds of jobs yielded the **job characteristics model,** which is illustrated in Exhibit 12.8. The model consists of three major parts: core job dimensions, critical psychological states, and employee growth-need strength.

Core Job Dimensions. Hackman and Oldham identified five dimensions that determine a job's motivational potential:

1. *Skill variety.* The number of diverse activities that compose a job and the number of skills used to perform it. A routine, repetitive assembly-line job is low in variety, whereas an applied research position that entails working on new problems every day is high in variety.

2. *Task identity.* The degree to which an employee performs a total job with a recognizable beginning and ending. A chef who prepares an entire meal has more task identity than a worker on a cafeteria line who ladles mashed potatoes.

3. *Task significance.* The degree to which the job is perceived as important and having impact on the company or consumers. People who distribute penicillin and other medical supplies during times of emergencies would feel they have significant jobs.

4. *Autonomy.* The degree to which the worker has freedom, discretion, and self-determination in planning and carrying out tasks. A house painter can determine how to paint the house; a paint sprayer on an assembly line has little autonomy.

5. *Feedback.* The extent to which doing the job provides information back to the employee about his or her performance. Jobs vary in their ability to let workers see the outcomes of

work redesign
the altering of jobs to increase both the quality of employees' work experience and their productivity.

job characteristics model
a model of job design that comprises core job dimensions, critical psychological states, and employee growth-need strength.

EXHIBIT 12.8

The Job Characteristics Model

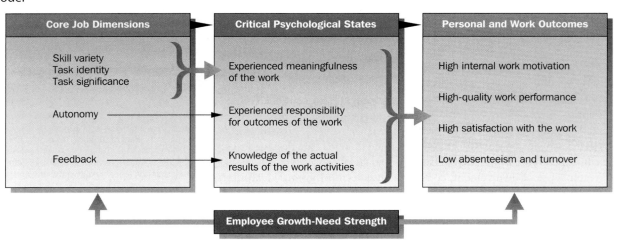

SOURCE: Adapted from J. Richard Hackman and G.R. Oldham, "Motivation through the Design of Work: Test of a Theory," *Organizational Behavior and Human Performance* 16 (1976): 256.

their efforts. A football coach knows whether the team won or lost, but a basic research scientist may have to wait years to learn whether a research project was successful.

The job characteristics model says that the more these five core characteristics can be designed into the job, the more the employees will be motivated and the higher will be performance, quality, and satisfaction.

Critical Psychological States. The model posits that core job dimensions are more rewarding when individuals experience three psychological states in response to job design. In Exhibit 12.8, skill variety, task identity, and task significance tend to influence the employee's psychological state of *experienced meaningfulness of work.* The work itself is satisfying and provides intrinsic rewards for the worker. The job characteristic of autonomy influences the worker's *experienced responsibility.* The job characteristic of feedback provides the worker with *knowledge of actual results.* The employee thus knows how he or she is doing and can change work performance to increase desired outcomes.

Personal and Work Outcomes. The impact of the five job characteristics on the psychological states of experienced meaningfulness, responsibility, and knowledge of actual results leads to the personal and work outcomes of high work motivation, high work performance, high satisfaction, and low absenteeism and turnover.

Employee Growth-Need Strength. The final component of the job characteristics model is called *employee growth-need strength*, which means that people have different needs for growth and development. If a person wants to satisfy low-level needs, such as safety and belongingness, the job characteristics model has less effect. When a person has a high need for growth and development, including the desire for personal challenge, achievement, and challenging work, the model is especially effective. People with a high need to grow and expand their abilities respond favorably to the application of the model and to improvements in core job dimensions.

One interesting finding concerns the cross-cultural differences in the impact of job characteristics. Intrinsic factors such as autonomy, challenge, achievement, and recognition can be highly motivating in countries such as the United States. However, they may contribute little to motivation and satisfaction in a country such as Nigeria, and might even lead to *demotivation.* A recent study indicates that the link between intrinsic characteristics and job motivation and satisfaction is weaker in economically disadvantaged countries with poor governmental social welfare systems, and in high power distance countries, as defined in Chapter 3.[54] Thus, the job characteristics model is expected to be less effective in these countries.

Innovative Ideas for Motivating

Despite the controversy over carrot-and-stick motivational practices discussed in the Spotlight on Skills box earlier in this chapter, organizations are increasingly using various types of incentive compensation as a way to motivate employees to higher levels of performance. Exhibit 12.9 summarizes several popular methods of incentive pay.

Variable compensation and forms of "at risk" pay are key motivational tools and are becoming more common than fixed salaries at many companies. These programs can be effective if they are used appropriately and combined with motivational ideas that also provide employees with intrinsic rewards and meet higher-level needs. Effective managers don't use incentive plans as the sole basis of motivation. At steelmaker Nucor, for example, the amount of money employees and managers take home depends on company profits and how effective the plants are at producing defect-free steel. However, as described in the preceding example, Nucor doesn't rely on incentives alone. The company has created one of the most motivated and dynamic workforces in the United States by meeting people's higher level needs.

 **TAKE ACTION**

Go to the ethical dilemma on page 474 that pertains to the use of incentive compensation as a motivational tool.

EXHIBIT 12.9

New Motivational Compensation Programs

Program	Purpose
Pay for performance	Rewards individual employees in proportion to their performance contributions. Also called *merit pay*.
Gain sharing	Rewards all employees and managers within a business unit when predetermined performance targets are met. Encourages teamwork.
Employee stock ownership plan (ESOP)	Gives employees part ownership of the organization, enabling them to share in improved profit performance.
Lump-sum bonuses	Rewards employees with a one-time cash payment based on performance.
Pay for knowledge	Links employee salary with the number of task skills acquired. Workers are motivated to learn the skills for many jobs, thus increasing company flexibility and efficiency.
Flexible work schedule	*Flextime* allows workers to set their own hours. *Job sharing* allows two or more part-time workers to jointly cover one job. *Telecommuting*, sometimes called *flex-place*, allows employees to work from home or an alternative workplace.
Team-based compensation	Rewards employees for behavior and activities that benefit the team, such as cooperation, listening, and empowering others.
Lifestyle awards	Rewards employees for meeting ambitious goals with luxury items, such as high-definition televisions, tickets to big-name sporting events, and exotic travel.

Some organizations give employees a voice in how pay and incentive systems are designed, which boosts motivation by increasing people's sense of involvement and control.[55] Managers at Premium Standard Farms' pork-processing plant hired a consultant to help slaughterhouse workers design and implement an incentive program. Annual pay-outs to employees in one recent year were around $1,000 per employee. More important, though, is that workers feel a greater sense of dignity and purpose in their jobs, which has helped to reduce turnover significantly. As one employee put it, "Now I have the feeling that this is my company, too."[56] The most effective motivational programs typically involve much more than money or other external rewards. Two recent motivational trends are empowering employees and framing work to have greater meaning.

EMPOWERING PEOPLE TO MEET HIGHER NEEDS

One significant way managers can meet higher motivational needs is to shift power down from the top of the organization and share it with employees to enable them to achieve goals. **Empowerment** is power sharing, the delegation of power or authority to subordinates in an organization.[57] Increasing employee power heightens motivation for task accomplishment because people improve their own effectiveness, choosing how to do a task and using their creativity.[58] Most people come into an organization with the desire to do a good job, and empowerment releases the motivation that is already there. Research indicates that most people have a need for *self-efficacy*, which is the capacity to produce results or outcomes to feel that they are effective.[59] By meeting this higher-level need, empowerment can provide powerful motivation.

Empowering employees involves giving them four elements that enable them to act more freely to accomplish their jobs: information, knowledge, power, and rewards.[60]

1. *Employees receive information about company performance.* In companies where employees are fully empowered, all employees have access to all financial and operational information. At Reflexite Corporation, for example, which is largely owned by employees,

empowerment
the delegation of power and authority to subordinates.

**Nucor: Giving
People a Stake
in the Business**

ince Daniel R. DiMicco took over as CEO of Nucor in 2000, sales jumped from $4.6 billion to $12.7 billion in 2005, income grew from $311 million to $1.3 billion for the same period, and the company shipped more steel in 2005 than any other company in the United States. Yet DiMicco, a 23-year veteran of Nucor, keeps everyone focused on long-term success, not short-term results. Nucor's goal is to be "the safest, highest quality, lowest cost, most productive, and most profitable steel-products company in the world," he says. To realize that goal, the Charlotte, North Carolina-based mini mill follows the path blazed by its legendary CEO, the late F. Kenneth Iverson. Iverson's employee-centered, egalitarian management philosophy helped the floundering company he inherited in 1965 not only survive the implosion of the U.S. steel industry that began in the 1970s but also emerge as one of the largest, most profitable steel producers in the country. Under his leadership, Nucor created an empowered workforce and devised a radical, performance-based compensation system.

Nucor searches for job candidates with an entrepreneurial bent. Once hired, the nonunionized workers join teams in a decentralized, flattened, four-level organization. With most decision-making authority pushed down to the division level, employees run their part of the business as if it were their own. Managers continue to practice Iverson's approach: "Instead of telling people what to do and then hounding them to do it, our managers focus on shaping an environment that frees employees to determine what they can do and should do, to the benefit of themselves and the business. We've found that their answers drive the progress of our business faster than our own."

Under Nucor's performance-based compensation system, all employees, from the CEO on down, have both responsibility for performance and an unusual chance to share in corporate wealth. Essentially, as Iverson explained, "The more they produce, the more they earn. They have a simple stake in the business." Nucor measures performance in clear-cut ways. For the rank and file, Nucor determines productivity weekly by measuring defect-free steel output against plant equipment capabilities. For department managers, professional, and clerical personnel, the company gauges performance against return on assets; for senior executives, it looks at annual return on equity. Although base pay at Nucor is relatively low, weekly bonuses based on production can average 80 to 150 percent of a steelworker's base pay, and a manager's annual bonus can amount to roughly 80 percent of his or her salary. Even though base pay starts at about $10 an hour, for example, the average Nucor steelworker took home approximately $100,000 in 2005. In a bad year, everyone—the CEO included—shares the pain. In addition, because a plant manager's bonus depends on the entire corporation's performance, the system fosters a companywide team mind-set.

The results speak for themselves. Nucor led the United States in steel shipments in 2005 as well as boasted a five-year 387 percent return on equity and 7 to 10 percent profit margins. And it accomplishes these achievements with a work environment that longtime employees (including engineers, not usually given to flights of fancy) have called magical.

SOURCES: Nanette Byrnes with Michael Arndt, "The Art of Motivation," *BusinessWeek* (May 1, 2006): 57; "About Us," www.nucor.com/indexinner.aspx?finpage= aboutus (accessed June 20, 2006); Patricia Panchak, "Putting Employees First Pays Off," *Industry Week* (June 2002): 14; and "Nucor CEO: Instill Your Culture, Empower Workers to Reach Goal," *Charlotte Business Journal* (November 22, 2002), http://charlotte.bizjournals.com/charlotte/stories/2002/11/25/editorial2.

managers sit down each month to analyze data related to operational and financial performance and then share the results with employees throughout the company. In addition to these monthly updates, employees have access to any information about the company at any time they want or need it.[61]

2. *Employees have knowledge and skills to contribute to company goals.* Companies use training programs to help employees acquire the knowledge and skills they need to contribute to organizational performance. For example, when DMC, which makes pet supplies, gave employee teams the authority and responsibility for assembly-line shutdowns, it provided extensive training on how to diagnose and interpret line malfunctions, as well as data related to the costs of shutdown and start-up. People worked through several case studies to practice decision making related to line shutdowns.[62]

3. *Employees have the power to make substantive decisions.* Empowered employees have the authority to directly influence work procedures and organizational performance, such as through quality circles or self-directed work teams. At Venezuela's Aluminio del Caroní,

employees participate in roundtable discussions and make recommendations to management regarding new equipment purchases or other operational matters. In addition, workers vote to elect managers and board members.[63] The Brazilian manufacturer Semco pushes empowerment to the limits by allowing its employees to choose what they do, how they do it, and even how they get compensated for it. Many employees set their own pay by choosing from a list of 11 different pay options, such as a set salary or a combination of salary and incentives.[64]

4. *Employees are rewarded based on company performance.* Organizations that empower workers often reward them based on the results shown in the company's bottom line. For example, at Semco, in addition to employee-determined compensation, a company profit-sharing plan gives each employee an even share of 23 percent of his or her department's profits each quarter.[65] Organizations may also use other motivational compensation programs described in Exhibit 12.9 to tie employee efforts to company performance.

Many of today's organizations are implementing empowerment programs, but they are empowering workers to varying degrees. At some companies, empowerment means encouraging workers' ideas while managers retain final authority for decisions; at others it means giving employees almost complete freedom and power to make decisions and exercise initiative and imagination.[66] Current methods of empowerment fall along a continuum, as illustrated in Exhibit 12.10. The continuum runs from a situation in which front-line

EXHIBIT 12.10

A Continuum of Empowerment

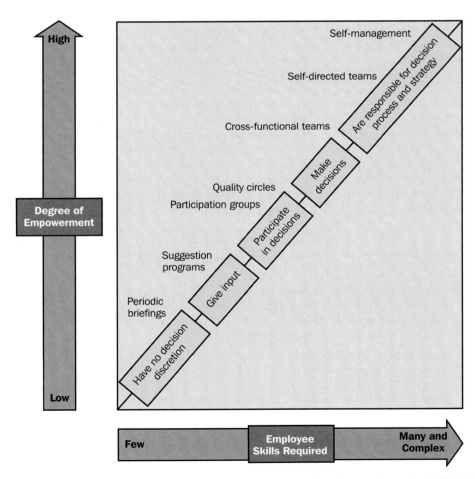

SOURCES: Based on Robert C. Ford and Myron D. Fottler, "Empowerment: A Matter of Degree," *Academy of Managment Executive 9*, no. 3 (1995): 21–31; Lawrence Holpp, "Applied Empowerment," *Training* (February 1994): 39–44; and David P. McCaffrey, Sue R. Faerman, and David W. Hart, "The Appeal and Difficulties of Participative Systems," *Organization Science 6*, no. 6 (November–December 1995): 603–627.

workers have almost no discretion, such as on a traditional assembly line, to full empowerment, where workers even participate in formulating organizational strategy. Studies indicate that higher-level empowerment programs, where employees have input and decision-making power related to both everyday operational issues and higher-level strategic decisions, are still relatively rare.[67]

GIVING MEANING TO WORK

Another way to meet higher-level motivational needs and help people get intrinsic rewards from their work is to instill a sense of importance and meaningfulness. *Fortune* magazine finds that one of the primary characteristics shared by companies on its annual list of "The 100 Best Companies to Work For" is that they are *purpose-driven*, that is, people have a sense that what they are doing matters and makes a positive difference in the world.[68] Consider the motivation of employees at Patagonia, which has been a frequent inhabitant of that yearly list.

It is easy to understand why employees at Patagonia feel they are serving an important cause. But managers in any organization can tap into people's desire to contribute and make a difference. Former Coca-Cola CEO Roberto Goizueta spent a lot of time talking to employees about the company's charitable work and emphasized that millions of small merchants could make a living because they sold Coca-Cola. Employees at FedEx take pride in getting people the items they need on time, whether it is a work report that is due, a passport for a holiday trip to Jamaica, or an emergency order of medical supplies.[69]

Another example is Les Schwab Tire Centers, where employees feel like partners united toward a goal of making people's lives easier. Stores fix flats for free, and some have been known to install tires hours before opening time for an emergency trip. Employees frequently stop to help stranded motorists. Schwab rewards people with a generous profit-sharing plan for everyone and promotes store managers solely from within. However, these external rewards only supplement, not create, the high motivation employees feel.[70]

Benchmarking

Patagonia

Even with two MBAs and a coveted internship in Europe, when Californian Scott Robinson returned from France, he rejected chances for well-paying corporate jobs and instead *begged* for a job as a stock handler at outdoor-clothing and equipment manufacturer Patagonia Inc. "I wanted to work for a company that's driven by values," he said simply. When he got back home, he read *Let My People go Surfing*, part memoir, part manifesto, by Patagonia's founder Yvon Chouinard, whose goal for the company is "to produce the highest-quality products while doing the least possible harm to the environment." This mission is a constant inspiration for all of Patagonia's 1,274 employees, all the way from Chouinard to the headquarters' receptionist, a guy who wears flip-flops. The mission guides every decision and management practice. Says the founder, "Most people want to do good things, but don't. At Patagonia, it's an essential part of your life."

Rather than being fear-based or mainly making employees feel good, Patagonia embraces a fourth way: stressing continuous improvement to become much better than the competition, as well as making employees feel comfortable. In Patagonia's 39 stores (in seven countries) and its headquarters, it offers on-site day care, full health insurance even to part-timers, and, when the surf is up, Chouinard encourages people to hit the beach. And people get fired who aren't up to the task. Chouinard sees outdoor activities as essential for employees, as they are either testing equipment or coming up with improvements. Yet, the company also demands creativity, collaboration, hard work, and results.

No one works there for the money, as pay rates are just barely above market rate. One of the best rewards, though, is a full-pay program allowing employees to take two months off to work for environmental groups. The culture is a magnet for top talent, and they get about 900 resumes for each job opening. The reason is simple, as described by one worker: "It's easy to go to work when you get paid to do what you love to do."

SOURCE: Steve Hamm, "A Passion for the Plan," *BusinessWeek* (August 21/28, 2006): 92–94.

In recent years, managers have focused on employee *engagement*, which has less to do with extrinsic rewards such as pay and much more to do with fostering an environment in which people can flourish. Engaged employees are more satisfied and motivated because they feel appreciated by their supervisors and the organization, and they thrive on work challenges rather than feeling frustrated by them.[71] Engaged employees are motivated, enthusiastic, and committed employees. In addition, there is a growing recognition that it is the behavior of managers that makes the biggest difference in whether people feel engaged at work. When David A. Brandon took over as CEO of Domino's Pizza, he commissioned research to identify the factors that contributed to a store's success. What he learned was that the quality of the manager and how he or she treats employees has a much greater impact than neighborhood demographics, packaging, marketing, or other factors.[72] Indeed, a Gallup Organization study conducted over 25 years found that the single most important variable in whether employees feel good about their work is the relationship between employees and their direct supervisors.[73]

The role of today's manager is not to control others but to organize the workplace in such a way that each person can learn, contribute, and grow. Good managers channel employee motivation toward the accomplishment of organizational goals by tapping into each individual's unique set of talents, skills, interests, attitudes, and needs. By treating each employee as an individual, managers can put people in the right jobs and provide intrinsic rewards to every employee every day. Then, managers make sure people have what they need to perform, clearly define the desired outcomes, and get out of the way.

One way to evaluate how a manager or a company is doing in engaging employees by meeting higher-level needs is a metric developed by the Gallup researchers called the Q12. When a majority of employees can answer these 12 questions positively, the organization enjoys a highly motivated and productive workforce:

1. Do I know what is expected of me at work?
2. Do I have the materials and equipment that I need to do my work right?
3. At work, do I have the opportunity to do what I do best every day?
4. In the past seven days, have I received recognition or praise for doing good work?
5. Does my supervisor, or someone at work, seem to care about me as a person?
6. Is there someone at work who encourages my development?
7. At work, do my opinions seem to count?
8. Does the mission or purpose of my company make me feel that my job is important?
9. Are my co-workers committed to doing quality work?
10. Do I have a best friend at work?
11. In the past six months, has someone at work talked to me about my progress?
12. This past year, have I had opportunities to learn and grow?[74]

Results of the Gallup study show that organizations where employees give high marks on the Q12 have less turnover, are more productive and profitable, and enjoy greater employee and customer loyalty.[75] Many companies have used the Q12 to pinpoint problems with motivation in the organization. Best Buy, for example, uses the survey and includes employee engagement as a key item on each manager's scorecard. Eric Taverna, the general manager of a Best Buy store in Manchester, Connecticut, took to heart the finding that his employees didn't think their opinions mattered. Taverna responded by implementing significant changes based on employee ideas and suggestions. The Manchester store's engagement levels improved significantly, as did the store's financial performance, while turnover has been substantially reduced.[76] When employees are more engaged and motivated, they—and their organizations—thrive.

Summary

This chapter introduced a number of important ideas about the motivation of people in organizations. Rewards are of two types: intrinsic rewards that result from the satisfactions a person receives in the process of performing a job, and extrinsic rewards such as promotions that are given by another person. Managers work to help employees receive both intrinsic and extrinsic rewards from their jobs. The content theories of motivation focus on the nature of underlying employee needs. Maslow's hierarchy of needs, Alderfer's ERG theory, Herzberg's two-factor theory, and McClelland's acquired needs theory all suggest that people are motivated to meet a range of needs. Process theories examine how people go about selecting rewards with which to meet needs. Equity theory says that people compare their contributions and outcomes with others' and are motivated to maintain a feeling of equity. Expectancy theory suggests that people calculate the probability of achieving certain outcomes. Managers can increase motivation by treating employees fairly and by clarifying employee paths toward meeting their needs. Goal-setting theory indicates that employees are more motivated if they have clear, specific

goals and receive regular feedback concerning their progress toward meeting goals. Still another motivational approach is reinforcement theory, which says that employees learn to behave in certain ways based on the use of reinforcements.

The application of motivational ideas is illustrated in job design and other motivational programs. Job design approaches include job simplification, job rotation, job enlargement, job enrichment, and the job characteristics model. Managers can change the structure of work to meet employees' high-level needs. The recent trend toward empowerment motivates by giving employees more information and authority to make decisions in their work while connecting compensation to the results. Managers can instill employees with a sense of importance and meaningfulness to help them reap intrinsic rewards and meet higher-level needs for esteem and self-fulfillment. Managers create the environment that determines employee motivation. One way to measure the factors that determine whether people have high levels of engagement and motivation is the Q12, a list of 12 questions about the day-to-day realities of a person's job.

Discussion Questions

1. In response to security threats in today's world, the U.S. government federalized airport security workers. Many argued that simply making screeners federal workers would not solve the root problem: bored, low-paid, and poorly trained security workers have little motivation to be vigilant. How might these employees be motivated to provide the security that travel conditions now demand?

2. One small company recognizes an employee of the month, who is given a parking spot next to the president's space near the front door. What theories would explain the positive motivation associated with this policy?

3. Campbell Soup Company reduces accidents with a lottery. Each worker who works 30 days or more without losing a day for a job-related accident is eligible to win prizes in a raffle drawing. Why has this program been successful?

4. If an experienced secretary discovered that she made less money than a newly hired janitor, how would she react? What inputs and outcomes might she evaluate to make this comparison?

5. What intrinsic rewards do you experience in your role as a student? Extrinsic rewards? Are intrinsic or extrinsic rewards generally more important motivators for you?

6. Would you rather work for a supervisor high in need for achievement, need for affiliation, or need for power? Why? What are the advantages and disadvantages of each?

7. A survey of teachers found that two of the most important rewards were the belief that their work was important and a feeling of accomplishment. Is this consistent with Hackman and Oldham's job characteristics model? Explain.

8. The teachers in question 7 also reported that pay and benefits were poor, yet they continue to teach. Use Herzberg's two-factor theory to explain this finding.

9. What theories explain why employees who score high on the Q12 questionnaire are typically highly motivated and productive?

10. How can empowerment lead to higher motivation? Could a manager's empowerment efforts sometimes contribute to demotivation as well? Discuss.

11. Why might intrinsic factors such as achievement and recognition be less motivating in a poor country such as Nigeria than they are in the United States?

Dear Dr. Dorothy

The other supervisors and myself go out to lunch together every week or so. It's time well spent because we not only resolve some work issues, but it also gives us time to bond. Because I am the newest one, I am still trying to figure out how everything works and what the norms are. The first time we went, they decided to go to a rather expensive restaurant, so I only ordered a cup of soup. I am still paying off student loans, so I have to watch every penny. Everyone else was ordering the most expensive items on the list, including $45 glasses of wine. When I saw what they were ordering, I couldn't imagine spending that much on one meal. Then the waiter came and asked if we wanted separate checks. Being the newest one, I did what I learned and observed others. Imagine my surprise when the ones who had ordered the priciest selections called out, "One check please, we'll just split it evenly." At the next outing, I ordered like everyone else, only this time they asked for separate checks. I've figured out they mostly (though not always) do the shared costs when two particular people are there and when we eat at expensive places. It's really important that I go to these lunches, but I can't afford those high-flying days, and it's nerve-wracking not to know which is which. What should I do?

Broke in Tacumseh

Dear Broke,

It wouldn't be so bad if you could predict which type of payment was coming which day, but this group has too many loose cantaloupes. You are on the wrong end of equity theory here, as there is little fairness in how the payment system operates. If you were all equals—which in theory you are, as managers of similar rank, but as the newest person, you are still no doubt low on the totem-pole—Dr. Dorothy would recommend you bring it up to the group. In this case, though, what would happen is the higher-ranking (socially, though Dr. Dorothy believes they must really be low in class), free-spending loose cannons would dominate the conversation, eloquently explaining why their method is more sensible (even if it really makes no sense at all). Therefore, you should go to one person whom you trust, who likes and respects you, and who is respected by this group, and you should calmly and matter-of-factly share your concerns. Dr. Dorothy cautions you not to get overheated during this explanation. Then ask the trusted colleague for advice and, if it feels appropriate, you could ask this person to bring the topic up with some of the others, people you don't feel as close to, while you talk to the ones you are comfortable with. Because this nonequitable practice has been going on for a while, and because your group has what Dr. Dorothy thinks are bullies in sheep's clothing, this is definitely not a topic to bring up in the entire group. That is, until you do your networking. Remember decision-making theory. This is not a G2 decision. But Dr. Dorothy speaks with confidence that this is a gee-whiz situation.

Self Learning

What Motivates You?

Indicate how important each characteristic is to you. Answer according to your feelings about the most recent job you had or about the job you currently hold. Circle the number on the scale that represents your feeling—1 (very unimportant) to 7 (very important).

1. The feeling of self-esteem a person gets from being in that job
   1 2 3 4 5 6 7

2. The opportunity for personal growth and development in that job
   1 2 3 4 5 6 7

3. The prestige of the job inside the company (i.e., regard received from others in the company)
   1 2 3 4 5 6 7

4. The opportunity for independent thought and action in that job
   1 2 3 4 5 6 7

5. The feeling of security in that job
   1 2 3 4 5 6 7

6. The feeling of self-fulfillment a person gets from being in that position (i.e., the feeling of being able to use one's own unique capabilities, realizing one's potential)
   1 2 3 4 5 6 7

7. The prestige of the job outside the company (i.e., the regard received from others not in the company)

1 2 3 4 5 6 7

8. The feeling of worthwhile accomplishment in that job

1 2 3 4 5 6 7

9. The opportunity in that job to give help to other people

1 2 3 4 5 6 7

10. The opportunity in that job for participation in the setting of goals

1 2 3 4 5 6 7

11. The opportunity in that job for participation in the determination of methods and procedures

1 2 3 4 5 6 7

12. The authority connected with the job

1 2 3 4 5 6 7

13. The opportunity to develop close friendships in the job

1 2 3 4 5 6 7

Scoring and Interpretation

Score the exercise as follows to determine what motivates you:

Rating for question 5 = _____.
Divide by 1 = _____ security.
Rating for questions 9 and 13 = _____.
Divide by 2 = _____ social.
Rating for questions 1, 3, and 7 = _____.
Divide by 3 = _____ esteem.
Rating for questions 4, 10, 11, and 12 = _____.
Divide by 4 = _____ autonomy.
Rating for questions 2, 6, and 8 = _____.
Divide by 3 = _____ self-actualization.

Your instructor has national norm scores for presidents, vice presidents, and upper middle-level, lower middle-level, and lower-level managers with which you can compare your mean importance scores. How do your scores compare with the scores of managers working in organizations?

SOURCE: Lyman W. Porter, *Organizational Patterns of Managerial Job Attitudes* (New York: American Foundation for Management Research, 1964): 17, 19. Used with permission.

Group Learning

Work vs. Play

1. Form groups of three to four members. Answer this question: What drives you to expend energy on a play activity? For leisure, why do you choose the activities you do? (Don't discuss the particular activities but rather *why* you choose them.) Select one of your group members as presenter.

2. Each group presents its main points to the class. The instructor will draw on the board a table, similar to the following, based on information from the class presentations.

Activities	Outcome #1	Outcome #2	Outcome #3	Outcome #4	Outcome #5	Outcome #6
Example: #1 Soccer	high-energy	team-bonding	fitness			
#2						
#3						
#4						

3. Questions for class discussion:
    a. How can you build some of these motives for play into a work environment?
    b. What prevents you from making work more intrinsically motivating, as play is?

c. Which motivation theories are relevant here?

SOURCE: Developed by Phil Anderson, University of St. Thomas, Minneapolis. Used with permission.

Action Learning

1. Interview four people who've had at least three jobs (maybe part-time) in their lives.

2. Ask them which jobs they liked the best, at which did they work the hardest. Why did they like that job, and why did they work harder?

3. Try to find patterns in the answers of the four people. Compare your outcomes to the motivation theories in this chapter. Which theories are confirmed or disconfirmed based on your interviews?

4. Your instructor may ask you to write a report on your findings, or meet in small groups to discuss patterns among all the interviewees. You may then be asked to either present your findings in class and/or write a group report.

Ethical Dilemma

To Renege or Not to Renege?

Federico Garcia, vice president of sales for Tacoma, Washington-based Puget Sound Building Materials, wasn't all that surprised by what company president Michael Otto and CFO James Wilson had to say during their meeting that morning.

Last year, launching a major expansion made sense to everyone at Puget, a well-established company that provided building materials as well as manufacturing and installation services to residential builders in the Washington and Oregon markets. Puget looked at the record new housing starts and decided it was time to move into the California and Arizona markets, especially concentrating on San Diego and Phoenix, two of the hottest housing markets in the country. Federico carefully hired promising new sales representatives and offered them hefty bonuses if they reached the goals set for the new territory over the next 12 months. All of the representatives had performed well, and three of them had exceeded Puget's goal—and then some. The incentive system he'd put in place had worked well. The sales reps were expecting handsome bonuses for their hard work.

Early on, however, it became all too clear that Puget had seriously underestimated the time it took to build new business relationships and the costs associated with the expansion, a mistake that was already eating into profit margins. Even more distressing were the most recent figures for new housing starts, which were heading in the wrong direction. As Michael said, "Granted, it's too early to tell if this is just a pause or the start of a real long-term downturn. But I'm worried. If things get worse, Puget could be in real trouble."

James looked at Federico and said, "Our lawyers built enough contingency clauses into the sales reps' contracts that we're not really obligated to pay those bonuses you promised. What would you think about not paying them?" Federico turned to the president, who said, "Why don't you think about it, and get back to us with a recommendation?"

Federico felt torn. On the one hand, he knew the CFO was correct. Puget wasn't, strictly speaking, under any legal obligation to pay out the bonuses, and the eroding profit margins were a genuine cause for concern. The president clearly wanted to not pay the bonuses. But Federico had created a first-rate sales force that had done exactly what he'd asked them to do. He prided himself on being a man of his word, someone others could trust. Could he go back on his promises?

What Would You Do?

1. Recommend to the president that a meeting be arranged with the sales representatives entitled to a bonus and tell them that their checks are going to be delayed until Puget's financial picture clarifies. The sales reps would be told that the company has a legal right to delay payment and that it may not be able to pay the bonuses if its financial situation continues to deteriorate.

2. Recommend a meeting with the sales representatives entitled to a bonus and tell them the company's deteriorating financial situation triggers one of the contingency clauses in their contract so that the company won't be issuing their bonus checks. Puget will just

have to deal with the negative impact on sales rep motivation.

3. Recommend strongly to the president that Puget pay the bonuses as promised. The legal contracts and financial situation don't matter. Be prepared to resign if the bonuses are not paid as you promised.

Your word and a motivated sales team mean everything to you.

SOURCE: Based on Doug Wallace, "The Company Simply Refused to Pay," *Business Ethics* (March–April 2000): 18; and Adam Shell, "Over-Heated Housing Market Is Cooling," *USA Today* (November 2, 2005), www.usatoday.com/money/economy/housing/2005-11-01-real-estate-usat_x.htm.

Case for Critical Analysis

Kimbel's Department Store

Frances Patterson, Kimbel's CEO, looked at the latest "Sales by Manager" figures on her daily Web-based sales report. What did these up-to-the-minute numbers tell her about the results of Kimbel's trial of straight commission pay for its salespeople?

A regional chain of upscale department stores based in St. Louis, Kimbel's faces the challenge shared by most department stores these days: how to stop losing share of overall retail sales to discount store chains. A key component of the strategy the company formulated to counter this long-term trend is the revival of great customer service on the floor, once a hallmark of upscale stores. Frances knows Kimbel's has its work cut out for it. When she dropped in on several stores incognito a few years ago, she was dismayed to discover that finding a salesperson actively engaged with a customer was rare. In fact, finding a salesperson when a customer wanted to pay for an item was often difficult.

About a year and a half ago, the CEO read about a quiet revolution sweeping department store retailing. At stores such as Bloomingdale's and Bergdorf Goodman, managers put all salespeople on straight commission. Frances decided to give the system a year-long try in two area stores.

Such a plan, she reasoned, would be good for Kimbel's if it lived up to its promise of attracting better salespeople, improving their motivation, and making them more customer-oriented. It could also potentially be good for employees. Salespeople in departments such as electronics, appliances, and jewelry, where expertise and highly personalized services paid off, had long worked solely on commission. But the majority of employees earn an hourly wage plus a meager 0.5 percent commission on total sales. Under the new scheme, all employees earn a 7 percent commission on sales. When she compared the two systems, she saw that a new salesclerk in women's wear would earn $35,000 on $500,000 in sales, as opposed to only $18,000 under the old scheme.

Now, with the trial period about to end, Frances notes that while overall sales in the two stores have increased

modestly, so also has employee turnover. When the CEO examined the sales-by-manager figures, it was obvious that some associates had thrived and others had not. Most fell somewhere in the middle.

For example, Juan Santore is enthusiastic about the change—and for good reason. He works in women's designer shoes and handbags, where a single item can cost upwards of $1,000. Motivated largely by the desire to make lots of money, he's a personable, outgoing individual with an entrepreneurial streak. Ever since the straight commission plan took effect, he has put even more time and effort into cultivating relationships with wealthy customers, and it shows. His pay has increased an average of $150 per week.

It's a different story in the lingerie department, where even luxury items have more modest price tags. The lingerie department head, Gladys Weinholtz, said salespeople in her department are demoralized. Several valued employees had quit, and most miss the security of a salary. No matter how hard they work, they cannot match their previous earnings. "Yes, they're paying more attention to customers," conceded Gladys, "but they're so anxious about making ends meet, they tend to pounce on the poor women who wander into the department." Furthermore, lingerie sales associates are giving short shrift to duties such as handling complaints or returns that don't immediately translate into sales. "And boy, do they ever resent the sales superstars in the other departments," said Gladys.

The year is nearly up. It's time to decide. Should Frances declare the straight commission experiment a success on the whole and roll it out across the chain over the next six months?

Questions

1. What theories about motivation underlie the switch from salary to commission pay?

2. What needs are met under the commission system? Are they the same needs in the shoes and handbag department as they are in lingerie? Explain.

3. If you were Frances Patterson, would you go back to the previous compensation system, implement the straight commission plan in all Kimbel's stores, or devise and test some other compensation method? If you decided to test another system, what would it look like?

SOURCES: Based on Cynthia Kyle, "Commissions question—to pay . . . or not to pay?" *Michigan Retailer* (March 2003), www.retailers.com/news/retailers/03mar/mr0303commissions.html; "Opinion: Effective Retail Sales Compensation," *Furniture World Magazine* (March 7, 2006), www.furninfo.com/absolutenm/templates/NewsFeed.asp?articleid=6017; Terry Pristin, "Retailing's Elite Keep the Armani Moving Off the Racks," *The New York Times* (December 22, 2001): D1; Francine Schwadel, "Chain Finds Incentives a Hard Sell," *Wall Street Journal* (July 5, 1990): B4; and Amy Dunkin, "Now Salespeople Really Must Sell for Their Supper," *BusinessWeek* (July 31, 1989): 50–52.

BIZ FLIX

For Love of the Game

Billy Chapel (Kevin Costner), a 20-year veteran pitcher with the Detroit Tigers, learns just before the season's last game that the team's new owners want to trade him. He also learns that his partner Jane Aubrey (Kelly Preston) intends to leave him. Faced with these daunting blows, Chapel wants to pitch a perfect final game. Director Sam Raimi's love of baseball shines through in some striking visual effects.

This scene is a slightly edited version of the "Just Throw" sequence, which begins the film's exciting closing scenes in which Chapel pitches his last game. In this scene, the Tigers' catcher Gus Sinski (John C. Reilly) comes out to the pitching mound to talk to Billy.

What to Watch for and Ask Yourself

1. What is Billy Chapel's level of esteem needs at this point in the game?

2. Do you expect Gus Sinski's talk to have any effect on Chapel? If it will, what will be the effect?

3. What rewards potentially exist for Billy Chapel? Remember, this is the last baseball game of his career.

VIDEO CASE

Motivation at Washburn Guitar

"It's a labor of love," said Gil Vasquez, Washburn Guitar production manager.

"It's a piece of art," says Eric Karol, Washburn floor manager. "I tell them to treat each guitar they're working on like they're making it for themselves."

"I would say 95% of the employees that work at U.S. Music (parent of Washburn Guitar) play an instrument and it really improves the quality of all of our instruments because they have a passion for what they are doing." said Kevin Lello, Washburn Guitar VP of marketing.

Having a motivated workforce is essential because guitar making is labor intensive, and requires attention to detail. Quality materials combined with quality craftsmanship are necessary to produce quality guitars. The Washburn Guitar workforce is motivated because they love music and care about the instruments.

Founded in the late 1800s in Chicago, Washburn boasts a rich tradition of fine instrument making. Today they sell more than 50,000 guitars annually, totaling about $40 million in revenue. Washburn Guitar produces a wide variety of acoustic and electric guitars.

Over the years an impressive list of artists have played Washburn guitars, including: Greg Allman, George Harrison, and Robert Plant. Today, Washburn artists include members of Weezer, Rascal Flats, Fall Out Boy, All American Rejects, and Modest Yahoo. Washburn also produces signature guitars for leading guitarists. For example, Washburn's Maya Pro DD75 is made for Dan Donegan, the lead guitarist for Disturbed, a popular hard-rock band.

Signature models like the Maya Pro confirm Washburn's capability for producing quality and style. It also strengthens Washburn's relationship with Dan Donegan, his band Disturbed, and their huge fan base. It also motivates their staff. Employees get more satisfaction out of creating these special guitars.

"Some are motivated by the fact of music, and some are motivated by being able to work on an instrument." Gil Vasquez says "One of the biggest motivational factors for me is when you're done with a guitar . . . you've taken it from the drawing board to the manufacturing point, given it to the artist . . . watching him play it on stage, it's like validation."

Washburn craftsman also enjoy making custom guitars. In recent years their custom shop production has grown dramatically from 20 guitars per month to 300 guitars per month.

Questions

1. What motivates most Washburn Guitar employees?
2. What kinds of guitars do employees most like to produce?
3. What is the connection between quality guitars and work-force motivation?

chapter 13

Communication

Learning Objectives

After studying this chapter, you should be able to:

1. Explain why communication is essential for effective management and describe how nonverbal behavior and listening affect communication among people.

2. Explain how managers use communication to persuade and influence others.

3. Describe the concept of channel richness, and explain how communication channels influence the quality of communication.

4. Explain the difference between formal and informal organizational communications and the importance of each for organization management.

5. Identify how structure influences team communication outcomes.

6. Explain why open communication, dialogue, and feedback are essential approaches to communication in a turbulent environment.

7. Identify the skills managers need for communicating during a crisis situation.

8. Describe barriers to organizational communication, and suggest ways to avoid or overcome them.

New Manager's Questions

Please circle your opinion below each of the following statements.

Assess Your Answer

1 Most communication is really rather simple.

1	2	3	4	5

strongly agree   strongly disagree

2 E-mailing is an efficient and effective tool for communicating.

1	2	3	4	5

strongly agree   strongly disagree

3 People are generally good listeners.

1	2	3	4	5

strongly agree   strongly disagree

Effective communication, both within the organization and with people outside the company, is a major challenge and responsibility for managers. Although in most companies, poor communication doesn't risk people's lives, as it does in hospital operating rooms, ineffective communication can cause significant problems, including poor employee morale, lack of innovation, decreased performance, and a failure to respond to new threats or opportunities in the environment. Many managers are trying to improve their communications knowledge and skills.

To stay connected with employees and customers and shape company direction, managers must excel at personal communications. At Dallas-based Brinker International, CEO Doug Brooks set up numerous processes to make sure he stays in touch with employees, including surveys, leadership discussion groups, and small quality circles that involve people from all levels of the company. Guidant Corporation, now owned by Eli Lilly, has a "reverse mentoring" program in which each top manager is assigned a mentor from lower organizational levels to help them stay in touch with what's going on in the organization. James E. Rogers, CEO of Cinergy Corp., encourages employees to send him e-mails, and he reads every one. They often alert him to such issues as festering problems in the organization, what the competition is doing, or pending legislation that could affect energy prices. Rogers is by no means alone. A survey for the *Wall Street Journal* found that 39 out of 44 companies responding said their CEOs personally read and answer employees' e-mails.[1]

Nonmanagers often are amazed at how much energy successful executives put into communication. Consider the comment about Robert Strauss, former chairman of the Democratic National Committee and former ambassador to Russia:

> One of his friends says, "His network is everywhere. It ranges from bookies to bank presidents. . . ."

TAKE ACTION ▶

As a manager, keep in touch with all your employees, find out what's going on, and learn to listen.

He seems to find time to make innumerable phone calls to "keep in touch"; he cultivates secretaries as well as senators; he will befriend a middle-level White House aide whom other important officials won't bother with. Every few months, he sends candy to the White House switchboard operators.[2]

This chapter explains why executives such as Robert Strauss, Doug Brooks, and James Rogers are effective communicators. First, we examine communication as a crucial part of the manager's job and describe a model of the communication process. Next, we consider the interpersonal aspects of communication, including communication channels, persuasion, listening skills, and nonverbal communication that affect managers' abilities to communicate. Then, we look at the organization as a whole and consider formal upward, downward, and horizontal communications as well as personal networks and informal communications. We discuss the importance of keeping multiple channels of communication open and examine how managers can effectively communicate during times of turbulence, uncertainty, and crisis. Finally, we examine barriers to communication and how managers can overcome them.

Communication and the Manager's Job

How important is communication? Consider this: Managers spend at least 80 percent of every working day in direct communication with others. In other words, 48 minutes of every hour is spent in meetings, on the telephone, communicating online, or talking informally while walking around. The other 20 percent of a typical manager's time is spent doing desk work, most of which is also communication in the form of reading and writing.[3]

Exhibit 13.1 illustrates the crucial role of managers as communication champions. Managers gather important information from both inside and outside the organization and then distribute appropriate information to others who need it. Managers' communication is *purpose-directed,* in that it directs everyone's attention toward the vision, values, and

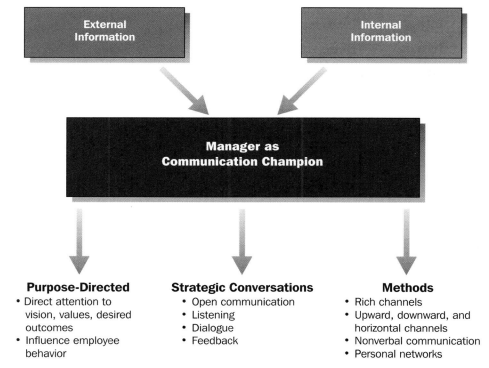

EXHIBIT 13.1

The Manager as Communication Champion

SOURCES: Adapted from Henry Mintzberg, *The Nature of Managerial Work* (New York; Harper and Row, 1973); and Richard L. Daft, *The Leadership Experience*, 3rd ed. (Cincinnati, OH: South-Western, 2005): 346.

desired goals of the team or organization and influences people to act in a way to achieve the goals. Managers facilitate *strategic conversations* by using open communication, actively listening to others, applying the practice of dialogue, and using feedback for learning and change. **Strategic conversation** refers to people talking across boundaries and hierarchical levels about the team or organization's vision, critical strategic themes, and the values that help achieve important goals.[4] For example, at Royal Philips Electronics, president Gerald Kleisterlee defined four strategic technology themes that he believes should define Philips's future in the industry: display, storage, connectivity, and digital video processing. These themes intentionally cross technology boundaries, which requires that people communicate and collaborate across departments and divisions to accomplish goals.[5] Effective managers use many communication methods, including selecting rich channels of communication; facilitating upward, downward, and horizontal communication; understanding and using nonverbal communication; and building informal communication networks that cross organization boundaries.

Communication permeates every management function described in Chapter 1.[6] For example, when managers perform the planning function, they gather information; write letters, memos, and reports; and meet with other managers to formulate the plan. When managers lead, they communicate to share a vision of what the organization can be and motivate employees to help achieve it. When managers organize, they gather information about the state of the organization and communicate a new structure to others. Communication skills are a fundamental part of every managerial activity.

WHAT IS COMMUNICATION?

A professor at Harvard once asked a class to define communication by drawing pictures. Most students drew a manager speaking or typing on a computer keyboard. Some placed

TAKE ACTION

As a manager, make it a point to find out what's happening from people who aren't in your group; don't stay in your own clique.

strategic conversation
dialogue across boundaries and hierarchical levels about the team or organization's vision, critical strategic themes, and the values that help achieve important goals.

"speech balloons" next to their characters; others showed pages flying from a printer. "No," the professor told the class, "none of you has captured the essence of communication." He went on to explain that communication means "to share"—not "to speak" or "to write."

Communication thus can be defined as the process by which information is exchanged and understood by two or more people, usually with the intent to motivate or influence behavior. Communication is not just sending information. Honoring this distinction between *sharing* and *proclaiming* is crucial for successful management. A manager who does not listen is like a used-car salesperson who claims, "I sold a car—they just did not buy it." Management communication is a two-way street that includes listening and other forms of feedback. Effective communication, in the words of one expert, is as follows:

> When two people interact, they put themselves into each other's shoes, try to perceive the world as the other person perceives it, try to predict how the other will respond. Interaction involves reciprocal role-taking, the mutual employment of empathetic skills. The goal of interaction is the merger of self and other, a complete ability to anticipate, predict, and behave in accordance with the joint needs of self and other.[7]

It is the desire to share understanding that motivates executives to visit employees on the shop floor, hold small informal meetings, or eat with employees in the company cafeteria. The things managers learn from direct communication with employees shape their understanding of the organization.

THE COMMUNICATION PROCESS

Many people think communication is simple. After all, we communicate every day without even thinking about it. However, communication usually is complex, and the opportunities for sending or receiving the wrong messages are innumerable. No doubt, you have heard someone say, "But that's not what I meant!" Have you ever received directions you thought were clear and yet still got lost? How often have you wasted time on misunderstood instructions?

To more fully understand the complexity of the communication process, note the key elements outlined in Exhibit 13.2. Two essential elements in every communication situation are the sender and the receiver. The *sender* is anyone who wants to convey an idea or concept to others, to seek information, or to express a thought or emotion. The *receiver* is the person to whom the message is sent. The sender **encodes** the idea by selecting symbols with which to compose a message. The **message** is the tangible formulation of the idea that is sent to the receiver. The message is sent through a **channel,** which is the communication carrier. The channel can be a formal report, a telephone call or e-mail message, or a face-to-face meeting. The receiver **decodes** the symbols to interpret the meaning of the message.

TAKE ACTION ▸

As a new manager, be a communication champion by communicating across boundaries, actively listening to others, and using feedback to make improvements.

communication
the process by which information is exchanged and understood by two or more people, usually with the intent to motivate or influence behavior.

encode
to select symbols with which to compose a message.

message
the tangible formulation of an idea to be sent to a receiver.

channel
the carrier of a communication.

decode
to translate the symbols used in a message for the purpose of interpreting its meaning.

EXHIBIT 13.2
A Model of the Communication Process

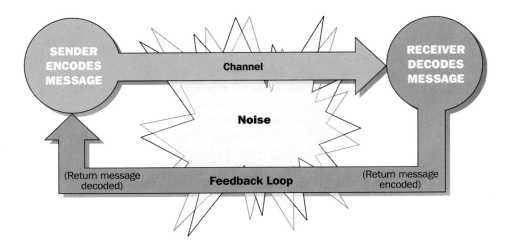

Encoding and decoding are potential sources for communication errors because knowledge, attitudes, and background act as filters and create *noise* when translating from symbols to meaning. Finally, **feedback** occurs when the receiver responds to the sender's communication with a return message. Without feedback, the communication is *one-way;* with feedback, it is *two-way.* Feedback is a powerful aid to communication effectiveness because it enables the sender to determine whether the receiver correctly interpreted the message.

Managers who are effective communicators understand and use the circular nature of communication. Consider Nortel Networks' *Virtual Leadership Academy,* a monthly televised program hosted by Dan Hunt, president of Nortel's Caribbean and Latin American operations, and Emma Carrasco, vice president of marketing and communications. Hunt and Carrasco use a talk-show format to get people talking. Employees from about 40 different countries watch

CONCEPT CONNECTION

Videoconferencing systems, such as the Polycom high-definition system shown here, use increasingly sophisticated hardware and software to transmit both visual and verbal cues and provide feedback. On large screens in the front of the room, managers not only see and hear colleagues thousands of miles away, but they can also scrutinize displays of relevant information. These new systems provide **channel richness** that was once characteristic of only face-to-face meetings. Analysts expect that terrorism threats, possible pandemics, and expensive business travel will fuel at least a 20 percent annual increase in spending on videoconferencing systems in the foreseeable future.

the show from their regional offices and call in their questions and comments. "We're always looking for ways to break down barriers," says Carrasco. "People watch talk shows in every country, and they've learned that it's okay to say what's on their minds."[8] The television program is the channel through which Hunt and Carrasco send their encoded message. Employees decode and interpret the message and encode their feedback, which is sent through the channel of the telephone hookup. The communications circuit is complete.

1 Most communication is really rather simple.

 Assess Your Answer

ANSWER: Communication *seems* simple, but is far more complicated—which is why we keep saying, "That's not what I meant." Effective communication requires sensitivity to the speaker, the ability to truly listen, and giving/receiving feedback, among other essentials.

Communicating Among People

The communication model in Exhibit 13.2 illustrates the components of effective communication. Communications can break down if sender and receiver do not encode or decode language in the same way.[9] We all know how difficult it is to communicate with someone who does not speak our language, and today's managers are often trying to communicate with people who speak many different native languages. However, communication breakdowns can also occur between people who speak the same language.

feedback
a response by the receiver to the sender's communication.

Many factors can lead to a breakdown in communications. For example, the selection of communication channel can determine whether the message is distorted by noise and interference. The listening skills of both parties and attention to nonverbal behavior can determine whether a message is truly shared. Thus, for managers to be effective communicators, they must understand how factors such as communication channels, nonverbal behavior, and listening all work to enhance or detract from communication.

COMMUNICATION CHANNELS

Managers have a choice of many channels through which to communicate to other managers or employees. A manager may discuss a problem face-to-face, make a telephone call, use instant messaging, send an e-mail, write a memo or letter, or put an item in a newsletter, depending on the nature of the message. Research has attempted to explain how managers select communication channels to enhance communication effectiveness.[10] The research has found that channels differ in their capacity to convey information. Just as a pipeline's physical characteristics limit the kind and amount of liquid that can be pumped through it, a communication channel's physical characteristics limit the kind and amount of information that can be conveyed through it. The channels available to managers can be classified into a hierarchy based on information richness.

The Hierarchy of Channel Richness.   **Channel richness** is the amount of information that can be transmitted during a communication episode. The hierarchy of channel richness is illustrated in Exhibit 13.3. The capacity of an information channel is influenced by three characteristics: (1) the ability to handle multiple cues simultaneously; (2) the ability to facilitate rapid, two-way feedback; and (3) the ability to establish a personal focus for the communication. Face-to-face discussion is the richest medium because it permits direct experience, multiple information cues, immediate feedback, and personal focus. Face-to-face discussions facilitate the assimilation of broad cues and deep, emotional understanding of the situation. Telephone conversations are next in the richness hierarchy.

channel richness
the amount of information that can be transmitted during a communication episode.

EXHIBIT 13.3

The Pyramid of Channel Richness

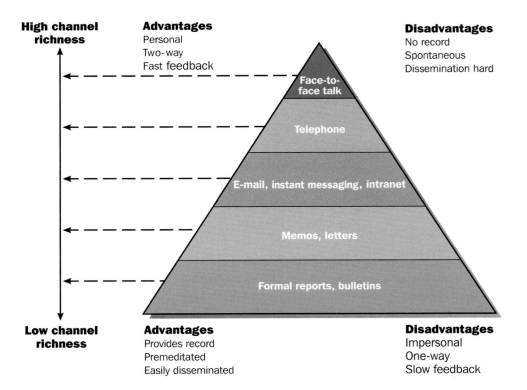

Benchmarking

Sean John

"There will be only three 'Sean John' T-shirts in the coming collection," Sean John Combs (aka Diddy) said to his designers at his $400 million company, Sean John. Some of the designers were not happy because clothing bearing "Sean John" makes up a large part of the company's revenues. "I'm putting you on rations," he laughed. "From now on, I want people to read the name without seeing the name. You get me?" Though most of the sales now are from baggy-to-the-crotch pants and noticeably branded shirts and hooded sweatshirts, P. Diddy or Puffy, wants to expand beyond the so-called urban market. "When it comes to my brand, my focus is on structure and longevity," he says.

Other hip-hop artists have ventured into the fashion field. Among them are Beyonce and Snoop Dog, but analysts say Combs has the greatest chance of success, partly because he had learned a lot about management and strategy, and partly because

he keeps control of his own company, being engaged in day-to-day operations. Unlike many other companies, Sean John makes 70 percent of its own clothing. Combs has learned the hard way: 1) with flat clothing sales as the urban look has peaked; and 2) from being distracted running an empire that includes restaurants and music publishing. To address these issues, he fired long-time business associate and friend, Jeffrey Tweedy, replaced by former Joseph Aboud Apparell CEO Robert J. Wichser. Combs vowed at the recent meeting with his closely directed designers that he would focus more on the clothing line.

After a two-year lull, clothing sales are up again, but the future depends on the new women's line Combs is launching. Because of his celebrity status, he's able to gain more attention in the marketplace than many other brands. But this "personality muscle" doesn't help much in HR or the boardroom. "You have to invest in executive talent in order to one day own or be part of a Fortune 500 company," he said. "I'm more mature now. I understand. It's all right to need people."

SOURCE: Patricia Hurtado, "The Rap on Puffy," *The New York Times* (July 24, 2005): A 1 and 3; Polly M. Sanders, "Hip Hop Hustlers$: Ka-Ching May Risk Street Cred," *New York Post* (April 17, 2007): 37.

Although eye contact, posture, and other body language cues are missing, the human voice can still carry a tremendous amount of emotional information. P. Diddy has learned that face-to-face and direct communication is necessary for business success, as shown in the Benchmarking box.

Electronic messaging, such as e-mail and instant messaging, is increasingly being used for messages that were once handled via the telephone. However, in a survey by researchers at The Ohio State University, most respondents said they preferred the telephone or face-to-face conversation for communicating difficult news, giving advice, or expressing affection.[11] Because e-mail messages lack both visual and verbal cues and don't allow for interaction and feedback, messages can sometimes be misunderstood. Using e-mail to discuss disputes, for example, can lead to an escalation rather than a resolution of conflict.[12] Studies have found that e-mail messages tend to be much more blunt than other forms of communication, even other written communications. This bluntness can cause real problems when communicating cross-culturally because some cultures consider directness rude or insulting.[13] Instant messaging alleviates the problem of miscommunication to some extent by allowing for immediate feedback.

Instant messaging (IM) allows users to see who is connected to a network and share short-hand messages or documents with them instantly. A growing number of managers are using IM, indicating that it helps people get responses faster and collaborate more smoothly.[14] Overreliance on e-mail and IM can damage company communications because people stop talking to one another in a rich way that builds solid interpersonal relationships. However, some research indicates that electronic messaging can enable reasonably rich communication if the technology is used appropriately.[15] Organizations are also using interactive meetings over the Internet, sometimes adding video capabilities to provide visual cues and greater channel richness.

Still lower on the hierarchy of channel richness are written letters and memos. Written communication can be personally focused, but it conveys only the cues written on paper

◄ TAKE ACTION

Don't use e-mail when you need to send a message that is emotionally charged or complicated; instead have a face-to-face interaction.

instant messaging (IM)
electronic communication that allows users to see who is connected to a network and share information instantly.

and is slower to provide feedback. Impersonal written media, including fliers, bulletins, and standard computer reports, are the lowest in richness. These channels are not focused on a single receiver, use limited information cues, and do not permit feedback.

Selecting the Appropriate Channel. It is important for managers to understand that each communication channel has advantages and disadvantages, and that each can be an effective means of communication in the appropriate circumstances.[16] Channel selection depends on whether the message is routine or nonroutine. *Nonroutine messages* typically are ambiguous, concern novel events, and involve great potential for misunderstanding. They often are characterized by time pressure and surprise. Managers can communicate nonroutine messages effectively by selecting rich channels. *Routine* messages are simple and straightforward. They convey data or statistics or simply put into words what managers already agree on and understand. Routine messages can be efficiently communicated through a channel lower in richness, such as e-mail or memorandum. Written communications should also be used when the communication is official, and a permanent record is required.[17] E-mail is used so commonly that people often forget to use correct grammar when sending a message for a business reason, as described next.

Consider the alert to consumers issued by the FDA following a widespread e.coli outbreak in September 2006. Tainted bagged spinach sickened 199 people in at least 26 states and resulted in one death. Grocers immediately pulled the product from shelves, and widespread news coverage warned the public not to consume any bagged spinach until the cause of the contamination could be identified. An immediate response was critical. This type of nonroutine communication forces a rich information exchange. The group will meet face-to-face, brainstorm ideas, and provide rapid feedback to resolve the situation and convey the correct information. If, in contrast, an agency director is preparing a press release about a routine matter such as a policy change or new department members, less information capacity is needed. The director and public relations people might begin developing the press release with an exchange of memos, telephone calls, and e-mail messages.

The key is to select a channel to fit the message. During a major acquisition, one firm decided to send top executives to all major work sites of the acquired company, where most of the workers met the managers in person, heard about their plans for the company, and had a chance to ask questions. The results were well worth the time and expense of the

Spotlight on Skills

E-mail grammar

"I need help," started the unpunctuated e-mail to a business writing professor. "i am writing essay on writing i work for this company and my boss want me to help improve the workers writing skills can yall help me with some information thank you." Dr. Craig Hogan gets hundreds of messages a month like this, as people are required to do more and more writing on the job and are basically messing up. "E-mail is a party to which English teachers have not been invited. It has companies tearing their hair out."

Corporations report that one-third of employees in top companies are poor writers, costing $3.1 billion per year on remedial training. These employers aren't asking for Tolstoy, just clear, understandable writing.

Dr. Hogan, who started his online writing course a decade ago, says that use of multiple exclamation points (!!) are okay for personal e-mails but not for business use. Ditto the overuse of capital letters. HR departments are having to reteach people how to write professionally.

"E-mail has erupted like a weed, and instead of considering what to say when they write, people now just let their thoughts drool out onto the screen," says Hogan.

SOURCE: Sam Dillon, "What Corporate American Can't Build: A Sentence," *The New York Times* (Dec. 7, 2004): 23; Henrietta Clancy, "Do's and Don'ts," *New Statesman* (May 28, 2007): 58.

2 E-mailing is an efficient and effective tool for communicating.

ANSWER: E-mail is best used for more routine, unambiguous, and nonemotional messages. When there is uncertainty, fear, danger of being misunderstood, and any emotional component, talking directly (face-to-face or phone) is preferable.

personal face-to-face meetings because the acquired workforce saw their new managers as understanding, open, and willing to listen.[18] Communicating their nonroutine message about the acquisition in person prevented damaging rumors and misunderstandings. The choice of a communication channel can also convey a symbolic meaning to the receiver; in a sense, the medium becomes the message. The firm's decision to communicate face-to-face with the acquired workforce signaled to employees that managers cared about them as individuals.

NEW MANAGER SELF TEST

Personal Assessment of Communication Apprehension

The following questions are about your feelings toward communication with other people. Indicate the degree to which each statement applies to you by marking (5) Mostly True, (4) Agree, (3) Are undecided, (2) Disagree, or (1) Mostly False with each statement. There are no right or wrong answers. Many of the statements are similar to other statements. Do not be concerned about this. Work quickly and just record your first impressions.

	Mostly True				Mostly False
1. When talking in a small group of acquaintances, I am tense and nervous.	5	4	3	2	1
2. When presenting a talk to a group of strangers, I am tense and nervous.	5	4	3	2	1
3. When conversing with a friend or colleague, I am calm and relaxed.	5	4	3	2	1
4. When talking in a large meeting of acquaintances, I am calm and relaxed.	5	4	3	2	1
5. When presenting a talk to a group of friends or colleagues, I am tense and nervous.	5	4	3	2	1
6. When conversing with an acquaintance or colleague, I am calm and relaxed.	5	4	3	2	1
7. When talking in a large meeting of strangers, I am tense and nervous.	5	4	3	2	1
8. When talking in a small group of strangers, I am tense and nervous.	5	4	3	2	1
9. When talking in a small group of friends or colleagues, I am calm and relaxed.	5	4	3	2	1

(Continued)

10. When presenting a talk to a group of acquaintances, I am calm and relaxed.	**5 4 3 2 1**	
11. When conversing with a stranger, I am tense and nervous.	**5 4 3 2 1**	
12. When talking in a large meeting of friends, I am tense and nervous.	**5 4 3 2 1**	

SCORING: This questionnaire permits computation of four subscores and one total score. Subscores relate to communication apprehension in four common situations: public speaking, meetings, group discussions, and interpersonal conversations. To compute your scores, add or subtract your scores for each item as indicated next.

Subscore/Scoring Formula
For each subscore, start with 18 points. Then add the scores for the plus (+) items and subtract the scores for the minus (–) items.

Public Speaking
18 + scores for items 2 and 5; – scores for item 10. Score = _____

Meetings
18 + scores for items 7 and 12; – scores for item 4. Score = _____

Group Discussions
18 + scores for items 1 and 8; – scores for item 9. Score = _____

Interpersonal Conversations
18 + score for 11; – scores for items 3 and 6. Score = _____

Total Score
Sum the four scores above for the Total Score _____

INTERPRETATION: This personal assessment provides an indication of how much apprehension (fear or anxiety) you feel in a variety of communication settings. Total scores may range from 60 to 108. Scores above 86 indicate that you are more apprehensive about communication than the average person. Scores above 95 indicate a very high level of communication apprehension. Scores below 72 indicate a very low level of apprehension. These extreme scores (below 72 and above 95) are generally outside the norm. They suggest that the degree of apprehension you may experience in any given situation may not be associated with a realistic response to that communication situation.

Scores on the subscales can range from a low of 15 to a high of 27. Any score above 18 indicates some degree of apprehension. For example, if you score above 18 for the public speaking context, you are like the overwhelming majority of people.

To be an effective communication champion, you should work to overcome communication anxiety. The interpersonal conversations create the least apprehension for most people, followed by group discussions, larger meetings, and then public speaking. Compare your scores with another student. What aspect of communication creates the most apprehension for you? How do you plan to improve it?

SOURCES: J. C. McCroskey, "Measures of Communication-Bound Anxiety," *Speech Monographs* 37 (1970): 269–277; J. C. McCroskey and V. P. Richmond, "Validity of the PRCA as an Index of Oral Communication Apprehension," *Communication Monographs* 45 (1978): 192–203; J. C. McCroskey and V. P. Richmond, "The Impact of Communication Apprehension on Individuals in Organizations," *Communication Quarterly* 27 (1979): 55–61; J. C. McCroskey, *An Introduction to Rhetorical Communication*, Prentice Hall, Englewood Cliffs, NJ: Prentice Hall, 1982.

COMMUNICATING TO PERSUADE AND INFLUENCE OTHERS

Communication is not just for conveying information but also to persuade and influence people. Although communication skills have always been important to managers, the ability to persuade and influence others is even more critical today. Businesses are run largely by cross-functional teams who are actively involved in making decisions. Issuing directives is no longer an appropriate or effective way to get things done.[19]

Valuedance

When Susan Cramm was asked by a client to help persuade the client's boss to support an initiative she wanted to launch, Cramm readily agreed. They scheduled a meeting with the boss, and then held a series of planning sessions where the two discussed the current situation at the client's firm, weighed the options, and decided on the best approach for launching the initiative. Filled with enthusiasm and armed with a PowerPoint presentation, Cramm was sure the client's boss would see things their way.

An agonizing 15 minutes later, she was out the door, PowerPoint deck and all, having just had a lesson about the art of persuasion. What went wrong? Cramm had focused on the hard, rational matters and ignored the soft skills of relationship building, listening, and negotiating that are so critical to persuading others. "Never did we consider the boss's views," Cramm said later about the planning sessions she and her client held to prepare for the meeting. "Like founding members of the 'it's all about me' club, we fell upon our swords, believing that our impeccable logic, persistence, and enthusiasm would carry the day."

With that approach, the meeting was over before it even began. The formal presentation shut down communications because it implied that Cramm had all the answers and the boss was just there to listen and agree.[20]

To persuade and influence, managers have to communicate frequently and easily with others. Yet some people find interpersonal communication experiences unrewarding or difficult and thus tend to avoid situations where communication is required. The term **communication apprehension** describes this avoidance behavior and is defined as "an individual's level of fear or anxiety associated with either real or anticipated communication." With training and practice, managers can overcome their communication apprehension and become more effective communicators.

Effective persuasion doesn't mean telling people what you want them to do; instead, it involves listening, learning about others' interests and needs, and leading people to a shared solution.[21] Managers who forget that communication means *sharing,* as described earlier, aren't likely to be as effective at influencing or persuading others, as the founder and president of the executive coaching firm Valuedance learned the hard way.

As this example shows, people stop listening to someone when that individual isn't listening to them. By failing to show interest in and respect for the boss's point of view, Cramm and her client lost the boss's interest from the beginning, no matter how suitable the ideas they were presenting. To effectively influence and persuade others, managers have to show they care about how the other person feels. Persuasion requires tapping into people's emotions, which can only be done on a personal, rather than a rational, impersonal level.

Managers who use symbols, metaphors, and stories to deliver their messages have an easier time influencing and persuading others. Stories draw on people's imaginations and emotions, which helps managers make sense of a fast-changing environment in ways that people can understand and share. If we think back to our early school years, we may remember that the most effective lessons often were couched in stories. Presenting hard facts and figures rarely has the same power.

Evidence of the compatibility of stories with human thinking was demonstrated by a study at Stanford Business School.[22] The point was to convince MBA students that a company practiced a policy of avoiding layoffs. For some students, only a story was used. For others, statistical data were provided that showed little turnover compared to competitors. For other students, statistics and stories were combined, and yet other students were shown the company's official policy statements. Of all these approaches, the students presented with a vivid story alone were most convinced that the company truly practiced a policy of avoiding layoffs. Managers can learn to use elements of storytelling to enhance their communication.[23] Stories need not be long, complex, or carefully constructed. A story can be a joke, an analogy, or a verbal snapshot of something from the manager's own past experiences.[24]

TAKE ACTION

When trying to persuade someone, try using a compelling story rather than merely facts and information.

communication apprehension
an individual's level of fear or anxiety associated with interpersonal communications.

NONVERBAL COMMUNICATION

Managers also use symbols to communicate what is important. Managers are watched, and their behavior, appearance, actions, and attitudes are symbolic of what they value and expect of others.

Most of us have heard the saying that "actions speak louder than words." Indeed, we communicate without words all the time, whether we realize it or not. **Nonverbal communication** refers to messages sent through human actions and behaviors rather than through words.[25] Most managers are astonished to learn that words themselves carry little meaning. A significant portion of the shared understanding from communication comes from the nonverbal messages of facial expression, voice, mannerisms, posture, and dress.

Nonverbal communication occurs mostly face to face. One researcher found three sources of communication cues during face-to-face communication: the *verbal,* which are the actual spoken words; the *vocal,* which include the pitch, tone, and timbre of a person's voice; and *facial expressions.* According to this study, the relative weights of these three factors in message interpretation are as follows: verbal impact, 7 percent; vocal impact, 38 percent; and facial impact, 55 percent.[26] To some extent, we are all natural *face readers,* but facial expressions can be misinterpreted, suggesting that managers need to ask questions to make sure they're getting the right message. Managers can hone their skills at reading facial expressions and improve their ability to connect with and influence followers. Studies indicate that managers who seem responsive to the unspoken emotions of employees are more effective and successful in the workplace.[27]

This research also strongly implies for managers that "it's not what you say but how you say it." Nonverbal messages and body language often convey our real thoughts and feelings with greater force than do our most carefully selected words. Thus, while the conscious mind may be formulating a vocal message such as "Congratulations on your promotion," body language may be signaling true feelings through blushing, perspiring, or avoiding eye contact. When the verbal and nonverbal messages are contradictory, the receiver will usually give more weight to behavioral actions than to verbal messages.[28]

A manager's office sends nonverbal cues as well. For example, what do the following seating arrangements mean? (1) The supervisor stays behind her desk, and you sit in a straight chair on the opposite side. (2) The two of you sit in straight chairs away from her desk, perhaps at a table. (3) The two of you sit in a seating arrangement consisting of a sofa and easy chair. To most people, the first arrangement indicates, "I'm the boss here," or "I'm in authority." The second arrangement indicates, "This is serious business." The third indicates a more casual and friendly, "Let's get to know each other."[29] Nonverbal messages can be a powerful asset to communication if they complement and support verbal messages. Managers should pay close attention to nonverbal behavior when communicating. They can learn to coordinate their verbal and nonverbal messages and at the same time be sensitive to what their peers, subordinates, and supervisors are saying nonverbally.

TAKE ACTION ▶

Always remember how important nonverbals are. If you smirk while giving a positive comment, the positive thought gets lost.

LISTENING

One of the most important tools of manager communication is listening, both to employees and customers. Most managers now recognize that important information flows from the bottom up, not the top down, and managers had better be tuned in.[30] This chapter's "Unlocking Innovative Solutions Through People" box describes how a new managing director and human resources director transformed Kwik-Fit Financial Services by listening to employees who were tired of feeling as though no one in the organization cared about them. Some organizations use innovative techniques for finding out what's on employees' and customers' minds. Cabela's, a retailer for outdoor enthusiasts, lets employees borrow

nonverbal communication
a communication transmitted through actions and behaviors rather than through words.

and use any of the company's products for a month, as long as they provide feedback that helps other employees better serve customers. The employee fills out a form detailing the product's pros and cons, gives a talk to other employees or customers about the product, and provides feedback in the form of "Item Notes" that are fed into a knowledge-sharing system.[31]

In the communication model in Exhibit 13.2, the listener is responsible for message reception, which is a vital link in the communication process. **Listening** involves the skill of grasping both facts and feelings to interpret a message's genuine meaning. Only then can the manager provide the appropriate response. Listening requires attention, energy, and skill. Although about 75 percent of effective communication is listening, most people spend only 30 to 40 percent of their time listening, which leads to many communication errors.[32] One of the secrets of highly successful salespeople is that they spend 60 to 70 percent of a sales call letting the customer talk.[33] However, listening involves much more than just not talking. Many people do not know how to listen effectively. They concentrate on formulating what they are going to say next rather than on what is being said to them. Our listening efficiency, as measured by the amount of material understood and remembered by subjects 48 hours after listening to a 10-minute message, is, on average, no better than 25 percent.[34]

What constitutes good listening? Exhibit 13.4 gives 10 keys to effective listening and illustrates a number of ways to distinguish a bad from a good listener. A good listener finds areas of interest, is flexible, works hard at listening, and uses thought speed to mentally summarize, weigh, and anticipate what the speaker says. Good listening means shifting from thinking about self to empathizing with the other person and thus requires a high degree of emotional intelligence, as described in Chapter 10. Dr. Robert Buckman, a cancer specialist who teaches other doctors, as well as businesspeople, how to break bad news, emphasizes the importance of listening. "The trust that you build just by letting someone say what they feel is incredible," Buckman says.[35]

CONCEPT CONNECTION

About a year ago, Hillary Johnson became the editor of a small newspaper in California. Describing her new responsibilities, Johnson emphasizes the importance of **listening.** "Whenever someone walks into my office with a knitted brow and an open mouth, I say, preemptively, 'Would you like a cup of tea?' Whatever the answer, this creates a pause and sets the tone for the discussion to follow." Johnson is convinced that listening to employees, although time consuming, is essential to her success as a manager.

listening
the skill of receiving messages to accurately grasp facts and feelings to interpret the genuine meaning.

3 People are generally good listeners.

 Assess Your Answer

ANSWER: Most people don't listen well enough, which leads to many communication errors. Learning to listen effectively can be a long struggle for many, but is a very worthwhile endeavor.

Few things are as maddening to people as not being listened to. Executives at health-insurer Humana Inc. realized they could grab a bigger share of the Medicare drug benefits business simply by listening to America's senior citizens.

Keys	Poor Listener	Good Listener
1. Listen actively.	Is passive, laid back	Asks questions, paraphrases what is said
2. Find areas of interest.	Tunes out dry subjects	Looks for opportunities, new learning
3. Resist distractions.	Is easily distracted	Fights or avoids distraction, tolerates bad habits, knows how to concentrate
4. Capitalize on the fact that thought is faster.	Tends to daydream with slow speakers	Challenges, anticipates, mentally summarizes; weighs the evidence; listens between the lines to tone of voice
5. Be responsive.	Is minimally involved	Nods, shows interest, give and take, positive feedback
6. Judge content, not delivery.	Tunes out if delivery is poor	Judges content; skips over delivery errors
7. Hold one's fire.	Has preconceptions, starts to argue	Does not judge until comprehension is complete
8. Listen for ideas.	Listens for facts	Listens to central themes
9. Work at listening.	Shows no energy output; fakes attention	Works hard, exhibits active body state, eye contact
10. Exercise one's mind.	Resists difficult material in favor of light, recreational material	Uses heavier material as exercise for the mind

SOURCES: Adapted from Sherman K. Okum, "How to Be a Better Listener," *Nation's Business* (August 1975): 62; and Philip Morgan and Kent Baker, "Building a Professional Image: Improving Listening Behavior," *Supervisory Management* (November 1985): 34–38.

EXHIBIT 13.4

Ten Keys to Effective Listening

Humana, Inc.

Sixty-eight-year-old Helen Arnold tells how she spent hours trying to research a Medicare drug benefit plan over the phone without ever being able to get through to a person. "This recorded voice just kept giving me all these numbers to punch," she said, her voice rising as she recalled the frustration. It's a frustration that was shared by seniors all over the United States as they struggled to comprehend the new Medicare plans.

Arnold is part of a consumer gripe session, sponsored by Humana, Inc., the nation's number 5 health insurer. Humana decided to take an approach unique in the health insurance industry—listening to what customers want and designing products and services around their needs. The company holds consumer focus groups, solicits the input of employees, and observes people in their homes as they make health-care decisions. Humana learned, for example, that many people got frustrated researching the new Medicare plans online or over the phone, so it set up kiosks at Wal-Marts, hired sales representatives to sell the plans in people's homes, and made a deal with 17,000 State Farm insurance agents to offer Humana's Medicare plans through their offices.

Listening has paid off. In early 2006, Humana had signed up 2.4 million people to its Medicare plans, second only to the much-larger United Health Group. The company is using listening to better serve other customers as well, such as by setting up kiosks at employers' offices so people can talk to someone face to face.[36]

Humana is the first major health insurer to create a culture that emphasizes actively listening to customers. Consumer products company Procter & Gamble effectively used these techniques for finding out what people want. P&G also learned that listening to employees translates into business success. Managers emphasize the importance of listening to both internal as well as external customers. "Gaining the hearts and minds of every employee . . . is no small challenge, and it's one that managers have to wrestle with every day to succeed," says P&G's global marketing officer James Stengel. "That's what we do with our customers—and now we're making sure we do it with our own employees."[37]

Organizational Communication

Another aspect of management communication concerns the organization as a whole. Organization-wide communications typically flow in three directions—downward, upward, and horizontally. Managers are responsible for establishing and maintaining formal channels of communication in these three directions. Managers also use informal channels, which means they get out of their offices and mingle with employees.

FORMAL COMMUNICATION CHANNELS

Formal communication channels flow within the chain of command or task responsibility defined by the organization. The three formal channels and the types of information conveyed in each are illustrated in Exhibit 13.5.[38] Downward and upward communications are the primary forms of communication used in most traditional, vertically organized companies. However, many of today's organizations emphasize horizontal communication, with people continuously sharing information across departments and levels.

Electronic communication such as e-mail and instant messaging have made it easier than ever for information to flow in all directions. For example, the U.S. Army is using technology to rapidly transmit communications about weather conditions, the latest intelligence on the insurgency, and so forth to lieutenants in the field in Iraq. Similarly, the Navy uses instant messaging to communicate within ships, across Navy divisions, and even back to the Pentagon in Washington. "Instant messaging has allowed us to keep our crew members on the same page at the same time," says Lt. Cmdr. Mike Houston, who oversees the Navy's communications program. "Lives are at stake in real time, and we're seeing a new level of communication and readiness."[39]

Downward Communication. The most familiar and obvious flow of formal communication, **downward communication,** refers to the messages and information sent from top management to subordinates in a downward direction.

Managers can communicate downward to employees in many ways. Some of the most common are through speeches, messages in company newsletters, e-mail, information leaflets tucked into pay envelopes, material on bulletin boards, and policy and procedures

formal communication channel
a communication channel that flows within the chain of command or task responsibility defined by the organization.

downward communication
messages sent from top management down to subordinates.

EXHIBIT 13.5
Downward, Upward, and Horizontal Communication in Organizations

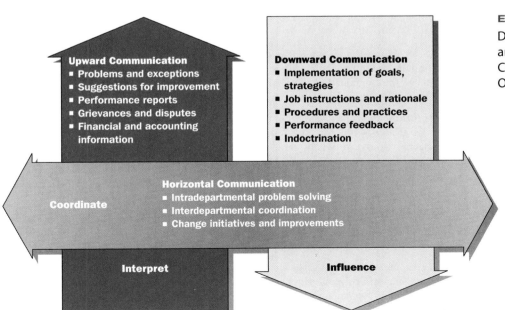

Upward Communication
- Problems and exceptions
- Suggestions for improvement
- Performance reports
- Grievances and disputes
- Financial and accounting information

Downward Communication
- Implementation of goals, strategies
- Job instructions and rationale
- Procedures and practices
- Performance feedback
- Indoctrination

Horizontal Communication
- Intradepartmental problem solving
- Interdepartmental coordination
- Change initiatives and improvements

Coordinate

Interpret

Influence

Business Blooper

Wal-Mart

Wal-Mart prides itself in selling books at steep discounts, and it screens both books and movies for appropriate content suitable for families. What a surprise when Wal-Mart started selling *How Wal-Mart Is Destroying America and*

the World and What You Can Do About It, for $3.40 off the list price, or only $7.55. The policy for suitable material must not have been communicated down clearly to the censors. That is, until links to the product page started turning up on many blogs. Finally, Wal-Mart removed the book from its inventory.

SOURCE: Adam Horowitz, Mark Athitakis, Mark Lasswell, and Owen Thomas, "101 Dumbest Moments in Business," *Business 2.0* (Jan/Feb. 2005): 103–110.

manuals. Managers sometimes use creative approaches to downward communication to make sure employees get the message. Mike Olson, plant manager at Ryerson Midwest Coil Processing, noticed that workers were dropping expensive power tools, so he hung price tags on the tools to show the replacement cost. Employees solved the problem by finding a way to hook up the tools so they wouldn't be dropped. Olson's symbolic communication created a climate of working together for solutions.[40]

Managers also have to decide what to communicate about. It is impossible for managers to communicate with employees about everything that goes on in the organization, so they have to make choices about the important information to communicate.[41] Unfortunately, many U.S. managers could do a better job of effective downward communication. The results of one survey found that employees want open and honest communication about both the good and the bad aspects of the organization's performance. But when asked to rate their company's communication effectiveness on a scale of 0 to 100, the survey respondents' score averaged 69. In addition, a study of 1,500 managers, mostly at first and second management levels, found that 84 percent of these leaders perceive communication as one of their most important tasks, yet only 38 percent believe they have adequate communications skills.[42]

Managers can do a better job of downward communication by focusing on specific areas that require regular communication. Recall our discussion of purpose-directed communication from early in this chapter. Downward communication usually encompasses these five topics:

1. *Implementation of goals and strategies.* Communicating new strategies and goals provides information about specific targets and expected behaviors. It gives direction for lower levels of the organization. *Example:* "The new quality campaign is for real. We must improve product quality if we are to survive."

2. *Job instructions and rationale.* These directives indicate how to do a specific task and how the job relates to other organizational activities. *Example:* "Purchasing should order the bricks now so the work crew can begin construction of the building in two weeks."

3. *Procedures and practices.* These messages define the organization's policies, rules, regulations, benefits, and structural arrangements. *Example:* "After your first 90 days of employment, you are eligible to enroll in our company-sponsored savings plan."

4. *Performance feedback.* These messages appraise how well individuals and departments are doing their jobs. *Example:* "Joe, your work on the computer network has greatly improved the efficiency of our ordering process."

5. *Indoctrination.* These messages are designed to motivate employees to adopt the company's mission and cultural values and to participate in special ceremonies, such as picnics and United Way campaigns. *Example:* "The company thinks of its employees as family and would like to invite everyone to attend the annual picnic and fair on March 3."

A major problem with downward communication is *drop off,* the distortion or loss of message content. Although formal communications are a powerful way to reach all employees, much information gets lost—25 percent or so each time a message is passed from one person to the next. In addition, the message can be distorted if it travels a great distance from its originating source to the ultimate receiver. The following is a tragic historical example:

> A reporter was present at a hamlet burned down by the U.S. Army 1st Air Cavalry Division in 1967. Investigations showed that the order from the Division headquarters to the brigade was: "On no occasion must hamlets be burned down."
>
> The brigade radioed the battalion: "Do not burn down any hamlets unless you are absolutely convinced that the Viet Cong are in them."
>
> The battalion radioed the infantry company at the scene: "If you think there are any Viet Cong in the hamlet, burn it down."
>
> The company commander ordered his troops: "Burn down that hamlet."[43]

Information drop off cannot be completely avoided, but the techniques described in the previous sections can reduce it substantially. Using the right communication channel, consistency between verbal and nonverbal messages, and active listening can maintain communication accuracy as it moves down the organization.

Upward Communication. Formal **upward communication** includes messages that flow from the lower to the higher levels in the organization's hierarchy. Most organizations take pains to build in healthy channels for upward communication. Employees need to air grievances, report progress, and provide feedback on management initiatives. Coupling a healthy flow of upward and downward communication ensures that the communication circuit between managers and employees is complete.[44] Five types of information communicated upward are the following:

1. *Problems and exceptions.* These messages describe serious problems with and exceptions to routine performance to make senior managers aware of difficulties. *Example:* "The printer has been out of operation for two days, and it will be at least a week before a new one arrives."

2. *Suggestions for improvement.* These messages are ideas for improving task-related procedures to increase quality or efficiency. *Example:* "I think we should eliminate step 2 in the audit procedure because it takes a lot of time and produces no results."

3. *Performance reports.* These messages include periodic reports that inform management how individuals and departments are performing. *Example:* "We completed the audit report for Smith & Smith on schedule but are one week behind on the Jackson report."

4. *Grievances and disputes.* These messages are employee complaints and conflicts that travel up the hierarchy for a hearing and possible resolution. *Example:* "The manager of operations research cannot get the cooperation of the Lincoln plant for the study of machine use."

5. *Financial and accounting information.* These messages pertain to costs, accounts receivable, sales volume, anticipated profits, return on investment, and other matters of interest to senior managers. *Example:* "Costs are 2 percent over budget, but sales are 10 percent ahead of target, so the profit picture for the third quarter is excellent."

Many organizations make a great effort to facilitate upward communication. Mechanisms include suggestion boxes, employee surveys, open-door policies, management information system reports, and face-to-face conversations between workers and executives. Consider how one entrepreneur keeps the upward communication flowing.

In today's fast-paced world, many managers find it hard to maintain constant communication. Ideas such as the Five-Fifteen help keep information flowing upward so managers get feedback from lower levels.

upward communication
messages transmitted from the lower to the higher levels in the organization's hierarchy.

Pat Croce, Entrepreneur

Pat Croce is involved in several business ventures, including the development of Pirate Soul, "the ultimate pirate museum," in Key West, Florida. Like many entrepreneurs, Croce spends a lot of time on the road, traveling all across the country from his home office in Philadelphia.

To make sure he stays in touch with what's going on in his various businesses, Croce implemented a key communication tool he calls the Five-Fifteen. Each Friday, all employees and managers take 15 minutes to write brief progress reports and forward them to their immediate supervisors. Within a few days, all the information trickles up to Croce in a sort of "corporate Cliff Notes" version. The idea is that the reports take Croce only five minutes to read (hence the name Five-Fifteen). Croce says the Five-Fifteens have enabled him to keep in touch with the little details that make a big difference in the success of his businesses.

Employees typically look at the Five-Fifteens as a chance to be heard, and Croce looks at them as a way to keep his finger on the pulse of each business. In addition, the reports give him a chance to compliment and thank people for their accomplishments and offer questions or suggestions in areas that need improvement.[45]

horizontal communication
the lateral or diagonal exchange of messages among peers or co-workers.

Despite these efforts, however, barriers to accurate upward communication exist. Managers might resist employee feedback because they don't want to hear negative information, or employees might not trust managers sufficiently to push information upward.[46] At *The New York Times*, for example, poor upward communication was partly to blame for the Jayson Blair scandal. Some people in the newsroom knew or suspected that the rising reporter was fabricating elements of his news stories, but the environment of separation between reporters and editors prevented the information from being transmitted upward.[47] Innovative companies search for ways to ensure that information gets to top managers without distortion. A report reviewing the Blair scandal at the *Times*, for instance, recommended techniques such as cross-hierarchical meetings, office hours for managers, and informal brainstorming sessions among reporters and editors to improve upward communication.[48] At Golden Corral, a restaurant chain with headquarters in Raleigh, North Carolina, top managers spend at least one weekend a year in the trenches—cutting steaks, rolling silverware, setting tables, and taking out the trash. By understanding the daily routines and challenges of waiters, chefs, and other employees at their restaurants, Golden Corral executives increase their awareness of how management actions affect others.[49]

Horizontal Communication. Horizontal communication is the lateral or diagonal exchange of messages among peers or co-workers. It may occur within or across departments. The purpose of horizontal communication is not only to inform but also to request support and coordinate activities. Horizontal communication falls into one of three categories:

1. *Intradepartmental problem solving.* These messages take place among members of the same department and concern task accomplishment. *Example:* "Kelly, can you help us figure out how to complete this medical expense report form?"

2. *Interdepartmental coordination.* Interdepartmental messages facilitate the accomplishment of joint projects or tasks.

CONCEPT CONNECTION

The National Oceanic and Atmospheric Administration (NOAA)—a decentralized, geographically dispersed agency with a mission to observe and describe changes in the entire earth's ecosystem—serves other coastal resource management groups with information, technology, and training. NOAA recently established the Office of Program Planning and Integration to improve **horizontal communication** and create a more coherent organization.

Example: "Bob, please contact marketing and production and arrange a meeting to discuss the specifications for the new sub-assembly. It looks like we might not be able to meet their requirements."

3. *Change initiatives and improvements.* These messages are designed to share information among teams and departments that can help the organization change, grow, and improve. *Example:* "We are streamlining the company travel procedures and would like to discuss them with your department."

Horizontal communication is particularly important in learning organizations, where teams of workers are continuously solving problems and searching for better ways of doing things. Recall from Chapter 7 that many organizations build in horizontal communications in the form of task forces, committees, or even a matrix or horizontal structure to encourage coordination.

TEAM COMMUNICATION CHANNELS

A special type of horizontal communication is communicating in teams. Teams are the basic building block of many organizations. Team members work together to accomplish tasks, and the team's communication structure influences both team performance and employee satisfaction.

Research into team communication has focused on two characteristics: the extent to which team communications are centralized and the nature of the team's task.[50] The relationship between these characteristics is illustrated in Exhibit 13.6. In a **centralized network,** team members must communicate through one individual to solve problems or make decisions. In a **decentralized network,** individuals can communicate freely with other team members. Members process information equally among themselves until all agree on a decision.[51]

In laboratory experiments, centralized communication networks achieved faster solutions for simple problems. Members could simply pass relevant information to a central person for a decision. Decentralized communications were slower for simple problems because information was passed among individuals until someone finally put the pieces together and solved the problem. However, for more complex problems, the decentralized communication network was faster. Because all necessary information was not restricted to one person, a pooling of information through widespread communications provided greater input into the decision. Similarly, the accuracy of problem solving was related to problem

TAKE ACTION

If you have a complex task, make sure members of the team can all communicate easily to one another.

centralized network
a team communication structure in which team members communicate through a single individual to solve problems or make decisions.

decentralized network
a team communication structure in which team members freely communicate with one another and arrive at decisions together.

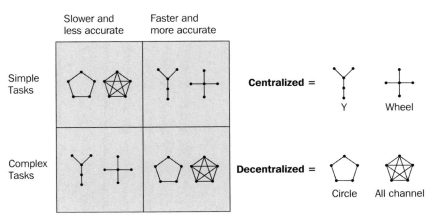

Slower and less accurate — Faster and more accurate

Simple Tasks / Complex Tasks

Centralized = Y, Wheel
Decentralized = Circle, All channel

EXHIBIT 13.6
Effectiveness of Team Communication Networks

SOURCES: Adapted from A. Bavelas and D. Barrett, "An Experimental Approach to Organization Communication," *Personnel* 27 (1951): 366–371; M. E. Shaw, *Group Dynamics: The Psychology of Small Group Behavior* (New York: McGraw–Hill, 1976); and E. M. Rogers and R. A. Rogers, *Communication in Organizations* (New York: Free Press, 1976).

complexity. The centralized networks made fewer errors on simple problems but more errors on complex ones. Decentralized networks were less accurate for simple problems but more accurate for complex ones.[52]

The implication for organizations is as follows: In a highly competitive global environment, organizations typically use teams to deal with complex problems. When team activities are complex and difficult, all members should share information in a decentralized structure to solve problems. Teams need a free flow of communication in all directions.[53] Teams that perform routine tasks spend less time processing information, and thus communications can be centralized. Data can be channeled to a supervisor for decisions, freeing workers to spend a greater percentage of time on task activities.

PERSONAL COMMUNICATION CHANNELS

Personal communication channels exist outside the formally authorized channels. These informal communications coexist with formal channels but may skip hierarchical levels, cutting across vertical chains of command to connect virtually anyone in the organization. In most organizations, these informal channels are the primary way information spreads and work gets accomplished. Three important types of personal communication channels are *personal networks, management by wandering around,* and the *grapevine.*

Developing Personal Communication Networks. Personal
networking refers to the acquisition and cultivation of personal relationships that cross departmental, hierarchical, and even organizational boundaries.[54] Smart managers consciously develop personal communication networks and encourage others to do so. In a communication network, people share information across boundaries and reach out to anyone who can further the goals of the team and organization. Exhibit 13.7 illustrates a communication network. Some people are central to the network, whereas others play only a peripheral role. The key is that relationships are built across functional and hierarchical boundaries.

The value of personal networks for managers is that people who have more contacts have greater influence in the organization and get more accomplished. For example, in Exhibit 13.7, Sharon has a well-developed personal communication network, sharing information and assistance with many people across the marketing, manufacturing, and engineering departments. Contrast Sharon's contacts with those of Mike or Jasmine. Who do you think is likely to have greater access to resources and more influence in the

personal communication channels
communication channels that exist outside the formally authorized channels and do not adhere to the organization's hierarchy of authority.

personal networking
the acquisition and cultivation of personal relationships that cross departmental, hierarchical, and even organizational boundaries.

EXHIBIT 13.7
An Organizational Communication Network

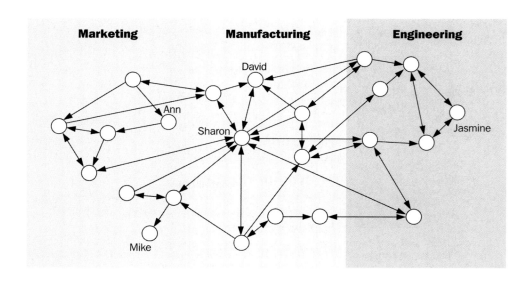

NEW MANAGER SELF TEST

Personal Networking

How good are you at personal networking? Having sources of information and support helps a new manager gain career traction. To learn something about your networking, answer the following questions. Please indicate whether each item is Mostly True or Mostly False for you in school or at work.

	Mostly True	Mostly False
1. I learn early on about changes going on in the organization and how they might affect me or my position.	_____	_____
2. I network as much to help other people solve problems as to help myself.	_____	_____
3. I am fascinated by other people and what they do.	_____	_____
4. I frequently use lunches to meet and network with new people.	_____	_____
5. I regularly participate in charitable causes.	_____	_____
6. I maintain a list of friends and colleagues to whom I send Christmas cards.	_____	_____
7. I maintain contact with people from previous organizations and school groups.	_____	_____
8. I actively give information to subordinates, peers, and my boss.	_____	_____

INTERPRETATION AND SCORING: Many good things flow from active networking, which will build a web of personal and organizational relationships for a new manager. Networking builds social, work, and career relationships that facilitate mutual benefit. People with active networks tend to be more effective managers and have broader impact on the organization.

Give yourself 1 point for each item marked as Mostly True. A score of 6 or higher suggests active networking and a solid foundation on which to begin your career as a new manager. If you scored 3 or less, you may want to focus more on building relationships if you are serious about a career as a manager.

---

organization? Here are a few tips from one expert networker for building a personal communication network:[55]

1. *Build it before you need it.* Smart managers don't wait until they need something to start building a network of personal relationships—by then, it's too late. Instead, they show genuine interest in others and develop honest connections.

2. *Never eat lunch alone.* People who excel at networking make an effort to be visible and connect with as many people as possible. Master networkers keep their social as well as business conference and event calendars full.

3. *Make it win-win.* Successful networking isn't just about getting what *you* want; it's also about making sure other people in the network get what *they* want.

 TAKE ACTION

Use your lunches and break times to develop closer relationships and communications with colleagues.

4. *Focus on diversity.* The broader your base of contacts, the broader your range of influence. Build connections with people from as many different areas of interest as possible (both within and outside of the organization).

Most of us know from personal experience that "who you know" sometimes counts for more than what you know. By cultivating a broad network of contacts, managers can significantly extend their influence and accomplish greater results.

The Grapevine. One type of informal, person-to-person communication network that is not officially sanctioned by the organization is referred to as the **grapevine**.[56] The grapevine links employees in all directions, ranging from the CEO through middle management, support staff, and line employees. The grapevine will always exist in an organization, but it can become a dominant force when formal channels are closed. In such cases, the grapevine is actually a service because the information it provides helps makes sense of an unclear or uncertain situation. Employees use grapevine rumors to fill in information gaps and clarify management decisions. One estimate is that as much as 70 percent of all communication in a firm is carried out through its grapevine.[57] The grapevine tends to be more active during periods of change, excitement, anxiety, and sagging economic conditions. For example, a survey by professional employment services firm Randstad found that about half of all employees reported first hearing of major company changes through the grapevine.[58] Consider what happened at Jel, Inc., an auto supply firm that was under great pressure from Ford and GM to increase quality. Management changes to improve quality—learning statistical process control, introducing a new compensation system, buying a fancy new screw machine from Germany—all started out as rumors, circulating days ahead of the actual announcements, and were generally accurate.[59]

Surprising aspects of the grapevine are its accuracy and its relevance to the organization. About 80 percent of grapevine communications pertain to business-related topics rather than personal gossip. Moreover, from 70 to 90 percent of the details passed through a grapevine are accurate.[60] Many managers would like the grapevine to be destroyed because they consider its rumors to be untrue, malicious, and harmful, which typically is not the case. Managers should be aware that almost five of every six important messages are carried to some extent by the grapevine rather than through official channels. In a survey of 22,000 shift workers in varied industries, 55 percent said they get most of their information via the grapevine.[61] Smart managers understand the company's grapevine. They recognize who's connected to whom and which employees are key players in the informal spread of information. In all cases, but particularly in times of crisis, executives need to manage communications effectively so that the grapevine is not the only source of information.[62]

Management by Wandering Around. The communication technique known as **management by wandering around (MBWA)** was made famous by the books *In Search of Excellence* and *A Passion for Excellence*.[63] These books describe executives who talk directly with employees to learn what is going on. MBWA works for managers at all levels. Managers mingle and develop positive relationships with employees and learn directly from them about their department, division, or organization. The president of ARCO had a habit of visiting a district field office. Rather than schedule a big strategic meeting with the district supervisor, he would come in unannounced and chat with the lowest-level employees. In any organization, both upward and downward communications are enhanced with MBWA. Managers have a chance to describe key ideas and values to employees and, in turn, learn about the problems and issues confronting employees.

When managers fail to take advantage of MBWA, they become aloof and isolated from employees. For example, Peter Anderson, president of Ztel, Inc., a maker of television switching systems, preferred not to personally communicate with employees. He

grapevine
an informal, person-to-person communication network of employees that is not officially sanctioned by the organization.

management by wandering around (MBWA)
a communication technique in which managers interact directly with workers to exchange information.

managed at arm's length. As one manager said, "I don't know how many times I asked Peter to come to the lab, but he stayed in his office. He wasn't that visible to the troops." This formal, impersonal management style contributed to Ztel's troubles and eventual bankruptcy.[64]

Using the Written Word. Not all manager communication is face-to-face, or even verbal. Managers frequently have to communicate in writing, via memorandums, reports, or everyday e-mails. The memo, whether it is sent on paper or electronically, remains a primary way of communicating within companies, and e-mail has become the main way most organizations communicate with customers and clients. Yet evidence shows that the writing skills of U.S. employees and managers in general are terrible. One study found that at least a third of workers in the United States don't have the writing skills they need to perform their jobs. A report from The National Commission on Writing says that states spend nearly $250 million a year on remedial writing training for government workers.[65]

Good writing matters. Consider this story told by the president of Opus Associates, a written communications consulting company: After attorney Brian Puricelli won a major case for a client, he petitioned the court to recover his fees. Magistrate Judge Jacob Hart agreed, but he deemed the petition so full or errors and misspellings that he declared it disrespectful to the court and slashed the amount due to Puricelli by nearly $30,000.[66]

Managers can learn to be good writers. Here are a few tips from experts on how to effectively communicate in written form:[67]

- *Respect the reader.* The reader's time is valuable; don't waste it with a rambling, confusing memo or e-mail that has to be read several times to try to make sense of it. Pay attention to your grammar and spelling. Sloppy writing indicates that you think your time is more important than that of your readers. You'll lose their interest—and their respect.

- *Know your point and get to it.* What is the key piece of information that you want the reader to remember? Many people just sit and write, without clarifying in their own mind what it is they're trying to say. To write effectively, know what your central point is and write to support it.

- *Write clearly rather than impressively.* Don't use pretentious or inflated language, and avoid jargon. The goal of good writing for business is to be understood the first time through. State your message as simply and as clearly as possible.

- *Get a second opinion.* When the communication is highly important, such as a formal memo to the department or organization, ask someone you consider to be a good writer to read it before you send it. Don't be too proud to take their advice. In all cases, read and revise the memo or e-mail a second and third time before you hit the send button.

A former manager of communication services at consulting firm Arthur D. Little Inc. has estimated that around 30 percent of all business memos and e-mails are written simply to get clarification about an earlier written communication that didn't make sense to the reader.[68] By following these guidelines, you can get your message across the first time.

Communicating During Turbulent Times

During turbulent times, communication becomes even more important. To build trust and promote learning and problem solving, managers incorporate ideas such as open communication, dialogue, and feedback and learning. In addition, they develop crisis communication skills for communicating with both employees and the public in exceptionally challenging or frightening circumstances.

OPEN COMMUNICATION

A recent trend that reflects managers' increased emphasis on empowering employees, building trust and commitment, and enhancing collaboration is open communication.

TAKE ACTION

As a manager, remember that organizational secrets don't often remain that way; therefore, be open and tell the truth from the beginning.

open communication
sharing all types of information throughout the company, across functional and hierarchical levels.

dialogue
a group communication process aimed at creating a culture based on collaboration, fluidity, trust, and commitment to shared goals.

Open communication means sharing all types of information throughout the company, across functional and hierarchical levels. Many companies, such as Springfield Remanufacturing Corporation, AmeriSteel, and Whole Foods Markets, are opening the financial books to workers at all levels and training employees to understand how and why the company operates as it does. At Wabash National Corporation, one of the nation's leading truck-trailer manufacturers, employees complete several hours of business training and attend regular meetings on the shop floor to review the company's financial performance.[69]

Open communication runs counter to the traditional flow of selective information downward from supervisors to subordinates. By breaking down conventional hierarchical barriers to communication, the organization can gain the benefit of all employees' ideas. The same ideas batted back and forth among a few managers do not lead to effective learning or to a network of relationships that keep companies thriving. New voices and conversations involving a broad spectrum of people revitalize and enhance organizational communication.[70] Open communication also builds trust and a commitment to common goals, which is essential in organizations that depend on collaboration and knowledge-sharing to accomplish their purpose. Fifty percent of executives surveyed report that open communication is a key to building trust in the organization.[71]

DIALOGUE

Another popular means of fostering trust and collaboration is through dialogue. The "roots of dialogue" are *dia* and *logos,* which can be thought of as *stream of meaning*. **Dialogue** is a group communication process in which together people create a stream of shared meaning that enables them to understand each other and share a view of the world.[72] People may start out at polar opposites, but by talking openly, they discover common ground, common issues, and shared goals on which they can build a better future.

A useful way to describe dialogue is to contrast it with discussion (see Exhibit 13.8). The intent of discussion, generally, is to deliver one's point of view and persuade others to adopt it. A discussion is often resolved by logic or "beating down" opponents. Dialogue, by contrast, asks that participants suspend their attachments to a particular viewpoint so that a deeper level of listening, synthesis, and meaning can evolve from the group. A dialogue's focus is to reveal feelings and build common ground. Both forms of communication—dialogue and discussion—can result in change. However, the result of discussion is limited to the topic being deliberated, whereas the result of dialogue is characterized by group unity, shared meaning, and transformed mind-sets. As new and deeper solutions are developed, a trusting relationship is built among team members.[73]

CRISIS COMMUNICATION

Over the past few years, the sheer number and scope of crises have made communication a more demanding job for managers. Organizations face small crises every day, such as charges of racial discrimination, a factory fire, or a flu epidemic. Moreover, acts of intentional evil, such as bombings or kidnappings, continue to increase, causing serious repercussions for people and organizations.[74] Managers can develop four primary skills for communicating in a crisis.[75]

CONCEPT CONNECTION

When an extortionist claimed to have placed seven pesticide-contaminated candy bars in Sydney area stores, manufacturer MasterFoods Australia-New Zealand's response was a textbook example of effective **crisis communication.** President Andy Weston-Webb announced, "It's not safe to eat Mars or Snickers bars" and immediately activated recall plans. MasterFoods launched a public relations campaign, which included interviews with Weston-Webb, full-page newspaper ads, a company hotline, and media access to the burial of 3 million candy bars in a deep pit. The two-month absence of the popular snacks cost the company more than $10 million. But MasterFoods emerged with its reputation intact. During the first week of the products' return, sales surged 300 percent.

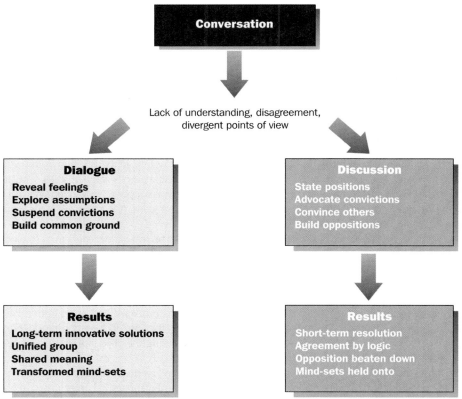

EXHIBIT 13.8
Dialogue and
Discussion: The
Differences

SOURCE: Adapted from Edgar Schein, "On Dialogue, Culture, and Organizational Learning," *Organizational Dynamics* (Autumn 1993): 46.

- *Maintain your focus.* Good crisis communicators don't allow themselves to be overwhelmed by the situation. Calmness and listening become more important than ever. Managers also learn to tailor their communications to reflect hope and optimism at the same time they acknowledge the current difficulties.

- *Be visible.* Many managers underestimate just how important their presence is during a crisis.[76] As we discussed in Chapter 1, people need to feel that someone is in control. A manager's job is to step out immediately, both to reassure employees and respond to public concerns. Face-to-face communication with employees is crucial for letting people know that managers care about them and what they're going through.

- *Get the awful truth out.*[77] Effective managers gather as much information as they can, do their best to determine the facts, and tell the truth to employees and the public as soon as possible. Getting the truth out quickly prevents rumors and misunderstandings.

- *Communicate a vision for the future.* People need to feel that they have something to work for and look forward to. Moments of crisis present opportunities for managers to communicate a vision of a better future and unite people toward common goals.

FEEDBACK AND LEARNING

Feedback occurs when managers use evaluation and communication to help individuals and the organization learn and improve. It enables managers to determine whether they have been successful in communicating with others. Recall from Exhibit 13.2 that feedback is an important part of the communication process. However, despite its importance, feedback is often neglected. Giving and receiving feedback is typically difficult for both managers and employees. Yet, by avoiding feedback, people miss a valuable opportunity to help one another learn, develop, and improve.[78]

 TAKE ACTION

When someone gives you negative feedback, rather than defending yourself and proving them wrong, just listen quietly and say, "thank you for the information" and nothing more.

U.S. Army

At the National Training Center just south of Death Valley, U.S. Army troops engage in a simulated battle: The "enemy" has sent unmanned aerial vehicles (UAVs) to gather targeting data. When the troops fire on the UAVs, they reveal their location to attack helicopters hovering just behind a nearby ridge. After the exercise, unit members and their superiors hold an *after-action review* to review battle plans, discuss what worked and what didn't, and talk about how to do things better. Gen. William Hertzog suggests that inexpensive decoy UAVs might be just the thing to make a distracted enemy reveal its location. The observation became a "lesson learned" for the entire army, and UAVs became an important part of battle operations in Iraq.

Many researchers attribute the transformation of the army from a demoralized, dysfunctional organization following the Vietnam War into an elite force capable of effectively accomplishing Operation Iraqi Freedom to this unique feedback and learning system. In the U.S. Army, after-action reviews take just 15 minutes, and they occur after every identifiable event—large or small, simulated or real. The review involves asking four simple questions: What was supposed to happen? What actually happened? What accounts for any difference? What can we learn? It is a process of identifying mistakes, of innovating, and of continually learning from experience.

The lessons are based not only on simulated battles but also on real-life experiences of soldiers in the field. The Center for Army Lessons Learned (CALL) sends experts into the field to observe after-action reviews, interview soldiers, and compile intelligence reports. Leaders in all army divisions are currently engaged in a detailed analysis of lessons learned during Operation Iraqi Freedom and Operation Enduring Freedom. The lessons will be used to train soldiers and develop action plans for resolving problems in future conflicts. For example, many of the problems and issues from a similar process following Operation Desert Storm had been resolved by the time of Operation Iraqi Freedom. A primary focus for current leaders is to improve training regarding the difficult shift from offensive operations to humanitarian and relief efforts.[79]

In this example, the organization is learning by communicating feedback about the consequences of field operations and simulated battles. Compiling what is learned and using communication feedback create an improved organization. After-action reviews are also used in corporate America. Steelcase Inc., an office furniture manufacturer, and oil giant BP are among the companies adapting the army's system to create a process of continuous learning and improvement. BP credits the feedback system for $700 million in cost savings and other gains.[80]

Successful managers focus their feedback to help develop the capacities of subordinates, and they encourage critical feedback from employees. When managers enlist the whole organization in reviewing the outcomes of activities, they can quickly learn what works and what doesn't and use that information to improve the organization. Consider how the U.S. Army's feedback system promotes whole-system learning.

Managing Organizational Communication

Many of the ideas described in this chapter pertain to barriers to communication and how to overcome them. Exhibit 13.9 lists some of the major barriers to communication, along with some techniques for overcoming them.

BARRIERS TO COMMUNICATION

Barriers can be categorized as those that exist at the individual level and those that exist at the organizational level.

Individual Barriers. First, *interpersonal barriers* include problems with emotions and perceptions held by employees. For example, rigid perceptual labeling or stereotyping prevents people from modifying or altering their opinions. If a person's mind is made up before the communication starts, communication will fail. Moreover, people with different backgrounds or knowledge may interpret a communication in different ways.

EXHIBIT 13.9
Communication Barriers and Ways to Overcome Them

Barriers	How to Overcome
Individual	
Interpersonal dynamics	Active listening
Channels and media	Selection of appropriate channel
Semantics	Knowledge of other's perspective
Inconsistent cues	MBWA
Organizational	
Status and power differences	Climate of trust, Dialogue
Departmental needs and goals	Development and use of formal channels
Lack of formal channels	Encouragement of multiple channels, formal and informal
Communication network unsuited to task	Changing organization or group structure to fit communication needs
Poor coordination	Feedback and learning

Second, *selecting the wrong channel* or *medium* for sending a communication can be a problem. When a message is emotional, it is better to transmit it face to face rather than in writing. E-mail can be particularly risky for discussing difficult issues because it lacks the capacity for rapid feedback and multiple cues. On the other hand, e-mail is highly efficient for routine messages.

Third, *semantics* often causes communication problems. **Semantics** pertains to the meaning of words and the way they are used. A word such as *effectiveness* may mean achieving high production to a factory superintendent, but to a human resources staff specialist, it might mean employee satisfaction. Many common words have an average of 28 definitions; thus, communicators must take care to select the words that will accurately encode ideas.[81] Language differences can also be a barrier in today's organizations. This chapter's Spotlight boxed feature offers some guidelines for how managers can better communicate with people who speak a different language.

Fourth, sending *inconsistent cues* between verbal and nonverbal communications will confuse the receiver. If a person's facial expression does not reflect his or her words, the communication will contain noise and uncertainty. The tone of voice and body language should be consistent with the words, and actions should not contradict words.

Organizational Barriers. Organizational barriers pertain to factors for the organization as a whole. One of the most significant barriers relates to *status and power differences*. Low-power people may be reluctant to pass bad news up the hierarchy, thus giving the wrong impression to upper levels.[82] High-power people may not pay attention or may think that low-status people have little to contribute.

Second, *differences across departments in terms of needs and goals* interfere with communications. Each department perceives problems in its own terms. The production department is concerned with production efficiency, whereas the marketing department's goal is to get the product to the customer in a hurry.

Third, the *absence of formal channels* reduces communication effectiveness. Organizations must provide adequate upward, downward, and horizontal communication in the form of employee surveys, open-door policies, newsletters, memos, task forces, and liaison personnel. Without these formal channels, the organization cannot communicate as a whole.

Fourth, the *communication flow* may not fit the team's or organization's task. If a centralized communication structure is used for nonroutine tasks, not enough information will be circulated to solve problems. The organization, department, or team is most efficient when the amount of communication flowing among employees fits the task.

TAKE ACTION
Go to the ethical dilemma on page 512 that pertains to individual barriers to communication.

TAKE ACTION
As a manager, solicit bad information from below, so you can avoid problems erupting.

semantics
the meaning of words and the way they are used.

Spotlight on Skills

Leaping Over Language Barriers

In today's global business environment, odds are good you'll find yourself conversing with an employee, colleague, or customer who has limited skills in your native language. Here are some guidelines that will help you speak—and listen—more effectively.

1. **Keep your message simple.** Be clear about what you want to communicate, and keep to the point.
2. **Select your words with care.** Don't try to dazzle with your vocabulary. Choose simple words, and look for opportunities to use cognates—that is, words that resemble words in your listener's language. For example, *banco* in Spanish means "bank" in English. Assemble those simple words into equally simple phrases and short sentences. And be sure to avoid idioms, slang, jargon, and vague terminology such as *soon, often,* or *several.*
3. **Pay close attention to nonverbals.**
   - Don't cover your mouth with your hand. Being able to see your lips helps your listener decipher what you're saying.
   - Speak slowly and carefully. In particular, avoid running words together. "Howyadoin?" won't make any sense to someone still struggling with the English language, for example.
   - Allow for pauses. If you're an American, your culture has taught you to avoid silence whenever possible, but

pauses give your listener time to take in what you've said, ask a question, or formulate a response.
   - Fight the urge to shout. Speaking louder doesn't make it any easier for someone to understand you. It also tends to be intimidating and could give the impression that you're angry.
   - Pay attention to facial expressions and body language, but keep in mind that the meaning of such cues can vary significantly from culture to culture. For example, Americans may view eye contact as a sign you're giving someone your full attention, but the Japanese consider prolonged eye contact rude.
4. **Check for comprehension frequently, and invite feedback.** Stop from time to time and make sure you're being understood, especially if the other person laughs inappropriately, never asks a question, or continually nods and smiles politely. Ask the listener to repeat what you've said in his or her own words. If you find the other person hasn't understood you, restate the information in a different way instead of simply repeating yourself. Similarly, listen carefully when the nonnative person speaks, and offer feedback so the person can check your understanding of his or her message.

Above all, when communicating with someone who doesn't speak your language well, be patient with yourself and the listener, be encouraging, and be persistent.

SOURCES: "How to Communicate with a Non Native English Speaker," wikiHow, www.wikihow.com/Communicate-With-a-Non-Native-English-Speaker; Sondra Thiederman, "Language Barriers: Bridging the Gap," www.thiederman.com/articles_detail.php?id=39; "Communicating with Nonnative Speakers," Magellan Health Services, www.magellanassist.com/mem/library/default.asp?TopicId=95&CategoryId=0&ArticleId=5.

A final problem is *poor coordination*, so that different parts of the organization are working in isolation without knowing and understanding what other parts are doing. Top executives are out of touch with lower levels, or departments and divisions are so poorly coordinated that people do not understand how the system works together as a whole.

OVERCOMING COMMUNICATION BARRIERS

Managers can design the organization to encourage positive, effective communications. Designing involves both individual skills and organizational actions.

Individual Skills. Perhaps the most important individual skill is *active listening*. Active listening means asking questions, showing interest, and occasionally paraphrasing what the speaker has said to ensure accurate interpretation. Active listening also means providing feedback to the sender to complete the communication loop.

Second, individuals should select the *appropriate channel* for the message. A complicated message should be sent through a rich channel, such as face-to-face discussion or telephone. Routine messages and data can be sent through memos, letters, or e-mail because the risk of misunderstanding is lower.

Third, senders and receivers should make a special effort to *understand* each other's perspective. Managers can sensitize themselves to the information receiver so they can better target the message, detect bias, and clarify misinterpretations. When communicators understand others' perspectives, semantics can be clarified, perceptions understood, and objectivity maintained.

The fourth individual skill is *management by wandering around*. Managers must be willing to get out of the office and check communications with others. Glenn Tilton, the CEO of United Airlines, takes every opportunity to introduce himself to employees and customers and find out what's on their minds. He logs more airplane time than many of his company's pilots, visits passenger lounges, and chats with employees on concourses, galleys, and airport terminals.[83] Through direct observation and face-to-face meetings, managers like Tilton gain an understanding of the organization and are able to communicate important ideas and values directly to others.

Organizational Actions. Perhaps the most important thing managers can do for the organization is to create a *climate of trust and openness*. Open communication and dialogue can encourage people to communicate honestly with one another. Subordinates will feel free to transmit negative as well as positive messages without fear of retribution. Efforts to develop interpersonal skills among employees can also foster openness, honesty, and trust.

Second, managers should develop and use *formal information channels* in all directions. Scandinavian Design uses two newsletters to reach employees. Dana Corporation has developed innovative programs such as the "Here's a Thought" board—called a HAT rack—to get ideas and feedback from workers. Other techniques include direct mail, bulletin boards, and employee surveys.

Third, managers should encourage the use of *multiple channels*, including both formal and informal communications. Multiple communication channels include written directives, face-to-face discussions, MBWA, and the grapevine. For example, managers at GM's Packard Electric plant use multimedia, including a monthly newspaper, frequent meetings of employee teams, and an electronic news display in the cafeteria. Sending messages through multiple channels increases the likelihood that they will be properly received.

Fourth, the structure should *fit communication needs*. An organization can be designed to use teams, task forces, project managers, or a matrix structure as needed to facilitate the horizontal flow of information for coordination and problem solving. Structure should also reflect information needs. When team or department tasks are difficult, a decentralized structure should be implemented to encourage discussion and participation.

A system of organizational *feedback and learning* can help overcome problems of poor coordination. Harrah's created a *Communication Team* as part of its structure at the Casino/Holiday Inn in Las Vegas. The team includes one member from each department. This cross-functional team deals with urgent company problems and helps people think beyond the scope of their own departments to communicate with anyone and everyone to solve those problems.

CONCEPT CONNECTION

"I've taken an oath to serve and protect all in my county," says Clark County, Ohio, Sheriff Gene Kelly. He uses the Phraselator P2, shown here, to overcome **barriers to communication** with the county's growing Spanish-speaking population. The Phraselator is a PDA-sized translation device originally developed by Maryland-based VoxTec for the military. The handheld computer translates English phrases such as "Halt" or "Show me where it hurts" and then broadcasts them in one of approximately 60 languages. Troops and medical personnel in Afghanistan, Iraq, Haiti, and Southeast Asia use Phraselators, and they're beginning to make their way into U.S. emergency rooms and county health departments in addition to law enforcement agencies.

 **TAKE ACTION**

As a manager, you can develop a climate of trust by becoming more trustworthy.

Summary

This chapter described several important points about communicating in organizations. Communication takes up at least 80 percent of a manager's time. Managers' communication is purpose-directed, in that it unites people around a shared vision and goals and directs attention to the values and behaviors that achieve goals. Communication is a process of encoding an idea into a message, which is sent through a channel and decoded by a receiver. Communication among people can be affected by communication channels, nonverbal communication, and listening skills. An important aspect of management communication is persuasion. The ability to persuade others to behave in ways that help accomplish the vision and goals is crucial to good management. Managers frequently use symbols, stories, and metaphors to persuade and influence others.

At the organizational level, managers are concerned with managing formal communications in a downward, upward, and horizontal direction. Good writing skills have become even more important with the increased use of e-mail for communication.

Informal communications also are important, especially management by wandering around, developing personal networks, and understanding the grapevine. Moreover, research shows that communication structures in teams and departments should reflect the underlying tasks. Open communication, dialogue, feedback, and learning are important communication mechanisms, especially in times of turbulence and uncertainty. In addition, today's managers have to develop effective crisis communication skills. Four important skills for communicating in a crisis are to remain calm and focused, be visible, "get the awful truth out," and communicate a vision for a brighter future.

The final part of this chapter described several individual and organizational barriers to communication. These barriers can be overcome by active listening, selecting appropriate channels, engaging in MBWA, using dialogue, developing a climate of trust, using formal channels, designing the correct structure to fit communication needs, and using feedback for learning. Status and power differences can be a significant barrier to communications.

Discussion Questions

1. Lee's Garage is an internal Wal-Mart Web site that CEO H. Lee Scott uses to communicate with the company's 1.5 million U.S. employees. A public relations associate screens employee questions, and Scott dictates his responses to an aide, who then posts them on the Web. What would you predict are the advantages and potential problems to this method of upper-level management's connecting with employees?

2. Describe the elements of the communication process. Give an example of each part of the model as it exists in the classroom during communication between teacher and students.

3. Why do you think stories are more effective than hard facts and figures in persuading others?

4. Try to recall an incident at school or work when information was passed primarily through the grapevine. How accurate were the rumors, and how did people react to them? How can managers control information that is processed through the grapevine?

5. What is the difference between a discussion and a dialogue? What steps might managers take to transform a discussion into a constructive dialogue?

6. What do you think are the major barriers to upward communication in organizations? Discuss.

7. What is the relationship between group member communication and group task? For example, how should communications differ in a strategic planning group and a group of employees who stock shelves in a grocery store?

8. Some senior managers believe they should rely on written information and computer reports because these yield more accurate data than do face-to-face communications. Do you agree? Why or why not?

9. Why is management by wandering around considered effective communication? How might managers encourage open and honest communication, as opposed to polite conversation and best behavior, when engaging in MBWA?

10. Assume that you have been asked to design a training program to help managers become better communicators. What would you include in the program?

Dear Dr. Dorothy

Although I've been a manager less than a year, I am proud to say I've totally streamlined the communications in my department. We used to have weekly meetings, and then I'd often have to talk to various people during the week, but I've managed to move almost everything to e-mail. It is so much quicker and much more efficient. Something troubles, me, though. Last week my boss sent me to a New Manager seminar, and the presenter was saying supervisors rely too heavily on e-mail. When I tried to explain what I've done, she just cut me off and said I wasn't focused on people enough. I say she was rude. What do you think?

Modernizer in Moline

Dear Modern,

Dr. Dorothy is reminded of the manager taking a high-speed train to the wrong city. The ride was very efficient but got him to the wrong place. Your management repertoire is as thin as Donald Trump's hair. Need Dr. Dorothy remind you some of the lessons you no doubt learned in business school? That doing things in the most effective way is not necessarily the most efficient. In your haste to save time (so you can leave early and go skateboarding, per chance?), you have violated a vital management edict: To remember your subordinates are *people* and should be accorded some measure of respect, even when you feel uninclined to do so. Simple messages can go by e-mail, but anything complicated or emotional requires more, shall we say, decorum. Not to mention sending several e-mails a day to employees right next door to your office might feel streamlined, but Dr. Dorothy believes it is rude. Go into the hallway, or my goodness, into their offices and *talk* to them, as if you were both human beings. Dr. Dorothy suggests that you might ultimately save time by doing so, as you will prevent some problems and misunderstandings. Communication isn't only about *sending*, but it's also about listening and trying to understand. Stop doing one-way communication before you are shown the way to the door.

Self Learning

Do You Love Your Company?

Open, honest, and authentic communication can help create the kind of organization that employees love. Here's an instrument to determine which of five key principles your company does best.

	Strongly Agree	Somewhat Agree	Neutral	Somewhat Disagree	Strongly Disagree
Capture the Heart					
1. We have a written vision that is know to all and lived every day.	1	2	3	4	5
2. We seek creative, low-cost ways to balance work and family.	1	2	3	4	5
3. We love to celebrate and find innovative ways to inject fun into the workplace.	1	2	3	4	5
Open Communication					
1. It is obvious that management considers internal listening a priority.	1	2	3	4	5
2. Attention is given to using multiple communication channels more than just using memos and e-mail.	1	2	3	4	5

	Strongly Agree	Somewhat Agree	Neutral	Somewhat Disagree	Strongly Disagree
3. Employees receive feedback in real time (immediate, direct, positive) rather than merely occasional performance appraisals.	1	2	3	4	5

Create Partnerships

	Strongly Agree	Somewhat Agree	Neutral	Somewhat Disagree	Strongly Disagree
1. There are few, if any, status barriers between employees (i.e., reserved parking, bonuses only for top management, special benefits).	1	2	3	4	5
2. We actively share financial numbers, ratios, and company performance measures with all employees.	1	2	3	4	5
3. Management visibly serves the front-line, customer-contact employees first (providing tools, resources, and training) before asking the front-line employees to serve us with reports, paperwork, and so on.	1	2	3	4	5

Drive Learning

	Strongly Agree	Somewhat Agree	Neutral	Somewhat Disagree	Strongly Disagree
1. We guarantee lifelong employability (rather than lifetime employment) through offering extensive training, cross-training, and work variety.	1	2	3	4	5
2. Special attention is given to creating visible, activity-filled programs that help drive learning through all levels of the organization: up, down and laterally.	1	2	3	4	5
3. We actively support a philosophy of lifelong learning for our employees that goes beyond focusing only on today's job needs.	1	2	3	4	5

Emancipate Action

	Strongly Agree	Somewhat Agree	Neutral	Somewhat Disagree	Strongly Disagree
1. We allow employees the freedom to fail and try again.	1	2	3	4	5
2. Constant attention is given to creating freedom from bureaucracy, unnecessary sign-offs, outdated procedures, and office politics.	1	2	3	4	5
3. All employees are encouraged to openly challenge the status quo to help find better, faster, more profitable ways to serve our customers.	1	2	3	4	5

Summary Score: The higher the score (on any of the five principles), the more you believe this principle is alive and well in your organization. The lower the score, the more your organization needs to address this principle.

Questions

1. Which of the items are directly or indirectly related to communications?

2. How are emotional issues (capturing the heart), partnerships, and learning related to communication in organizations?

SOURCE: Jim Harris, "The partnership facade: What's your love quotient?" *Management Review* (April 1996): 45–48.

Group Learning

Storytelling

1. Form groups of three to four members. Decide on a scenario you will use to write a story. Choose a struggle or conflict at your university, that is, a head coach in ethics violation, a fraternity censured for wild parties, students involved in racist activities, some student groups feeling discriminated against or marginalized, conflicts between well-known faculty and the administration, student cheating scandals, and so on. Then write a story that is meant to illustrate some concept or value. Here's what the story must have:

   a. A protagonist or hero (or anti-hero). Start with a real person so the conflict is more interesting to the listeners.

   b. Describe the moment when the hero's conflicts start.

   c. Bring in other players (these are all real people in the situation) who complicate the situation, who create even more conflicts.

   d. Show the ups and downs, the wins and losses along the way.

   e. Describe how the hero and those around the hero resolve the problems and what they had to overcome.

   f. Make sure you include some adages such as, "a stitch in time saves nine," "the early bird catches the worm," and so on.

   g. Detail the concept or value your story is based on.

   h. Make sure the story is written in a way that would help the powers that be see how important it is to help resolve the problem or prevent further problems in the future.

2. Each group shares its story with the class. Class members guess what the concept or value is of each story.

3. As a class, discuss: How can storytelling help managers to solve problems?

Action Learning

1. Form into pairs. You will be studying organizational communications at your university (or another company, which one of you may or may not work at).

2. Go to the "Organizational Communication" section, especially referring to the sections on downward communication and upward communication. Become familiar with the two lists of communication channels in both upward and downward communication.

3. Go to the university website (or the company) and find the places relevant to faculty and students. Look for examples of upward and downward communication. Write them down.

4. What is the purpose of each of these communications? What, in reality, do you expect the actual consequence of each communication to be?

5. If you were hired as a consultant to this organization, what would you recommend they change in their upward and downward communications? Why?

6. The instructor may ask you to either bring your findings to class for a discussion or to hand in a written report.

Ethical Dilemma

On Trial

When Werner and Thompson, a Los Angeles business and financial management firm, offered Iranian-born Firoz Bahmani a position as an accountant assistant one spring day in 2002, Bahmani felt a sense of genuine relief, but his relief was short-lived.

With his degree in accounting from a top-notch American university, he knew he was more than a little over-qualified for the job. But time after time, he'd been rejected for suitable positions. His language difficulties were the reason most often given for his unsuccessful candidacy. Although the young man had grown up speaking both Farsi and French in his native land, he'd only begun to pick up English shortly before his arrival in the United States a few years ago. Impressed by his educational credentials and his quiet, courtly manner, managing partner Beatrice Werner overlooked his heavy accent and actively recruited him for the position, the only one available at the time. During his interview, she assured him he would advance in time.

It was clear to Beatrice that Firoz was committed to succeeding at all costs. But it soon also became apparent that Firoz and his immediate supervisor, Cathy Putnam, were at odds. Cathy was a seasoned account manager who had just transferred to Los Angeles from the New York office. Saddled with an enormous workload, she let Firoz know right from the start, speaking in her rapid-fire Brooklyn accent, that he'd need to get up to speed as quickly as possible.

Shortly before Cathy was to give Firoz his three-month probationary review, she came to Beatrice, expressed her frustration with Firoz's performance, and suggested that he be let go. "His bank reconciliations and financial report preparations are first-rate," Cathy admitted, "but his communication skills leave a lot to be desired. In the first place, I simply don't have the time to keep repeating the same directions over and over again when I'm trying to teach him his responsibilities. Then there's the fact that public contact is part of his written job description. Typically, he puts off making phone calls to dispute credit card charges or ask a client's staff for the information he needs. When he does finally pick up the phone . . . well, let's just say I've had more than one client mention how hard it is to understand what he's trying to say. Some of them are getting pretty exasperated."

"You know, some firms feel it's their corporate responsibility to help foreign-born employees learn English," Beatrice began. "Maybe we should help him find an English-as-a-second-language course and pay for it."

"With all due respect, I don't think that's our job," Cathy replied, with barely concealed irritation. "If you come to the United States, you should learn our language. That's what my mom's parents did when they came over from Italy. They certainly didn't expect anyone to hold their hands. Besides," she added, almost inaudibly, "Firoz's lucky we let him into this country."

Beatrice had mixed feelings. On one hand, she recognized that Werner and Thompson had every right to require someone in Firoz's position be capable of carrying out his public contract duties. Perhaps she had made a mistake in hiring him. But as the daughter of German immigrants herself, she knew firsthand both how daunting language and cultural barriers could be and that they could be overcome in time. Perhaps in part because of her family background, she had a passionate commitment to the firm's stated goals of creating a diverse workforce and a caring, supportive culture. Besides she felt a personal sense of obligation to help a hardworking, promising employee realize his potential. What will she advise Cathy to do now that Firoz's probationary period is drawing to a close?

What Would You Do?

1. Agree with Cathy Putnam. Despite your personal feelings, accept that Firoz Bahmani is not capable of carrying out the accountant assistant's responsibilities. Make the break now, and give him his notice on the grounds that he cannot carry out one of the key stated job requirements. Advise him that a position that primarily involves paperwork would be a better fit for him.

2. Place Firoz with a more sympathetic account manager who is open to finding ways to help him improve his English and has the time to help him develop his assertiveness and telephone skills. Send Cathy Putnam to diversity awareness training.

3. Create a new position at the firm that will allow Firoz to do the reports and reconciliations for several account managers, freeing the account assistants to concentrate on public contact work. Make it clear that he will have little chance of future promotion unless his English improves markedly.

SOURCES: Mary Gillis, "Iranian Americans," *Multicultural America*, www.everyculture.com/multi/Ha-La/Iranian-Americans.html (accessed September 19, 2006); and Charlene Marmer Solomon, "Managing Today's Immigrants," *Personnel Journal* 72, no. 3 (February 1993): 56–65.

Case for Critical Analysis

Hunter-Worth

Christmas was fast approaching. Just a short while ago, Chuck Moore, national sales manager for Hunter-Worth, a New York–based multinational toy manufacturer, was confident the coming holiday was going to be one of the company's best in years. At a recent toy expo, Hunter-Worth unveiled a new interactive plush toy that was cuddly, high-tech, and tied into a major holiday motion picture expected to be a smash hit. Chuck had thought the toy would do well, but frankly, the level of interest took him by surprise. The buyers at the toy fair raved, and the subsequent pre-order volume was extremely encouraging. It had all looked so promising, but now he couldn't shake a sense of impending doom.

The problem in a nutshell was that the Mexican subsidiary that manufactured the toy couldn't seem to meet a deadline. Not only were all the shipments late so far, but they also fell well short of the quantities ordered. Chuck decided to e-mail Vicente Ruiz, the plant manager, about the situation before he found himself in the middle of the Christmas season with parents clamoring for a toy he couldn't lay his hands on.

In a thoroughly professional e-mail that started with a friendly "Dear Vicente," Chuck inquired about the status of the latest order, asked for a production schedule for pending orders, and requested a specific explanation as to why the Mexican plant seemed to be having such difficulty shipping orders out on time. The reply appeared within the hour, but to his utter astonishment, it was a short message from Vicente's secretary. She acknowledged the receipt of his e-mail and assured him the Mexican plant would be shipping the order, already a week late, in the next 10 days.

"That's it," Chuck fumed. "Time to take this to Sato." He prefaced his original e-mail and the secretary's reply with a terse note expressing his growing concern over the availability of what could well be this season's must-have toy. "Just what do I have to do to light a fire under Vicente?" he wrote. He then forwarded it all to his supervisor and friend, Michael Sato, the executive vice president for sales and marketing.

Next thing he knew, he was on the phone with Vicente—and the plant manager was furious. "Signor Moore, how dare you go over my head and say such things about me to my boss?" he sputtered, sounding both angry and slightly panicked. It seemed that Michael had forwarded Chuck's e-mail to Hunter-Worth's vice president of operations, who had sent it on to the Mexican subsidiary's president.

That turn of events was unfortunate, but Chuck wasn't feeling all that apologetic. "You could have prevented all this if you'd just answered the questions I e-mailed you last week," he pointed out. "I deserved more than a form letter—and from your secretary, no less."

"My secretary always answers my e-mails," replied Vicente. "She figures that if the problem is really urgent, you would pick up the phone and talk to me directly. Contrary to what you guys north of the border might think, we do take deadlines seriously here. There's only so much we can do with the supply problems we're having, but I doubt you're interested in hearing about those." And Vicente hung up the phone without waiting for a response.

Chuck was confused and disheartened. Things were only getting worse. How could he turn the situation around?

Questions

1. Based on Vicente Ruiz's actions and his conversation with Chuck Moore, what differences do you detect in cultural attitudes toward communications in Mexico as compared with the United States? Is understanding these differences important? Explain.

2. What was the main purpose of Chuck's communication to Vicente? To Michael Sato? What factors should he have considered when choosing a channel for his communication to Vicente? Are they the same factors he should have considered when communicating with Michael Sato?

3. If you were Chuck, what would you have done differently? What steps would you take at this point to make sure the supply of the popular new toy is sufficient to meet the anticipated demand?

SOURCES: Based on Harry W. Lane, *Charles Foster Sends an E-mail*, (London, Ontario: Ivey Publishing, 2005); Frank Unger and Roger Frankel, *Doing Business in Mexico: A Practical Guide on How to Break into the Market* (Council on Australia Latin America Relations and the Department of Foreign Affairs and Trade, 2002): 24–27; and Ignacio Hernandez, "Doing Business in Mexico—Business Etiquette—Understanding U.S.–Mexico Cultural Differences," *MexGrocer.com*, www.mexgrocer.com/business-in-mexico.html (accessed September 18, 2006).

Patch Adams

Hunter "Patch" Adams (Robin Williams), a maverick medical student, believes that laughter is the best medicine. The rest of the medical community believes that medicine is the best medicine. Unlike traditional doctors who remain aloof, Patch Adams wants to be close to his patients. Williams's wackiness comes through clearly in this film, which is based on a true-story.

This scene comes from the film's early sequence "The Experiment," which takes place after the students' medical school orientation. Patch Adams and fellow medical student Truman Schiff (Daniel London) leave the University Diner. They begin Patch's experiment for changing the programmed responses of people they meet on the street. Along the way, they stumble upon a meat packers' convention where this scene occurs.

What to Watch for and Ask Yourself

1. What parts of the communication process appear in this scene? Note each part of the process that you see in the scene.

2. What type of communication does this scene show: small group, large audience, or persuasive?

3. Do you think Patch Adams is an effective communicator? Why or why not?

Communication at Navistar International

The decision to dedicate the resources needed to fund and support the Department of Communications within Navistar International sends a signal that Corporate Communication is seen as vital to the health of this $12 billion truck and engine manufacturing and financial services corporation.

The Department of Communications functions as a business partner with the three major business units. Each plant has a communications manager or communicator who dual reports to the plant manager and the Corporate Director of the Department of Communications. The role of the Communications Manager is to drive the message to the target audience. They use different approaches depending on the audience and the direction of the message, whether it's heading up or down the corporate ladder, or across business units.

Typically, in any successful business organization, skilled and talented people within each business unit develop and execute planning, production, and measurement with precision. Skill and talent within the business unit does not always translate into skill and talent for communicating outside the business unit, across business units, or up and down the corporate ladder. In a business organization, lack of communication, poor communication, or miscommunication can be deadly and costly.

This is where skilled and talented communications professionals can add value to the organization. High quality corporate communication needs to be clearly and accurately delivered. Choosing and using the right combination of channels and media to create the best climate for reception and response is the province of communications professionals.

Some channels of communication require multiple senses to receive the message. Face-to-face communication is one channel of communication that uses several senses, but it may not assure accurate recall, and a conversation cannot be mass distributed without some kind of recording. Other channels of communication like telephone, TV, radio, email, memos, letters, formal reports, and bulletins enable effective recall and mass distribution, but involve fewer senses and learning styles.

Communications professionals are skilled and trained to know how to mix and match all the available communication media to the learning and communication styles and needs of the variety of audiences within the corporation. The customary communication styles that are effective within a business unit are often not the same styles that are required to communicate across business units or up and down the corporate ladder. The customary communication styles that are effective in everyday work situations are often not the same styles that are required to resolve conflict or manage crisis situations. This is the value add within Navistar International that results from the role the Department of Communications plays in the corporation.

Questions

1. Explain why the communication skills and techniques used within a business unit (department) are not always effective in communicating across business units or up and down the corporate ladder.

2. Explain why conflict resolution communication skills are not always present in everyday workplace situations and how a skilled communications professional would add value to that workplace.

3. How would a Communications Plan effectively handle a crisis in the workplace, such as violence, sexual abuse, scandal, etc? What would likely happen in a crisis situation without a communications plan in place?

chapter 14

Teamwork

Learning Objectives

After studying this chapter, you should be able to:

1 Identify the types of teams in organizations.

2 Discuss new applications of teams to facilitate employee involvement.

3 Identify roles within teams and the type of role you could play to help a team be effective.

4 Explain the general stages of team development.

5 Identify ways in which team size and diversity of membership affects team performance.

6 Explain the concepts of team cohesiveness and team norms and their relationship to team performance.

7 Understand the causes of conflict within and among teams and how to reduce conflict, including the importance of negotiation.

8 Define the outcomes of effective teams and how managers can enhance team effectiveness.

Please circle your opinion below each of the following statements.

Assess Your Answer

1 Team is just another word for group.

1	2	3	4	5
strongly agree				strongly disagree

2 It's better if team members are all in the same location.

1	2	3	4	5
strongly agree				strongly disagree

3 The best team members are those who encourage other members.

1	2	3	4	5
strongly agree				strongly disagree

chapter outline

Teams at Work
What Is a Team?
Model of Work Team Effectiveness

Types of Teams
Formal Teams
Self-Directed Teams
Teams in the New Workplace

Team Characteristics
Size
Diversity
Member Roles

Team Processes
Stages of Team Development
Team Cohesiveness
Team Norms

Managing Team Conflict
Balancing Conflict and Cooperation
Causes of Conflict
Styles to Handle Conflict
Negotiation

Work Team Effectiveness
Productive Output
Satisfaction of Members
Capacity to Adapt and Learn

In recent years, teams have become the primary way in which many companies accomplish their work, from the assembly line to the executive suite. Hypertherm, Inc., a maker of metal-cutting equipment in Hanover, New Hampshire, uses teams of researchers, engineers, marketers, and salespeople focused on updating and improving the company's five product lines.[1] Cirque du Soleil's top executives, including the CEO, COO, CFO, and vice president of creation, function as a team to coordinate, develop, and oversee 13 acrobatic troupes that travel to 100 cities on 4 continents.[2] And Lassiter Middle School in Jefferson County, Kentucky, uses teams of teachers to prepare daily schedules and handle student discipline problems.

Employees at United Airlines have suffered years of declining organizational performance, resulting in a demoralizing bankruptcy that cut wages, laid off thousands of employees, and forced remaining workers to do more with less. Ramp workers, those who wave in jets, load baggage, and push planes around with tractors and tow bars, have one of the toughest—and often one of the most underappreciated—jobs in the industry. At United, ramp workers typically work in teams of four. The work can be chaotic, with missing equipment, lousy weather, machinery breakdowns, and potentially dangerous debris on the tarmac. If someone calls in sick, an understaffed team has to handle the myriad ramp chores in the allotted time to get planes back in the air. Unfortunately, even fully staffed teams at United have trouble turning planes quickly.[3]

United took an innovative approach to team-building and sent more than 1,200 "lead" ramp workers through training at "Pit Crew U," where they learned the split-second techniques and teamwork practices of NASCAR pit crews. At Pit Instruction & Training LLC, in Mooresville, North Carolina, teams of people who had never before worked together had to quickly coalesce into a high-performing team to handle the various pit exercises thrown their way. The training course emphasizes the importance of teamwork, preparedness, and safety, issues that are as important on an airport tarmac as they are in a NASCAR pit. United wants people to translate what they learned into helping build cohesive teams that can quickly reach the performing stage of team development. At the same time, top executives are striving to improve relationships between management and workers, so that teams will be more likely to establish high-performance norms. With a combination of more cohesive teams and high-performance norms, United hopes to cut the time it takes to turn a plane by eight minutes and allow it to run more daily flights without buying new planes, thus increasing revenues and helping to pull United out of its slide.

Some companies use global virtual teams composed of managers and employees working in different countries.[4] Steelcase International, a furniture manufacturer based in Strasburg, France, has 14,000 employees and manufacturing facilities in 20 countries. Steelcase has been using teams for 30 years. In the past, they were aligned according to geography, with U.S. teams for the United States, French teams for France, and so on. Today, though, Steelcase teams have evolved into cross-functional and cross-geographical virtual teams that communicate and collaborate electronically.[5]

However, as at United Airlines, teams aren't always effective. In a survey of manufacturing organizations, about 80 percent of respondents said they used some kind of teams, but only 14 percent of those companies rated their teaming efforts as highly effective. Just over half of the responding manufacturers said their efforts were only "somewhat effective," and 15 percent considered their efforts not effective at all.[6]

This chapter focuses on teams and their applications within organizations. We define various types of teams, explore the stages of team development, and examine how characteristics such as size, cohesiveness, diversity, and norms influence team effectiveness. We also discuss how individuals can make contributions to teams, look at techniques for managing team conflict, and describe how negotiation can facilitate cooperation and teamwork. The final sections of the chapter focus on the outcomes of effective work teams within organizations. Teams are a central aspect of organizational life, and the ability to manage them is a vital component of manager and organization success.

Teams at Work

Some organizations have had great success with teams, including increased productivity, quality improvements, greater innovation, and higher employee satisfaction. FedEx, for example, cut service problems such as incorrect bills and lost packages by 13 percent by using teams. At Xerox, production plants using teams reported a 30 percent increase in productivity.[7] A study of team-based organizations in Australia supports the idea that teams provide benefits to both employees and organizations.[8] However, simply organizing people into teams does not guarantee their effectiveness. Managers are responsible for creating and nurturing the conditions and processes that enable teams to be successful.

In this section, we first define teams and then discuss a model of team effectiveness that summarizes the important concepts.

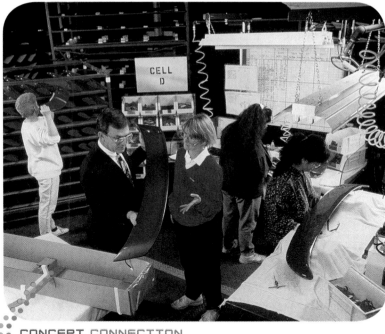

CONCEPT CONNECTION

Teams are emerging as a **powerful management tool** and are popping up in the most unexpected places, such as this manufacturing cell at TRINOVA'S Aeroquip Inoac facility in Fremont, Ohio. The facility uses more than 40 teams that cross operations and job functions, helping the company eliminate non-value-added activities, lower costs, improve customer responsiveness, and increase quality.

WHAT IS A TEAM?

A **team** is a unit of two or more people who interact and coordinate their work to accomplish a specific goal.[9] This definition has three components. First, two or more people are required. Teams can be quite large, although most have fewer than 15 people. In the survey of manufacturing organizations referred to earlier in the chapter, for example, the average size of teams decreased from 12.7 in 2003 to 10.5 in 2004.[10] Second, people in a team have regular interaction. People who do not interact, such as when standing in line at a lunch counter or riding in an elevator, do not compose a team. Third, people in a team share a performance goal, whether to design a new handheld computing device, build a car, or write a textbook. Students often are assigned to teams to do class assignments, in which case, the purpose is to perform the assignment and receive an acceptable grade.

Although a team is a group of people, the two terms are not interchangeable. An employer, a teacher, or a coach can put together a *group* of people and never build a *team*.

Exhibit 14.1 lists the primary differences between groups and teams.

TAKE ACTION

Remember that it takes work to turn a group of people into a team. The team concept implies a sense of shared mission and collective responsibility.

team
a unit of two or more people who interact and coordinate their work to accomplish a specific goal.

1 Team is just another word for group.

ANSWER: A group is not necessarily a team, which generally has a shared purpose and collective responsibility.

 Assess Your Answer

One example of a true team comes from the military, where U.S. Navy surgeons, nurses, anesthesiologists, and technicians make up eight-person forward surgical teams that operated for the first time ever in combat during Operation Iraqi Freedom. These teams were

EXHIBIT 14.1

Differences Between
Groups and Teams

Group	Team
• Has a designated strong leader	• Shares or rotates leadership roles
• Holds individuals accountable	• Holds team accountable to each other
• Sets identical purpose for group and organization	• Sets specific team vision or purpose
• Has individual work products	• Has collective work products
• Runs efficient meetings	• Runs meetings that encourage open-ended discussion and problem solving
• Measures effectiveness indirectly by influence on business (such as financial performance)	• Measures effectiveness directly by assessing collective work
• Discusses, decides, delegates work to individuals	• Discusses, decides, shares work

SOURCE: Adapted from Jon R. Katzenbach and Douglas K. Smith, "The Discipline of Teams," *Harvard Business Review* (March–April 1995): 111–120.

scattered over Iraq and were able to move to new locations in four trucks and be set up within an hour. With a goal of saving the 15 to 20 percent of wounded soldiers and civilians who will die unless they receive critical care within 24 hours, members of these teams smoothly coordinated their activities to accomplish a critical shared mission.[11]

The sports world also provides many examples of the importance of teamwork. The 2004 U.S. Olympic basketball team was made up entirely of superstar players, yet the members never coalesced as a team, instead functioning as a group of individual players. The team came in third and lost to Lithuania. In contrast, the 1980 U.S. hockey team that beat the Soviets to win gold at the Lake Placid Olympics consisted of a bunch of no-name players. Coach Herb Brooks picked players based on their personal chemistry—how they worked together as a team—rather than on their individual abilities and egos.[12] Creating more effective teams is a goal not always reached, as described in the following Business Blooper.

MODEL OF WORK TEAM EFFECTIVENESS

Some of the factors associated with team effectiveness are illustrated in Exhibit 14.2. Work team effectiveness is based on three outcomes—productive output, personal satisfaction, and the capacity to adapt and learn.[13] *Satisfaction* pertains to the team's ability to meet the personal needs of its members and hence maintain their membership and commitment. *Productive output* pertains to the quality and quantity of task outputs as defined by team goals. *Capacity to adapt and learn* refers to the ability of teams to bring greater knowledge and skills to job tasks and enhance the potential of the organization to respond to new threats or opportunities in the environment.

Business Blooper

Burger King

Many companies have team-building experiences for employees, to provide bonding. Burger King gave new meaning to "flame-broiled" when it asked 100 managers to be part of a fire-walking exercise and totter over 1200-degree hot coals, in the hopes of them learning that reaching beyond normal limits, they could achieve almost anything. One achievement: 12 employees suffered first- and second-degree burns on their feet.

SOURCES: "Bruising Bonding," *The Times* (May 26, 2004): 19.

EXHIBIT 14.2
Work Team
Effectiveness Model

The factors that influence team effectiveness begin with the organizational context.[14] The organizational context in which the team operates is described in other chapters and includes such factors as structure, strategy, environment, culture, and reward systems. Within that context, managers define teams. Important team characteristics are the type of team, the team structure, and team composition. Managers must decide when to create permanent teams within the formal structure and when to use a temporary task team. Factors such as the diversity of the team in terms of gender and race, as well as knowledge, skills, and attitudes, can have a tremendous impact on team processes and effectiveness.[15] Team size and roles also are important. Managers strive for the right mix of knowledge and skills for the task to be performed and consider whether a team is the best way to accomplish the task. If costs outweigh benefits, managers may want to assign an individual employee to the task.

These team characteristics influence processes internal to the team, which, in turn, affect output, satisfaction, and the team's contribution to organizational adaptability. Good team leaders understand and manage stages of team development, cohesiveness, norms, and conflict to build an effective team. These processes are influenced by team and organizational characteristics and by the ability of members and leaders to direct these processes in a positive manner.

The model of team effectiveness in Exhibit 14.2 is the basis for this chapter. In the following sections, we will examine types of organizational teams, team structure, internal processes, and the benefits of effective work teams.

Types of Teams

Many types of teams can exist within organizations. The easiest way to classify teams is in terms of those created as part of the organization's formal structure and those created to increase employee participation.

FORMAL TEAMS

Formal teams are created by the organization as part of the formal organization structure. Two common types of formal teams are vertical and horizontal, which typically represent vertical and horizontal structural relationships. These two types of teams are illustrated in Exhibit 14.3. A third type of formal team is the special-purpose team.

Vertical Team. A **vertical team** is composed of a manager and his or her subordinates in the formal chain of command. Sometimes called a *functional team* or a *command team*, the vertical team may in some cases include three or four levels of hierarchy within a

formal team
a team created by the organization as part of the formal organization structure.

vertical team
a formal team composed of a manager and his or her subordinates in the organization's formal chain of command.

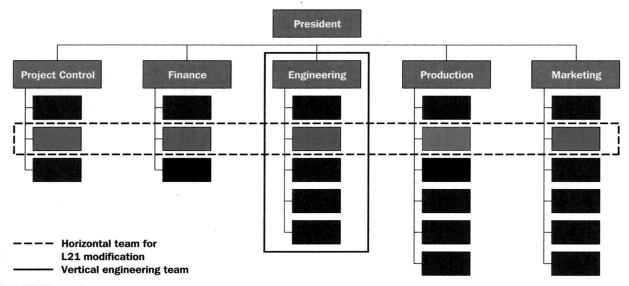

— — — — **Horizontal team for
L21 modification**
——————— **Vertical engineering team**

EXHIBIT 14.3

Horizontal and
Vertical Teams in an
Organization

functional department. Typically, the vertical team includes a single department in an organization. The third-shift nursing team on the second floor of St. Luke's Hospital is a vertical team that includes nurses and a supervisor. A financial analysis department, a quality control department, an accounting department, and a human resource department are all vertical or command teams. Each is created by the organization to attain specific goals through members' joint activities and interactions.

Horizontal Team. A **horizontal team** is composed of employees from about the same hierarchical level but from different areas of expertise.[16] A horizontal team is drawn from several departments, is given a specific task, and may be disbanded after the task is completed. The two most common types of horizontal teams are cross-functional teams and committees.

As described in Chapter 7, a *cross-functional team* is a group of employees from different departments formed to deal with a specific activity and existing only until the task is completed. Sometimes called a *task force,* the team might be used to create a new product in a manufacturing organization or a new history curriculum in a university. Georgetown Preparatory School created a task force made up of teachers, coaches, administrators, support staff, and outside consultants to develop a preparedness plan to address the threat of seasonal influenza and other potentially devastating epidemics.[17] When several departments are involved, and many views have to be considered, tasks are best served with a horizontal, cross-functional team.

A **committee** generally is long-lived and may be a permanent part of the organization's structure. Membership on a committee usually is decided by a person's title or position rather than by personal expertise. A committee often needs official representation, compared with selection for a cross-functional team, which is based on personal qualifications for solving a problem. Committees typically are formed to deal with tasks that recur regularly. For example, a grievance committee handles employee grievances; an advisory committee makes recommendations in the areas of employee compensation and work practices; and a worker-management committee may be concerned with work rules, job design changes, and suggestions for work improvement.[18]

As part of the horizontal structure of the organization, cross-functional teams and committees offer several advantages: (1) They allow organization members to exchange

TAKE ACTION ⊙➤

As a manager, periodically form cross-functional teams to have new people in conversations; otherwise, the same people will likely produce the same outcome.

horizontal team
a formal team composed of employees from about the same hierarchical level but from different areas of expertise.

committee
a long-lasting, sometimes permanent team in the organization structure created to deal with tasks that recur regularly.

information; (2) they generate suggestions for coordinating the organizational units that are represented; (3) they develop new ideas and solutions for existing organizational problems; and (4) they assist in the development of new organizational practices and policies.

Special-Purpose Team. **Special-purpose teams,** sometimes called *project teams,* are created outside the formal organization structure to undertake a project of special importance or creativity. Special-purpose teams focus on a specific purpose and expect to disband after the specific project is completed.[19] Examples include the team that developed the first IBM ThinkPad and the project team for the Motorola RAZR cell phone. A special-purpose team still is part of the formal organization and has its own reporting structure, but members perceive themselves as a separate entity.[20]

Many of today's companies are using special-purpose teams to dramatically speed up development of a special product or execute a highly important project. These *fast-cycle teams,* as described in Chapter 8, are set up to work on projects that top management deems highly important. They are provided the freedom and resources to bring projects to closure quickly.[21]

SELF-DIRECTED TEAMS

Employee involvement through teams is designed to increase the participation of workers in decision making and the conduct of their jobs, with the goal of improving performance. Employee involvement started out simply with techniques such as information sharing with employees or asking employees for suggestions about improving the work. Gradually, companies moved toward greater autonomy for employees, which led first to problem-solving teams and then to self-directed teams.[22]

Problem-solving teams typically consist of 5 to 12 hourly employees from the same department who voluntarily meet to discuss ways of improving quality, efficiency, and the work environment. Recommendations are proposed to management for approval. Problem-solving teams usually are the first step in a company's move toward greater employee participation. The most widely known application is *quality circles,* first used by Japanese companies, in which employees focus on ways to improve quality in the production process. USX adopted this approach in several of its steel mills, recognizing that quality takes a team effort. Under the title All Product Excellence program (APEX), USX set up APEX teams of up to 12 employees who met several times a month to solve quality problems.[23]

As a company matures, problem-solving teams can gradually evolve into self-directed teams, which represent a fundamental change in how work is organized. Self-directed teams enable employees to feel challenged, find their work meaningful, and develop a strong sense of identity with the company.[24] **Self-directed teams** typically consist of 5 to 20 multiskilled workers who rotate jobs to produce an entire product or service or at least one complete aspect or portion of a product or service (e.g., engine assembly, insurance claim processing). The central idea is that the teams themselves, rather than managers or supervisors, take responsibility for their work, make decisions, monitor their own performance, and alter their work behavior as needed to solve problems, meet goals, and adapt to changing conditions.[25] For example, at Ralston Foods plant in Sparks, Nevada, which produces cereals, production workers are divided into teams of about 10 people. Some of the teams function entirely without designated leaders and handle all issues and problems that arise in their areas, including hiring and firing, scheduling, budgeting, quality, and disciplinary problems. Other teams have leaders assigned by management as they continue to learn how to work in a team environment, but the teams that have progressed to total self-direction actually outperform teams with assigned leaders.[26]

Self-directed teams are permanent teams that typically include the following elements:

- The team includes employees with several skills and functions, and the combined skills are sufficient to perform a major organizational task. A team may include members from

special-purpose team
a team created outside the formal organization to undertake a project of special importance or creativity.

problem-solving team
typically 5 to 12 hourly employees from the same department who meet to discuss ways of improving quality, efficiency, and the work environment.

self-directed team
a team consisting of 5 to 20 multiskilled workers who rotate jobs to produce an entire product or service, often supervised by an elected member.

the foundry, machining, grinding, fabrication, and sales departments, with members cross-trained to perform one another's jobs. The team eliminates barriers among departments, enabling excellent coordination to produce a product or service.

- The team is given access to resources such as information, equipment, machinery, and supplies needed to perform the complete task.
- The team is empowered with decision-making authority, which means that members have the freedom to select new members, solve problems, spend money, monitor results, and plan for the future.[27]

TAKE ACTION ⏩

As a manager, make sure you allow self-directed teams to be truly self-directed but with enough management support to achieve their goals.

In a self-directed team, team members take over managerial duties such as scheduling or ordering materials. They work with minimum supervision, perhaps electing one of their own as supervisor, who may change each year. The most effective self-directed teams are those that are fully empowered. In addition to having increased responsibility and discretion, empowered teams are those that have a strong belief in their team's capabilities, find value and meaning in their work, and recognize the impact the team's work has on customers, other stakeholders, and organizational success.[28]

Managers create the conditions that determine whether self-directed teams are empowered by giving teams true power and decision-making authority, complete information, knowledge and skills, and appropriate rewards. The manager to whom the team and team leaders report, sometimes referred to as the *external leader,* has a tremendous impact on the team's success. In addition to creating conditions for empowerment, effective external leaders serve as an active link between the team and the organization, building constructive relationships and getting the team what it needs to do its best work.[29] An interesting example of the use of self-directed teams is the Orpheus Orchestra of New York City.

The Orpheus Orchestra has found that using self-directed teams provides a number of advantages. The greater information flow and diverse artistic input contributes to a superb performance. In addition, members typically feel a high degree of commitment, and turnover is quite low. One business organization that succeeds with teamwork is Consolidated Diesel's engine factory in Whitakers, North Carolina. In its 20 or so years of operation as a team-based organization, the plant has had higher revenues, lower turnover, and significantly lower injury rates than the industry average. In addition, while most plants average 1 supervisor for every 25 workers, Consolidated Diesel has 1 for every 100 employees because the plant workers themselves handle many supervisory duties. The difference yields a savings of about $1 million a year.[30]

TEAMS IN THE NEW WORKPLACE

Some exciting new approaches to teamwork have resulted from advances in information technology, shifting employee expectations, and the globalization of business. Two types of teams that are increasingly being used are virtual teams and global teams.

Orpheus Orchestra

Most orchestras are strongly hierarchical and structured around a conductor who wields almost complete power and control. Not Orpheus, a world-renowned chamber orchestra started in the 1970s by a small group of musicians committed to democratic power sharing.

Orpheus operates completely without a conductor! Teams of musicians determine the repertoire, schedule concerts, select new musicians, interpret musical works, and handle all the other artistic and performance duties a conductor usually controls. The instrument sections constitute natural, specialized self-directed teams. Leadership rotates among different members, who are elected by their teammates.

The actual structure of teams at Orpheus is quite complex and is designed to facilitate participative leadership, avoid hierarchical control, and allow everyone to participate in decision making.[31]

Virtual Teams. A **virtual team** is made up of geographically or organizationally dispersed members who are linked primarily through advanced information and telecommunications technologies.[32] Although some virtual teams may be made up of only organizational members, virtual teams often include contingent workers, members of partner organizations, customers, suppliers, consultants, or other outsiders. Team members use e-mail, instant messaging, voice mail, videoconferencing, Internet and intranet technologies, and various types of collaboration software to perform their work, although they might also sometimes meet face to face. Many virtual teams are cross-functional teams that emphasize solving customer problems or completing specific projects. Others are permanent self-directed teams. A new kind of virtual team predicts certain outcomes, as shown in the following example.

With virtual teams, team leadership is typically shared or rotated, depending on the area of expertise needed at each stage of the project.[33] In addition, team membership in virtual teams may change fairly quickly, depending on the tasks to be performed. One of the primary advantages of virtual teams is the ability to rapidly assemble the most appropriate group of people to complete a complex project, solve a particular problem, or exploit a specific strategic opportunity.

CONCEPT CONNECTION

When commercial air traffic was grounded immediately after September 11, 2001, Dreamworks CEO Jeffrey Katzenbach had to assemble a **virtual team** of creative designers. He discovered that existing videoconferencing technology didn't allow team members to hold multiple conversations or get a good look at an object's details. The experience inspired the animation studio to join forces with Hewlett-Packard to produce the Halo Collaboration Studio, pictured here. In addition to HP, companies such as Cisco Systems and Polycom are now offering these high-end "telepresence" systems that use studio-quality cameras and sound equipment, high-speed data transmission, and rooms carefully designed to be identical, giving geographically dispersed teams a lifelike virtual meeting room.

2 It's better if team members are all in the same location.

Assess Your Answer

ANSWER: A growing trend in organizations is virtual teams, some members of which actually never meet face-to-face because they are in far-flung locations. Virtual teams can be very effective, if managed properly.

Virtual teams present unique challenges. Managers as team leaders should consider these critical issues when building virtual teams:[34]

- *Select the right team members.* The first step is creating a team of people who have the right mix of technical and interpersonal skills, task knowledge, and personalities to work in a virtual environment. Interviews with virtual team members and leaders indicate that the ability to communicate and a desire to work as a team are the most important personal qualities for virtual team members.[35]

- *Manage socialization.* People need to get to know one another and understand the appropriate behaviors and attitudes. Smart team leaders establish team norms and ground rules for interaction early in the team's formation.

virtual team
a team made up of members who are geographically or organizationally dispersed, rarely meet face to face, and do their work using advanced information technologies.

- *Foster trust.* Trust might be the most important ingredient in a successful virtual team. Teams that exhibit high levels of trust tend to have clear roles and expectations of one another, get to know one another as individuals, and maintain positive action-oriented attitudes.

- *Effectively manage communications.* Frequent communication is essential. Team leaders need to understand when and how to use various forms of communication to best advantage. Some experts suggest regular face-to-face meetings, whereas others believe virtual teams can be successful even if they interact only electronically. One time when face-to-face communication might be essential is when misunderstandings, frustrations, or conflicts threaten the team's work.[36]

Global Teams. Virtual teams are also sometimes global teams. **Global teams** are cross-border work teams made up of members of different nationalities whose activities span multiple countries.[37] Generally, global teams fall into two categories: intercultural teams, whose members come from different countries or cultures and meet face-to-face, and virtual global teams, whose members remain in separate locations around the world and conduct their work electronically.[38] For example, global teams of software developers at Tandem Services Corporation coordinate their work electronically so that the team is productive around the clock. Team members in London code a project and transmit the

global team
a work team made up of members of different nationalities whose activities span multiple countries; may operate as a virtual team or meet face-to-face.

Spotlight on
Technology

MySQL: Creating a Twenty-First-Century Global Team

How do you instill esprit de corps in a far-flung virtual team? It's a challenge managers at MySQL, a Swedish software maker, face daily. MySQL, which produces a database management system used in Web applications, employs about 320 people scattered in 25 countries. The majority of them work from home.

For MySQL, building an effective virtual global team begins with hiring the right people. Interestingly, though, managers don't consider being a "team player" in the conventional sense all that important. What the company looks for are people with the right technical skills and a real love for their work. It doesn't mean all aspects of teamwork are ignored, however. It just looks different. Thomas Basil, MySQL's director of support, works in a basement office next to his family's washing machine, so he knows from experience that people working virtually can feel isolated. When he signs in to the MySQL chat room each day, he greets each support team member by name. Basil even staged an online Christmas party, gathering staffers from places as far apart as Russia, England, and Germany into a cyber

get-together, where he played Santa and dispensed virtual drinks and gifts. "When a company is as spread out as this one," he points out, "you have to think of virtual ways to imitate the dynamics of what goes on in a more familiar work situation." Occasionally, top executives get the entire MySQL staff together online through a system dubbed "Radio Sakila," which combines a typical conference call with instant messaging.

MySQL managers have built-in numerous communication channels to keep people talking across time and space. Team leaders recognize the limitations of text-based electronic communication, such as how easily miscommunication can occur in the absence of nonverbal cues. It's their responsibility to help people develop and follow guidelines for communication. As Basil found, sometimes an old-fashioned telephone conversation works best. "Voice is more personal than text and more helpful in building real understanding," he points out.

Managers have to think about performance evaluation and feedback differently too. Controls such as weekly performance reports keep people focused on tasks, yet managers have to be comfortable with the informality and loose structure of a virtual environment. "I'm not the kind of CEO who needs to see everybody sweat and work hard," says CEO Mårten Mickos. "These are passionate people who aren't going to stop because somebody isn't looking."

SOURCES: Josh Hyatt, "The Soul of a New Team," *Fortune* (June 12, 2006): 134–143; and Victoria Murphy Barret, "A Chat With . . . Oracle's New Enemy," *Forbes.com* (February 15, 2006), www.forbes.com/technology/2006/02/15/oracle-yahoo-googlecz_vmb_0215Mysql.html.

code each evening to members in the United States for testing. U.S. team members then forward the code they've tested to Tokyo for debugging. The next morning, the London team members pick up with the code debugged by their Tokyo colleagues, and another cycle begins.[39] The trend toward creating virtual teams that cross geographical boundaries has grown tremendously in recent years. In some organizations, such as open-source software maker MySQL, discussed on the previous page, most employees are scattered around the world and never see one another face-to-face.

Global teams present enormous challenges for team leaders, who have to bridge gaps of time, distance, and culture. In some cases, members speak different languages, use different technologies, and have different beliefs about authority, decision making, and time orientation. For example, some cultures, such as the United States, are highly focused on "clock time," and tend to follow rigid schedules, whereas many other cultures have a more relaxed, cyclical concept of time. These different cultural attitudes toward time can affect work pacing, team communications, and the perception of deadlines.[40] Members from different countries may also have varied attitudes about teamwork itself. Multinational organizations have found that many team phenomena are culture-specific. Some countries, such as Mexico, value high power distance, as described in Chapter 3, meaning that differences in power and status are seen as appropriate and desirable. This viewpoint conflicts with the American idea of teamwork, which emphasizes shared power and authority. Thus, the acceptance and effectiveness of team-based systems can vary widely across different cultures, which makes implementing and evaluating teams quite complex.[41]

Organizations using global teams invest the time and resources to adequately educate employees. Managers make sure all team members appreciate and understand cultural differences, are focused on goals, and understand their responsibilities to the team. For a global team to be effective, all team members must be willing to deviate somewhat from their own values and norms and establish new norms for the team.[42] As with virtual teams, carefully selecting team members, building trust, and sharing information are critical to success.

Team Characteristics

The next issue of concern to managers is designing the team for greatest effectiveness. One factor is *team characteristics,* which can affect team dynamics and performance. Characteristics of particular concern are team size, diversity, and member roles.

SIZE

More than 30 years ago, psychologist Ivan Steiner examined what happened each time the size of a team increased, and he proposed that team performance and productivity peaked at about five—a quite small number. He found that adding additional members beyond five caused a decrease in motivation, an increase in coordination problems, and a general decline in performance.[43] Since then, numerous studies have found that smaller teams perform better, although most researchers say it's impossible to specify an optimal team size.

One recent investigation of team size based on data from 58 software development teams found that the five best-performing teams ranged in size from 3 to 6 members.[44] Results of a recent Gallup poll in the United States show that 82 percent of employees agree that small teams are more productive.[45]

Teams need to be large enough to incorporate the diverse skills needed to complete a task, enable members to express good and bad feelings, and aggressively solve problems. However, they should also be small enough to permit members to feel an intimate part of the team and to communicate effectively and efficiently. In general, as a team increases in size, it becomes harder for each member to interact with and influence the others.

TAKE ACTION
Remember, smaller teams are more nimble and tend to function more effectively.

A summary of research on group size suggests the following:[46]

1. Small teams (two to five members) show more agreement, ask more questions, and exchange more opinions. Members want to get along with one another. Small teams report more satisfaction and enter into more personal discussions. They tend to be informal and make few demands on team leaders.

2. Large teams (10 or more) tend to have more disagreements and differences of opinion. Subgroups often form, and conflicts among them occur. Communication becomes more difficult, and demands on leaders are greater because of the need for stronger coordination, more centralized decision making, and less member participation. Large teams also tend to be less friendly. Turnover and absenteeism are higher in a large team, especially for blue-collar workers. Because less satisfaction is associated with specialized tasks and poor communication, team members have fewer opportunities to participate and feel like an important part of the team.

3. As teams increase in size, so does the number of *free riders*. The term **free rider** refers to a team member who attains benefits from team membership but does not actively participate in and contribute to the team's work. The problem of free riding has likely been experienced by people in student project groups, where some students put more effort into the group project, but everyone benefits from the result. Free riding is sometimes called *social loafing* because members do not exert equal effort.[47] A classic experiment by German psychologist Ringelmann found that the pull exerted on a rope was greater by individuals working alone than by individuals in a group.[48] Similarly, experiments have found that when people are asked to clap and make noise, they make more noise on a per-person basis when working alone or in small groups than they do in a large group.[49]

free rider
a person who benefits from team membership but does not make a proportionate contribution to the team's work.

As a general rule, large teams make need satisfaction for individuals more difficult; thus, people feel less motivation to remain committed to their goals. Large projects can be split into components and assigned to several smaller teams to keep the benefits of small team size. At Amazon.com, CEO Jeff Bezos established a "two-pizza rule." If a team gets so large that members can't be fed with two pizzas, it needs to be split into smaller teams.[50]

DIVERSITY

Because teams require a variety of skills, knowledge, and experience, it seems likely that heterogeneous teams would be more effective than homogeneous ones. In general, research supports this idea, showing that diverse teams produce more innovative solutions to problems.[51] Diversity in terms of functional area and skills, thinking styles, and personal characteristics is often a source of creativity. In addition, diversity may contribute to a healthy level of disagreement that leads to better decision making. At Southern Company, a new CIO made a conscious effort to build a diverse senior leadership team, recruiting people to build in gender, racial, educational, religious, cultural, and geographical diversity. "The differences we bring to the table sometimes mean we have long, heated discussions," says Becky Blalock.

CONCEPT CONNECTION

"As demographic shifts sweep our nation and our community, **diversity** in public relations is not just a good thing to do but a necessary business reality," declares Judy Iannaccone, Rancho Santiago Community College District communications director. Her professional organization agrees. The Public Relations Society of America (PSRA) promotes inclusion among work teams with a diversity tool kit, career website, and speakers list. Each year, the Society recognizes individual chapters for outstanding diversity promotion efforts. The Orange County, California, PSRA diversity committee was one of the 2005 recipients. Iannaccone, a committee member, is second from the right.

"But once we make a decision, we know we've viewed the problem from every possible angle."[52]

Research studies have confirmed that both functional diversity and gender diversity can have a positive impact on work team performance.[53] Racial, national, and ethnic diversity can also be good for teams, but in the short term, these differences might hinder team interaction and performance. Teams made up of racially and culturally diverse members tend to have more difficulty learning to work well together, but with effective leadership, the problems fade over time.[54]

MEMBER ROLES

For a team to be successful over the long run, it must be structured to both maintain its members' social well-being and accomplish its task. In successful teams, the requirements for task performance and social satisfaction are met by the emergence of two types of roles: task specialist and socioemotional.[55]

People who play the **task specialist role** spend time and energy helping the team reach its goal. They often display the following behaviors:

- *Initiate ideas.* Propose new solutions to team problems.
- *Give opinions.* Offer opinions on task solutions; give candid feedback on others' suggestions.
- *Seek information.* Ask for task-relevant facts.
- *Summarize.* Relate various ideas to the problem at hand; pull ideas together into a summary perspective.
- *Energize.* Stimulate the team into action when interest drops.[56]

People who adopt a **socioemotional role** support team members' emotional needs and help strengthen the social entity. They display the following behaviors:

- *Encourage.* Are warm and receptive to others' ideas; praise and encourage others to draw forth their contributions.
- *Harmonize.* Reconcile group conflicts; help disagreeing parties reach agreement.
- *Reduce tension.* Tell jokes or in other ways draw off emotions when group atmosphere is tense.
- *Follow.* Go along with the team; agree to other team members' ideas.
- *Compromise.* Will shift own opinions to maintain team harmony.[57]

task specialist role
a role in which the individual devotes personal time and energy to helping the team accomplish its task.

socioemotional role
a role in which the individual provides support for team members' emotional needs and social unity.

3 The best team members are those who encourage other members.

ANSWER: Although encouragement is important, other skills are needed as well, such as seeking information, giving opinions, initiating ideas, energizing the group, reducing tensions, compromising, and so on.

Assess Your Answer

Exhibit 14.4 illustrates task specialist and socioemotional roles in teams. When most individuals in a team play a social role, the team is socially oriented. Members do not criticize or disagree with one another and do not forcefully offer opinions or try to accomplish team tasks because their primary interest is to keep the team happy. Teams with mostly socioemotional roles can be satisfying, but they also can be unproductive. At the other extreme, a team made up primarily of task specialists will tend to have a singular concern

Task Specialist Role Focuses on task accomplishment over human needs Important role, but if adopted by everyone, team's social needs will not be met		**Dual Role** Focuses on task and people May be a team leader Important role, but not essential if members adopt task specialist and socioemotional roles
Nonparticipator Role Contributes little to either task or people needs of team; also called free riding Not an important role—if adopted by too many members, team will disband		**Socioemotional Role** Focuses on people needs of team over task Important role, but if adopted by everyone, team's tasks will not be accomplished

High / Low — Member Task Behavior

Low — Member Social Behavior — High

EXHIBIT 14.4
Team Member Roles

for task accomplishment. This team will be effective for a short period of time but will not be satisfying for members over the long run. Task specialists convey little emotional concern for one another, are unsupportive, and ignore team members' social and emotional needs. The task-oriented team can be humorless and unsatisfying.

As Exhibit 14.4 illustrates, some team members may play a dual role. People with **dual roles** both contribute to the task and meet members' emotional needs. Such people often become team leaders. A study of new-product development teams in high-technology firms found that the most effective teams were headed by leaders who balanced the technical needs of the project with human interaction issues, thus meeting both task and socioemotional needs.[58] Exhibit 14.4 also shows the final type of role, called the **nonparticipator role,** in which people contribute little to either the task or the social needs of team members. These people are free riders, as defined earlier and typically are held in low esteem by the team.

The important thing for managers to remember is that effective teams must have people in both task specialist and socioemotional roles. Humor and social concern are as important to team effectiveness as are facts and problem solving. Managers also should remember that some people perform better in one type of role; some are inclined toward social concerns and others toward task concerns. A well-balanced team will do best over the long term because it will be personally satisfying for team members as well as permit the accomplishment of team tasks.

Team Processes

Now we turn our attention to internal team processes. Team processes pertain to those dynamics that change over time and can be influenced by team leaders. In this section, we discuss the team processes of stages of development, cohesiveness, and norms. The fourth type of team process, conflict, will be covered in the next section.

STAGES OF TEAM DEVELOPMENT

After a team has been created, it develops through distinct stages.[59] New teams are different from mature teams. Recall a time when you were a member of a new team, such as a fraternity or sorority pledge class, a committee, or a small team formed to do a class assignment. Over time, the team changed. In the beginning, team members had to get to know one another, establish roles and norms, divide the labor, and clarify the team's task. In this way, each member became part of a smoothly operating team. The challenge for leaders is to understand the stages of team development and take action that will help the group improve its functioning.

dual role
a role in which the individual both contributes to the team's task and supports members' emotional needs.

nonparticipator role
a role in which the individual contributes little to either the task or members' socioemotional needs.

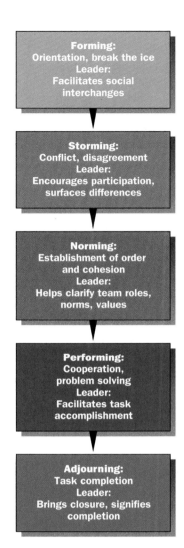

EXHIBIT 14.5
Five Stages of Team
Development

Research findings suggest that team development is not random but evolves over definitive stages. One useful model for describing these stages is shown in Exhibit 14.5. Each stage confronts team leaders and members with unique problems and challenges.[60]

Forming. The **forming** stage of development is a period of orientation and getting acquainted. Members break the ice and test one another for friendship possibilities and task orientation. Team members find which behaviors are acceptable to others. Uncertainty is high during this stage, and members usually accept whatever power or authority is offered by either formal or informal leaders. Members are dependent on the team until they find out what the ground rules are and what is expected of them. During this initial stage, members are concerned about such things as "What is expected of me?" "What is acceptable?" "Will I fit in?" During the forming stage, the team leader should provide time for members to get acquainted with one another and encourage them to engage in informal social discussions.

Storming. During the **storming** stage, individual personalities emerge. People become more assertive in clarifying their roles and what is expected of them. This stage is

forming
the stage of team development characterized by orientation and acquaintance.

 **TAKE ACTION**
Remember, when you are on a team that is having conflicts in the early stages, that is a normal part of the developmental process.

marked by conflict and disagreement. People may disagree over their perceptions of the team's mission. Members may jockey for position, and coalitions or subgroups based on common interests may form. One subgroup may disagree with another over the total team's goals or how to achieve them. Unless teams can successfully move beyond this stage, they may get bogged down and never achieve high performance. During the storming stage, the team leader should encourage participation by each team member. Members should propose ideas, disagree with one another, and work through the uncertainties and conflicting perceptions about team tasks and goals.

Norming. During the **norming** stage, conflict is resolved, and team harmony and unity emerge. Consensus develops concerning who has the power, who are the leaders, and what are the members' roles. Members come to accept and understand one another. Differences are resolved, and members develop a sense of team cohesion. This stage typically is of short duration. During the norming stage, the team leader should emphasize unity within the team and help to clarify team norms and values.

Performing. During the **performing** stage, the major emphasis is on problem solving and accomplishing the assigned task. Members are committed to the team's mission. They are coordinated with one another and handle disagreements in a mature way. They confront and resolve problems in the interest of task accomplishment. They interact frequently and direct their discussions and influence toward achieving team goals. During this stage, the leader should concentrate on managing high task performance. Both socioemotional and task specialists contribute to the team's functioning.

Adjourning. The **adjourning** stage occurs in committees and teams that have a limited task to perform and are disbanded afterward. During this stage, the emphasis is on wrapping up and gearing down. Task performance is no longer a top priority. Members may feel heightened emotionality, strong cohesiveness, and depression or regret over the team's disbandment. They may feel happy about mission accomplishment and sad about the loss of friendship and associations. At this point, the leader may want to signify the team's disbanding with a ritual or ceremony, perhaps giving out plaques and awards to signify closure and completeness.

The five stages of team development typically occur in sequence. In teams that are under time pressure or that will exist for only a short period of time, the stages may occur quite rapidly. The stages may also be accelerated for virtual teams. For example, bringing people together for a couple of days of team building can help virtual teams move rapidly through the forming and storming stages. McDevitt Street Bovis, one of the country's largest

---

TAKE ACTION ▶

As a new manager, help people on a new team get to know one another, clarify expectations, work out differences, and learn to work together.

storming
the stage of team development in which individual personalities, roles, and resulting conflicts emerge.

norming
the stage of team development in which conflicts developed during the storming stage are resolved, and team harmony and unity emerge.

performing
the stage of team development in which members focus on problem solving and accomplishing the team's assigned task.

adjourning
the stage of team development in which members prepare for the team's disbandment.

Business Blooper

Student Loan Xpress

One way for a student loan company to co-opt financial aid officers at universities: Make them part of your team. In other words, put them on paid advisory boards, hire some as consultants, and sell stock to others. This was done to the founders of Student Loan Xpress, in order for their company to be placed on the sought-after lists of recommended lenders for students. The strategy worked, as within five years Student Loan Xpress was in the top eight of student loan lenders. The jig is up, though. The New York Attorney General is looking into these "deceptive business practices" because the company put student loan officials into a conflict of interest. As a result of these investigations, a number of people have lost their jobs, and many more have been humiliated, perhaps ruining their careers.

SOURCE: Jonathan D. Glater and Sam Dillon, "Student Lender Planned to Woo Officials," *The New York Times* (April 10, 2007): A1.

T he team-building process at McDevitt Street Bovis is designed to take teams to the performing stage as quickly as possible by giving everyone an opportunity to get to know one another; explore the ground rules; and clarify roles, responsibilities, and expectations. The company credits this process for quickly and effectively unifying teams, circumventing damaging and time-consuming conflicts, and preventing lawsuits related to major construction projects.

Rather than the typical construction project characterized by conflicts, frantic scheduling, and poor communications, Bovis wants its collection of contractors, designers, suppliers, and other partners to function like a true team—putting the success of the project ahead of their own individual interests. The team is first divided into separate groups that may have competing objectives—such as the clients in one group, suppliers in another, engineers and architects in a third, and so forth—and asked to come up with a list of their goals for the project. Although interests sometimes vary widely in purely accounting terms, common themes almost always emerge. By talking about conflicting goals and interests, as well as what all the groups share, facilitators help the team gradually come together around a common purpose and begin to develop shared values that will guide the project. After jointly writing a mission statement for the team, each party says what it expects from the others, so that roles and responsibilities can be clarified. The intensive team-building session helps take members quickly through the forming and storming stages of development. "We prevent conflicts from happening," says facilitator Monica Bennett. Leaders at McDevitt Street Bovis believe building better teams builds better buildings.[61]

McDevitt Street Bovis

construction management firms, uses an understanding of the stages of team development to put teams on a solid foundation.

TEAM COHESIVENESS

Another important aspect of the team process is cohesiveness. **Team cohesiveness** is defined as the extent to which members are attracted to the team and motivated to remain in it.[62] Members of highly cohesive teams are committed to team activities, attend meetings, and are happy when the team succeeds. Members of less cohesive teams are less concerned about the team's welfare. High cohesiveness is normally considered an attractive feature of teams.

Determinants of Team Cohesiveness.
Characteristics of team structure and context influence cohesiveness. First is *team interaction*. The greater the contact among team members and the more time spent together, the more cohesive the team. Through frequent interactions, members get to know one another and become more committed to the team.[63] Second is the concept of *shared goals*. If team members agree on goals, they will be more cohesive. Agreeing on purpose and direction binds the team together. Third is *personal attraction to the team*, meaning that members have similar attitudes and values and enjoy being together. Complete the following New Manager Self Test to determine how cohesive your team is.

Consequences of Team Cohesiveness.
The outcome of team cohesiveness can fall into two categories—morale and productivity. As a general rule, morale is higher in cohesive teams because of increased communication among members, a friendly team climate, maintenance of membership because of commitment to the team, loyalty, and member participation in team decisions and activities. High cohesiveness has almost uniformly good effects on the satisfaction and morale of team members.[64]

With respect to team performance, research findings are mixed, but cohesiveness may have several effects.[65] First, in a cohesive team, members' productivity tends to be more uniform. Productivity differences among members are small because the team exerts pressure toward conformity. Noncohesive teams do not have this control over member behavior and therefore tend to have wider variation in member productivity.

team cohesiveness
the extent to which team members are attracted to the team and motivated to remain in it.

Is Your Group a Cohesive Team?

Think about a student group with which you have worked. Answer the questions below as they pertain to the functioning of that group.

	Mostly True				Mostly False
1. Group meetings were held regularly and everyone attended.	1	2	3	4	5
2. We talked about and shared the same goals for group work and grade.	1	2	3	4	5
3. We spent most of our meeting time talking business, but discussions were open-ended and active.	1	2	3	4	5
4. We talked through any conflicts and disagreements until they were resolved.	1	2	3	4	5
5. Group members listened carefully to one another.	1	2	3	4	5
6. We really trusted each other, speaking personally about what we really felt.	1	2	3	4	5
7. Leadership roles were rotated and shared, with people taking initiative at appropriate times for the good of the group.	1	2	3	4	5
8. Each member found a way to contribute to the final work product.	1	2	3	4	5
9. I was really satisfied being a member of the group.	1	2	3	4	5
10. We freely gave each other credit for jobs well done.	1	2	3	4	5
11. Group members gave and received feedback to help the group do even better.	1	2	3	4	5
12. We held each other accountable; each member was accountable to the group.	1	2	3	4	5
13. Group members really liked and respected each other.	1	2	3	4	5

SCORING AND INTERPRETATION

The questions here are about team cohesion. Add your scores for all 13 questions to obtain your total score: _____. If you scored 52 or greater, your group experienced authentic teamwork. Congratulations! If you scored between 39 and 51, there was a positive group identity that might have been developed even further. If you scored between 26 and 38, group identity was weak and probably not very satisfying. If you scored below 26, it was hardly a group at all, resembling a loose collection of individuals.

Remember, teamwork does not happen by itself. Individuals like you have to understand what a team is and then work to make it happen. What can you do to make a student group more like a team? Do you have the courage to take the initiative?

Two factors in the team's context also influence group cohesiveness. The first is the presence of competition. When a team is in moderate competition with other teams, its cohesiveness increases as it strives to win. Finally, team success and the favorable evaluation of the team by outsiders add to cohesiveness. When a team succeeds in its task and others in the organization recognize the success, members feel good, and their commitment to the team will be high.

	Team Cohesiveness	
High **Team Performance Norms** **Low**	**Moderate Productivity** Weak norms in alignment with organization goals	**High Productivity** Strong norms in alignment with organization goals
	Low/Moderate Productivity Weak norms in opposition to organization goals	**Low Productivity** Strong norms in opposition to organization goals
	Low Team Cohesiveness **High**	

EXHIBIT 14.6

Relationship Among Team Cohesiveness, Performance Norms, and Productivity

With respect to the productivity of the team as a whole, research findings suggest that cohesive teams have the potential to be productive, but the degree of productivity depends on the relationship between management and the working team. Thus, team cohesiveness does not necessarily lead to higher team productivity. One study surveyed more than 200 work teams and correlated job performance with their cohesiveness.[66] Highly cohesive teams were more productive when team members felt management support and less productive when they sensed management hostility and negativism. Management hostility led to team norms and goals of low performance, and the highly cohesive teams performed poorly, in accordance with their norms and goals.

The relationship between performance outcomes and cohesiveness is illustrated in Exhibit 14.6. The highest productivity occurs when the team is cohesive and also has a high performance norm, which is a result of its positive relationship with management. Moderate productivity occurs when cohesiveness is low because team members are less committed to performance norms. The lowest productivity occurs when cohesiveness is high and the team's performance norm is low. Thus, cohesive teams are able to attain their goals and enforce their norms, which can lead to either very high or very low productivity. A good example of team cohesiveness combined with high performance norms occurred at Motorola, where a highly cohesive team created a new cell phone that revived the company.

At Motorola, a combination of team cohesiveness and management support that created high performance norms led to amazing results. The phone wasn't originally conceived to be a blockbuster, but it proved to be just that. Between the time the RAZR was launched in late 2004 and mid-2006, the stylish phone sold almost as many units as the red-hot Apple iPod.[68]

TAKE ACTION

As a team leader, build a cohesive team by focusing on shared goals, giving members time to know one another and enjoy being together as a team, and making explicit statements to help develop norms of productivity.

Motorola Razr

The mood inside Motorola was bleak. Managers and engineers alike knew the company needed a hot new product to regain its reputation—and maybe even some of its lost market share. In the concept phone unit, engineers started talking about building an impossibly thin clamshell phone that would be as beautiful as a piece of fine jewelry and just as desirable—and they wanted it done in a year.

Engineer Roger Jellicoe aggressively promoted himself to lead the team and quickly put together a group of engineers, designers, and other specialists who were fired up by the ambitious project. The "thin clam" team, as they came to be known, rapidly became viewed almost as a rebellious cult within Motorola. The team worked at a facility 50 miles from Motorola's central research unit and kept the details of the project top-secret, even from their colleagues within the company. The need for secrecy and speed, as well as the relative isolation, contributed to the quick, tight bond that developed among team members. Time and again, the thin clam team flouted Motorola's rules for developing new products and followed their own instincts. Top management looked the other way. They wanted the team to have the freedom to be creative and take chances. Because Motorola badly needed a hit, money was not an object; top management gave the team whatever they needed in terms of support and resources to accomplish their goal.

The result was the RAZR, named as such based on the team's humorous reference to it as *siliqua patula*, Latin for razor clam. Unlike any other cell phone the world had seen, the RAZR wowed the industry and consumers alike—and rejuvenated the company in the process.[67]

TEAM NORMS

A **team norm** is a standard of conduct that is shared by team members and guides their behavior.[69] Norms are informal. They are not written down, as are rules and procedures. Norms are valuable because they define boundaries of acceptable behavior. They make life easier for team members by providing a frame of reference for what is right and wrong. Consider norms associated with the grueling three-week-long Tour de France. Each team is out to win the 2,700-mile bike race, but cooperation among competing teams is necessary for survival. When a team leader crashes, informal norms dictate that everyone slows down and waits. And when someone calls for a bathroom break, no formal rule says other riders have to pull to the side or slow down, but norms suggest they do so. When Dante Coccolo decided instead to go on the attack, putting a large time gap between him and the group, he learned the power of norms. When it came his own turn for a break, several other riders slowed down—but their purpose was to grab Coccolo's bike and toss it into a ditch. The chastened rider finished second to last, and never again rode in the Tour de France.[70]

Norms identify key values, clarify role expectations, and facilitate team survival. Norms begin to develop in the first interactions among members of a new team.[71] Thus, it is important for leaders, especially those of virtual teams, to try to shape early interactions that will lead to norms that help the team succeed. Leader Bill Franzblau sets norms through becoming a role model to team members, as described in the Benchmarking box.

team norm
a standard of conduct that is shared by team members and guides their behavior.

Benchmarking

Franzblau Media

Broadway musicals take the same planning and hard work as any other new venture. Producer Bill Franzblau creates a tight system to deliver a quality product (the musical) and give backers a comfortable return on their financial investment.

A successful show requires a strong team, and Franzblau starts by hiring people who are better than he is in their jobs. "He pulls together not-necessarily-team-playing creative people and fosters an environment where they become valuable contributors," says frequent collaborator New York PR executive Bill Hoffstetter. By gaining confidence through listening without ego, and by honoring talent while not having to take credit, Franzblau inspires dedication and excellent results. Anyone's ideas are given consideration, but if it doesn't work, he says so. "He's that rare person in theater who says what he feels," notes Tony Award-winning playwright and composer Rupert Holmes, Franzblau's collaborator on the award-winning Broadway hit, *Say Goodnight Gracie.* "He doesn't employ spin," he states. "While others embellish or cover up, Bill uses the unorthodox tactic of telling the kind truth." Tony-winning director and choreographer Hinton Battle elaborates further, "If he says he will do it, he will do it. He doesn't talk out of the side of his mouth and that is worth a LOT."

Franzblau knows chemistry is important in building a team and is wary of hiring divas. His finely-tuned sense of justice never lets temperamental members create situations of blatant unfairness, says Holmes. By not giving into outrageous demands, no matter how big the star, people learn to treat one another with respect.

Still, problems do erupt, and Franzblau handles them right away. "If ignored, business problems only fester and get worse, costing more financially and emotionally," he says. Crises often occur in shows, notes Battle, who worked with Franzblau on *Evil Dead: The Musical* and *RESPECT* (originally produced by Bob Cuillo) and says, "The difference is Bill knows how to put out fires and still keep people interested. This is not a skill many producers have."

One of Franzblau's cardinal rules: You must lead by example. If the producer/leader is wild and crazy, others follow suit. So he remains calm, saving any sharpness in tone for those rare every-four-years-or-so extreme situations. And he never takes anything personally. "Look," he says, "What we do is make people laugh. We are about singing and dancing and telling jokes. We aren't opening up anyone's chest cavity for open-heart surgery, nor are we curing cancer. At the end of the day, we are entertainers, and we need to remember that. It helps maintain balance and a sense of proportion."

"Bill's a real gentleman," says Hofstetter. "We would do anything for him." Battle concurs. "He's one of the good ones."

SOURCES: Hinton Battle, personal interview, July 2007; Bill Franzblau, personal interview, July 2007; Bill Hofstetter, personal interview, July 2007; Rupert Holmes, personal interview, July 2007.

EXHIBIT 14.7
Four Ways Team
Norms Develop

Norms that apply to both day-to-day behavior and employee output and performance gradually evolve, letting members know what is acceptable and directing their actions toward acceptable performance. Four common ways in which norms develop for controlling and directing behavior are illustrated in Exhibit 14.7.[72]

Critical Events. Often, *critical events* in a team's history establish an important precedent. One example occurred when an employee at a forest products plant was seriously injured while standing too close to a machine being operated by a teammate. This incident led to a norm that team members regularly monitor one another to make sure all safety rules are observed. Any critical event can lead to the creation of a norm.

Primacy. *Primacy* means that the first behaviors that occur in a team often set a precedent for later team expectations. For example, at one company, a team leader began his first meeting by raising an issue and then "leading" team members until he got the solution he wanted. The pattern became ingrained so quickly into an unproductive team norm that members dubbed meetings the "Guess What I Think" game.[73]

Carryover Behaviors. *Carryover behaviors* bring norms into the team from outside. One current example is the strong norm against smoking in many management teams. Some team members sneak around, gargling with mouthwash, and fear expulsion because the team culture believes everyone should kick the habit. Carryover behavior also influences small teams of college students assigned by instructors to do class work. Norms brought into the team from outside suggest that students should participate equally and help members get a reasonable grade.

Explicit Statements. With *explicit statements*, leaders or team members can initiate norms by articulating them to the team. Explicit statements symbolize what counts and thus have considerable impact. Making explicit statements can be a highly effective way for leaders to influence or change team norms.

One division of ABB was about to go bankrupt partly because team members had developed norms of politeness that made people hesitant to express disagreement or bring

TAKE ACTION

As a manager, consider developing a list of values and norms and sharing those with the group and new members as they join the group.

up negative information. The unit's leader turned things around by making an explicit statement that everyone was expected to speak their minds about problems. Similarly, Ameritech CEO Bill Weiss established a norm of cooperation and mutual support among his top leadership team by telling them bluntly every week that if he caught anyone trying to undermine the others, the guilty party would be fired.[74]

Managing Team Conflict

The final characteristic of team process is conflict. Of all the skills required for effective team management, none is more important than handling the conflicts that inevitably arise among members. Conflict can arise among members within a team or between one team and another. **Conflict** refers to antagonistic interaction in which one party attempts to block the intentions or goals of another.[75] Competition, which is rivalry among individuals or teams, can have a healthy impact because it energizes people toward higher performance.[76]

Whenever people work together in teams, some conflict is inevitable. Bringing conflicts out into the open and effectively resolving them is one of the team leader's most challenging jobs. For example, studies of virtual teams indicate that how they handle internal conflicts is critical to their success, yet conflict within virtual teams tends to occur more frequently and take longer to resolve because people are separated by space, time, and cultural differences. Moreover, people in virtual teams tend to engage in more inconsiderate behaviors such as name-calling or insults than do people who work face-to-face.[77]

BALANCING CONFLICT AND COOPERATION

TAKE ACTION ▶

As a manager, keep the right balance between conflict and cooperation; too much conflict is harmful, but too little squelches ideas and creativity.

TAKE ACTION ▶

Go to the ethical dilemma on page 552 that pertains to team cohesiveness and conflict.

Some conflict can actually be beneficial to teams.[78] A healthy level of conflict helps to prevent **groupthink,** in which people are so committed to a cohesive team that they are reluctant to express contrary opinions. Author and scholar Jerry Harvey tells a story of how members of his extended family in Texas decided to drive 40 miles to Abilene on a hot day when the car's air conditioning didn't work. Everyone was miserable. Later, each person admitted they hadn't wanted to go but went along to please the others. Harvey used the term *Abilene paradox* to describe this tendency to go along with others for the sake of avoiding conflict.[79] Similarly, when people in work teams go along simply for the sake of harmony, problems typically result. Thus, a degree of conflict leads to better decision making because multiple viewpoints are expressed. Among top management teams, for example, low levels of conflict have been found to be associated with poor decision making.[80]

However, conflict that is too strong, that is focused on personal rather than work issues, or that is not managed appropriately can be damaging to the team's morale and productivity.

Too much conflict can be destructive, tear relationships apart, and interfere with the healthy exchange of ideas and information.[81] Team leaders have to find the right balance between conflict and cooperation, as illustrated in Exhibit 14.8. Too little conflict can decrease team performance because the team doesn't benefit from a mix of opinions and ideas—even disagreements—that might lead to better solutions or prevent the team from making mistakes. At the other end of the spectrum, too much conflict outweighs the team's cooperative efforts and leads to a decrease in employee satisfaction and commitment, hurting team performance. A moderate amount of conflict that is managed appropriately typically results in the highest levels of team performance.

CAUSES OF CONFLICT

Several factors can cause people to engage in conflict, as described in the following sections.[82]

conflict
antagonistic interaction in which one party attempts to thwart the intentions or goals of another.

groupthink
the tendency for people to be so committed to a cohesive team that they are reluctant to express contrary opinions.

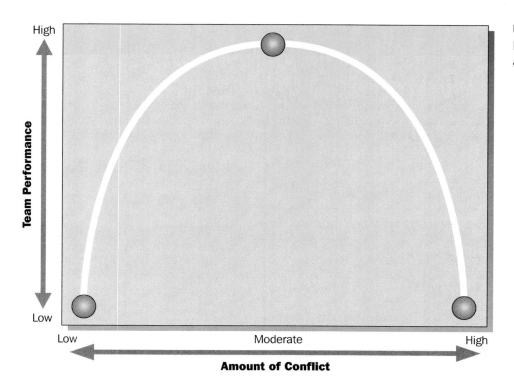

EXHIBIT 14.8
Balancing Conflict
and Cooperation

Scarce Resources. Resources include money, information, and supplies. Whenever individuals or teams must compete for scarce or declining resources, conflict is almost inevitable. The introduction of fast-cycle teams, as described earlier, for example, frequently leads to conflict because it creates a new competition for resources.[83] Some projects may be delayed because managers reallocate resources to fast-cycle projects, potentially creating conflicts.

Communication Breakdown. Poor communication results in misperceptions and misunderstandings of other people and teams. In some cases, information is intentionally withheld, which can jeopardize trust among teams and cause long-lasting conflict. Faulty communication can occur in any team, but virtual and global teams are particularly prone to communication breakdowns. For one thing, the lack of nonverbal cues, as described in the previous chapter, leads to more misunderstandings among virtual team members. In addition, trust issues are a major source of conflict in virtual teams because members may fear that they are being left out of important communication interactions.[84]

Personality Clashes. A personality clash occurs when people simply do not get along or do not see eye-to-eye on any issue. Personality clashes are caused by basic differences in personality, values, and attitudes. In one study, personality conflicts were the No. 1 reported cause preventing front-line management teams from working together effectively.[85] Some personality differences can be overcome. However, severe personality clashes are difficult to resolve. Often, it is a good idea to simply separate the parties so that they need not interact with one another.

Goal Differences. Conflict often occurs simply because people are pursuing conflicting goals. Goal differences are natural in organizations. Individual salespeople's targets

TAKE ACTION

As a manager, make sure team members know each other's responsibilities; this can be done through written roles and plenty of conversations amongst members to discuss assumptions.

NEW MANAGER SELF TEST

Managing Conflict

Conflicting opinions and perspectives occur in every team. The ability to handle conflict and disagreement is one mark of a successful new manager. To understand your approach to managing conflict, think about disagreements you have had with people on student teams or in other situations, and then answer each of the following items as Mostly True or Mostly False for you.

	Mostly True	Mostly False
1. I typically assert my opinion to win a disagreement.	_____	_____
2. I often suggest solutions that combine others' points of view.	_____	_____
3. I prefer to not argue with team members.	_____	_____
4. I raise my voice to get other people to accept my position.	_____	_____
5. I am quick to agree when someone makes a good point.	_____	_____
6. I tend to keep quiet rather than argue with other people.	_____	_____
7. I stand firm in expressing my viewpoints during a disagreement.	_____	_____
8. I try to include other people's ideas to create a solution they will accept.	_____	_____
9. I like to smooth over disagreements so people get along.	_____	_____

SCORING AND INTERPRETATION: Three categories of conflict-handling strategies are measured in this instrument: competing, accommodating, and collaborating. By comparing your scores you can see your preferred conflict-handling strategy.

Give yourself 1 point for each item marked Mostly True.

Competing: Items 1, 4, 7

Accommodating: Items 2, 5, 8

Collaborating: Items 3, 6, 9

For which conflict-handling strategy do you score highest? New managers may initially be accommodating to get along with people until they size up the situation. A too-strong competing style may prevent subordinates from having a say in important matters. The collaborating style tries for a win-win solution and has the long-run potential to build a constructive team. How would your strategy differ if the other people involved in a disagreement were family members, friends, subordinates, or bosses?

may put them in conflict with one another or with the sales manager. Moreover, the sales department's goals might conflict with those of manufacturing. When team members don't have a clear understanding of and commitment to the team goal and how their individual tasks contribute, they may be pursuing their own agendas, which can lead to conflicts.

STYLES TO HANDLE CONFLICT

Teams as well as individuals develop specific styles for dealing with conflict, based on the desire to satisfy their own concern versus the other party's concern. A model that describes five styles of handling conflict is shown in Exhibit 14.9. The two major dimensions are the extent to which an individual is assertive versus cooperative in his or her approach to conflict.

Effective team members vary their style of handling conflict to fit a specific situation. Each of these five styles is appropriate in certain cases.[86]

1. The *competing style* reflects assertiveness to get one's own way, and should be used when quick, decisive action is vital on important issues or unpopular actions, such as during emergencies or urgent cost cutting.

2. The *avoiding style* reflects neither assertiveness nor cooperativeness. It is appropriate when an issue is trivial, when there is no chance of winning, when a delay to gather more information is needed, or when a disruption would be costly.

3. The *compromising style* reflects a moderate amount of both assertiveness and cooperativeness. It is appropriate when the goals on both sides are equally important, when opponents have equal power and both sides want to split the difference, or when people need to arrive at temporary or expedient solutions under time pressure.

4. The *accommodating style* reflects a high degree of cooperativeness, which works best when people realize that they are wrong, when an issue is more important to others than to oneself, when building social credits for use in later discussions, and when maintaining harmony is especially important.

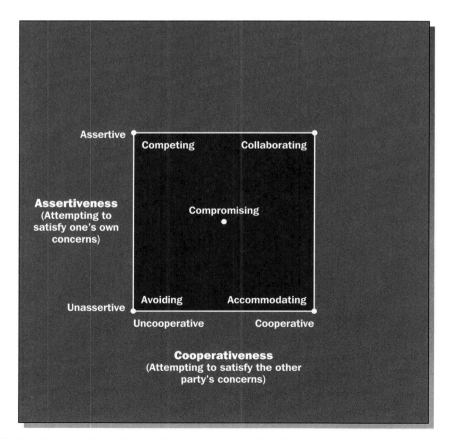

EXHIBIT 14.9

A Model of Styles to Handle Conflict

SOURCE: Adapted from Kenneth Thomas, "Conflict and Conflict Management," in *Handbook of Industrial and Organizational Behavior*, ed. M. D. Dunnette (New York: John Wiley, 1976): 900.

5. The *collaborating style* reflects both a high degree of assertiveness and cooperativeness. The collaborating style enables both parties to win, although it may require substantial bargaining and negotiation. The collaborating style is important when both sets of concerns are too important to be compromised, when insights from different people need to be merged into an overall solution, and when the commitment of both sides is needed for a consensus.

These various styles of handling conflict are especially effective when an individual disagrees with others. But what does a manager or team leader do when a conflict erupts among others within a team or among teams for which the manager is responsible? Research suggests that several techniques can be used as strategies for resolving conflicts among people or departments. These techniques might also be used when conflict is formalized, such as between a union and management.

Superordinate Goals. The larger objective that cannot be attained by a single party is identified as a **superordinate goal.**[87] It is similar to the concept of vision. A powerful vision often compels people to overcome conflicts and cooperate for the greater good. Similarly, a superordinate goal requires the cooperation of conflicting team members for achievement. People must pull together. To the extent that employees can be focused on team or organization goals, the conflict will decrease because they see the big picture and realize they must work together to achieve it.

Mediation. Using a third party to settle a dispute is referred to as **mediation.** A mediator could be a supervisor, a higher-level manager, an outside consultant, or someone from the human resource department. The mediator can discuss the conflict with each party and work toward a solution. If a solution satisfactory to both sides cannot be reached, the parties might be willing to turn the conflict over to the mediator and abide by his or her solution.

NEGOTIATION

One distinctive type of conflict management is **negotiation,** whereby people engage in give-and-take discussions and consider various alternatives to reach a joint decision that is acceptable to both parties. Conflicting parties may embark upon negotiation from different perspectives and with different intentions, reflecting either an *integrative* approach or a *distributive* approach.

Integrative negotiation is based on a win-win assumption, in that all parties want to come up with a creative solution that can benefit both sides of the conflict. Rather than viewing the conflict as a win-lose situation, people look at the issues from multiple angles, consider trade-offs, and try to "expand the pie" rather than divide it. With integrative negotiation, conflicts are managed through cooperation and compromise, which fosters trust and positive long-term

superordinate goal
a goal that cannot be reached by a single party.

mediation
the process of using a third party to settle a dispute.

negotiation
a conflict-management strategy whereby people engage in give-and-take discussions and consider various alternatives to reach a joint decision that is acceptable to both parties.

integrative negotiation
a collaborative approach to negotiation that is based on a win-win assumption, whereby the parties want to come up with a creative solution that benefits both sides of the conflict.

CONCEPT CONNECTION
The closing of the pulp mill in Port Alice on Canada's Vancouver Island put 350 people out of work in a community of only 700. "There was no one in the village who didn't suffer," said employee Stu Roper. In late 2005, foreign investors bought the plant after British Columbia absolved the new owners of responsibility for past environmental damage, the community approved a five-year reduction in property taxes, and union members and Neucel management, pictured here, reached an agreement after contentious **distributive negotiation.** The newly christened Neucel mill will produce high-purity cellulose used in a variety of industries.

relationships. Distributive negotiation, on the other hand, assumes the "size of the pie" is fixed, and each party attempts to get as much of it as they can. One side wants to win, which means the other side must lose. With this win-lose approach, distributive negotiation is competitive and adversarial rather than collaborative and does not typically lead to positive long-term relationships.[88]

In recent years, books, software, newsletters, and training seminars on negotiating have proliferated. Most emphasize the value of integrative negotiation for today's collaborative business environment. That is, the key to effectiveness is to see negotiation not as a zero-sum game but as a process for reaching a creative solution that benefits everyone.[89]

Rules for Reaching a Win-Win Solution.

Achieving a win-win solution through integrative negotiation is based on four key strategies:[90]

1. Separate the people from the problem. For successful integrative negotiation, people stay focused on the problem and the source of conflict rather than attacking or attempting to discredit each other.

2. Focus on interests, not current demands. Demands are what each person wants from the negotiation, whereas interests are why they want them. Consider two sisters arguing over the last orange in the fruit bowl. Each insisted she should get the orange and refused to give up (demands). Then, the girls' aunt walks in and asks each of them *why* they want the orange (interests). As it turned out, one wanted to eat it and the other wanted the peel to use for a class project. By focusing on the interests, the sisters arrived at a solution that got each person what she wanted.[91] Demands create yes-or-no obstacles to effective negotiation. Interests present problems that can be solved creatively.

3. Generate many alternatives for mutual gain. Both parties in an integrative negotiation come up with a variety of options for solving the problem and engage in give-and-take discussions about which alternatives can get each side what it wants.

4. Insist that results be based on objective standards. Each party in a negotiation has its own interests and would naturally like to maximize its outcomes. Successful negotiation requires focusing on objective criteria and maintaining standards of fairness rather than using subjective judgments about the best solution.

In the Bargaining Zone.

The bargaining zone is the zone between one party's minimum reservation point (the point beyond which the party is willing to accept a deal) and the other party's maximum reservation point. Exhibit 14.10 illustrates the bargaining zone for two students negotiating for the purchase of a used textbook.

distributive negotiation
a competitive and adversarial negotiation approach in which each party strives to get as much as it can, usually at the expense of the other party.

bargaining zone
the range between one party's minimum reservation point (the point beyond which the party is willing to accept a deal) and the other party's maximum reservation point.

EXHIBIT 14.10
The Bargaining Zone

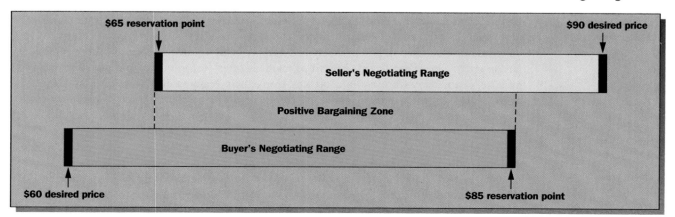

SOURCE: "Negotiation: Distributive Bargaining," Culture at Work, www.culture-at-work.com/distribute.html.

Samantha wants to buy a used *Health Standards* textbook. She would like to get one for $60 but is willing to pay up to $85. Bailey has advertised a used book for sale at $90. He knows he can sell it back to the bookstore for $65, so he won't go lower than that price. As shown in the exhibit, the bargaining zone is the range between $65 (the lowest Bailey will accept) and $85 (the highest Samantha is willing to pay). It is a *positive bargaining zone* because the reservation points overlap by a $20 amount, allowing room for negotiation.[92]

A *negative bargaining zone* occurs when the ranges do not overlap, for instance, if Bailey would not accept less than $65 and Samantha would go no higher than $60. This situation leaves no room for negotiation, and the parties have to fall back on their best alternative to a negotiated agreement, or BATNA. Prior to negotiation, each party decides what it will do if a mutual agreement cannot be reached. In the example of Samantha and Bailey, Samantha's BATNA might be to check out a copy of the textbook from the library and share a text with a classmate. Bailey's BATNA might be to wait for another buyer who will pay a higher price or sell the book to the bookstore for $65.

A key aspect of any negotiation is for each party to determine its BATNA and to ascertain the other party's reservation point. With a positive bargaining zone, successful negotiation is possible if both parties follow the strategies for effective integrative negotiation.

Work Team Effectiveness

Teams are the building blocks of today's organizations, but not all teams are effective. Teams often do not live up to their potential or to the dreams managers have for them. Good leaders help teams be successful.

In this section, we look at the positive outcomes of effective teams. By assessing teams in terms of productive output, personal satisfaction, and the capacity to adapt and learn, managers can better identify actions that will enhance work team effectiveness.[93]

PRODUCTIVE OUTPUT

One aspect of effectiveness relates to whether the team's output (such as decisions, products, or services) meets the requirements of customers or clients in terms of quality, quantity, and timeliness. An IBM team made up of members in the United States, Germany, and the United Kingdom, for example, used collaboration software as a virtual meeting room to solve a client's technical problem resulting from Hurricane Katrina within the space of just a few days.[94] Whether online or in physical space, effective meetings are essential to effective teamwork. The upcoming Benchmarking feature gives some tips for running a great meeting.

Effective employee teams often unleash enormous energy and creativity from workers. Research has found that working in a team often increases an individual's motivation and performance. **Social facilitation** refers to the tendency for the presence of others to enhance one's motivation and performance. Simply being in the presence of other people has an energizing effect.[95] This benefit of teams is often lost in virtual and global teams because people are working in isolation from their teammates. Organizations such as MySQL, described earlier, build in communication mechanisms that keep team members interacting.

SATISFACTION OF MEMBERS

Another important question is whether the team experience contributes to the well-being, personal satisfaction, and development of its members. Effective teams provide multiple opportunities for people to satisfy their individual needs and to develop both personally and professionally.[96] Employees have needs for belongingness and affiliation, and working in teams can help meet these needs. Participative teams can also reduce

TAKE ACTION ▸▸

As a manager, use participative teams whenever it is practical, to increase productivity and reduce boredom.

BATNA
the "best alternative to a negotiated agreement"; a previously determined choice of what a party will do if an acceptable agreement cannot be reached through negotiation.

social facilitation
the tendency for the presence of others to influence an individual's motivation and performance.

boredom, increase individuals' feeling of dignity and self-worth, and contribute to skill development because the whole person is employed. At Radius, a Boston restaurant, for example, two-person kitchen teams have full responsibility for their part of a meal, which gives them a greater sense of accomplishment and importance and enables them to expand their culinary and organizational skills.[97] People who have a satisfying team environment cope better with stress, enjoy their jobs, and have a higher level of organizational commitment.

Spotlight on Skills

How to Run a Great Meeting

A recent survey of nearly 700 employees in the United States and Britain found that people spend an average of 5.6 hours a week in meetings. Unfortunately, too much of this time is wasted in meetings where people doodle, drink coffee, tap away on their laptops, and think about what they could be doing back in their offices.

Effective meetings help people process important information, solve problems, and most importantly, feel actively involved in the organization's tasks or goals. But good meetings don't just happen. They are the result of careful planning. Here are a few tips from the experts.

Prepare in Advance

Advance preparation is the single most important tool for running an efficient, productive meeting. Advance preparation should include the following:

- *Define the purpose.* Not all meetings have the same purpose. Their goal can be to draw on participants' expertise and skills; elicit their commitment to a project, program, or goal; teach them new skills; or coordinate the efforts required to accomplish a specific task. The leader needs to be clear about what the meeting's purpose is and then communicate it clearly to others. Remember, if a meeting isn't essential, don't have it.
- *Prepare an agenda.* The agenda, a simple list of the topics to be discussed, is important because it lets people know what to expect and keeps the meeting focused.
- *Issue invitations selectively.* If the group gets too big, the meeting will not be productive. However, be sure every department with a stake in the topic is represented.
- *Set a strict time limit.* Announce the ending time for the meeting in advance, and then make sure the discussion stays on track.

Bring Out the Best During the Meeting

During the meeting, certain techniques will bring out the best in people and ensure a productive session:

- *Start on time.* Although this sounds obvious, many meetings get started 10 or 15 minutes late. Starting on time has symbolic value because it tells people that the topic is important and that the leader values their time.
- *Outlaw cell phones, Blackberry devices, and laptops.* A ringing cell phone can throw a meeting completely off-track. Ban laptops unless they'll be used during a meeting activity.
- *State the purpose, and review the agenda.* Begin by stating the meeting's explicit purpose and clarifying what should be accomplished by its conclusion.
- *Create involvement.* If the leader merely wants to present one-way information, he or she should send a memo. Some subtle techniques go a long way toward getting people involved.
- *Give everyone a voice.* Good leaders draw out the silent and control the talkative so that the meeting isn't dominated by one or two assertive people. One organization has a rule called NOSTUESO (No one speaks twice until everyone speaks once).
- *Encourage the clash of ideas.* A good meeting is a cross-current of discussion and debate. The leader listens, guides, mediates, stimulates, and summarizes this discussion.
- *Stick to the purpose.* Encouraging a free flow of ideas does not mean allowing participants to waste time by sidetracking the meeting into discussions of issues not on the agenda.

Attend to the End as Much as the Beginning

Review and follow-up is important to summarize and implement agreed-upon points.

- *End with a call to action.* Review the decisions made during the meeting, and make sure everyone understands his or her assignments.
- *Follow up.* Send a short memo to summarize the meeting's key accomplishments, outline agreed-upon activities, and suggest schedules for implementation.

SOURCES: Based on Phred Dvorak, "Corporate Meetings Go Through a Makeover," *Wall Street Journal* (March 6, 2006): B3; Richard Axelrod, Emily M. Axelrod, Julie Beedon, and Robert Jacobs, "Creating Dynamic, Energy-Producing Meetings," *Leader to Leader* (Spring 2005): 53–58; Antoney Jay, "How to Run a Meeting," *Harvard Business Review* (March–April 1976): 120–134; Edward Michaels, "Business Meetings," *Small Business Reports* (February 1989): 82–88; and Jeffrey L. Seglin, "We've Got to Start Meeting Like This," *CIO* (March 1, 2001): 168–170.

CAPACITY TO ADAPT AND LEARN

A professor of management at Santa Clara University analyzed 14 years of National Basketball Association results and found that teams that had played together longer won more games. By playing together over a period of time, members learned to anticipate their teammates' moves and adapt their own behavior to defeat the competition.[98] The same thing happens in effective work teams, where members can anticipate one another's actions and respond appropriately. A good example is the emergency room trauma team at Massachusetts General Hospital, which functions so smoothly that the team switches leaders seamlessly depending on the crisis at hand. With each new emergency, direction may come from a doctor, nurse, intern, or technician—whoever is particularly experienced with the problem.[99] Over time, effective teams learn from experience and use that learning to revitalize and regenerate themselves, smoothly adapting to shifting organizational and competitive demands.[100]

Summary

Several important concepts about teams were described in this chapter. Organizations use teams both to achieve coordination as part of the formal structure and to encourage employee involvement. Formal teams include vertical teams along the chain of command and horizontal teams such as cross-functional teams and committees. Special-purpose teams are used for special, large-scale creative projects. Employee involvement via teams is designed to bring lower-level employees into decision processes to improve quality, efficiency, and job satisfaction. Companies typically start with problem-solving teams, which may evolve into self-directed teams that take on responsibility for management activities. Innovative approaches to teamwork include virtual teams and global teams.

Most teams go through systematic stages of development: forming, storming, norming, performing, and adjourning. Team characteristics that influence organizational effectiveness are size, diversity, cohesiveness, norms, and members' roles. All teams experience some conflict because of scarce resources, ambiguous responsibilities, communication breakdown, personality clashes, power and status differences, and goal conflicts. Some conflict is beneficial, but too much can hurt the team and the organization. Techniques for managing and resolving conflicts include superordinate goals, bargaining, mediation, and negotiation. To identify ways to improve work team effectiveness, managers can assess teams in terms of productive output, personal satisfaction, and the capacity to adapt and learn.

Discussion Questions

1. Volvo went to self-directed teams to assemble cars because of the need to attract and keep workers in Sweden, where pay raises are not a motivator (high taxes) and many other jobs are available. Are these factors good reasons for using a team approach? Discuss.

2. Trust is an important characteristic of a successful team. If you were a team leader, how would you go about building a culture of trust?

3. What factors in today's environment are contributing to an increasing use of virtual teams and global teams? Would you like to be part of a virtual team? Why or why not?

4. Suppose you are the leader of a team that has just been created to develop a new registration process at your college or university. How can you use an understanding of the stages of team development to improve your team's effectiveness?

5. Imagine yourself as a potential member of a team responsible for designing a new package for breakfast cereal. Do you think interpersonal skills would be equally important if the team is organized face-to-face versus a virtual team? Why or why not? Might different types of interpersonal skills be required for the two types of teams? Be specific.

6. If you were the leader of a special-purpose team developing a new computer game, and conflicts arose related to power and status differences among team members, what would you do? How might you use the various conflict-resolution techniques described in the chapter?

7. When you are a member of a team, do you adopt a task specialist or socioemotional role? Which role is more important for a team's effectiveness? Discuss.

8. Some people argue that the presence of an outside threat correlates with a high degree of team cohesion. Would you agree or disagree? Explain your answer. What is the relationship between team cohesiveness and team performance?

9. Describe the advantages and disadvantages of teams. In what situations might the disadvantages outweigh the advantages?

10. One company had 40 percent of its workers and 20 percent of its managers resign during the first year after reorganizing into teams. What might account for this dramatic turnover? How might managers ensure a smooth transition to teams?

Dear Dr. Dorothy

After I got promoted two months ago to a management position, I've scheduled weekly meetings with our group, so we can go over what we accomplished during the past week and what our goals are for next week. Sometimes the meetings go over time, but it's REALLY IMPORTANT for everyone to participate and get their ideas out. Many meetings are actually quite exciting, with lots of new ideas being proposed and brainstormed. The problem is one of my employees keeps complaining that the meetings are "not focused" and they get "too touchy-feely." He says there are no action items and no follow-through at the next meeting. I definitely DO NOT agree. How can you have a good team if you don't pay attention to people's ideas and also their feelings? People NEED to be HEARD and APPRECIATED. How do I make this guy see we can't just have FACTS ONLY meetings?

Team-Builder in Toronto

Dear Builder,

Dr. Dorothy can see you have yourself convinced of the rightness of your actions. But beware the self-righteous outlook! Your troublesome employee may actually be your godsend (isn't that often the case that your calamity is your providence?) and help you to see the error of your ways. Ah, you are shocked that Dr. Dorothy would suggest such a preposterous notion? Consider that your idea of total participation, with lots of brainstorming and being focused on listening to all and appreciating everyone could, in fact, lead to chaos. The fact that your employee does not see action items or follow-through concerns Dr. Dorothy. Yes, she agrees, you do need to consider people's emotional needs, but without follow-up, your meetings are little more than verbal revelry. Lots of fun, but no work accomplished. So Dr. Dorothy asks you to listen to this employee, just as you do to others in the meetings. Listen without defensiveness. Then follow his suggestions. Also, and this Dr. Dorothy tells you from the bottom of her heart, please try writing without an obsession to capitalize.

Self Learning

Team Self-Assessment

At the beginning of a team's existence, it is hard to be sure where you stand in relation to the others on the team. This is best done with an ongoing team or with a group working on a project.

Rate the <u>honest opinions</u> you hold <u>right now</u> about you and your team by circling a number next to each statement.

I. Why am I here?

	Strongly disagree						Strongly agree	Don't know
1. I am confident I belong in this group.	1	2	3	4	5	6	7	10
2. The team's task is important and useful.	1	2	3	4	5	6	7	10
3. The team can do this task as well as or better than one individual could.	1	2	3	4	5	6	7	10
4. I am confident that my skills will be used.	1	2	3	4	5	6	7	10
5. I am confident that I can influence the team's direction and outcome.	1	2	3	4	5	6	7	10

II. How Much Do I Trust You?
("You" means all your fellow team members.)

	Very concerned				Very confident			Don't know
6. You can be relied upon.	1	2	3	4	5	6	7	10
7. You know your craft (as related to the team's work).	1	2	3	4	5	6	7	10
8. You can maintain confidentiality.	1	2	3	4	5	6	7	10
9. You are genuinely dedicated to the team's task.	1	2	3	4	5	6	7	10
10. You have no ulterior motives.	1	2	3	4	5	6	7	10
11. You will accept my idea of all that it means to be a member of this team.	1	2	3	4	5	6	7	10

Rate how easy or challenging it will be for you to perform the following team behaviors.

III. My Team Abilities

	Very easy				Very challenging			Don't know
12. Expect uncertainty early in the group's existence and tolerate that uncertainty.	1	2	3	4	5	6	7	10
13. Be interested in learning how groups develop.	1	2	3	4	5	6	7	10
14. Encourage other members.	1	2	3	4	5	6	7	10
15. Be willing to give honest feedback to others, even when it may feel uncomfortable to do so.	1	2	3	4	5	6	7	10
16. Be patient with people and the process.	1	2	3	4	5	6	7	10
17. Plan on conflict arising, and think of it as an indication of progress.	1	2	3	4	5	6	7	10
18. Assist in confining conflict to issues such as tasks, roles, and responsibilities, and discourage those about personalities.	1	2	3	4	5	6	7	10
19. Be open to yielding on certain troublesome issues, while striving to find creative solutions that are sensitive to others' views.	1	2	3	4	5	6	7	10
20. Complete in a timely manner all tasks that I agree to do.	1	2	3	4	5	6	7	10
21. Don't be a passive observer but take responsibility for what is happening, even when it doesn't affect me directly.	1	2	3	4	5	6	7	10
22. Suggest from time to time that the group take stock of how it is functioning.	1	2	3	4	5	6	7	10
23. Show up and really be present to what is going on.	1	2	3	4	5	6	7	10

Scoring:
Add up the total for the three parts.

	Total Score	Max. Possible	High Score
I. Why am I here?	_____	50	35+
II. How much do I trust you?	_____	60	45+
III. My team abilities	_____	120	90+

Look at which scores are relatively higher and lower for your team.

1. What are the strengths of your team? What are the weaknesses?

Optional group discussion:

2. After every member has done the self-assessment privately, divide into your teams.

3. Have a group discussion about your responses. In compiling all the results, the group should see where the average answer is low, indicating general concern. Also helpful is a discussion on answers where one person indicates a 2 and another a 6 or 7.

4. Under results on Abilities, discuss how members can complement each other, and also identify areas where the group may have collective deficiencies. For example, if everyone has trouble acknowledging conflict, then the group as a whole will probably avoid dealing with conflict directly.

5. (optional) Instructor may choose to debrief the exercise.

SOURCE: Developed by Kent Fairfield, Fairleigh Dickinson University. Used with permission. Adapted from Alan Drexler, David Sibbet, & Russell Forrester, "The Team Performance Mode," and Susan Wheelan, *Creating Effective Teams*. Thousand Oaks, CA: Sage Publications, 2005.

Group Learning

Grandma's Bakery Case Study

A graduate class in management consulting has received permission to study Grandma's Bakery. The employees of the bakery identify with the company, and things always seem to work well. Most of the staff members have been with the company for over 10 years. The owner is very supportive of his employees. He has an equalitarian attitude and respects the workers as individuals. He continually refers to his staff as "My family." From the employee's perspective, Grandma's Bakery is an ideal small business.

The class assignment is to observe the bakery operation and suggest any noted recommendations for improvement. In one area, the class notes that the task of bagging assorted cookies seems inefficient. The job involves eight staff members. Each stands in front of cartons filled with assorted cookies. A bag is held in the left hand. The right hand has to make an extended reach to pick up the cookies and place them in the bag. The staff works at a relaxed, informal pace. The tasks do not align with principles of motion economy. For example, the staff members do not use both hands simultaneously, and each hand works in opposite directions.

In addition, they do not have materials prepositioned for ease of reach.

When the graduate students suggest highly structured changes to accommodate efficiency, the owner graciously rejects their recommendations. The students are confused by his reaction.

1. Form groups and answer the following questions:

Grandma's Bakery
Why did the owner reject the recommendations?
What elements regarding team motivation were overlooked in the study?
What steps would you take as a group if you were studying Grandma's Bakery?

2. As a class, discuss the answers of each group. What did you learn about team effectiveness?

SOURCE: Unknown. If anyone knows the author, please contact publisher.

Action Learning

Teams on TV

1. Form into groups of three to five members. As a group, choose a TV show where teams are central to the plot. Examples include *The Office*, *Law & Order* (any of them), *CSI*, *Boston Legal*, *House*, *Prison Break*, *Friends*, and so on. Make sure the instructor agrees with your choice of TV show.

2. Watch several shows (make sure group members watch the same shows) and study team behavior. Use the Team Roles on pages 531–532 of this textbook and also the Stages of Team Development on pages 532–535. Take notes on which characters perform which role(s) and what stages of development the group is in during a particular show.

3. As a group, come to an agreement on which roles and stages were present in those shows.

4. Your instructor will tell you whether to prepare either a group presentation or group paper on your findings.

5. What did you learn about teams from this assignment? Were there some surprises?

Ethical Dilemma

One for All and All for One?

Melinda Asbel watched as three of her classmates filed out of the conference room. Then she turned back to the large wooden table and faced her fellow members (a student and three faculty members) of the university's judiciary committee.

The three students—Joe Eastridge, Brad Hamil, and Lisa Baghetti—had just concluded their appeal against a plagiarism conviction stemming from a group project for an international marketing course. Melinda, who happened to be in the class with the students on trial, remembered the day the professor, Hank Zierden, had asked Joe, Brad, and Lisa, along with the group's leader, Paul Colgan, to stay after class. She happened to walk by the classroom a half hour later to see four glum students emerge. Even though Paul had a chagrined expression on his face, Joe was the one who looked completely shattered. It didn't take long for word to spread along the ever-active grapevine that Paul had admitted to plagiarizing his part of the group paper.

At the hearing, the students recounted how they'd quickly and unanimously settled on Paul to lead the group. He was by far the most able student among them, someone who managed to maintain a stellar GPA even while taking a full course load and holding down a part-time job. After the group worked together for weeks analyzing the problem and devising a marketing plan, Paul assigned a section of the final paper to each member. With the pressure of all those end-of-the-semester deadlines bearing down on them, everyone was delighted when Paul volunteered to write the company and industry background, the section that typically took the most time to produce. Paul gathered in everyone's contributions, assembled them into a paper, and handed out the final draft to the other members. They each gave it a quick read. They liked what they saw and thought they had a good chance for an A.

Unfortunately, as Paul readily admitted when Professor Zierden confronted them, he had pulled the section he'd contributed directly off the Internet. Pointing out the written policy he had distributed at the beginning of the semester stating that each group member was equally responsible for the final product, the professor gave all four students a zero for the project. The group project and presentation counted for 30 percent of the course grade.

Joe, Brad, and Lisa maintained they were completely unaware that Paul had cheated. "It just never occurred to us

Paul would ever need to cheat," Brad said. They were innocent bystanders, the students argued. Why should they be penalized? Besides, the consequences weren't going to fall on each of them equally. Although Paul was suffering the embarrassment of public exposure, the failing group project grade would only put a dent in his solid GPA. Joe, on the other hand, was already on academic probation. A zero probably meant he wouldn't make the 2.5 GPA he needed to stay in the business program.

At least one of the faculty members of the judiciary committee supported Professor Zierden's actions. "We're assigning more and more group projects because increasingly that's the way these students are going to find themselves working when they get real jobs in the real world," he said. "And the fact of the matter is that if someone obtains information illegally while on the job, it's going to put the whole corporation at risk for being sued, or worse."

Even though she could see merit to both sides, Melinda was going to have to choose. If you were Melinda, how would you vote?

What Would You Do?

1. Vote to exonerate the three group project members who didn't cheat. You're convinced they had no reason to suspect Paul Colgan of dishonesty. Exonerating them is the right thing to do.

2. Vote in support of Hank Zierden's decision to hold each individual member accountable for the entire project. The professor clearly stated his policy at the beginning of the semester, and the students should have been more vigilant. The committee should not undercut a professor's explicit policy.

3. Vote to reduce each of the three students' penalties. Instead of a zero, each student will receive only half of the possible total points for the project, which would be an F. You're still holding students responsible for the group project but not imposing catastrophic punishment. This compromise both undercuts the professor's policy and punishes "innocent" team members to some extent but not as severely.

SOURCE: Based on Ellen R. Stapleton, "College to Expand Policy on Plagiarism," *The Ithancan Online* (April 12, 2001), www.ithaca.edu/ithacan/articles/0104/12/news/0college_to_e.htm.

Case for Critical Analysis

Acme Minerals Extraction Company

Several years ago, Acme Minerals Extraction Company introduced teams in an effort to solve morale and productivity problems at its Wichita plant. Acme used highly sophisticated technology, employing geologists, geophysicists, and engineers on what was referred to as the "brains" side of the business, as well as skilled and semiskilled labor on the "brawn" side to run the company's underground extracting operations. The two sides regularly clashed, and when some engineers locked several operations workers out of the office in 100-degree heat, the local press had a field day. The company hired Suzanne Howard to develop a program that would improve productivity and morale at the Wichita plant. The idea was that it would then be implemented at other Acme sites.

In Wichita, Howard had a stroke of luck in the form of Donald Peterson, a long-time Acme employee who was highly respected at the Wichita plant and was looking for one final challenging project before he retired. Peterson had served in just about every possible line and staff position at Acme over his 39-year career, and he understood the problems workers faced on both the brains and the brawn sides of the business. Howard was pleased when Peterson agreed to serve as leader for the Wichita pilot project.

Three functional groups at the Wichita plant included operations, made up primarily of hourly workers who operated and maintained the extracting equipment; the "below ground" group, consisting of engineers, geologists, and geophysicists who determined where and how to drill; and the "above ground" group of engineers in charge of cursory refinement and transportation of the minerals. Howard and Peterson decided the first step was to get these different groups talking to one another and sharing ideas. They instituted a monthly "problem chat," an optional meeting to which all employees were invited to discuss unresolved problems. At the first meeting, Howard and Peterson were the only two people who showed up. However, people gradually began to attend the meetings, and after about six months, the meetings became lively problem-solving discussions that led to many improvements. For example, a maintenance worker complained that a standard piece of equipment failed repeatedly due to high levels of heat and sand contamination. Peterson listened carefully and then drew a facilities engineer into the discussion. The engineer came up with a new configuration better suited to the conditions, and downtime virtually disappeared.

Next, Howard and Peterson introduced teams to "select a problem and implement a tailored solution," or SPITS. These ad hoc groups were made up of members from each of the three functional areas. They were formed to work on a specific problem identified in a chat meeting and were then disbanded when the problem was solved. Acme gave SPITS the authority to address problems without seeking management approval. Some rocky moments occurred when engineers resented working with operations personnel, and vice versa. However, over time, and with Peterson's strong leadership, the groups eventually began to come together and focus on the issues rather than spending most of their time arguing.

Eventually, workers in Wichita were organized into permanent cross-functional teams that were empowered to make their own decisions and elect their own leaders. After a year and a half, things were really humming. The different groups weren't just working together; they had also started socializing together. At one of the problem chats, an operations worker jokingly suggested that the brains and the brawn should duke it out once a week to get rid of the tensions so they could focus all their energy on the job to be done. Several others joined in the joking, and eventually, the group decided to square off in a weekly softball game. Peterson had T-shirts printed up that said BRAINS and BRAWN. The softball games were well attended, and both sides usually ended up having a few beers together at a local bar afterward. Productivity and morale soared at the Wichita plant, and costs continued to decline.

The company identified the Lubbock plant as the next facility where Suzanne Howard and her team needed to introduce the cross-functional teams that had proven so successful in Kansas. Howard's team felt immense pressure from top management to get the team-based productivity project up and running smoothly and quickly at Lubbock. Top executives believed the lessons learned at Wichita would make implementing the program at other sites less costly and time-consuming. However, when Howard and her team attempted to implement the program at the Lubbock plant, things didn't go well. Because people weren't showing up for the problem chat meetings, the team made attendance mandatory. However, the meetings still produced few valuable ideas or suggestions. Although a few of the SPITS teams solved important problems, none of them showed the kind of commitment and enthusiasm Howard had seen in Wichita. In addition, the Lubbock workers refused to participate in the softball games and other team-building exercises that the team developed for them. Howard finally convinced some workers to join in the softball games by bribing them with free food and beer.

"If I just had a Donald Peterson in Lubbock, things would go a lot more smoothly," Howard thought. "These workers don't trust us the way workers in Wichita trusted him." It seemed that no matter how hard Howard and her team tried to make the project work in Lubbock, morale continued to decline, and conflicts between the different groups of workers actually seemed to increase.

Questions

1. Suzanne Howard and Donald Peterson phased in permanent cross-functional teams in Wichita. What types of teams are the "problem chats" and SPITS groups? What stage or stages of team development did these groups evolve through?

2. What role did Donald Peterson play in the success of the Wichita team-based productivity project? What style did he employ to help reduce conflict between labor and the professionals? Do you agree with Suzanne

Howard that if she just had a Donald Peterson in Lubbock, the project would succeed? Explain your answer.

3. What advice would you give Suzanne Howard and her team for improving the employee involvement climate, containing costs, and meeting production goals at the Lubbock plant?

SOURCES: Based on Michael C. Beers, "The Strategy That Wouldn't Travel," *Harvard Business Review* (November–December 1996): 18–31.

BIZ FLIX

Apollo 13

This film re-creates the heroic efforts of astronaut Jim Lovell (Tom Hanks), his crew, NASA, and Mission Control to return the damaged Apollo spacecraft to earth. Examples of both problem solving and decision making occur in almost every scene. See the earlier Biz Flix exercise for more information about this film and a discussion of another scene.

This scene takes place during day five of the mission about two-thirds of the way through the film. Early in Apollo 13's mission Jack Swigert (Kevin Bacon) stirred the oxygen tanks at the request of Mission Control. After this procedure, an explosion occurred, causing unknown damage to the command module. Before the scene takes place, the damage has forced the crew to move into the LEM (Lunar Exploration Module), which becomes their lifeboat for return to earth.

What to Watch for and Ask Yourself

1. What triggers the conflict in this scene?
2. Is this intergroup conflict or intragroup conflict? What effects can such conflict have on the group dynamics on board Apollo 13?
3. Does mission commander Jim Lovell successfully manage the group dynamics to return the group to a normal state?

VIDEO CASE

Teamwork at Cold Stone Creamery

Freshly baked brownies and cones, handmade ice cream in a pantheon of flavors, and an array of toppings from cookies to fruit, sprinkles to marshmallow, all folded together into the perfect blend. This Ultimate Ice Cream Experience is not the work of one person, but the many teams that make up Cold Stone Creamery.

From the crew members to the managers to the franchisees, area developers, and Creamery members, Cold Stone Creamery is focused on facilitating teamwork. Their list of core values includes the statement "Win as a Team." Doug Ducey, CEO and chairman, is in charge of guiding the future direction of the business. As a leader, he is willing to embrace change and think creatively. He empowers people and believes in his team, challenging them to perform and deliver results. For Doug, individual success is measured by success of the team as a whole. It is through the building of teams that Cold Stone creates a cohesive, unified workforce committed to making Cold Stone Creamery the No. 1 selling ice cream in the U.S. by 2010. The front line of Cold Stone's service are the in-store crew members, mostly 17 year olds in their first job. Huge amounts of effort and the team norming go into supporting these employees and ensuring they have all of the knowledge and skill to make the next customer happy.

Within Cold Stone are a series of team structures: vertical, horizontal, special purpose, and global. Vertical teams include members from the Creamery down to the managers, who together strategize about the newest efforts to make Cold Stone No. 1. Within the store, crew members form horizontal teams based on different specialties, including entertainment, daily prep, fruit prep, and baking. Together, they create the celebratory experience customers enjoy within the store. As part of the Pyramid for Success, 2010, special-purpose teams have been assembled to help develop more stores, increase the customer base, adapt marketing, and, ultimately, increase sales. With stores in Japan, South Korea, Taiwan, Mainland China, and the Middle East, many global teams must meet and work virtually to deliver the Ultimate Ice Cream Experience internationally.

Cold Stone Creamery's use of teams has brought them extensive success. They have amplified the effort of their employees, unleashing their creative energies; increased employee satisfaction; expanded job knowledge; and augmented organizational responsiveness. The company has an excellent shot at making Cold Stone #1. And a little extra hot sauce does not hurt.

Questions

1. What are some norms that might be important to develop in a Cold Stone team?

2. Describe a situation in which conflict might arise in a horizontal team of Crew Members.

3. What might be some of the challenges in creating a global team?

PART 6

Controlling

Unlike analog signals, data in the Internet age travels in both directions. This simple fact has important implications for the revolutionary new types of feedback now available to Web-based entertainment businesses.

Amazon.com founder Jeff Bezos realized early on that the unprecedented data collection made possible by the Web means Amazon can track consumer behavior with extraordinary speed and accuracy. But tracking behavior is just the beginning. Amazon developed one of its best known (and most often copied) innovations: the recommendation system. The company uses individuals' search and purchase history to suggest books, DVDs, music, and other products on their personalized home pages. Those recommendations help customers find products before they even know they want them.

The Internet music streaming Web site, Pandora.com, uses listener feedback to actually personalize its product. Listeners begin creating individualized playlists by entering a favorite artist or song on Pandora's Web page. Pandora then streams tracks with similar characteristics and solicits the customer's feedback. That feedback triggers corrections designed to make the playlist better suit the individual's taste.

This remarkable two-way digital communication capability helps organizations meet their customer satisfaction and growth goals far more effectively.

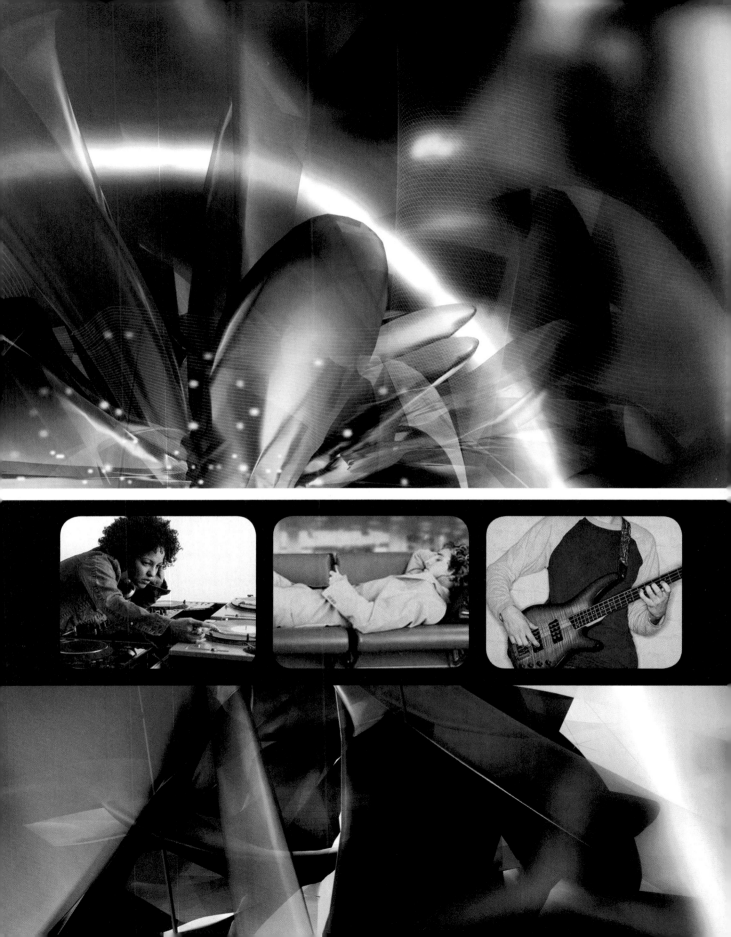

chapter 15

Productivity through Quality Control Systems

New Manager's Questions

Please circle your opinion below each of the following statements. **Assess Your Answer**

1 Controls are for bean counters.

1	2	3	4	5
strongly agree				strongly disagree

2 When there's a problem, a good manager finds out who is at fault.

1	2	3	4	5
strongly agree				strongly disagree

3 Total quality management is just another fad.

1	2	3	4	5
strongly agree				strongly disagree

Control is an important issue facing every manager in every organization. At Rochester Independent Practice Association, administrators have implemented new systems for cutting costs and increasing efficiency, but they also need to find new ways to maintain the quality of care, including the quality of the doctor-patient relationship. Other organizations face similar challenges, such as improving product quality, minimizing the time needed to resupply merchandise in retail stores, decreasing the number of steps needed to process an online merchandise order, or improving the tracking procedures for overnight package delivery. Control, including quality control, also involves office productivity, such as elimination of bottlenecks and reduction in paperwork mistakes. In addition, every organization needs basic systems for allocating financial resources, developing human resources, analyzing financial performance, and evaluating overall profitability.

This chapter introduces the basic mechanisms for controlling the organization. We begin by summarizing the basic structure and objectives of the control process. Then we discuss the changing philosophy of control, today's approach to total quality management (TQM), and recent trends such as ISO certification, economic value-added systems, and market value-added systems. The chapter concludes with a discussion of control systems for a turbulent environment, including the use of open-book management and the balanced scorecard, and looks at some special control problems in today's workplace.

The Meaning of Control

It seemed like a perfect fit. In the chaotic aftermath of 2005's Hurricane Katrina, the American Red Cross needed private-sector help to respond to the hundreds of thousands of people seeking emergency aid. Spherion Corp., a staffing company based in Fort Lauderdale, Florida, had the expertise to hire and train temporary workers fast, and the company had a good track record working with the Red Cross. Yet Red Cross officials soon noticed that an unusually large number of Katrina victim money orders, authorized by employees at the Spherion-staffed call center, were being cashed near the call center itself—in Bakersfield, California. A federal investigation found that some call-center employees were issuing money orders to fake hurricane victims and cashing them for themselves. Fortunately, the fraud was discovered quickly, but the weak control systems that allowed the scam to occur got both the Red Cross and Spherion into a public relations and political mess.[1]

A lack of effective control can seriously damage an organization's health, hurt its reputation, and threaten its future. Consider Enron, which was held up as a model of modern management in the late 1990s but came crashing down a couple of years later.[2] Numerous factors contributed to Enron's shocking collapse, including unethical managers and an arrogant, free-wheeling culture. But it ultimately comes down to a lack of control. No one was keeping track to make sure managers stayed within acceptable ethical and financial boundaries. Although former chairman and CEO Kenneth Lay claimed he didn't know the financial shenanigans were going on at the company, a Houston jury disagreed and found him guilty, along with former CEO Jeffrey Skilling, of conspiracy and fraud.[3] Some still believe that Lay—who died of a heart attack less than six weeks after the verdict—was telling the truth. However, at a minimum, he and other top leaders neglected their

Assess Your Answer

1 Controls are for bean counters.

ANSWER: Without adequate controls in an organization, disorganization and chaos often occur, so it is essential to have varying types of management and financial controls.

responsibilities by failing to set up and maintain adequate controls on the giant corporation. Since Enron, numerous organizations have established more clear-cut standards for ethical conduct and more stringent control systems regarding financial activities.

Organizational control refers to the systematic process of regulating organizational activities to make them consistent with the expectations established in plans, targets, and standards of performance. In a classic article on the control function, Douglas S. Sherwin summarizes the concept as follows: "The essence of control is action which adjusts operations to predetermined standards, and its basis is information in the hands of managers."[4] Thus, effectively controlling an organization requires information about performance standards and actual performance, as well as actions taken to correct any deviations from the standards.

To effectively control an organization, managers need to decide what information is essential, how they will obtain that information (and share it with employees), and how they can and should respond to it. Having the correct data is essential. Managers decide which standards, measurements, and metrics are needed to effectively monitor and control the organization and set up systems for obtaining that information. For example, an important metric for a pro football or basketball team might be the number of season tickets, which reduces the organization's dependence on more labor-intensive box-office sales.[5]

TAKE ACTION

As a manager, always measure your goals and standards against the actual results.

Organizational Control Focus

Control can focus on events before, during, or after a process. For example, a local automobile dealer can focus on activities before, during, or after sales of new cars. Careful inspection of new cars and cautious selection of sales employees are ways to ensure high quality or profitable sales even before those sales take place. Monitoring how salespeople act with customers is considered control during the sales task. Counting the number of new cars sold during the month or telephoning buyers about their satisfaction with sales transactions constitutes control after sales have occurred. These three types of control are formally called *feedforward*, *concurrent*, and *feedback*, and are illustrated in Exhibit 15.1.

organizational control
the systematic process through which managers regulate organizational activities to make them consistent with expectations established in plans, targets, and standards of performance.

EXHIBIT 15.1

Organizational Control Focus

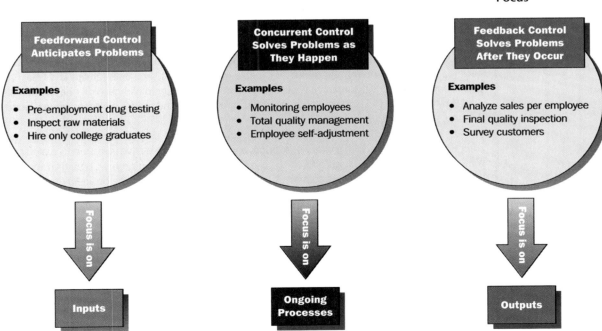

FEEDFORWARD CONTROL

Control that attempts to identify and prevent deviations before they occur is called **feedforward control.** Sometimes called *preliminary* or *preventive control*, it focuses on human, material, and financial resources that flow into the organization. Its purpose is to ensure that input quality is high enough to prevent problems when the organization performs its tasks. Tamara Mellon understands the importance of saying "no" at the right times, to avoid wasting company resources, as shown next.

Feedforward controls are evident in the selection and hiring of new employees. Organizations attempt to improve the likelihood that employees will perform up to standards by identifying the necessary skills, using tests and other screening devices to hire people who have those skills, and providing necessary training to upgrade important skills. The problems at Spherion and the Red Cross, referred to earlier, resulted primarily from weak feedforward controls. Severe time pressure and a sincere desire to get aid to the storm victims as quickly as possible caused Spherion to put new people in the call center before it completed all of its usual background checks and other tests. Numerous nursing homes and assisted living centers have come under fire in recent years due to lax feedforward controls, such as failing to ensure that workers have the appropriate skills or providing them with the training needed to adequately care for residents. Brookside Gables, an assisted living center in the Panhandle region of Florida, eventually closed after a resident died because caregivers didn't have basic skills in first aid and emergency procedures.[6]

> **feedforward control**
> control that focuses on human, material, and financial resources flowing into the organization; also called *preliminary* or *preventive* control.

Jimmy Choo Shoes

When Tamara Mellon was a little girl she loved shoes, really loved them. On a trip with her kindergarten convent school, she begged a nun to buy her some cowboy boots. After college, she worked at British *Vogue*, and her boss soon realized Tamara had an obsession with extraordinarily stylish shoes. When she traveled to Nepal and needed to trek for miles, she was nearly neurotic about which boot was best to wear. Her attention to detail on shoes, fashion layouts, and photographs was quite unusual.

She needed to find the perfect Greek Sandal for a layout and found London's East End cobbler, Jimmy Choo, who had such clients as Princess Diana. After Tamara was promoted to *Vogue*'s accessories editor, she and Jimmy Choo worked closely together. When she decided to go out on her own, she saw an opportunity to exploit: luxury shoes, which had no real competitor to Manolo Blahnik. Convincing her father to invest $250,000, she would run the company while Jimmy Choo and his fashion school-educated niece, Sandra Choi, would design and make the shoes. It was a typical start-up, working out of a basement, no computer. A larger problem surfaced. Though Jimmy Choo was a nice man and a decent cobbler, he was incapable of designing a shoe line. Tamara and Choi had never done it either. But Tamara realized they had one thing Manolo Blahnik didn't have: a female CEO. So they made shoes that Tamara loved because she was the model customer: young, good-looking, style-conscious, and rich.

Tamara and her father had visions of opening 35 stores, but Jimmy Choo was nervous. He was, after all, a working man, with a family to support, and these wild speculative investments scared him. When Equinox Luxury Holdings offered to buy a controlling interest in Jimmy Choo, they took the $100 million, allowing Jimmy Choo himself to bow out with $25 million. The business grew further, and they expect to have 50 stores open worldwide within two years, as the Asian market develops.

A careful businesswoman and manager, Tamara doesn't let her success keep her from making sound decisions. When a group of fragrance-branders were trying to woo her and the company name, she pointedly asked them, "What went wrong with Patrick Cox?" (a shoe designer whose foray into fragrances was not successful). That's the kind of thinking that has made her Britain's highest profile female executive and her company into a household name. It's all about smart decision making and high-heeled courage, which helped her in 2007 to sell the business she built from scratch for $364 million. That's a lot of shoes.

SOURCE: Evgenia Peretz, "The Lady and the Heel," *Vanity Fair* (Aug. 2005): 134–136 and 172–175; Zarah Crawford, "And So the Fantasy Goes," *The New York Times* (July 12, 2007): E4.

Another type of feedforward control is forecasting trends in the environment and managing risk. In tough economic times, for example, consulting companies such as A. T. Kearney stay in close touch with clients to monitor how much business and money will be coming in. The fashion company Liz Claiborne gathers information about consumer fads to determine what supplies to purchase and inventory to stock. Banks typically require extensive documentation before approving major loans to identify and manage risks.[7]

CONCURRENT CONTROL

Control that monitors ongoing employee activities to ensure they are consistent with performance standards is called **concurrent control.** Concurrent control assesses current work activities, relies on performance standards, and includes rules and regulations for guiding employee tasks and behaviors.

Many manufacturing operations include devices that measure whether the items being produced meet quality standards. Employees monitor the measurements; if they see that standards are not met in some area, they make a correction themselves or signal the appropriate person that a problem is occurring. Technology advancements are adding to the possibilities for concurrent control in services as well. For example, retail stores such as Beall's, Sunglass Hut, and Saks use cash-register-management software to monitor cashiers' activities in real time and help prevent employee theft. Trucking companies such as Schneider National and Covenant use computers to track the position of their trucks and monitor the status of deliveries.[8] This chapter's Spotlight feature describes the widespread practice of monitoring employees' e-mail and Web use as a means of concurrent control.

Other concurrent controls involve the ways in which organizations influence employees. An organization's cultural norms and values influence employee behavior, as do the norms of an employee's peers or work group. Concurrent control also includes self-control, through which individuals impose concurrent controls on their own behavior because of personal values and attitudes. Use of both feedforward and concurrent methods is used by Tokyopop, as shown next.

concurrent control
control that consists of monitoring ongoing activities to ensure that they are consistent with standards.

Tokyopop Manga

The biggest marketer of *manga*—animated Japanese novels—is Los Angeles-based Tokyopop, the brainchild of Georgetown Law Grad Stuart Levy. Without any publishing experience, Levy turned *manga* into a $100 million industry. How did an American guy do such a great job selling a uniquely Asian product to Americans? After graduating, he went to Japan, largely because of his love for sushi. There he saw the magnetism *manga* had on the population and believed the same would happen in North America. "I never liked comic books," he says, "but fell in love with Manga. They're so visual and have such a broad subject range—they are more like TV or film." And while comics are mostly for teenage boys, *manga* appeals to both genders in a wider age range.

Levy saw how *anime* TV shows (cartoons of Japanese style) were catching on the late 90s, so he used that info to pitch his ideas to mainstream booksellers, such as Barnes & Noble. To make it easier to sell, Levy designed the books so that each one would be a 5 × 7.5-inch paperback with a cost of $10, simplifying the display problem.

Getting story ideas to book has been systemized: 1) A committee in Japan comes up with basic stories they think Americans will like, and they send them on to the Los Angeles office; 2) employees who don't speak Japanese evaluate the story's appeal from a text summary and graphics; 3) the company quantifies reader interest through e-mails to its 100,000 fan base, as well as chat rooms and newsgroups; 4) an in-house translator adds American slang to the story. While the story is in development, it is available on Tokyopop's intranet to any U.S. or Tokyo employee, who can monitor its progress. Tokyopop has new visions: selling in Europe and taking some of the stories and finding customers back in Japan. And it has new products, including novels that help build vocabulary to prep for ACT and SAT exams. Test preparation sure isn't what it used to be.

SOURCE: Julie Boornstin, "Small & Global: License for Adventure," *FSB* (June 2004): 38–39; Nora Froeschle, "Defeating Exam Horrors," *Tulsa World* (July 17, 2007): A9.

Business Blooper

Wonder Bread

Ever wonder why Wonder Bread tastes, so, well, dull? Interstate Bakeries, which makes both Wonder Bread and Twinkies filed for bankruptcy last year, blaming its demise on the low-carb mania. But word got out that's not the way the bread was sliced, as they say. Turns out Interstate was trying to save money. So instead of cooking its books, like some other companies have, it tinkered with its Wonder Bread recipe to lengthen shelf life and reduce waste. But consumers knew the difference. The bread they had loved now tasted stale and gummy, so they quit buying it, and the company had a net loss last year of $26 million. That's a lot of dough.

SOURCE: Adam Horowitz, Mark Athitakis, Mark Lasswell, and Owen Thomas, "101 Dumbest Moments in Business," *Business 2.0* (Jan/Feb. 2005): 103–110.

TAKE ACTION

Periodically review your own performance at school or on the job—that way you are using control mechanisms to improve your own performance.

FEEDBACK CONTROL

Sometimes called *postaction* or *output control*, **feedback control** focuses on the organization's outputs—in particular, the quality of an end product or service. An example of feedback control in a manufacturing department is an intensive final inspection of a refrigerator at an assembly plant. In Kentucky, school administrators conduct feedback control by evaluating each school's performance every other year.

They review reports of students' test scores as well as the school's dropout and attendance rates. The state rewards schools with rising scores and brings in consultants to work with schools whose scores have fallen.[9] Performance evaluation is also a type of feedback control. Managers evaluate employees' work output to see whether people are meeting previously established standards of performance.

Besides producing high-quality products and services and meeting other goals, businesses need to earn a profit, and even nonprofit organizations need to operate efficiently to carry out their missions. Therefore, many feedback controls focus on financial measurements. Budgeting, for example, is a form of feedback control because managers monitor whether they have operated within their budget targets and make adjustments accordingly. Most organizations also have outside audits of their financial records. The U.S. government set up a special office to investigate the reconstruction effort in Iraq, which includes auditing how funds are being spent.

Feedback Control Model

All well-designed control systems involve the use of feedback to determine whether performance meets established standards. In this section, we will examine the key steps in the feedback control model and then look at how the model applies to organizational budgeting.

STEPS OF FEEDBACK CONTROL

Managers set up control systems that consist of the four key steps illustrated in Exhibit 15.2: establish standards, measure performance, compare performance to standards, and make corrections as necessary.

feedback control
control that focuses on the organization's outputs; also called *postaction* or *output control*.

Establish Standards of Performance. Within the organization's overall strategic plan, managers define goals for organizational departments in specific, operational terms that include a *standard of performance* against which to compare organizational activities. A standard of performance could include "reducing the reject rate from 15 to 3 percent,"

Spotlight on Skills

Cyberslackers Beware: The Boss is Watching

When employees have access to the Internet's vast resources, and the ability to communicate quickly via e-mail and instant messaging with anyone in the world, that's got to be good for productivity, right?

Not necessarily, as many organizations are discovering. Many companies are experiencing a growing problem with "cyberslackers," people who spend part of their workday sending personal e-mails, shopping, or downloading music and videos that hog available bandwidth and sometimes introduce viruses. In addition, it takes just a few bad apples engaging in harmful and possibly illegal activities, such as harassing other employees over the Web, to cause serious problems for their employers. So it's not surprising that since 2001, the use of increasingly sophisticated software to both block employees' access to certain sites and monitor their Internet and e-mail use has grown exponentially.

A certain degree of vigilance is clearly warranted. However, enlightened managers strive for a balanced approach that protects the organization's interests while at the same time maintains a positive, respectful work environment. Surveillance overkill can sometimes cost more than it saves, and it can also have a distinctly negative impact on employee morale. At the very least, employees may feel as though they're not being treated as trustworthy, responsible adults.

Here are some guidelines for creating an effective but fair "acceptable use policy" for workplace Internet use.

- *Make sure employees understand that they have no legal right to privacy in the workplace.* The courts so far have upheld an organization's right to monitor any and all employee activities on computers purchased by an employer for work purposes.

- *Create a written Internet policy.* Make sure you clearly state what qualifies as a policy violation by giving clear, concrete guidelines for acceptable use of e-mail, the Internet, and any other employer-provided hardware or software. For example, spell out the types of Websites that are never to be visited while at work and what constitutes acceptable e-mail content. Are employees ever permitted to use the Web for personal use? If so, specify what they can do, for how long, and whether they need to confine their personal use to lunchtime or breaks. List the devices you'll be checking and tell them the filtering and monitoring procedures you have in place. Get employees to sign a statement saying they've read and understand the policy.
- *Describe the disciplinary process.* Give people a clear understanding of the consequences of violating the organization's Internet and electronic use policy. Make sure they know the organization will cooperate if a criminal investigation arises.
- *Review the policy at regular intervals.* You'll need to modify your guidelines as new technologies and devices appear.

Managers should remember that monitoring e-mail and Internet use doesn't have to be an all-or-nothing process. Some organizations use continuous surveillance; others only screen when they believe a problem exists, or they disseminate a policy and leave enforcement to the honor system. Look carefully at your workforce and the work they're doing, and assess your potential liability and security needs. Then come up with a policy and monitoring plan that makes sense for your organization.

Sources: Lorraine Cosgrove Ware, "People Watching," www.cio.com (August 15, 2005): 24; Art Lambert, "Technology in the Workplace: A Recipe for Legal Trouble," *Workforce.com* (February 14, 2005), www.workforce.com/archive/article/23/95/08.php?ht=lambert%20lambert; Technical Resource Group, "Employee E-mail and Internet Usage Monitoring: Issues and Concerns," www.picktrg.com/pubs/EmployeeMonitoring_WP062804.pdf; Pui-Wing Tam, Erin White, Nick Wingfield, and Kris Maher, "Snooping E-Mail by Software Is Now a Workplace Norm," *Wall Street Journal* (March 9, 2005): B1; and Ann Sherman, "Firms Address Worries over Workplace Web Surfing," *Broward Daily Business Review* (May 17, 2006): 11.

"increasing the corporation's return on investment to 7 percent," or "reducing the number of accidents to one per each 100,000 hours of labor." Managers should carefully assess what they will measure and how they will define it. For example, at pharmaceutical companies such as Wyeth, getting more productivity from research and development has become a top priority, so Wyeth's R&D chief Robert Ruffolo set firm targets for how many compounds must move forward at each stage of the drug development process. The clear standards have helped Wyeth boost the number of potentially hot products in its drug pipeline.[10]

Tracking such matters as customer service, employee involvement, and turnover is an important supplement to traditional financial and operational performance measurement, but many companies have a hard time identifying and defining nonfinancial

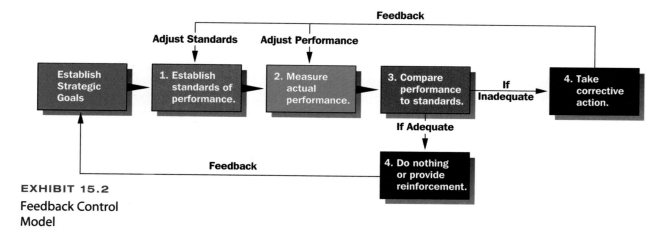

EXHIBIT 15.2

Feedback Control
Model

measurements.[11] To effectively evaluate and reward employees for the achievement of standards, managers need clear standards that reflect activities that contribute to the organization's overall strategy in a significant way. Standards should be defined clearly and precisely so employees know what they need to do and can determine whether their activities are on target.[12] George Clooney's standard of making socially relevant films was not enough to keep his production company afloat, as described in Chapter 11's Business Blooper.

Measure Actual Performance. Most organizations prepare formal reports of quantitative performance measurements that managers review daily, weekly, or monthly. These measurements should be related to the standards set in the first step of the control process. For example, if sales growth is a target, the organization should have a means of gathering and reporting sales data. If the organization has identified appropriate measurements, regular review of these reports helps managers stay aware of whether the organization is doing what it should.

In most companies, managers do not rely exclusively on quantitative measures. They get out into the organization to see how things are going, especially for such goals as increasing employee participation or improving customer satisfaction. Managers have to observe for themselves whether employees are participating in decision making and have opportunities to add to and share their knowledge. Interaction with customers is necessary for managers to really understand whether activities are meeting customer needs.

Compare Performance to Standards. The third step in the control process is comparing actual activities to performance standards. When managers read computer reports or walk through the plant, they identify whether actual performance meets, exceeds, or falls short of standards. Typically, performance reports simplify such comparisons by placing the performance standards for the reporting period alongside the actual performance for the same period and by computing the variance—that is, the difference between each actual amount and the associated standard. To correct the problems that most require attention, managers focus on variances.

CONCEPT CONNECTION

Is it possible to make scientific discovery efficient? Managers at pharmaceuticals company Wyeth think so. They devised a streamlined research and development system driven by ambitious, quantifiable **standards of performance.** Managers routinely **compare performance to standards** and issue automated scorecards for each individual. Wyeth ties compensation to accomplishment of these all-or-nothing targets. "If the goal was to discover 12 drugs, 11 drugs are worth no points," says Wyeth Research President Robert Ruffolo Jr., who oversaw the reengineering effort. So far, the approach has yielded impressive results. With no additional investment, Wyeth has seen the number of new drugs that emerge from the early discovery phase increase fourfold.

When performance deviates from a standard, managers must interpret the deviation. They are expected to dig beneath the surface and find the cause of the problem. If the sales goal is to increase the number of sales calls by 10 percent, and a salesperson achieved an increase of 8 percent, where did the salesperson fail to achieve the goal? Perhaps several businesses on the route closed, additional salespeople were assigned to the area by competitors, or the salesperson needs training in making cold sales calls more effectively. Managers should take an inquiring approach to deviations to gain a broad understanding of factors that influence performance. Effective management control involves subjective judgment and employee discussions, as well as objective analysis of performance data.

TAKE ACTION

As a new manager, apply the feedback control model: Define clear standards of performance, measure outcomes regularly, and work with team members to take corrective actions when necessary.

Assess Your Answer

2 When there's a problem, a good manager finds out who is at fault.

ANSWER: Comparing a standard to performance means the manager looks for what happened that caused the performance to below par. But focusing on blaming a person is usually not productive and deflects away from analyzing the problem.

Take Corrective Action. Managers also determine what changes, if any, are needed. In a traditional top-down approach to control, managers exercise their formal authority to make necessary changes. Managers may encourage employees to work harder, redesign the production process, or fire employees. In contrast, managers using a participative control approach collaborate with employees to determine the corrective action necessary.

In some cases, managers may take corrective action to change performance standards. They may realize that standards are too high or too low if departments continually fail to meet or routinely exceed standards. If contingency factors that influence organizational performance change, performance standards may need to be altered to make them realistic and to provide continued motivation for employees.

TAKE ACTION

As a manager, you must correct deficiencies; it's not enough to just measure.

---

eBay

One of Meg Whitman's guiding rules is: "If you can't measure it, you can't control it." As CEO of eBay, Whitman runs a company that is obsessed with performance measurement. She personally monitors a slew of performance metrics, including standard measurements such as site visitors, new users, and time spent on the site, as well as the ratio of eBay's revenues to the value of goods traded.

Managers and employees throughout the company also monitor performance almost obsessively. Category managers, for example, have clear standards of performance for their auction categories (such as sports memorabilia, jewelry and watches, health and beauty, fashion, etc.). They are constantly measuring, tweaking, and promoting their categories to meet or outperform the targets.

Whitman believes getting a firm grip on performance measurement is essential for a company to know where to spend money, where to assign more personnel, and which projects to promote or abandon. But performance measurement isn't just about numbers. At eBay, "it's all about the customer," and gauging customer (user) satisfaction requires a mix of methods, such as surveys, monitoring eBay's discussion boards, and personal contact. Whitman gets her chance to really connect with users at the annual eBay Live conference. There, she wanders the convention-hall floor talking with anyone and everyone about their eBay experiences.

By defining standards, using a combination of measurement approaches, and comparing performance to standards, eBay managers are able to identify trouble spots and move quickly to take corrective action when and where it's needed.[13]

Is Your Budget in Control?

By the time you are in college, you are in charge of at least some of your own finances. How well you manage your personal budget may indicate how well you will manage your company's budget on the job. Respond to the following statements to evaluate your own budgeting habits. If the statement doesn't apply directly to you, respond the way you think you would behave in a similar situation.

	Mostly True	Mostly False
1. I spend all my money as soon as I get it.	____	____
2. At the beginning of each week (or month, or term), I write down all my fixed expenses.	____	____
3. I never seem to have any money left over at the end of the week (or month).	____	____
4. I pay all my expenses, but I never seem to have any money left over for fun.	____	____
5. I can't pay all my bills.	____	____
6. I have a credit card, but I pay the balance in full each month.	____	____
7. I take cash advances on my credit card.	____	____
8. I know how much I can spend on eating out, movies, and other entertainment each week.	____	____
9. I pay cash for everything.	____	____
10. I lend money to friends whenever they ask, even if it leaves me short of cash.	____	____
11. I never borrow money from friends.	____	____
12. I am putting aside money each month to save for something that I really need.	____	____

SCORING AND INTERPRETATION

Mostly True responses to statements 2, 8, 9, 11, and 12 point to the most disciplined budgeting habits; Mostly True responses to 4 and 6 reveal adequate budgeting habits; Mostly True responses to 1, 3, 5, 7, and 10 indicate the poorest budgeting habits. If you have answered honestly, chances are you'll have a combination of all three. Look to see where you can improve your budgeting.

Managers may want to provide positive reinforcement when performance meets or exceeds targets. For example, they may reward a department that has exceeded its planned goals or congratulate employees for a job well done. Managers should not ignore high-performing departments at the expense of taking corrective actions elsewhere. The online auction company eBay provides a good illustration of the feedback control model.

APPLICATION TO BUDGETING

Budgetary control, one of the most commonly used methods of managerial control, is the process of setting targets for an organization's expenditures, monitoring results and comparing them to the budget, and making changes as needed. As a control device, budgets are reports that list planned and actual expenditures for cash, assets, raw materials, salaries, and other resources. In addition, budget reports usually list the variance between the budgeted and actual amounts for each item.

A budget is created for every division or department within an organization, no matter how small, as long as it performs a distinct project, program, or function. The fundamental unit of analysis for a budget control system is called a responsibility center. A **responsibility center** is defined as any organizational department or unit under the supervision of a single person who is responsible for its activity.[14] A three-person appliance sales office in Watertown, New York, is a responsibility center, as is a quality control department, a marketing department, and an entire refrigerator manufacturing plant. The manager of each unit has budget responsibility. Top managers use budgets for the company as a whole, and middle managers traditionally focus on the budget performance of their department or division. Budgets that managers typically use include expense budgets, revenue budgets, cash budgets, and capital budgets.

Budgeting is an important part of organizational planning and control. Many traditional companies use **top-down budgeting,** which means that the budgeted amounts for the coming year are literally imposed on middle- and lower-level managers.[15] These managers set departmental budget targets in accordance with overall company revenues and expenditures specified by top executives. Although the top-down process provides some advantages, the movement toward employee empowerment, participation, and learning means that many organizations are adopting **bottom-up budgeting,** a process in which lower-level managers anticipate their departments' resource needs and pass them up to top management for approval.[16] Companies of all kinds are increasingly involving line managers in the budgeting process. At the San Diego Zoo, scientists, animal keepers, and other line managers use software and templates to plan their department's budget needs because, as CFO Paula Brock says, "Nobody knows that side of the business better than they do."[17] Each of the 145 zoo departments also does a monthly budget close and reforecast so that resources can be redirected as needed to achieve goals within budget constraints. Thanks to the bottom-up process, for example, the Zoo was able to quickly redirect resources to protect its valuable exotic bird collection from an outbreak of a highly infectious bird disease, without significantly damaging the rest of the organization's budget.[18]

Financial Control

In every organization, managers need to watch how well the organization is performing financially. Not only do financial controls tell whether the organization is on sound financial footing, but they can be useful indicators of other kinds of performance problems. For example, a sales decline may signal problems with products, customer service, or sales force effectiveness.

FINANCIAL STATEMENTS

Financial statements provide the basic information used for financial control of an organization. Two major financial statements—the balance sheet and the income statement—are the starting points for financial control.

The **balance sheet** shows the firm's financial position with respect to assets and liabilities at a specific point in time. An example of a balance sheet is presented in Exhibit 15.3. The balance sheet provides three types of information: assets, liabilities, and owners' equity. *Assets* are what the company owns, and they include *current assets* (those that can be converted into cash in a short time period) and *fixed assets* (such as buildings and equipment

 **TAKE ACTION**

As a manager, regularly review your balance sheet.

responsibility center
an organizational unit under the supervision of a single person who is responsible for its activity.

top-down budgeting
a budgeting process in which middle- and lower-level managers set departmental budget targets in accordance with overall company revenues and expenditures specified by top management.

bottom-up budgeting
a budgeting process in which lower-level managers budget their departments' resource needs and pass them up to top management for approval.

balance sheet
a financial statement that shows the firm's financial position with respect to assets and liabilities at a specific point in time.

New Creations Landscaping
Consolidated Balance Sheet
December 31, 2007

Assets			Liabilities and Owners' Equity		
Current assets:			Current liabilities:		
Cash	$ 25,000		Accounts payable	$200,000	
Accounts receivable	75,000		Accrued expenses	20,000	
Inventory	500,000		Income taxes payable	30,000	
Total current assets		$ 600,000	Total current liabilities		$ 250,000
Fixed assets:			Long-term liabilities:		
Land	250,000		Mortgages payable	350,000	
Buildings and fixtures	1,000,000		Bonds outstanding	250,000	
Less depreciation	200,000		Total long-term liabilities		$ 600,000
Total fixed assets		1,050,000	Owners' equity:		
			Common stock	540,000	
			Retained earnings	260,000	
			Total owners' equity		800,000
Total assets		$1,650,000	Total liabilities and net worth		$1,650,000

EXHIBIT 15.3
Balance Sheet

that are long term in nature). *Liabilities* are the firm's debts, including both *current debt* (obligations that will be paid by the company in the near future) and *long-term debt* (obligations payable over a long period). *Owners' equity* is the difference between assets and liabilities and is the company's net worth in stock and retained earnings.

The **income statement,** sometimes called a profit-and-loss statement or P&L for short, summarizes the firm's financial performance for a given time interval, usually one year. A sample income statement is shown in Exhibit 15.4. Some organizations calculate the income statement at three-month intervals during the year to see whether they are on target for sales and profits. The income statement shows revenues coming into the organization from all sources and subtracts all expenses, including cost of goods sold, interest, taxes, and depreciation. The *bottom line* indicates the net income—profit or loss—for the given time period.

income statement
a financial statement that summarizes the firm's financial performance for a given time interval; sometimes called a profit-and-loss statement.

EXHIBIT 15.4
Income Statement

New Creations Landscaping
Statement of Income
For the Year Ended December 31, 2007

Gross sales	$3,100,000	
Less sales returns	200,000	
Net sales		$2,900,000
Less expenses and cost of goods sold:		
Cost of goods sold	2,110,000	
Depreciation	60,000	
Sales expenses	200,000	
Administrative expenses	90,000	2,460,000
Operating profit		440,000
Other income		20,000
Gross income		460,000
Less interest expense	80,000	
Income before taxes		380,000
Less taxes	165,000	
Net income		$ 215,000

The owner of Aahs!, a specialty retailing chain in California, used the income statement to detect that sales and profits were dropping significantly during the summer months.[19] He immediately evaluated company activities and closed two money-losing stores. He also began a training program to teach employees how to increase sales and cut costs to improve net income. This use of the income statement follows the control model described in the previous section, beginning with setting targets, measuring actual performance, and then taking corrective action to improve performance to meet targets.

The Changing Philosophy of Control

Managers' approach to control is changing in many of today's organizations. In connection with the shift to employee participation and empowerment, many companies are adopting a *decentralized* rather than a *bureaucratic* control process. Bureaucratic control and decentralized control represent different philosophies of corporate culture, which was discussed in Chapter 2. Most organizations display some aspects of both bureaucratic and decentralized control, but managers generally emphasize one or the other, depending on the organizational culture and their own beliefs about control.

Bureaucratic control involves monitoring and influencing employee behavior through the extensive use of rules, policies, hierarchy of authority, written documentation, reward systems, and other formal mechanisms.[20] In contrast, decentralized control relies on cultural values, traditions, shared beliefs, and trust to foster compliance with organizational goals. Managers operate on the assumption that employees are trustworthy and willing to perform effectively without extensive rules and close supervision.

Exhibit 15.5 contrasts the use of bureaucratic and decentralized methods of control. Bureaucratic methods define explicit rules, policies, and procedures for employee behavior. Control relies on centralized authority, the formal hierarchy, and close personal supervision. Responsibility for quality control rests with quality control inspectors and supervisors rather

bureaucratic control
the use of rules, policies, hierarchy of authority, reward systems, and other formal devices to influence employee behavior and assess performance.

EXHIBIT 15.5

Bureaucratic and Decentralized Methods of Control

Bureaucratic Control	Decentralized Control
Uses detailed rules and procedures; formal control systems	Limited use of rules; relies on values, group and self-control, selection and socialization
Top-down authority, formal hierarchy, position power, quality control inspectors	Flexible authority, flat structure, expert power, everyone monitors quality
Task-related job descriptions; measurable standards define minimum performance	Results-based job descriptions; emphasis on goals to be achieved
Emphasis on extrinsic rewards (pay, benefits, status)	Extrinsic and intrinsic rewards (meaningful work, opportunities for growth)
Rewards given for meeting individual performance standards	Rewards individual and team; emphasis on equity across employees
Limited, formalized employee participation (e.g., grievance procedures)	Broad employee participation, including quality control, system design, and organizational governance
Rigid organizational culture; distrust of cultural norms as means of control	Adaptive culture; culture recognized as means for uniting individual, team, and organizational goals for overall control

Sources: Based on Richard E. Walton, "From Control to Commitment in the Workplace," *Harvard Business Review* (March–April 1985), 76–84; and Don Hellriegel, Susan E. Jackson, and John W. Slocum, Jr., *Management*, 8th ed. (Cincinnati, Ohio: South-Western, 1999), 663.

than with employees. Job descriptions generally are specific and task related, and managers define minimal standards for acceptable employee performance. In exchange for meeting the standards, individual employees are given extrinsic rewards such as wages, benefits, and possibly promotions up the hierarchy. Employees rarely participate in the control process, with any participation being formalized through mechanisms such as grievance procedures. With bureaucratic control, the organizational culture is somewhat rigid, and managers do not consider culture a useful means of controlling employees and the organization. Technology often is used to control the flow and pace of work or to monitor employees, such as by measuring how long employees spend on phone calls or how many keystrokes they make at the computer.

Bureaucratic control techniques can enhance organizational efficiency and effectiveness. Many employees appreciate a system that clarifies what is expected of them, and they may be motivated by challenging, but achievable, goals.[21] However, although many managers effectively use bureaucratic control, too much control can backfire. Employees resent being watched too closely, and they may try to sabotage the control system. One veteran truck driver expressed his unhappiness with electronic monitoring to a *Wall Street Journal* reporter investigating the use of devices that monitor truck locations. According to the driver, "It's getting worse and worse all the time. Pretty soon they'll want to put a chip in the drivers' ears and make them robots." He added that he occasionally escapes the relentless monitoring by parking under an overpass to take a needed nap out of the range of the surveillance satellites.[22]

In addition, some managers take bureaucratic control to an extreme, hovering over employees and micromanaging every detail, which is inefficient as well as damaging to morale and motivation.[23] The Qwest call center in Idaho Falls was about to go under partly as a result of overcontrolling front-line supervisors, until a new manager arrived with a different philosophy, as described a bit later in this chapter.

Decentralized control is based on values and assumptions that are almost opposite to those of bureaucratic control. Rules and procedures are used only when necessary. Managers rely instead on shared goals and values to control employee behavior. The organization places great emphasis on the selection and socialization of employees to ensure that workers have the appropriate values needed to influence behavior toward meeting company goals. No organization can control employees 100 percent of the time, and self-discipline and self-control are what keep workers performing their jobs up to standard. Empowerment of employees, effective socialization, and training all can contribute to internal standards that provide self-control.

With decentralized control, power is more dispersed and is based on knowledge and experience as much as position. The organizational structure is flat and horizontal, as discussed in Chapter 7, with flexible authority and teams of workers solving problems and making improvements. Everyone is involved in quality control on an ongoing basis. Job descriptions generally are results-based, with an emphasis more on the outcomes to be achieved than on the specific tasks to be performed. Managers use not only extrinsic rewards such as pay but also the intrinsic rewards of meaningful work and the opportunity to learn and grow. Technology is used to empower employees by giving them the information they need to make effective decisions, work together, and solve problems. People are rewarded for team and organizational success as well as their individual performance, and the emphasis is on equity among employees. Employees participate in a wide range of areas, including setting goals, determining standards of performance, governing quality, and designing control systems.

TAKE ACTION ➡

As a manager, determine whether you need organizational controls or whether the values and goals can shape employee behavior.

decentralized control
the use of organizational culture, group norms, and a focus on goals, rather than rules and procedures, to foster compliance with organizational goals.

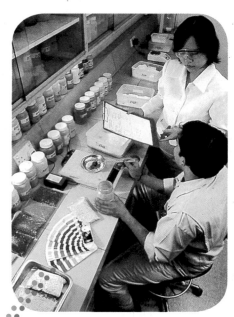

CONCEPT CONNECTION

For more than a decade, managers at General Electric have been dedicated to **decentralized control** through a program called "Work Out." Work Out is an ongoing effort to achieve what former CEO Jack Welch called boundaryless behavior—behavior that "ends all barriers of rank, function, geography, and bureaucracy in an endless pursuit of the best idea." With boundaries diminished, GE launched **Six Sigma,** a disciplined methodology that focuses on quality for every process that affects the GE customer. Cindy Lee and S. Mani were part of a Six Sigma team at the color lab of the GE Plastics plant in Singapore. The team reduced the lead time for matching colors of GE resins to customer requirements by 85 percent, providing a distinct competitive advantage in the fast-paced global market for plastics.

Spotlight on Skills

Controlling with Love, Not Fear

"I would think of any reason not to go to work," says Chyanne Smith about her job at Qwest Communication's Idaho Falls call center. "I would think, 'Somebody hit me with a truck. I do not want to go to work today.'" Smith wasn't alone in her feelings. The environment at the call center, one of 11 Qwest Communications centers around the United States, was bleak. Doors slamming. People crying on the phone to their friends. Rumors that the center would soon close.

When Larry Walters, a 13-year Qwest veteran, took on the daunting challenge of pulling the Idaho Falls operation back from the brink of extinction, he realized the center was clear proof that control through fear and intimidation just doesn't work. One of Walters's first moves was to bring in the six so-called "coaches," front-line managers who supervised teams of 10 to 12 telephone representatives. Walters made it clear that these supervisors had to live up to the title of coach by helping people be their best. Four of the managers simply refused to go along with the new approach and were fired, sending a clear signal to the reps that it was a new day in Idaho Falls.

An important aspect of Walters's transformation was focusing people on clear performance standards, being consistent and direct about what he wanted, and letting people know how they were doing. Within the first week, Walters posted the call center's results on the walls for all to see, showing how the center ranked for sales, customer service, and attrition compared to other Qwest centers. "I wanted to start building that sense of pride in our center . . .," Walters says. "I was actually showing people, 'Do you realize we're last in sales right now? Does that bother you?'"

This focus on results could have landed flat, except for Walters's genuine concern for rank-and-file employees. His first question to an employee in the morning wouldn't be "How are your numbers?" but "How was your son's Little League game?" or "Did you have a fun weekend?" Walters got out on the floor and got to know people by name. He listened to their frustrations and made changes to alleviate them where he could. He dressed up in silly costumes. He stood on a desk in the middle of the building and told people he loved them and believed they could accomplish great things.

Before long, people were accomplishing great things. The center buzzed with activity and enthusiasm as figures for sales and customer service consistently went up. Sales productivity skyrocketed 68 percent. Within less than two years, the Idaho Falls center not only exceeded its sales target but was ranked number 1. Senior executives were so impressed that they decided to expand the center. Walters cried along with other managers and employees as the announcement was made.

Down to just 65 people and with the lights out in half of the building when Walters arrived in April 2003, the Idaho Falls center employed about 400 in two buildings by early 2005 and was the largest Qwest call center in the country. And what about Chyanne Smith? "I'm proud to come to work," she says, "and I'm proud to say I'm a Qwest employee."

SOURCE: Rodd Wagner, "Becoming the Best at Qwest," *Gallup Management Journal* (January 13, 2005), http://gmj.gallup.com/content/default.aspx?ci=14593&pg=3.

With decentralized control, the culture is adaptive, and managers recognize the importance of organizational culture for uniting individual, team, and organizational goals for greater overall control. Ideally, with decentralized control, employees will pool their areas of expertise to arrive at procedures that are better than managers could come up with working alone.

Managing Productivity

Productivity is significant because it influences the well-being of the entire society as well as of individual companies. The only way to increase the output of goods and services to society is to increase organizational productivity.

LEAN MANUFACTURING

Many of the concepts we have discussed, including just-in-time inventory and an emphasis on quality, are central to the philosophy of lean manufacturing. Today's organizations are trying to become more efficient, and implementing the lean manufacturing philosophy is one popular approach to doing so. **Lean manufacturing,** sometimes called *lean production,* uses highly trained employees at every stage of the production process who take a painstaking approach to details and problem solving to cut waste and improve quality and

lean manufacturing
manufacturing process using highly trained employees at every stage of the production process to cut waste and improve quality.

productivity. Lean manufacturing was pioneered by Toyota, and the concept has spread around the world to both manufacturing and service organizations.

The heart of lean manufacturing is not machines or technology but employee involvement. Employees are trained to "think lean," and empowered to make changes to attack waste and strive for continuous improvement in all areas.[24] The system combines techniques such as just-in-time inventory, continuous-flow production, quick changeover of assembly lines, continuous improvement, and preventive maintenance with a management system that encourages employee involvement and problem solving. Any employee can stop the production line at any time to solve a problem. In addition, equipment is often designed to stop automatically so that a defect can be fixed.[25]

MEASURING PRODUCTIVITY

One important question when considering productivity improvements is: What is productivity, and how do managers measure it? In simple terms, **productivity** is the organization's output of goods and services divided by its inputs. This means that productivity can be improved by either increasing the amount of output using the same level of inputs or reducing the number of inputs required to produce the output. Sometimes a company can even do both. Ruggieri & Sons, for example, invested in mapping software to help it plan deliveries of heating fuel. The software plans the most efficient routes based on the locations of customers and fuel reloading terminals, as well as the amount of fuel each customer needs. When Ruggieri switched from planning routes by hand to using the software, its drivers began driving fewer miles but making 7 percent more stops each day—in others words, burning less fuel to sell more fuel.[26]

The accurate measure of productivity can be complex. Two approaches for measuring productivity are total factor productivity and partial productivity. **Total factor productivity** is the ratio of total outputs to the inputs from labor, capital, materials, and energy:

$$Total\ factor\ productivity = \frac{Output}{Labor + Capital + Materials + Energy}$$

Total factor productivity represents the best measure of how the organization is doing. Often, however, managers need to know about productivity with respect to certain inputs. **Partial productivity** is the ratio of total outputs to a major category of inputs. For example, many organizations are interested in labor productivity, which is measured as follows:

$$Labor\ productivity = \frac{Output}{Labor\ dollars}$$

Calculating this formula for labor, capital, or materials provides information on whether improvements in each element are occurring. However, managers often are criticized for relying too heavily on partial productivity measures, especially direct labor.[27] Measuring direct labor misses the valuable improvements in materials, work processes, and quality. Labor productivity is easily measured but may show an increase as a result of capital improvements. Thus, managers will misinterpret the reason for productivity increases.

---

productivity
the organization's output of products and services divided by its inputs.

total factor productivity
the ratio of total outputs to the inputs from labor, capital, materials, and energy.

partial productivity
the ratio of total outputs to the inputs from a single major input category.

TAKE ACTION ▶

As a manager, remember that productivity means you are adding value to the raw materials and making something economically valuable.

CONCEPT CONNECTION

For Anadarko, **productivity** is measured by the amount of oil and natural gas it can locate and extract from deep inside the earth. To measure the company's productivity, the cost of inputs (which includes exploration and drilling costs) must be measured against the value of the outputs (the oil and natural gas it can produce). Recent productivity has been very high for Anadarko, due mainly to its use of cutting-edge technology and exploration techniques. For instance, while exploring in a part of Algeria that bigger competitors had given up on, these Anadarko workers used an unorthodox imaging technique to discover a three-billion barrel field of oil.

Total Quality Management (TQM)

One popular approach based on a decentralized control philosophy is **total quality management (TQM),** an organization-wide effort to infuse quality into every activity in a company through continuous improvement. Managing quality is a concern for every organization. The Yugo was the lowest-priced car on the market when it was introduced in the United States in 1985, yet four years later, the division went bankrupt, largely as a result of quality problems in both products and services.[28] In contrast, Toyota has steadily gained market share over the past several decades and will likely soon overtake General Motors as the world's top-selling auto maker.[29] The difference comes down to quality. Toyota is a model of what happens when a company makes a strong commitment to TQM.

TQM became attractive to U.S. managers in the 1980s because it had been successfully implemented by Japanese companies, such as Toyota, Canon, and Honda, which were gaining market share and an international reputation for high quality. The Japanese system was based on the work of such U.S. researchers and consultants as Deming, Juran, and Feigenbaum, whose ideas attracted U.S. executives after the methods were tested overseas.[30] The TQM philosophy focuses on using teamwork, increasing customer satisfaction, and lowering costs. Organizations implement TQM by encouraging managers and employees to collaborate across functions and departments, as well as with customers and suppliers, to identify areas for improvement, no matter how small. Each quality improvement is a step toward perfection and meeting a goal of zero defects. Quality control becomes part of the day-to-day business of every employee, rather than being assigned to specialized departments.

The implementation of TQM is similar to that of other decentralized control methods. Feedforward controls include training employees to think in terms of prevention, not detection, of problems and giving them the responsibility and power to correct errors, expose problems, and contribute to solutions. Concurrent controls include an organizational culture and employee commitment that favor total quality and employee participation. Feedback controls include targets for employee involvement and for zero defects.

TQM TECHNIQUES

The implementation of TQM involves the use of many techniques, including quality circles, benchmarking, Six Sigma principles, reduced cycle time, and continuous improvement.

Quality Circles. One technique for implementing the decentralized approach of TQM is to use quality circles. A **quality circle** is a group of 6 to 12 volunteer employees who meet regularly to discuss and solve problems affecting the quality of their work.[31] At a set time during the workweek, the members of the quality circle meet, identify problems, and try to find solutions. Circle members are free to collect data and take surveys. Many companies train people in team building, problem solving, and statistical quality control. The reason for using quality circles is to push decision making to an organization level at which recommendations can be made by the people who do the job and know it better than anyone else.

Benchmarking. Introduced by Xerox in 1979, benchmarking is now a major TQM component. **Benchmarking** is defined as "the continuous process of measuring products, services, and practices against the toughest competitors or those companies recognized as industry leaders to identify areas for improvement."[32] The key to successful benchmarking lies in analysis. Starting with its own mission statement, a company should honestly analyze its current procedures and determine areas for improvement. As a second step, a company *carefully* selects competitors worthy of copying. For example, Xerox studied the order fulfillment techniques of L.L.Bean, the Freeport, Maine, mail-order firm, and learned ways to reduce warehouse costs by 10 percent. Companies can emulate internal processes and procedures of competitors but must take care to select companies whose methods are

total quality management (TQM)
an organization-wide commitment to infuse quality into every activity through continuous improvement.

quality circle
a group of 6 to 12 volunteer employees who meet regularly to discuss and solve problems affecting the quality of their work.

benchmarking
the continuous process of measuring products, services, and practices against major competitors or industry leaders.

NEW MANAGER SELF TEST

Freedom Versus Regulation

What is your attitude toward organizational regulation and control? Organizations have to control people to survive, yet control should be the right amount and type. Companies are often less democratic than the society of which they are a part. Think honestly about your beliefs toward the regulation of other people and answer each item that follows as Mostly True or Mostly False.

	Mostly True	Mostly False
1. I believe people should be guided more by feelings and less by rules.	_____	_____
2. I think employees should be on time to work and to meetings.	_____	_____
3. I believe efficiency and speed are not as important as letting everyone have their say when making a decision.	_____	_____
4. I think employees should conform to company policies.	_____	_____
5. I let my significant other make the decision and have his/her way most of the time.	_____	_____
6. I like to tell other people what to do.	_____	_____
7. I am more patient with the least capable people.	_____	_____
8. I like to have things running "just so."	_____	_____

SCORING AND INTERPRETATION: Give yourself 1 point for each Mostly True answer for the odd-numbered questions and 1 point for each Mostly False answer to the even-numbered questions. A score of 6 or above suggests you prefer decentralized control for other people in organizations. A score of three or less suggests a preference for more control and bureaucracy in a company. Enthusiastic new managers may exercise too much of their new control and get a negative backlash. However, too little control may mean less output. The challenge for new managers is to strike the right balance for the job and people at hand.

SOURCE: Adapted from J. J. Ray, "Do Authoritarians Hold Authoritarian Attitudes?" *Human Relations* 29 (1976): 307–325.

TAKE ACTION

When starting a new venture or bringing change, go out and benchmark successful programs that are similar.

Six Sigma
a quality control approach that emphasizes a relentless pursuit of higher quality and lower costs.

compatible. Once a strong, compatible program is found and analyzed, the benchmarking company can then devise a strategy for implementing a new program.

Six Sigma. Six Sigma quality principles were first introduced by Motorola in the 1980s and were later popularized by General Electric, where former CEO Jack Welch praised Six Sigma for quality and efficiency gains that saved the company billions of dollars. Based on the Greek letter *sigma*, which statisticians use to measure how far something deviates from perfection, Six Sigma is a highly ambitious quality standard that specifies a goal of no more than 3.4 defects per million parts. That essentially means being defect-free 99.9997 percent of the time.[33] However, Six Sigma has deviated from its precise definition to become a generic term for a quality-control approach that takes nothing for granted and emphasizes a

Benchmarking

Universal Studios

Six Sigma—rigorous business methods with quantifiable results—hasn't exactly been the Hollywood Way. Now that $134 billion corporate giant General Electric, which makes everything from medical imaging equipment to jet engines, has bought Universal Studios, there are frequent trips to GE offices in New York. Both sides talk about quarterly budget reviews and strategic planning, topics that were discussed before but not with such intensity or results-orientation. Marketing people are teamed with counterparts at GE's network, NBC. Previously the studio hadn't been partnered with a TV network. Agents and producers are being told by executives to hold the line on budgets.

Though GE has approved Universal's $1 billion budget to make about 16 movies this year, they are coming down on cost-control, and producers already are feeling it. They've clamped down on smaller expenses. Universal's president Ron Meyer has taken notice, producing solid, though less-than blockbusters such as *Knocked Up*, *The Break Up*, and *The Inside Man*, and even some hits, including the *Bourne* series and *King Kong*. But Meyer tries to make money rather than lose it, whereas much of Hollywood is in the "go for broke" mode.

"You gain stature and bragging rights by having big budgets," said entertainment analyst Harold Vogel. "Not too many up-and-coming filmmakers are motivated by saying, 'Gee, I just did a modestly budgeted picture for Universal.'" But the higher-ups at the studio are fine with the strategy. "We've been very, very pleased to be right in the middle of the pack of market share and have strong growth in profitability," said CEO Jeff Zucker. "People mistake market share for profitability. We're interested in running a very sound business and having discipline in doing so."

SOURCE: Laura M. Holson, "Six Sigma: A Hollywood Studio Learns the GE Way," *The New York Times* (Sept. 27, 2004): C1; "Chief of Universal Finds Success at the Back of the Pack," *The New York Times* (July 16, 2007): C1.

disciplined and relentless pursuit of higher quality and lower costs. The discipline is based on a five-step methodology referred to as *DMAIC* (Define, Measure, Analyze, Improve, and Control, pronounced "de-May-ick" for short), which provides a structured way for organizations to approach and solve problems.[34] GE bought a Hollywood studio and is trying to implement a form of Six Sigma, as shown in the Benchmarking box.

Effectively implementing Six Sigma requires a major commitment from top management because Six Sigma involves widespread change throughout the organization. Hundreds of organizations have adopted some form of Six Sigma program in recent years. Highly committed companies, including ITT Industries, Motorola, General Electric, Allied Signal, ABB Ltd., and DuPont & Co., send managers to weeks of training to become qualified as Six Sigma "black belts." These black belts lead projects aimed at improving targeted areas of the business.[35] Although originally applied to manufacturing, Six Sigma has evolved to a process used in all industries and affecting every aspect of company operations, from human resources to customer service. Exhibit 15.6 lists some statistics that illustrate why Six Sigma

99 Percent Amounts to:	Six Sigma Amounts to:
117,000 pieces of lost first-class mail per hour	1 piece of lost first-class mail every two hours
800,000 mishandled personal checks each day	3 mishandled checks each day
23,087 defective computers shipped each month	8 defective computers shipped each month
7.2 hours per month without electricity	9 seconds per month without electricity

EXHIBIT 15.6

The Importance of Quality Improvement Programs

SOURCE: Based on data from *Statistical Abstract of the United States*, U.S. Postal Service, as reported in Tracy Mayor, "Six Sigma Comes to IT: Targeting Perfection," *CIO* (December 1, 2003): 62–70.

is important for both manufacturing and service organizations. Cox Communications, Inc., based in Atlanta, Georgia, used Six Sigma to improve the "time to answer" metric for the company's help desk. According to Tom Guthrie, vice president of operations, the process enabled Cox to reduce staffing by 20 percent, saving big bucks, while also cutting the abandon rate (the number of calls abandoned before being answered) by 40 percent.[36]

Reduced Cycle Time. Cycle time has become a critical quality issue in today's fast-paced world. **Cycle time** refers to the steps taken to complete a company process, such as teaching a class, publishing a textbook, or designing a new car. The simplification of work cycles, including dropping barriers between work steps and among departments and removing worthless steps in the process, enables a TQM program to succeed. Even if an organization decides not to use quality circles or other techniques, substantial improvement is possible by focusing on improved responsiveness and acceleration of activities into a shorter time. Reduction in cycle time improves overall company performance as well as quality.[37]

L.L.Bean is a recognized leader in cycle time control. Workers used flowcharts to track their movements, pinpoint wasted motions, and completely redesign the order-fulfillment process. Today, a computerized system breaks down an order based on the geographic area of the warehouse in which items are stored. Items are placed on conveyor belts, where electronic sensors re-sort the items for individual orders. After orders are packed, they are sent to a FedEx facility on site. Improvements such as these have enabled L.L.Bean to process most orders within two hours after the order is received.[38]

Continuous Improvement. In North America, crash programs and designs have traditionally been the preferred method of innovation. Managers measure the expected benefits of a change and favor the ideas with the biggest payoffs. In contrast, Japanese companies have realized extraordinary success from making a series of mostly small improvements. This approach, called **continuous improvement,** or *kaizen,* is the implementation of a large number of small, incremental improvements in all areas of the organization on an ongoing basis. In a successful TQM program, all employees learn that they are expected to contribute by initiating changes in their own job activities. The basic philosophy is that improving things a little bit at a time, all the time, has the highest probability of success. Innovations can start simple, and employees can build on their success in this unending process.

cycle time
the steps taken to complete a company process.

continuous improvement
the implementation of a large number of small, incremental improvements in all areas of the organization on an ongoing basis.

CONCEPT CONNECTION
University of Miami public safety officers used to take a hit-or-miss approach to auto theft. The result: Cars continued to disappear. To upgrade their tactics, a **continuous improvement** team collected data, analyzed it, and pinpointed exactly where and when thieves were most likely to strike. Now a marked patrol car and security guards on bicycles, similar to the ones being assembled by Smith & Wesson employees here, patrol known campus "hot spots." Car thefts dropped by approximately 75 percent. The continuous improvement effort continues because "10 auto thefts may seem like a small number, but it is 10 more than we want."

TQM SUCCESS FACTORS

Despite its promise, TQM does not always work. A few firms have had disappointing results. In particular, Six Sigma principles might not be appropriate for all organizational problems, and some companies have expended tremendous energy and resources for little

Positive Factors	Negative Factors
• Tasks make high skill demands on employees.	• Management expectations are unrealistically high.
• TQM serves to enrich jobs and motivate employees.	• Middle managers are dissatisfied about loss of authority.
• Problem-solving skills are improved for all employees.	• Workers are dissatisfied with other aspects of organizational life.
• Participation and teamwork are used to tackle significant problems.	• Union leaders are left out of QC discussions.
• Continuous improvement is a way of life.	• Managers wait for big, dramatic innovations.

EXHIBIT 15.7

Quality Program Success Factors

payoff.[39] Many contingency factors (listed in Exhibit 15.7) can influence the success of a TQM program. For example, quality circles are most beneficial when employees have challenging jobs; participation in a quality circle can contribute to productivity because it enables employees to pool their knowledge and solve interesting problems. TQM also tends to be most successful when it enriches jobs and improves employee motivation. In addition, when participating in the quality program improves workers' problem-solving skills, productivity is likely to increase. Finally, a quality program has the greatest chance of success in a corporate culture that values quality and stresses continuous improvement as a way of life.

3 Total quality management is just another fad.

ANSWER: TQM has been implemented in many countries over the course of decades and has led to many organizational improvements, more efficiency, and lower costs for consumers.

Assess Your Answer

Trends in Quality Control

Many companies are responding to changing economic realities and global competition by reassessing organizational management and processes—including control mechanisms. Some of the major trends in quality and financial control include international quality standards and economic value-added and market value-added systems.

INTERNATIONAL QUALITY STANDARDS

One impetus for TQM in the United States is the increasing significance of the global economy. Many countries have adopted a universal benchmark for quality assurance, **ISO certification,** which is based on a set of international standards for quality established by the International Standards Organization in Geneva, Switzerland.[40] Hundreds of thousands of organizations in 150 countries, including the United States, have been certified to demonstrate their commitment to quality. Europe continues to lead in the total number of certifications, but the greatest number of new certifications in recent years has been in the United States. One of the more interesting organizations to recently become ISO certified was the Phoenix, Arizona, Police Department's Records and Information Bureau. In today's environment, where the credibility of law enforcement agencies has been called into question, the Bureau wanted to make a clear statement about its commitment to quality and accuracy of information provided to law enforcement personnel and the public.[41]

ISO certification
certification based on a set of international standards for quality management, setting uniform guidelines for processes to ensure that products conform to customer requirements.

TAKE ACTION ➡

As a new manager, be aware of current trends in quality control. Learn quality principles, new financial control systems, and open-book management and apply what works for you.

ISO certification has become the recognized standard for evaluating and comparing companies on a global basis, and more U.S. companies are feeling the pressure to participate to remain competitive in international markets. In addition, many countries and companies require ISO certification before they will do business with an organization.

Economic Value-Added (EVA).   Hundreds of companies, including AT&T, Quaker Oats, the Coca-Cola Company, and Philips Petroleum Company, have set up **economic value-added (EVA)** measurement systems as a new way to gauge financial performance. EVA can be defined as a company's net (after-tax) operating profit minus the cost of capital invested in the company's tangible assets.[42] Measuring performance in terms of EVA is intended to capture all the things a company can do to add value from its activities, such as run the business more efficiently, satisfy customers, and reward shareholders. Each job, department, process, or project in the organization is measured by the value added. EVA can also help managers make more cost-effective decisions. At Boise Cascade, the vice president of IT used EVA to measure the cost of replacing the company's existing storage devices against keeping the existing storage assets that had higher maintenance costs. Using EVA demonstrated that buying new storage devices would lower annual maintenance costs significantly and easily make up for the capital expenditure.[43]

Innovative Control Systems for Turbulent Times

As we have discussed throughout this text, globalization, increased competition, rapid change, and uncertainty have resulted in new organizational structures and management methods that emphasize information sharing, employee participation, learning, and teamwork. These shifts have, in turn, led to some new approaches to control. Two additional aspects of control in today's organizations are open-book management and use of the balanced scorecard.

OPEN-BOOK MANAGEMENT

In an organizational environment that promotes information sharing, teamwork, and the role of managers as facilitators, executives cannot hoard information and financial data. They admit employees throughout the organization into the loop of financial control and responsibility to encourage active participation and commitment to goals. A growing number of managers are opting for full disclosure in the form of open-book management. **Open-book management** allows employees to see for themselves—through charts, computer printouts, meetings, and so forth—the financial condition of the company. Second, open-book management shows the individual employee how his or her job fits into the big picture and affects the financial future of the organization. Finally, open-book management ties employee rewards to the company's overall success. With training in interpreting the financial data, employees can see the interdependence and importance of each function. If they are rewarded according to performance, they become motivated to take responsibility for their entire team or function, rather than merely their individual jobs.[44] Cross-functional communication and cooperation are also enhanced.

The goal of open-book management is to get every employee thinking and acting like a business owner. To get employees to think like owners, management provides them with the same information owners have: what money is coming in and where it is going. Open-book management helps employees appreciate why efficiency is important to the organization's success as well as their own. Open-book management turns traditional control on its head. Development Counsellors International, a New York City public relations firm, found an innovative way to involve employees in the financial aspects of the organization.

Managers in some countries have more trouble running an open-book company because prevailing attitudes and standards encourage confidentiality and even secrecy concerning financial results. Many businesspeople in countries such as China, Russia, and Indonesia, for

TAKE ACTION ➡

As a manager, consider letting subordinates know what is going on and what is in the financial statements.

economic value-added (EVA)
a control system that measures performance in terms of after-tax profits minus the cost of capital invested in tangible assets.

open-book management
sharing financial information and results with all employees in the organization.

W hen Andrew Levine took over as president of Development Counsellors International (DCI), the public relations firm founded by his father in 1960, he was eager to try open-book management. His first step was to add a financial segment to the monthly staff meeting, but employees just seemed bored. Most of them had no interest or skills in finance, statistics, and ratios.

Rather than providing standard training, Levine had an idea: Why not appoint a different staffer each month to be CFO for the day. That person would be required to figure out the financials and then present the financial reports at the monthly staff meeting. His first appointment was the receptionist, Sergio Barrios, who met with Levine and the company's CFO to go over the figures, look at any unusual increases or decreases in revenue or expenses, and talk about ideas to spark discussion. Levine was astounded by the reaction of staffers at the monthly meeting. Unlike Levine or another manager, Barrios was new to accounting and consequently explained things in a way that any layperson could understand. In addition, employees wanted to support Barrios as "one of their own," so they paid more attention and asked more questions.

At each monthly meeting, the CFO of the day goes through a breakdown of the company's sales and expenses, points out irregularities and trends in the numbers, takes questions from other staff members, and sparks discussion of current financial issues. At the end of the report, the person reveals the bottom line, indicating whether the company met its profit goal for the month. Each time DCI's accumulated profit hits another $100,000 increment during the course of the year, 30 percent is distributed to employees.[45]

DCI has been profitable ever since Levine began the CFO-of-the-day program. In addition, employees are happier with their jobs, so turnover has decreased. Clients tend to stick around longer too because employees put more effort into building relationships. "Nobody wants to see a zero next to their client in the income column," Levine says.[46]

Development Counsellors International

example, are not accustomed to publicly disclosing financial details, which can present problems for multinational companies operating there.[47] Exhibit 15.8 lists a portion of a recent *Opacity Index,* which offers some indication of the degree to which various countries are open regarding economic matters. The higher the rating, the more opaque, or hidden, the economy of that country. In the partial index in Exhibit 15.8, Indonesia has the highest opacity rating at 59, and Finland the lowest at 13. The United States has an opacity rating of 21, which is fairly low on the index of countries. In countries with higher ratings, financial figures are

EXHIBIT 15.8

International Opacity Index: Which Countries Have the Most Secretive Economies?

Country	Opacity Rating
Indonesia	59
Venezuela	51
China	50
India	48
Russia	46
Mexico	44
Turkey	43
Korea	37
Thailand	35
Taiwan	34
Japan	28
Singapore	24
Canada	23
United States	21
Hong Kong	20
United Kingdom	19
Finland	13

The higher the opacity rating, the more secretive the national economy, meaning that prevailing attitudes and standards discourage openness regarding financial results and other data.

SOURCE: Joel Kurtzman, Glenn Yago, and Triphon Phumiwasana, "The Opacity Index, 2004," published by *MIT Sloan Management Review* (October 2004), www.opacityindex.com (accessed on July 7, 2006).

typically closely guarded and managers may be discouraged from sharing information with employees and the public. Globalization is beginning to have an impact on economic opacity in various countries by encouraging a convergence toward global accounting standards that support more accurate collection, recording, and reporting of financial information.

balanced scorecard
a comprehensive management control system that balances traditional financial measures with measures of customer service, internal business processes, and the organization's capacity for learning and growth.

THE BALANCED SCORECARD

Another recent innovation is to integrate the various dimensions of control, combining internal financial measurements and statistical reports with a concern for markets and customers as well as employees.[48] Whereas many managers once focused primarily on measuring and controlling financial performance, they are increasingly recognizing the need to measure other, intangible aspects of performance to assess the value-creating activities of the contemporary organization.[49] Many of today's companies compete primarily on the basis of ideas and relationships, which requires that managers find ways to measure intangible as well as tangible assets.

One fresh approach is the balanced scorecard. The **balanced scorecard** is a comprehensive management control system that balances traditional financial measures with operational measures relating to a company's critical success factors.[50] A balanced scorecard contains four major perspectives, as illustrated in Exhibit 15.9: financial performance, customer service, internal business processes, and the organization's capacity for learning and growth.[51] Within these four

EXHIBIT 15.9
The Balanced Scorecard

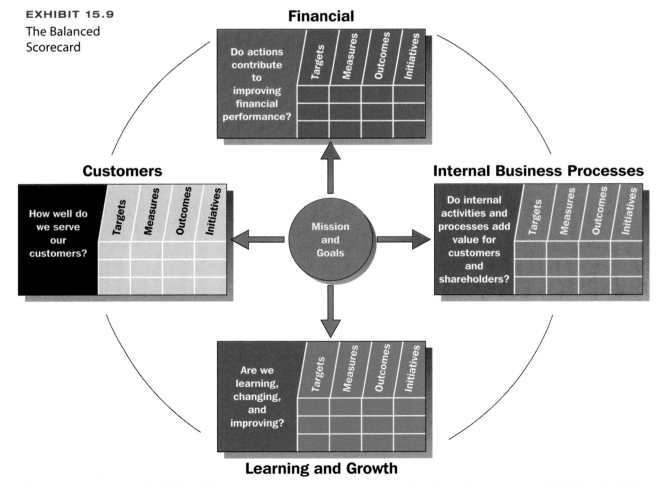

Sources: Based on Robert S. Kaplan and David P. Norton, "Using the Balanced Scorecard as a Strategic Management System," *Harvard Business Review* (January–February 1996): 75–85; and Chee W. Chow, Kamal M. Haddad, and James E. Williamson, "Applying the Balanced Scorecard to Small Companies," *Management Accounting* 79, no. 2 (August 1997): 21–27.

areas, managers identify key performance metrics that the organization will track. The *financial performance* perspective reflects a concern that the organization's activities contribute to improving short- and long-term financial performance. It includes traditional measures such as net income and return on investment. *Customer service* indicators measure such things as how customers view the organization, as well as customer retention and satisfaction. *Business process* indicators focus on production and operating statistics, such as order fulfillment or cost per order. The final component looks at the organization's *potential for learning and growth,* focusing on how well resources and human capital are being managed for the company's future. Metrics may include such things as employee retention and the introduction of new products. The components of the scorecard are designed in an integrative manner, as illustrated in Exhibit 15.9.

Managers record, analyze, and discuss these various metrics to determine how well the organization is achieving its strategic goals. The balanced scorecard is an effective tool for managing and improving performance only if it is clearly linked to a well-defined organizational strategy and goals.[52] At its best, use of the scorecard cascades down from the top levels of the organization, so that everyone becomes involved in thinking about and discussing strategy.[53] The scorecard has become the core management control system for many organizations, including well-known organizations such as Bell Emergis (a division of Bell Canada), ExxonMobil, Cigna Insurance, British Airways, Hilton Hotels Corp., and even some units of the U.S. federal government.[54] British Airways clearly ties its use of the balanced scorecard to the feedback control model we discussed early in this chapter. Scorecards are used as the agenda for monthly management meetings. Managers focus on the various elements of the scorecard to set targets, evaluate performance, and guide discussion about what further actions need to be taken.[55] As with all management systems, the balanced scorecard is not right for every organization in every situation. The simplicity of the system causes some managers to underestimate the time and commitment that is needed for the approach to become a truly useful management control system. If managers implement the balanced scorecard using a *performance measurement* orientation rather than a *performance management* approach that links targets and measurements to corporate strategy, use of the scorecard can actually hinder or even decrease organizational performance.[56]

In addition, the scorecard has evolved from a system that places equal emphasis on the four categories of performance management illustrated in Exhibit 15.9 into a cause-effect relationship that calls attention to how organizations achieve higher performance. This adapted approach to the scorecard, illustrated in Exhibit 15.10, indicates that financial results are the final outcome of other processes within the company. The foundation of high financial performance is learning and growth, which reflects that it is an organization's people and culture that cause excellent business processes. Excellent business processes in turn cause customers to be satisfied. And happy customers lead to financial success. Thus, the components of the scorecard can be organized into a pyramid, indicating that each level shown in Exhibit 15.10 reinforces the level above it. Thus, high financial performance is an outgrowth of success in other areas, starting with a firm commitment to developing human capital and internal business processes.

NEW WORKPLACE CONCERNS

Managers in today's organizations face some difficult control issues. The matter of control has come to the forefront in light of the failure of top executives and corporate directors to provide adequate oversight and control at companies such as Enron, HealthSouth, Adelphia, and WorldCom. Thus, many organizations are moving toward increased control, particularly in terms of **corporate governance,** which refers to the system of governing an organization so that the interests of corporate owners are protected. The financial reporting systems and the roles of boards of directors are being scrutinized in organizations around the world. At the same time, top leaders are also keeping a closer eye on the activities of lower-level managers and employees.

In a fast-moving environment, *undercontrol* can be a problem because managers can't keep personal tabs on everything in a large, global organization. Consider, for example,

corporate governance
the system of governing an organization so the interests of corporate owners are protected.

EXHIBIT 15.10

A New Approach
to the Balanced
Scorecard

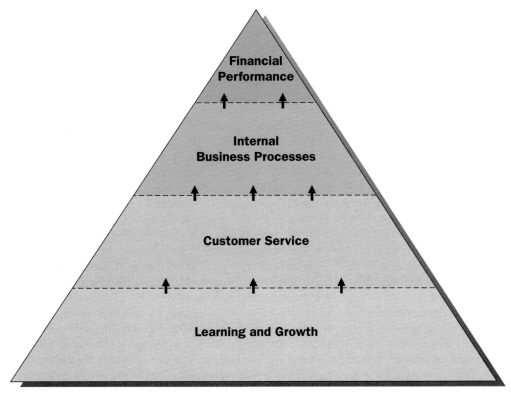

SOURCE: Based on Robert S. Kaplan and David P. Norton, *Strategy Maps: Converting Intangible Assets into Tangible Outcomes* (hardcover), (Boston: Harvard Business School Press, February 2, 2004).

TAKE ACTION

As a new manager, keep in mind that overcontrol can be just as detrimental to your team's performance as undercontrol. People resent being watched too closely. To keep a contemporary team working smoothly, find a balance between oversight and control on the one hand and mutual trust and respect on the other. Go to the ethical dilemma on page 588 that pertains to new workplace control issues.

that many of the CEOs who have been indicted in connection with financial misdeeds have claimed that they were unaware that the misconduct was going on. In some cases, these claims might be true, but they reflect a significant breakdown in control. In response, the U.S. government enacted the Sarbanes-Oxley Act of 2002, often referred to as SOX, which requires several types of reforms, including better internal monitoring to reduce the risk of fraud, certification of financial reports by top leaders; improved measures for external auditing; and enhanced public financial disclosure. SOX has been unpopular with many business leaders, largely because of the expense of complying with the act. In addition, some critics argue that SOX is creating a culture of overcontrol that is stifling innovation and growth. Even among those who agree that government regulation is needed, calls for a more balanced regulatory scheme that requires transparency and objectivity without restraining innovation are growing.[57]

Overcontrol of employees can be damaging to an organization as well. Managers might feel justified in monitoring e-mail and Internet use, as described earlier in the Spotlight feature, for example, to ensure that employees are directing their behavior toward work rather than personal outcomes, and to alleviate concerns about potential racial or sexual harassment. Yet employees often resent and feel demeaned by close monitoring that limits their personal freedom and makes them feel as if they are constantly being watched. Excessive control of employees can lead to demotivation, low morale, lack of trust, and even hostility among workers. Managers have to find an appropriate balance, as well as develop and communicate clear policies regarding workplace monitoring. Although oversight and control are important, good organizations also depend on mutual trust and respect among managers and employees.

Summary

This chapter introduced a number of important concepts about organizational control. Organizational control is the systematic process through which managers regulate organizational activities to meet planned goals and standards of performance. The focus of the control system may include feedforward control to prevent problems, concurrent control to monitor ongoing activities, and feedback control to evaluate past performance. Well-designed control systems include four key steps: establish standards, measure performance, compare performance to standards, and make corrections as necessary.

The feedback control model also applies to budgeting, which is one of the most commonly used forms of managerial control. Other financial controls include use of the balance sheet and income statement. Besides monitoring financial results, organizations control the quality of their goods and services. The application of total quality management (TQM) includes techniques such as quality circles, benchmarking, Six Sigma, reduced cycle time, and continuous improvement.

The philosophy of controlling has shifted to reflect changes in leadership methods. Traditional bureaucratic controls emphasize establishing rules and procedures, and then monitoring employee behavior to make sure the rules and procedures are followed. With decentralized control, employees assume responsibility for monitoring their own performance.

Recent trends in control include the use of international quality standards, economic value-added (EVA) and market value-added (MVA) systems, and activity-based costing (ABC). Other important aspects of control in today's turbulent environment are open-book management and use of the balanced scorecard. In addition, concerns such as corporate governance and employee monitoring are significant issues for today's managers.

Discussion Questions

1. You're a manager who employs a participative control approach. You've concluded that corrective action is necessary to improve customer satisfaction, but first you need to convince your employees that the problem exists. What kind of evidence do you think employees will find more compelling: quantitative measurements or anecdotes from your interactions with customers? Explain your answer.

2. How might a public school system use feedforward control to identify the best candidates for its teaching positions?

3. What are some examples of feedback control that might be used in a family-style restaurant? In a large hospital?

4. Think of a class you've taken in the past. What standards of performance did your professor establish? How was your actual performance measured? How was your performance compared to the standards? Do you think the standards and methods of measurement were fair? Were they appropriate to your assigned work? Why or why not?

5. Some critics argue that Six Sigma is a collection of superficial changes that often result in doing a superb job of building the wrong product or offering the wrong service. Do you agree or disagree? Explain.

6. In what ways could a university benefit from bureaucratic control? In what ways might it benefit from decentralized control? Overall, which approach do you think would be best at your college or university? Why?

7. Some companies are using both lean manufacturing and Six Sigma methods simultaneously to improve their operations. How do you think the two approaches might complement or conflict with each other? Explain.

8. Why is benchmarking an important component of total quality management (TQM) programs? Do you believe a company could have a successful TQM program without using benchmarking?

9. Why do you think today's managers would want to use the balanced scorecard to measure and control organizational performance? Think of two different kinds of organizations. Do you think the balanced scorecard approach is equally suitable for them both? Why or why not?

Dear Dr. Dorothy

I am the new restaurant manager in a hotel/convention center. We have a fabulous and highly rated facility, and I aim to keep it that way. The reason I am writing is that my direct reports, all supervisors, can't seem to get it right, no matter how many meetings we have going over all their mistakes. The restaurant sometimes takes 90 minutes to bring a meal to the table, room service sends the wrong food, and meeting-refreshment orders get confused. My boss has told me to come down hard on them and I have, and he's very proud of how strong I've become. But in one of our daily meetings, they just weren't being responsive to the continuing problems of getting the work done adequately. So I told them right there they had to work six-day weeks until they start to do their jobs right. All they did was balk at this command, even though I told them not showing up on Saturday would be the same as resigning. I just don't get how they can be so good on some days and so awful on the others. Should I fire them all and start over?

Wit's End in Wichita

Dear Wit,

Who assigned you to be the Punitive Parent to your employees? Oh, Dr. Dorothy forgot: your boss. The two of you are colluding and creating a hostile work environment, though Dr. Dorothy sees clearly that you two feel like the victims here. Does Dr. Dorothy have to remind you about the terrible teachers you had in high school, who humiliated you in front of the class, and how discombobulated you became, making it more difficult to get your work done? Your job is not to humiliate but to solve the problems at hand. It does not help the situation that your boss seems to be the reincarnation of Machiavelli. Here are some ideas from Dr. Dorothy: During the next meeting ask questions, find out what is going on, where the breakdowns occur. Ask your people what they would do to design a better system. You are too quick to admonish. Dr. Dorothy suggests that good managers rarely need to raise their voices to a higher decibel. Here is her formula, which you should memorize: More questions equals less yelling. Now if Dr. Dorothy could only get your boss to learn this, too.

Self Learning

What Is Your Attitude Toward Productivity?

Complete the following questions based on how you think and act in a typical work situation. For each item, circle the number that best describes you.

	Disagree Strongly				Agree Strongly
1. I spend time developing new ways of approaching old problems.	1	2	3	4	5
2. As long as things are done correctly and efficiently, I prefer not to take on the hassle of changing them.	1	2	3	4	5
3. I always believe the effort to improve something should be rewarded, even if the final improvement is disappointing.	1	2	3	4	5
4. A single change that improves things 30 percent is much better than 30 improvements of 1 percent each.	1	2	3	4	5
5. I frequently compliment others on changes they have made.	1	2	3	4	5
6. I let people know in a variety of ways that I like to be left alone to do my job efficiently.	1	2	3	4	5
7. I am personally involved in several improvement projects at one time.	1	2	3	4	5
8. I try to be a good listener and be patient with what people say, except when it is a stupid idea.	1	2	3	4	5
9. I am always proposing unconventional techniques and ideas.	1	2	3	4	5
10. I usually do not take risks that would create a problem for me if the idea failed.	1	2	3	4	5

Scoring and Interpretation

Subtract each of your scores for questions 2, 4, 6, 8, and 10 from the number 6. Then, using the adjusted scores, add the scores from all 10 items for your total score: _____

This scale indicates the extent to which your orientation toward productivity is based on *efficiency* or *continuous improvement*. Efficiency sometimes can be maximized by eliminating change. This may be appropriate in a stable organizational environment. Continuous improvement is an attitude that productivity can always get better and you take personal responsibility to improve it. This attitude is appropriate for a quality-conscious company experiencing frequent change.

A score of 40 or higher indicates that you take personal responsibility for improving productivity and frequently initiate change. A score of 20 or less indicates you make contributions through efficient work in a stable environment. Discuss the pros and cons of the efficiency versus continuous improvement orientations for organizations and employees.

Group Learning

Making Rules

1. Divide into groups of three to five members, and discuss the following questions, either in or out of class, depending on the instructor's assignment.

2. As a group, develop a list of policies for the groups in your class. You will turn in the list of policies to your instructor.

3. Be prepared to defend your choices to the rest of the class.

As a way of figuring out what rules and policies make sense for your organization, you might start by deciding how your group would handle each of these scenarios. Based on your discussion, you will be able to formulate a good working rule.

1. Your team agreed to meet at 1 p.m. Wednesday for two hours to work on the project. Jane doesn't show up until 1:20.

2. Your team divided up the tasks of the project and set up a meeting for each person to report on his or her progress. When it's Fred's turn to present, he says that he didn't have time to complete his part.

3. When decisions need to be made during your team's meetings, Chris often says, "It doesn't matter what we do. Let's just hurry up and get it done and turn it in."

4. Your team members reported on the work each had been doing, but it was clear that Frank had not put much effort into his part.

5. The teams are given the next class period to work on their project. Sandy doesn't show up for class; she has all of your team's materials.

6. Phil frequently interrupts other team members during meetings.

7. Once Connie has an idea in her head, she won't listen to anyone else's opinions.

8. Bob takes over team meetings. Others rarely get a chance to talk.

9. Sarah is a popular student. It seems that other team members agree with what she says regardless of the quality of her idea.

10. Tom comes to all the team's meetings but rarely says anything.

11. During your meeting, Carolyn starts talking about things unrelated to the project, like what's happening in other classes and upcoming parties.

12. Stan and Beth have very different opinions of how your team's work should progress. They seem to be at odds with each other most of the time. They argue during team meetings.

13. In your group, half the members are Asian, and half are Caucasian. The Asian students don't say very much, and the Caucasian students dominate the group.

14. In your group, three members belong to the same sorority. They arrive and leave together, take breaks together, and spend time in the group talking about sorority activities.

After you've made your list of rules, discuss the following as a group:

1. Why are policies important?

2. What happens when there are no rules or policies?

3. Can you have too many policies?

SOURCE: Developed by Karen Harlos, McGill University, karen.harlos@mcgill.ca.

Action Learning

Schoolwork Standards

1. Interview four students, besides yourself, who are not taking this same course right now. Make sure two of them are top grade-earners and two are about average. Tell the students you will keep their information confidential, that you will only be reporting results in a paper you will write, and that you will not divulge any names. Stick to that promise.

2. Ask them questions about how they study, how much they read, how they manage to work on and finish a project or paper, how they feel about grades, and so on.

3. Determine if they use any of the control mechanisms described in this chapter: feedforward, concurrent, or feedback.

4. Have they developed standards for their work? Do they compare the actual performance to the standard? What happens when the performance is less than expected, for example, they don't get as high a grade?

5. Write a report for your instructor, comparing the top students to the others. Make sure you don't mention the students' names in your report, but you keep it anonymous.

6. Your instructor may lead a class discussion on the findings. Again, do not mention anyone's names. If you want to talk about your own experiences as a student, that would be fine.

Ethical Dilemma

The Wages of Sin?

Chris Dykstra, responsible for loss prevention at Westwind Electronics, took a deep breath before he launched into making his case for the changes he was proposing in the company's shoplifting policy. He knew convincing Ross Chenoweth was going to be a hard sell. Ross, the president and CEO, was the son of the founder of the local, still family-owned consumer electronics chain based in Phoenix, Arizona. He'd inherited not only the company but also his father's strict moral code.

"I think it's time to follow the lead of other stores," Chris began. He pointed out that most other retailers didn't bother calling the police and pressing charges unless the thief had shoplifted merchandise worth more than $50 to $100. In contrast, Westwind currently had the zero-tolerance policy toward theft that Ross's father had put in place when he started the business. Chris wanted to replace that policy with one that only prosecuted individuals between 18 and 65, had stolen more than $20 worth of goods, and had no previous history of theft at Westwind. In the case of first-time culprits under 18 or over 65, he argued for letting them off with a strict warning regardless of the value of their ill-gotten goods. Repeat offenders would be arrested.

"Frankly, the local police are getting pretty tired of having to come to our stores every time a teenager sticks a CD in his jacket pocket," Chris pointed out. "And besides, we just can't afford the costs associated with prosecuting everyone." Every time he pressed charges against a shoplifter who'd made off with a $10 item, Westwind lost money. The company had to engage a lawyer and pay employees overtime for their court appearances. In addition, Chris was looking at hiring more security guards to keep up with the workload. Westwind was already in a battle it was losing at the moment with the mass retailers who were competing all too successfully on price, so passing on the costs of its zero-tolerance policy to customers wasn't really an option. "Let's concentrate on catching dishonest employees and those organized theft rings. They're the ones who are really hurting us," Chris concluded.

There was a long pause after Chris finished his carefully prepared speech. Ross thought about his recently deceased father, both an astute businessman and a person for whom honesty was a key guiding principle. If he were sitting here today, he'd no doubt say that theft was theft, that setting a minimum was tantamount to saying that stealing was acceptable just as long as you don't steal too much. He looked at Chris. "You know, we've both got teenagers. Is this really a message you want to send out, especially to kids? You know as well as I do that there's nothing they like better than testing limits. It's almost an invitation to see if you can beat the system." But then Ross faltered as he found himself glancing at the latest financial figures on his desk—another in a string of quarterly losses. If Westwind went under, a lot of employees would be looking for another way to make a living. In his heart, he believed in his father's high moral standards, but he had to ask himself just how moral could Westwind afford to be?

What Would You Do?

1. Continue Westwind's zero-tolerance policy toward shoplifting. It's the right thing to do—and it will pay off in the end in higher profitability because the chain's reputation for being tough on crime will reduce overall losses from theft.

2. Adopt Chris Dykstra's proposed changes, and show more leniency to first-time offenders. It is a more cost-effective approach to the problem than the current policy, plus it stays close to your father's original intent.

3. Adopt Chris Dykstra's proposed changes with an even higher limit of $50 or $100, which is still less than the

cost of prosecution. In addition, make sure the policy isn't publicized. That way you'll reduce costs even more and still benefit from your reputation for prosecuting all shoplifters.

SOURCE: Based on Michael Barbaro, "Some Leeway for the Small Shoplifter," *The New York Times* (July 13, 2006): section C, 1.

Case for Critical Analysis

Lincoln Electric

Imagine having a management system that is so successful people refer to it with capital letters—the Lincoln Management System—and other businesses benchmark their own systems by it. That is the situation of Ohio-based Lincoln Electric. For a number of years, other companies have tried to figure out Lincoln Electric's secret—how management coaxes maximum productivity and quality from its workers, even during difficult financial times. Lately, however, Lincoln Electric has been trying to solve a mystery of its own: Why is the company having such difficulty exporting a management system abroad that has worked so well at home?

Lincoln Electric is a leading manufacturer of welding products, welding equipment, and electric motors, with more than $1 billion in sales and 6,000 workers worldwide. The company's products are used for cutting, manufacturing, and repairing other metal products. Although it is now a publicly traded company, members of the Lincoln family still own more than 60 percent of the stock.

Lincoln uses a diverse control approach. Tasks are precisely defined, and individual employees must exceed strict performance goals to achieve top pay. The incentive and control system is powerful. Production workers are paid on a piece-rate basis, plus merit pay based on performance. Employees also are eligible for annual bonuses, which fluctuate according to the company's profits, and they participate in stock purchase plans. A worker's bonus is based on four factors: work productivity, work quality, dependability, and cooperation with others. Some factory workers at Lincoln have earned more than $100,000 a year.

However, the Lincoln system succeeds largely because of an organizational culture based on openness and trust, shared control, and an egalitarian spirit. To begin with, the company has earned employee trust with its no layoff policy. In fact, the last time it laid off anyone was in 1951. Although the line between managers and workers at Lincoln is firmly drawn, managers respect the expertise of production workers and value their contributions to many aspects of the business. The company has an open-door policy for all top executives, middle managers, and production workers, and regular face-to-face communication is encouraged. Workers are expected to challenge management if they believe practices or compensation rates are unfair. Most workers are hired right out of high school, then trained and cross-trained to perform

different jobs. Some eventually are promoted to executive positions because Lincoln believes in promoting from within. Many Lincoln workers stay with the company for life.

One of Lincoln's founders felt that organizations should be based on certain values, including honesty, trustworthiness, openness, self-management, loyalty, accountability, and cooperativeness. These values continue to form the core of Lincoln's culture, and management regularly rewards employees who manifest them. Because Lincoln so effectively socializes employees, they exercise a great degree of self-control on the job. Each supervisor oversees 100 workers, and less tangible rewards complement the piece-rate incentive system. Pride of workmanship and feelings of involvement, contribution, and esprit de corps are intrinsic rewards that flourish at Lincoln Electric. Cross-functional teams, empowered to make decisions, take responsibility for product planning, development, and marketing. Information about the company's operations and financial performance is openly shared with workers throughout the company.

Lincoln emphasizes anticipating and solving customer problems. Sales representatives are given the technical training they need to understand customer needs, help customers understand and use Lincoln's products, and solve problems. This customer focus is backed by attention to the production process through the use of strict accountability standards and formal measurements for productivity, quality, and innovation for all employees. In addition, a software program called Rhythm helps streamline the flow of goods and materials in the production process.

Lincoln's system worked so well in the United States that senior executives decided to extend it overseas. Lincoln built or purchased 11 plants in Japan, South America, and Europe, with plans to run the plants from the United States using Lincoln's expertise with management control systems. Managers saw the opportunity to beat local competition by applying manufacturing control incentive systems to reduce costs and raise production in plants around the world. The results were abysmal and nearly sunk the company. Managers at international plants failed to meet their production and financial goals every year—they exaggerated the goals sent to Lincoln's managers to receive more resources, especially during the recession in Europe and South America. Many overseas managers had no innate desire to increase sales, and workers were found sleeping on benches because not enough work was available. The European labor culture was hostile to the piecework and bonus control system. The huge losses in the international plants, which couldn't seem to adopt Lincoln's vaunted control systems, meant the company would have to borrow money to pay U.S. workers' bonuses, or forgo bonuses for the first time in Lincoln's history. Top managers began to wonder. Had they simply done a poor job of applying the Lincoln Management System to other cultures, or was it possible that it simply wasn't going to work abroad?

Questions

1. What types of control described in the chapter—feedforward, concurrent, or feedback—are illustrated in this case? Would you characterize Lincoln's control approach as primarily bureaucratic or decentralized? Explain your answers.

2. Based on what you've just read, what do you think makes the Lincoln System so successful in the United States?

3. What is the problem with transporting Lincoln's control systems to other national cultures? What suggestions would you make to Lincoln's managers to make future international manufacturing plants more successful?

4. Should Lincoln borrow money and pay bonuses to avoid breaking trust with its U.S. workers? Why or why not?

Sources: Based on Herb Greenberg, "Why Investors May Do Well with Firms That Avoid Layoffs," *Wall Street Journal* (September 9, 2006): B4; Mark Gottlieb, "Feeding the Dragon," *Industry Week* 251, no. 1 (February 2002): 54–55; Donald Hastings, "Lincoln Electric's Harsh Lessons from International Expansion," *Harvard Business Review* (May–June, 1999): 3–11; and Joseph Maciariello, "A Pattern of Success: Can This Company Be Duplicated?" *Drucker Management* 1, no. 1 (Spring 1997): 7–11.

BIZ FLIX

Casino

Martin Scorsese's lengthy, complex, and beautifully filmed *Casino* offers a close look at the gambling casinos of Las Vegas and their organized crime connections in the 1970s. It completes his trilogy that began with *Mean Streets* (1973) and continued with *Goodfellas* (1990). In *Casino*, ambition, greed, drugs, and sex ultimately destroy the mob's gambling empire. The film includes strong performances by Robert De Niro, Joe Pesci, and Sharon Stone. The violence and expletive-filled dialogue give *Casino* an R rating.

This scene, which comes from the beginning of "The Truth about Las Vegas" sequence, opens the film and establishes important background about casino operations. Listen carefully to Sam Rothstein's (De Niro) voice-over. He quickly describes the casino's operation and explains how it tries to reach its goals.

What to Watch for and Ask Yourself

1. What type of operations management does this scene show—manufacturing operations management or service operations management?

2. Are the customers directly involved in this operation? If they are, in what way? What likely effects does their involvement have on the casino's operation and its management?

3. Does the casino have independent or interdependent operations processes?

SOURCE: J. Craddock, Ed. *VideoHound's Golden Movie Retriever*, (Farmington Hills, MI: The Gale Group, Inc.), 2000.

VIDEO CASE

Managerial and Quality Control at Honda

In 1982 when Honda announced they were building the first Japanese auto assembly plant in North America, many Japanese were skeptical that North American labor could produce the same quality as their Japanese counterpart. Quality had been the key strategic factor for the Japanese, who were rebuilding their industry following World War II. W. Edwards Deming was the architect behind the quality-based strategy and was honored by having the nation's highest award named after him. The strategy was simple: build a better product and build it right the first time. The Japanese spent many years perfecting this concept and were not optimistic that it could be easily transplanted to another culture, especially one like the United States.

By having assembly plants in North America, Honda not only saved transportation costs, but was also insulated from changing exchange rates that were raising the price of goods sourced from Japan. But could the small Japanese company hold on to the market share it earned from its reliable and well-made Civics and Accords? While not a large factor in the Japanese auto market, Honda had done very well exporting their cars to the United States. This success was due primarily to the extremely high reputation Honda had for reliability and quality. If they lost that edge, they were probably out of business.

Honda realized that quality is a systemic process. By creating the right systems and infusing the culture of quality, there was no reason why the quality in North America should be any different that Japan. Sam Kennedy was given the responsibility of managing quality at Honda's Marysville plant. Some of the tools Sam uses are weekly manager's meetings; daily quality circle meetings, statistical process control, and a philosophy of continuous improvement. But the key factor was a systematic discipline for measuring quality, correcting procedure to improve quality, and making sure every employee knew that quality was Honda's biggest priority.

Honda's success has been enormous. They will open their sixth plant in North America this year. Their employment numbers in North America have grown to over 25,000, but the reputation for quality is unchanged. Honda was the first Japanese company to build a plant in North America and now every Japanese, German, and Korean automotive company has facilities in North America. Quality has been and will continue to be Honda's competitive advantage.

Questions

1. How has Honda used quality to promote its products?
2. What are some of the techniques used by Honda to ensure quality?
3. What is a QC circle?

Appendix A

Continuing Case

Costco: Join the Club

If 25 years ago a pair of entrepreneurs aspired to the ranks of Fortune 500 retailers by following unconventional and counterintuitive strategies, investors and colleagues would have likely dismissed the effort or perhaps even advised the idealistic greenhorns to consider other careers. Yet as James Sinegal and Jeffrey Brotman mark their 25th anniversary as co-founders of Costco Wholesale Corporation, the iconoclastic businessmen are the envy of retailers everywhere. By offering a limited selection of merchandise at rock bottom prices, setting razor-thin profit margins, establishing lofty ethical standards, and rewarding workers with premium wages and healthcare benefits, the enterprising duo defied conventional wisdom and created the No.1 membership warehouse club in the world.

In the years since the co-founders opened their first low-price retail warehouse just miles from its current headquarters in Issaquah, Washington, Costco has grown to over 488 locations serving 48 million enthusiastic cardholders in eight countries. With annual sales of over $50 billion and a workforce of nearly 125,000 highly motivated and famously well-paid employees, Costco is the top warehouse club and fourth-largest retailer in the nation.

The story of Costco's rise from a single Seattle store in 1983 to a multinational chain of enormously profitable warehouses is a tale of exemplary leadership in a rapidly-changing retail world. Under the artful direction of Sinegal and Brotman, Costco Wholesale Corp. developed and perfected the warehouse-club formula pioneered in the 1970s by Sol Price, founder of California retailer Price Club. Initially a protégé to Price, young Jim Sinegal learned his mentor's high volume low-cost trade secrets, but later left Price Club to launch a competing company—Costco. The two businesses eventually merged in 1993, and Sinegal went on to eclipse Sol Price in the art of getting the right product in the right place for the right price.

The most visible emblem of Sinegal and Brotman's retail strategy is the Costco warehouse itself. With its bare concrete floors, fluorescent lights, and pallets of merchandise piled to the rafters, the colossal 150,000-square-foot theater of retail is worthy of the "big box" appellation. Visitors are immediately struck by the conspicuous absence of signs and displays throughout the massive structures, and the self-checkout lanes and dispersed sales associates betray Costco's barebones, no-frills approach to reducing costs to the absolute minimum.

But if Costco's atmospherics are generic and uninspiring, the company's merchandising mix is anything but. While Wal-Mart stands for low prices and Target is the master of cheap chic, Costco is a treasure hunt. Among the high-end merchandise moving through stores are Waterford crystal, Coach leather goods, Fila jackets, Dom Pérignon Champagne, Apple Video iPods, and Prada sunglasses. Sinegal's quest to offer luxury goods to his characteristically upscale customers has inspired Costco merchandisers to source some unusual surprises: rare Picasso drawings and 10.6-carat yellow-diamond rings priced at $180,000. Yet in a single shopping cart, such pricy merchandise can be found alongside bulk items like 2,250-count Q-Tip packs and vats of mayonnaise—or beside the many products sold under Costco's own Kirkland Signature private label. Of the 4,000 items offered in Costco warehouses, approximately 1,000 are these upscale treasure-hunt goods that come and go at a moment's notice, creating an urgency to buy before it's too late.

Managing warehouses of ever-changing merchandise requires an organization that is flat, fast, and flexible. Sinegal fancies each warehouse a minicorporation, and each warehouse manager a de facto CEO. These "local CEOs" make rapid, independent merchandising decisions based on knowledge of their customers' wants and needs. Likewise, lower level employees are expected to make decisions guided by the organization's mission and values and based on widely distributed inventory and sales information.

To develop a highly-trained and knowledge driven workforce, Sinegal and other leaders atop Costco's managerial hierarchy abandon the old command-and-control mindset and emphasize coaching, motivation, and empowerment instead. Sinegal famously spends about 200 days a year visiting his company's warehouses—often dressed in casual attire. During these warehouse tours, Sinegal is at once a monitor, figurehead, leader, and disturbance handler. As the CEO strolls around the "racetrack"—the U-shaped path along the perimeter of the facility—he checks whether stocks are replenished and positioned to sell, discusses sales with warehouse managers, and observes how workers are sharing knowledge and solving problems. This "management-by-walking around" routine creates a bond of trust and loyalty between Sinegal and his employees.

Costco's benevolent and motivational management approach manifests itself dramatically in wages and benefits paid to workers. The company pays employees an average hourly wage of $17—the highest among discount retailers—while also picking up 92 percent of health-insurance premium costs. The result is high performance and low turnover. Costco's workforce has a reputation for being the most productive and loyal in all of retail.

A winning retail strategy, flexible organization, exemplary leadership, and well-compensated employees—these are the unique qualities that place Costco Wholesale Corporation at the head of its class. As you progress through your course in management, you'll continue to read about the extraordinary leadership of Costco's founders and encounter the innovative planning, organizing, leading, and controlling methods the company uses to outstrip competitors and steer the organization toward future success.

Questions

1. Which of the three management-skill categories do you think Costco CEO James Sinegal draws upon most during his year-round visits to local Costco warehouses? Explain.

2. What aspects of Costco's business model exemplify the transition from "the old workplace" to the "new workplace," and why?

3. How does Costco's high worker-retention rate help the warehouse club maintain low prices?

SOURCES: Matthew Boyle, "Why Costco is So Damn Addictive," Fortune, October 30, 2006; Alan B. Goldberg and Bill Ritter, "Costco CEO Finds Pro-Worker Means Profitability," ABC News, August 2, 2006, http://abcnews.go.com, accessed November 8, 2006; Doug Desjardins, "Bulking Up Sales Through Sales in Bulk," Retailing Today, September 25, 2006; Daren Fonda, "Jim Sinegal: Costco's Discount CEO," Time, May 8, 2006; Alyce Lomax, "Most Foolish CEO: Jim Sinegal," The Motley Fool, September 28, 2006, http://www.fool.com, accessed November 6, 2006.

James Sinegal, The Conscience of a Corporation

Entrepreneurs face enormous challenges in today's complex business world. To succeed in the 21st century, these aspiring business owners must be able to identify global trends, provide ethical leadership, develop effective corporate cultures, and manage the various environments in which they operate. Like jugglers in a circus, entrepreneurs are expected to balance the often-conflicting demands of customers, employees, shareholders, and other stakeholders to whom they are responsible. The ones that rise to the occasion make enormous contributions to society and reap rewards beyond their wildest dreams.

Transforming a startup into a multinational corporation often begins with the vision, drive, and perseverance of a single individual. The entrepreneurial impetus that catapulted Costco Wholesale Corp. from a Seattle warehouse to the nation's top warehouse club chain originated with James Sinegal, the Pittsburgh native and grandfather-like figure who co-founded Costco and now serves as its chief executive. The son of a steelworker, Sinegal embarked on his retail journey early in life. In 1954, at the age of 18, Sinegal took a job unloading mattresses for Fed-Mart, a new San Diego discount store launched by Sol Price, an early pioneer of the warehouse-club concept. Sinegal worked hard and became Price's protégé, eventually achieving the head manager position at Fed-Mart's flagship store. In the 1970s, Price sold Fed-Mart and launched a new warehouse store, one bearing his name: Price Club. Though Sinegal followed his mentor to the new warehouse establishment, it was only a matter of time before Price's star pupil would venture out on his own. That time came in 1983 when Sinegal founded Costco with business partner and lawyer Jeffrey Brotman, the company's current chairman. Their efforts helped launch an era of "big-box retailers" typified by companies like Wal-Mart, BJ's Wholesale Club, and Target.

From the beginning, Sinegal's vision for Costco was guided by a set of values and priorities now expressed in the company's five-point code of ethics. The Costco Code of Ethics indicates that, to achieve its mission of providing members with quality goods and services at the lowest possible prices, Costco must (1) obey the law, (2) take care of its customers, (3) take care of employees, and (4) respect its suppliers. If the organization follows these four guidelines, it will accomplish its fifth and ultimate goal: reward shareholders.

To ensure that these ethical standards would become the guiding principles for all Costco business operations, Sinegal developed a vibrant corporate culture that embodied and reinforced the co-founders' values and beliefs. One of the most visible and often discussed aspects of Costco's corporate culture is its generous-yet-proportional employee compensation. Convinced that happy workers are productive workers, Sinegal saw to it that his team was lavishly compensated with a livable wage and premium benefits. In 2006, Costco workers made an average hourly wage of $17, an astounding 42 percent higher than rival Sam's Club. Richard Galanti, Costco's executive vice president and chief financial officer, believes the pro-worker wages policy makes good business sense: "It's important to pay people a fair living wage. If you do, and it's better than everybody else, you're going to get better people—and they're going to stick around longer." Despite complaints on Wall Street that Costco's employee-remuneration program functions at the expense of profits and share prices, Sinegal is committed to the long-range benefits of a generous compensation strategy: "On Wall Street, they're in the business of making money between now and next Thursday . . . but we can't take that view. We want to build a company that will still be here 50 and 60 years from now."

Though Costco's employees and first-line managers are the best paid in retail, leaders atop the managerial hierarchy earn a humble living, relative to their peers. Sinegal's salary hovers around $350,000—chump change compared to the greenbacks flooding the wallets of most Fortune 500 bosses. Even with bonuses, Sinegal's annual compensation ranks among the lowest ten percent of chief executives. The worker centric leader is unapologetic, viewing his company's executive pay policy in terms of distributive justice: "I just think that if you're going to try to run an organization that's very cost-conscious, then you can't have those disparities. Having an individual who is making 100 or 200 or 300 times more than the average person working on the floor is wrong."

The egalitarian-minded CEO reinforces this culture of inclusion and proportionality in other ways, as well. Sinegal dons a Costco Kirkland Signature dress shirt instead of a suit. He wears an ID nametag like other employees, answers his own phones, and spends 200 days each year visiting warehouses and teams. Even his corner office is welcoming: with no door or window, the Costco general's quarters are covered with photographs of family members and store openings. In ways large and small, Sinegal sends the message that employees are the company's most valuable commodity.

Costco's commitment to ethics and social responsibility has not been without challenges, however. In 2006, a stock-options backdating scandal tainted hundreds of businesses, forcing the ouster of dozens of top executives. When an internal investigation at Costco uncovered "imprecisions" in the company's executive options plan, officers proactively cancelled executive bonuses for the year, withholding payouts of up to $200,000. This dramatic act of self-regulation was suggested by the two leaders who had the most to lose: James Sinegal and Richard Galanti. Costco has been accused of other lapses, such as impeding the advancement of female workers to senior-level positions and displaying environmental and cultural insensitivity during its Mexico expansion, but Sinegal & Co. have thus far emerged unscathed.

Despite occasional allegations, Costco has managed to maintain its squeaky-clean reputation. And so long as Jim Sinegal continues serving as the conscience of the corporation, there is every reason to believe it will stay that way.

Questions

1. What are the motivations and personality traits that compel individuals like James Sinegal to strike out on their own, preferring the risks of entrepreneurship to the relative safety of working for others? Does Sinegal qualify as a social entrepreneur? Why or why not?

2. In what way does the carefully crafted order of Costco's five-point Code of Ethics represent a rejection of the profit-maximizing approach to evaluating corporate social performance?

3. Which of the four types of corporate cultures best describes Costco? Identify ways that James Sinegal exhibits cultural leadership to create and maintain a high-performance organization?

SOURCES: Mike Duff, "The Sinegal Factor: Thriving with a Handson Approach," *DSN Retailing Today*, December 19, 2005; Doug Desjardins, "Culture of Inclusion: Where Top Executives Lead by Example and Honesty and Frugality Are Valued Virtues," *DSN Retailing Today*, December 19, 2005; Chris Noon, "No Bonuses For You Two," *Forbes*, October 20, 2006; Alyce Lomax, "Most Foolish CEO: Jim Sinegal," *The Motley Fool*, September 28, 2006, *http://www.fool.com*, accessed November 6, 2006; David Pinto, "Costco Named Retailer of the Year, *MMR*, January 9, 2006; Steve Greenhouse, "How Costco Became the Anti-Wal-Mart," *The New York Times*, July 17, 2005; Mike Troy, "A Model Business: Long-term Vision Benefits Customers, Employees,"*DSN Retailing Today*, December 19, 2005; Matthew Boyle, "Why Costco is So Damn Addictive," *Fortune*, October 30, 2006; "Code of Ethics," Costco Investor Relations Web site, *http://phx.corporate-ir.net/phoenix.zhtml?c=83830&p=irol-irhome*, accessed November 14, 2006.

Costco Turns 500

November 22, 2006, marks a major milestone in the history of Costco Wholesale Corporation. On that date, in the city of La Quinta, California, the world's top warehouse-club operator opened its 500th location since pioneering the discount warehouse concept in the 1970s and '80s.

Throngs of customers, city planners, and interested observers gathered in the Southern California suburb to celebrate the store's grand opening, days before the onset of the 2006 holiday shopping season. At 8 A.M., the boxy 148,000 square-foot facility threw open its doors, welcoming hundreds of enthusiastic bargain hunters giddy at the prospect of buying the year's hottest merchandise at rock-bottom prices. As the morning hours passed, Xbox 360s, Panasonic plasma TVs, and AG brand jeans began beeping briskly through the checkouts—a sure sign that holiday stockings across the Greater Palm Springs area would soon be filled with gift-giving cheer.

The landmark opening of Costco's 500th warehouse was not only a sign of good things to come for local residents or for La Quinta officials anticipating a one-million-dollar boost to the city's annual tax revenues; for Costco CEO James Sinegal and his team of strategic planners, breaking the 500 barrier was confirmation that Costco's long-term growth plan was working. In the 25 years since Sinegal and Costco co-founder Jeffrey

Brotman broke ground on their first archetypal no-frills warehouse in Seattle, Washington, Costco has consistently executed its mission to build warehouse clubs that provide quality goods and services at the lowest possible prices. The general merchandise retailer has grown at an average of 20 warehouses per year and now ranks No.1 among discount warehouse chains.

For some businesses, reaching the top might seem like a time for self-congratulation. But for Sinegal & Co., success is handled with a kind of "business asusual" modesty. Far from causing Costco's top brass to rest on their laurels, hitting the 500 marker has emboldened management to set even more aggressive expansion goals. During an August 2006 conference call, CFO Richard Galanti announced plans for 35 to 40 new stores, with a target of 700 U.S. locations—a sizable increase over previous goals.

Launching new storefronts is central to any major retailer's grand strategy. First and foremost, adding locations is about increasing revenues and profits. A typical Costco warehouse averages $128 million in annual sales. By raising expansion projections for 2007, the Issaquah, Washington-based retailer has set itself on track for double-digit percentage revenue growth beyond its record $60 billion achieved in 2006.

Costco doesn't throw warehouses up just anywhere, however. Sinegal's strategic planning effort involves the careful identification of sites that provide a good fit between the organization and its environment. A majority of Costco store openings target suburban commercial districts, where suburban customers like their bulk-packaged soup, toilet paper, and peanut butter under a single roof with computers, copiers, hot tubs, and grand pianos. But in Costco's urban outlets, such as the tower-complex location in the heart of downtown Vancouver, Canada, merchandise caters to downtown demographics. The club's urban-tailored product mix features upscale Louis Vuitton fashion goods and a hearty deli selection of home-ready meals—a nod to Vancouver's many downtown condo dwellers. "It is the most unique Costco in the world," says Regional Marketing Director Robin Ross, reflecting on the store's uncommon placement within big-city surroundings. "This is a place where you can buy tires *and* a two carat diamond ring for $19,699."

Though revenue generation and demographic fit are primary goals for all Costco locations, certain warehouses also serve as testing labs for new ventures. One such idea incubator is Costco's 205,000 square-foot superstore in Hillsboro, Oregon, near Portland. The store's footprint was designed 40% larger than typical stores to test out a mini-version of Costco Home, the retailer's high-end home furnishings chain store. "It gives us lots of extra space where we can test some things and it's close enough where we can keep an eye on it," said Galanti.

Management's strategy of designating certain locations for test marketing purposes has proven successful, especially in light of the fact that most of Costco's present ancillary businesses began in such warehouses before being rolled out nationwide. The company's $2 billion-in-sales pharmacy division began as an experiment in a Portland store in 1986. More recently, in 2006, Costco's drive-through Car Wash business made its test-market debut at the famous Fourth Avenue store in south Seattle.

But as Costco implements expansion plans in locations ranging from Manhattan and Mexico to Taiwan, the discounter's big box concept faces challenges from numerous forces in the external environment. Various stakeholders—including unions, local governments, and anti-globalization groups—are engaged in a contentious dispute over the rapid growth of big boxes. Though city developers and state officials typically view superstores as a preferred means of filling government coffers with millions in tax revenues, labor and anti-growth forces see the priceslashing mega-stores as detrimental to their interests. The debate is growing particularly acrimonious in California, where arguments rage over whether superstore retailers belong in a neighborhood and legislative bills threaten a severe restriction of big box expansion.

Keen to the threat from outside forces, and dedicated to his team's plan for growth, Sinegal sets course and asserts his rock-steady leadership. To Costco's seasoned founder and chief, the company's growth from one single Seattle store into a 500-warehouse retail chain is a powerful motivator for future performance. "We still take pictures of that original building and show it at our manager's meetings and then show the contrast to what our businesses look like today," Sinegal says. "If we are going to continue to prosper as a company, we had better be as creative in the next twenty years as we have been in the past twenty years. It is an imperative that you continue to be creative and build your business."

Questions

1. What strategy formulation tools might top management at Costco use to assess opportunities and threats to the company's future expansion?

2. Explain how Costco's select test-market warehouses demonstrate cooperation and connectedness between the different levels of planning and strategy throughout an organization.

3. How does James Sinegal's recounting of Costco's history using early warehouse photographs at manager's meetings illustrate the role of corporate culture in supporting an organization's strategy and performance?

SOURCES: Marcel Honore, "Valley's Second Costco Lands in La Quinta," *The Desert Sun*, November 21, 2006; Will Fifield, "500 and Counting," *The Costco Connection*, November 2006; Doug Desjardins, "Bulking Up Sales Through Sales in Bulk," *Retailing Today*, September 25, 2006; Gillian Shaw, "Costco Opens Yaletown Warehouse Store," *Vancouver Sun*, November 10, 2006; John Howard, "Big Box Debate," *Capitol Weekly*, November 16, 2006; "Ancillary Businesses Continue to Drive Through Sales," *Retailing Today*, September 25, 2006; Doug Desjardins, "Retailer's Largest Store a Learning Lab," *Retailing Today*, November 6, 2006; Mac Greer, "Is Costco Giving Away the Store?," *The Motley Fool*, November 22, 2006, *http://www.fool.com*.

Costco's Generous Pay Yields Generous Profits

Attracting and retaining a loyal and productive workforce is essential to the success of any business. But in retailing, where employee turnover can nearly outpace rapidly churning inventories, a stable and satisfied workforce can be of critical importance. When it comes to cultivating human capital, Costco Wholesale Corp. stands heads and shoulders above its discount retailing peers. The No. 1 membership warehouse chain boasts the highest-paid, most dependable workforce in the industry. This distinction stands in sharp contrast to prevalent labor trends, where many businesses have abandoned the lifetime-employee concept and are engaged in a lower-wages race to the bottom. When viewed against this backdrop, Costco's strategy for developing a loyal and empowered labor force is at once the most innovative and most controversial in retailing today.

Costco's unconventional approach to human resource management is immediately apparent in the recruitment of its warehouse workers. In keeping with the company's bare-bones, cost-cutting ethic that eliminates overhead and passes the savings to its customers, the big-box discounter doesn't retain outside recruiters, and the human resource staff doesn't participate in hiring. When a new warehouse is being built in a location, regional and local managers pitch office tents onsite to take applications and place helpwanted ads in area newspapers. After conducting interviews with job candidates, managers select hires and schedule training sessions, where the recruits are assigned a mentor. For their first assignment, trainees go on a scavenger hunt for information about their new company, gathering facts and reporting their discoveries to managers within the month. Once acclimated to the Costco way, the new workers finish their orientation and prepare for the store's grand opening. The entire process is carried out on a shoestring budget, in keeping with Costco's no-frills, low-budget operations philosophy.

Bolstering Costco's recruitment effort is one of the most generous compensation packages in retail. Costco's workers earn an average of $17 per hour—42 percent more than employees at rival Sam's Club and high above U.S. retail industry averages. Employees at this pay level are eligible for bonuses of between $2,000 and $3,000, and, after four years, full-time hourly employees earn $40,000 annually. Equally alluring are Costco's premium health benefits that are the envy of many American workers. Costco employees, whether part- or full-time, pay only 8 percent of healthcare costs, compared to the retail average of 25 percent. Topping it off is Costco's 401(k) program for new hires that eventually matches up to 9 percent of workers' annual pay.

The expense on such lavish compensation adds up: Costco's labor and benefit costs make up about 70 percent of its operating expenses, a lofty number that troubles some analysts who say the $60-billion-a-year retailer is showering benefits at the shareholders' expense. But CEO James Sinegal maintains that his company's investment in human capital is good business, not corporate altruism. "It absolutely makes good business sense," Sinegal states. "Most people agree that we're the lowest-cost provider. Yet we pay the highest wages. So it must mean we get better productivity . . . you get what you pay for." Costco financial chief Richard Galanti sees things in a similar light: "One of the things Wall Street chided us on is that we're too good to our employees . . . we don't think that's possible."

The numbers speak for themselves—Costco's workers stay longer and produce more than workers of competing retailers. After the first year, only 6 percent of Costco employees leave, compared with 21 percent at Sam's. With recruitment and training costs estimated at around $2,500 per trainee, a sizable retention rate means sizable savings. Moreover, Costco workers generate $918 in per square foot of retail space annually, outstripping worker productivity at other major retailers. Sam's Club employees yield $552 in sales per foot of space, and Wal-Mart and Target staffs produce $438 and $307 per foot, respectively.

Costco displays the same pro-worker mindset with the recruitment of top management. Sinegal has claimed that up to 98 percent of managerial positions are filled from within the company—in fact, most upper-level managers worked their way up the ladder starting at the warehouse floor. This official policy of promoting from within fosters loyalty and helps to develop warehouse managers, buyers, and executives who have thorough knowledge of the company. When sourcing such talent, recruiters look for leaders with people skills, smarts, and an entrepreneurial love of merchandising. The company has been accused of lacking diversity among top management, however. Sinegal admits that having 17 percent of management jobs occupied by women is low: "We don't let ourselves off the hook on that," he says. "We think we can do better. We know we can do better."

Costco's success proves that low prices for customers don't have to come at the expense of wages and benefits for workers. Sinegal chooses to save money elsewhere in the business while generating ample revenues through membership fees and high volume sales. Reflecting Sinegal's labor-oriented values, Costco's top brass views people as a competitive advantage, not another expense to be reduced to the minimum. "Some companies control these expenses by figuring out how little they must pay their employees and how much of the health care cost they can pass on to their employees," Galanti remarks. "While we agree with the idea of cost efficiency, we believe the rest of that stuff is mostly about sacrificing the well-being of your employees in order to increase profits; we don't buy that. We believe you can do both."

Questions

1. What sacrifices does Costco make so that it may pay employees higher wages?

2. What are the benefits of promoting from within? What might be possible drawbacks to having a high internal promotion rate?

3. What steps could Costco take to foster greater diversity among its management, particularly as it relates to the promotion of women?

SOURCES: Michelle V. Rafter, "Welcome to the Club–Parts 1 & 2; Costco Employees Enjoy Some of the Most Generous Wages and Benefits Among U.S. Retailers" *Workforce Management*, April 1, 2005; Matthew Boyle, "Why Costco is So Damn Addictive," *Fortune*, October 30, 2006; S. Holmes and W. Zellner, "The Costco Way: Higher Wages Mean Higher Profits. But Try Telling Wall Street," *Business Week*, April 12, 2004; Steven Greenhouse, "How Costco Became the Anti-Wal-Mart," *The New York Times*, July 17, 2005; Nina Shapiro, "Company For the People," *Seattle Weekly*, December 15, 2004; Jim Underwood, *What's Your Corporate IQ?: How the Smartest Companies Learn, Transform, Lead,* Chicago, Ill.: Dearborn Trade, 2004, quoted in Cecil Johnson, "Treating Employees Well Is One Key to Firm's Success, Professor Writes," *Fort Worth Star-Telegram*, October 7, 2004.

Providing Leadership in Bulk

When Costco Wholesale procured land to construct a new warehouse in Cuernavaca, Mexico in 2001, it had no idea that the purchase would spark a two-year clash between anti-globalization protesters and senior management. The leading U.S. warehouse club operator was looking to continue its international expansion, and the Mexican government's auctioning of a site occupied by a dilapidated hotel and casino known as the *Casino de la Selva* presented a strategic opportunity.

But what started out as a business-as-usual transaction for Costco soon turned into a public relations crisis. Opponents of the land development staged human blockades to stop chainsaw crews from clearing the way for the superstore and surrounding facilities. Numerous protestors were arrested, and the conflict received widespread media attention.

Despite overwhelming support in Cuernavaca for the new Costco store and its promise of new jobs and economic prosperity, accusations that Costco was paving a parking lot overtop the city's civic, artistic, and national heritage were beginning to create the perception of Costco as an insensitive multinational corporation. To demonstrate environmental and cultural sensitivity to the citizens of the region, and to offer an olive branch to anti-growth opponents, Costco set aside millions of dollars beyond its original budget to preserve much of the area's natural landscape and to restore the dilapidated murals of the *Casino de la Selva*, the site's once-thriving hotel and gaming casino. In cooperation with the Mexican National Institute of Fine Arts and Literature, the Vergel Foundation, and regional city planners, Costco built a cultural center and museum that now displays the hotel frescos as well as the esteemed Gelman Collection of Mexican art, featuring works by Frida Kahlo and Diego Rivera. Today, the site serves as a valuable international attraction for Cuernavaca, preserving the city's cultural heritage and providing a boost to the city's economy.

The Cuernavaca story illustrates the exemplary moral leadership that has come to characterize Costco's senior management. From the very beginning, Costco had a different way of seeing its own mission. While many businesses measure success in strictly financial terms— Are we profitable?—the world's leading membership warehouse chain has always gauged achievement according to broader criteria: Are we creating greater value for the consumer? Are we more efficient? Are we doing the right thing for employees and other stakeholders? This holistic approach to business has made Costco not only wildly profitable but also vitally relevant to the issues and trends shaping the future of business today.

Led by co-founder and CEO James Sinegal, Costco forged a new model of retailing that combined wholesale-styled bulk efficiencies with brand-name merchandising, delivering high-end products to club members at the lowest possible prices. As a result of Sinegal's strong leadership and vision, Costco finds itself at the forefront of big box retailing, occupying a seat among top chains like Wal-Mart, Target, and Home Depot.

On its way to becoming the No. 1 warehouse club in the nation, Costco launched timely ancillary businesses that changed the way people shop. To its core warehouse club business Costco has added gas stations, home furnishing stores, pharmacies, drive through car washes, optical centers, photo labs, fresh-food departments, and business centers. These ancillary businesses have contributed $7 billion to Costco's $60 billion in annual sales and stimulated a growing market demand for one-stop shopping.

In some instances, Costco's side ventures have risen to the top of their associated retail categories. In 2006, Costco's fast-growing pharmacy division generated sales of $2.6 billion, making Costco one of the nation's largest pharmacy chains—an astounding accomplishment that took only 20 years. With their staggering prescription drug sales and recent entry into low-priced generic drugs, Costco pharmacies are turning up the heat on category leaders CVS Corp. and Walgreen Co. and demonstrating effective positioning to meet the needs of the aging baby-boomer population.

Costco's innovative leadership has also extended to the private label enterprise. At a time when many retailers are struggling to sell private labels alongside national brands, Costco's Kirkland Signature label has evolved into one of the most successful and recognized own-brands in the country. Designed to be of equal or better quality than national brands, Kirkland Signature products make up 400 of Costco's approximately 4,000 SKUs, with items ranging from diapers manufactured by Kimberly-Clark to tires produced by Michelin—offered at a minimum of 20 percent savings compared to leading national brands. Applying highvolume leverage on the distribution channel helped to create Kirkland Signature's more-for-less reputation—Costco buyers famously exclude suppliers that fail to meet their demands. "This is not the Little Sisters of the Poor," Sinegal declares with usual dry wit. "We have to be competitive in the toughest marketplace in the world against the biggest competitor in the world. We cannot afford to be timid."

From its development of Cuernavaca to its transformational impact upon the retail industry, Costco's legacy of innovation and success is owed to the company's motivational leadership, and especially to James Sinegal, a visionary CEO that *Time* magazine named as one of the 100 most influential people of 2006.

Questions

1. What is moral leadership, and why is it increasingly important for global business?

2. What types of leadership are necessary for leading change? In what ways has Costco's management demonstrated such leadership?

3. What motivational impact might Costco's handling of the Cuernavaca expansion have on employees, both in Mexico and internationally? Explain.

SOURCES: Mya Frazier, "The Private Label Powerhouse; With Booming Kirkland Signature Line, Costco Controls National Brands Like No Other Retailer," *Advertising Age*, August 21, 2006; Mike Duff, "A Private Label Success Story," *DSN Retailing Today*, December 19, 2005; Doug Desjardins, "Presence Builds Rapidly Amid Rx Top Tier," *Retailing Today*, November 6, 2006; David Pinto, "Costco Named Retailer of the Year," *MMR*, January 9, 2006; "Costco to Match $4 Generics Price as Rx Sales Continue to Rise," *Drug Store News*, November 6, 2006; Investor Relations Web site, *http://phx.corporate-ir.net/phoenix.zhtml?c=83830&p=irol-irhome*, accessed November 21, 2006; "Ancillary Businesses Continue to Drive Through Sales," *Retailing Today*, September 25, 2006; "Mix Includes Everything From Cosmetics to Caskets," *MMR*, January 9, 2006; Alyce Lomax, "Most Foolish CEO: Jim Sinegal," *The Motley Fool*, September 28, 2006, *http://www.fool.com*; Mya Frazier, "Chic Costco beauty line displayedin cardboard; Warehouse chain offers Borghese, undercutting department store rivals," *Advertising Age*, May 22, 2006; Steven Greenhouse, "How Costco Became the Anti-Wal-Mart," *The New York Times*, July 17, 2005; Mac Greer, "Is Costco Giving Away the Store?" *The Motley Fool*, November 22, 2006, *http://www.fool.com*; "A Culture of Commitment: The Story of Costco in Cuernavaca," Company Web site, *http://www.costco.com/Service/FeaturePage.aspx?ProductNo=11004800*; Daren Fonda, "Jim Sinegal: Costco's Discount CEO," Time, May 8, 2006.

Costco's Whopper of a Fish Tale

Continuous improvement isn't a mere buzzword at Costco Wholesale: it's a *modus operandi*. To offer high-quality products at rock-bottom prices, the $60-billion-a-year warehouse club must manage its daily operations and supply chain with ever-increasing efficiency and innovation. Without this commitment, selling stacks of AG dark-rinse jeans and Canon high performance digital cameras at deep discounts would be a losing business proposition.

When illustrating Costco's ongoing quest for an ever-higher standard of quality and efficiency, senior executives recount an old fish tale—fortunately, this is not about the one that got away. The story begins with a salmon fillet that Costco's seafood department once sold for $5.99 per pound. At the time, shoppers saw nothing unusual or impressive about the fish—the pinkish-orange tender fillets lined the seafood aisle, complete with skin, bones, fins, and belly fat. One day, merchandisers began looking for a way to boost the fish's $200,000-per-week sales. Their objective was to improve the product while lowering its price. In a breakthrough procurement effort, staffers located a salmon-jerky manufacturer in Japan that could deliver the fish trimmed and stripped of bones, after retaining the belly fat for its jerky product. The new leaner salmon fillet sold for $5.29 per pound, producing a 20 to 30 percent rise in sales. After additional improvements, Costco offered a fully trimmed, skinless and boneless fillet for $4.99 per pound. At this price point, sales of the salmon jumped from about $850,000 per week to $1.4 million. The higher volume sales now enabled Costco's buyers to source the product directly from salmon farms in Canada and Chile, creating even greater cost savings. The final result of Costco's fishing expedition: a $3.99-per-pound salmon delicacy generating over $2 million in weekly revenues.

This salmon story has come to symbolize Costco's unique operating philosophy—so much so that it is now tightly woven throughout the company's corporate culture. The oft-recounted tale has given rise to the Salmon Awards, the company's annual achievement program that recognizes the merchant or vendor who does the most to improve a product's quality while lowering its cost. In addition, Costco's Issaquah, Washington headquarters prominently displays a statue of spawning salmon—a shrine dedicated to the cherished Pacific Northwest fish and to Costco's value-driven merchandising.

Establishing cost-saving partnerships with suppliers requires the resourcefulness of Costco's dedicated managers, but maintaining these relationships on a day-to-day basis is made possible through cutting edge technology. For example, coordinating the order, transport, and replenishment of inventories would be nearly impossible without computerized information systems like the Costco Collaborative Retail Exchange (CRX), a high-tech program that creates an electronic link between Costco and its vendors. The program gives manufacturers, suppliers, and other partners constant visibility of Costco's warehouse management to effectively reduce out-of-stocks, increase new product introduction success, and manage item performance. With Costco CRX, vendors gain direct, interactive access to Costco's warehouse-specific, item-level data—in real time. "The CRX program is our approach to providing our vendor community with standard, secure access to current and detailed information about their business at Costco Wholesale," said Ed Maron, executive vice president at Costco. Maron added that CRX transforms Costco's point-of-sale information into actionable business insights for retail partners.

Other Costco business operations depend on technology as well. As a result of having many retail partners, Costco must manage thousands of communications in and out of the company each day. The warehouse club operator can't afford to get bogged down in delayed responses to purchase orders, debit memos, or invoices. To streamline processing of the nearly 30,000 documents exchanged between Costco and its suppliers daily—6.7 million each year—the company employs a document imaging system that scans documents for digital storage and retrieval. The system facilitates fast, effective communication between Costco and outside firms, resulting in improved service to warehouse, depot, and vendor customers.

Though high-tech coordination with suppliers has played a vital role in Costco's past, it also holds the key to Costco's future. Nowhere is this more evident than with Costco.com, the company's e-commerce division.

Costco.com offers about 4,000 items for sale online, and nearly 70 percent of products ordered through the site are shipped directly from external suppliers to the customer. By connecting outside vendors and manufacturers to its e-supply chain, Costco saves millions of dollars in warehousing, inventory, and shipping expenses. The retailer's Internet-based strategy is paying off: in 2005, Costco.com ranked 27 among online retailers, boasting sales of $534 million. Looking ahead, the e-business division is projected to generate over $1 billion annually.

Whether the objective is to offer customers the best salmon product at the lowest possible price or to implement state-of-the-art technologies that streamline daily business processes, Costco Wholesale is dedicated to keeping continuous improvement at the center of its business. After more than 25 years of retailing success, the No.1 warehouse club is as determined as ever to lead the way to the future with ever-increasing efficiency, profitability, and success.

Questions

1. How does Costco's famous and oft-recounted salmon story help management create a culture of performance and quality?

2. What role does the Salmon Awards program play in Costco's system of control?

3. How does Costco reduce its operating expenses by investing in technologies that enable outside suppliers to manage inventories and ship orders directly to customers?

SOURCES: Tim Craig, "Impressed by Costco? Join the Club," *DSN Retailing Today*, December 19, 2005; Mike Duff, "Innovation Has Its Own Reward," *DSN Retailing Today*, December 19, 2005; "Salmon Tells the Costco Story," *MMR*, August 23, 2004; "Costco Makes It Easier for Suppliers," *MMR*, December 12, 2005; "Costco Keeps Prices Low with Document Imaging," *Transform*, December 2004; Mya Frazier, "What Long Tail," *Advertising Age*, August 21, 2006.

Appendix B

Small Business Start Ups

What Is Entrepreneurship?

Entrepreneurship is the process of initiating a business venture, organizing the necessary resources, and assuming the associated risks and rewards.[1] An entrepreneur is someone who engages in entrepreneurship. An entrepreneur recognizes a viable idea for a business product or service and carries it out by finding and assembling the necessary resources—money, people, machinery, location—to undertake the business venture. Entrepreneurs also assume the risks and reap the rewards of the business. They assume the financial and legal risks of ownership and receive the business's profits.

A good example of entrepreneurship is Andra Rush, who quit her nursing job to start a trucking company in 1984. Using her savings and a loan from her parents, Rush bought two used trucks and a new one and maxed out her credit cards to start the business. She couldn't afford a cell phone or an office manager, so she forwarded calls to her grandmother's house while she was out drumming up business. She learned how to do her own truck repairs and made an impression on customers by specializing in emergency shipping, even if she had to get up at 2 A.M. to deliver the load herself. The early days were rough, and Rush made a lot of sacrifices to succeed, but today Rush Trucking has 350 full-time employees and makes 1,400 shipments a day with 1,000 trucks. The

company generated $132 million in revenue in 2003. Rush was willing to take the risks and is now reaping the rewards of entrepreneurship.[2]

Successful entrepreneurs have many different motivations, and they measure rewards in different ways. One study classified small business owners in five different categories, as illustrated in Exhibit B.1. Some people are *idealists*, who like the idea of working on something that is new, creative, or personally meaningful. *Optimizers* are rewarded by the personal satisfaction of being business owners. Entrepreneurs in the *sustainer* category like the chance to balance work and personal life and often don't want the business to grow too large, while *hard workers* enjoy putting in the long hours and dedication to build a larger, more profitable business. The *juggler* category includes entrepreneurs who like the chance a small business gives them to handle everything themselves. These high energy people thrive on the pressure of paying bills, meeting deadlines, and making payroll.[3]

Compare the motivation of Paula Turpin to that of Greg Littlefield. Turpin borrowed a few thousand dollars to start a hair salon, Truly Blessed Styles, in Shirley, New York. She does all the cutting, styling, and coloring herself, while her mother helps schedule appointments and keeps the books. Turpin likes the flexibility and freedom of working for herself. Although she hopes to expand by adding beauty supplies, she doesn't want the

EXHIBIT B.1

Five Types of Small Business Owners

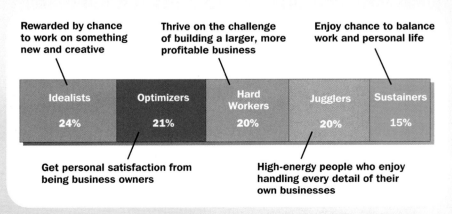

SOURCE: Study conducted by Yankelovich Partners, reported in Mark Henricks, "Type-Cast," *Entrepreneur* (March 2000): 14–16.

headaches of managing a large business. Greg Littlefield quit his management job and started a cleaning service because he reasoned that it would never lack customers. From the beginning, when he was working two part-time jobs and cleaning buildings by himself at night, Littlefield had plans for expansion. Within a decade, Littlefield's firm, Professional Facilities Management, grew into a 900-employee company providing a range of services including housekeeping, landscaping, minor maintenance, and security services.[4] Greg Littlefield reflects the motivation of a *hard worker*, whereas Paula Turpin's motivation is more that of a *sustainer*.

Sometimes people start new businesses when they lose their jobs due to corporate downsizing. The major layoffs in the early 2000s provided just the push some latent entrepreneurs needed to strike out on their own. Some experts think an economic downturn is actually the best time to start a business. For one thing, a downturn opens up lots of opportunities because people are looking for lower costs and better ways of doing things. The economic climate also enables the new business to hire good people, forces the entrepreneur to keep costs in line, and provides the time needed to build something of lasting value rather than struggling to keep pace with rapid growth.[5]

Many people also regard entrepreneurship as a better use of their time, talent, and energy. Women and minorities, who have sometimes found their opportunities limited in the corporate world, are often seeing entrepreneurship as the only way to go. Hispanic and African American entrepreneurship is on the rise. The National Federation of Women Business Owners reports that Hispanic women are starting companies in the United States at four times the national growth rate. "The [corporate] work environment is not friendly to Latinas," says Alma Morales Fiojas, CEO of Mana, a National Latina Organization. "Sometimes the best avenue . . . is to go into your own business, where there is more flexibility and you can accomplish more."[6]

Entrepreneurship and the Environment

Not so long ago, scholars and policy makers were worrying about the potential of small business to survive. The turbulence in the technology sector and the demise of many dot-com start-ups heightened concerns about whether small companies can compete with big business. However, entrepreneurship and small business, including high-tech start-ups, are vital, dynamic, and increasingly important parts of the U.S. economy. Small businesses grew from 19 million in 1992 to 24.7 million in 2004.[7] These firms account for a tremendous portion of the goods and services provided. Entrepreneurship in other countries is also booming. The list of the most entrepreneurial countries, shown in Exhibit B.2, is intriguing. A project monitoring entrepreneurial activity around the world reports that an estimated 25 percent of adults age 18 to 64 in Venezuela are either starting up or managing new enterprises. The percentage in Thailand is 20.7 percent, and in Jamaica 17 percent. China and New Zealand also show higher rates of entrepreneurial activity than the U.S. rate of 12.4 percent.[8] Japan, which shows a low rate of only 2.2 percent, is attempting to spur entrepreneurial activity with a new law that makes it possible to start a business with capital of just 1 yen.[9] Structural reforms in Russia spurred a jump in small business formation in that country, and one economic study predicts a doubling of small business as a part of Russia's gross domestic product between the years of 2004 and 2009.[10]

ENTREPRENEURSHIP TODAY

Small business is such a dynamic part of today's economy for a number of reasons, including economic changes, globalization and increased competition, advancing technology, and new market niches.[11]

Economic Changes. Today's economy is fertile soil for entrepreneurs. The economy changes constantly, providing opportunities for new businesses. The demand for services is booming, and 97 percent of service firms are small, with fewer than 100 employees. Landscaping, for example, is one of the fastest growing small businesses, spurred by a surge in housing and office construction.[12] The trend toward outsourcing work to companies that can do it cheaper has also given entrepreneurs new openings. Ogio, a small company based in Bluffdale, Utah, engineers and manufactures innovative golf bags for Callaway, helping the smaller firm's sales skyrocket from $8 million to $47 million in five years.[13]

EXHIBIT B.2
The World's Most Entrepreneurial Countries

Country	Percentage of Individuals Age 18 to 64 Active in Starting or Managing a New Business, 2005
Venezuela	25.00
Thailand	20.70
New Zealand	17.60
Jamaica	17.00
China	13.70
United States	12.40
Brazil	11.30
Chile	11.10
Australia	10.90
Iceland	10.70
Argentina	9.50
Canada	9.30
Singapore	7.20
Latvia	6.60
Croatia	6.10
Average of countries surveyed	8.40

SOURCE: Global Entrepreneurship Monitor, "Table 2: Prevalence Rates of Entrepreneurial Activity Across Countries, 2005." *2005 GEM Tables and Figures*, Babson College and the London Business School, (March 14, 2006): www.gemconsortium.org/category_list.asp.

Globalization and Increased Competition. Even the largest of companies can no longer dominate their industry in a fast changing global marketplace. Globalization demands entrepreneurial behavior and gives an advantage to the flexibility and fast response that small business can offer rather than to huge companies with economies of scale. Rather than being hurt by the globalization of today's business world, many entrepreneurs are finding new opportunities. Stefanie Heiter started a four-person consulting business called Heiter-Connect that helps global managers communicate, collaborate, and motivate across borders.[14] Bill Weiller bought a nearly bankrupt company called Purafil, which was then focused exclusively on making air filters for U.S. pulp and paper factories, and transformed it into a global powerhouse. Purafil now sells filters in 11 industries to companies in 50 countries. Sixty percent of Purafil's revenues come from overseas.[15]

Technology. Rapid advances and dropping prices in computer technology spawned whole new industries, as well as entirely new methods of producing goods and delivering services. Unlike technological progress of the past, these advances are within the reach of companies of all sizes. The explosive growth of the Internet created tremendous opportunities for entrepreneurs. For every story of a failed dot-com business, numerous other small companies are successfully using the Web to sell products and services, to improve productivity, communications, and customer service, or to obtain information and market their services. Intranets.com (previously named Intranetics), for example, found new uses for its Web-based data- and document-management systems, such as helping NASA keep track of data after the 2003 Columbia space shuttle explosion.[16] Jeff Fluhr started a company called StubHub Inc., which is a leading Internet player in the burgeoning market of ticket reselling.[17] Thos. Moser Cabinetmakers, a Maine-based business that makes and sells handcrafted furniture, uses the Web as an online catalog, enabling the small company to reach people it could never reach before the advent of the Internet, which leads to lots of new buyers.[18]

Improvisation

Do you have what makes an entrepreneur tick? It is not for the faint of heart. An entrepreneur faces many demands. Do you have the proclivity to start and build your own business? To find out, consider the extent to which each of the following statements characterizes your behavior. Please answer each of the following items as Mostly True or Mostly False for you.

	Mostly True	Mostly False
1. Give me a little information and I can come up with a lot of ideas.	_____	_____
2. I like pressure in order to focus.	_____	_____
3. I don't easily get frustrated when things don't go my way.	_____	_____
4. I identify how resources can be recombined to produce novel outcomes.	_____	_____
5. I enjoy competing against the clock to meet deadlines.	_____	_____
6. People in my life have to accept that nothing is more important than the achievement of my school, my sport, or my career goals.	_____	_____
7. I serve as a role model for creativity.	_____	_____
8. I think "on my feet" when carrying out tasks.	_____	_____
9. I am determined and action oriented.	_____	_____

INTERPRETATION AND SCORING: Each question pertains to some aspect of **improvisation,** which is a correlate of entrepreneurial intentions. Entrepreneurial improvisation consists of three elements. Questions 1, 4, and 7 pertain to **creativity/ingenuity,** the ability to produce novel solutions under constrained conditions. Questions 2, 5, and 8 pertain to working under **pressure/stress,** the ability to excel under pressure filled circumstances. Questions 3, 6, and 9 pertain to **action/persistence,** the determination to achieve goals and solve problems in the moment. If you answered "Mostly True" to at least two of three questions for each subscale or six of nine for all the questions, then consider yourself an entrepreneur in the making with the potential to manage your own business. If you scored one or fewer "Mostly True" on each subscale or three or fewer for all nine questions, you might want to consider becoming a manager by working for someone else.

SOURCES: Based on Keith M. Hmieleski and Andrew C. Corbett, "Proclivity for Improvisation as a Predictor of Entrepreneurial Intentions," *Journal of Small Business Management* 44, no. 1 (January 2006): 45–63; and "Do You Have an Entrepreneurial Mind?" *Inc.com* (October 19, 2005).

Other technological advances also provide opportunities for small business. Biotechnology, aided by recent work in genomics, is a growing field for small businesses. Five Prime Therapeutics, for example, developed a protein-screening process that can accelerate the development of hit drugs for diseases such as cancer, Type 2 diabetes, and rheumatoid arthritis.[19] Research into microelectromechanical systems (MEMS), tiny machines used in numerous applications from biotechnology and telecommunications to the auto industry, is being conducted primarily by small companies.

New Opportunities and Market Niches.

Today's entrepreneurs are taking advantage of the opportunity to meet changing needs in the marketplace. Tapping into the growing *sustainability* movement, for example, Ron Warnecke founded NitroCision, a company that mops up radioactive and industrial waste without the use of chemicals.[20] Stampp Corbin spotted an opportunity in the growing need for companies to dispose of outdated equipment such as personal computers, printers, and servers. His company, RetroBox, wipes the machines clean of all data, refurbishes and sells any that are still useful, and makes sure others are disposed of safely. With organizations continually upgrading, Corbin's business grows each year, with revenue climbing to $14 million in 2004.[21]

DEFINITION OF SMALL BUSINESS

The full definition of *small business* used by the U.S. Small Business Administration (SBA) is detailed and complex, including 37 different benchmarks that define 1,151 industries and 13 sub industries across the United States. In general, a small business is considered to be "one that is independently owned and operated and which is not dominant in its field of operation."[22] Exhibit B.3 gives a few examples of how the SBA defines small business for a sample of industries.

However, the definition of small business is currently under revision in response to concerns from small business owners. After nationwide public hearings in 2005, the SBA determined that standards should be changed in light of shifting economic and industry conditions. Redefining small business size standards is a daunting task, but SBA leaders agree that the standards need to be more flexible in today's world. The SBA's definition has been revised a number of times over the years to reflect changing economic conditions.[23]

Exhibit B.3 also illustrates general categories of businesses most entrepreneurs start: retail, manufacturing, and service. Additional categories of small businesses are construction, hospitality, communications, finance, and real estate.

EXHIBIT B.3

Examples of SBA Definitions of Small Business

Manufacturing	
Soft-drink manufacturing	Number of employees does not exceed 500
Electronic computer manufacturing	Number of employees does not exceed 1,000
Prerecorded CD, tape, and record producing	Number of employees does not exceed 750
Retail (Store and Nonstore)	
Sporting goods stores	Average annual receipts do not exceed $6.0 million
Electronic auctions	Average annual receipts do not exceed $21.0 million
Vending machine operators	Average annual receipts do not exceed $6.0 million
Miscellaneous Internet Services	
Internet service providers	Average annual receipts do not exceed $21.0 million
Web search portals	Average annual receipts do not exceed $6.0 million
Internet publishing and broadcasting	Number of employees does not exceed 500

IMPACT OF ENTREPRENEURIAL COMPANIES

The impact of entrepreneurial companies on the U.S. economy is astonishing. According to the Small Business Administration, businesses with fewer than 500 employees represent 99.7 percent of all firms with employees in the United States, employ more than 50 percent of the nation's nonfarm private sector workers, and generate more than 50 percent of the nation's nonfarm gross domestic product (GDP). In addition, small businesses represent 97 percent of America's exporters and produce 26 percent of all export value.[24] In 2000, the status of the SBA administrator was elevated to a cabinet-level position in recognition of the importance of small business in the U.S. economy.[25]

Inspired by the growth of companies such as eBay, Google, and Amazon.com, entrepreneurs are still flocking to the Internet to start new businesses. In addition, demographic and lifestyle trends create new opportunities in areas such as environmental services, lawn care, computer maintenance, children's markets, fitness, and home health care. Entrepreneurship and small business in the United States is an engine for job creation and innovation.

Job Creation. Researchers disagree over what percentage of new jobs is created by small business. Research indicates that the *age* of a company, more than its size, determines the number of jobs it creates. That is, virtually *all* new jobs in recent years have come from new companies, which include not only small companies but also new branches of huge, multinational organizations.[26] However, small companies still are thought to create a large percentage of new jobs in the United States. The SBA reports that small businesses create 65 percent or more of America's new jobs. Jobs created by small businesses give the United States an economic vitality no other country can claim. However, as we discussed earlier, other countries are also finding new ways to encourage entrepreneurial economic activity.

Innovation. According to Cognetics, Inc., a research firm run by David Birch that traces the employment and sales records of some 9 million companies, new and smaller firms have been responsible for 55 percent of the innovations in 362 different industries and 95 percent of all radical innovations. In addition, fast-growing businesses, which Birch calls *gazelles*, produce twice as many product innovations per employee as do larger firms. Consulting firm CHI Research, which tracks innovation in both small and large firms, found that among 1,270 "highly innovative" firms, the number of small businesses rose from 33 percent in 2000 to 40 percent in 2002. Small firms that file for patents typically produce 13 to 14 times more patents per employee than large patenting firms.[27]

Among the notable products for which small businesses can be credited are WD-40, the jet engine, and the shopping cart. Virtually every new business represents an innovation of some sort, whether a new product or service, how the product is delivered, or how it is made.[28]

Many of today's new products from giant corporations were originated by small companies. Consider the popular Crest Spin Brush from Procter & Gamble. The product was originally created by a tiny start-up. P&G bought the company and brought in the entrepreneurial leaders to head up the new division.[29] Entrepreneurial innovation often spurs larger companies to try new things. The giant greeting card companies Hallmark and American Greetings, for example, now include lines of cards for nontraditional families, pet owners, and culturally diverse consumers, all of which were first developed and marketed by small greeting card makers.[30] Small business innovation keeps U.S. companies competitive, which is especially important in today's global marketplace.

Who Are Entrepreneurs?

The heroes of American business—Henry Ford, Steve Jobs, Sam Walton, Bill Gates, Michael Dell, Oprah Winfrey, Larry Page, and Sergey Brin—are almost always entrepreneurs. Entrepreneurs start with a vision. Often they are unhappy with their current jobs and see an opportunity to bring together the resources needed for a new venture. However, the image of entrepreneurs as bold pioneers probably is overly romantic. A survey of the CEOs of the nation's fastest-growing small firms found that these entrepreneurs could be best characterized as hardworking and practical, with great familiarity with their market and industry.[31] For example, Nancy Rodriguez was a veteran R&D manager at Swift Foods before she started Food Marketing Support Services. Rodriguez started the firm in the mid-1980s when Swift and other big food companies were cutting staff and R&D budgets. Large companies can now take a rough new product idea to Food Marketing, which fully develops the concept, creates prototypes, does taste testing, and so forth. American Pop Corn, which makes Jolly Time Pop Corn, allocated 100 percent of its new-product development dollars to the 20-person firm, which does about $5 million in business a year.[32]

DIVERSITY OF ENTREPRENEURS

Entrepreneurs often have backgrounds and demographic characteristics that distinguish them from other people. Entrepreneurs are more likely to be the firstborn within their families, and their parents are more likely to have been entrepreneurs. Children of immigrants also are more likely to be entrepreneurs.[33] Consider Hector Barreto Jr., whose parents were both Mexican immigrants and ran several successful businesses in Kansas City, Missouri, including a restaurant, an import-export business, and a construction firm. After a four-year stint as an area manager for Miller Brewing Company, Hector moved to California and started Barreto Financial Services. Later, he started another firm to provide technical assistance to small businesses. Barreto's next step was into the head office of the Small Business Administration, where he became the first entrepreneur to lead the government agency.[34]

Entrepreneurship offers opportunities for individuals who may feel blocked in established corporations. Women-owned and minority-owned businesses may be the emerging growth companies of the next decade. In 2005, women owned 6.5 million U.S. businesses that generated $950.6 billion in revenues and employed more than 7 million workers. In Canada as well, women entrepreneurs are thriving. Since 1989, the rate of small businesses started by women in Canada grew 60 percent faster than the growth in the number of small businesses started by men.[35] Statistics for minorities in the United States are also impressive, with minorities owning 4.1 million firms that generated $694 billion in revenues and employed 4.8 million people.[36] The number of new firms launched by minorities is growing about 17 percent a year, with African American businesses growing at a rate of about 26 percent a year. African American males between the ages of 25 and 35 start more businesses than any other group in the country. Moreover, the face of entrepreneurship for the future will be increasingly diverse. When Junior Achievement (an organization that educates young people about business) conducted a poll of teenagers ages 13 to 18, it found a much greater interest among minorities than whites in starting a business, as shown in Exhibit B.4.[37]

EXHIBIT B.4

A Glimpse of Tomorrow's Entrepreneurs

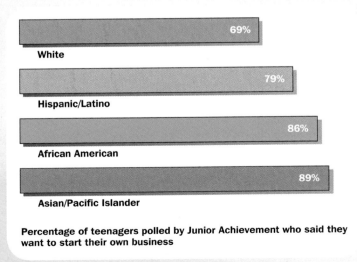

White — 69%

Hispanic/Latino — 79%

African American — 86%

Asian/Pacific Islander — 89%

Percentage of teenagers polled by Junior Achievement who said they want to start their own business

SOURCE: Junior Achievement Survey results reported in Cora Daniels, "Minority Rule," *FSB* (December 2003–January 2004): 65–66.

The types of businesses launched by minority entrepreneurs are also increasingly sophisticated. The traditional minority-owned mom-and-pop retail store or restaurant is being replaced by firms in industries such as financial services, insurance, and media. For example, Pat Winans, an African American who grew up in a Chicago ghetto, started Magna Securities, a successful institutional brokerage firm in New York City, with just $5,000. Ed Chin, a third-generation Chinese American, founded AIS Corporation to offer small and midsized companies the kind of sophisticated insurance packages usually available only to large companies. Chin originally found a niche by catering to the Asian marketplace, but word-of-mouth has helped his company expand beyond that market.[38]

PERSONALITY TRAITS

A number of studies investigated the personality characteristics of entrepreneurs and how they differ from successful managers in established organizations. Some suggest that entrepreneurs in general want something different from life than do traditional managers. Entrepreneurs seem to place high importance on being free to achieve and maximize their potential. Some 40 traits are identified as associated with entrepreneurship, but 6 have special importance.[39] These characteristics are illustrated in Exhibit B.5.

Internal Locus of Control. The task of starting and running a new business requires the belief that you can make things come out the way you want. The entrepreneur not only has a vision but also must be able to plan to achieve that vision and believe it will happen. An internal locus of control is the belief by individuals that their future is within their control and that external forces have little influence. For entrepreneurs, reaching the future is seen as being in the hands of the individual. Many people, however, feel that the world is highly uncertain and that they are unable to make things come out the way they want. An external locus of control is the belief by individuals that their future is not within their control but rather is influenced by external forces. Entrepreneurs are individuals who are convinced they can make the difference between success and failure; hence, they are motivated to take the steps needed to achieve the goal of setting up and running a new business.

High Energy Level. A business start-up requires great effort. Most entrepreneurs report struggle and hardship. They persist and work incredibly hard despite traumas and obstacles. A survey of business owners reported that half worked 60 hours or more per week. Another reported that entrepreneurs worked long hours, but that beyond 70 hours little benefit was gained. The data in Exhibit B.6 show findings from a survey conducted by the National Federation of Independent Business. New business owners work long hours, with only 23 percent working fewer than 50 hours, which is close to a normal workweek for managers in established businesses.

Need to Achieve. Another human quality closely linked to entrepreneurship is the need to achieve, which means that people are motivated to excel and pick situations in which success is likely.[40] People who have high

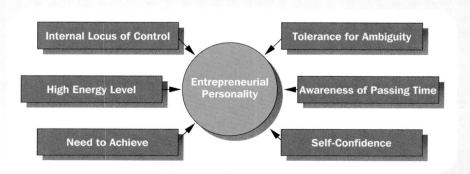

EXHIBIT B.5

Characteristics of Entrepreneurs

SOURCE: Adapted from Charles R. Kuehl and Peggy A. Lambing, *Small Business: Planning and Management* (Ft. Worth: The Dryden Press, 1994): 45.

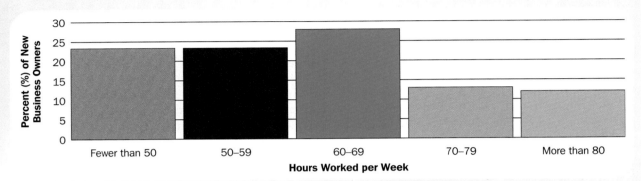

EXHIBIT B.6

Reported Hours
per Week Worked
by Owners of New
Businesses

SOURCE: National Federation of Independent Business. Reported in Mark Robichaux, "Business First, Family Second," *The Wall Street Journal* (May 12, 1989): B1.

achievement needs like to set their own goals, which are moderately difficult. Easy goals present no challenge; unrealistically difficult goals cannot be achieved. Intermediate goals are challenging and provide great satisfaction when achieved. High achievers also like to pursue goals for which they can obtain feedback about their success.

Self-Confidence. People who start and run a business must act decisively. They need confidence about their ability to master the day-to-day tasks of the business. They must feel sure about their ability to win customers, handle the technical details, and keep the business moving. Entrepreneurs also have a general feeling of confidence that they can deal with anything in the future; complex, unanticipated problems can be handled as they arise.

Awareness of Passing Time. Entrepreneurs tend to be impatient; they feel a sense of urgency. They want things to progress as if there is no tomorrow. They want things moving immediately and seldom procrastinate. Entrepreneurs seize the moment.

Tolerance for Ambiguity. Many people need work situations characterized by clear structure, specific instructions, and complete information. Tolerance for ambiguity is the psychological characteristic that allows a person to be untroubled by disorder and uncertainty.

This trait is important, because few situations present more uncertainty than starting a new business. Decisions are made without clear understanding of options or certainty about which option will succeed.

These personality traits and the demographic characteristics discussed earlier offer an insightful but imprecise picture of the entrepreneur. Successful entrepreneurs come in all ages, from all backgrounds, and may have a combination of personality traits. No one should be discouraged from starting a business because he or she doesn't fit a specific profile. One review of small business suggests that the three most important traits of successful entrepreneurs in today's turbulent environment are realism, flexibility, and passion. Even the most realistic entrepreneurs tend to underestimate the difficulties of building a business, so they need flexibility and a passion for their idea to survive the hurdles.[41]

Social Entrepreneurship: An Innovative Approach to Small Business

In today's shifting business and social environment, a new breed of entrepreneur has emerged—the social entrepreneur. Social entrepreneurs are leaders who are committed to both good business and positive social change. They create new business models that meet critical human needs and solve important problems that remain unsolved by current economic and social institutions.[42] Consider John Wood, who quit his job as an executive with Microsoft's Asian operations to start Room to Read, which works collaboratively with villagers in Southeast Asia to build schools and libraries. Earl Martin Phalen founded BELL (Building Educated Leaders for Life) out of his Boston living room in 1992 to provide after-school and summer support services to low-income students in grades K–6. As an African American growing up in the state's foster care system, Bell understood first-hand how the right kind of support can change lives and communities. "To know that [somebody] supported me, and all of a sudden, it took my life from going to jail to going to Yale," he says of his motivation to start BELL. All 20 of the students in BELL's first class went on to college.[43]

Social entrepreneurship combines the creativity, business smarts, passion, and hard work of the traditional entrepreneur with a mission to change the world for the better. One writer referred to this new breed as a cross between Richard Branson, the high-powered CEO of Virgin Airlines, and Mother Teresa, a Catholic nun who dedicated her life to serving the poor.[44] Social entrepreneurs have a primary goal of improving society rather than maximizing profits, but they also emphasize solid business results, high performance standards, and accountability for results. The organizations created by social entrepreneurs may or may not make a profit, but the bottom line for these companies is always social betterment rather than economic return.

Social entrepreneurship is not new, but the phenomenon blossomed over the past 20 or so years. Exact figures for the number of social entrepreneurs are difficult to verify, but estimates number in the tens of thousands working around the world. The innovative organizations created by social entrepreneurs are defying the traditional boundaries between business and welfare.[45] One good illustration is Project Impact, founded by David Green. Project Impact helped start a factory in India that makes inexpensive plastic lenses used in cataract surgery. The factory provides lenses, some at no cost, for 200,000 poor Indians a year. It also makes money—30 percent profit margins in 2003—and has captured 10 percent of the global market for intraocular lenses. Green expanded his approach to other parts of the world, as well as the United

States, and is adding hearing aids to the product mix.[46] As another example, ACCIÓN International is a leader in the *microfinance* industry. ACCIÓN developed a network of lending institutions that give tiny loans and business training to poor people to start modest businesses in developing countries. One Bolivian woman used a $100 loan to start a bread-making business using the mud oven in her one-room home. Six years later, she borrowed $2,800 to expand to five mud ovens and a backyard storefront. ACCIÓN now operates in 23 countries and boasts a 97 percent repayment rate on loans of some $7.6 billion.[47]

Launching an Entrepreneurial Start-Up

Whether one starts a socially oriented company or a traditional for-profit small business, the first step in pursuing an entrepreneurial dream is to come up with a viable idea and then plan like crazy. Once someone has a new idea in mind, a business plan must be drawn and decisions must be made about legal structure, financing, and basic tactics, such as whether to start the business from scratch and whether to pursue international opportunities from the start.

STARTING WITH THE IDEA

To some people, the idea for a new business is the easy part. They do not even consider entrepreneurship until they are inspired by an exciting idea. Other people decide they want to run their own business and set about looking for an idea or opportunity. Exhibit B.7 shows the most important reasons that people start a new business and the source of new business ideas. Note that 37 percent of business founders got their idea from an in-depth understanding of the industry, primarily because of past job experience. Interestingly, almost as many—36 percent—spotted a market niche that wasn't being filled.[48]

The trick for entrepreneurs is to blend their own skills and experience with a need in the marketplace. Acting strictly on one's own skills may produce something no one wants to buy. On the other hand, finding a market niche that one does not have the ability to fill doesn't

Reasons for Starting a Business

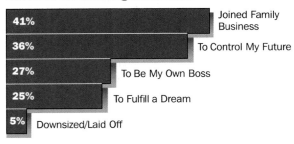

41%	Joined Family Business
36%	To Control My Future
27%	To Be My Own Boss
25%	To Fulfill a Dream
5%	Downsized/Laid Off

Source of New Business Ideas

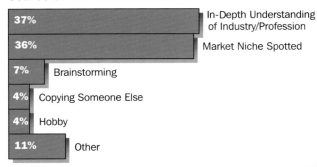

37%	In-Depth Understanding of Industry/Profession
36%	Market Niche Spotted
7%	Brainstorming
4%	Copying Someone Else
4%	Hobby
11%	Other

EXHIBIT B.7

Sources of Entrepreneurial Motivation and New-Business Ideas

SOURCES: "The Rewards," *Inc.* (May 29, 2001): 50–51; and Leslie Brokaw, "How to Start an *Inc.* 500 Company," *Inc.* 500 (1994): 51–65.

work either. Both personal skill and market need typically must be present.

WRITING THE BUSINESS PLAN

Once an entrepreneur is inspired by a new business idea, careful planning is crucial. A business plan is a document specifying the business details prepared by an entrepreneur prior to opening a new business. Planning forces the entrepreneur to carefully think through the issues and problems associated with starting and developing the business. Most entrepreneurs have to borrow money, and a business plan is absolutely critical for persuading lenders and investors to participate in the business. Studies show that small businesses with a carefully thought-out, written business plan are much more likely to succeed than those without one.[49] To attract the interest of venture capitalists or other potential investors, the entrepreneur should keep the plan crisp and compelling.

The details of a business plan may vary, but successful business plans generally share several characteristics:[50]

- Demonstrate a clear, compelling vision that creates an air of excitement.

- Provide clear and realistic financial projections.

- Profile potential customers and the target market.

- Include detailed information about the industry and competitors.

- Provide evidence of an effective entrepreneurial management team.

- Pay attention to good formatting and clear writing.

- Keep the plan short—no more than 50 pages.

- Highlight critical risks that may threaten business success.

- Spell out the sources and uses of start-up funds and operating funds.

- Capture the reader's interest with a killer summary.

The business plan should indicate where the product or service fits into the overall industry and should draw on concepts that will be discussed throughout this book.

CHOOSING A LEGAL STRUCTURE

Before entrepreneurs begin a business, and perhaps again as it expands, they must choose an appropriate legal structure for the company. The three basic choices are proprietorship, partnership, or corporation.

Spotlight on Skills

Helpful Hints for Writing the Business Plan

The Summary
- Make it no more than three pages.
- Summarize the what, how, why, where, and so on.
- Complete this part *after* the finished business plan has been written.

  The summary is the most crucial part of your plan because it must capture the reader's interest.

The Business Description Segment
- List the name of the business.
- Provide a background of the industry with history of the company (if any).
- Describe clearly the potential of the new venture.

The Marketing Segment
- Convince investors that sales projections and competition can be met.
- Use and disclose market studies.
- Identify target market, market position, and market share.
- Evaluate *all* competition and specifically cover why and how you will be better than the competitors.
- Identify all market sources and assistance used for this segment.
- Demonstrate pricing strategy; your price must penetrate and maintain a market share to *produce profits*. Thus the lowest price is *not* necessarily the "best" price.
- Identify your advertising plans with cost estimates to validate the proposed strategy.

The Research, Design, and Development Segment
- Cover the *extent* of and *costs involved* in needed research, testing, or development.
- Explain carefully what has been accomplished *already* (prototype, lab testing, early development).
- Mention any research or technical assistance provided for you.

The Manufacturing Segment
- Provide the advantages of your location (zoning, tax laws, wage rates).
- List the production needs in terms of facilities (plant, storage, office space) and equipment (machinery, furnishings, supplies).
- Describe the access to transportation (for shipping and receiving).
- Explain proximity to your suppliers.
- Mention the availability of labor in your location.
- Provide estimates of manufacturing costs, but be careful because too many entrepreneurs underestimate their costs.

The Management Segment
- Provide résumés of all key people in the management of the venture.
- Carefully describe the legal structure of the venture (sole proprietorship, partnership, or corporation).
- Cover the added assistance (if any) of advisers, consultants, and directors.
- Provide information on how everyone is to be compensated (how much, also).

The Critical Risks Segment
- Discuss potential risks *before* investors point them out. Some examples follow:
- Price cutting by competitors
- Potentially unfavorable industry wide trends
- Design or manufacturing costs in excess of estimates
- Sales projections not achieved
- Product development schedule not met
- Difficulties or long lead times encountered in the procurement of parts or raw materials
- Larger-than-expected innovation and development costs to stay competitive
- Name alternative courses of action.

The Financial Segment
- Provide statements.
- Describe the needed sources for your funds and the uses you intend for the money.
- Provide a budget.
- Create stages of financing for the purpose of allowing evaluation by investors at various points.

The Milestone Schedule Segment
- Provide a timetable or chart to demonstrate when each phase of the venture is to be completed in order to show the relationship of events and provide a deadline for accomplishment.

SOURCE: Donald F. Kuratko, Ray V. Montagno, and Frank J. Sabatine, *The Entrepreneurial Decision* (Muncie, IN: The Midwest Entrepreneurial Education Center, Ball State University, 1997): 45–46. Reprinted with permission.

Sole Proprietorship.

A sole proprietorship is defined as an unincorporated business owned by an individual for profit. Proprietorships make up the majority of businesses in the United States. This form is popular because it is easy to start and has few legal requirements. A proprietor has total ownership and control of the company and can make all decisions without consulting anyone. However, this type of organization also has drawbacks. The owner has unlimited liability for the business, meaning that if someone sues, the owner's personal as well as business assets are at risk. Also, financing can be harder to obtain because business success rests on one person's shoulders.

Partnership.

A partnership is an unincorporated business owned by two or more people. Partnerships, like proprietorships, are relatively easy to start. Two friends may reach an agreement to start a graphic arts company. To avoid misunderstandings and to make sure the business is well planned, it is wise to draw up and sign a formal partnership agreement with the help of an attorney. The agreement specifies how partners are to share responsibility and resources and how they will contribute their expertise. The disadvantages of partnerships are the unlimited liability of the partners and the disagreements that almost always occur among strong-minded people. A poll by *Inc.* magazine illustrated the volatility of partnerships. Fifty-nine percent of respondents considered partnerships a bad business move, citing reasons such as partner problems and conflicts. Partnerships often dissolve within five years. Respondents who liked partnerships pointed to the equality of partners (sharing of workload and emotional and financial burdens) as the key to a successful partnership.[51]

Corporation.

A corporation is an artificial entity created by the state and existing apart from its owners. As a separate legal entity, the corporation is liable for its actions and must pay taxes on its income. Unlike other forms of ownership, the corporation has a legal life of its own; it continues to exist regardless of whether the owners live or die. And the corporation, not the owners, is sued in the case of liability. Thus, continuity and limits on owners' liability are two principal advantages of forming a corporation. For example, a physician can form a corporation so that liability for malpractice will not affect his or her personal assets. The major disadvantage of the corporation is that it is expensive and complex to do the paperwork required to incorporate the business and to keep the records required by law. When proprietorships and partnerships are successful and grow large, they often incorporate to limit liability and to raise funds through the sale of stock to investors.

GETTING FINANCING

Most entrepreneurs are particularly concerned with financing the business. A few types of businesses can still be started with a few thousand dollars, but starting a business usually requires coming up with a significant amount of initial funding. An investment is required to acquire labor and raw materials and perhaps a building and equipment. High-tech businesses, for example, typically need from $50,000 to $500,000 just to get through the first six months, even with the founder drawing no salary.[52] Forrester Research estimates that the total cost to get a business up and running on the Internet ranges from $2 million to $40 million.[53]

Many entrepreneurs rely on their own resources for initial funding, but they often have to mortgage their homes, depend on credit cards, borrow money from a bank, or give part of the business to a venture capitalist.[54] The financing decision initially involves two options—whether to obtain loans that must be repaid (debt financing) or whether to share ownership (equity financing).

Debt Financing.

Borrowing money that has to be repaid at a later date in order to start a business is referred to as debt financing. One common source of debt financing for a start-up is to borrow from family and friends. Increasingly, entrepreneurs are using their personal credit cards as a form of debt financing. Another common source is a bank loan. Banks provide some 25 percent of all financing for small business. Sometimes entrepreneurs can obtain money from a finance company, wealthy individuals, or potential customers. A typical source of funds for businesses with high potential is through angel financing. Angels are wealthy individuals, typically with business experience and contacts, who believe in the idea for the start-up and are willing to invest their personal funds to help the business get started. Significantly, angels also provide advice and assistance as the entrepreneur is developing the company. The entrepreneur wants angels who can make business contacts, help find talented employees, and serve as all-around advisors.

Another form of loan financing is provided by the Small Business Administration (SBA). Staples, which started with one office supply store in Brighton, Massachusetts, in 1986, got its start toward rapid growth with the assistance of SBA financing. Today, Staples is the country's largest operator of office superstores, with more than 1,500 stores and 58,000 employees worldwide.[55] The SBA is especially helpful for people without substantial assets, providing an opportunity for single parents, minority group members, and others with a good idea but who might be considered high-risk by a traditional bank. The percentage of SBA loans to women, Hispanics, African Americans, and Asian Americans increased significantly in recent years.[56]

Equity Financing. Any money invested by owners or by those who purchase stock in a corporation is considered equity funds. Equity financing consists of funds that are invested in exchange for ownership in the company.

A venture capital firm is a group of companies or individuals that invests money in new or expanding businesses for ownership and potential profits. This form of capital is a potential for businesses with high earning and growth possibilities.

Venture capitalists are particularly interested in high-tech businesses such as biotechnology, innovative online ventures, or telecommunications because they have the potential for high rates of return on investment.[57] The venture capital firm Lighthouse Capital Partners, for example, provided some of the early funding for Netflix, the online DVD rental service.[58] Venture capitalists also usually provide assistance, advice, and information to help the entrepreneur prosper. A growing number of minority-owned venture capital firms, such as Provender Capital, founded by African American entrepreneur Fred Terrell, are ensuring that minorities have a fair shot at acquiring equity financing.[59]

TACTICS FOR BECOMING A BUSINESS OWNER

Aspiring entrepreneurs can become business owners in several different ways. They can start a new business from scratch, buy an existing business, or start a franchise. Another popular entrepreneurial tactic is to participate in a business incubator.

Start a New Business. One of the most common ways to become an entrepreneur is to start a new business from scratch. This approach is exciting because the entrepreneur sees a need for a product or service that has not been filled before and then sees the idea or dream become a reality. Ray Petro invested his $50,000 life savings and took out a $25,000 loan to launch Ray's Mountain Bike Indoor Park after learning from other mountain biking enthusiasts of their frustration with not being able to ride during the winter months. Taryn Rose started her shoe company, Taryn Rose International, after searching for stylish shoes that wouldn't destroy her feet while working long hours as an orthopedic surgeon.[60] The advantage of starting a business is the ability to develop and design the business in the entrepreneur's own way. The entrepreneur is solely responsible for its success. A potential disadvantage is the long time it can take to get the business off the ground and make it profitable. The uphill battle is caused by the lack of established clientele and the many mistakes made by someone new to the business. Moreover, no matter how much planning is done, a start-up is risky, with no guarantee that the new idea will work. Some entrepreneurs, especially in high-risk industries, develop partnerships with established companies that can help the new company get established and grow. Others use the technique of outsourcing—having some activities handled by outside contractors—to minimize the costs and risks of doing everything in-house.[61] For example, Philip Chigos and Mary Domenico are building their children's pajama business from the basement of their two-bedroom apartment, using manufacturers in China and Mexico to produce the goods and partnering with a local firm to receive shipments, handle quality control, and distribute finished products.[62]

Buy an Existing Business. Because of the long start-up time and the inevitable mistakes, some entrepreneurs prefer to reduce risk by purchasing an existing business. This direction offers the advantage of a shorter time to get started and an existing track record. The entrepreneur may get a bargain price if the owner wishes to retire or has other family considerations. Moreover, a new business may overwhelm an entrepreneur with the amount of work to be done and procedures to be determined. An established business already has filing systems, a payroll tax system, and other operating procedures. Potential disadvantages are the need to pay for goodwill that the owner believes exists and the possible existence of ill will toward the business. In addition, the company may have bad habits and procedures or outdated technology, which may be why the business is for sale.

Buy a Franchise. Franchising is perhaps the most rapidly growing path to entrepreneurship. The International Franchise Association reports that the country's 320,000 franchise outlets account for about $1 trillion in annual sales.[63] According to some estimates, 1 out of every 12 businesses in the United States is franchised, and a franchise opens every eight minutes of every business day.[64] Franchising is an arrangement by which the owner of a product or service allows others to purchase the right to distribute the product or service with help from the owner. The franchisee invests his or her money and owns the business but does not have to develop a new product, create a new company, or test the market. Franchises exist for weight-loss clinics, pet-sitting services, sports photography, bakeries, janitorial services, auto repair shops, real estate offices, and numerous other types of businesses, in addition to the traditional fast-food outlets. Exhibit B.8 lists five franchise concepts that have been popular in recent years, according to *The Wall Street Journal*. The exhibit lists the type of business, the number of franchisees as of late 2003, and the initial costs. Initial franchise fees can range from $1,000 to $250,000, and that doesn't count the other start-up costs the entrepreneur will have to cover. A study by an economics professor several years ago found that the typical franchise costs $94,886 to open.[65] For a casual restaurant such as Buffalo Wild Wings Grill & Bar, listed in the exhibit, the cost is much higher, $969,500 and up, depending on the restaurant location.

The powerful advantage of a franchise is that management help is provided by the owner. For example, Subway, the second fastest growing franchise in the country, does not want a franchisee to fail. Subway has regional development agents who do the research to find good locations for Subway's sandwich outlets. The Subway franchisor also provides two weeks of training at company headquarters and ongoing operational and marketing support.[66] Franchisors provide an established name and national advertising to stimulate demand for the product or service. Potential disadvantages are the

EXHIBIT B.8

Five Hot Franchise Concepts for Today

Franchise	Type of Business	Number of Outlets	Initial Costs
Curves for Women	Exercise, weight loss centers	5,646	$30,625, not including real estate
Cruise Planners	Selling ocean cruises	389	$2,095–$18,600
Buffalo Wild Wings Grill & Bar	Sports bar	145	$969,500+
Jani-King	Building cleaning, maintenance	7,843	$11,300–$34,100
Comfort Keepers	Nonmedical home care for seniors	386	$39,700–$65,100

SOURCE: Richard Gibson, "Small Business (A Special Report); Where the Buzz Is: Five of the Hottest Franchise Concepts Out There—and Their Chances of Becoming the Next Big Thing," *The Wall Street Journal* (December 15, 2003): R7.

lack of control that occurs when franchisors want every business managed in exactly the same way. In some cases, franchisors require that franchise owners use certain contractors or suppliers that might cost more than others would. In addition, franchises can be expensive, and the high start-up costs are followed with monthly payments to the franchisor that can run from 2 percent to 15 percent of gross sales.[67]

Entrepreneurs who are considering buying a franchise should investigate the company thoroughly. The prospective franchisee is legally entitled to a copy of franchisor disclosure statements, which include information on 20 topics, including litigation and bankruptcy history, identities of the directors and executive officers, financial information, identification of any products the franchisee is required to buy, and from whom those purchases must be made. The entrepreneur also should talk with as many franchise owners as possible, because they are among the best sources of information about how the company really operates.[68] Exhibit B.9 lists some specific questions entrepreneurs should ask about themselves and the company when considering buying a franchise. Answering such questions can improve the chances for a successful career as a franchisee.

Participate in a Business Incubator.

An attractive option for entrepreneurs who want to start a business from scratch is to join a business incubator. A business incubator typically provides shared office space, management support services, and management and legal advice to entrepreneurs. Incubators also give entrepreneurs a chance to share information with one another about local business, financial aid, and market opportunities. A recent innovation is the *virtual incubator,* which does not require that people set up on-site. These virtual organizations connect entrepreneurs with a wide range of experts and mentors and offer lower overhead and cost savings for cash-strapped small business owners. Christie Stone, co-founder of Ticobeans, a coffee distributor in New Orleans, likes the virtual approach because it gives her access to top-notch advice while allowing her to keep her office near her inventory.[69]

The concept of business incubators arose about two decades ago to nurture start-up companies. Business incubators have become a significant segment of the small business economy, with approximately 1,100 in operation in the United States in 2005.[70] During the dot-com boom, a tremendous jump in the number of

EXHIBIT B.9

Sample Questions for Choosing a Franchise

Questions about the Entrepreneur	Questions about the Franchisor	Before Signing the Dotted Line
1. Will I enjoy the day-to-day work of the business?	1. What assistance does the company provide in terms of selection of location, setup costs, and securing credit; day-to-day technical assistance; marketing; and ongoing training and development?	1. Do I understand the risks associated with this business, and am I willing to assume them?
2. Do my background, experience, and goals make this opportunity a good choice for me?	2. How long does it take the typical franchise owner to start making a profit?	2. Have I had an advisor review the disclosure documents and franchise agreement?
3. Am I willing to work within the rules and guidelines established by the franchisor?	3. How many franchises changed ownership within the past year, and why?	3. Do I understand the contract?

SOURCES: Based on Thomas Love, "The Perfect Franchisee," Nation's Business (April 1998): 59–65; and Roberta Maynard, "Choosing a Franchise," Nation's Business (October 1996): 56–63.

for-profit incubators ended as many of them went out of business when the tech economy crashed.[71] The incubators that are thriving are primarily not-for-profits and those that cater to niches or focus on helping women or minority entrepreneurs. These incubators include those run by government agencies and universities to boost the viability of small business and spur job creation. The great value of an incubator is the expertise of a mentor, who serves as advisor, role model, and cheerleader, and ready access to a team of lawyers, accountants, and other advisors. Incubators also give budding entrepreneurs a chance to network and learn from one another.[72] Incubators are an important part of the international entrepreneurial landscape, as well. For example, Harmony is a global network support system for business incubators. Harmony was started in 1998—with partners in Germany, France, Spain, Finland, Switzerland, Australia, Japan, and the United States—to provide training and support for both new and established incubators worldwide, enabling them to better serve clients and improve the success of small businesses.[73]

Managing a Growing Business

Once an entrepreneurial business is up and running, how does the owner manage it? Often the traits of self-confidence, creativity, and internal locus of control lead to financial and personal grief as the enterprise grows. A hands-on entrepreneur who gave birth to the organization loves perfecting every detail. But after the start-up, continued growth requires a shift in management style. Those who fail to adjust to a growing business can be the cause of the problems rather than the solution.[74] In this section, we look at the stages through which entrepreneurial companies move and then consider how managers should carry out their planning, organizing, leading, and controlling.

STAGES OF GROWTH

Entrepreneurial businesses go through distinct stages of growth, with each stage requiring different management skills. The five stages are illustrated in Exhibit B.10.

EXHIBIT B.10

Five Stages of Growth for an Entrepreneurial Company

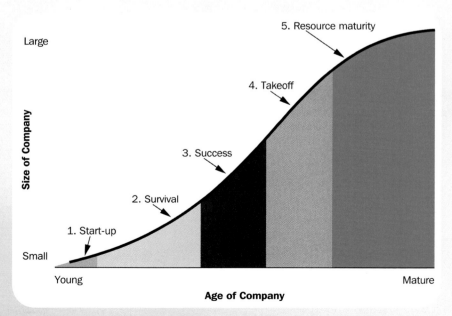

SOURCE: Based on Neil C. Churchill and Virginia L. Lewis, "The Five Stages of Small Business Growth," *Harvard Business Review* (May–June 1993): 30–50.

1. *Start-up.* In this stage, the main problems are producing the product or service and obtaining customers. Several key issues facing managers are: Can we get enough customers? Will we survive? Do we have enough money? Burt's Bees was in the start-up stage when Roxanne Quimby was hand-making candles and personal care products from the beeswax of Burt Shavitz's bees and selling them at craft fairs in Maine.

2. *Survival.* At this stage, the business demonstrates that it is a workable business entity. It produces a product or service and has sufficient customers. Concerns here involve with finances—generating sufficient cash flow to run the business and making sure revenues exceed expenses. The organization will grow in size and profitability during this period. Burt's Bees reached $3 million in sales by 1993, and Quimby moved the business from Maine to North Carolina to take advantage of state policies that helped her keep costs in line.

3. *Success.* At this point, the company is solidly based and profitable. Systems and procedures are in place to allow the owner to slow down if desired. The owner can stay involved or consider turning the business over to professional managers. Quimby chose to stay closely involved with Burt's Bees, admitting that she's a bit of a control freak about the business.

4. *Takeoff.* Here the key problem is how to grow rapidly and finance that growth. The owner must learn to delegate, and the company must find sufficient capital to invest in major growth. This period is pivotal in an entrepreneurial company's life. Properly managed, the company can become a big business. However, another problem for companies at this stage is how to maintain the advantages of "smallness" as the company grows. In 2003, Quimby sold 80 percent of Burt's Bees to AEA Investors, a private equity firm, for more than $175 million. She continued as CEO and focuses on continuing to grow the business.

5. *Resource maturity.* At this stage, the company's substantial financial gains may come at the cost of losing its advantages of small size, including flexibility and the entrepreneurial spirit. A company in this stage has the staff and financial resources to begin acting like a mature company with detailed planning and control systems.

PLANNING

In the early start-up stage, formal planning tends to be nonexistent except for the business plan described earlier. The primary goal is simply to remain alive. As the organization grows, formal planning usually is not instituted until the success stage. Recall that planning means defining goals and deciding on the tasks and use of resources needed to attain them. Chapters 5 and 6 described how entrepreneurs can define goals and implement strategies and plans to meet them. It is important that entrepreneurs view their original business plan as a living document that evolves as the company grows or the market changes.

One planning concern for today's small businesses is the need to be Web-savvy. For many small companies today, their Web operations are just as critical as traditional warehouse management or customer service operations. The growing importance of e-business means entrepreneurs have to plan and allocate resources for Internet operations from the beginning and grow those plans as the company grows. Of the small companies that have Web sites, more than half say the site has broken even or paid for itself in greater efficiency, improved customer relationships, or increased business.[75]

ORGANIZING

In the first two stages of growth, the organization's structure is typically informal with all employees reporting to the owner. At about stage 3—success—functional managers often are hired to take over duties performed by the owner. A functional organization structure will begin to evolve with managers in charge of finance, manufacturing, and marketing. Another organizational approach is to use outsourcing, as described earlier. Method, a company launched by two 20-something entrepreneurs to develop a line of nontoxic cleaning products in fresh scents and stylish packaging, contracted with an industrial designer for the unique dish soap bottle and uses contract manufacturers in every region of the country to rapidly make products and get them to stores.[76]

During the latter stages of entrepreneurial growth, managers must learn to delegate and decentralize authority. If the business has multiple product lines, the owner may consider creating teams or divisions responsible for each line. The organization must hire competent managers and have sufficient management talent to handle fast growth and eliminate problems caused by increasing size. As an organization grows, it might also be characterized by greater use of rules, procedures, and written job descriptions. For example, Tara Cronbaugh started a small coffeehouse in a college town, but its success quickly led to the opening of three additional houses. With the rapid growth, Cronbaugh found that she needed a way to ensure consistency across operations. She put together an operations manual with detailed rules, procedures, and job descriptions so managers and employees at each coffeehouse would be following the same pattern.[77] Chapters 7, 8, and 9 discussed organizing in detail.

LEADING

The driving force in the early stages of development is the leader's vision. This vision, combined with the leader's personality, shapes corporate culture. The leader can signal cultural values of service, efficiency, quality, or ethics. Often entrepreneurs do not have good people skills but do have excellent task skills in either manufacturing or marketing. By the success stage of growth, the owner must either learn to motivate employees or bring in managers who can. Rapid takeoff is not likely to happen without employee cooperation. Stepping from the self-absorption of the early days of a company to the more active communication necessary for growth can be tricky for entrepreneurs. Stan and Bob Lee built a successful business making spare parts for the corrugated box industry, but as the company grew, the two entrepreneurs had trouble shifting to more active leadership and communication. One consultant joked that the two seemed to fear that sales might actually increase if they listened to their staff.[78] The president of Foreign Candy Company of Hull, Iowa, saw his company grow rapidly when he concentrated more on employee needs and less on financial results. He made an effort to communicate with employees, conducted surveys to learn how they were feeling about the company, and found ways to involve them in decision making. His shift in leadership style allowed the company to enter the takeoff stage with the right corporate culture and employee attitudes to sustain rapid growth.

Leadership also is important because many small firms have a hard time hiring qualified employees. Labor shortages often hurt small firms that grow rapidly. A healthy corporate culture can help attract and retain good people.[79] You learned more about leadership in Chapters 10 through 14.

CONTROLLING

Financial control is important in each stage of the entrepreneurial firm's growth. In the initial stages, control is exercised by simple accounting records and by personal supervision. By stage 3—success—operational budgets are in place, and the owner should start implementing more structured control systems. During the takeoff stage, the company will need to make greater use of budgets and standard cost systems and use computer systems to provide statistical reports. These control techniques will become more sophisticated during the resource maturity stage.

As Amazon.com grew and expanded internationally, for example, entrepreneur and CEO Jeff Bezos needed increasingly sophisticated control mechanisms. Bezos hired a computer systems expert to develop a system to track and control all of the company's operations.[80] Chapter 15 discussed controlling in detail.

Appendix Summary

This appendix explored entrepreneurship and small business management. Entrepreneurs start new businesses, and entrepreneurship plays an important role in the economy by stimulating job creation, innovation, and opportunities for minorities and women. An entrepreneurial personality includes the traits of internal locus of control, high energy level, need to achieve, tolerance for ambiguity, awareness of passing time, and self-confidence. A new breed of entrepreneur, the *social entrepreneur*, is committed to both good business and positive social change. The organizations started by social entrepreneurs sometimes blur the line between business and social activism.

The U.S. economy is ripe for entrepreneurial ventures, but entrepreneurial activity is also booming in other countries, with some of the highest rates in developing nations. Starting an entrepreneurial firm requires a new-business idea. At that point a comprehensive business plan should be developed and decisions made about legal structure and financing. Tactical decisions for the new venture include whether to start, buy, or franchise, and whether to participate in a business incubator.

After a business is started, it generally proceeds through five stages of growth: start-up, survival, success, takeoff, and resource maturity. The management functions of planning, organizing, leading, and controlling should be tailored to each stage of growth.

Appendix C

Solutions to Chapter Three's Manager's Workbook

1. China (1.3 b)

   India (1.0 b)

   US (278 m)

   Indonesia (228 m)

   Brazil (174 m)

   Russia (145 m)

2. 1. Mandarin (15.0%)

   2. English (5.5%)

   3. Spanish (5.0%)

   4. Arabic (3.3%)

   5. Hindi (3.2%)

   6. Bengali (3.0%)

3. c. 6,800

4. b. 193

5. 300%

6. 77 million

7. a. decreased from 980 million in 1970 to 780 million in 2000.

8. c. $17 trillion

9. c. 2/3

10. 66%

11. 50%

12. 1/10

13. b. 20%

14. 35%

15. Mexico City

16. 42 trillion

17. 19,000% from 376,000 to 73.4 million

18. 27.9 percent in South Africa, 25 percent in Zimbabwe, 39 percent in Botswana. The greatest decrease was in Uganda, which went from 30% in 1992 to 2007's 4.1%, because of aggressive public health education programs.

19. 4.98 billion

20. b. Cleaning their teeth with the tap running is the right answer. The United Nations says that in the world's 40 poorest countries, people have access to only an average of 30 liters or less per day each. The absolute minimum for well-being is considered to be 50 liters per day.

21. c. Poverty is the main reason for girls not attending school. In many communities daughters are valued less than sons, and their education consequently is considered a waste of time and money.

22. a. The United States gives the least aid as a proportion of GDP. Although the United States gives more foreign aid in absolute terms than any other country, it amounts to only 0.1% of its GDP. The US gives $11 billion a year in aid and announced in 2006 an increase of $5 billion over the next three years.

23. ___60___ would be Asian

   ___80___ would be non-white

   ___67___ would be non-Christian

   ___25___ would live in substandard housing

   ___17___ would be illiterate

   ___2___ would have a college education

   ___4___ would own a computer

24. False. All regions of the world are going through a profound transformation. As mortality rates and fertility rates have fallen and life expectancy has increased, the population is aging.

25. b. 25%

26. a. Canada

27. c. 1 billion

28. c. Tokyo

29. c. $20 billion

Glossary

360-degree feedback a process that uses multiple raters, including self-rating, to appraise employee performance and guide development.

accountability the fact that the people with authority and responsibility are subject to reporting and justifying task outcomes to those above them in the chain of command.

achievement culture a results-oriented culture that values competitiveness, personal initiative, and achievement.

adaptability culture a culture characterized by values that support the company's ability to interpret and translate signals from the environment into new behavior responses.

adjourning the stage of team development in which members prepare for the team's disbandment.

administrative model a decision-making model that describes how managers actually make decisions in situations characterized by nonprogrammed decisions, uncertainty, and ambiguity.

administrative principles the design and functioning of the organization as a whole.

affirmative action a policy requiring employers to take positive steps to guarantee equal employment opportunities for people within protected groups.

ambiguity a condition in which the goals to be achieved or the problem to be solved is unclear, alternatives are difficult to define, and information about outcomes is unavailable.

application form a device for collecting information about an applicant's education, previous job experience, and other background characteristics.

assessment center a technique for selecting individuals with high managerial potential based on their performance on a series of simulated managerial tasks.

attitude a cognitive and affective evaluation that predisposes a person to act in a certain way.

attributions judgments about what caused a person's behavior—either characteristics of the person or of the situation.

authoritarianism the belief that power and status differences should exist within the organization.

authority the formal and legitimate right of a manager to make decisions, issue orders, and allocate resources to achieve organizationally desired outcomes.

B2B marketplace an electronic marketplace set up by an intermediary where buyers and sellers meet.

balance sheet a financial statement that shows the firm's financial position with respect to assets and liabilities at a specific point in time.

balanced scorecard a comprehensive management control system that balances traditional financial measures with measures of customer service, internal business processes, and the organization's capacity for learning and growth.

bargaining zone the range between one party's minimum reservation point (the point beyond which the party is willing to accept a deal) and the other party's maximum reservation point.

BATNA the "best alternative to a negotiated agreement"; a previously determined choice of what a party will do if an acceptable agreement cannot be reached through negotiation.

behavior modification the set of techniques by which reinforcement theory is used to modify human behavior.

behavioral sciences approach a subfield of the humanistic management perspective that applies social science in an organizational context drawing from economics, psychology and other disciplines.

behaviorally anchored rating scale (BARS) a rating technique that relates an employee's performance to specific job-related incidents.

benchmarking the continuous process of measuring products, services, and practices against major competitors or industry leaders.

Big Five personality factors dimensions that describe an individual's extroversion, agreeableness, conscientiousness, emotional stability, and openness to experience.

blog web log that allows individuals to post opinions and ideas.

bottom-up budgeting a budgeting process in which lower-level managers budget their departments' resource needs and pass them up to top management for approval.

boundary-spanning roles roles assumed by people and/or departments that link and coordinate the organization with key elements in the external environment.

bounded rationality the concept that people have the time and cognitive ability to process only a limited amount of information on which to base decisions.

brainstorming a technique that uses a face-to-face group to spontaneously suggest a broad range of alternatives for decision making.

bureaucratic control the use of rules, policies, hierarchy of authority, reward systems, and other formal devices to influence employee behavior and assess performance.

business-to-business e-commerce (B2B) electronic transactions between organizations.

business-to-consumer e-commerce (B2C) sell products and services to consumers over the Internet.

centralization the location of decision authority near top organizational levels.

centralized network a team communication structure in which team members communicate through a single individual to solve problems or make decisions.

ceremony a planned activity at a special event that is conducted for the benefit of an audience.

certainty the situation in which all the information the decision maker needs is fully available.

chain of command an unbroken line of authority that links all individuals in the organization and specifies who reports to whom.

change agent an OD specialist who contracts with an organization to facilitate change.

changing the intervention stage of organization development in which individuals experiment with new workplace behavior.

channel the carrier of a communication.

channel richness the amount of information that can be transmitted during a communication episode.

charismatic leader a leader who has the ability to motivate subordinates to transcend their expected performance.

chief ethics officer a company executive who oversees ethics and legal compliance.

classical model a decision-making model based on the assumption that managers should make logical decisions that will be in the organization's best economic interests.

classical perspective a management perspective that emerged during the nineteenth and early twentieth centuries that emphasized a rational, scientific approach to the study of management and sought to make organizations efficient operating machines.

coalition an informal alliance among managers who support a specific goal.

code of ethics a formal statement of the organization's values regarding ethics and social issues.

coercive power power that stems from the authority to punish or recommend punishment.

cognitive dissonance a condition in which two attitudes or a behavior and an attitude conflict.

collaboration cooperating with other firms rather than competing with them.

collaborative relationships staying connected to employees and customers.

collectivism a preference for a tightly knit social framework in which individuals look after one another, and organizations protect their members' interests.

committee a long-lasting, sometimes permanent team in the organization structure created to deal with tasks that recur regularly.

communication the process by which information is exchanged and understood by two or more people, usually with the intent to motivate or influence behavior.

communication apprehension an individual's level of fear or anxiety associated with interpersonal communications.

compensation monetary payments (wages, salaries) and nonmonetary goods/commodities (benefits, vacations) used to reward employees.

compensatory justice the concept that individuals should be compensated for the cost of their injuries by the party responsible and also that individuals should not be held responsible for matters over which they have no control.

competitive advantage what sets the organization apart from others and provides it with a distinctive edge for meeting customer needs in the marketplace.

competitors other organizations in the same industry or type of business that provide goods or services to the same set of customers.

concurrent control control that consists of monitoring ongoing activities to ensure that they are consistent with standards.

conflict antagonistic interaction in which one party attempts to thwart the intentions or goals of another.

consideration a type of behavior that describes the extent to which the leader is sensitive to subordinates, respects their ideas and feelings, and establishes mutual trust.

consistency culture a culture that values and rewards a methodical, rational, orderly way of doing things.

consumer-to-consumer (C2C) an Internet-based business acts as an intermediary between and among consumers.

content theories a group of theories that emphasize the needs that motivate people.

contingency one thing depends on other things, and for organizations to be effective, there must be a "goodness of fit" between their structure and the conditions in their external environment.

contingency approach a model of leadership that describes the relationship between leadership styles and specific organizational situations.

contingency plans plans that define company responses to specific situations, such as emergencies, setbacks, or unexpected conditions.

contingent workers people who work for an organization but not on a permanent or full-time basis, including temporary placements, contracted professionals, or leased employees.

continuous improvement the implementation of a large number of small, incremental improvements in all areas of the organization on an ongoing basis.

continuous process production a type of technology involving mechanization of the entire work flow and nonstop production.

continuous reinforcement schedule a schedule in which every occurrence of the desired behavior is reinforced.

controlling the management function concerned with monitoring employees' activities, keeping the organization on track toward its goals, and making corrections as needed.

coordination the quality of collaboration across departments.

core competence something the organization does especially well in comparison to its competitors.

corporate governance the system of governing an organization so the interests of corporate owners are protected.

corporate social responsibility the obligation of organization management to make decisions and take actions that will enhance the welfare and interests of society as well as the organization.

corporate university an in-house training and education facility that offers broad-based learning opportunities for employees.

cost leadership strategy an aggressive attempt to seek efficient facilities, pursue cost reductions, and use tight cost controls to produce products more efficiently than competitors.

countertrade the barter of products for other products rather than their sale for currency.

courage the ability to step forward through fear and act on one's values and conscience.

creativity the generation of novel ideas that might meet perceived needs or offer opportunities for the organization.

crisis management plan (CMP) a detailed, written plan that specifies the steps to be taken, and by whom, if a crisis arises.

cross-functional teams a group of employees from various functional departments that meet as a team to resolve mutual problems.

cultural intelligence (CQ) a person's ability to use reasoning and observation skills to interpret unfamiliar gestures and situations and devise appropriate behavioral responses.

cultural leader a manager who uses signals and symbols to influence corporate culture.

culture the set of key values, beliefs, understandings, and norms that members of an organization share.

culture change a major shift in the norms, values, attitudes, and mindset of the entire organization.

culture shock feelings of confusion, disorientation, and anxiety that result from being immersed in a foreign culture.

customer relationship management (CRM) systems that collect and manage large amounts of data about customers and make them available to employees,

enabling better decision making and superior customer service.

customer relationship management (CRM) systems systems that help companies track customers' interactions with the firm and allow employees to call up information on past transactions.

customers people and organizations in the environment who acquire goods or services from the organization.

cycle time the steps taken to complete a company process.

data raw, unsummarized, and unanalyzed facts and figures.

decentralization the location of decision authority near lower organizational levels.

decentralized control the use of organizational culture, group norms, and a focus on goals, rather than rules and procedures, to foster compliance with organizational goals.

decentralized network a team communication structure in which team members freely communicate with one another and arrive at decisions together.

decision a choice made from available alternatives.

decision making the process of identifying problems and opportunities and then resolving them.

decision styles differences among people with respect to how they perceive problems and make decisions.

decode to translate the symbols used in a message for the purpose of interpreting its meaning.

delegation the process managers use to transfer authority and responsibility to positions below them in the hierarchy.

departmentalization the basis on which individuals are grouped into departments and departments into the total organization.

descriptive an approach that describes how managers actually make decisions rather than how they should.

devil's advocate a decision-making technique in which an individual is assigned the role of challenging the assumptions and assertions made by the group to prevent premature consensus.

diagnosis the step in the decision-making process in which managers analyze underlying causal factors associated with the decision situation.

dialogue a group communication process aimed at creating a culture based on collaboration, fluidity, trust, and commitment to shared goals.

differentiation strategy an attempt to distinguish the firm's products or services from others in the industry.

digital technology technology characterized by use of the Internet and other digital processes to conduct or support business operations.

direct investing an entry strategy in which the organization is involved in managing its production facilities in a foreign country.

discretionary responsibility organizational responsibility that is voluntary and guided by the organization's desire to make social contributions not mandated by economics, law, or ethics.

discrimination the hiring or promoting of applicants based on criteria that are not job relevant.

distributive justice the concept that different treatment of people should not be based on arbitrary characteristics. In the case of substantive differences, people should be treated differently in proportion to the differences among them.

distributive negotiation a competitive and adversarial negotiation approach in which each party strives to get as much as it can, usually at the expense of the other party.

diversity ethnically and racially generational

divisional structure an organization structure in which departments are grouped based on similar organizational outputs.

downsizing intentional, planned reduction in the size of a company's workforce.

downward communication messages sent from top management down to subordinates.

dual role a role in which the individual both contributes to the team's task and supports members' emotional needs.

$E \rightarrow P$ expectancy expectancy that putting effort into a given task will lead to high performance.

e-business any business that takes place by digital processes over a computer network rather than in physical space.

e-business the work an organization does by using electronic linkages (including the Internet) with customers, partners, suppliers, employees, or other key constituents.

e-commerce business exchanges or transactions that occur electronically.

e-commerce refers specifically to business exchanges or transactions that occur electronically.

economic dimension the dimension of the general environment representing the overall economic health of the country or region in which the organization operates.

economic forces the availability, production, and distribution of resources in a society.

economic value-added (EVA) a control system that measures performance in terms of after-tax profits minus the cost of capital invested in tangible assets.

effectiveness the extent to which the organization achieves a stated goal.

efficiency the use of minimal resources—raw materials, money, and people—to produce a desired volume of output.

electronic brainstorming bringing people together in an interactive group over a computer network to suggest alternatives; sometimes called *brainwriting*.

electronic data interchange (EDI) a network that links the computer systems of buyers and sellers to allow the transmission of structured data primarily for ordering, distribution, and payables and receivables.

employment test a written or computer-based test designed to measure a particular attribute such as intelligence or aptitude.

empowerment the delegation of power and authority to subordinates.

empowerment unleashing the power and creativity of employees by giving them the freedom, resources, information, and skills to make decisions and perform effectively.

encode to select symbols with which to compose a message.

enterprise resource planning (ERP) systems that weave together all of a company's major business functions, such as order processing, product design, purchasing, inventory, manufacturing, distribution, human resources, receipt of payments, and forecasting of future demand.

equity theory a process theory that focuses on individuals' perceptions of how fairly they are treated relative to others.

equity a situation that exists when the ratio of one person's outcomes to inputs equals that of another's.

ERG theory a modification of the needs hierarchy theory that proposes three categories of needs: existence, relatedness, and growth.

escalating commitment continuing to invest time and resources in a failing decision.

ethical dilemma a situation that arises when all alternative choices or behaviors are deemed undesirable because of potentially negative consequences, making it difficult to distinguish right from wrong.

ethics the code of moral principles and values that governs the behaviors of a person or group with respect to what is right or wrong.

ethics committee a group of executives assigned to oversee the organization's ethics by ruling on questionable issues and disciplining violators.

ethics training training programs to help employees deal with ethical questions and values.

ethnocentrism a cultural attitude marked by the tendency to regard one's own culture as superior to others.

ethnocentrism the belief that one's own group or subculture is inherently superior to other groups or cultures.

ethnorelativism the belief that groups and subcultures are inherently equal.

euro a single European currency that has replaced the currencies of 12 European nations.

event-driven planning evolutionary planning that responds to the current reality of what the environment and the marketplace demand.

exchange rate the rate at which one country's currency is exchanged for another country's.

exit interview an interview conducted with departing employees to determine the reasons for their termination.

expectancy theory a process theory that proposes that motivation depends on individuals' expectations about their ability to perform tasks and receive desired rewards.

expert power power that stems from special knowledge of or skill in the tasks performed by subordinates.

exporting an entry strategy in which the organization maintains its production facilities within its home country and transfers its products for sale in foreign countries.

extranet an external communications system that uses the Internet and is shared by two or more organizations.

extrinsic reward a reward given by another person.

fast-cycle team a multifunctional team that is provided with high levels of resources and empowerment to accomplish an accelerated product development project.

feedback a response by the receiver to the sender's communication.

feedback control control that focuses on the organization's outputs; also called *postaction* or *output control.*

feedforward control control that focuses on human, material, and financial resources flowing into the organization; also called *preliminary* or *preventive* control.

femininity a cultural preference for relationships, cooperation, group decision making, and quality of life.

first-line managers who are at the first or second management level and are directly responsible for the production of goods and services.

flat structure a management structure characterized by an overall broad span of control and relatively few hierarchical levels.

focus strategy concentration on a specific regional market or buyer group.

force-field analysis the process of determining which forces drive and which resist a proposed change.

formal communication channel a communication channel that flows within the chain of command or task responsibility defined by the organization.

formal team a team created by the organization as part of the formal organization structure.

forming the stage of team development characterized by orientation and acquaintance.

franchising a form of licensing in which an organization provides its foreign franchisees with a complete package of materials and services.

free rider a person who benefits from team membership but does not make a proportionate contribution to the team's work.

frustration-regression principle the idea that failure to meet a high-order need may cause a regression to an already satisfied lower-order need.

functional structure the grouping of positions into departments based on similar skills, expertise, and resource use.

fundamental attribution error the tendency to underestimate the influence of external factors on another's behavior and to overestimate the influence of internal factors.

general environment the layer of the external environment that affects the organization indirectly.

glass ceiling an invisible barrier that separates women and minorities from top management positions.

global outsourcing engaging in the international division of labor so as to obtain the cheapest sources of labor and supplies regardless of country; also called *global sourcing.*

global team a work team made up of members of different nationalities whose activities span multiple countries; may operate as a virtual team or meet face-to-face.

goal a desired future state that the organization attempts to realize.

goal-setting theory a motivation theory in which specific, challenging goals increase motivation and performance when the goals are accepted by subordinates and these subordinates receive feedback to indicate their progress toward goal achievement.

grapevine an informal, person-to-person communication network of employees that is not officially sanctioned by the organization.

groupthink the tendency for people to be so committed to a cohesive team that they are reluctant to express contrary opinions.

halo effect a type of rating error that occurs when an employee receives the same rating on all dimensions regardless of his or her performance on individual ones.

halo effect an overall impression of a person or situation based on one characteristic, either favorable or unfavorable.

hero a figure who exemplifies the deeds, character, and attributes of a strong corporate culture.

hierarchy of needs theory a content theory that proposes that people are motivated by five categories of needs—physiological, safety, belongingness, esteem, and self-actualization—that exist in a hierarchical order.

high-performance culture a culture based on a solid organizational mission or purpose in which adaptive values guide decisions and business practices and encourage individual employee ownership of both bottom-line results and the organization's cultural backbone.

horizontal communication the lateral or diagonal exchange of messages among peers or co-workers.

horizontal linkage model an approach to product change that emphasizes shared development of innovations among several departments.

horizontal team a formal team composed of employees from about the same hierarchical level but from different areas of expertise.

human capital the economic value of the knowledge, experience, skills, and capabilities of employees.

human resource information system an integrated computer system designed to provide data and information used in HR planning and decision making.

human resource management (HRM) activities undertaken to attract, develop, and maintain an effective workforce within an organization.

human resource planning the forecasting of HR needs and the projected matching of individuals with expected job vacancies.

human resources perspective combines prescriptions for design of job tasks with theories of motivation.

human skills the ability to work with and through other people and to work effectively as a group member.

humility being unpretentious and modest rather than arrogant and prideful.

hygiene factors factors that involve the presence or absence of job dissatisfiers, including working conditions, pay, company policies, and interpersonal relationships.

idea champion a person who sees the need for and champions productive change within the organization.

idea incubator an in-house program that provides a safe harbor where ideas from employees throughout the organization can be developed without interference from company bureaucracy or politics.

implementation the step in the decision-making process that involves using managerial, administrative, and persuasive abilities to translate the chosen alternative into action.

income statement a financial statement that summarizes the firm's financial performance for a given time interval; sometimes called a profit-and-loss statement.

individualism a preference for a loosely knit social framework in which individuals are expected to take care of themselves.

individualism approach the ethical concept that acts are moral when they promote the individual's best long-term interests, which ultimately leads to the greater good.

influence the effect a person's actions have on the attitudes, values, beliefs, or behavior of others.

information data that have been converted into a meaningful and useful context for the receiver.

information technology (IT) the hardware, software, telecommunications, database management, and other technologies used to store, process, and distribute information.

infrastructure a country's physical facilities that support economic activities.

initiating structure a type of leader behavior that describes the extent to which the leader is task oriented and directs subordinate work activities toward goal attainment.

instant messaging (IM) electronic communication that allows users to see who is connected to a network and share information instantly.

integrative negotiation a collaborative approach to negotiation that is based on a win-win assumption, whereby the parties want to come up with a creative solution that benefits both sides of the conflict.

interactive leadership a leadership style characterized by values such as inclusion, collaboration, relationship building, and caring.

internal environment the environment that includes the elements within the organization's boundaries.

international dimension the portion of the external environment that represents events originating in foreign countries, as well as opportunities for U.S. companies in other countries.

international management the management of business operations conducted in more than one country.

Internet a global collection of computer networks linked together for the exchange of data and information.

intranet an internal communications system that uses the technol-ogy and standards of the Internet but is accessible only to people within the organization.

intrinsic reward the satisfaction received in the process of performing an action.

intuition the immediate comprehension of a decision situation based on past experience but without conscious thought.

involvement culture a culture that places high value on meeting the needs of employees and values cooperation and equality.

ISO certification certification based on a set of international standards for quality management, setting uniform guidelines for processes to ensure that products conform to customer requirements.

job analysis the systematic process of gathering and interpreting information about the essential duties, tasks, and responsibilities of a job.

job characteristics model a model of job design that comprises core job dimensions, critical psychological states, and employee growth-need strength.

job description a concise summary of the specific tasks and responsibilities of a particular job.

job design the application of motivational theories to the structure of work for improving productivity and satisfaction.

job enlargement a job design that combines a series of tasks into one new, broader job to give employees variety and challenge.

job enrichment a job design that incorporates achievement, recognition, and other high-level motivators into the work.

job evaluation the process of determining the value of jobs within an organization through an examination of job content.

job rotation a job design that systematically moves employees from one job to another to provide them with variety and stimulation.

job satisfaction a positive attitude toward one's job.

job simplification a job design whose purpose is to improve task efficiency by reducing the number of tasks a single person must do.

job specification an outline of the knowledge, skills, education, and physical abilities needed to adequately perform a job.

joint venture a strategic alliance or program by two or more organizations.

joint ventures separate entities created with two or more active firms as sponsors, and the organizations share the associated risks and costs.

justice approach the ethical concept that moral decisions must be based on standards of equity, fairness, and impartiality.

knowledge management efforts to systematically find, organize, and make available a company's intellectual capital and to foster a culture of continuous learning and knowledge sharing so that a company's activities build on what is already known.

knowledge management the process of systematically gathering knowledge, making it widely available throughout the organization, and fostering a culture of learning.

knowledge management portal a single point of access for employees to multiple sources of information that provides personalized access on the corporate intranet.

labor market the people available for hire by the organization.

large-group intervention an approach that brings together participants from all parts of the organization (and may include key outside stakeholders as well) to discuss problems or opportunities and plan for major change.

law of effect the assumption that positively reinforced behavior tends to be repeated, and unreinforced or negatively reinforced behavior tends to be inhibited.

leadership the ability to influence people to adopt the new behaviors needed for strategy implementation.

leadership the ability to influence people toward the attainment of organizational goals.

leadership grid a two-dimensional leadership theory that measures the leader's concern for people and for production.

leading the management function that involves the use of influence to motivate employees to achieve the organization's goals.

lean manufacturing manufacturing process using highly trained employees at every stage of the production process to cut waste and improve quality.

learning a change in behavior or performance that occurs as the result of experience.

learning organization an organizational climate that values experimentation and risk taking, applies current technology, tolerates mistakes and failure, and rewards nontraditional thinking and the sharing of knowledge.

legal-political dimension the dimension of the general environment that includes federal, state, and local government regulations and political activities designed to influence company behavior.

legitimate power power that stems from a formal management position in an organization and the authority granted to it.

licensing an entry strategy in which an organization in one country makes certain resources available to companies in another to be able to participate in the production and sale of its products abroad.

line authority a form of authority in which individuals in management positions have the formal power to direct and control immediate subordinates.

listening the skill of receiving messages to accurately grasp facts and feelings to interpret the genuine meaning.

locus of control the tendency to place the primary responsibility for one's success or failure either within oneself (internally) or on outside forces (externally).

long-term orientation a greater concern for the future and high value on thrift and perseverance.

Machiavellianism the tendency to direct much of one's behavior toward the acquisition of power and the manipulation of other people for personal gain.

management the attainment of organizational goals in an effective and efficient manner through planning, organizing, leading, and controlling organizational resources.

management by objectives (MBO) a method of management whereby managers and employees define goals for every department, project, and person and use them to monitor subsequent performance.

management by wandering around (MBWA) a communication technique in which managers interact directly with workers to exchange information.

management information system (MIS) a computer-based system that provides information and support for effective managerial decision making.

market entry strategies organizational strategies for entering a foreign market.

masculinity a cultural preference for achievement, heroism, assertiveness, work centrality, and material success.

mass production a type of technology characterized by the production of a large volume of products with the same specifications.

matching model an employee selection approach in which the organization and the applicant attempt to match each other's needs, interests, and values.

matrix approach an organization structure that uses functional and divisional chains of command simultaneously in the same part of the organization.

matrix boss the product or functional boss, responsible for one side of the matrix.

mediation the process of using a third party to settle a dispute.

merger the combining of two or more organizations into one.

message the tangible formulation of an idea to be sent to a receiver.

middle manager managers who work at the mid-levels of the organization and are responsible for major departments.

mission the organization's reason for existence.

mission statement a broadly stated definition of the organization's basic business scope and operations that distinguishes it from similar types of organizations.

modular approach the process by which a manufacturing company uses outside suppliers to provide large components of the product, which are then assembled into a final product by a few workers.

monoculture a culture that accepts only one way of doing things and one set of values and beliefs.

moral leadership distinguishing right from wrong and choosing to do right in the practice of leadership.

moral-rights approach the ethical concept that moral decisions are those that best maintain the rights of those people affected by them.

most favored nation a term describing a GATT clause that calls for member countries to grant other member countries the most favorable treatment they accord any country concerning imports and exports.

motivation the arousal, direction, and persistence of behavior.

motivators factors that influence job satisfaction based on fulfillment of high-level needs such as achievement, recognition, responsibility, and opportunity for growth.

Myers–Briggs Type Indicator (MBTI) personality test that measures a person's preference for introversion versus extroversion, sensation versus intuition, thinking versus feeling, and judging versus perceiving.

negotiation a conflict-management strategy whereby people engage in give-and-take discussions and consider various alternatives to reach a joint decision that is acceptable to both parties.

neutralizer a situational variable that counteracts a leadership style and prevents the leader from displaying certain behaviors.

new-venture fund a fund providing resources from which individuals and groups can draw to develop new ideas, products, or businesses.

new-venture team a unit separate from the mainstream of the organization that is responsible for developing and initiating innovations.

nonparticipator role a role in which the individual contributes little to either the task or members' socioemotional needs.

nonprogrammed decision a decision made in response to a situation that is unique, is poorly defined and largely unstructured, and has important consequences for the organization.

nonverbal communication a communication transmitted through actions and behaviors rather than through words.

normative an approach that defines how a decision maker should make decisions and provides guidelines for reaching an ideal outcome for the organization.

norming the stage of team development in which conflicts developed during the storming stage are resolved, and team harmony and unity emerge.

office automation systems systems that combine modern hardware and software to handle the tasks of publishing and distributing information.

on-the-job training (OJT) a type of training in which an experienced employee "adopts" a new employee to teach him or her how to perform job duties.

open communication sharing all types of information throughout the company, across functional and hierarchical levels.

open innovation extending the search for and commercialization of new ideas beyond the boundaries of the organization.

open-book management sharing financial information and results with all employees in the organization.

operational goals specific, measurable results expected from departments, work groups, and individuals within the organization.

operational plans plans developed at the organization's lower levels that specify action steps toward achieving operational goals and that support tactical planning activities.

operations information system a computer-based information system that supports a company's day-to-day operations.

opportunity a situation in which managers see potential organizational accomplishments that exceed current goals.

organization a social entity that is goal-directed and deliberately structured.

organization chart the visual representation of an organization's structure.

organization development (OD) the application of behavioral science techniques to improve an organization's health and effectiveness through its ability to cope with environmental changes, improve internal relationships, and increase learning and problem-solving capabilities.

organization structure the framework in which the organization defines how tasks are divided, resources are deployed, and departments are coordinated.

organizational behavior an interdisciplinary field dedicated to the study of how individuals and groups tend to act in organizations.

organizational change the adoption of a new idea or behavior by an organization.

organizational citizenship work behavior that goes beyond job requirements and contributes as needed to the organization's success.

organizational commitment loyalty to and heavy involvement in one's organization.

organizational control the systematic process through which managers regulate organizational activities to make them consistent with expectations established in plans, targets, and standards of performance.

organizational environment all elements existing outside the organization's boundaries that have the potential to affect the organization.

organizing the deployment of organizational resources to achieve strategic goals.

organizing the management function concerned with assigning tasks, grouping tasks into departments, and allocating resources to departments.

outsourcing contracting out selected functions or activities to other organizations that can do the work more cost-efficiently.

P → O expectancy expectancy that successful performance of a task will lead to the desired outcome.

partial productivity the ratio of total outputs to the inputs from a single major input category.

partial reinforcement schedule a schedule in which only some occurrences of the desired behavior are reinforced.

path–goal theory a contingency approach to leadership specifying that the leader's responsibility is to increase subordinates' motivation by clarifying the behaviors necessary for task accomplishment and rewards.

pay-for-performance incentive pay that ties at least part of compensation to employee effort and performance.

peer-to-peer (P2P) file-sharing swapping music, movies, software, and other files.

people change a change in the attitudes and behaviors of a few employees in the organization.

perception the cognitive process people use to make sense out of the environment by selecting, organizing, and interpreting information.

perceptual defense the tendency of perceivers to protect themselves by disregarding ideas, objects, or people that are threatening to them.

perceptual distortions errors in perceptual judgment that arise from inaccuracies in any part of the perceptual process.

perceptual selectivity the process by which individuals screen and select the various stimuli that vie for their attention.

performance the organization's ability to attain its goals by using resources in an efficient and effective manner.

performance appraisal the process of observing and evaluating an employee's performance, recording the assessment, and providing feedback to the employee.

performance gap a disparity between existing and desired performance levels.

performing the stage of team development in which members focus on problem solving and accomplishing the team's assigned task.

permanent teams a group of participants from several functions who are permanently assigned to solve ongoing problems of common interest.

personal communication channels communication channels that exist outside the formally authorized channels and do not adhere to the organization's hierarchy of authority.

personality the set of characteristics that underlies a relatively stable pattern of behavior in response to ideas, objects, or people in the environment.

personal networking the acquisition and cultivation of personal relationships that cross departmental, hierarchical, and even organizational boundaries.

person–job fit the extent to which a person's ability and personality match the requirements of a job.

plan a blueprint specifying the resource allocations, schedules, and other actions necessary for attaining goals.

planning the act of determining the organization's goals and the means for achieving them.

planning the management function concerned with defining goals for future organizational performance and deciding on the tasks and resources needed to attain them.

planning task force a group of managers and employees who develop a strategic plan.

pluralism an environment in which the organization accommodates several subcultures, including employees who would otherwise feel isolated and ignored.

point-counterpoint a decision-making technique in which people are assigned to express competing points of view.

political forces the influence of political and legal institutions on people and organizations.

political instability events such as riots, revolutions, or government upheavals that affect the operations of an international company.

political risk a company's risk of loss of assets, earning power, or managerial control as a result of politically based events or actions by host governments.

power the potential ability to influence others' behavior.

power distance the degree to which people accept inequality in power among institutions, organizations, and people.

pressure group an interest group that works within the legal-political framework to influence companies to behave in socially responsible ways.

problem a situation in which organizational accomplishments have failed to meet established goals.

problem-solving team typically 5 to 12 hourly employees from the same department who meet to discuss ways of improving quality, efficiency, and the work environment.

procedural justice the concept that rules should be clearly stated and consistently and impartially enforced.

process an organized group of related tasks and activities that work together to transform inputs into outputs and create value.

process control system a computer system that monitors and controls ongoing physical processes, such as temperature or pressure changes.

process theories a group of theories that explain how employees select behaviors with which to meet their needs and determine whether their choices were successful.

product change a change in the organization's product or service outputs.

productivity the organization's output of products and services divided by its inputs.

programmed decision a decision made in response to a situation that has occurred often enough to enable decision rules to be developed and applied in the future.

project manager a person responsible for coordinating the activities of several departments on a full-time basis for the completion of a specific project.

projection the tendency to see one's own personal traits in other people.

quality circle a group of 6 to 12 volunteer employees who meet regularly to discuss and solve problems affecting the quality of their work.

realistic job preview (RJP) a recruiting approach that gives applicants all pertinent and realistic information about the job and the organization.

recruiting the activities or practices that define the desired characteristics of applicants for specific jobs.

reengineering the radical redesign of business processes to achieve dramatic improvements in cost, quality, service, and speed.

referent power power that results from characteristics that command subordinates' identification with, respect and admiration for, and desire to emulate the leader.

refreezing the reinforcement stage of organization development in which individuals acquire a desired new skill or attitude and are rewarded for it by the organization.

reinforcement anything that causes a given behavior to be repeated or inhibited.

reinforcement theory a motivation theory based on the relationship between a given behavior and its consequences.

responsibility the duty to perform the task or activity an employee has been assigned.

responsibility center an organizational unit under the supervision of a single person who is responsible for its activity.

reward power power that results from the authority to bestow rewards on other people.

risk a situation in which a decision has clear-cut goals, and good information is available, but the future outcomes associated with each alternative are subject to chance.

risk propensity the willingness to undertake risk with the opportunity of gaining an increased payoff.

role a set of expectations for one's behavior.

role ambiguity uncertainty about what behaviors are expected of a person in a particular role.

role conflict incompatible demands of different roles.

satisficing to choose the first solution alternative that satisfies minimal decision criteria, regardless of whether better solutions are presumed to exist.

scenario building looking at trends and discontinuities and imagining possible alternative futures to build a framework within which unexpected future events can be managed.

schedule of reinforcement the frequency with which and intervals over which reinforcement occurs.

scientific management precise procedures developed after careful study of individual situations.

selection the process of determining the skills, abilities, and other attributes a person needs to perform a particular job.

self-directed team a team consisting of 5 to 20 multiskilled workers who rotate jobs to produce an entire product or service, often supervised by an elected member.

self-serving bias the tendency to overestimate the contribution of internal factors to one's successes and the contribution of external factors to one's failures.

semantics the meaning of words and the way they are used.

servant leader a leader who works to fulfill subordinates' needs and goals as well as to achieve the organization's larger mission.

service technology technology characterized by intangible outputs and direct contact between employees and customers.

short-term orientation a concern with the past and present and a high value on meeting social obligations.

single-use plans plans that are developed to achieve a set of goals that are unlikely to be repeated in the future.

situation analysis an evaluation that typically includes a search for SWOT—strengths, weaknesses, opportunities, and threats—that affect organizational performance.

situational theory a contingency approach to leadership that links the leader's behavioral style with the task readiness of subordinates.

Six Sigma a quality control approach that emphasizes a relentless pursuit of higher quality and lower costs.

skunkworks a separate small, informal, highly autonomous, and often secretive group that focuses on breakthrough ideas for the business.

slogan a phrase or sentence that succinctly expresses a key corporate value.

small-batch production a type of technology that involves the production of goods in batches of one or a few products designed to customer specification.

social contract the unwritten, common rules and perceptions about relationships among people and between employees and management.

social facilitation the tendency for the presence of others to influence an individual's motivation and performance.

social forces those aspects of a culture that guide and influence relationships among people.

social networking online interaction in a community format where people share personal information and photos, produce and share all sorts of information and opinions, or unify activists and raise funds.

sociocultural dimension the dimension of the general environment representing the demographic characteristics, norms, customs, and values of the population within which the organization operates.

socioemotional role a role in which the individual provides support for team members' emotional needs and social unity.

span of management the number of employees reporting to a supervisor; also called *span of control.*

special-purpose team a team created outside the formal organization to undertake a project of special importance or creativity.

staff authority a form of authority granted to staff specialists in their area of expertise.

stakeholder any group within or outside the organization that has a stake in the organization's performance.

standing plans ongoing plans that are used to provide guidance for tasks performed repeatedly within the organization.

stereotyping placing an employee into a class or category based on one or a few traits or characteristics.

stereotyping the tendency to assign an individual to a group or broad category and then attribute generalizations about the group to the individual.

storming the stage of team development in which individual personalities, roles, and resulting conflicts emerge.

story a narrative based on true events that is repeated frequently and is shared among organizational employees.

strategic conversation dialogue across boundaries and hierarchical levels about the team or organization's vision, critical strategic themes, and the values that help achieve important goals.

strategic goals broad statements of where the organization wants to be in the future; they pertain to the organization as a whole rather than to specific divisions or departments.

strategic management a specific type of planning in for-profit business organizations; typically pertains to competitive actions in the marketplace.

strategic plans the action steps by which an organization intends to attain strategic goals.

strategy plan of action that describes resource allocation and activities for dealing with the environment, achieving a competitive advantage, and attaining the organization's goals.

strategy formulation the planning and decision making that lead to establishment of the firm's goals and development of a specific strategic plan.

strategy implementation the use of managerial and organizational tools to direct resources toward accomplishing strategic results.

stress a physiological and emotional response to stimuli that place physical or psychological demands on an individual.

substitute a situational variable that makes a leadership style unnecessary or redundant.

superordinate goal a goal that cannot be reached by a single party.

suppliers people and organizations who provide the raw materials the organization uses to produce its output.

supply chain management managing the sequence of suppliers and purchasers, covering all stages of processing from obtaining raw materials to distributing finished goods to consumers.

survey feedback a type of OD intervention in which questionnaires on organizational climate and other factors are distributed among employees and their results reported back to them by a change agent.

sustainability economic development that meets the needs of the current population while preserving the environment for the needs of future generations.

symbol an object, act, or event that conveys meaning to others.

synergy a joint effect that is greater than the sum of the parts acting alone.

tactical goals goals that define the outcomes that major divisions and departments must achieve for the organization to reach its overall goals.

tactical plans plans designed to help execute major strategic plans and to accomplish a specific part of the company's strategy.

tall structure a management structure characterized by an overall narrow span of management and a relatively large number of hierarchical levels.

task environment the layer of the external environment that directly influences the organization's operations and performance.

task force a temporary team or committee formed to solve a specific short-term problem involving several departments.

task specialist role a role in which the individual devotes personal time and energy to helping the team accomplish its task.

team a unit of two or more people who interact and coordinate their work to accomplish a specific goal.

team-based structure structure in which the entire organization is made up of horizontal teams that coordinate their activities and work directly with customers to accomplish the organization's goals.

team building a type of OD intervention that enhances the cohesiveness of departments by helping members learn to function as a team.

team cohesiveness the extent to which team members are attracted to the team and motivated to remain in it.

team norm a standard of conduct that is shared by team members and guides their behavior.

technical complexity the degree to which complex machinery is involved in the production process to the exclusion of people.

technological dimension the dimension of the general environment that includes scientific and technological advancements in the industry and society at large.

technology change a change that pertains to the organization's production process.

telecommuting using computers and telecommunications equipment to perform work from home or another remote location.

top leader the overseer of both the product and functional chains of command, responsible for the entire matrix.

top-down budgeting a budgeting process in which middle- and lower-level managers set departmental budget targets in accordance with overall company revenues and expenditures specified by top management.

total factor productivity the ratio of total outputs to the inputs from labor, capital, materials, and energy.

total quality management (TQM) an organization-wide commitment to infuse quality into every activity through continuous improvement.

total quality management (TQM) focuses on managing the total organization to deliver quality to customers.

traits distinguishing personal characteristics, such as intelligence, values, and appearance.

transactional leader a leader who clarifies subordinates' role and task requirements, initiates structure, provides rewards, and displays consideration for subordinates.

transaction-processing system (TPS) a type of operations information system that records and processes data resulting from routine business transactions such as sales, purchases, and payroll.

transformational leader a leader distinguished by a special ability to bring about innovation and change.

two-boss employees employees who report to two supervisors simultaneously.

Type A behavior behavior pattern characterized by extreme competitiveness, impatience, aggressiveness, and devotion to work.

Type B behavior behavior pattern that lacks Type A characteristics and includes a more balanced, relaxed lifestyle.

uncertainty the situation that occurs when managers know which goals they want to achieve, but information about alternatives and future events is incomplete.

uncertainty avoidance a value characterized by people's intolerance for ambiguity and the resulting support for beliefs that promise certainty and conformity.

unfreezing the stage of organization development in which participants are made aware of problems to increase their willingness to change their behavior.

upward communication messages transmitted from the lower to the higher levels in the organization's hierarchy.

utilitarian approach the ethical concept that moral behaviors produce the greatest good for the greatest number.

valence the value or attraction an individual has for an outcome.

validity the relationship between an applicant's score on a selection device and his or her future job performance.

value the combination of benefits received and costs paid.

vertical team a formal team composed of a manager and his or her subordinates in the organization's formal chain of command.

virtual network structure an organization structure that disaggregates major functions to separate companies that are brokered by a small headquarters organization.

virtual team a team made up of members who are geographically or organizationally dispersed, rarely meet face to face, and do their work using advanced information technologies.

vision an attractive, ideal future that is credible yet not readily attainable.

Vroom-Jago model a model designed to help managers gauge the amount of subordinate participation in decision making.

wage and salary surveys surveys that show what other organizations pay incumbents in jobs that match a sample of "key" jobs selected by the organization.

whistle-blowing the disclosure by an employee of illegal, immoral, or illegitimate practices by the organization.

work redesign the altering of jobs to increase both the quality of employees' work experience and their productivity.

work specialization the degree to which organizational tasks are subdivided into individual jobs; also called division of labor.

workforce optimization implementing strategies to put the right people in the right jobs, make the best use of employee talent and skills, and develop human capital for the future.

World Wide Web (WWW) a collection of central servers for accessing information on the Internet.

Chapter 1

Innovative Management for Turbulent Times

1. Daniel Roth," Catch Us If You Can," *Fortune* (February 9, 2003): 64–74; Ian Austen, "Downloading Again," *The New York Times* (May 3, 2004): C12; Christie Eliezer, "Kazaa Case Grinds on in Australia," *Billboard* (April 17, 2004): 60; and Steve Knopper, "Tower in Trouble," *Rolling Stone* (March 18, 2004): 26.

2. Ian Mitroff and Murat C. Alpaslan, "Preparing for Evil," *Harvard Business Review* (April 2003): 109–115.

3. Darrell Rigby and Barbara Bilodeau, "The Bain 2005 Management Tool Survey," *Strategy & Leadership* 33, no. 4 (2005): 4–12.

4. Susan Spielberg, "The Cheesecake Factory: Heather Coin," *Nation's Restaurant News* (January 26, 2004): 38–39.

5. David Carr, "Media Age Business Tips from U2," *The New York Times*, (November 28, 2005): www.nytimes.com

6. Geoffrey Colvin, "What Makes GE Great? "*Fortune* (March 6, 2006): 90–96; and Betsy Morris, "The GE Mystique," *Fortune* (March 6, 2006): 98–104.

7. James A. F. Stoner and R. Edward Freeman, *Management*, 4th ed. (Englewood Cliffs, NJ: Prentice Hall, 1989).

8. Peter F. Drucker, *Management Tasks, Responsibilities, Practices* (New York: Harper & Row, 1974).

9. Louis Uchitelle, "Ready for an Upturn. Not Ready to Spend," *The New York Times* (June 23, 2002): Section 3, 1, 13.

10. Martha Brannigan and Eleena De Lisser, "Cost Cutting at Delta Raises the Stock Price But Lowers the Service," *Wall Street Journal* (June 20, 1996): A1.

11. Robert L. Katz, "Skills of an Effective Administrator," *Harvard Business Review 52* (September–October 1974): 90–102.

12. Eileen Sheridan, "Rise: Best Day, Worst Day," *The Guardian* (September 14, 2002): 3.

13. Heath Row," Force Play" (Company of Friends column), *Fast Company* (March 2001): 46

14. Charles Fishman, "Sweet Company," *Fast Company* (February 2001): 136–145.

15. Based on Sydney Finkelstein, "7 Habits of Spectacularly Unsuccessful Executives," *Fast Company* (July 2003): 84–89; Ram Charan and Jerry Useem, "Why Companies Fail," *Fortune* (May 27, 2002).

16. Ibid.

17. Matthew Rose and Laurie P. Cohen, "Man in the News: Amid Turmoil, Top Editors Resign at New York Times," *Wall Street Journal* (June 6, 2003): A1, A6; and Jena McGregor, "Gospels of Failure," *Fast Company* (February 2005): 61–67.

18. For a review of the problems faced by first-time managers, see Loren B. Belker and Gary S. Topchik, *The First-Time Manager: A Practical Guide to the Management of People*, 5th ed.

(New York: AMACOM, 2005); J. W. Lorsch and P. F. Mathias, "When Professionals Have to Manage," *Harvard Business Review* (July–August 1987): 78–83; R. A. Webber, *Becoming a Courageous Manager: Overcoming Career Problems of New Managers* (Englewood Cliffs, NJ: Prentice Hall, 1991); D. E. Dougherty, *From Technical Professional to Corporate Manager: A Guide to Career Transition* (New York: Wiley, 1984); J. Falvey, "The Making of a Manager," *Sales and Marketing Management* (March 1989): 42–83; M. K. Badawy, *Developing Managerial Skills in Engineers and Scientists: Succeeding as a Technical Manager* (New York: Van Nostrand Reinhold, 1982); and M. London, *Developing Managers: A Guide to Motivating and Preparing People for Successful Managerial Careers* (San Francisco: Jossey-Bass, 1985).

19. Erin White, "Learning to Be the Boss; Trial and Error Is the Norm as New Managers Figure Out How to Relate to Former Peers," *Wall Street Journal* (November 21, 2005): B1.

20. Based on Linda A. Hill, *Becoming a Manager: How New Managers Master the Challenges of Leadership*, 2nd. ed. (Boston, MA: Harvard Business School Press, 2003): 6–8.

21. See also Boss's First Steps, sidebar in White, "Learning to Be the Boss," Note 19; and Belker and Topchik, *The First-Time Manager*, Note 18.

22. Spielberg, "The Cheesecake Factory," Note 4.

23. Geoffrey Colvin, "The Bionic Manager," *Fortune* (September 16, 2005).

24. Henry Mintzberg, "Managerial Work: Analysis from Observation," *Management Science* 18 (1971): B97–B110.

25. Based on Carol Saunders and Jack William Jones, "Temporal Sequences in Information Acquisition for Decision Making: A Focus on Source and Medium," *Academy of Management Review* 15 (1990): 29–46; John P. Kotter, "What Effective General Managers Really Do," *Harvard Business Review* (November–December 1982): 156–167; and Mintzberg, "Managerial Work," Note 24.

26. Mintzberg, "Managerial Work," Note 24.

27. Anita Lienert, "A Day in the Life: Airport Manager Extraordinaire," *Management Review* (January 1995): 57–61.

28. Lance B. Kurke and Howard E. Aldrich, "Mintzberg Was Right!: A Replication and Extension of *The Nature of Managerial Work*," *Management Science* 29 (1983): 975–984; Cynthia M. Pavett and Alan W. Lau, "Managerial Work: The Influence of Hierarchical Level and Functional Specialty," *Academy of Management Journal 26* (1983): 170–177; and Colin P. Hales, "What Do Managers Do? A Critical Review of the Evidence," *Journal of Management Studies* 23 (1986): 88–115.

29. Henry Mintzberg, "Rounding Out the Manager's Job, "*Sloan Management Review* (Fall 1994): 11–26.

30. Edward O. Welles, "There Are No Simple Businesses Anymore," *The State of Small Business* (1995): 66–79.

31. This section is based largely on Peter F. Drucker, *Managing the Non-Profit Organization: Principles and Practices* (New York:

HarperBusiness, 1992); and Thomas Wolf, *Managing a Nonprofit Organization* (New York: Fireside/Simon & Schuster, 1990).

32. Christine W. Letts, William P. Ryan, and Allen Grossman, *High Performance Nonprofit Organizations* (New York: Wiley & Sons, 1999): 30–35.

33. Carol Hymowitz, "In Sarbanes-Oxley Era, Running a Nonprofit Is Only Getting Harder," *The Wall Street Journal* (June 21, 2005): B1; and Bill Birchard, "Nonprofits by the Numbers," *CFO* (June 2005): 50–55.

34. This section is based on Harry G. Barkema, Joel A. C. Baum, and Elizabeth A. Mannix, "Management Challenges in a New Time," *Academy of Management Journal* 45, no. 5 (2002): 916–930; "The New Organization: A Survey of the Company," *The Economist* (January 21, 2006); Michael Harvey and M. Ronald Buckley, "Assessing the 'Conventional Wisdoms' of Management for the 21st Century Organization," *Organizational Dynamics* 30, no. 4 (2002): 368–378; and Toby J. Tetenbaum, "Shifting Paradigms: From Newton to Chaos," *Organizational Dynamics* (Spring 1998): 21–32.

35. Caroline Ellis, "The Flattening Corporation," *MIT Sloan Management Review* (Summer 2003): 5.

36. Cliff Edwards, "Wherever You Go, You're on the Job," *Business Week* (June 20, 2005).

37. Barkema, Baum, and Mannix, "Management Challenges in a New Time," Note 34.

38. Keith H. Hammonds, "Smart, Determined, Ambitious, Cheap: The New Face of Global Competition," *Fast Company* (February 2003): 91–97.

39. Toby J. Tetenbaum, "Shifting Paradigms: From Newton to Chaos," *Organizational Dynamics* (Spring 1998): 21–32.

40. Jennifer Reingold, "What We Learned in the New Economy," *Fast Company* (March 2004): 57–66.

41. Timothy L. O'Brien, "Not Invented Here: Are U.S. Innovators Losing Their Competitive Edge?" *The New York Times* (November 13, 2005), 1.

42. Kevin Maney, "'Must-Win' Attitude Gets Motorola Back on the Hip Track," *USA Today* (January 18, 2006): B3; and Roger O. Crockett, with Cliff Edwards and Spencer E. Ante, "How Motorola Got Its Groove Back," *BusinessWeek* (August 8, 2005): 68–70.

43. Erick Schonfeld, "GE Sees the Light," *Business 2.0* (July 2004): 80–86; Colvin, Note 23; and Colvin, "What Makes GE Great?" (Note 6); Patricia Sellers, "P&G: Teaching an Old Dog New Tricks," *Fortune* (May 31, 2004): 167–180; and Bettina von Stamm, "Collaboration with Other Firms and Customers: Innovation's Secret Weapon," *Strategy & Leadership* 32, no. 3 (2004): 16–20.

44. Scott Kirsner, "Every Day, It's a New Place," *Fast Company* (April–May 1998): 130–134; Peter Coy, "The Creative Economy," *BusinessWeek* (August 28, 2000): 76–82; and Jeremy Main, "The Shape of the New Corporation," *Working Woman* (October 1998): 60–63.

45. Bill Carter, "ABC Says it was Outbid by NBC for Paris Hilton Interview," *The New York Times*, (June 22, 2007): C1 & C4.

46. This section is based on Loretta Ucelli, "The CEO's 'How To' Guide to Crisis Communications," *Strategy & Leadership* 30, no. 2 (2002): 21–24; Eric Beaudan, "Leading in Turbulent Times," *Ivey Business Journal* (May–June 2002): 22–26; Christine Pearson, "A Blueprint for Crisis Management," *Ivey Business Journal* (January–February 2002): 68–73; Leslie Wayne and Leslie Kaufman, "Leadership, Put to a New Test," *The New York Times* (September 16, 2001): Section 3, 1, 4; Jerry Useem, "What It Takes," *Fortune* (November 12, 2001): 126–132; and Andy Bowen, "Crisis Procedures That Stand the Test of Time," *Public Relations Tactics* (August 2001): 16.

47. June Kronholz and Stefan Fatsis, "Obstacle Course; After Hurricane, Tulane University Struggles to Survive," *Wall Street Journal* (September 28, 2005): A1, A8.

48. Beaudan, "Leading in Turbulent Times," Note 45.

49. Dennis Cauchon, "The Little Company That Could," *USA Today* (October 9, 2005): www.usatoday.com

50. Paul Argenti, "Crisis Communication: Lessons from 9/11," *Harvard Business Review* (December 2002): 103–109.

51. Allison Fass, "Duking It Out," *Forbes* (June 9, 2003): 74–76.

52. Ronald A. Heifetz and Donald L. Laurie, "The Leader as Teacher: Creating the Learning Organization," *Ivey Business Journal* (January–February 2003): 1–9.

53. Peter Senge, *The Fifth Discipline: The Art and Practice of Learning Organizations* (New York: Doubleday/Currency, 1990).

54. Art Kleiner, "Our 10 Most Enduring Ideas," *Strategy Business*, no. 41 (December 12, 2005): 36–41.

55. Khoo Hsien Hui and Tan Kay Chuan, "Nine Approaches to Organizational Excellence," *Journal of Organizational Excellence* (Winter 2002): 53–65; Leon Martel, "The Principles of High Performance—And How to Apply Them," *Journal of Organizational Excellence* (Autumn 2002): 49–59; and Jeffrey Pfeffer, "Producing Sustainable Competitive Advantage through the Effective Management of People," *Academy of Management Executive* 9, no. 1 (1995): 55–69.

56. Alex Markels, "The Wisdom of Chairman Ko," *Fast Company* (November 1999): 258–276.

57. Edward O. Welles, "Mind Gains," *Inc.* (December 1999): 112–124.

58. Kevin Kelly, *New Rules for the New Economy: 10 Radical Strategies for a Connected World* (New York: Viking Penguin, 1998).

59. Nick Wingfield, "In the Beginning...," *Wall Street Journal* (May 21, 2001): R18.

60. Andy Reinhardt, "From Gearhead to Grand High PoohBah," *BusinessWeek* (August 28, 2000): 129–130.

61. Julia Angwin, "Used Car Auctioneers, Dealers Meet Online," *Wall Street Journal* (November 20, 2004): B1, B13; William J. Holstein and Edward Robinson, "The ReEducation of Jacques Nassar," Business2.Com (May 29, 2001): 60–73.

62. Definition based on Steven A. Melnyk and David R. Denzler, *Operations Management: A Value Driven Approach* (Burr Ridge, IL: Richard D. Irwin, 1996): 613.

63. Bernard Wysocki, Jr., "Corporate Caveat: Dell or Be Delled," *Wall Street Journal* (May 10, 1999): A1.

64. Michelle Singletary, "Beating a Path to the Power Sellers," *Washington Post* (August 7, 2005): F1; and Patricia Sellers, "EBay's Secret," *Fortune* (October 18, 2004): 160–178.

65. Amber Chung, "Music Retailers Face Tough Times as File-Sharing Grows," *Taipei Times* (February 10, 2004): 11; www.taipeitimes.com (accessed on February 10, 2004).

66. Geoffrey Colvin, "Managing in the Info Era," *Fortune* (March 6, 2000), F6–F9.

67. Jeffrey Zygmont, "The Ties That Bind," *Inc. Tech* no. 3, (1998): 70–84; and Nancy Ferris, "ERP: Sizzling or Stumbling?" *Government Executive* (July 1999): 99–102.

68. Harrington, "The Big Ideas." Also see Peter Drucker, *Post-Capitalist Society*, (Oxford: Butterworth Heinemann, 1993): 5.

69. Based on Andrew Mayo, "Memory Bankers," *People Management* (January 22, 1998): 34–38; William Miller, "Building the Ultimate Resource," *Management Review* (January 1999): 42–45; and Todd Datz, "How to Speak Geek," *CIO Enterprise*, Section 2 (April 15, 1999): 46–52.

70. Rigby and Bilodeau, "The Bain 2005 Management Tool Survey," and Edward Prewitt, "CRM Gains Ground as Management Tool," *CIO* (September 1, 2005): 28.

71. Daniel A. Wren, *The Evolution of Management Thought*, 2d ed. (New York: Wiley, 1979): 6–8. Much of the discussion of these forces comes from Arthur M. Schlesinger, *Political and Social History of the United States, 1829–1925* (New York: Macmillan, 1925); and Homer C. Hockett, *Political and Social History of the United States, 1492–1828* (New York: Macmillan, 1925).

72. Based on Stephanie Armour, "Generation Y: They've Arrived at Work with a New Attitude," *USA Today* (November 6, 2005): www.usatoday.com/money/workplace/2005-11-06-gen-y_x.htm; and Marnie E. Green, "Beware and Prepare: The Government Workforce of the Future," *Public Personnel Management* (Winter 2000): 435+.

73. This section is based heavily on Thomas Petzinger, Jr., "So Long Supply and Demand," *Wall Street Journal* (January 1, 2000): R31.

74. Petzinger, "So Long Supply and Demand," Note 72.

75. Darrell Rigby and Barbara Bilodeau, "The Bain 2005 Management Tool Survey," *Strategy & Leadership* 33, no. 4 (2005): 4–12; and Darrell Rigby, "Management Tools Survey 2003: Usage Up as Companies Strive to Make Headway in Tough Times," *Strategy & Leadership* 31, no. 5 (2003): 4–11.

76. See Daniel James Rowley, "Resource Reviews," *Academy of Management Learning and Education* 2, no. 3 (2003): 313–321; Jane Whitney Gibson, Dana V. Tesone, and Charles W. Blackwell, "Management Fads: Here Yesterday, Gone Today?" *SAM Advanced Management Journal* (Autumn 2003): 12–17; David Collins, *Management Fads and Buzzwords: Critical-Practices Perspective* (London, UK: Routledge, 2000); Timothy Clark, "Management Research on Fashion: A Review and Evaluation," *Human Relations* 54, no. 12 (2001): 1650–1661; Brad Jackson, *Management Gurus and Management Fashions* (London: Routledge, 2001); Patrick Thomas, *Fashions in Management Research: An Empirical Analysis* (Aldershot, UK: Ashgate, 1999).

77. Daniel A. Wren, "Management History: Issues and Ideas for Teaching and Research," *Journal of Management* 13 (1987): 339–350.

78. Business historian Alfred D. Chandler, Jr., quoted in Jerry Useem, "Entrepreneur of the Century," *Inc.* (20th Anniversary Issue, 1999): 159–174.

79. Useem, "Entrepreneur of the Century."

80. The following is based on Wren, *Evolution of Management Thought*, Chapters 4, 5; and Claude S. George, Jr., *The History of Management Thought* (Englewood Cliffs, NJ.: Prentice-Hall, 1968): Ch 4.

81. Alan Farnham, "The Man Who Changed Work Forever," *Fortune* (July 21, 1997): 114; Charles D. Wrege and Ann Marie Stoka, "Cooke Creates a Classic: The Story Behind F. W. Taylor's Principles of Scientific Management," *Academy of Management Review* (October 1978): 736–749; Robert Kanigel, *The One Best Way: Frederick Winslow Taylor and the Enigma of Efficiency* (New York: Viking, 1997); and "The X and Y Factors: What Goes Around Comes Around," in "The New Organisation: A Survey of the Company," *The Economist* (January 21–27, 2006): special section pp. 17–18.

82. Quoted in Ann Harrington, "The Big Ideas," *Fortune* (November 22, 1999), 152–154.

83. Kelly Barron, "Logistics in Brown," *Forbes* (January 10, 2000): 78–83; Scott Kirsner, "Venture Vérité: United Parcel Service," *Wired* (September 1999): 83–96; "UPS," *Atlanta Journal and Constitution* (April 26, 1992): H1; and Kathy Goode, Betty Hahn, and Cindy Seibert, "United Parcel Service: The Brown Giant" (unpublished manuscript, Texas A&M University, 1981).

84. "IBM: The Open Door," vignette in Matthew Boyle, "How the Workplace Was Won," *Fortune* (January 22, 2001): 139; and Thomas A. Stewart, Alex Taylor III, Peter Petre, and Brent Schlender, "The Businessman of the Century," *Fortune* (November 22, 1999): 108–128.

85. Curt Tausky, *Work Organizations: Major Theoretical Perspectives* (Itasca, IL: F. E. Peacock, 1978): 55.

86. Douglas McGregor, *The Human Side of Enterprise* (New York: McGraw-Hill, 1960): 16–18.

87. Samuel Greengard, "25 Visionaries Who Shaped Today's Workplace," *Workforce* (January 1997): 50–59; and Harrington, "The Big Ideas," Note 81.

88. Mauro F. Guillen, "The Age of Eclecticism: Current Organizational Trends and the Evolution of Managerial Models," *Sloan Management Review* (Fall 1994): 75–86.

89. Jeremy Main, "How to Steal the Best Ideas Around," *Fortune* (October 19, 1992): 102–106.

90. Rigby and Bilodeau, The Bain 2005 Management Tool Survey," Note 3.

Chapter 2

The Environment and Corporate Culture

1. Robert A. Guth and Kevin J. Delaney, "Default Lines; Pressuring Microsoft, PC Makers Team Up with Software Rivals," *Wall Street Journal* (February 7, 2006): A1, A25.

2. Ann Carns, "Point Taken; Hit Hard by Imports, American Pencil Icon Tries to Get a Grip," *Wall Street Journal* (November 24, 1999): A1, A6.

3. George S. Day and Paul J. H. Schoemaker, "Scanning the Periphery," *Harvard Business Review* (November 2005): 135–148.

4. Christopher Joyce, reporter, transcript of "Analysis: International Panel Says U.S. Department of Agriculture Should Take Further Steps to Protect the U.S. from Mad Cow Disease," *NPR: All Things Considered* (February 5, 2004): 1; Sue Kirchhoff, "Natural Beef Industry Might See Boost from Mad Cow Fears," *USA Today* (January 12, 2004): www. usatoday. com/money/industries/food/2004-01-12-organic_x.htm; June Kronholz, "Kindergarten Crisis: By Federal Order, Snail Races Are Over," *Wall Street Journal* (February 11, 2004): A1.

5. This section is based on Richard L. Daft, *Organization Theory and Design*, 8th ed. (Cincinnati, OH: South-Western, 2004): 136–140.

6. Pete Engardio, "A New World Economy," *BusinessWeek* (August 22–29, 2005): 52–58.

7. Robert Rosen, with Patricia Digh, Marshall Singer, and Carl Phillips, *Global Literacies: Lessons on Business Leadership and National Cultures* (New York: Simon and Schuster, 2000).

8. Engardio, "A New World Economy."

9. Cliff Edwards, "Wherever You Go, You're On the Job," *BusinessWeek* (June 20, 2005): 87–90.

10. Stephen Baker and Adam Astor, "The Business of Nanotech," *BusinessWeek* (February 14, 2005): 64–71.

11. William B. Johnston, "Global Work Force 2000: The New World Labor Market," *Harvard Business Review* (March–April 1991): 115–127.

12. U.S. Census Bureau statistics reported in "Minorities Should Be Very Close to Majority by 2050, Census Projection Says," AP Story in *Johnson City Press* (March 18, 2004): 5A; and Peter Coy, "The Creative Economy," *BusinessWeek* (August 28, 2000): 76–82.

13. Peter Coy, "Old. Smart. Productive," *BusinessWeek* (June 27, 2005): 78–86; Danielle Sacks, "Scenes from the Culture Clash," *Fast Company* (January–February 2006): 73–77; and Ellyn Spragins, "The Talent Pool," *FSB* (October 2005): 93–102.

14. U.S. Census, *www.census.gov/*

15. Michelle Conlin, "UnMarried America," *BusinessWeek* (October 20, 2003): 106–116.

16. Sebastian Moffett, "Senior Moment: Fast-Aging Japan Keeps Its Elders on the Job Longer," *Wall Street Journal* (June 15, 2005): A1.

17. Julie Dunn, "Restaurant Chains, Too, Watch Their Carbs," *The New York Times* (January 4, 2004); Brian Grow with Gerry Khermouch, "The Low-Carb Food Fight Ahead," *BusinessWeek* (December 22, 2003): 48; and Laura Crimaldi, "Girl Scout Numbers Drop," *Boston Herald* (March 11, 2005): 7.

18. Samuel Loewenberg, "Europe Gets Tougher on U.S. Companies," *The New York Times* (April 20, 2003): Section 3, 6.

19. Jeremy Caplan, "Paper War," *Time* (January 2006): A11.

20. Linda Himelstein and Laura Zinn, with Maria Mallory, John Carey, Richard S. Dunham, and Joan O. C. Hamilton, "Tobacco: Does It Have a Future?" *BusinessWeek* (July 4, 1994): 24–29; Bob Ortega, "Aging Activists Turn, Turn, Turn Attention to Wal-Mart Protests," *Wall Street Journal* (October 11, 1994): A1, A8.

21. Jessi Hempel, "The MySpace Generation," *BusinessWeek* (December 12, 2005): 86–94.

22. John Simons, "Stop Moaning About Gripe Sites and Log On," *Fortune* (April 2, 2001): 181–182.

23. Rick Brooks, "Home Depot Turns Copycat in Its Efforts to Stoke New Growth," *Wall Street Journal* (November 21, 2000): A1; Dan Sewell, "Home Depot, Lowe's Building Up Competition," *Lexington Herald-Leader*: Business Profile Supplement (December 8, 1997): 3.

24. Julia Angwin and Motoko Rich, "Inn Fighting: Big Hotel Chains Are Striking Back Against Web Sites," *Wall Street Journal* (March 14, 2003): A1.

25. Paul Glader, "Steel-Price Rise Crimps Profits, Adds Uncertainty," *Wall Street Journal* (February 23, 2004): A1.

26. John R. Wilke and Kathy Chen, "Planned Economy; As China's Trade Clout Grows, So Do Price-Fixing Accusations," *Wall Street Journal* (February 10, 2006): A1.

27. Olga Kharif, "Nortels's New Lease on Life," *BusinessWeek Online* (January 26, 2006); Roger O. Crockett,"Nortel: Desperately Seeking Credibility," *BusinessWeek* (January 17, 2005): 60–61; Bernard Simon, "A Bright New Day for the Telecom Industry, If the Public Will Go Along," *The New York Times* (January 12, 2004): C3; Mark Heinzl, "Nortel's Profit of $499 Million Exceeds Forecast," *Wall Street Journal* (January 30, 2004): B4; Joseph Weber with Andy Reinhardt

and Peter Burrows, "Racing Ahead at Nortel," *BusinessWeek* (November 8, 1999): 93–99; Ian Austen, "Hooked on the Net," *Canadian Business* (June 26–July 10, 1998): 95–103; "Nortel's Waffling Continues; First Job Cuts, Then Product Lines, and Now the CEO. What's Next?" *Telephony* (May 21, 2001): 12.

28. Robert B. Duncan, "Characteristics of Organizational Environment and Perceived Environmental Uncertainty," *Administrative Science Quarterly 17* (1972): 313–327; and Daft, *Organization Theory and Design*, Note 6.

29. Sarah Moore, "On Your Markets," *Working Woman* (February 2001): 26; and John Simons, "Stop Moaning about Gripe Sites and Log On," *Fortune* (April 2, 2001): 181–182.

30. Tom Duffy, "Spying the Holy Grail," *Microsoft Executive Circle* (Winter 2004): 38–39.

31. Edwin M. Epstein, "How to Learn from the Environment about the Environment—A Prerequisite for Organizational Well-Being," *Journal of General Management 29*, no. 1 (Autumn 2003): 68–80.

32. Mark McNeilly, "Gathering Information for Strategic Decisions, Routinely," *Strategy & Leadership* 30, no 5 (2002): 29–34.

33. Day and Schoemaker, "Scanning the Periphery."

34. Stephan M. Wagner and Roman Boutellier, "Capabilities for Managing a Portfolio of Supplier Relationships," *Business Horizons* (November–December 2002): 79–88; Peter Smith Ring and Andrew H. Van de Ven, "Developmental Processes of Corporate Interorganizational Relationships," *Academy of Management Review* 19 (1994): 90–118; Myron Magnet, "The New Golden Rule of Business," *Fortune* (February 21, 1994): 60–64; and Peter Grittner, "Four Elements of Successful Sourcing Strategies," *Management Review* (October 1996): 41–45.

35. Patricia Sellers, "The Business of Being Oprah," *Fortune* (April 1, 2002): 50–64.

36. Yoash Wiener, "Forms of Value Systems: A Focus on Organizational Effectiveness and Culture Change and Maintenance," *Academy of Management Review* 13 (1988): 534–545; V. Lynne Meek, "Organizational Culture: Origins and Weaknesses," *Organization Studies* 9 (1988): 453–473; John J. Sherwood, "Creating Work Cultures with Competitive Advantage," *Organizational Dynamics* (Winter 1988): 5–27; and Andrew D. Brown and Ken Starkey, "The Effect of Organizational Culture on Communication and Information," *Journal of Management Studies 31*, no. 6 (November 1994): 807–828.

37. Joanne Martin, *Organizational Culture: Mapping the Terrain* (Thousand Oaks, CA: Sage Publications, 2002); Ralph H. Kilmann, Mary J. Saxton, and Roy Serpa, "Issues in Understanding and Changing Culture," *California Management Review* 28 (Winter 1986): 87–94; and Linda Smircich, "Concepts of Culture and Organizational Analysis," *Administrative Science Quarterly* 28 (1983): 339–358.

38. Based on Edgar H. Schein, *Organizational Culture and Leadership*, 2nd ed. (San Francisco: Jossey-Bass, 1992): 3–27.

39. Michael G. Pratt and Anat Rafaeli, "Symbols as a Language of Organizational Relationships," *Research in Organizational Behavior* 23 (2001): 93–132.

40. Christine Canabou, "Here's the Drill," *Fast Company* (February 2001): 58.

41. Alex Frangos, "In Office Mock-Up, Real Workers Put Layout Ideas to Test," *Wall Street Journal* (December 1, 2004).

42. Patrick M. Lencioni, "Make Your Values Mean Something," *Harvard Business Review* (July 2002): 113–117.

43. Robert E. Quinn and Gretchen M. Spreitzer, "The Road to Empowerment: Seven Questions Every Leader Should Consider," *Organizational Dynamics* (Autumn 1997): 37–49.

44. Martin, *Organizational Culture*: 71–72, Note 37.

45. Terrence E. Deal and Allan A. Kennedy, *Corporate Cultures: The Rites and Rituals of Corporate Life* (Reading, MA: Addison-Wesley, 1982).

46. Patricia Jones and Larry Kahaner, *Say It and Live It: 50 Corporate Mission Statements That Hit the Mark* (New York: Currency Doubleday, 1995).

47. Harrison M. Trice and Janice M. Beyer, "Studying Organizational Cultures Through Rites and Ceremonials," *Academy of Management Review 9* (1984): 653–669.

48. Brent Schlender, "Wal-Mart's $288 Billion Meeting," *Fortune* (April 18, 2005): 90–106.

49. Jennifer A. Chatman and Karen A. Jehn, "Assessing the Relationship Between Industry Characteristics and Organizational Culture: How Different Can You Be?" *Academy of Management Journal* 37, no. 3 (1994): 522–553.

50. John P. Kotter and James L. Heskett, *Corporate Culture and Performance* (New York: Free Press, 1992).

51. This discussion is based on Paul McDonald and Jeffrey Gandz, "Getting Value from Shared Values," *Organizational Dynamics* 21, no. 3 (Winter 1992): 64–76; Daniel R. Denison and Aneil K. Mishra, "Toward a Theory of Organizational Culture and Effectiveness," *Organization Science* 6, no. 2 (March–April 1995): 204–223; and Richard L. Daft, *The Leadership Experience*, 3rd ed. (Cincinnati, OH: South-Western, 2005): 570–573.

52. Lucas Conley, "Rinse and Repeat," *Fast Company* (July 2005): 76–77.

53. Robert Hooijberg and Frank Petrock, "On Cultural Change: Using the Competing Values Framework to Help Leaders Execute a Transformational Strategy," *Human Resource Management* 32, no. 1 (1993): 29–50.

54. Lencioni, "Make Your Values Mean Something," Note 42; and Melanie Warner, "Confessions of a Control Freak," *Fortune* (September 4, 2000): 130–140.

55. Janet Guyon, "The Soul of a Moneymaking Machine," *Fortune* (October 3, 2005): 113–120.

56. Rekha Balu, "Pacific Edge Projects Itself," *Fast Company* (October 2000): 371–381.

57. Jeffrey Pfeffer, *The Human Equation: Building Profits by Putting People First* (Boston: Harvard Business School Press, 1998).

58. Jeremy Kahn, "What Makes a Company Great?" *Fortune* (October 26, 1998): 218; James C. Collins and Jerry I. Porras, *Built to Last: Successful Habits of Visionary Companies* (New York: HarperCollins, 1994); and James C. Collins, "Change Is Good—But First Know What Should Never Change," *Fortune* (May 29, 1995): 141.

59. Andrew Wahl, "Culture Shock," *Canadian Business* (October 10–23, 2005): 115–116.

60. Jennifer A. Chatman and Sandra Eunyoung Cha, "Leading by Leveraging Culture," *California Management Review* 45, no. 4 (Summer 2003): 20–34.

61. This section is based on Jeff Rosenthal and Mary Ann Masarech, "High Peformance Cultures: How Values Can Drive Business Results," *Journal of Organizational Excellence* (Spring 2003): 3–18.

62. Rosenthal and Masarech, "High-Performance Cultures," Note 61.

63. Katherine Mieszkowski, "Community Standards," *Fast Company* (September 2000): 368; Rosabeth Moss Kanter, "A More Perfect Union," *Inc.* (February 2001): 92–98; Raizel Robin, "Net Gains" segment of "E-Biz That Works," *Canadian Business* (October 14–26, 2003): 107.

64. Reggie Van Lee, Lisa Fabish, and Nancy McGaw, "The Value of Corporate Values: A Booz Allen Hamilton/Aspen Institute Survey," *Strategy + Business* 39 (Spring 2005): 52–65.

65. Lucas Conley, "Cultural Phenomenon," *Fast Company* (April 2005): 76–77.

66. Rosenthal and Masarech, "High-Performance Cultures," Note 61.

67. John P. Kotter and James L. Heskett, *Corporate Culture and Performance* (New York: Free Press, 1992); Eric Flamholtz and Rangapriya Kannan-Narasimhan, "Differential Impact of Cultural Elements on Financial Performance," *European Management Journal* 23, no. 1 (2005): 50–64. Also see J. M. Kouzes and B. Z. Posner, *The Leadership Challenge: How to Keep Getting Extraordinary Things Done in Organizations*, 3rd ed. (San Francisco: Jossey-Bass, 2002).

68. Micah R. Kee, "Corporate Culture Makes a Fiscal Difference," *Industrial Management* (November–December 2003): 16–20.

69. Rosenthal and Masarech, "High-Performance Cultures," Note 63; Lencioni, "Make Your Values Mean Something," Note 44; and Thomas J. Peters and Robert H. Waterman, Jr., *In Search of Excellence* (New York: Warner, 1988).

70. Jenny C. McCune, "Exporting Corporate Culture," *Management Review* (December 3, 1999): 52–56.

71. Lencioni, "Make Your Values Mean Something," Note 42.

72. Andrew Wahl, "Culture Shock," *Canadian Business* (October 10–23, 2005): 115–116; and Calvin Leung, Michelle Magnan, and Andrew Wahl, "People Power," *Canadian Business* (October 10–23, 2005): 125–126.

73. Guyon, "The Soul of a Moneymaking Machine," Note 55; and Geoff Colvin, "The 100 Best Companies to Work For 2006," *Fortune* (January 23, 2006).

Chapter 3

Managing in a Global Environment

1. Evan Ramstad, "Lenova Picks Turin for 'Coming-Out Party': Chinese PC Maker Uses Games to Move Beyond IBM Brand," *Asian Wall Street Journal* (February 10, 2006): 26; Louise Lee with Peter Burrows and Bruce Einhorn, "Dell May Have to Reboot in China," *BusinessWeek* (November 7, 2005): 46; Evan Ramstad and Gary McWilliams, "Computer Savvy; For Dell, Success in China Tells Tale of Maturing Market," *Wall Street Journal* (July 5, 2005): A1, A8; and Charles Forelle, "Lenova Taps Dell's Asia Chief as CEO for Next Growth Phase," *Wall Street Journal* (December 21, 2005): B2.

2. Lee et al., "Dell May Have to Reboot in China"; and Ramstad and McWilliams, "Computer Savv," Note 1.

3. David Kirkpatrick, "One World—For Better or Worse," *Fortune* (November 26, 2001): 74–75.

4. Nilly Ostro-Landau and Hugh D. Menzies, "The New World Economic Order," in *International Business 97/98, Annual Editions*, Fred Maidment, ed. (Guilford, CT: Dushkin Publishing Group, 1997): 24–30; and Murray Weidenbaum, "American Isolationism versus the Global Economy," in *International Business 97/98, Annual Editions*, Fred Maidment, ed. (Guilford CT: Dushkin Publishing Group, 1997): 12–15.

5. Jason Dean, "Upgrade Plan: Long a Low-Tech Player, China Sets Its Sights on Chip Making," *Wall Street Journal* (February 17, 2004): A1.

6. Pete Engardio, "A New World Economy," *BusinessWeek* (August 22–29, 2005): 52–58.

7. Joseph B. White, "There Are No German or U.S. Companies, Only Successful Ones," *Wall Street Journal* (May 7, 1998): A1.

8. Ted C. Fishman, "How China Will Change Your Business," *Inc. Magazine* (March 2005): 70–84; and Stephen Baker, "The Bridges Steel is Building," *BusinessWeek* (June 2, 1997): 39.

9. Figures provided by CXO Media, reported in Steve Ulfelder, "All the Web's a Stage," *CIO* (October 1, 2000): 133–142; and Pete Engardio, "A New World Economy," Note 6.

10. Jena McGregor, "A Foreign Affair," *Fast Company* (December 2005): 67–68.

11. Justin Martin, "The Global CEO: Overseas Experience Is Becoming a Must on Top Executives' Resumes," *Chief Executive* (January–February 2004): 24.

12. Christopher Bartlett, *Managing Across Borders*, 2d ed. (Boston: Harvard Business School Press, 1998)

13. Daniel W. Drezner, "The Outsourcing Bogeyman," *Foreign Affairs* (May–June 2004).

14. Engardio et al.,"Is Your Job Next?" Elisabeth Malkin, "Backlash," *BusinessWeek* (April 24, 2000): 38–44; Pete Engardio, "A New World Economy," Note 6.

15. Jean Kerr, "Export Strategies, "*Small Business Reports* (May 1989): 20–25.

16. Fishman,"How China Will Change Your Business," Note 8.

17. Pete Engardio, "A New World Economy," Note 6.

18. David Wighton, "Indian Growth for JPMortan," *Financial Times* (December 5, 2005): 1, 18.

19. James Flanigan, "Now, High-Tech Work Is Going Abroad," *The New York Times* (November 17, 2005): C6.

20. Cited in Gary Ferraro, *Cultural Anthropology: An Applied Perspective*, 3d ed. (Belmont, CA: West/Wadsworth, 1998): 68.

21. Jim Holt, "Gone Global?"*Management Review* (March 2000): 13.

22. Ibid.

23. "Slogans Often Lose Something in Translation," *The New Mexican* (July 3, 1994): F1, F2.

24. Louis S. Richman, "Global Growth Is on a Tear," in *International Business 97/98, Annual Editions*, Fred Maidment, ed. (Guilford, CT: Dushkin Publishing Group, 1997): 6–11.

25. Amal Kumar Jaj, "United Technologies Looks Far from Home for Growth," *Wall Street Journal* (May 26, 1994): B4.

26. Engardio," A New World Economy," Note 6.

27. Andrew E. Serwer, "McDonald's Conquers the World," *Fortune* (October 17, 1994): 103–116.

28. David W. Conklin,"Analyzing and Managing Country Risks," *Ivey Business Journal* (January–February 2002): 37–41.

29. Bruce Kogut, "Designing Global Strategies: Profiting from Operational Flexibility," *Sloan Management Review* 27 (Fall 1985): 27–38.

30. Ian Bremmer, "Managing Risk in an Unstable World," *Harvard Business Review* (June 2005): 51–60; and Mark Fitzpatrick, "The Definition and Assessment of Political Risk in International Business: A Review of the Literature," *Academy of Management Review* 8 (1983): 249–254.

31. Bremmer, "Managing Risk in an Unstable World," Note 30.

32. Kevin Sullivan, "Kidnapping Is Growth Industry in Mexico; Businessmen Targeted in Climate of Routine Ransoms, Police Corruption," *Washington Post* (September 17, 2002): A1.

33. Brian O'Keefe, "Global Brands," *Fortune* (November 26, 2001): 102–110.

34. Conklin," Analyzing and Managing Country Risks," Note 28.

35. Ibid.

36. Geert Hofstede,"The Interaction between National and Organizational Value Systems," *Journal of Management Studies* 22 (1985): 347–357; and Geert Hofstede, "The Cultural Relativity of the Quality of Life Concept," *Academy of Management Review* 9 (1984): 389–398.

37. Geert Hofstede, "Cultural Constraints in Management Theory," *Academy of Management Executive* 7 (1993): 81–94; and G. Hofstede and M. H. Bond, "The Confucian Connection: From Cultural Roots to Economic Growth," *Organizational Dynamics* 16 (1988): 4–21.

38. "Retrospective: *Culture's Consequences*," a collection of articles focusing on Hofstede's work, appeared in *The Academy of Management Executive* 18, no. 1 (February 2004): 72–93. See also Michele J. Gelfand, D. P. S. Bhawuk, Lisa H. Nishii, and David J. Bechtold, "Individualism and Collectivism," in R. J. House et al., eds., *Culture, Leadership and Organizations: The Globe Study of 62 Societies* (Thousand Oaks, CA: Sage, 2004).

39. Robert J. House, Paul J. Hanges, Mansour Javidan, Peter W. Dorfman, and Vipin Gupta, *Culture, Leadership, and Organizations: The GLOBE Study of 62 Societies* (Thousand Oaks, CA: Sage Publications, 2004); M. Javidan and R. J. House, "Cultural Acumen for the Global Manager: Lessons from Project GLOBE," *Organizational Dynamics* 29, no. 4 (2001): 289–305; and R. J. House, M. Javidan, Paul Hanges, and Peter Dorfman, "Understanding Cultures and Implicit Leadership Theories Across the Globe: An Introduction to Project GLOBE," *Journal of World Business* 37 (2002): 3–10.

40. Chantell E. Nicholls, Henry W. Lane, and Mauricio Brehm Brechu, "Taking Self-Managed Teams to Mexico," *Academy of Management Executive* 13, no. 2 (1999): 15–27; Carl F. Fey and Daniel R. Denison, "Organizational Culture and Effectiveness: Can American Theory Be Applied in Russia?" *Organization Science* 14, no. 6 (November–December 2003): 686–706; Ellen F. Jackofsky, John W. Slocum, Jr., and Sara J. McQuaid, "Cultural Values and the CEO: Alluring Companions?" Academy of Management Executive 2 (1988): 39–49.

41. Terence Jackson, "The Management of People Across Cultures: Valuing People Differently," *Human Resource Management* 41, no. 4 (Winter 2002): 455–475.

42. Carol Hymowitz, "Companies Go Global, But Many Managers Just Don't Travel Well," *Wall Street Journal* (August 15, 2000): B1.

43. Orla Sheehan, "Managing a Multinational Corporation: Tomorrow's Decision Makers Speak Out," *Fortune* (August 24, 1992): 233; Jonathan Friedland and Louise Lee, "The Wal-Mart Way Sometimes Gets Lost in Translation Overseas," *Wall Street Journal* (October 8, 1997): A1, A12.

44. Michael R. Czinkota, Ilkka A. Ronkainen, Michael H. Moffett, and Eugene O. Moynihan, *Global Business* (Fort Worth, TX: Dryden Press, 1995): 151; and Robert D. Gatewood, Robert R. Taylor, and O. C. Ferrell, *Management* (Burr Ridge, IL: Irwin, 1995): 131–132.

45. "For Richer, for Poorer," *The Economist* (December 1993): 66; Richard Harmsen,"The Uruguay Round: A Boon for the World Economy," *Finance & Development* (March 1995): 24–26; Salil S. Pitroda, "From GATT to WTO: The Institutionalization of World Trade," *Harvard International Review* (Spring 1995): 46–47, 66–67; David H. Holt, *International Management: Text and Cases* (Fort Worth: Dryden, 1998); and www.wto.org (accessed on February 20, 2006).

46. This discussion of WTO is based on William J. Kehoe, "GATT and WTO Facilitating Global Trade," *Journal of Global Business* (Spring 1998): 67–76.

47. "The History of the European Union," www.europa.eu.int/ abc/history/index_en.htm (accessed on February 16, 2004)

48. Justin Fox, "Introducing the Euro," *Fortune* (December 19, 2001): 229–236.

49. Lynda Radosevich, "New Money," *CIO Enterprise*, Section 2 (April 15, 1998): 54–55.

50. Barbara Rudolph, "Megamarket," *Time* (August 10, 1992): 43–44.

51. Tapan Munroe, "NAFTA Still a Work in Progress," *Knight Ridder/Tribune News Service* (January 9, 2004); www. contracostatimes.com; and J. S. McClenahan, "NAFTA Works," *IW* (January 10, 2000): 5–6.

52. Amy Barrett, "It's a Small (Business) World," *BusinessWeek* (April 17, 1995): 96–101.

53. Eric Alterman, "A Spectacular Success?" *The Nation* (February 2, 2004): 10; Jeff Faux, "NAFTA at 10: Where Do We Go From Here?" *The Nation* (February 2, 2004): 11; Geri Smith and Cristina Lindblad, "Mexico: Was NAFTA Worth It? A Tale of What Free Trade Can and Cannot Do," *BusinessWeek* (December 22, 2003): 66; Jeffrey Sparshott, "NAFTA Gets Mixed Reviews," *Washington Times* (December 18, 2003): C10; and Munroe, "NAFTA Is Still Work in Progress," Note 51.

54. Munroe, "NAFTA Is Still Work In Progress," Note 51; Jeffrey Sparshott, "NAFTA Gets Mixed Reviews," *Washington Times* (December 18, 2003): C10; Amy Borrus, "A Free-Trade Milestone, with Many More Miles to Go," *BusinessWeek* (August 24, 1992): 30–31.

55. This review is based on Jyoti Thottam, "Is Your Job Going Abroad?" *Time* (March 1, 2004): 26–36; and Pete Engardio, Aaron Bernstein, and Manjeet Kripalani, "Is Your Job Next?" *BusinessWeek* (February 3, 2003): 50–60.

56. Reported in "IBM Data Give Rare Look at Sensitive 'Offshoring' Plans," *CNNMoney* (January 19, 2004); www.money.cnn.com (accessed on January 19, 2004)

57. Thottam, "Is Your Job Going Abroad?" Note 55.

58. Jerry Useem, "There's Something Happening Here," *Fortune* (May 15, 2000): Paul Magnusson, "Meet Free Traders' Worst Nightmare," *BusinessWeek* (March 20, 2000): 113–118; Elisabeth Malkin, "Backlash," *BusinessWeek* (April 24, 2000): 38–44.

59. See, for example, Alan Greenspan, "International Trade: Globalization vs. Protectionism," address printed in *Vital Speeches of the Day* (April 15, 2001): 386–388.

60. Michael Schroeder and Timothy Aeppel, "Skilled Workers Sway Politicians with Fervor Against Free Trade," *Wall Street Journal* (December 10, 2003): A1, A11.

61. Morgan W. McCall Jr. and George P. Hollenbeck, "Global Fatalities: When International Executives Derail," *Ivey Business Journal* (May–June 2002): 75–78.

62. The discussion of cultural intelligence is based on P. Christopher Earley and Elaine Mosakowski, "Cultural Intelligence," *Harvard Business Review* (October 2004): 139; Ilan Alon and James M. Higgins, "Global Leadership Success Through Emotional and Cultural Intelligence," *Business Horizons* 48 (2005): 501–512; P. C. Earley and Soon Ang, *Cultural Intelligence: Individual Actions Across Cultures* (Stanford, CA: Stanford Business Books); and David C. Thomas and Kerr Inkson, *Cultural Intelligence* (San Francisco: Berrett-Koehler, 2004).

63. These components are from Earley and Mosakowski, "Cultural Intelligence," Note 62.

64. Karl Moore, "Great Global Managers," *Across the Board* (May–June 2003): 40–43.

65. Richard E. Nisbett, *The Geography of Thought: How Asians and Westerners Think Differently . . . and Why* (New York: Free Press, 2003), reported in Sharon Begley, "East vs. West: One Sees the Big Picture, The Other Is Focused," *Wall Street Journal* (March 28, 2003): B1.

66. Robert T. Moran and John R. Riesenberger, *The Global Challenge* (London: McGraw-Hill, 1994): 251–262.

67. Valerie Frazee, "Keeping Up on Chinese Culture," *Global Workforce* (October 1996): 16–17; and Jack Scarborough, "Comparing Chinese and Western Cultural Roots: Why 'East Is East and . . . ,' "*Business Horizons* (November–December 1998): 15–24.

68. Mansour Javidan and Ali Dastmalchian, "Culture and Leadership in Iran: The Land of Individual Achievers, Strong Family Ties, and Powerful Elite," *Academy of Management Executive* 17, no. 4 (2003): 127–142.

69. Randall S. Schuler, Susan E. Jackson, Ellen Jackofsky, and John W. Slocum, Jr., "Managing Human Resources in Mexico: A Cultural Understanding," *Business Horizons* (May–June 1996): 55–61.

70. Xu Huang and Evert Van De Vliert, "Where Intrinsic Job Satisfaction Fails to Work: National Moderators of Intrinsic Motivation," *Journal of Organizational Behavior* 24 (2003): 159–179.

71. Shari Caudron, "Lessons from HR Overseas," *Personnel Journal* (February 1995): 88.

72. Reported in Begley, "East vs. West," Note 65.

Chapter 4

Ethics and Social Responsibility

1. Landon Thomas, Jr. "On Wall Street, A Rise in Dismissals Over Ethics," *The New York Times* (March 29, 2005), www. nytimes.com.

2. Bethany McLean, "Why Enron Went Bust," *Fortune* (December 24, 2001): 58–68; survey results reported in Patricia Wallington, "Honestly?!" *CIO* (March 15, 2003): 41–42.

3. Data from KPMG, reported in Muel Kaptein, "The Diamond of Managerial Integrity," *European Management Journal* 21, no. 1 (2003): 99–108.

4. Katie Hafner and Claudia H. Deutsch, "When Good Will Is Also Good Business," *The New York Times* (September 14, 2005): www.nytimes.com; Peter Asmus, "100 Best Corporate Citizens, 2005," *Business Ethics* (Spring 2005): 20–27; Michelle Conlin and Jessi Hempel, with Joshua Tanzer and David Polek, "Philanthropy 2003: The Corporate Donors," *BusinessWeek* (December 1, 2003): 92–96.

5. Gordon F. Shea, *Practical Ethics* (New York: American Management Association, 1988); and Linda K. Treviño, "Ethical Decision Making in Organizations; A Person-Situation Interactionist Model," *Academy of Management Review* 11 (1986): 601–617.

6. Thomas M. Jones, "Ethical Decision Making by Individuals in Organizations: An Issue-Contingent Model," *Academy of Management Review* 16(1991): 366–395.

7. John R. Emshwiller and Alexei Barrionuevo, "U.S. Prosecutors File Indictment Against Skilling," *Wall Street Journal* (February 20, 2004): A1, A13.

8. See Clinton W. McLemore, *Street-Smart Ethics: Succeeding in Business Without Selling Your Soul* (Louisville, KY: Westminster John Knox Press, 2003), for a cogent discussion of some ethical and legal issues associated with Enron's collapse.

9. Rushworth M. Kidder, "The Three Great Domains of Human Action," *Christian Science Monitor* (January 30, 1990).

10. Linda K. Treviño and Katherine A. Nelson, *Managing Business Ethics: Straight Talk About How to Do It Right* (New York: John Wiley & Sons, Inc. 1995): 4.

11. Jones, "Ethical Decision Making by Individuals in Organizations," Note 6.

12. Based on a question from a General Electric employee ethics guide, reported in Kathryn Kranhold, "U.S. Firms Raise Ethics Focus," *Wall Street Journal* (November 28, 2005): B4.

13. Based on information in Constance E. Bagley, "The Ethical Leader's Decision Tree," *Harvard Business Review* (February 2003): 18–19.

14. Based on information in Vadim Liberman, "Scoring on the Job," *Across the Board* (November–December 2003): 46–50.

15. This discussion is based on Gerald F. Cavanagh, Dennis J. Moberg, and Manuel Velasquez, "The Ethics of Organizational Politics," *Academy of Management Review* 6 (1981): 363–374; Justin G. Longenecker, Joseph A. McKinney, and Carlos W. Moore, "Egoism and Independence: Entrepreneurial Ethics," *Organizational Dynamics* (Winter 1988): 64–72; Carolyn Wiley, "The ABCs of Business Ethics: Definitions, Philosophies, and Implementation," *IM* (February 1995): 22–27; and Mark Mallinger, "Decisive Decision Making: An Exercise Using Ethical Frameworks," *Journal of Management Education* (August 1997): 411–417.

16. Michael J. McCarthy, "Now the Boss Knows Where You're Clicking," and "Virtual Morality: A New Workplace Quandary," *Wall Street Journal* (October 21, 1999): B1, B4; and Jeffrey L. Seglin, "Who's Snooping on You?" *Business 2.0* (August 8, 2000): 202–203.

17. Thomas M. Burton, "Red Flags; Amid Alarm Bells, A Blood Substitute Keeps Pumping," *Wall Street Journal* (February 22, 2006): A1, A12.

18. John Kekes, "Self-Direction: The Core of Ethical Individualism," in *Organizations and Ethical Individualism*, ed. Konstanian Kolenda (New York: Praeger, 1988): 1–18.

19. Tad Tulega, *Beyond the Bottom Line* (New York: Penguin Books, 1987).

20. Lynn Sharp Paine, "Managing for Organizational Integrity," *Harvard Business Review* (March–April 1994): 106–117.

21. This discussion is based on Treviño, "Ethical Decision Making in Organizations," Note 5.

22. L. Kohlberg, "Moral Stages and Moralization: The Cognitive-Developmental Approach," in *Moral Development and Behavior: Theory, Research, and Social Issues*, ed. T. Lickona (New York: Holt, Rinehart & Winston, 1976): 31–83; L. Kohlberg, "Stage and Sequence: The Cognitive-Developmental Approach to Socialization," in *Handbook of Socialization Theory and Research*, ed. D. A. Goslin (Chicago: Rand McNally, 1969); and Jill W. Graham, "Leadership, Moral Development, and Citizenship Behavior," *Business Ethics Quarterly* 5, no. 1 (January 1995): 43–54.

23. Carol Gilligan, *In a Different Voice: Psychological Theory and Women's Development* (Cambridge, MA: Harvard University Press, 1982).

24. See Thomas Donaldson and Thomas W. Dunfee, "When Ethics Travel: The Promise and Peril of Global Business Ethics," *California Management Review* 41, No. 4 (Summer 1999): 45–63.

25. Transparency International, "Transparency International Releases New Bribe Payers Index," www.transparency.org (accessed on February 24, 2004).

26. Paul Burnham Finney, "The Perils of Bribery Meet the Open Palm," *The New York Times* (May 17, 2005): www.nytimes.com.

27. Susan Pulliam, "Crossing the Line; At Center of Fraud, WorldCom Official Sees Life Unravel," *Wall Street Journal* (March 24, 2005): A1; and S. Pulliam, "Over the Line: A Staffer Ordered to Commit Fraud Balked, Then Caved," *Wall Street Journal* (June 23, 2003): A1.

28. Duane M. Covrig, "The Organizational Context of Moral Dilemmas: The Role of Moral Leadership in Administration in Making and Breaking Dilemmas," *Journal of Leadership Studies* 7, no. 1 (2000): 40–59; and James Weber, "Influences

Upon Organizational Ethical Subclimates: A Multi-Departmental Analysis of a Single Firm," *Organizational Science* 6, no. 5 (September–October 1995): 509–523.

29. Linda Klebe Treviño, "A Cultural Perspective on Changing and Developing Organizational Ethics," in *Research and Organizational Change and Development,* ed. R. Woodman and W. Pasmore (Greenwich, CT: JAI Press, 1990): 4.

30. *Ibid*; John B. Cullen, Bart Victor, and Carroll Stephens, "An Ethical Weather Report: Assessing the Organization's Ethical Climate," *Organizational Dynamics* (Autumn 1989): 50–62; and Bart Victor and John B. Cullen, "The Organizational Bases of Ethical Work Climates," *Administrative Science Quarterly* 33 (1988): 101–125.

31. Eugene W. Szwajkowski, "The Myths and Realities of Research on Organizational Misconduct," in *Research in Corporate Social Performance and Policy,* ed. James E. Post (Greenwich, CT: JAI Press, 1986): 9:103–122; and Keith Davis, William C. Frederick, and Robert L. Blostrom, *Business and Society: Concepts and Policy Issues* (New York: McGraw-Hill, 1979).

32. Douglas S. Sherwin, "The Ethical Roots of the Business System," *Harvard Business Review* 61 (November–December 1983): 183–192.

33. Nancy C. Roberts and Paula J. King, "The Stakeholder Audit Goes Public," *Organizational Dynamics* (Winter 1989): 63–79; Thomas Donaldson and Lee E. Preston, "The Stakeholder Theory of the Corporation: Concepts, Evidence, and Implications," *Academy of Management Review* 20, no. 1 (1995): 65–91; and Jeffrey S. Harrison and Caron H. St. John, "Managing and Partnering with External Stakeholders," *Academy of Management Executive* 10, no. 2 (1996): 46–60.

34. Clay Chandler, "The Great Wal-Mart of China," *Fortune* (July 25, 2005): 104–116; and Charles Fishman, "The Wal-Mart You Don't Know—Why Low Prices Have a High Cost," *Fast Company* (December 2003): 68–80.

35. David Wheeler, Barry Colbert, and R. Edward Freeman, "Focusing on Value: Reconciling Corporate Social Responsibility, Sustainability, and a Stakeholder Approach in a Networked World," *Journal of General Management* 28, no. 3 (Spring 2003): 1–28; James E. Post, Lee E. Preston, and Sybille Sachs, "Managing the Extended Enterprise: The New StakeholderView," *California Management Review* 45, no. 1 (Fall 2002): 6–28; and Peter Fritsch and Timothy Mapes, "Seed Money; In Indonesia, A Tangle of Bribes Creates Trouble for Monsanto," *Wall Street Journal* (April 5, 2005): A1, A6.

36. Max B. E. Clarkson, "A Stakeholder Framework for Analyzing and Evaluating Corporate Social Performance," *Academy of Management Review* 20, no. 1 (1995): 92–117.

37. Asmus, "100 Best Corporate Citizens," Note 4.

38. "The World We Serve," *Bristol-Myers Squibb 2002 Annual Report,* Bristol-Myers Squibb Company.

39. Mark A. Cohen, "Management and the Environment," *The Owen Manager* 15, no. 1 (1993): 2–6.

40. R. E. Freeman, J. Pierce, and R. Dodd, *Shades of Green: Business Ethics and the Environment* (New York: Oxford University Press, 1995).

41. Greg Toppo, "Company Agrees to Pay Record Pollution Fine," Associated Press, *Johnson City Press* (July 21, 2000): 9.

42. Andrew C. Revkin, "7 Companies Agree to Cut Gas Emissions," *The New York Times* (October 18, 2000): C1, C6.

43. This definition is based on Marc J. Epstein and Marie-Josée Roy, "Improving Sustainability Performance: Specifying, Implementing and Measuring Key Principles," *Journal of General Management* 29, no. 1 (Autumn 2003): 15–31, World Commission on Economic Development, *Our Common Future* (Oxford: Oxford University Press, 1987): and Marc Gunther, "Tree Huggers, Soy Lovers, and Profits," *Fortune* (June 23, 2003): 98–104.

44. Peter Asmus, "17th Annual Business Ethics Awards," *Business Ethics* (Fall 2005): 15–19.

45. Gunther, "Tree Huggers, Soy Lovers, and Profits, Note 43."

46. Brian Deagon, "New Technology Could Boost Efficiency and Green Image for UPS," *Investor's Business Daily* (December 10, 2003); and Charles Haddad with Christine Tierney, "FedEx and Brown Are Going Green," *BusinessWeek* (August 11, 2003): 60.

47. Gunther, "Tree Huggers, Soy Lovers, and Profits."

48. The discussion of ISO 14001 is based on Pratima Bansal, "The Corporate Challenges of Sustainable Development," *Academy of Management Executive* 16, no. 2 (2002): 122–131.

49. Karina Funk, "Sustainability and Performance," *MIT Sloan Management Review* (Winter 2003): 65–70; and "The Fast 50: Trendsetters," *Fast Company* (March 2002).

50. Mark S. Schwartz and Archie B. Carroll, "Corporate Social Responsibility: A Three-Domain Approach," *Business Ethics Quarterly* 13, no. 4 (2003): 503–530; and Archie B. Carroll, "A Three-Dimensional Conceptual Model of Corporate Performance," *Academy of Management Review* 4 (1979): 497–505. For a discussion of various models for evaluating corporate social performance, also see Diane L. Swanson, "Addressing a Theoretical Problem by Reorienting the Corporate Social Performance Model," *Academy of Management Review* 20, no. 1 (1995): 43–64.

51. N. Craig Smith, "Corporate Social Responsibility: Whether or How?" *California Management Review* 45, no. 4 (Summer 2003): 52–76.

52. Milton Friedman, *Capitalism and Freedom* (Chicago: University of Chicago Press, 1962): 133; and Milton Friedman and Rose Friedman, *Free to Choose* (New York: Harcourt Brace Jovanovich, 1979).

53. Umesh Kher, "Getting Smart at Being Good . . . Are Companies Better Off For It?" *Time* (January 2006): A1–A8.

54. Eugene W. Szwajkowski, "Organizational Illegality: Theoretical Integration and Illustrative Application," *Academy of Management Review* 10 (1985): 558–567.

55. Deborah Solomon and Anne Marie Squeo, "Crackdown Puts Corporations, Executives in New Legal Peril," *Wall Street Journal Online* (June 20, 2005): http:online.wsj.com.

56. Kurt Eichenwald, "U.S. Awards Tenet Whistle-Blowers $8.1 Million," *The New York Times* (January 8, 2004): www.nytimes.com.

57. David J. Fritzsche and Helmut Becker, "Linking Management Behavior to Ethical Philosophy—An Empirical Investigation," *Academy of Management Journal* 27 (1984): 165–175.

58. Kevin Kelly, "My Slithery Rivals," *FSB* (February 2005): 28–29; Reed Abelson, "Possible Conflicts for Doctors Are Seen on Medical Devices," *The New York Times* (September 22, 2005): www.nytimes.com.

59. Katie Hafner and Claudi H. Deutsch, "When Good Will Is Also Good Business," *The New York Times* (September 14, 2005): www.nytimes.com.

60. Saul W. Gellerman, "Managing Ethics from the Top Down," *Sloan Management Review* (Winter 1989): 73–79.

61. This discussion is based on Linda Klebe Treviño, Laura Pincus Hartman, and Michael Brown, "Moral Person and Moral Manager: How Executives Develop a Reputation for Ethical Leadership," *California Management Review* 42, no. 4 (Summer 2000): 128–142.

62. Muel Kaptein, "The Diamond of Managerial Integrity," *European Management Journal* 21, no. 1 (2003): 99–108.

63. Business Roundtable Institute for Corporate Ethics, www.corporate-ethics.org, and "Corporate Ethics: A Prime Business Asset," (February 1988): *The Business Roundtable*, 200 Park Avenue, Suite 2222, New York, NY 10166.

64. Michael Barrier, "Doing the Right Thing," *Nation's Business* (March 1998): 33–38; Joseph L. Badaracco, Jr., and Allen P. Webb, "Business Ethics: A View from the Trenches," *California Management Review* 37, no. 2 (Winter 1995): 8–28.

65. Gary R. Weaver, Linda Klebe Treviño, and Bradley Agle, "'Somebody I Look Up To:' Ethical Role Models in Organizations," *Organizational Dynamics* 34, no. 4 (2005): 313–330; and L. K. Treviño, G. R. Weaver, David G. Gibson, and Barbara Ley Toffler, "Managing Ethics and Legal Compliance: What Works and What Hurts?" *California Management Review* 41, no. 2 (Winter 1999): 131–151.

66. Treviño, Hartman, and Brown, "Moral Person and Moral Manager," Note 61.

67. Weaver, Treviño, and Agle, "Somebody I Look Up To," Note 65.

68. Ibid.

69. Dennis K. Berman, "Does Wall Street Finally Need an Ethics Code?" *Wall Street Journal* (March 10, 2005): C1.

70. Treviño et al., "Managing Ethics and Legal Compliance."

71. Carolyn Wiley, "The ABC's of Business Ethics: Definitions, Philosophies, and Implementation," *IM* (January–February 1995): 22–27; Badaracco and Webb, "Business Ethics: a View from the Trenches"; and Ronald B. Morgan, "Self- and Co-Worker Perceptions of Ethics and Their Relationships to Leadership and Salary," *Academy of Management Journal* 36, no. 1 (February 1993): 200–214.

72. Journal Communications—Code of Ethics, from Codes of Ethics Online, The Center for the Study of Ethics in the Professions, Illinois Institute of Technology, www.iit.edu/departments/csep/ PublicWWW/codes/index.html.

73. Alan Yuspeh, "Do the Right Thing," *CIO* (August 1, 2000): 56–58.

74. The Ethics and Compliance Officers Association, www.theecoa.org (accessed on February 27, 2006).

75. Beverly Geber, "The Right and Wrong of Ethics Offices," *Training* (October 1995): 102–118.

76. Kranhold, "U.S. Firms Raise Ethics Focus" and "Our Actions: GE 2005 Citizenship Report," General Electric Company, 2005.

77. Amy Zipkin, "Getting Religion on Corporate Ethics," *The New York Times*, (October 18, 2000): C1.

78. Marcia Parmarlee Miceli and Janet P. Near, "The Relationship among Beliefs, Organizational Positions, and Whistle-Blowing Status: A Discriminant Analysis," *Academy of Management Journal* 27 (1984): 687–705.

79. Eugene Garaventa, "*An Enemy of the People* by Henrik Ibsen: The Politics of Whistle-Blowing," *Journal of Management Inquiry* 3, no. 4 (December 1994): 369–374; Marcia P. Miceli and Janet P. Near, "Whistleblowing: Reaping the Benefits," *Academy of Management Executive* 8, no. 3 (1994): 65–74.

80. Jayne O'Donnell, "Blowing the Whistle Can Lead to Harsh Aftermath, Despite Law," *USA Today* (July 31, 2005): www.usatoday.com.

81. Jerry G. Kreuze, Zahida Luqmani, and Mushtaq Luqmani, "Shades of Gray," *Internal Auditor* (April 2001): 48.

82. George Stalk, "Warm and Fuzzy Doesn't Cut It," *Wall Street Journal* (February 15, 2005): B2.

83. Hafner and Deutsch, "When Good Will Is Also Good Business"; John A. Pearce II and Jonathan P. Doh, "The High Impact of Collaborative Social Initiatives," *MIT Sloan Management Review* (Spring 2005): 30–39; Carol Hymowitz, "Asked to Be Charitable, More CEOs Seek to Aid Their Businesses As Well," *Wall Street Journal* (February 22, 2005): B1.

84. Cristina Simón, Juan Luis Martínez, and Ana Agüero, "Solidarity Day at Unión Fenosa in Spain," *Business Horizons* 48 (2005): 161–168.

85. Homer H. Johnson, "Does It Pay to Be Good? Social Responsibility and Financial Performance" *Business Horizons* (November–December 2003): 34–40; Jennifer J. Griffin and John F. Mahon, "The Corporate Social Performance and Corporate Financial Performance Debate: Twenty-Five Years of Incomparable Research," *Business and Society* 36, no. 1 (March

1997): 5–31; Bernadette M. Ruf, Krishnamurty Muralidar, Robert M. Brown, Jay J. Janney, and Karen Paul, "An Empirical Investigation of the Relationship between Change in Corporate Social Performance and Financial Performance: A Stakeholder Theory Perspective," *Journal of Business Ethics* 32, no. 2 (July 2001): 143; Philip L. Cochran and Robert A. Wood, "Corporate Social Responsibility and Financial Performance," *Academy of Management Journal* 27 (1984): 42–56.

86. Paul C. Godfrey, "The Relationship Between Corporate Philanthropy and Shareholder Wealth: A Risk Management Perspective," *Academy of Management Review* 30, no. 4 (2005): 777–798; J. A. Pearce II and J. P. Doh, "The High Impact of Collaborative Social Initiatives"; Curtis C. Verschoor and Elizabeth A. Murphy, "The Financial Performance of Large U.S. Firms and Those with Global Prominence: How Do the Best Corporate Citizens Rate?" *Business and Society Review* 107, no. 3 (Fall 2002): 371–381; Johnson, "Does It Pay to Be Good?"; Dale Kurschner, "5 Ways Ethical Business Creates Fatter Profits," *Business Ethics* (March–April 1996): 20–23. Also see studies reported in Lori Ioannou, "Corporate America's Social Conscience," *Fortune* (May 26, 2003): S1–S10.

87. Verschoor and Murphy, "The Financial Performance of Large U.S. Firms," Note 86

88. Gretchen Morgenson, "Shares of Corporate Nice Guys Can Finish First," *The New York Times* (April 27, 2003): Section 3, 1.

89. Jean B. McGuire, Alison Sundgren, and Thomas Schneeweis, "Corporate Social Responsibility and Firm Financial Performance," *Academy of Management Journal* 31 (1988): 854–872; and Louisa Wah, "Treading the Sacred Ground," *Management Review* (July–August 1998): 18–22.

90. Vogel, "Is There a Market for Virtue?"

91. Daniel W. Greening and Daniel B. Turban, "Corporate Social Performance as a Competitive Advantage in Attracting a Quality Workforce," *Business and Society* 39, no. 3 (September 2000): 254.

92. "The Socially Correct Corporate Business," in Leslie Holstrom and Simon Brady, "The Changing Face of Global Business," *Fortune* (July 24, 2000): S1–S38.

93. Based on survey results from PricewaterhouseCoopers, *2002 Sustainability Survey Report,* reported in Ioannou, "Corporate America's Social Conscience."

Chapter 5

Managerial Planning and Goal Setting

1. Quoted in Oren Harari, "Good/Bad News about Strategy," *Management Review* (July 1995): 29–31.

2. Amitai Etzioni, *Modern Organizations* (Englewood Cliffs, NJ: Prentice Hall, 1984): 6.

3. Ibid.

4. Max D. Richards, *Setting Strategic Goals and Objectives,* 2d ed. (St. Paul, MN: West, 1986).

5. C. Chet Miller and Laura B. Cardinal, "Strategic Planning and Firm Performance: A Synthesis of More Than Two Decades of Research," *Academy of Management Journal* 37, no. 6 (1994): 1649–1685.

6. This discussion is based on Richard L. Daft and Richard M. Steers, *Organizations: A Micro/Macro Approach* (Glenview, IL: Scott, Foresman, 1986): 319–321; Herbert A. Simon, "On the Concept of Organizational Goals," *Administrative Science Quarterly* 9 (1964): 1–22; and Charles B. Saunders and Francis D. Tuggel, "Corporate Goals," *Journal of General Management* 5 (1980): 3–13.

7. Carol Hymowitz, "Big Companies Become Big Targets Unless They Guard Images Carefully," *Wall Street Journal* (December 12, 2005): B1; Robert Berner, "Can Wal-Mart Fit into a White Hat?" *BusinessWeek* (October 3, 2005): 94–96.

8. See "The 100 Best Companies to Work For, 2006," *Fortune* (January 23, 2006): 71–74; "2004 Special Report: The 100 Best Companies to Work For," *Fortune* (January 12, 2004): 56–80; and Kevin E. Joyce, "Lessons for Employers from *Fortune's* 100 Best," *Business Horizons* (March–April 2003): 77–84.

9. J. Lynn Lunsford, "Lean Times: With Airbus on Its Tail, Boeing Is Rethinking How It Builds Planes," *Wall Street Journal* (September 5, 2001): A1, A16.

10. Marc Gunther, "Tree Huggers, Soy Lovers, and Profits," *Fortune* (June 23, 2003): 98–104; Gary Fields and John R. Wilke, "The Ex-Files: FBI's New Focus Places Big Burden on Local Police," *Wall Street Journal* (June 30, 2003): A1, A12.

11. Paul Sloan, "The Sales Force That Rocks," *Business 2.0* (July 2005): 102–107.

12. Mary Klemm, Stuart Sanderson, and George Luffman, "Mission Statements: Selling Corporate Values to Employees," *Long-Range Planning* 24, no. 3 (1991): 73–78; John A. Pearce II and Fred David, "Corporate Mission Statements: The Bottom Line," *Academy of Management Executive* (1987): 109–116; Jerome H. Want, "Corporate Mission: The Intangible Contributor to Performance," *Management Review* (August 1986): 46–50; and Forest R. David and Fred R. David, "It's Time to Redraft Your Mission Statement," *Journal of Business Strategy* (January–February 2003): 11–14.

13. "Tennessee News and Notes from State Farm," State Farm Mutual Automobile Insurance Company, 2004.

14. Janet Adamy, "Father, Son, and Gum," *Wall Street Journal* (March 11–12, 2006): A1, A10.

15. Paul Meising and Joseph Wolfe, "The Art and Science of Planning at the Business Unit Level," *Management Science* 31 (1985): 773–781.

16. Based in part on information about 1-800-Flowers, in Jenny C. McCune, "On the Train Gang," *Management Review* (October 1994): 57–60.

17. "Study: IRS Employees Often Steer Taxpayers Wrong on Law Questions," *Johnson City Press* (September 4, 2003): 4A.

18. Geary A. Rummler and Kimberly Morrill, "The Results Chain," *TD* (February 2005): 27–35; and John C. Crotts, Duncan R. Dickson, and Robert C. Ford, "Aligning Organizational Processes with Mission: The Case of Service Excellence," *Academy of Management Executive* 19, no. 3 (August 2005): 54–68.

19. Karyll N. Shaw, "Changing the Goal-Setting Process at Microsoft," *Academy of Management Executive* 18, no. 4 (November 2004): 139–142.

20. Sayan Chatterjee, "Core Objectives: Clarity in Designing Strategy," *California Management Review* 47, no. 2 (Winter 2005): 33–49.

21. John O. Alexander, "Toward Real Performance: The Circuit-Breaker Technique," *Supervisory Management* (April 1989): 5–12.

22. Mark J. Fritsch, "Balanced Scorecard Helps Northern States Power's Quality Academy Achieve Extraordinary Performance," *Corporate University Review* (September–October 1997): 22.

23. Carol Hymowitz, "Readers Share Tales of Jobs Where Strategy Became Meeting Target," *Wall Street Journal* (March 22, 2005): B1; and Joy Riggs, "Empowering Workers by Setting Goals," *Nation's Business* (January 1995): 6.

24. Joel Hoekstra, "3M's Global Grip," *World Traveler* (May 2000): 31–34; and Thomas A. Stewart, "3M Fights Back," *Fortune* (February 5, 1996): 94–99.

25. Edwin A. Locke, Gary P. Latham, and Miriam Erez, "The Determinants of Goal Commitment," *Academy of Management Review* 13 (1988): 23–39.

26. George S. Odiorne, "MBO: A Backward Glance," *Business Horizons* 21 (October 1978): 14–24.

27. Jan P. Muczyk and Bernard C. Reimann, "MBO as a Complement to Effective Leadership," *The Academy of Management Executive* 3 (1989): 131–138; and W. Giegold, *Objective Setting and the MBO Process*, vol. 2 (New York: McGraw-Hill, 1978).

28. John Ivancevich, J. Timothy McMahon, J. William Streidl, and Andrew D. Szilagyi, "Goal Setting: The Tenneco Approach to Personnel Development and Management Effectiveness," *Organizational Dynamics* (Winter 1978): 48–80.

29. Brigitte W. Schay, Mary Ellen Beach, Jacqueline A. Caldwell, and Christelle LaPolice, "Using Standardized Outcome Measures in the Federal Government," *Human Resource Management* 41, no. 3 (Fall 2002): 355–368.

30. Eileen M. Van Aken and Garry D. Coleman, "Building Better Measurement," *Industrial Management* (July–August 2002): 28–33.

31. Curtis W. Roney, "Planning for Strategic Contingencies," *Business Horizons* (March–April 2003): 35–42; and "Corporate Planning: Drafting a Blueprint for Success," *Small Business Report* (August 1987): 40–44.

32. Ellen Florian Kratz, "For FedEx, It Was Time to Deliver," *Fortune* (October 3, 2005): 83–84.

33. Geoffrey Colvin, "An Executive Risk Handbook," *Fortune* (October 3, 2005): 69–70; and Syed H. Akhter, "Strategic Planning, Hypercompetition, and Knowledge Management," *Business Horizons* (January–February 2003): 19–24; and Steven Schnaars and Paschalina Ziamou, "The Essentials of Scenario Writing," *Business Horizons* (July–August 2001): 25–31.

34. Schnaars and Ziamou, "The Essentials of Scenario Writing," Note 33.

35. Colvin, "An Executive Risk Handbook, Note 33"; and Ian Wylie, "There Is No Alternative To . . . ," *Fast Company* (July 2002): 106–110.

36. Ian Mitroff with Gus Anagnos, *Managing Crises Before They Happen* (New York: AMACOM, 2001).

37. Ian Mitroff and Murat C. Alpaslan, "Preparing for Evil," *Harvard Business Review* (April 2003): 109–115.

38. This discussion is based largely on W. Timothy Coombs, *Ongoing Crisis Communication: Planning, Managing, and Responding* (Thousand Oaks, CA: Sage Publications, 1999).

39. Ian I. Mitroff, "Crisis Leadership," *Executive Excellence* (August 2001): 19; Andy Bowen, "Crisis Procedures that Stand the Test of Time," *Public Relations Tactics* (August 2001): 16.

40. Mitroff and Alpaslan, "Preparing for Evil."

41. Christine Pearson, "A Blueprint for Crisis Management," *Ivey Business Journal* (January–February 2002): 69–73.

42. See Mitroff and Alpaslan, "Preparing for Evil," Note 37, for a discussion of the "wheel of crises" outlining the many different kinds of crises organizations may face.

43. Grimsley, Kirsten, "Many Firms Lack Plans for Disaster," Washington Post (October 3, 2001: E01; Fonda, Daren, "Girding Against New Risks: Global Executives Are Working to Better Protect Their Employees and Businesses from Calamity," *Time* (October 8, 2001): B8+.

44. Mitroff, "Crisis Leadership, Note 39." Also see Loretta Ucelli, "The CEO's 'How To' Guide to Crisis Communications," *Strategy & Leadership* 30, no. 2 (2002): 21–24; and Paul Argenti, "Crisis Communication: Lessons from 9/11," *Harvard Business Review* (December 2002): 103–109, for tips on crisis communication.

45. Grimsley, "Girding Against New Risks," Note 42.

46. "After Katrina: New Lessons to Learn," *Fortune* (October 3, 2005): 87–88.

47. Harari, "Good News/Bad News about Strategy, Note 1."

48. This discussion of the importance of vision and mission is based on Khoo Hsien Hui and Tan Kay Chuan, "Nine Approaches to Organizational Excellence," *Journal of Organizational Excellence* (Winter 2002): 53–65; Gerald E. Ledford, Jr., Jon R. Wendenhof, and James T. Strahley, "Realizing a Corporate Philosophy," *Organizational Dynamics* (Winter 1995): 5–18; James C. Collins, "Building Companies to Last," *The State of Small Business* (1995): 83–86; James C. Collins and Jerry I. Porras, "Building a Visionary Company," *California Management Review* 37, no. 2 (Winter 1995): 80–100; and James C. Collins and Jerry I. Porras, "The Ultimate Vision," *Across the Board* (January 1995): 19–23.

49. Steven Kerr and Steffan Landauer," Using Stretch Goals to Promote Organizational Effectiveness and Personal Growth: General Electric and Goldman Sachs," *Academy of Management Executive* 18, no. 4 (November 2004): 134–138.

50. See Kenneth R. Thompson, Wayne A. Hockwarter, and Nicholas J. Mathys, "Stretch Targets: What Makes Them Effective?" *Academy of Management Executive* 11, no. 3 (August 1997): 48.

51. This discussion is based on Chuck Martin, "How to Plan for the Short Term," in Chuck Martin, *Managing for the Short Term* (New York: Doubleday, 2002), as quoted in *CIO* (September 15, 2002): 90–97.

52. Martin, "How to Plan for the Short Term," Note 50.

53. Doug Bartholomew, "Gauging Success," *CFO-IT* (Summer 2005): 17–19.

54. Jeffrey A. Schmidt, "Corporate Excellence in the New Millennium," *Journal of Business Strategy* (November–December 1999): 39–43.

55. Polly LaBarre, "The Company Without Limits," *Fast Company* (September 1999): 160–186.

56. Keith H. Hammonds, "Michael Porter's Big Ideas," *Fast Company* (March 2001): 150–156.

57. John E. Prescott, "Environments as Moderators of the Relationship between Strategy and Performance," *Academy of Management Journal* 29 (1986): 329–346; John A. Pearce II and Richard B. Robinson, Jr., *Strategic Management: Strategy, Formulation, and Implementation,* 2d ed. (Homewood, IL: Irwin, 1985); and David J. Teece, "Economic Analysis and Strategic Management," *California Management Review* 26 (Spring 1984): 87–110.

58. Jack Welch, "It's All in the Sauce," excerpt from his book, *Winning,* in *Fortune* (April 18, 2005): 138–144.

59. Michael E. Porter, "What Is Strategy?" *Harvard Business Review* (November–December 1996): 61–78.

60. Arthur A. Thompson, Jr., and A. J. Strickland III, *Strategic Management: Concepts and Cases,* 6th ed. (Homewood, IL: Irwin, 1992); and Briance Mascarenhas, Alok Baveja, and Mamnoon Jamil, "Dynamics of Core Competencies in Leading Multinational Companies," *California Management Review* 40, no. 4 ((Summer 1998): 117–132.

61. Michael V. Copeland, "Stitching Together an Apparel Power-house," *Business 2.0* (April 2005): 52–54.

62. "Gaylord Says Hotels Prosper by Becoming Destinations," *The Tennessean* (July 24, 2005): http://www.tennessean.com.

63. Chris Woodyard, "Big Dreams for Small Choppers Paid Off," *USA Today* (September 11, 2005), http://www.usatoday.com

64. Michael Goold and Andrew Campbell, "Desperately Seeking Synergy," *Harvard Business Review* (September–October 1998): 131–143.

65. Chris Woodyard, "FedEx Ponies Up $2.4B for Kinko's," *USA Today* (December 30, 2003); http://www.usatoday.com/money/

industries/2003-12-30-fdx-kinkos_x.htm (accessed January 2, 2004); and Claudia H. Deutsch, "FedEx Moves to Expand with Purchase of Kinko's," *The New York Times* (December 31, 2003): C1.

66. Wooley, "Best Leaders."

67. Kerry Capell, "IKEA: How the Swedish Retailer Became a Global Cult Brand," *BusinessWeek* (November 14, 2005): 96–106.

68. Milton Leontiades, "The Confusing Words of Business Policy," *Academy of Management Review* 7 (1982): 45–48.

69. Lawrence G. Hrebiniak and William F. Joyce, *Implementing Strategy* (New York: Macmillan, 1984).

70. Pallavi Gogoi,"The Heat in Kraft's Kitchen; Cheap Rivals and Demands for Leaner Fare Close In,"*BusinessWeek* (August 4, 2003): 82; and Shelly Branch,"Critical Curds; At Kraft, Making Cheese 'Fun'Is Serious Business," *The Wall Street Journal* (May 31, 2002): A1, A6.

71. Michael E. Porter, *Competitive Strategy* (New York: Free Press, 1980): 36–46; Danny Miller, "Relating Porter's Business Strategies to Environment and Structure: Analysis and Performance Implementations," *Academy of Management Journal* 31 (1988): 280–308; and Michael E. Porter, "From Competitive Advantage to Corporate Strategy," *Harvard Business Review* (May–June 1987): 43–59.

72. Michael E. Porter, "Strategy and the Internet," *Harvard Business Review* (March 2001): 63–78.

73. William C. Symonds, "Can Gillette Regain Its Edge?" *BusinessWeek* (January 26, 2004): 46.

74. Charles Fishman, "The Man Who Said No to Wal-Mart," *Fast Company* (January–February 2006): 66-71, excerpted from *The Wal-Mart Effect* (New York Penguin Press, 2006).

75. Thomas L. Wheelen and J. David Hunger, *Strategic Management and Business Policy* (Reading, MA: Addison-Wesley, 1989)

76. Andrew Park and Peter Burrows, "Dell, the Conqueror," *BusinessWeek* (September 24, 2001): 92–102; and Thompson and Strickland, *Strategic Management*, Note. 60.

77. "We Weren't Just Airborne Yesterday; A Brief History of Southwest Airlines," http://www.southwest.com/about_swa/airborne.html (accessed March 29, 2004); Micheline Maynard, "Are Peanuts No Longer Enough?" *The New York Times* (March 7, 2004): Section 3, 1; and Wendy Zellner with Michael Arndt, "Holding Steady," *BusinessWeek* (February 3, 2003): 66–68.

78. Richard Teitelbaum, "The Wal-Mart of Wall Street," *Fortune* (October 13, 1997): 128–130.

79. Joshua Rosenbaum, "Guitar Maker Looks for a New Key," *Wall Street Journal* (February 11, 1998): B1, B5.

80. Nitin Nohria, William Joyce, and Bruce Roberson, "What Really Works," *Harvard Business Review* (July 2003): 43–52.

81. Porter, "Strategy and the Internet," Note 71; Hammonds, "Michael Porter's Big Ideas," Note 56; and G. T. Lumpkin, Scott B. Droege, and Gregory G. Dess, "E-Commerce Strategies: Achieving Sustainable Competitive Advantage and Avoiding Pitfalls," *Organizational Dynamics* 30, no. 4 (2002): 325–340.

82. Lumpkin et al., "E-Commerce Strategies, Note 79.

83. Based on John Burton, "Composite Strategy: The Combination of Collaboration and Competition," *Journal of General Management* 21, no. 1 (Autumn 1995): 1–23; and Roberta Maynard, "Striking the Right Match," *Nation's Business* (May 1996): 18–28.

84. Alice Dragoon, "A Travel Guide to Collaboration," *CIO* (November 15, 2004): 68–75.

85. Don Tapscott, "Rethinking Strategy in a Networked World," Strategy & Business, no. 24 (Third Quarter, 2001): 34–41.

86. Nick Wingfield, "New Chapter; A Web Giant Tries to Boost Profits by Taking on Tenants," *Wall Street Journal* (September 24, 2003): A1, A10; and Nick Wingfield, "Amazon's eBay Challenge," *Wall Street Journal* (June 3, 2004): B1, B2.

87. Julia Angwin and Motoka Rich, "Inn Fighting: Big Hotel Chains Are Striking Back Against Web Sites," *Wall Street Journal* (March 14, 2003): A1, A7.

88. Tonya Vinas, "It Starts with Parts," *Industry Week* (September 2003): 40–43.

89. Dionne Searcey, Almar Latour, and Dennis K. Berman, "Wedding Bells; A Reborn AT&T to Bay BellSouth," *Wall Street Journal* (March 6, 2006): A1, A13.

90. Burton, "Composite Strategy: The Combination of Collaboration and Competition," Note 82.

91. Eric M. Olson, Stanley F. Slater, and G. Tomas M. Hult, "The Importance of Structure and Process to Strategy Implementation," *Business Horizons* 48 (2005): 47–54; L.J. Bourgeois III and David R. Brodwin, "Strategic Implementation: Five Approaches to an Elusive Phenomenon," *Strategic Management Journal* 5 (1984): 241–264; Anil K. Gupta and V. Govindarajan, "Business Unit Strategy, Managerial Characteristics, and Business Unit Effectiveness at Strategy Implementation," *Academy of Management Journal* (1984): 25–41; and Jeffrey G. Covin, Dennis P. Slevin, and Randall L. Schultz, "Implementing Strategic Missions: Effective Strategic, Structural, and Tactical Choices," *Journal of Management Studies* 31, no. 4 (1994): 481–505.

92. Rainer Feurer and Kazem Chaharbaghi, "Dynamic Strategy Formulation and Alignment," *Journal of General Management* 20, no. 3 (Spring 1995): 76-90; and Henry Mintzberg, *The Rise and Fall of Strategic Planning* (Toronto: Maxwell Macmillan Canada, 1994).

93. Olson, Slater, and Hult, Note 89.

94. Jay R. Galbraith and Robert K. Kazanjian, *Strategy Implementation: Structure, Systems and Process*, 2d ed. (St. Paul, MN: West, 1986); and Paul C. Nutt, "Selecting Tactics to Implement Strategic Plans," *Strategic Management Journal* 10 (1989): 145–161.

95. Spencer E. Ante, "The New Blue," *BusinessWeek* (March 17, 2003): 80–88.

96. James E. Skivington and Richard L. Daft, "A Study of Organizational 'Framework' and 'Process' Modalities for the Implementation of Business-Level Strategies" (unpublished manuscript), Texas A&M University, 1987).

97. Steve Hamm, "Beyond Blue," *BusinessWeek,* (April 18, 2005): 36–42.

98. Abby Ghobadian and Nicholas O'Regan, "The Link Between Culture, Strategy, and Performance in Manufacturing SMEs," *Journal of General Management* 28, no. 1 (Autumn 2002): 16–34.

99. Melvyn J. Stark, "Five Years of Insight into the World's Most Admired Companies," *Journal of Organizational Excellence* (Winger 2002):3–12.

100. Nitin Nohria, William Joyce, and Bruce Roberson, "What Really Works," *Harvard Business Review* (July 2003): 43–52; and Jeff Rosenthal and Mary Ann Masarech, "High Performance Cultures: How Values Can Drive Business Results," *Journal of Organizational Excellence* (Spring 2003): 3–18.

101. James E. Cashman, "Strategy Sustains Success," *Industrial Management* (September–October 2005): 25–19.

102. Lumpkin et al., "E-Commerce Strategies," Note 79.

103. Paulette Thomas, "Fighting the Giants with a Savvy Mix," *Wall Street Journal* (November 29, 2005): B12.

Chapter 6

Decision Making

1. Brooks Barnes, "Disney Will Offer Many TV Shows Free on the Web; ABC's Prime-Time Hits and Zap-Proof Commercials Are Pillars of Bold Strategy," *Wall Street Journal* (April 10, 2006): A1, A10.

2. Michael V. Copeland and Owen Thomas, "Hits (& Misses)," *Business 2.0* (January–February 2004): 126.

3. Michael V. Copeland, "Stuck in the Spin Cycle" *Business 2.0* (May 2005): 74–75; Adam Horowitz, Mark Athitakis, Mark Lasswell, and Owen Thomas, "101 Dumbest Moments in Business," *Business 2.0* (January–February 2004): 72–81.

4. Herbert A. Simon, *The New Science of Management Decision* (Englewood Cliffs, NJ: Prentice Hall, 1977): 47.

5. Monica Langley, Lee Hawkins Jr., and Dennis Berman, "GM Board Seeks Probe of Mistakes in Bookkeeping," *Wall Street Journal* (March 18–19, 2006): A1, A6; and Carol J. Loomis, "The Tragedy of General Motors," *Fortune* (February 20, 2005): 58–75.

6. Samuel Eilon, "Structuring Unstructured Decisions," *Omega 13* (1985): 369–377; and Max H. Bazerman, *Judgment in Managerial Decision Making* (New York: Wiley, 1986).

7. James G. March and Zur Shapira, "Managerial Perspectives on Risk and Risk Taking," *Management Science* 33 (1987): 1404–1418; and Inga Skromme Baird and Howard Thomas, "Toward a Contingency Model of Strategic Risk Taking," *Academy of Management Review* 10 (1985): 230–243.

8. Hugh Courtney, "Decision-Driven Scenarios for Assessing Four Levels of Uncertainty," *Strategy & Leadership* 31, no. 1 (2003): 14–22.

9. Janet Guyon, "Changing Direction," interview with Nancy McKinstry in "The Path to Power," *Fortune* (November 14, 2005): 145–156.

10. Michael Masuch and Perry LaPotin, "Beyond Garbage Cans: An AI Model of Organizational Choice," *Administrative Science Quarterly* 34 (1989): 38–67; and Richard L. Daft and Robert H. Lengel, "Organizational Information Requirements, Media Richness and Structural Design," *Management Science* 32 (1986): 554–571.

11. David M. Schweiger, William R. Sandberg, and James W. Ragan, "Group Approaches for Improving Strategic Decision Making: A Comparative Analysis of Dialectical Inquiry, Devil's Advocacy, and Consensus," *Academy of Management Journal* 29 (1986): 51–71; and Richard O. Mason and Ian I. Mitroff, *Challenging Strategic Planning Assumptions* (New York: Wiley Interscience, 1981).

12. Michael Pacanowsky, "Team Tools for Wicked Problems," *Organizational Dynamics* 23, no. 3 (Winter 1995): 36–51.

13. Boris Blai, Jr., "Eight Steps to Successful Problem Solving," *Supervisory Management* (January 1986): 7–9; and Earnest R. Archer, "How to Make a Business Decision: An Analysis of Theory and Practice," *Management Review* 69 (February 1980): 54–61.

14. Bernard Wysocki Jr., "The Rules: At One Hospital, a Stark Solution for Allocating Care," *The Wall Street Journal* (September 23, 2003): A1, A21.

15. Thomas H. Davenport and Jeanne G. Harris, "Automated Decision Making Comes of Age," *MIT Sloan Management Review* (Summer 2005): 83–89; and Stacie McCullough, "On the Front Lines," *CIO* (October 15, 1999): 78–81.

16. Srinivas Bollapragada, Prasanthi Ganti, Mark Osborn, James Quaile, and Kannan Ramanathan, "GE's Energy Rentals Business Automates Its Credit Assessment Process," *Interfaces* 33, no. 5 (September–October 2003): 45–56; Julie Schlosser, "Markdown Lowdown," *Fortune* (January 12, 2004): 40.

17. Srinivas Bollapragada, Hong Cheng, Mary Phillips, Marc Garbinas, Michael Scholes, Tim Gibbs, and Mark Humphreville, "NBC's Optimization Systems Increase Revenues and Productivity," *Interfaces* 32, no. 1 (January–February 2002): 47–60.

18. James G. March and Herbert A. Simon, *Organizations* (New York: Wiley, 1958).

19. Herbert A. Simon, *The New Science of Management Decision* (New York: Harper & Row, 1960): 5–6; and Amitai Etzioni, "Humble Decision Making," *Harvard Business Review* (July–August 1989): 122–126.

20. Herbert A. Simon, *Models of Man* (New York: Wiley, 1957): 196–205; and Herbert A. Simon, *Administrative Behavior*, 2d ed. (New York: Free Press, 1957).

21. Paul C. Nutt, "Expanding the Search for Alternatives During Strategic Decision Making," *Academy of Management Executive* 18, no. 4 (2004): 13–28.

22. Weston H. Agor, "The Logic of Intuition: How Top Executives Make Important Decisions," *Organizational Dynamics* 14 (Winter 1986): 5–18; and Herbert A. Simon, "Making Management Decisions: The Role of Intuition and Emotion," *Academy of Management Executive* 1 (1987): 57–64.

23. Study reported in C. Chet Miller and R. Duane Ireland, "Intuition in Strategic Decision Making: Friend or Foe in the Fast-Paced 21st Century?" *Academy of Management Executive* 19, no. 1 (2005): 19–30.

24. Gary Klein, *Intuition at Work: Why Developing Your Gut Instincts Will Make You Better at What You Do* (New York: Doubleday, 2002).

25. Malcolm Gladwell, *Blink: The Power of Thinking Without Thinking* (New York: Little Brown 2005); Sharon Begley, "Follow Your Intuition: The Unconscious You May Be the Wiser Half," *Wall Street Journal* (August 30, 2002): B1.

26. Thomas Stewart, "How to Think with Your Gut," *Business 2.0* (November 2002): http://www.business2.com; Thomas George, "Head Cowboy Gets Off His High Horse," *The New York Times* (December 21, 2003): Section 8, 1.

27. Chris Smith, "Chao, Baby," *New York* (October 18, 1993): 66–75; and "Chao in Charge," *Cablevision* (November 29, 1999): 24.

28. Miller and Ireland, "Intuition in Strategic Decision Making," and Eric Bonabeau, "Don't Trust Your Gut," *Harvard Business Review* (May 2003): 116ff.

29. Eugene Sadler-Smith and Erella Shefy, "The Intuitive Executive: Understanding and Applying 'Gut Feel' in Decision Making," *Academy of Management Executive* 18, no. 4 (2004): 76–91; and Ann Langley, "Between 'Paralysis by Analysis' and 'Extinction by Instinct,' " *Sloan Management Review* (Spring 1995): 63–76.

30. William B. Stevenson, Jon L. Pierce, and Lyman W. Porter, "The Concept of 'Coalition' in Organization Theory and Research," *Academy of Management Review* 10 (1985): 256–268.

31. George T. Doran and Jack Gunn, "Decision Making in High-Tech Firms: Perspectives of Three Executives," *Business Horizons* (November–December 2002): 7–16.

32. Stephanie N. Mehta and Fred Vogelstein, "AOL: The Relaunch," *Fortune* (November 14, 2005): 78–84.

33. Jonathan Harris, "Why Speedy Got Stuck in Reverse," *Canadian Business* (September 26, 1997): 87–88.

34. Daniel Golden and Steve Stecklow, "Crimson Tide; Facing War with His Faculty, Harvard's Summers Resigns," *Wall Street Journal* (February 22, 2006): A1, A13.

35. James W. Fredrickson, "Effects of Decision Motive and Organizational Performance Level on Strategic Decision Processes," *Academy of Management Journal* 28 (1985):

821–843; James W. Fredrickson, "The Comprehensiveness of Strategic Decision Processes: Extension, Observations, Future Directions," *Academy of Management Journal* 27 (1984): 445–466; James W. Dean, Jr., and Mark P. Sharfman, "Procedural Rationality in the Strategic Decision-Making Process," *Journal of Management Studies* 30, no. 4 (July 1993): 587–610; Nandini Rajagopalan, Abdul M. A. Rasheed, and Deepak K. Datta, "Strategic Decision Processes: Critical Review and Future Directions," *Journal of Management* 19, no. 2 (1993): 349–384; and Paul J. H. Schoemaker, "Strategic Decisions in Organizations: Rational and Behavioral Views," *Journal of Management Studies* 30, no. 1 (January 1993): 107–129.

36. Marjorie A. Lyles and Howard Thomas, "Strategic Problem Formulation: Biases and Assumptions Embedded in Alternative Decision-Making Models," *Journal of Management Studies* 25 (1988): 131–145; and Susan E. Jackson and Jane E. Dutton, "Discerning Threats and Opportunities," *Administrative Science Quarterly* 33 (1988): 370–387.

37. Richard L. Daft, Juhani Sormumen, and Don Parks, "Chief Executive Scanning, Environmental Characteristics, and Company Performance: An Empirical Study" (unpublished manuscript, Texas A&M University, 1988).

38. Jena McGregor, "Gospels of Failure," *Fast Company* (February 2005): 62–67.

39. C. Kepner and B. Tregoe, *The Rational Manager* (New York: McGraw-Hill, 1965).

40. Joseph B. White and Lee Hawkins Jr., "Harried Driver; At General Motors, Troubles Mount for Man Behind the Wheel," *Wall Street Journal* (November 11, 2005): A1; and Loomis, "The Tragedy of General Motors."

41. Paul C. Nutt, "Expanding the Search for Alternatives During Strategic Decision Making," *Academy of Management Executive* 18, no. 4 (2004): 13–28; and P. C. Nutt, "Surprising But True: Half the Decisions in Organizations Fail," *Academy of Management Executive* 13, no. 4 (1999): 75–90.

42. Pallavi Gogoi, "The Heat in Kraft's Kitchen; Cheap Rivals and Demands for Leaner Fare Close In," *BusinessWeek* (August 4, 2003): 82; and Shelly Branch, "Critical Curds; At Kraft, Making Cheese 'Fun' Is Serious Business," *Wall Street Journal* (May 31, 2002): A1, A6.

43. Peter Mayer, "A Surprisingly Simple Way to Make Better Decisions," *Executive Female* (March–April 1995): 13–14; and Ralph L. Keeney, "Creativity in Decision Making with Value-Focused Thinking," *Sloan Management Review* (Summer 1994): 33–41.

44. Janet Guyon, "The Soul of a Moneymaking Machine," *Fortune* (October 3, 2005): 113–120; Robert Levering and Milton Moskowitz, "And the Winners Are . . ." (The 100 Best Companies to Work For), *Fortune* (January 23, 2006): 89–108.

45. Mark McNeilly, "Gathering Information for Strategic Decisions, Routinely," *Strategy & Leadership* 30, no. 5 (2002): 29–34.

46. Ibid.

47. Suzanne Woolley, ed., "Best Leaders," *BusinessWeek* (December 19, 2005): 60–64.

48. Jenny C. McCune, "Making Lemonade," *Management Review* (June 1997): 49–53.

49. Based on A. J. Rowe, J. D. Boulgaides, and M. R. McGrath, *Managerial Decision Making* (Chicago: Science Research Associates, 1984); and Alan J. Rowe and Richard O. Mason, *Managing with Style: A Guide to Understanding, Assessing, and Improving Your Decision Making* (San Francisco: Jossey-Bass, 1987).

50. Marc Gunther, "Jeff Zucker Faces Life Without *Friends*," *Fortune Magazine* (May 12, 2003): 147 (9), 95.

51. V. H. Vroom and Arthur G. Jago, *The New Leadership: Managing Participation in Organizations* (Englewood Cliffs, NJ: Prentice Hall, 1988).

52. Victor H. Vroom, "Leadership and the Decision-Making Process," *Organizational Dynamics* 28, no. 4 (Spring 2000): 82–94.

53. R. H. G. Field, "A Test of the Vroom-Yetton Normative Model of Leadership," *Journal of Applied Psychology* (October 1982): 523–532; and R. H. G. Field, "A Critique of the Vroom-Yetton Contingency Model of Leadership Behavior," *Academy of Management Review* 4 (1979): 249–257.

54. Vroom, "Leadership and the Decision Making Process"; Jennifer T. Ettling and Arthur G. Jago, "Participation under Conditions of Conflict: More on the Validity of the Vroom-Yetton Model," *Journal of Management Studies* 25 (1988): 73–83; Madeline E. Heilman, Harvey A. Hornstein, Jack H. Cage, and Judith K. Herschlag, "Reactions to Prescribed Leader Behavior as a Function of Role Perspective: The Case of the Vroom-Yetton Model," *Journal of Applied Psychology* (February 1984): 50–60; and Arthur G. Jago and Victor H. Vroom, "Some Differences in the Incidence and Evaluation of Participative Leader Behavior," *Journal of Applied Psychology* (December 1982): 776–783.

55. Based on a decision problem presented in Victor H. Vroom, "Leadership and the Decision-Making Process," *Organizational Dynamics* 28, no. 4 (Spring 2000): 82–94.

56. Nathaniel Foote, Eric Matson, Leigh Weiss, and Etienne Wenger, "Leveraging Group Knowledge for High-Performance Decision Making," *Organizational Dynamics* 31, no. 3 (2002): 280–295.

57. Kathleen M. Eisenhardt, "Strategy as Strategic Decision Making," *Sloan Management Review* (Spring 1999): 65–72.

58. Major Chip Daniels, "Making Values-Based, Mission-Focused Decisions," *Leader to Leader* Special Supplement (May 2005): 48–59; Greg Jaffe, "Trial by Fire; On Ground in Iraq, Capt. Ayers Writes His Own Playbook," *Wall Street Journal* (September 22, 2004): A1.

59. See Katharine Mieskowski, "Digital Competition," *Fast Company* (December 1999): 155–162; Thomas A. Stewart, "Three Rules for Managing in the Real-Time Economy,"

Fortune (May 1, 2000): 333–334; and Geoffrey Colvin, "How to Be a Great eCEO," *Fortune* (May 24, 1999): 104–110.

60. R. B. Gallupe, W. H. Cooper, M. L. Grise, and L. M. Bastianutti, "Blocking Electronic Brainstorms," *Journal of Applied Psychology* 79 (1994): 77–86; R. B. Gallupe and W. H. Cooper, "Brainstorming Electronically," *Sloan Management Review* (Fall 1993): 27–36; and Alison Stein Wellner, "A Perfect Brainstorm," *Inc.* (October 2003): 31–35.

61. Wellner, "A Perfect Brainstorm"; Gallupe and Cooper, "Brainstorming Electronically."

62. Charles O'Reilly III and Jeffrey Pfeffer, *Hidden Value: How Great Companies Achieve Extraordinary Performance with Ordinary People* (Boston: Harvard Business School Press, 2000).

63. Michael V. Copeland, "Mistakes Happen," *Red Herring* (May 2000): 346–354.

64. Hans Wissema, "Driving Through Red Lights; How Warning Signals Are Missed or Ignored," *Long Range Planning* 35 (2002): 521–539.

65. Ibid.

66. Joshua Klayman, Richard P. Larrick, and Chip Heath, "Organizational Repairs," *Across the Board* (February 2000): 26–31.

67. Michael A. Roberto, "Making Difficult Decisions in Turbulent Times," *Ivey Business Journal* (May–June 2003): 1–7.

68. Eisenhardt, "Strategy as Strategic Decision Making"; and David A. Garvin and Michael A. Roberto, "What You Don't Know About Making Decisions," *Harvard Business Review* (September 2001): 108–116.

69. Roberto, "Making Difficult Decisions in Turbulent Times."

70. David M. Schweiger and William R. Sandberg, "The Utilization of Individual Capabilities in Group Approaches to Strategic Decision Making," *Strategic Management Journal* 10 (1989): 31–43; and "The Devil's Advocate," *Small Business Report* (December 1987): 38–41.

71. Doran and Gunn, "Decision Making in High-Tech Firms."

72. Eisenhardt, "Strategy as Strategic Decision Making."

73. Garvin and Roberto, "What You Don't Know About Making Decisions."

74. "The Web Smart 50," *BusinessWeek* (November 21, 2005): 82–112.

75. Christopher Palmeri, "Believe in Yourself, Believe in the Merchandise," *Continental* (December 1997): 49–51; Timothy J. Mullaney with Heather Green, Michael Arndt, Robert D. Hof, and Linda Himelstein, "The E-Biz Surprise," *Business Week,* (May 12, 2003): 60–68.

76. "The Web Smart 50"; Timothy J. Mullaney, "E-Biz Strikes Again," *BusinessWeek* (May 10, 2004): 80–82; and Mullaney et al., "The E-Biz Surprise."

77. Thomas L. Friedman, "It's a Flat World, After All," *The New York Times Magazine* (April 3, 2005): http://www.nytimes.com/2005/04/03/magazine.

78. Ibid.

79. Michael A. Fontaine, Salvatore Parise, and David Miller, "Collaborative Environments: An Effective Tool for Transforming Business Processes," *Ivey Business Journal* (May–June 2004).

80. "The Web Smart 50."

81. Matt Richtel, "The Long-Distance Journey of a Fast-Food Order," *The New York Times* (April 11, 2006): http://www.nytimes.com.

82. Liz Thach and Richard W. Woodman, "Organizational Change and Information Technology: Managing on the Edge of Cyberspace," *Organizational Dynamics* (Summer 1994): 30–46; and Elizabeth Horwitt, "Going Deep: Empowering Employees," *Microsoft Executive Circle* (Summer 2003): 24–26.

83. Greg Jaffe, "Tug of War: In the New Military, Technology May Alter Chain of Command," *Wall Street Journal* (March 30, 2001): A3, A6.

84. Meridith Levinson, "Business Intelligence: Not Just for Bosses Anymore," *CIO* (January 15, 2006): 82–86.

85. Tonya Vinas, "Surviving Information Overload," *Industry Week* (April 2003): 24–29.

86. Joseph McCafferty, "Coping with Infoglut," *CFO* (September 1998): 101–102.

87. Leonard M. Fuld, "The Danger of Data Slam," *CIO Enterprise* (September 15, 1998): 28–33.

88. Anya Kamenetz, "The Network Unbound," *Fast Company* (June 2006): 68ff; and Stephen Baker and Heather Green, "Blogs Will Change Your Business," *BusinessWeek* (May 2, 2005): 56–67.

89. Kamenetz, "The Network Unbound."

90. Michael Barbaro, "Wal-Mart Enlists Bloggers in P.R. Campaign," *The New York Times* (March 7, 2006), http://www.nytimes.com; Daniel McGinn, "Wal-Mart Hits the Wall," *Newsweek* (November 14, 2005): 42; Reed Abelson, "One Giant's Struggle Is Corporate America's, Too; Rewriting the Social Contract—The Wal-Mart Challenge," *The New York Times* (October 29, 2005): C1; http://www.walmartwatch.com; and Jerry Useem, "Should We Admire Wal-Mart?" *Fortune* (March 8, 2004): 118ff.

91. Baker and Green, "Blogs Will Change Your Business."

92. This discussion of social networks is based on Kamenetz, "The Network Unbound."

93. Kevin J. Delaney, "Garage Brand; With NBC Pact, YouTube Site Tries to Build a Lasting Business," *Wall Street Journal* (June 27, 2006): A1, A13.

94. Ibid.

95. Derek Slater, "Chain Commanders," *CIO Enterprise* (August 15, 1998): 29–30+.

96. Thomas H. Davenport and Jeanne G. Harris, "Automated Decision Making Comes of Age," *MIT Sloan Management Review* (Summer 2005): 83–89.

97. John P. Mello Jr., "Fly Me to the Web," *CFO* (March 2000): 79–84.

98. Heather Harreld, "Pick-Up Artists," *CIO* (November 1, 2000): 148–154; and Carol J. Loomis, "The Big Surprise Is Enterprise," *Fortune* (July 24, 2006): 140–150.

99. Jim Turcotte, Bob Silveri, and Tom Jobson, "Are You Ready for the E-Supply Chain?" *APICS–The Performance Advantage* (August 1998): 56–59.

100. "History of the Internet: Origin of World Wide Web," (Chapter 6 Excerpt), The Moschovitis Group, http://www.historyoftheinternet.com/chap6.html.

101. Steve Hamm with David Welch, Wendy Zellner, Faith Keenan, and Peter Engardio, "E-Biz: Down But Hardly Out," *BusinessWeek* (March 26, 2001): 126–130.

102. David Drickhamer, "EDI Is Dead! Long Live EDI!" *Industry Week* (April 2003): 31–38; Ian Mount, "Why EDI Won't Die," *Business 2.0* (August 2003): 68–69; and Marie-Claude Boudreau, Karen D. Loch, Daniel Robey, and Detmar Straud, "Going Global: Using Information Technology to Advance the Competitiveness of the Virtual Transnational Organization," *Academy of Management Executive* 12, no. 4 (1998): 120–128.

103. This discussion is based on Long W. Lam and L. Jean Harrison-Walker, "Toward an Objective-Based Typology of E-Business Models," *Business Horizons* (November–December 2003): 17–26; and Detmar Straub and Richard Klein, "E-Competitive Transformations," *Business Horizons* (May–June 2001): 3–12.

104. Tom Lowry, "In the Zone," *BusinessWeek* (October 17, 2005): 66–78; Tom Lowry, "TV's New Parallel Universe," *BusinessWeek* (November 14, 2005): 72–74.

105. Katharine Q. Seelye, "Reviving a Magazine with Ballast of a Web Site First," *The New York Times* (April 11, 2005): http://www.nytimes.com; and http://www.radarmagazine.com.

106. Russ Banham, "Old Dogs, New Clicks," *CFO-IT* (Summer 2005): 21–26.

107. Mullaney et al., "The E-Biz Surprise."

108. "The Web Smart 50."

109. Jonathan L. Willis, "What Impact Will E-Commerce Have on the U.S. Economy?" *Economic Review—Federal Reserve Bank of Kansas City* 89, no. 2 (Second Quarter 2004): 53ff; 2005 productivity gains reported in Mullaney et al., "The E-Biz Surprise."

110. Straub and Klein, "E-Competitive Transformations."

111. "The Web Smart 50."

112. This discussion of implementation approaches is based on Ranjay Gulati and Jason Garino, "Get the Right Mix of Bricks and Clicks," *Harvard Business Review* (May–June 2000): 107–114.

113. Ibid.

114. "Business: Surfing USA," *The Economist* (June 30, 2001): 58; and James R. Hagerty and James Hall, "British Supermarket Giant Cooks Up Plans to Go Global—Tesco's Move to Duplicate High Growth at Home Comes with Big Risks," *Wall Street Journal* (July 5, 2001): A9.

115. Banham, "Old Dogs, New Clicks."

116. This discussion is based on Mauro F. Guillén, "What Is the Best Global Strategy for the Internet?" *Business Horizons* (May–June 2002): 39–46; and Bob Tedeschi, "American Web Sites Speak the Language of Overseas Users," *The New York Times* (January 12, 2004): http://www.nytimes.com.

117. Statistic reported in Mullaney et al., "The E-Biz Surprise." This discussion is based on Pamela Barnes-Vieyra and Cindy Claycomb, "Business-to-Business E-Commerce: Models and Managerial Decisions," *Business Horizons* (May–June 2001): 13–20.

118. Reported in Hamm et al., "E-Biz: Down But Hardly Out."

119. "The Web Smart 50."

120. Robert D. Hof, "The eBay Economy," *BusinessWeek* (August 25, 2003): 124+.

121. Raizel Robin, "Net Gains," *Canadian Business* (October 14–October 26, 2003): 107.

122. Eric Young, "Web Marketplaces That Really Work," *Fortune/CNET Tech Review* (Winter 2001): 78–86.

123. Brian Caulfield, "Facing Up to CRM," *Business 2.0* (August–September 2001): 149–150; and "Customer Relationship Management: The Good. The Bad. The Future." *BusinessWeek* (April 28, 2003): 53–64.

124. Ellen Neuborne, "A Second Act for CRM," *Inc.* (March 2005): 40.

125. The discussion of collaborative customer experiences is based on Paul Greenberg, "Applied Insight: Move Over, Baby Boomers," *CIO* (March 1, 2006), http://www.cio.com.

126. Reported in Eric Seubert, Y. Balaji, and Mahesh Makhija, "The Knowledge Imperative," *CIO Advertising Supplement* (March 15, 2001): S1–S4.

127. Ryan K. Lahti and Michael M. Beyerlein, "Knowledge Transfer and Management Consulting: A Look at 'The Firm,'" *Business Horizons* (January–February 2000): 65–74.

128. Morten T. Hansen, Nitin Nohria, and Thomas Tierney, "What's Your Strategy for Managing Knowledge?" *Harvard Business Review* (March–April 1999): 106–116; Louisa Wah, "Behind the Buzz," *Management Review* (April 1999): 17–26; and Jenny C. McCune, "Thirst for Knowledge," *Management Review* (April, 1999): 10–12.

129. Seubert, Balaji, and Makhija, "The Knowledge Imperative."

130. Tony Kontzer with Melanie Turek, "Learning to Share," *Information Week* (May 5, 2003): 29–37.

Chapter 7

Organizing

1. Karen Chan, "From Top to Bottom," *Wall Street Journal* (May 21, 2001): R12.

2. Chuck Salter, "Ford's Escape Route," *Fast Company* (October 2004): 106–110; and Bernard Simon, "Ford Aims to Build on Hybrid's Success," *National Post* (January 26, 2005): FP–10.

3. Andrew Pollack, "Medical Companies Join Offshore Trend," *The New York Times* (February 24, 2005), www.nytimes.com; Saritha Rai, "Drug Companies Cut Costs with Foreign Clinical Trials," *The New York Times* (February 24, 2004), www.nytimes.com.

4. John Child, *Organization: A Guide to Problems and Practice*, 2d ed. (London: Harper & Row, 1984).

5. Adam Smith, *The Wealth of Nations* (New York: Modern Library, 1937).

6. This discussion is based on Richard L. Daft, *Organization Theory and Design*, 4th ed. (St. Paul, MN: West, 1992): 387–388.

7. C. I. Barnard, *The Functions of the Executive* (Cambridge, MA: Harvard University Press, 1938).

8. Thomas A. Stewart, "CEOs See Clout Shifting," *Fortune* (November 6, 1989): 66.

9. Michael G. O'Loughlin, "What Is Bureaucratic Accountability and How Can We Measure It?" *Administration & Society* 22, no. 3 (November 1990): 275–302; and Brian Dive, "When Is an Organization Too Flat?" *Across the Board* (July–August 2003): 20–23.

10. Gary L. Neilson and Bruce A. Pasternack, "The Cat That Came Back," *Strategy + Business*, no. 40 (August 17, 2005): 32–45.

11. Carrie R. Leana, "Predictors and Consequences of Delegation," *Academy of Management Journal* 29 (1986): 754–774.

12. Curtis Sittenfeld, "Powered by the People," *Fast Company* (July–August 1999): 178–189.

13. Barbara Davison, "Management Span of Control: How Wide Is Too Wide?" *Journal of Business Strategy* 24, no. 4 (2003): 22–29; Paul D. Collins and Frank Hull, "Technology and Span of Control: Woodward Revisited," *Journal of Management Studies* 23 (March 1986): 143–164; David D. Van Fleet and Arthur G. Bedeian, "A History of the Span of Management," *Academy of Management Review* 2 (1977): 356–372; and C. W. Barkdull, "Span of Control—A Method of Evaluation," *Michigan Business Review* 15 (May 1963): 25–32.

14. Gary Neilson, Bruce A. Pasternack, and Decio Mendes, "The Four Bases of Organizational DNA," *Strategy + Business*, 33 (December 10, 2003): 48–57.

15. Barbara Davison, "Management Span of Control"; Brian Dive, "When Is an Organization Too Flat?"; and Brian Dumaine, "What the Leaders of Tomorrow See," *Fortune* (July 3, 1989): 48–62.

16. Raghuram G. Rajan and Julie Wulf, "The Flattening Firm: Evidence from Panel Data on the Changing Nature of Corporate Hierarchies," working paper, reported in Caroline Ellis, "The Flattening Corporation," *MIT Sloan Management Review* (Summer 2003): 5.

17. Dennis Cauchon, "The Little Company That Could," *USA Today* (October 9, 2005), www.usatoday.com; Charles Haddad, "How UPS Delivered Through the Disaster," *BusinessWeek* (October 1, 2001): 66.

18. Brian O'Reilly, "J&J Is on a Roll," *Fortune* (December 26, 1994): 178–191; and Joseph Weber, "A Big Company That Works," *BusinessWeek* (May 4, 1992): 124–132.

19. Steffan M. Lauster and J. Neely, "The Core's Competence," *Strategy + Business*, 38 (April 15, 2005): 40–49.

20. Clay Chandler and Paul Ingrassia, "Just as U.S. Firms Try Japanese Management, Honda Is Centralizing," *Wall Street Journal* (April 11, 1991): A1, A10.

21. The following discussion of structural alternatives draws heavily from Jay R. Galbraith, *Designing Complex Organizations* (Reading, MA: Addison-Wesley, 1973); Jay R. Galbraith, *Organization Design* (Reading, MA: Addison-Wesley, 1977); Jay R. Galbraith, *Designing Dynamic Organizations* (New York: AMACOM, 2002); Robert Duncan, "What Is the Right Organization Structure?" *Organizational Dynamics* (Winter 1979): 59–80; and J. McCann and Jay R. Galbraith, "Interdepartmental Relations," in *Handbook of Organizational Design*, ed. P. Nystrom and W. Starbuck (NewYork: Oxford University Press, 1981): 60–84.

22. Based on the story of Blue Bell Creameries in Richard L. Daft, *Organization Theory and Design*, 9th ed. (Mason, OH: South-Western, 2007): 103.

23. Jay Greene, "Less Could Be More at Microsoft," *BusinessWeek* (October 3, 2005): 40; and Robert A. Guth, "Code Red: Battling Google, Microsoft Changes How It Builds Software," *Wall Street Journal* (September 23, 2005): A1, A14.

24. Eliza Newlin Carney, "Calm in the Storm," *Government Executive* (October 2003): 57–63; and www.irs.gov (accessed on April 20, 2004).

25. Robert J. Kramer, *Organizing for Global Competitiveness: The Geographic Design* (New York: The Conference Board, 1993): 29–31.

26. Maisie O'Flanagan and Lynn K. Taliento, "Nonprofits: Ensuring That Bigger Is Better," *McKinsey Quarterly*, no. 2 (2004): 112ff.

27. Lawton R. Burns, "Matrix Management in Hospitals: Testing Theories of Matrix Structure and Development," *Administrative Science Quarterly* 34 (1989): 349–368; Carol Hymowitz, "Managers Suddenly Have to Answer to a Crowd of Bosses," *Wall Street Journal* (August 12, 2003): B1.

28. Stanley M. Davis and Paul R. Lawrence, *Matrix* (Reading, MA: Addison-Wesley, 1977).

29. Susan Carey, "US Air 'Peon' Team Pilots Start-Up of Low-Fare Airline," *Wall Street Journal* (March 24, 1998): B1.

30. Charles Fishman, "Total Teamwork: Imagination Ltd.," *Fast Company* (April 2000): 156–168.

31. Melissa A. Schilling and H. Kevin Steensma, "The Use of Modular Organizational Forms: An Industry-Level Analysis," *Academy of Management Journal*, 44, no. 6 (December 2001): 1149–1169.

32. Susan G. Cohen and Don Mankin, "Complex Collaborations for the New Global Economy," *Organizational Dynamics* 31, no. 2 (2002): 117–133; David Lei and John W. Slocum Jr., "Organizational Designs to Renew Competitive Advantage," *Organizational Dynamics* 31, no. 1 (2002): 1–18.

33. Raymond E. Miles and Charles C. Snow, "The New Network Firm: A Spherical Structure Built on a Human Investment Philosophy," *Organizational Dynamics* (Spring 1995): 5–18; and Raymond E. Miles, Charles C. Snow, John A. Matthews, Grant Miles, and Henry J. Coleman, Jr., "Organizing in the Knowledge Age: Anticipating the Cellular Form," *Academy of Management Executive* 11, no. 4 (1997): 7–24.

34. Jena McGregor, with Michael Arndt, Robert Berner, Ian Rowley, Kenji Hall, Gail Edmondson, Steve Hamm, Moon Ihlwan, and Andy Reinhardt, "The World's Most Innovative Companies," *BusinessWeek* (April 24, 2006), http://www.businessweek.com.

35. Raymond E. Miles and Charles C. Snow, "Organizations: New Concepts for New Forms," *California Management Review* 28 (Spring 1986): 62–73; and "Now, The Post-Industrial Corporation," *BusinessWeek* (March 3, 1986): 64–74.

36. N. Anand, "Modular, Virtual, and Hollow Forms of Organization Design," working paper, London Business School (2000); Don Tapscott, "Rethinking Strategy in a Networked World," *Strategy & Business*, Issue 24 (Third Quarter 2001): 34–41.

37. Gregory G. Dess, Abdul M. A. Rasheed, Kevin J. McLaughlin, and Richard L. Priem, "The New Corporate Architecture," *Academy of Management Executive* 9, no. 3 (1995): 7–20.

38. Malcolm Wheatley, "Cycle Company with a Virtual Spin," *MT* (September 2003): 78–81.

39. Philip Siekman, "The Snap-Together Business Jet," *Fortune* (January 21, 2002): 104[A]–104[H].

40. Kathleen Kerwin, "GM: Modular Plants Won't Be a Snap," *BusinessWeek* (November 9, 1998): 168, 172.

41. Robert C. Ford and W. Alan Randolph, "Cross-Functional Structures: A Review and Integration of Matrix Organization and Project Management," *Journal of Management* 18, no. 2 (1992): 267–294; and Paula Dwyer with Pete Engardio, Zachary Schiller, and Stanley Reed, "Tearing Up Today's Organization Chart," *BusinessWeek/Twenty-First Century Capitalism*, 80–90.

42. These disadvantages are based on Michael Goold and Andrew Campbell, "Making Matrix Structures Work: Creating Clarity on Unit Roles and Responsibilities," *European Management Journal* 21, no. 3 (June 2003): 351–363; Hymowitz, "Managers Suddenly Have to Answer to a Crowd of Bosses"; and Dwyer et al., "Tearing Up Today's Organization Chart."

43. Geoff Keighley, "Massively Multinational Player," *Business 2.0* (September 2005): 64–66.

44. Dexter Filkins, "Profusion of Rebel Groups Helps Them Survive in Iraq," *The New York Times* (December 2, 2005), www.nytimes.com.

45. Scott Shane and Neil A. Lewis, "At Sept. 11 Trial, Tale of Missteps and Mismanagement," *The New York Times* (March 31, 2006), www.nytimes.com.

46. Raymond E. Miles, "Adapting to Technology and Competition: A New Industrial Relations System for the Twenty-First Century," *California Management Review* (Winter 1989): 9–28; and Miles and Snow, "The New Network Firm."

47. Dess et al., "The New Corporate Architecture"; Henry W. Chesbrough and David J. Teece, "Organizing for Innovation: When Is Virtual Virtuous?" *The Innovative Entrepreneur* (August 2002): 127–134; N. Anand, "Modular, Virtual, and Hollow Forms," and M. Lynne Markus, Brook Manville, and Carole E. Agres, "What Makes a Virtual Organization Work?" *Sloan Management Review* (Fall 2000): 13–26.

48. Laurie P. O'Leary, "Curing the Monday Blues: A U.S. Navy Guide for Structuring Cross-Functional Teams," *National Productivity Review* (Spring 1996): 43–51; and Alan Hurwitz, "Organizational Structures for the 'New World Order,'" *Business Horizons* (May–June 1996): 5–14.

49. Jay Galbraith, Diane Downey, and Amy Kates, *Designing Dynamic Organizations*, Chapter 4: Processes and Lateral Capability (New York: AMACOM, 2002).

50. Sara Lipka, "The Lawyer Is In," *The Chronicle of Higher Education* (July 1, 2005): A19, A21.

51. Lee Iacocca with William Novak, *Iacocca: An Autobiography* (New York: Phantom Books, 1984): 152–153.

52. Miriam Jordan and Jonathan Karp, "Machines for the Masses," *Wall Street Journal* (December 9, 2003): A1, A20.

53. William J. Altier, "Task Forces: An Effective Management Tool," *Management Review* (February 1987): 52–57.

54. "Task Forces Tackle Consolidation of Employment Services," *Shawmut News*, Shawmut National Corp. (May 3, 1989): 2.

55. Henry Mintzberg, *The Structure of Organizations* (Englewood Cliffs, NJ: Prentice Hall, 1979).

56. Gary Neilson, Bruce A. Pasternack, and Decio Mendes, "The Four Bases of Organizational DNA," *Strategy + Business* Issue 33 (December 10, 2003): 48–57.

57. Paul R. Lawrence and Jay W. Lorsch, "New Managerial Job: The Integrator," *Harvard Business Review* (November–December 1967): 142–151.

58. Ronald N. Ashkenas and Suzanne C. Francis, "Integration Managers: Special Leaders for Special Times," *Harvard Business Review* (November–December 2000): 108–116.

59. This discussion is based on Michael Hammer and Steven Stanton, "How Process Enterprises *Really* Work," *Harvard Business Review* (November–December 1999): 108–118; Richard L. Daft, *Organization Theory and Design,* 5th ed. (Minneapolis, MN: West Publishing Company, 1995): 238; Raymond L. Manganelli and Mark M. Klein, "A Framework for Reengineering," *Management Review* (June 1994): 9–16; and Barbara Ettorre, "Reengineering Tales from the Front," *Management Review* (January 1995): 13–18.

60. Hammer and Stanton, "How Process Enterprises *Really* Work."

61. Michael Hammer, definition quoted in "The Process Starts Here," *CIO* (March 1, 2000): 144–156; and David A. Garvin, "The Processes of Organization and Management," *Sloan Management Review* (Summer 1998): 33–50.

62. Frank Ostroff, *The Horizontal Organization: What the Organization of the Future Looks Like and How It Delivers Value to Customers* (New York: Oxford University Press, 1999).

63. Hammer and Stanton, "How Process Enterprises *Really* Work."

64. Richard Koonce, "Reengineering the Travel Game," *Government Executive* (May 1995): 28–34, 69–70.

65. John A. Byrne, "The Horizontal Corporation," *BusinessWeek* (December 20, 1993): 76–81.

66. Erik Brynjolfsson, Amy Austin Renshaw, and Marshall Van Alstyne, "The Matrix of Change," *Sloan Management Review* (Winter 1997): 37–54.

67. See Harold J. Leavitt, "Why Hierarchies Thrive," *Harvard Business Review* (March 2003): 96–102, for a discussion of the benefits and problems of hierarchies.

68. Michael E. Porter, *Competitive Strategy* (New York: Free Press, 1980): 36–46.

69. Eric M. Olson, Stanley F. Slater, and G. Tomas M. Hult, "The Importance of Structure and Process to Strategy Implementation," *Business Horizons* 48 (2005): 47–54.

70. Pam Black, "Finally, Human Rights for Motorists," *BusinessWeek* (May 1, 1995): 45.

71. Paul R. Lawrence and Jay W. Lorsch, *Organization and Environment* (Homewood, IL: Irwin, 1969).

72. Robert B. Duncan, "Characteristics of Organizational Environments and Perceived Environmental Uncertainty," *Administrative Science Quarterly* 17 (1972): 313–327; W. Alan Randolph and Gregory G. Dess, "The Congruence Perspective of Organization Design: A Conceptual Model and Multivariate Research Approach," *Academy of Management Review* 9 (1984): 114–127; and Masoud Yasai-Ardekani, "Structural Adaptations to Environments," *Academy of Management Review* 11 (1986): 9–21.

73. Tom Burns and G. M. Stalker, *The Management of Innovation* (London: Tavistock, 1961).

74. John A. Coutright, Gail T. Fairhurst, and L. Edna Rogers, "Interaction Patterns in Organic and Mechanistic Systems," *Academy of Management Journal* 32 (1989): 773–802.

75. Robert Pool, "In the Zero Luck Zone," *Forbes ASAP* (November 27, 2000): 85+.

76. Ibid.

77. Denise M. Rousseau and Robert A. Cooke, "Technology and Structure: The Concrete, Abstract, and Activity Systems of Organizations," *Journal of Management* 10 (1984): 345–361; Charles Perrow, "A Framework for the Comparative Analysis of Organizations," *American Sociological Review* 32 (1967): 194–208; and Denise M. Rousseau, "Assessment of Technology in Organizations: Closed versus Open Systems Approaches," *Academy of Management Review* 4 (1979): 531–542.

78. Joan Woodward, *Industrial Organizations: Theory and Practice* (London: Oxford University Press, 1965); and Joan Woodward, Management and Technology (London: Her Majesty's Stationery Office, 1958).

79. Woodward, *Industrial Organizations,* vi.

80. Peter K. Mills and Thomas Kurk, "A Preliminary Investigation into the Influence of Customer-Firm Interface on Information Processing and Task Activity in Service Organizations," *Journal of Management* 12 (1986): 91–104; Peter K. Mills and Dennis J. Moberg, "Perspectives on the Technology of Service Operations," *Academy of Management Review* 7 (1982): 467–478; and Roger W. Schmenner, "How Can Service Businesses Survive and Prosper?" *Sloan Management Review* 27 (Spring 1986): 21–32.

81. Richard B. Chase and David A. Tansik, "The Customer Contact Model for Organization Design," *Management Science* 29 (1983): 1037–1050; and Gregory B. Northcraft and Richard B. Chase, "Managing Service Demand at the Point of Delivery," *Academy of Management Review* 10 (1985): 66–75.

82. Michael Hammer in "The Process Starts Here"; and Emelie Rutherford, "End Game," (an interview with David Weinberger, coauthor of *The Cluetrain Manifesto*), *CIO* (April 1, 2000): 98–104.

83. Thomas A. Stewart, "Three Rules for Managing in the Real-Time Economy," *Fortune* (May 1, 2000): 333–334.

Chapter 8

Change and Innovation

1. Bruce Nussbaum, with Robert Berner and Diane Brady, "Get Creative," *BusinessWeek* (August 1, 2005): 60–68; Jena McGregor, Michael Arndt, Robert Berner, Ian Rowley, Kenji Hall, Gail Edmondson, Steve Hamm, Moon Ihlwan, and Andy Reinhardt, "The World's Most Innovative Companies," *BusinessWeek* (April 24, 2006), http://www.businessweek.com.

2. Keith Bracsher, "Newest Export Out of China: Inflation Fears," *The New York Times* (April 16, 2004), http://www.nytimes.com.

3. Scott Kirsner, "5 Technologies That Will Change the World," *Fast Company* (September 2003): 93–98; Peter Grant and Amy Schatz, "Battle Lines; For Cable Giants, AT&T Deal Is One

More Reason to Worry," *Wall Street Journal* (March 7, 2006): A1; Stuart F. Brown, "The Automaker's Big-Time Bet on Fuel Cells," *Fortune* (March 30, 1998): 122(B)–122(D); Alex Taylor III, "Billion-Dollar Bets," *Fortune* (June 27, 2005): 138–154.

4. Kirsner, "5 Technologies That Will Change the World."

5. Richard L. Daft, "Bureaucratic vs. Nonbureaucratic Structure in the Process of Innovation and Change," in *Perspectives in Organizational Sociology: Theory and Research,* ed. Samuel B. Bacharach (Greenwich, CT: JAI Press, 1982): 129–166.

6. Glenn Rifkin, "Competing Through Innovation: The Case of Broderbund," *Strategy + Business* 11 (Second Quarter 1998): 48–58; and Deborah Dougherty and Cynthia Hardy, "Sustained Product Innovation in Large, Mature Organizations: Overcoming Innovation-to-Organization Problems," *Academy of Management Journal* 39, no. 5 (1996): 1120–1153.

7. Adapted from Patrick Reinmoeller and Nicole van Baardwijk, "The Link Between Diversity and Resilience," *MIT Sloan Management Review* (Summer 2005): 61–65.

8. Teresa M. Amabile, "Motivating Creativity in Organizations: On Doing What You Love and Loving What You Do," *California Management Review* 40, no. 1 (Fall 1997): 39–58; Brian Leavy, "Creativity: The New Imperative," *Journal of General Management* 28, no. 1 (Autumn 2002): 70–85; and Timothy A. Matherly and Ronald E. Goldsmith, "The Two Faces of Creativity," *Business Horizons* (September–October 1985): 8.

9. Gordon Vessels, "The Creative Process: An Open-Systems Conceptualization," *Journal of Creative Behavior* 16 (1982): 185–196.

10. Robert J. Sternberg, Linda A. O'Hara, and Todd I. Lubart, "Creativity as Investment," *California Management Review* 40, no. 1 (Fall 1997): 8–21; Teresa M. Amabile, "Motivating Creativity in Organizations"; Leavy, "Creativity: The New Imperative"; and Ken Lizotte, "A Creative State of Mind," *Management Review* (May 1998): 15–17.

11. James Brian Quinn, "Managing Innovation: Controlled Chaos," *Harvard Business Review* 63 (May–June 1985): 73–84; Howard H. Stevenson and David E. Gumpert, "The Heart of Entrepreneurship," *Harvard Business Review* 63 (March–April 1985): 85–94; Marsha Sinetar, "Entrepreneurs, Chaos, and Creativity—Can Creative People Really Survive Large Company Structure?" *Sloan Management Review* 6 (Winter 1985): 57–62; and Constantine Andriopoulos, "Six Paradoxes in Managing Creativity: An Embracing Act," *Long Range Planning* 36 (2003): 375–388.

12. Cynthia Browne, "Jest for Success," *Moonbeams* (August 1989): 3–5; and Rosabeth Moss Kanter, *The Change Masters* (New York: Simon and Schuster, 1983).

13. Micheal A. Prospero, "Fast Talk: Creative to the Core," *Fast Company* (December 2005): 25–32.

14. Joann S. Lublin, "Nurturing Innovation," *Wall Street Journal* (March 20, 2006): B1; and Ben Elgin, "Managing Google's Idea Factory," *BusinessWeek* (October 3, 2005): 88–90.

15. David Kirkpatrick, "Throw It at the Wall and See If It Sticks," *Fortune* (December 12, 2005): 142–150.

16. Harold J. Leavitt, "Why Hierarchies Thrive," *Harvard Business Review* (March 2003): 96–102.

17. "Hands On: A Manager's Notebook," *Inc.* (January 1989): 106.

18. Sherry Eng, "Hatching Schemes," *The Industry Standard* (November 27–December 4, 2000): 174–175.

19. Ibid.

20. McGregor et al., "The World's Most Innovative Companies," *BusinessWeek* (April 24, 2006), http://www.businessweek.com.

21. Barry Jaruzelski, Kevin Dehoff, and Rakesh Bordia, "Money Isn't Everything," *Strategy + Business,* no. 41 (December 5, 2005): 54–67; William L. Shanklin and John K. Ryans, Jr., "Organizing for High-Tech Marketing," *Harvard Business Review* 62 (November–December 1984): 164–171; and Arnold O. Putnam, "A Redesign for Engineering," *Harvard Business Review* 63 (May–June 1985): 139–144.

22. Andrew H. Van de Ven, "Central Problems in the Management of Innovation," *Management Science* 32 (1986): 590–607; Daft, *Organization Theory*; and Science Policy Research Unit, University of Sussex, *Success and Failure in Industrial Innovation* (London: Centre for the Study of Industrial Innovation, 1972).

23. Daft, *Organization Theory.*

24. Ariane Sains and Stanley Reed, with Michael Arndt, "Electrolux Cleans Up," *BusinessWeek* (February 27, 2006): 42–43.

25. Brian Dumaine, "How Managers Can Succeed Through Speed," *Fortune* (February 13, 1989): 54–59; and George Stalk, Jr., "Time—The Next Source of Competitive Advantage," *Harvard Business Review* (July–August 1988): 41–51.

26. Steve Hamm, with Ian Rowley, "Speed Demons," *BusinessWeek* (March 27, 2006): 68–76; and John A. Pearce II, "Speed Merchants," *Organizational Dynamics* 30, no. 3 (2002): 191–205.

27. Hamm, "Speed Demons."

28. V. K. Narayanan, Frank L. Douglas, Brock Guernsey, and John Charnes, "How Top Management Steers Fast Cycle Teams to Success," *Strategy & Leadership* 30, no. 3 (2002): 19–27.

29. Hamm, "Speed Demons."

30. Timothy L. O'Brien, "Not Invented Here; Are U.S. Innovators Losing Their Edge?" *The New York Times* (November 13, 2005), http://www.nytimes.com; Darrell Rigby and Barbara Bilodeau, "The Bain 2005 Management Tool Survey," *Strategy & Leadership* 33, no. 4 (2005): 4–12; Ian Mount, "The Return of the Lone Inventor," *FSB (Fortune Small Business)* (March 2005): 18; McGregor et al., "The World's Most Innovative Companies;" Henry Chesbrough, "The Logic of Open Innovation: Managing Intellectual Property," *California Management Review* 45, no. 3 (Spring 2003): 33–58.

31. McGregor et al., "The World's Most Innovative Companies."

32. Robert D. Hof, "The Power of Us," *BusinessWeek* (June 20, 2005): 74–82.

33. Henry Chesbrough, "The Era of Open Innovation," *MIT Sloan Management Review* (Spring 2003): 35–41; Amy Muller and Liisa Välikangas, "Extending the Boundary of Corporate Innovation," *Strategy & Leadership* 30, no. 3 (2002): 4–9; and Navi Radjou, "Networked Innovation Drives Profits," *Industrial Management* (January–February 2005): 14–21.

34. Sarah Ellison, "Focus Group; P&G Chief's Turnaround Recipe: Find Out What Women Want," *Wall Street Journal* (June 1, 2005): A1, A16.

35. G. Gil Cloyd, "P&G's Secret: Innovating Innovation," *Industry Week* (December 2004): 26–34; McGregor et al., "The World's Most Innovative Companies"; Bettina von Stamm, "Collaboration with Other Firms and Customers: Innovation's Secret Weapon," *Strategy & Leadership* 32, no. 3 (2004): 16–20; Robert Berner, "Why P&G's Smile Is So Bright," *BusinessWeek* (August 12, 2002): 58–60; Robert D. Hof, "Building an Idea Factory," *BusinessWeek* (October 11, 2004): 194–200; Patricia Sellers, "P&G: Teaching an Old Dog New Tricks," *Fortune* (May 31, 2004): 167–180; Ian Mount, "The Return of the Lone Inventor," *FSB* (March 2005): 18; and Hof, "The Power of Us."

36. Mitsuru Kodama, "Case Study; How Two Japanese High-Tech Companies Achieved Rapid Innovation Via Strategic Community Networks," *Strategy & Leadership* 33, no. 6 (2005): 39–47; Radjou, "Networked Innovation Drives Profits."

37. Katy Koontz, "How to Stand Out from the Crowd," *Working Woman* (January 1988): 74–76.

38. Jane M. Howell, "The Right Stuff: Identifying and Developing Effective Champions of Innovation," *Academy of Management Executive* 19, no. 2 (2005): 108–119.

39. George Anders, "Hard Cell," *Fast Company* (May 2001): 108–122.

40. Harold L. Angle and Andrew H. Van de Ven, "Suggestions for Managing the Innovation Journey," in *Research in the Management of Innovation: The Minnesota Studies,* ed. A. H. Van de Ven, H. L. Angle, and Marshall Scott Poole (Cambridge, MA: Ballinger/Harper & Row, 1989).

41. Robert I. Sutton, "The Weird Rules of Creativity," *Harvard Business Review* (September 2001): 94–103.

42. C. K. Bart, "New Venture Units: Use Them Wisely to Manage Innovation," *Sloan Management Review* (Summer 1988): 35–43; Michael Tushman and David Nadler, "Organizing for Innovation," *California Management Review* 28 (Spring 1986): 74–92; Peter F. Drucker, *Innovation and Entrepreneurship* (New York: Harper & Row, 1985); and Henry W. Chesbrough, "Making Sense of Corporate Venture Capital, *Harvard Business Review* (March 2002), http://www.hbsp.harvard.edu.

43. Joseph Weber, with Stanley Holmes and Christopher Palmeri, "'Most Pits' of Creativity," *BusinessWeek* (November 7, 2005): 98–100.

44. McGregor et al., "The World's Most Innovative Companies."

45. Christopher Hoenig, "Skunk Works Secrets," *CIO* (July 1, 2000): 74–76; and Tom Peters and Nancy Austin, *A Passion for Excellence: The Leadership Difference* (New York: Random House, 1985).

46. Hoenig, "Skunk Works Secrets."

47. Sutton, "The Weird Rules of Creativity."

48. Alan Deutschman, "Building a Better Skunkworks," *Fast Company* (March 2005): 69–73.

49. McGregor et al., "The World's Most Innovative Companies"; Interview with Craig Barrett in Ellen Florian, "CEO Voices: 'I Have a Cast-Iron Stomach,'" *Fortune* (March 8, 2004); and Eng, "Hatching Schemes."

50. E. H. Schein, "Organizational Culture," *American Psychologist* 45 (February 1990): 109–119; Eliza Newlin Carey, "Calm in the Storm."

51. Rosabeth Moss Kanter, "Execution: The Un-Idea," sidebar in Art Kleiner, "Our 10 Most Enduring Ideas," *Strategy + Business*, no. 41 (December 12, 2005): 36–41.

52. Diane Brady, "The Immelt Revolution," *BusinessWeek* (March 28, 2005): 64.

53. Michelle Conlin, "Tough Love for Techie Souls," *BusinessWeek* (November 29, 1999): 164–170.

54. Alix Nyberg, "Kim Patmore," profile in "The Class of 2000," *CFO* (October 2000): 81–82.

55. M. Sashkin and W. W. Burke, "Organization Development in the 1980s," *General Management* 13 (1987): 393–417; and Richard Beckhard, "What Is Organization Development?" in *Organization Development and Transformation: Managing Effective Change,* Wendell L. French, Cecil H. Bell, Jr., and Robert A. Zawacki, eds. (Burr Ridge, IL: Irwin McGraw-Hill, 2000): 16–19.

56. Wendell L. French and Cecil H. Bell, Jr., "A History of Organization Development," in French, Bell, and Zawacki, *Organization Development and Transformation,* 20–42; and Christopher G. Worley and Ann E. Feyerherm, "Reflections on the Future of Organization Development," *The Journal of Applied Behavioral Science* 39, no. 1 (March 2003): 97–115.

57. Paul F. Buller, "For Successful Strategic Change: Blend OD Practices with Strategic Management," *Organizational Dynamics* (Winter 1988): 42–55; Robert M. Fulmer and Roderick Gilkey, "Blending Corporate Families: Management and Organization Development in a Postmerger Environment," *The Academy of Management Executive* 2 (1988): 275–283; and Worley and Feyerherm, "Reflections on the Future of Organization Development."

58. W. Warner Burke, "The New Agenda for Organization Development," *Organizational Dynamics* (Summer 1997): 7–19.

59. This discussion is based on Kathleen D. Dannemiller and Robert W. Jacobs, "Changing the Way Organizations Change: A Revolution of Common Sense," *The Journal of Applied Behavioral Science* 28, no. 4 (December 1992): 480–498; and Barbara Benedict Bunker and Billie T. Alban, "Conclusion: What Makes Large Group Interventions Effective?" *The Journal of Applied Behavioral Science* 28, no. 4 (December 1992): 570–591.

60. Bunker and Alban, "What Makes Large Group Interventions Effective?"

61. Kurt Lewin, "Frontiers in Group Dynamics: Concepts, Method, and Reality in Social Science," *Human Relations* 1 (1947): 5–41; and E. F. Huse and T. G. Cummings, *Organization Development and Change*, 3rd ed. (St. Paul, MN: West, 1985).

62. Based on John Kotter's eight-step model of planned change, which is described in John Kotter, *Leading Change* (Boston: Harvard Business School Press, 1996): 20–25, and "Leading Change: Why Transformation Efforts Fail," *Harvard Business Review* (March–April, 1995): 59–67.

63. Andre L. Delbecq and Peter K. Mills, "Managerial Practices that Enhance Innovation," *Organizational Dynamics* 14 (Summer 1985): 24–34.

64. Steven Gray, "Beyond Burgers; McDonald's Menu Upgrade Boosts Meal Prices and Results," *Wall Street Journal* (February 18–19, 2006): A1, A7.

65. Interview with Art Collins in Ellen Florian, "CEO Voices: 'I Have a Cast-Iron Stomach,'" *Fortune* (March 8, 2004).

66. Robert A. Guth, "Code Red; Battling Google, Microsoft Changes How It Builds Software," *Wall Street Journal* (September 23, 2005): A1, A14.

67. Daniel Del Re, "Pushing Past Post-Its," *Business 2.0* (November 2005): 54–56.

68. Neal E. Boudette, "Shifting Gears; Chrysler Gains Edge by Giving New Flexibility to Its Factories," *Wall Street Journal* (April 11, 2006): A1, A15.

69. Vanessa Fuhrmans, "Bedside Manner; An Insurer Tries a New Strategy: Listen to Patients," *Wall Street Journal* (April 11, 2006): A1.

70. John P. Kotter, *Leading Change* (Boston: Harvard University Press, 1996): 20–25; and "Leading Change: Why Transformation Efforts Fail," *Harvard Business Review* (March–April, 1995): 59–67.

71. Almar Latour, "Trial by Fire: A Blaze in Albuquerque Sets Off Major Crisis for Cell-Phone Giants," *Wall Street Journal* (January 29, 2001): A1, A8.

72. Attributed to Gregory Bateson in Andrew H. Van de Ven, "Central Problems in the Management of Innovation," *Management Science* 32 (1986): 595.

73. J. P. Kotter and L. A. Schlesinger, "Choosing Strategies for Change," *Harvard Business Review* 57 (March–April 1979): 106–114.

74. Interview with Fred Smith in Ellen Florian, "CEO Voices."

75. G. Zaltman and Robert B. Duncan, *Strategies for Planned Change* (New York: Wiley Interscience, 1977).

76. Leonard M. Apcar, "Middle Managers and Supervisors Resist Moves to More Participatory Management," *Wall Street Journal* (September 16, 1985): 25.

77. Dorothy Leonard-Barton and Isabelle Deschamps, "Managerial Influence in the Implementation of New Technology," *Management Science* 34 (1988): 1252–1265.

78. Kurt Lewin, *Field Theory in Social Science: Selected Theoretical Papers* (New York: Harper & Brothers, 1951).

79. Paul C. Nutt, "Tactics of Implementation," *Academy of Management Journal* 29 (1986): 230–261; Kotter and Schlesinger, "Choosing Strategies"; R. L. Daft and S. Becker, *Innovation in Organizations: Innovation Adoption in School Organizations* (New York: Elsevier, 1978); and R. Beckhard, *Organization Development: Strategies and Models* (Reading, MA: Addison-Wesley, 1969).

80. Rob Muller, "Training for Change," *Canadian Business Review* (Spring 1995): 16–19.

81. Gerard H. Seijts and Grace O'Farrell, "Engage the Heart: Appealing to the Emotions Facilitates Change," *Ivey Business Journal* (January–February 2003): 1–5; John P. Kotter and Dan S. Cohen, *The Heart of Change: Real-Life Stories of How People Change Their Organizations* (Boston: Harvard Business School Press, 2002); and Shaul Fox and Yair AmichaiHamburger, "The Power of Emotional Appeals in Promoting Organizational Change Programs," *Academy of Management Executive* 15, no. 4 (2001): 84–95.

82. Taggart F. Frost, "Creating a Teamwork-Based Culture within a Manufacturing Setting," *IM* (May–June 1994): 17–20.

83. Dean Foust with Gerry Khermouch, "Repairing the Coke Machine," *BusinessWeek* (March 19, 2001): 86–88.

84. Joy Persaud, "Strongest Links," *People Management* (May 29, 2003): 40–41.

Chapter 9

Human Resources and Diversity

1. Results of a McKinsey Consulting survey, reported in Leigh Branham, "Planning to Become an Employer of Choice," *Journal of Organizational Excellence* (Summer 2005): 57–68.

2. Robert L. Mathis and John H. Jackson, *Human Resource Management: Essential Perspectives,* 2nd ed. (Cincinnati, OH: South-Western Publishing, 2002): 1.

3. Keith H. Hammonds, "Handle with Care," *Fast Company* (August 2002): 103–107; and Branham, "Planning to Become an Employer of Choice."

4. Hammonds, "Handle with Care"; and Branham, "Planning to Become an Employer of Choice."

5. Joy Persaud, "Game On," *People Management* (September 25, 2003): 40–41.

6. Jonathan Poet, "Schools Looking Overseas for Teachers," *Johnson City Press* (April 20, 2001): 6; and Jill Rosenfeld, "How's This for a Tough Assignment?" *Fast Company* (November 1999): 104–106.

7. See James C. Wimbush, "Spotlight on Human Resource Management," *Business Horizons* 48 (2005): 463–467; Jonathan

Tompkins, "Strategic Human Resources Management in Government: Unresolved Issues," *Public Personnel Management* (Spring 2002): 95–110; Noel M. Tichy, Charles J. Fombrun, and Mary Anne Devanna, "Strategic Human Resource Management," *Sloan Management Review* 23 (Winter 1982): 47–61; Cynthia A. Lengnick-Hall and Mark L. Lengnick-Hall, "Strategic Human Resources Management: A Review of the Literature and a Proposed Typology," *Academy of Management Review* 13 (July 1988): 454–470; Eugene B. McGregor, *Strategic Management of Human Knowledge, Skills, and Abilities,* (San Francisco: Jossey-Bass, 1991).

8. Edward E. Lawler III, "HR on Top," *Strategy + Business,* no. 35 (Second Quarter 2004): 21–25.

9. Tompkins, "Strategic Human Resource Management in Government: Unresolved Issues"; and Wimbush, "Spotlight on Human Resource Management."

10. Mark A. Huselid, Susan E. Jackson, and Randall S. Schuler, "Technical and Strategic Human Resource Management Effectiveness as Determinants of Firm Performance," *Academy of Management Journal* 40, no. 1 (1997): 171–188; and John T. Delaney and Mark A. Huselid, "The Impact of Human Resource Management Practices on Perceptions of Organizational Performance," *Academy of Management Journal* 39, no. 4 (1996): 949–969.

11. D. Kneale, "Working at IBM: Intense Loyalty in a Rigid Culture," *Wall Street Journal* (April 7, 1986): 17.

12. Jeffrey Pfeffer, "Producing Sustainable Competitive Advantage Through the Effective Management of People," *Academy of Management Executive* 9, no. 1 (1995): 55–72; and Harry Scarbrough, "Recipe for Success," *People Management* (January 23, 2003): 32–25.

13. James N. Baron and David M. Kreps, "Consistent Human Resource Practices," *California Management Review* 41, no. 3 (Spring 1999): 29–53.

14. Cynthia D. Fisher, "Current and Recurrent Challenges in HRM," *Journal of Management* 15 (1989): 157–180.

15. See Dave Ulrich, "A New Mandate for Human Resources," *Harvard Business Review* (January–February 1998): 124–134; Philip H. Mirvis, "Human Resource Management: Leaders, Laggards, and Followers," *Academy of Management Executive* 11, no. 2 (1997): 43–56; Richard McBain, "Attracting, Retaining, and Motivating Capable People," *Manager Update* (Winter 1999): 25–36; and Oren Harari, "Attracting the Best Minds," *Management Review* (April 1998): 23–26.

16. Floyd Kemske, "HR 2008: A Forecast Based on Our Exclusive Study," *Workforce* (January 1998): 46–60.

17. This definition and discussion is based on George Bollander, Scott Snell, and Arthur Sherman, *Managing Human Resources,* 12th ed. (Cincinnati, OH: South-Western, 2001): 13–15; and Scarbrough, "Recipe for Success."

18. Griffith, "Winning Hearts and Minds."

19. Mark C. Bolino, William H. Turnley, and James M. Bloodgood, "Citizenship Behavior and the Creation of Social Capital in Organizations," *Academy of Management Review* 27, no. 5 (2002): 505–522.

20. Victoria Griffith, "Winning Hearts and Minds at Home Depot" *Strategy + Business,* Issue 38 (First Quarter 2005): 61–71; and Lawler, "HR on Top."

21. Ellen A. Ensher, Troy R. Nielson, and Elisa Grant-Vallone, "Tales from the Hiring Line: Effects of the Internet and Technology on HR Processes," *Organizational Dynamics* 31, no. 3 (2002): 224–244.

22. Section 1604.1 of the EEOC Guidelines based on the Civil Rights Act of 1964, Title VII.

23. Charles F. Falk and Kathleen A. Carlson, "Newer Patterns in Management for the Post–Social Contract Era," *Midwest Management Society Proceedings* (1995): 45–52.

24. A. S. Tsui, J. L. Pearce, L. W. Porter, and A. M. Tripoli, "Alternative Approaches to the Employee-Organization Relationship: Does Investment in Employees Pay Off?" *Academy of Management Journal* 40 (1997): 1089–1121; D. Wang, A. S. Tsui, Y. Zhang, and L. Ma, "Employment Relationships and Firm Performance: Evidence from an Emerging Economy," *Journal of Organizational Behavior* 24 (2003): 511–535.

25. Richard Pascale, "The False Security of 'Employability,'" *Fast Company* (April–May 1996): 62, 64; and Louisa Wah, "The New Workplace Paradox," *Management Review* (January 1998): 7.

26. Douglas T. Hall and Jonathan E. Moss, "The New Protean Career Contract: Helping Organizations and Employees Adapt," *Organizational Dynamics* (Winter 1998): 22–37.

27. Based on Branham, "Planning to Become an Employer of Choice."

28. Ibid.

29. Sean Donahue, "New Jobs for the New Economy," *Business 2.0* (July 1999): 102–109.

30. The discussion of temporary employment agencies is based on David Wessel, "Capital: Temp Workers Have a Lasting Effect," *Wall Street Journal* (February 1, 2001): A1.

31. Brenda Paik Sunoo, "Temp Firms Turn Up the Heat on Hiring," *Workforce* (April 1999): 50–54; H. Lancaster, "Some Veteran Bosses Find More Excitement in Doing Temp Work," *Wall Street Journal* (November 17, 1998): B1; and J. Thottam, "When Execs Go Temp," *Time* (April 26, 2004): 40–41.

32. Jaclyn Fierman, "The Contingency Workforce," *Fortune* (January 24, 1994): 30–31.

33. Nancy B. Kurland and Diane E. Bailey, "Telework: The Advantages and Challenges of Working Here, There, Anywhere, Anytime," *Organizational Dynamics* (Autumn 1999): 53–68.

34. Kevin Voigt, "For 'Extreme Telecommuters,' Remote Work Means Really Remote," *Wall Street Journal* (January 31, 2001): B1.

35. Ibid.

36. John Challenger, "There Is No Future for the Workplace," *Public Management* (February 1999): 20–23; Susan Caminiti, "Work-Life," *Fortune* (September 19, 2005): S1–S17.

37. Stephanie Armour, "GenerationY: They've Arrived at Work With a New Attitude," *USA Today* (November 6, 2005), http://www.usatoday.com; Ellyn Spragins, "The Talent Pool," *FSB* (October 2005): 92–101; and Caminiti, "Work-Life."

38. B. Nussbaum, "Where Are the Jobs?" *BusinessWeek* (March 22, 2004): 36–37.

39. James R. Morris, Wayne F. Cascio, and Clifford Young, "Downsizing After All These Years: Questions and Answers About Who Did It, How Many Did It, and Who Benefited From It," *Organizational Dynamics* (Winter 1999): 78–86; William McKinley, Carol M. Sanchez, and Allen G. Schick, "Organizational Downsizing: Constraining, Cloning, Learning," *Academy of Management Executive* 9, no. 3 (1995): 32–42; and Brett C. Luthans and Steven M. Sommer, "The Impact of Downsizing on Workplace Attitudes," *Group and Organization Management* 2, no. 1 (1999): 46–70.

40. Effective downsizing techniques are discussed in detail in Bob Nelson, "The Care of the Un-Downsized," *Training and Development* (April 1997): 40–43; Shari Caudron, "Teaching Downsizing Survivors How to Thrive," *Personnel Journal* (January 1996): 38; Joel Brockner, "Managing the Effects of Layoffs on Survivors," *California Management Review* (Winter 1992): 9–28; and Kim S. Cameron, "Strategies for Successful Organizational Downsizing," *Human Resource Management* 33, no. 2 (Summer 1994): 189–211.

41. James G. March and Herbert A. Simon, *Organizations* (New York: Wiley, 1958).

42. Richard McBain, "Attracting, Retaining, and Motivating Capable People: A Key to Competitive Advantage," *Manager Update* (Winter 1999): 25–36.

43. Dennis J. Kravetz, *The Human Resources Revolution* (San Francisco: Jossey-Bass, 1989).

44. J. W. Boudreau and S. L. Rynes, "Role of Recruitment in Staffing Utility Analysis," *Journal of Applied Psychology* 70 (1985): 354–366.

45. Megan Santosus, "The Human Capital Factor," *CFO-IT* (Fall 2005): 26–27.

46. Brian Dumaine, "The New Art of Hiring Smart," *Fortune* (August 17, 1987): 78–81.

47. Nanette Byrnes, "Star Search," *BusinessWeek* (October 10, 2005): 68–78.

48. This discussion is based on Mathis and Jackson, *Human Resource Management*, Chapter 4, 49–60.

49. Victoria Griffith, "When Only Internal Expertise Will Do," *CFO* (October 1998): 95–96, 102.

50. J. P. Wanous, *Organizational Entry* (Reading, MA: Addison-Wesley, 1980).

51. Samuel Greengard, "Technology Finally Advances HR," *Workforce* (January 2000): 38–41; and Scott Hays, "Hiring on the Web," *Workforce* (August 1999): 77–84.

52. Jessica Mintz, "Online Tools Aid Job Recruiters in Search of 'Passise' Prospects," *Wall Street Journal* (July 12, 2005): B6.

53. Kathryn Tyler, "Employees Can Help Recruit New Talent," *HR Magazine* (September 1996): 57–60.

54. Scott Westcott, "Scenes from the Talent Wars," *Inc.* (January 2006): 29–31.

55. Ron Stodghill, "Soul on Ice," *FSB* (October 2005): 129–134.

56. Ann Harrington, "Anybody Here Want a Job?" *Fortune* (May 15, 2000): 489–498.

57. Milt Freudenheim, "More Help Wanted: Older Workers Please Apply," *The New York Times* (March 23, 2005), http://www.nytimes.com.

58. "Bank of America to Hire 850 Ex-Welfare Recipients," *Johnson City Press* (January 14, 2001): 29; E. Blacharczyk, "Recruiters Challenged by Economy, Shortages, Unskilled," *HR News* (February 1990): B1; Victoria Rivkin, "Visa Relief," *Working Woman* (January 2001): 15.

59. Wimbush, "Spotlight on Human Resource Management."

60. P. W. Thayer, "Somethings Old, Somethings New," *Personnel Psychology* 30 (1977): 513–524.

61. J. Ledvinka, *Federal Regulation of Personnel and Human Resource Management* (Boston: Kent, 1982); and Civil Rights Act, Title VII, 42 U.S.C. Section 2000e *et seq.* (1964).

62. Studies reported in William Poundstone, "Impossible Questions," *Across the Board* (September–October 2003): 44–48.

63. Anne S. Tsui and Joshua B. Wu, "The New Employment Relationship Versus the Mutual Investment Approach: Implications for Human Resource Management," *Human Resource Management* 44, no. 2 (Summer 2005): 115–121.

64. Bohlander, Snell, and Sherman, *Managing Human Resources*, 202.

65. Powers, "Finding Workers Who Fit."

66. Bohlander, Snell, and Sherman, *Managing Human Resources*.

67. Meridith Levinson, "How to Hire So You Don't Have to Fire," *CIO* (March 1, 2004): 72–80.

68. "Assessment Centers: Identifying Leadership through Testing," *Small Business Report* (June 1987): 22–24; and W. C. Byham, "Assessment Centers for Spotting Future Managers," *Harvard Business Review* (July–August 1970): 150–167.

69. Mike Thatcher, "'Front-line Staff Selected by Assessment Center," *Personnel Management* (November 1993): 83.

70. Bernard Keys and Joseph Wolfe, "Management Education and Development: Current Issues and Emerging Trends," *Journal of Management* 14 (1988): 205–229.

71. "2005 Industry Report," *Training* (December 2005): 14–28; "Pinpointing Inside Up-and-Comers," sidebar in Nanette Byrnes, "Star Search," *BusinessWeek* (October 10, 2005): 68–78.

72. William J. Rothwell and H. C. Kazanas, *Improving On-the Job Training: How to Establish and Operate a Comprehensive OJT Program* (San Francisco: Jossey-Bass, 1994).

73. "2005 Industry Report."

74. Doug Bartholomew, "Taking the E-Train," *Industry Week* (June 2005): 34–37.

75. Jeanne C. Meister, "The Brave New World of Corporate Education" *The Chronicle of Higher Education* (February 9, 2001): B10; and Meryl Davids Landau, "Corporate Universities Crack Open Their Doors," *The Journal of Business Strategy* (May–June 2000): 18–23.

76. Meister, "The Brave New World of Corporate Education"; Edward E. Gordon, "Bridging the Gap," *Training* (September 2003): 30; and John Byrne, "The Search for the Young and Gifted," *BusinessWeek* (October 4, 1999): 108–116.

77. Bartholomew, "Taking the E-Train"; Joel Schettler, "Defense Acquisition University: Weapons of Mass Instruction," *Training* (February 2003): 20–27.

78. Gordon, "Bridging the Gap."

79. Jim Dow, "Spa Attraction," *People Management* (May 29, 2003): 34–35.

80. Scott Leibs, "Building a Better Workforce," *CFO-IT* (Fall 2005): 20–27; and Charles Forelle, "IBM Tool Dispatches Employees Efficiently," *Wall Street Journal* (July 14, 2005).

81. "Pinpointing Inside Up-and-Comers"; and Forelle, "IBM Tool Dispatches Employees Efficiently."

82. Spragins, "The Talent Pool."

83. Walter W. Tornow, "Editor's Note: Introduction to Special Issue on 360-Degree Feedback," *Human Resource Management* 32, no. 2–3 (Summer–Fall 1993): 211–219; and Brian O'Reilly, "360 Feedback Can Change Your Life," *Fortune* (October 17, 1994): 93–100.

84. Kris Frieswick, "Truth & Consequences," *CFO* (June 2001): 56–63.

85. This discussion is based on Dick Grote, "Forced Ranking: Behind the Scenes," *Across the Board* (November–December 2002): 40–45; Matthew Boyle, "Performance Reviews: Perilous Curves Ahead," *Fortune* (May 28, 2001): 187–188; Carol Hymowitz, "Ranking Systems Gain Popularity But Have Many Staffers Riled," *Wall Street Journal* (May 15, 2001): B1; and Frieswick, "Truth & Consequences."

86. Dick Grote, *Forced Ranking: Making Performance Management Work* (Boston: Harvard Business School Press, 2005); Jena McGregor, "The Struggle to Measure Performance," *BusinessWeek* (January 9, 2006): 26–28.

87. Hymowitz, "Ranking Systems Gain Popularity"; and Boyle, "Performance Reviews."

88. Reported in McGregor, "The Struggle to Measure Performance."

89. Ibid.

90. Catherine Edwards, "Called to Account," *People Management* (July 2004): 33–34.

91. V. R. Buzzotta, "Improve Your Performance Appraisals," *Management Review* (August 1988): 40–43; and H. J. Bernardin and R. W. Beatty, *Performance Appraisal: Assessing Human Behavior at Work* (Boston: Kent, 1984).

92. Lou Kaucic, "Finding Your Stars," *Microsoft Executive Circle* (Summer 2003): 14.

93. Ibid.

94. Richard I. Henderson, *Compensation Management: Rewarding Performance*, 4th ed. (Reston, VA: Reston, 1985).

95. L. R. Gomez-Mejia, "Structure and Process Diversification, Compensation Strategy, and Firm Performance," *Strategic Management Journal* 13 (1992): 381–397; and E. Montemayor, "Congruence Between Pay Policy and Competitive Strategy in High-Performing Firms," *Journal of Management* 22, no. 6 (1996): 889–908.

96. Renée F. Broderick and George T. Milkovich, "Pay Planning, Organization Strategy, Structure and 'Fit': A Prescriptive Model of Pay," paper presented at the 45th Annual Meeting of the Academy of Management, San Diego (August 1985).

97. E. F. Lawler, III, *Strategic Pay: Aligning Organizational Strategies and Pay Systems* (San Francisco: Jossey-Bass, 1990); and R. J. Greene, "Person-Focused Pay: Should It Replace Job-Based Pay?" *Compensation and Benefits Management* 9, no. 4 (1993): 46–55.

98. L. Wiener, "No New Skills? No Raise," *U.S. News and World Report* (October 26, 1992): 78.

99. Data from Hewitt Associates, Bureau of Labor Statistics, reported in Michelle Conlin and Peter Coy, with Ann Therese Palmer, and Gabrielle Saveri, "The Wild New Workforce," *BusinessWeek* (December 6, 1999): 39–44.

100. Brian Friel, "The Rating Game," *Government Executive* (August 2003): 46–52.

101. *Employee Benefits*, (Washington, DC: U. S. Chamber of Commerce, 1997): 7.

102. Danielle Sacks, "Not the Retiring Sort," *Fast Company* 94 (May 2005): 28.

103. Jay Greene, "Troubling Exits at Microsoft," *BusinessWeek* (September 26, 2005): 98–108.

104. Frank E. Kuzmits, "Communicating Benefits: A Double-Click Away," *Compensation and Benefits Review* 30, no. 5 (September–October 1998): 60–64; and Lynn Asinof, "Click and Shift: Workers Control Their Benefits Online," *Wall Street Journal* (November 27, 1997): C1.

105. Robert S. Catapano-Friedman, "Cafeteria Plans: New Menu for the '90s," *Management Review* (November 1991): 25–29.

106. Byrnes, "Star Search."

107. Mike Brewster, "No Exit," *Fast Company* (April 2005): 93.

108. Yvette Debow, "GE: Easing the Pain of Layoffs," *Management Review* (September 1997): 15–18.

109. M. Fine, F. Johnson, and M. S. Ryan, "Cultural Diversity in the Workforce," *Public Personnel Management* 19 (1990): 305–319.

110. Taylor H. Cox, "Managing Cultural Diversity: Implications for Organizational Competitiveness," *Academy of Management Executive* 5, no. 3 (1991): 45–56; and Faye Rice, "How to Make Diversity Pay," *Fortune* (August 8, 1994): 78–86.

111. Roy Harris, "The Illusion of Inclusion," *CFO* (May 2001): 42–50; C. J. Prince, "Doing Diversity: The Question Isn't Why to Do It—But How," *Chief Executive* (April, 2005): 46; and results of a study conducted by the Society for Human Resource Management and *Fortune* magazine, reported in "Diversity Hiring in 2005: Are You in the Minority?" *Fortune* (January 24, 2005): 57–58.

112. Val Singh and Sébastien Point, "Strategic Responses by European Companies to the Diversity Challenge: An Online Comparison," *Long Range Planning* 37 (2004): 295–318.

113. Survey results reported in "Diversity Initiatives Shown to Be Critical to Job Seekers," *The New York Times Magazine* (September 14, 2003): 100.

114. Results reported in "Diversity Hiring in 2005."

115. Lennie Copeland "Valuing Diversity, Part I: Making the Most of Cultural Differences at the Workplace," *Personnel* (June 1988): 52–60.

116. Lee Smith, "The Business Case for Diversity" in "The Diversity Factor," *Fortune* (October 13, 2003): S1–S12.

117. Lennie Copeland, "Learning to Manage a Multicultural Workforce," *Training* (May 25, 1988): 48–56; and D. Farid Elashmawi, "Culture Clashes: Barriers to Business," *Managing Diversity* 2, no. 11 (August 1993): 1–3.

118. Singh and Point, "Strategic Responses by European Companies to the Diversity Challenge."

119. Robert Doktor, Rosalie Tung, and Mary Ann von Glinow, "Future Directions for Management Theory Development," *Academy of Management Review* 16 (1991): 362–365; and Mary Munter, "Cross-Cultural Communication for Managers," *Business Horizons* (May–June 1993): 69–78.

120. Renee Blank and Sandra Slipp, "The White Male: An Endangered Species?" *Management Review* (September 1994): 27–32; Michael S. Kimmel, "What Do Men Want?" *Harvard Business Review* (November–December 1993): 50–63; and Sharon Nelton, "Nurturing Diversity," *Nation's Business* (June 1995): 25–27.

121. Marianne Bertrand and Sendhil Mullainathan, *Are Emily and Greg More Employable than Lakisha and Jamal?* National Bureau of Economic Research report, as reported in L. A. Johnson, "What's in a Name: When Emily Gets the Job Over Lakisha," *The Tennessean* (January 4, 2004): 14A.

122. N. Songer, "Workforce Diversity," *B&E Review* (April–June 1991): 3–6; Lee Smith, "Closing the Gap," *Fortune* (November 14, 2005): 211–218; Prince, "Doing Diversity."

123. M. Bennett, "A Developmental Approach to Training for Intercultural Sensitivity," *International Journal of Intercultural Relations* 10 (1986): 179–196.

124. Prince, "Doing Diversity."

125. Michael L. Wheeler, "Diversity: The Performance Factor," *Harvard Business Review* (March 2005): S1–S7.

126. Jason Forsythe, "Winning with Diversity," *The New York Times Magazine* (March 28, 2004): 65–72; Amy Aronson, "Getting Results: Corporate Diversity, Integration, and Market Penetration," special advertising section, *BusinessWeek* (October 20, 2003): 140–144; and Nixon and West, "America Addresses Work Force Diversity,"

127. Wheeler, "Diversity: The Performance Factor."

128. G. Pascal Zachary, "Mighty Is the Mongrel," *Fast Company* (July 2000): 270–284.

129. Kimberly L. Allers with Nadira A. Hira, "The Diversity List," *Fortune* (August 22, 2005); Elizabeth Wasserman, "A Race for Profits," *MBA Jungle* (March–April 2003): 40–41; Amy Aronson, "Getting Results."

130. Immigrant statistics from the U.S. Census Bureau reported in Chris Woodyard, "Multilingual Staff Can Drive Up Auto Sales," *USA Today* (February 21, 2005), http://www.usatoday.com.

131. Bureau of Labor Statistics data reported in Prince, "Doing Diversity."

132. Stephanie N. Mehta, "What Minority Employees Really Want," *Fortune* (June 10, 2000): 181–186.

133. Harris, "The Illusion of Inclusion."

134. Jennifer L. Knight, Michelle R. Hebl, Jessica B. Foster, and Laura M. Mannix, "Out of Role? Out of Luck: The Influence of Race and Leadership Status on Performance Appraisals," *The Journal of Leadership and Organizational Studies* 9, no. 3 (2003): 85–93.

135. Mehta, "What Minority Employees Really Want."

136. "Diversity in the Federal Government," report of a round-table discussion on "Addressing Diversity Issues in the Government," July 10, 2003, moderated by Omar Wasow, executive director of BlackPlanet.com, reported in *The New York Times Magazine* (September 14, 2003): 95–99.

137. Quoted in Lee Smith, "The Business Case for Diversity."

138. Bryan Gingrich, "Individual and Organizational Accountabilities: Reducing Stereotypes and Prejudice within the Workplace," *Diversity Factor* 8, no. 2 (Winter 2000): 14–20.

139. Alison Stein Wellner, "The Disability Advantage," *Inc. Magazine* (October 2005): 29–31.

140. Copeland, "Valuing Diversity, Part I: Making the Most of Cultural Differences at the Workplace"; Judy and D'Amico, *Workforce 2020;* and S. Hutchins, Jr., "Preparing for Diversity: The Year 2000," *Quality Process* 22, no. 10 (1989): 66–68.

141. Fred L. Fry and Jennifer R. D. Burgess, "The End of the Need for Affirmative Action: Are We There Yet?" *Business Horizons* (November–December 2003): 7–16.

142. Roosevelt Thomas, Jr., "From Affirmative Action to Affirming Diversity," *Harvard Business Review* (March–April 1990): 107–117; Nicholas Lemann, "Taking Affirmative Action Apart," *The New York Times Magazine* (July 11, 1995): 36–43; and Terry H. Anderson, *The Pursuit of Fairness: A History of Affirmative Action* (New York: Oxford University Press, 2004).

143. Robert J. Grossman, "Behavior at Work," *HR Magazine* 46, no. 3 (March 2001): 50+; Madeline E. Heilman, Caryn J. Block, and Peter Stathatos, "The Affirmative Action Stigma of Incompetence: Effects of Performance Information Ambiguity," *Academy of Management Journal* 40, no. 1 (1997): 603–625.

144. Fry and Burgess, "The End of the Need for Affirmative Action"; and Erika H. James, Arthur P. Brief, Joerg Dietz, and Robin R. Cohen, "Prejudice Matters: Understanding the Reactions of Whites to Affirmative Action Programs Targeted to Benefit Blacks," *Journal of Applied Psychology* 86, no. 6 (December 2001): 1120+.

145. Greg Winter, "After Ruling, 3 Universities Maintain Diversity in Admissions," *The New York Times* (April 13, 2004): A22.

146. "Race Relations Better But Bias Persists, Poll Finds," *Jet* (May 3, 2004): 10.

147. Sheila Wellington, Marcia Brumit Kropf, and Paulette R. Gerkovich, "What's Holding Women Back?" *Harvard Business Review* (June 2003): 18–19.

148. Julie Amparano Lopez, "Study Says Women Face Glass Walls as Well as Ceilings," *Wall Street Journal* (March 3, 1992): B1, B2; Ida L. Castro, "Q: Should Women Be Worried About the Glass Ceiling in the Workplace?" *Insight* (February 10, 1997): 24–27; Debra E. Meyerson and Joyce K. Fletcher, "A Modest Manifesto for Shattering the Glass Ceiling," *Harvard Business Review* (January–February 2000): 127–136; and Wellington, Brumit Kropf, and Gerkovich, "What's Holding Women Back?"; Finnegan, "Different Strokes."

149. Catalyst survey results reported in Forsythe, "Winning with Diversity."

150. Jory Des Jardins, "I Am Woman (I Think)," *Fast Company* (May 2005): 25–26; Lisa Belkin, "The Opt-Out Revolution," *The New York Times Magazine* (October 26, 2003): 43–47, 58; Annie Finnigan, "Different Strokes," *Working Woman* (April 2001): 42–48; and Meyerson and Fletcher, "A Modest Manifesto for Shattering the Glass Ceiling."

151. Statistics from the U.S. Census Bureau, Current Population Survey, 2004 Annual Social and Economic Supplement, as reported in "2003 Median Annual Earnings by Race and Sex," http://www.infoplease.com/ipa/A0197814.html; and "The Economics of Gender and Race: Examining the Wage Gap in the United States," The Feminist Majority Foundation Choices Campus Campaign, http://www.feministcampus.org.

152. Cliff Edwards, "Coming Out in Corporate America," *BusinessWeek* (December 15, 2003): 64–72; Belle Rose Ragins, John M. Cornwell, and Janice S. Miller, "Heterosexism in the Workplace: Do Race and Gender Matter?" *Group & Organization Management 28*, no. 1 (March 2003): 45–74.

153. Sylvia Ann Hewlett and Carolyn Buck Luce, "Off-Ramps and On-Ramps; Keeping Talented Women on the Road to Success," *Harvard Business Review* (March 2005): 43–54.

154. Belkin, "The Opt-Out Revolution."

155. John Byrne, "The Price of Balance," *Fast Company* (February 2004); Tischler, "Where Are the Women?" *Fast Company* (February 2004): 52–60; Patricia Sellers, "Power: Do Women Really Want It?" *Fortune* (October 13, 2003): 80–100.

156. C. J. Prince, "Media Myths: The Truth About the Opt-Out Hype," *NAFE Maazine* (Second Quarter 2004): 14–18; Sellers, "Power: Do Women Really Want It?"

157. Jia Lynn Yang, "Goodbye to All That," *Fortune* (November 14, 2005): 169–170.

158. Welllington et al., "What's Holding Women Back?"

159. The Leader's Edge/Executive Women Research 2002 survey, reported in "Why Women Leave," *Executive Female* (Summer 2003): 4.

160. Barbara Reinhold, "Smashing Glass Ceilings: Why Women *Still* Find It Tough to Advance to the Executive Suite," *Journal of Organizational Excellence* (Summer 2005): 43–55; Des Jardins, "I Am Woman (I Think)"; and Alice H. Eagly and Linda L. Carli, "The Female Leadership Advantage: An Evaluation of the Evidence," *The Leadership Quarterly* 14 (2003): 807–834.

161. Claudia H. Deutsch, "Behind the Exodus of Executive Women: Boredom," *USA Today* (May 2, 2005).

162. C. Soloman, "Careers under Glass," *Personnel Journal* 69, no. 4 (1990): 96–105; and Belle Rose Ragins, Bickley Townsend, and Mary Mattis, "Gender Gap in the Executive Suite: CEOs and Female Executives Report on Breaking the Glass Ceiling," *Academy of Management Executive* 12, no. 1 (1998): 28–42.

163. Eagly and Carli, "The Female Leadership Advantage: An Evaluation of the Evidence"; Reinhold, "Smashing Glass Ceilings"; Sally Helgesen, *The Female Advantage: Women's Ways of Leadership* (New York: Doubleday Currency, 1990); Rochelle Sharpe, "As Leaders, Women Rule: New Studies Find that Female Managers Outshine Their Male Counterparts in Almost Every Measure," *BusinessWeek*

(November 20, 2000): 5+; and Del Jones, "2003: Year of the Woman Among the Fortune 500?" (December 30, 2003): 1B.

164. Reported in Mary Beth Marklein, "College Gender Gap Widens: 57% Are Women," *USA Today* (October 19, 2005), http://www.usatoday.com.

165. Michelle Conlin, "The New Gender Gap," *BusinessWeek* (May 26, 2003): 74–82; and "A Better Education Equals Higher Pay."

166. Quoted in Conlin, "The New Gender Gap."

167. Kathryn M. Bartol, David C. Martin, and Julie A. Kromkowski, "Leadership and the Glass Ceiling: Gender and Ethnic Group Influences on Leader Behaviors at Middle and Executive Managerial Levels," *The Journal of Leadership and Organizational Studies* 9, no. 3 (2003): 8–19; Bernard M. Bass and Bruce J. Avolio, "Shatter the Glass Ceiling: Women May Make Better Managers," *Human Resource Management* 33, no. 4 (Winter 1994): 549–560; and Rochelle Sharpe, "As Leaders, Women Rule," *BusinessWeek* (November 20, 2002): 75–84.

168. Dwight D. Frink, Robert K. Robinson, Brian Reithel, Michelle M. Arthur, Anthony P. Ammeter, Gerald R. Ferris, David M. Kaplan, and Hubert S. Morrisette, "Gender Demography and Organization Performance: A Two-Study Investigation with Convergence," *Group & Organization Management* 28, no. 1 (March 2003): 127–147; Catalyst research project cited in Reinhold, "Smashing Glass Ceilings."

169. Deutsch, "Behind the Exodus of Executive Women."

170. Jonathan D. Glater, "In Washington, Taking the Express Lane to Diversity," *The New York Times* (July 22, 2005), http://www.nytimes.com.

171. Smith, "Closing the Gap."

172. E. G. Collins, "Managers and Lovers," *Harvard Business Review* 61 (1983): 142–153.

173. Sharon A. Lobel, Robert E. Quinn, Lynda St. Clair, and Andrea Warfield, "Love Without Sex: The Impact of Psychological Intimacy Between Men and Women at Work," *Organizational Dynamics* (Summer 1994): 5–16.

174. Carol Hymowitz and Joann S. Lublin, "Many Companies Look the Other Way at Employee Affairs," *Wall Street Journal* (March 8, 2005): B1; William C. Symonds with Steve Hamm and Gail DeGeorge, "Sex on the Job," *BusinessWeek* (February 16, 1998): 30–31.

175. "Sexual Harassment: Vanderbilt University Policy" (Nashville: Vanderbilt University, 1993).

176. Rachel Thompson, "Sexual Harassment: It Doesn't Go with the Territory," *Horizons* 15, no. 3 (Winter 2002): 22–26.

177. Statistics reported in Jim Mulligan and Norman Foy, "Not in My Company: Preventing Sexual Harassment," *Industrial Management* (September/October 2003): 26–29; also see *EEOC Charge Complaints,* http://www.eeoc.gov.

178. Jack Corcoran, "Of Nice and Men," *Success* (June 1998): 65–67.

179. Barbara Carton, "At Jenny Craig, Men Are Ones Who Claim Sex Discrimination," *Wall Street Journal* (November 29, 1994): A1, A11.

180. Thompson, "Sexual Harassment: It Doesn't Go with the Territory."

181. Richard W. Judy and Carol D'Amico, *Workforce 2020: Work and Workers in the 21st Century* (Indianapolis, IN: Hudson Institute, 1997).

Chapter 10
Dynamics of Behavior in Organizations

1. See Michael West, "Hope Springs," *People Management* (October 2005): 38ff; and Mark C. Bolino, William H. Turnley, and James M. Bloodgood, "Citizenship Behaviors and the Creation of Social Capital in Organizations," *Academy of Management Review* 27, no. 4 (2002): 505–522.

2. Reported in Del Jones, "Optimism Puts Rose-Colored Tint in Glasses of Top Execs," *USA Today* (December 15, 2005), http://www.usatoday.com.

3. Jerry Krueger and Emily Killham, "At Work, Feeling Good Matters," *Gallup Management Journal* (December 8, 2005).

4. John W. Newstrom and Keith Davis, *Organizational Behavior: Human Behavior at Work,* 11th ed. (Burr Ridge, IL: McGraw-Hill Irwin, 2002): Chapter 9.

5. S. J. Breckler, "Empirical Validation of Affect, Behavior, and Cognition as Distinct Components of Attitude," *Journal of Personality and Social Psychology* (May 1984): 1191–1205; and J. M. Olson and M. P. Zanna, "Attitudes and Attitude Change," *Annual Review of Psychology* 44 (1993): 117–154.

6. Jeffrey Zaslow, "Pursuits: Happiness, Inc.," *Wall Street Journal* (March 18, 2006): P-1.

7. M. T. Iaffaldano and P. M. Muchinsky, "Job Satisfaction and Job Performance: A Meta-Analysis," *Psychological Bulletin* (March 1985): 251–273; C. Ostroff, "The Relationship Between Satisfaction, Attitudes, and Performance: An Organizational Level Analysis," *Journal of Applied Psychology* (December 1992): 963–974; and M. M. Petty, G. W. McGee, and J. W. Cavender, "A Meta-Analysis of the Relationship Between Individual Job Satisfaction and Individual Performance," *Academy of Management Review* (October 1984): 712–721.

8. Sue Shellenbarger, "Companies Are Finding Real Payoffs in Aiding Employee Satisfaction," *Wall Street Journal* (October 11, 2000): B1.

9. "Worried at Work: Generation Gap in Workplace Woes," International Survey Research, http://www.isrsurveys.com (accessed May 19, 2004).

10. Tony Schwartz, "The Greatest Sources of Satisfaction in the Workplace Are Internal and Emotional," *Fast Company* (November 2000): 398–402.

11. William C. Symonds, "Where Paternalism Equals Good Business," *BusinessWeek* (July 20, 1998): 16E4, 16E6.

12. "The People Factor: Global Survey Shows That an Engaged Workforce Measurably Improves the Bottom Line—and How," *International Survey Research*, http://www.isrsurveys.com (accessed May 19, 2004).

13. "Employee Commitment; U.S.: Leader or Follower?" *International Survey Research*, http://www.isrsurveys.com (accessed May 19, 2004).

14. W. Chan Kin and Renée Mauborgne, "Fair Process: Managing in the Knowledge Economy," *Harvard Business Review* (January 2003): 127–136.

15. Survey results reported in Jones, "Optimism Puts Rose-Colored Tint in Glasses of Top Execs."

16. Jennifer Laabs, "They Want More Support—Inside and Outside of Work," *Workforce* (November 1998): 54–56.

17. For a discussion of cognitive dissonance theory, see Leon A. Festinger, *Theory of Cognitive Dissonance* (Stanford, CA: Stanford University Press, 1957).

18. D. A. Kravitz and S. L. Klineberg, "Reactions to Two Versions of Affirmative Action Among Whites, Blacks, and Hispanics," *Journal of Applied Psychology* 85 (2000): 597–611; and Robert J. Grossman, "Race in the Workplace" *HR Magazine* (March 2000): 41–45.

19. Jaclyne Badal, "Surveying the Field: Cracking the Glass Ceiling," *Wall Street Journal* (June 19, 2006): B3.

20. J. A. Deutsch, W. G.Young, and T. J. Kalogeris, "The Stomach Signals Satiety," *Science* (April 1978): 22–33.

21. Richard B. Chase and Sriram Dasu, "Want to Perfect Your Company's Service? Use Behavioral Science," *Harvard Business Review* (June 2001): 79–84.

22. H. H. Kelley, "Attribution in Social Interaction," in E. Jones et al. (eds.), *Attribution: Perceiving the Causes of Behavior* (Morristown, NJ: General Learning Press, 1972).

23. See J. M. Digman, "Personality Structure: Emergence of the Five-Factor Model," *Annual Review of Psychology* 41 (1990): 417–440; M. R. Barrick and M. K. Mount, "Autonomy as a Moderator of the Relationships Between the Big Five Personality Dimensions and Job Performance," *Journal of Applied Psychology* (February 1993): 111–118; and J. S. Wiggins and A. L. Pincus, "Personality: Structure and Assessment," *Annual Review of Psychology* 43 (1992): 473–504.

24. Del Jones, "Not All Successful CEOs Are Extroverts," *USA Today* (June 6, 2006), http://www.usatoday.com.

25. Joseph Nocera, "In Business, Tough Guys Finish Last," *The New York Times* (June 18, 2005): C1; Carol Hymowitz, "Rewarding Competitors Over Collaborators No Longer Makes Sense," *Wall Street Journal* (February 13, 2006): B1.

26. Tim Sanders, *The Likeability Factor: How to Boost Your L-Factor and Achieve the Life of Your Dreams* (New York: Crown, 2005).

27. Lisa Takeuchi Cullen, "SATs for J-O-B-S," *Time* (April 3, 2006): 89.

28. Michelle Leder, "Is That Your Final Answer?" *Working Woman* (December–January 2001): 18; "Can You Pass the Job Test?" *Newsweek* (May 5, 1986): 46–51.

29. Alan Farnham, "Are You Smart Enough to Keep Your Job?" *Fortune* (January 15, 1996): 34–47.

30. Cora Daniels, "Does This Man Need a Shrink?" *Fortune* (February 5, 2001): 205–208.

31. Julie Bennett, "Franchising: Do You Have What It Takes?" *Wall Street Journal* (September 19, 2005): R11.

32. Lori Gottlieb, "How Do I Love Thee?" *The Atlantic Monthly* (March 2006): 58–70.

33. Daniel Goleman, "Leadership That Gets Results," *Harvard Business Review* (March–April 2000): 79–90; Richard E. Boyatzis and Daniel Goleman, *The Emotional Competence Inventory–University Edition,* The Hay Group, 2001; and Daniel Goleman, *Emotional Intelligence: Why It Can Matter More than IQ* (New York: Bantam Books, 1995).

34. Farnham, "Are You Smart Enough to Keep Your Job?"

35. Hendrie Weisinger, *Emotional Intelligence at Work* (San Francisco: Jossey-Bass, 2000); D. C. McClelland, "Identifying Competencies with Behavioral-Event Interviews," *Psychological Science* (Spring 1999): 331–339; Daniel Goleman, "Leadership That Gets Results," *Harvard Business Review* (March–April 2000): 78–90; D. Goleman, *Working with Emotional Intelligence* (New York: Bantam Books, 1999); and Lorie Parch, "Testing . . . 1, 2, 3," *Working Woman* (October 1997): 74–78.

36. Goleman, "Leadership That Gets Results."

37. J. B. Rotter, "Generalized Expectancies for Internal versus External Control of Reinforcement," *Psychological Monographs* 80, no. 609 (1966).

38. Andy Serwer, "There's Something about Cisco," *Fortune* (May 15, 2000); Stephanie N. Mehta, "Cisco Fractures Its Own Fairy Tale," *Fortune* (May 14, 2001): 104–112.

39. See P. E. Spector, "Behavior in Organizations as a Function of Employee's Locus of Control," *Psychological Bulletin* (May 1982): 482–497.

40. T. W. Adorno, E. Frenkel-Brunswick, D. J. Levinson, and R. N. Sanford, *The Authoritarian Personality* (New York: Harper & Row, 1950).

41. Niccolo Machiavelli, *The Prince,* trans. George Bull (Middlesex: Penguin, 1961).

42. Richard Christie and Florence Geis, *Studies in Machiavellianism* (New York: Academic Press, 1970).

43. R. G.Vleeming, "Machiavellianism: A Preliminary Review," *Psychological Reports* (February 1979): 295–310.

44. Christie and Geis, *Studies in Machiavellianism.*

45. Carl Jung, *Psychological Types* (London: Routledge and Kegan Paul, 1923).

46. Alison Overhold, "Are You a Polyolefin Optimizer? Take This Quiz!" *Fast Company* (April 2004): 37.

47. Reported in Cullen, "SATs for J-O-B-S."

48. Mary H. McCaulley, "Research on the MBTI and Leadership: Taking the Critical First Step," keynote address, The Myers–Briggs Type Indicator and Leadership: An International Research Conference, January 12–14, 1994.

49. Charles A. O'Reilly III, Jennifer Chatman, and David F. Caldwell, "People and Organizational Culture: A Profile Comparison Approach to Assessing Person-Organization Fit," *Academy of Management Journal* 34, no. 3 (1991): 487–516.

50. Anna Muoio, "Should I Go .Com?" *Fast Company* (July 2000): 164–172.

51. Leder, "Is That Your Final Answer?"

52. David A. Kolb, "Management and the Learning Process," *California Management Review* 18, no. 3 (Spring 1976): 21–31.

53. De'Ann Weimer, "The Houdini of Consumer Electronics," *BusinessWeek* (June 22, 1998): 88, 92; and http://www.bestbuy.com (accessed June 19, 2006).

54. See David. A. Kolb, I. M. Rubin, and J. M. McIntyre, *Organizational Psychology: An Experimental Approach*, 3rd ed. (Englewood Cliffs, NJ: Prentice Hall, 1984): 27–54.

55. Stephanie Gruner, "Our Company, Ourselves," *Inc.* (April 1998): 127–128.

56. Ira Sager, "Big Blue's Blunt Bohemian," *BusinessWeek* (June 14, 1999): 107–112.

57. Paul Roberts, "The Best Interest of the Patient Is the Only Interest to be Considered," *Fast Company* (April 1999): 149–162.

58. T. A. Beehr and R. S. Bhagat, *Human Stress and Cognition in Organizations: An Integrated Perspective* (New York: Wiley, 1985); and Bruce Cryer, Rollin McCraty, and Doc Childre, "Pull the Plug on Stress," *Harvard Business Review* (July 2003): 102–107.

59. Ekramul Hoque and Mayenul Islam, "Contribution of Some Behavioural Factors to Absenteeism of Manufacturing Workers in Bangladesh," *Pakistan Journal of Psychological Research* 18, no. 3–4 (Winter 2003): 81–96; U.S. research study conducted by HERO, a not-for-profit coalition of organizations with common interests in health promotion, disease management, and health-related productivity research, and reported in Bruce Cryer, Rollin McCraty, and Doc Childre, "Pull the Plug on Stress," *Harvard Business Review* (July 2003): 102–107.

60. M. Friedman and R. Rosenman, *Type A Behavior and Your Heart* (New York: Knopf, 1974).

61. John L. Haughom, "How to Pass the Stress Test," *CIO* (May 1, 2003): 50–52; Quote from Cora Daniels, "The Last Taboo," *Fortune* (October 28, 2002): 137–144.

62. Haughom, "How to Pass the Stress Test."

63. Reported in "Work Stress Is Costly," *Morning Call* (October 18, 2005): E1.

64. Families and Work Institute survey, reported in "Reworking Work," *Time* (July 25, 2005): 50–55; Spherion survey, reported in Donna Callea, "Workers Feeling the Burn: Employee Burnout a New Challenge to Productivity, Morale, Experts Say," *News Journal* (March 27, 2006): A11; "Workplace Stress Now Causing Huge Loss of Working Days," *Birmingham Post* (April 19, 2006): 23; Vani Doraisamy, "Young Techies Swell the Ranks of the Depressed," *The Hindu* (October 11, 2005): 1.

65. Kris Maher, "At Verizon Call Center, Stress Is Seldom on Hold," *Wall Street Journal* (January 16, 2001): B1, B12.

66. Rama Lakshmi, "India Call Centers Suffer Storm of 4-Letter Words; Executives Blame American Anger Over Outsourcing," *The Washington Post* (February 27, 2005): A22.

67. Donalee Moulton, "Buckling Under the Pressure," *OH & S Canada* 19, no. 8 (December 2003): 36.

68. Claire Sykes, "Say Yes to Less Stress," *Office Solutions* (July–August 2003): 26; and Andrea Higbie, "Quick Lessons in the Fine Old Art of Unwinding," *The New York Times* (February 25, 2001): BU–10.

69. Rosabeth Moss Kanter, "Balancing Work and Life," *Knight-Ridder Tribune News Service* (April 8, 2005): 1.

70. Leslie Gross Klass, "Quiet Time at Work Helps Employee Stress," *Johnson City Press* (January 28, 2001): 30.

71. Moulton, "Buckling Under the Pressure."

72. David T. Gordon, "Balancing Act," *CIO* (October 15, 2001): 58–62.

Chapter 11

Leadership

1. Leigh Buchanan, "Pat McGovern . . . For Knowing the Power of Respect," segment in "25 Entrepreneurs We Love," *Inc Magazine* (April 2004): 110–147; Melanie Warner, "Confessions of a Control Freak," *Fortune* (September 4, 2000): 130–140.

2. Greg Jaffe, "Change of Command; A Marine Captain Trains Iraqi Colonel to Take Over Fight," *Wall Street Journal* (February 24, 2005): A1, A6; and Jackie Spinner, "Training a New Army from the Top Down; U.S. Military Struggles to 'Build Leaders,'" *Washington Post* (November 1, 2005): A19.

3. Kevin Kelleher, "How To . . . Spot Great Chief Executives," *Business 2.0* (April 2005): 42.

4. Gary Yukl, "Managerial Leadership: A Review of Theory and Research," *Journal of Management* 15 (1989): 251–289.

5. James M. Kouzes and Barry Z. Posner, "The Credibility Factor: What Followers Expect from Their Leaders," *Management Review* (January 1990): 29–33.

6. Joseph L. Badaracco, Jr. "A Lesson for the Times: Learning From Quiet Leaders," *Ivey Business Journal* (January–February 2003): 1–6; and Matthew Gwyther, "Back to the Wall," *Management Today* (February 2003): 58–61.

7. See J. Andrew Morris, Céleste M. Brotheridge, and John C. Urbanski, "Bringing Humility to Leadership: Antecedents and Consequences of Leader Humility," *Human Relations* 58, no. 10 (2005): 1323–1350; Linda Tischler, "The CEO's New Clothes," *Fast Company* (September 2005): 27–28; James C. Collins, *From Good to Great: Why Some Companies Make the Leap . . . And Others Don't* (New York: HarperCollins. 2001); Charles A. O'Reilly III and Jeffrey Pfeffer, *Hidden Value: How Great Companies Achieve Extraordinary Results with Ordinary People* (Boston, MA: Harvard Business School Press, 2000); Rakesh Khurana, "The Curse of the Superstar CEO," *Harvard Business Review* (September 2002): 60–66, excerpted from his book, *Searching for a Corporate Savior: The Irrational Quest for Charismatic CEOs* (Princeton University Press, 2002); and Joseph Badaracco, *Leading Quietly* (Boston, MA: Harvard Business School Press, 2002).

8. Jim Collins, "Level 5 Leadership: The Triumph of Humility and Fierce Resolve," *Harvard Business Review* (January 2001): 67–76; Collins, "Good to Great," *Fast Company* (October 2001): 90–104; A. J. Vogl, "Onward and Upward" (an interview with Jim Collins), *Across the Board* (September–October 2001): 29–34; and Jerry Useem, "Conquering Vertical Limits," *Fortune* (February 19, 2001): 84–96.

9. Alice H. Eagly and Linda L. Carli, "The Female Leadership Advantage: An Evaluation of the Evidence," *The Leadership Quarterly* 14 (2003): 807–834; Judy B. Rosener, *America's Competitive Secret: Utilizing Women as a Management Strategy* (New York: Oxford University Press, 1995); Rosener, "Ways Women Lead," *Harvard Business Review* (November–December 1990): 119–125; Sally Helgesen, *The Female Advantage: Women's Ways of Leadership* (New York: Currency/Doubleday, 1990); and Bernard M. Bass and Bruce J. Avolio, "Shatter the Glass Ceiling: Women May Make Better Managers," *Human Resource Management* 33, no. 4 (Winter 1994): 549–560.

10. Rochelle Sharpe, "As Leaders, Women Rule," *BusinessWeek* (November 20, 2000): 75–84.

11. Rosener, *America's Competitive Secret*, 129–135.

12. Sharpe, "As Leaders, Women Rule."

13. Alan Deutschman, "What I Know Now" (interview with Terri Kelly), *Fast Company* (September 2005): 96.

14. James E. Colvard, "Managers vs. Leaders," *Government Executive* 35, no. 9 (July 2003): 82–84.

15. G. A. Yukl, *Leadership in Organizations* (Englewood Cliffs, NJ: Prentice Hall, 1981); and S. C. Kohs and K. W. Irle, "Prophesying Army Promotion," *Journal of Applied Psychology* 4 (1920): 73–87.

16. R. Albanese and D. D. Van Fleet, *Organizational Behavior: A Managerial Viewpoint* (Hinsdale, IL: The Dryden Press, 1983).

17. Gary Yukl, Angela Gordon, and Tom Taber, "A Hierarchical Taxonomy of Leadership Behavior: Integrating a Half Century of Behavior Research," *Journal of Leadership and Organizational Studies* 9, no. 1 (2002): 13–32.

18. C. A. Schriesheim and B. J. Bird, "Contributions of the Ohio State Studies to the Field of Leadership," *Journal of Management* 5 (1979): 135–145; and C. L. Shartle, "Early Years of the Ohio State University Leadership Studies," *Journal of Management* 5 (1979): 126–134.

19. Joseph Weber, "Waging War on Hunger," *BusinessWeek* (May 16, 2005): 94, 96.

20. Patrick J. Sauer, "Are You Ready for Some Football Clichés?" *Inc.* (October 2003): 96–99.

21. P. C. Nystrom, "Managers and the High-High Leader Myth," *Academy of Management Journal* 21 (1978): 325–331; and L. L. Larson, J. G. Hunt, and Richard N. Osborn, "The Great High-High Leader Behavior Myth: A Lesson from Occam's Razor," *Academy of Management Journal* 19 (1976): 628–641.

22. R. Likert, "From Production- and Employee-Centeredness to Systems 1–4," *Journal of Management* 5 (1979): 147–156.

23. Robert R. Blake and Jane S. Mouton, *The Managerial Grid III* (Houston: Gulf, 1985).

24. Paul Hersey and Kenneth H. Blanchard, *Management of Organizational Behavior: Utilizing Human Resources*, 4th ed. (Englewood Cliffs, NJ: Prentice Hall, 1982).

25. Robert Tomsho and John Hechinger, "Crimson Blues; Harvard Clash Pits Brusque Leader Against Faculty," *Wall Street Journal* (February 18, 2005): A1, A8; and Ruth R. Wisse, "Cross Country; Coup d' Ecole," *Wall Street Journal* (February 23, 2006): A17.

26. Fred E. Fiedler, "Assumed Similarity Measures as Predictors of Team Effectiveness," *Journal of Abnormal and Social Psychology* 49 (1954): 381–388; F. E. Fiedler, *Leader Attitudes and Group Effectiveness* (Urbana, Ill.: University of Illinois Press, 1958); and F. E. Fiedler, *A Theory of Leadership Effectiveness* (New York: McGraw-Hill, 1967).

27. Fred E. Fiedler and M. M. Chemers, *Leadership and Effective Management* (Glenview, IL: Scott, Foresman, 1974).

28. Fred E. Fiedler, "Engineer the Job to Fit the Manager," *Harvard Business Review* 43 (1965): 115–122; and F. E. Fiedler, M. M. Chemers, and L. Mahar, *Improving Leadership Effectiveness: The Leader Match Concept* (New York: Wiley, 1976).

29. R. Singh, "Leadership Style and Reward Allocation: Does Least Preferred Coworker Scale Measure Tasks and Relation Orientation?" *Organizational Behavior and Human Performance* 27 (1983): 178–197; and D. Hosking, "A Critical Evaluation of Fiedler's Contingency Hypotheses," *Progress in Applied Psychology* 1 (1981): 103–154.

30. M. G. Evans, "The Effects of Supervisory Behavior on the Path–Goal Relationship," *Organizational Behavior and Human Performance* 5 (1970): 277–298; M. G. Evans, "Leadership and Motivation: A Core Concept," *Academy of Management Journal* 13 (1970): 91–102; and B. S. Georgopoulos, G. M. Mahoney, and N. W. Jones, "A Path–Goal Approach to Productivity," *Journal of Applied Psychology* 41 (1957): 345–353.

31. Robert J. House, "A Path–Goal Theory of Leader Effectiveness," *Administrative Science Quarterly* 16 (1971): 321–338.

32. M. G. Evans, "Leadership," in *Organizational Behavior*, ed. S. Kerr (Columbus, OH: Grid, 1974): 230–233.

33. Robert J. House and Terrence R. Mitchell, "Path–Goal Theory of Leadership," *Journal of Contemporary Business* (Autumn 1974): 81–97.

34. Jennifer Reingold, "Bob Nardelli Is Watching," *Fast Company* (December 2005): 76–83.

35. Charles Greene, "Questions of Causation in the Path–Goal Theory of Leadership," *Academy of Management Journal* 22 (March 1979): 22–41; and C. A. Schriesheim and Mary Ann von Glinow, "The Path–Goal Theory of Leadership: A Theoretical and Empirical Analysis," *Academy of Management Journal* 20 (1977): 398–405.

36. S. Kerr and J. M. Jermier, "Substitutes for Leadership: Their Meaning and Measurement," *Organizational Behavior and Human Performance* 22 (1978): 375–403; and Jon P. Howell and Peter W. Dorfman, "Leadership and Substitutes for Leadership among Professional and Nonprofessional Workers," *Journal of Applied Behavioral Science* 22 (1986): 29–46.

37. Anthony J. Mayo and Nitin Nohria, "Double Edged Sword," *People Management* (October 27, 2005).

38. The terms *transactional* and *transformational* come from James M. Burns, *Leadership* (New York: Harper & Row, 1978); and Bernard M. Bass, "Leadership: Good, Better, Best," *Organizational Dynamics* 13 (Winter 1985): 26–40.

39. Katherine J. Klein and Robert J. House, "On Fire: Charismatic Leadership and Levels of Analysis," *Leadership Quarterly* 6, no. 2 (1995): 183–198.

40. Jay A. Conger and Rabindra N. Kanungo, "Toward a Behavioral Theory of Charismatic Leadership in Organizational Settings," *Academy of Management Review* 12 (1987): 637–647; Walter Kiechel III, "A Hard Look at Executive Vision," *Fortune* (October 23, 1989): 207–211; and William L. Gardner and Bruce J. Avolio, "The Charismatic Relationship: A Dramaturgical Perspective," *Academy of Management Review* 23, no. 1 (1998): 32–58.

41. Robert J. House, "Research Contrasting the Behavior and Effects of Reputed Charismatic vs. Reputed Non-Charismatic Leaders" (paper presented as part of a symposium, "Charismatic Leadership: Theory and Evidence," Academy of Management, San Diego, 1985).

42. Robert J. House and Jane M. Howell, "Personality and Charismatic Leadership," *Leadership Quarterly* 3, no. 2 (1992): 81–108; and Jennifer O'Connor, Michael D. Mumford, Timothy C. Clifton, Theodore L. Gessner, and Mary Shane Connelly, "Charismatic Leaders and Destructiveness: A Historiometric Study," *Leadership Quarterly* 6, no. 4 (1995): 529–555.

43. Bernard M. Bass, "Theory of Transformational Leadership Redux," *Leadership Quarterly* 6, no. 4 (1995): 463–478; Noel M. Tichy and Mary Anne Devanna, *The Transformational Leader* (New York: John Wiley & Sons, 1986); and Badrinarayan Shankar Pawar and Kenneth K. Eastman, "The Nature and Implications of Contextual Influences on Transformational Leadership: A Conceptual Examination," *Academy of Management Review* 22, no. 1 (1997) 80–109.

44. Richard L. Daft and Robert H. Lengel, *Fusion Leadership: Unlocking the Subtle Forces that Change People and Organizations* (San Francisco: Berrett-Koehler, 1998).

45. Taly Dvir, Dov Eden, Bruce J. Avolio, and Boas Shamir, "Impact of Transformational Leadership on Follower Development and Performance: A Field Experiment," *Academy of Management Journal* 45, no. 4 (2002): 735–744.

46. Robert S. Rubin, David C. Munz, and William H. Bommer, "Leading from Within: The Effects of Emotion Recognition and Personality on Transformational Leadership Behavior," *Academy of Management Journal* 48, no 5 (2005): 845–858; and Timothy A. Judge and Joyce E. Bono, "Five-Factor Model of Personality and Transformational Leadership," *Journal of Applied Psychology* 85, no. 5 (October 2000): 751ff.

47. Rubin et al., "Leading from Within."

48. Paul Nadler, "The Little Things That Help Make Wells a Giant," *American Banker* (December 10, 2003): 4; John R. Enger, "Cross-Sell Campaign," *Banking Strategies* 77, no. 6 (November–December 2001): 34; Bethany McLean, "Is This Guy the Best Banker in America?" *Fortune* (July 6, 1998): 126–128; and Jacqueline S. Gold, "Bank to the Future," *Institutional Investor* (September 2001): 54–63.

49. Henry Mintzberg, *Power In and Around Organizations* (Englewood Cliffs, NJ: Prentice Hall, 1983); and Jeffrey Pfeffer, *Power in Organizations* (Marshfield, MA: Pitman, 1981).

50. George Anders, "Back to Class; How a Principal in New Orleans Saved Her School," *Wall Street Journal* (January 13, 2006): A1, A6.

51. Jay A. Conger, "The Necessary Art of Persuasion," *Harvard Business Review* (May–June 1998): 84–95.

52. D. Kipnis, S. M. Schmidt, C. Swaffin-Smith, and I. Wilkinson, "Patterns of Managerial Influence: Shotgun Managers, Tacticians, and Politicians," *Organizational Dynamics* (Winter 1984): 58–67.

53. These tactics are based on Kipnis et al., "Patterns of Managerial Influence"; and Robert B. Cialdini, "Harnessing the Science of Persuasion," *Harvard Business Review* (October 2001): 72–79.

54. Ibid.; and Pfeffer, *Managing with Power: Politics and Influence in Organizations* (Boston: Harvard Business School Press, 1992): Chapter 13.

55. Ibid.

56. V. Dallas Merrell, *Huddling: The Informal Way to Management Success* (New York: AMACOM, 1979).

57. Robert B. Cialdini, *Influence: Science and Practice,* 4th ed. (Boston: Pearson Allyn & Bacon, 2000).

58. Diane Brady, "The Immelt Revolution," *BusinessWeek* (March 28, 2005): 64–71.

59. Harvey G. Enns and Dean B. McFarlin, "When Executives Influence Peers, Does Function Matter?" *Human Resource Management* 4, no. 2 (Summer 2003): 125–142.

60. Daft and Lengel, *Fusion Leadership*.

61. Jim Collins, "The 10 Greatest CEOs of All Time," *Fortune* (July 21, 2003): 54–68.

62. Robert K. Greenleaf, *Servant Leadership: A Journey into the Nature of Legitimate Power and Greatness* (Mahwah, NJ: Paulist Press, 1977).

63. Anne Fitzgerald, "Christmas Bonus Stuns Employees," *The Des Moines Register* (December 20, 2003), http://www.desmoinesregister.com.

64. Collins, "The 10 Greatest CEOs of All Time."

65. Richard L. Daft, *The Leadership Experience*, 3rd ed. (Cincinnati, OH: South-Western, 2005): Chapter 6.

66. Badaracco, "A Lesson for the Times: Learning From Quiet Leaders."

67. Jim Collins, "The 10 Greatest CEOs of All Time."

Chapter 12

Motivation

1. David Silburt, "Secrets of the Super Sellers," *Canadian Business* (January 1987): 54–59; "Meet the Savvy Supersalesmen," *Fortune* (February 4, 1985): 56–62; Michael Brody, "Meet Today's Young American Worker," *Fortune* (November 11, 1985): 90–98; and Tom Richman, "Meet the Masters. They Could Sell You Anything," *Inc.* (March 1985): 79–86.

2. Richard M. Steers and Lyman W. Porter, eds., *Motivation and Work Behavior*, 3rd ed. (New York: McGraw-Hill, 1983); Don Hellriegel, John W. Slocum, Jr., and Richard W. Woodman, *Organizational Behavior*, 7th ed. (St. Paul, MN: West, 1995): 170; and Jerry L. Gray and Frederick A. Starke, *Organizational Behavior: Concepts and Applications*, 4th ed. (New York: Macmillan, 1988): 104–105.

3. Carol Hymowitz, "Readers Tell Tales of Success and Failure Using Rating Systems," *Wall Street Journal* (May 29, 2001): B1.

4. Alan Deutschman, "Can Google Stay Google?" *Fast Company* (August 2005): 62–68.

5. See Linda Grant, "Happy Workers, High Returns," *Fortune* (January 12, 1998): 81; Elizabeth J. Hawk and Garrett J. Sheridan, "The Right Stuff," *Management Review* (June 1999): 43–48; Michael West and Malcolm Patterson, "Profitable Personnel," *People Management* (January 8, 1998): 28–31; Anne Fisher, "Why Passion Pays," *FSB* (September 2002): 58; and Curt Coffman and Gabriel Gonzalez-Molina, *Follow This Path: How the World's Great Organizations Drive Growth By Unleashing Human Potential* (New York: Warner Books, 2002).

6. Steers and Porter, *Motivation*.

7. J. F. Rothlisberger and W. J. Dickson, *Management and the Worker* (Cambridge, MA: Harvard University Press, 1939).

8. Abraham F. Maslow, "A Theory of Human Motivation," *Psychological Review* 50 (1943): 370–396.

9. Sarah Pass, "On the Line," *People Management* (September 15, 2005).

10. Clayton Alderfer, *Existence, Relatedness, and Growth* (New York: Free Press, 1972).

11. Robert Levering and Milton Moskowitz, "2004 Special Report: The 100 Best Companies To Work For," *Fortune* (January 12, 2004): 56–78.

12. Jeff Barbian, "C'mon, Get Happy," *Training* (January 2001): 92–96.

13. Jena McGregor, "Employee Innovator; Winner: USAA," *Fast Company* (October 2005): 57.

14. Karol Rose, "Work-Life Effectiveness," *Fortune* (September 29, 2003): S1–S17.

15. W. Glaser, *The Control Theory Manager* (New York: Harper-Business, 1994); and John W. Newstrom, "Making Work Fun: An Important Role for Managers," *SAM Advanced Management Journal* (Winter 2002): 4–8, 21.

16. Newstrom, "Making Work Fun."

17. Frederick Herzberg, "One More Time: How Do You Motivate Employees?" *Harvard Business Review* (January 2003): 87–96.

18. David C. McClelland, *Human Motivation* (Glenview, IL: Scott, Foresman, 1985).

19. John Brant, "What One Man Can Do," *Inc.* (September 2005): 145–153.

20. David C. McClelland, "The Two Faces of Power," in *Organizational Psychology*, ed. D.A. Colb, I.M. Rubin, and J.M. McIntyre (Englewood Cliffs, NJ: Prentice Hall, 1971): 73–86.

21. J. Stacy Adams, "Injustice in Social Exchange," in *Advances in Experimental Social Psychology*, 2d ed., ed. L. Berkowitz (New York: Academic Press, 1965); and J. Stacy Adams, "Toward an Understanding of Inequity," *Journal of Abnormal and Social Psychology* (November 1963): 422–436.

22. "Study: The Brain Prefers Working Over Getting Money for Nothing," *TheJournalNews.com* (May 14, 2004), www.thejournalnews.com/apps/pbcs.dll/frontpage.

23. Ray V. Montagno, "The Effects of Comparison to Others and Primary Experience on Responses to Task Design," *Academy of Management Journal* 28 (1985): 491–498; and Robert P. Vecchio, "Predicting Worker Performance in Inequitable Settings," *Academy of Management Review* 7 (1982): 103–110.

24. Daniel Henninger, "How One School Found a Way to Spell Success," *Wall Street Journal* (October 14, 2005): A10.

25. James E. Martin and Melanie M. Peterson, "Two-Tier Wage Structures: Implications for Equity Theory," *Academy of Management Journal* 30 (1987): 297–315.

26. Jared Sandberg, "Why You May Regret Looking at Papers Left on the Office Copier," *Wall Street Journal* (June 20, 2006): B1.

27. Victor H. Vroom, *Work and Motivation* (New York: Wiley, 1964); B. S. Gorgopoulos, G. M. Mahoney, and N. Jones, "A Path-Goal Approach to Productivity," *Journal of Applied Psychology* 41 (1957): 345–353; and E. E. Lawler III, *Pay and*

Organizational Effectiveness: A Psychological View (New York: McGraw-Hill, 1981).

28. Studies reported in Tom Rath, "The Best Way to Recognize Employees," *Gallup Management Journal* (December 9, 2004).

29. Erin White, "Theory & Practice: Praise from Peers Goes a Long Way—Recognition Programs Help Companies Retain Workers as Pay Raises Get Smaller," *Wall Street Journal* (December 19, 2005): B3.

30. Richard L. Daft and Richard M. Steers, *Organizations: A Micro/Macro Approach* (Glenview, IL: Scott, Foresman, 1986).

31. See Edwin A. Locke and Gary P. Latham, "Building a Practically Useful Theory of Goal Setting and Task Motivation: A 35-Year Odyssey," *The American Psychologist* 57, no. 9 (September 2002): 705+; Gary P. Latham and Edwin A. Locke, "Self-Regulation through Goal Setting", *Organizational Behavior and Human Decision Processes* 50, no. 2 (1991): 212+; G. P. Latham and G. H. Seijts, "The Effects of Proximal and Distal Goals on Performance of a Moderately Complex Task," *Journal of Organizational Behavior* 20, no. 4 (1999): 421+; P. C. Early, T. Connolly, and G. Ekegren, "Goals, Strategy Development, and Task Performance: Some Limits on the Efficacy of Goal Setting," *Journal of Applied Psychology* 74 (1989): 24–33; E. A. Locke, "Toward a Theory of Task Motivation and Incentives," *Organizational Behavior and Human Performance* 3 (1968): 157–189; Gerard H. Seijts, Ree M. Meertens, and Gerjo Kok, "The Effects of Task Importance and Publicness on the Relation Between Goal Difficulty and Performance," *Canadian Journal of Behavioural Science* 29, no. 1 (1997): 54+.

32. Locke and Latham, "Building a Practically Useful Theory of Goal Setting and Task Motivation."

33. Edwin A. Locke, "Linking Goals to Monetary Incentives," *Academy of Management Executive* 18, no. 4 (2005): 130–133.

34. Brian Ellsworth, "Making a Place for Blue Collars in the Boardroom," *The New York Times* (August 3, 2005), www.nytimes.com.

35. J. M. Ivanecevich and J. T. McMahon, "The Effects of Goal Setting, External Feedback, and Self-Generated Feedback on Outcome Variables: A Field Experiment," *Academy of Management Journal* (June 1982): 359+; G. P. Latham and E. A. Locke, "Self-Regulation Through Goal Setting," *Organizational Behavior and Human Decision Processes* 50, no. 2 (1991): 212+.

36. Ellyn Spragins, "The Best Bosses," *FSB* (October 2004): 39–57.

37. Jyoti Thottam, "Reworking Work," *Time* (July 25, 2005): 50–55.

38. Thottam, "Reworking Work."

39. Gary P. Latham, "The Motivational Benefits of Goal-Setting," *Academy of Management Executive* 18, no. 4 (2004): 126–129.

40. Alexander D. Stajkovic and Fred Luthans, "A Meta-Analysis of the Effects of Organizational Behavior Modification on Task Performance, 1975–95," *Academy of Management Journal* (October 1997): 1122–1149; H. Richlin, *Modern Behaviorism* (San Francisco: Freeman, 1970); and B. F. Skinner, *Science and Human Behavior* (New York: Macmillan, 1953).

41. Stajkovic and Luthans, "A Meta-Analysis of the Effects of Organizational Behavior Modification on Task Performance, 1975–95," and Fred Luthans and Alexander D. Stajkovic, "Reinforce for Performance: The Need to Go Beyond Pay and Even Rewards," *Academy of Management Executive* 13, no. 2 (1999): 49–57.

42. Reported in Charlotte Garvey, "Meaningful Tokens of Appreciation," *HR Magazine* (August 2004): 101–105.

43. Kenneth D. Butterfield and Linda Klebe Treviño, "Punishment from the Manager's Perspective: A Grounded Investigation and Inductive Model," *Academy of Management Journal* 39, no. 6 (December 1996): 1479–1512; and Andrea Casey, "Voices from the Firing Line: Managers Discuss Punishment in the Workplace," *Academy of Management Executive* 11, no. 3 (1997): 93–94.

44. Gwendolyn Bounds, "Boss Talk: No More Squeaking By—WD-40 CEO Garry Ridge Repackages a Core Product," *Wall Street Journal* (May 23, 2006): B1.

45. Jaclyn Badal, "New Incentives for Workers Combine Cash, Fun," *Wall Street Journal* (June 19, 2006): B3.

46. L. M. Sarri and G. P. Latham, "Employee Reaction to Continuous and Variable Ratio Reinforcement Schedules Involving a Monetary Incentive," *Journal of Applied Psychology* 67 (1982): 506–508; and R. D. Pritchard, J. Hollenback, and P. J. DeLeo, "The Effects of Continuous and Partial Schedules of Reinforcement on Effort, Performance, and Satisfaction," *Organizational Behavior and Human Performance* 25 (1980): 336–353.

47. Amy Joyce, "The Bonus Question; Some Managers Still Strive to Reward Merit," *The Washington Post* (November 13, 2005): F6.

48. Survey results from World at Work and Hewitt Associates, reported in Karen Kroll, "Benefits: Paying for Performance," *Inc.* (November 2004): 46; and Kathy Chu, "Firms Report Lackluster Results from Pay-for-Performance Plans," *Wall Street Journal* (June 15, 2004): D2.

49. Barbian, "C'mon, Get Happy."

50. Norm Alster, "What Flexible Workers Can Do," *Fortune* (February 13, 1989): 62–66.

51. Christine M. Riordan, Robert J. Vandenberg, and Hettie A. Richardson, "Employee Involvement Climate and Organizational Effectiveness," *Human Resource Management* 44, no. 4 (Winter 2005): 471–488.

52. Glenn L. Dalton, "The Collective Stretch," *Management Review* (December 1998): 54–59.

53. J. Richard Hackman and Greg R. Oldham, *Work Redesign* (Reading, MA: Addison-Wesley, 1980); and J. Richard Hackman and Greg Oldham, "Motivation through the Design

of Work: Test of a Theory," *Organizational Behavior and Human Performance* 16 (1976): 250–279.

54. Xu Huang and Evert Van de Vliert, "Where Intrinsic Job Satisfaction Fails to Work: National Moderators of Intrinsic Motivation," *Journal of Organizational Behavior* 24 (2003): 157–179.

55. Ann Podolske, "Giving Employees a Voice in Pay Structures," *Business Ethics* (March–April 1998): 12.

56. Rekha Balu, "Bonuses Aren't Just for the Bosses," *Fast Company* (December 2000): 74–76.

57. Edwin P. Hollander and Lynn R. Offermann, "Power and Leadership in Organizations," *American Psychologist* 45 (February 1990): 179–189.

58. Jay A. Conger and Rabindra N. Kanungo, "The Empowerment Process: Integrating Theory and Practice," *Academy of Management Review* 13 (1988): 471–482.

59. Jay A. Conger and Rabindra N. Kanungo, "The Empowerment Process: Integrating Theory and Practice," *Academy of Management Review* 13 (1998): 471–482.

60. David E. Bowen and Edward E. Lawler III, "The Empowerment of Service Workers: What, Why, How, and When," *Sloan Management Review* (Spring 1992): 31–39; and Ray W. Coye and James A. Belohav, "An Exploratory Analysis of Employee Participation," *Group and Organization Management* 20, no. 1, (March 1995): 4–17.

61. William C. Taylor, "Under New Management; These Workers Act Like Owners (Because They Are)," *The New York Times* (May 21, 2006), www.nytimes.com.

62. Russ Forrester, "Empowerment: Rejuvenating a Potent Idea," *Academy of Management Executive* 14, no. 3 (2000): 67–80.

63. Ellsworth, "Making a Place for Blue Collars in the Boardroom."

64. Ricardo Semler, "How We Went Digital Without a Strategy," *Harvard Business Review* (September–October 2000): 51–58.

65. Podolske, "Giving Employees a Voice in Pay Structures."

66. This discussion is based on Robert C. Ford and Myron D. Fottler, "Empowerment: A Matter of Degree," *Academy of Management Executive* 9, no. 3 (1995): 21–31.

67. Bruce E. Kaufman, "High-Level Employee Involvement at Delta Air Lines," *Human Resource Management* 42, no. 2 (Summer 2003): 175–190.

68. Geoff Colvin, "The 100 Best Companies to Work For."

69. Colvin, "The 100 Best Companies to Work For"; Levering and Moskowitz, "And the Winners Are . . ."; and Daniel Roth, "Trading Places," *Fortune* (January 23, 2006): 120–128.

70. Cheryl Dahle, "Four Tires, Free Beef," *Fast Company* (September 2003): 36.

71. Jerry Krueger and Emily Killham, "At Work, Feeling Good Matters," *Gallup Management Journal* (December 8, 2005).

72. Erin White, "New Recipe; To Keep Employees, Domino's Decides It's Not All About Pay," *Wall Street Journal* (February 17, 2005): A1, A9.

73. This discussion is based on Tony Schwartz, "The Greatest Sources of Satisfaction in the Workplace are Internal and Emotional," *Fast Company* (November 2000): 398–402; Marcus Buckingham and Curt Coffman, *First, Break All the Rules: What the World's Greatest Managers Do Differently* (New York: Simon and Schuster, 1999); and Krueger and Killham, "At Work, Feeling Good Matters."

74. The Gallup Organization, Princeton, NJ. All rights reserved. Used with permission.

75. Curt Coffman and Gabriel Gonzalez-Molina, *Follow This Path: How the World's Greatest Organizations Drive Growth by Unleashing Human Potential* (New York: Warner Books, 2002), as reported in Anne Fisher, "Why Passion Pays," *FSB* (September 2002): 58.

76. Rodd Wagner, "'One Store, One Team'at Best Buy," *Gallup Management Journal* (August 12, 2004).

Chapter 13

Communication

1. Joann S. Lublin, "The 'Open Inbox'," *Wall Street Journal* (October 10, 2005): B1, B3.

2. Elizabeth B. Drew, "Profile: Robert Strauss," *The New Yorker* (May 7, 1979): 55–70.

3. Henry Mintzberg, *The Nature of Managerial Work* (New York: Harper & Row, 1973).

4. Phillip G. Clampitt, Laurey Berk, and M. Lee Williams, "Leaders as Strategic Communicators," *Ivey Business Journal* (May–June 2002): 51–55.

5. Ian Wylie, "Can Philips Learn to Walk the Talk?" *Fast Company* (January 2003): 44–45.

6. Fred Luthans and Janet K. Larsen, "How Managers Really Communicate," *Human Relations* 39 (1986): 161–178; and Larry E. Penley and Brian Hawkins, "Studying Interpersonal Communication in Organizations: A Leadership Application," *Academy of Management Journal* 28 (1985): 309–326.

7. D. K. Berlo, *The Process of Communication* (New York: Holt, Rinehart and Winston, 1960): 24.

8. Paul Roberts, "Live! From Your Office! It's . . . ," *Fast Company* (October 1999): 150–170.

9. Bruce K. Blaylock, "Cognitive Style and the Usefulness of Information," *Decision Sciences* 15 (Winter 1984): 74–91.

10. Robert H. Lengel and Richard L. Daft, "The Selection of Communication Media as an Executive Skill," *Academy of Management Executive* 2 (August 1988): 225–232; Richard L. Daft and Robert H. Lengel, "Organizational Information Requirements, Media Richness and Structural Design," *Managerial Science* 32 (May 1986): 554–572; and Jane

Webster and Linda Klebe Treviño, "Rational and Social Theories as Complementary Explanations of Communication Media Choices: Two Policy-Capturing Studies," *Academy of Management Journal* 38, no. 6 (1995): 1544–1572.

11. Research reported in "E-mail Can't Mimic Phone Calls," *Johnson City Press* (September 17, 2000): 31.

12. Raymond E. Friedman and Steven C. Currall, "E-Mail Escalation: Dispute Exacerbating Elements of Electronic Communication, www.mba.vanderbilt.edu/ray.friedman/pdf/emailescalation.pdf; Lauren Keller Johnson, "Does E-Mail Escalate Conflict?" *MIT Sloan Management Review* (Fall 2002): 14–15; and Alison Stein Wellner, "Lost in Translation," *Inc. Magazine* (September 2005): 37–38.

13. Wellner, "Lost in Translation"; Nick Easen, "Don't Send the Wrong Message; When E-Mail Crosses Borders, a Faux Pas Could Be Just a Click Away," *Business 2.0* (August 2005): 102.

14. Scott Kirsner, "IM Is Here. RU Prepared?" *Darwin Magazine* (February 2002): 22–24.

15. John R. Carlson and Robert W. Smud, "Channel Expansion Theory and the Experiential Nature of Media Richness Perceptions," *Academy of Management Journal* 42, no. 2 (1999): 153–170; R. Rice and G. Love, "Electronic Emotion," *Communication Research* 14 (1987): 85–108.

16. Ronald E. Rice, "Task Analyzability, Use of New Media, and Effectiveness: A Multi-Site Exploration of Media Richness," *Organizational Science* 3, no. 4 (November 1992): 475–500; and M. Lynne Markus, "Electronic Mail as the Medium of Managerial Choice," *Organizational Science* 5, no. 4 (November 1994): 502–527.

17. Richard L. Daft, Robert H. Lengel, and Linda Klebe Treviño, "Message Equivocality, Media Selection and Manager Performance: Implication for Information Systems," *MIS Quarterly* 11 (1987): 355–368.

18. Mary Young and James E. Post, "Managing to Communicate, Communicating to Manage: How Leading Companies Communicate with Employees," *Organizational Dynamics* (Summer 1993): 31–43.

19. Jay A. Conger, "The Necessary Art of Persuasion," *Harvard Business Review* (May–June 1998): 84–95.

20. Susan Cramm, "The Heart of Persuasion," *CIO* (July 1, 2005): 28–30.

21. Ibid.

22. J. Martin and M. Powers, "Organizational Stories: More Vivid and Persuasive than Quantitative Data," in B. M. Staw, ed., *Psychological Foundations of Organizational Behavior* (Glenview, IL: Scott Foresman, 1982): 161–168.

23. Bronwyn Fryer, "Storytelling that Moves People: A Conversation with Screenwriting Coach Robert McKee," *Harvard Business Review* (June 2003): 51–55.

24. Bill Birchard, "Once Upon a Time," *Strategy & Business* no. 27 (Second Quarter 2002): 99–104; and Laura Shin, "You

Can Be a Great Storyteller," *USA Weekend* (January 16–18, 2004): 14.

25. I. Thomas Sheppard, "Silent Signals," *Supervisory Management* (March 1986): 31–33.

26. Albert Mehrabian, *Silent Messages* (Belmont, CA: Wadsworth, 1971); and Albert Mehrabian, "Communicating without Words," *Psychology Today* (September 1968): 53–55.

27. Meridith Levinson, "How to Be a Mind Reader," *CIO* (December 1, 2004): 72–76; Mac Fulfer, "Nonverbal Communication: How to Read What's Plain as the Nose . . . ," *Journal of Organizational Excellence* (Spring 2001): 19–27; Paul Ekman, *Emotions Revealed: Recognizing Faces and Feelings to Improve Communication and Emotional Life* (New York: Time Books, 2003).

28. Sheppard, "Silent Signals."

29. Arthur H. Bell, *The Complete Manager's Guide to Interviewing* (Homewood, IL: Richard D. Irwin, 1989).

30. C. Glenn Pearce, "Doing Something about Your Listening Ability," *Supervisory Management* (March 1989): 29–34; and Tom Peters, "Learning to Listen," *Hyatt Magazine* (Spring 1988): 16–21.

31. Michael A. Prospero, "Leading Listener; Winner: Cabela's," *Fast Company* (October 2005): 53.

32. M. P. Nichols, *The Lost Art of Listening* (New York: Guilford Publishing, 1995).

33. "Benchmarking the Sales Function," a report based on a study of 100 salespeople from small, medium, and large businesses, conducted by Ron Volper Group Inc. Sales Consulting and Training, White Plains, NY (1996), as reported in "Nine Habits of Highly Successful Salespeople," *Inc. Small Business Success.*

34. Gerald M. Goldhaber, *Organizational Communication*, 4th ed. (Dubuque, IA: Brown, 1980): 189.

35. Curtis Sittenfeld, "Good Ways to Deliver Bad News," *Fast Company* (April 1999): 58, 60.

36. Vanessa Fuhrmans, "Bedside Manner; An Insurer Tries a New Strategy: Listen to Patients," *Wall Street Journal* (April 11, 2006): A1.

37. James R. Stengel, Andrea L. Dixon, and Chris T. Allen, "Listening Begins at Home," *Harvard Business Review* (November 2003): 106–116.

38. Richard L. Daft and Richard M. Steers, *Organizations: A Micro/Macro Approach* (New York: Harper Collins, 1986); and Daniel Katz and Robert Kahn, *The Social Psychology of Organizations*, 2d ed. (New York: Wiley, 1978).

39. Greg Jaffe, "Tug of War: In the New Military, Technology May Alter Chain of Command," *Wall Street Journal* (March 30, 2001): A3; and Aaron Pressman, "Business Gets the Message," *The Industry Standard* (February 26, 2001): 58–59.

40. Roberta Maynard, "It Can Pay to Show Employees the Big Picture," *Nation's Business* (December 1994): 10.

41. Phillip G. Clampitt, Robert J. DeKoch, and Thomas Cash-man, "A Strategy for Communicating about Uncertainty," *Academy of Management Executive* 14, no. 4 (2000): 41–57.

42. Reported in Louise van der Does and Stephen J. Caldeira, "Effective Leaders Champion Communication Skills," *Nation's Restaurant News* (March 27, 2006): 20.

43. J. G. Miller, "Living Systems: The Organization," *Behavioral Science* 17 (1972): 69.

44. Michael J. Glauser, "Upward Information Flow in Organizations: Review and Conceptual Analysis," *Human Relations* 37 (1984): 613–643; and "Upward/Downward Communication: Critical Information Channels," *Small Business Report* (October 1985): 85–88.

45. Pat Croce, "Catching the 5:15: A Simple Reporting System Can Help You Keep Tabs on Your Business," *FSB* (March 2004): 34.

46. Dennis Tourish, "Critical Upward Communication: Ten Commandments for Improving Strategy and Decision Making," *Long Range Planning* 38 (2005): 485–503; Mary P. Rowe and Michael Baker, "Are You Hearing Enough Employee Concerns?" *Harvard Business Review* 62 (May–June 1984): 127–135; W. H. Read, "Upward Communication in Industrial Hierarchies," *Human Relations* 15 (February 1962): 3–15; and Daft and Steers, *Organizations*.

47. Jena McGregor, "Gospels of Failure," *Fast Company* (February 2005): 61–67.

48. Ibid.

49. Barbara Ettorre, "The Unvarnished Truth," *Management Review* (June 1997): 54–57; and Roberta Maynard, "Back to Basics, From the Top," *Nation's Business* (December 1996): 38–39.

50. E. M. Rogers and R. A. Rogers, *Communication in Organizations* (New York: Free Press, 1976); and A. Bavelas and D. Barrett, "An Experimental Approach to Organization Communication," *Personnel* 27 (1951): 366–371.

51. This discussion is based on Daft and Steers, *Organizations*.

52. Bavelas and Barrett, "An Experimental Approach"; and M. E. Shaw, *Group Dynamics: The Psychology of Small Group Behavior* (New York: McGraw-Hill, 1976).

53. Richard L. Daft and Norman B. Macintosh, "A Tentative Exploration into the Amount and Equivocality of Information Processing in Organizational Work Units," *Administrative Science Quarterly* 26 (1981): 207–224.

54. This discussion of informal networks is based on Rob Cross, Nitin Nohria, and Andrew Parker, "Six Myths About Informal Networks," *MIT Sloan Management Review* (Spring 2002): 67–75; and Rob Cross and Laurence Prusak, "The People Who Make Organizations Go—or Stop," *Harvard Business Review* (June 2002): 105–112.

55. Tahl Raz, "The 10 Secrets of a Master Networker," *Inc.* (January 2003).

56. Keith Davis and John W. Newstrom, *Human Behavior at Work: Organizational Behavior*, 7th ed. (New York: McGraw-Hill, 1985).

57. Suzanne M. Crampton, John W. Hodge, and Jitendra M. Mishra, "The Informal Communication Network: Factors Influencing Grapevine Activity," *Public Personnel Management* 27, no. 4 (Winter 1998): 569–584.

58. Survey results reported in Jared Sandberg, "Ruthless Rumors and the Managers Who Enable Them," *Wall Street Journal* (October 29, 2003): B1.

59. Joshua Hyatt, "The Last Shift," *Inc.* (February 1989): 74–80.

60. Donald B. Simmons, "The Nature of the Organizational Grapevine," *Supervisory Management* (November 1985): 39–42; and Davis and Newstrom, *Human Behavior*.

61. Barbara Ettorre, "Hellooo. Anybody Listening?" *Management Review* (November 1997): 9.

62. Lisa A. Burke and Jessica Morris Wise, "The Effective Care, Handling, and Pruning of the Office Grapevine," *Business Horizons* (May–June 2003): 71–74; "They Hear It Through the Grapevine," in Michael Warshaw, "The Good Guy's Guide to Office Politics," *Fast Company* (April–May 1998): 157–178 (p. 160); and Carol Hildebrand, "Mapping the Invisible Workplace," *CIO Enterprise*, Section 2 (July 15, 1998): 18–20.

63. Thomas J. Peters and Robert H. Waterman Jr., *In Search of Excellence* (New York: Harper & Row, 1982); and Tom Peters and Nancy Austin, *A Passion for Excellence: The Leadership Difference* (New York: Random House, 1985).

64. Lois Therrien, "How Ztel Went from Riches to Rags," *BusinessWeek* (June 17, 1985): 97–100.

65. Reported in "Employers Want Better Writing," *News for You* (December 8, 2004): 2.

66. Jonathan Hershberg, "It's Not Just What You Say," *Training* (May 2005): 50.

67. Based on Michael Fitzgerald, "How to Write a Memorable Memo," *CIO* (October 15, 2005): 85–87; and Hershberg, "It's Not Just What You Say."

68. Mary Anne Donovan, "E-Mail Exposes the Literacy Gap," *Workforce* (November 2002): 15.

69. John Case, "Opening the Books," *Harvard Business Review*, (March–April 1997): 118–127.

70. Gary Hamel, "Killer Strategies That Make Shareholders Rich," *Fortune* (June 23, 1997): 70–84.

71. "What Is Trust?" results of a survey by Manchester Consulting, reported in Jenny C. McCune, "That Elusive Thing Called Trust," *Management Review* (July–August 1998): 10–16.

72. David Bohm, *On Dialogue* (Ojai, CA: David Bohm Seminars, 1989).

73. This discussion is based on Glenna Gerard and Linda Teurfs, "Dialogue and Organizational Transformation," in *Community Building: Renewing Spirit and Learning in Business,*

ed. Kazinierz Gozdz (Pleasanton, CA: New Leaders Press, 1995): 142–153; and Edgar H. Schein, "On Dialogue, Culture, and Organizational Learning," *Organizational Dynamics* (Autumn 1993): 40–51.

74. Ian I. Mitroff and Murat C. Alpaslan, "Preparing for Evil," *Harvard Business Review* (April 2003): 109–115.

75. This section is based on Leslie Wayne and Leslie Kaufman, "Leadership, Put to a New Test," *The New York Times* (September 16, 2001): Section 3, 1, 4; Ian I. Mitroff, "Crisis Leadership," *Executive Excellence* (August 2001): 19; Jerry Useem, "What It Takes," *Fortune* (November 12, 2001): 126–132; Andy Bowen, "Crisis Procedures That Stand the Test of Time," *Public Relations Tactics* (August 2001): 16; and Matthew Boyle, "Nothing Really Matters," *Fortune* (October 15, 2001): 261–264.

76. Stephen Bernhut, "Leadership, with Michael Useem," *Ivey Business Journal* (January–February 2002): 42–43.

77. Mitroff, "Crisis Leadership."

78. Jay M. Jackman and Myra H. Strober, "Fear of Feedback," *Harvard Business Review* (April 2003): 101–108; and Tourish, "Critical Upward Communication."

79. Thomas E. Ricks, "Army Devises System to Decide What Does, and Does Not, Work," *Wall Street Journal* (May 23, 1997): A1, A10; Stephanie Watts Sussman, "CALL: A Model for Effective Organizational Learning," *Strategy* (Summer 1999): 14–15; John O'Shea, "Army: The Leader as Learner-in-Chief," *The Officer* (June 2003): 31; Michael D. Maples, "Fires First in Combat—Train the Way We Fight," *Field Artillery* (July–August 2003): 1; Thomas E. Ricks, "Intelligence Problems in Iraq Are Detailed," *The Washington Post* (October 25, 2003): A1; and Richard W. Koenig, "Forging Our Future: Using Operation Iraqi Freedom Phase IV Lessons Learned," *Engineer* (January–March 2004): 21–22.

80. Thomas A. Stewart, "Listen Up, Maggots! You *Will* Deploy a More Humane and Effective Managerial Style!" *Ecompany* (July 2001): 95.

81. James A. F. Stoner and R. Edward Freeman, *Management*, 4th ed. (Englewood Cliffs, NJ: Prentice Hall, 1989).

82. Janet Fulk and Sirish Mani, "Distortion of Communication in Hierarchical Relationships," in *Communication Yearbook*, vol. 9, ed. M. L. McLaughlin (Beverly Hills, CA: Sage, 1986): 483–510.

83. "CEO Stopping Descent of Airline That's in Trouble," *Johnson City Press* (June 20, 2004): 7D.

Chapter 14

Teamwork

1. Scott Thurm, "Theory & Practice: Teamwork Raises Everyone's Game—Having Employees Bond Benefits Companies More Than Promoting 'Stars'," *Wall Street Journal* (November 7, 2005): B8.

2. Telis Demos, "Cirque du Balancing Act," *Fortune* (June 12, 2006): 114.

3. Susan Carey, "Racing to Improve; United Airlines Employees Go to School for Pit Crews to Boost Teamwork, Speed," *Wall Street Journal* (March 24, 2006): B1.

4. Traci Purdum, "Teaming, Take 2," *Industry Week* (May 2005): 41–43.

5. "Team Goal-Setting," *Small Business Report* (January 1988): 76–77; Frank V. Cespedes, Stephen X. Dole, and Robert J. Freedman, "Teamwork for Today's Selling," *Harvard Business Review* (March–April 1989): 44–55; Victoria J. Marsick, Ernie Turner, and Lars Cederholm, "International Managers as Team Leaders," *Management Review* (March 1989): 46–49; and Terry Adler, Janice A. Black, and John P. Loveland, "Complex Systems: Boundary-Spanning Training Techniques," *Journal of European Industrial Training* 27, no. 2–4 (2002): 111+.

6. Industry Week/Manufacturing Performance Institute's Census of Manufacturers for 2004, reported in Traci Purdum, "Teaming, Take 2."

7. J. D. Osburn, L. Moran, E. Musselwhite, and J. H. Zenger, *Self-Directed Work Teams: The New American Challenge* (Homewood, IL: Business One Irwin, 1990).

8. Linda I. Glassop, "The Organizational Benefits of Teams," *Human Relations* 55, no. 2 (2002): 225–249.

9. Carl E. Larson and Frank M. J. LaFasto, *TeamWork* (New-bury Park, CA: Sage, 1989).

10. Purdum, "Teaming, Take 2."

11. "'Golden Hour' Crucial Time for Surgeons on Front Line," *Johnson City Press* (April 1, 2003): 9.

12. Geoffrey Colvin, "Why Dream Teams Fail," *Fortune* (June 12, 2006): 87–92.

13. Eric Sundstrom, Kenneth P. DeMeuse, and David Futrell, "Work Teams," *American Psychologist* 45 (February 1990): 120–133.

14. Deborah L. Gladstein, "Groups in Context: A Model of Task Group Effectiveness," *Administrative Science Quarterly* 29 (1984): 499–517.

15. Dora C. Lau and J. Keith Murnighan, "Demographic Diversity and Faultlines: The Compositional Dynamics of Organizational Lease Groups," *Academy of Management Review* 23, no. 2 (1998): 325–340.

16. Thomas Owens, "Business Teams," *Small Business Report* (January 1989): 50–58.

17. Margaret Frazier, "Flu Prep," *Wall Street Journal* (March 25, 2006): A8.

18. "Participation Teams," *Small Business Report* (September 1987): 38–41.

19. Susanne G. Scott and Walter O. Einstein, "Strategic Performance Appraisal in Team-Based Organizations: One Size Does Not Fit All," *Academy of Management Executive* 15, no. 2 (2001): 107–116.

20. Larson and LaFasto, *TeamWork*.

21. V. K. Narayanan, Frank L. Douglas, Brock Guernsey, and John Charnes, "How Top Management Steers Fast-Cycle Teams to Success," *Strategy & Leadership* 30, no. 3 (2002): 19–27.

22. James H. Shonk, *Team-Based Organizations* (Homewood, IL: Business One Irwin, 1992); and John Hoerr, "The Payoff from Teamwork," *BusinessWeek* (July 10, 1989): 56–62.

23. Gregory L. Miles, "Suddenly, USX Is Playing Mr. Nice Guy," *BusinessWeek* (June 26, 1989): 151–152.

24. Jeanne M. Wilson, Jill George, and Richard S. Wellings, with William C. Byham, *Leadership Trapeze: Strategies for Leadership in Team-Based Organizations* (San Francisco: Jossey-Bass, 1994).

25. Ruth Wageman, "Critical Success Factors for Creating Superb Self-Managing Teams," *Organizational Dynamics* (Summer 1997): 49–61.

26. Daniel R. Kibbe and Jill Casner-Lotto, "Ralston Foods: From Greenfield to Maturity in a Team-Based Plant," *Journal of Organizational Excellence* (Summer 2002): 57–67.

27. Thomas Owens, "The Self-Managing Work Team," *Small Business Report* (February 1991): 53–65.

28. Bradley L. Kirkman and Benson Rosen, "Powering Up Teams," *Organizational Dynamics* (Winter 2000): 48–66.

29. Vanessa Urch Druskat and Jane V. Wheeler, "Managing from the Boundary: The Effective Leadership of Self-Managing Work Teams," *Academy of Management Journal* 46, no. 4 (2003): 435–457.

30. Curtis Sittenfeld, "Powered by the People," *Fast Company* (July–August 1999): 178–189.

31. Donald Vredenburgh and Irene Yunxia He, "Leadership Lessons from a Conductorless Orchestra," *Business Horizons* (September–October 2003): 19–24.

32. The discussion of virtual teams is based on Wayne F. Cascio and Stan Shurygailo, "E-Leadership and Virtual Teams," *Organizational Dynamics* 31, no. 4 (2002): 362–376; Anthony M. Townsend, Samuel M. DeMarie, and Anthony R. Hendrickson, "Virtual Teams: Technology and the Work-place of the Future," *Academy of Management Executive* 12, no. 3 (August 1998): 17–29; and Deborah L. Duarte and Nancy Tennant Snyder, *Mastering Virtual Teams* (San Francisco: Jossey-Bass, 1999).

33. Jessica Lipnack and Jeffrey Stamps, "Virtual Teams: The New Way to Work," *Strategy & Leadership* (January–February 1999): 14–19.

34. Based on Bradley L. Kirkman, Benson Rosen, Cristina B. Gibson, Paul E. Tesluk, and Simon O. McPherson, "Five Challenges to Virtual Team Success: Lessons from Sabre, Inc.," *Academy of Management Executive* 16, no. 3 (2002): 67–79; Wayne F. Cascio and Stan Shurygailo, "E-Leadership and Virtual Teams," *Organizational Dynamics* 31, no. 4 (2002): 362–376; Ilze Zigurs, "Leadership in Virtual Teams: Oxy-moron or Opportunity?" *Organizational Dynamics* 31, no. 4 (2002): 339–351; and Manju K. Ahuja and John E. Galvin, "Socialization in Virtual Groups," unpublished manuscript.

35. Kirkman et al., "Five Challenges to Virtual Team Success."

36. Terri L. Griffith and Margaret A. Neale, "Information Processing in Traditional, Hybrid, and Virtual Teams: From Nascent Knowledge to Transactive Memory," *Research in Organizational Behavior* 23 (2001): 379–421.

37. Vijay Govindarajan and Anil K. Gupta, "Building an Effective Global Business Team," *MIT Sloan Management Review* 42, no. 4 (Summer 2001): 63–71.

38. Charlene Marmer Solomon, "Building Teams Across Borders," *Global Workforce* (November 1998): 12–17.

39. Carol Saunders, Craig Van Slyke, and Douglas R. Vogel, "My Time or Yours? Managing Time Visions in Global Virtual Teams," *Academy of Management Executive* 18, no. 1 (2004): 19–31.

40. Saunders et al., "My Time or Yours?"

41. Cristina B. Gibson, Mary E. Zellmer-Bruhn, and Donald P. Schwab, "Team Effectiveness in Multinational Organizations: Evaluation Across Contexts," *Group and Organizational Management* 28, no. 4 (December 2003): 444–474.

42. Sylvia Odenwald, "Global Work Teams," *Training and Development* (February 1996): 54–57; and Debby Young, "Team Heat," *CIO* (September 1, 1998): 43–51.

43. Reported in Jia Lynn Yang, "The Power of Number 4.6," part of a special series, "Secrets of Greatness: Teamwork," *Fortune* (June 12, 2006): 122.

44. Martin Hoegl, "Smaller Teams—Better Teamwork: How to Keep Project Teams Small," *Business Horizons* 48 (2005): 209–214.

45. Reported in "Vive La Difference," box in Julie Connelly, "All Together Now," *Gallup Management Journal* (Spring 2002): 13–18.

46. For research findings on group size, see M. E. Shaw, *Group Dynamics*, 3d ed. (New York: McGraw-Hill, 1981); G. Manners, "Another Look at Group Size, Group Problem-Solving and Member Consensus," *Academy of Management Journal* 18 (1975): 715–724; and Martin Hoegl, "Smaller Teams—Better Teamwork: How to Keep Project Teams Small," *Business Horizons* 48 (2005): 209–214.

47. Robert Albanese and David D. Van Fleet, "Rational Behavior in Groups: The Free-Riding Tendency," *Academy of Management Review* 10 (1985): 244–255.

48. D. A. Kravitz and B. Martin, "Ringelmann Rediscovered: The Original Article," *Journal of Personality and Social Psychology* 50, no. 5 (1986): 936–941.

49. Baron, *Behavior in Organizations*.

50. Yang, "The Power of Number 4.6."

51. Warren E. Watson, Kamalesh Kumar, and Larry K. Michaelsen, "Cultural Diversity's Impact on Interaction Process and

Performance: Comparing Homogeneous and Diverse Task Groups," *Academy of Management Journal* 36 (1993): 590–602; Gail Robinson and Kathleen Dechant, "Building a Business Case for Diversity," *Academy of Management Executive* 11, no. 3 (1997): 21–31; and David A. Thomas and Robin J. Ely, "Making Differences Matter: A New Paradigm for Managing Diversity," *Harvard Business Review* (September–October 1996): 79–90.

52. Becky Blalock, "Peer to Peer: Playing Nice in the Sandbox," *CIO* (December 15, 2005): 32–34.

53. J. Stuart Bunderson and Kathleen M. Sutcliffe, "Comparing Alternative Conceptualizations of Functional Diversity in Management Teams: Process and Performance Effects," *Academy of Management Journal* 45, no. 5 (2002): 875–893; and Marc Orlitzky and John D. Benjamin, "The Effects of Sex Composition on Small Group Performance in a Business School Case Competition," *Academy of Management Learning and Education* 2, no. 2 (2003): 128–138.

54. Watson et al. "Cultural Diversity's Impact on Interaction Process and Performance."

55. George Prince, "Recognizing Genuine Teamwork," *Supervisory Management* (April 1989): 25–36; K. D. Benne and P. Sheats, "Functional Roles of Group Members," *Journal of Social Issues* 4 (1948): 41–49; and R. F. Bales, *SYMOLOG* Case Study Kit (New York: Free Press, 1980).

56. Robert A. Baron, *Behavior in Organizations*, 2d ed. (Boston: Allyn & Bacon, 1986).

57. Ibid.

58. Avan R. Jassawalla and Hemant C. Sashittal, "Strategies of Effective New Product Team Leaders," *California Management Review* 42, no. 2 (Winter 2000): 34–51.

59. Kenneth G. Koehler, "Effective Team Management," *Small Business Report* (July 19, 1989): 14–16; and Connie J. G. Gersick, "Time and Transition in Work Teams: Toward a New Model of Group Development," *Academy of Management Journal* 31 (1988): 9–41.

60. Bruce W. Tuckman and Mary Ann C. Jensen, "Stages of Small-Group Development Revisited," *Group and Organizational Studies* 2 (1977): 419–427; and Bruce W. Tuckman, "Developmental Sequences in Small Groups," *Psychological Bulletin* 63 (1965): 384–399. See also Linda N. Jewell and H. Joseph Reitz, *Group Effectiveness in Organizations* (Glenview, IL: Scott, Foresman, 1981).

61. Thomas Petzinger Jr., "Bovis Team Helps Builders Construct a Solid Foundation" *Wall Street Journal* (March 21, 1997): B1.

62. Shaw, *Group Dynamics*.

63. Daniel C. Feldman and Hugh J. Arnold, *Managing Individual and Group Behavior in Organizations* (New York: McGraw-Hill, 1983).

64. Dorwin Cartwright and Alvin Zander, *Group Dynamics: Research and Theory*, 3d ed. (New York: Harper & Row, 1968);

and Elliot Aronson, *The Social Animal* (San Francisco: W. H. Freeman, 1976).

65. Peter E. Mudrack, "Group Cohesiveness and Productivity: A Closer Look," *Human Relations* 42 (1989): 771–785. Also see Miriam Erez and Anit Somech, "Is Group Productivity Loss the Rule or the Exception? Effects of Culture and Group-Based Motivation," *Academy of Management Journal* 39, no. 6 (1996): 1513–1537.

66. Stanley E. Seashore, *Group Cohesiveness in the Industrial Work Group* (Ann Arbor, MI: Institute for Social Research, 1954).

67. Adam Lashinsky, "RAZR's Edge," *Fortune* (June 12, 2006): 124–132.

68. Ibid.

69. J. Richard Hackman, "Group Influences on Individuals," in *Handbook of Industrial and Organizational Psychology*, ed. M. Dunnette (Chicago: Rand McNally, 1976).

70. Paul Hochman, "Pack Mentality," *Fortune* (June 12, 2006): 145–152.

71. Kenneth Bettenhausen and J. Keith Murnighan, "The Emergence of Norms in Competitive Decision-Making Groups," *Administrative Science Quarterly* 30 (1985): 350–372.

72. The following discussion is based on Daniel C. Feldman, "The Development and Enforcement of Group Norms," *Academy of Management Review* 9 (1984): 47–53.

73. Wilson et al., *Leadership Trapeze*, 12.

74. Colvin, "Why Dream Teams Fail."

75. Stephen P. Robbins, *Managing Organizational Conflict: A Nontraditional Approach* (Englewood Cliffs, NJ: Prentice Hall, 1974).

76. Daniel Robey, Dana L. Farrow, and Charles R. Franz, "Group Process and Conflict in System Development," *Management Science* 35 (1989): 1172–1191.

77. Yuhyung Shin, "Conflict Resolution in Virtual Teams," *Organizational Dynamics* 34, no. 4 (2005): 331–345.

78. Dean Tjosvold, Chun Hui, Daniel Z. Ding, and Junchen Hu, "Conflict Values and Team Relationships: Conflict's Contribution to Team Effectiveness and Citizenship in China," *Journal of Organizational Behavior* 24 (2003): 69–88; C. De Dreu and E. Van de Vliert, *Using Conflict in Organizations* (Beverly Hills, CA: Sage, 1997); and Kathleen M. Eisenhardt, Jean L. Kahwajy, and L. J. Bourgeois III, "Conflict and Strategic Choice: How Top Management Teams Disagree," *California Management Review* 39, no. 2 (Winter 1997): 42–62.

79. Jerry B. Harvey, "The Abilene Paradox: The Management of Agreement," *Organizational Dynamics* (Summer 1988): 17–43.

80. Eisenhardt et al., "Conflict and Strategic Choice."

81. Koehler, "Effective Team Management"; and Dean Tjosvold, "Making Conflict Productive," *Personnel Administrator* 29 (June 1984): 121.

82. This discussion is based in part on Richard L. Daft, *Organization Theory and Design* (St. Paul, MN: West, 1992): Chapter 13; and Paul M. Terry, "Conflict Management," *The Journal of Leadership Studies* 3, no. 2 (1996): 3–21.

83. Narayanan et al., "How Top Management Steers Fast-Cycle Teams to Success."

84. Shin, "Conflict Resolution in Virtual Teams."

85. Clinton O. Longenecker and Mitchell Neubert, "Barriers and Gateways to Management Cooperation and Team-work," *Business Horizons* (September–October 2000): 37–44.

86. This discussion is based on K. W. Thomas, "Towards Multidimensional Values in Teaching: The Example of Conflict Behaviors," *Academy of Management Review* 2 (1977): 487.

87. Robbins, *Managing Organizational Conflict.*

88. "The Negotiation Process: The Difference Between Integrative and Distributive Negotiation," La Piana Associates Inc., www.lapiana.org/resources/tips/negotiations.

89. Rob Walker, "Take It or Leave It: The Only Guide to Negotiating You Will Ever Need," *Inc.,* (August 2003): 75–82.

90. Based on Roger Fisher and William Ury, *Getting to Yes: Negotiating Agreement Without Giving In* (New York: Penguin, 1983).

91. This familiar story was reported in "The Difference Between Integrative and Distributive Negotiation."

92. This discussion and example is adapted from "Distributive Bargaining," *Culture at Work,* www.culture-at-work.com/distribute/html.

93. Based in part on "A Note for Analyzing Work Groups," prepared by Linda A. Hill, Harvard Business School Publishing, www.hbsp.harvard.edu.

94. "Big and No Longer Blue," *The Economist* (January 21–27, 2006), www.economist.com.

95. R. B. Zajonc, "Social Facilitation," *Science* 149 (1965): 269–274; and Erez and Somech, "Is Group Productivity Loss the Rule or the Exception?"

96. Claire M. Mason and Mark A. Griffin, "Group Task Satisfaction; The Group's Shared Attitude to Its Task and Work Environment," *Group and Organizational Management* 30, no. 6 (2005): 625–652.

97. Gina Imperato, "Their Specialty? Teamwork," *Fast Company* (January–February 2000): 54–56.

98. Reported in Thurm, "Theory & Practice: Teamwork Raises Everyone's Game."

99. Kenneth Labich, "Elite Teams Get the Job Done," *Fortune* (February 19, 1996): 90–99.

100. "A Note for Analyzing Effective Work Groups."

Chapter 15

Productivity through Quality Control Systems

1. Yochi J.Dreazen, "More Katrina Woes: Incidents of Fraud at Red Cross Centers," *Wall Street Journal* (October 19, 2005): B1, B2.

2. John A. Byrne with Mike France and Wendy Zellner, "The Environment Was Ripe for Abuse," *BusinessWeek* (February 25, 2002): 118–120.

3. Bethany McLean and Peter Elkind, "The Enron Verdict: The Guiltiest Guys in the Room," *Fortune* (June 12, 2006): 26–28.

4. Douglas S. Sherwin, "The Meaning of Control," *Dunn's Business Review* (January 1956).

5. Russ Banham, "Nothin' But Net Gain," *eCFO* (Fall 2001): 32–33.

6. Kevin McCoy and Julie Appleby, "Problems with Staffing, Training Can Cost Lives," *USA Today* (May 26, 2004), www.usatoday.com

7. Carol Hymowitz, "As Economy Slows, Executives Learn Ways to Make Predictions," *Wall Street Journal* (August 21, 2001): B1.

8. Jennifer S. Lee, "Tracking Sales and the Cashiers," *The New York Times* (July 11, 2001): C1, C6; Anna Wilde Mathews, "New Gadgets Track Truckers' Every Move," *Wall Street Journal* (July 14, 1997): B1, B10.

9. Steve Stecklow, "Kentucky's Teachers Get Bonuses, But Some Are Caught Cheating," *Wall Street Journal* (September 2, 1997): A1, A5.

10. Amy Barrett, "Cracking the Whip at Wyeth," *BusinessWeek* (February 6, 2006): 70–71.

11. Richard E. Crandall, "Keys to Better Performance Measurement," *Industrial Management* (January–February 2002): 19–24; Christopher D. Ittner and David F. Larcker, "Coming Up Short on Nonfinancial Performance Measurement," *Harvard Business Review* (November 2003): 88–95.

12. Crandall, "Keys to Better Performance Measurement."

13. Adam Lashinsky, "Meg and the Machine," *Fortune* (September 1, 2003): 68–78.

14. Sumantra Ghoshal, *Strategic Control* (St. Paul, MN: West, 1986): Chapter 4; and Robert N. Anthony, John Dearden, and Norton M. Bedford, *Management Control Systems*, 5th ed. (Homewood, IL: Irwin, 1984).

15. Anthony, Dearden, and Bedford, *Management Control Systems.*

16. Participation in budget setting is described in a number of studies, including Neil C. Churchill, "Budget Choice: Planning versus Control," *Harvard Business Review* (July–August 1984): 150–164; Peter Brownell, "Leadership Style, Budgetary Participation, and Managerial Behavior," *Accounting Organizations and Society* 8 (1983): 307–321; and Paul J. Carruth and Thurrell O. McClandon, "How Supervisors React to 'Meeting the Budget' Pressure," Management Accounting 66 (November 1984): 50–54.

17. Tim Reason, "Budgeting in the Real World," *CFO* (July 2005): 43–48.

18. Ibid.

19. Bruce G. Posner, "How to Stop Worrying and Love the Next Recession," *Inc.* (April 1986): 89–95.

20. William G. Ouchi, "Markets, Bureaucracies, and Clans," *Administrative Science Quarterly* 25 (1980): 129–141; and B. R. Baligia and Alfred M. Jaeger, "Multinational Corporations: Control Systems and Delegation Issues," *Journal of International Business Studies* (Fall 1984): 25–40.

21. Sherwin, "The Meaning of Control."

22. Mathews, "New Gadgets Track Truckers' Every Move," B10.

23. Jared Sandberg, "Overcontrolling Bosses Aren't Just Annoying; They're Also Inefficient," *Wall Street Journal* (March 30, 2005): B1.

24. Art Kleiner, "Leaning Toward Utopia," *Strategy + Business,* no. 39 (Second Quarter 2005): 76–87; Fara Warner, "Think Lean," *Fast Company* (February 2002): 40, 42; and James P. Womack and Daniel T. Jones, *The Machine That Changed the World: The Story of Lean Production* (New York: HarperCollins, 1991).

25. Peter Strozniak, "Toyota Alters Face of Production," *Industry Week* (August 13, 2001): 46–48.

26. Emily Esterson, "First-Class Delivery," *Inc. Technology* (September 15, 1998): 89.

27. W. Bouce Chew, "No-Nonsense Guide to Measuring Productivity," *Harvard Business Review* (January–February 1988): 110–118.

28. John A. Parnell, C. W. Von Bergen, and Barlow Soper, "Profiting from Past Triumphs and Failures: Harnessing History for Future Success," *SAM Advanced Management Journal* (Spring 2005): 36–59.

29. Stephen Power and Guy Chazan, "Politics & Economics: Europe Auto Relations Get Testy; Car Makers' Friction with Workers Rises Over Plans to Relocate Jobs," *Wall Street Journal* (June 15, 2006): A8.

30. A.V. Feigenbaum, *Total Quality Control: Engineering and Management* (New York: McGraw-Hill, 1961); John Lorinc, "Dr. Deming's Traveling Quality Show," *Canadian Business* (September 1990): 38–42; Mary Walton, *The Deming Management Method* (New York: Dodd-Meade & Co., 1986); and J. M. Juran and Frank M. Gryna, eds., *Juran's Quality Control Handbook,* 4th ed. (New York: McGraw-Hill, 1988).

31. Edward E. Lawler III and Susan A. Mohrman, "Quality Circles after the Fad," *Harvard Business Review* (January–February 1985): 65–71; and Philip C. Thompson, *Quality Circles: How to Make Them Work in America* (New York: AMACOM, 1982).

32. D. J. Ford, "Benchmarking HRD," *Training and Development* (July 1993): 37–41.

33. Tracy Mayor, "Six Sigma Comes to IT: Targeting Perfection," *CIO* (December 1, 2003): 62–70; Hal Plotkin, "Six Sigma: What It Is and How to Use It," *Harvard Management Update* (June 1999): 3–4; Tom Rancour and Mike McCracken, "Applying 6 Sigma Methods for Breakthrough Safety Performance," *Professional Safety* 45, no. 10 (October 2000): 29–32; G. Hasek, "Merger Marries Quality Efforts," *Industry Week* (August 21, 2000): 89–92; and Lee Clifford, "Why You Can Safely Ignore Six Sigma," *Fortune* (January 22, 2001): 140.

34. Dick Smith and Jerry Blakeslee "The New Strategic Six Sigma," *Training & Development* (September 2002): 45–52; Michael Hammer and Jeff Goding, "Putting Six Sigma in Perspective," *Quality* (October 2001): 58–62; and Mayor, "Six Sigma Comes to IT."

35. Plotkin, "Six Sigma: What It Is"; Timothy Aeppel, "Nicknamed 'Nag,' She's Just Doing Her Job," *Wall Street Journal* (May 14, 2002): B1, B12; John S. McClenahen, "ITT's Value Champion," *IndustryWeek* (May 2002): 44–49.

36. M. Elisebeth Tyler, "Magic Number," *Microsoft Executive Circle* (Spring 2004): 31–32.

37. Philip R. Thomas, Larry J. Gallace, and Kenneth R. Martin, *Quality Alone Is Not Enough* (New York: American Management Association, August 1992).

38. Kate Kane, "L.L.Bean Delivers the Goods," *Fast Company* (August–September 1997): 104–113.

39. Clifford, "Why You Can Safely Ignore Six Sigma"; and Hammer and Goding, "Putting Six Sigma in Perspective."

40. Syed Hasan Jaffrey, "ISO 9001 Made Easy," *Quality Progress* 37, no. 5 (May 2004): 104; Frank C. Barnes, "ISO 9000 Myth and Reality: A Reasonable Approach to ISO 9000," *SAM Advanced Management Journal* (Spring 1998): 23–30; and Thomas H. Stevenson and Frank C. Barnes, "Fourteen Years of ISO 9000: Impact, Criticisms, Costs, and Benefits," *Business Horizons* (May–June 2001): 45–51.

41. David Amari, Don James, and Cathy Marley, "ISO 9001 Takes On a New Role—Crime Fighter," *Quality Progress* 37, no. 5 (May 2004): 57+.

42. Don L. Bohl, Fred Luthans, John W. Slocum Jr., and Richard M. Hodgetts, "Ideas That Will Shape the Future of Management Practice," *Organizational Dynamics* (Summer 1996): 7–14.

43. John Berry, "How to Apply EVA to I.T.," *CIO* (January 15, 2003): 94–98.

44. Perry Pascarella, "Open the Books to Unleash Your People," *Management Review* (May 1998): 58–60.

45. Nadine Heintz, "Everyone's a CFO," *Inc.* (September 2005): 42, 45.

46. Ibid.

47. Mel Mandell, "Accounting Challenges Overseas," *World Trade* (December 1, 2001).

48. This discussion is based on a review of the balanced scorecard in Richard L. Daft, *Organization Theory and Design,* 7th ed. (Cincinnati, OH: South-Western, 2001): 300–301.

49. "On Balance," a *CFO* Interview with Robert Kaplan and David Norton, *CFO* (February 2001): 73–78; and Bill Birchard, "Intangible Assets + Hard Numbers = Soft Finance," *Fast Company* (October 1999): 316–336.

50. Robert Kaplan and David Norton, "The Balanced Scorecard: Measures That Drive Performance," *Harvard Business Review* (January–February 1992): 71–79; and Chee W. Chow, Kamal M. Haddad, and James E. Williamson, "Applying the Balanced Scorecard to Small Companies," *Management Accounting* 79, no. 2 (August 1997): 21–27.

51. Based on Kaplan and Norton, "The Balanced Scorecard"; Chow, Haddad, and Williamson, "Applying the Balanced Scorecard"; and Cathy Lazere, "All Together Now," *CFO* (February 1998): 28–36.

52. Geert J. M. Braam and Edwin J. Nijssen, "Performance Effects of Using the Balanced Scorecard: A Note on the Dutch Experience," *Long Range Planning* 37 (2004): 335–349; Kaplan and Norton, "The Balanced Scorecard"; and Cam Scholey, "Strategy Maps: A Step-by-Step Guide to Measuring, Managing, and Communicating the Plan," *Journal of Business Strategy* 26, no. 3 (2005): 12–19.

53. Nils-Göran Olve, Carl-Johan Petri, Jan Roy, and Sofie Roy, "Twelve Years Later: Understanding and Realizing the Value of Balanced Scorecards," *Ivey Business Journal* (May–June 2004); Eric M. Olson and Stanley F. Slater, "The Balanced Scorecard, Competitive Strategy, and Performance," *Business Horizons* (May–June 2002): 11–16; and Eric Berkman, "How to Use the Balanced Scorecard," *CIO* (May 15, 2002): 93–100.

54. Ibid.; and Brigitte W. Schay, Mary Ellen Beach, Jacqueline A. Caldwell, and Christelle LaPolice, "Using Standardized Outcome Measures in the Federal Government," *Human Resource Management* 41, no. 3 (Fall 2002): 355–368.

55. Olve et al., "Twelve Years Later: Understanding and Realizing the Value of Balanced Scorecards."

56. Braam and Nijssen, "Performance Effects of Using the Balanced Scorecard."

57. "Business: The Trial of Sarbanes-Oxley; Regulating Business," *The Economist* (April 22, 2006): 69; and Maurice R. Greenberg, "Regulation,Yes; Stangulation, No," *Wall Street Journal* (August 21, 2006): A10.

Appendix B

Small Business Start Ups

1. Donald F. Kuratko and Richard M. Hodgetts, *Entrepreneurship: A Contemporary Approach,* 4th ed. (Fort Worth: The Dryden Press, 1998): 30.

2. Nadine Heintz, "Andra Rush: For Rolling Up Her Sleeves," *Inc.* (April 2004): 128–129.

3. Study conducted by Yankelovich Partners, reported in Mark Henricks, "Type-Cast," *Entrepreneur* (March 2000): 14–16.

4. Olson, "They May Be Mundane, But Low-Tech Businesses Are Booming."

5. Norm Brodsky, "Street Smarts: Opportunity Knocks," *Inc.* (February 2002): 44–46; and Hilary Stout, "Start Low," *The Wall Street Journal* (May 14, 2001): R8.

6. Kathleen Collins, "¡La Vida Próspera! Latin-Owned Businesses Explode," *Working Woman* (October 2000): 13.

7. Office of Advocacy of the U.S. Small Business Administration, reported in T. Shawn Taylor, "Kitchen Table CEOs," *Essence* (March 2004): 112; and www.sba.gov.

8. Global Entrepreneurship Monitor, "Table 2: Prevalence Rates of Entrepreneurial Activity Across Countries, 200,5" *2005 GEM Tables and Figures,* Babson College and the London Business School, (March 14, 2006): www.gemconsortium.org/category_list.asp.

9. "One-Yen Wonders," *The Economist* (June 28, 2003): 66.

10. Ovetta Wiggins, "Report: Small Business Set to Double By 2009," *The Moscow Times,* as reported on The America's IntelligenceWire, (March 2, 2004): www.themoscowtimes.com.

11. This section based on John Case, "The Wonderland Economy," *The State of Small Business* (1995): 14–29; and Richard L. Daft, *Management,* 3rd ed. (Fort Worth, Texas: The Dryden Press, 1992).

12. "Number of Small Businesses Continues to Grow; Nevada, Georgia Lead the Way," *The Network Journal* (March–April 2005): 54.

13. Susan Greco and Elaine Appleton Grant, "Innovation, Part III: Creation Nation," *Inc.* (October 2002): 72–80.

14. Alessandra Bianchi, "Erasing Borders," in Joshua Hyatt, "Small and Global," *FSB* (June 2004): 44–45.

15. Julia Boorstin, "Exporting Cleaner Air," in Joshua Hyatt, "Small and Global," *FSB* (June 2004): 44–45.

16. Elizabeth Olson, "Dot-Com Survivor Hits on Right Plan," *The New York Times* (February 5, 2004): C6.

17. Steve Stecklow, "StubHut's Ticket to Ride," *The Wall Street Journal* (January 17, 2006): B1.

18. George Mannes, "Don't Give Up on the Web," *Fortune* (March 5, 2001): 184[B]–184[L].

19. Brian Caulfield et al., "12 Hot Startups," *Business 2.0* (January–February 2004): 93–97.

20. Caulfield et al., "12 Hot Startups."

21. Christine Y. Chen, "The E-Recycler," *FSB* (May 2005): 93–94.

22. www.sba.gov.

23. Thuy-Doan Le Bee, "How Small Is Small? SBA Holds Hearings to Decide," *The Sacramento Bee* (June 29, 2005): D2.

24. Office of Advocacy, U.S. Small Business Administration, www.sba.gov/advo.

25. Barbara Benham, "Big Government, Small Business," *Working Woman* (February 2001): 24.

26. Research and statistics reported in "The Job Factory," *Inc.* (May 29, 2001): 40–43.

27. Ian Mount, "The Return of the Lone Inventor," *FSB* (March 2005): 18; Office of Advocacy, U.S. Small Business Administration, www.sba.gov/advo.

28. Kuratko and Hodgetts, *Entrepreneurship: A Contemporary Approach*, 4th ed. (Fort Worth: The Dryden Press, 1998): 11; and "100 Ideas for New Businesses," *Venture* (November 1988): 35–74.

29. Robert Berner, "Why P&G's Smile Is So Bright," *BusinessWeek* (August 12, 2002): 58–60.

30. Lorrie Grant, "Little Guys Take On Greeting Card Giants," *USA Today* (June 16, 2005): www.usatoday.com.

31. John Case, "The Origins of Entrepreneurship," *Inc.* (June 1989): 51–53.

32. Greco and Grant, "Innovation, Part III: Creation Nation."

33. Robert D. Hisrich, "Entrepreneurship-Intrapreneurship," *American Psychologist* (February 1990): 209–222.

34. Olson, "From One Business to 23 Million."

35. www.sba.gov; "CIBC Report Predicts Canada Will Be Home to One Million Women Entrepreneurs by 2010," *Canada NewsWire* (June 28, 2005): 1.

36. www.sba.gov.

37. Statistics reported in Cora Daniels, "Minority Rule," *FSB* (December 2003–January 2004): 65–66; Elizabeth Olson, "New Help for the Black Entrepreneur," *The New York Times* (December 23, 2004): C6; and David J. Dent, "The Next Black Power Movement," *FSB* (May 2003): 10–13.

38. Ellyn Spragins, "Pat Winans" profile, and Cora Daniels, "Ed Chin" profile, in "The New Color of Money," *FSB* (December 2003–January 2004): 74–87.

39. This discussion is based on Charles R. Kuehl and Peggy A. Lambing, *Small Business: Planning and Management,* 3rd ed. (Ft. Wort: The Dryden Press, 1994).

40. David C. McClelland, *The Achieving Society* (New York: Van Nostrand, 1961).

41. Paulette Thomas, "Entrepreneurs' Biggest Problems—and How They Solve Them" *The Wall Street Journal* (March 17, 2003): R1.

42. Definition based on Albert R. Hunt, "Social Entrepreneurs: Compassionate and Tough-Minded," *The Wall Street Journal* (July 13, 2000): A27; David Puttnam, "Hearts Before Pockets," *The New Statesman* (February 9, 2004): 26; and Christian Seelos and Johanna Mair, "Social Entrepreneurship: Creating New Business Models to Serve the Poor," *Business Horizons* 48 (2005): 241–246.

43. Cheryl Dahle, "Filling the Void: The 2006 Social Capitalist Award Winners," *Fast Company* (January–February 2006): 50–61.

44. Putnam, "Hearts Before Pockets."

45. Cheryl Dahle, "The Change Masters," *Fast Company* (January 2005): 47–58; David Bornstein, *How to Change the World: Social Entrepreneurs and the Power of New Ideas* (Oxford and New York: Oxford University Press, 2004).

46. Brian Dumaine, "See Me, Hear Me," segment in "Two Ways to Help the Third World," *Fortune* (October 27, 2003): 187–196.

47. Dahle, "Filling the Void"; and Cheryl Dahle, "Social Capitalists: The Top 20 Groups That Are Changing the World," *Fast Company* (January 2004): 45–57.

48. Leslie Brokaw, "How to Start an *Inc.* 500 Company," *Inc.* 500 (1994): 51–65.

49. Paul Reynolds, "The Truth about Start-Ups," *Inc.* (February 1995): 23; Brian O'Reilly, "The New Face of Small Businesses," *Fortune* (May 2, 1994): 82–88.

50. Based on Ellyn E. Spragins, "How to Write a Business Plan That Will Get You in the Door," *Small Business Success* (*Inc.* 2001); Linda Elkins, "Tips for Preparing a Business Plan," *Nation's Business* (June 1996): 60R–61R; Carolyn M. Brown, "The Do's and Don'ts of Writing a Winning Business Plan," *Black Enterprise* (April 1996): 114–116; and Kuratko and Hodgetts, *Entrepreneurship,* 295–397. For a clear, thorough step-by-step guide to writing an effective business plan, see Linda Pinson and Jerry Jinnett, *Anatomy of a Business Plan,* 5th ed. (Virginia Beach, VA: Dearborn, 2001).

51. The INC. FAXPOLL, *Inc.* (February 1992): 24.

52. MacVicar, "Ten Steps to a High-Tech Start-Up."

53. Reported in H. M. Dietel, P. J. Dietel, and K. Steinbuhler, *e-Business and e-Commerce for Managers* (Upper Saddle River, NJ: Prentice Hall, 2001): 58.

54. "Venture Capitalists' Criteria" *Management Review* (November 1985): 7–8.

55. "Staples Makes Big Business from Helping Small Businesses," *SBA Success Stories, www.sba.gov/successstories.html* (accessed on March 12, 2004).

56. Olson, "From One Business to 23 Million."

57. "Where the Venture Money Is Going," *Business 2.0* (January–February 2004): 98.

58. Gary Rivlin, "Does the Kid Stay in the Picture?" *The New York Times* (February 22, 2005): E1, E8.

59. Dent, "The Next Black Power Movement."

60. Kristen Hampshire, "Roll With It," *FSB* (November 2005): 108–112; Jennifer Maxwell profile in Betsy Wiesendanger, "Labors of Love," *Working Woman* (May 1999): 43–56; Jena McGregor, Taryn Rose profile in "25 Top Women Business Builders," *Fast Company* (May 2005): 67–75.

61. Wendy Lea, "Dancing With a Partner," *Fast Company* (March 2000): 159–161.

62. Matt Richtel, "Outsourced All the Way," *The New York Times* (June 21, 2005): www.nytimes.com.

63. Reported in Sheryl Nance-Nash, "More Are Betting the Franchise," *The New York Times* (February 29, 2004): Section 14 LI, 6.

64. Echo Montgomery Garrett, "The Twenty-First-Century Franchise," *Inc.* (January 1995): 79–88; Lisa Benavides, "Linking Up with a Chain," *The Tennessean* (April 6, 1999): 1E.

65. Henry Weil, "Business in a Box," *Working Woman* (September 1999): 59–64.

66. Quinne Bryant, "Who Owns 20+ Subway Franchises?" *The Business Journal of Tri-Cities Tennessee/Virginia* (August 2003): 42–43.

67. For a current discussion of the risks and disadvantages of owning a franchise, see Anne Fisher, "Risk Reward," *FSB* (December 2005–January 2006): 44.

68. Anne Field, "Your Ticket to a New Career? Franchising Can Put Your Skills to Work in Your Own Business," in *Business Week Investor: Small Business* section, *BusinessWeek* (May 12, 2003): 100+: and Roberta Maynard, "Choosing a Franchise," *Nation's Business* (October 1996): 56–63.

69. Darren Dahl, "Getting Started: Percolating Profits." *Inc.* (February 2005): 38.

70. Reported in Dahl, "Getting Started: Percolating Profits."

71. Harvard Business School, reported in Kimberly Weisul, "Incubators Lay an Egg," *BusinessWeek Frontier* (October 9, 2000): F14.

72. Oringel, "Sowing Success."

73. Peter Balan, University of South Australia, "Harmony: A Global Network Support System for Incubators," and "Harmony: A Network System to Support Innovation Commercialisation," http://business2.unisa.edu.au/cde/docs/HarmonyOverviewAndBenefits%2025Feb02.pdf.

74. Carrie Dolan, "Entrepreneurs Often Fail as Managers," *The Wall Street Journal* (May 15, 1989): B1.

75. Mannes, "Don't Give Up on the Web."

76. Finn, "Selling Cool in a Bottle."

77. Amanda Walmac, "Full of Beans," *Working Woman* (February 1999): 38–40.

78. Ron Stodghill, "Boxed Out," *FSB* (April 2005): 69–72.

79. Udayan Gupta and Jeffery A.Tannenbaum, "Labor Shortages Force Changes at Small Firms," *The Wall Street Journal* (May 22, 1989): B1, B2; "Harnessing Employee Productivity," *Small Business Report* (November 1987): 46–49; and Molly Kilmas, "How to Recruit a Smart Team," *Nation's Business* (May 1995): 26–27.

80. Saul Hansell, "Listen Up! It's Time for a Profit: A Front Row Seat as Amazon Gets Serious," *The New York Times* (May 20, 2001): Section 3, 1.

Photo Credits

This page constitutes an extension of the copyright page. We have made every effort to trace the ownership of all copyrighted material and to secure permission from copyright holders. In the event of any question arising as to the use of any material, we will be pleased to make the necessary corrections in future printings. Thanks are due to the following authors, publishers, and agents for permission to use the material indicated.

Name Index

Company Index

Subject Index